A Frontier Life

Jacob Hamblin portrait, possibly dating to around 1863.
Courtesy LDS Church History Library.

A FRONTIER LIFE

Jacob Hamblin, Explorer and Indian Missionary

Todd M. Compton

THE UNIVERSITY OF UTAH PRESS
Salt Lake City

This book is dedicated to Laura, Zachary, and Wesley—companions on the journey.

First paperback edition 2026.

LIBRARY OF CONGRESS CATALOGING-IN-PUBLICATION DATA

Compton, Todd, 1952–

A frontier life : Jacob Hamblin, explorer and Indian missionary / Todd M. Compton.

pages cm

Includes bibliographical references and index.

ISBN 978-1-60781-234-0 (cloth : alk. paper)

ISBN 978-1-64769-271-1 (paperback : alk. paper)

ISBN 978-1-60781-235-7 (ebook)

1. Hamblin, Jacob, 1819-1886. 2. Frontier and pioneer life—West (U.S.)—Biography. 3. Indians of North America—Missions. 4. Mormon Church. 5. Utah—Biography. I. Title. II. Title: Jacob Hamblin, explorer and Indian missionary.

F826.H2C58 2013

979.2'02092—dc23

[B]

2013009238

For EU safety / GPSR concerns:

Email: gpsr@mare-nostrum.co.uk

Physical address:

Mare Nostrum Group B.V.

Mauritskade 21D

1091 GC Amsterdam

The Netherlands

Errata and further information on this and other titles available at UofUpress.com.

Index by Andrew L. Christenson

Contents

Figures

Preface

Why another biography of Jacob Hamblin? some might ask. My short answer is that previous biographies—Paul Bailey's *Jacob Hamblin: Buckskin Apostle* (1948), Pearson Corbett's *Jacob Hamblin: Peacemaker* (1952), Juanita Brooks's *Jacob Hamblin: Mormon Apostle to the Indians* (1980), and Hartt Wixom's *Hamblin: A Modern Look at the Frontier Life and Legend of Jacob Hamblin* (1996)—often did an excellent job of dramatizing Hamblin's life. However, none of them took an academic approach, and none made full use of a wealth of primary documents that have become available in archives in Utah and other western libraries in recent decades. (And, of course, the books of Bailey and Corbett were published more than a half century ago.) I've also tried to place Jacob's life in the broader context of western history, not just in Mormon or Utah history. Hopefully, the drama of Jacob's life will also emerge from my documentary approach.

Jacob Hamblin left a published autobiography, ghost written by James Little and first published in 1881; a holograph autobiography; a number of diaries and account books that are sometimes quasi-autobiographical; and a number of letters, some in his own handwriting, some apparently dictated to friends, wives, or children. When quoting from holograph documents, I have added terminal punctuation and initial capitals for readability. Beyond that I have preserved the punctuation and spelling of the original. Jacob's handwriting and spelling were often rudimentary, which was common among many nineteenth-century Americans on the frontier. Sometimes I have noted that some words are difficult to read, but generally I have simply given the most likely reading, leaving more detailed renditions of the text to a critical edition.

I cite Jacob's published autobiography as Little, *Jacob Hamblin* (abbreviated to LJH), [page number]. I cite the holograph autobiography as "Autobiography."

Many proper names in this book were subjected to radically inconsistent orthography by many different writers in the primary sources. Even the names of Indian tribes have different spellings—Shoshone, Shoshoni, for example. For Indian names, I have simply chosen one common spelling and tried to use it consistently in this work (for example, I have used the following spellings for four prominent Indians: the Paiute Tutsegabits, the Hopi Tuuvi and his wife Talasnimki, and the Navajo Spaneshanks). However, I have mentioned variants in footnotes. In addition, Indians tended to have multiple names, including nicknames, within their own language and culture; then they often had names given to them by whites. Navajos, such as

Barboncito or Manuelito, often were most widely known (by whites) by their Spanish names. For recognition, I have chosen one name and used it consistently, though, again, I have often explained the individual's other names in footnotes.

For geographical places, I was torn between referring to the place as the pioneers did or by its modern name. I finally felt that, for recognition, it would be advisable to use the modern name. Thus I refer to the Kaibab Plateau, rather than Buckskin Mountain; to the Paria River rather than the Pahreah or Pahrear (though I retain the old spelling for the ghost town Pahreah); to Moenkopi, rather than Moencopi.

As Bernard DeVoto has noted, writing history is a cooperative enterprise. Philosophically and practically, this book seeks to build on the remarkable achievement of books such as Juanita Brooks's edition of John D. Lee's diaries and her biographies of John D. Lee and Dudley Leavitt; Charles Peterson's *Take Up Your Mission*; Wallace Stegner's *Beyond the Hundredth Meridian*; and John Alton Peterson's *The Utah Black Hawk War*. John Peterson, in addition, generously shared important Hamblin documents from the LDS Church Archives and the Utah State Historical Society with me.

I am also indebted to P. T. Reilly, both for his *Lee's Ferry* and for his massive collection of research files at the Cline Library in Northern Arizona University at Flagstaff. However, for some reason, he developed a pronounced animus against Jacob Hamblin, and I will often take issue with his interpretations of Hamblin in the following pages.

I would like to thank many good angels at the LDS Church Archives, including Michael Landon, William Slaughter, Ronald G. Watt, Scott R. Christensen, and Emily Utt. The staffs of the Harold B. Lee Library at Brigham Young University, the Marriott Library at the University of Utah, the Huntington Library in San Marino, California, the Sherratt Library at Southern Utah University, the Bancroft Library at the University of California at Berkeley, and the National Archives Library at San Bruno, California, have also been unfailingly helpful. The following have given me invaluable assistance, correcting myriads of small mistakes and suggesting new, important sources, and helping in many other ways: Laura Compton, Merlin Compton, Kenneth Beesley, Lavina Fielding Anderson, Waldo Perkins, John Alton Peterson, W. Paul Reeve, Gary Topping, E. Leo Lyman, Eric Olson, Will Bagley, Robert Briggs, Ronald W. Walker, Quincy Newell, William Shepherd, Jennifer Whitehorse, Janet Burton Seegmiller, Douglas Alder, Richard Rands, Charles Maxwell, Larry Burk, Joan Hamblin, Connell O'Donovan, Tina Compton, Tamara Hauge, Ladd Anderson, Terry Harward, Byron Harward, Peter DeLafosse, John Alley, and Virginia Hoffman. Corey Smallcanyon was kind enough to send me a copy of his excellent thesis on Tuba City, which opened up many fruitful avenues of research for me.

Any mistakes in this book, however, are entirely my own.

Introduction

On March 13, 1852, two men, one white and armed with a rifle, the other a Goshute Indian armed with bow and arrows, confronted each other in the Stansbury Mountains west of Tooele, a small two-year-old settlement some twenty-five miles west of Salt Lake City. The white man, Jacob Hamblin, a lieutenant in the Nauvoo Legion, Utah's pioneer military force, had been given specific instructions by his military and ecclesiastical superior to kill all Indians, as they had been raiding the whites' cattle.[1] However, when Hamblin and the Goshute faced each other in the mountains, neither could kill the other despite multiple arrows loosed at Hamblin and multiple rifle shots fired at the Indian. The Indian finally fled after Hamblin threw a stone at him. This was a tense, dangerous, yet almost comic confrontation that would profoundly shape Hamblin's subsequent life. He concluded that the incident was a sign from God that he should not kill Indians and that, if he followed this directive, he would never be killed by them.

He later wrote about this in his published autobiography:

> In my subsequent reflections, it appeared evident to me that a special providence had been over us, in this and the two previous expeditions, to prevent us from shedding the blood of the Indians. The Holy Spirit forcibly impressed me that it was not my calling to shed the blood of the scattered remnant of Israel [American Indians], but to be a messenger of peace to them. It was also made manifest to me that if I would not thirst for their blood, I should never fall by their hands.[2]

Thus, Hamblin changed from a militaristic soldier sent to kill Indians to a person who felt he had been specially directed to avoid killing and bloodshed when dealing with them. In October 1853, Brigham Young, president of the Church of Jesus Christ of Latter-day Saints (whose members are commonly known as Mormons), called Hamblin to be an Indian missionary in southern Utah, and he served in this capacity for the rest of his life. As part of this mission, he continually pioneered settlements on what Juanita Brooks called the "ragged edge" of the frontier. The small Indian farms he helped found, such as Santa Clara and Kanab, gradually became Mormon towns. In 1858, with a party of fourteen men that included a Paiute guide, he crossed the Colorado and visited the Hopis in Arizona; after that, exploring-missionary trips to the Hopis and Navajos became almost an annual occurrence for him. He became one of the important early explorers of the Grand Canyon and northern Arizona area, and when John Wesley Powell started his Grand Canyon explorations, Hamblin served as his guide and Indian interpreter (beginning with preparations for his second Colorado expedition, in 1870). For years he helped the Powell companies in their mapping and exploring expeditions. Hamblin thus served as a key pioneer who opened up the route from Utah to northern Arizona and made possible the Mormon colonization of the Little Colorado starting in 1876. He and his family became part of that migration to Arizona. Eventually, seeking to evade arrest and imprisonment for polygamy, Hamblin ended up living in western New Mexico and was apparently planning to move to the Mormon colonies in Old Mexico just before he died.

He lived a life of adventure, in one sense. He came to know the Indians of the Southwest so intimately that many of his friends described him as taking on the traits of Indians. His accomplishments, his exploring, his diplomacy with Indians, made him a legend in his own time.

But he also lived a life of paradox, as he tried to act both as an Indian missionary and as an explorer and colonizer. These roles sometimes conflicted; some might argue that they always conflict.

Jacob Hamblin has become a larger-than-life figure, a man who was viewed as impervious to danger, perfectly honest, and infallibly wise. While many important nineteenth-century Mormons languish without a biography, Hamblin has inspired three, not counting the short semifictional work by Juanita Brooks.[3] Two of them—Corbett's *Jacob Hamblin: Peacemaker* (1952) and Wixom's *Hamblin: A Modern Look at the Frontier Life and Legend of Jacob Hamblin* (1996)—are written from a conservative Mormon perspective. Corbett's book is in many ways a history written for Hamblin's family. Paul Bailey's *Jacob Hamblin: Buckskin Apostle* (1948) is a quasi-novel glorifying Hamblin as a frontiersman.[4] Hamblin's home in Santa Clara has been restored and Latter-day Saint missionaries give tours of it. He has even become the lead character in a musical, *Utah*.[5]

Jacob Hamblin as legend is not merely a Mormon phenomenon. As early as 1902, Frederick Dellenbaugh, who had been a member of the second Powell expedition, referred to Jacob as "the 'Leather-stocking' of Utah—a man who knew the Amerinds of Utah and northern Arizona better than anyone who ever lived."[6] "Leather-stocking" is a reference to James Fenimore Cooper's fully legendary, fictional character, the "pathfinder," Natty Bumpo. A number of authors, including McClintock, Hoffman Birney, and Wallace Stegner, also likened Jacob to this potent American mythical figure.[7]

Dellenbaugh's early reference clearly started the process of making Hamblin larger than life, and his successors have extended the process.[8] These non-Mormons responded to the exploring, pathfinding aspect of the Hamblin persona, while devout Mormons have tended to emphasize his religious, "Indian missionary" aspects.

Not surprisingly, this widespread heroicizing of Hamblin (the legend-making process was a characteristic of the American frontier) created its own backlash, beginning with the writings of John D. Lee in the 1860s and 1870s, which document a bitter feud between Hamblin and Lee.[9] Some historians, such as P. T. Reilly, author of *Lee's Ferry* (1999), have strongly taken Lee's side and portray Hamblin as manipulative and, in contrast to the view of Hamblin's honesty, as nearly a serial liar. Reilly almost seemed to be pursuing a personal vendetta against Hamblin. Will Bagley, in his history of the Mountain Meadows Massacre, *Blood of the Prophets: Brigham Young and the Massacre at Mountain Meadows* (2002), also gives a notably unsympathetic view of Hamblin.[10]

Charles Peterson, historian of the Little Colorado mission, offered a convincing revisionist evaluation of Hamblin in 1975, portraying him as an unsuccessful Indian missionary.[11] Juanita Brooks, despite early ambitions to write a full biography of Hamblin, never did, in part because her father dissuaded her, arguing that many of Hamblin's friends—including Juanita's grandfather, Dudley Leavitt—deserved as much or greater credit. "Uncle Jacob! Uncle Jacob! Everybody talks about Uncle Jacob!" Pa broke in bitterly. "When Uncle Jacob had a job that was too big for him, who did he send? Dudley Leavitt and Thales Haskell, or Dudley Leavitt and Ira Hatch!"[12] We should note that Jacob had married Dudley Leavitt's sister, so this was criticism from within the Leavitt-Hamblin clan. Dudley's son—possibly reflecting Dudley's own attitudes—was clearly upset that Hamblin got so much credit when the Leavitts, Haskells, and Hatches were ignored. Ammon Tenney, another close companion, at one point had a bitter break with Hamblin because he felt he was not being given sufficient credit for his own Indian missionary work.[13] These were friends and relatives, not anti-Mormon naysayers.

In fact, Hamblin was a real human being, somewhere between the all-wise omniscient legend and the manipulative, lying antihero. When Hamblin had weaknesses, I will not avoid bringing them into the story of his life, but I will also defend him when I think he deserves defense, as in the case of Reilly's treatment. I believe that the primary documents show a more nuanced view of Hamblin than the generally negative, almost melodramatic portrait Reilly presented.

This book will look for the primary evidence behind the legends, and will provide a scholarly treatment to supplement the previous biographies. As often occurs in history, the earliest documents sometimes tell substantially different stories than do later, retrospective accounts.

One could argue, as does Charles Peterson, that Hamblin did not achieve success as an Indian missionary, that his real successes were as explorer and colonizer,[14] Indian interpreter, and negotiator. One could also argue that he helped the LDS Church in its scapegoating of John D. Lee and cover-up of Mormon involvement in the Mountain Meadows Massacre. Some have stated that Hamblin neglected his large family while away on his frequent expeditions. No doubt he arguably made decisions that were wrong, in retrospect, when faced with difficulties and pressures while alone or with a few companions on the frontier.

Nevertheless, one could also argue that Hamblin's personal commitment to spare the lives of Indians and instead work with them through negotiation and understanding helped save the lives of many, both whites and Indians, on the Mormon-Indian frontier. His was a voice of moderation and compassion where, often, moderation and compassion were in short supply. Without Hamblin, there would probably have been more massacres of Indians in early Utah.

One issue that any Mormon historian must face is the concept of the supernatural. Jacob Hamblin was a deeply religious man. From his conversion to Mormonism in 1842 until his death in 1886, he was a devout and loyal member, subscribing fully to the characteristic Mormon ideology of literal biblical restorationism—modern prophets, prophecy, scripture, and "restorations" of many Old Testament institutions, such as temples, priesthood, and polygamy. Hamblin, like other Mormons, believed that the visionary realities and institutions of the Old and New Testaments were fully operative in the midst of the westward expansion of America throughout the nineteenth century.

Some aspects of Mormonism were intensely visionary, while others were practical and this-worldly. The LDS faithful came to have a deep sense of community, though sometimes they were so unified that they developed a polarized bunker mentality when dealing with non-Mormons. Unquestioning obedience to the church president, seen as a living prophet, is a cornerstone tenet of Mormon faith even today, and Hamblin revered Brigham Young, president and prophet of the LDS Church, and worked closely with him throughout his life. He believed in living prophets and was something of a prophet himself—a man of visions as well as a priest or shaman with special sensitivity to spiritual impressions and a special power to heal. Often, while on his journeys in the wilderness, he received spiritual impressions that affected his actions. He often interpreted dreams that he felt had been sent to him by God, and recounted occasions when God had answered his prayers quickly and seemingly miraculously. Once, after a life-threatening fall, he visited heaven and spoke with his long-dead father before returning to the earth. Another time, when he leaned toward making a wrong decision, the spirit of an ancestor visited him and admonished him to follow the right path.

Such miracle narratives are an issue the historian repeatedly faces when dealing with much of early Mormon history, and frequently in the life of Jacob Hamblin. Jacob's published autobiography appeared in "the Faith-Promoting Series," and its frequent miracles and visions justify that description. His friend Martha Cragun Cox reported that James Little, who cowrote the book, said that he was not able to use much of the material that Jacob gave him because it was too visionary![15] Cox also noted that Jacob felt a special connection with those peculiar figures in Mormon folklore, the Three Nephites, apostles from Christ's early church in America who had been given the special blessing of never tasting death and instead wandered the earth doing good. Jacob would unexpectedly leave his work at home to go on missions at the behest of these ancient, wandering, Indian apostles.[16]

Historians, when considering miracle stories, must weigh and balance sources, look for the best (usually the earliest) source, and be skeptical of a source that is late or in conflict with other evidence.[17] Some miracle stories will not stand up to detailed historical scrutiny while others remain ambiguous. Sometimes the earliest accounts of an incident do not include the supernatural aspects, the more visionary perspectives developing later. Hamblin's conversion to peaceful relations with Indians following his early fight with the Goshute is an example of an event in which the earliest records are relatively matter-of-fact, as Hamblin clearly developed his religious view of the incident afterward, when looking back and trying to make sense of it.

Miracle stories serve best as examples of Hamblin's beliefs, his ethical and cosmic ideology.[18] When Jacob Hamblin and Mormon pioneers are said to have been fed by quails in the wilderness on their exodus from Nauvoo to Salt Lake City, historians can neither prove nor disprove that the quails were miraculously sent by God. However, they can use this miracle story to show how early Mormons identified themselves as the children of Israel, rescued from death by the miracle of a God who was specially providing for them; they were reliving the Old Testament.

Another issue confronting historians of the Southwest is the complex interweaving of historical records from many traditions. Much Mormon and Utah history, both written and via collective oral memory, is characterized by the often justified heroicizing of LDS pioneers. The Mormon exodus to Utah was a unique accomplishment; the settlement of Utah, especially geographically isolated and forbidding southern Utah, was difficult and admirable.[19] One is continually impressed by the strong will, courage, intelligence, and endurance of the founding settlers of many towns in Utah, Nevada, and Arizona (not to mention the old and new Mexicos, in Hamblin's later life). After being driven out of Missouri and Illinois by lawless anti-Mormons (as the Mormons perceived the conflicts), the Latter-day Saints, under Brigham Young's strong leadership, were able to settle a large western territory (including much land that was far from inviting and fertile).[20] Hamblin's non-Mormon friend, Frederick Dellenbaugh, contrasted the industry, organization, and lack of crime in Mormon towns to many violent, chaotic settlements in the West. Stewart Udall has pointed to the quiet virtues of many early Mormon and non-Mormon settlers.[21] Wallace Stegner praised Mormon towns as models of cooperation in the harsh, arid environment of the West.[22]

In the Mormon narrative of settlement, Indians are sometimes seen as the object of missionary work, converts who help the pioneering Mormons. But they are also seen as a dangerous, frightening, troublesome element of the frontier—an obstacle to the early settlers. One common type of Indian story in Utah, as elsewhere, describes pioneers' near escapes from violent Indians. Of course, there were also Mormons who dehumanized Indians and participated in campaigns of "extermination" against them.[23]

The history of Indians in Utah, viewed from their perspective, presents a startling contrast to the Mormon history of settling town after successful town in the state. For the Indians, it is a story of loss and displacement, of eventual banishment from traditional homelands to a few limited reservations in uninviting territory not wanted by whites. Theirs is a story that often includes loss of water and food resources, hunger and starvation, and death from new and deadly diseases. Sometimes the Indian narrative includes outbreaks of open warfare with Mormons, but despite occasional victories, the Native Americans were doomed by the whites' superior technology, greater political cohesion, inherited resistance to the diseases they spread, and rapidly increasing numbers.

Indian history during the chronological compass of this book was recorded by Mormons, since Indians generally could not read or write when Mormons arrived in Utah. Sometimes we are fortunate to have some late oral histories told from the Indian perspective, but we have no early histories written by them. Often we are missing half of the story.

Nevertheless, this book, like many books in recent western history, will try to view events in Utah history through a dual lens, both from the Mormon and Indian perspective. My view of the Mormon settlement of Utah, therefore, will always be tinged with the tragedy of the displacement of Indians that resulted from it. As historian Patricia Limerick writes, "The clashes and conflicts of Western history will always leave the serious individual emotionally and intellectually unsettled."[24]

Whites, in addition to displacing Indians from their land, often practiced an ideological colonialism by requiring the Indians to give up their culture. Instead of being allowed to practice their traditional religions, a key part of their cultural heritage, they were expected to convert to Christianity, and more specifically in the case of Utah, to Mormon Christianity. Most Christian and LDS missionaries were utterly sincere in their attempts to share their religions with Indians, feeling they were offering them something precious.

While the Mormons were definitely the more powerful group in this conflict, the displacers and not the displaced, we cannot reduce the conflict to absolutes of good and evil. There was great complexity on both sides of this conflict, including people who strove to work generously and pragmatically with the other side, and others who tended to act quickly and harshly through the use of force. There were violent, destructive acts on both sides, and innocent victims. Just as whites had outlaws, so did Indians. In addition, there was no unified Indian side—different groups and tribes of Indians had warred against each other before the whites came, and often Indians welcomed the whites as allies in wars with neighboring tribes.[25] Sometimes Indians preyed upon each other—in Utah, the powerful horse-Indians, the Utes, stole women and children from the impoverished Paiutes and Goshutes and sold them into slavery in New Mexico, for example. Even within a tribe, there was often little political cohesion, and conflicts and raids between tribes and within different factions in a tribe were common.

The whites had much to offer Indians. The horse, the gun, European livestock—including the Navajos' prized sheep—are examples of elements of European culture that were successfully adopted and embraced by American Indians. Western techniques of farming and ranching proved helpful as they were forced to abandon their traditional methods of living. Learning to read and write became a valuable tool for Indians as they navigated the new, white-dominated West. (Unfortunately, the cultural chasm between white and Indian was so vast that Indians who could read and write, in Hamblin's lifetime, were almost unheard of, unless they had been raised in Mormon homes.)

Looking at Mormon and Indian history simultaneously forces us to recognize a central paradox in the life of Jacob Hamblin, a conflict he remarkably seems consciously aware of at times. On the one hand, in southern Utah and northern Arizona, he saw that the Mormons were taking the Paiutes' choicest lands and water sources, were destroying their precious seed supplies by cattle ranching, and that the Indians were being driven to the brink of starvation. He even looked at Indian thievery sympathetically for that reason, a remarkably empathetic perspective for a white, nineteenth-century pioneer. On the other hand, he actively worked throughout his life to help Brigham Young and other Mormons in their colonizing efforts and in opening up land for Mormon farming and stock-raising.

Perhaps this is one of the reasons that early Mormon missionary work to the Indians in Utah was not remarkably successful. The Saints became competitors to Indians, for land, water, and other resources, soon after they began to live among them and proselytize them. Given this sometimes tense and dangerous situation, the best Hamblin and other Indian missionaries could do would be to minimize violence between whites and Indians, through negotiation, when they could, as the Mormons gradually took over more and more Indian territory and disrupted the balance of water, plants, and game that Indians depended on for survival.

A Frontier Life

1

"A Vast Unsettled Wilderness"

Growing Up on the Frontier, 1819–1841

In his holograph autobiography, Hamblin wrote, "I was born in Salem Astahbuleh co Ohio April the 2 in the year of our Lord 1819. I was the oldest son of the family. My parents ware poor whose names ware Isiah and Dapheny Hamblin."[1] In 1819, Ohio was fully on the American frontier; Hamblin's youth is a history of westering America.[2]

Isaiah Hamblin, a dark-complexioned man who stood a commanding six feet six inches tall, had been born in Falmouth, Massachusetts, in 1790, but grew up mostly in Vermont. As a young man, he worked as a harpooner on two multiyear whaling voyages leaving from Nantucket. His famous son would later share his "mild and even temper."[3]

Isaiah possessed a noteworthy religious bent; he accepted Christianity and the Bible but was suspicious of formal religion. "He was naturally a pious man" a family history tells us, "but did not allow his children to attend church: holding that the preachers did not teach in accordance with the scriptures."[4] Widespread rejection of organized religions combined with a belief in God and the Bible provided a perfect seedbed for the primitivist, apocalyptic religions that were sweeping America and Britain: Adventism, Campbellitism, and Mormonism, along with the more mainstream Methodism, which had similar restorationist roots. All these religions sought to restore the original biblical purity of practice and vision.

On November 30, 1812, Isaiah, then twenty-two, married twenty-one-year-old Daphne Haynes at North Hero, Grand Isle County, Vermont. Daphne had been born in 1791 in North Hero; family traditions preserve very little about her.[5]

Isaiah served in the War of 1812 under General Henry Dearborn. In the middle of the war, Isaiah and Daphne began their large family, when Melissa Daphne Hamblin was born in North Hero on February 1, 1814. The next Hamblin child, Emily Haynes, was born on October 31, 1816. While living in North Hero, Isaiah worked as a lumber boss on the St. Lawrence River, about forty miles west of Vermont.

Isaiah and Daphne sold their land in North Hero to a Samuel Butler on January 18, 1817,[6] and that is the last we hear of them until Jacob was born on April 2, 1819, in

Salem (modern Conneaut), Ashtabula County, Ohio, a small farming town located in the extreme northeast corner of Ohio, bordered by Lake Erie on the north and Pennsylvania on the east.[7] Isaiah was sheriff in Salem in 1819.

The Hamblins subsequently settled in the town of Munson in Geauga County, just west of Ashtabula County,[8] where Olive Haynes was born on May 1, 1821, and Adeline Amarilla on September 18, 1823. Adeline would later be Jacob's only sister to go west to Utah. Jacob's first brother, Obed, was born on February 25, 1826, followed by Alson Haynes on April 28, 1828.

At some point, the Hamblins moved to the township of Bainbridge, southwest of Munson, where William Haynes ("Gunlock") Hamblin, probably the most famous Hamblin sibling after Jacob, was born on October 28, 1830.[9] The next brother, Oscar, was born on April 4, 1833.[10] Edwin, born two years later, on May 20, was the longest-lived of Jacob's siblings, dying in 1925 in St. George, Utah, at the age of eighty-nine.[11]

Clearing and working the land in Munson and Bainbridge was back-breaking work. Jacob, who lived in Ohio till he was seventeen, wrote that it took twenty days of hard labor to clear one acre and "render it fit for the harrow and a crop of wheat."[12]

Strengthened by such labors, Jacob grew into a tall young man—as an adult he stood about six feet tall.[13] He learned the rudiments of reading and writing but later confessed that his "education was very limited."[14] If he attended any formal schools, he probably did so rarely. His literary style is not polished, but the amount that he wrote is remarkable—diaries, autobiographies, and numerous letters. Many frontiersmen left no primary documentation at all.

Jacob's religious tendencies followed his father's: "Altho I was taught to respect my parents and reverance the god of heaven my mind and attencion was never confind to any one sect or party but to live learn all the good that I could," he wrote.[15] As a teenager, he often brooded about religion:

> I was fifteen or sixteen years of age of reflecting very seriously on what was then called religion or the plan of salvation and the blesings and the promises spoken of in the scriptures which I heard much and listend to the different preachers of the day. My father who despised priestcraft and superstition cautioned me about connecting my self with any sect or party. I began to observe thear clashing and thear discord as I advanced in years. In short I could see no beauty or comeliness in thear religion no promises of the gifts and blessings of the gospel. I could read of these blesings aintehely [anciently] and that was all.[16]

In all of Jacob's writing, his spiritual experiences will be a central theme. He is not simply writing a historical record; he is recording his inner spiritual struggles, and later, the frequent miracles in his life. This is typical of early American autobiography, and certainly of Mormon biography.[17]

One evening, in Ohio, while Jacob was reading and reflecting on religion, he decided that if he would pray for understanding, he would get it.

> Acordingly went by my self to call on the name of the Lord but I could not get confidence enough to belive my prayer would be answerd. When I retired to my bed I could not refrain from sheading tears for I felt condemed to think I had not prayd.[18]

But that night Jacob had a remarkable dream. Early Mormons viewed their dreams as revelations from beyond the veil, and frequently wrote of them in their diaries and autobiographies.[19] After falling asleep, he was "imedtilly [immediately] walking in a beautiful road in search of some one who could give me an understanding of these things." He met "a person of smiling countenance" who directed Jacob to follow him. At a building by a large river, Jacob's guide handed him two books and told him to read them. "I was almost overjoyed," Jacob wrote, but his joy was tempered by the appearance of a skeptic, his father, at the door of the house, who

> immeditatly inquird my bissness. I told him what I had got. I thought he spoke very feelin[g]ly saying that he did not want that I should bring trouble on my self by embraceing any eror and deprive my self of rights and priviliges. I told him I had the privlage of readin[g] two books. He took the book and lookd at it and said he belived it to be true.[20]

Of course, Hamblin later would have identified the two books as the Bible and the Book of Mormon. But he includes a contemporary misreading of the sacred dream. He recounted it to a Baptist friend, who interpreted the books as the Old and New Testament and encouraged Jacob to attend Baptist services, predicting that Isaiah would convert if he did. "I attended thear meetings became acquainted with thear articels and creeds which I did not like. I then made up my mind I would join no Church believing that univve[r]slist doctrin as nigh right as eney."[21] Universalism held that Jesus's atonement would save all men.[22] It was a popular alternative to the standard Christian sects of the day, which often emphasized hellfire and damnation in their camp meetings and the necessity of conversion and baptism before salvation could be obtained.

While Jacob was in the midst of this religious searching, unfortunately, Isaiah Hamblin's Ohio farm project did not succeed. Jacob writes: "My father now Commenctt Clearing up a heavey timber farm ~~whear~~ when he from hardships and exposure lost his health and having a family of small children to maintain he failed paying for his land which kept him in limited circumstances."[23] Isaiah was reduced to poverty but somehow managed to keep his family afloat on the frontier.

The next logical step? Look even farther to the west, where the backbreaking work of clearing land and plowing through roots could be taken up once again! Jacob wrote of his family's move to Wisconsin, "My father from the information he had received of Mishigan thought he could [help his] family by moving them. Acordingly he left his family to visit that Country takeing me with him in company with two of his nephews." Jacob was then seventeen.

"In traveling through we found the best locations all occupied," he wrote.[24] When one thinks of the vast wildernesses in Michigan and Wisconsin even today, one can see that these westering Americans were particular about good farmland. Some were willing to travel farther and farther west to obtain it. Jacob writes that his father,

> finding some of our company that was jest setting out for a still newer contery lying west of lake Mishigan [accompanied them]. This was a vast unsettled willderness inhabited only by a few Indians or lamenites.[25] Finding apla[c]e which suted us we settled about twenty five miles from rensene [Racine] on lake Michigan.[26]

Hamblin continued, "It was a beautiful prarie which we named spring prarie from the many springs which we found thear. We all began to cultivateing the ground."[27] Though there was some timber on the land, this prairie country in the southeastern corner of Wisconsin probably did not need to be as extensively cleared as had the Ohio land.

The Hamblins settled in modern Lafayette, which was originally connected with Spring Prairie, west of the modern town.[28] Isaiah Hamblin was among the first settlers of the area. The "Pilgrim Fathers of Walworth County"—about thirty men heading thirty-one families—included, in Lafayette, Isaiah Hamblin, Sylvanus Longdon, and Isaac Fuller (husband of Melissa) and their families.[29] The *History of Walworth County* tells us that "Isaiah Hamblin, first settler in the town" came to Lafayette in June of 1836.[30] When he had gathered enough logs, the inhabitants of nearby towns showed up to help him raise the first house in the town.

Isaiah returned to Ohio to bring the rest of the family to Wisconsin, while Jacob was left behind to keep the new farm going. Another chapter in his spiritual autobiography now unfolds: "In his absence I past meney lonesome hours as I had always lived at home with my Mother," he wrote. In September 1836 he cut his leg, then "took cold in it which made me all most dispair of seeing my parents again as it was badly swollin and mutch inflamed."[31] But he managed to drag himself into a hazel thicket and, for the first time in his life, pray: "I called on the Lord to hav mercy on me and spare my life."[32] A neighbor called at the house, saying she had felt impressed to stop, and when she saw Jacob's plight, said that she could bring the "swelling all out," which she did by some kind of steam treatment, and Jacob's life was spared.[33]

Isaiah and the greater part of the Hamblin family arrived at Spring Prairie in the late fall of 1836, while Daphne and the two youngest children joined them the following summer.[34] When Olive married Henry Johnson that August, it was Spring Prairie's first wedding.[35]

Isaiah and Daphne's next child, Francis Marion (Frank), was born in Spring Prairie on November 27, 1839.[36] The baby of the family, Frederick, was born on February 12, 1841.[37]

Life in Spring Prairie was not easy, and Jacob wrote, "I past through many hardships the two f[o]llowing years."[38] In early 1838 the eighteen-year-old Jacob, finding it necessary to pay for land he had claimed, packed a bundle of clothing and left the Hamblin household to work in the lead mines in Galena, (modern) Illinois, some seventy-five miles to the west.[39] Lead mining was extremely dangerous work.[40] Twice Jacob, working about a hundred feet underground, barely escaped being buried alive by cave-ins. Once, apparently in late 1838, he was working some two hundred feet beneath the surface when a rock fell unexpectedly and struck the man who was working next to him, killing him instantly. Jacob had to drag the mangled body along the tunnel and tie a rope around it to raise it to the surface. This grotesque experience so horrified him that he felt a total revulsion for mining, and that night he decided he would not go beneath the earth again.[41] He had enough money to buy his claim in Spring Prairie, and it was time to return.

He narrowly escaped death again on his journey home as he trudged along snow-covered paths in severely cold weather. At one point, "over come with hunger fategue and cold," he took shelter in an old cabin, and nearly froze to death. But "some power" was protecting him, and he suddenly realized his danger and started walking again. "Was exceeding thankful to my hevnly Father that I was not left to perish in the wilderness."[42] Looking back much later, Hamblin felt that his life was being continually spared by a higher power.

But Jacob would soon face a challenge greater than any he had encountered earlier: marriage.

> The third of oct 1839 I mared [married] Mis Lucinda Taylor young and little experiance[d] as I was my self. This was contrar[y] to the feelings of my Parence. When the Mariage Seremony was over I felt condmed for what I had don. I would of given all I possesed if I could of ben freed. Thus was I pead [paid] for my disobedience in that I had no joy in the wife I had taken.[43]

Three years younger than Jacob, Lucinda Taylor had been born on August 24, 1823, to Daniel Taylor and Sarah McCrumbie. She is a tragic figure, and the marriage was clouded from the beginning, at least as Jacob told the story in his later life. He wrote of Lucinda in a generally negative way, but some statements of his next wife, Rachel, balance his account with a more sympathetic portrait.

Soon he had an heir: "[On] jayuary 11th ~~1840~~ 1841 my wife was deliverd of a son," he wrote.[44] Duane Hamblin was the first of Hamblin's twenty-four biological children.[45] Two months later Jacob bought eighty acres of land in Walworth County.[46]

Up to this point, Jacob had lived a fairly unremarkable life on the American frontier—though still in the Midwest by modern standards. If Mormonism had not touched him, it is possible that he would have spent his life as a Wisconsin farmer. But soon a Mormon missionary would visit Walworth County, a contact that would lead Jacob to the far frontier of the American West, to a life of hardship, exploration, and danger in the deserts, mesas, high plateaus, and canyons of southern Utah and northern Arizona.

2

"He Preached What I Had Long Been Seeking For"

Mormonism, 1842–1849

Mormonism, which would transform Jacob Hamblin's life, began with the visions of the teenage Joseph Smith Jr., who came to be accepted by Mormons as a prophet.[1] According to Smith, an angel, Moroni, who had lived long ago as a prophet in America, appeared to him and directed him to unearth an ancient book written on golden plates buried not far from Smith's home in Manchester, New York. According to Mormon belief, Joseph was eventually able to obtain these plates and translate them with a combination of Old Testament divinatory and early American folk magic techniques. This became the Book of Mormon, published in 1830, the most important scripture in Mormonism, as Mormons believe that the Bible, while originally perfect, has been partially corrupted by flawed transmission.

Smith taught that, since there had been a universal apostasy of the early Christian church, it was necessary for the church to be restored by angels, including the restitution of an authoritative priesthood. In many ways, Mormonism became as authoritarian as the Catholic Church, rejecting the baptisms and authority of all other churches and religions. Early Christian rituals and gifts of the spirit, healing and speaking in tongues, were also restored. Mormonism, then, lies solidly in the tradition of early Christian primitivist, or restorationist, churches, such as Methodism, Campbellitism, and Adventism, that viewed themselves as restoring Biblical realities and institutions.[2]

Joseph Smith organized a church in 1830, which eventually came to be called the Church of Jesus Christ of Latter-day Saints, nicknamed Mormonism. After a period of change and development, the church's present organization crystallized; it was led by a prophet-president and two counselors (the three together forming the First Presidency), supported by a quorum of twelve apostles. Joseph Smith felt especially close to the Old Testament and restored many characteristic "Old Covenant" institutions, such as prophets, temples, and polygamy.

Early Mormons viewed their organization as not only a church, but as a political kingdom, which would grow and prepare for the second coming of Jesus Christ and would usher in a millennium of peace. Thus Mormon converts were called to "gather to Zion," wherever that was in early church history: in New York; Kirtland, Ohio; Far West, Missouri; Nauvoo, Illinois; or Salt Lake City, Utah. Wherever they settled, Joseph Smith and the Mormons experienced political and religious tensions with local non-Mormons, and sometimes they suffered violence from mobs, especially in Missouri and Illinois.

On October 7, 1841, Mormon elders Lyman Stoddard, who would become Hamblin's spiritual father, and Elisha H. Groves were sent on a mission to Wisconsin.[3] Stoddard, forty-seven, had converted to Mormonism in about 1836, gathered with his family to Kirtland and Nauvoo, and served a number of missions.[4] In February 1842, Lyman spoke at a house in the Spring Prairie area, and one of Jacob's neighbors suggested to Jacob that he go listen to him, as the Mormon had preached "more Bible doctrine" than anyone he had ever heard. This report interested Hamblin intensely, to the extent that he could barely attend to his regular daily routine after hearing it, and he made sure to attend the Mormon elders' next meeting.[5] As soon as he entered the house, Jacob felt electrified merely on seeing the Mormon elder's face and hearing his voice. Stoddard

> spoke of the privil[i]ges of the mormons or [Latterd]ay saints said in as m[u]tch as ~~or~~ anyone would ob[e]y the gospell that they should obtain knowledge and the gifts ~~of~~ and blessings spoken of in the Scripturs should follow. I thought from the many proovs he introduced if the gospel was [*illegible*] I ever herd he preacht it.[6]

Jacob was a seeker who had finally become a finder: "He preached what I had long been seeking for." As he listened, he was overcome by the "plain and natural" principles Stoddard taught (probably another reference to Mormonism's restoration of Biblical principles). Stoddard sat down, and Hamblin was entirely convinced of his message. But somehow he needed some further spiritual witness. How would he *know* that these things were true?

As if in answer to Hamblin's unspoken question, Stoddard rose to his feet again and said that if anyone in the congregation wanted to know whether these things were true, he should be baptized and have hands laid upon his head for the gift of the Holy Ghost. Then he would have a sure knowledge. Hamblin wrote that his mind was so "fired" by this challenge that he decided on the spot that he would be baptized, even if it meant losing his family and the loosing of "every earthly tie."[7]

When Jacob went home and told Lucinda of his decision, she replied that if he was baptized, she would leave him. Undeterred, Jacob went in search of Stoddard and found him late at night. He told him he wanted to be baptized and asked to see the "Mormon Bible." Stoddard, misunderstanding him, gave him a regular Bible, but Jacob explained that he wanted to see the "new" Bible. Stoddard handed him a Book of Mormon, the book that would shape Hamblin's view of American Indians for the rest of his life. Simply holding it in his hands caused Hamblin to feel a strong outpouring of the Holy Ghost: "I felt like opening my mouth and declaring it to be a revelation from God," he wrote.[8]

In the autobiography, Jacob writes that, "being fully convi[n]sed of the truth I couldnot rest in mind u[n]til I obeyd. I was baptised the 3d of march 1842."[9] In Little, Hamblin's published autobiography, Hamblin recounts that he had arisen early in the morning, and on the way to the pool of water where he would meet Stoddard, he had a momentary lapse of purpose as he thought of losing his entire family after becoming a Mormon. (He knew that his father would be strongly opposed to Mormonism.) But as his pace slackened, he felt a presence, his grandfather, descend from the sky and tell him: "Go on, my son; your heart cannot conceive, neither has it entered into your mind to imagine the blessings that are in store for you, if you go on and continue in this work." Strengthened by this message from beyond the veil, Hamblin hurried to the pool and was baptized.[10]

While Stoddard had been planning to leave the following day, Hamblin and other interested neighbors convinced him to stay, and Stoddard was able to organize a branch of the church in the Spring Prairie area.[11]

Hamblin had worried that he would lose his family after becoming a Mormon, but Lucinda did not pack up and leave. Isaiah's reaction was predictably negative: he came to visit at Jacob's house, but would not come in. From outside, he told Jacob that he had hoped he had raised his children in such a way that they would not be deceived by "priestcraft," then walked away.[12] Jacob's friends also turned against him: "I felt that I was hated by all my former acquaintances. This was a great mystery to me," he wrote.[13] Nevertheless, he predicted that he would baptize his father within two years.

A chain of miracles brought about Lucinda's conversion. Her father took great delight in abusing and insulting his son-in-law, and one day Jacob said in return, "You will not have the privilege of abusing me much more." A few days later, Daniel Taylor grew sick and died. This dark prophecy presages similar deaths Hamblin predicted, much later, in Indian territory.

One day Lucinda surprised Jacob by saying she was no longer an unbeliever, as her father had appeared to her in a dream and "told her not to oppose me any more as she had done; and that he was in trouble on account of the way he had used me."[14] Soon Lucinda was baptized, to Jacob's great joy.

Hamblin's entrance into the LDS Church was a fairly typical early Mormon conversion. He had always accepted the Bible, interpreted literally, and fully believed in God, but was also suspicious of ministers and established religions. He was fascinated by the idea of modern prophecy and scripture. Mormonism's restorationism, its new scripture and revelation, its authoritarianism, and its millennialism all were powerful attractions.[15] Three factors in Mormonism had special relevance to him. First, as we have seen, he believed thoroughly in the miraculous and felt that Biblical miracles had been restored in modern America. Fully accepting modern prophets as his spiritual leaders, he became something of a prophet himself, with visionary insight and special healing powers.

Second, he was an entirely typical Latter-day Saint in his acceptance of visionary apocalypticism.[16] This kind of millennial vision, which expected an imminent end of the world, was characteristic of many religions in early America; one historian wrote that Americans in the early nineteenth century were "drunk on the millennium."[17]

Third, Jacob would have been introduced to the Mormon concept of the American Indian as he first began to read the Book of Mormon, which told a history of Israelites, led at first by two prophets, Lehi and his son Nephi, who had departed from Jerusalem in 600 BC, traversed the ocean in ships, and settled in America. Thus Latter-day Saints viewed Indians of North and South America as descendants of Lehi, divided into two main groups, Nephites (light-skinned, originally more righteous) and Lamanites (dark-skinned, originally more wicked). Jesus visited the Nephites and Lamanites soon after his resurrection, bringing about a long period of righteousness in the Americas. However, the Nephites and Lamanites both fell away from the true gospel again and the Nephites, who had become exceptionally corrupt, were destroyed by the Lamanites after long, terrible wars.

Thus the Latter-day Saints accepted (and still accept) American Indians as "the scattered remnant of Israel"—descendants of the lost tribes of Israel. This was not an idea original to the Mormons, but no one else believed it with such fervor and intensity as did the Latter-day Saints, due to its prominence in the Book of Mormon.[18]

After his conversion, Hamblin was suddenly a component of a dynamic, tightly-knit community, the early Church of Jesus Christ of Latter-day Saints. He would look upon meetings with other Mormons as a special joy and privilege, and in February 1843, he attended a conference in Milwaukee County in which he was ordained an elder.[19]

Soon thereafter Hamblin visited his father's home and told him of his ordination and that "the signs followed my administrations." Isaiah ordered Jacob out of the house "for believing such nonsense." Not long after this Isaiah contracted spotted fever, and both Jacob and his mother feared that he would soon die, but Jacob felt that God would spare his father if he, Jacob, prayed for him. After a visit to Isaiah one night, Jacob retired to a place in the wilderness and prayed. When he returned to his parents' house, his mother was waiting for him at the door with good news. Isaiah had recovered and wanted to talk to him. He asked Jacob why he had visited and then departed, and Jacob confirmed that he had left to pray for his father's recovery. He was a believer in the signs of God, he said, and that they followed the true saints.

"Well," Isaiah replied, "if it is the gospel, I would like to know it; but if it is priestcraft, I want nothing to do with it." Isaiah held onto his distrust for any organized religion, but at least seemed willing to listen to his son for the first time.[20]

For nineteenth-century Mormons, conversion was not just psychological and spiritual, but geographical. New converts were called to gather with the main body of the Saints, now in Nauvoo, Illinois. For a thoroughgoing convert such as Jacob Hamblin, then, the centripetal attraction of Mormonism was an irresistible force, and he began to make plans to move to Nauvoo. But before this move, he records two miracles.

Shortly after his father's recovery from illness, Jacob was sent on a mission to the Indians at Lake Winnebago, but when he arrived, he found the men away hunting. Returning home, he found his wife with "hur fase badly swolen and in mutch pain from an efectted tooth." She asked Jacob to administer to her—a common Mormon rite in which the healer anoints the sick person with consecrated oil, lays hands on his or her head, then gives him or her a verbal blessing. Jacob did so and "the pain left in stantly."[21] Lucinda had apparently become thoroughly converted and now looked to Hamblin as a person with special spiritual power. Little Duane, who had been suffering an unspecified "lingrin[g] deces [disease]," was also healed.[22]

Finally, just as the Hamblins were preparing to leave Spring Prairie for Nauvoo, the branch president at nearby Burlington, Aaron Smith, sent his son to ask that Jacob come quickly as he, Aaron, was suffering from a fever and was near death. When Jacob arrived, Smith confessed that he had been negligent in his church duties and promised to reform if healed. "I Prayed and laid my ... hands on his head," wrote Hamblin. "The feaver left him. He thanked the Lord made great promices that he would bemore faithful &c."[23] Clearly, Jacob had become a spiritual leader in his community.

Anxious that his family receive the message of Mormon salvation, he found that his sister Melissa would listen to him, and he soon "convinsed hur of the truth of the gospel." The conversion of his family had begun. After she was baptized, Melissa, too, "manifested a great anxiety about our kinsfolks," and Jacob prophesied that they would join the church and that he would baptize some of them himself.[24]

On September 15, 1843, Jacob and Lucinda had their second child, Martha Adaline.[25] Later that month, Jacob, Lucinda, Duane, and newborn Martha bade Spring Prairie farewell, "leeving all that was near and drear [dear] to me by the ties of nature.... My feelings I cannot describe," wrote Jacob.[26] Family head Isaiah Hamblin was especially distraught at seeing his son caught up in Mormonism. According to Jacob, "My Father thinking I was desceived could not refrain from shedding teers."[27]

The Hamblins traveled west a hundred miles to the Mississippi, where they bought passage on a steamer to Nauvoo. En route, Jacob records another miracle: during his family's second night of travel, Martha "was taken sick with the feaver."[28] Seeing his wife's concern for her, Jacob isolated himself and prayed for the child, and she soon regained her health.

The Hamblins arrived in Nauvoo at night, and the next morning Jacob walked through the unique theocratic riverside town. In September 1843 it was a bustling metropolis of about ten thousand people, comparable in size to Chicago at the time. A number of impressive public buildings and private residences could be found in the city center, and the Nauvoo Temple was slowly rising on a hill to the east.[29]

Hamblin sought out the residence of Joseph Smith, the charismatic leader whom Mormons regarded as a prophet fully the equal of Abraham, Moses, Isaiah, or Peter. A boy told him where Smith lived, but warned him not to take any money with him or Smith would get it. Hamblin thought this was curious advice and asked the boy if he was a Mormon. He affirmed that he was, and the son of a high priest.

At Smith's home, Jacob immediately sensed that a "tall, noble-looking man" standing outside talking with another man was the prophet. As Jacob observed him, a man came to Smith and asked him to repay money he had loaned him, and Smith replied that he would try to get the money that day. Hamblin approached and offered the prophet money, but Smith replied, as Hamblin later remembered the exchange, "Keep your money. I will not borrow until I try to get what is owing me. If you have just come in and wish to pay your tithing, you can pay it to Brother Hyrum; he sees to that."[30] Jacob had seen and spoken with the prophet, always a memorable moment for Mormon newcomers to Nauvoo.

However, Jacob may have had trouble finding work in Nauvoo, for he spent the winter chopping wood on an island in the Mississippi, twenty miles north of the Mormon city.[31] Presumably, Lucinda and the children lived there with him.

Hamblin probably visited Nauvoo periodically and apparently heard a sermon by Joseph Smith in which he preached that the time had come when the promises of Malachi would be fulfilled, when the hearts of the fathers would turn to the children and the children to their fathers. He challenged the Saints to pray until they received this spirit. Hamblin, a true believer, obeyed; he repeatedly sought privacy early in the morning to pray for the spirit of Malachi. In reply to his prayers, he felt an "influence" that showed him his own absolute nothingness before God. Hamblin, weighed down before this overwhelming vision, for a time almost wished he had never been born. However, he then received a witness that man could receive the highest salvation but that a person must walk by the fullest obedience to attain eternal life.[32] This realization drew him up out of the existential blackness of his initial feelings.

Years later, he told a friend in Utah that he had actually received a call from Joseph Smith to serve a mission among Indians. Passing the house of Smith's father, Joseph Smith Sr., one day, Joseph Smith Jr. came out and asked Hamblin's name.

When Jacob told him, he invited him inside and told him that he "wanted to set him apart to his mission among the tribes of the Lamanites." The two Smiths, Jr. and Sr., together performed this ordinance.[33] Jacob then asked when he would leave on this mission. Joseph reportedly replied, "You will commence in the thirty-fifth hour."

According to Hamblin, Smith also told him there was a hollow in the North Pole, where a part of the earth had been removed when the ten tribes were taken, and when the ten tribes' part of the planet was returned, the earth would reel like a drunkard. This kind of freewheeling, otherworldly speculation was characteristic of the Mormon prophet.[34] For early Mormons, the apocalyptic vision was never far away.

Jacob would soon be able to support Joseph Smith in a concrete way. Smith, thoroughly disenchanted with the political parties of America and their leaders, became a candidate for the presidency of the United States in January 1844. He produced a pamphlet with his views and prepared to mobilize Mormon elders as his political supporters throughout the United States. Historians have debated whether Smith thought he could actually win the election or became a candidate merely to publicize his views and to educate America on the Mormons' situation and message. In any event, during April conference, the apostles, in charge of missionary work, sent a small army of elders out to America.[35] "I felt anxious to go on sutch amission," wrote Hamblin, and submitted his name.[36] For the state of Maryland, the three missionaries assigned were Jacob Hamblin, Patrick Norris, and Lyman Stoddard.[37] Apparently, Hamblin was now ordained a seventy, the second of three ranks in the higher, Melchizedek priesthood.[38] Apostles George A. Smith and Amasa Lyman performed the rite, both of whom would soon have extensive histories in western and southwestern America. Smith, who had been called to be an apostle in 1839, would become a close friend of Hamblin. A monumental (270 pounds) and jovial man, he was well loved among the saints. He led the Iron Mission in southern Utah in 1851.[39] He served as Church Historian in Salt Lake, and as a result, pioneers in southern Utah, including Jacob Hamblin, often sent him letters and reports.

Before Jacob left for the east, he decided to visit his family in Wisconsin first and try again to convert them. But when he arrived at Spring Prairie, he found that his father and one of his brothers-in-law (possibly Isaac Fuller, husband of Melissa) had moved once more, buying land thirty miles from Nauvoo. On the way back to Nauvoo Jacob tried to find them, even though he had no idea what their exact location might be. Near Burlington in Warren County, Iowa, he "took acourse back in to the contry as I was directted by the Spirit," and in the evening he found his relatives "in a scirt of timber halling [hauling] house logs." To his surprise, he found that his brother-in-law had become a Mormon, and, to his probable amazement, his father was also "a believeing," though he was not yet fully converted. It must have been a joyful reunion, and the next morning Hamblin returned to Nauvoo elated.[40]

There, Hamblin found that Stoddard and Norris had been reassigned and instead John Myers, a thirty-year-old convert of eight years from England, would be his companion in Maryland. They left Nauvoo on May 21. Hamblin's autobiography suddenly begins to record dates and places—clearly, he was now copying from a missionary journal, which records the typical vicissitudes of a Mormon missionary traveling without purse or script, meeting opposition at times, and preaching to profoundly interested listeners at other times.

After traveling south and east by steamboat, they reached Pittsburgh and set out through Pennsylvania for Maryland. At "Mecanics town" (possibly Mechanicsburg in south-central Pennsylvania), there was "an excitement" and Hamblin and Myers were threatened with "a coat of tar and feathers." Nevertheless, they "still travaild about throu[gh] the diferant Townes preaching whare ever we could get the chance. We ware pursecutted for the gospels Sake sometimes cast forth and compelled to ly on the ground and in the open air."[41]

But the mission would soon end in shock and mourning. Back in Nauvoo, tensions between Mormons and non-Mormons had heightened, Joseph and Hyrum Smith were arrested, and on June 27 were killed by a mob while imprisoned in nearby Carthage. The news did not reach the eastern United States quickly, but Hamblin and Myers were told of the Smiths' lynching by non-Mormons sometime around July 4.[42] Jacob found it hard to believe this news but was depressed by the report nevertheless. For many early Mormons, the violent death of a living prophet equivalent to a Moses or Isaiah would be almost unbelievable. "I know I felt very meloncoly and my spirits deprest," he wrote. When he offered to preach in Mechanicsburg, the non-Mormons "manifested a spirit of exultation" and Hamblin "felt more like weeping than preaching."

On July 14, Hamblin wrote, while on his way to Hagerstown to fulfill an appointment, "I asertaind from a privet letter the truth that the Prophet and Patriarch ware Marterd. My feelings I will not attempt to describe for a moment all was lost." The overwhelming burden of working through cognitive dissonance descended on this young Mormon convert, and he thought of his appointment that night:

> I thought I could not Preach and that I was under no obligation to in as mutch [inasmuch] as they had kiled the man that God had sent to restore all things. I couldnot refrain from weeping. I turned aside to giv vent to my feelings. As I was a bout to leeve the Road I met two or three purson[s]. One of them observed I wonder what will become of Elder Hamblins Morman President. I could heardly restrain myself. I felt as ~~if I coul~~ if I could be ani~~lated th~~ annilated it would be a great blesing to me. I stopt ~~my~~ under a tree. The thoughts

> that the Prophet was dead was more than I could well endure. Thare apeard to be the wate of a Mountain on me. I thought it would crush me to deth.[43]

But as often, Hamblin turned to prayer: "At length believing it must be the power of the Devel an[d] knowing that there was something rong I Prayd to my Hevnly father for the Holy Spirit. After alittle all was wright." That night Hamblin met with Myers and they concluded that they should return home after meeting all of their scheduled appointments.[44] They left Hagerstown on August 5; at Pittsburgh, Hamblin was low on money and wondered how he would obtain passage back to Nauvoo. He happened upon a Mormon woman whose daughter had scarlet fever and he gave her a blessing, after which she was much better. The woman's non-Mormon husband was so grateful that he offered Jacob passage and even extra money if he needed it. So, with a confluence of miracles, Jacob's needs were taken care of on the journey home.[45] He arrived at Nauvoo on August 24th.[46]

The problem of who would succeed Smith as church president now faced both the church and Hamblin. Smith had not left a definite successor in case of his death, and the current LDS practice of the senior member of the Quorum of Twelve Apostles automatically becoming president was not yet in place. So the main struggle was between Sidney Rigdon, a brilliant but unstable leader who had been first counselor in the first presidency, and the forceful Brigham Young, the senior apostle in the Quorum of the Twelve. Hamblin heard Rigdon speak but was not impressed: "I listened afew minits and said in my hart [that it] was not the vois of the trew S[h]ep herd."[47]

Therefore, Hamblin chose to follow Brigham Young rather than any of the groups that stayed in the Midwest. He subsequently developed a close bond with Young and gave him his loyalty throughout his life (though at times there were tensions between them). Hamblin would stay with the group of Latter-day Saints who would settle the mountains, deserts, and canyons of the far West.

After a brief stay in Nauvoo, Hamblin reunited with Lucinda and the children, who were living with Jacob's sister, Melissa Fuller, probably near Burlington.[48]

The succession crisis having resolved, to a large extent, the next major obstacle facing the church was the continued conflict with non-Mormons in Illinois. This was a chaotic period in LDS history, sometimes called a war. Though there were no actual battles, non-Mormons carried out numerous vigilante actions that resulted in tremendous destruction of Mormon property.[49] Mormon militarism was carried out by a force named the Nauvoo Legion (a group and name that would survive through the years and be a factor in the history of early Utah). Hamblin was recruited to become "one of the minit men to assist in watching the movements of the enemy" and served in this paramilitary or spy group throughout the following winter.[50]

During this time Hamblin's brother, Obed, possibly living near Burlington, was near death with malaria and sent for Jacob. Jacob "Praid for him and anointed him" and told him he would recover. Soon Obed was up and about, and a week later visited Jacob in Nauvoo.[51]

The healing so impressed Jacob's parents that Isaiah attended April conference in Nauvoo "to here for him self." When conference ended, both of Jacob's parents asked to be baptized. Isaiah told his son, "It is your privilege to baptize your parents, for you have prayed for them in secret and in public; you never gave them up; you will be a Joseph to your father's house."[52] And so, on April 17, Jacob wrote, "I Baptised my Father and Mother."[53] Isaiah explained to Jacob that no one's preaching had convinced him of Mormonism, but God had shown him its truth in dreams.[54] Despite Isaiah's antisectarian, skeptical tendencies, he had a visionary side, like Jacob. Undoubtedly, this was a season of rejoicing for Jacob and his clan. Another cause for celebration was the birth of another child in Jacob and Lucinda's family, Maryette Magdaline, on May 17.[55]

In the summer of 1845 Hamblin worked on the temple, doing any jobs required of him.[56] But the conflict with non-Mormons continued to escalate, and anti-Mormon vigilantes closed in around Nauvoo, burning and looting. Jacob once again became a "minute man," serving both in a horse company and a rifle company.[57] After taking part in a major Nauvoo Legion action, possibly in September 1845,[58] Jacob returned to Nauvoo and immediately "was taken very sick with the billious feaver"—fever combined with severe nausea, vomiting, and diarrhea. Some of Hamblin's relatives gave him up for dead, but "by the blessings of the Lord I recoverd," he wrote.[59]

Even before his death, Joseph Smith had made vague plans to lead the Mormons westward. Brigham Young and the Twelve continued these intentions and plans, but it was uncertain exactly when the Saints would leave Nauvoo and where they would go. By summer 1845, they had chosen the Salt Lake Valley, in modern Utah, as their destination.[60]

In September, with mobs destroying outlying Mormon communities and causing these terrorized Mormons to gather to Nauvoo for protection, Brigham Young and the Twelve made the decision to abandon Nauvoo in spring 1846.[61] After the Mormons formally agreed to depart, an uneasy truce with the non-Mormon vigilantes prevailed. Preparations for the journey west began in earnest in early October 1845, while the Saints were still struggling to finish the temple. Hamblin helped to obtain timber to make wagons for their impending exodus.[62]

In December 1845 the temple was sufficiently finished that many thousands of Mormons were able to do their "endowments," or temple rites, there.[63] These few months of temple ritual were a Pentecostal moment of religious triumph for the Mormons before their exodus into the wilderness. Jacob and Lucinda took part, receiving their endowments on January 5, 1846.[64]

Hamblin left his family in Nauvoo in February 1846 and "went with the church as Pyeonee[r] about 4 weeks."[65] "Pioneer," in this early stage of the Mormon exodus, meant those who went ahead and prepared the way for the main body of Mormon travelers, improving roads and camps, and looking out for dangers.[66] Going ahead before the migrations of the saints would be the role Hamblin would play for the rest of his life.

Jacob then returned to Nauvoo for Lucinda and the children—Duane, five, Martha, two, and Maryette, about eight months old—and brought them to "Pisgey," Mount Pisgah, one of the Mormon way stations in Iowa, about two miles west of modern Thayer.[67] Apparently, Jacob's parents and siblings also traveled with him. His mother was in bad health before leaving Nauvoo, so the family delayed leaving for two weeks. However, she seemed to rally, and so the Hamblins started to cross Iowa with her. But she apparently could not tolerate the bad weather and difficult travel—she died quietly in the night near Mount Pisgah and was buried beside the trail. Jacob sadly wrote, "My mother ... died on the road from Nauvoo."[68]

At Pisgah, Jacob lacked financial resources, so he decided to backtrack a hundred miles to work in non-Mormon settlements "for flower [flour] and other nessiceries."[69] By early August 1846, he was living in Bloomfield, Iowa, near Fox River, about forty miles west of Nauvoo, where he was stricken with malaria, which combined onsets of sudden coldness and rigor with episodes of high fever and head and back pains and lasted for months. "I was thare taken sick ... with the chilles and feaver and could scarcely walk," he wrote.[70]

Jacob and his family were delayed in Bloomfield for a year and a half, living in "a miserable hut," suffering intermittent attacks of malaria, which sometimes struck the whole family and which once kept Jacob from working for half a year. Interspersed with these trials were moments of Pentecostal exaltation and miracles. One day he wrote, "I was blest with the power of the spirit. My Wif S[p]oke in toungs. The same was interpeted to us that we should all liv o[n]ly be faithful." The ecstatic gift of speaking in tongues was common practice in early Mormonism; it was generally followed, as in this case, by another member giving the interpretation.[71] Another day, quails fed the Hamblins, just as they had fed the children of Israel during the Exodus.[72] Jacob's last child with Lucinda, Lyman Stoddard Hamblin, was born in Bloomfield on March 11, 1848.[73]

But scraping together the resources to come west to Utah seemed almost impossible. Finally, with the help of Jacob's brother Obed, Jacob and Lucinda left Bloomfield. They arrived at Council Bluffs, on the Iowa side of the Missouri River, on April 11, 1848, where Jacob found his father, seven brothers, and one sister "in good helth. This was a great comfort to me," he wrote.[74] Council Bluffs, which the Mormons renamed Kanesville, served as the setting-off point for Mormon pioneers traveling west to Utah between 1846 and 1852. Apostle Orson Hyde presided over this town of some 350 log cabins, two log tabernacles, and numerous commercial buildings.[75] Jacob built a house "within half a mild [mile] of the Counsill house"—a square log meetinghouse close to Brigham Young's home. Jacob and his family would stay in the Kanesville area two years, probably time they needed to prepare financially for the journey to Utah.

In the autobiography, Jacob now takes almost ten pages to describe the breakup of his marriage with Lucinda, indicating a compelling need to justify and explain the divorce. This is painful reading, as Hamblin is harshly critical of his former wife and we do not have her side of the story.

Jacob started his time in Kanesville looking forward to close contact with fellow believers. "As I had ben absent or deprivd of the privileges of meeting with the Church for a long time I antisipated great comfort and satisfacion of again being with the Church," he wrote.[76] However, this moment of peace was not to be, due to tensions with Lucinda, who, according to Jacob, began telling falsehoods about Jacob to church leaders and his own children. In addition, he accused her of depleting family finances by selling everything in the household. "I saw that such a course of thing[s] was Sertin ruin to me and my children," he wrote, so he took his clothes and his three oldest children and left the house, leaving baby Lyman with her.[77]

Church leaders, including Lyman Stoddard, tried to counsel Jacob and Lucinda to restore the marriage, but despite another attempt at living together, Jacob eventually felt he had no choice but to made a complete break with his wife. Formal complaints were submitted to Apostle Orson Hyde, and Jacob finally received a divorce and custody of all the children. Hyde, he wrote, "gave me writing to take my childrin and leave the house to my wife. The next morning I took them and left."[78] This separation from Lucinda, which occurred in February 1849, was final.[79]

This story is primarily from Hamblin's holograph autobiography. From Hamblin family traditions a somewhat different, or perhaps complementary, view of the breakup emerges. Lucinda, who must have had terrible experiences in Bloomfield and now was probably living in very primitive circumstances in Kanesville, wanted to find a permanent place to live and feared the journey west to Utah. According to family traditions, Jacob's next wife, Rachel, said that Lucinda "was not a bad woman, she was just weak. As the time to go west came on, she felt she couldn't face it; we were all still badly under-nourished. She had a way to return to her home and plenty, and she took it. I do not entirely condemn her."[80] Faced with the daunting prospect of settling the far frontier, Lucinda turned back, by this account.

Now with four children to care for as a single parent, Hamblin also faced the challenge of working and accumulating resources to cross the plains. "My childrin ware shifted from plase to plas four or five times in course of the sumer," he wrote. "I done my best to keep them as becometh a Father but I couldnot in my situacion." No doubt, family members assisted in caring for the children, but he really needed a wife to help raise them. In the autobiography, he writes, "I then made upe my mind to get maried if I could find a woman that would suit me. I then went to see Mrs. Rachel Hendersowon an amiable woman. I found this woman was of a mild jentle disposition."[81]

The red-headed Rachel had been born on September 15, 1821, to Arza Judd and Lucinda Adams, in Bastard township (modern Rideau Lakes township), Leeds County, Eastern Ontario, Canada.[82] Her family converted to Mormonism and became stalwart members. One of her younger brothers was Zadok Knapp Judd, who would be a Mormon Battalion participant, and later an exploring companion of Jacob Hamblin.[83] She had apparently been married twice previously. The second husband was early Mormon apostle John E. Page, who had also married Rachel's sister Mary; Rachel became his plural wife.[84] Rachel left him when he became estranged from the church. The second husband was shoemaker James Henderson, "a fine man," a widower with two young sons and a daughter. Unfortunately, he died within a year of the marriage.[85] Rachel had had no children with either of these men, so concluded that she could not bear children.

An account of Jacob and Rachel's first meeting, given in the words of Rachel as remembered by Dudley Leavitt, shows that she and Jacob felt an immediate attraction. "We both liked each other instantly," said Rachel. "I gave him a chair, and he told me his story. I wanted to marry him, but I thought I should be fair with him." She then told Jacob she hadn't been able to bear children, and he replied, "You shall not only bear a child, but you shall bear children ... and like Jacob and Rachel of Old, our sons shall be Joseph and Benjamin."[86] Jacob, as was typical of early Mormons, was consciously assimilating himself and Rachel to events from Biblical, Old Testament times.

The couple was married on September 30, 1849, by Lyman Stoddard at Indian Creek, Iowa.[87] They combined her three stepchildren, William, John, and Eunice Henderson,[88] and Jacob's four children. Hamblin later wrote, "I hav had pease at home or in my family ever cence I hav livd with this kind eff[e]ctionate companion. I hav tasted the bitter I know well how to apresciate the sweet."[89]

3

"My Wife Violently Attacted with Colery"

Cholera Country: Crossing the Plains, 1850

Jacob and Rachel lived in the Indian Creek branch nine miles outside of Kanesville during the winter of 1849–1850.[1] Hoping to travel to Utah the following spring, he began preparations for the journey. In his published autobiography, these preparations involve a miracle. To make the overland journey, one had to acquire a wagon and a team of oxen to draw it, as well as a supply of provisions. However, one morning in the spring of 1850, Jacob's team had disappeared, along with other animals he had acquired, and he was unable to find them. This was a major disaster, and Jacob reluctantly decided he would have to wait till the following year to cross the plains.

But he began to have dreams in which he saw his team in the wilderness. After the vision was repeated three times, he rode off in search of the location he had seen. When he found it, there were his oxen and other animals. "These kind providences, with strict economy," allowed Jacob to start for Utah on schedule.[2]

This was one of the great years of Mormon overland emigration. According to one estimate, some eight hundred wagons and about twenty-one hundred Latter-day Saints crossed the plains in 1850.[3] That was also a year of tragedy for the pioneer companies, as cholera was endemic on the overland journey among both Mormons and non-Mormons.

Jacob wrote, "In May 29 1850 I started for the vally of the great Salt Lake." Evidently he and his family joined a camp of pioneers on this date. Then, on June 2, Apostle Orson Hyde made a major organization of the entire company. Hamblin was assigned to the company of Aaron Johnson, later well known as the bishop of Springville, Utah County. According to Hamblin, this company consisted of a hundred wagons, with three to nine persons to a wagon.[4] One hundred was the standard number for a Mormon company, which was then divided into fifties and tens. Hamblin was apparently in the first fifty, under forty-year-old Tennessee native Elijah Averett—later a southern Utah stalwart—as Jacob mentions Averett frequently in his diary.[5]

In Hamblin's family group, besides himself, were Rachel, Hamblin's four children with Lucinda—Duane, nine, Martha Adaline, six, Marryette Magdaline, five, and

Lyman, two—and Rachel's three Henderson stepchildren, all in their teens.[6] He had a small wagon, a yoke of oxen, and two cows.[7] In addition, members of Hamblin's extended family were in the Johnson company, including patriarch Isaiah Hamblin and Jacob's brothers Bill, twenty, Oscar, seventeen, Edwin, fifteen, Frank, eleven, and Fred, nine.

A week later, the actual overland journey began.[8] "I c[r]osed the Missourie River with my family the 8th of June," wrote Hamblin.[9] Emma Guymon Kearnes, eight years old at the time, remembered crossing the river peacefully on a flat boat, trailing her hand along in the water, as the cattle were swum across the river.[10] Hamblin, however, was almost killed during the crossing. His cattle were not swum across, but were put on the ferry, and during the crossing they gathered on one side of the flat boat and it capsized. While some Saints were able to hold onto the boat, or even climb up on its upended bottom, Hamblin tried to swim to a nearby landing but was swept past it by a strong current. Things looked bleak for him, as the following three miles offered only a perpendicular bank on his side of the river and the water was filled with whirlpools and eddies. However, he noticed a place where a path had been cut through to the river, and a woman was standing there at the riverbank. He swam as close to her as he could, reached out, and she was able to take his hand. "With a great effort, I was saved from the surging water," he wrote.[11] He had been lucky; accidents while crossing rivers or creeks were a common cause of death for overland travelers.[12] It was not the last time that Hamblin and his family would face death on this journey.

In the next few days, the journey began in earnest, with the Johnson company meeting the Oto-Missouri Indians (Southern Sioux, who required a ten-cent tariff for each wagon that passed through their territory) and passing through "butifel prairie country," as Hamblin wrote. In this first part of the trek westward, Mormons followed the standard Oregon Trail route along the Platte River.

But on June 14, just past Salt Creek, some of the company members began exhibiting symptoms of cholera.[13] The next day Hamblin wrote: "Travaild ten miles. Brother John Shipley died with the colery and Willis Johnson and some two or three others." Willis, twenty-two, was a son of Aaron Johnson.[14] Hamblin continues: "This was truly a mournfull scene to see women mourning for thare Husbands and childrin for thare Fathers but we were oblige[d] to leav them on the plaines burying them as desent as we could."[15] The sudden, shocking deaths; the intense mourning; the makeshift graves; the subsequent tension and fear—this was now cholera country.

Asiatic cholera had been brought to the overland trail from the eastern United States, but also from Asia up the Mississippi, and was flourishing at the time of the Gold Rush, an estimated 2,500 pioneers falling victim to this "ruthless destroyer" in 1850.[16] That summer, overland traveler Abraham Sortore wrote that along the Platte he was "scarcely out of sight of grave diggers" because of cholera.[17]

This disease, which was especially prevalent in the hot months of July and August, was caused by unsanitary conditions and infected water (which were typical of the camps of many rushed gold-seekers). The symptoms of cholera began with extreme, severe diarrhea, involving what pioneer doctors called "rice-water evacuations," followed by violent vomiting. Then there was a complete physical collapse or prostration. The pulse lessened to near imperceptibility; the eyes seemed to sink into the face; the skin wrinkled, turning blue or purple; the body was cool to the touch. This was followed by a violent cramping of muscles in the limbs and abdomen. If the victim survived the first day or two of cholera, he or she would regain warmth in the body and normal flesh color in the face.[18]

It is difficult to convey the panic caused by the speed, violence, and lethal nature of cholera attacks during an outbreak in a group, town, or pioneer company. When a person was struck by the disease, the family of the victim might be held in suspense for days, to see if they would also contract it. In the family of Horace Spafford, in the Aaron Johnson company, six members of a family of twelve died in the space of four days.[19]

Cholera transformed the overland route visually. Elijah Averett wrote, "We saw a great many gentile graves on the road. The cholera had Slayed them terribly. There was wagons, tires, clothing, guns, bedding, boots and shoes scattered along the road."[20] In Little, Hamblin describes passing the bodies of non-Mormon travelers, many from Missouri, who had been ravaged by the disease. These bodies had usually been lightly buried, sometimes with crude boards marking the graves, and wolves had often dug them up and devoured them, leaving bones behind. There were days when human bones were visible through most of the day.[21]

Hamblin's diary continues to record rough mileage, brief descriptions of the territory, and cholera. On the sixteenth, Thomas Kirk, a Mormon Battalion veteran, died, and the following day Hamblin wrote that "several [were] atacted with colery." The suddenness and violent nature of the disease is expressed vividly in Hamblin's laconic sentence. "Capt [Elijah] Evrits and Martha Meacham was violant[ly] attacted with colery" four days later, but "ware held [healed] by the blessing of God."

On the twenty-fourth, the company struggled through eight miles of rain and mud, then witnessed even more deaths: "Abel J Sarjent and Son died of Colery. 2 childrin died also. Several taken sick." Faced with this crisis, Aaron Johnson called a meeting in which the chaplain of the company, Daniel D. Hunt, chose "two from the Company to offer Prayr to God for the welfaire of the Saints."[22] Hunt, Elijah Averett, Aaron Johnson, and Isaac Hill "went out in the prarie and prayed that the Lord would stop the Cholery, and we had a testimony that it would stop," wrote Averett.[23] But the deaths only continued.

The following days, after the company slogged nine miles through mud and rain, cholera began to touch the Hamblin family, beginning with Jacob who suddenly had a severe pain in his side.[24] That night, at three in the morning, the "ruthless destroyer" seized Rachel with all its savagery: "My wife violently attacted with Colery," Jacob wrote.[25] She called out, "O Lord, help, or I die!"[26] However, Hamblin "prayd for hur and anointed hur in the name of the Lord. Coled [called] on Bro [George] Pectal and [Isaac] Hill to administer. She was relievd immediately."[27] The angel of death had passed by them.

Others in the company were not so fortunate. In a harrowing night, Polly Zerviah Johnson, Aaron Johnson's first wife, aged forty-two, and forty-eight-year-old Susan Davis Hunt, wife of Chaplain Daniel Hunt, both succumbed to cholera.[28] Jacob assisted at Susan's burial.

Nevertheless, the company "travaild fourteen miles through mud and water" that day, and camped within three miles of "Ft Chiles." Fort Childs, situated on the south bank of the Platte, in central Nebraska, was later called Fort Kearny (or Kearney). This was a famous meeting point of all trails west.[29] But the Mormons stayed a cautious three miles away from the fort, with its Gentile influences, and traveled nine miles away from it the next day.

At this point, Hamblin's marital past made a surprising reappearance. He wrote in his diary, "Saw Lucinda the Mother of my Childrin. She was the same old six pense as She said." One can only imagine Lucinda's awkwardness as she met her former husband and his new wife, and had a sad, affectionate reunion with her children. What Lucinda was doing so far west is unknown.

The cholera continued without mercy. On the same day that he met Lucinda, Hamblin wrote, "Bro. ~~Fora~~ Fords Child died."[30] The next day, June 29, Jacob himself was called to face death: "I was attacted with the colery," he wrote. "It was rebuked under the hands of my Father & Br Pictel [Pectol]." But if Jacob survived the first onset, it apparently led to another sickness. The next day, he wrote, "I found my Self ~~under the~~ attacted with a burning feaver. When the Company s[t]opt I was baptised by B[r]other Johnson. The feaver was rebuked."[31] This was a "baptism for health," a ritual often practiced in early Mormonism.[32]

Calling a halt, the company had a rest and a Sunday morning meeting, baptizing children (including Duane, Jacob's oldest), listening to preaching, and no doubt singing. Then they cleaned their wagons, spreading the contents out in the sunshine. This was the social culture, the texture of life, of the Mormon trail: religious meetings, with preaching and singing, combined with the most down-to-earth, practical occurrences. Emma Guymon fondly remembered singing round the campfires in the 1850 company, and also collecting the buffalo chips that fueled those fires.[33]

But the cholera was relentless. The day after the meeting, Hamblin, still suffering from fever, wrote, "Capt Hills wife died. One of Capt Johnsons family died. travaild 20 miles."[34]

Jacob's fever continued unabated the next day, during which the company forged ahead some twenty miles. On July 3, he was advised to ride in the wagon, and his son Duane took the whip to guide the oxen. Then another typical overland accident occurred, followed by a believer's miracle—Duane, struggling to handle a heavy outfit, pitched forward onto the ground, and both wheels on the left side of the wagon ran over him. When Jacob looked out of the wagon and saw him, he wrote, "The blood was runing out of his mouth. At first I gave him up for lost." But then a Mormon administration, presided over by Isaiah Hamblin, took place and Duane "was immediately heeled," according to Jacob. The boy stood up and said he was not hurt.[35]

On August 6, Jacob wrote, "12 miles. Helth increasing." And with those words his overland diary ends. Little records that Lyman, Jacob's youngest, suffered an attack of cholera. Once again, patriarch Isaiah administered to him, "rebuked the destroyer, and commanded him to depart from him, from the family and from the company." Isaiah commands "him," not "it." Apparently, Hamblin and his family saw cholera as the devil personified.[36]

According to George Pectol, the company passed Fort Laramie, in eastern Wyoming on July 25; four days later, Pectol survived a bout of "colery Morbus." On August 3, they crossed the Platte at Deer Creek, near modern Glenrock, Wyoming.[37] Averett writes, "It rained pretty hard on us, and in crossing the North Platt[e] some of our wagons swam, but we got across all right."[38] Crossing rivers during overland journeys was always dangerous. Drownings and losing wagons or livestock to quicksand were common.

The company now would have left the Platte to follow a tributary, the Sweetwater River, for about a hundred miles, ascending the seemingly endless foothills and mountains of the Rockies, to cross the continental divide at South Pass, in western Wyoming. They left the Oregon Trail at Fort Bridger (on the Blacks Fork of the Green River, in southwestern Wyoming) and followed the "Mormon trail" into northern Utah.

In late August, the company came to the Wasatch Mountains. They would have worked their way slowly through the difficult Echo Canyon, and soon these weary Mormon pioneers would have first caught sight of the Great Salt Lake, impressive in the distance, and its expansive valley—the new Mormon Zion, as Isaiah had prophesied in Old Testament times.

Finally, members of the Aaron Johnson company wended their way down Emigration Canyon, east of Salt Lake City, and completed their hegira: "We arived in the Citty [of "the Great Salt Lake"] the 6th of Sept," wrote Hamblin.[39] It wasn't really a city yet—Emma Kearnes remembered just a "little town" with a few houses.[40] But it was the new center of sacred gravity for the Mormons. Doubtless Jacob, Rachel, their children, and Jacob's father and siblings rejoiced.

4

"When I Herd the Schreems of the Chirldin"

Becoming a "Messenger of Peace" in Tooele, 1850–1853

After arriving in Salt Lake City, Mormons could not count on settling in the comparatively urbanized Salt Lake City area, as Brigham Young was an active colonizer. By 1850, there were Mormon settlements in Ogden and Provo, respectively about fifty miles north and south of Salt Lake City, and Tooele, about twenty-five miles west of the city.[1]

On September 20, Jacob and family were assigned to the one-year-old "Toela settlement."[2] A week later, Hamblin "reneud the gospel covenant together with my family," a reference to the practice of rebaptism that new arrivals in Utah often performed.[3] Just as traveling across the plains was a sacred event, an exodus carried out by the new children of Israel, so the arrival in the new Zion had to be sacralized by ritual. This was a new beginning.

Tooele, at the mouth of Settlement Canyon, was situated in southeast Tooele Valley, which is about twenty-five miles long and fifteen miles wide, separated from Salt Lake Valley by the Oquirrh Mountains; it is bounded on the north by the Great Salt Lake and on the west by the Stansbury Mountains. West beyond this range is Skull Valley, and farther west still lie the Cedar Mountains. Beyond these mountains lie sixty miles of the most forbidding salt desert in the United States. These valleys, mountains, and deserts were the home of the Goshute Indian tribe.

Early descriptions of Tooele Valley emphasize its grasslands.[4] Philip De La Mare, an early Tooele settler, described the valley as "a waving mass of grass three to four feet high."[5] This was not verdant farmland, as water supplies were limited, but it supplied excellent forage for cattle, and Mormons were using Tooele Valley for grazing as early as 1848.[6] An early settler, John Rowberry, was sent there in December 1849 to winter Apostle Ezra T. Benson's herd of cattle.[7] Cattle were important in the Mormon economy from the earliest period of Utah settlement; by 1850, there were some 12,000 head of cattle in Utah.[8]

Though Hamblin is known for his missions, explorations, and diplomacy in southern Utah and Arizona, Tooele was the place where he first began to interrelate with Indians, first as a soldier sent to punish them, later as a friend and negotiator. The story of the relationship of Mormon and Native American in early Utah history is complex and riddled with ambiguities.[9] In the Book of Mormon, the resurrected Christ predicts that the descendants of Lehi, not the European Gentiles, will inherit the Americas. Nevertheless, the Mormons will bring "a great and marvellous work" to the scattered remnant of Israel, the Lamanites, "after they have dwindled in unbelief because of iniquity."[10] Then the righteous Gentiles and the restored Lamanites will fight together in apocalyptic wars (destroying unrighteous Gentiles). It was expected that Lamanites, with the Saints of European descent, would build a New Jerusalem in America.

Thus, from the beginning, Mormon views of the American Indian have been remarkably positive, from one point of view. The Latter-day Saints viewed Indians as descendants of the pure blood of Israel; and in their central scripture, at least, there was the prophecy that Lamanites—Native Americans—would take a leading role in inheriting the Americas. The conversion of Indians in America would be one of the main events that would accomplish the restoration of Israel and the second coming of Christ in Mormon eschatology.[11]

Thus it is not surprising that from the beginning, the Mormon Church has made missions to Indians a priority. Given Latter-day Saint views of the high Israelite heritage of Indians and their exalted destiny, one might expect the Mormon record of coexistence with Indians on the western frontier would be exceptionally far-seeing, Christian, and understanding. In fact, one could argue that the Mormons' record was better than that of most whites of the period.[12] Typical whites in nineteenth-century America often viewed Indians as subhuman, "wolves to be exterminated or curs to be kicked aside, verminous and beggarly and treacherous pests."[13] For one newspaper editor in 1867, Indians were "a set of miserable, dirty, lousy, blanketed, thieving, lying, sneaking, murdering, graceless, faithless, gut-eating skunks as the Lord ever permitted to infect the earth, and whose immediate and final extermination all men, except Indian agents and traders, should pray for."[14] The great majority of Mormons were far removed from such attitudes toward Indians, and many influential Mormons sincerely sought for the good of the Indians that they lived near.

Nonetheless, Mormons often did not know how to bridge the yawning cultural divide between white and Indian in Utah. Even friendly Indians who were baptized Mormons did not always understand what membership in the LDS Church meant for whites.[15] Robert Utley has written, "The frontier condemned them [whites and Indians] to physical union, while a great cultural chasm condemned them never to really see or understand each other."[16] Of Brigham Young, Leonard Arrington writes that "as for countless other white men, the attempt to fit the Indians into the mold he desired had not succeeded."[17]

4.1. Brigham Young, second president of the LDS Church. An energetic colonizer, he often sent Jacob on his missions and exploratory expeditions. Courtesy Library of Congress.

This was also generally true of Protestant missions to Indians, as "missionary directors and patrons saw millennial hopes dashed upon the stubborn reality of culture conflict and misunderstanding," according to historian Robert F. Berkhofer Jr.[18] He suggests that the Protestant missions failed because they did not see that European civilization and Christianity had to be taught together—Indians could not suddenly become good Christians without understanding the basics of Western culture. In addition, Indians who did convert were often not accepted as equal due to American racial attitudes.[19]

When Indians did not convert quickly to Mormonism and European culture, as the Mormons had hoped, and in fact sometimes acted with hostility, some Mormons viewed them as decadent and cursed, "a dark, and loathsome, and a filthy people" (1 Nephi 12:23), "an idle people, full of mischief and subtlety" (2 Nephi 5:24), especially since they were regarded as descendants of Lehi's two wicked sons, Laman and Lemuel.[20]

Thus the Saints in Utah in Hamblin's day sometimes developed typically American negative attitudes toward Indians—pursuing the policy of harsh punitive actions against them whenever it was deemed necessary.[21]

Brigham Young has been regarded by some historians as a generous friend to the Utah Indians, and his saying that it was cheaper to feed Indians than to fight them is often quoted.[22] Mormons certainly were not responsible for genocidal massacres of Indians, such as occurred in other parts of the West.[23] For good and practical reasons, Young wanted Indians to be allies and friends. Nevertheless, his colonization of Utah and the Southwest, brilliantly carried out from one point of view, consistently pushed Indians from their traditional homelands and away from precious water resources. Mormon settlements and herds made progressively ruinous inroads into ecosystems on which Indians relied. Historian John Alton Peterson comments: "Often conducting themselves more like conquerors than missionaries, the Latter-day Saints displaced native societies and colluded with federal officials to place them on reservations."[24] Peterson remarks on the tragic irony that the Mormons, a displaced people, were now themselves displacing a people.

If Young was moderate in his policies concerning Indians on the whole, historian Howard Christy has portrayed him as initially more punitive than conciliatory with Utah's Indians, using a "mailed fist" as well as an "open hand."[25] Although historian Ronald W. Walker has argued that Christy's conclusions need tempering, nevertheless some of the primary documents Christy relies on in fact show that many Mormons—including Young in this early period—dealt harshly with Indians, who were admittedly sometimes hostile to Mormons.[26] Historians Floyd O'Neil and Stanford J. Layton write,

> Although the rhetoric of Brigham Young, Heber C. Kimball, and others contained the promise of accommodation and respect for the Indians, at that moment Young was pursuing a policy of extermination against the Utes of Utah Valley. Under his direction, and extending well beyond his tenure as superintendent, the Mormons continued to crowd the Indians off choice land, using force as necessary, until 1869 when the Utes were finally relocated to the Uintah Reservation and the other Indians were expelled from the territory or confined to its remote corners.[27]

Though "extermination" seems a harsh characterization, LDS leaders actually used the word in their dealing with Indians. Apostle Willard Richards stated, in a January 31, 1850, meeting dealing with Indian conflicts in Utah Valley: "My voice is for war, & exterminate them [the Indians]." Later in the same meeting, Brigham Young articulated an equally combative position: "I say go & kill them." Those present voted in support of this plan.[28] On February 14, 1850, Young advised military leader Daniel H. Wells: "If the Indians sue for peace grant it to them, according to your discretionary Judgment in the case.—If they continue hostile pursue them until you use them up—<u>Let it be peace with them or extermination</u>."[29]

Thus, when Hamblin arrived in Tooele on September 20, 1850, his arrival coincided with a period of the "mailed fist" in Mormon-Indian relations.

The first words describing Tooele in Hamblin's holograph autobiography are a bit surprising, coming as they do from the man renowned for his sympathy for Indians: "Here we ware pesterd with the Indians. They ware continualy coming out from the mountains which was their lurking plases and steeling Cattle and horses. There was several attempts maid to stop them but to no affect."[30] Hamblin's language—"pestered," "lurked," and later, "depredations"—reflects the typical white view of Indians as dangerous annoyances. Such language fails to recognize that the Mormons were settling permanently in traditional Indian lands, often occupying the best camping sites near reliable creeks or springs, hunting in the Indians' hunting grounds, and grazing their stock on meadowlands, often rendering them unfit for sustaining the animals and plants used by the Indians. In fact, the Mormons were encroaching on a complex and delicate ecosystem that supported the already destitute Goshutes. It would never be the same again.

Thus, though Jacob Hamblin was more sympathetic to Indians than the typical Mormon or non-Mormon white settler and, throughout his life, strove to deal with them through negotiation rather than violence, he nevertheless had many of the biases of the white settlers throughout the West—especially the bias that the white man had full rights to settle wherever he wanted. This view was perhaps even more pronounced among Mormons, who had their own Biblical version of Manifest Destiny, regarding wherever they settled as a Zion—a promised land given to them by God.

The Goshutes of Tooele were much less powerful and wealthy than the dominant tribe in Utah, the Utes, who lived in central Utah and Colorado, and had some Plains Indians cultural traits, such as possession of the horse.[31] North of Salt Lake Valley, the Shoshonis lived in northern Utah, Idaho, and Wyoming, and also had Plains Indian characteristics.[32]

The Goshutes lived in Tooele, west of Salt Lake City, and their territory extended west into present-day Nevada. Both the Goshutes and the Paiutes of southern Utah were known as "Diggers" because they dug for roots, often in desert areas.[33] Rabbits, lizards, groundhogs, insects, and seeds were also among their food staples. Sometimes, but apparently rarely, the Goshutes would kill an antelope. Neither group used horses as a general rule; the southern Paiutes would often eat any horses that fell into their hands, perhaps driven by hunger. Some sources indicate that the Goshutes did not keep horses because they would have eaten the grasses that the Goshutes depended upon for their own survival.[34] Adding to the oppressed states of the Goshutes and Paiutes was the fact that the Utes would raid into their territories, capture women and children, and sell them to the residents of New Mexico.[35]

Many complexities blur clear lines of tribal demarcation. The Pahvants, a band considered Utes who lived by Sevier Lake in modern Millard County in midwestern Utah, apparently had alliances with the Goshutes in the north and the Paiutes in the south.[36] Some central Utah Utes intermarried with Goshutes, including the Ute chief Black Hawk, who later led the Black Hawk War (1865–1872).[37]

While the Goshutes thus had ties with the Utes, they were even more closely connected with the Shoshoni.[38] Anthropologist Julian Steward stated that their language and culture were entirely Shoshoni, despite their poverty and the fact that they

4.2. "Go-Shoot Habitation, Pleasant Valley." Jacob's first dealings with Indians were with the Goshute Indians in northern Utah. Water painting by J. J. Young from sketch by H.V.A. von Beckh. James H. Simpson Expedition, 1859. Used by permission, Utah State Historical Society, all rights reserved.

had to adapt to an arid basin and range environment, though he granted that they did intermarry with the Utes somewhat. (The Goshutes in Tooele Valley may have had closer ties with Utes than the more western Goshutes.) Historian Brigham Madsen estimates that there were about nine hundred Goshutes in the 1840s; they had no strong tribal organization at that time and were living in small family groups.[39]

Early observers of the Goshutes were struck by their poverty. As early as 1827, Jedediah Smith, mountain man and explorer, described Goshutes as "Indians who appeared the most miserable of the human race, having nothing to subsist on (nor any clothing), except grass seed, grasshoppers, etc."[40] Howard Stansbury described two Goshutes on June 12, 1850, as nearly naked, with a child who, though plump, was "almost famished."[41] On May 9, 1859, James Simpson described the "Go-shoot Indians" as "the most wretched I have ever seen, and I have seen great numbers in various portions of our country."[42] Both men and women wore a cape made of strips of rabbit skins, which extended just below the hips and offered little substantial protection for the body. They did not wear leggings or moccasins. Young children wore no clothes at all, although it was so cold that Simpson's company was still wearing overcoats. Clearly, the Goshutes were struggling to survive in a marginal desert environment.

The Goshutes lived in wickiups make from cedar branches arranged in a circle, which served as a windbreak.[43] They subsisted on "rats, lizards, snakes, insects, grass-seed, and roots, and their largest game is the rabbit, it being seldom that they kill an antelope." Perhaps their main weapon, the bow and arrow, was not suited for killing antelope. Guns were rare among the Goshutes. When Simpson visited a Goshute village, the primary game brought in by hunters was "rats"—probably prairie dogs or ground squirrels. They also made cakes of seeds and roots.[44] They carried or stored water, seeds, and roots in willow baskets.[45]

Their religious leaders were shamans who treated them for sickness, had prophetic knowledge, and could give personal guidance. The Goshute religious tradition included the typical round dances of Utah Indians and myths of Hawk and the feared Coyote.[46]

"Fear of capture"—apparently fear of Utes stealing their children—caused them to avoid living too close to water. They were, Simpson wrote, "a suspicious, secretive set."[47] A mail agent named Faust characterized the Goshutes to Simpson as "of a thievish disposition, the mail company having lost by them about 12 head of cattle and as many mules." However, such thefts might have been a result of the Goshutes' daily struggle for survival: "They steal them for food."[48]

Many of these early descriptions of the Goshutes are written from a non-Indian perspective; they certainly missed some of the dignity, poetry, cultural depth, and positive values in the Goshute way of life. Nevertheless, they give early firsthand accounts showing that, in comparison with other Indians, the Goshutes were impoverished, lacked guns and horses, and subsisted on a diet of seeds, roots, and small animals.

Goshute historian Dennis Defa describes Mormon colonization in Tooele as "plac[ing] the Goshutes in a desperate situation. The Indians had long been accustomed to placing their camps near streams and canyons to take advantage of the water and food supply there.... These white settlers brought with them the idea of exclusive use of natural resources and robbed the Goshute of many of the things they needed to survive."[49]

Mormons and Goshutes found themselves immediately competing for water resources. Novelist, historian, and environmentalist Wallace Stegner famously wrote that "the primary unity of the West is a shortage of water."[50] In the arid Great Basin, and later the even more arid Southwest, Mormons would need to found towns and cities near springs and streams, and became famed for their skillful irrigation.[51] Historian Donald Worster writes that Mormons took the beehive as a symbol for their industry, "but a more appropriate one would have been the beaver, for control over water became the ecological basis of their society."[52] In his view, power over water became an important way in which the hierarchical, nondemocratic nature of Mormonism could express itself. Often Mormons settled permanently in places that had been extensively used by Indians as seasonal camps.

Grasslands were also an important locus of resource competition. If it is true that the Goshutes did not keep horses because their grazing would destroy the grass and seeds that were their dietary staples, the Mormons' widespread cattle grazing undoubtedly catastrophically impacted the Goshute environment.

The culture clash of white and Indian, and the competition for resources of survival, were inevitable, given the underlying assumptions of both Native American and Mormon communities. Although Brigham Young was comparatively moderate in his dealings with Utah's Indians, he was an energetic colonizer who saw the intermountain West as the core of the Mormon homeland and endeavored to plant many permanent Mormon settlements throughout the West and Southwest, at the most strategic and fertile locations possible, on streams and rivers. The two least prosperous groups of Utah Indians—the Goshutes and the Paiutes—were hardest hit by Mormon incursions into their territory.

When Goshutes, sometimes allied with Utes, stole from Mormon herds, many Mormons viewed them with typical American cultural views, seeing Indians as uncivilized, idle, thieving, and indistinguishably bad. They felt that only harsh reprisals, including summary executions, could control them and make them respect Mormon property.

A passage from James Dunn, an early local historian of Tooele, shows this demonization of the Indian:

> When the mean rascals had the chance they would rather steal than hunt: and that is the reason they went into the wholesale stealing of cattle, both in this valley and Salt Lake Valley until the settlers in both valleys joined together and killed a few of the red thieves; and that helped in a great measure to stop the killing of men and stealing of stock.[53]

However, the early primary sources flatly contradict this stereotype of the Goshutes of making an easy living based on hunting. Territorial Indian Agent Garland Hurt wrote in 1855: "The Indians claim that we have eaten up their grass and thereby deprived them of its rich crop of seed which is their principal subsistence during winter. They say too that the long guns of the white people have scared away the game and now there is nothing left for them to eat but ground squirrels and pisants."[54] Modern Tooele historian George Tripp notes, in the Mormons' defense, that they probably had little idea that their increasing farming and livestock grazing were destroying the Goshute winter food supply.[55]

Dunn implies that the Mormon reprisals were carried out to "stop the killing of men"; but the Goshutes killed very few Mormons (none during Jacob Hamblin's time in Tooele), while Mormons killed a number of Goshutes. In addition to the motivation of hunger for the Goshutes' "thefts," it is also possible that their cattle raids were not, in their own cultural terms, stealing. Tripp writes,

> The Gosiutes regarded the land, water and food resources both vegetable and animal as belonging to everyone, not in the sense of communal ownership, but [as] no ownership at all.... Therefore, until the Indians were taught

> otherwise by their Mormon neighbors, livestock running free on the open range was regarded the same as any game animal available to whoever bagged them.... In good years [for the Goshutes] there was usually not much more than just enough food for survival, and in times of scarcity only the strongest survived.[56]

The early primary sources support this point of view.

The early "war" with the Goshutes in Tooele, beginning in 1849, is little known in Utah history. These Indians were considerably less dangerous and deadly than the well-mounted and more aggressive Utes, although Utes were apparently sometimes involved in the Tooele conflicts. In Tooele, Indians stole livestock from Mormons, and the Mormons responded with military reprisals. While the loss of livestock was certainly a serious matter to the whites, the reprisals often ended in deaths for the Goshutes.

As we have seen, Mormons were herding cattle in Tooele by 1848, and the first cattle were lost to Indian raids in late February 1849.[57] These raiders herded the cattle southeast to Utah Valley, which suggests that they were Utes, or Utes and Goshutes working together. The raids, and attempted reprisals, continued periodically thereafter.[58]

Jacob Hamblin may have witnessed one of these brutal reprisals first hand.[59] He wrote:

> There was several attempts maid to stop them [the Indian raids] but to no affect. There was one expedicion under the command of Capt Porter Rockwell. He took [captured] some 20 or 30 Eutaws nere a fresh Lake 7 or 8 miles from our Settlement. While comeing in an affrey took plase in which ~~one~~ Mr Custer was kiled an Emigrant. The Prisioners maid their escape and fled except 5. They ware taken out and shot.[60]

This incident began when some non-Mormons were helping Mormons build a dam for Apostle Benson's mill in Richville (northwest of the town of Tooele). On about April 21, 1851, Indians stole their horses.[61] The Tooele residents quickly notified authorities in Salt Lake City and on the same day, General Daniel Wells sent out a company of volunteers under the leadership of Porter Rockwell, the legendary Mormon gunman, to recover the horses.[62] On April 22, the posse, consisting of Salt Lake volunteers, Tooele volunteers, and some non-Mormons, came to Rush Lake, about seventeen miles southwest of Tooele. They "evidently mistook the route the marauders had taken" and came instead upon a "band of Indians with their familes"—Utes, according to Hamblin and other sources.[63] They had apparently not been involved in the horse raid,[64] but Rockwell, in a questionable decision, ordered that thirty should be taken as prisoners to Tooele.[65] They were not disarmed.

As the group approached Tooele at about twilight, some Indians hung back and began to scatter. W. R. Dickinson, one of the non-Mormons working at Benson's mill, wrote, in a letter, that a non-Mormon named Custer "spured his horse to git Rounde them. He then puild his revolver pointed at the ingine. Shot. A nother ingine got Custer. I shot the ingine that shot Custer."[66] In other words, Custer fired the first shot, and another Indian returned his fire, killing him.[67]

Evidently the Indians scattered, and Rockwell was only able to keep four or five prisoners. The next day he and his men took them across the Stansbury Mountains into Skull Valley. They found no horses, and the prisoners stated, apparently with utter truthfulness, that they knew nothing about the theft. Rockwell, thus faced with the problem of five captive Utes, solved it neatly with summary execution. As Jacob Hamblin wrote, "They ware taken out and shot." Tullidge, in a notorious bit of special pleading, writes, "Rockwell and his men not finding any trace of the stolen horses, deemed it unwise to turn the thieves in their power loose to commit more depredations and perhaps shed the blood of some useful citizens, and they were sacrificed to the natural instincts of self-defense."[68] This brutal execution of unarmed, innocent Indians was thus scrubbed clean and turned into "self-defense."

Rockwell may have been following policy. On February 9, 1850, Daniel H. Wells wrote to George D. Grant, "Take no hostile Indians as prisoners" and "let none escape but do the work up clean."[69] Thus, killing captive Indians was not just allowed, but was sometimes ordered. Negotiations were often not even attempted; instead, the adversarial military point of view prevailed, which judged success by body count.

Hamblin remembers that "this act"—presumably Custer's death, not the murder of the Utes—"alarmed the Settlers of Toela. They asked for council." In this council, the Tooelans decided to move their homes into a fort arrangement and organize an armed guard for their livestock and fields.[70] This early fort was built around the middle of May 1851.[71] However, as Hamblin writes, even though "we managed in this way for 18 months," nevertheless the Indians continued "takeing our cattle whenever opertunity presented."[72]

In early summer of 1851, a month or two after the fort was built, Indians rustled about a hundred cattle from Charles White's herd and drove them through the Stansbury Mountains, past Skull Valley, and into the Cedar Mountains. In response, fourteen men were sent from Salt Lake City under Captain William McBride on June 13, but they were driven back by the Indians in the Cedar Mountains, and so they sent home for reinforcements and supplies.[73] On June 21, forty men arrived, supplemented by ten men from Tooele, possibly including Jacob Hamblin.[74] McBride wrote to Daniel Wells on June 24, asking for "a pound of arsenic" to poison the Indians' wells, and strychnine to poison their meat.[75] It is hard to assess the tone of this request; it may have been only rough, grotesque humor.[76]

On June 25, after "morning prayer was offered to the God of the armies of Isreal" by Mormon Battalion veteran, adjutant James Ferguson, the Mormon party attacked the Indians, caught them by surprise, and killed eight to eleven of them, including a woman with a baby.[77] There were no Mormon casualties.

In these campaigns, the Indians in Tooele had not killed any whites (with the exception of Custer, who had fired first), but the Mormons had taken a typical white view of "Indian problems": the best solution was a quick, harsh attack.

By 1852, Hamblin was an active participant in these military actions—a "first lieutenant" in the company of Captain Phineas Wright, a thirty-five-year-old Mormon Battalion veteran who served as Tooele's military captain. They made "several expeditions against the thieves, but without accomplishing much good."[78] Jacob left accounts of numerous contacts with Goshutes in Tooele.

His first military expedition against Indians apparently took place about a month before March 13, 1852. Wright sent him with fourteen men "to asertain Something with regard to them [the Indians] if posible."[79] The group rode to Willow Creek (Grantsville), where they learned that a light, presumably from an Indian camp, had been seen in the Stansbury Mountains. Jacob investigated with Grantsville resident Harrison Severe, and at about midnight, they, too, saw the light. Hamblin quickly organized a raid on the camp, split his forces into two groups, and at dawn sent them up parallel canyons to take the camp by surprise. However, they found only two families, who ran up the canyon shrieking, expecting to be shot. "We run in a hed of them and they stopt. Thare was several shots fird at them. None took affect. When I herd the schreems of the chirldin I could not bare the thought of killing one of them," wrote Hamblin.[80] Apparently, the whites had been planning to kill the Goshutes, but Hamblin's tenderness toward children changed his intent. He wrote that he "felt inspired" to prevent his company from shooting the Indians.[81]

In Little, which emphasizes the miraculous, Jacob wrote that a headman stepped toward him talking in Goshute and Jacob somehow understood him to say, "I never hurt you, and I do not want to. If you shoot, I will; if you do not, I will not.'" "Such an influence came over me," Jacob wrote, "that I would not have killed one of them for all the cattle in Tooele Valley."[82] Jacob was turning into an odd kind of military commander: one who prevented his men from shooting at the enemy.

He brought some of the Indians back to Tooele, "gave them p[r]ovisions blankets and treated them k[i]ndley," he wrote in the autobiography.[83] He assured the frightened Indians that they would be safe, but his military superior, either John

Rowberry or Phineas Wright, ignored this promise and in keeping with the "take no prisoners" policy, ordered that they should be executed. Hamblin replied that he "did not care to live" if he saw the Indians whose safety he had guaranteed murdered, "and as it made but little difference with me, if there were any shot I should be the first," and he stepped in front of the captive Goshutes. Rowberry or Wright backed down, and the Indians were freed.[84]

Hamblin went on to confess that he came to doubt his nonviolent attitude toward the Indians. "From the feelings manifested by the Bishop [Rowberry] and the people generally, I thought that I might possibly be mistaken in the whole affair," he wrote. "The people had long suffered from the depredations of these Indians, and they might be readily excused for their exasperated feelings, but, right or wrong, a different feeling actuated me."[85] Rowberry, in addition to his ecclesiastical office, was a major in the territorial militia,[86] and Phineas Wright, Hamblin's direct military superior, was Rowberry's first counselor in the bishopric. From Missouri onward, Mormon militarism was closely tied to ecclesiastical leadership.

Hamblin's autobiography adds, "[T]he manner we had tretd the Lamanites that we had taken prisoners had good influence in that trib[e]. In three months from that time the hole tribe came in and wanted to liv with us and be brothers promiceing to s[t]eel nomore."[87] "Whole tribe" is probably overstatement, but perhaps a band of Goshutes, a group of families, came to Tooele.

This incident shows Hamblin beginning to turn away from the psychology of the Indian fighter for whom Indian deaths are seen as military trophies, to someone who avoided killing. His sensitivity to the terrified Goshute children seems to have forcibly struck him with their shared humanity.

All of these incidents, as well as the actual brutal killings of Goshutes that Hamblin may have witnessed (five in the Rockwell expedition, eight in the McBride expedition), were steps toward the confrontation with a Goshute that took place on March 13, 1852. A military report by Phineas Wright, probably written directly from a report by Jacob Hamblin, begins: "March the 12th we received an express from Grants vill that the Gosutes Indians were in the Tooile vally fresh tracks being seen also being told by the Indian that lives at Grants ville."[88] Jacob identified these Indians as part of the same band that had stolen cattle before.[89]

This time, Major Rowberry specifically ordered Hamblin "to take another company of men, go after the Indians, to shoot all we found, and bring no more into the settlement."[90] The particularity of these orders shows that Rowberry was probably still angered by Hamblin's taking prisoners and intervening to stop their execution in the previous expedition.

The military report lists the twelve Mormon members of the expedition, not including the friendly Indian, Jack, who accompanied them. Jacob Hamblin, "3 Lieut.," was the leader. Also included were Jacob's brother Oscar; twenty-two-year-old Dudley Leavitt, who became a major figure in the settlement of southern Utah and Nevada, and whose sister, Priscilla, would marry Hamblin in 1857;[91] Ensign Riggs, also twenty-two, who had recently married Jacob's sister Adeline and who would also help pioneer southern Utah; Cyrus Tolman, one of Tooele's founders; English convert George Atkin, another Tooele stalwart; and Harrison Severe of Grantsville.

The company set out at midnight,[92] came to Grantsville, where they "refreshed" themselves and their horses, and set out again before daylight.[93] At dawn they found the Indians' trail and followed it about ten miles.[94] The tracks came down to the valley, but then turned back when snow made tracking them possible.[95] Then the Mormon posse found a large cache of roots that the Indians had buried, and Jack told Hamblin that the Indians would be found at the next water hole.[96]

At about ten a.m., the Mormons "came upon the Indians 6 in number camped on the side of the mountain," eighteen miles west of Grantsville, on the east side of the Stansbury Mountains.[97] The camp's sentinel saw them when they were still a half mile away, "which gave the Indians a chance to scater on the mountain before our men could git to them or Break of[f] there Retreat."[98] The Goshutes had been drying themselves by a fire when the whites attacked them. "They left their legins mogisons and fled among the rocks."[99] Hamblin apparently divided his company to pursue the scattering Goshutes and keep them from reaching the mountains.[100]

Jack opened fire on one Indian, who "was skulking behind some rocks," but missed, and the hostile Indian "sprung after Jack with a volly of arrows."[101] Jack ran toward Hamblin, who had hidden "behind a rock in a narrow pass."[102] When the Goshute was about twenty-five feet away, he saw Hamblin taking aim at him.[103]

"As I raised my gun to fire the poor fellow begd for mercy," Hamblin wrote. He was obviously offering to surrender, but Hamblin, under strict orders from Rowberry, "thought it would be a neglect of duty if I let him pas." Hamblin pulled the trigger, "but my gun mist [missed] fire."[104] Hamblin's "cap lock" gun could not be reloaded quickly,[105] and the Goshute, convinced his life was in danger, "as quick as thought…threw an arow at me but fo[r]tunately it struck the gard of my gun." Both men sprang for a stone that lay between them. Hamblin, strong and tall, wrested it free. The Goshute leaped backward, then shot three more arrows at the white: one pierced his hat, another whizzed by his head, and still another penetrated his coat but missed his body.[106] Jacob hurled the stone at the Indian, hitting him in the chest. As the Goshute reeled backward, Hamblin reloaded and "burnt two more caps at him but my gun would not go, and so he past by."[107]

Hamblin returned to his company and found that "several of the company had fair shots clost by but their guns mist fire."[108] There was only one white casualty, a slight arrow wound.[109] "We felt vexed at ~~our~~ first of all our ill success as we killed none of them," wrote Hamblin in the autobiography, reflecting a military perspective.

Similarly, the Wright/Hamblin report summarizes: "However the rest of the company were Blaseing [blazing] away at them the Best they could and some of the Indians was Badly wounded so suposed by the Blood on the rocks as they followed them some 5 miles. In there flight they left there moccacines all but one and took there flight Barefooted."[110] Thus Wright/Hamblin apparently wanted to emphasize a degree of military success (wounding some of the Indians).

But Jacob and his men soon saw divine intercession in their lack of military success: "We ~~finnly~~ concluded it was all wright that the Lord had youse [use] for them so we returnd home."[111] In subsequent weeks, months, and years, Hamblin's antiviolent convictions deepened as a result of this incident, causing him to revise his sense of mission with regard to Utah's Indians. In the Little autobiography, published in 1881, Hamblin writes:

> In my subsequent reflections, it appeared evident to me that a special providence had been over us, in this and the two previous expeditions, to prevent us from shedding the blood of the Indians. The Holy Spirit forcibly impressed me that it was not my calling to shed the blood of the scattered remnant of Israel [Americans Indians], but to be a messenger of peace to them. It was also made manifest to me that if I would not thirst for their blood, I should never fall by their hands. The most of the men who went on this last expedition, also received an impression that it was wrong to kill these Indians.[112]

This miraculous "guarantee" of safety, contingent on his own peaceful intentions, became a significant psychological support for Hamblin in his future relations with all Indians.

It is not clear exactly how soon after the actual confrontation in the mountains Hamblin's "conversion" to nonviolence took place, and it may have taken months to crystallize. The "conversion" is first explicitly attested in Little in 1881, but the holograph autobiography, written after 1854, probably twenty to thirty years earlier than Little, contains a suggestion of the conversion.

Hamblin's next clash with Indians suggests that he was not immediately fully converted to pacifism, as he tried to kill, and was nearly killed by, an Indian named "Big Foot."[113] Once again, Hamblin was part of an expedition (he calls it the fourth expedition) that surprised a camp of Goshutes in the mountains. Once again, he witnessed the Indian women and children fleeing in terror, cutting their feet on rocks and leaving trails of blood. Again, this piteous sight moved him to work with Indians "in a different way," not through military reprisal and massacre.

However, when he saw the tracks of the Indian leader "Big Foot," he felt that this was a very dangerous Indian who perhaps deserved to be killed. As Jacob followed the trail through the snow along high ridges, he came to a juniper with low foliage, but instead of investigating it, he wrote, "a feeling came over me not to go near it." After he ascended a steep hill and could look back at the tree, he saw that "no trail had passed on." He circled around to get the Indian in sight, but Big Foot was able to somehow slip off unobserved.

Later, Hamblin came to know this Big Foot personally, and he told Jacob that if he had walked up to the cedar tree, the Indian would have buried an arrow in him "up to the feather." Again, Hamblin felt that a divine providence kept him from shedding the blood of an Indian, and from being killed. "I thanked the Lord, as I often felt to do, for the revelations of His Spirit," wrote Hamblin.[114] Thus, it is probable that Hamblin's nonviolence crystallized in the months following the incident in the mountains in which his gun would not shoot, not immediately after it.

While Hamblin's miraculous safety among Indians cannot be proven historically or scientifically, he himself deeply believed in it. That conviction partially accounts for his willingness to go on many expeditions, often alone, among hostile natives, far from the safety of white settlements. In his own view, he was not risking his life. Hamblin relied on this "promise" that he would not die at the hands of Indians when visiting angry, vengeful Navajos in 1874.[115] Martha Cragun Cox, a woman who knew him when she was a child, mentioned to him that the men who had gone with him on the mission to the Navajos had said that "braver man never lived, than Jacob Hamblin," but Hamblin strongly denied this: "I had the assurance from the Holy Spirit—a promise given direct from the heavens that so long as I did not desire to shed the blood of the Lamanite or did not shed the blood of any, my blood should not be shed by them. It was not so hard for me to be brave when I knew they could not kill me."[116]

Hamblin's conversion to nonviolence is all the more remarkable given its setting in a period when Mormons tended to deal harshly with Indians—during the time of Howard Christy's "mailed fist," when some Mormons carried out punitive raids on Indians and executed Indian prisoners. It is worth noting that Hamblin's nonviolent feelings and reluctance to kill put him in explicit rebellion against his local military and ecclesiastical leaders, John Rowberry and Phineas Wright. The misfiring of Hamblin's gun, Hamblin's interpretation of the incident as a promise of protection, and his conversion to a form of pacifism, present a stark contrast to other Mormons' willingness to employ harsh militaristic solutions while confronting the vast culture gap that yawned between white and Indian in early Utah.

Furthermore, although this confrontation was a conversion experience of sorts for Hamblin, he had demonstrated sympathy for Indians in military expeditions before this one. Thus, the conversion was a culmination rather than a complete about-face. Nevertheless, his feelings of doubt about his own nonviolence, due to criticism from his military-ecclesiastical leaders, show that he was conflicted on the issue before the conversion.

The next incident in this story, in which we see Hamblin the visionary, shows his gradual metamorphosis into a pacifist, and a quasi-Indian himself. After returning home from this fourth expedition, he had a dream that was repeated three nights running, in which he was west of Tooele, where he and the other Mormons had been trying to destroy the Goshute bands. Yet in the dream, he walked with them as a friend, and suddenly saw "a lump of shining substance" which he bent down and picked up. When he tried to brush it from his fingers, some of it stuck, and his attempts to brush it off only made it brighter.[117]

As we have seen, early Mormons—like many religious early Americans (and religious persons throughout history)—often viewed their dreams as supernatural messages. So Hamblin interpreted this dream as a call for him to spend time with his enemies. He took bare survival necessities, blankets and gun, and traveled alone into Goshute territory.

This was not at all a safe undertaking, for a white alone could easily be killed by Indians who had grudges against them, and Indians had been killed by Mormons. However, Jacob fell in with some Goshutes who were willing to befriend him, and he spent several days with them. They hunted deer and duck together, and occasionally Jacob loaned them his rifle. He also communicated with them as best he could, advising peaceful coexistence with Mormons. Jacob came to feel a kinship with these Indians, and they came to accept and trust him.

An April 2, 1853, editorial in the *Deseret News*, which quotes from a letter to the *News* from Hamblin dated March 5, shows him taking days away from his farming to explore and hunt with local Goshutes.[118] On about February 12, he left Tooele with three Goshutes, who planned to explore streams in northeast Skull Valley, then called Spring Valley.

> They told me they would "never steal any more from the Mormons, for they talked good talk, and they wanted to be brothers; that they had stole many cattle and horses, but they should never steal any more; that a part of their tribe had left them, and gone many sleeps south-west." "I asked why they did not come in with them?" Their excuse was trivial, and a brief answer satisfied them. No doubt those referred to, were some of the bad ones of the clan, and have gone a few moons off to keep out of the way of their deserts. When the subject was explained, the Indians present thought some of them would return before another snow, as they had had a talk with them.

Here we have classic Hamblin, talking with Indians about peace and coexistence. Nevertheless, he admits the presence of "bad Indians." "I traveled 3 days on the east side of the valley, saw plenty of cedar timber, but water scarce, that could be used for irrigating purposes."This is again typical Hamblin; in his traveling, hunting, and bonding with Indians, he always kept his eyes open for possible sites for further Mormon settlements.

One day, while hunting duck, he noticed smoke two miles away, and when he visited it he found an Indian boy, whose Indian name meant "hungry,"[119] sitting near a fire. He asked him in Goshute if he had a father. Silence. When Jacob asked him where his wickiup was, he pointed, and Jacob saw his mother sitting in a hut. As he approached her, he saw that "[e]verything bespoke their wretchedness and want; they had not clothing enough then to make a shirt. They said they had been there 5 moons, living on roots, having no shelter from the storms, but partially from the wind." Jacob asked the woman to give him the boy, and she refused. But the next day, Jacob and his friends were still in the area, and she came and "pressed" Jacob to take him. Jacob agreed, "and gave her a blanket, buiscuits &c., as she had suffered much from hunger, cold, &c., the past winter."

Jacob brought the boy home and renamed him Albert. He wrote to the *Deseret News* that, "The Indian boy is much pleased with his situation.—As soon as it is light, he wants the whip to bring up the cattle. I find him very faithful in everything I ask of him."

Thus, we have a firm date for the entrance of Albert into the Hamblin family: February 12–15, 1853.

In an 1860 letter to Brigham Young, Hamblin referred to Albert as "of the Sho Shone desent—I got him of the Toso Wich or White Knife band ranging west of Tooele."[120] This band made knives and other utensils of white rock from a quarry in their territory, about fifty miles east of Winnemucca, Nevada.[121] In the same letter, Hamblin describes dealing with Albert's band, not just his mother. The White Knife Shoshonis "said that the Mormons kiled his Father and they wanted me to be a father to him which I hav had to be every [ever] since." Indeed, Albert later referred to Jacob as "father" and to Isaiah Hamblin as "grandfather." As the *Deseret News* letter states, Albert became a herdsman in the family economy.[122]

Hamblin now admonishes his Mormon "brethren" to try to work with Indians:

> I would say to the brethren, don't be afraid of talking and teaching them to do good. If the Lord is not working in the hearts of this people, I am greatly deceived. The Indians in this valley are manufacturing rope, or cord, from the coat of the Milk-weed, and baskets from the Willow. The brethren generally are anxious to encourage industry and honesty among them, in buying their baskets and ropes whether they need them or not. The Indians appear anxious

> to raise a crop of wheat and potatoes this season; they ask a great many questions about the Mormons; I have had some good talk with them of late.

In Little, Hamblin also tells the story of the adoption of Albert, which adds a theological overlay not found in the earlier account.[123] The story of economic exchange, giving presents to Albert's impoverished mother, is left out, and we have a full-fledged miracle story, as Jacob and Albert recognize each other through some mysterious power: "As soon as I saw the boy, the Spirit said to me, 'Take that lad home with you; that is part of your mission here, and here is the bright substance which you dreamed of picking up.'" So finding Albert is the fulfillment of Hamblin's sacred dream.

In Little, Jacob asks Albert if he will go with him and the boy immediately agrees. However, when Hamblin talked with the boy's mother, she only reluctantly assented to her son's departure. Albert promptly took his bow and arrow and followed Jacob, but the mother must have set up a keen of mourning, so Hamblin told Albert to go back to her. The boy refused to do so.

That night the mother showed up where Hamblin and Albert were camping with his Goshute friends; she was still probably mourning for her child. However, after she talked to the other Indians and they praised Hamblin, she felt differently, and the next morning told Jacob, "the boy could go with me if I would always be his father and own him as my son." Hamblin assured her that he would.

Later, Jacob asked Albert why he had come with him so quickly, and the boy told him that he had had a dream the night before telling him that he should leave with a man (possibly white) who would come to his mother's lodge. When Albert saw Hamblin at a distance, he knew he was the man in the dream, and actually built a fire to attract Jacob to his mother's lodge.

The nearly contemporary 1853 account is more matter-of-fact, including the economic detail that Hamblin traded for Albert. The 1881 account provides Hamblin's later theological interpretation of the event.

Jacob's last adventure with Indians in Tooele probably took place in about 1853. After Goshutes had stolen some cattle, a posse of men, including Hamblin, one of his brothers, and Frank Lougy, an eighteen-year-old stepson of Phineas Wright, pursued them into Rush Valley, about twelve miles south of Tooele.[124] However, the two Hamblin siblings ended up in a heated argument, and finally Jacob decided to return to Tooele. The men in the posse sent Lougy back with Jacob for safety and the two men left the next morning.

Jacob and Lougy decided to hunt duck on the east side of Rush Lake on the way back home, and set some grass afire near springs at modern Slagtown. Looking up

Soldier's Canyon on the east, they saw three Indians jogging quickly down from the hills, apparently to cut off their northern escape route. Hamblin and Lougy immediately began to run and were able to stay north of the Indians and avoid being headed off. However, the Indians approached them and raised their bows and arrows. Hamblin and Lougy leveled their guns at them. The Indians lowered their bows and arrows, but followed them for some distance, occasionally raising their bows, but lowering them when the Mormons trained their guns on them. "Hamblin (who was an experienced Scout) and older than Lougy, told Lougy, 'Don't you shoot until I tell you to.'" Walking backward, the two men saw what looked like the heads of three more Indians looking over "the tops of the sagebrush" up where they had first confronted the three Indians.

However, after this tense standoff, the three Indians apparently retreated, and Hamblin and Lougy were able to travel back to Tooele without further incident. Later, an Indian named Dick Mooni told Lougy that he had been one of the three Indians in the sagebrush. He said that the group of six Indians (including two boys) had been gathering pine nuts among the cedars in Soldier Canyon when they saw the smoke from the duck hunt and decided to try to get the guns of the white hunters. Only one of the Indians had a gun, and they stationed him to cut off the two whites. However, when this Indian saw two whites with guns, he decided that the odds were not good for an attack, and let Hamblin and Lougy pass by.

This is a typical story of Indian danger barely survived, with no theological coloring. Lougy is probably the source for it.

While this narrative has concentrated on Hamblin's relations with Indians, his daily life in early Tooele, a small, close-knit pioneer community, was also an important part of his experience. Settling here was not easy; the pioneers struggled to obtain adequate food, and sometimes resorted to eating local seeds and roots, like the Goshutes. Nevertheless, the small community bonded in hardship. Hamblin's third wife, Sarah Priscilla Leavitt, would later remember participating in square dances, molasses candy pulls, and many kinds of games and contests in the fledgling settlement.[125] Early accounts of Tooele emphasize the communal unity of the pioneer town. Priscilla wrote that "[e]veryone was so good to each other and there was very little gossip and contention."[126] On March 25, 1852, John Rowberry wrote to the *Deseret News*, "We have had no law suits, nor bishop's court to contend with; peace and goodwill prevail in our midst."[127]

In the middle of the town was a twenty-four-foot-square meeting house, which probably served as church on Sundays and a school on weekdays, as well as a political meeting place.

The main occupation of the townspeople was farming, though millwrights, herders, and ranchers also lived in Tooele. In his March 1852 letter, Rowberry wrote that members of his community were busy planting grain at the time. Hamblin would have been one of these farmers. He probably had an assigned plot in the "Big Field" located northwest of Tooele city, and received an allotment of the water from Settlement Canyon Creek that was used for irrigation. If he was a typical early Tooele farmer, he used fairly primitive farm utensils, harvesting grain with handmade cradles, pitchforks, and wooden rakes. The grain was struck by flails or trampled by cattle, then was hand-winnowed.[128] Tooele, like Salt Lake City, was periodically invaded by swarms of "grasshoppers" (probably Rocky Mountain locusts) and crickets (probably the large shieldbacked katydid now known as the Mormon cricket) eating anything green they could find. Jacob undoubtedly had to deal with these menaces to priceless crops.[129]

Jacob was not one of the main ecclesiastical or political leaders (often identical in early Utah) of Tooele, yet was a valued member of the community. On August 2, 1852, he was elected to the position of treasurer of Tooele County.[130] He was also a member of the Sixth Quorum of Seventies.[131]

Happily, it turned out that Rachel was not sterile, and bore a child in Tooele, Lois, on June 15, 1851.[132]

In spring 1852, Tooelans (possibly including Jacob) had begun to leave their first fort and spread out. About a year later, a town site was surveyed by Jesse W. Fox, which eventually became modern Tooele, and people began to build on their town lots.[133] However, at the beginning of the Walker War (named from the Ute Wakara, lasting from July 1853 to approximately May 1854),[134] Brigham Young advised all settlers to "fort up," "enclose theor biltings with good substantials walls," as Hamblin puts it, and avoid leaving settlements except in large parties. Jacob wrote, "Tharefore I was employd moveing my houces and putting them up again and cultivating the Earth."[135] So he evidently moved his home into Tooele proper, and the Tooele inhabitants began to erect a mud wall around their town, with bastions at each corner.[136]

In the midst of these events, on October 6, 1853,[137] Hamblin may have been attending General Conference in Salt Lake City when he heard the clerk announce that Brigham Young had called a number of men on "a mishion to open up the Gospell to the Lamanittes" in southern Utah, in the spring.[138] To his surprise, Jacob heard his name called out. (Or possibly, the calling was relayed to him in Tooele after the announcement.) He would immediately begin preparing for this new mission.

Tooele had been an education, an apprenticeship, a first call to live with and understand Indians, to change from a soldier to a diplomat. His life's main calling, among the Paiutes, Hopis, Navajos, and other Indians of southern Utah and Arizona, was approaching.

5

"*We Ware Mormans Thare White Brothers*"

The Southern Utah Indian Mission, 1854

From October 1853 to April 1854, Hamblin would have put his affairs in Tooele in order, planting his crops in March and making arrangements for his older children (Duane and Martha were now thirteen and eleven; Albert might have been a little younger) and siblings to care for his farmland. His mission would last a year or two, as far as he knew, and he expected that he would return to live permanently in Tooele.

According to Thomas Brown, who left a superb journal of the southern Indian mission, some twenty-five men had been called to the southern Utah Indian mission on October 6, 1853, with Apostle Parley P. Pratt named to lead the group.[1] Among these missionaries were such later worthies of Southern Utah history as Ira Hatch, Isaac Riddle, Lorenzo Roundy, Samuel Knight, and Thales Haskell. Juanita Brooks describes them as "young men, with twelve of them under thirty and the oldest of the group forty-six. Five were still in their teens; at least eight were unmarried." They were frontiersmen, "men who knew the out-of-doors and who were hardy and resourceful," but like Hamblin, they were generally devout.[2]

On April 10, 1854, apostles Orson Hyde, Parley Pratt, Wilford Woodruff, Erastus Snow, Lorenzo Snow, and Ezra T. Benson set apart sixteen of the missionaries (probably including Hamblin) for their mission. New York native Rufus Allen was called to serve as captain of the group. Though only twenty-six years old, he had already participated in the epic trek of the Mormon Battalion, then had accompanied Parley P. Pratt on an expedition to southern Utah and South America from 1849 to 1852.[3]

Kentucky-born David Lewis, called as first lieutenant, was a seasoned forty years of age. A survivor of the Haun's Mill Massacre in Missouri, he described himself as black-haired, blue-eyed, and six foot one.[4] Twenty-nine-year-old Connecticut native Samuel Frink Atwood was called to be second lieutenant,[5] and Thomas Brown acted as clerk and recorder. Brown, a Scotch schoolteacher and a skilled writer, had converted to Mormonism in 1844. Five years later, he was in Kanesville where he worked as a storekeeper; he followed the same occupation in Salt Lake City by 1852, before being called to the southern Indian mission.[6]

The apostles instructed the missionaries that their purpose was "to civilize &

instruct the Indians in this region, that they might come up to inherit the blessings pertaining to them because of the works & promises of their Fathers"—that is, their ancestors in the Book of Mormon.[7] They should take substantial provisions–two hundred pounds of flour each, farming implements, and seed corn and wheat. After the Latter-day Saint faith, perhaps the main cultural skill the Mormons hoped to teach the "Lamanites" was farming.

The main company of missionaries, which may have included Jacob, left Salt Lake on the morning of April 14 with six wagons. Jacob shared a wagon with Elnathan Eldridge and Robert Ritchie (who would later help Jacob settle Santa Clara) on the southward journey; between them they had four horses, six hundred pounds of flour, one plow, two guns, one cow, two bushels of wheat and one of corn, and a good quantity of "Fixings & Notions"—which may have included knick-knacks to trade with Indians.[8]

The band of missionaries pursued a leisurely course south, stopping at settlements and visiting friends, who often gave them contributions to help them in their mission. They passed through Utah Valley, just south of Salt Lake Valley, following the "California Road," as Jacob Hamblin referred to it, south through the mountain valleys of the Wasatch Range.[9] They arrived at Fillmore, then the state capital, in the vast Pahvant Valley in central Utah, on April 22, where they spent two snowy days. On the twenty-fifth, at Corn Creek south of Fillmore, they "met the Pahvants Chief and some of his braves," Hamblin wrote. "[We] gave them some ~~little~~ Presants and went on." The chief was probably Chuick, though Kanosh, later a friend of Hamblin and the Mormons, was a rising leader in the tribe.[10] Brown noted that the Mormons were creating a farm for the Indians at Corn Creek, "& if possible teaching the Walker band to labor." This might have been Hamblin's first substantial introduction to central Utah Utes. He would not be primarily concerned with Utes in his long career as frontiersman in southern Utah and Arizona, but the Utes of central Utah often visited southern Utah, and for many years kidnapped or bought Paiute children to sell to the New Mexicans. The visits of the powerful, well-mounted Utes often impacted local tribal politics.

By this time, the missionaries had left the mountain ranges of north and central Utah and were beginning to traverse the high plateaus of southern Utah. On the twenty-sixth, the company camped at Pine Creek, about thirteen miles north of the modern town of Beaver (not yet founded in 1854). "We her[e] met a compeny from Sanbanedeno," wrote Hamblin. San Bernardino, California, had been a Mormon colony since 1851, and travelers to and from it often passed through southern Utah.[11] With the group was Wakara, who had fought against Mormons in the "Walker War," but by this time he was seeking peace.[12]

After passing Beaver Valley, the company began an ascent to a pass leading to "Little Salt Lake Valley" (where Parowan and Cedar City were located). Then a steep descent down a stony, difficult mountain trail led to "wearisome miles of barren land, thickly covered with sage brush." One traveler described this road as "the devil's own pass."[13]

As the missionaries came to the Little Salt Lake Valley, they saw the Black Mountains looming to the west, and the Hurricane Cliffs to the east; Little Salt Lake, now dry but formerly fed by springs, lay to the west. They camped at Red Creek, the site of the town of Paragonah, which had been abandoned at the beginning of the Walker War.

Little Salt Lake Valley, now called Parowan Valley, had been settled by Mormons in January 1851, a colonization effort known as the Iron Mission. Parley P. Pratt's exploration party had discovered iron in the valley a year earlier, and Brigham Young decided to establish a settlement there to process the ore. About 120 men were called to the mission, and Apostle George A. Smith first presided over it. Parowan was the first town settled. In November 1851, when coal was discovered nineteen miles south of Parowan, Cedar City, first known as the Coal Creek settlement, was founded. A blast furnace was located here because of the proximity of coal. While a limited amount of iron ore was processed at the Iron Mission, as time went on the Saints unfortunately learned that iron production was not economically feasible, and in 1858 the blast furnace was shut down. Nevertheless, Parowan and Cedar City became important Mormon communities in Brigham Young's outer ring of Utah settlements.[14] While Jacob Hamblin would never live in Parowan or Cedar City, he often passed through the area and had frequent dealings with the residents of these towns.

On April 29, after ten miles' journey, the Indian missionaries reached Fort Parowan, "whare the Brotherin made us welcome," wrote Hamblin. In 1853, Parowan, situated at the base of the Hurricane Cliffs, contained about a hundred pink adobe homes, which were organized in a square. Gardens and trees surrounded the houses, and there was a large agricultural area outside the town itself, called "The Field."[15]

Jacob probably stayed with Zadok Knapp Judd, brother of his wife Rachel. Zadok, now about twenty-seven years old, had served in the Mormon Battalion, after typical Mormon migrations from Canada to Missouri and Nauvoo. He and his wife Mary would later help Jacob settle Santa Clara.[16] The next night the missionaries were put up in Cedar City, larger than Parowan but built after precisely the same pattern, where "the Saints of that plase allso gladly received us," according to Hamblin.[17]

The missionaries had been instructed to travel to the southernmost Mormon colony, and on the second of May, after traveling about twenty-five miles southwest of Cedar City, they "arived in Harmony our destind plase," as Hamblin wrote. Harmony, a small fort on Ash Creek nestled beneath the spectacular Hurricane Cliffs to the east, with their sculpted red sandstone formations, was the first town "over the rim" of the great basin.[18] Ash Creek, a large creek with a rocky bottom, drained southward to the Virgin River.[19]

Arriving in Harmony, Jacob soon met John D. Lee, the leader of Harmony, a man who would be his ally and friend for many years.[20] Lee was one of the dominating figures of Southern Utah history, for his leadership in early Utah, his remarkable journals, and his role in the Mountain Meadows Massacre. Aside from his involvement in that horrific event, Lee was a devout, loyal Mormon, an adopted son of Brigham Young, the husband of some nineteen wives, and an accomplished pioneer. Lee's forcefulness rubbed many people the wrong way, and when the missionaries came to Harmony, Thomas Brown disliked him almost instantly.

There were actually three different locations for Harmony, which I will refer to as Harmony I, Harmony II, and Harmony III (or New Harmony). The missionaries arrived at Harmony I (Brown calls it "the old fort"), near the present Ash Creek Reservoir, which had been settled by Lee and others in spring 1852.[21] By March 1853, Harmony I included at least fifteen men and their families (including six of Lee's plural wives), a schoolhouse, and a corral. Friendly Paiutes had helped build the fort.[22] When the missionaries arrived, there were some thirty men living here, and there was apparently an area of farmland about four miles away. Brown wrote that the land in this first Harmony would not be adequate for the missionaries,[23] so Lee and the missionary leaders—after some initial uncertainty as to who should be in charge, Lee or Allen—decided the missionaries should move to another settlement site, which was not yet precisely located. However, the leaders tentatively chose the location of the "new farming ground," the New Harmony Flat, and the new settlement.[24] Brigham Young was scheduled to visit in mid-May and he would make the final decisions on the location of Harmony II.

Hamblin writes: "Here we stopt and commensed prepareing a plase to plant the seeds which we had brought. We examinded the valley. We found that by makeing 6 miles of water ditch we could water 400 or 500 acres of good land. So we commensed leighbor [labor] with plows spaids shovles ho[e]s and other tooles makeing the water ditch." Brown's diary describes the laborious project of excavating the ditch in detail. In addition, each missionary had two acres of land which he had to grub—clear for planting—often removing sagebrush, greasewood, and other plants. On May 9, Thomas Brown grubbed with an axe until his hands "were much blistered, broke, and bled."[25]

A number of Paiutes were living near Harmony, and this would have been Hamblin's first exposure to this tribe; now he would have begun to learn their language.[26] The Parowan–Cedar City–Harmony Paiutes had close ties to the Pahvants and Utes of central Utah, and, in fact, sometimes the Paiutes in Dixie regarded them as Utes.[27] Cal-o-e-chipe, the Paiute leader in Cedar Valley, was closely related to Wakara.[28]

In mid-May, Brigham Young made one of his periodic visits to outlying settlements in southern Utah, with a large entourage, including Parley P. Pratt (who had apparently been released from his assignment to lead the southern mission).[29] The Young company first met with the Harmony saints on May 19.[30]

The moment when authority was apportioned was a tense one in the meeting. One Harmony resident nominated Lee to be president of the entire community, which Young agreed to, but then Brown stood and requested that the missionaries have "another President to Bror Lee." Rufus Allen immediately stood and agreed that they did not want Lee as their leader. So Young told the missionaries to keep "your present organization," while Lee would preside over the Harmony branch.[31] It must have been an embarrassing moment for Lee, but apparently the missionaries were relieved.

Young's counsel to the Indian missionaries was eminently sensible:

> You are to save the remnants of Israel in these mountains.... You are sent, not to farm,... not to help white men, but to save the red ones, learn their language, and you can do this more effectually by living among them, as well as writing down a list of words, go with them where ~~you~~ they go, live with them & when they rest let them live with you, feed them, clothe them and teach them as you can, & being thus with you all the time, you will soon be able to teach them in their own language, they are our brethren, we must seek after them.[32]

Hamblin wrote that Brigham Young preached that the missionaries should "be on hand to hunt up the Lamanits from the Dens and caves and holes of the Earth." This advice would have been very welcome to Hamblin, who had enjoyed living and hunting with the Goshutes in Tooele.

Young's emphasis on learning the Indian languages was remarkably wise counsel for Indian missionaries. One historical question that is difficult to answer is, how well did the early Mormon Indian missionaries learn the Indian languages? One can acquire the basics of some languages fairly quickly, but it takes years of experience to gain a full, idiomatic mastery of a language and its associated culture. The Mormon missionaries were not grammarians; they often did not speak or write English grammatically. But many long-time Indian missionaries, such as Jacob Hamblin and Ira Hatch, reputedly learned to speak Paiute expertly.

During this meeting, Brigham Young gave the dimensions for the "New Fort Harmony," and the next day, May 20, he dug the foundation for the southeast corner of this new fort, two hundred feet square, three feet thick. Its cornerstones are still extant near Highway 144, the road connecting I-15 and New Harmony.

On the twenty-first Parley P. Pratt emphasized that the Saints should treat Indians with kindness. "If you cannot yet talk with them, there is one language that all can understand and feel—kindness—sympathy." He seconded Brigham Young's language advice, and encouraged the local Mormons to "feed, clothe, instruct them; win, save the remnants of the house of Israel." But for Pratt, if Indians were literal Hebrews, they were also cursed: "They have suffered hell enough here and this for generations because of the rebellion of their fathers...abuse & suffering has followed their rejection of the Priesthood, and such will ever be the reward of them that follow a similar course & it will be on their children after them."[33]

After this meeting, Brigham Young went north "with all his Braves," and the Indian missionaries continued their work. The next day, Brown wrote, "after dinner we moved to the new settlement." This might record the first settlement of Harmony II, often referred to now as "old Fort Harmony."

The missionaries held a meeting two days later which shows that Jacob Hamblin was anxious to spend time with the Indians in southernmost Utah, but that Rufus Allen was somewhat reluctant to send his missionaries there. David Lewis proposed journeying south to meet "Toker, the chief of the Piede band," who lived near modern Toquerville. In about August 1852, Toquer, with thirty of his men, had visited Harmony and implored Lee and the Mormons to settle among them, so they could both learn Mormon farming techniques and work for the Mormons.[34]

Allen objected to Lewis's suggestion, proposing that the missionaries should attend to watering their grain first. But Lewis insisted that a party should go at that time, carrying seed with them, and Allen finally acquiesced. Hamblin had also spoken privately to Allen on this subject.

But in an evening meeting, Rufus Allen "made some remarks on some being overanxious about going out on a trip south." This brought a quick response from Hamblin, according to Brown:

> His remarks hurt the feelings of J. Hamblin, who said he felt them to be too personal, he had spoken his mind in private to Bror Allen, & next day had it thrown in his teeth while on the Canal publicly. If this whole body meet & seek the mind of the Lord did not think they would err much in appointing men to go out and visit the Indians. Did not like so many private meetings.[35]

Jacob was here criticizing both the policy of not going south to the Indians he regarded as his real mission, and the leadership style of Rufus Allen.

However, Allen was conciliatory, gave an explanation and an apology, and this "restored 'Harmony,'" as Brown wrote.

This interchange evidences Jacob's focus on spending time with Indians, at the expense of practical concerns, but it also shows that he could stand up to his ecclesiastical leaders on occasion, a pattern we have already seen in Tooele.

He participated in an abortive exploring trip in late May, in which the missionaries met no Paiutes and wandered lost in the mountains for days, though they did see the Virgin River for the first time.[36] But on June 7, the moment Jacob had been waiting for arrived: his first trip south to visit and teach the Toquerville and Santa Clara Indians. In the company, aside from Jacob, were Rufus Allen, Lorenzo Roundy, William Hennefer, Thomas Brown, Augustus P. Hardy, Amos G. Thornton, Thales Haskell, Henry Evans, and two Paiutes, the elderly Tso, and Queets ("Dick").[37] A few of these became close companions of Jacob throughout his life. New York native Lorenzo Roundy, virtually a senior missionary at age thirty-five, had crossed the plains in 1847. He later become a long-time bishop of Kanarraville, near Harmony, and would help Jacob explore Arizona.[38] Augustus Poor ("Gus" or "A.P.") Hardy, a twenty-three-year-old native of Massachusetts, had been baptized a Mormon in August 1846 and crossed the plains four years later. Quiet, steady, and reliable, he had married in March 1854, just before leaving on the southern Utah mission. Thales Haskell, a twenty-year-old native of Massachusetts, had crossed the plains with his mother in 1847, then settled in Salt Lake City. He would go on many expeditions and endure many hardships with Jacob, but always responded courageously and good-naturedly to calls. "On very rare occasions," a friend wrote of him, "he imbibed a bit freely, but those who will reflect a moment will readily account for this in taking into account the many, many years he had spent among the Indians away from family and civilization," and he became one of the "real peace makers" in southern Utah history.[39]

The party of missionaries followed Ash Creek southward, passing by "rolling ridges of sand and rocky bolders alternately," as Brown wrote. The Hurricane Cliffs rose to the east, and Pine Valley Mountains to the west. Here Jacob and his friends had to make their way past the Black Ridge, with its volcanic rocks, a point of legendary difficulty on the Ash Creek Canyon road. In 1857 George A. Smith described the road from Harmony to Washington as "the most desperate piece of road that I ever traveled in my life."[40] They may have also descended Peter's Leap, the precipitous cliff where wagons later had to be lowered by windlass, and which still must have been unnerving to these missionaries as they walked down an Indian path, leading horses or mules. The farther south they went, the hotter the climate became, and the mountains on the east became blacker, the result of igneous formations. Then at sunset, Brown wrote, "after passing over some rough rocky steep hills & large boulders we come to see the smoke of The Chief Toquer's Wickeups." This community was not far from modern Toquerville, which Mormons would settle in 1858 and name after this chief. Toquer means "black," and the community is located near a mountain that possesses striking black rock formations.

The missionaries received a warm welcome from the Paiute chief. "Toker Peads or the Black Captan was very glad to see us," Hamblin wrote. "He sat by a narow pass in the rocks and huged [hugged] each one of us [as] w[e] pased by." When he learned that Rufus Allen was their leader, "the two big men embraced each other very

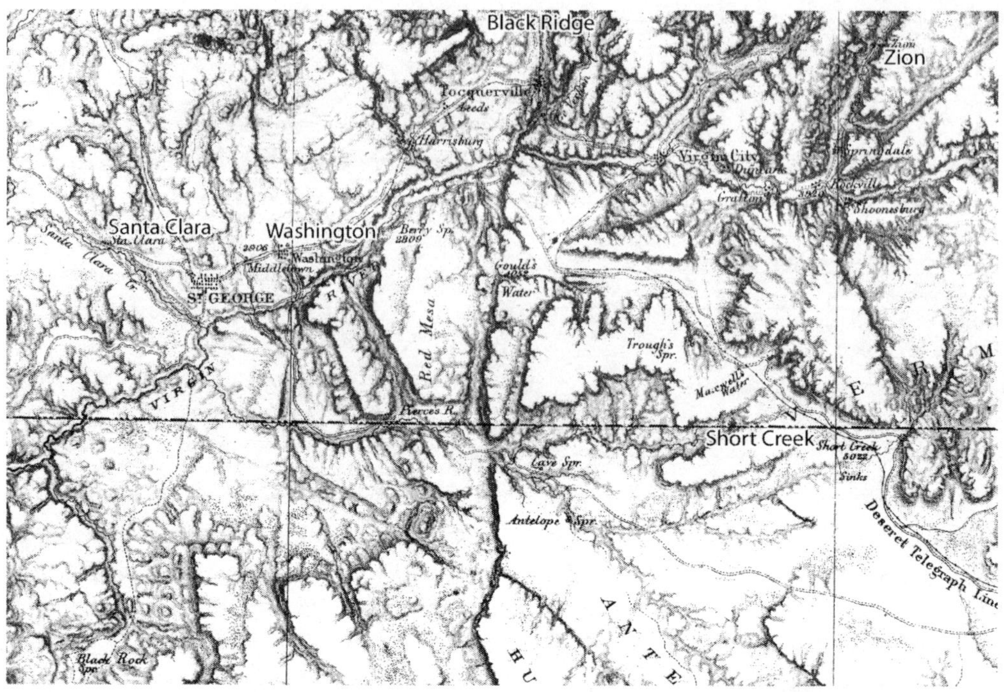

5.1. Southern Utah. Detail from Map 67, dated 1876, from G. M. Wheeler, *Topographical Atlas.* Courtesy David Rumsey Historical Map Collection.

affectionately." Brown described Toquer as "a small broad old man," about fifty years old, with a broad forehead, flat nose, dark skin, and a long thin beard. Toquer also had "the long straight black hair of Israel's race."[41]

Hamblin was struck by the Paiutes' poverty: "They ware the most destitute People I ever saw[,] naked excep[t] the ~~Male~~ adults had a strip about thare loins. The Maile Childrin had not Smutch [as much] as that. They had nothing to eat except a few grass seeds and roots. We gave them some bread ~~for~~ which pleased them very mutch."[42] Brown, however, reports a fair amount of food in the camp, and describes women grinding seeds by moonlight and boiling a large pot of pottage of a "darkish grey color with litle chunks of bacon in it."[43] The chunks, it turned out, were actually bunches of matted ants. A roasted head of porcupine and a roasted "sand lark" completed the feast.

The Toquer Paiutes, like many southern Paiutes, were farmers. Brown records that Toquer's band had "small stripes of corn, squash, potatoes, &c., all scratched in with their hands, for miles along ash creek and seem very industrious." All the southern Indians Hamblin would meet in this trip practiced agriculture by the banks of creeks and rivers.[44] The irrigation of the Paiutes, their canals and dams, were comparatively sophisticated. Their use of the entire ecology of the region—such as beaver

5.2. Paiutes in St. George, Utah, of various bands, in conference with the U.S. Commission in 1873. John Wesley Powell stands to the left. Hamblin spent much of his life dealing with Paiutes in southern Utah, Nevada, and northern Arizona. Photograph by John K. Hillers. Courtesy National Anthropological Archives, Smithsonian Institution, GN-01662a.

dams and irrigation encouraging edible wild plants—created an environment that the Paiutes had utilized carefully for generations.[45]

This was Jacob's first introduction to the Paiutes of Dixie, with whom he would live for about fifteen years. They were often called Piedes (especially the Paiutes near Cedar City and Harmony). The word "Paiute," of uncertain origin, was a name other tribes, and early white explorers, used to refer to them.[46] Paiutes called themselves *Nuwuvi*, "the people." Even though they were often farmers, they were nevertheless highly mobile, and would migrate regularly to take advantage of seasonal food opportunities—harvesting pine nuts and grass seeds, hunting in Pine Valley in the fall, sometimes gathering with other Paiutes and Utes at Fish Lake (modern Panguitch

Lake) when fish were plentiful.[47] Headmen led bands, but they generally worked by seeking consensus in councils, rather than by authoritative fiat. The shaman, called *paugant*, was a religious leader—guided by an animal spirit helper, he could heal friends through long ceremonies or curse enemies and cause them to die.[48] In the winter, the Paiutes told stories of their gods and mythical figures, especially the noble Wolf and the evil or irresponsible Coyote. They also believed in a dominant spirit being, "one who made the earth."[49] However, in their view, supernatural power was not something that was always far away, but also resided in many inanimate objects. They had a ceremonial system that often included round dances.[50]

The Southern Paiutes have been divided into some sixteen bands or subgroups, based on where they lived, covering a territory from eastern Utah and Arizona, along the Arizona strip and in southern Utah, in country southeast of the Colorado (the San Juan Paiutes), to southern Nevada and the lower Colorado.[51] Thus each band was located in a traditional hereditary territory. John Wesley Powell remarked on the Paiutes' remarkable knowledge of every minute detail of their environment. He had thought himself to be a keen observer of landscapes, but found that the Southern Paiute far surpassed him in this respect.[52]

The missionaries had a group prayer, then spread out their buffalo robes and slept. The next day, Brown, and probably the missionary leadership, visited Toquer at his wickiups and inspected his "farm," which covered three acres and was watered by "a good irregating canal some 1/2 mile long."[53] All digging and planting had been done with sticks that looked like axe handles.

That afternoon two Paiutes from Santa Clara arrived; they struck Brown as taller, "more intellectual," "handsomer and more intelligent" than the Toquerville Indians. The missionaries held a council with Toquer and the new arrivals from Santa Clara that night. The Indians' main theme, which they would repeat in subsequent councils, was: "We are hungry often, we want food, we are naked we want shirts pants and hats." They had seen the clothing that the Coal Creek Piedes had received as payment for their work, and hoped to gain the same status.

The next day, June 9, the missionaries said farewell to Toquer and his people and continued down Ash Creek. In about two miles they reached the Virgin River, a swift running river about eleven feet wide and two feet deep, which the Indians called "Parouse" or "Pawdoos," meaning white water, or rapid water.[54] Its headwaters, in two forks, lay northeast, in modern Zion Canyon and Long Valley; after passing through southern Utah, it emptied into the Colorado in Nevada.

The missionaries traveled about fourteen miles west on the bank of the Virgin, past bluffs and what Brown called "elevated benches" covered with sand. Prickly pear, cactus, and "tall ouse," a kind of yucca, were plentiful. The missionaries camped that night near modern Washington, just east of modern St. George.[55]

Hamblin wrote that "the guide we had with us went out and [brought] some 5 or Six of the Piedes to our camp whare we had a good talk." The first of these was "Capt. Tsatwouts or Tatsigobits or 'Amos'"—this is Tutsegabits, dominant headman of Paiutes on the Santa Clara River and reportedly beyond; he would soon become a firm ally of Hamblin. Indian missionary Richard Robinson described him as the tallest Paiute he had seen, and stern and sober in appearance: "He looks as though he would be a friend whilst friendly and a fearful enemy whilst at enmity."[56]

Jacob records that these Indians also invited the Mormons to come live with them:

> The Pieds ware mutch p[l]eased with our visit. They said they wanted the Mormans to comed [come] among them and sho them how to get corn and wheet and make shirts for they s[u]ferd much with hunger and cold and many of their Women and Childrin [suffered] for want of something to eat. They said they had herd of the Mormans and that they ware freinds to the Pieds.

The next day the Santa Clara Indians traveled with the missionaries west along the south bank of the Virgin, "and seemed to be all most over joyd with our company," writes Hamblin. Their path took them over difficult hilly land, but they passed through an opening in these hills to arrive at a "fine table land south and east of the Rio virgin." Here, some women and children were gathering berries. Brown and William Hennefer approached a Paiute woman, who trembled in fear, and other missionaries went to investigate smoke by a stand of cottonwoods, where some Paiute men were clearing land for more farming.

Near some willows the missionaries saw a few Paiute families; they were nearly naked, and very frightened for their children. The whites crossed the Virgin here and camped on the north side of a bend in the river. For the rest of the day, curious Indians from the Santa Clara River dropped by. That night thirteen Indians slept near the eight missionaries.

On the eleventh, the missionaries reached the confluence of the Santa Clara and the Virgin, near modern St. George. The Santa Clara, which has its headwaters in the Pine Valley Mountains, was called *Tonequint* (or *Tuunukwinte*, "Black Stream" or "Black Flowing") in Paiute, and the local Paiutes called themselves, *Tonaquint-its*, "Those who live by the Tonequint," or *Too'nookweentseng*, "Black Flowing People."[57] After following the Santa Clara north for half an hour, the missionaries came to a cottonwood grove and camped.

Hamblin was greatly impressed by the Santa Clara Paiutes' agriculture: "Here the Pieds had quite extensive fields of wheet and corn. Some of the wheet was wripe," he wrote. Brown noted many patches of wheat on the Santa Clara, and beaver dams every few rods. The water often overflowed, which rendered the banks "good grazing patches."

Once again, Hamblin noted the intense shyness of the local Indians: "I well remember of entring many of there lodges of seeing thare women cetch up thare Childrin and run and hide for feer we had come to steel thare childrin but the news soon spred among them that we ware mormans thare white Brothers," wrote Hamblin proudly. "So all feer was banish[ed]."

After supper, five missionaries went to the wickiup of an Indian named Matruprenup for a meeting. There were eight or ten Paiute men there, two women, and a female child. The Indians were "in great fear," and grew pale and trembled at first. An old Paiute fled on the approach of the Mormons, and did not return, even when his friends called him. But, Brown writes, "Jacob Hamblin a quiet man went out and found him rolled up in his rabbit mantlet, like a rabbit hid in an old wickeup, he patted him on the shoulder, looked kindly upon him & told him the Mormons were 'toojee ticaboo toinab' very friendly & the same as the Pahutes, finally he came & [sat] down beside me all trembling. After smoking with us he became more composed."[58] Jacob's sincere sympathy for Indians is at the fore here, and his early use of the Paiute language.

In the following days, the missionaries preached and sang to the Indians, ate with them, traded with them, talked with them in their rudimentary Paiute, and had their interpreters preach to them. Jacob wrote with satisfaction, "The women would bring thare Childrin and set them down by me to sho to me thare confidence. They said the Eutahs had practis[ed] steeling thare childrin as they come on horse back. They ware a fraid of us until they lernt who we was." The Ute raids on the Paiutes, carried out on horseback and with guns, had had a devastating impact on the southern Utah Indians.[59] Utes (as well as Navajos) stole or bought Paiute children, then sold them to white Catholic Mexicans in New Mexico, who felt they were helping the children by raising them as Christians but who often simply used them as slaves.

On the thirteenth, the missionaries traveled up the Santa Clara, finally reaching Tutsegabits's wickiup, the capital of the Santa Clara Paiute homeland, as it were, where they again camped. This day marked an epoch in Hamblin's life; he would spend the next fifteen years of his life in the town that would later be known as Tonaquint Station, Fort Clara, or Santa Clara, located close to Tutsegabits's settlement. After a meeting with some forty Tonaquint-its, the missionaries went with Tutsegabits to see local "improvements"—especially a substantial dam seventeen feet wide crossing the Santa Clara. There were ten acres cultivated here, and ten more at a settlement just south of this one. "All along this river are small indian patches of 2 to 10 acres cultivated," Brown wrote. The Indians raised, among other things, wheat, now ripening, much corn, and beans.

The next day, Thales Haskell and Henry Evans, who were running low on provisions, left for Harmony with an Indian guide. Some thirty Paiute men and five or six women met with the missionaries in their camp that night. The Mormons sang hymns, "smoked the pipe of peace," and gave talks. Brown notes that Lorenzo Roundy and Hamblin's "feelings were full & longed for the day when they could express their sympathies in the native Indian language."[60] Tutsegabits and the missionaries' interpreter, Dick, both spoke at length. Brown noted that "The Captain" (Tutsegabits) had two wives and five or six children.

Brown awoke on the sixteenth to find eight women and twelve children in camp, all very curious to see how the missionaries attended to washing and cooking. The women were dressed in "mantillas" of "silver grey rabbit skin," which were hung on left and right shoulder alternately. Brown observed that Paiute women were viewed by the men as lesser beings: "The men always kept them in the rear & seem to esteem them as of but little account."[61]

At about noon, Brown received news that a trading expedition led by a Mormon, Colonel John Reese, had arrived nearby on the California Road. It was on its way back to Utah after a visit to California. Brown immediately began walking and arrived at the traders' camp an hour after sunset. Reese and his brother Enoch were proprietors of an early Salt Lake City store, dating from 1850, and they later set up a trading post in Carson Valley, Nevada.[62] This was the first freighting expedition from Salt Lake to California, and not a very successful one.[63]

The missionaries traded food, then camped with the Reese company, and apparently Rufus Allen decided that the missionaries should continue on with the company and return home to Harmony.

The next morning, June 17, as the Mormons started up the Santa Clara, they met a band of Paiutes led by a "smart, shrewd little Indian" named Macoovcooks (Jim), who requested baptism. Reese wanted to witness this event, and so he halted his company. First, the missionaries administered to Jim's brother, Oreump (Amos), who was seriously ill, then they baptized not just one, but eleven Indians. "Ten of them demanded baptisam. We tryed to pursuade them to wate until they understood more about it. They incisted on baptisiam then. So we baptised them," wrote Jacob.[64]

Oreump felt much better after receiving his blessing and baptism—Jacob writes that he was "heeled...allmos[t] instantly." After the baptism, there was a time of gift-giving, and Colonel Reese gave Macoovcooks pants and a shirt.

Rufus Allen then asked Jacob and William Hennefer to stay and visit more Paiute villages.[65] Hennefer, a thirty-year-old English blacksmith and barber, had been converted to Mormonism in 1844 and emigrated to America four years later.[66] He and Jacob would stay with the Paiutes for only a few more days.

At one Paiute village, a young woman asked the Mormon elders to help heal her mother, who was isolated in a wickiup, undergoing treatment from a Paiute shaman.[67] Jacob and Hennefer visited her and indeed found her near death. However, she wanted traditional Paiute treatment instead of Mormon prayers. The medicine man "was thare singin to the great spirit so that he would pity the sick woman and drive the Evle spirit away which was trying to kill hur," Jacob wrote. Paiutes often believed that serious illnesses derived from malevolent witchcraft.[68] Evil shamans, or ghosts, caused objects to enter the sufferer's body, "object intrusions." The healing shaman typically treated the sick person in his or her wickiup, as here, in a night-long treatment session attended by family and friends. The shaman, who had been chosen in dreams and had an animal guardian, brought regalia that often included eagle feathers.[69] Here, the shaman displayed a "medicine bow," and placed eagle feathers on his head.[70]

A shaman would typically sing songs that would be repeated by those present, and would walk or dance back and forth. Aided by his spirit guardian, he would diagnose the cause of the sickness—moral or ceremonial infractions on the part of the sufferer, visitation by spirits in dreams, a ghost entering the body (or loss of soul which had been stolen by a ghost), or malevolent witchcraft directed against him or her. Finally, he would lie under the patient and suck the foreign object from his or her body. Often the small object was exhibited to onlookers, then was buried.[71] Jacob noted that the medicine man placed "his mouth to the woman's, in order to drive away the evil spirits, and charm away the pain."[72]

But the woman's condition steadily worsened, and at sundown Paiutes sent for the Mormons. Hennefer thought it would not do any good to visit the woman, but Jacob convinced him to go. They "went and sung and prayd and laid our hands upon hur and she was instantly heled. They was all amased to see hur get up and ask for some thing to eat. They said she had not eat anything for 3 days."

If the Paiutes had supernatural healers, so did the Mormons. This must have been the beginning of Hamblin's reputation as a healer among the Paiutes.

On the nineteenth, Hamblin and Hennefer visited Tutsegabits and found the Paiutes of his village busy harvesting wheat with short sticks. Hamblin joined in, cutting off wheat heads with a knife and filling some of the women's baskets. "This rather diverted them," he wrote. The next day the Paiutes' dam broke, and Hamblin helped them repair it.

The two missionaries decided to return to Harmony two days later. They set out without Indian guides, evidently judging that they could find their way back via the Virgin and Ash Creek route they had taken before. Even at night, the heat was blistering, and they were buffeted by "scorchin winds from the desert," as Hamblin wrote. Against Jacob's advice, Hennefer set out in the dark along the trail that led away from the Virgin. Soon they were wandering helplessly over "burning sand," far from any possible resting place; it must have been a terrifying experience. Fortunately, Hamblin found a patch of grass and the trail leading through it. They traveled on through the night, rested in the morning, then visited Toquer again the next day, and by the twenty-third were back in Harmony.

5.3. Baptism of Shivwits Paiutes in 1875. Daniel D. McArthur baptizes Quituss, a Shivwits headman; Augustus Poor Hardy, one of the founders of Santa Clara, stands on the bank to the right and interprets. Photograph by C. R. Savage. Courtesy LDS Church History Library.

The historic journey was done. But it had only whetted Hamblin's appetite to live among the Paiutes at Santa Clara.

David Lewis soon led another company to the Santa Clara, without Hamblin, returning on June 30, after baptizing at least eighty-nine Paiutes, apparently including Tutsegabits.[73] This is the first of a number of mass baptisms of Paiutes in southern Utah history.[74]

Back in Harmony, Hamblin must have renewed his efforts to build Harmony: continuing to build the irrigation ditch, the fort, a corral, as well as looking after his own crops. But he was restless, and on June 28, 1854, he departed for Parowan with Prime Coleman,[75] and July 3 found them in the mountains east of Harmony hunting with local Piedes—a continuation of a favorite Tooele occupation. However, he noted ruefully, "game very scars."[76] He took the opportunity to learn the Paiutes' language as thoroughly as possible and obtain "an insight into their character."[77] Perhaps this is the expedition mentioned by Thales Haskell with his characteristic humor: "Jacob Hamblin, Amos Thornton, and I went with half a dozen Indians hunting deer. The Indian guide led us over the rocks, brush, high ledges and mountains until we were all tired out. We had to camp without water, saw one deer but did not kill it, so we returned much wiser if not better men."[78]

On the seventeenth, the Indian missionaries held a council and decided that since it was very hot south of the basin, and as their farming in Harmony had not been a great success, they would allow some missionaries to return home to northern Utah, spend some time there, then "beredy to go south when cold [called] on," as Hamblin put it.[79] The next day, he departed for Tooele, accompanied by Lorenzo Roundy, Isaac Riddle, and Augustus Hardy.[80] Twenty-four-year-old Isaac Riddle, a native of Kentucky, later lived in Pine Valley and Antimony, following the trade of miller and rancher. He would accompany Hamblin in a number of his journeys south of the Colorado.[81]

Jacob arrived in Tooele on July 26, 1854; it must have been a joyful reunion. "I found my Family all well," Jacob wrote, "for which I felt very thankful to my Father in Heven. The Brotherin of Tuela had jest commenced thare Wheet harvest."[82] He worked in Tooele till early September, when it was time to return south. Since he expected to be gone from Tooele for a long time, he decided to call his family together and bless them, in Old Testament fashion. Isaiah Hamblin also gave Jacob a blessing:

> Jacob. I lay my hands upon your head and Bless you with the Blesings of Abraham Isaac & Jacob.... The Lord will hav his eye over you on your presant mission and will bring you safe throu all difficiltys. Hundreds and thousands of the scatterd Remnants of the House of Israel shall be brought to the fold of good through your Preaching.

On this pentecostal day, Jacob wrote, "the Lord Pord [poured] out his spirit upon me. I felt to regoyc [rejoice] in the Lord and giv thanks to his Holy name."[83]

He was ready to return to southern Utah.

On about September 13, 1854, Jacob left Tooele for Salt Lake, and soon he traveled south with Hardy, Riddle, Roundy, and newcomers George Johnson and Clark Ames, arriving in Harmony on the twenty-eighth. They were pleased to find that late rains had saved their corn and vegetables, which had looked on the point of drying up when they went north. "I gethered my corn and such other things as the Lord had given me," wrote Hamblin, "and put it in as saf condicion as I. could." He also worked on the construction of the new Fort Harmony.[84]

On October 6, in Tooele, Rachel bore her second child, Joseph.[85]

5.4. Ira Hatch, early settler of Santa Clara, and companion of Hamblin on many journeys. He married a daughter of Navajo headman Spaneshanks. From McClintock, *Mormon Settlement in Arizona* (1921).

The next expedition that Hamblin participated in, led by David Lewis, set out on October 23. The plan was to visit Chief Toquer again, pass on to the Virgin, then travel east and northeast, following the Virgin to its headwaters and visiting Indians as they traveled. Then they would seek the Sevier River and Fish Lake (modern Panguitch Lake) near Parowan and pass over the mountains to that town.[86]

The company also included Sam Atwood, Gus Hardy, Ira Hatch, Clark Ames, Hyrum Burgess, Peter Shirts, and two Indian guides and interpreters, Queets (Dick) and Naguts. New York native Ira Hatch, then just eighteen years old, would also be a frequent companion with Hamblin on his journeys, and became a legendary explorer and Indian interpreter in his own right.[87] Peter Shirts, now about forty-six, helped found Iron City (west of Cedar City); Pahreah in Kane County; Montezuma Creek in San Juan County; and Las Vegas, Nevada. "Peter's Leap," on the road from Harmony to Washington, was named after him.[88] He was not a member of the Southern Indian Mission, but had a taste for unknown territory and seemed to prefer living far from any substantial town.[89]

The two sources for this expedition south and east of Cedar City, journals by Hamblin and Lewis, sometimes seem to describe entirely different expeditions, though their reports coincide occasionally.[90] If Lewis carried through on his plan to follow the Virgin to its headwaters, then find the headwaters of the Sevier and pass on to Panguitch Lake, the company must have traveled more or less along the east fork of the Virgin, through the spectacular narrows of Parunuweap Canyon, possibly following the east fork northeast through Long Valley between the Pink Cliffs to the west and the Paunsaugunt Plateau to the east. The weird and beautiful rock formations of southern Utah greatly impressed Lewis: "lofty turrets; temple spires; elevated ramparts; forts inaccessible; bastions & outworks impregnable!" he wrote. The east fork of the Virgin passes through the lower part of Zion National Park—this may be the first written description of the Zion area.[91]

There had once been many Paiutes living here, Paiutes told them, "but the land had become bad and the Piedes all died but a few."[92] Possibly this records one of the epidemics that decimated the Paiute population.

As they neared the Panguitch area, David Lewis, the Indian guides, and the missionaries were uncertain where exactly they were and in what direction to travel, though they knew that Fish Lake was near. The irascible Peter Shirts lost his patience with the company and left them to find the lake on his own. Lewis conferred with Hamblin, Sam Atwood, and Gus Hardy, then they set out. In an hour they could see the lake and soon camped near it. Shirts wandered in an hour later, Hamblin noted with satisfaction.

Toward the end of their expedition, as they were crossing the mountains east of Parowan, they braved a nerve-racking trail to meet some Indians who had hailed them from a mountaintop. At one point they had to make their horses jump from one cliff to another, and Jacob's nearly lost its balance and hurtled hundreds of feet to rocks below.

They introduced these mountain-dwelling Paiutes to white culture and Mormonism, exchanging shirts, cups, and knives for pine nuts. We might view this exchange as economic, Indian trading; or it might be regarded as mutual gift giving, a ritualized ethical practice in Paiute culture.[93] Hamblin would continue such Indian trading throughout his later career. Some modern historians have viewed his trading unsympathetically, but it was probably typical of many friendly white-Indian meetings in the American West.[94] By all accounts, he was generous in his dealings with Indians.

On about November 3, the missionaries arrived in Parowan, and soon were back in Harmony.

The next entry in Hamblin's journal is dramatic: "A few days after that I bought an Indian boy about six years old. Gave a gun and blanket some amunicion [for him]. Bro A. P. Hardy took him to Paroan and let Bro. Judd hav him." This is probably Zadok Knapp Judd, Jacob's brother-in-law. "Bro Hardy was offerd a horse for him by a Jentile. The Boy had ben Stolen from a small trybe so I baugh[t] him that I might let a good Man hav him that would try and make him youseful."[95] This is one of the earliest records of Mormons trading for Indian children, which were then raised in Mormon settlements.

Of course, Hamblin already had Albert, and other adopted Indian children, in his own family. In southern Utah, he became active in purchasing and raising Native

American children.[96] Mormons felt that they redeemed children—from Indians who had kidnapped or bought them—to prevent them from being sold into slavery to New Mexicans, and to prevent them from being abused by their captors. They regarded themselves as buying the children into freedom and argued that they were also educating the children and teaching them useful trades. These goals fit well with their religious mission to convert the people they considered "Lamanites" to Mormonism.

Non-Mormons in Utah viewed this situation less positively.[97] Sondra Jones argues that the Mormons enslaved Indians when they adopted them and treated their Indian charges no better or worse than Catholics, who enslaved Indians in New Mexico. When the legislature adopted an indenture procedure in 1852, it allowed some Mormons to regard Indians as property, until the Native Americans paid back their purchase price through labor. Jones writes: "As with any indenture, these children could be, and often were, traded and bartered between families. And occasionally they were purchased and carried for trade into other communities."[98] Van Hoak counters that the Mormons were certainly "more benevolent than New Mexicans" with Indian children. In New Mexico, enslavement of Native Americans was open and legal, while in Utah it was illegal.[99]

The Mormons of early Utah would have strongly disagreed with Sondra Jones's analysis. Indians were less slaves in Mormon homes than they were adopted children. They were taught to work hard, but so were white children. Undoubtedly, a minority of Indian children were ill-treated, or were treated as property, but in most cases they became members of the family. Albert referred to Jacob Hamblin as "Father."[100]

The slave trade declined after the Walker War. Utes still continued the slave trade with the New Mexicans (often exchanging children for guns), but Mormon settlements among the Paiutes effectively stopped the Ute raids for children.[101]

In November Rufus Allen sent Hamblin, by himself, to the Santa Clara Paiutes to use his influence "to keep them from disturbing the travelers on the southern route to California."[102] While there he witnessed a "squaw fight," his first exposure to a phenomenon that he encountered many times thereafter. In this case, an Indian who had claimed a woman was required to pass between two files of Indians, leading her along. As Hamblin watched, one of the Indians who had gotten the worst of a fight called on Hamblin for assistance. Hamblin did not want to get involved in local disputes and refused, but the Paiutes began to accuse him of cowardice, calling him a "squaw." Hamblin, feeling that his standing as a leader and friend might be undermined, agreed to enter the fight, but only on his terms—if any Paiutes were hurt by him, they could not hold that against him. The Paiutes agreed.

So Hamblin took the woman by the hand and led her down the two files of men. Only one Paiute disputed his claim, and, Hamblin wrote, "With one blow I stretched him on the ground." However, he also kicked him, which was against Paiute rules, and he had to pay a fine in recompense. Nevertheless, he was awarded the woman and immediately turned her over to the man she had preferred. "This was my first and last fight for a squaw," wrote Hamblin. "It gave me a prestige among them that greatly added to my subsequent influence."[103]

6

"The Chief Shed Teers When He Saw Our Women and Children"

Founding Santa Clara, 1854–1856

Jacob Hamblin's approach to Indian missionary work was total immersion—living with Indians, hunting with them, learning their language, using white technology to benefit them, sometimes participating in their religion and ritual, finding points of contact in religious viewpoints, talking with them when there were conflicts with whites. This was an approach he had followed even in Tooele, before he had been called on a formal mission. But he could not follow this policy with the Santa Clara Paiutes when he was living and farming in Harmony and only visiting Santa Clara periodically.

However, toward the end of summer 1854, the leaders at Harmony realized that there wasn't enough water there to sustain a large settlement, and it was decided to send some missionaries south to live on the Santa Clara. Rufus Allen and his counselors selected Hamblin, Thales Haskell, Ira Hatch, Samuel Knight, and Gus Hardy to found the new settlement.[1] Hamblin must have been overjoyed, as now he would be actually living in the midst of hundreds of Tonaquint Paiutes.

And he could not have selected better companions for this adventure. We have met all except Samuel Knight. Now twenty-two, he would also accompany Hamblin on a number of his expeditions and would spend many years with him in Santa Clara, which, unlike many Indian missionaries, he never left, except for brief periods.[2]

Three of these missionaries, Hamblin, Haskell, and Hardy, departed for the Santa Clara on December 1, and the next night camped near the Clara, where they found some Clara Paiutes hunting, including the chief Tutsegabits.[3] "They ware mutch pleesed to see us," Hamblin wrote. "I. told them that we ware going to stay with them now and learn them to build Houses and raise grain. This pleased them verymutch." The missionaries traveled on and camped near Tutsegabits's lodge, at his request.

The next day the Paiutes were "mu[tch] alarmed. They said the Eutahs ware acoming to steel [t]hare Childrin that night." They asked Hamblin and his companions if they would fight for them, and Hamblin, after counseling with Haskell and

6.1. Samuel Knight, early settler of Santa Clara, who accompanied Jacob Hamblin on many of his expeditions. Unlike many Santa Clara founders, Knight spent the rest of his life in the town. Courtesy Robert Briggs.

Hardy, agreed, and gave ammunition to the Indians. However, no Utes arrived that night, so in the morning Jacob and his friends traveled eight miles downriver, where they had planned to settle.

On December 14, Rufus Allen and Hyrum Burgess arrived from Harmony, and the next day the five men began cutting logs for a cabin. "One chopt them. I cared [carried] [them] to the building as thare was plenty of cottenwood timber thare," Hamblin wrote. "We soon had a comfortable cabin." They also made two cabins for the Indians. Tonaquint Station, the modern town of Santa Clara, had begun.

Two days later, on the seventeenth, the powerful Ute Sanpitch arrived at the Santa Clara. He was a brother or close relative of chiefs Wakara and Arapeen and would become one of the Indian leaders of the Black Hawk War.[4] Approaching the missionaries, he abruptly asked them what they intended to do on the Santa Clara. They (presumably Rufus Allen is the main spokesman) responded that they were going to live there in a settlement. Sanpitch told them that they must not build houses there, and that Wakara "the Big Chief" said they must leave the Santa Clara. "The Snakes [a branch of the Shoshoni] had ben kiling Eutahs at Provo and the mormans was glad," he informed them, implying that the Mormons were enemies of the Utes.

The missionaries told Sanpitch that Brigham Young, "our Chief," had sent them to the Santa Clara, and they would stay until he told them to leave. As for the Mormons in Utah Valley, "They had ben good to the Eutahs and gave them presants. The Eutahs in return had ben meen and if some of the Eutahs ware kiled it would learn the others a leson." After this bold statement, Sanpitch smiled.[5] The Mormons then asked Tutsegabits whether the Tonaquint Paiutes "wished us to stay, or leave. He said that the water and land are ours, and we wish you to stay."[6] "Go ahead," Sanpitch then replied, "It is all wright. I wanted to know if you ware braves. Use but logs for 2 cabins." So the Mormons and Paiutes continued with their work.

Sanpitch stayed with the Paiutes about a week and a half, and he stole no Paiute children, though he traded for some. Hamblin gives a fascinating, detailed account of this transaction. The Paiutes sold Sanpitch three children for one horse, two guns, and many beads. One of the Paiutes had bought two of these children from "a more distant Trybe," paying one gun for them. He in turn sold them to Sanpitch for two guns and the beads. "The Indian said the Girls Father and Mother cryd to see them go but they had nothing to eat and it would be beter for the childrin thanto stay and starve," Hamblin noted. And with the gun, they could obtain food. Hamblin saw "the teers fall fast from the eyes" of the oldest of the three children, perhaps the local Paiute, who was about ten. Then he editorializes: "I felt hart sick to see them dragd from thare homes to become slaves to the Jentiles"—that is, the New Mexicans.

While one can sympathize with the plight of the slaves, one can also see why basic economic considerations would be a strong motivation for the Utes to trade in children. An Indian child could be sold for a few hundred dollars, a monumental sum for Utah Indians.[7] Hamblin then inserts his thoughts (obviously retrospective) on the plight of the Indian and his mission to the Indians. It is a remarkable, quasi-poetic meditation.

> I saw the necesity of the Elders doing all they could to amelyerate the condicion of this miserable people. I felt that thus far I had don all that I could and still feel determind to. I hav sufferd many privations since I started on this Micion. Sometimes I step on the scorchig sand of the Desart at other times on the snow capt. Mts. The Mother Earth was our bead [bed]. The canopy of Heaven was our covering except a few blankets. I. hav many times had my feelings hurt to see the cold indiference with which the Elders hav ben treted by some of the Southern Setlers but I hav ben greatly blest of the Lord. He has all ways herd my prayres in times of trouble and deliverd me.

One of the challenges the Indian missionary faced was the "cold indiferance" of many fellow white settlers. This would be a constant in Jacob's coming life experience.

In the following days, Hamblin reported that he "had many a good talk" with Sanpitch, and reported Sanpitch's synthesis of Indian myth and Christianity, an unwise "Sun of God" who returned to his wise father, but would come again "and destroy evrything that was not good on the fase of the hole Earth" (including "the mosquitoes, snakes, wolves, etc."). So the Mormon and Indian found a common apocalyptic vision to share.

On the day before Christmas, Hamblin, Gus Hardy, and Thales Haskell left Santa Clara to return to Harmony for a time. While camping on the way home, an Indian who had just come from Harmony stopped by. He said that he had heard that the "Americans" did not want Brigham Young to be "Captain" any longer, and that the Americans "was agoing to send an American Capt. here. He said if the

Americans ever came here to fight the Mormans the Piedes would all help the Mormans." While this was just a rumor at this point, it shows graphically the triangulation of power in Utah: Mormons and Americans were enemies, to a certain extent; Mormons wanted Indians on their side in any possible conflicts with the Americans.[8] However, this triangulation (never entirely straightforward) was further confused by tensions and alliances between tribes. We have seen Hamblin siding with the Paiutes against the Utes but then striking up a friendship with Sanpitch. When Mormons had serious conflicts with Indians, on the other hand, they would be reluctant to go to the American army for help. The tensions between Mormons and the U.S. government would result in the "Utah War" of 1857–1858, and served as an important backdrop for the Mountain Meadows Massacre. During the Black Hawk War, Black Hawk used the lack of unity between Mormons and Americans skillfully to further his objectives.

Apparently spending little time in Harmony, Hamblin continued on to Cedar City and then Parowan, where he visited the nearby camp of Wakara to inquire about a woman who had been stolen from the Santa Clara Paiutes. Wakara said he knew nothing of the woman and that he also had tried to find out what had happened to her, without success.

That night Hamblin had a Christmas dinner with brother-in-law Zadok Judd, and the next day he visited the camps of the local Paiutes, all of whom said they knew nothing about the missing woman. But apparently Hamblin came to understand that Wakara did know something. Returning to the chief's tent, he ordered him to tell the truth. "He then said the Piedes [the Paiutes in Little Salt Lake Valley] had sold hur to the Eutahs un benone [unbeknown] to Walker [Wakara] and they had taken hur away." At this point, Hamblin apparently felt he could do no more, and returned to Harmony.

As Jacob's health was not good, he remained in Harmony for another week and a half. During this time he witnessed an altercation between the Mormon settlers in Little Salt Lake Valley and the Utes, an incident that shows the complex relationship between Utes, Paiutes, and Mormons at the time. The "Eutahs kiled a cow in Harmony" and apparently butchered and ate it. This angered "the settlers" (presumably the permanent settlers of Harmony, rather than the Indian missionaries) and "some wanted to fight." At this point, the Utes, instead of traveling north to their traditional territory, went south to the Santa Clara. Some of the Indian missionaries, however, desiring to prevent bloodshed, followed the Utes to the Santa Clara and "had a good talk with them." The Utes promised to return to Harmony and pay for the cow.

They did return, and did pay for the cow, by giving the Mormons a horse as a trade. But when they left they started to drive the horse off with them. John D. Lee, angry, "caled on the Brotherin to go with thare guns and fetch the horse back s[o] we went and met them," wrote Hamblin. A confrontation ensued, in which the Mormons were badly outnumbered. "Th[e] Piedes getherd around us two to one," wrote

Hamblin, and "some of the Boys got mutch alarmed." He calls the Indians "Piedes," that is, Paiutes, but there must have been Utes among them. No violence occurred, however, as Lee traded a shirt for the stolen horse.[9] The Mormons were discovering the limits of their alliance with the Paiutes: sometimes they would side with the Utes when the Utes and Mormons had a conflict, which angered the Mormons.

On January 11, Hamblin and Ira Hatch started for Tonaquint Station, and on the way were overtaken by a Paiute who had supported the Utes the day before, as Hamblin noted with a hint of anger. The Paiute said he "was agoing two days travail to the East in surch of his squaw that had run away." However, Hamblin thought that the probable cause of his leaving Harmony was to escape punishment for stealing sheep. The Paiute asked Hamblin to give him bread and matches. Hamblin's anger surged to the surface now: "I felt like thrashing the ground with him. I thought that would not do." Why, asked Hamblin, did he want to fight the Mormons yesterday then ask them for bread today?

The Paiute answered that he was afraid that Lee "was agoing to shoot the Eutahs" and then Wakara would return and kill all the whites in Harmony. Hamblin told him that he lied, that Wakara would not come to Little Salt Lake Valley to fight, and that the Paiutes "was fools to [threaten to] shoot thare friends." If the Paiutes had killed just one Mormon, Hamblin told him, all of the Indians would have been killed in retribution. The Paiute "said he did not want me to say any more for it would make him crye."

Hamblin now, as was typical of him, tried to create a bond with the local Indians, even after they had offended him. "I thought it was not best to through [throw] the P[i]edes away that lived about harmony," he wrote. So he told the Paiute that he had no bread to spare, but gave him some matches, with instructions to "talk good to all the Piedes he found whare he went." The Paiute agreed. They shook hands "and parted with better feelings than when we met." This is typical of Hamblin, in that he rose above initial irritation and feelings of enmity to seek a general long-term solution to a problem.

Hamblin and Hatch arrived at the settlement on the Santa Clara on the twelfth, meeting with Hardy and Haskell, who had preceded them, and immediately called a meeting of the local Indians to warn them against following the Cedar City Paiutes' example. "A good spirit prevailed I think," wrote Hamblin. "It was a good thing we come here be fore the minds of the Toneyquints ware prejudicet."

Hamblin and Hatch visited the various villages on the Clara, talking with the Paiutes, making them ax helves and doing "all the good we could."

They were invited to an "Indian weding" on the seventeenth, arrived at the village of nine or ten lodges where it would take place, and spent time talking with the local Indians as they waited for the event. Hamblin recorded two conversations in particular.

First, when Hamblin entered the lodge of the local chief, the man gave Jacob his hand but said, "I no talk. I am sick and sore. One of my daughters died last summer. I had to sell the other to the Eutahs to keep them from fighting us." This forced sale had occurred only a few days before. Hamblin responded that he would try to buy the girl back if he could, which pleased the chief. "He said if I would by hur and bring hur to the Toneyquint the[y] would be very glad to see hur once more."[10]

The other conversation introduced Hamblin to a new kind of Indian: the Moapats, Paiutes who lived in the sun-scorched deserts around what is now known as the Muddy River in southern Nevada. Just as the Indians on the Tonaquint took their name from the river they lived by, so the Moapats lived by the Moapa River—Moapa meaning "muddy."

Hamblin described the Moapat Paiute as "a tall fierce looking Indian." He had apparently journeyed to Santa Clara to meet these new white men living among the Indians: "He come to see his White Brothers." The Moapats had occasionally harassed and attacked whites passing through southern Nevada on the "California Road." This Moapat "said in time past he kiled white Men. Now he did not want to throw away any more blood."

Hamblin was a visionary man, and enjoyed talking about otherworldly things with his Indian friends. He reported that this Moapat told him that "great Spirits" lived near his land.

> He had seen them. Thare was 5 of them. He represented them as being about. 10 feet high [with] long bushy hair hanging down about there shouldiers. They ware great Chiefs and very Wise. One of them brought. game. The others brought all kinds of fruit corn. oos. [yucca] yant [agave] greaps [grapes]. salt and other things for the Piedes.[11]

But these spirits were not always beneficent. One of them became enraged when the Moapat killed a deer, and "chased him with a big speer and wounded him in the back." The Indian showed Hamblin a huge scar on his back to authenticate his story.

Hamblin now describes some Indian weddings or "squaw fights" at length, and it is a bleak account, which emphasizes the brutalization of the woman. According to Hamblin, "[W]hen a Piede squaw is old enough to Mary thare is from six to twenty wanting hur for a wife so they get together and fight for hur until they are all whipt but one. He taks the bride." Presumably, there were from six to twenty men competing for one young woman, in part because of the slave trade carried out by the Utes of Utah and the whites of New Mexico, which focused on children and women.

Multiple men fighting for a woman seems to have a certain clear logic, as does the next step in the process: each combatant could bring friends and allies to fight on his side. Thus if one of the combatants was smaller in stature than the other, he could nevertheless win the bride if his friends fought courageously. This enlarged the battle to include substantial groups of Indians—Hamblin says he witnessed fifty to a hundred fighters at one of these events. These fights left many contestants injured for life.[12]

Women were an anxious audience at these conflicts; when they felt the fight had gotten too violent they would sometimes throw burning coals into the fray to stop it. At some point, it was apparently accepted that the young woman in question might play a part in the battle, and she could be dragged from one party of combatants to another. This must have been extremely painful for the woman. Hamblin describes one woman, after hours of being dragged back and forth, as looking dead, or near death.[13] In 1861, Anthony W. Ivins witnessed a squaw fight near the Santa Clara fort in which the woman was dragged back and forth and lost consciousness.[14] Jacob explained to him that he had witnessed a squaw fight in which the woman had been so brutalized that her brother could not endure it any longer, and killed her with a knife to stop her agony.[15]

The main combat Hamblin witnessed, on January 24, was not a simple fight for an unmarried young woman. About a year previously, an Indian from a different area had stolen a married woman and taken her to his home.[16] After a while, she apparently accepted marriage with this second man, but at one point she wanted to see her family and friends in her home village again, and she and her husband came back to visit. However, her former husband claimed her and the local headman, perhaps Tutsegabits, ruled that the two men should fight for her. On the twenty-fourth, about fifty fighters gathered by the Clara, naked except for a strip around their loins, and with their hair tied back. The two husbands began to fight, "bruseing each others fases to a horible rate," Jacob wrote. One fell, and a friend took his place. Eventually, all the men had fought and become badly bruised. They then apparently rested, and "rupet [rubbed] thare fases and rubed and puled thare fingers a short time," a curious regimen, in order to recuperate.

At this point, one of the men took the contested woman by the arm and "puled hur along." This signaled the beginning of another round of the fight. Another man confronted the man leading her and the man-to-man combat started again. Then they began to drag and "haul" her around. At one point, some men began to cross the river with the woman, and she broke free and ran to where Hamblin was standing on the bank. She asked Hamblin to pull her up, which he did. However, a Paiute man then confronted Hamblin aggressively, and the missionary said he did not want to fight. The Paiute said that Hamblin should not take hold of the woman if he did not want to fight. Hamblin said he did not understand, and "it past off." "I was glad to get out of it with out a brused fase," he wrote.

The combatants dragged the woman over the river near a grouping of five or six lodges, and the two claimants to the woman fought for her again. One grabbed the hair of the other, which evidently was against the rules, and one of the friends of the offended man struck the other. At this, "they all commenced fighting like someny Bull Dogs," wrote Hamblin. "This presented a sight and sound that I cannot describe the Women and Childrin heloing and schreeming." At this point the women began throwing hot coals onto the fighting men and whipping their heads with long sticks. The "bride" was trampled underfoot.

The fighting continued until an hour after sundown. Two of the men dragged the woman—who had fainted and appeared lifeless, with blood issuing from her mouth—behind one of the lodges, tore her buckskin shirt off her, and fought over the shirt until they were exhausted. Then the man who ended up with the shirt slept on it.

The next day the number of combatants had doubled. They organized at a place near the fires of the lodges, and after they had talked for some time, "they mad[e] a jeneral rush at ech other," wrote Hamblin, "and beet each other until thare fases ware all covered with blood." The curious interlude of rubbing faces and pulling fingers then was repeated, and they began pulling the woman around and fighting again. They finished at three o'clock in the afternoon.

On the following day, there was another squaw fight, about eight miles down the river, and the Paiutes invited Hamblin to witness it. They began fighting in the morning, and at about noon, they began pulling and dragging the woman. A few hours later, they dragged her to the lodges, even though, Hamblin wrote, "I could see no sines of life in the Woman."

On the twenty-sixth, Hamblin evidently returned to the original squaw fight. After the day's fight, one of the claimants had won her "fair and square"—evidently her original husband. But she threw a monkey wrench into the situation when she would not accept the resolution, wanting instead to stay with her present husband, and would not sleep with the winner.

The next night, the main combatants and their supporters fought again for about two hours. The side that had won previously was infuriated that the woman would not accept the defeat of her second husband. This fight was especially difficult for Hamblin to watch, as they stripped the woman naked and "dragd hur about and abused hur in the most s[h]ameful manner," dragging her body over sagebrush and greasewood. When they began to drag the woman into the river, Hamblin could tolerate no more. "I run before them talked all the Indian words I could make of any Survice," he wrote. The Paiutes stopped the proceedings and carried the apparently lifeless woman back to the camp.

Hamblin went to the chief—perhaps Tutsegabits—and said he would not stay with the Paiutes if they continued such conduct. "He said that was the way they got thare Women." Hamblin said that there was a better way—"if a Man wanted a Wife and he could find a Women [*sic*] that wanted him he should Mary them and they should love thare Women." He also stated that he wanted to write favorably about the Paiutes to "the great Morman Chief," but he would have to report the abusive nature of the squaw fights unless the Paiute chief tried to stop it now.

The chief and his principal counselors discussed the situation that night. The next morning, the chief came to Hamblin and said that "he did not want me to say any thing about what had ben don. They was a shaimd of it themselves. He wanted me to throwe away all that I had seen and they would stop such fights that night."

Later that day, Hamblin wrote that he "preacht to them from the house top"—perhaps literally, for they now had log cabins. Hamblin felt encouraged that he had begun to gain influence among the Paiutes: "I felt to rejoice in the Lord my Father in Heavan that his work had commenced among his people that I was a yousefull instrament in his hand in getherin Israel."

On February 2, Sam Knight and Amos Thornton arrived at Tonaquint Station with "spaids hose [hoes] picks and some other tools" donated by the Saints in Cedar City, and the next day, the missionaries, together with the Paiutes, began to build a stone dam across the Santa Clara—which would "enable many of the Piedes to raise there one [own] bread." In the following week, they worked hard on the dam.[17] The Paiutes brought stones with their bare hands, and the missionaries were able to use an old axe the Paiutes had to break the larger stones down. When completed, the dam was eighty feet long, fourteen feet high, and three feet thick—an impressive achievement (though it would eventually fall victim to flooding).

The Paiutes, after contributing much labor to the dam, had been suspicious that they would not receive an equal share of water, but were delighted to find that an equal amount of water flowed into their ditch.[18]

On the eighteenth, Hamblin was struck by a severe sickness, caused by "hard labor and exposure."[19] "I went to the Dore [door] was taken with a gidyness could not see," he wrote. "I attempted to go in to the House when I fell prostrate on the ground. Bros Hardy. and. Hascal helpt me on the bead [bed]. They then bathed my head and brest in cold water. I was attacted with a violent Feaver." This was probably malaria, which would plague pioneers living by the Santa Clara and Virgin Rivers in Mormon Dixie for many years.[20] Both fellow missionaries and Paiutes were concerned. "The Piedes crouded in around me. They was afraid I would dye," Jacob wrote. Sam Knight and Gus Hardy administered to Hamblin, and the fever left him, but he was too weak to move. That night, "3 Chiefs got together and cryed and made a mornful nois all the fore part of the night." Hardy was apparently sent back to Harmony for provisions at about this time.

Jacob convalesced slowly and could not leave his bed the following week. On Friday or Saturday, Tutsegabits, probably about to set off on one of the Paiutes' seasonal journeys, came to bid Jacob good bye. "He said he wanted me to get well quick. He and the other Chiefs cryed until midnight for me." By Sunday, February 25, Hamblin was improving, but he continued to endure "a sevier pain in my elbose and knees. I. could not sleep knights nor but little days."[21] His diet was inadequate, only bitter corn meal, which had disagreed with him even before he had become ill. He endured "rather lonesome times" alone in his bed.

The next day, Hamblin noted that Hardy had not returned as expected. He prayed in his journal:

> I do not complain or murmer. It is all wright. I feel anxious to do mutch for this people to bring them from thare loe [low] degraded condicion. I desire to soon get my helth and strength to go a bout my Masters buisness that I may be free from pain which blessings may the Lord my Hevnly Father grant. I asket [ask it] in the name of. Jesus. Christ. Amen.

On Tuesday the twenty-seventh, Hardy and Sam Atwood arrived with food, after having been delayed by a week of severe storms in Harmony. Jacob was so overcome with relief when he saw them that he could barely speak.

Hardy's return marked the beginning of another chapter in southern Utah history: the Dixie cotton mission. While he was visiting in Parowan, a Sister Nancy Pace Anderson, who had lived in the southern states, gave him about a quart of cotton seed, which was the first cotton seed to be brought south of Parowan. This was planted in Santa Clara, tended with care, and produced enough cotton for thirty yards of cloth, created by Caroline Beck Knight, Maria Woodbury Haskell, and Charlotte Curtis.[22]

Hardy and Atwood advised Hamblin to return to Harmony where he could receive better treatment for his lingering illness, and two days later Jacob managed to mount a horse and, accompanied by Atwood, start the journey back to Harmony. They camped near a stream that night and the horses wandered away, so Atwood went to recover them, leaving Hamblin alone and untended. "When he was gon I was ver[y] sick high feaver sevier pain in [my body]," he wrote. "I lay in heerin[g] of the water could not get it." Atwood finally returned with the horses late at night. He had no vessel to bring water to Hamblin, but carried water to him in one of his holsters. "It was Heaven to get all I wanted of" the water, wrote Jacob.

The next day, the two men rose at sunrise and once again Hamblin, weak with fever and with only a few bites of bread for breakfast, somehow managed to stay on his horse. "I believe the Lord strengthened me from time to time as I was enabled to sit on the horse until I arived at the Ft," he wrote.

At Harmony, Robert Ritchie took Hamblin into his home and gave him a bed and nourishment. "May th[e] Lord bless him for his kindness for I was sick and afflicted and he took me in," Jacob journalized. He convalesced through February and early March, apparently never regaining his health completely, though it improved. On March 22 he was able to accompany Thales Haskell and Gus Hardy, newly arrived from Tonaquint, to Cedar City to pick up vegetables and flour that had been donated to them.

By March 26, Jacob had recovered enough to return to Santa Clara, with five other missionaries, Haskell, Hardy, Sam Knight, Clark Ames, and Lyman Curtis, as well as "6. Horces. 2. Mules. one yoak of oxen. 2. pigs. 10. chickens 2 wagons laded with provisions and seeds and one. Plow." Slowed down by the animals, they did not arrive at Tonaquint Station until April 1. During the journey there was some heated "plain talk" between Ames and Curtis, and when they got to Tonaquint, they brought their dispute to Hamblin. As Curtis had been a Mormon much longer than Jacob, he felt somewhat uncomfortable being placed in the position of adjudicator. Nevertheless, "They in sisted on my speeking my mind. I then spoke my mind freely. The dificilty was setled. A good feeling prevailed." Hamblin was gradually taking hold of the reins of leadership in Tonaquint Station.

On April 2, the missionaries plowed "a gardin spot," assisted by Paiutes. "Many of the Piutes come to see us throwe the dirt as they caled Plowing," wrote Hamblin. The Indians assisted in cutting the sagebrush and clearing the land, and the Mormons fed the workers. The missionaries also gave five bushels of potatoes to the Paiutes to use for seed. The missionaries raised a good crop of beans, corn, and squash and watermelon that season.[23]

Hamblin was pleased with the work done. "A good sp[i]rit seemed to prevail," he wrote. Nevertheless, the challenge of converting and educating the Paiutes daunted him; he was starting to face the vast cultural chasm between whites and Paiutes unencumbered by European education and tradition. "I reialise the task of sivialiseing this People," he wrote. "They are in avery low degraced condicion in deed lothesome and filthey beyond descripsion." This language was probably influenced by the Book of Mormon, in which the prophet Mormon writes that the Lamanites "shall become a dark, a filthy, and a loathsome people, beyond the description of that which ever hath been amongst us" (Mormon 5:15). Hamblin continues:

> I hav wished many times for the moment that my lot was cast a mong a more cleanly People whare thare could befound something desirable something cheering to a purson accustomed to a civilised life. As yet we hav manage[d] to gain mutch influance among them. As for my self I hav saught the Lord mutch for understanding.

Hamblin remarks that nothing has been stolen from the missionaries by local Indians, even though they have often left their cabin unattended. The missionaries *had* been challenged on a few occasions. Once, three Paiutes came into the cabin and attempted to insult or "run over" the missionaries. "I jirked one kuffed another and told the thurd to go out [the] Doar," Hamblin wrote. "He said he would not so I led him out by the hair of his head and took my foot from his seet of honor which gave him to think I ment what I said." The next day this Paiute came running aggressively toward Hamblin with a gun in his hand, but Hamblin, who was riding a horse, faced him down.

Thales Haskell wrote that the biggest problem facing the Santa Clara missionaries was traveling bands of Indians who constantly "invaded our camp" and the local Paiute camps. They would use trading as a pretext but would actually be planning thefts. When animals were taken, the missionaries would try to preserve good relations with the Indians while reclaiming the stolen animals, a delicate tightrope act. "Oftimes we would follow a renegade bunch for days before we were able to contact them and convince them that we were friends who came to live among them," Haskell wrote.[24] He characterized life in early Santa Clara as "one continual round of privation and hardship."[25]

After a meeting of eight missionaries at what Hamblin called the "lower station," on April 29, Chief Tutsegabits came to Hamblin and said he would move up the Tonaquint to plant corn now. Since one of his sons had died here in the previous year, he did not want to plant and harvest the same land so soon after this event. "I and all of the Yanawants [local Paiutes] lov the Mormans all the time," he told Hamblin. "We do not love a little and get mad but we are friends all the time. I want you to prey for me and my ~~band~~ men that we ned [need] not die. The Pieutes are not wise at coal crick [Cedar City] they steel and die all the time." Tutsegabits thus understood that the Cedar City Paiutes were dying, perhaps from some epidemic, because they had stolen from the Mormons.[26]

Hamblin clearly was touched by this speech, and wrote that he believed the Paiutes were "as good as they know how to be."

The next day Hamblin started for the northern settlements with Hardy and Knight, probably to pick up supplies. They arrived in Harmony on the first of May, then visited Cedar City and Parowan, where Jacob attended church, trying to sit in the back, unnoticed, because his clothes were not suited for church. But the presiding leader rose, said that he understood Brother Hamblin was here from the Santa Clara settlement, and called him to the stand to speak. Jacob acquiesced. "I had a good flo [flow] of the spirit for which I felt thankful," he wrote. "I spoke of my leighbors among the Lamanites and of thare low degraded condicion. The congregacion seemed well pleased with my remarks." Religious oratory was one of the great pleasures of early Mormon culture, and Hamblin clearly enjoyed participating. A carpenter named

Elijah Elmer called Hamblin aside after the service and donated three chairs to the Santa Clara community.

Jacob arrived back at Tonaquint Station on April 13 but did not stay long, returning to Little Salt Lake Valley with Knight, Hardy, and Thales Haskell, since Brigham Young was about to visit. Clark Ames at this point sold out his share in the Santa Clara farms and gave up on the Tonaquint mission. He "said he was agoing to plant some potatoes whare he had some one to cook them," wrote Hamblin. He was clearly used to steady, predictable meals, which he was not getting at Santa Clara. He said that "if he got out of this snap [predicament] he would not be cetched in another very soon." This lively language again shows that settling in Santa Clara was a continual struggle, and that the missionaries often did not eat well. Many who were called to Dixie did not stay.

Hamblin and his friends arrived in Harmony on May 18 and heard Brigham Young, Heber C. Kimball, and George A. Smith preach in Cedar City two days later. Hamblin's health must have continued to be poor, for in the days following the conference, Rufus Allen counseled him to return to Tooele and regain his health with his family. On the thirtieth, Gus Hardy went to Tonaquint Station to bring back his and Hamblin's horses, and soon after his return they departed for northern Utah.

Hamblin arrived at his Tooele home on June 20, 1855. The reunion with Rachel and the children was undoubtedly joyful, but the family's prospects were not promising. "Grasshoppers" (locusts) had eaten all Hamblin's wheat and most of his vegetables that spring, and there was "evry prospect of a famin."[27] He worked hard to get his family situated so he could leave them and take up his mission in the south again.

However, at some point, according to Hamblin himself, he met with Brigham Young, who told him "to take my family and go south and not neglect my Micion when I got them thare." Or, as a December 1855 letter puts it, "to take my Family and .4. or .5. others if I could fin[d] thos that would go and do write [right] and go on a Micion with me on the Staclara."[28] This was a significant change in policy. (Apparently, there may have been some kind of miscommunication between Hamblin and Young on this point.) The idea had been for the Indian missionaries, without their families, to spend a year or two in the south, then return and take up their farms and labors in the comparatively civilized north again. Now Hamblin was taking his family to the south, which would make it much easier to put down roots there. It would also make his total immersion policy with the Paiutes easier—he would not have to visit Tooele periodically. Jacob also recruited his brother Oscar and Dudley Leavitt, with their families, to accompany him. Before he left Tooele, Jacob deeded all his property—including some seventy head of livestock, two wagons, and household

6.2. Dudley Leavitt, early settler of Santa Clara, who accompanied Jacob Hamblin on many of his expeditions. One of his sisters married Jacob Hamblin, and two others married Jacob's brother William ("Gunlock"). From Brooks, *Dudley Leavitt, Pioneer to Southern Utah* (1942).

furniture, altogether worth $1,600—to "Brigham Young, Trustee in Trust" for the Mormon Church.[29] A number of people consecrated their surplus property to the church at this time, but these consecrations apparently were never acted upon by church leadership.[30]

Jacob and his family left northern Utah on September 11, accompanied by Oscar, Dudley Leavitt, and their families, with wagons and livestock. Oscar, twenty-two, was fourteen years younger than Jacob; he had married Mary Ann Corbridge the previous year, and the couple had one child. Dudley Leavitt would become a close companion of Hamblin in southern Utah, and one of Dixie's legendary pioneers. Though only twenty-five, Dudley had already married two wives.[31]

In addition, two remarkable, strong-minded females followed Dudley south the next spring: his mother, fifty-seven-year-old widow Sarah Studevant Leavitt, and his youngest sibling, Sarah Priscilla, just fourteen. The latter had already become a close friend and helper to Rachel Hamblin in Tooele; she would eventually become her sister wife. They travelled south with Dudley's brothers Jeremiah and Lemuel, arriving at Harmony on May 22, 1856.[32]

When the September 1855 caravan of Hamblins and Leavitts stopped in Parowan for Rachel to visit her brother Zadok, Jacob invited him to join the new settlement. "I was anxious to go," wrote Judd. He counseled with his bishop, who advised him to stay in Parowan as he doubted Jacob's authority to call settlers to Tonaquint Station. However, "[t]he love of a warm climate and my anxiety to go overcame the advice of the Bishop," wrote Judd, "and I consented to go."[33] So for one early pioneer, the die was cast for Dixie. The Judds came to Santa Clara within the year.

Jacob's group probably arrived in Harmony in mid-October. At some point before reaching Harmony, Hamblin apparently conferred with Rufus Allen, told him of Young's instructions, and Allen said he would set apart Oscar and Dudley for their missions when he returned from a visit north. In Harmony, Jacob talked with Allen's counselor, Sam Atwood, who said he would inform local stake president Isaac Haight of Hamblin's plans.

The Hamblin company arrived at Santa Clara on October 18, and "ware kindley receivd by the Lamanites," wrote Hamblin in his diary. "They was all most overd joud to see our Women and childrin. We had many good talks with our read [red] friends." In the December 1855 letter to Young, Hamblin wrote that many Santa Clara Paiutes traveled six to eight miles to meet them. Tutsegabits "shed teers when he saw our women and childrin wagons catle and sheep. He said now he believ[ed] what we had told him." That is, now he believed that Hamblin and the Mormons would make a permanent settlement on the Clara.

The issue of trafficking in children came up again. "We tol[d] them they must not sell there Childrin to the Eutahs unles they wanted to," Hamblin wrote to Young. And, in fact, on November 14, prominent Ute headman Ammon, a brother or close relative of Wakara, Sanpitch, and Arapeen, arrived to buy children from the Santa Clara Paiutes.[34] Ammon and local Paiutes met in a council, to which Hamblin was invited. The Paiutes told Ammon that Hamblin had told them not to sell their children, and Ammon turned to Hamblin and asked if he had indeed given the Paiutes such an instruction. "This plased me in a peculier fix," wrote Hamblin. He replied that he had told the Paiutes not to sell their children "if they did not want to." Evidently, Ammon did not react with anger, and Hamblin developed a friendship with him. In fact, Ammon even "preached mutch to the Piutes," and was an influential speaker.[35]

Ammon and two Utes who traveled with him were also planning to visit the Hopis and requested that Hamblin accompany them. If they met other Utes, he said, they might be angry that Ammon was not bringing children to trade, and he wanted Hamblin on hand to explain why he had discouraged the child trafficking. The Paiutes, in their turn, wanted Hamblin to visit the Hopis and to trade for blankets and sheep. Hamblin agreed to go, taking some wheat as a gift to the Hopis.[36] When they had been gone a week, however, the Utes decided they would stop and hunt for a few weeks, and Jacob turned back, arriving home on November 25.[37]

He was expecting the arrival of Rufus Allen, but when he did not show up, became concerned and decided to visit Harmony, arriving there on December 16. He was stunned to find that Allen "and his council was mutch dissatisfide with me"—both for starting on the journey to the Hopis without authorization, and also for bringing his family to the south, as Allen informed Hamblin that Young had told him he did not want families in the Santa Clara settlement. Hamblin must have felt at a total loss, as he had understood that Young explicitly advised him to take his family, and a few other suitable families, south. Perhaps Young gave instructions to

Jacob that the missionary misunderstood, or he simply gave instructions at different times that were contradictory.

Erastus Snow, an apostle who must have been visiting Harmony, advised Hamblin to write to Young and make sure that he had not misunderstood his instructions.[38] Hamblin did write, and queried Young, "Could I of misunderstoo[d] you. when you told me how to manage with the Indians...and many other things?" He mentioned that he had four Indian children living in his family, three of them female, and he had promised two of them that they would live on the Santa Clara. He wrote that he thought bringing other missionaries with skills would be a great benefit for the Tonaquint community. He ended, "If I have gon contrary to yur councell the so[o]ner I know it the beter."[39]

Jacob returned to Santa Clara, accompanied by Rufus Allen, who intended to ask the missionaries to bring their wives and children back to Harmony, but Jacob convinced Allen that the families had had "a good influence" on the Paiutes, "which might seriously have been interrupted by any sudden move." After Allen told them to remain until he received further guidance from Young, he returned to Harmony, where he received a letter from Young that evidently requested that the families of the missionaries leave Santa Clara and return to northern settlements. However, it may have left open the possibility that the families could stay, provided that provisions for their safety were made.

Allen, Jacob, a Brother Pugmire, and three others met in council, apparently in Harmony, to discuss the situation. After reading letters that Young had written to Jacob as well as to Allen, and discussing the matter freely, the council decided that the families might stay if a fort was built to protect them. Allen wrote to Brigham Young,

> We came to the conclusion to strengthen that station for a short time, and commence a fort, which with the aid of a few masons from these parts, and probably 50 or 60 indians & the facility of getting good rock naturally cut in squares close by, we think we can finish within 3 weeks at farthest.

The Paiutes were interested in helping to build the fort so that they could be protected from the Utes, and so that they could use it for storage of their grain.

Allen concluded his letter:

> I am satisfied that Bro. Hamblin went down there believing he was doing your will in good faith; at first...he went by my Counsel then, & since has ever been ready to do as we counselled him, & I believe has the welfare of the remnants of Israel continually in his mind. & his error is one of judgement not of will. When Bro Hamblin came down I was north. I did not think it according to your general counsel, that families should gather. & further believed if you had so ordered it, you would have advised me of it.[40]

Thus it was decided to allow the families of the missionaries to stay, but to build Fort Clara as protection for them and for the local Indians.

Four stone masons from Cedar City, including Elias Morris, volunteered to help with the fort, and in the early months of 1856, the Clara and Pinto Creek residents, with the help of local Paiutes, built it. Hamblin wrote, "We commenced quaren [quarrying] rock and halling and in three weeks 12 men built a Fort 100 feet square 2 feet thick. 8 feet 6 inc[h] high. The Lord blesed us excedingly in our undertakeing for which we felt to thank and to praise his holy name."[41]

In reference to the three Indian girls mentioned in Jacob's letter to Young—it is well-known that Jacob and his wives brought up three Indian girls in his family, named Eliza, Ellen, and Fanny. In 1857, an Indian agent spoke of two girls in the Hamblin household; when they were adopted in 1853, they were about six and eight years old, and Rachel soon started to train them in the art of weaving.[42] So at least two girls were adopted in Tooele, and were probably Goshute or Shoshoni, like Albert.

In February 1856 there had been Indian trouble in the Iron Mission towns, so in March Rufus Allen ordered the missionaries at the new Fort Clara to return to Harmony, which they did, Hamblin says, only reluctantly. However, they decided to take a new route through the mountains, even though they had heard that it was impassable for wagons. But, "we all felt like trying it," wrote Jacob—an attitude typical of those pioneers.[43]

The standard route to Harmony followed the Santa Clara River northwest until it met the "California Road" (and Old Spanish Trail); it then continued by the Santa Clara north past modern Gunlock. It branched off to follow a tributary of the Santa Clara, Magotsu Creek, then angled northeast and north through Mountain Meadows until it reached Pinto (near modern Newcastle). At Pinto, the route left the California Road and led southeast through the Pine Valley Mountains to Harmony.[44]

Now, however, this intrepid group of pioneers apparently followed roughly the modern route north, through modern St. George, and then up Ash Creek, by modern Toquerville, past the fearsome Black Ridge, and on to the Little Salt Lake Valley. They made it to Harmony, with wagons, in only four days, to the surprise of many Harmony saints. Mary Judd gives a vivid description of this mini-epic:

> We washed our clothes and packed up and started over the mountaines where...no wagon had ever travelled before and went thrue misqueet [Mesquite] flatt where the sity of saint geor[ge] now standes and thrue the sand onto the riovergin and camped that knite and so on the next day with no road Br knite and Colman thales hascal riding a head to serch out the best track for us to follow. So we travelled on untill we came to fort harmony. Here

> we stoped to fix up as we had torne our close [clothes] terably travling thrue brush and rockes with no road of any kinde.[45]

This was a far cry from the relaxing hour-long drive from Santa Clara to Cedar City on the highways that we enjoy today.

Jacob once again returned to Tooele, where he found his father very sick, reportedly of calculus (kidney stones).[46] Isaiah told Jacob that he wanted to come south, in the hopes that the hot weather there would improve his health, and Jacob agreed. They left Tooele on April 26, 1856, and after a cold, snowy journey, arrived in Harmony on May 7. Three days later Jacob and Isaiah started for Fort Clara (Oscar Hamblin and Zadok Judd, with their families, had already moved back to the fort), arriving there on the fourteenth.

Then Hamblin left his father at the fort, returned to Harmony, and took Rachel, about seven months pregnant, and the children, to Pine Valley, at the headwaters of the Santa Clara in the Pine Valley Mountains, where a few missionaries were building a sawmill. He probably wanted to spare Rachel the oppressive heat at Fort Clara; however, he could do no more than set up a tent for her at Pine Valley.[47] Isaac Riddle had discovered this place when he was searching for a stray cow, and he settled it with Jehu Blackburn and Robert Richey in summer 1855.[48] Located some twelve miles southwest of Harmony, it later provided much of the lumber in southern Utah, and also offered plentiful forage for sheep and cattle, which is what attracted Hamblin. After making a deal with the sheepherders of Harmony, he brought their flocks to Pine Valley.

On May 17, Jacob wrote a letter to Brigham Young, mentioning that George Armstrong, the Indian agent, had visited two days earlier and had left welcome farming implements and clothes for the local Paiutes. These were, he wrote, "strictley honest the most so of any People. I ever knew." He described Tutsegabits as "the Chief of all the Tribes or bands of Indians East of the Colerado and west to the great Desert including the big mudy Indians." Modern historians doubt that Tutsegabits's influence reached that far, but a number of sources repeat this.[49] He is Hamblin's prize convert—"as good a man as he knows how to be," Jacob wrote to Young. "He preaches a great deel to his peopl and preaches as good as any Elder in Israel could do." Oratory was one of the art forms of the Paiutes, as well as other Indian tribes. Often a man became a leader in a band because of his persuasive skill.

Jacob once again affirmed that he hadn't meant to go against President Allen's counsel or find fault with him. He also said that the local Indians had requested that he go among the Hopis and buy sheep, and the Hopis had sent messages requesting that he go, but he said that he would not go unless given permission.

He described the Indians in his household: "I hav redeemed .2. boys and .4. girls or bought them of the Lamanites. One of the boys is keeping sheep. He is about 14 years old [a] very trusty usful boy." This was Albert. "The squaws are carding spining and lurning to read."

He closed the letter, "I rejoice to think I hav ben an instrument in the hand of the Lord in comencing this great work among this People and for the influance. I hav gained. It is my meet and my drink."[50]

In summer 1856 Brigham Young advised Hamblin to choose more settlers to come to Fort Clara, and three more of Jacob's brothers, Alsen, now twenty-eight, Frank, seventeen, and Frederick, fifteen, along with two Leavitts and Andrew S. Gibbons, joined the community.[51] Andrew Smith Gibbons was a young man always ready for adventure. Born in 1825 in Ohio, his parents died when he was a child, and he was raised by a Mormon family named Smith. He converted, and lived in Kirtland and Nauvoo as a young man. He married Rizpah Knight in 1846 and in the following year crossed the plains in the first company to arrive in the Salt Lake Valley. He would accompany Hamblin on a number of his expeditions.[52]

On June 2, 1856, the county court awarded Hamblin an eight-mile square tract of land to use as "herd-grounds"; it was located on the California trail, about six miles from the Pinto Creek settlement, and included the area known as "Mountain Meadows."[53] This beautiful valley, running north to south about four miles, bisected by the rim of the basin, would later become famous as the site of the Mountain Meadows Massacre. It had springs at its northern and southern ends and was covered with grass. Hamblin went on to build a ranch at the northern end of the valley, and the small town that grew up around it was named Hamblin.[54]

On June 15, Hamblin returned to Fort Clara to find a crisis awaiting him—the Santa Clara River, often little more than a creek, had nearly dried up and the Paiute farmers were anxious. Tutsegabits confronted Hamblin. "The Tonequint [Santa Clara River] is ded," said the Paiute chief.

> You said you told us if we would hear your talk and plant corn the Lord would Bless us. My corn is Dying for water. What will I feed my childrin next winter? The Mormans are youseing the water in Pine Vally. You said they would not youse it thare onley for cutting pine logs. We once could feed our childrin on Rabits when they was hungry. Now thare is no Rabits for us. What do you think about it?

At this early point in the southern Utah Indian mission, the missionaries, though few, were already competing with the local Paiutes for water.

Hamblin replied that he did not believe the Paiutes "would starve. It ma[y] be the Lord will send us rain so we can watter our crops."

The chief replied that he believed the Lord would "send wrain if the Mormans prey for it." He asked Hamblin to pray, and he, in his turn, "would send an old man to the Mts. to make a cloud and he believe[d] the rain would come." In his autobiography, Hamblin specifies that "the old man" was a medicine man, and says that he saw the cloud of smoke this shaman created up on Pine Mountain.[55] Tutsegabits's religious outlook was clearly a synthesis of the ancient traditional ways and the new Mormon faith.

Hamblin "felt some wo[r]ked up" in his feelings when he saw the Paiutes' "child like ways and their faith they had in us." He asked his brethren at the Fort to let the Indians have all the Santa Clara water available, which they agreed to, then he returned to Pine Valley to be near Rachel. While there, his conversation with Tutsegabits "rested with Ponderous [force]" on his mind. The next morning he prayed "to the God of Abraham Isaac and Jacob that the Hevnes might giv rain that we could hav water to water the porcions of Earth that was cultivated and hav an abundant harvest." While he was still on his knees, drops began to fall on him. "I arose up," he wrote, "and felt that my Prayr was heard and felt that all was wright."

The next night a rainstorm answered his prayers—and possibly the prayers of the Paiute shaman in the mountains—and filled the Santa Clara. There was an abundance of water that summer and fall, and a plentiful harvest of corn, beans, and squash.[56]

In his autobiography, Hamblin wrote that from that time, the Paiutes looked upon Mormons as being able to influence the clouds, and also having the power to bring sickness upon them. Though the missionaries strove to "have them understand these things in their true light...this was difficult on account of their ignorance and superstitions."[57] As we have seen, Indians often viewed sickness as the result of witchcraft, an attack by something alien and supernatural that entered their bodies. If they viewed Mormons as having supernatural powers, as medicine men or shamans, they would believe that they would have power to cause sickness, as well as cure it.[58]

On August 3, Rachel, after a short labor—she "was sick but 2 houars through the blessings of the Lord," Jacob wrote—gave birth to Rachel Tamar Hamblin, known as the first white child born in Pine Valley.[59] Six days later, Hamblin moved his family from Pine Valley to a settlement on Pinto Creek, which had been founded by missionaries from Harmony that summer, about twelve miles north of Pine Valley and not far from Harmony.[60] Hamblin moved his family, surprisingly, because of competition between Paiutes and Mormons for water rights on the Santa Clara, with Hamblin taking the Indian side. This made him *persona non grata* in Pine Valley. "The Brotheren in Pine Vally would rather hav my room than my company," he wrote, explaining the move. "I was surprised at the course they had taken be[i]ng sent to the Lamanites to teach them to cultivate the Earth and then rob them of the water. I cum out against such a course which ofended them very mutch." In his autobiography, Hamblin states that moving his family at this time saved their lives and his own.[61]

George F. Hendrix wrote a virulent letter to Brigham Young, dated June 23, 1860, which paints the actions of Hamblin and other Santa Clara Mormons in the worst possible light.[62] In this letter Hendrix described a personal conflict between Hamblin and Robert Richey at Pine Valley. As Hendrix tells the story, after Richey and Riddle had been granted the area of Pine Valley in order to build and operate a sawmill, Hamblin asked if he could bring his family and herds there also. Richey and Riddle agreed, provided that Hamblin and his herds stayed in the upper part of the valley, as they had grain growing in the lower part. However, after Hamblin and his family and herds moved in, according to Hendrix, Richey found that Hamblin's cattle were allowed to "run at large" in just a few days and began grazing on Richey's grain. Richey, says Hendrix, was forced to sleep in his fields at night, gun in hand, to save his crop.

Muddled charges and countercharges followed. Hamblin stated that Richey had taken the name of the Lord in vain and had said that he should have shot some of Hamblin's cattle. Finally, Richey and Hamblin decided to reconcile. According to Hendrix, Hamblin said, "I knew that report about you killing the cattle...was a lie when I told it, and if you are willing to compromis[e], those difficulties and live in friendship, I am."[63]

It is hard to know what to make of this story. As always, one would like to hear about the conflict from Hamblin's perspective.

After the move to Pinto Creek, Hamblin left Rachel and the children there and returned to Fort Clara "to attend to my Micion." Jacob came back to Pinto Creek on September 15 to find his family in good health, except for an Indian girl that he had bought the previous winter.

Three weeks later, on October 5, Jacob was preparing to move his family to Fort Clara when he received news that his father was very ill, possibly dying. Jacob rode quickly back to the fort, arriving there the next day, and as he entered the cabin he heard his father saying, "I am afraid Jacob will be to[o] late geting here. I want to see him before I go." Jacob stepped quickly to the bed and the old man joyfully seized his hand.

"Jacob I am agoing to leve you," he said, "but I am not afraid to die. I never ronged a man in my life. I once dreded the grave. I now hail it as a pleasyr [pleasure]."

Jacob answered, "I was in hopes you would of got your helth when I left."

Isiaiah replied, somewhat impatiently,

> "Jacob, what is the youse of my suffering in this old Tabernicle any longer. I comprehend Mormonism. I know the worth of the Gospel of Jesus Christ. I now apoint you to act as Patriarch over my Family. You are older than your Brothers council them in all important maters. Doe as I tell you and it will be of more worth to you than all the gold of Calafornia."

Jacob, recognizing that his father "had sufferd much," gave him a ritual laying on of hands, and instead of praying that Isaiah be healed, he "asked the Lord that he mite be freed from pane and depart in pease."

The old man slept comfortably that night, and the next day, October 7, he died at the age of sixty-six.[64] Jacob was now the patriarch of the Hamblin clan.

While he had been fortunate in having Tutsegabits, who arguably served as a sort of overchief among the bands of Paiutes in southern Utah and Nevada, as an ally, Jacob now faced the challenge of other Paiute headmen opposing him, killing Mormon livestock, and acting as possible leaders for similarly minded Paiutes. Hamblin tells these stories, as was typical of him, as miracle stories in the tradition of the Bible, in this case the deaths of Ananias and Saphira in Acts. He dates these events roughly to the winter of 1856–1857.

There are three sources for these stories, sometimes contradictory: a March 2, 1857, letter to Brigham Young, Hamblin's diary, and Little.[65] According to the letter, the two chiefs rebelled against Tutsegabits in fall 1856, and "finaly againsed the Sain[t]s at the Fort and went to the Mountains. They thretned to kill me or some of my Family and drive off our cattle." They took about a hundred Indians, old and young, with them, a substantial political group in the context of Santa Clara Paiutes. They "became dissatisfide...kiled Cattle and thretned our lives."[66] The second angry chief, Ag-ara-poots, was greatly feared by the local Paiutes, as he had recently killed two men.[67]

The first chief led a small band east of the Santa Clara. He came to Fort Clara and ridiculed the Indians for ignoring the meat readily available to them (the missionaries' flocks) and, to emphasize his point, killed an ox.[68]

As was typical of Hamblin, he went to talk to this chief, rather than taking a military force into the mountains as some of the other Mormons advised. In his interview with the chief, Hamblin emphasized that the chief had done them an injustice, because Hamblin and the missionaries only wanted to help the Paiutes. The chief answered with insults; he "wanted to know if I wished to kill him, or if I could make medicine strong enough to kill him. I told him that he had made his own medicine, and that some evil would befall him before he got home."[69]

Dealing with Ag-ara-poots would be more difficult, as he was the more "headstrong" of the two chiefs. He had asked Hamblin to administer to his son, and the missionary instructed him to wash his son first. The father refused, and when the son subsequently died, the Indian and some Paiutes who followed him burned their lodges and a lodge storing food (a powerful symbolic gesture), retreated to the mountains, and threatened Jacob's life.[70]

Nevertheless, as was typical for Hamblin, he wanted to simply talk to him. He first approached Tutsegabits to accompany him to Ag-ara-poots's camp, but the overchief turned him down and advised Jacob to leave the angry headman alone.[71] Hamblin then asked for a fellow missionary volunteer to come visit Ag-ara-poots with him; only Thales Haskell was willing to go.[72] They tracked the large group of Indians into the mountains and found them at nightfall. "They was mutch surprised to see us," wrote Hamblin.[73] He asked them to get the two missionaries something to eat, then went to see the chief.

Ag-ara-poots was sitting in an apparently surly mood, his face blackened in mourning.[74] Hamblin stated that he asked Ag-ara-poots "if he wanted my blood. [I] toled him I was a shaimmed of him. I had p[l]owed land for him and we ben friends solong. He was a fool for actin so."[75]

Ag-ara-poots denied threatening Jacob's life, but said that he had been, and still was, mad that Hamblin had allowed his son to die. Hamblin said that the chief himself had killed his own child by not allowing the Lord to heal him through washing. He then told the Paiute that they could not eat with a man who was mad and had no food, and the three men left the lodge.[76]

But just as they came out, Ag-ara-poots was stricken to the ground—"he trembled like aleef and reeled like a druncan man," wrote Hamblin.[77] The other Indians gathered around the fallen chief (who did not die) and Hamblin advised them all to come back to the river, where food was available for them. Most of the Indians who heard him did so, apparently including Ag-ara-poots.[78]

Nevertheless, the more headstrong Paiute—presumably Ag-ara-poots—returned to his "evle ways and sneerd at our instrucions," and the other dissident Paiute apparently followed his lead. One of two chiefs—presumably the first one—died within two weeks.[79] This did not sober the other chief—he said "he was stout and hard," and boasted that "[t]he Mormans could not Prey him to deth."[80] Tutsegabits suggested that Hamblin should, in fact, pray for him to die, as he had always been a bad man. Jacob prayed that Ag-ara-poots would not have the power to shed the blood of any missionaries,[81] and "[t]his wicked chief was taken sick the next day lingerd a few months and died."[82]

The story of the deaths spread among the Paiutes. "This gave us great influance among the diferante bands," wrote Hamblin.[83]

Another Indian, apparently one of the Muddy Paiutes in modern Nevada, proclaimed that the Mormons had no supernatural power, and said he would steal stock from the first Mormon he met. He followed through on his promise, stole a cow, killed it, and was in the process of skinning it when he became sick and soon died.[84]

In Little, Hamblin adds a fourth story of a Paiute killing Mormon cattle, then being struck dead. "He talked and acted in such a rascally manner that I was disgusted. I told him that he was in the hands of the Lord; if He would forgive him, I would, but I did not believe that He would." This man died a few days after this confrontation.[85]

This fully established the missionaries' influence among the Paiutes. "From this time forth the Mision prosprd," Hamblin wrote, and "the influance of the Misionarys spread among the diferante bands."[86]

The Paiutes, like most southwestern Indians, strongly believed in witchcraft. The Las Vegas Paiutes executed a shaman accused of witchcraft as late as 1910.[87] Undoubtedly the Santa Clara Paiutes would take such sudden deaths as Hamblin describes very seriously, and think twice before opposing the missionaries again. According to Paiute belief, sorcery was often used to cause sickness or death, and illness caused by sorcery was greatly dreaded.[88] The death of these dissident chiefs would be viewed by Hamblin within a context of Biblical retribution, while the Paiutes would regard it within the ideological framework of malevolent, if perhaps morally justified, sorcery. Whatever the ideological context, the deaths would serve to further the cause of the missionaries among the Paiutes.

Thus, the missionaries seemed to be making progress with the Santa Clara Paiutes. At this time, "The men ceased to abuse their families, and they did as well as could be expected of people in their low condition," wrote Hamblin.[89] In 1855 and 1856, some two hundred Paiutes were baptized, adding to the large number of Paiute baptisms in 1854.[90]

When Paiutes were sick, they greatly valued administration by the missionaries, and Hamblin recalls that the administrations were always successful. The elders encouraged the Paiutes to work and promise to be honest. If a thief was caught, he either made complete restitution or he was tied to a tree and whipped. The Indians generally did the whipping, while Hamblin prescribed the number of lashes.[91] Hamblin and the missionaries were careful and humane in their dealings with the Paiutes, Hamblin wrote, and "[t]hey soon learned to regard our words as law."[92]

Sometimes Jacob adjudicated between whites and Indians. Once a Paiute sold a spring to a Mormon for a horse and a blanket (a typical example of a white gaining valuable Indian property for a small price). The horse died, the blanket wore out, and the Paiute came to Jacob and complained that he had not been treated justly. Jacob then reportedly tried to arrange a compromise between the white and the Indian.[93]

But despite the missionaries' apparent successes, the cultural chasm between Mormon and Indian, white and red man, continued to yawn, deeply discouraging Hamblin.

One problem was blood feuds between bands and tribes. If one band killed an Indian of another band, a life was required to make recompense, sometimes the life of a relative or a member of the same band.[94] To whites, used to centuries of sophisticated British or European justice, in which a murderer was captured, investigated, convicted on good evidence, and punished, the Indian justice seemed ad hoc and harsh.

Tensions between the Moapats, in modern Nevada, and the Santa Clara Paiutes occasionally erupted into violence. One day in summer 1856 a Moapat killed a Santa Clara Paiute near Fort Clara, and Santa Clara Paiutes further up the river somehow captured a Moapat woman, tied her to a tree, and burned her alive, working quickly so that Hamblin would not be able to stop them. A messenger alerted him to the action, but when he arrived the woman was dead.

When Hamblin talked to the killers, they cried and said that they had to carry out this punishment by the laws of their culture—"that is, they were so bound up in their traditions and customs, that what they had done was a necessary duty," Jacob wrote.[95]

Hamblin's reaction was to blame the Paiutes for their non-American, non-Christian culture. "They appeared so childlike, and so anxious to have me think that what they had done was all right, that I said nothing, but felt that I would be truly thankful if I should ever be so fortunate as to be called to labor among a higher class of people," he wrote. Mormons seemed to expect Indians to convert like American or European Saints had converted; after baptism, these Europeans were often fully active Mormons, quickly integrated into Mormon community, ideology, and mores. But Indians, the early Mormon missionaries found, could not convert like that. At one moment they appeared to be childlike and teachable, but the next moment they appeared to be living by incomprehensible patterns. Sometimes the two cultures could find points of contact, as when Tutsegabits viewed Hamblin as a weather shaman like the old Paiute medicine man on the mountain, or when he interpreted the deaths of Paiute dissidents as the result of sorcery. But at other times, the two cultures seemed to lack a basis for comprehending each others' actions. The Mormons did not understand that to convert the Indian to Mormonism, they would first have to convert them to at least the basics of centuries of European culture—reading, writing, math, modern agriculture, medicine, law, politics, city planning, the Bible and Christianity.

Their ethical systems also differed. Sometimes the Indian system seemed harsh, by white standards; Ute and Paiute culture often called for a strict "eye for an eye" retaliation.[96] At other times, the Paiute social system seemed too permissive to puritanical Mormons. No Indians lived by the purely Western system of sexual morality. Once a young man eloped with a sub-chief's daughter, then when he returned refused to marry her. The sub-chief took the boy and girl to Tutsegabits for adjudication of the matter. The Paiute leader asked the girl if she had enjoyed herself, and when she answered in the affirmative, he said, "Girl look alright—boy look alright—no harm done; case dismissed." This angered the sub-chief, who came to Jacob and complained. "Jacob took the mater up with the Piede Chief and had the trouble straightened out." Paiutes were sometimes more tolerant of premarital sexual relations than were Mormons.[97] They had no formal marriages or divorces; marriages began when partners started to live together.[98]

Soon after the burning of the Moapat woman, Hamblin and Ira Hatch journeyed to Cedar City. The Cedar City Paiutes had also been carrying on a feud with the Muddy Indians, and a group of them had gone to the Muddy and stolen two women. However, the Moapats pursued them, killed a chief in the party, and wounded two other Cedar Indians. Furious, the Cedar Indians stole horses from Santa Clara on the way back home. According to Little, Hamblin, using his spiritual insight, told Ira where to go to find and recover the stolen horses.[99] This raiding and violence between the different bands of the Paiutes clearly depressed Hamblin.

In late 1856 or early 1857, some Paiutes came to Hamblin and said, according to Jacob, "We cannot be good; we must be Piutes. We want you to be kind to us. It may be that some of our children will be good, but we want to follow our old customs."[100] Then, Hamblin wrote, he watched as the men began to paint their faces again and beat their women, as they had before the Mormons arrived.

It would be generations before Paiutes would become acculturated to the European way of life. The early Mormons, especially the more idealistic Indian missionaries, had hoped for a miraculous, instant conversion, especially since the Indians were of the blood of Israel. It was not to be.[101]

7

"I was Apointed to Take Charge of the Mision"

Marriage and Massacre during the Utah War, 1857

1857 was a tumultuous year for the Mormons, as the "Utah War" began in May. After the Saints in northern Utah had allegedly threatened federal appointees and driven them out of Utah, and after one judge accused Brigham Young of ignoring federal law as a virtual religious dictator, U.S. president James Buchanan decided to replace Brigham Young as governor of the territory and send an army of twenty-five hundred soldiers with the new governor to enforce his will. This military action was called "Buchanan's Blunder" and there was considerable mismanagement, misunderstanding, and extremism on both sides of the Mormon-U.S. standoff, which would last until July 1858.[1] As the U.S. Army neared Utah in fall 1857, Mormon military units harassed it, driving off civilian-contracted supply trains, without coming into open conflict with the actual military. Meanwhile, behind the scenes, leaders of the Mormons and the U.S. government, especially Thomas L. Kane, worked to negotiate a peace.

Certainly the greatest disaster of the war was the Mountain Meadows Massacre, which took place from September 7–11, 1857, in the southern part of the valley in which Hamblin had a ranch. This almost inexplicable outbreak of frontier violence, orchestrated by Isaac Haight and William Dame, stake presidents in the Cedar City and Parowan area, and John D. Lee, has darkened southern Utah and Mormon history ever since. Mormons, aided by some Paiutes, killed some 120 to 140 innocent members of the Fancher-Baker company traveling from Arkansas to southern California, including women and children over the age of six. The emigrants were murdered in a brutal, deceptive way; many of the Mormons involved in the event, following the orders of their ecclesiastical superiors, lived with guilt and horrific memories of the atrocity the rest of their lives.[2]

Jacob Hamblin was in Salt Lake City at the time of the massacre and later told Frederick Dellenbaugh, a member of the second Powell company, that "if he had been at home the Mountain Meadows Massacre would not have occurred."[3] Could Hamblin have stood up to Haight and Dame, his ecclesiastical and military superiors, and tamped down the collective war hysteria that had swept southern Utah (partially as a result of war sermons by George A. Smith) and helped cause the event? It is difficult to assess such alternate possible histories. Dellenbaugh, however, had no hesitations in answering the question: "I have no doubt that he [Hamblin] would have prevented the slaughter," he wrote.

While Hamblin was not present at the massacre, he was an important player in its aftermath. No one in Mormonism, including Brigham Young and Jacob Hamblin, came away from the Mountain Meadows Massacre unscathed, even if they were not personally involved in it. After it occurred, the Mormon people collectively attempted to deny Mormon involvement in it, and Young and Hamblin were part of this effort.[4]

For Jacob Hamblin personally, 1857 was a landmark year, for in August his leadership at Santa Clara was expanded to the whole southern Indian mission. He also became a polygamist in September, marrying young Priscilla Leavitt on a trip north in which he accompanied Tutsegabits and other Indians to Salt Lake City to meet the "Great Chief" of the Mormons, Brigham Young.

On March 2, Hamblin wrote a letter to Young that begins rather abruptly with this harbinger of changes in his domestic situation: "I hav felt imprest by the spirit of late that it was not onely my privilege but my duty to take more wives. I hav but one. President Allen advised me to do so. I now ask permicion and council from you."[5] In addition, there was another marital matter to be broached: "Bro Ira Hatch bought a young squaw and promiced to Mary hur if the great Morman Chief was willing. It has givin him more influance among the Indians than any thing els he could of done."

Hamblin folklore states that Brigham Young once advised Hamblin to marry an Indian woman, but Hamblin told him that his influence over the Indians would immediately be lost if he did this.[6] This March 2 letter, a contemporary source, directly contradicts such traditions. Here, Hamblin stated that Hatch's offer of marriage to an Indian woman gave him *more* influence than he could have obtained otherwise.

Hamblin ends the letter by mentioning that the Iats—Mohaves, living on the lower Colorado south of modern Las Vegas, "the enemy of the Santa Clara Indians"—"sent for him [Hatch] to come and see them." Apparently Hatch had met some Mohaves previously. Their subsequent reception of him and Dudley Leavitt was far from friendly.

On April 7, Young replied to these marital questions, giving Hamblin permission to expand his family in one remarkably concise sentence: "It is your privilege to increase." In the case of Ira Hatch, he was not opposed to the marriage, and he gave him permission to proceed, granted that the girl's parents agreed, that the community of Indians would not object, and that she was old enough "to bear children without injury." However, he ended by saying he was "rather inclined to think the girl is too young at present," from reports he had heard.[7] Hatch reportedly did not marry an Indian wife until October 1859.[8]

An important event in the history of Dixie took place in April and May—the founding of Washington, on the Virgin River. In early 1857, about ten families were called to found a town on the Virgin that would specialize in raising cotton—part of Brigham Young's ambitious plans for the Mormons to be entirely self-sufficient economically. This first group arrived in April. At about the same time, Young called an additional twenty-eight families and a number of young men to follow the first group, and these fifty men and their families arrived in May. Washington was suddenly the largest town below the rim of the basin, and soon was the county seat. John D. Lee built a big house there, dividing his time between Washington and New Harmony.[9]

Brigham Young was beginning to be interested in Dixie for economic and strategic reasons, not just as an Indian mission.

Settling Washington was not at all an easy task. When Mormons from San Bernardino came to Dixie later in the year, Brigham asked fifty of them to settle in Washington, but only one of that number eventually stayed in town.[10] The residents of Washington were easy prey for malarial mosquitoes, and, four years later, when the founders of St. George passed through Washington, they were shocked at the sickly complexions of the residents of the town. Robert Gardner wrote that they had clothes that were dyed blue, and their faces were as blue as their clothes:

> The aperance of thos brothern and there wives and childern was rather discourageing. Nerly all of them had the fevour and agu or chiles as they ar caled in this country....This tryed me harder than any thing I had se[e]n, in my mormon exspearance. thinking that my wives and children, from the nature or the climate would have to look as sickly as those now surrounding me. But I said we will trust in God and go a head.[11]

The residents of Santa Clara endured the same malarial fever and chills and had the same blue complexion at times.[12]

In June, one of the tragic events in Santa Clara history occurred.[13] Thales Haskell and his wife, Maria, had befriended a Paiute "chore boy," who had disappeared from Santa Clara for a period, but on the twenty-first, when Thales was ten to fifteen miles north, unblocking beaver dams, the boy had arrived unexpectedly at the Haskell home. Maria was nervous about his presence in the house, so began to prepare a meal for him, hoping he would leave after he had eaten.[14] The boy, according to his own account, started to examine a gun and it went off, accidentally shooting Maria.[15] After this, he ran away. Mary Dart Judd wrote,

> As I herd the shot I went to the door and saw her [Maria] come to her door holding her handes to her brist. I went to her and askid what was the mater. She said she thaught she was shot but did not know. By this time she was quite faint and Br Oscar and wife Mary Ann Hamblin came to her hous and we put her on the bead.[16]

The other men were harvesting about two miles away. Mary Judd ran down to tell them of the tragedy, and they sent Indian runners north to bring Thales back, and other runners to Washington where a doctor lived. The women examined the wound and found that the bullet had entered through Maria's hip on the left side and then had "gone through the abdomen and now lay just under the skin on the right side."[17] Maria asked for them to remove the bullet, and Rachel Hamblin bathed the wound in turpentine, and was just going to operate with a razor when Jacob Hamblin showed up, and he was able to remove the bullet.[18]

Thales arrived that night, and the following day the doctor came. Mary Judd wrote,

> We done all we could for her. She did not bleed outwerdley but the Doctor said she bled inwardly. She was quite uneasy and wanted to be mooved about so she was taken from one shade tree to another untill about 2 oclock when she was anxious to have on some clean garments and so we chainged her and then she Died before we got on her clean garments. We saw the change and she died with out a grone. So quiet a nature she was in life the same in Death.[19]

The funeral, performed in haste because of intense heat, followed.[20] Thales wrote,

> We made a rough casket from the boards taken from a wagon box and laid her away with the babe in her arms as comfortably as we could at a grave site in the red sand soil of the Santa Clara. She was the first white person to lose her life in that desolate location so far from home, former friends, and relatives.[21]

This incident shows the complexity of the interrelationship of Indian and Mormon culture in early Santa Clara: the Paiute coming into the woman's house unexpectedly when her husband was far away; the white woman at a loss what to do; the

Indian's lack of technical knowledge of guns. Some of the Paiutes felt that a life must be given for a life in this case, and so the boy must die. But Thales Haskell believed his story, that the gun had gone off accidentally, and refused to have him executed. He never saw the boy again, and years later asked local Paiutes if they knew where he was, and they said they knew where his bones were.[22] Possibly the fiercely Mosaic Paiute law of eye for an eye was more harsh than was European law as administered by the Indian missionaries in this case. Or perhaps the Paiutes did not understand an accident as purely accidental, as we do, but felt that the boy was cursed or had destructive powers. In any event, Haskell understood that the local Paiutes had killed him.

Hamblin's tensions with Rufus Allen continued. In July, the missionaries had a meeting in which Allen reproved Hamblin "very roughly for some little thing that did not suit him," as Jacob wrote. This left the Indian missionary feeling "grieved and vext" at the unjust rebuke.[23] Soon after this Jacob had a prayer meeting with Sam Knight and Ira Hatch in which they prayed that God would appoint a man to preside over them in whom they could have confidence. At this point Hamblin "felt the influance of the spirit resting on [him]," and told Knight and Hatch that Allen would not preside over them long. "Doe you Provicy that asked the Brotheren. I answerd yes. They said, we believe it will be fullfilled. A few Days after I was apointed to take charge of the Mision."[24]

A July 25 letter by Cedar City stake president Isaac Haight (soon to be infamous for his role in the Mountain Meadows Massacre) to Brigham Young gives background for the change:

> I have the best of feelings towards Br Allen but he has not the confidence of the Brethren of the Mission neither of the Indians that a man ought to have that stands as he does.... If he could be more useful in some other feeld of laibor and Br Jacob Hamlin have charge of the Mission I think would much advance the intrest of the Mission.[25]

Young appointed Hamblin in a letter dated August 4, 1857, which is also an important Utah War document. The church president wrote, "You are hereby appointed to succeed Elder R. C. Allen (whom I have released as President of the Santa Clara Indian Mission). I wish you to enter upon the duties of your calling immediately." Young gave typical counsel with regard to the Indians: "Continue the conciliatory policy toward the Indians, which I have ever recommended and seek by words of righteous to obtain their love and confidence."

Then Young reflects the current political situation in Utah, as he writes that the Indians "must learn that they have either got to help us, or the United States will kill us both." He then went on to describe the Utah war in scathing terms. The intent of the invading troops "is entirely peaceful. The current report is that they somewhat query whether they will hang me with or without a trial. There are about 20 others they intend to deal with.... We feel first rate about all this." He repeated the usual ban on selling grain or ammunition to non-Mormons.[26]

This letter was probably delivered by Apostle George A. Smith, who visited Santa Clara in mid-August during his famous tour of the Mormon settlements in southern Utah in which he whipped local members to a white-hot passion on Utah War issues.[27] The record of his visit to "Hamblin's Fort" noted that the Clara had dried up and that the townspeople were raising corn, cotton, indigo, melons, peaches, and grapes, all adversely affected by the lack of water.[28] The clerk counted thirteen Indian cornfields between Santa Clara and Mountain Meadows and repeated what became a common joke about the heat in Dixie: "Ther 103° in shade & 136 in sun. The people called it cool."

Jacob was now president of the southern Indian mission, with Dudley Leavitt and Samuel Knight as his counselors.[29] War clouds were gathering in northern and southern Utah. It was at this time that he decided to add another wife to his family.

Sarah Priscilla Leavitt, born in Nauvoo on May 8, 1841, to Jeremiah and Sarah Sturdevant Leavitt, was the last child in a family of twelve children. She reportedly had "a heavy head of coal-black hair," blue eyes, and was tall and slender.[30] The Leavitts had converted to Mormonism in Canada in 1837, so Priscilla grew up in the LDS faith. Jeremiah died in August 1846, and the family crossed the plains fatherless in 1850, when Priscilla was nine.[31]

Priscilla remembers that Rachel was already a near invalid, often bedridden, during her Tooele years from 1850 to 1855, so Priscilla often tended the six children in the Hamblin household—seven after Jacob adopted Albert in 1853, when he was about ten years old. So already in Tooele, Jacob knew that Priscilla was a hard worker and a willing helper for Rachel.

Priscilla and her mother had come south to Santa Clara soon after Dudley had accompanied Jacob south in fall 1855. So Priscilla probably continued tending Rachel and her children whenever they were in the same town. (As we have seen, Jacob moved his family to Pine Valley, Pinto, and Mountain Meadows at various times of the year.)

As in Rachel's case, Jacob's marriage to Priscilla is well documented. In her memoirs, Priscilla stated that on one occasion, Jacob was sitting on Rachel's bed talking to her. Then, "she told him to ask me to be his wife so that he would have someone to care for his children when she was gone. Calling me to them, Rachel put my hand in Jacob's and Jacob asked me to become his wife."[32] If Priscilla's memories

7.1. Sarah Priscilla Leavitt Hamblin, Jacob Hamblin's third wife and first plural wife. She was a midwife and a tireless worker. Reproduced by permission of The Huntington Library, San Marino, California.

are correct, this proposal was another almost instantaneous one, although Jacob had known Priscilla for years.[33]

According to Leavitt traditions, Hamblin asked Sarah Leavitt for sixteen-year-old Priscilla's hand. Sarah replied, "She is too young, Jacob. Give her a chance to grow up."

Hamblin replied, "Why don't we ask her? Call her in and let's talk to her about it." Priscilla came in at that point. "Priscilla, I have just asked your mother's permission to marry you," said Jacob, "and she is leaving the decision up to you. Could you marry an old man like me [he was thirty-eight] who loves and honors you very much?"

She replied, "Oh, yes. Yes, I can."

Jacob was planning a visit to Salt Lake in the near future, where they could be married in the Endowment House; but he said they could get married locally in a month if Priscilla preferred. Priscilla chose the marriage in Salt Lake.[34]

Priscilla thus decided that she "loved this family well enough to help them, and to give them my love and care."[35] Thus, she fell in love with a family, not just a man. Priscilla entered the family with her eyes wide open: "Since Brother Jacob had to be away from home so much on church business and missionary work with the Indians, I felt very humble in accepting this great responsibility," she wrote.[36] Hamblin's absences from home might have been a practical reason for wanting to have a young, energetic wife in his family. In his May 17, 1856, letter to Brigham Young, he wrote that he had not slept in his house "five nites in a month since I brought my Family here. I have spent my time whare the dutyes of my Micion requird."

Jacob Hamblin and Priscilla Leavitt traveled north to Salt Lake City, with George Albert Smith and a number of Indian chiefs, and planned to wed in the Endowment House there. So as the Fancher party was traveling south on their doomed journey toward the Mountain Meadows, the Hamblin-Smith party was going north and away from the massacre.

As we have seen, Jacob had been awarded the Mountain Meadows valley for grazing purposes. In 1857, his family was living at Fort Clara during the winter and Mountain Meadows, in a primitive "board shanty," during the summer.[37] Before the trip, Hamblin situated Rachel and the children in the shanty, and Samuel Knight and his wife Caroline, pregnant and nearly due, were living nearby in a wagon. Hamblin made arrangements with Knight and another man, probably David Tullis, to build Rachel a more substantial cabin.[38] When Knight became caught up in the events of the massacre, however, he had no time to build Rachel's cabin.

Hamblin's "diary" now takes up the story, but at this point it is entirely autobiographical rather than a daily record. He writes: "I started for G. S. L. C. in company with Thales Hascal and Tutsegarvats the Yanawant Chief. He had felt anxious for a long time to visit Brigham Young. We fel in company with George. A Smith." They apparently left Parowan on August 24.[39]

The next day, this group met the Fancher group about ten miles south of Fillmore.[40] "We encampd on Corn Creek while on our way nere a company of emigrants from Arcan Saw on thare way to Calafornia," Hamblin wrote. "Thare was a strang atmosphere serounded them. George A spoke of it. [He] said he believd some evle would be fall them before they got through."[41] Unfortunately, this is a retrospective account, not a contemporary diary. Historians who believe that Young, through George Smith, had ordered the Mountain Meadows Massacre, take this statement as evidence that Smith knew what the fate of the Fancher party would be.

Several members of the Fancher party asked Jacob about the condition of the roads, possible dangers from Indians, and the best places to stop. He recommended that they stay at Mountain Meadows, as springs in the north and south provided good water for livestock and the whole valley had excellent grass for forage. "I recommended this spring, and the grazing about here, four miles south of my house, as the place where they should stop," he later said.[42]

As the Hamblin-Smith party proceeded northward, they picked up Indian chiefs until they ended up with about a dozen leaders, including Kanosh, the Pahvant chief;[43] Ammon, Jacob's friend, brother of Wakara;[44] a wife of Ammon; and Youngwuds, a "Piede Chief" from the Harmony area.[45] This group had been invited to go north because Brigham Young wanted to talk to them and firm up their support for the Mormon cause during the Utah War.

They arrived in Salt Lake City on September 1, and Young met with them for about an hour.[46] Presumably Hamblin was present as an interpreter. Dimick Huntington, a prominent Indian interpreter, was also at this interview and wrote that he, undoubtedly carrying out Brigham Young's policy, "gave" the livestock of "American" emigrant companies on the southern California trail to the Indians. "It made them open their eyes," wrote Huntington. When they protested that they had been taught by Huntington that they should not steal, he replied that he had indeed taught this, but that now the American armies were coming and when "they kill us they will kill you."[47]

Indian policy was an important consideration during the Utah War. Brigham Young felt he could use the Indians as his allies, and that while previously he had shielded "Americans" from Indian attacks, now, given the present military circumstances, he would no longer protect non-Mormons. In fact, as the Huntington diary shows, he apparently went a step further and encouraged Indians to attack and drive off stock from emigrant parties passing through Utah.[48]

Hamblin and Priscilla did not get married for a week and a half—they were finally sealed in the President's Office, by Brigham Young himself, on September 11, 1857, the same day that the Mountain Meadows Massacre occurred in southern Utah.[49]

During his time in Salt Lake, Hamblin showed the Indian chiefs, especially Tutsegabits, around Salt Lake City, which must have been a remarkable culture shock for the Paiutes. Jacob wrote, "The Chiefs was treted with mutch res[p]ect. [They] was taken to the work shops gardens orchards and other plases to shoe [show] them the advantages of industry and incourag ~~them to the same~~ or induce them to labor for a living."[50]

At some point, Tutsegabits received an extraordinary honor: he was ordained an elder by Brigham Young himself. This event was recorded in three different primary sources, though each source gives a different date for the event.[51]

Jacob wrote that he attended several councils of the leading brethren while in Salt Lake City. "While I was in the citty I was several times invited into the council of the first presidency and questioned concerning the mision and cashing [caching]." Brigham Young was interested in storing caches of grain during the Utah War.[52] Hamblin was present at the historic meeting when James Haslam arrived as a messenger from the southern Utah church leaders, asking if they should attack the Fancher train. Hamblin remembered that "the spirit of the Express, rather or the expressman asked the privilege to chastize them." But Brigham Young quickly answered, "No, They have a perfect right to pass. when I want Marshal Law proclaimed, ~~I will let you know~~ You will know it!"[53]

Back in southern Utah, on the date of the massacre, Rachel, about four miles north of the Fancher train encampment, heard the shooting. She was tending Caroline Knight, Samuel Knight's wife, who was recovering from a difficult childbirth Rachel had midwived. Then Sam Knight drove up in a wagon containing the seventeen children who had survived the massacre,[54] including a girl about one or two years of age who had been "shot through one of her arms below the elbow by a large ball, breaking both bones and cutting the arm half off."[55] All of the children were probably suffering from acute shock after having witnessed the murder of their parents at the hands of whites and Indians. Rachel cleaned and bound the wound of the one-year-old, held and comforted the child, then fed mush to the rest of the children. She prayed with them, laid straw on the floor, put blankets over it, and got them to sleep, including the wounded girl. Then she returned to caring for Caroline, who had gone into hysterics when she saw blood on her husband's clothes.[56]

Rachel ended up keeping the wounded one-year-old and her two sisters, aged six or seven and about three—Rebecca, Louisa, and Sara Dunlap—in her home until they were returned to Arkansas.[57] After the massacre, John D. Lee wanted to break up the group of sisters, sending them to different homes, but Rachel convinced Lee to let the three sisters stay together.[58]

Army officer James Carleton interviewed Rachel in 1859 and stated that her testimony on the massacre seemed to be dependent on her husband's.[59] However, he added, "when she told of the 17 orphan children who were brought by such a crowd to her house of one small room there in the darkness of night, two of the children cruelly mangled and the most of them with their parents' blood still wet upon their clothes, and all of them shrieking with terror and grief and anguish, her own mother heart was touched. She at least deserves kind consideration for her care and nourishment of the three sisters, and for all she did for the little girl" whose arm had been wounded. Rachel, never very healthy, was also caring for her own large household.

There are some reports that Jacob Hamblin was at the Mountain Meadows Massacre. Rebecca Dunlap, one of the seventeen child survivors and one of the three who stayed with Rachel, stated in an interview that she hid with her sisters in some sagebrush:

> She remained here until she saw a white man, who proved to be Jacob Hamblin. She went up to him and begged him to save her and her little sisters. She says that Hamblin was the only white man that she saw who belonged to the massacring party. She remembers distinctly that Hamblin was dressed in a suit of green jeans.[60]

This passage shows how treacherous memory can be. Historian Will Bagley suggests that Dunlap mistook one of Hamblin's brothers for Jacob Hamblin, which is possible, but at the time of the massacre, the Arkansans did not know any local Mormons.[61] Undoubtedly, Jacob Hamblin was a Mormon male Dunlap came to know fairly well, after staying in his home, and I believe it is likely that years later she simply accused someone she knew.

Since Hamblin suggested that the Fancher-Baker party camp at Mountain Meadows, some non-Mormons concluded that he was part of the plot to kill them.[62] Those who believe that George A. Smith brought orders from Brigham Young to attack the Fancher-Baker company might accept this idea. Those who believe that evidence shows that the massacre was primarily instigated by local leaders in Parowan, Harmony, and Cedar City will disagree.[63] In addition, the first plan was to attack the Fancher party in a canyon south of Mountain Meadows, not at Mountain Meadows itself.[64]

Hamblin—presumably with Tutsegabits, Haskell, and Priscilla—left Salt Lake City on September 19.[65] There is a major discrepancy in dating here, as Hamblin later stated (incorrectly, I believe) that he left Salt Lake City on about September 14 and arrived at his ranch on about September 18.[66] A number of primary sources, including Hamblin's own 1871 letter, conclusively document a later dating for his journey—Hamblin leaving Salt Lake City on the nineteenth and arriving at his home on the twenty-ninth, possibly stopping along the way to visit friends.

Jacob was carrying two important documents from Brigham Young: his proclamation of martial law, dated September 15, and a military order for the southern Saints to muster troops on October 10.[67]

On the way back home, Hamblin heard a rumor that the Fancher-Baker party had been massacred by Indians at Mountain Meadows, which was the cover story that Haight, Lee, and Dame had put out.[68] This must have been a shock to Hamblin, as he would have considered the generally peaceful Paiutes to be incapable of such an aggressive action. He was probably skeptical of the story.

Then on the twenty-fourth he met John D. Lee at springs a few miles south of Fillmore,[69] who modified the story—Indians attacked the company, but Lee and some other whites "joined them in the perpetration of the deed," as Hamblin writes in his autobiography.[70] This still suggests that the massacre was an Indian action with a minority of Mormons involved. In the second Lee trial, Hamblin testified that Lee told him that he, Lee, had helped carry out the massacre because he had been ordered to do so by church leaders in Cedar City and Parowan.[71]

According to Hamblin, Lee told him that "the afore mentioned Emigrants were all wiped out excepting a few Children, ~~and that the Bretheren help[ed] to do it~~. I asked—what was that for? He said they were enemies to us, & that this was the beginning of great and important events."[72] This last phrase frames the massacre in an apocalyptic context; for Lee and other Mormons at the time, it was part of the judgments against the wicked in the last days. It also shows that Lee was explaining white involvement in the massacre; he was not describing it to Hamblin as a purely Indian affair. Perhaps he realized that portraying the southern Utah Paiutes as solely responsible for a major massacre would not be convincing for someone like Hamblin, who knew them intimately.

Hamblin met some Saints from the Cedar area at Wild Cat Canyon, about ten miles north of Beaver,[73] including William Dame, stake president of Parowan and militia leader of southern Utah, and with Lee and Cedar City stake president Isaac Haight, one of the three men most responsible for the massacre. Dame, like Lee, gave him some of the details of the massacre, and Hamblin "spoke emphatically against such proceedings." Dame said,

> John D. L. & the Indians had commenced it, a bad Job!. and it had to be done ~~or~~ for if it should come to the ears of President Bucanan, it would endanger the lives of the Bretheren. I answered: I had rather that James Bucanan, and all of his Cabinet would know the Indians had killed & wounded a few men, than for the Lord Almighty to know that I had consented to the death of Women & Children. The answer was but I tell you it had to be did to save the lives of the Bretheren.[74]

In other words, Dame stated that since Lee and other had begun the killing, the rest of the company had to be killed to preserve the lives of "the Bretheren"—presumably church leaders and members in southern Utah.

Dame also told Hamblin that he had heard that Indians on the Muddy were gathering to "wipe out" a company of Americans that was following in the tracks of the Fancher-Baker company, the Dukes-Turner company,[75] and gave Jacob an "express" to catch up with them and protect them if he could.[76] So Jacob left Priscilla and Tutsegabits with Thales Haskell at Beaver and rode ahead in haste, changing horses several times.

On September 25, Jesse N. Smith, traveling from Parowan to Salt Lake City, met Jacob one day north of Parowan, coming south.[77] The Indian missionary reached Parowan the following day.[78]

Jacob stopped briefly at Cedar City, then pressed on toward Mountain Meadows. At Pinto Creek, he found his counselors in the Indian mission, Dudley Leavitt and Samuel Knight, who confirmed that the Dukes-Turner company was in great danger. Leavitt "told me it was true, and that all the Indians in the southern country were greatly excited and 'all hell' could not stop them from killing or from at least robbing the other train of its stock."[79] So Hamblin, exhausted, sent Leavitt and Knight ahead to protect the wagon company while he rested.[80] "I instructed these men to make every possible effort to save the company and their effects, and to save their lives at all hazards," he wrote.[81] He slept a few hours at Pinto Creek, then arrived at his ranch probably about September 27.[82]

He found his wife and family still in the primitive shanty, "living out of doors exposed to wind and rain," he wrote in his diary. And in addition to caring for his own large family, Rachel also was tending the three child survivors from the Fancher party. Fortunately, Priscilla would soon be there to help.

That afternoon, Albert, who had either witnessed the massacre or had been a participant, took Hamblin to view the remains of the Fancher-Baker company. It must have been an astoundingly horrific sight. The bodies had been buried in three large "heaps": "The wolves had dug open the heaps," Hamblin wrote, "dragged out the bodies, and were then tearing the flesh from them. I counted 19 wolves at one of these places.... The most of the bodies were stripped of all their clothing, [and] were then in a state of putrefaction."[83]

According to Hamblin's testimony at the second Lee trial, Albert took him aside and showed him the bodies of two teenage girls, whom John D. Lee and an Indian chief had reportedly killed in cold blood.[84]

As he witnessed the remains of the company, Hamblin would have been told by Albert what he saw of the massacre. Perhaps the whole revelation of the dominant white involvement in the massacre was made clear to him at this time, which would have been an additional horror. "My feelings, upon this occasion, I will not attempt to describe," Hamblin wrote. "The gloom, that seemed to diffuse itself through the air and cast a shade over the hills and vales, was dismal in the extreme. This was one of the gloomiest times I ever passed through."[85] Reading a good account of the massacre is still a horrific, depressing experience; one can only imagine what it would have been like to see the bodies, half eaten by wolves, some stripped and mutilated, so soon after the event.

In the 1871 letter to Young, Hamblin records a conversation with Rachel about the massacre. She asked him if he thought the massacre was "right" and carried out under the directions from the General Authorities in Salt Lake. "I told her no; that it was one of the worst massacre's on the annals of History."

Not only was he witnessing the aftermath of an atrocity, but members of his own church, people he had accounted as Christians and saints, had carried it out. Some of his closest friends and relatives had some involvement in it and events connected to it, such as his brother Oscar, Sam Knight, and Ira Hatch. Some reports included Albert as a full participant;[86] Albert himself told Carleton that he was merely a witness.[87] Dudley Leavitt's involvement is ambiguous.

The next event described in Hamblin's "journal" is the return of Dudley Leavitt from his encounter with the Dukes-Turner company. The events connected with this wagon train have been shrouded in controversy and contradictory evidence from the time they occurred until the present.[88] One can only attempt a reconstruction.

The Dukes-Turner company—named after William C. Dukes and Nicholas Turner—numbered about fifty-four adults and forty-six children.[89] It had had Indian conflicts in the relatively safe town of Beaver in central Utah;[90] the company was in danger from Indian attack both because of this and because the Indians in southern Utah and Nevada were thirsting for more plunder after the Mountain Meadows

Massacre. In addition, the desert in Nevada was a dangerous place for travelers under any circumstances.

The company reached Cedar City on September 14,[91] where they hired about eight Mormons to guide them safely through southern Utah and Nevada, including Ira Hatch, Oscar Hamblin, and Nephi Johnson. They paid them $1,815, a huge sum at that time.[92]

When Leavitt and Knight arrived among the Nevada Paiutes, the Indian missionaries found them in war paint and feathers, in a bloodthirsty mood, preparing to attack the train.[93] Leavitt later stated that going among the Muddy Indians then was very dangerous: "It was like taking our lives in our hands. If any one but the servants of God had asked me to go on that trip, I would have refused." But he talked with them and convinced them to take the cattle only, and "let the company go on in peace." Then Leavitt tied a red bandana around his head, and "giving a mighty whoop, he led the stampede himself."[94] The other Mormon guides might have helped Leavitt and the Paiutes in this raid of approximately three hundred head of stock, which took place about seven miles west of the Muddy River, in a place near deep ravines, in early October.[95] Though some Mormon accounts later described this as an Indian raid with no Mormon involvement, according to Leavitt, he was not only involved, but led the operation.[96] However, by doing this, he felt that he saved the Duke-Turner company from probable massacre, and had to follow Hamblin's instructions to save the company at all costs.

Paiutes took about two hundred head of cattle and distributed them to various bands, while Leavitt and the other Mormons saved about a hundred head and brought them to Hamblin at Mountain Meadows.[97] The Dukes-Turner company traveled safely on to California, where many of them were furious at the Mormons for not preventing the loss of their stock.

Hamblin was not sure what to do with the hundred head of cattle. He wrote Young on October 14, telling him, "The Indians here are very hostile to all strangers allmost ungovernable. I dar[e] not go to[o] far with them or to[o] much against the spirit of them for feir of loosing influance and govermant ove[r] them."[98] The Utah War and the Mountain Meadows Massacre, not surprisingly, had had a general negative impact on Indian relations in Utah.[99] He continued, stating that Paiutes had "brought 100 cows to us to keep to rase calves. If any movements we have taken does not meet your aprobacion please let us know."

Non-Mormon John Aiken states that on October 16, he overheard a conversation between Hamblin and Ira Hatch about the cattle. In addition, Jacob sold a steer to a Mormon at Fort Clara that was in bad condition because it had been driven to the Muddy and back. He concluded from the tracks that a herd of three hundred cattle came to Hamblin's possession, which appears to be a wild overestimate.[100]

Evidently, Brigham did not reply to Hamblin's October 14 request, so Hamblin asked again on December 26:

> The cattle taken by the Indians at the Muddy, they turned over to me near a hundred, and they are now in my care, I had concluded to divid them out among the Missionary company, there being about twenty, to milk and rear the ofspring, to be accountable for old and young and if any were used, to be used for Indian purposes. If this meat your mind, you will please inform me accordingly. The Indians both at the Muddy and this place, are much opposed to their removal, but wish them to remain under my care that they may increase & becom numerous, for if they had retained them they would soon eat them all up. I have thought best to give you an understanding, on this subject that you might not be mistaken with regard to our intentions.[101]

Definitely, Hamblin did not want to keep the stolen cattle without Young's approval. Here he argues that the Indians are "much opposed" to anyone but himself taking care of the animals, which would be used to help the Indians.

Evidently, there was no reply from Young, so once again, on February 14, 1858, Hamblin wrote:

> The catle the Mudy Indians took last fall a porcian of them was given into my hands to keep. The condicions they giv them up was that they and the Misionarys should have the benefit of them in time of troubl. If evryone and no one has controle over them the catl will begon and it will prove a curse to the Micion in sted of a blessing. A word from you will set all to wright.

Hamblin emphasizes that he and the missionaries are holding the cattle, in part, for the Indians.

Young finally responded to Hamblin on March 5, 1858: "In regard to the cattle you should control them and use them for the best interest of both the missionaries and the Indians." Young also advised Hamblin to educate the Indians on raising stock.[102] Hamblin and Young apparently viewed the hundred head of cattle as legitimate spoils at a time when the Mormons were at war.

While some might conclude that Hamblin's acceptance of the cattle would be something that he kept secret from non-Mormons, this was not the case. He openly mentioned the cattle in a December 1858 letter to non-Mormon Indian agent Jacob Forney: "I saved nearly one hundred cows from being killed and wasted last fall, that were taken from the emigrants on the Big Muddy."[103] Also, in his interview with army officer James H. Carleton, he openly admitted getting a hundred cattle, though he gave the impression that only Indians drove off the cattle.[104]

In 1859, someone from the Dukes-Turner company, apparently Joseph Lane mentioned in the Honea interview, came to recover stock from the Mormons.[105] In February 1859, Zadok Judd wrote, "Mr Lane one of the emigrant stockowners that was robed by the indians just when leaving the Muddy (it was said by them that the

Mormons had a hand in it) has been here [Santa Clara] & found 25 head of his cattle which the indians left here a year ago last fall. Mr. Lane went away feeling well."[106] It's hard to imagine Lane feeling that positive about so few cattle, though he perhaps had twenty-five more cattle than he expected. Jacob also reported turning some cattle over to Lane, though his account conflicts with Judd's in some ways.[107]

Mountain Meadows Massacre historian Will Bagley, following one line of interpretation, argues that Hamblin probably arranged with Leavitt and Knight to plunder the Dukes-Turner company and enrich themselves with the stock of the company, just as John D. Lee and the people in Cedar and Harmony appropriated the cattle of the Fancher-Baker company.[108] Juanita Brooks gives this perspective some support, observing that stealing cattle, rather than attacking their owners, was a typical Utah war tactic.[109] She also points to Hamblin "editing" out problematic points in the story, which would not have been necessary if he had been proud of the part he and Mormons had played in driving off the stock.

If Hamblin and other Mormons regarded the hundred head of cattle as legal plunder in the context of the Utah war, it would explain why they felt they were justified in keeping the greater part of them. After the Utah War had passed, driving off the herd and giving only part of it to Lane did not look as justifiable, so the story gradually began to be told differently.

Overland Trail historian E. Leo Lyman disagrees with Bagley's overall interpretation, arguing that Leavitt and Knight may have saved the Dukes-Turner company from a massacre.[110] According to Leavitt, he had risked his life to go among the hostile Indians and avert an open, bloody conflict. He felt that he was forced to make the deal with them that they could have the loose stock, and this agreement allowed the Mormons to prevent the destruction of the company. For the Dukes-Turner company "to have left that region at all at that explosive time was a major accomplishment and a tribute to Hamblin and his men," Lyman writes. He does admit that the Mormons ended up with some of the cattle, though he points out that they also returned some of them.[111]

So depending on your point of view, Dame, Hamblin, Leavitt, and Knight went out of their way, Leavitt and Knight risking their lives, to save a company of non-Mormons; or Hamblin, Leavitt, and other Mormons carefully plotted to steal the cattle, after agreeing to safeguard them and receiving a huge sum as payment. Physical events in history can sometimes be fairly well documented, but motivations are difficult to prove, absent a full, frank confession or candid diary.

Hamblin, as president of the southern Utah Indian mission, now decided to send missionaries to many bands of Paiutes, on the Santa Clara and on the Muddy in modern southern Nevada. "Bro Hatch and 4 or 5 others will start for the vagos and Muddy in a few days," he wrote to Young on October 14. He also sent Hatch and Dudley Leavitt to visit the Mohaves, known to the Paiutes and Mormons as Iyats or Yats, on the Colorado. "The Iats and coats on the Colerado hav sent several invitacions for us to come among them," Hamblin wrote to Young, mentioning that Ira Hatch had talked to some of them.[112]

Hamblin described the Yats as "large in sta[t]ure, being from six to seven feet high, well proportioned."[113] George Washington Bean, after mentioning a number of Paiute tribes in Nevada and southern Utah, writes of the Mohaves that they were "a more intelligent industrious tribe located at Cottonwood Island, on the Colorado river, eighty or ninety miles below our settlement [Las Vegas] where they raised cotton, grain and other products."[114] The Mohaves were farmers, but they also had a strongly militaristic ideology, curiously mixed with dream mysticism.[115]

Unfortunately, there were tensions between Mohaves, whites, and other Indians at this time, and Hamblin was unwittingly sending Hatch and Leavitt into a hornet's nest.[116]

Hamblin himself began to make preparations to visit the Hopis, east of the Colorado, traveling to Cedar City with a cow to trade for flour.[117] While he himself had long desired to visit the Hopi mesas, apparently Brigham Young had either ordered or sanctioned the journey, which would also create a route for crossing the Colorado into modern Arizona. In a letter to Young dated December 26, 1857, Hamblin said, "Nariguats an Indian Chief is ready to Pilot us through to the Moquich nacion so soon as the Brotheren arive that are agong [a-going] from the citty." Apparently, Young was planning to send some men to accompany Hamblin on the journey.

In Harmony on October 25, Jacob spoke in church, saying that "he engoyed himself first rate since he had been with prest Young. He spoke encouriging of the Indian Mission said the Lord was working through them."[118]

The Hopi expedition was quickly set aside for another task from Young. At Pinto Creek, on about November 15, Hamblin met Isaac Haight traveling with William Bell, a leader of a company traveling south.[119] Haight relayed instructions from Brigham Young "to call on me as a guide for the company, requesting me to use my best endeavors to get them and their effects safe through," Hamblin wrote.[120] Bell promised Hamblin three hundred dollars as payment, and Jacob agreed to take the job, then returned to Fort Clara to prepare for the journey.

The Bell company, including about fifteen travelers and some five wagons, was on its way to California; it had left Salt Lake City on November 7.[121] The group was dominated by businessmen seeking to avoid the Utah War; William Bell, for example, represented the firm Livingston & Kinkead.

We have a memoir of a participant in the company, John L. Ginn's "Mormon and Indian Wars"; unfortunately it is sensationalized and sometimes thoroughly unreliable.[122] "Ginn's story reads like a Wild West thriller," writes Juanita Brooks, stating that Ginn's description of the Mountain Meadows massacre site is "sheerest nonsense."[123] As an example of one of Ginn's major historical mistakes, he affirms that Jacob Hamblin was involved in the Aiken murders, which took place near Nephi in northern Utah on November 25 and 28, though Hamblin was apparently with the Bell company in southern Utah and Nevada at the time of the murders.[124] According to Ginn, Hamblin joined the Bell company in Salt Lake City—again, this seems to be incorrect.[125] Such discrepancies cause one to lose confidence in Ginn as a witness, though the parts of his memoir that appear to be based on his actual memories are useful and historically valuable.[126]

At Fort Clara, Hamblin enlisted Tutsegabits to accompany him to the Muddy,[127] since "the southern Indians were very much excited and eager for spoil."[128] Although Hamblin expected to meet the company fairly close to Fort Clara, he found that they had gone on ahead. As Hamblin and Tutsegabits followed them, they came upon two local Indians with a white captive, who had been trying to reach the Bell company to accompany them out of Utah, and whom they had stripped and were planning to torture. The intended victim told Hamblin that if he would save him, even though he was a non-Mormon, he would serve him the rest of his life, but Hamblin replied that he expected no reward and would do all he could to help him. He instructed the Indians to return his clothes, and the three men continued on.[129]

At sundown they caught up with the Bell company where the Santa Clara flows into the Virgin, near modern St. George, and found them surrounded by about a hundred Indians who "manifested rather a hostile appearance."[130]

"They were highly pleased to see us, as they had no Interpreter," wrote Hamblin. The company leaders told him, "The Ship is now in your hand, do not stear her too near land," and indicated that they had many presents for Indians that he could bargain with.[131] Jacob and Tutsegabits spent the night talking with the Indians, making sure that the Bell company would be allowed to proceed. According to Ginn, Tutsegabits dressed down the threatening Indians and allayed any possible trouble.[132]

Hamblin astutely made use of the Indian code of hospitality to safeguard the company's stock. When the company asked him what to do with their animals, Hamblin told them he knew where good grass was available, and he would turn the cattle over to two Indians, who would be paid a supper and a shirt each to tend to them. The company leaders refused, but Hamblin told them that if he guided the company they needed to follow his advice. So they reluctantly agreed. The cattle were returned intact the next morning, though a pair of lead lines were missing. Hamblin notified the Indian leaders as they set out west, and three miles later Indians rode up with the lines.[133]

When the company had traveled about sixty miles, an Indian told Hamblin that the Moapat Paiutes were planning to attack the company at the Muddy. He woke at dawn the next day and rode ahead in a buggy.[134] At the Muddy, the Indians were indeed gathered for an ambush, believing they could kill the men in the small party with ease.[135] According to Ginn, some five hundred warriors—apparently local

Paiutes—were at the ford of the Muddy, "and as they knew of our coming they had made every preparation to kill us before we reached the ford." They were armed with "buck-horn bows and arrows."[136] Though this account is exaggerated—the count of five hundred warriors is highly improbable—it does support Hamblin's story in its main outlines.

Hamblin had brought along tobacco, and he asked for a powwow with the Indian leaders. As they smoked together, he asked, "You have listened to my talk in times past; you believe that it is good to hear, and to do what I say?"

The Indians answered, "Yes."

"I am going through to California with some friends, Americans and merchants," Hamblin continued, "and we have brought along many blankets, shirts, and other articles. I hope you will see that none of the animals are stolen, and if any stray, that you will bring them into camp."[137]

The Indian leaders reluctantly agreed, but a minority of the Indians wanted to carry out the attack anyway. As an extra security measure, Hamblin asked for the Indians to bring out their women and children, as women and children were usually hidden before a battle.[138]

Ginn writes that after Hamblin conferred with the two main chiefs, whose Mormon names were Isaac and Thomas,[139] they decided to allow the train through. He describes Indian messengers sent on ahead and bringing in Indians hidden in the "jungle of tules and willows."[140] The Bell company made it to the Muddy safely.

In addition, Hamblin met two Indian missionaries from Cedar City living at the Muddy, probably Perry Liston and Jehiel McConnell, who posed the next threat to the Bell company.[141] They told Hamblin that they had instructions to massacre the company and enrich themselves with its goods. Hamblin informed them that Brigham Young had commissioned him to bring the company through the desert safely. To his amazement, they told him that they had secret instructions that Hamblin knew nothing about and intended to continue with their plan, presumably with Hamblin's help. After a long, heated argument, Hamblin finally "told them that words were to convey ideas, and that I had written instructions from Brigham Young to take this company through safe, and that I would stand by them to the last." Liston and McConnell finally backed down.[142]

In December, Hamblin wrote Young that Bell's trip was "attended with some difficulty in consequence of certain personsons [*sic*] having been sent to the Muddy, not belonging to this Mission, and there giving the Indians such instructions as we know nothing about."[143] Possibly one of the Cedar City leaders sent them to the Muddy and gave them their bloody directives.

When some Indians came to the merchants' camp that evening, Hamblin again made use of the code of hospitality to protect the company, making the Indians some mush; then he "got them to dance by joining with them."[144] This is a vivid example of how Hamblin had almost become part of Indian culture in order to establish bonds with them. "This begat a good spirit in them," he wrote. Ginn also describes a feast with the Indians and dancing.[145] More and more Indians streamed into the camp for the festivities, and by morning, feelings were entirely amicable "so that we were enabled to persue our journey without molestation," as Hamblin writes.[146]

Ginn reports that "all of the 500 bucks" and many of their "squaws" were at this party, and that Hamblin fed them all, though he provides no explanation how Hamblin and the small pack train could have fed so many.

After passing a dreaded fifty-five-mile stretch of waterless desert, the company approached Las Vegas—"the Vagas," as Hamblin calls it—the famous oasis with springs and trees that was greatly valued by overland travelers as they traversed the great Mohave desert. This site had been well known to the Spanish (who gave it the name Las Vegas, "The Meadows"), to explorers, to trappers, and to travelers to and from southern California (and of course to the Indians before any whites), but Mormons were the first to actually build a town there, in June 1855. Led by William Bringhurst, these settlers had been called on an Indian mission much as had Hamblin and company in Santa Clara. Ironically, devout Mormon missionaries founded Las Vegas. They built a fort (one wall of which is still standing) and began to teach the Indians and cultivate the land. But the mission was plagued by internal disputes (in part because Brigham Young sent some men to work a lead mine that had been discovered near there), and Las Vegas had been mostly abandoned by the Mormons earlier that year.[147]

As he guided the Bell company, Hamblin was on the alert for news of Hatch and Leavitt among the Mohaves. Three miles from Las Vegas he met three young Indians and asked them for news of his fellow missionaries, and was stunned when they told him that the Mohaves had killed them. He asked the smallest Indian to ride with him and tell him the details of the deaths. The boy confirmed the news: "It is truth, they are killed."

"This shocked me like a thunderbolt," wrote Hamblin, "as these two men had been faithful on the Mission, and I partly blamed myself for sending them there. I, with difficulty, refrained from weeping."

But as the boy saw Hamblin's barely concealed grief, he softened, and told him, "Your friends are not killed—they are over there in a Muskeet grove by the spring."[148] When the Bell company reached Vegas, Hamblin made arrangements for the Indians to take care of the stock, then had the boy take him to the mesquite grove where Hatch and Leavitt were waiting. Soon the three friends were joyfully embracing and shaking hands.

Why did the Indians tell Hamblin that his friends were dead? Ginn, despite his usual embellishments of the truth, may shed some light on this question.[149] Apparently, the Indians at Las Vegas still held hopes of attacking the Bell company, and felt that Ira Hatch, who had great prestige among them, might prevent them if he was allowed to speak to Hamblin.

Ginn describes the stay at Las Vegas as another tense confrontation with dangerous, demonic Indians. He reports that Hamblin went to find Hatch because he had "great influence with the chief and all the Vegas band, as well as with the 130 Muddy Indians who had joined them." Ginn confirms that the Native Americans at first lied to Hamblin about Hatch's and Leavitt's whereabouts and survival. According to Ginn, Hamblin was not led to the mesquite grove: he found Ira Hatch by pure luck. And then, even Hatch could not at first dissuade the local chief from attacking the train, until Hatch promised the chief that he would succeed Tutsegabits as "chief of chiefs" of the Paiutes.

If there was danger, when it was over, Hamblin sat down with Hatch and Leavitt to hear their story. He could tell from their emaciated, sunburned faces that their mission had not been easy.[150]

Hatch and Leavitt had traveled south from Las Vegas with a few trusted Paiutes. As the missionaries came to the lower Colorado, they at first met a village of "half-breeds, so called, Piutes & Iats, these speak the Piute & Iat Languages," who received them hospitably.[151] These are probably the Chemehuevi, Paiutes whom the Mohaves had invited to live near them at one point.[152] They warned Hatch and Leavitt that if they went to the main village, where the war chief lived, they were afraid they would be killed.[153] The tribe had recently been at war with whites and had taken two white scalps a few days before this.[154]

While there were tensions between whites and Mohaves throughout the 1850s, a military disaster the tribe had recently suffered at the hands of Indians east of the Colorado might have left them enraged and inclined to take out their fury on any chance passers-by. An alliance of Mohave and Yuma warriors, numbering between four and six hundred men, had in the summer or early fall of 1857 made a hostile incursion eastward into the territory of the Pima and Maricopa Indians.[155] After an initial attack, they had been surrounded by the Pimas and Maricopas and their forces were almost entirely destroyed.[156]

Thus Hatch and Leavitt were arriving at a very dangerous time, and were heading toward the locus of Mohave frustration and rage. The war chief was undoubtedly part of a special group of military leadership among the Mohaves, called *kwanami*, who in wars dreamed what would occur in the upcoming conflicts, then planned and led the raids.[157] Hatch and Leavitt were about to enter an enclave of *kwanami*, just after the group had suffered a disastrous defeat. The Mohaves had divided between a war party and a peace party; the war party wanted to show that they were not afraid of whites and could kill them with impunity.[158] Killing Hatch and Leavitt would allow them to make their point.

Despite the warnings of their Paiute and Chemehuevi friends, Hatch and Leavitt continued south; Hatch was possibly relying on the earlier friendly contacts he had had with Mohaves.[159] When they reached the main village, the Indians led them to the war chief. The meeting did not go well, and soon the Paiutes told the missionaries that the Mohaves were planning to kill them. The Mohaves confiscated the missionaries' horses, told them they could not leave, and apparently killed and ate Leavitt's horse.[160]

Hatch and Leavitt then found a Mohave who could speak some English. They told him that they were friends and had traveled a long way to come visit them. "White men are mean and dishonest and are not our friends," the Indian answered coldly.[161] A number of Mohaves gathered around the two whites in a threatening manner. The Paiutes began pleading with the Mohaves to spare the missionaries' lives, but to no avail. One of the Moapat Indians came to Hatch and said, "We told you last night they would kill you if you came here" and burst into tears.[162]

In his diary, Hamblin quoted Hatch as saying: "The Cheif then called a vote to see who would sanction ~~their~~ our death. All of the Iyats formed themselves in single file with their chief at their head, showing by this that they sanctioned our death." Weeping, the Paiutes relayed the death sentence to their friends.

In the letter to Young, Hamblin wrote,

> Hach replied they will not be so foolish as to kill their best friends, and asked the privilege of praying, this being granted, the two brethren knelt in their midst, the Piutes their friends on one side, and Iats on the other armed with their war clubs the only wepon of defence used. Ira prayed in the piute language, they interpreted to the Iats.

Hatch asked his Heavenly Father "'to soften the hearts of the indians that they might spare their lives, and that they might know they came here to do them good and not harm.'"

The letter continues: "At the close of which, the Iat Chief steped between his wariors and their intended victims—took them our brethren under his care untill they left, through the influence of that prayer our brethren were saved."[163] The chief, named Chah-ne-wants, and his daughter pleaded for the lives of the missionaries.[164] Then the chief rushed them into his lodge, built a fire there, and personally stood guard over them through the night. Indians brought the missionaries' surviving animal, a somewhat broken-down mule, and tied it to the doorpost, but a Paiute came and told the missionaries that many Mohaves still hoped to kill them before they left.

Nevertheless, Hatch and Leavitt spent the evening giving the chief "much good instruction—telling him things that must shortly come to pass with the indians." Mormons always loved the apocalyptic vision, and what better time than now to share it with their Native American brothers? Evidently, the chief was impressed, because he continued to protect the Mormons.

The next morning they were allowed to leave.[165] But they apparently had no food at all, and the only plant food the country offered was mesquite pods, though they were gone by this time of the year. So they killed and ate lizards, snakes, and chipmunks. They debated boiling and eating their moccasins, but decided instead to push on as best they could.[166] Amasa Lyman later described the stretch from Vegas to the Colorado as "barren and desolate in the extreme." There were no springs, very little grass, and an abundance of extremely annoying cactus and prickly pear bushes.[167] Nevertheless, Hatch and Leavitt kept walking and somehow stumbled into the safety of Las Vegas.

Hamblin added a prayer of thanksgiving for the miracle of his friends' deliverance:

> I consider the preservation of the lives of these two men a remarkable intervention of Providence. Many other mericles, mercies and blessings have been manifested, under my observation, towards the brethren on this mission, for which I feel to thank the Lord, my Heavenly Father, and his son Jesus Christ. To whom be glory and honor for ever and ever, Amen.[168]

Evidently, Hatch and Leavitt then traveled east to Fort Clara, while Hamblin and the Bell company pushed on into the desert. They had no further major Indian troubles as they continued down to southern California. Hamblin planned to accompany the group to San Bernardino, but he began hearing from friendly travelers that non-Mormons in southern California blamed him both for the Mountain Meadows Massacre and for the loss of the stock in the Turner-Dukes company. Therefore, if he set foot in San Bernardino, they claimed that they "would hang me the first sight they got of me without Judge or Jury."[169] So when he reached the head of the Mojave, in the San Bernardino Mountains, he turned back, after being paid by Bell and the other merchants.[170] The company reached San Bernardino six days after leaving Las Vegas.[171]

On reaching the Muddy, Hamblin found that it was in "rather a precarious situation" because the missionaries there (Perry Liston and Jehiel McConnell again?) "felt very impatient to take squaws" in marriage. Hamblin wrote that this caused the young men of the surrounding Indian bands to become very jealous of the whites and they even made some attempts on their lives.

Hamblin probably arrived at Fort Clara not long before December 26, when he wrote to Brigham Young. Soon after this, he sent Ira Hatch to preside over the missionaries on the Muddy. "Br Hach is now on his way there to correct those errors & set things to wright as soon as possible," Hamblin wrote to Young.[172] He was also to help Mormons traveling to Utah from southern California. Hamblin eventually sent Thales Haskell to assist him, because "the indians were very troublesome."[173] "This was a very arduous task and hard to be endured and it tried the faith and patience of these two men but they endured it without a murmer," wrote Hamblin. Hatch and Haskell returned near the end of February.[174] Hamblin wrote that he also spent much time that winter on the road between Fort Clara and Las Vegas, assisting the Saints who were moving to Utah.[175]

Hamblin's 1857 diary-autobiography ends with a vision. Soon after he returned from piloting the Bell company through to California, one of his wives told him that Albert had been very solemn in recent days and wanted to talk to him. That night the boy told Hamblin that a few days before, as he was bringing his herd of sheep home, he saw someone standing by the side of the road, "dressed in a white robe that shown so brilliant that I could not look at it long." Albert stopped, frightened, but the figure approached him and told him "not to be afraid, but to be a good boy and there was many blessings for me."

Soon, Albert said, in a marvelous phrase, "the air came under me," and he went up "where there was butiful buildings—the most butiful that I ever saw." The messenger on the road was still at Albert's side and instructed him to enter the largest of the buildings, but Albert was afraid to because "it looked so much like fire." This is a classic apocalyptic pattern, in which a heavenly messenger guides a prophet up into heaven.

The messenger led the young man to another "department," where Albert saw "my grandfather, (meaning my father that had been dead one year)"—Isaiah Hamblin—dressed in a white robe hanging to his ankles, and looking younger and more handsome than Albert remembered him in life.

Albert was then taken to a different "department" and was

> shown the situation of the indians, or as they told me, "My people." This person told me that I must come back and some day bear witness to all the indians on the earth and try and bring them to occupy the same sphere that this glorious personage did that I was with.

Albert was told he could not stay long away from earth, but the boy could not bear the thought of leaving this heavenly place with buildings that shone like fire. The messenger had to lead him out and back down to the fields near Santa Clara.[176]

A Mormon visiting heaven, then returning, is a standard trope in the Mormon historical record, and we see by this narrative that Albert had become a true Mormon and his adopted father's son in his visionary ways.[177]

In Hamblin's private life, the major event of 1857 was the introduction of Priscilla into the family. She would be a rock of stability and energy in the Hamblin family for the rest of her life. Since Rachel's health would only decline in the coming years, Priscilla must have done her own work and often Rachel's as well. While the history of polygamy contains many examples of tension between older and younger wives, in this case the two wives became very close: "She gave me her wisdom and help, and I returned to her my trust and love," wrote Priscilla.[178] According to family tradition, Priscilla once offered Jacob especially good and plentiful food, and he promised her a reward. Rachel whispered, "Tell him he can give you that [large] piece of dark blue dress goods." Each woman got a dress as a result.[179] So sometimes these two would join forces in dealing with their husband.

Women shared fully in the dangers of living on southern Utah's frontier. Thales Haskell wrote that during these times, Fort Clara was frequently without men and without firearms, and in fact, some local Indians boasted that they could massacre the inhabitants of the fort and ransack it before word could reach the men. The missionaries, on leaving Fort Clara, always advised the people left behind not to leave possible weapons or dangerous tools lying around within easy reach of visitors. "But the women were as full of courage as the men. Every night the axes were put inside the fort where they could easily be reached if an Indian attempted to break in at a window or a door."[180]

Once, when Jacob was on a mission and the Santa Clara men were working in the fields, some Indians unexpectedly entered Fort Clara. Rachel, quick-witted and courageous, offered them bread to eat in her home; and while they were distracted, she secretly dispatched a boy to alert the men working nearby. The Indians promptly left when they discovered that help was on the way.[181]

One time when Jacob was absent, a group of "painted Indians" on horseback approached the Hamblin house in the fort. One rode right up the steps, across the front porch, through the door, and into Priscilla's kitchen. However, when he reached out for a biscuit, Priscilla beat the horse on its head, and it backed out of the house, almost throwing its rider. "Hump! Jacob has heap brave squaw!" the man reportedly said.[182]

It is possible that the Indians meant no harm, but these incidents show the real fears and isolation that women on the frontier often felt. Historian Julie Jeffrey observes,

> Friendly Indians had the unnerving habit of appearing silently [in a home], wanting food or just a look at a white woman and her children. Many white women believed that native men were particularly aggressive when white husbands were away from the homestead. They found the Indians' scavenging for food frightening, especially when the men carried weapons.... Not surprisingly, women often reacted aggressively.[183]

This is just one of many examples of the cultural divide between whites and Indians in the far West.

Priscilla became renowned as a healer and nurse, and she followed her mother in becoming a midwife. She was well known for a special relationship she had with one of the Indian girls living in the Hamblin family. Three Indian girls were adopted into the Hamblin household early; from the time they were very young, one (Eliza) lived with Rachel and one (Ellen) with Priscilla.[184] In 1857, George W. Armstrong reported to Brigham Young that Jacob had four "apprenticed Pied children" in his house, and that the two girls (aged ten and twelve) "had spun sufficient wool during the spring to make forty yards of cloth, besides attending to other household duties, such as milking."[185]

One day Ellen stepped on a sharp chaparral stick that was covered with tarantula poison, and the foot became badly infected. Priscilla constantly tended her as her foot worsened, and eventually Ellen absolutely refused to let Priscilla leave her room. One night Priscilla, sleeping in the same room, awoke and Ellen's bed was empty.[186]

> Looking around, she saw Ellen curled up in a little ball on the floor at her feet. The Indian girl loved her so much and had such confidence in her that she had wanted to be as near her as possible. Ellen suffered greatly before death finally came, and Priscilla could never speak of her without emotion. "She was just a little dusky diamond," she often said.[187]

Undoubtedly, Priscilla's sympathy and kindness were valued equally with her medical skills.

8

"The Gentiles are Fiting Up Steamers to Explore the Colerado"

Encounter with Ives on the Lower Colorado, 1858

At this time, Hamblin's history dovetails with one of the famous explorations of the Southwest, the steamboat expedition of Joseph Christmas Ives up the Lower Colorado. The Hamblin and Ives groups met on March 16, 1858, during the polarized era of the Utah War (which lasted till July). As a result, the Mormons and the American soldiers viewed each other with paranoia and suspicion. We have accounts of the confrontation from both sides, and both accused the other of sinister plotting.

In this meeting, Hamblin was certainly acting as an information gatherer for Brigham Young, though whether he received actual instructions from Young is not known. The Indian missionary knew about the Ives expedition by December 26, 1857, when he wrote to Young, "The Government is now puting up an iron Steemer to penetrate the Colerado as far as possible, then send pack trains through to the Southern settlements of the Saints. Whatever course you would wish me to take in reference to this operation, would be gladly received as soon as possible."[1] About a month and a half later, Hamblin repeated the news in another letter to Young, telling him that the Mohave Indians had told him that "the Gentiles are fiting up Steamers to explore the colerado to find whare they can get suplys to an army."[2]

Hamblin was correct in asserting that the steamboat exploration of the Colorado had a military purpose. The Ives expedition was commissioned by the secretary of war, John B. Floyd, and had as its main purpose "to ascertain how far the river was navigable for steamboats," according to Ives's diary-memoir. And the secretary of war wanted to know the limits of navigation on the Lower Colorado in order to discover whether it "might prove an avenue for the economical transportation of supplies to the newly occupied stations," wrote Ives.[3]

In summer 1857, Floyd assigned Ives, his niece's husband but also a lieutenant and topographical engineer in the U.S. Army, to start the expedition at the mouth of the Colorado on about December 1 (when the water was lowest). There were already two steamboats on the Lower Colorado at Fort Yuma, but Ives decided he did not want to use them and instead chose to have a steamboat built on the East Coast, then disassembled and shipped to the West at considerable expense.[4]

His company unloaded and reconstructed the steamboat, named *The Explorer*, at the mouth of the Colorado, beginning on December 4, 1857. While he was assembling his ship, Ives received a letter from Floyd, through an intermediary, informing him that since the Mormons had begun "open hostilities" with the U.S. troops in Utah, the "War Dept. may wish to send a strong force to Great Salt Lake by the Colorado river & Virgin River." He instructed Ives to take a "strong escort with a howitzer," as he might face dangers from the Mormons.[5] Ives did indeed fit out his steamboat with a howitzer, which was certainly overkill, granted the total nonexistence of a Mormon navy or army on the Colorado. The fifty-four-foot-long steamboat was constructed and ready to go on December 30, and the Ives company steamed out northward.[6]

Ives's published report, an edited diary, chronicles the expedition as it sailed up the Colorado, with maps and careful descriptions of the flora, fauna, and local Indians, especially the Yumas and Mohaves. Ives found that it was possible for a steamboat to ascend the Colorado to Black Canyon, near today's Davis Dam, just north of Laughlin, a point about sixty miles from Las Vegas and twenty miles from the "Mormon road." Ives arrived at this "head of navigation" on March 8, when he hit a rock which damaged the steamship.[7] He subsequently took a skiff five miles upstream to Las Vegas Wash, which he mistakenly thought might be the Virgin River, arriving there on March 12.[8] Then he returned to the steamboat, which had been repaired, and the company began to sail downriver. Ives had made arrangements to meet a pack train from Fort Yuma, then to set out across Arizona toward the Hopi mesas and Fort Defiance in eastern Arizona.

Hamblin met Apostle Amasa Lyman a day's journey east of the Muddy River in modern Nevada on January 17, 1858.[9] Lyman, who had been a leader at San Bernardino in California, wrote to Brigham Young on this day, "The Indians have brought us the news that the 'Americats' are coming up the Colorado to kill off the Mormons and Indians." He suggested that a party of twenty men and four missionaries should be sent to the Colorado to verify this rumor.[10] Lyman also spoke with a Major George Blake, who had helped with some crossings of the Lower Colorado, on January 31, and Blake told him of the two steamboat missions on the Colorado. Then, apparently trying to bluff the Mormon leader, "He also hinted that 3000 men w[ould] be sent up that way."[11] Lyman had no reason to suspect that he was bluffing, and the apostle met with Thomas Kane, who was acting as a mediator in resolving the Utah War, on his way to Salt Lake City, in early February, and traveled with him northward.[12] After conferring with Lyman on February 25,[13] Brigham Young agreed to his plan to lead a party of twenty men to the Lower Colorado to investigate rumors of troops approaching in that direction, and sent a letter to Jacob Hamblin instructing him to help Lyman in any way he could.[14] Lyman left Salt Lake City on March 8.[15]

Hamblin had already decided to visit the Mohaves on the Lower Colorado—perhaps to also keep an eye on the Gentiles in their steamboat exploration. "We hav heard from the Yats several times. They are anxious to see us," he wrote to Brigham Young on February 14. "They hav seen the treatment the Lamanites hav receivd below them and want we should come thare believieng we are there Friends. The way is opened for the work to comence among them." The Indians "below" the Mohaves were the Yumas, who had been thoroughly subjugated by the U.S. Army. Fort Yuma, across the river from modern Yuma, Arizona, had been founded in 1850.[16] The Mohaves had by now entirely repented of their rough treatment of Hatch and Leavitt the previous year.

In the February 14 letter to Young, Hamblin also gave an overview of the Indian mission: "The Micion prospers [more] than I had any anticipacion when I saw you last. The brotheren are all younited. If thare has ben a desenting word among them I am not aware of it. . . . Bro. Hulse[17] at the vagos. Bros. Hatch. and Hascal at the Mudy. Bros Samuel. Knites. Dudley Levit. Oscar. and. Fredric Hamblin has gone to the Lead mines to secure lead."

Jacob left Fort Clara with trusted companions Dudley Leavitt, Ira Hatch, Sam Knight, and Thales Haskell on March 6.[18] They reached Las Vegas four days later, and, without Hatch, set out for the Lower Colorado, taking with them Patsarump, a headman of the Vegas Indians.[19] On the fifteenth, they arrived at a small village of Mohaves on the Colorado, and were received hospitably. The next day Indians from bigger villages in the south arrived and "said that the Americans were coming up the river; and that they were afraid that they would take their lands."[20] In Ives's view, the Mormons had implanted that belief among the Indians who had formerly been friendly to Ives; according to Hamblin's account, the Indians had arrived at this fear entirely on their own. Ives may have underestimated the complexity of attitudes among the Mohaves at the time; many of them had sincere anti-American feelings, while others were more friendly.

The Mohaves led the Mormons to Cottonwood Valley, where the steamer had stopped for the evening, and an Indian told Hamblin that "there was a great many whites coming up the river, on horse back and on foot." Since the Utah War had not yet ended, this was alarming news. (The Indian probably was referring to the pack train from Fort Yuma that was coordinating with Ives.) "Knowing, as I did, the feelings of the parrent government towards this people," wrote Hamblin, "I felt anxious to know the business of this boat and, if possible, to get some information in relation to the opperations of the Government of this river."[21] Therefore, he assigned Thales Haskell to contact the men on the steamboat and board it if possible. The Mormons viewed this as something of a cloak and dagger operation, and Hamblin gave Haskell a cover story: "he need not tell them that he was a mormon, but if they asked him to tell them that he had relations belonging to the church." He should say that he was on his way to California, but as Indians were very dangerous on "the Old Spanish Trail," he was keeping close to the river. As Ives notes, the idea that someone on the way to California would detour all the way to the Colorado is a somewhat outlandish story. "This was my first real experience at espionage," Haskell later wrote. And not a very promising start.

Nevertheless, Haskell hailed the Americans, and Ives and company sent a yawl over to take him aboard, while Hamblin, Dudley Leavitt, and Sam Knight hid in a willow thicket and watched. That night Leavitt and Knight felt forebodings that Haskell would be held prisoner, but Hamblin predicted that he would return to them the next morning, which in fact is what happened. Haskell told them that a Lieutenant Ives of the U.S. Army commanded the ship, and that he had treated Haskell "like a gentleman." Ives told Haskell that he was exploring the river "to see if supplies might not be brought to Utah up this river cheaper than they could be brought over the Plains." This was a half-truth at best. Secretary of War Floyd had also requested him to see if "a strong force" could be brought to Utah via the Colorado.

Ives expressed worries that Mormons "might interfere with his expedition," but Haskell, posing as a non-Mormon, "told him that he need not have any fears upon that point as the mormons had enough to keep them busy to keep the Troops back on the east side of the Territory."[22]

Ives wrote that one of his men had been in Utah, and immediately recognized Haskell as a Mormon bishop (although Haskell had not been a bishop). Ives wrote:

> For some reason he chose to make a mystery of his personality, and told a clumsily contrived and impossible story; representing himself and companions as California emigrants en route to Los Angelos. He said they had taken this detour of a couple of hundred miles to avoid meeting Indians—and, according to his own account, they had already passed all of the Indians that were to be encountered on the regular trail,—and by coming to the Colorado would be obliged to run the gauntlet of one or two thousand more. This and several similar discrepancies did not argue well for the bishop's sanctity; but we gave him a night's lodging—that is, a pair of blankets to sleep upon—and entertained him as well as the corn and beans would permit.[23]

Haskell's reminiscences, on the other hand, portray the men on the steamboat as completely taken in by his story, and telling him anti-Mormon tales through the night. "I appeared as innocent as I could and listened to their horrible stories about the Mormons and what they intended to do to them."[24] In other words, this account completely contradicts the Ives story.

In any event, the encounter ended without bloodshed, but in the aftermath of the meeting, both sides suspected the other side of dark plotting. Ives felt that the Mormons had turned the local Indians against him—by stating that the Ives company was going to take over their land—after he had worked hard to develop a good relationship with them.[25]

The four Mormons decided to split up now. Leavitt and Knight were anxious to return home, so they went north with all four horses, and Hamblin and Haskell went south on foot, presumably to obtain more information on the Ives expedition. They met several Mohaves "who told us that the Americans would kill us if they saw us." Jacob and Haskell saw a number of soldiers coming up the river, and suspected the worst. They began to "feel deprest and heavy in spirits as if there was something wrong," and turned back north to where they had parted from Leavitt and Knight. There they saw several skyrockets shot into the air, which were answered by skyrockets from the pack train down the river. It all seemed sinister to the Mormons. Could Ives be warning the approaching "army" of the presence of the Mormons? After a night of foreboding dreams, Hamblin and Haskell felt "strongly impressed by the Spirit" to leave, and set out for home.[26]

That night, the eighteenth, Indians came to camp and said that the American soldiers "had offered a large reward for our skalps." This was probably a wild exaggeration by the Indians or Mormons, but it vividly shows the atmosphere of paranoia that Mormons, Indians, and soldiers felt during the Utah War. Indians told Hamblin that the men in the steamboat offered blankets and other goods for the capture of any Mormon. Leavitt and Knight also said that they had seen soldiers following the Mormons' tracks down to the river.[27]

At Las Vegas, Hamblin and Haskell found that a guard from Lieutenant Ives had followed them with an Indian guide. The soldier had questioned Leavitt and Knight rudely, and the Indian guide had talked with local Indians, which would have demolished Haskell's already paper-thin cover story. "This revealed to us the meaning of the Skyrockets; and had we remained there another day we would have been in trouble," wrote Hamblin. These, the last words in Hamblin's account of the Ives encounter, give sinister meaning to the mysterious skyrockets, as somehow meant to encourage the death of the Mormons.

The Ives company suspected that Mormons had performed deeds equally sinister. After describing his encounter with Haskell, Ives wrote, "It was afterwards ascertained that he had incited some Mohave Indians to make an attack on the expedition."[28] Hamblin would have certainly denied this. Ives does describe how the Mohave Indians cooled toward him and his expedition after the Mormons had tried to "excite the hostility" of the Mohaves "in every way" against the U.S. Army.[29] Even though he was convinced by the report of Yuma and Mohave Indians, Ives wrote, "I feel reluctant to believe that any white men could be guilty of such unprovoked rascality." (Of course, Hamblin reports that the Indians were concerned about the "Americats" taking their land even before he and the other missionaries arrived, and would also have accused the Ives expedition of trying to capture and kill him and his friends.)

Ives set out east from the Colorado on March 23, and has a claim to be the first non-Hispanic white man to witness the Grand Canyon from the south. He visited the Hopi mesas, went on to Fort Defiance and Albuquerque, then returned to Fort Yuma.[30]

Though the main company of Latter-day Saints had abandoned Las Vegas by March 1857, a few missionaries under Hamblin's supervision struggled on there. He now called a meeting of all the Mormons to discuss the fate of the settlement, and they decided that Las Vegas would be discontinued as a community, and nearly all the Latter-day Saints would leave. However, they left Oscar Hamblin to help the Indians with their crops.

Lead had been discovered near Mountain Springs, some thirty miles southwest of Las Vegas, and this metal now had strategic importance, as Mormons felt it might be needed as ammunition in the Utah War.[31] Rather than return to Utah immediately, Jacob Hamblin decided to take Dudley Leavitt with him, visit the nearby lead mine, and obtain a load of lead. They went thirty-five miles southwest of Vegas, found the mine on the side of a mountain, and smelted a load. That night, however, Hamblin went up to look at the mine one more time, and when he came down the mountain, the horses were gone, and all the two men ever saw of them afterward were their tracks, and the tracks of the Indian who had led them off.[32] Without other horses, Jacob and Leavitt had no means of pursuit.[33]

So the two men decided that Leavitt should walk to Las Vegas to get Oscar to come with a team to take the load of lead back. Jacob, alone in the desert, would wait for help. When days passed with no sign of his brother, Jacob, having run out of food, began walking back. That night he slept in a cave and collected some cactus pods to roast for supper. However, this was a variety with scarlet spots, which he had never seen before. As he ate them, they did not taste right, and he felt a burning sensation in his stomach and pain in the glands of his mouth and throat. He had eaten a poisonous plant, he concluded (and Indians later confirmed that this was correct). The pain increased and dizziness overwhelmed him.

Thinking he was close to death, the Indian missionary knelt and asked God to spare his life, as he had many times before. Afterward, he vomited and then felt great thirst. He quickly drank the little water he had remaining in his canteen, which he "soon ejected." But then he felt some relief and was able to sleep.

In the morning he continued walking through the desert, famished and now with no water. At noon, he met Oscar coming to his relief. "It was a welcome sight," he wrote, with understatement.[34]

The brothers returned to get the load of lead, but then decided that they would travel twenty-five miles farther west to pick up some iron at a spring on a byroad where wagons were often abandoned. They did not find as much iron as they'd hoped, but loaded what there was.

At this point, Jacob had a waking vision. Albert, with Hamblin's wagon and team, had accompanied a man named Calvin Read to San Bernardino about three months earlier, and now Jacob "saw" Albert and his company at a spring about twenty miles west of where Jacob and Oscar were; he even saw Albert herding animals near the spring. Jacob wanted to go meet the company, but Oscar objected that he had not heard of any water west of the spring where they were. However Jacob was persistent, so Oscar reluctantly agreed, complaining that Jacob was "a visionary man, and always seeing something."[35]

As is necessary for a miracle story, Hamblin's vision was entirely confirmed, and Jacob and Oscar found Albert tending the animals where Hamblin had envisioned him. The members of the company were pleased, because they were not on the main road and did not know how to get to Las Vegas. The Hamblin brothers, after stopping to pick up their iron and lead, directed the company to "the Vagas," and Jacob, Oscar, and Albert soon returned to Fort Clara.

On April 2 Amasa Lyman and his company of twenty men, seeking intelligence on any troops being brought up the Colorado, showed up at Santa Clara.[36] Lyman conferred with Jacob, and Ira Hatch was deputed to accompany the party. After fulfilling this mission on the Lower Colorado, Lyman met "br. Hamlin" (probably Jacob) near Las Vegas on the twenty-eighth with two other brethren, on their way to the lead mines. They turned back with the Lyman party, which arrived at Fort Clara on May 3.[37] As Lyman had found no evidence of any troops bound for Utah, this ended the military actions in the Lower Colorado theater of the Utah War—such as they were.[38]

Hamblin was back at Las Vegas in early May, when John Ray Young stopped there while traveling from California to Utah.[39] John, a son of Lorenzo Dow Young, Brigham's brother, would settle in Santa Clara and later Kanab, accompany Jacob on a number of his journeys, and have a remarkable career in the Mormon Southwest.

Jacob later testified that in spring 1858, he and Albert gathered up any visible bones of the victims of the Mountain Meadows Massacre and reburied them.[40] Just as he was fated to bury the massacre victims, he was also called to play a central role in the aftermath of the LDS Church's reactions to this atrocity. For unknown reasons, he made a trip to Salt Lake City in June 1858. "I had occasion to go to Salt Lake City," he writes vaguely.[41] He arrived in Salt Lake just after the Utah War had ended, and all of upper Utah must have been in commotion. The U.S. Army was entering the city and many Salt Lake residents, who had fled to Utah County, were returning. President Buchanan had pardoned Mormons who had taken part in the war, so Mormon leaders were in no immediate legal or military danger, especially since Utah's new governor,

Alfred Cumming, was inclined to work amicably with the Mormons. Though having the despised U.S. Army in northern Utah, and having a non-Mormon governor, were bitter pills for Mormons to swallow, they could have come out of the Utah War in a much worse situation, given that they had arguably been in a state of open rebellion against the United States government.

There would still be tensions between Mormons and non-Mormons in Utah, but the paranoia, white-hot rhetoric, and occasional flashpoints of violence of the Utah War era would now lessen. In the coming years, Jacob would work well with non-Mormon Indian agents appointed by the federal government, and sometimes served as a subagent in southern Utah.

However, one serious problem that still faced Brigham Young was the Mountain Meadows Massacre. With the U.S. government assigning new, non-Mormon judges to Utah, there was the possibility of further investigation of this and other Utah War–era acts of violence. If Mormon involvement in the massacre became definitively known, the reputation of the LDS Church would suffer enormously, and church leaders, not excepting Brigham Young, might eventually face legal liability.

While in Salt Lake City, Jacob was involved in one event that places him at the center of the story of how the institutional LDS Church would deal with the Mountain Meadows Massacre: he was one of the first Mormons to tell Brigham Young the full story of Mormon involvement in the massacre. When John D. Lee had described the massacre to Young half a month after it occurred, he apparently did not include Mormon involvement in his narrative, portraying it as an Indian massacre.[42]

In the second Lee trial in 1877, Hamblin stated that he spoke to Young and Apostle George A. Smith "pretty soon after it [the massacre] happened" and when he was asked if he had given them "the whole facts" on the event, said, "I gave them some more than I have here, because I recollected more of it."[43] The attorney asked Hamblin why he did not tell anyone else, since a great crime had been committed. Hamblin agreed that "a great crime had been committed. But Brigham Young told me that 'as soon as we can get a court of justice, we will ferret this thing out, but till then don't say anything about it.'"[44]

However one judges Young's sincerity in wanting an impartial legal court to investigate and try those responsible for the Mountain Meadows Massacre, in the second part of this sentence he was directing Hamblin to participate in a cover-up of Mormon involvement in the massacre, for the time being. Hamblin followed Young's counsel, and for many years he told the Mountain Meadows Massacre story without white involvement.

After this, George Smith took Jacob to meet the new governor of the territory, Alfred Cumming. Brigham Young had asked Smith to visit Cumming to see what he thought of the Mountain Meadows Massacre, and to assure him that the Mormons would give him their full assistance in investigating it. Smith introduced Jacob,

> as a man who was well informed regarding Indian matters in Southern Utah, and would impart to him any information required that I might be in possession of. He also urged upon Governor Cumming the propriety of an investigation of this horrid affair, that, if there were any white men engaged in it, they might be justly punished for their crimes.[45]

Yet Hamblin had recently told Young and Smith the story of the massacre including Mormon participation; Smith knew that Mormon leaders in southern Utah had been involved. So even as Smith was suggesting that Cumming investigate the massacre to see if Mormons were involved, he already knew that they were.

According to Hamblin, Cumming stated that President Buchanan had issued a blanket pardon of the Mormon people, and he did not want to pursue any crimes committed during the Utah War further. Smith reportedly disagreed, stating that the massacre was "exclusively personal in its character" and did not involve "the general officers of the Territory" and therefore should be investigated. Again Cumming stated that he refused to take any further steps in view of the president's pardon. Smith replied, according to Hamblin, "If the business had not been taken out of our hands by a change of officers in the Territory, the Mountain Meadow affair is one of the first things we should have attended to when a United States court sat in Southern Utah. We would see whether or not white men were concerned in the affair, with the Indians."[46] Once again, Smith and Hamblin knew full well that white men were involved.

Stating that Mormon leaders wanted to prosecute Mormon leaders involved in the Mountain Meadows Massacre, but that the new administration would not do so, is a defense of the Mormon Church's response to the massacre that was used as early as 1869 and is still being used today.[47] Yet, granted that Young and Smith knew of significant Mormon involvement in the massacre at least by June 1858, this defense is not entirely convincing. After the Utah War, Young was now purely an ecclesiastical leader, though he clearly had great influence among Mormons in all aspects of their lives. Presumably, he would have dealt with the matter in an ecclesiastical setting, after a thorough internal investigation. Then culpable church leaders would have been removed from office, and any members guilty of plotting mass murder would have faced the most serious ecclesiastical punishments possible. But no Mormons were subjected to church discipline until many years after the massacre—in fact, John D. Lee and Isaac Haight were excommunicated only in 1870, after their roles in the massacre became well known among non-Mormons. Dame was never excommunicated, and remained president of Parowan stake for decades after the massacre. According to John D. Lee, Young approved of the massacre, though he regretted the deaths of the women and children.[48]

As was said earlier, no Mormons connected with the Mountain Meadows Massacre came away from it unscathed. They were usually either involved in the massacre itself, or were involved in an extended cover-up that was in some ways surprisingly successful, among Mormons.[49]

Cumming must have been impressed with Jacob, for he recommended him to new Indian agent Jacob Forney,[50] and Forney hired the Indian missionary as a sub-agent.[51] On June 22, Jacob told Forney the story of the massacre, once again portraying it as wholly an Indian affair, and stated that the Mormons repeatedly warned the Fancher party that the Indians were planning to attack.[52]

Charles Mix, the acting commissioner of Indian affairs, had asked Forney to locate the children who had survived the Mountain Meadows Massacre and recover them,[53] and Jacob told Forney that the children had been taken by Indians, but that Mormons had bought and recovered fifteen of them "with considerable effort," and these were in Mormon homes in southern Utah, including one living with Rachel.[54] However, Jacob also informed him that some children were still among the Indians.[55]

In actuality, the Indians had apparently never had any of the seventeen survivors of the massacre, so Hamblin was using a standard massacre cover story here. Yet some of the people who were housing the children, with astounding audacity, asked the government to reimburse them for the money they spent buying the children from the Indians.[56] James Lynch, who later traveled south with Forney, affirmed, "He [Lee] and other white men had these children, and they never were in the hands of the Indians, but in those that murdered them, and Jacob Hamlin and Jacob Forney know it."[57] It's odd that Lynch accuses Forney of covering up here, as Forney, in his reports, also stated that the children had never been among the Indians.

In any event, Forney deputized Hamblin to locate and collect the children. He wrote to Hamblin on August 4 and stated that Jacob's first task as Indian agent would be to find the children of the massacre: "All such must be recovered whether among white or Indians at any sacrifice."[58]

Hamblin later stated that he had heard some massacre survivors were still among Indians. The seventeen children who were eventually recovered said that they had never been among Indians, and Lee and other massacre perpetrators would have known this. However, it is possible that there really were rumors that Indians had taken one or two of the children, and Hamblin felt, in all good conscience, that he had to check out these stories. He certainly described rumors that some children had been taken by the Indians, though it is impossible to prove whether he believed them.[59] Some historians have concluded that Young and Hamblin knew that all the massacre survivors were in Mormon hands in Southern Utah but were trying to get federal money to help finance an exploring and missionary trip to the Navajos and Hopis.[60] On the other hand, one cannot discount the possibility that Hamblin had heard a rumor somewhere (possibly from Indians) that one or two children had ended up among Indians and had been sold in Arizona.

In late July and early August, two apostles, George A. Smith and Amasa Lyman, traveled to southern Utah to investigate the Mountain Meadows Massacre and related problems. They visited all the settlements, including Santa Clara, and undoubtedly talked with Jacob. Their most important investigatory meetings were at Cedar City and Parowan.[61]

As a result, Smith cowrote a report on the massacre on August 6, and submitted another report to Young on August 17.[62] In these reports, Smith portrayed the massacre as carried out entirely by Indians, though a few Mormons visited the scene of the combat. For example, in the August 17 letter, Smith actually portrayed Dame and Haight as hoping to stop the Indian massacre but arriving too late to help. "On the 9th Major Haight, with a party of about 50 men, started from Cedar City to endeavor to relieve the emigrants, and arriving at Mountain Meadows the next morning, found the Indians had killed the entire company, with the exception of a few small children, who were with difficulty, obtained from them. The Indians were pillaging and destroying the property and driving off the cattle in every direction; each one endeavoring to secure to himself the most plunder." According to Hamblin's testimony, at least, both Smith and Young knew that what Smith wrote was incorrect.

Historian Thomas Alexander concludes that on August 6, "the apostles' investigation to that point led them to believe Lee rather than Hamblin."[63] In my view, the dynamics of the situation do not support such an interpretation. If Smith, Lyman, and Young felt Hamblin had been lying, and had been accusing local church leaders falsely of a horrific crime, then he presumably would have been brought to account and disciplined. In fact, nothing like this happened. No one—not Haight, Dame, Lee, Klingensmith, or Hamblin—was disciplined at this time. Stake President Isaac Haight and Bishop Philip Klingensmith were removed from office a year later, in July 1859, as the Cedar City stake was reorganized, but apparently Haight had requested his own release.[64] Lee was allowed to be a branch president in Harmony from 1861 to 1864.[65] It is hard to escape the conclusion that Young and Smith knew, beginning in June 1858, that Mormons were involved in the massacre but decided to portray it as an Indian massacre. As Juanita Brooks writes, the August 6 and 17 reports were the first official church reports on the massacre.[66] Smith, not Young, wrote the August 6 and 17 reports, but Young accepted the August 17 report then passed it on to important non-Mormons, such as Thomas L. Kane, describing it as "the most reliable [account]" then available.[67]

Jacob was in Salt Lake City again on August 5,[68] where he met with Jacob Forney and told him he had discovered ten of the Fancher children and thought there were more. Forney told him to collect the ten children and keep them at his house—a tall order for Rachel and Priscilla. He gave Jacob written instructions, telling him to "endeavor with all diligence to discover the remainder of the children, supposed to be living all such must be recovered whether among whites or Indians, at any sacrifice."[69] Thus he still was under the impression that the Indians had some of the children. He told Jacob to tell chiefs from Fillmore to southern Utah that he, Forney, would visit them in January, and to distribute a few presents "with care and discretion." He gave Jacob a written document giving him the authority to search for the children and collect them.[70]

For the rest of the year, Jacob would be in Santa Clara (in fall 1858 numbering thirty-seven male Indian missionaries and nine male "settlers," some from San Bernardino)[71] and surrounding areas, collecting more of the massacre survivors and continuing his work as president of the Indian mission, which obligated him to officiate in both spiritual and practical ways.

As a church leader on the Dixie frontier, Jacob would sometimes help found new settlements. On February 9, 1858, John D. Lee had visited Fort Clara with Joseph Horne, who had been sent with eighteen men to find a location for a settlement that would grow cotton using experimental methods. Horne, Lee, and Hamblin rode downriver and located the site for the town of Heberville (later Price City) in a valley about two miles southwest of the confluence of the Santa Clara and Virgin rivers.[72]

Hamblin was also an economic leader in Santa Clara and acted as stockman and storekeeper. As he and Lee rode south on their exploration trip, he agreed to sell Lee ten "year old steers"—apparently from the Dukes-Turner train. On May 31, Lee bought sixty dollars' worth of "Store goods" from Hamblin, paying him in gold. Hamblin also held political office in Dixie, as he was appointed to be a selectman, part of an administrative board for a town or entity, on December 2, 1856, at the fourth session of county court at Fort Harmony, and such appointments continued through the years.[73]

On September 9, Jacob wrote Forney and informed him of a conversation he had had with the Pahvant Kanosh. He gave him presents from Forney—tobacco, ammunition, shirts, and a spade—but apparently held back other presents that he wanted to give directly to the Pahvant tribe. At this, Kanosh "was somewhat cross and wanted all I had or nothing. I...told him he was foolish and talked like a child, and left him not in a very good humor."[74] Jacob stated that he had fourteen of the surviving children from the massacre living at his home, and that two more had been "taken to the Crabes a wealthy tribe of Indians East of the Colorado"—Crabes is probably a copyist's mistake for Orabes, Hopis living in Oraibi. Jacob was planning on leading a company east of the Colorado to find these children and visit the Hopis.[75] He said that he also looked forward to traveling with Forney and the fourteen massacre survivors west to California.

Part of the reason Jacob was looking hopefully to the intriguing pueblo-dwelling Hopis was his continuing disillusionment with Paiutes. After he had returned home from Salt Lake City in June, he had heard rumors that the Tonaquint Paiutes had killed a Mormon named Freestone, an elderly Englishman. Jacob and Ira Hatch questioned the local Indians at length, and they denied all knowledge of the old man's death. But finally, Tutsegabits admitted to Jacob that two of his men had killed the elderly Mormon. He said that his band had "teased" him for a long time "to let them kill one Mormon to goe with thare ded friend."[76]

In Paiute death customs, when a person died, often someone would be killed to accompany him on his journey.[77] Hamblin does not state who the dead friend was, but it is possible that it was a Paiute who apparently had been recently killed by Isaac Riddle in Pine Valley (for unknown reasons). In any event, Tutsegabits agreed to allow them to kill a Mormon, because Riddle had killed the Paiute, "and the mormons went around with thare heads down and done nothing about it," as Tutsegabits told Jacob. The Paiutes observed local Mormons closely and selected Freestone, as he was an old man without wife or children, and was "not worth anything." Depending on one's point of view, this was either a compassionate or a brutal choice for a victim.

Tutsegabits came to have second thoughts about the planned killing and realized that allowing the retaliation was wrong. He followed the two men who were going to waylay Freestone, and as he stood on top of a hill, saw them approach the old man. Tutsegabits "belood [bellowed] at them not to kill him for it was wrong," and ran down the hill, but before he could reach them, the two Paiutes had broken Freestone's skull with a large rock. Tutsegabits was furious and beat the two men with a large stick.

Jacob asked Tutsegabits and one of the killers to take him to Freestone's body so they could bury it. The Paiutes admitted that they now realized they had done wrong; however, Tutsegabits said that if the two Paiutes who killed Freestone were executed, then Isaac Riddle should be executed in the same way. This incident shows the Paiutes' rough sense of justice; if one of their people was killed by a Mormon, one of the Mormons—but not necessarily the killer—should also die.[78]

Nevertheless, the murder left Jacob feeling deeply disturbed and disillusioned with his native converts. "Many of the Brethren," he wrote, "feel discouraged in trying to doe any thing with the Piutes." He also recognized that there were criminal whites going unpunished in the area, perhaps a reference to the Riddle killing. "I feel anxious for the time to come when we can punish offenses her[e] whether among Indians or whites men," he wrote to Smith. "Thare is some few scampes that run over the writes [rights] of others with impunity."[79]

The more western Paiutes were also troublesome. On September 10, Hamblin wrote to George A. Smith again, reporting the decision to pull missionaries back from Las Vegas and the Muddy because the "Brotheren and Indians maturd nere 40 acres of corn and wheet. The Indians from the .Mts. stole or robd them of the entire crop. We think that it would [be good] to let them swet a while."[80] This was apparently a case of Paiutes stealing from Paiutes as well as from Mormons.

In the face of these disillusionments, rather than stay at the Clara and work with local Indians, Hamblin started to look to other Indians in the Southwest who might be more suitable for proselytizing. "Thare is a great opening for the Mision to extend East among the more noble trybes of Indians," he wrote to Smith. The work with the Paiutes was preparatory: "If I ever rejoiced in this work it is now. The Elders hav had experiance a mong these Piutes enough to prepare them to goe to a more noble race of them [Indians]." Jacob's references to Indians "more noble" than the Paiutes, so jarring to modern readers, once again reflect the vast cultural divide between whites and Indians on the American frontier. As it turned out, Mormons would also become disillusioned with the Hopis.

Hamblin also mentioned the two white children to Smith as a motivation for the trip across the Colorado: "We intend to visit the Moquich. Navaho. Orabes and as many other of the Trybs as is necessary to find those unfortunate Children."[81] So he was gearing up for the first visit to the Hopis.

In a two-week period in fall 1858, two children were added to the Hamblin family. Benjamin, Rachel's fourth child, was born on September 29, in Santa Clara,[82] and Sarah Olive, Priscilla's first, arrived on October 15.[83]

9

"In & through the Roughefist Country It Has Ever Been My Lot to Travel"

Crossing the Colorado, Visiting the Hopis, Late 1858

Jacob Hamblin's first expedition across the Colorado to the Hopi mesas, which took place from October 28 to December 26, 1858, was one of the great adventures in western history. It included the first known crossing of the Colorado by whites at the "Crossing of the Fathers," El Vado de los Padres, since Fathers Escalante and Domínguez crossed it in 1776 and Antonio Armijo in 1829, and an early reconnaissance of some of the territory of northern Arizona.[1] It was a journey into country that was absolutely unknown to the Mormons—it is not surprising that the expedition teetered on the edge of disaster at times. On the one hand, the participants witnessed landscapes that were spectacularly beautiful and made contact with one of the most unique tribes of Indians in America. On the other hand, they almost died of starvation and thirst and also risked freezing to death. As they witnessed breathtaking, vast formations of rock carved out by water and wind, they had to struggle to keep their balance on trails that were nearly nonexistent and which were a casual misstep away from spectacular drop-offs.

This was far from a pleasant, relaxed tourist jaunt. Ammon Tenney writes, "The sorrows and hardships on that journey would shock the readers of history. The strength of some of our company reached beyond the endurance of mortal man. [We suffered] Starvation, sickness, without clothing to cover our weak and worn bodies, disentery followed with Hemmorage."[2] The expedition also attained mythic status because many geographical points received their names during the journey—notably Pipe Spring, Badger Creek, and Soap Creek.[3]

This journey would become a major test of Jacob Hamblin's leadership. Originally, he may have viewed it as he had his hunting and exploration expeditions with Goshute and Paiute Indians; after all, he was only going over a route that Utes and Paiutes traversed frequently. However, he would find it would be much more difficult than anything he had experienced previously.

To a large extent, this was a missionary journey, as Brigham Young sent Hamblin and company to preach to the Hopis.[4] Young had been intrigued by reports that the Hopis were white, like the Nephites of the Book of Mormon, and were "the first Lamanites known, up to that date, to live in permanent villages."[5]

Other purposes of the journey were less straightforward. As we have seen, Utah Indian agent Jacob Forney had given Hamblin the responsibility of locating all the child survivors of the Fancher party after the Mountain Meadows Massacre, and Paranigat Paiutes in modern Nevada had told Hamblin that "Pey Utes" had taken two children east of southern Utah, possibly to the Hopis or Navajos. "I could not feel satisfied in my mind until I had visited those two tribes," he wrote.[6] As a result the U.S. government may have contributed $318 to this expedition.[7] Some historians believe that Hamblin concocted the story of these two Mountain Meadows Massacre survivors in order to receive funding from the government, but it is entirely possible that there were rumors of massacre survivors among Indians, and Hamblin simply felt it was worthwhile to check on these rumors, even though they turned out to be wrong.[8]

Another purpose of the expedition, according to Ammon Tenney, was to find a possible place for the Saints to retreat if the United States armies in the Utah War drove the Mormons out of northern Utah.[9] While the Utah War had concluded by June 1858, Brigham Young may have been planning this journey before then, or he may have considered the underlying Utah War conflict to be ongoing, even though the standoff had officially terminated.

In addition, the expedition was supposed to find out if the Hopis were, in fact, descendants of the Welsh, in western Britain. Young and other Mormons were intrigued by the Welsh Indian theory (which held that Welshmen had sailed to America soon after 1170 A.D. and became the ancestors of certain tribes of Indians) and therefore wondered if the Hopis—whose culture seemed so different from other, mostly nomadic Indians—might be "descendants of Nephi or of Welsh."[10] Dan Jones, a Welsh convert to Mormonism, was an enthusiastic advocate for the Welsh Indian theory and had written a letter to Brigham Young on the subject in 1845. He became a member of the Parley P. Pratt expedition to southern Utah in 1849 and 1850, partially to serve as the Welsh linguist needed to identify any pockets of American Indians speaking Welsh![11]

On September 26, 1858, Hamblin and his party met in a missionary meeting, and six men were called to stay among the Hopis and Navajos for a year.[12] The members of the expedition were: three Hamblins, Jacob, William (called to the Hopis), and the youngest of the family, Frederick. Then there were two Leavitts, Dudley and Thomas (also called to the Hopis). Four southern Utah stalwarts from Santa Clara

9.1. Ammon Meshach Tenney, who at the age of thirteen, had accompanied Jacob on his first mission to the Hopis (1858) as Spanish interpreter. He later served many missions as explorer, settler, and Indian missionary in Utah, Arizona, and Mexico. From McClintock, *Mormon Settlement in Arizona* (1921).

were part of the group: Ira Hatch, Samuel Knight, Andrew S. Gibbons, and Thales Haskell (the last three of whom were called to the Navajos).

Then there were Santa Clara resident Lucius (Luke) Hubbard Fuller; Englishman Benjamin Knell, one of the founders of Pinto (also called to the Navajos); and two linguists, a Welshman, James George "Dariris" Davis, from Harmony, who would hopefully confirm that a lost tribe of Welshmen had settled in the desolate mesas of southwest America; and Spanish-speaking Ammon Tenney,[13] who was only thirteen, was in poor health, and weighed less than ninety pounds.[14] At this tender age he started a long career of travel, exploration, and missionary work among the Indians in the far West. He was a crucial member of the team, as he had learned to speak fluent Spanish as a boy in Mormon San Bernardino, and Spanish was spoken by many southwest Indians. Tenney gives a moving account of his last moments with his family before the trip. After a final meal, "around the family alter [altar] every knee bowed while the quivering lips of my father uttered a short but feeling prayr." Ammon's mother followed: "My loving mother…being more eloquent circumscribed my pathway from the threshhold of our door to my return thereto with the blessings of heaven & earth combined."[15] The family probably sensed the real dangers Ammon would face.

Most of these men were in their early or mid-twenties; Jacob was now thirty-nine.

Later, the Paiute Naraguats would join the group as guide, along with other unnamed Paiutes.[16] This brings the tally of the group to fourteen named participants, thirteen whites and one Indian.[17]

This company of thirteen men left Santa Clara on October 28, 1858, with pack mules and supplies for thirty days' travel.[18] Hamblin, in his December 1858 letter

9.2. Pipe Spring, for centuries an Indian oasis and camping ground, became an important stop on the Utah-Arizona wagon road after Jacob Hamblin's 1858 expedition. Brigham Young built this fort, "Winsor's Castle," directly over the spring in 1871–1872. Sketch by Albert Tissandier, 1886. Courtesy Utah Museum of Fine Arts.

to Young, describes the first part of the journey as travel over "a contry destitute of water," except for water in rock hollows. Their first major obstacle would have been the Hurricane Cliffs, which they probably surmounted near the eventual site of Fort Pearce. From here they traveled southeast and entered into the territory of Arizona.

On the third day out they reached the oasis that Paiutes called Red Rock Spring, and which Hamblin describes as "alarg spring."[19] It had been used by Indians for centuries, and after 1858 would become an important way station for travelers between Arizona and Utah. It became known as Pipe Spring because of an incident that occurred as the missionaries rested here in 1858. As Ammon Tenney tells the story, Bill Hamblin and the Leavitt brothers, all excellent marksmen, were taking target practice at a silk handkerchief, and were all missing it. James Davis laughed and said, "You can't hit my hat 25 yards away." They declined to shoot at this target, but offered to shoot the bottom out of the pipe Davis was smoking at the time. He set it up for target practice, then sure enough, one of them—reputedly Bill Hamblin, nicknamed "Gunlock" for his expertise with guns—paced off the twenty-five yards then aimed, shot, and "did tear the entire back of the pipe out without breaking the edges of the mouth."[20]

Some Paiutes were camping at the springs, and one of them took Jacob to see the bones of Nahguts, who had killed Jacob's ox on the Clara. He had come to Pipe Spring, turned blind, and died.[21]

9.3. William "Gunlock" Hamblin, Jacob's brother, one of the founders of Gunlock, Utah, north of Santa Clara. His marksmanship gave Pipe Spring its name on the first expedition to the Hopis (1858). From Andrews (1902).

A day and a half later, the company reached the foot of modern Kaibab Plateau, soon to be called Buckskin Mountain,[22] and which Hamblin called "Deer mountain" in his 1858 letter to Young. There the missionaries met the "Minepats or Pine ites Indians a small band of Piutes with hoom we ware acquainte[d]," as Hamblin writes. "Naraguots the chief [who] was some acquainted with the Moquiches and the rout[e] we engaged to Pilot us throu[gh]." The Mormons and Paiutes feasted together on rabbits and bread that night.[23] Hamblin noticed one Paiute sitting alone, brooding, and sat down beside him and asked what the trouble was—an action characteristic of Hamblin. "I am thinking of my brother, whom you killed with bad medicine," was the straightforward and chilling response. Hamblin would have been on his guard, knowing the code of retaliation among the Paiutes. He told Nahguts's brother that Nahguts "made his own medicine" and had brought a curse on himself when he killed Hamblin's ox. He responded to an implied threat with one of his own: he advised the Paiute to eat with the company "and not make any bad medicine and kill himself." The Indian did take a piece of bread and the confrontation was defused.[24]

The next morning, the group, now with Naraguats and possibly a few other Paiutes, set out over the Kaibab Plateau. Hamblin described this as "nere 29 mls a high or elivated country covered with Pine no water for 60 miles." "Kaibab" derives from the Paiute word *Kai-vav-wi*, which means "mountain lying down," an astute description of the plateau. Aside from the pine Hamblin mentions, this formation is covered with spruce, fir, juniper, and aspen trees; its elevation sometimes reaches 9,300 feet, but much of it is 7,000 or 8,000 feet high. Approaching from the west, it slopes gently upwards, but on the east, it drops down in steep slopes and escarpments to House Rock Valley. Two of the early names of the formation, Deer Mountain and Buckskin Mountain, attest to the prevalence of deer on the plateau—this was an important Indian hunting ground.[25] Tenney wrote of "the gorges of mountain, where ... the foot of civilized man had never trod."[26]

The Kaibab slopes might have been covered with snow at this time and were

9.4. The Crossing of the Fathers, where Fathers Domínguez and Escalante crossed the Colorado in 1776. Hamblin used this crossing from 1858 to 1862. Lithograph from a sketch made by John E. Weyss in 1872. Courtesy David Rumsey Historical Map Collection, www.davidrumsey.com.

certainly very cold. "Alas cold & bleak indeed was the knight," wrote Tenney. He was called to take his share of guard duty at one camp, and the company's horses somehow managed to get loose, which caused "quite a rumpass" in the morning.[27] However, the group managed to track down and recover their mounts.

The company probably followed a trail up modern Jacob Canyon as they ascended the Kaibab, then may have followed Ridge Trail Canyon down off the plateau.[28] After this descent, the missionaries would have passed modern House Rock Valley and continued traveling southeast near the beautiful Vermilion Cliffs, which rose above them on their left. Then, at the southern point of the Paria Plateau, they would have turned northeast. The Vermilion Cliffs would have continued on their left; to their right, still unseen, lay the Grand Canyon and the Colorado.

According to Tenney, the group passed modern Soap and Badger Creeks (flowing through canyons into the Colorado; they received these names on the expedition's return journey), then "camped in the Bottom where now stands Bro Johnsons house and enjoyed the roaring of the Colorado River."[29] Tenney is referring to ferryman Warren Johnson, and thus the site of modern Lee's Ferry, near where the Paria River flows into the Colorado. This was the first documented visit by whites to Lee's Ferry since it had baffled Escalante in 1776. Jacob did not try to cross here, but he saw that the Colorado might be traversed by boat at this site at some future time, and that such a crossing might save the traveler a substantial amount of precious time and supplies.

The only practical place for crossing the river on foot or horseback was a three-day march northeastward, the "Crossing of the Fathers," known to Hamblin as the Ute Ford. To get there, the men would have to surmount the northeast wall of Paria Canyon, then, far above the Colorado River, work their way back down to the river. Ammon Tenney merely says that the missionaries continued up the river, then over a mountain.[30] These three days of travel were nerve-racking, as the men climbed "dangerous cliffs" and crossed "extensive fissures in the rocks."[31]

Escalante, Domínguez, and company (and presumably the later Mormon company) traveled three miles up Paria Canyon, then took a rough path four hundred feet up to a sloping bench with areas of red sand. They climbed this until they were about a thousand feet above the Paria, then had to ascend another very steep slope. About three hundred feet from the top, they switchbacked over sandstone ledges "that were not only narrow but were dangerously rounded on the outside edge." They came to the summit via "a shallow notch about 150 yards long."[32] Escalante and Domínguez (and, presumably, Hamblin and company) then passed modern Castle Rock, Navajo Creek Canyon, Warm Creek, and Gunsight Canyon.[33]

The Ute Ford, Hamblin wrote, "being [shut in] with rock hundreds of feet high all of the inlets being in the same fix made the road crooked and dificuilt to travail with pack Animals." The Escalante diary parallels this description precisely.[34]

Jacob and company passed Gunsight Canyon then probably took Gunsight Pass, a narrow passage northwest of Gunsight Butte. This may be what Gibbons referred to as "The Devil's Gate," where the trail passed between "steep, perpindicular rocks."[35] This led to a winding Indian path on the north side of the canyon. The Escalante and Domínguez party went south of Gunsight Butte and then had to make a steep descent into Navajo Canyon on the south side of the canyon, carving steps into the slickrock. As the Hamblin company had Indian guides, they probably took the less precipitous trail on the north side, though steps have also been carved out here as well.[36]

The Ute Ford was simply a place where the Colorado, at certain times of the year, was shallow and gentle enough to ford; one simply walked or rode one's horse across it, following sandbars when possible. Wallace Stegner referred to "fantastic erosional forms" there and the "moonlike loneliness" of the spot.[37]

This historic crossing took place on the tenth day after the group left Santa Clara—approximately November 7, 1858.[38] The company did not cross directly across the river, which was about three-quarters of a mile in width;[39] they had to slant southeast before reaching the opposite bank.[40] According to Tenney, nineteen Paiutes helped the Mormons across, holding hands to make a hundred foot line, "so that they could aid and help to hold up the one or more [men or horses] who found it hard to swim the water." The missionaries stayed behind this line and followed the men who had reached shallower water in front of them, which allowed them to maneuver their horses when they were not swimming. "Our suspense was lowered a little on reaching the eastern bank," wrote Tenney, probably a considerable understatement.[41]

Thus these Indian missionaries repeated what the Escalante and Domínguez expedition had done eighty-two years earlier—curiously enough, on the same day of the year, November 7.[42] Both expeditions were primarily evangelical, religious in nature—one animated by Old World Catholicism, the other by New World Mormonism.

Hamblin and company now probably continued to follow the Ute Trail, as had the Domínguez-Escalante expedition, setting out over a no-man's-land of mesas, buttes, and washes, a territory even now little populated, and with very little water. First, the trail led just west of Padre Butte, then followed the Domínguez Buttes and reached the dramatic Tse Tonte formation. It came to another major natural barrier, "Cottonwood Creek," probably Navajo Creek and Canyon, after one day's journey south of the Colorado, twenty-five miles, traveling southwest. Crossing this canyon required a dangerous descent by the minimal Ute trail, with frightening drop-offs just inches away. The trail weaves a course through small canyons leading to the main canyon, winding "through side gulches, around isolated mini-buttes, and across precipitous ledges," as historian Ted Warner writes.[43] At points, Indians had "fixed" the trail with "loose stones and sticks," according to Escalante.[44] Crossing this by foot was a challenge; crossing it with animals was extremely difficult; and crossing it with a wagon would be impossible.

At the bottom there was welcome water, as Jacob and friends came to the confluence of Navajo and Kaibito Creeks. Now the Ute trail followed the Kaibito and led the missionaries up the east face of Chaol Canyon. Here again the journey was nerve-racking: Escalante wrote that his company climbed upward "by a precipitous and rocky ridge-cut…making many turns and passing some rocky shelves which are perilous and improvable only by dint of crowbars."[45]

Tenney wrote, "our rout lay in & through the roughefist country it has ever been my lot to travel."[46] It was hard going but beautiful, and Hamblin was overwhelmed by the scenery. In his December 18, 1858, letter to Young he wrote,

> On either Side of the River is sand, plains, rocks or small mountains perpendicular on all sides which has the aperance of domes, pyramids and castles. These rocks look to be from 500 to 1000 feet high. The aperance of these was the most grand and sublime of any thing I ever saw. We travailed ocasiso[nal]ly on bare rocks for miles.

Judging by the route of the 1859 company, the 1858 expedition, after crossing Navajo Canyon, traveled thirty miles southeast to what the missionaries would call "Rock Basin," then the following day another twenty-three miles southeast to "flat rock," where there were some "ancient ruins"—modern Wildcat Peak (which had natural features that looked like fortified walls), just south of White Mesa.[47] Continuing southeast another twenty-two miles brought them to water in Blue Canyon, on the Moenkopi Wash, part of which the Paiutes called Quichintoweep, meaning "Buffalo Flats." From here, it was about thirty-five miles to Oraibi.

During this trek, in 1858, the expedition was faced with a near-disaster three days after crossing the Colorado: a pack mule "ran off with our dried meet and flower," Jacob wrote. "This he done jest at Dusk."[48] The men searched unsuccessfully for the animal with his precious cargo through the night. Since Naraguats did not expect

9.5. Oraibi, the Hopi town which Jacob first visited in 1858, on the Third Mesa. It is one of the oldest continuously inhabited towns in the United States. Photograph by John K. Hillers, in the 1870s. Hillers first traveled to the Hopi mesas with Jacob Hamblin in 1872. Courtesy Wikimedia Commons/National Archives.

water for a full three days, they "were oblige[d] to travail without food" (and water). Hamblin left two men to search for the mule while the other twelve soldiered on.

On the third day after the split, at noon, some of the men, desperate with hunger, roasted and ate a cowhide they had with them.[49] But finally, "after many days we began to see signs of men & beasts," wrote Tenney, which must have been a welcome sight to the starving men.[50] At about this time, Naraguats and the other Paiutes left the Mormons, as they did not believe they would be needed at the mesas. However, the Mormons commissioned one of the Paiutes to hunt antelope for them and meet them with food on their return journey.

At four o'clock on about November 14, the missionaries saw a place where sheep had been herded and a garden of onions, peppers, and other vegetables on the side of the mountain, under a cliff, and watered from a small spring (probably the Hotevilla Spring), eight miles northwest of Oraibi.[51] On the top of a cliff they found a withered squash which looked abandoned.[52] The men lost no time in carving it up and devouring it. "It tasted delicious," wrote Hamblin, and they thought it was a variety of squash they had never tasted before, but they subsequently found that hunger had made it sweet.[53]

Thus fortified by feasts of cowhide and one squash, the missionaries staggered on. When they reached the summit of a ridge, they found it was "pasturd with sheep and goats." They followed a trail five miles and found themselves below old Oraibi, on the westernmost of the three Hopi mesas.

The Hopis and their villages on mesas are of course one of the most unique cultures and sights in southwest America.[54] Hamblin wrote that "The Oribie Town" was "built on an eminance or high rock perpendicular except a narow enterance. [It] consists of about .500. dwelling plases built of morter and small rock."[55]

The missionaries were met by "guards" on horses whose appearance was most striking to young Ammon Tenney. Their "netely comed" hair was "tied in a bow behind their heads," except for some bangs over the forehead. They had saddles whose headpieces holding the bridle bit were covered with silver ornaments.[56]

A brief parley with the village leaders ensued, and fortunately for the starving men, they were treated most hospitably. "We ware invited in to Town," wrote Hamblin, and were led up into Oraibi, ascending via a narrow, difficult entrance on the east side of the mesa.[57]

As they passed through the gates of the town, "hundreds could be seen from the house tops where they had congregated to see the white face of which they knew nothing except by tradition," as Tenney writes.[58] This is an exaggeration, but whites at the mesas were certainly rare at this time. The missionaries were taken to a large room, and their animals were unpacked and fed. Then each of the missionaries was assigned to a different family. A Hopi signaled to Hamblin, and he followed him through a few streets. He noticed that the houses were usually three stories high, with the second and third stories set back from the first, so that the lower stories looked like terraces. Entrances to the dwellings were on the roof of the first level, so Hamblin was led up a ladder to reach the roof of his host's home, then climbed a ladder down into the house. Inside, the room was furnished with sheepskins, blankets, earthen cooking utensils, and water urns. It seemed like a palace to Hamblin, after his last four days of exhaustion and hunger.[59]

The Hopis now gave Jacob a meal which he remembered with great fondness: blue cornbread tortillas (called *piki*), boiled meat, bean soup, and a pudding of stewed peaches "of luxerant flavor." He "partook with agoo[d] relish thanking the Lord that he had onc[e] more plased me in a land of plenty having pertakeing very little for four days previous." The woman of the house, seeing that Hamblin was uncertain how to eat the soup, dipped her fingers in it and raised them to her mouth. He quickly followed her example.[60]

The next day, he was relieved when the two men he'd left to find the runaway pack mule showed up at the mesas with the recalcitrant animal.

The following day, perhaps November 13, the Mormons visited what Hamblin called "Moquis Town," about eighteen miles from Oraibi, which was apparently Sichomovi on the First Mesa.[61] It took the missionaries a half-hour to climb up to the town. Here they found some Navajos, though many of these had fled in fear at seeing whites, as Americans had "drove them out of thare Town and took many of thare horses sheep and goats," Hamblin wrote.[62]

Using Ammon Tenney as interpreter, Hamblin did talk to one Navajo who

9.6. First Mesa at Hano (Tewa), looking south at Sichomovi and Walpi. With three Hopis in the right foreground, and a child on a kiva ladder behind them. Hamblin and his friends often visited the First Mesa. Photograph by William Henry Jackson, 1875. Courtesy U.S. Geological Survey.

knew Spanish.[63] The missionaries also met a Spanish-speaking Hopi, who invited them to a dance and feast. Hamblin testified that even though he had been to many Indian dances, "this surpased any I ever witnessed."[64] Many visitors to the Hopis have been similarly overwhelmed at the beauty of their ceremonial cycles, with their elaborately symbolic costumes, dances, and ritual actions.

The next day, the Mormons visited Mishongnovi, on the Second Mesa, where they "maid strict inquiry for the lost childrin and could here of non[e] among the Moquiches." However, they found a white child, whom the Hopis said they had obtained from Comanches. As the child was sick, the missionaries decided they could not even attempt to bring it back with them.[65]

In his autobiography, which emphasizes the miraculous, Jacob mentions a conversation with a Hopi about a prophecy that Jacob felt he and his companions had fulfilled.

> A very aged man said that when he was a young man, his father told him that he would live to see white men come among them, who would bring them great blessings, such as their fathers had enjoyed, and that these men would come from the west. He believed that he had lived to see the prediction fulfilled in us.[66]

Many sources do record that the Hopis had a Messianic tradition that a White Brother, the Pahana, would visit them and help good Hopis at some time, while punishing (often beheading) bad Hopis.[67] However, the Hopis also explicitly believed that some whites would be corrupt and deceptive, so whites who visited the mesas would need to be carefully tested. Earlier, the Hopis had met with the Spanish, but came to explicitly reject them as the messianic white visitors.

Hamblin also reports two Mormon-related Hopi prophecies. First, when the Mormons invited the Hopis to live in Utah with them, the Hopis declined to cross the Colorado River because "they had a tradition from their fathers that they must not cross that river until the three prophets who took them into the country they now occupy, should visit them again."[68] According to the second prophecy, Hamblin wrote, "their chief men also prophesied that the 'Mormons' would settle in the country south of them, and that their route of travel would be up the Little Colorado. This looked very improbable to us at that time, but all has since been fulfilled."[69] This second prophecy has no known parallel in the Hopi tradition.

Historian Armin Geertz's "Catalogue and Typology of Hopi Prophecies" provides exhaustive documentation for Hopi prophecy that we can consider as background for these passages.[70] Hamblin's 1858 reference (published in 1881) is quite important, as it is the earliest documentation in the historical record for this kind of Hopi prophecy. Hamblin is placed at the beginning of Geertz's "Catalogue and Typology of Hopi Prophecies," and historian Peter Whiteley states that Hamblin's reference is the earliest Hopi Messianic prophecy that he has found.[71]

Despite this, there are some anomalies in Hamblin's references,[72] the most important of which is the idea that the Pahana or Pahanas would come from the west. The Hopi traditions almost without exception looked to the east for the messianic white or whites.[73] For example, according to one Hopi, they would have to endure much from whites until the gods recalled "Our Great White Brother from the East to deliver us."[74] Because the Pahana will come from the east, Hopis are buried with their faces toward the east to watch for him.[75] In 1872, Hopis would daily send a ritual group of emissaries to the east to look for the Pahana.[76]

Another unique detail is Hamblin's reference to three prophets. This has no known parallel in Hopi prophecy.

Hamblin did not mention these prophecies in his 1858 letter to Brigham Young, as one would expect, but there is a reference to the prophets coming from the west in the Wilford Woodruff diary at February 3, 1863, about three years after the first visit to the Hopi. Woodruff, reporting a conversation with Hamblin and three Hopis, with Hamblin as translator, writes, "They have had a tradition that some good men will Come from the west and bring them the truth and they think we are the people and they have Come as ambasadors to see the people & to see if we are the people they have been looking for."[77]

In addition, in May 1863, Hamblin wrote to Brigham Young, after describing how Hopis witnessed U.S. soldiers raping Navajo women:

> These things all tend to confirm the Moquis in the traditions of their forefathers; that white and bearded men would come from the East and try to destroy them, therefore, they ought to have as little as possible to do with them; but white and bearded men would come from the west who would have a good spirit and would bless them and try to save them; the tradition teaches that when these from the west should appear they were to be taken into the houses and supplied with the best fare they had to give. This tradition is deeply rooted in the minds of the Moquis. Many of the old men say their fathers told it to them, hence, when they meet us they meet us as good men and friends.[78]

In summary, scholars have noted that the Southwest Pueblo Indians had Messianic myths and expectations that "fused" with Christian beliefs.[79] It is possible that Hamblin was viewing Hopi prophecy through the lens of Mormon eschatology—thus creating a "fusion" of LDS and Hopi beliefs. Hamblin's reference to "three prophets" reminds the Latter-day Saint of classic Mormon folklore of the Three Nephites—Book of Mormon apostles who were called upon to never die, but roam the earth doing good.[80] Hamblin, a thoroughgoing believer in the miraculous, apparently felt that the Three Nephites often appeared to him and gave him guidance.[81]

When it came time for the main party to return to Utah, the Mormons decided to leave four missionaries (Bill Hamblin, Andrew Gibbons, Tom Leavitt, and Ben Knell) at the Hopi mesas and none among the Navajos, as the Hopis advised them not to visit the Navajos, "as they was mad at all white fases."[82]

The Hopi reports were entirely correct. A major war between the U.S. Army and the Navajos had begun on September 8 and would not end until November 20.[83] This would begin about eight years of brutal, destructive, tragic war between the U.S. Army and the Navajos, a period characterized by typical mismanagement and militaristic harshness from U.S. administrators and soldiers, and by sporadic deadly attacks by the Navajos. Though the U.S. Army was handicapped by the desert terrain of the Navajo homeland (which often did not supply water and forage needed for horses and mules), by the Navajos' thorough knowledge of their territory, and by their mobility, nevertheless, the army made many destructive incursions into Navajo territory. They eventually subjugated the Navajos through a scorched earth policy that targeted their agriculture and flocks. Sometimes they captured hundreds or thousands of sheep, which dealt a severe blow to the Navajo way of life.

The Navajos would have a major impact on southern Utah history, and on the lives of Jacob Hamblin and the early Indian missionaries.[84] They lived in the Four Corners area, and knew the mesas and deserts of Arizona and New Mexico intimately. Unlike the Goshutes and Paiutes, many Navajos were comparatively wealthy, often herding large numbers of sheep and goats. They were skilled horsemen and used European rifles as well as bows and arrows. Before the arrival of the whites, conflicts with Utes, Pueblo Indians, and Apaches taught them to become skilled raiders.

The Navajos were not a politically unified nation. Divided into clans, or extended families, they had strong local leaders, often shamans or raiding leaders, who had great prestige, but they did not have a centralized authority or leader.

The Navajos had an elaborately developed ritual cycle, including multi-night "sings" for various ritual occasions.[85] They believed deeply in witchcraft and destructive magic. Their mythology was extensive and complex, starting with "origin" stories, and telling of a "First Man" and "First Woman" who created the four sacred mountains of the Navajo: Blanca Peak in Colorado (in the east), Mount Taylor in New Mexico (in the south), the San Francisco Peaks in Arizona (in the west), and Hesperus Peak in Colorado (in the north).

"First Man" and "First Woman" raised "Changing Woman," an ancestor of the Navajos. Impregnated by the Sun, she gave birth to twins, Monster Slayer and Born for Water, who helped destroy the monsters who still infested the earth in those days. This made the earth safe for humans. Changing Woman created the first four Navajo clans, and these clans migrated back to the land of the four sacred mountains.[86]

The Navajos practiced agriculture extensively, raising corn, and when the Spaniards brought horses, sheep, goats, cattle, and peaches to the Southwest, these became integral to modern (historical) Navajo culture.

The Spaniards introduced the Navajos to European civilization, and many learned to speak Spanish, read, and write. But the New Mexicans also captured Navajo children and raised them as slaves, teaching them to be Catholics. The Navajos retaliated by conducting raids on the settlements of New Mexico, in which they expertly drove off herds of sheep or cattle and also took captives. In a few years, pressed by the U.S. Army in Arizona and New Mexico, the Navajos would turn their skills in raiding to southern Utah.

Having arranged for the four missionaries to stay at the mesas, the rest of the company prepared for the difficult homeward trek. Though the starving Mormons had been kindly received by the Hopis, nevertheless, Tenney describes a persistent "jealousy" that some Hopis felt toward the Mormons. As the missionaries began seeking to buy food and supplies for the trip back to Santa Clara, the Hopis seemed to charge exorbitant prices. This left the missionaries "powerless" and thus forced to set out for home facing a serious risk that they would not be able to find sufficient food for themselves or their animals.[87] It is possible that the Hopis were still recovering from a severe smallpox plague and drought in 1853–1855.[88] Thus Hamblin and eight of the missionaries left the mesas on November 18 without sufficient supplies.[89] The larger group of missionaries left their brethren with some apprehension, given the "jealousy" and high rates for food that the Hopis were demanding.

The first camp of the homecoming missionaries—possibly at Quichintoweep—was stamped in Ammon Tenney's memory because Navajos repeatedly tried to steal the missionaries' horses through the night.[90] A bitter north wind also blew on them, but they did not dare light any fires.[91]

The missionaries expected to have desperately needed antelope meat waiting for them now, but the Paiute hunter apparently did not make an appearance, so they continued on their way on very short rations—"unlevened bread, beans and occasionally a little meat with salt, so by the time we reached the [Colorado] river we had nothing left but crums a few Buns & salt," wrote Tenney. The men often traveled on foot because their horses were "exausted from hardships."[92] Despite these adverse conditions, they pressed forward as quickly as possible because they wanted to surmount the Kaibab Plateau before any major snowstorms arrived.[93]

After crossing the Colorado, they retraced their steps, passing by modern Lee's Ferry. As they trudged on in the shadow of the Vermilion Cliffs, Jacob Hamblin killed a badger, and soon thereafter they reached a creek and camped on it, with "our Horses worn out and us fainting for want of food," Tenney wrote.[94] The missionaries "put [the badger] to boiling but it proved so tough and tasted so strong we decided to carry it and try it agin the following night."[95]

They camped the next night on another creek, where they began to boil the badger meat and buns. But "no sooner did the kittle begin to boil when there arose a foam that smelt like soap and within the space of two hours it had curdled so much like soap that the mess could not be eaten," wrote Tenney. "Thus the names of Bagger & Soap Creek."[96] These names have stuck up to the present day.

Next they sampled some crabapples, but these sickened and weakened them instead of strengthening them.[97] "By this time we were allmost starving to death," wrote Tenney. But they were temporarily saved when they met some Paiutes who took them to their camp, "where the squaws mixed up grass suds in cold watter and we drank it." This typical Indian food allowed the missionaries to regain some strength and begin their dangerous winter journey over the Kaibab Plateau. They reached what Tenney called "the warrior's camp" where they had cached fifty pounds of flour. "The natives ... were true to their trust," Tenney wrote, "but alas what was 50 lbs for starving men?" They could only push onward.

On November 27, the men "crosed the mountains s[n]owe knee deep," Jacob wrote. The following day, the weather seemed to conspire against them: "A snow storm set in upon us. We ware unable to travail as we could not see our course this storm having lasted .2. days and nites." Two of the men, very anxious to get back to civilization, pushed on ahead, against Hamblin's advice. He soon felt that it had been a mistake to let them separate, so the main company of missionaries "packed up and persude [pursued] after them." After following their trail about two hours, they overtook the two men in a cedar grove. "Thare feet [were] nerely frosen. The snowe was then knee deep and the storm increasing. We stopt under those cedars which partley shelterd us from the storm. We had then ben 5 days racioned on lesse than a pint of beans a day to the man. Our provisions had now given out." In addition to facing possible death by starvation, the men were menaced by the severe cold: "It was all most imposible to ceep [keep] from freasing [even] with a larg fire," Hamblin wrote.[98]

We should not imagine these men crossing the winter mountain with solid, substantial boots. "Ear [ere] we reached Pipe Springs we were realing like drunken men for want of food and the snow falling fast," Tenney wrote. "Our shoes had been worn out and our poor feet larcerated by rocks thorns & ice."[99]

Dudley Leavitt reports that during this time Jacob seemed to withdraw into himself; undoubtedly the burdens of leadership were weighing on him. Not only was he facing starvation and freezing weather himself, but he was responsible for the well-being of his company as they were facing these grim circumstances.

The missionaries somehow managed to descend the mountain and come to Pipe Spring but the storm continued. They set out from Pipe Spring but at some point Samuel Knight was ill and had to dismount and stay behind. Tenney states that Knight had to "release a few Oose apples [a yucca fruit that was generally eaten raw or roasted over coals] which demanded of him their entire and unconditional freedom. He was so weakened by the disloyalty of the only nourishment he had received for some passed days that he couldn't mount his horse."[100] The rest of the company covered only eight miles, to Cedar Ridge, then sent two men back to help Knight. "He was not able to remount and had the two men been 30 minutes longer they would have found him frozen stiff," writes Tenney.[101]

This was the darkest moment of their entire journey, as the storm refused to relent. They were only able to start a fire with great difficulty, "for the sleet, ice and snow was falling all day and the snow lay two feet deep while our poor horses stumbled and reeled like drunkards."[102] Finally the starving men were forced to look to their precious mounts for food. "The knaweings of hunger induced us to kill one of our animils," wrote Hamblin. "We chose the flesheyest one, a 4 year old mare."[103]

As Dudley Leavitt tells the story, he and Luke Fuller began saddling their horses to try to ride ahead, but Jacob came up to them and told them they would never make it. "I see no way but to kill one of the horses for food," he said. In response, Dudley simply pulled the saddle from his mare and motioned for Fuller to shoot it. Jacob turned away in tears. Dudley later remembered that "some of the men had steaks cut

9.7. Andrew Smith Gibbons, diarist from the first expedition to the Hopis (1858). He continued to serve as Indian missionary in Utah and Arizona. From McClintock, *Mormon Settlement in Arizona* (1921).

out of the hind quarters of that horse almost before it stopped kicking. No meat has ever tasted so good since."[104] Jacob agreed. "We boiled the flesh on the coles and eat it without salt and to me it was the sweetest meat I ever et. I think thare was not a man in camp that eat less than 5 lbs. of that meat."[105]

After this meal they were able to lie down and sleep through the night, and in the morning "the storm was abated and we felt strengthened and persuid our journey at a raped rate," wrote Jacob. They had survived the last crisis.

On December 4, the missionaries arrived "at the coton Farm on the Riovergin," the town of Washington on the Virgin River, "wharc the Brotheren Blessed us with such good things as the Lord Blessed them with."[106] For these nine men, the great adventure was over.

Meanwhile, the four missionaries back at Sichomovi were not making good progress in their mission, and in fact, though they had been expecting to stay a year, departed less than a month after the main company, mostly because of the difficulty they had obtaining food in the mesas, despite their best efforts to work, hunt, and even beg. They managed to obtain some supplies for their return journey only with great difficulty, but as they were getting ready to depart for Utah, in a touching moment, a Hopi leader took one of their sacks around Oraibi, filling it with *piki*. He also brought a small pony to exchange for a mare the missionaries had that was so "reduced in flesh" that she probably would not make it home. After receiving this last unexpected double gesture of kindness, the Mormons set off on December 8, plodding through a foot of snow.

The trip home was probably even more difficult for these four than that of the main group of missionaries, because the weather was colder and there was more snow on the ground.[107] For example, on December 9, Gibbons wrote, "Made our beds on the snow. Suffered considerable from cold." Four days later, the men "had considerable difficulty in keeping from freezing our feet." In addition, the path was often hard to see because of snow, and the four missionaries wasted precious time wandering as they searched for it.

They somehow managed to bring their animals down Navajo Canyon (which fortunately was not snowy), but at the bottom of the canyon, at Navajo Creek, one of their animals was "strained...very bad," and could not be used after this.

On the fourteenth, they reached the Colorado and found pieces of ice floating in it. When they crossed the river early the next day, they found the river shallower than it had been on the trip out, but it was bitterly cold and they had to watch for dangerous pieces of floating ice. Gibbons had a lame knee, so rode a horse across, but the other three men waded across safely, though they were probably half-frozen when they reached the northwest side.

The travel through the cold and snow continued, and the missionaries' provisions were nearly gone. By the seventeenth, the four men were reduced to killing and eating a crow. As they approached the Kaibab Plateau, they fired their guns to attract friendly Paiutes, and when these came, they begged them "to bring us some ground grass seed, on which we mad[e] our supper." The Paiutes also gave them some seed for the trail ahead.

The snow on the Kaibab Plateau was very deep, especially where it drifted against stands of timber. Fortunately, two Indians had passed over the mountain the day before, so the four missionaries at least did not get lost. When they camped on the twentieth, the cold was "verry severe," Gibbons wrote. The next day, running out of food, they met some Indians, who gave them two small rabbits and some oose. They roasted and devoured the rabbits, but unfortunately, Gibbons and party had the same experience with oose that Knight had had a month earlier: it turned out to be "very injurious to persons not used to eating it," Gibbons wrote, as the missionaries discovered only after "eating a hearty supper of it." Vomiting or diarrhea was probably the result.

After descending the west flank of the Kaibab on the twenty-second, they camped in a small hollow, but that night their beds "swam in mud and water." They reached Pipe Spring the next day at midday and watered their thirsty animals, who had had nothing but melted snow to drink since the Ute Ford. They did not stop but pushed ahead. That night they were weak, having had nothing but oose to eat in recent days, and amazingly, they made exactly the same decision that the main group of missionaries had made, and in about the same place—they would have to kill and eat a horse to survive. They shot the lame animal, and made "a sumptuous supper on horse meat which relished well," Gibbons wrote.

The next day, the twenty-fourth, they traveled all day through deep snow without any trail. But a supper of horse meat kept them strong and active. On Christmas day, they found the trail of the main group at midday, which would have heartened them, and ate the rest of their horse meat, as they expected to arrive at Washington in about twenty-four hours. They sent Tom Leavitt ahead on their best horse and the remaining three men traveled on about six miles before camping. They "suffered much from cold" that Christmas night.

The next day they traveled some six miles and reached the bluff overlooking the Virgin Valley, at which sight they "rejoiced much." After traveling on three or four more miles, they had reached the limits of their strength, and lay down exhausted. Soon after this they saw "the brethren comeing to our relief," as Gibbons wrote. "The feelings that pervaded our bosoms is much easyer felt than described." The men from Washington gave them hearty handshakes of welcome, and the three men wept openly from joy and relief.

After arriving back at Fort Clara the next day, Gibbons wrote a fitting coda to their improbable trek: "After a Journey of 19 days in the dead of winter, travling a distance of 350 miles through a section of country little known by the white man we all feel to acknowledge the miraculous power of God being made manifest in our deliverance from the many dangers that we were exposed to." The survival of the fourteen Indian missionaries was not a certain thing at many points.

Subsequent expeditions over the Colorado would still be difficult and dangerous, but at least Hamblin and others knew that the journey was possible, and they knew the route in a general way. In addition, they had made some friends in the Hopi mesas.

One striking aspect of this story is the importance of Paiutes in helping Hamblin and his men make this journey. They guided the Mormons along Indian trails and over an Indian ford; then fed them traditional Indian foods of rabbit, oose, and grass seed as they faced starvation on their trip back. The good relations that Hamblin and the Mormons had developed with these natives served them well in this journey.

This epic story has been overshadowed by the explorations of Fathers Escalante and Domínguez, Joseph Christmas Ives, and John Wesley Powell.[108] Without taking anything away from the remarkable explorations and writings of those men, the first trip to the Hopis by Hamblin and his thirteen companions, guided by the Paiute Naraguats, deserves to stand in their company. Aside from the accomplishment of this company in surviving such a difficult winter journey, the 1858 expedition to the Hopis marked the beginning of the important Utah-Arizona road, one of the major arteries in southwestern history.

10

"Mr. Hamblin Has Discharged His Duty"

Collecting the Children and Second Expedition to the Hopis, 1859–1860

After surviving the late 1858 trip across the Colorado, Jacob and his companions would have returned to daily life in Dixie, farming, ranching, helping local Paiutes. In early 1859, between thirty and sixty white families were living at Santa Clara, while Paiutes, "living in the adjacent rocks," as one observer put it, tended several Indian farms.[1] Santa Clarans were leaving the fort and building homes outside it. A log footbridge crossed the stream, and a narrow lane, lined with orchards, gardens, and some houses, continued south.[2] Jacob had a gristmill, located across the Clara just south of the fort, which was not yet in operation, and he intended to have a threshing machine ready for the year's wheat harvest.[3]

Apostle Amasa Lyman toured Dixie in about mid-March and wrote that at Fort Clara, Jacob was "improving his residence in the Fort." He noted that expert gardener Walter E. Dodge, whom Lyman would have known in San Bernardino, was starting a "fruit garden, orchard and nursery."[4] Santa Clara was apparently perfectly adapted for growing fruit. According to Zadok Knapp Judd, you could plant a peach pit and have it grow eight to ten feet the first year, the second year it would blossom, and the third it would bear fruit.[5] Jacob's peach orchards became well known.

Santa Clara continued to be very much part of the Cotton Mission, and the Zadok Judd family took a special interest in it. It was hard work, growing cotton, ginning it, carding it, and spinning it. Mary Dart Judd wrote proudly that "I spun the first peas of cloth that was made of cotton raised in the mountaines of Utah and the misionaries raised the seed that stocked all southern Utah."[6] In her autobiography, she interspersed her spinning achievements among important life events: "Jan 14 [1858] I had a daughter born. I made a long peas of lincy cloth. My baby died aged 9 monthes. We baught an indian girl Matilda in March 19."[7] This reference shows how an Indian baby might be added to the family after the loss of a child.

In June 1859, it was decided that Jacob Hamblin was so constantly away on Indian assignments that a local ecclesiastical leader was needed. Santa Clara was organized into a ward and Zadok Judd, now thirty-two, was set apart as a bishop by

Apostles George A. Smith and Amasa Lyman.[8] He called as his counselors James Richie and John William Young, but Richie was soon replaced by Hiram Judd, Zadok's brother.

Jacob continued as an active member of the community in 1859, serving as a selectman for Washington County, and also as a member of a board to examine schoolteachers. His Mountain Meadows rights were renewed, and he was also given land at Shoal Creek, later called Hebron, near modern Enterprise. The county ordered that roads be built between Santa Clara, Pine Valley, and Harmony.[9]

In the sphere of Indian relations, Hamblin continued to act as judge of Paiute wrongdoers. In February, he consulted with John D. Lee in dealing with an Indian, Enos, who had stolen a horse. The surprising punishment was to send him on a mission.[10] In August, Hamblin had local Paiutes whip six Indians under his direction, for stealing.[11]

George Hendrix's anti-Hamblin letter to Young also supplies a very negative portrait of Santa Clara.[12] In June 1859, Hendrix states, Zadok Judd, newly called as bishop, authorized Lucius Fuller—one of the participants of the first expedition to the Hopis—to marry the fifteen-year-old Ann Lay without the knowledge or consent of her parents.[13] When Lay's parents learned of the marriage, they preferred charges against Judd before Jacob Hamblin, but Hamblin supported his brother-in-law, which angered the Lays and Robert Richey. On July 25 and 26, Apostles George A. Smith and Amasa Lyman visited to address the conflict.[14] While we do not know exactly how Smith and Lyman resolved the situation, we know that Fuller and Ann Lay stayed together and had four children by 1870.[15]

Hendrix also offers a worm's eye visual snapshot of the Fort Clara community as it spread outside the fort, describing it as unplanned, and mixing residential houses and animal pens in an unpleasant way. He also described numerous animal corpses rotting in the streets throughout the winter!

While at Fort Clara, apostles Smith and Lyman encouraged Hamblin to lay out the town in a more organized way, to create lots and streets. Hamblin and Judd did this, but, according to Hendrix, took this opportunity to run Richey and Hendrix out of town. Hendrix viewed Hamblin as totally corrupt, and Judd as his agent. Hendrix's view is extremely partisan. One would need to have the Hamblin and Judd version of events in order to assess the situation in a more balanced way. However, his letter does show one thing incontrovertibly: Hamblin had become a man of stature in southern Utah, and had made enemies.

Forney wrote Hamblin on January 28, 1859, telling him of his plans to visit the south in mid-February, and that he would take the children back to Salt Lake City, not to California, at which point they could be transported to relatives in Arkansas.[16]

Hamblin wrote the Indian agent on February 4, reporting that the Mohave Indians had met with the Paiutes of southern Utah and had agreed to stop all travelers going through their territory. As a result, seven men had been killed on the Santa Clara River. However, Hamblin visited these Indians and convinced them to stop this policy. With reference to the children, he wrote, "I would like to get those children off my hands as soon as possible."[17]

Hamblin was still rounding up children on March 2, when he took a child from the home of John D. Lee in Washington. With astounding effrontery, Lee, a wealthy man, then made out a bill to the government for the expenses he had incurred in sheltering Christopher "Charles" Fancher.[18]

Forney left Salt Lake City for the south toward the end of March, 1859.[19] He had two or three main objectives in this journey. First, he would collect the surviving children from the Fancher party and take them back to Salt Lake City. Second, he would visit Indians in central and southern Utah and become acquainted with them and their circumstances. Third, he would investigate the Mountain Meadows Massacre, per the instructions of Alexander Wilson, U.S. Attorney in Utah.[20]

After visiting Mountain Meadows on April 14 with Ira Hatch as his guide, he was in Santa Clara the following day. He wrote, in a May 5, 1859, letter:

> Here (Santa Clara) myself and party were kindly treated during our stay—two days. These children [survivors of the massacre], sixteen in number, I have now in my possession.... I am pleased to say that Mr. Hamblin has discharged his duty in relation to the collection and keeping of those children.... Mr. Hamblin has good reasons for believing that a boy about 8 years and belonging to the party in question is among the Navajo Indians, at or near the Colorado river....
>
> Mr. Jacob Hamblin and others, of Santa Clara, expressed much anxiety to bring the guilty to justice.[21]

Forney wrote that the children "were in a better condition than children generally in the settlements in which they lived."[22] This directly contradicts a report by his assistant, James Lynch, who later stated that the sixteen children "when we first saw them, were in a most wretched and deplorable condition; with little or no clothing, covered with filth and dirt."[23]

In a later interview, Lynch also stated that Hamblin told him and Forney that the children were still with the Indians, and refused to turn them over; however, Lynch ordered the federal officers to direct their rifles on Hamblin, saying, "Produce them or we kill you."[24] Then Hamblin magically found them and delivered them to Lynch and Forney. Again, this appears to be a fabrication. It is clearly documented that Hamblin started collecting the children long before Forney and Lynch came south, and had arranged with Forney to turn them over. In Forney's writings there is not a hint of such a dramatic showdown as this. Forney, in fact, wrote positively of Hamblin's actions as he collected the children.

Forney and Hamblin visited the home of John D. Lee on April 22 and 23. On the morning of the twenty-third, Lee came to Forney's tent and Hamblin introduced the two men. After breakfast, Forney questioned Lee about the Mountain Meadows Massacre, and Lee responded with a long harangue on the corruption of Gentiles in Utah and the forbearance of Brigham Young, who kept the Mormons from destroying the invading army.[25]

Forney, having obtained the sixteen child survivors of the massacre, talked with Indians in the area and obtained information on the Mountain Meadows Massacre; he then began his return to Salt Lake City. However, near Fillmore he heard from some Paiutes and the Pahvant chief Kanosh that there were still two other child survivors of the massacre in Cedar City,[26] so he sent one of his assistants, William H. Rogers, back south, and Rogers was able to learn of a child in Pocketville, modern Virgin City, some forty or fifty miles away from Cedar City. He sent Jacob to pick up this child,[27] then gave Jacob the job of bringing him north to Salt Lake City. Jacob decided to take Rachel north with him, perhaps to help care for the child.

By May 1, Forney had brought the sixteen children to Spanish Fork in northern Utah,[28] and three days later, they were in Salt Lake City.[29]

At about this time, late April or May, federal judge John Cradlebaugh traveled to southern Utah, with a military escort of some two to three hundred men led by a Capt. Reuben P. Campbell, trying to obtain information for the possible prosecution of those responsible for the Mountain Meadows Massacre.[30] He especially wanted to apprehend John D. Lee, who had gone into hiding. Hamblin had reportedly asked local Indians where Lee was, but when he came to Lee's campground, found that he had disappeared. On about May 8, Cradlebaugh and the soldiers were at Santa Clara to request that Hamblin employ Indians to track down Lee. Hamblin told Cradlebaugh what he knew generally about Lee's whereabouts, but refused to use Indians to arrest Lee, stating that that would go against his instructions as an Indian agent.[31]

According to a secondhand story in the John D. Lee diary, the Indian Enos came to Washington and said that Gen. Albert Sidney Johnston had offered five hundred dollars for Lee's scalp, but that Enos had refused the offer. However, other Indians said that Enos indeed was trying to collect the scalp and the money. A William Freem contacted Jacob Hamblin, and Hamblin reportedly "wrote to the authorities at washington to take 20 men & surround the [Paiute] Encampment, demand Enos & shoot [him] down before their Eyes." Enos heard about this plan and fled.[32] There are reasons to doubt this story. First, it would go against Hamblin's policy of strictly avoiding bloodshed with Indians; second, Enos later had a good relationship with Hamblin and accompanied him on his third visit to the Hopis.[33]

Meanwhile, another military officer arrived in southern Utah, James Henry Carleton, "Brevet Major, United States Army, Captain, First Dragoons," whose military superior had ordered him to bury the massacre victims; he also sought to investigate how the massacre took place. Carleton later gained fame as the man who subdued the Navajos through a scorched earth policy and sent them on their long, grim walk to Bosque Redondo in northeastern New Mexico in 1864, forcing them to endure a disastrous residence in the reservation there for four years.[34] He was generally a capable, forceful officer, despite his catastrophic mismanagement of the Navajos at Bosque Redondo.

Carleton met the Campbell company at Fort Clara, then the two groups traveled together to Mountain Meadows beginning on May 16.[35] On May 19, Jacob met Major Carleton and accompanied him to his camp. Carleton interviewed Jacob, Rachel, and Albert Hamblin the following day.[36] Jacob told the story of the massacre entirely without Mormon involvement. Carleton noted that Judge Cradlebaugh felt that Jacob was telling the truth, by his lights. But by Jacob's own testimony in the second trial of John D. Lee, this was not true; he had full knowledge of Mormon involvement in the massacre at this time. But Mormon leaders were adamantly sticking to the Indian massacre cover story, and Jacob did also.[37]

Carleton described Jacob as "a man of considerable importance and noted among the Mormons in the southern part of the Territory. He is about 50 years of age"—he was forty—"and although with but little education, is a shrewd, intelligent, thinking man."[38] This is an insightful analysis of Hamblin; some non-Mormons passed him off as a simple country bumpkin. Jacob also showed the soldiers where many bodies were buried or half-buried.[39]

Carleton wrote that Rachel "evidently looks with the eyes of her husband at everything"—he felt that she was following Jacob in giving less than the whole truth about the massacre—but said that "she at least deserves kind consideration for her care and nourishment of the three [Dunlap] sisters," especially for her nursing and care of the wounded child. Once again, if the massacre children had been naked and filthy, as Lynch accused, Carleton would not have commended her in this way.

Other interviews that Carleton conducted convinced him that Mormons were indeed at the massacre and in fact had orchestrated it. He wrote his report on May 25, 1859; it is one of the key early documents for the Mountain Meadows Massacre.

On the nineteenth, Rachel brought the Pocketville child to Carleton's encampment and the following day, Jacob, Rachel, and the boy started out for Salt Lake City.[40] Jacob told Rogers that he had recently learned more about the massacre than he had known previously, and that many people were involved in the massacre whom he never would have suspected could have been involved. This was probably entirely true, though Jacob had known that Mormons were involved. When Rogers asked for names, however, he said he was sworn to secrecy, and would divulge the information only to Governor Cumming. Rogers said that he later checked with Cumming and found that Jacob had given him none of this information.[41]

By June 2, 1859, Jacob had delivered the Miller boy to Forney in Salt Lake City.[42] James Lynch, who had traveled with Forney, then took responsibility for the children, delivering them to Senator William Mitchell at Fort Leavenworth in Kansas Territory.

Hamblin dropped by the Church Historian's office on the same day, and submitted a history of the Santa Clara settlement.[43] On the third, he wrote an affidavit at the Historian's Office concerning his recent actions in the hunt for John D. Lee.[44] The following day he delivered a "History of his travels among the Lamanites."[45]

Hamblin was still in Salt Lake City on June 15, when he, George A. Smith, and a young man named Marion Shelton, who was interested in Indians, went to the president's office and talked to Young about the Hopis.[46] He dictated another affidavit the next day, concerning a conversation he had overheard in Jacob Forney's office, in which a Major Lyons spoke of his wish to goad the Mormons to open warfare.[47] Jacob and George Smith had an interview with Brigham Young the following day, in which Young reportedly told Hamblin "that as soon as a Court of Justice could be held, so that men could be heard without the influence of the military he should advise the accused men to come forward and demand trial on the charges preferred against them for the Mountain Meadows Massacre."[48] All of these affidavits and interviews relating to the massacre show that Hamblin had become a key figure in the aftermath of the event: he had not been present, so was not tainted by direct complicity, yet he was an Indian expert and a leader in southern Utah who had been able to learn about the event through interviews with family, friends, and participants, including John D. Lee and William H. Dame.

The U.S. government reimbursed Hamblin generously for his work gathering the children: $600.56 for taking care of the three Dunlap girls from September 10, 1857, to April 18, 1858; $318.00 for searching for a child (presumably the journey to the Hopis); $350.00 for caring for massacre children from December 1, 1858, to June 30, 1859; and $1,693.20 for boarding, clothing, and schooling massacre children from August 1, 1858, to April 18, 1859: in total, $2,961.76. Jacob probably divided this money among those who had helped him.[49]

On August 10, Jacob Forney wrote a letter to attorney Wilson, reporting on his investigation into the Mountain Meadows Massacre. Though short, it is a remarkably accurate portrayal of the event. He said that the massacre was "concocted" by whites, then carried out by whites and Indians combined. He listed eight guilty parties, the first four of whom were Isaac Haight, John D. Lee, Philip Klingensmith, and John Higbee (he does not list Dame, which is a major omission). Then as witnesses for this report, which remarkably portrays the massacre as planned by Mormons, he lists only two names: "Mrs. Jacob Hamblin" and "Jacob Hamblin, at Santa Clara."[50] It is hard to imagine that he would name them as witnesses if they were still denying

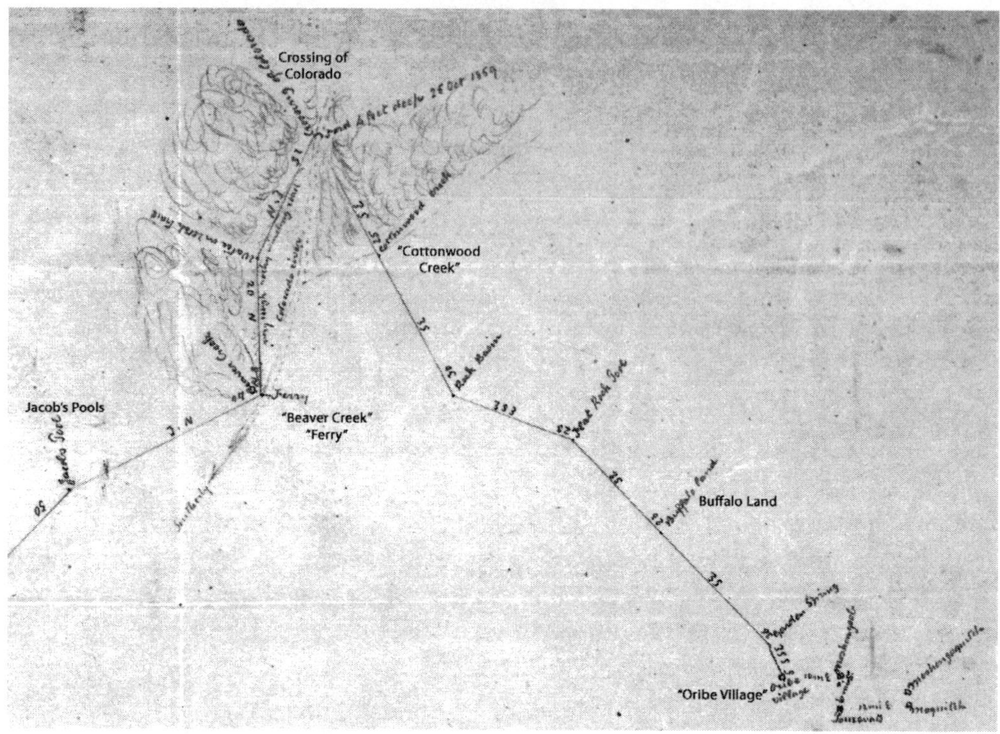

10.1. Map of 1859 expedition to the Hopis, by Thomas Bullock from Jacob Hamblin's description, 1860, detail. From Jacob's Pools to "Oribe Village." Including the mouth of the Paria, "Beaver Creek," "Crossing of Colorado" (the Crossing of the Fathers), "Buffalo Land" (Quichintoweep), and Moquitch (probably Sichomovi). Courtesy LDS Church History Library, CR 100 310, fd2.

that whites had been involved in planning and carrying out the massacre. This letter is open to multiple interpretations, but it raises the possibility that Jacob and Rachel had opened up to Forney, in private.

Hamblin must have returned to Fort Clara, but he was back in Salt Lake City on August 26,[51] when Brigham Young asked him to visit the Hopis again, taking Marion Shelton with him, and leave him there to learn the Hopi language, along with an experienced Indian missionary. Shelton, a twenty-six-year-old Illinois native who had broad experience visiting Indians, had converted to the Mormon faith the previous year and had been living in Harmony and Santa Clara.[52] Young also donated some sixty dollars worth of goods to share with the Hopis.[53] Hamblin and Shelton returned to Dixie and in October started out on this second trip to the Hopis.

This journey is brought to life for us by a delightful and insightful diary by Thales Haskell.[54] Jacob Hamblin also gave a short account of the journey in Little,

10.2. Thales Hastings Haskell, early settler of Santa Clara, companion of Hamblin on many journeys, irrepressible diarist of the second expedition to the Hopis (1859). Used by permission, Utah State Historical Society, all rights reserved.

and made a map of the expedition's route.[55] In addition, Marion Shelton wrote letters about the journey to George A. Smith and Brigham Young, one of which is a valuable travel diary.[56]

The company included seven men: Jacob Hamblin, Marion Shelton, Thales Haskell, Benjamin Knell (both of whom had also gone on the first visit to the Hopis), John William Young, Taylor Crosby, and James Pearce.[57] Young and Crosby would soon become Jacob's sons-in-law—Young, a thirty-one-year-old native of Illinois, and no relation to Brigham, would marry Maryette Magdaline, on April 1, 1861, as a plural wife,[58] and Taylor Crosby, a twenty-three-year-old from Athens, Mississippi, would marry Martha Adaline on January 28, 1860.[59]

James Pearce, a twenty-year-old native of Fulton, Mississippi, and one of the founders of Washington, had been a reputed participant in the Mountain Meadows Massacre.[60] His father, Harrison Pearce, also present at the massacre, would give his name to Pearce's Ferry on the Colorado, south of St. George, in 1876.

Thales Haskell's diary of this expedition is full of the mishaps of exploring—getting lost collectively or as separated groups (in which case the groups would have to fire guns to locate each other). The party had no Paiute guide this time, so, while Hamblin, Haskell, and Knell could remember the main routes, the local landmarks of the journey, including where water might be found, were often unknown. As a result, in some ways this expedition was as difficult as the first visit to the Hopis. Haskell's diary is also an amusing record of the problems of dealing with animals on an exploring trip; they would often escape during the night and a member of the party would have to ride back many miles to recover them. Haskell also eloquently recorded the humor, friendship, and bonhomie of these Mormon friends as they worked together on this challenging, physically exhausting expedition. The diary also vividly shows the friendly relations that Mormons and Paiutes shared.

On October 11, just beyond Washington, Jacob, Shelton, and Crosby met Haskell, Knell, Riddle, and Young struggling with a cart and two oxen.[61] "Br Hamblin thought we looked rather low spirited. We told him [the] cart was a bad egg and that we did not think it would make the riffle," wrote Haskell. The next day the party split up as backtracking animals needed to be rounded up, and Jacob, Shelton, and Young took the cart ahead to "the mountain"—probably Hurricane Fault. When Haskell caught up with them at the base of the cliffs, the cart indeed would not go up the incline, so Shelton and Knell were sent back to the Mormon settlements to replace it with mules.

Haskell now described a few animals, in particular a mule appropriately named Devil, since "he seemed to take great delight in all kinds of mulish deviltry—for instance Jumping stifleged—turning his pack—geting tangled in the riging &c." Taylor Crosby's mule tried to buck him off, but "getting pretty well aquainted with a pair of American spurs concluded to give up and be gentle." Jacob's packhorse somehow threw a sack of beans onto the ground, which burst, and the beans had to be reloaded.

Such passages remind us how dependent these exploring expeditions were on animals, and the close synergy between nineteenth-century pioneers and their horses and mules. The mule was enormously important for Jacob in this and later expeditions. Though it could be temperamental at times (as Haskell notes in his colorful fashion), the Spanish mule was a superb pack animal and could go farther on little water and forage than a horse. In addition, it was a sure-footed, intelligent traveler on difficult, steep trails.[62] Kit Carson always rode a mule, and Jacob leaned toward mules, also. Family history states that he rode a mule called Bowlegs, and once was going on a trip with a group of men, and they thought that he would never make it on Bowlegs, who looked almost crippled. Jacob fussed with his pack while they went ahead; and when they came to their destination, he and Bowlegs were there waiting for them.[63]

At the end of the day, the party got to the top of the mountain and pushed on through sand and sagebrush landscapes to "Rock Canyon"—this is perhaps the same Rock Canyon that is known today, across the Arizona border, about fifteen miles from Washington, where a small stream with grass and wood offered a good campsite.[64] After staying here a few days, waiting for stragglers, the party set out over the forty-mile desert leading to Pipe Spring. During this trek, the group had an unending struggle with recalcitrant mules and horses. One would spook, snort, plunge wildly, scatter his pack in all directions, and run off, which would in turn spook the other animals.

One night the missionaries formed a circle around the campfire and relaxed, "gasing smoking spinning yarns about old times." But Shelton, who had been walking around, came with some bad news: the oxen had departed, and the men had to search for them in the dark—unsuccessfully. So the men returned to camp to sleep. Just before daylight, all the mules stampeded! Eventually all animals were recovered.

The group reached Pipe Spring on the eighteenth, and talked with several friendly Paiutes who were there. However, the Indian whom Jacob had counted on as a guide—probably Naraguats—was hunting in the mountains, and Jacob could not convince any of the other Indians to go with him. The best he could do was to get them to explain the route ahead, emphasizing the locations of water holes.

On the twentieth, they continued on over "an immense plain covered with splendid grass," as Shelton wrote. In the ensuing days, they had difficulty finding the trails and water holes the Paiutes had told them about. After twelve miles they came to a wash where the Indians had told them water was available, but it turned out to be dry, so they traveled another fifteen miles, but finally were forced to camp without water. The next day was very hot, and everyone suffered from thirst. As they followed a trail down a steep ledge of rocks, the mood of the company darkened. Some of the men started quoting Shakespeare, but "one of the boys remarked that he wished that Shakspeare was in hell and he was with him if they had such a commodity as water there." Haskell states that he recorded this "to show how savage men feel traveling in the sand without water."

Eventually the group arrived at the base of the Kaibab Plateau, where they could rest under cedars, and where they soon found water. They reached the top of the Kaibab, and that night, as they were "spinning yarns" again around the campfire, suddenly "br Shelton's pants caught fire causing him to jump and dance in such a manner as to set the rest of us into a roar of laughter." Unfortunately, Shelton burned his hands putting out the fire, which tempered the merriment somewhat.

Jacob, while on guard that night, killed a badger and roasted it; the subsequent guards managed to eat it. Badger evidently was never a delicacy.

The party lost their way the next day, the twenty-fourth, but turned down a canyon and successfully descended the Kaibab Plateau. They found a camp with a very good spring that night, close to the Vermilion Cliffs, and decided to slaughter one of their oxen there. The men spent the next day cutting and drying the beef. They "dug out and walled up" the spring and decided to call it Jacob's Pools, after Jacob Hamblin, and it became one of the important landmarks of the Utah-Arizona trail. Fred Dellenbaugh, of the second Powell expedition, mentioned two pools here, each about seven or eight feet long.[65]

Shelton described the land from the Kaibab Plateau to the Crossing of the Fathers as "a Desert, barren rocks, and sand."[66] Soon the company came to what Shelton called "Beaver Creek," probably the Paria.[67] Some Indians visited, once again telling Hamblin that the guide he had been counting on was unavailable. Jacob had been hoping to perhaps cross the Colorado at the mouth of the Paria (modern Lee's Ferry) with a raft, but now decided they had no alternative but to take the "old Ute trail" all the way to the Crossing of the Fathers again. "Br Hamblin gave the head and entrails of the beef to the Indians and stuffing themselves to their hearts content they all left except one old gent who honored us with his presence over night," wrote Haskell. The next day, a young Paiute arrived with some antelope skins to trade, and Jacob gave him some ammunition in exchange for them.

On the thirty-first, they ascended a "very steep sandy rocky mountain" which was difficult for the animals, but they had no mishaps. As they ate dinner, they saw a smoke signal, which Hamblin answered, and soon two Indians arrived at the camp, one of whom had never seen whites before and was very timid. "We gave them some meat which they seemed to relish very much," wrote Haskell. One agreed to act as guide for the Mormons, which must have been a relief to Hamblin.

The next day they came to the "Utah trail," which led them to a pass with towering rocks just wide enough to allow mules to pass single file. Then they came to "a deep mudy nasty ravine leading to the Colerado," which was most difficult. "After wading through much tribulation in the shape of mud water willows bulrushes &c.," the group finally made it to the Crossing of the Fathers.

Now came their next challenge, for their two Indian guides said the water was too high for a crossing and refused to take the lead. Since they alone knew where the water was shallowest, this was a disappointment. Nevertheless, the missionaries attempted the crossing, but it turned into a fiasco, as they "got into deep water, floundered around a while," and had to turn back, which left them half drenched and in a foul mood. Thales rebuked the two friendly Indians with gusto, but they merely said that they were afraid.

The next morning, Jacob and "some of the other boys" were sick as a result of the previous night's exposure. Their guides said that an Indian who lived on the other side of the river and knew the crossing better than they did would be there soon. He did show up, with several others, but he also pronounced the water too high, and advised the missionaries to wait eight to ten days till it lowered. Then all the Indians vanished!

Jacob thought that a couple of the missionaries should try to ford the river on horseback, so Haskell and Shelton made the attempt, expecting to be drenched as their horses swam. But they evidently hit the right route for crossing and forded the river easily.

The rest of the company packed up and started across the river with all the animals. But the remaining ox, who missed his companion and had not been cooperative since she had been slaughtered, stopped halfway across and would not budge. The missionaries had to let him return to the northwest shore. They had almost reached the far shore, but wandered a little to the left of the route of Haskell and Shelton so that some of the mules had to swim. One mule, heavily packed with dried meat, lost its balance "and went rolling over and over down stream." It looked like the animal and its precious load would be lost, as it hit the bottom and lay with its feet sticking up and kicking, its head underwater. Everyone had given it up for dead, when suddenly it "made a desperate strugle raised up, and come to shore much to the satisfaction of all concerned."

Shelton and Pearce went across the river again to try to bring over the ox and pack, but as they returned with him, partway across, the ox turned back and nothing they could do would turn him. They left him till the next day, November 3.

Haskell wandered a bit after breakfast, and when he returned to camp found that he had been selected to bring the ox across. He chose Young to help him, and they managed to goad the ox across with a spike attached to a pole. Everyone sighed with relief.

The next morning, they had breakfast, packed, and started south, but after they had covered a mile, someone noticed that the ox was not with them. They returned to the Colorado and found that it had crossed back to the other side of the river. This time Hamblin and Young went to bring him back while the rest of the group forged ahead. That night, as they rested in a camp in Navajo Canyon, Hamblin and Young showed up with the errant ox.

They camped at a place called Rock Basin the night of the fifth. The next night they made camp after dark and saw a large fire not far away, and Hamblin and James Pearce went onto a high rock and lit a fire to alert the Indians. Soon some Paiutes came to their camp and told them there was plentiful water at their camp, so Hamblin, Haskell, and Taylor Crosby went to water the animals and fill their canteens. They found much good water in a rock basin, and wood and grass at this place, which they called Flat Rock.[68]

The next day, one of the Indians agreed to guide them farther, and after a twenty-two-mile jaunt, they camped at Quichintoweep, apparently Paiute for "Buffalo Flats."[69] As the guide warned them that they were now in Navajo country, and that they had better guard their animals carefully, they drove them up onto a "rocky bench" that was only accessible in one place and was otherwise surrounded by steep cliffs.

Two days later, they camped near "a small spring and the Oriba gardens," and on November 10 they arrived at Oraibi.[70]

The Oraibi Hopis were once again hospitable to the missionaries and offered them a room to stay in. However, before moving in, the Mormons wanted to butcher their ox, so Haskell and the other missionaries, leaving Hamblin and Young in Oraibi, found a place with water about a half mile down the mesa, killed the ox, and set the meat out to dry.

The next day, they finished cutting up the meat, and when they returned to

Oraibi, Haskell wrote, they found Hamblin and Young "surrounded by something less than a thousand Indians trading."

After dinner Hamblin asked Thales if he could speak to him privately. He told him that Brigham Young had asked him (Hamblin) to find a seasoned Indian missionary to leave with Shelton at the mesas for a year, and Hamblin, in a less than ideal leadership maneuver, had delayed asking anyone to do this. Now he asked Haskell if he would fulfill the assignment.[71] He knew that Haskell had been on Indian assignments constantly, but knew of no one else with sufficient experience whom he could ask. True to form, Haskell agreed to accept the mission.

Hamblin took Young, Crosby, Knell, and Pearce to visit "the Moquitch vilage," apparently Sichomovi on the First Mesa, and "Moshamineel," probably Mishongnovi on the Second Mesa, while Haskell and Shelton stayed at Oraibi to settle in.[72] They found a room with a Hopi named Thuringwa, and Shelton commenced learning Hopi and trying to teach the Hopis the Deseret Alphabet.[73]

On the fifteenth, Hamblin and company returned with the sobering news that a Navajo had stolen Crosby's saddle, revolver, and knife. In addition, trading had not gone well because the Hopis, who had been given gifts by the U.S. Army, also expected gifts, instead of trading, from the Mormons. Young, Crosby, Knell, and Pearce left the next day, while Hamblin stayed because he'd heard that some of the U.S. Army was going to visit;[74] in addition, he traded for *piki* and dried peaches. The army rumor turned out to be false, and so Hamblin decided to leave on the seventeenth. He was getting ready to go when he found his horse's bridle was gone. Haskell generously lent him his own bridle and promised to look for Hamblin's while he was among the Hopis. "He now bid br Shelton adieu and started," wrote Haskell. "I went about a half mile with him. He gave me [a] tent to trade for provisions and we shook hands and parted."

Now the weight of his isolation descended on the ebullient Haskell:

> Sloly and sorrowfuly I wended my way back to the village. Such a feeling of utter loneliness I never experienced before for search the wide world over I do not believe a more bleak lonsome heart sickening place could be found on the earth where human beings dwell. And here we are Br Shelton and me with strange Indians who talk a strange language situated far from the busy haunts of men. Who but Mormons would do it. Who but Mormons could do it. Make up their minds to stay here a year.

Hamblin and his four companions left Oraibi on about November 17 and arrived back at Fort Clara on about December 1.[75]

Thales Haskell's Hopi diaries are pure Haskell: lively, straightforward, incisive. Though not an anthropologist by any means, his descriptions of Hopi culture and festivals are perceptive. Once the Hopi danced wearing gourds and turtle shells that rattled "[so] that every time the person steps in dancing they rattle scandilous."[76] On January 12, 1860, he became an early interpreter of Kachina dolls, which were considered gods to help in hunting, farming and collecting food, but they were somehow emanations of a supreme deity, the sun, or some great spirit.

His opinion of the visiting Navajos is not high; he attributes numerous thefts of missionary property to them, never to Hopis. The Hopis in turn warned them never to travel alone, as the Navajos would rob and kill them. However, on December 10, two Navajos ended up passing the night in the missionaries' hut. One of them, "Spanishyank"—also known as Spaneshanks—was a Navajo headman who became a good friend of Haskell, Ira Hatch, and Jacob Hamblin.[77] He reportedly came from a leading Navajo family, and was a brother or close relative of Barboncito, one of the prominent Navajo headmen. According to Mormon oral traditions, Spaneshanks had gone against Navajo custom by marrying a Paiute woman, so he moved to Kaibab Paiute territory near modern Kanab. He became friendly with Ira Hatch and gave one of his daughters to him; Hatch, in turn, gave her to another family to raise. A few years later Hatch married her.[78] After Spaneshanks's Paiute wife died, he moved back to Navajo territory (the Navajo Mountain, in San Juan County, straddling the Utah-Arizona border),[79] where he rejoined his Navajo people and remarried.[80]

In April 1855, Mormons had founded a settlement near modern Moab, Grand County, in southeastern Utah (called the Elk Mountain Mission), and Spaneshanks had become an ally of the Saints. However, the Elk Mountain Mission ended in September of the same year, when local Utes killed some of the Mormons and stole cattle from them. Spaneshanks and his band evidently reclaimed some of the cattle, drove them fourteen miles, and gave them back to the Mormons.[81] Haskell described him as an "old gray headed fellow." Another Mormon said he was "odd looking...very short and stout, with an extra large head."[82]

Spaneshanks spoke Ute and Paiute, and said he had traveled four "sleeps" to talk to the Mormons. He "was uncomon hungry for tobacco," but the missionaries had none, though they shared mush with the Navajos. Spaneshanks said that "he was not much of a friend to the americans" as he had been to Fort Defiance, where they would not give him any presents because of his friendship with Mormons.

"The old gent said he would talk good for us to his people and would like the Mormons to come and trade with them next summer," wrote Haskell. Spaneshanks would play a major part in the next expedition across the Colorado, in 1860.

Haskell and Shelton met another prominent Indian while at the mesas, the Ute Arapeen, on November 21. The interview started inauspiciously, with the chief tongue-lashing the missionaries for saying that Utes sold children, but then he relaxed, and he and the Mormons ended up in a mellow mood. "We smoked and chatted with

10.3. Tuuvi and Talasnimki, friends of Jacob who accompanied him to Utah on multiple occasions and later became Mormon converts. Tuba City, now in the Navajo Reservation, was named after Tuuvi. From Beadle, *The Undeveloped West* (1873).

him somtime," wrote Haskell, "when he got in an uncomon good humor and when we left gave us some coffee and two plugs of tobacco." Arapeen would die a year later, on December 4, 1860.[83]

However, Haskell and Shelton's main mission was to the Hopis. They became good friends with their landlord, Thuringwa, but the most important Hopi contact they made was a man named Tuuvi, who later became a Mormon convert and a good friend of Hamblin, Ira Hatch, and other Mormons.[84] Christian Christensen, who knew Tuuvi in the 1880s, said that the Hopi came to regard Jacob Hamblin "as a Special Messenger" to his people.[85] Tuuvi's name devolved into "Tuba," the version of his name found in the town named after him, Tuba City, ironically now one of the major towns in the western Navajo Reservation.

On December 16, 1859, Thales watched as a Navajo stole a roll of red cloth from a Hopi woman and started to ride away; but "a tall noble looking Oriba"—Tuuvi—leapt on the horse of the Navajo's friend, and was able to catch up with the thief and wrest the cloth from him, to Thales's satisfaction.

In the following weeks, a friendship developed between Tuuvi and the Mormons, for on February 26, 1860, Haskell wrote that they had a talk "with our friend Tuby." About a week later, Tuuvi gave Thales a pony as a present, and the missionary almost had to force him to take something in return. "I prevailed on him to except my gun.... He said when he made his friend a present he did not wish anything in return." These were two extraordinarily kind and generous men.[86]

"Tuuvi" was a nickname; his real name was "Qötswayma," according to one source, or "Woo Pah," according to another.[87] Most sources say he was born into the Piikyas, or Young Corn clan.[88] Mormons often referred to him as a chief, but if he was, he was definitely not the village chief of Oraibi; possibly he was a leader of his clan.[89]

According to missionary C. L. Christensen, in Tuuvi's childhood he experienced the oppression of the Spaniards who conquered the Southwest, and was involved in a violent conflict with a Spaniard when one of them wanted to appropriate a Hopi girl who apparently had royal blood of some sort. After a duel in which the Spaniard killed the girl's champion through a cowardly trick, Tuuvi threw a spear into the ribs of the Spaniard, killing him. He married the young woman, named Talasnimki.[90] Hopi historian Peter Whiteley states that she was from the Eagle clan and that she was a leading officer in the "*Lakon* society," a woman's society in charge of certain important rituals.[91]

According to some sources, Tuuvi left Oraibi because of tensions with leading Hopis, and he was called Tuuvi ("outcast") for this reason. He was reportedly despised because of his friendship with the Mormons, but his skill as a rainmaker still gave him authority in Hopi society.[92] However, Haskell calls him Tuuvi on meeting him, so it is certain that he was called "outcast" before developing close friendships with Mormons.

In the summers, Tuuvi often farmed at Moenkopi (the Hopi word is Mùnqapi, "Flowing Water Place"), an oasis some fifty miles west of Oraibi, now just southeast of Tuba City. It is presently regarded as a Third Mesa village, the only one not on or near the mesas. According to one source, the Oraibi chief asked Tuuvi to farm there to extend Oraibi's domain.[93] Haskell and Shelton visited Moenkopi on March 5, 1860, possibly at Tuuvi's invitation. "This is a small stream where the Oribes raise cotton," Haskell wrote, "and they reccomended it to us as a good place to build a mill and for the Mormons to make a small settlement." Moenkopi was used by the Hopis as a place for summer gardening, but Navajo attacks had caused them to give up actual residence there. Tuuvi, along with Mormons, later helped turn it into a permanent settlement. This is the beginning of an important nineteenth-century Mormon community and way station near the Hopi mesas. Hamblin would spend a great deal of time there.[94]

Haskell and Shelton left the mesas to return home on March 9, 1860. There are no hints in the diary as to why they left before their one-year goal. Hamblin, in Little, ascribes the departure to Hopi prophecy, but Haskell does not mention this in his diary.[95] Haskell's description of his and Shelton's return home is extremely brief, with just a few dates and places noted. They reached the Colorado on the fourteenth, and, finding it low, crossed it easily. "Felt to return thanks to our Father in heaven, for we realized His kindness unto us continually," Haskell wrote.

On the eighteenth, they arrived at Jacob's Pools and three days later came to Pipe Spring. They reached Washington on the twenty-fourth and the next day came to Fort Clara. Haskell and Shelton attended meeting at the fort and reported on their Hopi mission. "Br Jacob requested all who felt that we had done our duty to raise their right hands and I believe that every hand was raised," Haskell wrote. He arrived home at Pinto on March 27; Shelton must have returned to northern Utah.

While Haskell and Shelton were not able to stay at the mesas as long as they had planned, nevertheless on the second trip across the Colorado their accomplishments were substantial. Haskell had met and developed solid relationships with two important Indian leaders, the Navajo Spaneshanks and the Hopi Tuuvi. Tuuvi would become an important ally of Hamblin and the Mormons in upcoming years. Haskell and Shelton were also the first Mormons to visit Moenkopi and, at Tuuvi's urging, assess its possibilities as a possible Mormon settlement. The Mormon presence in Arizona would slowly, gradually increase.

11

"Your Son . . . Partially Arose and Said Here I am Shot"

Murder on the Trail and Flight from Quichintoweep, 1860

The American West was a violent place. Hampton Sides, historian of the Navajo wars, said that in the nineteenth-century West, "You couldn't travel anywhere without fearing for your life.... There was no law, and thus no outlaws. Anyone who feels nostalgia for this period is naïve."[1] Indians killed many white travelers and explorers in the American West, and on the other hand, amoral or militaristic whites often massacred innocent Indians. On both sides, innocents would often be killed as retaliation for earlier killings.[2] The Gunnison expedition was killed in eastern Utah in 1853 by vengeful Pahvants. Three members of the first Powell Colorado River expedition who quit the expedition in 1869 would be killed as they set out for Mormon settlements, by Paiutes who were generally not dangerous.[3] Unexpected death could strike at any time in the West.

In Hamblin's third trip across the Colorado, in October and November 1860, which marked his first major exposure to the Navajo tribe, the missionaries met a large group of Navajos on the far side of the Colorado, and violence resulted. This incident shows the repercussions for the Mormons of the continuing war between the Navajos and the U.S. Army and New Mexican volunteers in New Mexico and Arizona. It would be many years before Mormon-Navajo relations stabilized.

The first part of 1860 was fairly uneventful for Hamblin. On January 15 and 16, he met with local church leaders, including John D. Lee, in Washington and organized a small company to form a settlement at the mouth of the Clara "for Farming purposes," appointing James Richey to preside over the settlement. This was apparently Tonaquint, a town that would not survive the combined flooding of the Santa Clara and Virgin. At this time, Lee stressed Hamblin's friendship with him: "Bishop Lunt,

Judd, Wood & Pres. J. Hamblin brakefasted with me. Pres. Hamblin invitd me to come to the Clara & Preach to the Saints the foll[ow]ing Sund. & when ever I could."[4] For many years, Lee and Hamblin were firm allies.

Jacob was in Salt Lake City on February 18 and reported on the second trip to the Hopis. The recorder in the Historian's Office found the peaches Jacob brought from the mesas especially noteworthy. According to Hamblin, the Hopis had said that the U.S. soldiers had brought gifts to them, then had encouraged them to kill any Mormons who visited.[5] This does not seem credible, but it does show that Mormon-U.S. antagonism was still intense in Utah and Arizona. Hamblin arrived back from Salt Lake on March 10, in the company of former San Bernardino bishop William Crosby, Dudley Leavitt, and Leavitt's new bride, Janet, his fourth wife, a Paiute who had been adopted into a Mormon family.[6]

About nine o'clock in the morning on June 13, at Fort Clara, Hamblin began to trim branches from a large cottonwood near his home that was putting too much shade on a vineyard. Suddenly he lost his balance and fell some thirty or forty feet to the ground, which knocked him unconscious.[7] In his account of the events that followed, he rose up as a spirit and looked down on the earth, which had the appearance of a "dark ball." But the heavenly place he arrived at was bright and filled with an infinite variety of color. It was divided into "compartments" by walls covered with ivy and flowers. He saw his father in one of the compartments but was not able to pass into it. In agony, he asked why he was barred from entering, and his father said, "Your work is not yet done."

Jacob started to speak again, but Isaiah motioned with his hand that he should leave, and suddenly he was back on earth: "I saw the brethren carrying my body along, and it was loathsome to me in appearance," he wrote. They carried him to his home where he lay unconscious throughout the day.[8]

Ascending to heaven as a spirit while the body is close to death is a persistent motif in Mormon culture. Common themes are detailed descriptions of heaven, meetings with departed loved ones, and deep reluctance to return to earth and one's body.[9]

Hamblin regained consciousness about eight p.m. and immediately coughed up a quantity of blood. In a letter to Brigham Young, he reported that the accident "resulded in brusing my body in a chocking maner. For the first week I had to be handelt with a blanket could not move my hand nor feet but am now fast recovering. My under jaw is broken in three or four p[l]esis [places]."[10] He also knocked out several teeth, bruised his shoulder and thigh, severely injured the joint of his neck, and seriously hurt his chest.[11]

His family transported him up to Mountain Meadows, where, nursed on goat's milk, he began to recuperate.[12] A couple weeks later, George A. Smith was visiting the south and on June 18 stopped at Hamblin's ranch to see him. He was still an invalid, but could walk with a crutch. George A. wanted to see the site of the Mountain

11.1. George A. Smith, apostle and counselor to Brigham Young, was a close friend of Jacob Hamblin. A jovial, well-loved church leader, he helped settle southern Utah. Used by permission, Utah State Historical Society, all rights reserved.

Meadows Massacre, so Hamblin was put in a cart, while George's son, George A. Smith Jr., rode Hamblin's horse, and Hamblin showed the massacre site to them. George Jr. would play an important, tragic role in Jacob's next trip across the Colorado.

On June 23 Hamblin wrote to Brigham that his wounds were "dificuilt to heal. But throug[h] the blessing of the Lord I hope so[o]n to go forth and do good among the Lamonites."[13] On July 12, he was still recovering slowly from his fall.[14]

At about this time, Jacob sent Albert, now about seventeen, north with a letter to Brigham Young, and much of it is about Albert.[15] Since he had been adopted by Hamblin, he had accepted Mormonism and, as we have seen, had become a visionary person. "He says he knows that there is such a being as Jesus Crist for he has sean and talked with him several times," Hamblin wrote. On the other hand, Albert had been tried by seven devils, and told Hamblin their names and when they would arrive. Jacob said he had been with him when the seventh one left.[16]

Albert had always hoped to take Mormonism to his tribe, the White Knife Shoshonis, and now he felt the time had come. So Jacob sent him to Brigham Young: "I could do no more nor less than send him to you for your aproveal or disaproval," he wrote. Brigham ordained Albert an elder and gave him a letter of recommendation.[17]

On October 8, Hamblin again wrote to Brigham Young about Albert, and asked him to "take the over sight of this boy Albert for one year" and help arrange for his lodging and education. He confessed that Albert had not been to school as much as he should have and had not made much progress in reading and writing. Nevertheless, "as to the Boys morality I never saw his equal. If he ever told a falsehood I hav no knowlage of it." Hamblin offered to pay for Albert's lodging. "Please be a Father to the boy and care for him until I see you which will be next fall confrance if the Lord will," he wrote.[18] Apparently, Albert did stay in Salt Lake City and Brigham Young did help him.

In late summer, Hamblin visited Pine Valley and Pinto Creek. He went to Heberville (Price), a couple miles south of modern St. George, three or four times, as some unspecified problem involving stealing had to be resolved.[19]

On August 17, Hamblin was in Salt Lake City again and conferred with Young on the matter of "improving the Indians."[20] He may have received his assignment to visit the Hopis once again during this visit, and when he returned to Fort Clara, he and his companions would have begun to prepare for the expedition.

One of the unusual aspects of this trip was the presence of women—the young Indian wives of Jacob Hamblin and Ira Hatch—in the company. Apparently Jacob married an Indian girl, Eliza, perhaps in October, in preparation for the third trip to the Hopis. The evidence for Hamblin's marriage to Eliza (and possibly other Indian women) is convincing, but there are still elements of ambiguity in those relationships. Some of his relatives have denied that he married an Indian or Indians, while others have freely admitted it. Unfortunately, Eliza did not bear any children with Hamblin, and apparently separated from him, so she did not become as closely attached to his family history and genealogy as did his other wives.

Historian Richard Kitchen has shown that in the early years of Mormon settlement marriages with Native Americans were encouraged and accepted; but as time went on, these intermarriages became rarer, and a cultural silencing resulted, in which relatives of men who married Indian women minimized or denied those relationships.[21] For example, Priscilla Leavitt Hamblin, in a late reminiscence, denied that Jacob married any Indian wives and quoted him as telling Brigham Young that he would lose his influence among Indians if he did so.[22] However, Jacob, in an 1857 letter, spoke of Ira Hatch *increasing* his influence with Indians because he was willing to marry an Indian wife.[23]

Philosophically, Brigham Young was entirely in favor of Mormon-Indian intermarriage, under the right circumstances—he had recommended such marriages to Saints living among Indians as early as 1847.[24] Ten years later, Young told Jacob and Tutsegabits that "he w [wished?] the Elders to marry the squaws of the Tribes to fulfill the commandment of God &c."[25] In the Salmon River mission in Idaho, in a conference on May 10, 1857, Young's counselor Heber C. Kimball called upon the missionaries to marry Indian women, and Young spoke after him, seconding Kimball's counsel.

Some missionaries felt that it was their duty to obey and took Shoshoni wives soon after the conference.[26]

Mormon men were somewhat unlike typical western settlers in their willingness to marry Indian wives (though some non-Mormon white explorers, traders, and settlers, such as Kit Carson, married or had relationships with Indian women).[27] For Indian missionaries, one of the motivations for such marriages would be to create ties with Indian leaders (and so often the Indian women that missionaries married were daughters of chiefs). However, another motivation was the belief that such marriages would help redeem the Lamanites by giving the children European education and Mormon religious training, and making their children's skin lighter. Brigham Young, in 1847, said that Mormons "would yet take their [the Indians'] squaws wash & dress them up teach them our language...& raise up children by them & teach the Children & not many generations Hence they will become A white & delightsome people & in no other way will it be done."[28] Naturally, the Mormon practice of polygamy would make it easier for men to marry Native American women and cement alliances with local Indians, while at the same time remaining married to one or more white women.

A number of sources refer to Hamblin's marriage to one or more Indian women. First, there is a temple record of Hamblin's marriage to Eliza in 1863.[29] An Ira Hatch family biography tells us that Jacob, "like Ira Hatch, married an Indian woman whom he loved devotedly."[30] According to this source, both Hamblin and Ira Hatch brought Indian wives with them on the third mission across the Colorado.[31] Hamblin, in a somewhat ambiguous passage in his autobiography, admits that one of the young Indian women was his wife.[32] Dellenbaugh reports that Hamblin was married to Paiute women in Kanab.[33]

According to reminiscences of Anthony Ivins, when he first visited Santa Clara with his father in late 1861, Jacob had an "Indian wife" who fed them delicious cornmeal mush. She lived inside the fort, and had been won by Jacob in one of the Paiute squaw fights. "Jacob had entered the lists and after knocking down several opponents defied the remainder of the band to come and take her. No one accepted the challenge and he took the woman into the fort....The Indians recognized her as Jacobs squaw....Several Indian women were recognized as the wives of Jacob," wrote Ivins. Nevertheless, he stated that Jacob much later told him that he "had never lived with them as wives, not believing it right to do so."[34] If the latter statement it true, it is possible that Jacob's Indian wives—at least the wives that Ivins knew about in 1861—had lesser status in his family than his white, childbearing wives.[35]

Ira Hatch's marriage to Sarah is fairly well documented. Her father was reportedly Spaneshanks,[36] the old tobacco-loving Navajo chief whom Thales Haskell and Marion Shelton entertained in the second visit to the Hopis, while her mother was a Kaibab Paiute.[37] They had one child, a girl, Asun Natoni. However, Spaneshanks's Paiute wife died when Asun was about seven years old, and the Navajo, who had developed a close friendship with Ira Hatch, decided to give his daughter to him. Ira gave Spaneshanks a gun "to show he appreciated the gift," then gave Asun to his close friends Andrew and Rizpah Gibbons to raise.[38] She was renamed Sarah.

According to Hatch family traditions, in October 1859 Apostle Charles Rich was visiting in the southern settlements, and very late one night arrived at Fort Clara. Calling Hatch, Hamblin, and Andrew Gibbons to confer with him at Hamblin's home, he told them that Brigham Young had specifically requested that Hatch marry Sarah. Though Hatch had recently married a young Anglo woman in Salt Lake City, Amanda Pace, he said he was agreeable, if Sarah was. She was asleep at the Gibbons home, so they went over and woke her up. Would she consent to marry Ira Hatch? Sleepy-eyed, she asked if it couldn't wait till morning. They told her that Apostle Rich wanted to perform the marriage, and he had to leave at the break of dawn. Sarah agreed to the marriage, there was a brief ceremony, and then she went back to bed.[39] Even by Mormon standards, this would be considered a fairly brief courtship and marriage! Sarah must have awakened the next day and wondered if she'd dreamed the whole thing.

Ira reportedly was now faced with the uncomfortable prospect of explaining to his first wife that she now had a Navajo-Paiute sister-wife. Amanda and Sarah were not sister-wives long, as Amanda died in April 1861.[40] Ira and Sarah reportedly had a very successful, loving marriage, and had five children.[41]

It is possible that the brethren, through Apostle Rich, also encouraged Jacob Hamblin to marry a young Indian woman in 1859 or 1860. Eliza had been bought at an unknown time and raised in the Hamblin home. Neither the names of her parents nor her birth name have been preserved, but she evidently was connected with the Shivwits. In her 1863 "temple sealing" to Hamblin, she is reported as born in 1846 in the Piute Nation, New Mexico (presumably meaning modern Arizona).[42] This would be Shivwits territory in 1863, which extended south of the St. George and Santa Clara to the Shivwits Plateau and the Colorado.[43]

Eliza was probably close to Ellen, another Indian adopted by the Hamblins; Eliza was apparently raised by Rachel and Ellen by Priscilla. As we have seen, in 1857, the Hamblin family had two Indian girls, one about twelve and the other about ten, and two Indian boys, according to a visiting Indian agent, who added that Hamblin had obtained them four years earlier.[44] Probably the two girls were Eliza and Ellen. In 1860, they would have been about fifteen and thirteen.[45]

In December of 1861, John Lee Jones of Cedar City helped guide Swiss immigrants over the difficult wagon road from Iron County to the Santa Clara settlement. Jones wrote that in Santa Clara "we found a Small Fort built of Adobies & was first Founded by Bro '*Jacob Hamlin*' who had one of the Indian Squas or a Female Lamanit for a wife, This was quite a Novel Circimstance to Me."[46]

Pearson Corbett only reluctantly admits that Hamblin married Eliza and expresses skepticism about Jones's account because Jones says adobes were used in the stone Santa Clara Fort.[47] However, adobe was a common fort material in Utah and could be readily combined with stone.[48]

According to Leavitt family tradition, Eliza "resented Rachel's supervision and would not obey her. 'I am as much his wife as you are,' she said one day."[49] This is the first sign of tension in Eliza's story, and it may indicate that Rachel did not know that Hamblin had married Eliza.

Hamblin, with eleven companions, left Santa Clara for the Hopi mesas on October 10.[50] Aside from the novelty of having two women in the company, the teenage son of Apostle George A. Smith was another extraordinary member of the group. George A. Smith Jr., born in 1842 in Nauvoo, was a thoroughly likable young man who had had wayward moments. Now, however, he was enthusiastically entering into a unique mission to the southwest Indians. "I went with my father to bid President Young good bye," he had written in his diary on September 4. "He blessed me in the name of the Lord & said I should do a good work if I would be humble & faithful. [I] shook hands with him, Brs [Heber C.] Kimball & [Daniel H.] Wells." The presence of the son of a close friend and apostle would be another burden of leadership that Hamblin would have to shoulder.

The other members of the company were Thales Haskell, Jehiel McConnell, Ira Hatch, Isaac Riddle, Amos Thornton, Francis "Frank" M. Hamblin, James Pearce, and Enos, the Indian who had served a mission as punishment for horse thievery in 1859. He had associations with both the Pahvant Utes and the Cedar City Paiutes. John D. Lee had a low opinion of him, calling him "the litle notorious thief,"[51] and in fact, it appears that other Mormons and Indians shared this outlook. Arapeen, talking to Navajos before the expedition, had told them that neither the Utes nor the Mormons liked Enos. Nevertheless, Arapeen said, Enos "had a <u>Big Heart</u> and they must not kill him."[52] He would play a crucial part in the expedition.

Jehiel McConnell, an Indiana-born schoolteacher, was now some forty-six years old. He had developed a special empathy for Utah Indians as a resident of modern Lehi in Utah County. Called to southern Utah in 1853, he had settled in Cedar City, where he bought and adopted a number of Indian children.[53] An incident from a family history gives an idea of his qualities. One night, in Cedar City, he was fast asleep when he heard a woman's screams nearby. He leapt out of bed and found that a young woman in a neighboring house was being attacked by a wolf. Jehiel immediately seized the wolf by its jaws and pried it loose from the woman, breaking its jaws. Unfortunately, the woman died of rabies, but fortunately for Jehiel, he was not infected.[54] He would accompany Hamblin on a number of his journeys.

Amos Griswold Thornton, about twenty-eight years of age, was one of the founders of Pinto. A native of Pickering, Ontario, Canada, he had fought in the Walker War and reportedly had been present at the Mountain Meadows Massacre.[55]

The purpose of the expedition, which had been specifically called by Brigham Young, was to leave men with the Hopis and Navajos for a year to learn their languages and do missionary work with them.[56] In addition, according to George A. Smith Sr., they had been given the task of exploring the area with a view to opening up a road between the southern Utah Mormon settlements and western New Mexico.[57] In order to shorten the journey, Hamblin wanted to try a boat crossing at the mouth of the Paria, and Isaac Riddle, in Pine Valley, was commissioned to build a boat for this attempt.[58] It had to be transported on a wagon, which would make the journey to the Colorado that much more difficult.

Hamblin's mission was thus twofold: there was the obvious mission to the Indians, but also the assignment to explore, create roads through impassible country, find a place to cross the Colorado that was closer than the Vado de los Padres, and make further Mormon settlement possible.

On October 10, Jacob wrote, "Started for the moquicts. Went to Washington 12 miles."[59] The journey had begun. The ten men, two Indian women, with twenty horses and mules, and three "beeves," would have made a striking procession as they passed through the Dixie settlements.[60] The company soon arrived in Toquerville, where Jacob wrote a letter to George A. Smith Sr., saying that his son was "in fine Spirits and so is all of the company." Jehiel McConnell wrote that on the outward journey "all were buoyant with hope at the prospects before us."[61]

By the twelfth, the missionaries were at Virgin City, on the Virgin River, and the following day they camped at the foot of a mountain.[62] Here, the young men cast lots to see who would serve as "captain of the guard," and George Jr. received that responsibility, "which duty he performed to the entire satisfaction of the company," wrote McConnell.[63]

The next day, the men discovered that two animals had decided to return home, and George Jr. and James Pearce were sent to bring them back. They were entirely unsuccessful at this, so Frank Hamblin and Enos were sent on the same mission and returned with the recalcitrant animals on the fifteenth.

The company traveled twenty-five miles and reached Pipe Spring the following day. On the eighteenth, they arrived at the foot of Kaibab Plateau and camped. Some of the men evidently tried to prepare a road up a canyon for the boat and wagon, while other men took the animals to water.[64]

They crossed the Kaibab Plateau the next day and started down the east side of the mountain on the twentieth. This was "the roufest road I ever saw a wagon taken," wrote Jacob. They traveled ten miles and "crost a narow valy. Found water in the side of the red rock mountain"—possibly House Rock Springs, near the Vermilion Cliffs. Here there was good wood and feed, and they killed one of the cattle. They spent the next couple days drying the meat, greasing their saddles, and exploring. On the twenty-second, Hamblin sent Amos Thornton, James Pearce, and a Paiute to find a likely "crosing of the Colerado," specifically a place where they could make a wagon road down to the river. Meanwhile the main group traveled twelve miles to Jacob's Pools. Thornton and Pearce met them there the next day, reporting that they had not been able to find an adequate wagon route down to a crossing site. On the twenty-fourth the company decided that they could not get the boat down to the river, and that they would have to leave it and the wagon at the Pools.

The next morning, the guard, James Pearce, was missing and the missionaries, examining tracks, concluded that the remaining cattle had escaped and Pearce had gone after them, which is in fact what happened. He found them at House Rock Springs and led them back.[65]

The company descended to the Colorado and made a camp, apparently at modern Lee's Ferry, where the Paria flows into the Colorado. The next day, the twenty-sixth, Hamblin's journal records what was perhaps the first modern crossing of the Colorado at Lee's Ferry. "Made a raft. 8 of us crosed the River and found that animils could [not] come out from the River quickSand no ford." The men could cross on a raft, but apparently the animals could not because of quicksand. James Pearce remembers that one horse drowned during this experiment.[66] So the Mormons would be forced to detour northeast to the Ute Ford again, losing precious days.

Nevertheless, this was a historic event, the first crossing of the Colorado via boat near the mouth of the Paria. In John Wesley Powell's 1874 report on his geographical survey, he correctly stated that Lee's Ferry "had been discovered by Jacob Hamlin, a Mormon missionary."[67] At least, Hamblin was the leader of the group that first visited the ferry site and first crossed the river. Mormons would later find places where animals could cross to the opposite side easily.

On October 27, the group ascended the sandy Domínguez Pass trail (or, as Jacob wrote, "Climb the big mountain"). James Pearce remembered that this canyon ascent was "so steep that the horses could hardly get up. They could not have climbed it if it had been any steeper."[68] "All gotup safe except Sarah hatch," Jacob wrote; she was "throde on the rocks," and her horse stepped on her foot. Despite this accident, the company reached the "Eutah Trail" at sunset.

The next day, when the men awoke, their horses were gone, and they had to travel back nine miles from camp to recover them. After this late start, they were able to "clim down the rocks safe to the River." As they made this descent, George Jr. and McConnell reminisced about their past lives. George confessed that he had been a "wild boy" but affirmed that he knew "this work to be true & President Young to be a Prophet of God." He told McConnell that when they reached camp, he wanted to share with him a blessing that he had been given by First Presidency Counselor Heber C. Kimball.[69]

Finally, the group reached the Crossing of the Fathers. While "the boys went down to the waters edge to wash," McConnell wrote, he borrowed George Jr.'s diary and read his blessing. He also added, in his letter to George A. Smith Sr., that his son "never declined leading in prayer both evening & morning in his turn, also in giving thanks for our food."[70] This touch shows the piety of these early Indian missionaries, despite their rough edges.

Though it was late in the day, Hamblin decided to cross the Colorado immediately. His account is confusing, but apparently a friendly Paiute who was traveling with them, named Puskish, "could not see the ford." The missionaries started the crossing anyway, at the best place they could find, but soon they were in very deep water. Hamblin was riding on a horse with "the Indian gurll"—presumably Eliza—and the horse fell down, turned over, and could not right itself. Two packs on the animal were lost. Jacob jumped into the water as the animal capsized and was able to help Eliza off. He "held hur until the horse got up," he wrote. "Helpt her on then got on myself." All the missionaries crossed over safely.

The next day was a relaxing day of recovery: the missionaries "la [lay] by to dry our blankets and other articles."

On the thirtieth, the missionaries traveled twenty miles "over some of the most dangerous rocks and narow pases on the rout," according to Jacob. He is probably describing the descent into Navajo Canyon. At one particularly dangerous point, on a narrow trail with a dropoff to one side, one of Jacob's pack mules slipped and Jacob thought he was going over the cliff, but "he re~~stored~~ gained his standin[g] and past in safty to camp." The camp was located at Cottonwood Creek, modern Navajo Creek, at the bottom of Navajo Canyon. Jacob went back two miles to help Jehiel McConnell and "the Indian girl," who "had ben atacted with a shake of the ague" and could neither ride a horse or walk. The three travelers passed a place Jacob called "the narows" after dark.

An incident that occurred the next day shows Jacob's gentle nature. As the group was climbing out of a deep gulch over craggy rocks, a wild goose suddenly flew a few yards over their heads then landed nearby. Jacob shot at it three times, and two others also shot at it, before killing it. "I felt hurt in my feelings when it was kiled believeing it was rong too killet [kill it]," wrote Jacob. Not the sentiments of the typical frontiersman.

An hour after sundown the group arrived at Basin Rock but found no water there. This was the beginning of the chain of events that would lead inexorably to tragedy. Places that had had water in Hamblin's earlier journeys to the Hopis did not have it now. Apparently, water was only found in holes in the rocks at this point in the journey, and the Mormons later found out that such water had been "used entirely up by the Navahoes" who had unexpectedly been in the area.[71]

The missionaries needed water urgently, and Hamblin decided to travel on through the night. Near dawn they stopped and slept for two hours.[72]

When they woke up, on November 1, they found the ground covered with the trails of men, horses, goats, and probably sheep.[73] Navajos had been traveling through this area with their herds. The missionaries packed up their animals and continued on. Two men were sent ahead to "flat rock" to look for water, but found none. Hamblin then sent two more ahead to another small spring, which was also dry. "We then went on as fast as our animils could travail expecting to find water to Bufalo creek" (Quichintoweep), which was about fifteen miles away.[74] The company was now desperate for water.

After they had traveled about seven miles, they were suddenly overtaken by five or six Navajos, who told Hamblin that the party "must goe back."[75]

Hamblin asked, "Who says we must goe back?"

They answered, "Panisank." Hamblin, in a letter to Brigham Young, explained that Panisank was "the name of a Navajo chief with hoom I was some acquainted." This is Spaneshanks, whom Thales Haskell had met at the Hopi mesas the previous year, and Sarah Hatch's father.

The Indians said that they had been watching for them at the trail for seven days, but the Mormons had passed them in the night and got a long way ahead of them before they knew they had gone by. As Jacob explained the conversation, "They had run thare horses nerly down to overtake us. Thare chief wanted us to come back and traid with him. He had plenty of horses and blankets. If we went to Bufalo Creek we would be kiled for the Americans had ben killing Navajos and drove them out and they was mad at the Palefases."[76]

Hamblin and the missionaries knew that Spaneshanks was eager to trade with them and suspected that he was concocting a story to get them to take a detour to visit him.[77] Hamblin and Hatch probably would have willingly traded with Spaneshanks, but felt they needed to get water soon or their horses would die. "It was along distance to water in that direcion and our animils [were] neer famishing," wrote Jacob. Therefore, "We did not comply with the request."

The November 25 letter from Hamblin to Young also states that the group was worried that they would have to trade all their goods with Spaneshanks, and then they would not have adequate supplies to trade with the Hopis, their mission objective. Jacob also reasoned that they were five miles from water and within one day of the Hopi mesas.

The missionaries were faced with a difficult choice; if they went ahead to water, they might meet dangerous Navajos. But if they turned back without water, their horses and mules, carrying their precious supplies, might simply collapse. And perhaps Spaneshanks's men were exaggerating the threat of the Navajos at Buffalo Creek.[78]

So Hamblin told the group of friendly Navajos that the missionaries would continue on and water their animals at Buffalo Creek and do some trading with them there.[79] This place, also called Quichintoweep or Low Land,[80] was a camping place about twenty miles northwest of Oraibi in Blue Canyon, in the Moenkopi Wash.[81]

Not knowing the full extent of the ongoing war between the Navajos and U.S. Army and brutal volunteers of New Mexico, which had driven desperate, angry, starving Navajos west into the country surrounding the Hopi mesas, the company pushed on ahead.

Hamblin and Haskell had camped at Quichintoweep in previous years, and knew of the high ground nearby that would be a good place to protect their animals. Hamblin described the area as "an narow ridge 2 or 3 rods wide leeding on too some 40 acers of land surounded by a purpendicular rock."[82] There were indeed Navajos at Quichintoweep, camped on the other side of the wash in a meadow shaded by cottonwoods.[83] When the Mormons got close to the creek, Hamblin instructed Thales Haskell to take the company to the Moenkopi Creek, water the animals there, and set up camp on the narrow passage in Quichintoweep that led to the broad, enclosed area.[84] Meanwhile, Hamblin, McConnell and Enos would stay in the rear and talk to the Navajos, "which ware gethering in quite fast."

Hamblin and Enos were able to parley with a Navajo chief, "who said the White Fases had kiled all of his Familey not many Days before and hundreds of others." Either the chief or Hamblin was exaggerating here, as Navajo military historians estimate that, at most, dozens of Navajos had been killed. It is certain that many Navajos were captured and enslaved, herds of livestock were confiscated, and the Navajos were driven to the brink of starvation. And it is entirely possible that the chief's family might have been killed.

The Indian leader asked Hamblin why the missionaries were traveling through that country. Hamblin replied that "we ware agoeng to the Moquiches to traid." This did not please him, understandably, as the Hopis were traditional enemies of the Navajo. "He said we had got to traid with him." Hamblin promised him that the missionaries "would let him hav all the traid we had in the morning." The chief apparently agreed, and his group of Navajos "built a larg Fire nere our camp and a good feeling prevaild for some time," Jacob wrote, as they talked for hours.[85]

However, the missionaries concluded that night that the Navajos would not allow them to reach the Hopi mesas, so decided that they would trade all of their supplies with the Navajos in the morning and return to Utah.[86]

At about nine or ten o'clock at night, the mood of the Navajos changed, as "a larg numbr of the Navajose had colected" around the missionaries—some two to three hundred.[87]

"I did not like [the] Spirit they manifested," wrote Hamblin. Soon the Navajos flung wild accusations at the Mormons. "They said the Mormans had joind with the Americans and kiled many of thare People that they [the Americans] kiled all of the women and childrin they come to." This is entirely unlikely; the New Mexican volunteers would have been inclined to capture and sell women and children. But it may represent rumors drifting in times of war. It is a fact that a group of soldiers, presumably non-Mormons, had marched from Camp Floyd in Utah to join the Navajo wars.[88]

Some Navajos began threatening the Mormon missionaries, and one faction wanted to massacre the entire party; but the majority of the Navajos rejected this plan.[89] The Mormons were able to spend a peaceful night at their camp, though the threats and anger of many of the Navajos were profoundly unsettling.

The next morning, at about ten o'clock, the Navajos brought two hundred head of horses and mules, blankets and goat meat to trade, and negotiations started. At about noon, some of the missionaries took the company's livestock to water near their camp.[90] As they were bringing the animals back, George A. Smith Jr.'s gray mare suddenly ran back toward the Navajos' horses.[91] George jumped on Amos Thornton's horse and "road quite slow ovr a hill out of sight of camp" to recover his mount.[92] Haskell also emphasizes Smith's slow movement, which suggests that he had no idea he was in any danger.[93] Jacob remembered advising Smith not to go alone, but Smith "made an indifferent reply," then something distracted Hamblin's attention, and he did not see Smith riding out by himself.[94]

After riding for about a half mile to a mile, Smith came suddenly upon six Navajos.[95] According to one account, they were actually leading George's horse back to him and appeared to be friendly. However, when they came close to George, suddenly "one of them snatched his [George's] pistol from his belt, and commenced shooting at him; others fired arrows."[96] Smith, when he saw his own revolver aimed directly at his head, ducked, trying to avoid the shot, which caused him to fall off the horse.[97] The Navajos shot him repeatedly, putting four bullets in "the lower part of his Body" and three arrows in his chest.[98] Three balls hit him in the back near the kidneys and another passed through one of his thighs. One of the bullets, penetrating his hip, caused his lower limbs to be paralyzed.[99]

After Smith was thoroughly helpless, the Navajos stripped his buckskin shirt off him but disturbed him no further. Smith pulled the three arrows out of his chest before his friends could reach him.[100]

John D. Lee, whose diary supplies the earliest record of the third trip across the Colorado, gives an account of the murder that is remarkably different from the other versions. In his retelling, Smith, on Amos Thornton's horse, came upon the Navajos, and one of them, himself mounted, was leading Smith's horse away with a lasso. "Geo. rode up abruptly & caught the Bridle of the Indians horse & yanked it severely, insomuch that it made his Mouth Bleed," wrote Lee. "This raised the Ire of the Indian who shot his [Smith's] horse from under him & shot 3 arrows in Geo. He was surround[e]d, his revolver taken from him & with it he was Shot 4 time[s] in the Back." In this version, the Navajo murderer did not suddenly seize George's gun, then shoot him unexpectedly. George, in fact, did something to anger the Indian, though he was understandably trying to recover his horse.

Jacob's account, in Little, is quite similar, but he also stated that the Navajo who had been leading Smith's horse asked to see his revolver, Smith passed it to him, then it was passed to another Indian, who shot the boy three times. After he fell from his horse, Indians shot him in the back with arrows. However, it is hard to imagine, given the circumstances, that Smith would thoughtlessly pass his gun to a Navajo in this way. Lee's version, the Indians shooting him with arrows first, then taking the gun from him, seems more plausible.

At least one tradition supports the story that Smith passed the gun to the Indian in friendship. Christensen wrote that George Jr. "was Mortaley Wounded by *Black Horse* a Black Dwarf of a Navijo Who Said he did it accidently as He had never seen or Handled a Pistol before."[101] This does not explain the arrows in Smith's body.

In later years, the Navajo chief Peokon claimed to have killed George A. Smith Jr.[102] Peokon was Spaneshanks's son, according to some sources, and had a ranch close to where George A. was killed.[103] If this is true, then it would be tragic and ironic that George A. would be killed by Ira Hatch's brother-in-law.

Back in camp, the missionaries heard the gunshots and Hamblin sent McConnell and Haskell to investigate.[104] Smith was about a mile from camp, near the trail, but when they came close to him, they initially didn't see him; when he heard them, he "partially arose and said here I am shot."[105]

Smith, lying on his side, told his friends that he had lost all feeling from his hips downward, "and before starting to carry him to the camp he wished us to turn him partially, upon his back to see ~~if~~ whether he could get any ease from his pains, which appeared to be the greatest in his right hip & near the left kidney." They did this, and he felt a moderate amount of relief.

Meanwhile, back at camp, all the Navajos suddenly disappeared, hurriedly driving off their own horses and mules. Jacob asked the last Indian leaving what this departure meant. "He said thare was a Man kiled over thare." Hamblin immediately saddled a horse and rode over the hill, meeting Haskell coming to tell him the news. When Hamblin came to Smith, the young man "had no youse of his limbs but talked with apparent ease. Said he would like some water soon as he could get it. Said he did not like to ride on [a] horse."[106]

The three Mormons put George Jr. on a blanket, then Hamblin asked for help from Navajos that were nearby. Strangely enough, about a dozen came over; one helped carry George and another led Hamblin's horse back to camp. When they had George halfway to camp, he said he wanted to rest so they put him down near a greasewood bush.[107] He asked for water, and Hamblin went ahead for some.

Hamblin now knew that his expedition was in crisis mode. The four Navajos from Spaneshanks's band, who probably had heard the local Navajos speaking among themselves, said that "we must get out of thare or thare would be more kiled."[108] According to Warren, "Bro. Hamlin prayed to the Lord a short prayer and said to the brethren we have just time to escape with our lives." In Little, Hamblin says the he "asked the Lord to be merciful, and pity us in our miserable and apparently helpless condition, and to make known to me what to do and say to extricate us from our difficulties."[109]

Jacob sent James Pearce to inform McConnell and Haskell that they had to leave immediately to avoid being killed, and evidently they were able to get Smith to camp.[110]

The four friendly Navajos brought up the Mormons' horses and mules, and the missionaries began to pack in great haste. Just then, between fifty and a hundred Navajos "came in to camp took most of our provisions and cared [carried] off maney other things such as they could lay thare hands on," wrote Hamblin. Since there were about a hundred more Navajos between the Mormons and the Hopi mesas, Hamblin knew they must retreat: "Thare was no other Shoe [show] only for us to take the back track."[111]

Hamblin asked the Navajos why, after they had promised that they would trade peacefully with the Mormons, they had broken their promise and killed a man.[112] The Navajos ignored this accusation and now offered Hamblin terms by which he could save some of his party: Enos translated that the Navajos "wanted to kill 3 men take the 2 Indian girls and we mite goe back."[113] Two of the men, Thales Haskell and Isaac Riddle, "looked like two of the Merican Captains that kiled So Many of their Squaws & Papoose,"[114] so they, along with George Jr., would make up the three.[115] This count of three Navajos dying at the hands of the army or volunteers is much more believable than the reports of a thousand Navajos being massacred.

After the Navajos' request for two more men to kill, "Enos asked me what I thaught of that," wrote Hamblin. "I said we will not giv up one of our company."[116] He said that instead the group would fight to the end. The Navajos "had kiled one man & that was Enough," he said, "& before we would consent to give up an other, we would fight till we would all die togeather."[117] And, Hamblin warned, "You ... can kill all of us but at the same time we can kill some of you."[118]

Regarding the two Indian girls, Hamblin, in Little, states: "We had taken two Indian women with us, thinking that they might be a great help in introducing something like cleanliness in cooking, among the people we were going to visit." He does not explicitly say that he and Hatch had taken their two Indian wives. "The Navajos said we might go home if we would leave them. I directed the interpreter to tell them that one of the women was Brother Hatch's wife, and the other was mine." One reading of this is that Hamblin was instructing the interpreter to tell an untruth (i.e., that Eliza was his wife); but according to Hatch's biographer, Ezra Robinson, what he said was literally true.[119]

According to Christensen—not a first-hand witness, but a friend of Ira Hatch—some of the younger, more aggressive Navajos felt that they had explicit right to take Sarah Hatch as she had a Navajo father, and they made an attempt to seize her.[120] Ira Hatch, in a quick and probably instinctual response, "hit one of the Indians over the face with a heavy rawhide quirt until the blood squirted in a stream." If this happened—it is mentioned in none of the early accounts—it was a bold act, as the Mormons were surrounded by Navajos.[121] But according to Christensen, the older Navajos cried out, "He is worthy of his wife; see him fight for her!" After this, the older Navajos reportedly fell into place behind the Mormons, which prevented the younger Navajos from attacking, and allowed the missionaries to leave.[122]

George Smith Jr., half paralyzed and in despair, told the company to push on, leave him, and try to save themselves, but Jehiel McConnell told him that before they would do that they would all die together.[123]

In addition, Enos pleaded with the Navajos, telling them that the missionaries "were good men & had never shed Indian Blood."[124] Warren's informants told him that Enos "was instrumental in saving the brethren,s lives, it is said that he stood between the brethren and Navahoes and preached to them a long time, and at last by stratagem dissuaded them from an attack."[125] Pendleton wrote, "Enos was with our boys and through the whole affair acted with great decision and courage, declaring that if the party was slain they must kill him too."[126] Jacob told Lee that Enos "Saved there Lives."[127]

An accidental gift to the Navajos reportedly gave the missionaries a chance to leave. A pack mule spooked, kicked his pack off, and "strung the Indian Notions in every direction."[128] According to Riddle, the mule scattered trinkets in the grass as it ran in a circle of about a half mile. Many hostile Indians followed the mule and dived for the goods, began arguing about them, and a fistfight ensued.[129] Now, Lee wrote, "some of the friendly Indians got between the Brethren & the Crowd & helped them away."[130] This supports the view that the Navajos were divided, and that many of them worked to save the Mormons from younger, more vengeful warriors.[131]

The twelve Mormons set off, riding as quickly as they could,[132] with George Jr. riding on a mule behind Jehiel McConnell. Two Spaneshanks Navajos rode in front of the Mormons, and two in the rear. Two miles out of camp, the enemy Navajos "was getheren together on the trail [a] little behind us," wrote Hamblin,[133] "dogging close after" their party.[134] So the Mormons had to stop and confront them again. Hamblin gave a bundle of trinkets to Enos, and told him to "take them and traid or giv them away and doe the best he could to stop the Indians folowing."[135]

At this point, a Navajo approached, boldly riding Amos Thornton's horse. This especially outraged the leader of the Spaneshanks Navajos,[136] who turned back, took a gun out of the hands of the Indian on the stolen horse, "shot the horse and broak the gun over the head of the thief"![137] The Spaneshanks Navajo said that this felled Navajo "should not kill his friends nor have their effects."[138] This evidently started a considerable disturbance—"I saw that quite a row had commenced among them," wrote Jacob,[139]—which allowed the missionaries to set off again.

They rode as fast as they could for a long time, and George Jr. continued to lose precious blood during the forced retreat. About an hour before sunset, he told

McConnell and Ira Hatch that he was losing his sight. McConnell looked at his eyes "& discovered that they presented a very glossy appearance, & the sights entirely scattered."[140] A little before sundown, George Jr. turned to Hamblin and said, "O, Jacob, do Stop, for I am dying."[141]

Hamblin asked the leader of the Spaneshanks Navajos to stop, but the Navajo advised against it. "You cannot doe the dyeing man any good," he said. "You can help more [and avoid] geting in the same fix if you will goe on. I am mad at you now because you would not here [listen] to me yesterday and then this man would not of ben kiled."[142] Indeed, a remarkable part of this story is the extraordinary loyalty that Spaneshanks and his followers showed toward the Mormon missionaries. Of course, Sarah Hatch was apparently Spaneshanks's daughter, and Ira Hatch his son-in-law, though none of the accounts touch on these relationships.

George Jr. died soon after this, "precisely at sunset," while still riding his mule.[143] The "wild boy" turned Indian missionary passed to the other side. McConnell carried the body in front of him till it was dark, "when br Hamblin took him from my arms and laid him by the road side having no way of burying him."[144] They had no time to bury or dress the body, wrote Warren, as Navajos were still hotly pursuing them.[145] This event occurred about ten miles north of Quichintoweep, possibly near modern Tonalea.[146]

Hamblin wrote that the group traveled into the night, then hid in sheltering rocks and junipers.[147] This, writes Lee, "decoyed their Persuers."[148] They made a camp and tried to sleep.

The weight of George Jr.'s death suddenly fell on Jacob, and he could not sleep, as he imagined the body devoured by vultures or wolves, or Navajos dancing with his scalp.[149] And the most dreaded task of all awaited him when he arrived home: he would have to notify George Jr.'s father, mother, and sister of the violent death. This realization "pierced me like barbed arrows," he wrote.[150]

At dawn the missionaries took up their journey again, and at two p.m., November 3, they came to Spaneshanks's camp, where they were made welcome.[151] The immediate danger was past, though an Indian runner brought a message that encouraged Spaneshanks to kill the Mormons. He ignored it.[152]

Hamblin talked with Spaneshanks through the afternoon and well into the night. The chief was very interested in the Mormon religion. "He profesed to know something about…our faith by dreems and some thing he had seen," Jacob wrote. In fact, he said that he "believd Mormonism." But like the Navajos that had led Hamblin to Spaneshanks, he rebuked Hamblin strongly for not following the advice of his men. He said that the Ute Arapeen had told him that a few Mormons would be passing on the Ute trail on their way to the Hopis, and that Spaneshanks must keep them from going to the mesas, for all or some of them would be killed by the angry Navajos if they tried to go in that direction. The Navajo chief accordingly sent men to watch for the Mormons for nine days. "He said he felt vext at me to think I would not stop when he told me and we never stopt to traid with him."

Hamblin asked Spaneshanks why the Navajos had been so murderous at this time, when they had been friendly a year ago. The chief replied that the Navajos believed that the Mormons—or "some me[n] from Salt Lake Citty"—had "joined in with the Amerians and help[ed] kil the Navajos men women and childrin." Hamblin explained that this was false, at least with respect to Mormons.[153] Jacob later learned that the Navajos at Quichintoweep had previously lived near Fort Defiance, and had been driven west.[154]

The chief again offered to trade with the Mormons, saying the he had plenty of horses and blankets. Hamblin told him that if he would help his company depart safely, he would come back as soon as possible and trade with them. "I made this promice so we would run no more [risk] of life," Hamblin later wrote Young. "I think it would be well perhaps to fullfil the promice. He kep[t] his with me."[155]

The next day, November 4, the missionaries left Spaneshanks's camp and traveled swiftly west. The following day they crossed the Colorado safely, and a few days later, as they were running out of food on the Kaibab Plateau, Paiutes brought them a large supply of pine nuts.[156] Hamblin's group reached the settlements on November 9, after another difficult march.[157]

George A. Smith Sr. did not receive the news of his son's death until the end of the month, for unknown reasons. The first letter he received was the November 21 letter from William Warren in Cedar City. Hamblin wrote Smith a full account of the expedition that has not survived. On November 25, at Fort Clara, he wrote his letter to Brigham Young.

Two days after this George Smith Sr., received news of his son's death:

> At sundown, Sam. Clark brought me a letter, which stated that my son George Albert Smith had been murdered by the Navahoe indians. He was shot with 3 arrows & 4 balls. The Postmaster brought me a letter from W. J. Warren given some particulars of my son's death but it was second-handed information. The evening was occupied with tears mourning & lamentation. I could not cry.[158]

Hamblin, in Little, gives a final visionary perspective to place this tragic story in a religious context. He says that when he later talked with George A. Smith Sr., the apostle said that at first, he was shocked when his son was killed; but as time went on, he came to believe that God had taken George Jr. for a specific reason at a specific time. And Hamblin noted that President Young felt the same way.[159]

We have seen that the Mormons, repeating what friendly Navajos told them, stated that the reason that George A. Smith Jr.'s murderers were so violent was that U.S. troops had perpetrated massacres on the Navajos, killing women and children, and driving off sheep and cattle. Some of the specific charges found in the Mormon documents are certainly inflated (whether by Navajo informants or by Mormons themselves). For example, George Smith Sr. wrote,

> The Navajoe party had just received the intelligence that Lieutenant-Colonel Ruggles of the United States Army, with a detachment of soldiers, had burned their village, two hundred miles east, had massacred two hundred and fifty squaws and papooses, and killed forty thousand of their sheep. The receipt of this news by the war party was the cause of the murder of George A., Jr.[160]

Two hundred and fifty is actually conservative, compared to other Mormon accounts. Warren (in his letter to Smith) and Smith himself (in a letter to Amasa Lyman) both say that a thousand Navajos were massacred. These are wildly inflated numbers; in addition, women and children would likely be sold into slavery, not massacred.

But in fall and winter 1860, Navajos certainly suffered a disastrous invasion into their territory by the U.S. Army and a force of New Mexican "volunteers."

As was recounted earlier, a war had broken out between the Navajos and the U.S. troops in 1858. After Colonel Dixon Miles's campaign against the Navajos that year, a peace treaty was signed, but like most Navajo-U.S. treaties, it did not last. After Navajo raids on the Pueblo Indians, reportedly led by young warriors against the advice of older leaders, Maj. John Simonson was sent on an expedition to Navajo country in June 1859.[161] Simonson reported that the great majority of Navajos wanted peace, were not involved in raiding, and continued to suffer greatly from raids of the New Mexicans in their territory, who were especially interested in abducting children or women to serve as slaves.

Simonson was moderate and sympathetic to the Navajos, but his military superiors, including Col. Benjamin L. E. de Bonneville, influenced by New Mexicans, were more harsh. On October 22, 1859, Bonneville ordered that the army march against the Navajos at Chusca Valley, and "kill four or five at least of this tribe."[162] The army obeyed; on November 1, they marched into Navajo country and simply opened fire on the first Navajos they met, killing from five to ten Indians.

The Navajos, not surprisingly, regarded this as a declaration of war on their tribe. Navajo reprisals against New Mexican settlements followed, as the Navajo peace party was rendered powerless by the American or American-sanctioned aggression. This in turn raised anti-Navajo feelings in New Mexico to new heights. In addition, in early 1860 Navajos began raiding the herds and killing herdsmen at Fort Defiance. These attacks culminated in a full-scale attack on the fort by about a thousand Navajos on April 30, 1860, led by dominant war chiefs Barboncito and Manuelito. Though the

Navajo warriors outnumbered the soldiers in the fort five to one, the soldiers had much superior firepower, and the Navajos could not take the fort.[163]

Even though the Navajos immediately sued for peace after this setback, the audacity of the Indian attack led Secretary of War John B. Floyd, back in Washington, to order a winter campaign against the Navajos.[164] He explicitly forbade volunteers from New Mexico taking part in the campaign.

The campaign, scheduled for winter 1860 to 1861, was given to moderate, efficient Brev. Lt. Col. Edward Canby, who would head one of three regular U.S. Army companies used in the invasion of Navajo territory.[165] The other companies would be led by Brev. Maj. Henry H. Sibley and Capt. Lafayette McLaws.

As was mentioned previously, troops from Camp Floyd, Utah, were transferred to Fort Defiance to help with this campaign.[166] Here we have a direct link with a Mormon tradition, for Isaac Riddle states, "We learned later that the real reason these Indians"—the Navajos who killed George Jr. and threatened the entire company—"were so unfriendly was because a company of United States soldiers from Camp Floyd had passed through their land sometime previous, and for some trifle had killed an entire band of Navajos."[167]

Against the orders of the military, a battalion of New Mexican volunteers, 448 men, was organized; it would be led by "lieutenant colonel" Manuel A. Chaves. This group boldly entered the field without authorization. They did not have the discipline of the regular army (none too gentle itself), and would be looking for captives to sell into slavery.

The campaign began in mid-October, as Canby, Sibley, McLaws, and Chaves pressed west into eastern Arizona. Canby and Sibley met at Marsh Pass on October 26, hoping to trap a major group of Navajos there. While it was not the trap they had expected, it did force many Navajos west toward the Hopi mesas. Canby, whose horses were famishing in the Navajo desert, decided to return immediately to Fort Defiance.[168]

While Canby and Sibley were concentrating on Marsh Pass, the volunteer battalion ranged westward to the area of the Hopi villages. McNitt writes, "The Chaves battalion had cut swathes through Navajo cornfields, captured thousands of their livestock, and returned with about one hundred Navajo women and children euphemistically referred to as captives."[169] The Chaves battalion mustered out on December 3.

The regular army killed twenty-eight Navajos and captured 360 horses and 2,000 sheep, by historian Frank McNitt's accounting. It is not known how many Navajos the volunteers killed, but McNitt estimates that "the casualties were probably severe."[170]

This background, the U.S. Army and the battalion of volunteers pushing the Navajos westward toward Pueblo Colorado (modern Ganado), Navajo Mountain, Shonto, and the Hopi mesas,[171] shows why there were so many Navajos on the usually deserted wastelands between the Crossing of the Fathers and the Hopi mesas. It also explains why the Hamblin company could not find the usual water in hollows of rocks; the Navajos and their livestock had drunk it.

The Navajos called the years from 1860 to 1868 *Nahondzod*, the "fearing time." As McNitt notes, "A state of constant warfare was contrary to Navajo nature and totally disruptive of normal Navajo life." The army kept the Navajos perpetually on the move and when winter arrived many of them were nearing starvation.[172] Peace talks began on January 12, 1861—long after the killing of George Smith Jr. The Mormon expedition, by bad luck, had arrived in Navajo territory during a major disruption in Navajo life, during which whites, especially the brutal, extremist, New Mexico volunteers, had driven the Indians to the very territory the Mormons had to pass over to reach the mesas. It is probably a tribute to the older, more peaceable element among the Navajos at Quichintoweep that eleven of the twelve Mormons made it back to southern Utah alive.

12

"I Want You to Give Dilligent Heed to This Letter"

Gathering the Bones, 1861

Hamblin's fourth trip across the Colorado, in early 1861, was an assignment from Brigham Young, as were most of his visits to Arizona. Young wrote to Hamblin on January 8:

> I would be much pleased to have you, as soon as possible, arrange to go or have some other suitable person go, with a few white men and Indians, and endeavor to recover the body of George A. Smith Jun., for which, if it can be done, I would not begrudge paying a reasonable amount, and for the delivery of the body in this city, which can be done while it remains cold weather. Your brother in the Gospel, Brigham Young.

And, as if he wanted to make sure he had made himself clear, Young added a postscript: "I want you to give dilligent heed to this letter and God bless you in so doing. B. Y."[1]

Hamblin received the letter from the hands of George A. Smith Sr., who visited Santa Clara on February 8 and preached with Joseph A. Young at the new Santa Clara schoolhouse.[2] Jacob immediately began to prepare for the expedition, traveling to Cedar City and Parowan to recruit men for what promised to be a difficult and dangerous journey.[3] One wonders at Young and Smith's judgment: they were sending Hamblin and others back to the far side of the Colorado, a difficult journey in the best of conditions; but now they were sending them into the territory of hostile, angry Navajos who had almost massacred a Mormon party a few months before. Despite these real risks, Hamblin's response was typical: immediate unquestioning obedience.

Though the primary purpose of the journey was clear, the expedition also had an exploratory dimension. In the Church Historian's Office Journal, which is based on an interview with Hamblin and is one of our main sources for the journey, the scribe referred to the fourth trip across the Colorado as "an exploring expedition."[4]

The members of the party were: from Santa Clara, Frank Hamblin, Sam Knight, Hiram Judd, Luke Fuller, Lemuel Leavitt, Charles Searle, Amos Thornton, and Jacob Hamblin; from Cedar City, Jehiel McConnell, William C. Stewart, Thomas Walker, and John Hunter; and from Parowan, William C. Mitchell, William M. West, Sidney R. Burton, David Ward, and William Robb Jr.[5] In addition, two Indians, Enos and Tutsegabits, accompanied the whites. Thus, there were nineteen men, thirty-four animals, "and a good fit out" on this expedition.[6] The men from Parowan left that town on February 21,[7] and the group collected in Santa Clara. They set out on their journey five days later.[8]

They took a new route to the Colorado, which included a spring at the 110-mile point which supplied a good campground with water and feed. The Colorado at the Vado de los Padres was lower than they had ever seen it before, and they crossed it "circuitously," probably a reference to the diagonal route they had to follow while crossing.[9]

On the other side of the river, Hamblin and his company met Paiutes who told him that there were many more Navajos than when he had been there previously, so it would be dangerous to go personally to gather George Jr.'s remains. They said all that was left was a few bones. Enos asked these Indians to go gather the young man's bones and bring them to their camp. The company also sent messengers to Spaneshanks.

The local Paiutes said that the Navajos, though plentiful in the area now, were not unified and were fighting with each other; one had been killed the previous day. They had also "disagreed about killing him [George Jr.], some believing that in doing so they had forfeited the friendship of the Saints," and that this was a major mistake.[10]

Traveling on "very bad rocky roads," they came to Navajo Canyon, which had water.[11] Jacob mentions their trail sometimes "ran along the almost perpendicular sides of deep rock fissures, narrow with frequent short turns." Sometimes these rocks were icy, and the men had to hack away the ice to continue their journey.

Once, as they were waiting for the morning sun to melt frost and ice on a steep rock so that they could emerge from a gulch up to a plain above, Jacob's pack mule slipped, then rolled down an incline to within a yard of a deep chasm. The men were able to fasten a rope to the animal and haul it and its pack back to the path.[12]

That night, at their camp, they melted snow to water their animals. The next day they took a new route, which led them southeast toward the Shonto area—they must have followed the general direction of Navajo Canyon.

According to the official report, in the evening local Indians "brought in Geo. A. Jun.'s Skull without the jaw, and his thigh bone which were partly knawed, being all they could find of Geo. A.'s remains."[13] Jehiel McConnell, however, records that the skull, with part of its hair, was complete, except for one tooth, and that two thigh bones were found, not one. Wolves had gnawed at the bones.[14]

On the third day past the Colorado, the expedition found brackish water in pools, and came to ruins in Navajo Canyon, not too far from the well-known Inscription House ruins:

> The Company discovered in the shelving rocks a place or fort about forty feet wide and ninety long, divided off by walls built by rock and cement, into four different rooms. port holes on the outside walls, a large overhanging rock projects over the fort. ~~with~~ steps cut out of the stone to go up into the fort, and also larger steps cut up the mountain to go up the mountain out from the fort. In this fortified position amid the shelving rocks a small spring of water trickles down the rocks.[15]

Remarkably, at this cliff dwelling, called NA5642 by archaeologists, two of the Hamblin company left inscriptions: "W. C. Mitchell 1861" and "W. C. Stewart / [*illegible*] / Cedar City Ward / 1861."[16] This gives us a certain point of travel for the expedition.

Though the Mormons was fascinated by this cliff fort, they decided to camp elsewhere. Apparently, they pushed into Nitsin Canyon, a tributary to Navajo Canyon, and about half a mile from Navajo Canyon came to the extensive archaeological site now called the Inscription House ruins, a major cliff dwelling site with some seventy rooms. Here one of the men made another inscription. Much of it is illegible, but it included a date, which for many years was read as 1661, and was taken as evidence for a visit from Spanish Americans in the seventeenth century (and which gave the site its name). However, later researchers have read the date as "1861 Anno D.," and have convincingly argued that someone in Hamblin's company made it.[17]

The party eventually camped in a canyon that was shut in except for its entrance, and which supplied good feed for the company's animals.[18]

According to Jehiel McConnell, the first Navajos who visited were not friendly. They suspected that the party of Mormons and Paiutes had come to avenge George Smith's death, and felt special enmity toward Enos. They gathered around him, drew their bows and said they were going to kill him—but he showed no fear, and they eventually lowered their bows and decided to talk with him.[19]

The next morning, just after sunrise, Spaneshanks and four companions arrived at the Mormon camp.[20] They brought news that many Navajos had been displaced from their villages because the U.S. Army was building a new fort where they had been living.[21] Forced to leave their hogans and cornfields, they were "living upon their sheep & horses."

Navajos, reassured that the Mormons had not come for vengeance, continued coming to the Mormon camp, but now "they wished to return the friendship of the Mormons, to which many of the Pi Utes bore testimony." They requested the Mormons to stay till the following morning so that they could "have a talk and have a good understanding." The Navajos were especially interested in trading for flour.

Enos, Tutsegabits, and Spaneshanks—three Mormon converts—preached all night to the local Paiutes and Navajos, who continued to gather into the camp throughout the night.

At daybreak, an old Navajo arrived who evidently admitted to having given the order to kill George Jr. He would not give his name, but wanted to shake hands with Jacob Hamblin. Jacob refused, and when Spaneshanks asked why, "Jacob replied, that he was thinking on Geo. A. Jun. whom they killed."[22]

Yes, Spaneshanks said, they killed a Mormon; but at the time, they didn't know the true character of Mormons, and now were very sorry for the action.[23] According to McConnell, a man who had scalped Smith was also present and wished to trade with the Mormons. They were reluctant, but Spaneshanks took his part. The volatile Navajo requested a red blanket, flew into a rage when the Mormons did not produce one, and finally Thomas Walker gave him a blanket. Jacob also distributed some fifty dollars' worth of goods among the leading Navajos, "which damped the passion."[24]

Jacob invited Spaneshanks and other friendly Indians to come live closer to the Mormon settlements, though the Navajo headman, like the Oraibi Hopis, never did accept this invitation.[25]

Soon after this, some of the local Paiutes warned Hamblin to be cautious, and not let any of his party wander away alone. Since Jacob had himself started to feel uncomfortable with the Navajos' demeanor, he told the brethren he felt it would be advisable for the company to begin their journey back to Utah. Some of the members of the party said that they were sure there was no danger, and wanted to trade with the Navajos; this "only inspired Jacob with greater fear," and the company left in the early morning.[26] After they started, Spaneshanks caught up to them with some Navajos who had just arrived and wanted to trade. The Mormons gave Enos some goods and left him to carry out the trade while they pushed ahead.[27]

The Historian's Office account says that the party was gone twenty-three days. As they left Santa Clara on February 26, they would have returned on about March 21. The "Parowan boys" got back to that town on March 23.[28] McConnell states that the parley near Navajo Canyon took place from a Saturday to a Tuesday—possibly March 9–12.

The Parowan members of the expedition described it as a "very hard trip."[29] This was par for the course in these early forays across the Colorado. McConnell and Stewart, in their sacrament meeting missionary reports, emphasized the danger from hostile Navajos: "There are many who would have taken our lives but the Lord would not permit it," said Stewart.[30] Jacob had accomplished another dangerous, difficult expedition.

He soon began his journey north with the remains of George Jr. He arrived in Salt Lake City on April 7, and reported to George A. Smith and Brigham Young. Two days later, Smith and Hamblin visited Young, who offered to pay Hamblin and his party for their trip to find George Jr.'s bones. Hamblin replied "that the party had taken that matter into consideration and agreed that they should perform the mission at their own expenses."[31]

Perhaps now Jacob achieved some degree of closure after the nightmare of George A. Smith Jr.'s death.

Hamblin must have returned to southern Utah as quickly as possible, for Priscilla was eight and a half months pregnant. He had left his family at Mountain Meadows with plenty of flour, but on returning home found that they'd generously lent much of it to needy neighbors, and they now had none. Because the roads at the Meadows were impassible with late snow, he had to use a hand sled to obtain fuel and flour for them.[32] Priscilla bore her second child, Melissa, on April 22, in Santa Clara.[33] Earlier in the year, on January 27, Rachel had borne her fifth and last child, Ariminda, in Santa Clara. Ariminda would not live long, dying in 1862.

Albert, back in Santa Clara, wrote a letter to Brigham Young on February 6 that suggests that he had been supported financially by Young in Salt Lake City, and regarded him as a kind of uncle.[34] The letter also shows that the boy had learned to read and write while in the city. Albert confided to Young that he was going to school with a Brother Slack, who, he wrote, "takes an interes in learning me."

The main topic of the letter is a squaw fight, which had demanded Jacob's intervention: "The Indians hav comenced thare old customes abuseing thare squaws" that "the Misionarys had stopt for .4. years," Albert wrote. "They fit [fought] ove[r] one Squaw here all day stabd hur 3 times. Father and some of the Boys stop the fuss."

Albert ended his letter, "We will be glad to see you when you come here I hope you will stop to my Fathers house when you come.... I prey most evrey day a lone as you told me."

Brigham Young did come to Southern Utah.[35] On February 22 and 23 he and his party were in Parowan, where Young fulminated against Mormons who were trading with the army and Gentiles, including local bishop William Warren. They passed through Mountain Meadows and "Jacob's Twist," the narrow rocky pass between the California Road and Santa Clara, which James Martineau had named in honor of Jacob Hamblin,[36] coming to Santa Clara on the twenty-sixth. As this was a Sunday, two meetings were held in Santa Clara, no doubt at the schoolhouse, and Young, George A. Smith, Daniel H. Wells, John Taylor, and Bishop Edward Hunter preached—a rare treat for the Santa Clara Saints.

The scribe took the opportunity to describe Santa Clara as a community of thirty-four men and thirty houses, with 250 acres in cultivation. It was situated on "a very fertile bottom although it is a bed of sand." He described extensive orchards and vineyards, Walter Dodge's nursery, and a flourishing cotton field, and estimated that the Santa Clara saints would have a thousand bushels of peaches this year, half

12.1. Erastus Snow was for many years the apostle-leader of Southern Utah and sent Jacob Hamblin on many missions. Used by permission, Utah State Historical Society, all rights reserved.

of which would be from Jacob's orchards. In addition, there were herds of livestock outside the town, and more than half of the Santa Clara men had gone into the fields to tend their flocks.

Soon after this tour of the south, Brigham Young made a decision that would deeply impact Jacob Hamblin and his fellow Indian missionaries in Santa Clara. Young envisioned increased economic production from southern Utah, especially in cotton,[37] and decided to found a major settlement between Santa Clara and Washington. He had always encouraged Mormons to become entirely self-sufficient; the outbreak of the Civil War in the East in 1861 apparently motivated him to try to make southern Utah a major cotton-producing region. In addition, Young planned for St. George to produce wine, olive oil, castor oil, indigo, molasses, and sugar, as well as tobacco, figs, and almonds.[38]

At October conference in Salt Lake, Young had the names of some three hundred heads of families read out, and they were called to found a new city at the present site of St. George, as part of the "Cotton Mission."[39] Two apostles, Erastus Snow and Orson Pratt, would accompany the new settlers and live with them. Pratt did not stay in Dixie long, but Snow became a St. George resident, and Hamblin had frequent dealings with him. A native of Vermont, he had joined the church in 1832, at the age of fourteen, and experienced the vicissitudes of the Mormon communities in Ohio, Missouri, and Nauvoo. He crossed the plains in 1847, and was called to be an apostle two years later. A polygamist, he had eight wives and thirty-six children throughout his life. He was known as a capable, level-headed, "colonizer" apostle.[40]

In addition, in 1861, some ninety Saints from Switzerland were called to settle at Santa Clara and raise vineyards and other crops there. And a year later, two hundred more families were called at October conference to move south to Dixie and help build up the cotton mission.[41]

George A. Smith wrote Jacob a letter on October 16, giving him some of the details of the impending migration. He told him that after the names of the settlers were called out in conference, there was "no small excitement in this City"; two hundred men, with their families, would be in Dixie by fall. He instructed Jacob to keep the Pine Valley mill going night and day to supply lumber for the new settlers.[42]

All of this would turn Jacob's world upside down. There had been competition for resources between the Paiutes and the Mormons on the Clara, and between the different communities of Mormons. Now, that competition would be greatly exacerbated. Cotton needs a great deal of water to be grown successfully—one of the chief factors that would eventually make raising cotton in Utah's Dixie economically unfeasible.[43] But before the Cotton Mission would be abandoned, the cotton fields would require an enormous amount of irrigation water.

While before, the Mormons and Paiutes had lived in a delicate symbiosis in Dixie, now the Mormons would start to equal or exceed the local Indians in number, and they would be living in politically powerful unified, permanent settlements. Santa Clara, and all of Dixie, had been settled first as an Indian mission, but now Santa Clara and the suddenly dominant St. George would be full-fledged Mormon communities with a specific economic mission: to raise cotton and other economically important crops.

The old Indian missionary settlers of Santa Clara would suddenly find themselves far outnumbered by Swiss emigrants in their own town; and the Swiss would understandably be far less interested in preaching to Paiutes than in planting their crops and farming successfully. Missionary work to the Indians or learning their language was not part of their calling; if there were Indian troubles, they would send for Hamblin or Ira Hatch or Andrew Gibbons to help them. Their primary mission was agricultural.

One part of Hamblin's mission was undoubtedly that of Indian missionary; but now another part of his life's calling would come to the fore, the persona of explorer, pioneer, and Indian expert keeping peace for Mormon pioneering settlements. He served as explorer of new country for possible Mormon settlements, then he worked to smooth the way for the new settlements by coming to know the local Indians and working with them through negotiation, rather than with violence. This is not the same as pure missionary work. Hamblin certainly felt divided about this. He came to see the settlement of St. George and the Swiss influx into Santa Clara as disastrous for the Paiutes.[44]

Nevertheless, he gradually found himself more and more functioning as explorer and first settler for Brigham Young in his colonization of southern Utah and Arizona, rather than as Indian missionary in the fullest sense. Understandably, he was more an advocate for his own people and religion than he was for the Indians and their culture, though he was divided and sympathized with the Indians' plight. He worked to cause Mormons to moderate anti-Indian attitudes as they settled southern Utah and Arizona.

So Hamblin and the local Paiutes were about to endure a major social upheaval. In addition, in one of those moments of dark synchronicity that occur in history, a major upheaval in nature was about to engulf both of them.

13

"The Last Vestige of the Fort . . . Had Disappeared and in [Its] Place Roar Now the Wild Torrents of the River"

The Big Washout, January 1862

The great flood that swept much of Santa Clara away in January 1862, including the solid rock fort, was one of the epic moments in southern Utah history, complete with the adventure, hair-raising escapes, humor, tragedy, and heroism that epic requires.[1] Jacob Hamblin was a major character in the drama and struggle for survival. The story that emerges from both the earliest and retrospective sources shows the cohesiveness of Santa Clara's residents, who somehow survived as their homes, mills, and orchards were swept away and their solid fort fell stone by stone into a monstrously swollen river. The "old" settlers of Fort Clara had just been joined by ninety immigrants from the unlikely country of Switzerland when the flood occurred. Working together, the two groups survived and then resettled together in the new town of Santa Clara, about a half mile below the older settlement. The old community had been entirely washed out; the new one began immediately.

The fate of the Paiute Indian settlements located on the opposite side of the river is not recorded in the white historical record. However, the probable destruction of their villages and farms, coupled with other problems caused by the recent Mormon settlement in southern Utah, must have had a devastating impact on their way of life.

The date of the Santa Clara flood—January 17–19, 1862—has been disputed by some local historians and writers. For example, Jacob himself, in Little, dates the flood in mid-February, while Santa Clara residents have often dated the flood as early as January 1.[2] However, a letter by Daniel Bonelli (captain of the Swiss immigrants who had arrived in Santa Clara in late November 1861) to Brigham Young, written on January 19, 1862, gives the correct date for the flood and conclusively resolves the debate.

By 1861, there were from twenty to thirty families, some hundred people, living in Santa Clara.[3] Aside from houses in the fort, there were about seven homes built outside it, and a schoolhouse and Jacob Hamblin's grist mill on the other side of the stream.[4]

The settlers of St. George arrived there in late November and early December, and the ninety Swiss immigrants arrived at Fort Clara from November 24 to 28, at first camping around the adobe meetinghouse then putting up shelters around it.[5] Some of the Swiss Saints moved into the fort. The George and Sophia Staheli family, with a pregnant mother and seven children aged two to twelve, moved into the second floor of the Ira Hatch home in the fort's southwest corner.[6]

Settlement leaders decided that the Swiss saints should be permanently located on the "lower flat" on the "Big Bend" of the Santa Clara about a half mile to a mile southeast of the fort.[7] This site would eventually become the hub of modern Santa Clara. The Swiss moved onto their apportioned lots and began to live in their wagon boxes or construct crude shelters.[8]

On Christmas day, three significant events occurred. First, Barbara Staheli was born to George and Sophia Barbara Staheli in the upstairs room of the Hatch home in the fort. The Stahelis had moved into the fort to accommodate the childbirth, and since Sophia was ill for weeks after the birth, they stayed in the fort after Christmas. Second, the Swiss settlers finished their diversion dam and irrigation ditches leading to their lots. And third, it began to rain.[9] According to early sources, the rain continued, with temporary respites, for some forty days, which would be about six weeks or until about February 8, 1862.[10]

Farther to the north, in Pine Valley and elsewhere, heavy rain and snow fell on the upper Santa Clara, which soon swelled the lower Santa Clara beyond recognition. Before the flood, according to many early reminiscences, the Santa Clara was more aptly termed a creek that, under normal circumstances, one could walk across in places.[11] In the weeks following Christmas 1861, the creek became a river in full flood, with banks widening continually and the water level always rising.

The flood came "as a thief in the night," in John R. Young's words, early in the morning of Friday, January 17.[12] When the flood struck, the once-meek Santa Clara indeed presented a fearsome sight. John Young remembered a "wall of water" ten to fifteen feet high.[13] Daniel Bonelli was impressed by the eerie sight of cottonwood trees and huge logs careening down the Clara, rushing along "like arrows upon the turbid current." This presented "a spectacle of dreadful magnificence."[14] In addition, the flood uprooted trees at Santa Clara "with astounding rapidity."[15] Jesse W. Crosby wrote on the seventeenth that the Virgin and the Santa Clara "became mighty rivers, and both man and beast fled from them terrified." In fact, a number of horses, mules, and cattle were drowned.[16] Jacob remembered the awesome sound of the flood: "the roar of the water awakened most of the inhabitance in and about Ft Clara."[17] Mary Judd wrote that the flood "looked like the sea as it came out of the kanion and spread over the bottoms from hill to hill."[18] Bonelli wrote that the river "overflew nearly the whole of the bottoms, destroying orchards and field."[19]

On the other side of the river, the angry current swept away Jacob Hamblin's grist mill. When the flood struck on early Friday morning, the elderly miller Solomon Chamberlain and his grandchildren, who lived near the mill, were rudely awakened by a stream of water pouring into their dugout. They managed to escape this deathtrap and climb a nearby tree, where they spent a miserable and terrifying night. "Old Father Chamberlen grandson and daughter ware in a long tree surounded by the floods," Hamblin wrote.[20] They stayed in the tree until Friday afternoon when the floods abated, and then the Chamberlains retreated to a high spot on the millrace.[21] Soon after this, the tree in which they had taken refuge was swept away in the still-raging current. "Chamberlen had decended from his tree but a few minits when it...was hauld into the distructiv element," according to Hamblin.[22] However, they were now safe, and John Young reports that three days later he and Ira Hatch were able to cross the river and bring Chamberlain and his grandchildren back to the main settlement with them.[23]

By about midday on Friday the flood water in the bottoms had retreated to the river channel. Daniel Bonelli wrote, "During the forenoon the floods seemed to abate and returned to the deeper washing bed of the river." Hamblin wrote that on that afternoon the river had receded to its banks, but the channel of the river was eight feet deeper than it had been, and now "the banks [were] sliding in with great rapidity undermining houses stacks of grain orchards and nurserys."[24] According to one local history, "The mad river was slashing into the bank, carving out pieces as big as a house."[25]

The Santa Clara pioneers evidently felt that the fort and houses near to it were safe. Hamblin, in his autobiography, wrote, "Our fort, constructed of stone...with walls twelve feet high and two feet thick, stood a considerable distance north of the original bed of the creek...and we had considered it safe from the flood."[26] On Saturday night, Priscilla warned Jacob that the situation was dangerous. "Priscilla, you are too concerned," he responded, and went to bed.[27]

Later that night, the flood waters began making inroads beneath the southwest corner of the fort, where the Hatches and Stahelis were living.[28] The Santa Clarans realized they might lose the fort, and quick evacuation was necessary. Someone knocked on Jacob's door: "Jake, are you going to lay there and be washed away?" was his brusque question. That got Hamblin out of bed.[29]

John Young described the waters hitting the west wall of the fort and dividing the flood water north and south. While the walls of the fort held for a time, the water on the north soon streamed into the entrance of the fort. A sheet of water four or five feet deep "swept through the gate like a mill race, flooding the inside of the fort to a man's armpits."[30]

A rescue mission to save people and remove the settlement's possessions from the fort was quickly organized. The rescuers must have presented an eerie spectacle;

while the chaos of the river roared, a black unseen monster, human forms moved about in near darkness, lit only by a few torches or makeshift lanterns.

Their first priority was to take women and children to higher ground. However, just outside the entrance to the fort a dangerously strong current was flowing that could easily sweep people away. To provide safe passage through the rushing water, the men tied a strong rope to a post inside the fort and to a tree higher up the hill.[31]

Thus, the women and children were evacuated, some clinging to the necks and riding on shoulders of men as they held onto the rope.[32] Many of the refugees took shelter in a "stone corell" that Hamblin had built higher up the hill. Mary Judd later remembered "a city of tentes and shanties around that stone fort."[33]

Following the evacuation of the women and children, the men turned to saving what supplies they could. There were two hundred bushels of wheat stored in the northwest corner of the fort, and the men started to move the wheat, while John Young held a lantern and kept an eye on the flood. "We barly saved the grain that was stord in the Fort lard[er]," wrote Hamblin.[34] When they had removed 175 bushels, Young gave a warning, and soon after this the northwest corner of the fort fell into the raging Santa Clara waters.

At about this time a near disaster occurred, as the Saints realized that most of George Staheli's family was still inside the fort. (George Staheli had been attempting to rake wood out of the creek's channel and did not realize that the fort was being evacuated.) Hamblin headed the rescue even as the back part of the fort was falling away "piece by piece." Judd, Hamblin, and others waded through the water and were able to get to the Stahelis in time while George Staheli attempted to take his wife through the wild current north of the fort, but "the depth and swiftness of the water prevented him" from escaping from the rapidly disintegrating structure.[35] Hamblin, a large, tall man came to the rescue. "I then took the sick woman on my back and by the help of Bro Young and the roap conveyed hur safe to the shore," he wrote.[36] According to one account, Hamblin nearly lost his own life while trying to save Sophia Staheli. Just as he and Sophia were nearly safe, the pole at the fort on which the rope was tied "gave way and tore the rope loose." Someone was able to seize Sophia even as Hamblin was being swept away in the rushing water. A quick-thinking Indian threw a rope to Hamblin who seized it and the Santa Clara men dragged him to safety.[37]

In Hamblin's autobiography, he tells the story somewhat differently. Midway through the most dangerous part of the rescue, Sophia Staheli's arms pressed so heavily on his throat that he was nearly strangled. "It was a critical moment, for if I let go the rope we were sure to be lost, as the water was surging against me," he wrote. However, he was able to persevere, and reached safety "to the great joy of the husband and children."[38] The other Staheli children were rescued by other men, with great difficulty. Just after the Stahelis were saved, the entire south wall of the fort collapsed into the water.[39]

According to Mary Judd, Jacob Hamblin nearly lost his life while bringing his own wife to safety: "[B]r Jacob Hamblin came near going down to[o] trying to git out his wife."[40]

John R. Young reports another close shave for Hamblin (or another version of the fall described above). After the rescue of the people in the fort and the wheat, Hamblin asked Young to hold the lantern while he moved some cordwood to higher ground. While he was engaged in this task, the section of earth on which he stood fell into the river. Young shouted for help, and Joseph Knight came running with the rope they had used to evacuate the fort. As Young tried to direct the light down the bank to where Hamblin was struggling to hold onto "snapping roots," Knight made a noose and threw it down, lassoing Jacob with it.[41] Hamblin seized the rope and Knight and Young pulled him from certain death, for, as Young later wrote, "no man could have lived long in that torrent of mud and water."[42]

By three a.m. Sunday morning, the fort had been entirely swept away, along with the schoolhouse, and seven houses close to the fort.[43] There has been a local tradition that a wall of the fort still stood, and Jacob Hamblin used the rock from the wall of the fort to build his new home. However, in his February 2, 1862, letter to George A. Smith, Hamblin convincingly contradicts this: "by the next morning thare was not a single rock of the old fort to be seen but a chanel whare it once stood, [and] the schoolhouse and 7 other houses above the Fort had [also] disappeared and in their place roar now the wild torrents of the river." The Santa Clara orchards, vineyards, and Brother Dodge's prize nursery were also entirely gone.

As the sun arose on Sunday morning, January 19, the Santa Clara residents, camping out in the rain at Jacob Hamblin's stone corral at the top of the bluff, must have witnessed a heartbreaking panorama of apocalyptic grandeur. Their fort, town, orchards, and vineyards were entirely gone. In their place was a river "one hundred and fifty yards wide the banks on the north side of the creek 25 feet high."[44]

Many accounts of the flood emphasize how the old town of Fort Clara was washed away, and even old settlers, along with the Swiss newcomers, had to make a new beginning. The flood "changed the prospects and circumstances of all to a great extent, reducing the first settlers to almost the position of new beginners," writes James Bleak.[45] After the flood, the area even looked different, aside from the obvious lack of the fort and schoolhouse, homes, and orchards; the flood "gave a very different aspect to the country."[46] This transition from destruction to new beginnings possibly provides a reason for the persistent misdating of the flood to January 1. It may have simply felt right that the flood should occur when the old year was ending and the new year was beginning.[47]

Erastus Snow, in St. George, wrote to Brigham Young in March that because of the flood and rains, "the whole country seemed as if the bottom had fallen out." Cattle had become mired on "the high black ridges," and grass, which cattle depended upon, had bleached.[48]

In the days and weeks following the flood, the men and women of Santa Clara set to work to provide themselves and their families with dry clothing, hot meals, and temporary homes as the forty-day rain continued. Priscilla Hamblin believed in a gospel of work, and now it was time to practice it. "There was no time for self-pity," Priscilla later said. "There was work to be done and much of it; shelters were made, and the mothers had to make them pleasant to live in."[49]

Priscilla had just washed and ironed the clothes of the large Hamblin family on Friday and had put them on a rack on a side wall inside the fort to dry. In the rush of evacuation, her clothes were forgotten and washed away. Later Priscilla said, "I only owned two aprons [at the time of the flood], I was wearing the old one, and my good one was buried in the red Santa Clara flood."[50]

Some things that had washed downriver were recovered. St. George resident Robert Gardner helped salvage pieces of Jacob's grist mill, four miles down the Clara.[51] Apparently, Jacob, Zadok Judd, and Walter Dodge also recovered a good portion of their peach trees and gardens.[52]

Though the great rains and flood were a harsh welcome to the new Swiss arrivals at Santa Clara, they were actually somewhat fortunate. "On the 'lower flat,'" Mary Ann Hafen wrote, "we were untouched by the flood."[53] However, their new dams and ditches were entirely washed away and had to be rebuilt.[54]

Remarkably, no lives were lost during the "big washout" at Santa Clara, though Hamblin, Judd, Solomon Chamberlain and his children, and the Stahelis all had brushes with death. Elsewhere, the Lee family at Fort Harmony, about forty-five miles away, was not so fortunate, as John D. Lee lost two children to a cave-in just as they were preparing to finally evacuate the fort.[55] The survival of the entire Santa Clara community in the face of a sudden, violent challenge from nature is a tribute to the cohesiveness of the little Mormon town, which had recently received a major, quite alien infusion of population—many of whom could not even speak English.

Nevertheless, the great flood took its toll; a few people who were already ill obviously would not have been helped by the unavoidable exposure to cold, rain, and flood waters of the Clara. There were a few later deaths that were attributed to the flood. John Terry Young, the two-year-old son of John R. and Albina Terry Young, died on February 22, 1862, and John senior wrote, "During the damp and rainy weather that accompanied the flood, our little son, John T., took the croup, and after several days of terrible suffering, died. This was our first life sorrow, and the blow was a heavy one."[56] Sophia Barbara Staheli, the mother of the child born in Fort Clara on Christmas day, died of typhoid fever on June 3, 1862.[57] Her son wrote, "Barbara was never well after the night of the flood."[58]

Rachel Hamblin died four years later, in 1865, and family traditions report that her health, already poor, was worse after the flood.[59] Caroline Beck Knight, the wife of Samuel Knight, likewise had poor health before the flood and was eight months pregnant when it occurred. She bore her second child, Leonora, on February 8, while all the Santa Clara settlers were undoubtedly living in crude shelters of some sort.

The forty-day rain may have continued up through the date of the birth. Caroline died eight years later, at the age of thirty-nine, and the flood may have worsened her sickly condition.

There is a persistent tradition that Brigham Young had advised the Santa Clara residents to move to higher ground before the flood. In Andrew Karl Larson's account of the flood in Santa Clara, he quotes the LDS Church's monumental daily scrapbook, the Journal History, which in this case draws from the more primary "History of Brigham Young." The Journal History has Brigham Young giving this advice on May 26, 1861, when he visited Santa Clara. This tradition suggests that old Santa Clara was destroyed partly as the result of the heedlessness and disobedience of the settlers there.[60]

However, in the Journal History, the statement by Young is written in pencil, while the main text is typed. The advice is thus a later addition to the Journal History. In the actual "History of Brigham Young," the sentence on Young advising the move is not there.[61]

Other sources for this tradition do not come from Santa Clara residents. In his January 20, 1862, letter to the Deseret News, St. George resident Jesse W. Crosby records this advice, but Crosby was not in Santa Clara when Brigham Young visited the community in May 1861.[62] James Bleak, another St. George resident, stated that "President Brigham Young in his visit...advised the people of Santa Clara to move to higher ground."[63] However, this statement appears in the 1859 section of Bleak's work, and Brigham Young did not visit Dixie in 1859 but in 1861. The text in "Annals" continues, giving Brigham Young's well-known prophecy of St. George, which occurred in 1861. So Bleak was probably referring to Young's 1861 visit to Santa Clara, and, as we have seen, there is no record of a warning from Young in the "History of Brigham Young."

In addition, at one point, Brigham Young declared Fort Clara to be "the best Fort in Utah."[64] It would be hard to imagine him praising it in such glowing terms if he felt it had been built in a dangerous place.

My conclusion is that Brigham Young did not advise the Santa Clara Saints to abandon Fort Clara, though this tradition came to be accepted by some who were not early residents of Santa Clara.

Undoubtedly, the Santa Clara flood also impacted the Paiute Indian community, not only near Fort Clara but up and down the Santa Clara River. As has been noted, the Paiutes were known for their remarkable agricultural accomplishments,[65]

and one wonders how the flood affected their farms and villages. However, the Paiutes were not writing history, and their fate during and after the great flood is not recorded in any substantial way. There are only a few references to Indians during this time period.

John Staheli recalled that when he and the others first settled at Santa Clara there were about three hundred Indians camped by the creek below the fort. For a time "they were troublesome" but Staheli and the other settlers were "fortunate ... having Jacob Hamblin with us, since he was able to assist us in settling most of our troubles. However at times we had unpleasant encounters. Often Indians would come begging for bread and would not believe that we could not supply them, even when assured we had neither bread nor flour for ourselves."[66] The white settlers did indeed undergo great difficulties in the months and years after the flood, but this reference suggests that the Paiutes may have been placed in an even worse position.

The Swiss settlers were alarmed when the Paiutes in the Indian village burned their wickiups throughout December, and Samuel Knight explained to them that Indians were dying, and the living were trying to ward off the ghosts of evil men who had recently died. This describes the Paiutes before the flood, and may indicate an epidemic.[67]

Sometimes Mormons mentioned Indian memories of a previous comparable flood. Chapman Duncan in Virgin City wrote, "The Indians say their fathers told them there was a similar flood in this country many years ago."[68]

These few references tell us very little about how the Paiutes were impacted by the flood. Common sense argues that it must have had a devastating effect on their agriculture. If the Santa Clara changed from a creek you could step across to a river twenty-five feet deep and a hundred fifty yards across, then the Paiutes' traditional fields and gardens, which they depended on at certain times of the year, must have been swept away in many places.

Another serious blow to the Paiutes and their gardens was the appearance of sizable groups of new settlers in Santa Clara and St. George at about the same time as the rains and great flood, as has been discussed previously.[69] The great flood, combined with the major influx of new Mormon settlers with their need for irrigation water and land for cattle grazing, must have been a major catastrophe for the Paiutes.

There is one piece of evidence showing the devastation that the flood caused for the Santa Clara Paiutes, a heartbreaking story of loss of Paiute cultural and family ties by a child adopted by Mormons. In early 1862, Jacob rode into St. George with a five-year-old Paiute girl sitting ahead of him on his saddle. Her parents, who had lost everything in the flood, "desired to sell the child to obtain necessities." Eliza Jane Dykes Burgess, wife of Hyrum Burgess, immediately wanted the girl, and Hyrum bought her for fifty dollars. The Paiute parents would come to visit the girl at first, but she would hide when they visited (either because she resented having been sold, or because she had become acclimated to her new family), and they eventually stopped coming.[70] Like many adopted Paiute children, she entirely entered white culture.

The 1862 flood, though one of the worst floods in nineteenth-century Utah history, was in some ways typical of the Mormon pioneer experience in southern Utah and Nevada, though the Santa Clara Saints were fortunate in that they apparently were not periodically subject to ruinous flooding, as was the case in the Virgin River settlements.[71] Joseph W. Young wrote in 1868, "The floods come now and then, and wash away these rich bottoms, carrying down with its foaming currents houses, corrals, vineyards, and all one has, and the toiling man feels almost disheartened."[72]

It must have been especially disheartening, for "desert saints," to see the more fertile bottomland swept away. Historian W. Paul Reeve interprets these constant destructive floods as a winnowing agent in southern Utah history. Many settlers left, but those who stayed were firmly committed to their mission.[73] Ann Woodbury wrote of the town Shuneburg, as late as 1891, "If they ever had any land to farm worth speaking of, the floods of the last few years have taken it away, leaving the people with but poor prospects for the future; they certainly deserve credit for their staying qualities."[74] Floods tested the "staying qualities" of the saints in Santa Clara, and in most of southern Utah.

Two towns that Jacob would later help settle, Kanab and Pahreah, in Utah, as well as the Little Colorado settlements in Arizona, would also be subject to periodic destructive floods.[75]

14

"The Rocks Stand Up Biding Defiance to Wind and Weather in All Manner of Shapes"

Circling the Grand Canyon, 1862

Documentation is meager on the Santa Clara settlers' recovery from the flood. Jacob and his family undoubtedly participated in the day-to-day struggle for a return to normalcy—rebuilding houses, gathering and preparing food, combing the retreating waters of the Santa Clara and Virgin for trees, implements, pieces of buildings. Hamblin must have reclaimed a number of trees, for he had a substantial peach orchard when Brigham Young visited Santa Clara the following September.

His first major task after the rain and the flooding stopped was to build a house for his substantial family—possibly three wives (Rachel, Priscilla, and Eliza), his children, and adopted Indian children. The new Hamblin house was built on the northwestern edge of what was then the new community of Santa Clara (now dominated, at least numerically, by the Swiss), southeast of the site of the old fort. This home still stands, a major historical landmark in Santa Clara, a substantial two-story stone building, built against a hill. On the first floor, there is a vestibule/front room with dining table and chairs; to the left and right of this are Rachel's and Priscilla's rooms with beds and matching fireplaces. In the back is a room in which food and implements were stored.

On the second floor is a large family and workroom, with a spinning wheel. Evidently this was used as a community meeting room, a school, and a church meeting place. Behind this is a bedroom for the Hamblin children.

There is little contemporary documentation for the building of Jacob's Santa Clara house. However, a number of people who lived in Santa Clara and St. George remembered working on the building. A biography of carpenter David Canfield portrays him as the main builder, moving with his family to Santa Clara while the house was being constructed, hauling timber from Pine Valley, and quarrying rock with his sons.[1] Another Santa Clara resident, Luke Syphus, has also been identified as one of the main builders of the structure. He turned to stone masonry as a trade after the

14.1. The Jacob Hamblin home in Santa Clara, built after the 1862 flood, still standing. With unidentified persons in front. From Andrews, *The Hamlin Family* (1902).

flood, and in his diary, he wrote, "I laid up the walls of the Jacob Hamblin home in Santa Clara."[2] It was also reported that Elias Morris worked on Jacob's home.[3]

Some believe that building the home was a community project, as it was used as a meeting place in the years following the flood. Rosina Brachman wrote, "My father helped quarrie the rocks for the house of Jacob Hamblin. In return for his work they gave him cattle."[4] "They" could mean the Hamblin family, the Canfield family as contractors, or the Santa Clara community.

On March 22 and 23, the "first conference of the Southern Utah Mision," as James Bleak termed it, was held in a bowery at St. George, with Apostles Erastus Snow and Orson Pratt presiding.[5] Jacob spoke on the second day of this historic conference, and "very interestingly related some of his experience among the Lamanites. He exhorted the people to be united that great good might result."[6]

In September Brigham Young visited Dixie again, and on the thirteenth he was in Santa Clara. He and his entourage walked around the settlement, viewed the effects of the flood, and inspected Hamblin's peach orchard, which would produce a thousand bushels of fruit that year.[7]

Hamblin may have accompanied the Young party home, for on September 30 he was in Salt Lake City, and he and George A. Smith discussed Indian matters with James Duane Doty, superintendent of Indian affairs since the previous December, and Governor Stephen S. Harding.[8]

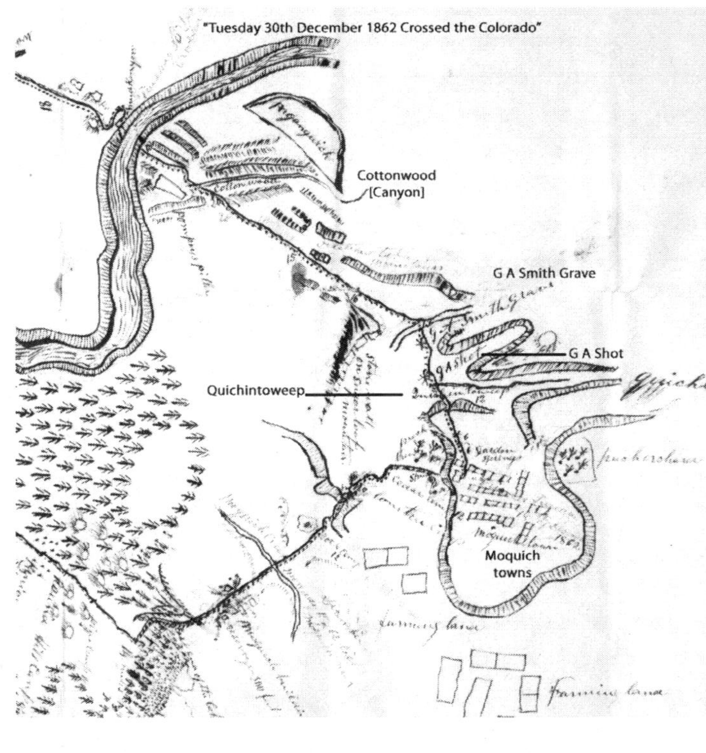

14.2. Map of 1862 expedition, by John Steele, detail. Steele notes Quichintoweep, where George Smith Jr. was shot, and his grave about ten miles north. Also marked are the Crossing of the Fathers, Navajo ("Cottonwood") Canyon, and "Moquichtown" (probably Sichomovi). Courtesy LDS Church History Library, MS 15320.

Brigham Young, during his September visit to Dixie, told Hamblin that "it was time for him to extend his labors among the Lamanites." He wanted him to visit the Hopi mesas again, but by a different route—he should cross the Colorado south of St. George, at the Grand Wash, "and explore the country in that direction; with the view of finding a more feasible route than the one we had before traveled."[9] The Crossing of the Fathers was not a practical wagon route to Arizona, so Young was looking elsewhere. This passage shows the symbiosis between Young and Hamblin; it also shows how closely connected were Hamblin's roles as Indian missionary and explorer in the Southwest. The two men were preparing the way for the Mormon settlement of Arizona and Mexico.

The foundational document for this expedition is an excellent diary by forty-one year old Mormon Battalion veteran John Steele.[10] A native of Ireland, he had been called to the Iron Mission, Parowan, in 1850, and later became one of the early settlers of Las Vegas. When that mission was abandoned, he relocated in Toquerville. His son wrote that John stood "about 5 ft. 8 in. tall, weighed about 150 lbs.," and was "hard and resilient as a steel spring. He never seemed to tire. He had a fiery temper, and keen sense of right and wrong, and the man never lived that he feared." He practiced a number of occupations in his lifetime: sailor, soldier, mason, shoemaker, and surveyor.[11]

This journey around the Grand Canyon was another epic accomplishment, as Jacob and company set out over northwestern and north-central Arizona without maps (unless he had the Ives maps, published in 1861) and often without Indian guides. Steele, author of the one diary we have for the trip, later wrote, "This has been one of the hardest trips I ever took."[12] These early trips across the Colorado were grueling, plodding accomplishments in which the participants were often desperate for water or food or both. Simply the number of horses that dropped dead during this trip, exhausted, thirsty, and famished, shows how grim the conditions were. In addition, this was a winter journey that was often in high mountainous country, and the cold must have been severe.

Steele blamed Hamblin for the hardships of the journey, writing: "We were nearly starved to death by the improvident management of Jacob Hamblin." He felt that Hamblin should have required them to bring more food; in addition, Hamblin always had Indians traveling with them, which further depleted food supplies. Finally, he had cached food at the Grand Wash on the Colorado on the way out, but on the return crossed the river at the Crossing of the Fathers instead.[13] My personal view is that Steele underestimated how difficult it was to prepare for these trips across the Colorado. They teetered on the edge of disaster because the territory was often forbidding, and because these early trips were explorations. One perpetual challenge these missionaries faced was obtaining supplies for the trip home at the Hopi mesas. The Hopis were extremely hospitable, but seemed unwilling to trade for food to help travelers, possibly because they had no excess food themselves. In addition, given the difficulty of the journey via the Grand Wash, Jacob may have felt it wiser to travel home via the comparatively well-known Crossing of the Fathers route.

The participants of the expedition were given a fairly typical Mormon mission call. On the morning of October 26, Hamblin spoke at the second St. George conference, recounting his first visit to the Hopi mesas. He apparently mentioned, or stated obliquely, that Brigham Young wanted him to travel there again. Apostle Orson Pratt followed Hamblin and said that he wanted twenty or twenty-five men to be ready to go on an expedition to the Hopis with Hamblin, with the target date of departure November 17.

The conference participants were given all of lunch time to mull over this possible call, then returned to conference for the afternoon session, only to hear their names read out from the pulpit as members of the company: Jacob Hamblin, as president, Taylor Crosby, Lucius Fuller, Frank Hamblin, Ira Hatch, Zadok K. Judd, and Joseph Knight, from Santa Clara; Thales Haskell from Pinto; Jehiel McConnell, William Stewart, and Thomas Walker from Cedar City; Nathan C. Tenney and William B. Maxwell from Grafton; John Steele from Toquerville; Samuel Newton Adair from Washington;[14] James Pearce, William P. Lytle, and Alexander McIntire from St. George; and Benjamin Redd from Harmony.

14.3. William Bailey Maxwell in Nauvoo Legion uniform, about 1865. He holds a sword in his left hand and places his right hand on the Book of Mormon. A founder of the outlying southern Utah town, Short Creek, he accompanied Jacob on many of his expeditions and married his daughter Maryette. Courtesy Charles H. Maxwell.

John A. Lytle of St. George and Isaac Riddle of Pinto were called to help bring a baggage wagon and a boat to the Colorado.[15]

From other sources, we know that Hamblin's adopted Indian son Albert was part of the company, as well as Mosiah Hancock, Hiram Judd, and Thomas J. Clark.[16] Hamblin and Hancock also mention James Andrus.[17] Andrew Gibbons went with the expedition as far as the Colorado.[18]

Among the new names in this list is Illinois-born William Bailey Maxwell, a Mormon Battalion veteran. Now about forty-one years of age, he had lived in Payson and Santaquin in Utah County, and worked to negotiate peace with the Utes at those places. Brigham Young had sent him to Dixie in 1862, and he soon began ranching at Short Creek, near the present Utah-Arizona border. Maxwell would have many dealings with Hamblin in the upcoming years, and in fact would take Hamblin's daughter Maryetta as a plural wife in 1867.[19]

Also notable is Ammon Tenney's father, Nathan, a forty-five-year-old native of New York, formerly a bishop at San Bernardino, who was now following his son to the Hopi mesas.[20] James Andrus would become a major military leader in the upcoming Navajo–Black Hawk wars.

The missionaries were given a list of items that each man would need for the journey, and this list gives a valuable perspective on the material culture of these early trips across the Colorado. Each man was to take a "riding animal" (usually a horse) and a "pack animal" (usually a mule) with pack saddle; a lasso and a pair of hobbles would be needed for both animals. There were no lightweight sleeping bags in 1862; instead, each man was told to take "a comfortable supply of blankets." For defense and hunting, each man should have a revolver or light rifle or both, with at least twelve rounds of ammunition for each gun. For food, the main staple would be seventy-five pounds of flour or "hard bread." Then, twelve pounds of dried beef or bacon was required, as well as twelve pounds of beans and a pound of salt. Some luxuries were recommended: "Tea, sugar, Coffee, molasses and as many comforts as each person may deem necessary to make himself comfortable." Tea, tobacco, coffee, and alcohol, in moderation, were well within the nineteenth-century Mormon Church's interpretation of the Word of Wisdom, though individual views of this revelation varied.[21] Required implements included a two-quart canteen, a cup, a knife and scabbard, and a tin plate.[22]

The company met in St. George on November 16 and 17 to receive instruction from Apostles Amasa Lyman, Orson Pratt, and Erastus Snow and to be set apart on their mission.[23] The apostles told the company "that this was one of the greatest Misions that ever had ben given to any set of men," wrote Hamblin. "Bro Erastus Snow said thare is .24. of you jest as meny besides the Lamanit [Albert]...as John saw around the Throne of God. Whatsoever you attempt to doe being you-nited you shal acomplish."[24]

Hamblin then asked the company to pack up as soon as they could, and on the afternoon of the seventeenth, they traveled down to the Virgin and camped there. The party numbered twenty-five men and fifty animals, though at least three men would turn back at the Colorado.[25]

The company then split into the main group, in front, and the "boat group," behind. On the morning of the eighteenth, Hamblin sent the main company ahead and waited for the boat. Crossing rivers was always a challenge in the Old West, and while the boat company was crossing the Virgin River with a wagon, "the taem [team] dropt in to the quick sand," and the men had to unharness the horses, extricate them from the quicksand, and carry the load across by hand. The next day, the boat group "let down our wagon into a deep rocky canon withe our lasows and [pursued] our journey." But when they came to camp, "the wagon was broak." On the twentieth, Hamblin wrote, the wagon "was lashed up with cow hide and brought on. We had much dificilt[y] labor and toil. We got the..." At this point, Hamblin's diary unfortunately breaks off.

The missionaries were now facing one of the true hinterlands in the Southwest, the Grand Wash Cliffs Wilderness in the modern Grand Canyon–Parashant National Monument. The westernmost area in the Arizona Strip, this represents a transition between the Colorado Plateau to the south and the Basin and Range country to the northwest. It is arid and mountainous, but there are springs in the area, and Jacob's Paiute informants directed him along a route in which water would be accessible.

If we compare Steele's map and diary with the later road to Pearce's Ferry, we can perhaps approximate the route Jacob and company took in 1862.[26] After crossing the Virgin, they probably went south via the Mokaac Wash, then came to modern Wolf Hole. On the nineteenth, the main company climbed a "rocky kanyon" and reached "the tops of the mountains," where they camped and spent the next day.[27] This is probably the area near Mustang Knoll.

On the twenty-first, they passed the high point of the mountain and began descending into Hobble Canyon. They came to "Canes Springs," west of Hobble Canyon, the following day. From there they could follow Pocum Wash south. Two days later, they came to the Grand Wash, with the Grand Wash Cliffs rising to the east, which served as a direct highway to the Colorado. After passing Seven Springs, they finally reached the river, just west of the western termination of the Grand Canyon. Here they camped.[28] A road could be made on this wash, they concluded. The wagon with the boat was still behind them, so they had to wait overnight for it.

On the twenty-fifth, the party looked for a good place to cross the river, and found one about a mile from their camp. At noon the boat arrived, and Steele, Bill Stewart, and Mosiah Hancock "set to work to fit her for the water" and were done by sunset. Hamblin, Steele, and Isaac Riddle got into it and enjoyed an experimental sail.

The next day, a historic event took place: the first successful, practical crossing of the upper Colorado by boat, with animals, in modern times. At the place of crossing, they unpacked their animals and Steele got into the boat, leading his horses into the water, and it "was then pushed into the River and Andrew Gibbons and Broth Riddle rowed the Boat. We soon landed on the other side. All the rest of our Horses was driven in and swam after my horse making 52 in all."[29] The boat was used for luggage, and the animals were able to swim, which would become a standard pattern.[30] Andrew Gibbons, stripped to the waist, helped guide all the animals across the river.[31]

By two p.m., the exploring party was safely landed on the southeast side of the Colorado. Andrew Gibbons and "the boat Company" started back to the settlements,[32] taking a letter from Jacob to Erastus Snow in which he stated that he had received news that Tutsegabits, on a mission to the Indians, had preached to "a small band of the Opaches"[33]—probably Hualapai Indians, who were sometimes referred to as Apaches.[34] Jacob also wrote that "The Piutes have so far given a very truthful account of the country so far as they knew," which shows that Jacob and his friends were following Paiute directions and trails to the Colorado.

The next morning the group started (counterintuitively) west, traveling over very rough places, "rocky points and breaks of the mountains." While ascending one of these points, Hamblin's horse lost its footing, fell over backwards, and rolled three times. However, the missionaries were able to right it, and Hamblin, unhurt, rode on.

The group turned east to follow a bend of the river and arrived at a camping place at noon. They turned their horses loose to drink from the Colorado; Steele felt that this would be a good place for a ferry, as there was a "large wide wash of a kanyon" which led "into the tops of the rolling upland." Logically, this would have been Grapevine Wash—on Steele's map, he writes, "8 miles grape vines." They camped at a spring some eight miles up the canyon.[35]

On the twenty-eighth, they traveled east up the canyon, camping at "Grass Springs." The next day, the group mounted ridges, saw a valley to the east, came upon a camp of Shivwits Paiutes and convinced one to accompany them as a guide "through this broken country."[36] Hancock described these Shivwits Indians:

> Their heads were quite shaggy, and they spoke a sort of Piute dialect. They were low in their deportment, and many of them were quite badly deformed. They were naked, and when they first got sight of us, would run like wild deer until stopped by the guides. They would stop and look at us until, by chance, we might drop a cracker, then they would scramble for it. They were not farmers; all they seemed to comprehend was to keep out of our way, and to eat cedar berries. I saw no other food among them. There were many of them not far from the river.[37]

On the thirtieth, while surmounting a divide, the missionaries saw a mountain far off to the east—the San Francisco Peaks?—that the previous Hopi missionaries said was near the Hopi mesas.

The Mormons had now entered the territory of the Hualapais, or Walapais, "people of the tall pine," who inhabited a hundred-mile territory south of the Grand Canyon, extending to the Bill Williams River and San Francisco Peaks. The Hualapais spoke a language related to that of the Yumas and Mohaves at the Colorado on the west, and the Havasupai and Yavapai to the east. Their lands were arid and diverse—forests at high elevations contrasted with desert valleys and basins. Though there were some streams that emptied into the Colorado in Hualapai land, its general aridity prevented extensive farming. However, wildlife—antelope, deer, rabbits, and rodents—was plentiful, and the Hualapais were skillful hunters. After the discovery of gold in Prescott in 1863, there would be significant incursions of whites into this area, and a "Walapai War," with miners, settlers, and U.S. troops, which lasted from 1865 to 1868, resulted, in which the Hualapai were finally forced to surrender.[38]

As the missionaries continued to travel east in broken, mountainous country the following day, they came to a place that had good running water and a peach tree.[39] According to Samuel Adair, even though there was only one peach tree, before leaving Hamblin said, "Let's call this place Peach Springs."[40] This is apparently the modern Peach Springs, the main town in the Hualapai Indian Reservation, on Route

66 about fifty miles northeast of Kingman. Hamblin's name for the place survived. This would be the last running water the missionaries would see for nearly two weeks.

Soon the missionaries met some Indians, presumably Hualapais. One of their leaders, according to Steele,

> made us a long speech; layed down his bow and told us that we might come in from all directions and pass and repass, lengthways of his bow, and they would be friendly with us. He finished his speech and sung us a song of his very best, which was certainly very interesting to us, for we could not understand one word.

Possibly the Shivwits guide could do some rough translation. Indians were often skillful at communicating through gestures and maps drawn in the ground.

After this, "Many more sermons were preached" and were "sanctioned by shaking hands and a good piece of cake."[41]

The next day was snowy, windy, and very cold. The missionaries passed from mountainous country to a stretch of desert, and the day after traveled through thirty miles of "rolling prairie," camping at night near "Tutsegabits's spring" in a beautiful country filled with pine and oak.[42] The men were expecting to meet Enos at this place, but found that he had gone off hunting. However, his wife visited the camp and was happy to see the Mormon company.

At this point, the Shivwits guide refused to go any farther, as he did not know the territory they were approaching.[43] However, he knew that there was no water in the land ahead, for about four days' travel, and he predicted that if the Mormons tried to continue eastward, they would die in the desert![44] Having shared these cheerful prognostications, he departed, and the missionaries were left on their own. Jacob and his friends looked to the east, and decided they could reach the San Francisco foothills, so continued on.

They were now entering the Coconino Plateau, in the southwest part of the Colorado Plateau, an area in which high plateaus with forests of pine and juniper alternated with deserts. (Steele's map shows them traveling among trees in this part of the journey.) On December 4, the Mormons traveled over "high points of rolling spurs of mountains," among pines and oak, in a southeasterly direction. They came upon a herd of antelope and killed one, which was "quite a treat," Steele wrote.[45] However, this fresh meat acted as a laxative, "which caused some uneasiness to some of the Boys through the night."[46]

The next day, they had gone three days without water—the Shivwits' prophecy of four days without water was proving true. Mosiah Hancock had broken his canteen when a "wild mare" he was riding collided with a tree, and he tells a vivid anecdote of begging for water from his companions. As no one else had much water, he put some pebbles in his mouth and soldiered on.[47] He remembered praying late one night, then hearing a voice, seeing a light, and finding "a great many holes in the Limestone full of water."

> I thanked the Lord and took a drink I went and placed my hand on Jacob Hamblin and he was awake in an instant. All the camp were in a profound slumber apparently. We awoke several so as to get the Canteens filled before the horses were taken to befowl the water.[48]

Eventually, they came to snow and were able to melt it to drink. They now had a good view of the "Cohoneny, or Cosninas," Mountain, modern San Francisco Peaks, covered with snow. This massive volcanic mountain is a prominent feature of northeastern Arizona, a holy place to the Hopi, Navajo, and other nearby tribes. Its highest peak, Humphreys Peak, rises to 12,643 feet above sea level (though only 6,000 feet above the surrounding country, as it is on the Colorado Plateau), and is the highest mountain in Arizona.

The following day, after covering twenty-two miles over more rolling prairie, they camped without water in "Rock Canyon," and on the seventh they traveled eight miles to "Round Hill" camp, where they melted snow to water their animals, which were "jaded" from exhaustion and lack of good water. The next two days they traveled through "beautiful pine groves," then camped at the foot of San Francisco Mountain.[49] Wilford Woodruff summarized this part of the journey with an eye to Mormon expansion, writing that the missionaries "passed through a vary good Country for a settlement well timbered with tall white pine also white oak & Cedar good soil & grass a[nd] plenty of gaim such as wild Turkies, Deer, Antilope also wild Honey."[50]

The next day the company traveled east eight miles and killed an antelope. They had seen thousands of them, Steele says. They woke up on the eleventh to find four of their horses gone, and wasted half a day tracking them down. They packed and had traveled only four miles when a major snowstorm overtook them, which kept them in camp the following day. Hamblin and others went on a hunt but could shoot nothing.

On the thirteenth, the storm had abated, and they left the San Francisco Peaks area, traveling northeast through "beautiful looking country covered with volcanic rock and gravel." After many days in a wilderness, Steele wrote, they were now entering a desert.

As the Mormon company descended toward a valley, they found "ruins of ancient grandeur" that Steele ascribed to ancestors of the Hopis.[51] The party traveled twenty-five miles and arrived at "Moquis Creek"—the first running water they had seen since Peach Springs. This was apparently the Little Colorado River.[52] The company waved their hats, gave three cheers, and watered their thirsty animals. Hancock remembers striking the Little Colorado near the Black Falls:

> We were tollerable thirsty. Some of the Boys Cryed when they saw the water and some lay down and drank till they belched it up again—A couple horses here drank to much and died—one got in the stream with its pack on. I secured mine and washed them and gave them a little by little.[53]

However, this water brought bad luck to Jacob, as his horse wandered into quicksand and drowned in the night.[54] Quicksand was a characteristic of the Little Colorado that Mormon settlers would later experience all too frequently. Ives had taken this same approximate route from the San Francisco Peaks to the Hopi mesas a few years earlier, in 1858, and wrote of the Little Colorado, "The banks and bottom are composed of quicksand, and we have been unable to find a ford."[55] The military company finally crossed the river only with great difficulty.

The Mormons were lucky to reach the Little Colorado at the Black Falls because this was a natural crossing. They rested at the creek the next day, and on the fifteenth, set out in a northeasterly direction again.

Ives, after telling how their journey had worn down their mules till they were nothing but "slightly animated skeletons," described the country just east of the Little Colorado as "a flat table-land" with occasional canyons and low bluffs:

> The scene was one of utter desolation. Not a tree nor a shrub broke its monotony. The edges of the mesas were flaming red, and the sand threw back the sun's rays in a yellow glare. Every object looked hot and dry and dreary. The animals began to give out. We knew that it was desperate to keep on, but felt unwilling to return, and forced the jaded brutes to wade through the powdery impalpable dust for fifteen miles. The country, if possible, grew worse.[56]

He did, however, note that the desert was not devoid of life, for that night scorpions, spiders, rattlesnakes, and centipedes emerged from their daytime places of shelter to join the military party in their campground.

The Mormon horses and mules must have also become "animated skeletons" by this point. On this day's journey, Bill Maxwell's horse "gave out" and they had to leave it behind. The next day they ascended a rocky area and came to "sand mountains," where another horse dropped dead. It is remarkable that these horses failed immediately after a rest day with plentiful water. (Of course, the Little Colorado water is notoriously akaline.)

On the seventeenth, the missionaries followed a winding road up a mountain, traveling east and southeast. They could now see a large mountain on the Colorado, which Steele called Pagangwich Kibe (probably Navajo Mountain), and the mountains near the Hopi mesas.

The next day, after traveling over "rolling ridges," they saw Oraibi "standing upon a high prominent point of rocks."[57] As they traveled the final seven miles to the village, they realized that the Hopis had seen them and were mobilizing for a battle. Navajos had recently stolen many flocks of sheep and goats from them, and they at first mistook the missionaries for their enemies. However, Thales Haskell went ahead and "as soon as they saw him they commenced shaking hands with him and fear gave place to joy among them," Steele wrote. The missionaries ascended the mesa to Oraibi, and the Hopis gave them *piki* bread and water, showed them a house where they could lay their packs, and invited them to visit their workshops.

The Mormons found themselves in a familiar position—short on supplies before their trip back to southern Utah. They sought to trade with the Hopis the next day, but once again found that the Indians would rather give a little food than sell it. Due in part to the thefts of the Navajos—which were caused in their turn by the invasions of the U.S. Army and New Mexico volunteers—some forty-six Hopis had died of starvation in the last two years. The Mormons were able to obtain only a little food to take with them on the long, grueling homeward march to Utah.

They were thinking of returning immediately, but the Hopis told them that they were observing a festival and invited the Mormons participate. So the missionaries stayed at Oraibi from December 18 to 20, to celebrate "a feasting and dancing time," correlated with the new moon, intended to bring down snow from the heavens.[58] This may have been the Soyal Ceremony, which celebrates the winter solstice. In this rite, kachinas, supernatural spirits, are welcomed back to the mesas for a half year, and Hopis dance in kachina costumes. The sun is prevented from leaving the sky, and rites intended to bring a bountiful agricultural year are performed.[59]

On the nineteenth, the Hopis spent the night "running to and fro," and the Mormons were asked not to watch, so some spent the night in a cellar, while others stayed in the pack room with windows covered. On the last day, the Mormons could enter any house in the town, and "we were presented with victuals and enjoyed ourselves as well as could be expected," wrote Steele.

The culminating rite of the festival took place now; it was "performed in a large cellar"—the famous Hopi *kiva*—and was esoteric. However, according to Mosiah Hancock, some of the Mormons who had especially impressed the Hopis—Hamblin, Bill Maxwell, John Steele, Ira Hatch, Jehiel McConnell, Thales Haskell, and Hancock—were invited "down into their Council Hall," where they were allowed to witness a "performance," a circular dance of prayer for snow and a bountiful harvest.[60]

In another part of the ritual, the Hopis gave the Mormons a painted stick with feathers tied on—the well-known Hopi prayer stick, *paho*—"and a handfull of consecrated meal which was distributed among us." Then the missionaries, with Thales Haskell leading them, marched through town. This must have been a remarkable sight, Mormons with beards and hats in a Hopi ceremonial procession in old Oraibi. At a certain ritual site outside, the missionaries stuck the pahos in the ground, and each Mormon sprinkled cornmeal on the stick. "This was done to incorporate our faith with theirs," wrote Steele, "in order that snow might come down to water their land. Several of them had their hair wet and meal sprinkled on, in imitation of snow."[61] This *paho* planting may be one of the "blessing rites" at the end of Soyal, in which at dawn families "take the prayer sticks to a shrine at the edge of the mesa, plant them firmly, and draw a cornmeal path from them to the east."[62]

Hamblin invited some of the Hopis to return with him to Utah, but none agreed to do so, due to their religious taboo against crossing the Colorado.[63] Thales Haskell, Jehiel McConnell, and Ira Hatch were left at the mesas to continue long-term missionary work. Unfortunately, Haskell left no diary for this stay at the mesas, but Mormon folklore does preserve one anecdote that reflects Haskell's well-known predilection for strong drink. One day, as they sat on a ledge "pondering their lot," Haskell told his companions that he had decided why the three had been chosen for the Hopi mission.

> He was immediately queried why, to which he replied: "You, Ira Hatch, are more Indian than white anyway having chosen an Indian wife, and you McConnel, have long been known to have more zeal than good judgement, and I was chosen by Brother Young so that the Dixie wine would get one year older."[64]

The Hopis told Hamblin that the Navajos had retreated from the country between the mesas and the Colorado, so he decided to return to Utah via the fairly well-known route of the Crossing of the Fathers, rather than face the uncertainties of the western route again in mid winter. On December 21, Jacob and his group departed. The next day, another massive snowstorm delayed them; they traveled only six miles, then sought shelter in a cave.[65] Then, to their surprise, five Hopis appeared at the mouth of the cave; four of them had decided to return to Utah with the Mormons, with the permission of Hopi leaders.[66] This was surprising, given the tribal taboos on crossing the Colorado, but it heartened the Mormons. The names of the four Hopis were Lye,[67] Ta-wa-ho-we, La-mo-e, and Tu-wa-wat.[68] One of these Hopis was a priest, as it was customary for the Hopis to send a religious leader with any group of Hopis leaving the mesas.[69]

Two days later the party came to the place of George Smith Jr.'s death, Quichintoweep, and the missionaries passed by in a somber mood.

On the twenty-fourth, Steele described another Indian ruin on "Sugar Loaf Mountain," which has been identified as Wildcat Peak. This has natural dikes on it that look man-made, but are actually igneous formations.[70] The missionaries traveled fifteen miles on Christmas day and camped at a "Rock Pool," possibly Rock Basin. They were running short of food, and Hancock wrote that "some of the Boys growled some for the prospect of nothing but corn. Says Jacob 'Boys you will find it a hard matter to starve on raw corn.' He often chewed dried corn as he traveled.

Hamblin sent six men—Steele, Lucius Fuller, James Andrus, Nephi Johnson, Mosiah Hancock, and one unknown person—ahead to find Indians from whom they could trade for provisions.[71] They traveled some twenty miles and met some Paiutes and Navajos who had sheep they could trade for, so they waited for the main party to reach them. The next day, the main party arrived, and they feasted on mutton. Some of the Indians were "friendly to our people," writes Steele, and he was surprised that nothing in camp was stolen. Spaneshanks visited, so this must have been a joyful reunion.[72]

The company set out again on the twenty-seventh, only to be overtaken by the Navajos with more meat. The next day, Steele wrote that they were "in the worst kind of a broken country." He marveled at the danger of the path as it wound around cliffs. "This is one of the worst kind of roads or places for a trail. It takes the best kind of sure footed mules, as one miss step would plunge the horse and pack, at many points, into an abiss of 500 feet." He is probably describing the dangerous descent into and ascent out of Navajo Canyon.

One of the challenges of these expeditions was tensions between men who were being pushed to the limit physically. At about this time, John Steele had a dispute with Tom Walker about flour in a pack, and the men almost drew guns on each other. Hancock wrestled Walker to the ground, James Andrus tackled Steele, and violence was averted.[73]

On the twenty-ninth, the company reached the Crossing of the Fathers. Steele left an astute description of the country:

> This country looks as if mighty eruptions had taken place. The table mountains stand detached from one another all over the country. Some of them more than 500 feet high. There is a regular formation, at other places the hills are rolled up edgeways, at other places as though the ground had sunk. On the banks of the river the mountains stand certainly 1000 feet high.

And, in Steele's holograph diary: "The Rocks stand up biding [bidding] defiance to wind and weather in all manner of shapes. It looks as though Natur had some wonderful freaks about this River."

The group had lost eight horses by the time they reached the Colorado, and the surviving horses were worn out and could not travel quickly.[74] It seems that, despite their best efforts to plan ahead, every time the missionaries traveled back from a trip across the Colorado, their circumstances were grim.

The next day the missionaries began to look for the best ford across the river.[75] Hamblin suspected that the four Hopis would turn back when actually faced with the sight of the dreaded Colorado, so sent their packs and gear across the river by the first missionaries that crossed over. And in fact, the Hopis, looking at the size of the river, were about to turn back to the mesas, but Hamblin pointed out that their gear was already across the river.[76] So they placed some feathered *pahos* at the river's edge and sprinkled consecrated meal on them and on the water, praying that they would not be drowned.[77] When they arrived at especially deep water, they "sprinkled more meal upon the water." They were able to cross the Colorado without mishap, and "thanked the Lord for bringing them over safe."[78] Hamblin sent the six "pioneers" ahead again to try to obtain more food or bring back help to the company.[79]

On December 31, Steele, in the advance company, looked down on the Colorado and saw that it was now "covered with floating ice." He felt greatly relieved that there had been no ice the day before, as he didn't see how the horses could have crossed the river under those conditions. The advance party managed, with great difficulty, to get their horses up a "mud kanyon," and then ascended a rocky path that was almost too steep for horses; "and by winding back and forth about six miles traveling to all points of the compass, we made one mile ahead. Came on through gaps, gorges, kanyons, etc., and at last got fairly under way and made Little Cottonwood Creek."[80]

The main company also had great difficulty at "Mud Canyon," having to lay willows on the trail to allow their animals to cross it. Then they "had to Climb out about 400 feet by Cutting steps in the rocks in a Zigzag Course. Seven of the animals missed the steps & fell down the mountains some 50 feet."[81]

Once they had surmounted the canyon, they could follow the well-worn Ute path. On New Year's Day the six pioneers camped on the Paria.[82] The following day, they found their usual pass up the eastern flank of Buckskin Mountain washed out; they were able to find another pass, but it was muddy, and they had to use butcher knives to cut mud out of the rocks. Then they were able to climb the mountain.[83]

According to Hancock, "some of the animals had given out," and the pioneers decided to leave Mosiah to watch them. Totally without food, he unsuccessfully tracked a wolf, then managed to kill a buzzard, and began to boil it in a stew. Just as the buzzard began to get "a little tender" and Mosiah was looking forward to a real meal, of sorts, Bill Maxwell walked into camp. He immediately begged for some of the food:

> "Mosiah, for God sakes, have you anything to eat? I haven't had a bite for three days!" Said I, "I have a turkey buzzard most done—let us hurry, for I haven't had a bite for three days either." So we downed it, and I did not think there was a stink to it, for I had licked the bowl clean; but when the company came up, some of them wanted to know, "What in hell stank so!"[84]

On January 3, one of Steele's horses "gave out." The five pioneers made it to Kanab Stream—"a beautiful little stream good land and plenty of grass." This is probably the first time that the word Kanab is found in the historical record. Kanab Creek—the name Kanab is from the Paiute *Kanav 'uip*, "willow canyon"[85]—flows from Long Valley down to the Colorado, and had long been an important resource for the Kaibab Paiutes, who raised crops along its banks.

The group then traveled another sixteen miles. The next day, the fourth,[86] they came to Pipe Spring, then traveled fifteen more miles to "Brother Tinney and Maxwell's herd ground" at Short Creek, where another horse dropped by the wayside. Apparently, the five men now made contact with herders bringing in cattle, and initiated rescue efforts for the main party behind them. They were so weak, Steele wrote, that they "could scarcely stick to" their saddles.[87] They arrived at the Tenney and Maxwell ranch houses, and Sister Tenney and Maxwell treated them to a good supper. "After being so long on quarter rations," Steele wrote, "it seemed as though we could not get enough."

On January 5, a rescue party including Lucius Fuller departed eastward.

Hamblin and his group, after getting up the Mud Canyon, finally came to the Paria, where they rested a day and killed crows for food.[88] Then they climbed the road that the six pioneers had dug out with knives on east Buckskin, crossed the mountain, and finally came to Kanab Stream. They were very hungry, as they had eaten their last food the day before.

> And there brother Lucious Fuller...one of our party, in company with two of the brethren met them with fresh horses and provisions. It was a joyful meeting and the brethren gave thanks to God, and their brethren for their kindness, and even the Lamanites [the Hopis] thanked God and the Mormons, and said surely God has heard our prayers and the Mormons love one another.[89]

Fuller had with him a dressed sheep and some bread and flour, and the missionaries were soon feasting on it.[90]

Hancock tells the story with a more folkloric tone. Before Fuller arrived, the company had just decided to kill a horse and were deciding between two sorry-looking candidates.

> They called me to give my judgment. I looked to the southwest, saying, "Let some of us go yonder and get that white-tailed deer." They all looked, but there was a man instead—a man on horseback leading a pack horse. It was Lucas Fuller, popping his lariat with his left hand. He had stopped at the Maxwell ranch, and Sister Maxwell had sent 60 lbs. of flour and a mutton out to us. Luke Fuller being one of the Mormon boys, knew no fear when in danger, and feeling no fatigue when he saw his brethren were suffering, came forth again with his noble help. I can assure all that the 60 lbs. of flour and the sheep were all cleaned up at one meal![91]

However, not long after this moment of collective joy, as Hamblin felt overwhelming relief that he and his group had survived the ordeal of a trans-Colorado expedition once again, one of the men who came with Fuller took Jacob aside and shared with him some shattering news—one of his sons had been killed the previous month, on December 17, in an accident while working on an irrigation ditch. The man named Lyman, but it was actually Duane, Hamblin's first-born child, not long married and just twenty-one years old.

The Clara had suddenly dried up at Santa Clara, so Duane took a Swiss man and a couple others to find where the river had "broken away" and return it to its normal bed. "That day about 11 or 12 oclock the news came to us that the bankes had caved in on the men and buried them," Mary Minerva Dart Judd wrote. One man, Brown Crow, was rescued, "but Duane Hamblins neck it was broken." The body was brought to Santa Clara, and a funeral was held under a tent. "Oh what sorrow it was to see him there with his fase so black and blue. A good young man about 22 years old just maried and to go and leave her in side of one year or even six monthes and we buried him there be side of his Grandfather."[92]

Duane's wife, Elizabeth Russell Hamblin, was pregnant, and bore a child, also named Duane, on July 17, 1863.

So Jacob's sense of relief at returning to the settlements would have been quickly transformed into intense grief.

Hancock says that the main party continued on to Pipe Spring that day, the seventh, and on the tenth arrived in Short Creek and Virgin City, where they were given "a feast of royal proportions." Jacob probably arrived home at Santa Clara on January 11 or 12, 1863, where he must have grieved with his family for Duane's loss.[93]

Jacob and his companions had survived another brush with starvation and extreme exhaustion as they effected the first circling of the Grand Canyon, by whites, in history, a stunning achievement. Hamblin had explored western and central Arizona for Brigham Young, and John Steele had provided a detailed itinerary of the journey. In addition, the missionaries had opened up friendly relations with Shivwits and Hualapai Indians south of the Colorado.

And remarkably, Jacob had brought back Hopis to see Utah. His next task would be to take them to Salt Lake City to meet Brigham Young and the leading brethren of the church.

15

"The Hight of the Rock and Its Smooth Surfis on Each Side P[r]esented the Seenery Grand and Sublime"

Founding Pearce's Ferry, 1863

The visit of the three Hopis to Utah was certainly one of the earliest visits by Hopis to American settlements and culture. It must have been a profoundly alien experience for these mesa-dwellers, probably intensely interesting, but possibly very disconcerting, also. Mormons, in their turn, were intrigued by these unwarlike, town-dwelling Indians.

After arriving back in Fort Clara, Hamblin showed the Hopis the local sights, then in late January he headed north for Salt Lake City with Ta-wa-ho-we, La-mo-e, and Tu-wa-wat. Hamblin also decided to take Eliza and Ellen with him to marry them for eternity in the Endowment House (the earlier marriage to Eliza had probably not been performed for eternity). So the young women, and apparently Rachel, were part of the company, as was Bill Maxwell.[1]

The group arrived in Salt Lake on February 3.[2] The following day they had a formal interview with Brigham Young; George A. Smith, Hamblin, and Maxwell also were present. The church president "seemed pleased with the interview," Apostle Wilford Woodruff wrote, and gave each Hopi an apple, "which they Eat with a good relish." Woodruff described the Hopis as very intelligent and light in complexion. "There are some with blue Eyes & Hazel Eyes and vary light hair but they have never mixed blood with any white men or other Indian tribes."[3]

Brigham Young immediately suggested that a hundred Mormon volunteers should settle in the verdant San Francisco Peaks area, and that they should "take the same Number of Moquitchs with them to plant and built & prepare to move their families there." A Mormon colony in Arizona did not occur till much later, but Young's spontaneous enthusiasm for settling Arizona is remarkable, especially given that he had only recently received a sketchy first view of this territory.[4]

After leaving Young's office, Woodruff took the Hopis (and presumably Hamblin and Maxwell) to the printing office and telegraph office, and had dinner with them at his home. In the evening, Hamblin took them to stores and even to the

15.1. Three Hopis from Oraibi, Ta-wa-ho-we, La-mo-e, and Tu-wa-wat, brought to Salt Lake City by Jacob Hamblin, were photographed on February 5, 1863, at the Savage Studio, possibly by Charles R. Savage. This is the first photograph of Hopis in history. Courtesy National Anthropological Archives, Smithsonian Institution, GN 01843.

theater. One wonders what the Hopi, with their immemorial traditions of sacred drama and ritual, thought of Western drama.

On February 11, Hamblin talked with George A. Smith and Brigham Young again, and Young once more suggested a Mormon-Hopi colony on Hopi land.[5]

Maxwell and the Hopis started for southern Utah on February 14,[6] while Jacob stayed in Salt Lake City, and married Eliza on the fourteenth, in the Endowment House. Daniel H. Wells officiated, and Apostle Woodruff stood as one of the witnesses.[7] According to family tradition, Ellen chose not to marry him at the last minute.[8] Jacob, Eliza, Ellen, and Rachel left the city on the fifteenth and probably caught up with Maxwell and the Hopis as they traveled south.[9]

The first purpose of Jacob's next trip to the mesas was to take the Hopis back to their homes and bring Haskell, McConnell, and Hatch back to southern Utah. But in addition, as we have seen, Young hoped to create a permanent Mormon-Hopi colony south of the Colorado. In a letter to Erastus Snow dated February 15, 1863, which was read publicly on March 1, George A. Smith told of Young's plans to create this settlement, which would guard the Hopis, "should they see proper to be gathered under the wings of Israel's Eagles."[10]

Young himself wrote a parallel letter to Hamblin dated February 16,[11] in which he outlined an ambitious plan for a major Mormon-Hopi colony in Arizona. He asked Jacob to recruit about a hundred men for the settlement[12] and create a wagon road to the Colorado, with fortified stone houses built at water sources on the road. A ferry should be established on the Colorado, again protected by a stone house. The settlement itself should be made at a site that had "good soil, timber and water-power," as close to the Colorado as possible, and should be protected by a substantial fort enclosing thirty to forty acres[13] to defend against "fierce Navajo or Apache war parties."[14] From this fort missionaries could be sent to the various Indian tribes.[15]

The Hopis would be invited to inhabit this fort, and with the "appurtenances of civilized life" they would be able to develop their "native ingenuity" more fully, "while the protection of 100 brave generous and high minded missionaries would render their flocks and their herds, as well as their scalps, comparatively safe." Here they would obtain the moral and religious training which would be required "to make the descendants of Lehi, Ishmael and Zoram, a white and delightsome people."[16]

However, half a month later, on March 6, Young sent Hamblin a letter in which he put off any settlements south or east of the Colorado until the following fall. He directed Hamblin, "at his earliest convenience," to find a few other men who could travel with him, and "make an exploring trip" to Arizona, "and report the facilities and adaptation for settlements there. After your report, we shall be better able to determine what will be best to be done in that region."[17] In this letter, Young also authorized the missionaries to marry Hopi women, though no such marriages have been recorded. Hamblin might have asked for guidance on the subject.

Young had specifically asked Hamblin to explore the territory around the San Francisco Peaks.[18] Thus, as usual, this would be a combined missionary and exploration journey, but Young emphasized the exploration.

Mormon leaders continued to be interested in the southern route to the Colorado, via the Grand Wash. On March 6, Erastus Snow directed three Mormons, Hyrum Burgess, William Pulsipher, and G. G. R. San Giovanni, with Tutsegabits, to "explore a wagon-route from St. George, south to the Colorado."[19] The Paiutes had told the Mormons that they visited the Colorado by that route and only had one dry camp when they traveled with their women. Not much is known of this preliminary expedition, but it shows how Mormons often based their explorations on close contacts with local Indians.

Jacob's expedition, which would take the southern route again, would leave in mid-March.[20] As he was preparing to leave, he mentioned to his adopted son Albert that the peach trees had begun to bloom and it would be warmer soon.

"Yes," Albert replied, "and I shall bloom in another place before you get back. I shall be on my mission!"

"What do you mean by that?" asked Jacob.

"That I shall be dead and buried when you get back," said Albert.[21] Jacob hoped he was wrong.

The members of this expedition, as listed in Hamblin's journal, were Jacob's siblings, Gunlock Bill and Frank; Andrew Gibbons; "Clinghams Smith" (Philip Klingensmith), well known for his participation in the Mountain Meadows Massacre; Llewellyn Harris (as Spanish and Welsh interpreter); and the three Hopis. (Lye decided to stay on with Bill Maxwell.)[22] A listing in Bleak's "Annals" adds John W. Freeman, one of the founders of Washington, to the group.[23] And remarkably, a non-Mormon would join them soon after they started.

Klingensmith, a Pennsylvania native and an accomplished blacksmith, was now forty-seven years old, had been one of the early settlers of the Iron Mission, and was a bishop in Cedar City from 1852 to 1859. He stayed a faithful LDS Church member for a number of years after the Mountain Meadows Massacre, but finally left Mormonism and Utah, and testified openly about the massacre in the first John D. Lee trial in 1875, in which he was the central witness.[24]

Llewellyn Harris was a thirty-one-year-old Welshman who would serve a number of Indian missions in the southwest. He is most famous for a mission he would serve among the Zunis in 1878.[25]

There is evidence that Jacob was able to use Ives's "Map No. 2" during this expedition.[26]

On March 18, the group departed for the Colorado crossing south of St. George, presumably retracing their steps of the journey the year before. On the twenty-first, they traveled "over the sumit betwen the Virgin and Colrado Rivers," probably Mustang Knoll, and the next day began descending the Pocum and Grand Washes.[27]

They reached the Colorado on the twenty-third and found their cache of food from the previous expedition undisturbed, though spoiled. The following day they built a raft of dry wood, and Jacob and Bill Hamblin crossed the Colorado, "found the scif whare we cashed it last fall," and returned with the boat.

At this point, a rather unexpected event occurred: a non-Mormon stranger showed up with a letter of introduction from Erastus Snow. It was Louis Greeley, nephew of the famous journalist Horace Greeley, wanting to join the expedition, little knowing the dangers and ordeals he would soon be facing. He was warmly accepted.

The missionaries spent that day looking for a good ferry site—or as Hamblin puts it, "Bro Gibons Mr Grely and myself went up the River... to hunt the... best plase for crosing." To do this, they passed through a "perpendicular cut" in the mountains.[28] They found the desired crossing site about five miles east of the mouth of the Grand

15.2. Pearce's Ferry, looking east at the western termination of the Grand Canyon. Jacob Hamblin and companions first crossed the Colorado here in 1863. Ruins of one of the ferry buildings can be seen in the bottom foreground. Photograph by Eugene C. LaRue, 1923. Courtesy U.S. Geological Survey.

Wash.[29] "Found a good plase for a farry allso good goeing to and from the River at the same plase. This crosing was one mild [mile] and half below whare the River run through a mountain," wrote Hamblin. In this general area Pearce's (or Pierce's) Ferry was eventually located; it was named after Harrison Pearce, who made it a commercial ferry in 1876.[30] Hamblin made a number of subsequent trips south of the Colorado by this crossing, which apparently was originally called "Jacob's Crossing."[31]

On the way back, they came to some falls or rapids. "The Brotheren said it was dangerous," wrote Hamblin, but he thought it looked passable in the boat, asked for a volunteer to accompany him, and the non-Mormon stepped forward. "We went over the falls safely. The Boat dipt water once," Hamblin wrote.

Andrew Gibbons and some of the other men were sent back to the mouth of Grand Wash to pick up baggage and animals. Returning the next morning, the twenty-sixth, Gibbons reported that they had found a good route for a road. The way from Grand Wash (and St. George) to Pearce's Ferry was complete.

The company crossed the river then traveled southeast up a wash, probably Grapevine Wash, for a few days. They passed through country rich in grass, cedar, and springs, then ascended a mountain, and when they reached the summit, had a stunning view of the countryside. They could see the "harmony mountains the country we had lef[t] 9 days before and a vast distance in evry direcions." And when the Hopis looked east, one of them said that he recognized a mountain. "They aperd much pleased at the prospect of geting home," wrote Jacob.

March 30 saw the beginning of an unfortunate adventure. One of the Hopis found five loose horses with Spanish brands, seemingly without owners. "As they apeard to be animils that had ben stray of for some months," Hamblin wrote in his diary, "we gav ~~them~~ one to each of the Indians." That left the missionaries "a mare and colt for the trip" back "if we found no o[w]ners."[32] They camped that night at Peach Springs, in the heart of Hualapai country.

On April 2, the missionaries consulted with some Paiutes and the Hopis, and decided to take a new trail, northeast of their former route.[33] They were probably following what looked like a promising Indian trail, which, unbeknownst to Hamblin and company, was apparently the Hualapai trail to Havasu Canyon. The next day they traveled "through some of the best country I have saw," Hamblin wrote. "The most grass and of the best and most luxurious kind with open places... surounded with tawl pine timber." This is Hamblin the explorer writing, evaluating sites for possible settlements.

On the fourth, the missionaries thought they were close to the Little Colorado and started northeast following a wash, when suddenly the wash was "interrupted by purpendicular rock" and the Mormons found themselves in a deep canyon, "the trail takeing the side of the canion which was very steep and dificilt to folow leeding around presipecipeses." The canyon that Hamblin and his friends had wandered into was Havasu or Cataract Canyon, which continues north till it meets the Colorado, one of the most beautiful canyons leading into the Grand Canyon. Whites had first encountered it in 1776, when Father Francisco Garcés came there; Joseph Ives had visited more recently, in 1857.

Jacob wrote that this path—probably the Hualapai Trail—"was the most dangerous and difficult [trail] I ever travailed wit[h] pack animils," which, for Jacob, was saying something. Indeed, in 1854 Lieutenant A. W. Whipple, with a group of soldiers, attempted to descend into this canyon and turned back, regarding the path to be too difficult and dangerous.[34]

Joseph Ives, halfway down the Hualapai Trail, riding a mule, had a sudden memorable moment of recognition. The trail seemed to end, and it looked as if even a mountain goat could not have continued, but on closer inspection, there was a path that "though narrow and dizzy, had been cut with some care into the surface of the cliff." Then Ives suddenly noticed that the bottom of the canyon was much lower than he had realized:

> Glancing down the side of my mule I found that he was walking within three inches of the brink of a sheer gulf a thousand feet deep; on the other side, nearly touching my knee, was an almost vertical wall rising to an enormous altitude. The sight made my head swim, and I dismounted and got ahead of the mule, a difficult and delicate operation, which I was thankful to have safely performed. A part of the men became so giddy that they were obliged

> to creep upon their hands and knees, being unable to walk or stand. In some places there was barely room to walk, and a slight deviation in a step would have precipitated one into the frightful abyss.[35]

Ives did not make it all the way to the bottom of the canyon, but retraced his steps up to Hualapai country.

When the party of General Crook visited the canyon in 1884, one of the pack mules stumbled and fell from the path, dropped a long ways, and died a violent but quick death.[36] Hamblin and company, facing this same challenge, continued on, "asending and decending steep and dangerous rocks," until, at one o'clock, they "came to a purpendicular rock and in sight of a butiful streem of water 1000 feet below."

Indians were farming on the stream, but when they caught sight of the Mormons, the women and children fled into rocks to hide, while the men came running armed with bows and arrows and a few "old rusty flint-lock muskets." However, one of the Hopis called out to them and allayed their fears. The Havasupai showed the party their horse trail, and two hours later, after much "fategue and toil, we found our selves and animils on the banks of the creek [which] is 2. rods wide 2 feet deep clear as cristal." Hamblin wrote, "I was so fatigued that I could scarsely step."

They were also ravenous with hunger, for they had eaten no breakfast, "as we thought we ware neer the little colerado when we started." This suggests that Hamblin and company entered Cataract Canyon purely by accident. Though the three Hopis knew about the canyon, they probably had never approached it from the west.[37]

The Hopis told Hamblin that these were the "Co-ho-ni-na" Indians, the Hopi term for the Havasupais, linked by language and culture to the Hualapais to the west. The creek that Hamblin refers to as "clear as cristal" is Havasu or Cataract Creek, famous for its blue, crystalline water. In fact, Havasupai means "people of the blue green waters."[38]

The Havasupais had chosen this location for its defensive advantages, Hamblin wrote. Conflicts with the Yavapais and Apaches must have driven them into the canyon, though they often emerged to hunt. Using irrigation, they were raising corn, beans, Indian squash, and peaches. One of the Indians, who spoke Ute, invited Hamblin to his "cave" where there were eight or ten lodges. He told him that he had visited the Hopi mesas recently and that Haskell, McConnell, and Hatch were doing well.

Some Havasupai arrived from downstream and "inquired rather sharply why we were there," writes Hamblin. However, "They were soon satisfied with our explanations." They asked Hamblin not to lead anyone to Havasupai Canyon, especially strangers, without asking their permission.[39]

The following day, the missionaries rested, repaired packs, tightened horseshoes, and traded with the Havasupai.[40]

Now the next development in the story of the five horses occurred, as some of the Havasupai recognized them and told the missionaries that they were the property of the Hualapais at Peach Springs, and that if the missionaries wanted to turn them over to them (the Havasupai), they would return them to the Hualapais in three days. The Hopis and missionaries agreed, and let the Havasupai take the animals.[41]

On April 6, the missionaries started traveling upstream. "This was shut in on eather side with the hiest perpendicular rock I ever saw," Hamblin wrote. "The hight of the rock and its smooth surfis on each side p[r]esented the seenery grand and sublime." They passed a battle site where the Havasupais had killed a number of "Euches" (Yavapais, another group related to the Hualapais and Havasupais). Some two hundred Yavapais had invaded Havasupai Canyon around 1862, but had been driven away.[42]

Then the missionaries climbed out of the canyon in two or three hours, an ascent "attended with mutch difficulty and hardship." However, the hike out of Havasu Canyon was certainly much less steep than the descent; the party probably followed Topocoba Trail or Moqui Trail up Lee Canyon, a standard route on the east.

Havasupai historian Stephen Hirst reports that Hamblin visited the Havasupai and tried to preach to them, but that the Indians were suspicious, ushered him out of the canyon, and told him not to come back on pain of death.[43] This does not tally with the account in Hamblin's diary, and indeed, when one consults Hirst's source, Frank Cushing's memoir, "The Nation of the Willows," there is no reference to Hamblin. It is the "celebrated Lee" who preaches to the Havasupai.[44] Dobyns and Euler are closer, correctly putting Hamblin's visit in the year 1863, but they incorrectly refer to Hamblin as being "turned back."[45]

The next day, as the company drew nearer to the Hopi homeland, two of the Hopis decided to hurry ahead to the mesas, leaving one with the Mormons as a guide.[46] However, when the Mormons came to a fork in the path, the remaining Hopi said the other two had apparently taken the "ucha trail" by mistake. As he felt they would not find water and might be killed by the dangerous Yavapais, he decided to go in pursuit of them. Because he was the priest, he first performed some religious ceremonies, then gave the Mormons directions—go to the left and follow the first trail they came to—and rushed off to help his friends.[47]

The Mormons followed the directions as best they could, traveling through "firtile country," which included "pine and cedar turkey bare [bear] and deer." When they stopped to rest their animals in the afternoon, however, the Hopi guide showed up, so thirsty that he quickly emptied one of their canteens, saying that he had not been able to find his friends. He also told the Mormons that they had taken the wrong path, and were now also on a Yavapai trail. At sundown, they camped at a pool of water not far from the Little Colorado. Fortunately, the hostile Yavapais never made an appearance.

The next day, according to the grammatical diary, the other two Hopis showed up, "in a state of great exhaustion, having been absent one night and two days and most of the time without water."

On the tenth, the missionaries and Hopis reached the Little Colorado, though it was in a deep gulch,[48] and two days later, they "arrived to the Oribes. Met brothers Thal Hascal. Maconel. and Ira Hacth 2 miles from the Oribe town in good spirits."[49] It must have been a joyful reunion.

In the days following, Hamblin and the other missionaries enjoyed their visit to the Hopis, with its friendships, hospitality, and festivities. "Had an interesting time with the Brotheren and the Oribies," wrote Hamblin. The missionaries had more invitations to dine than they could accept. The Hopis "were much pleased with the report of their 'Ambassadors.'"

On the fourteenth, the Hopis "had a sprea [spree] caled the Chochema," or Chochina, as the grammatical diary puts it, and the missionaries attended. There are no major Hopi ceremonials in spring, but many dances;[50] possibly this was a Kachina dance, and "Chochina" may simply be Hamblin's transliteration of "Kachina."

Both the Hopis and some visiting Navajos sorely wanted to trade for the Mormons' surplus ammunition, but Hamblin decided they would only trade with the Hopis.

In his May 18, 1863, letter to Young, Hamblin wrote,

> A great change has taken place among the Oribas within the last few months. Fort Defiance is burnt,[51] and as there is no trading post east, the Navajos cannot obtain ammunition, and are trading their guns to the Oribas for hoes to farm with. We traded our surplus ammunition to the Oribas, who then felt perfectly secure against the assaults of their enemies. They are no longer the depressed passive beings we first found them to be, but manifest a spirit of self-reliance and resistance to oppression. While there I saw a couple of Navajos kicked out of the houses for their rudeness.[52]

Some of the Navajos asked for Hamblin to leave a Mormon to live among them. "They wish for friends…saying 'we are not all thieves, we once had chiefs to govern us, now we have none.'" Hamblin replied that missionaries to the Navajos would have to be sent by President Young.[53]

When the U.S. troops and New Mexico volunteers had conquered the Navajos, the Hopis told Hamblin, the Hopis had sent a deputation to visit the Americans. But they, "flushed with success, damned them, saying 'damn you get out of here, we intend to drive every G-d damned Indian and Mormon together.'"[54]

The Hopis said that when they were at "the captured fort"—possibly Fort Wingate—"they saw the soldiers ravishing the Navajo and other Indian women; they described the poor women as crying piteously; but the brutal soldiers only made mock of their distress." For all the paternalism in the Mormons' attitudes toward the Indian, the contrast between them and such soldiers is stark. Hamblin wrote to Young that such sights caused the Hopis to view the U.S. Army as the bad white and bearded men from the east, while the Mormons would be regarded as the good white and bearded men from the west.[55]

Hamblin and his friends departed from the mesas on April 15, traveling southwest, as Hamblin had been asked by Young to explore near the San Francisco Peaks on this journey. They reached the Little Colorado River on the seventeenth, passed through a country of "sinders or wash from the volcanic peeks," and arrived at the "bench" of the San Francisco mountains the next day.

On the nineteenth, as they ascended this bench, they traveled through a pine forest and saw antelope and wild turkeys. The ground was "coverd with a thicke luxerous [luxurious] grass." The next day, as they proceeded south of the mountain, the company split up to find water and make "such other discoveres as we could," and Louis Greeley "discoverd a pond of water on a sugar loaf mountain." This was apparently the crater of a sizable volcanic peak, containing "not far from 10 acers" of water.[56] There are a number of well-known craters in this area, such as Sunset Crater; many of them are "cinder cones," extinct volcanoes that now are crater lakes.

The company continued in the discovery mode for the following two days, as they "explored in diferent direcions," and discovered a wagon road that they concluded had to be "Beals rout." This is Edward Fitzgerald Beale, who from August to October 1857 helped lay out a thousand-mile wagon road from eastern Arizona to Fort Mojave on the lower Colorado.[57] The Beale expedition is famous for its use of imported camels. Modern Route 66 and Interstate 40 lie roughly on the Beale road, which follows the 35th parallel and passes directly through modern Flagstaff south of the San Francisco Peaks. To the east, it then passes directly through the eventual site of the first Mormon settlements on the Little Colorado. Beale's report was published in 1858, and it is possible that Hamblin had seen it.[58]

Hamblin described one valley in glowing terms. It was "skirted all around with dense forests of Pine. Grass is in the valley waist-high and very abundant on the hills around. Cowslips and wild onions grown plentifully among the grass in the valley. We found fish worms in the soil indicating that the ground is kept moist during the summer."[59] Perhaps this would be his recommendation for the site of the Mormon-Hopi colony.

The company set out westward on the twenty-fourth, following the wagon road and stopping at a series of beautiful valleys. They then veered south to visit Bill Williams Mountain, twenty miles west of modern Flagstaff, which they reached on the twenty-sixth. Hamblin, again, keeps careful note of likely settlement spots. At the foot of the mountain was "a very fertile valley containing 500 acres of Meadow land and one or two permanent springs. This is a delightful country! Plenty of Bear, Elk, Antelope, Deer and Turkeys. And considerable Black Walnut timber."[60]

They then traveled north on "the old over land mail road," which the grammatical version of the diary calls "the old Butterfield road," possibly a mistake, as the Butterfield Overland Stage road passed through southern Arizona.[61] As the road they were on turned south, the missionaries decided to leave it and travel west to Seep Springs. They had a dry camp that night, and the next day found no water. Hamblin's entry for his activities this evening is unusually personal:

> Stopt at sunset at the foot of a small shugar loaf mountain. No water. Men and animils suferd alike. Our canteens ware empty. We had not brought a larg suply as we expected to of got water the night before which we mised. I discoverd a trail leeding to a brake in the mountain on the East side of the valy. I followed it in hopes to find water.

It terminated at a rock that protected a deep well lined with rocks.

> I got in to the well thrust my hand to the botom. Thare was nothing but mud. I then hunted my way back to camp. It was late at night. Men ware asleep and animils tied or hobled clost to prevent them from stampedeing in surch of water that mutch needed element. I was hungry and fatiegued and my mouth parched with thurs[t]. I took my canteen putit to my lips but I had drained it empty. I l[a]y down and dreamed of water.[62]

They struggled on the next day without water and at about noon, they had gone fifty-six hours without water—approaching three days, the point at which human survival is threatened. Symptoms of acute dehydration can include delirium and weakness, and inability to move. Jehiel McConnell could not speak above a whisper.

However, at two or three o'clock, they arrived at Seep Springs. "This with a little cleening out afforded plenty of pure cool water for our selves and animils. This was very exceptable to all," Hamblin wrote. The crisis was over. They stayed at the spring and rested.

At least there was no shortage of food on this route: "Kiled a big turkey had a splended supper."

The next day, May 1, they rested at the spring and explored north and west. There were no "durable springs" but plenty of game—bear, deer, antelope, and turkey. They traveled what must have been an exhausting fifty miles to Peach Springs on the second, arriving there at two a.m. They were thus in the heart of Hualapai country, where they had appropriated the five horses on the journey out.

The next day they started for Milk Weed Springs at noon and traveled twenty miles, but lost the trail at night "among the cedars and rocks." They decided to stay there and rest their animals, which they hobbled. "As all [missionaries] were excessively fatigued no guard was put on duty," wrote Hamblin. During the night, "thare was some[thing] hurd that did not sound as so all was wright," the howl of a wolf.[63] The men suspected that this was an Indian signal, so despite their exhaustion immediately began looking for their animals. Many of them had disappeared. Jacob found a trail leading away from the camp and as he followed it by moonlight, recognized "2 Indian tracks folowing the animils." At dawn, he was eight miles from camp and decided that he had better turn back.

At camp, he found that the Hualapais had taken ten horses, which left only eight for the missionaries. Five missionaries were still gone, trying to reclaim the lost animals. As Hamblin waited at camp, two men returned, saying that they had met two Paiutes who were helping them track the missing horses. The three men at camp packed the remaining animals and set out after the three absent missionaries, who did not return till after sunset. They said that the Paiutes had talked with the rustlers

> and found that the Hualpais claimed that we had stolen 5 of their animals and they had laid their plans to take 2 for each 1, or blood. This made us all feel glad that no guard had been put out on the night of the 3rd; this feeling was increased as we discovered that one of the ten missing animals, being hobbled and close to where we were sleeping, had been shot with a poisoned arrow, which speedily terminated his existence.[64]

This incident shows clearly the Indian ethic of retaliation.[65]

The Paiutes gave some hope that two of the stolen horses might be recovered, so the missionaries waited in camp, but in vain. Finally, the missionaries gave up all hope of recovering any of their horses, and on the sixth they packed up all their baggage on their eight remaining animals and set off for home, apparently on foot. "Travailed late at nite. Blisterd my feet," wrote Hamblin. "Kiled antelope. A beter and more humble spirit in camp than when we had our animils." Losing ten horses was a major disaster; nevertheless, on the bright side, there had been no loss of life.

Twenty-five Paiutes came into camp on the seventh, and the missionaries and Indians feasted together. The Paiutes offered to recover the horses or take "the blood of the Hualpais" but Hamblin forbade this. He did say that he would like to talk to the Hualapais at some point, and subsequently found that the Havasupais had not returned the horses to them.[66]

The next day at noon, the party arrived at Grapevine Springs, rested during the afternoon, then arrived at the Colorado, "much fategued," with feet badly blistered.[67] They "felt to realise the worth of our animils the Indians had taken from us."[68]

On the ninth they crossed the river safely, then traveled fifteen miles to Cottonwood Spring. "This is a larg spring [that] gushes out of the side of the hill," wrote Hamblin, supplying "enough to water 50 acres of land. This is a butiful streem in a thurstey land."[69]

The next day they crossed "a desert looking bench intercepted with deep ravines" that was "dry and baren as an ash heep." At the bottom of the Grand Wash, they saw mud, and a mule started pawing at the ground. They dug down three feet and found an abundance of water. "There has been water there ever since, and it is called White Spring," Jacob wrote.[70] On the eleventh they reached Cane Springs, and as they were "feet-sore hungry thurstey and tired," they stopped there for the day.

They walked twenty miles to Rock Springs the following day, where they traded with Paiutes, a spade for an animal skin. The day after, the thirteenth, they pushed themselves to cover thirty-five miles, arriving at St. George late at night.[71]

Hamblin and company had completed another major expedition. They had founded a ferry site on the Colorado south of St. George (which made crossing the Colorado feasible all year round), had delivered the three Hopis to the mesas, and had brought back the Mormon missionaries who had been living there. Hamblin had explored a route eastward south of the Colorado and accomplished one of the early visits of whites down Havasu Canyon. On the way home he had explored the territory around the San Francisco Peaks and Bill Williams Mountain, linking up with the Beale Road. Bleak wrote that Hamblin and his group had "explored a practicable route as a wagon road from St George to the Little Colorado."[72] This information would be invaluable to Brigham Young as he planned the Mormon colonization of Arizona. Once again, the company had endured exhaustion, dehydration, cold, dangerous trails (especially in Havasu Canyon), and danger from Indians in Hualapai country.

But, as in his last homecoming from the mesas, Hamblin received devastating personal news when he arrived home. Albert, as the boy himself had predicted, had died. Not much is known about his death, but Priscilla linked it to the Mountain Meadows Massacre, if only by conjecture. "Because Albert had been the main eyewitness to the terrible massacre for Jacob and other authorities, he had a hard time adjusting to life again," she wrote. "I have always felt that some of those involved in the terrible tragedy were the ones who made sure that Albert didn't live to testify at the court trial. He was found dead in a cactus patch."[73] According to Corbett, however, Albert died of pneumonia after suffering from a cold for several days.[74] Hamblin eulogized him: "For a number of years he had charge of my sheep, horses and cattle, and they had increased and prospered in his hands. He was a faithful Latter-day Saint; believed he had a great work to do among his people; had many dreams and visions, and had received his blessings in the house of the Lord."[75]

In addition, little Araminda was also gone. "My daughter Arminda had died in my ab[s]ence a promiceing girl nearly 3 years of age," Hamblin wrote in his diary.

Family traditions hold that Eliza of the Shivwits left Hamblin not long after her marriage to him in Salt Lake City. If that is true, then she might have departed from the Hamblin household at about this time. Tradition says that, after leaving the Hamblin home, she married a Shivwits man named Polunkin or Poinkum, and bore him at least one child.[76] This must have been a blow to Jacob, who was reportedly very attached to Eliza, and who had made a permanent affirmation of the marriage by the eternal sealing.

No information has been preserved about Eliza's thoughts and feelings, or about her experiences in returning to her native culture, from which she had probably been separated for a decade or more. Had she gotten used to "European" food and customs? In a Shivwits village, was there enough to eat, as there had been in Jacob's household? How was she treated as a woman and a wife? After the culture shock of entering into American Mormon culture when she was small, how much of a shock was her reentry into Paiute life?[77]

Those questions remain unanswered. There is a family tradition that Eliza, with her child, asked to rejoin the Hamblin household, but Jacob refused.[78] Possibly she was one of those unfortunate Indians who was caught between two cultures, not fitting into either one.[79]

Alice Rich wrote that wandering groups of Paiutes often came to New Harmony, "always peaceable and friendly," trading baskets, pine nuts, and buckskins for food and clothing. "One family that I shall always remember [was] Poeinkum, Liza, and their two sons, Winey [Wiley] and Puss. Lisa was blind in her last days," she wrote.[80] If this is Eliza, who had been Jacob's wife, we are fortunate to have a window into her last days, traveling with Poinkum and her two sons, blind in her old age.

This Poinkum was apparently well known in southern Utah. Another New Harmony resident wrote that he was "a good Indian. He almost joined the church. Poinkum had a boy name Puss and another boy named Wiley."[81]

However, Jean Holbrook, a resident of Cove Fort, remembered an Indian, Sussic, who lived near the fort and had two wives, one of whom, Eliza, had been raised by the Jacob Hamblin family. "The two wives would do any heavy work though Eliza was better at it. She learned quicker and stayed at it longer than Ruth. They would scrub floors, peel potatoes, bake, polish knives, and forks and do laundry work."[82]

For Jacob, the shock of two deaths, and the possible divorce, were balanced by a birth: Lucy, third child of Priscilla, had been born on May 11.[83] On reaching his home in Santa Clara on the fifteenth, he was greeted by Priscilla, who held up the four-day-old baby: "I want you to meet your daughter, 'Lucy,'" she said.[84]

On May 18, Hamblin wrote to Brigham Young, reporting on the new ferry site and the road from St. George to the ferry.[85] He said that there was only one hill that would have to be worked on, at minimal expense, to create a workable road to the Colorado. He stated that some thirty-five miles south of the ferry site was "the Butterfield road"—again, he is probably mistaken on this; he apparently meant Beale's road.[86] After recounting how Mormons were regarded by some Hopis as good white and bearded saviors who had been prophesied of generations earlier, Hamblin pleaded with Young that missionaries to the Hopis would be sincerely focused on Indians, instead of merely wanting good Arizona land.

> This causes one to earnestly desire that whoever may be sent among this people may be men of integrity in carrying out your will in instituting a righteous form of government, and otherwise carrying out the purposes of God in gathering and saving Israel, instead of hunting for a country where they could live in affluence and ease.[87]

This passage shows the tension in Jacob between Indian missionary and explorer—he had become a key man in Young's Southwest explorations and colonizing. In Santa Clara, he had come to the country as an Indian missionary, and in fact had been invited by the Paiutes. Now the Virgin and Santa Clara area had been settled by a great majority of Mormons whose aims were economic and agricultural. And Jacob was working largely as an explorer, though the jobs of explorer and Indian missionary overlapped somewhat.

Jacob then described the country south of the San Francisco and Bill Williams mountains. It had many springs, many fertile valleys, large stands of pines, with other woods.

> This country appears to be in an almost Paradisaical state. The Bear, Elk, Deer, Antelope, and Turkeys in great abundance, roam apparently without fear of molestation. I have been diverted by seeing antelope follow us apparently surprised at our appearance. I did not suffer any game to be shot but what we actually needed.

In 1863, Jacob continued his farming and civic duties at Santa Clara. George A. Smith toured the south in July, and wrote that Jacob "exhibited the largest bunch of grapes that we have seen," estimated to weigh a hundred pounds.[88] In September, he was appointed to a committee to apportion timber to three mills in Pine Valley.[89]

In the October 26–27, 1862, conference, Edward Bunker, who was then living in Toquerville, had been called to be bishop of Santa Clara, with Marius Ensign as a counselor.[90] Tensions between the "old settlers" of Santa Clara and the newly arrived

Swiss had developed, and church leaders evidently felt that an outsider would serve best as bishop, instead of Jacob's brother-in-law, Zadok Judd. The conflicts lessened.

Tensions with the residents of St. George would be a bigger challenge for the Santa Clarans. The inhabitants of St. George began to farm in a large field south of the town of Santa Clara, and claimed an equal part of the water of the Santa Clara for their fields.[91] However, there was not sufficient water for both towns from the small creek. In an October 31–November 1, 1863, conference in St. George, Bunker reported that "the crops are light through lack of water; they would not average more than a quarter of a crop."[92] This caused many of the old settlers of Santa Clara, including Bill Hamblin, Ira Hatch, and Dudley Leavitt, to move away from the settlement to found Clover Valley and Panaca in what is now southeast Nevada. (At the time, these towns were part of Utah.)[93] Water rights would continue to be a bone of contention between the inhabitants of Santa Clara and St. George, not to mention the communities higher on the Clara.[94]

In such an intense conflict for the water of the Santa Clara, the rights and divisions of water for the Paiutes are never mentioned. One senses that they were no longer regarded as a major, permanent factor on the Clara.

16

"A Raft was Built on Which Bro Hamblin and Dayton Crossed"

Founding Lee's Ferry and Callville, 1864

One of the key exploring years for Jacob Hamblin was 1864, as his company crossed the Colorado at the mouth of the Paria successfully on March 22 of that year. Thus began the practical use of Lee's Ferry, which would be the main artery between southern Utah and Arizona until 1928, when the Navajo Bridge was completed five miles west of the Paria. Lee's Ferry opened up an important road that many Mormon colonists of Arizona would later travel. It became an important locus of passage and cultural exchange between Mormons and non-Mormons, Indians and whites, geographers, geologists, authors, financiers, outlaws, tourists, and prospectors.

Hamblin was asked to visit the Hopis in spring 1864 for two reasons. First, he was to attempt to reclaim horses that Navajos had stolen from the new settlement of Kanab, in modern Kane County, and from other Mormon settlements. Second, following up on Young's vision of a joint Mormon-Hopi colony, Hamblin would try once again to convince the Hopis to leave their mesas and live and work with the Mormons.

Kanab was a town less than a year old, and undoubtedly owed its founding to Jacob's trips to the Hopis. On January 3, 1863, John Steele had written, "Got…as far as Kanab….This is a beautiful little stream. Good land and plenty of grass, wood timber can be got at Buckskin Mountain fifteen or twenty miles off." Clearly, this is diarist as potential settler writing. Steele added, in a note to George A. Smith: "(This is the place I told you of once before.)"[1] It seems he had known about Kanab even before the 1862–1863 expedition.

In spring 1863, some eight to fourteen saints, including Ezra Strong and Levi Savage Jr., made the bold move of settling at Kanab Creek, far from any other sizable settlements.[2] In theory this was not a dangerous place for a settlement, as the local

Paiutes were quite friendly. Navajo raids into southern Utah, however, would make Kanab a prime target.

Navajos plundering stock in Mormon settlements north of the Colorado was a grim new development, and Hamblin would spend much of his time in the upcoming years dealing with incursions of Navajos (and with the Utes, Paiutes, and Apaches they took as their allies) on raiding expeditions in southern Utah. The continuing Navajo Wars in New Mexico and Arizona had an enormous impact on southern Utah settlements. After General Edward Canby and the New Mexico volunteers' invasion of Navajo territory in fall and winter 1860, the Navajos were driven to peace talks in January 1861. But this lull lasted only a few months. In September 1861, twelve Navajos were killed at Fort Fauntleroy, New Mexico, at what has been called the Fauntleroy Massacre.[3] Col. Manuel Chaves, a leader of the New Mexico volunteers, was commanding the fort at the time and narrowly escaped court-martial for his part in the massacre. Relations between the Navajos and the U.S. Army, never good at the best of times, quickly disintegrated.

While the army in New Mexico was distracted by the Civil War and Confederate operations in Texas, Arizona, and New Mexico, Navajos raided New Mexico settlements, and were raided in turn by New Mexicans and Indian enemies of the Navajos such as the Utes.

In August 1862, General Canby was replaced by Brig. Gen. James Henry Carleton,[4] whom we met in 1859, investigating the massacre and interring the dead at Mountain Meadows, near Hamblin's ranch. After Confederate operations in New Mexico had failed, Carleton was able to turn his attention to "the Navajo problem."

Hampton Sides, author of *Blood and Thunder*, a history of Kit Carson and the Navajo Wars, describes Carleton as "a man who thought of everything and whose perfectionism seldom gave him an occasion to apologize. But also an officer of rare excellence, rigid ethics, fine manners, and multifaceted competence."[5] Nevertheless, in an interview, Sides described Carleton as the "real villain" of his book, though Kit Carson was a subsidiary hero or antihero. Carleton "wanted Carson to be more ruthless. He was a Calvinist New Englander, an insufferable disciplinarian, who thought he knew what was right for the Indians and just rammed it down their throats."[6]

Carleton at first focused on subduing the Mescalero Apaches, and developed policies of subjugation and relocation for them that he would use with the Navajos. In March 1863, after a brutal five-month campaign, he moved the remnants of the Mescalero Apaches, about four hundred of them, to Bosque Redondo on the Pecos River in east central New Mexico, Fort Sumner. It was expected that the Apaches would become farmers and good Christians in short order.

Carleton then pursued the same kind of campaign against the much more numerous Navajos, with the intent of removing them from their traditional lands and placing them with the Apaches (their traditional enemies) at the Bosque Redondo reservation. On June 15, 1863, he ordered Kit Carson to "prosecute a vigorous war upon the men of this tribe until it is considered at these Head Quarters that they have been effectually punished for their long continued atrocities."[7]

Carleton offered the Navajos this message: "Go to Bosque Redondo, or we will pursue and destroy you. We will not make peace with you on any other terms."[8] Kit Carson carried out a campaign that attacked the Navajos when possible but sought to destroy all the Navajos' sources of food, culminating in a destructive invasion of Canyon de Chelly. The soldiers captured herds of sheep, destroyed cornfields, and cut down thousands of peach trees.[9] About three-fourths of the ten thousand Navajos surrendered and made the grim Long Walk to Bosque Redondo in New Mexico, beginning in February 1864.[10] And there, as it turned out, Carleton's experiment in turning Indians into sedentary farmers and good Christians was a disastrous failure, for a number of reasons: inadequate food, crop failure, disease. Many Navajos died of starvation, sickness, and exposure.

Meanwhile, a sizable number of Navajos refused to surrender and retreated northward into southeastern Utah and westward into Arizona. These were often the more aggressive, wealthy Navajos.[11] Since they had by definition been turned into outlaws by Carleton, and since he had done his best to destroy their food supplies, they continued raiding to survive, making forays into New Mexico, but also crossing the Colorado to begin rustling Mormon herds—especially at outlying settlements and ranches such as Kanab and Pipe Spring.

Sometimes these Navajos allied with local Utes and Paiutes (though Utes were traditional enemies).[12] As Mormon settlements increased throughout Utah, Utes and Paiutes began to see their choicest lands settled by Mormons, saw the grasslands they depended on for seed become pastures for Mormon herds, saw creeks and springs depleted by Mormon irrigation. These tensions caused the Black Hawk War from 1865 to 1872, and sometimes Navajos were involved in this conflict, riding with Black Hawk in southern and central Utah.[13]

Navajos reportedly began to steal Mormon stock in fall 1863.[14] According to Erastus Snow, Spaneshanks and members of his band came to the eastern Mormon settlements—presumably Short Creek, Pipe Spring, and Kanab—at this time, and were hospitably received. But when they left they rustled a number of horses from Kanab.[15] Though Snow identified Spaneshanks as the leader of the group, it is probable that one of his sons had recently replaced his father as headman.[16] This is the beginning of at least a decade of Mormon-Navajo tensions and conflicts.

Hamblin, in Little, wrote, "I was requested"—probably by Erastus Snow—"to go over the Colorado, and, if practicable, have a talk with them [the Navajos], and recover the stolen horses."[17] Spaneshanks sent Hamblin a message through a Paiute telling him that he "entirely disapproved" of the recent raid on Kanab, and said that he might be able to get some of the animals back.[18]

The main source for this expedition is a literate, full diary by James Bleak.[19] Bleak, now thirty-four years old, later wrote that irreplaceable compendium of southern Utah history, "Annals of the Southern Utah Mission." A native of England, he received the call to St. George in 1861 and spent the rest of his life in Dixie. He served as recorder for the St. George Temple, postmaster, and patriarch.[20]

The members of the company were: Jacob Hamblin, Ira Hatch, and Taylor Crosby (from Santa Clara); Isaac Riddle (from Pine Valley); Llewellyn Harris, Lysander Dayton, James G. Bleak, David H. Cannon, and Benjamin F. Woods (from St. George); and George Petty, Mosiah Behunin, Thomas J. Clark, Andrew J. Kirby, and Lye, the Hopi who had come to Utah with Hamblin in the winter of 1862–1863—fourteen men in all.[21]

Notable among these were: David H. Cannon, a twenty-six-year-old native of England, and brother of prominent Mormon leader George Q. Cannon. He was called to St. George in 1861, and went on a number of Indian missions. He is famous for being photographed while baptizing a large group of Shivwits Paiutes in 1875.[22] He was president of the St. George Temple for some thirty years.

Mosiah Behunin, twenty, had been born in Nauvoo. He would spend much of his life working with Indians in Utah, and served as a translator in the Black Hawk War. His father, Isaac, was one of the early settlers of Zion's Canyon.[23]

The Bleak diary starts *in medias res* on what looks like the first day of the journey, March 10. There was a great deal of confusion in the following days, due to animals "taking the backward track," and the group split up, with Hamblin going ahead to Pipe Spring (which had recently been claimed as a ranch by James Whitmore).

The group united there on March 14 and read a letter from Apostle Erastus Snow. Following his advice, they chose Hamblin as "Pres. & Captain of the Company," David H. Cannon as captain of the guard, and Bleak as "Chaplain and clerk of the mission." Snow also gave practical camp advice (practice vigilance in guarding animals), religious advice ("live humble and prayerful") but also a warning to the Navajos: "Tell the Navajos not to let their thiefes visit us again unless they make satisfaction for the horses they have stolen from our people, lest some of our angry men slay them."[24]

The company left Pipe Spring on the fifteenth and began the ascent of Kaibab Plateau the following day. They found a good camping spot and most of the missionaries went hunting, but as night fell, Mosiah Behunin did not return. Though the company actively searched for the young man, no one found him that night or for the better part of the next day. Some expert trackers found his trail but could not locate him. In the evening he suddenly walked into camp, exhausted but alive.

On the eighteenth, the company reached the summit of Buckskin and rested there. A friendly Paiute showed up and talked with Hamblin, saying that there were many Navajos on the other side of the Colorado but the missionaries need not be

16.1. The mouth of the Paria River emptying into the Colorado, later known as Lee's Ferry. Hamblin first visited here in 1858, and crossed the Colorado here in 1864, opening up a major artery between Utah and Arizona. John D. Lee's cabin and a fence, although hard to see here, are near the river. Across the Colorado is the beginning of the dreaded road, Lee's Backbone. Photograph taken by William Bell or Timothy O'Sullivan, of the George M. Wheeler Geographical Survey, in 1872. Courtesy Wikimedia Commons/National Archives.

afraid of them. After continuing their journey, the company camped at Jacob's Pools, which Bleak called "a seepe from Red Bluff"—the Vermilion Cliffs—which was "a very good drinking place for horses." They found the boat that the missionaries had abandoned there on the ill-fated 1860 trip, untouched by the Paiutes.

The next morning the same Paiute, with two companions, showed up with pine nuts to trade for ammunition and rawhide. Jacob was nominated to handle the trading, and asked the Indians how much they wanted for the nuts. They "threw down their little sacks and told him to do what he thought right." When the trade was finished, they seemed very pleased with the outcome, Bleak reports. As we have seen, trading with Indians was always a factor in these early expeditions, as they were generally interested in acquiring white goods, especially ammunition.

The company traveled through a "barren and desolate looking country" that day—sand and clay and rocks, with little vegetation. They often had to keep near the base of the Vermilion Cliffs to avoid "deep and abrupt ravines" dropping off to the Colorado.

On the twentieth, they reached the Colorado at the mouth of the Paria, modern Lee's Ferry, where the Colorado's width was about two hundred yards.[25] They searched for a favorable place for crossing, and Isaac Riddle and Taylor Crosby noticed a point where the "Navajo Trail" led down to the river, then started again on the other side, so it was decided that this would be the place where they would attempt a crossing. (Once again, white explorers were simply following paths and crossings that had been used by Indians for centuries.)

Jacob and the whole company, except for a camp guard, went to find material for a raft. Though driftwood was scarce, the company was able to collect enough to construct a crude raft. In the afternoon Hamblin and Lysander Dayton crossed the Colorado in it, and found that there was indeed a trail on the other side of the river, with signs that Navajos and animals had been there recently. The day was finished with a religious meeting at which the company "enjoyed a goodly portion of the Holy Spirit."[26]

The next day, Jacob cached some provisions, then the company transported their baggage to the south side of the river, via the raft. In the late afternoon, they made two attempts to swim the horses across the river—both unsuccessful. (As in the 1863 expedition, the method for swimming the animals was for the men to ride on the raft, holding the horses as the animals swam beside it.)

On the twenty-second, the missionaries again tried to swim the horses and mules across the river, this time with more success, though this turned out to be a difficult, dangerous task. While David Cannon, on the raft, held a horse near, the terrified animal somehow twisted and a hoof struck him a blow on his arm, which was severely bruised, but fortunately, no bones were broken.

Thus Hamblin and company finished the historic crossing of the Colorado with baggage and animals. They had cut some six to eight days of dangerous, exhausting travel from their journey (including difficult descents into Crossing of the Fathers and Navajo Canyon). This was a triumph simply from the viewpoint of logistics: precious food supplies would go further, and the necessity of eating horses or mules (or badgers or crows) on a return journey could hopefully be avoided. From this time on, the Paria crossing became the main crossing point on the upper Colorado.

The next morning, the party followed a trail up the bluff. "Some parts were very steep," wrote Bleak. This may have been Lee's Backbone, later widely known for the difficulty of its road. They continued through "a broken country" till they were opposite Jacob's Pool on the other side of the Grand Canyon, at which point they followed an Indian trail—Riddle calls it "the old Ute trail"[27]—up a steep mountain, then made a dry camp on the summit.

The next morning they turned east toward Basin Rock, traveling through pine and cedar. This would put them on their former well-known route to the mesas. Both Navajo Mountain (to the northeast) and the San Francisco Peaks (to the southeast) were well in view. They reached Basin Rock at five p.m.—only to find no water there.

Jacob asked Isaac Riddle if he could find the spring where Spaneshanks had been camped when they first met him, and Riddle said he would try. They continued heading northeast, and after an hour and a half they came to a "high, steep mountain," and Riddle decided to climb up it to see if he could recognize any landmarks. He managed to crawl to the summit, where he was pleasantly stunned to find three large pools of rainwater.

He called down that there was plenty of water up where he was, in holes in rocks. He found that descending the mountain on another side was easy, and the missionaries could lead their horses up to the large pool. "And when we drunk our fill, and attended to our horses we knelt down and returned thanks to God for our deliverance," Riddle wrote.[28] The place was named Isaac's Rock in his honor.[29]

The party traveled through thirty miles of rocky, broken country the next day, still in Spaneshanks's direction, as Jacob wanted to discuss the stolen horses that Spaneshanks had said he would try to recover. The next morning, Jacob sent smoke signals to Spaneshanks, but when no one appeared at the camp, the party turned southwest and continued on its way. On March 25, they passed Flat Rock and Wildcat Peak, and the following day, the place where Jacob had left the body of George A. Smith Jr. They nooned at Quichintoweep, at the Moenkopi Wash, and the veterans of the 1860 expedition pointed out to Bleak where Smith Jr. had been shot.

They continued on the Ute trail till they came to Rock Cave, which sheltered them from snow that night. They reached Oraibi at about two p.m. on March 27. Unfortunately, the leading man of Oraibi and of other mesas had gone to visit the Zunis, in modern northwestern New Mexico, and would not be back for some time.

Bleak gave a standard visitor's description of the Hopis and Oraibi. For him, the keynote of Oraibi culture was hospitality. He wrote, "Whenever you enter, food is placed before you," especially *piki* and parched corn. At family meals, on the other hand, the main dish was a stew of boiled, parched corn and beans, to which corn dumplings were sometimes added. All ate the stew out of the same dish, with fingers. If the Hopi family had any spoons, they give them to the visitors to use. The dumplings were apparently similar to Mexican tamales, with "pulverized white corn rolled up in corn shucks and neatly tied," then boiled and served in the shucks.

This was clearly a diet greatly dependent on corn (of many varieties and colors, not simply modern yellow sweet corn). Bleak wrote that "the sound of grinding corn can be heard long before daylight and continues most of the forenoon."

On the evening of the twenty-eighth, the company had a meeting and decided that Hamblin, Hatch, Dayton, and Bleak would visit Shungopavi, on the Second Mesa, the next day, while the balance of the company would return to the spring four miles from Oraibi. So the next morning, Hamblin with three companions set out for Shungopavi, and on the way there met a chief from that town who had "an intelligent and very cheerful countenance," in Bleak's estimation. He told the Mormons that he was glad they were visiting his town, but his people "would surely not leave the homes of their fathers."

Shungopavi turned out to be about a third smaller than Oraibi, with cleaner streets and people who were better dressed. However, Bleak judged them to be "less hospitable and less cheerful" than the Oraibi dwellers. There were not many men left in the village (some had joined with the U.S. Army to fight against the Navajos), but the missionaries spoke to some Hopis in a private house. The Mormons then returned to Oraibi, where the chief had not returned.

On the thirtieth, the four missionaries called the people of Oraibi together and, with Lye acting as interpreter, invited them to accompany them to the new colony. "The most profound attention was given," Bleak wrote. However,

> before the close of the meeting one of the old men arose and told of the instructions that the Oribas had received from their forefathers to the effect that they were never to leave their homes for any other place or country. That if they remained in their rocky fastnesses in due time their enemies around them would be destroyed and game should again abound in their neighborhood.

Bleak emphasized that this was not spoken in "the spirit of opposition," but to explain why they could not "accept any proposition to leave the rock houses of their forefathers."

Hamblin and company also had to decide how to pursue the Navajo side of their mission. "We did not succeed in recovering the stolen horses," wrote Hamblin in his autobiography. "We were informed by the Moquis that the old Navajoe chief, the friendly Spaneshanks, had been discarded by his band, that his son had succeeded him as chief, and that he [the son] was disposed to raid at any favorable opportunity. For these reasons we thought it would be useless and perhaps dangerous to go into their country."[30] Once again, the Mormons were not able to visit and develop friendships with the Navajos, and in fact, their one close Navajo friend, the headman Spaneshanks, had suddenly lost status in his band.

Having fulfilled their mission to the extent they could, given the Oraibi chief's absence, Hamblin and his three companions turned homeward, leaving the Hopi town at noon and meeting their friends at the spring. On the way back home, they reached Isaac's Rock, where there had been plentiful water on the way to the mesas; unfortunately, only about five gallons could be found there now. As several animals were already very weak with thirst and Navajo Springs was forty-five miles away, they faced a "gloomy prospect." The missionaries decided to rest their horses for a while, then travel at night.

Not long after this, at about twilight, "the cry was raised" that six horses were missing, and a general search began. Two horses were quickly found, but four were still missing, so the company had no alternative but to make camp for the night where they were.

The next day, April 2, the four wandering horses were found soon after dawn. Then it began to snow, filling the holes in the rocks with welcome moisture. The crisis had ended. After the animals were watered, the company continued on its way.[31]

In Little, Hamblin tells this story as a miracle tale. When there was no water at places they expected it, he ascended a nearby hill and prayed earnestly for guidance. As he prayed he happened to look toward the Colorado River, forty miles away, and saw a small cloud that rapidly became bigger and bigger. In a half hour, "we were enveloped in a heavy snowstorm," he wrote. "The snow melted and ran into the cavities of the rocks, until there was an abundance of water." However, when the group started on its way, they found that the ground was dry a mile and a half from camp. "I thanked the Lord that He had sent us relief in our great need," wrote Hamblin.[32]

The company reached the Colorado on the fourth and were able to ferry their luggage and swim their horses across in only five hours. They passed Jacob's Pool the following day, then trekked through deep snow and camped on the Kaibab Plateau. They reached Pipe Spring on April 8. One senses that this part of the journey was almost a matter of course now, especially since there were settlers at Kanab, Pipe Spring, and Short Creek.

James Whitmore's ranch at Pipe Spring shows the rapid pace of Mormon colonization of southern Utah. Just six years earlier, the two divisions of Hamblin's company each had to kill a horse near Pipe Spring to avoid starvation as they made their last desperate marches home. Now, there was a ranch at the spring, and the owner was sympathetic to their cause. "We were out of meat and Bro. J. M. Whitmore who owns the ranch at the springs very kindly gave us a sheep to eat," wrote Bleak.[33]

This journey was in a way emblematic of Hamblin's dual persona, as missionary and explorer. It was a historic success as the first crossing of the Colorado by a company at Lee's Ferry. But in their main objectives, Hamblin and company had made no headway at all; despite their friendship with five or six prominent Hopis, they had not convinced them to join with them in a settlement outside of the mesas. And they had not even talked with any Navajos about the stolen horses.

Back in southern Utah, Jacob faced problems with local Indians in a number of places. According to Little, in 1864, Indians gathered between St. George and

Harrisburg, about seven miles northeast of Washington, "for the purpose of carrying out their threat to destroy some of the settlements the first favorable opportunity." Hamblin handled the situation in typical fashion. He took one man with him, George Adair, and no weapons.[34] When he reached the Indians, who had hidden their women and children in preparation for war, he asked them to bring them out again. By talking with the Indians, he wrote, "a better influence came over them, and the spirit of peace triumphed over irritation and a sense of wrong."[35]

Another flash moment of conflict with Indians occurred in summer 1864, seventy-five miles west of St. George—in modern Nevada, considered part of Utah at the time. According to Little, a band of Paiutes had joined with a band of Indians who had been driven out of California, and they threatened the new Mormon colonies of Meadow Creek (modern Panaca, in Lincoln County, a few miles south of Pioche), Clover Valley (twenty miles southeast of Panaca),[36] and Shoal Creek (near eventual Hebron, near modern Enterprise, in Utah).[37] According to Hamblin, the Mormons had killed two Indians, and the Indians had left their cornfields and retreated to the mountains in preparation for war.

Hamblin took Andrew Gibbons with him, sent out word for the Indians to come in for a talk and a feast, and killed an ox. "In a general talk, they told over their grievances," Hamblin wrote. "They said that they felt justified in what they had done, and also in what they intended to do." Hamblin, surprisingly, said he could not blame them, "viewing matters from their standpoint." He even "rather justified them in what they expected to do"—presumably attack the Mormon settlements in Nevada. However, he warned them that "in the end it would be worse for them to carry out their plans than to drop them, and smoke the pipe of peace." The Paiutes protested that Mormon cattle had eaten grass that produced seeds that Paiutes depended upon. Hamblin agreed with them on that point. "But if they would be friendly," he reasoned, "they could get more food by gleaning our fields than they had before we came into their country." After hours of talk, Hamblin wrote, "The difficulty was settled and we returned home."[38]

It is hard to place this incident exactly in the history of Panaca and Clover Valley. The existing historical record shows that Hamblin was involved in trying to resolve southeast Nevada Indian difficulties, but it does not seem to show such a neat resolution of the problems.

Jacob's brother, Bill "Gunlock" Hamblin, was a key figure in Nevada's Mormon history. He befriended an Indian, known as Moroni, and in 1863, the Paiute led him and another Mormon, William Pulsipher, to rocks filled with shiny metal—silver. After investigation, Hamblin, who had spent two years mining in California, had the rocks tested, then laid a preliminary claim to the site.[39]

Bill did not keep his claim secret, and Brigham Young and Erastus Snow became interested in securing and developing it, but did not follow through on laying a solid claim. Non-Mormons found out about the rich silver lode, and soon the area was swarming with miners. Legal difficulties arose over conflicting claims.[40]

In spring 1864, Panaca was settled in Meadow Valley, and Samuel Lee became its first presiding elder.[41] Pioche, a non-Mormon mining town, sprang up close by, and when the area's silver mines began to be successful, it became a boomtown mining community, legendary for its vice and violence.

The Mormons in Nevada at first had good relations with the local Paiutes, but the influx of miners and more Mormons destabilized Mormon-Indian relations, and the local Paiutes started troubling the Saints—intimidating women while men were in the fields, and stealing cattle.[42] A serious conflict with local Indians erupted, possibly caused by a large band of Paiutes attempting to drive off Mormon cattle in August 1864,[43] and five Indians were taken prisoner by Mormons. Though the evidence is contradictory, and Mormon accounts stated that the Indians were killed while trying to escape,[44] the earliest evidence suggests that at least three of the Indians were executed as unarmed prisoners. "I deeply regret the necessity for killing your Indian prisoners," Erastus Snow wrote to local settlers in August. "I fear it will render conciliation more difficult. I recommended to Brother Bunker the policy of taking no prisoners, but of killing thieves when taken in the act."[45] This reminds us of "take-no-prisoners" military policy in early Tooele and Utah Valley. Snow also referred to the "killing five of the Indians by the settlers of Panaca, three of them after they had been made prisoners and disarmed."[46] The local Paiutes were understandably furious and threatened war.

In response, Erastus Snow sent a "detachment of militia" commanded by John D. L. Pearce to the area. On August 27, Erastus Snow wrote to Pearce, Meltiar Hatch (Ira's brother), and Samuel Lee,

> If there is indeed a combined movement of a large number of warriors to attack Panaca, as these letters represent, I would advise that your women and children be at once sent to Pinto Creek, or elsewhere, beyond danger... and for men to remain to secure the crops, complete the stockade and entrench themselves if necessary.... You ask my advice in relation to the policy to be pursued toward these hostile Indians in the event of Bro. Hamblin failing to restore peace.[47]

So Jacob was indeed in Nevada acting as diplomat at the time. On August 29, he and Tutsegabits returned from Nevada and reported to Snow. The apostle wrote to Brigham Young, on that day, "Bro Hamlin accompanied by Indian Tutsigavit came in and by conversing with them, I feel confirmed in my previous opinion that the threatened evil may be turned aside by the exercise of common prudence, and just forbearance towards the natives."[48] Jacob and Tutsegabits clearly reported that the settlers had not been practicing "prudence" and "forbearance."

Jacob probably had a tempering impact on this dispute, but the historical record shows no decisive conclusion for the conflict. When Pearce and his militia left the area, half of the residents left with him, and Paiutes continued to attack Mormon settlements and herds in early 1865 and 1866.[49] Historian John Alton Peterson connects these conflicts with the Black Hawk War.[50]

Using an unfortunate passive construction, Bleak writes, "It was suggested"—by whom? Erastus Snow seems the likely suggester—"that the remaining settlers of Meadow Valley leave for a safer locality."[51] However, some of the Lees and a few others decided to remain.

On November 4 Erastus Snow, in a conference, assigned Jacob to help Meltiar Hatch and other Mormons "re-commence the settlement" of Eagle Valley with their stock, "provided that they take such measures and precautions as not to embroil themselves with the Indians."[52] Ira Hatch and Fred Hamblin also were part of the Eagle Valley resettlement.[53]

Bill Hamblin and other Mormon claimants sold their silver mine holdings to non-Mormons.[54] At some point, Bill was excommunicated from the LDS Church—possibly because of his dealings with non-Mormon mining developers.[55] Mormon leaders were somewhat ambivalent about mining, most often condemning it and associating it with non-Mormons and apostates (former Mormons, often antagonistic to the LDS Church), though at other times they actively sought for precious metals to help build up Zion.[56]

In 1872, Bill Hamblin was called to testify in a law case related to his former mine, and while in Pioche, his coffee was poisoned before he could testify.[57] Mortally sick, he was rebaptized on May 6, then died two days later at the age of forty-two—a tragically untimely death.

Brigham Young and Erastus Snow continued to seek new roads into Arizona. On June 11, the High Council in St. George deemed it advisable "to explore for a more direct wagon-road from St. George to the head of navigation on the Colorado and especially for a distance of twenty miles, or so, from St. George in a S. W. direction," according to Bleak. Jacob Hamblin, Isaac Duffin, a resident of Toquerville,[58] David H. Cannon, and Leonard H. Conger, who had ridden the Pony Express on the Utah-California road, were appointed to carry out this exploration, with power to call others to help them.[59] Presumably this expedition took place, but there are no other extant references to it.

In late 1864, Young took definite steps to create a settlement on the lower Colorado. In February, merchant William P. Hardy had created a commercial landing on the lower Colorado seven miles north of Fort Mohave. He wrote to the Mormons and suggested that they trade with him, or rather, trade with California through him. The Mormons were interested, but decided to also create their own settlement on the Colorado, with a warehouse, at the Colorado's "head of navigation." Brigham Young and some Mormon commercial leaders gave the assignment to Anson Call, a trusted agent for Young then living in northern Utah.[60] The purpose of the new landing would be partly commercial, but in addition Young hoped that European Mormons might immigrate via Panama and the Gulf of California up the Colorado to the Mormon landing.[61]

In the November 4 conference, Erastus Snow read Hardy's letter, then proposed that some men "make further exploration on the Colorado," in search of "a road to the head of navigation"—that is, the highest point that boats could travel north and northeast on the Colorado. In addition, they should visit Hardy's Landing and make arrangements for trade with Hardy. Snow designated Jacob Hamblin, Hamblin's son Lyman, James M. Whitmore (the Pipe Spring rancher), David H. Cannon, and Angus M. Cannon (another brother of George Q. Cannon) to be members of this exploring team.[62] In addition, Brigham Young had specifically asked Jacob to help lay out the path of a road to the Colorado.[63]

On November 25, Call, relative James Davids, Angus Cannon, and Whitmore (David Cannon for some reason had dropped out), arrived in Santa Clara, and picked up Jacob and Lyman.[64] In a meeting the next day, Call appointed Hamblin "Interpreter and Guide," while Angus Cannon was named clerk. The company traveled west and southwest, past Joshua Canyon, then visited Beaver Dams (which would become a Mormon settlement within a year) and the farm of "Indian Thomas."[65] Call described this area as a good place for Mormon settlement. The next day, with high mountains on their left all day, they crossed the Virgin River. They reached "Virgen Hill," where the California Road leaves the Virgin, five miles west of modern Bunkerville, on the thirtieth.[66] They left the road and traveled fifteen miles down the Virgin, reaching the mouth of the Muddy, the site of the soon-to-be-founded Muddy Mission town of St. Thomas. "To-day we saw many Indians," wrote Call. "We were struck with the respect they showed towards Br. Hamblin."

On December 1, the company crossed the Virgin and traveled along the Muddy for a while. Call felt that this valley was ripe for colonization. The company then returned to the Virgin and traveled along it for twelve miles, afterward turning into a wash, which they named Echo Wash. "Our Guide [Hamblin] talked with many of the Indians met by us to-day," wrote Call. "They are anxious for us to settle their country, and are willing for our cattle to eat their grass, if we will employ them that they may have clothes to wear and food to eat when their grass seed is all used." This is a remarkable statement—it shows that Mormon colonists were well aware that their cattle herds would destroy the precious seeds that Indians depended upon. It also shows how substantially southern Utah Mormons depended on ranching, not just on farming.

On December 2, the group apparently continued to follow the wash and came to the Colorado "a mile below the narrows above the mouth of Black kanyon." This was about two and a half miles north of the mouth of Las Vegas Wash. Close to the mouth of the wash, they discovered the site of future Callville, or Call's Landing. "We found a black rocky point which we considered a suitable locality for the erection of a warehouse above high-water mark; here we considered the best landing could be established," Call wrote.[67] They camped on an extensive bottom that they considered good land, which would become the projected site for Callville.[68] The next day, they traveled to Las Vegas Wash, then followed it up to Las Vegas, where about five men, apparently non-Mormons, were ranching.

On the fifth, the company set out south, ascended a summit, then descended into "Eldorado kanyon," where they came upon a miner's camp. The next day, they continued their descent, turned to the right, and "followed a tortuous trail over rocky ridges and gulches" for twenty-five miles, finally reaching the Colorado. They came to Cottonwood Island, which, along with a bottom on the west side of the river, was "farmed by Indians after the river floods subside," Call wrote. However, "white adventurers"—apparently miners—had claimed both the island and the fertile land on the west.

The party then traveled twenty-three miles over a trail that was, if anything, worse than the previous day's, then arrived at Hardy's Landing, which was on the west side of the river. As they were on the east side, they had to hail a boat moored at the landing, but the boat owners were happy to ferry the Mormons across the river. By bad luck, Hardy was absent on a visit to Prescott, Arizona's capitol, but the Mormons were warmly received by Hardy's agent.

Call now decided to split up the company; he, Whitmore, and Cannon would stay at Hardy's Landing and hope that Hardy would return soon, while the rest of the party—presumably the two Hamblins and James Davids—would return to the site of Call's Landing and start creating roads there.

Call and his group waited until the thirteenth, but Hardy did not return, so they departed northward again and camped at lower Cottonwood Island. "Here we were much troubled by mosquetoes, which are very large," Call wrote. That must have been a restless night.

On the seventeenth they reached the mouth of Las Vegas Wash then traveled on to the new landing, where they must have met Jacob, Lyman, and Davids. Call claimed the settlement as "Agent for President Brigham Young, Trustee in Trust in, and for, The Church of Jesus Christ of Latter Day Saints."[69] They measured off forty lots for the new community, then the next day they departed, leaving Lyman Hamblin and James Davids to dig the foundation for a warehouse. They camped at Salt Mountain on the nineteenth, two miles from the mouth of the Muddy.

The next day, they "more thoroughly examined the facilities for forming a settlement on the Muddy" and found the site more promising than they had previously realized. The Muddy Mission would be founded in less than a month; the Mormons expected that these settlements would serve as a way station for projected immigrants and commercial travelers on their way to and from Callville.[70]

After this, the company explored a new route back to St. George, as the present route was not only extremely sandy, but had to cross the Virgin in twenty-three places, and quicksand was often found at those crossings.

The company therefore turned east toward modern Pearce's Ferry. They ascended the mountains via the Grand Wash, reached a summit, then arrived at St. George on the evening of December 24. Call wrote that this route was ten miles shorter than the Virgin River route, and to create a road here would cost six thousand dollars. Hamblin was also enthusiastic, though he thought that the road would need considerable work north at the "summit," which was probably near Mustang Knoll. For various reasons, this road was never built, though a primitive road to the Colorado via the Grand Wash eventually was used to reach Pearce's Ferry in the 1870s.

The three expeditions Hamblin went on this year are evidence of his importance to the expanding Mormon community as explorer and guide. He had come to know both the lower and upper Colorado quite well, along with the territory south of the upper Colorado, and Brigham Young and Erastus Snow assigned him to help found towns, locate and start laying out roads, and open up commercial opportunities for Mormon interests. In one sense, Jacob's seventh trip across the Colorado was a special triumph, given that he had now made a practical crossing of the great barrier of the Colorado, at future Lee's Ferry, and opened up the pathway to future Mormon colonies in Arizona, New Mexico, and old Mexico. However, in another sense, Jacob's missions to the Hopis and Navajos on that trip were not successful. The Navajos would continue raiding in southern Utah, and the Hopis would for the most part stay in or near their mesas.

17

"Why She Ever Married 'Old Jacob' Was a Mystery"

The Death of Rachel and Marriage to Louisa, 1865

Since Callville had been founded the previous December, Erastus Snow and Anson Call continued to call upon Jacob's skills as frontiersman and missionary as they sought to make the new settlement a commercial success. Young and Snow wondered if they could set up a boating route down the Virgin "with a view to accelerate building a warehouse at Mormon Landing on the Colorado." Hamblin was called upon to try this experiment.[1] A flatboat (named "Virgen Adventurer") was built and on January 17, Hamblin set out on this mission, accompanied by one L. J. Utley—apparently fifty-nine-year-old Little John Utley, a longtime resident of Tooele who had moved to Dixie.[2] The Virgin was unusually low, six to eight inches deep, due to freezing in the mountains, but Jacob and Utley had no trouble for their first two miles of their trip. Then they reached modern Virgin River Gorge, the beautiful, dramatic canyon which all travelers on the I-15 highway from St. George to southern Nevada now drive through. Here, the water became even more shallow, and five miles into the canyon, Hamblin and Utley had to leave their boat and "carry their bedding and provisions, crossing and recrossing the water a great many times."

One recorder of this journey, Daniel Bonelli, now succumbed to the beauty of the canyon:

> The acute angles of the current's course, together with the great bowlders and cliffs therein, the towering walls of dingy basalt on either side, the unbroken silence of this desert region, except the rushing of the water breaking over the rocks, combine to make this spot one of the cheariest loveliness—the most inexpressible desolation.[3]

It is not clear if Jacob and Utley merely traveled through the Virgin Canyon, or if they followed the Virgin all the way to the Colorado. Bonelli gave Jacob's conclusion:

"Br. Hamblin thinks, in times of high water, a downward trip could be made easily and rapidly."

Jacob returned to Santa Clara by February 8 at the latest. Rachel was fading fast, but Jacob was apparently called away again soon after this. Priscilla, in her autobiography, writes that at the time of Rachel's death, "Jacob was away."[4]

After listing a series of deaths in the family, Priscilla wrote, "Rachel, my precious friend and advisor, was next. I had sat up at night with her for a week."[5] As Priscilla nursed her, Rachel "would express her thanks to her over and over."[6] Finally, when she saw her death approaching, "she said to Priscilla, 'Priscilla, you have been so kind to me. After I die and am resurrected I hope you're the first one I meet.' Priscilla answered, 'The load will be easy if you stand true to your trust and depend on the Lord.'" Priscilla was pregnant, and Rachel told her the baby would be a son and to name it Jacob. Rachel died on February 18, in Priscilla's arms.[7] "The place would never be the same again without this one of God's angels, whom He had called to leave us," Priscilla later wrote.[8] The closeness of their bond must have compensated on some level for Jacob's many absences.[9]

Rachel was buried three days later, on the twenty-first.[10] A month later, on March 21, Priscilla gave birth to the promised son, who was named Jacob Jr., as Rachel had requested.[11]

When Jacob returned, he must have been devastated to find his second wife gone, Rachel who had been so loyal and kind after his stormy first marriage. But there was a new boy, a namesake, as some sort of recompense.

Priscilla, now twenty-three, was raising her own children (Olive, Melissa, Lucy, and Jacob Jr.), as well as all of Rachel's (Lois, Joseph, Tamar, and Benjamin), by herself during Jacob's absences. But she would not remain Hamblin's only wife for long.

We have seen that the capable, articulate Daniel Bonelli was a leader of the Swiss Saints in Santa Clara.[12] His parents and siblings followed him to Santa Clara, probably in 1864, and Jacob Hamblin came to know the whole family, George and Anna Bonelli, and Daniel's twenty-two-year-old, small, black-haired, blue-eyed sister, Louisa.[13] The young Swiss woman reportedly turned down multiple prospective suitors before her marriage to Jacob. When Jacob asked her father for permission to marry her, George had reservations concerning the difference in age (Hamblin was now forty-six) and the polygamous household Louisa would marry into. "But Louisa begged her father to agree to the marriage, and eventually he gave his consent."[14] Thus, family tradition sees Louisa as eager for the marriage.

Non-Mormon Frederick Dellenbaugh wrote that it was a mystery why "she ever married 'Old Jacob'" at all, "for she was not old and was rather attractive in her personal appearance."[15] While it was common for older men to marry younger women of

17.1. Louisa Bonelli Hamblin, Jacob Hamblin's fifth wife. Born in Switzerland, she lived with Jacob in Santa Clara and Kanab, Utah, and in Pleasanton, New Mexico. This image was taken about the time she married Hamblin. Courtesy International Society Daughters of Utah Pioneers.

childbearing age in Utah,[16] Louisa may have felt a bit of hero worship for the prominent Indian missionary, a spiritual leader in the community. Hamblin was also comparatively well-to-do in Santa Clara.

Jacob and Louisa were married on November 18, 1865, in Salt Lake City, in the Endowment House, with Apostle George Q. Cannon officiating.[17]

Louisa had been born on October 28, 1843, in Weingarten, Switzerland, near Bern, to Hans Georg and Anna Maria Ammann Bonelli (originally Bommelli).[18] According to a short biography that preserves some of Louisa's own statements, she learned the value of physical labor early, and did all the knitting for a family of eight.[19] "She never had time to play but would watch the other children while she sat knitting."[20]

In 1854, when Louisa was eleven, her family was baptized into the LDS Church, reportedly through a hole broken in the ice on a day so cold their baptismal clothes froze to their bodies.[21] Louisa suffered persecution for her Mormonism in her local school, so her parents sent her to Bern, where she could attend school with other Mormons. The Bonellis began saving to emigrate.

Three years later, when Louisa was a young teenager, she, her parents, and two of her sisters, Susanna and Elizabeth, traveled to Liverpool, then sailed on the *George Washington* to Boston.[22] "I wasn't at all seasick and did not have sense enough to be afraid on the ship," Louisa said later. "I would stand on the deck and watch the great waves roll up and sometimes they would wash across me but I hung on to the post and enjoyed it."[23]

The Bonellis arrived at the Missouri River in May 1857 and traveled in the Sixth Handcart Company, led by Israel Evans, departing May 22.[24] Louisa remembered the journey as idyllic: "The weather was warm and lovely. I walked all the 1,300 miles to the Salt Lake Valley, helping to pull a cart most of the way." Louisa wore wooden shoes, which would often get stuck in the mud. "In the company was a crippled girl about eight years of age. She had to be carried all the way. I had my turn at carrying her on my back."[25] She fondly remembered gathering buffalo chips for campfires at the end of the day.

The Bonellis arrived at Salt Lake on September 11, and Hans Bonelli started a spinning and weaving business—Louisa was an expert spinner. The move to Santa Clara, probably in 1864, and the marriage to Hamblin followed.

Having a new wife did not turn Jacob into more of a homebody and he still spent "most of the time amongst the Indians."[26] Louisa, as she started to have children, would find that she was often left to herself to deal with family necessities. Louisa's relationship with Priscilla was not as close as Rachel's had been, but family traditions preserve no accounts of major tensions between them.

Once Louisa asked Jacob why he was always talking to himself, and Jacob joked: "Well, in the first place, I like to hear a smart man talk, and in the second place, I like to talk to a smart man."[27] While some accounts portray Jacob as unsmiling and humorless, his family did not remember him that way. According to his youngest daughter, Amarilla (who must have heard stories from her siblings, as she was only two when he died), he "loved a joke." She wrote that one day he asked his son, Oscar, "Is the old mare tied up good?" The boy replied, "Yes, I guess so, you tied her up." Jacob "laughed heartily" and replied, "Well, I'm glad I have a son who has confidence in me."[28]

In mid-winter, in December, Jacob and James Whitmore visited Las Vegas, the Muddy Mission, and the Lower Colorado.[29] "I was called on this trip to accompany Doctor Whitmore on special business to the Vegas," wrote Hamblin. It is not known precisely what that business was.

At Beaver Dam (Millersburg), which had been settled earlier in the year, a spring had been discovered that made irrigation feasible. Daniel Bonelli was now a resident of this town, though he would not stay there long.[30]

Next Hamblin and Whitmore visited the new settlements on the Muddy.[31] St. Thomas, the first town of the Muddy Mission, had been founded at the junction of the Muddy and Virgin in January, and St. Joseph, eight miles up the Muddy, had been settled in June.[32] These communities, founded in enormously dry and difficult territory, were intended to be links to Callville in the grand scheme to bring immigrants and goods to Utah by way of the lower Colorado, and it was also hoped that they could produce cotton. According to Hamblin, these towns had been weakened by the men being absent on trips north for supplies and by "the depredations of the Indians upon their crops"; nevertheless, "the chances are ample for large and flourishing settlements."[33]

At Callville, Hamblin and Whitmore found two non-Mormons living in the warehouse, with "two Mohave Pied squaws"—probably Chemehuevi women—housekeeping for them. One of the men had collected about eighty cords of driftwood, and Hamblin thought that similar wood salvage projects might provide a good source for steamboat fuel. At this point, Bonelli (it seems his voice here) rhapsodizes on the bright future of the Callville project. "Energy and enterprize are all that is needed to make this natural highway to the commerce of the world yield its advantages to our secluded home," he wrote.[34]

Hamblin and Whitmore found Las Vegas inhabited by five non-Mormons who had planted forty acres of wheat and were raising stock, making a good living selling these products to western travelers. "We partook of the hospitality of the occupants," wrote Hamblin and Bonelli. "The swearing propensity apparent here reminded us of being 'from home,' though at meal time we were honored with the office of 'saying grace,' as it had transpired that we were Mormons, who, it appears, are allowed to be conversant with this practice."[35]

Hamblin and Whitmore also visited the Chemehuevis and Mohaves on the lower Colorado, returning to Santa Clara on December 18.[36]

Dr. Whitmore reported that a few of the settlers on the notoriously difficult Muddy settlements had moved on to California and that "but little business" was being done at Call's Landing.[37] This last datum, more realistic than the Hamblin and Bonelli letter, points to Callville's eventual fate. The settlement never took off as a commercial venture (or as a site for Mormon immigration), for a number of reasons.[38] While Callville was at the "head of navigation," the Colorado was rough and dangerous at many places between Hardy's Landing and Callville, and building roads from St. George to Call's Landing would have been enormously expensive. Furthermore, when a transcontinental railroad was completed in Utah in 1869, the lower Colorado transport route became unnecessary.[39] Presently, Callville is a "drowned town," submerged beneath Lake Mead.

18

"I Never Was So Ashamed of Anything in My Life"

Murder and Massacre at Pipe Spring, 1866

A military company from St. George and other Mormon towns massacred eight unarmed Paiutes near Pipe Spring in January 1866, after another group of Indians, probably Navajos, had killed two Mormons, rancher James Whitmore, and his herdsman, Robert McIntyre, near the same site.[1] Hamblin started out as the group's Indian interpreter, but severe illness caused him to turn back. Nevertheless, he subsequently made important comments on the incident, based on his interviews with Indian and Mormon participants, and for this reason, and because the "Pipe Spring Massacre" is a significant event in southern Utah Mormon-Indian relations, it will be treated here. It is a complex story, and much of the evidence for it is conflicting. As is typical in the Mormon historical record when it treats conflicts with Indians, some sources are thoroughly partisan and portray the Mormon actions as justified and even heroic. Other Mormon sources were entirely sympathetic to the Paiutes and were revolted by the actions of the military, which were interpreted by these eyewitnesses as unjustified, vengeful, and bloodthirsty.

The story begins in 1863, when James Whitmore started a cattle ranch at Pipe Spring, now in Arizona, on the trail from the Dixie settlements to Hopi and Navajo country.[2] Whitmore, a thirty-six-year-old native of Tennessee, moved with his family to Texas when he was a child, and his family farmed and raised cattle on 160 acres of land. James became interested in medicine, served in the medical corps in the Mexican War, and thereafter was called "Doctor." He and his brother Franklin joined the Texas Rangers and fought with Indians and outlaws for a time, then returned to ranching. The Whitmores were converted to Mormonism, and James and Franklin made a unique hegira to Utah—driving more than a thousand Texas longhorn cattle before them. James came to St. George with five hundred cattle in 1861 and must have immediately begun looking for a place to situate them. He built a home in St. George, where his wife and children lived permanently.[3]

At Pipe Spring he built a comfortable dugout, fenced in eleven acres, and planted grapevines and apple and peach trees.[4] He divided his time between St. George and Pipe Spring, and in addition to his cattle, he also kept a sizable herd of sheep there.

Starting this ranch was a bold move, as it was not close to other major Mormon settlements—though Short Creek was a few miles to the west and Kanab was a few miles to the east, they were not substantial towns. Pipe Spring had been an important Indian water source and meeting place since time immemorial. Nevertheless, the local Indians did not seem to be a threat. Whitmore had good relations with the Kaibab Paiutes, and reportedly often would slaughter a steer to share with them and would help doctor their sick and injured.[5]

But a number of circumstances put outlying Mormon settlements and ranches such as Whitmore's in a precarious position at this time. First, as we have seen, the Navajo wars in New Mexico and Arizona ended with most of the Navajo nation sent to Bosque Redondo in 1864, while the remnant who refused to go were the more dangerous element, who were placed in desperate circumstances and became, in effect, outlaws. Many of these Navajos, expert horsemen and adept at stealing cattle and sheep from New Mexican settlements, now turned these skills to raids on Mormon settlements northwest of the Colorado.[6]

Second, the Black Hawk War, a response by Utes to the U.S. government and the Mormons trying to force them from their ancestral homelands and onto a reservation, had begun in spring 1865. Black Hawk led a band of renegades and outlaws that conducted raids on Mormon settlements, especially on towns in Sanpete County in central Utah. But the conflict also had repercussions in southern Utah, as Black Hawk's Utes often allied with Navajos and Paiutes to carry out raids in Mormon settlements in Long Valley, the Kanab area, and Dixie. Black Hawk often lived in southeastern Utah.

Third, as has been noted previously, the major influx of Mormons into southern Utah in 1861, and the foundation of a number of new settlements there, began to crowd Paiutes from their traditional water sources and hunting grounds, and cattle grazing began to destroy the delicate ecosystem that the Paiutes depended upon. Before the Mormons came, they were on the edge of starvation; now, many of them actually starved to death. In addition, exposure to white man's diseases increasingly killed many Indians. Placed in a desperate situation, many Paiutes turned to theft—Hamblin in fact wrote that their situation forced them into theft.

Because of all these factors, many Indians—Utes and Navajos, sometimes allied with Paiutes and Apaches[7]—attacked Pahreah, Kanab, and Pipe Spring in December 1865.[8] They reportedly drove off a number of Whitmore's cattle, and he came to Pipe Spring to investigate in early January 1866.

The next chapter in the Pipe Spring Massacre involves another outlying community, Pahreah, which the Shirts family, Peter and Margaret Murch Shirts, their son Don Carlos, a daughter, and Ezra Meeks, had settled in 1865, high on the Paria River—a typical Shirts settlement on the outlying fringes of the Mormon frontier. Peter built a solid defensive house from sandstone, nestled against a cliff, presumably modern Rock House Cove, and the settlement became known as Rockhouse or Pahreah (I refer to it as Pahreah I). It was located about four miles south of the eventual location of the town of Pahreah II. The Shirts family and Meeks planted crops, tended herds, and prospected for precious metals.[9] Clearly, they did not see the local Indians as a threat, and we have seen that Hamblin, in his trips through Kaibab Paiute territory, always viewed them as friends.

Nevertheless, tensions with Indians developed here, as a mixture of Utes, Paiutes, and Navajos, began to steal food from Rockhouse fields and appropriate the community's livestock. According to a Paiute oral tradition, one day, when Don Carlos Shirts found that Indians had stolen some of his corn, he placed a curse on the Indians who were responsible, and the "hexed men" indeed suffered "lingering and mysterious" deaths. The informant emphasized to Palmer that both Paiutes and Navajos felt "anger and fright" as a result (which confirms that Navajos were part of the corn-raiding party). Both Paiutes and Navajos were terrified of witchcraft and were known to kill suspected witches.[10]

Sometime in 1865, church leaders in St. George sent word to Rockhouse that Indian troubles were looming and that outlying settlers should return to secure towns. Apparently Ezra Meeks complied with this directive, but the eccentric Peter Shirts and his family, a wife and four children, refused or, according to some accounts, were not able to leave safely. They stayed in their rock house, something of a house fort, through the winter, while Indians drove off all Peter's cattle and took all the food in his fields.[11] There is a legend that a Mormon military force came to rescue him in the spring, only to find him plowing the ground with Paiutes harnessed in his plow.[12] However, Peter left Rockhouse in February,[13] at a time of deep snows, so it is unlikely that this legend is true.

According to Paiute oral tradition, the raid of Whitmore's ranch was a partial result of a desire for vengeance after the two hexed Indians died.[14]

Later, Hopis at Oraibi informed Jacob that a Paiute had led Navajos to the Whitmore ranch:

> Oribes said that it was 3 Piutes that led the theveing bands of Navajose. One of the Paiutes was Patnish.... He took Lasae [?] with him and led the[m] to the Pipe Spring. When Whitmore was kiled then went back to the Buckskins Mts and wated and wated [?] for the Navajose and went back with them. He is thare [their] leder.... Thare is 2 others. One by the name of Uncop. The other Shanap.[15]

Patnish was a formidable headman of the San Juan Paiutes, who lived across the Colorado near Navajo Mountain.[16] Frederick Dellenbaugh, a member of the second Powell company in 1871 and 1872, described Patnish as a dangerous Ute chief who led a band of renegade Utes and Navajos.[17] But Anthony Ivins, who met Patnish in 1875, described him as a Navajo, culturally:

> About sundown Pahtnish the Ute Chief and nine of his men rode up to our camp they were well armed and were the hardest looking lot of men I ever saw. Pahtnish is a Ute by birth was raised among the Navajoes and finaly got to be chief over a small band of desperadoes part Navajoes and part Pah Utes. He is said to be the man who led the party that killed Bros. Whitmore and McIntire at Pipe Spring.[18]

Patnish is a classic example of the occasional difficulty in making exact tribal identifications of Indians in the American Southwest. First, it was often difficult to distinguish between the Weeminuche Utes in the Four Corners area and San Juan Paiutes.[19] Second, he was probably a Paiute captive raised by Navajos, thus was culturally entirely a Navajo. Third, the group he led was a combination of Utes, Paiutes, and Navajos.

Thus, according to Hopi friends of Jacob Hamblin, a Paiute (though not a local Paiute) and a band of Navajos, south of the Colorado, planned the raid on Whitmore's ranch. Perhaps they had been involved in raids on Rockhouse, so had felt they had been hexed by Carlos Shirts. The Paiute and the Navajos decided on James Whitmore and his herdsman to satisfy the blood debt, undoubtedly because Whitmore's herds offered raiding opportunities as well as vengeance. After Patnish led the Navajos to Pipe Spring, he retired to the Kaibab Plateau to await their return.

Some early Mormons felt that local Paiutes helped the Navajos in the killing. David Chidester, a member of the St. George military expedition, stated that the Navajos would often cross the Colorado "and compel the less powerful tribe to do their bidding." On this occasion, some Navajos "compelled the Shevete's [Shivwits Paiutes] who were camped in the neighborhood to assist in the killing."[20] One very early source, John Steele's January 22 letter, states that Paiutes alone committed the murder—in Steele's view, they had been "stealing all the time and laying the blame on the Navajoes."[21] Actually, it is well documented that Navajos were raiding in Mormon settlements, so Steele's general perspective can be discounted.

However, Jacob Hamblin, and Kaibab Paiute traditions, laid the murders directly at the door of the Navajos: "In the winter...Dr. Whitmore and his herder, young McIntyre, were killed...by the Navajoes, who also drove off their sheep and some cattle," Jacob wrote.[22] In other words, he knew that Patnish was complicit in the planning of the raid, but felt that neither he nor any Paiutes actually committed the murder.

In 1866, a Paiute headman in Parowan named "Owannup" insisted "that

Whitmore and Macintire were murdered and the Ranch robbed by Navajoes and that the Pah Edes played only a secondary part being fools and begging some of the spoils."[23] Cedar City Paiutes, including a survivor of the massacre, "declared very stoutly that the Paiutes did not kill Whitmore and McIntire; that Navajoes did that."[24] Another Paiute, a son and grandson of massacre victims, stated, "The trouble started when the Navajos killed" Whitmore.[25] Historian John Alton Peterson places the Pipe Spring murder and massacre in the context of the Black Hawk War, in which Navajos were allied with Utes.[26]

Erastus Snow reported that Navajos from Spaneshanks's band were part of the group that killed Whitmore and McIntyre.[27] Though Snow was not a firsthand witness, this is entirely credible.

On the morning of January 8, 1866, James Whitmore and Robert McIntyre left the dugout to hunt horses on the range, telling Whitmore's eleven-year-old son, James Jr., that they would be back for dinner. They took no food or bedding with them.[28] They were never seen alive by whites again.

We have no good account of the murder of Whitmore and McIntyre. Only the condition of the bodies, when they were discovered on the twentieth, gives us hints of how they died. Each man received one gunshot wound "from the left side," and had been shot by multiple arrows—Whitmore had eight arrow wounds and McIntyre sixteen.[29]

The Navajos then stripped the bodies of their outer clothing and hid them in the wilderness, and a heavy snow subsequently covered them. They were apparently killed or buried about four miles southeast of the dugout.[30]

The Navajos then took Whitmore and McIntyre's mounts, rode them back to the sheep corral, not far from the dugout, and took the sheep, as well as a horse and a mule at the ranch.[31] Whitmore's eleven-year-old son was at the ranch headquarters, but though the Indians came to the area, he hid in the dugout and was not noticed or killed.[32]

According to Paiute traditions, the Navajos, leading the stock away, traveled south to Bull Rush Wash, which empties into Kanab Creek about six miles southeast of Pipe Spring, where they found a band of local Paiutes and camped with them.[33] They told them that they had killed the two men at Pipe Spring, indicated where the bodies were located, and advised them to move far from their present camp.[34] "They...gave them some of the clothing stripped from the bodies. They also killed two sheep for meat and gave her people the two pelts and some of the meat."[35] Two of the local Paiute boys, with one or two men, went to see the bodies.

The Navajos then continued in haste to modern Lee's Ferry or to the Crossing of the Fathers, and safety on the other side of the Colorado. The Paiutes who had been camping at Bull Rush moved "down to Grammer Canyon,"—probably Grama Canyon, which leads into Kanab Canyon—about six miles away.[36]

Whitmore's son, or a friendly Paiute, brought the news of the disappearance of Whitmore and McIntyre to nearby communities.[37] Local Mormons investigated Pipe Spring on the eleventh and found the ranch deserted and the stock mostly gone.[38] Bill Maxwell, at Short Creek, immediately went to St. George,[39] and forty-four volunteers from St. George and surrounding towns set out for Pipe Spring on the twelfth. This group was headed by Col. Daniel D. McArthur, a pillar of the St. George community, and included another prominent military leader, Col. James Andrus (who had accompanied Jacob on the 1862–1863 journey across the Colorado).[40] Hamblin started out in the group to serve as Indian interpreter, but was stricken by a painful attack of calculus, kidney stones,[41] so he had to return to Santa Clara, and was apparently replaced by Andrew S. Gibbons as interpreter.[42] So Hamblin's moderating voice was lost to this Mormon military group.

McArthur's party arrived at Pipe Spring on the sixteenth, then set up headquarters at Moccasin Springs, about two miles north. After a period of preliminary scouting, on the nineteenth a group of Mormons led by Andrus came upon two young local Paiutes slaughtering a beef and questioned them.[43] These were apparently the same two boys from the Bull Rush Paiute camp who had come to see the bodies. Edwin D. Woolley Jr., however, remembered an older Paiute (afflicted by epilepsy) and a younger Paiute. When questioned about the deaths of Whitmore and McIntyre, the older Paiute was terrified and immediately fell down in an epileptic seizure.[44]

Though they were reluctant to talk about the Whitmore-McIntyre killings, death threats and possible physical intimidation[45] convinced these Paiutes to communicate what they knew, and, in a somewhat cryptic fashion, they revealed that Navajos had murdered the two Mormons. On the twentieth, at about ten a.m., one of the boys directed part of the company (led by McArthur) to the site of Whitmore and McIntyre's bodies.[46] The corpses were covered by snow, but a horse accidentally uncovered Whitmore's elbow. Then the Indian led the men to the site of McIntyre's corpse.

The other boy led Andrus and his group to the band of Paiutes (presumably still at Grama Canyon) who had camped with the Navajos—this group of Paiutes comprised six or seven men, two or three women, and two children.[47] The Mormons, arriving at sunrise on the twentieth,[48] found in the possession of the Paiutes Whitmore and McIntyre's clothes, some money, new sheepskins[49] and Whitmore's saddle[50]—these items sealed the fate of these Paiute men. Two of the Paiutes were killed at this camp—reportedly because they resisted the Mormon soldiers.[51] Bleak writes that while the whites were searching the camp, one Indian refused to move from his sitting position when asked to do so. Charles Lytle tried to make him move, and the Indian reportedly "drew an arrow with the evident intention of shooting." Captain

James Andrus accordingly shot and killed the Indian, and Whitmore's clothes were found beneath him.[52]

Bleak continues that the Indians "were now called upon to deliver their arms." However, one Indian "after doing so, made three attempts to wrest a gun from some of the boys, his desperation increased to such a degree that it was necessary to kill him." Anson Winsor tells a similar story: "Then an other repenting [of having given up his weapon] Sprung fore one of the boys and tried to get his gun failing he tried another and so-on till one of the boys Struck him over the head with his revolver and broke his Skull in then they killed him."[53]

Edwin D. Woolley Jr. tells a much different story, in which the Indians told the Mormons that they had not committed the murders, but the Navajos had forced them to help drive off the sheep. However, the Mormons "found Whitmore's overcoat on one of the Indians, another was wearing McIntyre's pants." Andrus took this as conclusive proof of the guilt, so "commenced firing upon them, the women and children were mixed up with the men. Killed 2 or 3 and took 4 prisoners."[54] Here there is no rationale of resisting arrest or seizing guns—the Mormon militia simply fired into the group of Paiutes, male, female, and children.

Woolley adds one grim, unforgettable detail. One Paiute had been up on a ledge when he was shot; he then fell "off the ledge head first in snow doubled up like a jack-knife."

One Paiute, an elderly man, was severely wounded in the thigh, and his wife stayed with him to tend him. According to one report, other women and the children ran for safety.[55] Two teenagers were hunting and so were not present when the Mormons arrived.[56]

Though the Paiutes had some items belonging to Whitmore, they did not have any of Whitmore's live sheep or cattle—the Navajos had taken them, which is evidence that the Navajos were the thieves. In addition, Paiute oral traditions are adamant that the Navajos, not Paiutes, killed Whitmore and McIntyre.

By Bleak's account, this left four male Paiutes alive. The Mormons brought them, as well as the guide, to the site of the Whitmore and McIntyre bodies. When the five Paiutes arrived, according to McArthur's official report, "This meeting was too much for the brethren to stand, so they turned the prisoners loose and shot them on the ground where the murdered bodies lay. Thus did retribution overtake them on the scene of their crime."[57] McArthur's tone is approving. He views punishing Indians as a mission from God: "We have heard of a large band of Indians, camped on the Pahreah, and as soon as our supplies come up, we shall march on to them, with prayers in our hearts that the Lord will use us as a means in His hands to punish them for their crimes."

Bleak reports that the five Paiutes arrived when the Mormons were lifting the bodies of Whitmore and McIntyre into a wagon. "The boys on seeing the bodies of their dead brethren, lost their patience, they turned the four Indian prisoners and the guide loose, and then shot them."[58]

Winsor, on the other hand, portrays the Paiutes as attempting an escape: "James Andrews and Company Came up and the pieds with them seeing the bodes broke to run, the boys fired on them and Spoted the groung [ground] with them, or the Snow which maid Several of them killed that had had a hand in killing our breathren."[59] However, both McArthur and Bleak report that the Mormons intentionally freed the Paiutes in order to shoot them as they ran away.[60]

McArthur's report seeks to justify the killing of the five Paiutes as an act of passion. However, the fact that the Paiutes were brought to the site of Whitmore and McIntyre's burial suggests that they had been brought for execution. Another account by a participant in this massacre, Seth E. Johnson, tends to confirm this. Johnson reported that the Indians were given explicit promises that if they surrendered they would not be hurt.

> It was well known that the raiders wer the Navajoes from across the river but there were a few half Starved piutes whose home was in that part of the country & they were wandering around to keep from freezing to death & many of the more Ignorant part of the Company [of Mormons] who came out [thought] that because they were Indians they of course were the guilty parties....[These Paiutes were blamed] just because they were Indians & Indians had done the mischief never thinking whether they were the guilty ones or not & now the Indians were questioned carefully & they told a Strange Story. They said that while they were away on a hunt the Navajoes from over the river came & done the Killing & Stealing & they knew nothing of it until after it was done[61] & now a council [of the posse] was called to decide what they Should [do] with these Indians & after much more deliberation it was decided that they Should be Shot & he [Seth] was ordered to so Inform them. All kinds of arguments were brought up by the men & among others was why were they [the Kaibab Paiutes] here & Seth very soon informed them [the Mormons] that the reason was it was their [the Kaibab Paiutes'] land & home. As soon as they were told of the Sentence they [the Kaibab Paiutes] gathered around Seth clinging to him & pleading that their lives might be spared until the snow was gone when they would Show them the tracks of the real guilty ones & Said...only let us live to Show to them that we are innocent. But all to no purpose they were shot down like dogs after promising them their lives.[62]

This unofficial account strikingly contradicts the official reports by McArthur and Bleak, which portray a quick emotional killing of the Paiutes regarded as guilty; Johnson's narrative shows that there was a formal council of the military party, and only after "much more deliberation" was it decided that the Paiutes should be shot. This suggests that the military leaders decided on the executions.

Edwin Woolley Jr., also describes an execution. The Mormons "took 4 prisoners, brought them back to where the bodies [of Whitmore and McIntyre] were found, stood them up in a row about 100 pases [paces] from where the bodies lay, saved the Ind. that had given information but stood boy up with the 4 prisoners and shot them, they all fell on their faces in the snow, not one made a struggle."[63]

An early account from a participant, John Steele's letter of January 22, offers another variant. He writes that eight Paiutes were found at the Grama Canyon site, and that seven were killed because they acted aggressively. "They [the Paiutes] shoed fight and our men killed seven of them and have reserved the other for [illegible] after consideration."[64] If Seth Johnson and Edwin Woolley can be believed, as early as this, two days after the Paiutes were massacred, Mormon participants were attempting to sanitize this military execution of unarmed, innocent Paiutes.

This is a typical account of whites executing unarmed Indians, but portraying it as a defensive response to Indian attacks. It is strikingly similar to Rockwell's execution of unarmed prisoners in the Tooele area. And it is possible that McArthur and Andrus felt they were following accepted procedures.[65]

David Chidester writes in the same vein: "The Indians refused to be taken prisoners and put up a fight, which resulted in seven of them being killed."[66] A moral failure has been turned into a heroic act of defense.

Paiute Tony Tillohash later said that five brothers were killed at Bullrush, one of whom was his grandfather.[67]

One more execution adds an exclamation point to this already grim tale of unjust execution: the following day, a group of Mormons came across the old wounded Paiute, who had a broken thighbone; his wife had been carrying him for miles. The Mormons left the couple, but began to debate whether the elderly man should also be killed. Some men felt that they should spare him, but the leaders argued that they should execute him, too, so that he could not tell the story of the execution of the five other Paiutes. Two members of the group eagerly volunteered to ride back to do the killing. Tom Clark, a Washington resident, said, "Damned if I wouldn't like to kill an Indian before I go." He raced John Ward, of Santa Clara, back to see who got to do the actual shooting. On arriving at the Indians, Clark shot first at the old man from close range, but missed, so Ward "blew his brains out." The elderly Paiute was killed in cold blood, while the woman tending him shrieked in agony and shock. "I never was so ashamed of anything in my life," wrote Edwin D. Woolley Jr., who had argued against the killing. "The whole thing was so unnecessary."[68]

Once again, the purported reason for this killing seems suspect. If silencing a witness had been the motive, the old man's wife would have had to be killed also, but instead, she was allowed to live. Clearly, this was one more execution-style killing to satisfy feelings of vengeance. Not surprisingly, this murder never made it into the official reports. Woolley later gave his account of it, but wrote, "the leaders"—he mentions Daniel D. McArthur, James Andrus, John D. L. Pierce, and Angus L. Cannon—"never say anything about it."

Here Mormon attitudes toward killing Indians (as evidenced by the murderers) are strikingly similar to common anti-Indian attitudes among whites on the frontier. There is no hint of Mormon sympathy for possible converts whom they regarded as a lost remnant of the tribes of Israel, and no hint of Christian principles of avoiding violence except as a last resort. McArthur, in his official report, wrote with religious and military fervor of hopefully killing another group of Paiutes—for him, at this point, all Indians were evidently guilty of the Whitmore-McIntyre murders.

However, another Mormon, Woolley, shows a sympathy for the wounded old man who was murdered and for his wife. In the face of conflict with Indians in early Utah, Mormon attitudes and responses varied, as the whole career of Jacob Hamblin shows.

So eight Paiutes, who did not commit the murders of Whitmore and McIntyre, were punished for their deaths. After having killed the Paiutes, the Mormons did not pursue the Navajos that the Paiutes had said committed the crime. Indeed, the Navajos were far from any possible capture now, in the badlands across the Colorado. Instead, the Mormon military killed the Indians who were available, generally peaceful Kaibab Paiutes—"half Starved piutes" who "were wandering around to keep from freezing to death" in Johnson's words—killing eight to balance out the two Mormons. They then returned home.

Seth Johnson later reported the incident to Hamblin ("Uncle Jacob Ha[m]blin the great Indian friend man"), and he was disgusted by it:

> Seth related to him the account of the killing ... & after a moments reflection he [Jacob Hamblin] answered I guess that it was all right that I was not there for if I had have been & those Indians had been killed it would have been done over my dead body.[69]

Jacob wrote: "We killed seven Piutes at a place near where a white man was killed; we killed the wrong Indians, not the Piutes who done the mischief. I was very sick at the time."[70]

Word spread quickly among the local Paiutes that Mormons had hastily and vengefully killed the wrong Indians. Paiutes told John D. Lee in February 1866 that Navajos had killed the two Mormons, and then had shared the booty with local Paiutes. When Mormons had killed the eight Paiutes, they were guilty of murder. They told Lee that "we [Mormons] do just as the Indians do; kill the first that we find—whether they are guilty or not." Not surprisingly, the local Paiutes were reportedly furious about this massacre. "I regret to find a spirit among the Brethren to kill every Indian that they find," wrote Lee.[71]

Seth Johnson says that the Berry murders, described below, were carried out in direct retaliation for the murder of these Kaibab Paiutes.[72]

The story of the Pipe Spring massacre of Paiutes is notable in that the people who performed the killing were in a military company, led by some of St. George's most distinguished citizens. Yet they committed an act of summary vengeance without taking prisoners and seriously investigating the incident, even when the Paiutes had insisted that the Navajos had done the killing.[73]

Indefensible as these revenge killings of innocent Paiutes were, and the propagandistic military dispatches that portrayed them as noble deeds, the minority reports by Mormons Edwin Woolley and Seth Johnson deserve enormous respect.

Indians later told Hamblin that the Navajo raiding party, after crossing the Colorado, divided their plunder; one company rode south toward San Francisco Peaks with sheep and a few cattle, while another company rode east with most of the cattle. Hopis, learning of these two Navajo parties, collected the twenty or thirty old guns that Hamblin and his friends had left them, followed the eastern party, and approached so close to the Navajos "that they could plainly hear them laughing, and jesting about killing the 2 white men," Hamblin wrote. The Hopis opened fire on the raiding company, killed eleven of sixteen Navajos, and captured all the horses and cattle.[74] Reportedly, the Navajo chief Manuelito was severely wounded in this encounter.[75] The Hopis later suffered harsh retaliation from the Navajos, but enjoyed this temporary triumph against their traditional enemies.

The chain of violence and innocent death continued: Navajos or Paiutes or Utes or a mixture of tribes killed Joseph and Robert Berry, two brothers, and Robert's wife, Isabella, west of Pipe Spring, on April 2, 1866.

The Berrys, after a trip to Northern Utah, were riding in a wagon en route to their home, Berryville in Long Valley, but were ambushed by about twenty-five Indians a few miles east of Short Creek. One of the men was severely wounded at this time. They quickly left their route and reached the road to Kanab, but the Indians followed them and were able to open fire on them again, soon killing the three Mormons. The Indians ransacked the wagon and departed, leaving the body of one of their number who had been killed by the Mormons. The Berrys were found by Mormons five days later. Bill Maxwell wrote that they had been "shot with Guns and arrows. It appears that the woman was the last to suffer. She was a bused all they wanted & then shot with a gun and arrows. They [the bodies] was neather skelped [scalped] nor striped [stripped]."[76]

Other later Mormon accounts, such as Woodbury's *History of Southern Utah*, give a portrait of the Paiutes torturing the woman and shooting arrows into her.[77] However, other early accounts record that the Berry brothers were killed by many arrows, while the woman was killed by a gunshot.[78] One 1872 report of the massacre—perhaps partly derived from Indian accounts of the event—states that the woman was shot while trying to unharness a horse and escape.[79] "The bodies were evidently not interfered with after death," James Bleak reported on April 13, which would suggest that they were not mutilated.[80] These sources suggest that the woman met a sudden death by gunshot, thus was not tortured or raped, and was not mutilated after death.

The Indian corpse was "an old grey headed Indian,"[81] and Bill Maxwell, who had accompanied Hamblin on his late 1862 journey to the Hopi mesas, recognized the body:

> Thare was one Navijo left on the ground which I am Satisfied is the Chief Banashaw known as Spanish Shanks by us. I have seen him when alive and when dead and it is the same. He was very noted as he was very gray & also had lost his upper front teeth which was the case with this one that was killed.[82]

This was a bitter, tragic end for a man who had been a loyal friend of the Mormons since the days of the Elk Mountain Mission. Now, he had become part of a murderous raiding party preying on Mormons—it is one of the ironies of fate that he should be killed by Mormons, whom he had befriended. However, we have seen that Spaneshanks had lost power in his tribe, and possibly was required to follow the raiding policy his son or sons had chosen.[83]

There are reports that Spaneshanks's relatives, especially his sons, vowed vengeance against the Mormons for his death.[84]

Terrible as these murders were, Paiute authority William Palmer points out that they were carried out by "tribesman" of the Paiutes executed unjustly by the Mormon military near Pipe Spring (which assumes that the killers of the Berrys were Paiutes or that Paiutes were assisting Navajos).[85] As was noted above, Seth Johnson held that the Berry murders were perpetrated as direct retaliation for the massacre of innocent Paiutes after the death of Whitmore and McIntyre.

However, Woodbury's informant suggested that the murders were carried out in revenge for three Indians killed by Mormons in Long Valley, north of Kanab, a male and his wife and baby.[86] Steele reports the local Paiutes said that Navajos carried out the attack, but Steele did not believe this, and felt that Paiutes killed the Berrys in "retaliation for the three [Paiutes] that were killed by Capt. James Andrews [Andrus]."[87] Other accounts state that Berry was targeted because he had turned a Paiute off his property.[88] Some say that Kaibab Paiute headman Timpenampats was responsible for the attack (and was the dead Indian, not Spaneshanks);[89] others say that Cedar City headman Coal Creek John was the instigator.[90]

In any event, the four deaths west of Pipe Spring show how relations between Mormons and Indians had broken down in early 1866 in southern Utah. Innocent Mormons had been killed, including James Whitmore who reportedly had been a good friend of the local Paiutes. Innocent Paiutes were killed in retaliation, and Hamblin's good friend Spaneshanks was killed while riding with a party of Navajos and Paiutes in a raid driven by revenge.

The Navajo raids on the Mormons are an unfortunate chapter in Navajo history, for Mormons, unlike whites in New Mexico, had never attacked the Navajos; had never raided into Navajo territory; and had never stolen their children and sold them into slavery. Mormons had not even made settlements in Navajo territory. However, the Navajos were arguably in a desperate situation. (And in fact, the Utes in the Black Hawk War swore that they were forced into the raids against the Mormons in that war to avoid starvation.)[91]

Historians Garrick and Roberta Bailey record that the Navajos simply carried out raids on all possible sources during this period—from Utes, Jicarilla Apaches, Mescalero Apaches, Pueblo Indians, Spanish Americans, Anglo Americans and Mormons. "Nobody was spared."[92] (And strangely enough, Navajo raiders also made allies of Utes and Apaches at times.)

Later Navajos came to feel that the Navajo propensity for morally questionable raiding was a cause of their severe punishment by the U.S. Army. For example, Helen Begay wrote that while some Navajos did not steal, others did—from their enemies, the New Mexicans, the Utes, and Comanches. "The Navajos brought the war [with the U.S. Army and allied Indians] on themselves," Begay said.[93] How much less were the raids on Mormons and Mormon herds justified.

Nevertheless, one might understand the Navajo actions as the product of desperate Indians allied with equally desperate Indians nearby, fighting against the reservation system that had driven the Utes and Paiutes to starvation, and that was now causing the deaths of many innocent Navajos in Bosque Redondo.[94]

Whatever our views of Navajo raiding, everyone agrees that they were expert at it. Thales Haskell, who spent many days searching for stolen livestock during this period, wrote that raiding Navajos would skin a calf, leaving its head and hoofs on, "get inside this hide and leisurely let down the bars of our fields and corrals and drive off our animals." Or they would uproot and use a small tree for cover. "Such is the experience of many of the early settlers of southern Utah, northern Arizona, New Mexico, and Colorado."[95]

19

"They Begged Him to be Their Big Chief, Saying That They Had No Captains Left"

Refounding Kanab and Boating on the Colorado, 1866–1868

Jacob Hamblin may not have realized it, but in 1867 a new chapter in his story was beginning. Santa Clara was no longer on the frontier (given the size of St. George and the number of Swiss settlers in Santa Clara itself) and Jacob's skills as diplomat and explorer were always needed on the ragged edge—especially during the times of the Black Hawk War and the Navajo raids. When Erastus Snow asked Hamblin to visit the Kaibab Paiutes near Kanab in 1867 or 1868 (partially so they could serve as a counterweight to the raiding Navajos), he was in effect sending him on a new mission. This was a significant turning point in Hamblin's life, as Kanab would gradually replace Santa Clara as his and his family's center of operations.

After Jacob retired from the Pipe Spring expedition, he remained seriously ill for months with "calculus" (kidney stones).[1] On January 27, 1866, James Bleak wrote to George A. Smith that Jacob, "who has been sick nigh unto death with the disease that killed his father (calculus), is very much better. Sitting up a little yesterday."[2] Despite Bleak's hopeful prognosis, Jacob did not improve significantly for some time. When Smith visited Santa Clara in late February, Jacob was still very sick.[3]

At one point, Jacob's friends thought he was dying, and he said that he was willing to depart this life, since he'd only been in their way for such a long time. "But my little children were crying around me, and the question came into my mind: What will they do if I am taken away? I could not bear the thought of leaving my family in so helpless a condition." So he prayed to God that he would live. He then felt a desire for food and asked for something to eat. "Some boiled beef and tea were brought me; I thought I had never before eaten anything that tasted so good," he wrote. He began to recover slowly.[4]

He was up and around again by October 1866, when he visited Salt Lake City to attend General Conference. While there he made an unfortunate business connection—he teamed up with two partners, Seth Blair and Elijah Thomas, to start

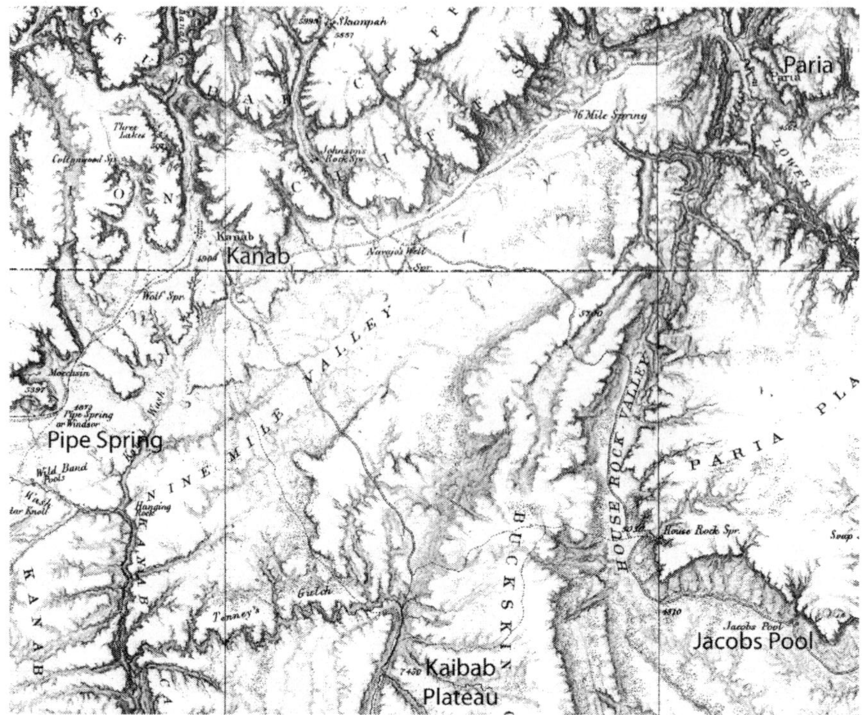

19.1. Kanab area. The Utah-Arizona road led from Pipe Spring to Kanab. Then it passed over the Kaibab Plateau (Buckskin Mountain) to House Rock Valley and Jacob's Pool. Detail from Wheeler, *Topographical Atlas*, Map 67, courtesy David Rumsey Historical Map Collection.

a company that would manufacture castor bean oil, both refined oil for drugs and crude oil for tanning and lubricating.[5] Blair, who had been a businessman in Illinois before his conversion to Mormonism, apparently sought out Jacob to provide capital for this venture, and while in Salt Lake City, the two men borrowed a thousand dollars from Charles Taylor, of Holladay and Halsey's Banking House, with Jacob's cattle pledged as security. The promissory note, signed by "Hamblin & Co" and by Blair, was dated October 15, 1866, and was due three months later, on January 16 of the new year.[6]

Corbett assumes that Hamblin and Blair were simply setting up a general store in St. George, but Hamblin had already been acting as a shopkeeper in Santa Clara since at least May 1858.[7] The *Deseret News* letter cited above suggests that the two men were focused on a more limited venture, the production of castor oil, and would need to operate a castor bean farm and set up some sort of factory to process the castor beans and bottle the oil.[8]

On January 16, 1867, the promissory note became due, and a protest document demanding payment was promptly lodged.[9] Unfortunately, "Hamblin & Co" did not have ready cash to pay. On the back of the document, it was noted that Blair paid two hundred dollars on March 9 (no year given), and it was not until a year later, on April 6, 1868, that the rest of the money was paid, by Hamblin.[10] According to family traditions, the Hamblin and Blair company had generated little profit, so Hamblin had to sell nearly his entire herd of cattle to raise the required hard money for repayment. As Priscilla watched the herd being driven away, she suddenly put her foot down and demanded that at least a couple milk cows be spared. She was allowed these.[11]

In July 1867, Hamblin kept something of a combined diary and account record for a time. As it is short, it deserves quotation. Much of it is enigmatic, and it is sometimes hard to read, but it gives a general sense of his business dealings:

> July 8. Bought this Book $1.
> [July] 10. let W M. Burges hav .28. lbs of cheas [cheese] at 35 cents per pound.
>
> [July] 13. took 1000 ft of lumbr at Burgs mill. Let him hav 52 lbs of mutton 10 cents per pound.
>
> Joseph Grange 45 lbs flower [flour].
>
> Westover .80. [lbs] flowr.
>
> Grange 14-1/2 lbs of mutton .12-1/2 cents per pound.
>
> Harcoet 23 lb flowr.
>
> Jacob Truman .24. [lbs] flower 2 lbs mutton.
>
> James Holt 86 lbs flower.
>
> Jacob Truman dr by 60 lbs flowr 2/1 doz pans x 9.00.
>
> July 14th paid Theel [?] 500 lbs flowr.
>
> Hamblin in co dr to Jacob Hamblin.
>
> 524 lbs flowr 8 cents per pound.
>
> Hamblin in e dr to Jacob Hamblin 18 seks of
>
> [July] 17th went to Ranch Vally. W M Maxwell took the tobacco. 1 pr [pair?] pants and over shurt.
>
> [July] 19th Grange dr by one shoulder mutton.
>
> 18 lbs mu [mutton] 10 cents per lb
>
> Hamblin in co dr to Jacob Hamblin one mutton $4.20.
>
> Canfield dr. to 33 lbs.

This brief window into Hamblin as merchant shows him dealing frequently in flour and mutton, and also in cheese, tobacco, and some clothing. These transactions were apparently simply a continuation of his "shopkeeper" dealings in Santa Clara. According to family traditions, Hamblin was not successful as a shopkeeper because he was entirely too willing to extend credit to friends, especially to Indians.[12]

Hamblin's business experiences show that his career as Indian missionary and explorer was not a paid occupation. He had to keep many practical irons in the fire to support his family during his long absences. He was a rancher, the proprietor of an extensive orchard, a businessman, and a shopkeeper. In addition, he sometimes carried mail.[13] It is not surprising that he would not be overwhelmingly successful in some of these occupations (notably in the castor oil business, or as shopkeeper), since his long absences would not allow him to focus on any one practical trade.

In April 1867 Hamblin was back in the saddle, on an exploring expedition to the lower Colorado, with Henry W. Miller and Jesse W. Crosby, testing the feasibility of a boat navigating between Grand Wash and Call's Landing. The three men left St. George on April 10, accompanied by Apostle Erastus Snow, James Andrus, Ira Hatch, and David Cameron, transporting a sixteen-foot skiff with them.[14] The sixty-year-old Miller, a native of New York, was known as a lawyer, farmer, and stockman. He had joined the church in 1839, had served in the Mormon Battalion, and had been called to settle Beaver Dam (Millersburg), which Jacob and Call had visited in 1864.[15] Crosby was a forty-six-year-old native of Nova Scotia who had helped settle St. George in 1861 and who specialized in producing molasses. He had gained some boating experience on Lake Erie and in Canada, which no doubt was the reason for his call on this mission.[16]

The company took the Grand Wash route to the Colorado, and from here, on the fifteenth, Snow, Andrus, Hatch, and Cameron set off on land for St. Thomas, one of the Muddy Mission settlements, agreeing to meet Hamblin, Crosby, and Miller there in two days.

Jacob and his two companions went upstream to the Pearce's Ferry site, a mile and a half above the Grand Wash, then set out down the Colorado. Jacob acted as steersman, while Crosby and Miller rowed. "We were on an unexplored part of the Colorado," wrote Miller, "and every sense had to be actively exercised," for in many places there were walls instead of river banks, and it would have been impossible to escape from the river in an emergency. About a mile below the Grand Wash, Miller wrote that the river was "hemmed in for a distance of thirty miles, with high black rocks." Occasionally there was a sandy bottom on one side of the river or the other, but the three men realized that it would be impossible to bring a road in to this thirty-mile stretch.[17]

The group passed several rapids, then arrived at the "Grand Rapids, whose roar is heard over a mile before reaching them." Here there was a drop-off of six to eight feet, and at these rapids—which Miller judged to be the actual "head of navigation on the Colorado"—the men lowered the skiff with lariats. When they set out again, constant eddies and whirlpools required energetic rowing to keep the skiff pointed in the right direction.

The scenery on this stretch of the river excited Miller's admiration, but there was no approach to the river and no substantial bottomland in the canyon.

About thirty miles from the Grand Wash, and fifteen miles short of the confluence with the Virgin, was a towering black rock on the northwest side of the canyon, rising some 650 feet above the river—"the most majestic rock I ever saw," Miller wrote. The three men named it Tower Rock and spent the night beneath it.

The next morning they set out at six a.m. and passed a few rapids. Then, according to Miller, "the river assumed a less dangerous appearance, and the country on the north side was filled with low gravely hills." These hills continued until the confluence with the Virgin, which at this point had become "a slow, sluggish stream, full of sand-bars and shallow water." Hamblin and company tried to row the skiff up the Virgin, with no success.

They continued down the Colorado, and eight miles later came to what they called Boulder Canyon, named for the large boulders in the river, which they were able to navigate around. Then they entered a portion of the canyon that stimulated a purple passage from Miller—it was "the most gloomily grand part of the river that we saw on the trip," he wrote.

> A deep gorge seemingly cut in the solid rock, from 1,200 to 1,500 feet deep, with the whole mass of waters compressed in a channel about ten rods wide, formed the bed of the river, and the great black walls rose up perpendicular, as it were into the heavens, shutting us in almost from light and hope, and filling us with a sensation akin to awe, as our frail skiff was carried down the silent stream, for the water moved slowly and silently along its gloomy channel. Away up above us a thin streak of light could be seen, looking like a rift in a mountain top...This cañon has to be passed through to have its wild sublimity realized.

After traversing about twelve miles of this canyon, they emerged from it, and a mile and a half later reached Callville. Of the sixty-five miles they had traveled, they stated that the forty-five miles from the Grand Wash to the Virgin had never been traversed by white man before, and there is no reason to dispute that assertion.[18] This expedition was indeed a remarkable accomplishment. One valuable aspect of the journey was that it showed that one could only realistically navigate on the Colorado as far north as the "Grand Rapids" Miller refers to.[19] For practical purposes, Callville and the confluence with the Virgin were the "head of navigation."

A diary of this journey was kept, possibly by Miller, unfortunately not extant. However, someone in Salt Lake City gave it to John Wesley Powell in 1869 and he took it with him on his historic exploration of the Colorado. It turned out to be of crucial help to him in the latter part of his expedition.[20]

Hamblin, Miller, and Crosby arrived at St. Thomas on the seventeenth, and presumably returned to Santa Clara and St. George with Erastus Snow and company.

After the Pipe Spring murders, Jacob now had to face the new landscape of Indian hostility brought about by the Black Hawk War and the Navajo War against the Mormons. He did this by trying to enlist local Paiutes to help the Mormons defend against Navajo-Ute raids. In May 1867, Bleak wrote, "Jacob Hamblin in his quiet, but persistent, manner has continued his peaceful ministry amongst the Indians in these southern and south eastern regions; and using the more friendly among them to assist in watching for marauding Navajos."[21]

In spring and summer 1867, Jacob wrote that he was called upon—presumably by Erastus Snow—to visit the Kaibab Indians, and then the Indians on the Sevier River, where Mormons had had to abandon a number of fledgling settlements.[22] He first visited Kanab, where he gathered some friendly Paiutes and with them planted corn and vegetables. Kanab had been deserted in March 1866, but the quasi fort and houses that had been built in the winter of 1865–1866 were still there.[23] Hamblin was arguably the founding pioneer of the city, based on the criteria of continuous occupation.

In 1869, Jacob Hamblin and John R. Young wrote to George A. Smith:

> When Bro Hamblin first came [to Kanab] in July last [1868], and told them [the local Paiutes] the burden of his mission, they begged him to be their Big Chief, saying that they had no Captains left, and they knew that he was their friend, they were willing to trust him and since then his word has been law, that they have cheerfully obeyed. We wish we could communicate truthfully to you the spirit that moves upon these low, degraded, persecuted people, but in this short letter it is not in our power.[24]

Possibly Jacob made an 1867 visit to Kanab that was preparatory, with his 1868 settlement being more permanent; or possibly he was a year off in Little. In any event, Jacob now would turn his attention to these Kaibab Paiutes for a number of years, and many of them became his faithful allies. They also became key resources that John Wesley Powell and his men relied upon when they conducted their geographical survey.[25] Like the Santa Clara Paiutes, they migrated seasonally, but they also practiced agriculture.[26] They made skillful use of plants and hunted rabbits and deer on the Kaibab Plateau. Before the coming of the Europeans, by one estimate, they numbered about 5,500; before 1863, their population had declined to 1,175.[27] These are very rough estimates, but probably give a general idea of their population. It is possible that disease had reduced their numbers significantly.

Hamblin next traveled north, crossed the rim of the basin, and passed through Sevier Valley. There he sought out the largest gatherings of Indians, and "had many long talks with them, which seemed to have a good effect," he wrote.[28] This is probably the Upper Sevier River, including Panguitch Valley, which had been a traditional wintering area for Paiutes.

In fall 1867, Hamblin knew that the Colorado would start to run low enough to allow Navajo-Ute raiders to cross at Vado de las Padres or at modern Lee's Ferry, so he made trips to "the eastern frontiers of Southern Utah" to try to monitor and deter Navajo incursions. "I met with quite a number of young Piutes when I first went into the country," wrote Hamblin. "They said they had dreamed that I was coming out into their country, and they proposed to assist me in watching the frontiers. They proved to be quite useful in watching the passes, and waylaid and shot several raiders [Navajos]."[29] In Little, Hamblin wrote that he spent 1868 in a similar fashion—watching the eastern frontiers of Dixie.[30]

The Black Hawk–Navajo War had put Hamblin in a situation where he was at war with Indians again—if he was not killing the Navajo raiders himself, his deputies were doing so. Certainly, many of the raiders were outlaws and had been involved in stealing Mormons flocks and killing Mormons. Nevertheless, Hamblin gradually came to sense that he was acting now against his "conversion" to pacifism in Tooele.[31]

In July Hamblin's diary offers a window into his agricultural activities. He had grown up farming, and was evidently a skilled farmer and orchard keeper. From the beginning, agriculture had been an essential component of his Indian mission. On July 15, he was growing corn for feed, and his "early york peaches" had begun to turn. His wheat was mostly cut. It began to rain in the mountains on the fifteenth, and soon it was raining at Santa Clara also. On the twentieth, Jacob noted that his peaches were ripe, his corn was ready for boiling, and his apricots were gone.

On August 9, he wrote, "replanted corn. Sowd one ~~acre~~ of buc wheet. Examined .200. buds I had set .10. days before. All looked well. This was my last weeks business." He seems to be keeping a weekly agricultural journal.

On the fifteenth, he planted three acres of corn and turnips. "Yesterday extremely hot," he wrote. "Some Isabella grapes ripe." This week's work included "seting fruit buds, watering land, repairing water ditches."

The Santa Clarans celebrated a harvest feast on the twentieth. On the twenty-second, there was an invasion, typical for Utah but always dreaded: "The grass hopers [Rocky Mountain locusts] come into our garden," Jacob wrote. Evidently, he smoked them out somehow, and "they mostley left the Clary field," but not before accomplishing major devastation, as they had destroyed all of Jacob's corn by eating the corn silk.[32]

In the first week of September, Jacob watered his land and dried peaches. He noted that the buckwheat was in bloom, about eight to ten inches high. On the twelfth, the Hamblin family dried fruit. Two days later, cool nights and enigmatic "Smokey days" began. In the following week, ending on the twentieth, Jacob and his family were "getheren grapes and peaches." He went to Mountain Meadows the week after that, and when he returned he "bought 5 goats of Moroni Canfield."

In the week ending October 3, he made some wine, slaughtered a cow, and worked about home. On the eighth, a frost killed some of his late corn.

In telling Hamblin's life story, we obviously focus on dramatic moments, but we should remember that much of his life was spent in daily farming activities such as these.

The Hamblin family continued to expand. Priscilla's fifth child, Ella Ann Hamblin, was born on June 11, 1867,[33] and Louisa's first, Walter Eugene, was born on April 15, 1868, both in Santa Clara.[34]

Hamblin was beginning to spend a great deal of time in Kanab, making a new "home away from home" among the Kaibab Paiutes. Priscilla was undoubtedly used to Jacob's frequent absences by now, but Louisa was probably still coming to terms with them. Jacob's religious mysticism could make his absences unpredictable. One of Jacob's "peculiar ways," family friend Martha Cox wrote, was that he would suddenly stop whatever he was doing, at home or while working in the field, take a flour sack and fill it with whatever food he found at home, then "hasten away into the Indian country many miles away. And I had heard also that he never made a trip in vain. There was sure to be trouble brewing when he reached his destination."

Martha protested to Jacob that this method of doing missionary work sounded "out of harmony with the regulations of the Church," but Jacob answered that his work was an "independent mission" but still directed by church leaders. In addition, "the Three Nephites mentioned in the B.M. [Book of Mormon] were his personal directors. When one of them appeared and told him he was needed with some distant or near Indian tribe it became his duty to lay everything aside and go out immediately."[35]

In some ways Jacob was a loyal messenger and representative of his most important leaders, Brigham Young and Erastus Snow; in other ways, he had an independent, mystical streak that might have perplexed them, and his family, at times.

20

"*Started for the Canab Mision*"

AT KANAB AND PAHREAH, 1869

The Navajo raids in southern Utah continued unabated. Navajo raiders reportedly had intimidated the smaller tribes south of the Colorado, and had "taken possession" of the country between the Colorado and St. George. According to one report, they were aided by whites, who provided them with guns and ammunition.[1] In the context of the Black Hawk War, this is not at all unlikely, as Black Hawk and his allied Navajos sold cattle to whites in the Four Corners area.[2]

In St. George on January 2, 1869, Erastus Snow wrote to Brigham Young that the Navajo raids were increasingly successful, and that "Jacob and his Piedes with the few whites he has, can do but little towards checking it." He explained the difficulty of Jacob's task, and stated that guardhouses on the Colorado, with thirty Mormons and twenty Indians each, might check the Navajo raids, but it would be difficult to recruit men for such guardhouses and to finance them. "It is not so easy in this scarce time," he wrote, "to gather up and forward supplies for maintaining such a force nor agreeable to men to lay on the rocks at the Colorado all winter," as Jacob had been doing. Snow wrote that he would not hesitate, however, if he had the financial resources that would be necessary to fund such an operation.[3] Snow was apparently hinting to Young that he needed funds from Salt Lake.

The Navajos made a major raid on St. George in late February, and the Mormons sent out three platoons under Capt. Willis Copeland to try to recover the livestock.[4]

On June 4, Jacob was in Salt Lake City and had a meeting with Young, who instructed him "to farm with the Indians at Pipe Springs" and donated twenty guns, including eight Ballard rifles (a single-shot gun that was widely used during America's westward expansion), to the cause.[5] Pipe Spring would serve as a "frontier protection to St. George. The Indians who lived there had always come and told Hamblin when the Navajoes intended to make raids."[6] Jacob in fact started Indian farms at Pipe Spring, Kanab, and Pahreah, with Kanab functioning as the central outpost.

Hamblin was clearly acting as Brigham Young's agent when he worked with Indians on the Kanab mission; he was directly instructed by Young to start farms with local Indians to facilitate renewed Mormon settlements in Kane County, and to help protect St. George and other southern Utah settlements.

On July 19, Jacob wrote in his journal, "Started for the canab mision." His work on the Arizona strip and Kane County was a mission, and Kanab was the headquarters. He stopped in St. George and talked with Apostle Snow, who asked Hamblin to meet him in Parowan on August 3. Jacob agreed, and Snow wrote to Brigham Young, on July 20, "Jacob Hamblin just started with 3 men to put in turnips and cut hay at pipe springs and Kanab and commence his Indian mission."[7] Jacob and his companions would also bring some sheep or cattle or both, with them.

The next day, Jacob left Washington with a Brother Packer and John Mangum, and traveled to Toquerville, where "Bro Savage"—probably Levi Savage, who had been the main colonist of Kanab—"was sent with us." John Mangum and his brother James were Alabamans who had helped settle Washington. Reputed participants in the Mountain Meadows Massacre, they would become important residents of Kanab and Pahreah, as would their nephew Joseph.[8]

Hamblin then stopped at Rockville, on the Virgin, near the entrance to Zion's Canyon, where he picked up two Paiutes ("Mose" and an old man) who had been recommended by a Brother Winsor—presumably Anson P. Winsor, bishop of Grafton, who would later give his name to "Winsor's Castle," at Pipe Spring. Jacob met the other members of the company at a goat ranch, then traveled on to Short Creek. Hamblin writes, "It was with mutch trouble we could get the stock along."[9]

On July 25, they came to Pipe Spring, where they planted some turnips and corn. Two days later they continued on to Kanab, where they prepared the ground for turnips, "burnt some cane patches," and presumably sowed the turnip seeds. On the thirtieth, they watered the turnips, and some local Paiutes arrived.

Hamblin left for Parowan the following day, and met Snow on August 3. "I spoak to some lent [length] on the policy that had ben practised towards the Read Men and of the policy that should be," he wrote.[10] While Hamblin was continually calling the Indians to repentance, he also often criticized Mormons for their treatment of Indians. Snow, in his letter to Young, explained the purpose of this part of Jacob's mission: he would travel "with friendly Indians on a mission of peace to the Red Lake Utes."[11]

The next day Hamblin apparently talked to local Indians, and gave instructions to messengers sent to the Red Lake Utes or "Read fishe Eateres," who were associated with Grass Valley and the west Fremont River area in Piute and Wayne County (Red Lake, no longer extant, was two miles south of Bicknell in Wayne County). The Red Lake Utes, closely allied to the Shiberetches and Elk Mountain Utes, who had been the backbone of Black Hawk's army during the Black Hawk War, had the reputation of being hostile to whites, and often would not allow them to pass through their territory.[12] They had "formerly preyed upon Circleville and latterly upon Beaver and Iron counties," according to Erastus Snow. He had sent Coal Creek John and other Indians as ambassadors to them, and they found some Elk Mountain Utes among them, advising "blood and plunder." However, one of Black Hawk's brothers was also there, counseling for peace.[13]

Hamblin sent some presents to the Red Lake Utes and a letter from Erastus Snow. "I told them it was a medicin letter," he wrote—that is, it had magical properties. "They must not steel nor shead blud any more." Now we see that Hamblin would explicitly threaten hostile Indians with supernatural death on occasion: "If they did they would be sick and some of them would die." This was a dangerous policy, for, as we have seen, Indians who felt they or their relatives were bewitched would often seek revenge. This passage also suggests that Jacob felt he had power to cause deaths, or at least power to predict deaths.[14]

Jacob then continued on to Cedar City. On August 5 he was in Kanarraville and Harmony, where he bought four horses and four guns from John D. Lee "for the Canab Mision." He waited for the horses to be brought, then on the eighth started for home. He attended a meeting in St. George two days later, then finally arrived at Santa Clara.

Jacob did not allow himself a long stay at home. The following day, he started for Kanab again with his son Lyman and John R. Young.[15] They visited Pipe Spring, where there was an old stone house, and where some brethren were cutting hay, then arrived at Kanab on the fifteenth, and "found Bros [John] Mangram and Packer well and doeing well. The turnips and corn that we had planted the .26. of August [July] looked well."[16] Mangum and Packer returned to Washington on the sixteenth, which left Young and the two Hamblins, "10 able bodied Indians and 24 old men squaws. & children" at Kanab. In John R. Young's August 15 letter to Erastus Snow, he discussed Jacob's plans to rebuild the Kanab fort, and described the local Paiutes as "anxious, and willing to work, they are doing good service in Cutting Cane with their Butcher knifes."[17]

Jacob and Young wrote a joint letter to Erastus Snow on the sixteenth, in which they asked him to send "ten good labouring men, prepared to put up Log Houses, and do some mason work, & to put in the Windows & doors," bringing as many carpenter tools with them as possible, in order to rebuild the Kanab fort. They also emphasized that food must be sent to them to supplement their farming, and a wagon.

> We see nothing to hinder a compleet success of this Mission, provideing there is a reasonable supply of Provisions afforded us. The native men all seem to be united, and say they [are] anxious to assist in watching or fighting the Navijoes, or opening up traid with them. They will do all the labour nessessary for raiseing a Crop, excepting Plowing. The natives have six Lodges here, twelve able bodied men, anxious to Labour for something to eat. By this you can

> readily perceive the necessity of haveing a good supply of bread stuf, to enable us to encourage the natives who gather around us to depend upon labour for a livelihood instead of the uncertainty of the chase.[18]

On the twenty-fourth, Jacob hunted a band of wild horses with two Paiutes south of Pipe Spring. It rained in the night and the next day, and he was "drenched thru" on his back, becoming so "Stif and laim" that he "could hardley get back to the foot of the mountain." The twenty-sixth found him in Kanab.[19]

Snow responded to Hamblin and Young's request for laborers by sending a group of workers from the southern settlements, including diarist Charles Walker, John Mangum, John W. Smith, Samuel Whittier (or Wittwer), and Warren Hardy, who arrived at Kanab on August 28.[20] Walker wrote that the Kanab fort was

> situated at the mouth of a Kanyon about 1 mile in width. On the east, west, and north are high red sandstone mountains [the Vermilion Cliffs] on which cedar and pinnion pine grow. On the south is a fine open country looking towards the Buckskin Mountains covered with grass in abundance. The stream is about 4 or 5 rods wide, good water but very shallow.[21]

The workers set in constructing walls and chimneys, and Jacob killed a beef on this day, perhaps for the workers. The next night, the men had a meeting, and "Br Hamlin gave us a very interesting account of his experience with the Indians," Walker wrote. Jacob left for Santa Clara on August 31, traveling with "Indian Mose," and found all well at home when he arrived.

About a week later, at Kanab, John R. Young thanked the workers and they returned to St. George and Washington.[22]

John Mangum liked the looks of Kanab, and returned with his family to live there, bringing his brother James and his family with him. A few other men, such as James Wilkins and George Ross, also moved to Kanab in 1869.[23]

In a September 12 letter to George A. Smith, Hamblin and Young described Kanab fort as "an area of 11 rods [about 60 yards] square enclosed with a substantial Cedar Stockade, and 13 log houses for us and the Native Brethren. There are two good stone guard houses, and one snug Commissary house."[24] The Kanabans had ten horses, a few milk cows, and plentiful hay. There was "an abundance of rich land" at Kanab.

John Mangum had been put in charge of agriculture, and was preparing to sow ten acres of wheat. In the spring the Mormons planned to sow corn, beans and potatoes. They had only one plow, and a few hoes and shovels, and needed more.

At this time, the Paiutes were thoroughly integrated into the community, even living in log houses in the fort. There were nearly fifty Indians at Kanab, "being the remnants of the Buckskin Mountain tribe." Undoubtedly there were other Kaibab Indians in other bands, but this is still a surprisingly small group of "remnants." "In all our labor the Red Brethren have given a helping hand, doing good service in cutting Hay, as well as watering crops, and working on the Fort," Young wrote. Hamblin had received "quite an out-fit" from the superintendent of Indian affairs, "but when he came to distribute it, to a naked nation it was but small."[25]

Jacob's son Benjamin described the Indians who worked with the Mormons in early Kanab:

> Eight or ten of these Indians grubbed brush from the land on the west side of the creek so that it could be planted for the white settlers when they came back from their forced evacuation. These Indians received their food from the church. The rations were issued by John Mangum. The other Indians hunted rabbits and wild game. At this time these friendly Indians lived in the fort for protection and so they could render assistance to the men on guard in case of a raid from Navajos.[26]

There was a real enmity between some Paiutes and the Navajos at this time.[27] Paiutes, apparently without Hamblin, discovered a party of Navajo raiders at Pahreah Pass and shot and wounded a Navajo who was a few hundred yards ahead of his company. They then apparently outnumbered the Navajos, who begged the Paiutes to let them go home. The Paiutes agreed if they would leave their booty, and the Navajos did so.

The next day Hamblin and a few Paiutes tracked the wounded Navajo, and near where he had been picked up by his friends, they found another camp of raiders. One of the Paiutes shot two of these and scalped one of them.[28]

On September 9, Hamblin was on another mission, perhaps in the Kanab area, though the location is not specified in his journal: "I spent the most of my time with the Inds," he wrote. At this time, he was apparently visited by a Paiute he knew, whose brother was severely wounded, and wanted Jacob to visit him. "One of the young men I had hope for...got acilydently shot in the thy [thigh]," wrote Hamblin. The thigh was "badly broken," and the bullet was still in his body.[29] The wounded Paiute "wanted to be brought for he thought he would die and he wanted to be buried like the Mormans s[o] that his dry bones would not rattle on top of the dry [?] ground." Paiutes typically cremated their dead, and did not bury the remains after cremation, though sometimes they put rocks on top of them.[30] So this shows how Paiutes were beginning to synthesize Paiute and Mormon belief and practice. Jacob would visit the wounded Paiute on his upcoming trip to the Hopi mesas.

Jacob summarizes the rest of this trip: "I travailed and taked [talked] mutch to...all I met with [saying that] they ware to change their way of living."

As relations with Navajos remained at a low point, church leaders decided that it might be good for some Saints to visit the Hopis to strengthen them as a counterweight against their traditional enemies. As usual, Hamblin was asked to lead the expedition, which took place in October 1869.[31]

In a letter to Jacob and the company, Snow and St. George stake president Joseph W. Young wrote that the purpose of the mission was to renew ties of friendship with the Hopis, and to promote friendly relations with all other Indians the company met with.[32] In addition, they were to take "a few guns and a little ammunition" to the Hopis, so they could defend themselves against Navajos or other hostile Indians.[33] Bleak wrote that Jacob had been sent to the Hopis "to talk with the people and learn if other than Navajos are engaged in the persistent raidings."[34]

On May 3, Brigham Young, on one of his visits to the South, had given another reason for the expedition: "I hear that the Moquiches want to Come & live with us. I think we had Better send word to Brother Hamblin to send word to them to Come & live with us."[35] Young and Hamblin continued to hope for this migration, to no avail.

Perhaps because of danger from Navajos, Young advised that this should be a substantial expedition, including about twenty Mormons and fifteen Indians. Known members were Bill Maxwell, Thales Haskell, Ira Hatch, Hyrum Judd, E. Strong, Horatio Morrill, Wesly Jolly, S. Adams, George Forsythe, William Harris and Ashton Nebeker; John R. Young, William Perkins, Ephraim Wilson, H. Canfield, George Whitmore, George Fawcett, O. Star, George Averett, and Leroy Beebee.[36] Fawcett also remembers John Rupaung, Bill Riges, and Eph[r]aem Wiltbank in the company.[37] Of note in this group is Ash Nebeker, a twenty-six-year-old Toquerville resident, who would go on a number of journeys with Hamblin and later became a controversial bishop at Tuba City, near Moenkopi, Arizona.[38]

On the Indian side, we have only five names: Panamitow; Coal Creek John, the well-known Cedar City Paiute leader; Quantuquackets, a Shivwits; Mannaradet [?]; and an Indian named George.[39]

It was a reunion of many previous visitors to the Hopis—Hamblin, Hatch, Haskell, Maxwell, with the addition of a number of first-time travelers.

On September 28, Hamblin wrote,

> Started for the Moquises. 21. Brotheren. and as meny Inds. I receivd a letter of instrucions from Bros E. Snow. and Joseph W. Young to bare the olive branch of peas to the Navajose and all I met with and to renew our friendley relacionship with the Moquises. The Bishops had furnished the company...the Inds. with provisions riding and pack animals all he would not or could not furnish them selves.[40] This was the best outfit I had ever had to travail this road

> and...to bare the olive branch. I felt humble and had a great desire to fill my Mision exceptable before the Lord.[41]

According to the anonymous diarist, the group met at Berry Springs, where "Ten Indian Warriaors under Panamitow (the Son of Tutsagavit) gathered with us."

The next day they traveled on to Virgin City, and Daniel D. McArthur, C. Lyttle, and Alma Spilsbury met them with two wagons "hauling our Bagage." Here more missionaries straggled in. On the thirtieth, the diarist wrote, "Our Company is begining to present a forminable [formidable] appearance. The indians on wild colts & [b]ronco mules, make no small amount of merriment." Paiutes generally did not own horses, and so may have had little experience riding them. The next day, "Capt. Maxwell amused us by drilling the Pieades, & they enjoyed it as mutch as we did."

They reached Pipe Spring on October 2, and the following day there was a meeting, at which a letter of encouragement from Apostle Snow was read. He recommended that Jacob serve as president of the company, Maxwell as captain, Thales Haskell as first lieutenant, and John R. Young as second lieutenant and clerk. Ira Hatch should assist Hamblin in managing the Indians who would be part of the company. The group was organized per Erastus Snow's directions. Daniel D. McArthur, Jacob Hamblin, and John R. Young blessed and set apart a number of brethren for this mission, then the expedition traveled to Kanab.[42]

The missionaries spent the day preparing for the upcoming journey—"fitting up saddles for the Indians. prepareing our own Packs & shoeing a few horses"—and in relaxing with target practice, trying out the Ballards Brigham Young had donated. After dinner, John R. Young, who had not yet been shooting, proposed a marksmanship contest with Bill Maxwell. As men were working near the target that had been used during the day, Maxwell "pointed to a small knot in the 2nd bottom Log of a Cabbin in the North West Corner of the fort," which Maxwell and Young understood was vacant. John R. called out twice to make sure no one was in the cabin, and when he received no reply, he and Maxwell fired, hitting the wood just above and below the knot. But Ira Hatch immediately emerged from the house, "supporting Thales Haskell, & called for healp, stateing that Haskell [was] shot in the head."

Hatch and Haskell, who had been standing guard, had gone unnoticed into the house to sleep, and evidently were in such a deep slumber that they had not heard Young's call.

Haskell now presented a frightening sight. Blood was streaming from his right temple, and his hair was clotted with crimson. Fortunately, however, as the missionaries examined him carefully, they found that he had only suffered a flesh wound. "The Ball from Bro. Young's gun passed through a log 5 inches thick, & 3 folds of an over Coat & the rim of his hat, inflicting the wound on his head." Then the bullet lodged in his coat. Though Haskell had no serious wound, this near fatality "cast a feeling of sadness over the whole Camp."[43]

Fawcett's laconic version of the tale is surprisingly moving: "Thales, jumping up, said to Ira Hatch, who was with him, 'I am shot.' After finding the ball in the sleeve of his coat he lit a cigarette and felt much better. John R. Young cried like a child he felt so bad. But he [Haskell] took good care of the wound and it got well."[44]

This must have been one of the more startling wake-up calls in Thales Haskell's experience as an Indian missionary.

On October 5, the Mormons and Indians departed from Kanab, leaving Lyman Hamblin, John Mangum, Hiram Judd, and John W. Smith there. After traveling eight miles over "table land covered with scruby Cedars," they traversed a valley and the "Buckskin Mountain Wash" for seven miles, and ten miles more brought them to the foot of Kaibab Plateau, where they camped at a water hole. A small band of Paiutes were encamped nearby, including the wounded Paiute and his brother. Jacob arranged for a wagon to come move them to Kanab. The Kaibabits offered Jacob ten men for the expedition, but he took only three.

The next day the expedition started over the Kaibab Plateau. "I was mutch pleased with this far famed Buckskin Mountain," the anonymous diarist wrote. "The western ascent is gradual." The mountain had "excellent groves of Pine Trees and saw timber."[45] On the seventh, the missionaries descended the east Kaibab and camped at Jacob's Pools under the Vermilion Cliffs.[46] They had been hoping to take the boat from 1860 to the Paria crossing but found that it had rotted away, so decided to give up on it and create a raft somehow to cross the Colorado.

The next day they traveled over a road that was "sandy & rolling with good grass part of the way" and crossed Soap Creek. After a lunch, they packed up and descended to the mouth of the Paria—modern Lee's Ferry—where they found the water very low.

On October 9, they built a raft of floatwood fastened by withes and crossed the river, swimming the horses alongside the raft, as before. They crossed the river eight times and had only one serious accident.[47] Bill Maxwell's horse got too far ahead of the raft, and one of the men, worried that he would get tangled in ropes, brought him back, but "sank the horse under the raft, causing the raft to go down stream." Fortunately they were able to regain control of the raft, and no men were killed, but Maxwell's horse drowned.[48] After this, according to Morrill, "We tried again & succede[d] better. The horses were driven in & swam or crossed without further loss."[49]

The next day, Morrill gave Maxwell his pack mare and added his pack to Strong's mule. Nine very rough miles south brought them to Navajo Springs, then they rode eight miles to Mineral Springs (presumably modern Bitter Springs), where the water was "scarce & bad," wrote Morrill. These both became landmarks on the Mormon Wagon Road.

On the eleventh they "passed over a steep & rough trail" to the top of a mountain (possibly Echo Cliffs), then traveled southeast to "Pokotow's Spring." They rested, then woke at midnight and covered fifteen miles in the dark over sand, stopping for breakfast at eight a.m. After resting an hour, they drove their tired, thirsty horses till three p.m., when they came upon "Hatche's Wells," water in holes in the rock which supplied plentiful water for both horse and man.[50]

Traveling east on the thirteenth, they "struck the Old Utah trail," an indentation three inches deep in sandstone, which led them southeast. They ate dinner at Quichintoweep in the Moenkopi Wash, then continued southeast, finding a camp with good grass but no water. Continuing southeast the following day, after seventeen miles' travel they arrived at Hoteville, which Morrill described as "several gardens one above another on the side hill." Then,

> One of the oribas made his appearance on the top of the hill. Ira Hatch went up to meet him & he came to our camp. Another ran to the village to tell the news. The one that came down felt glad that we had come to see them. He eat some breakfast with us & then started saying that he had got to take home a load of wood telling us to come on as soon as we were ready.

As they rode on about four miles, some Hopis met them with melons and peaches. They rode into Oraibi at two p.m.

Morrill does not give us any insight into Hamblin's talks with Hopi leaders, but his short diary does give us a valuable, concise description of early Oraibi.

> They farm without irrigation.... They obtain their water for town stock purposes from two wells down in the valley.... They raise a plenty of melons and peaches. They carry their firewood three or four miles on thier backs hence they burn very little fuel. They burn the manure fm thier sheep corrals in thier houses. They have no cattle. I saw two horses & quite a number of jackasses. The Women attend strictly to house hold duties. They fetch the water. That is all of the heavy ~~out~~ work that I saw them perform. The men carry the wood gather the crops and do the weaving. When any thing is carried into the house the woman takes care of it. If you tell a man that you want to buy some peaches or melons he will ask his wife or send you to her. They have a great many cats and dogs the latter they use for food. They also have chickens. Thier sheep have been drove off by maurauding bands of Spaniard[s] and Indians until they have but few left.... The men generally go naked with the exception of a shirt and breech clout. The women dress better. They are mostly clad in black loose frocks. The marraagable girls dress similar but wear thier hair in the shape of a rams horns on the side of their heads. The little boys run naked wh[i]le the girls dress respectable.... They try to be cleanly in thier habits.

The Hopis were "very liberal," Morrill wrote. John R. Young hired an Indian to make a quick census of the town, and found that there were only seven hundred residents in Oraibi, down from the twelve hundred when Hamblin first visited them.

The Hopis had a ring dance on the fifteenth, and a "grand dance & feast" the following day.[51] The Mormons witnessed a ceremony performed in a large well, in which a chief would sprinkle men dressed in fox skins, and pray for rain. Fawcett states, matter-of-factly, "Rain would always follow within 1 or 2 days of the prayer."[52] The Indian missionary has almost been converted to the native religion.

Hamblin himself felt that some of the Hopis received the Mormons "rather coldly." When some Hopi friends told them that the Navajos were planning a major raid on Mormon settlements soon, Jacob decided to hasten his departure.[53]

The company left Oraibi early on the eighteenth. They breakfasted at Hoteville and debated whether to return home by the Crossing of the Fathers, without making a final decision, then traveled to Quichintoweep after dark. The next morning, once again, they debated but did not decide which route to take home.[54] Perhaps at about this point, Jacob received a spiritual intuition that the company should cross the Colorado at the Crossing of the Fathers. While the Indians were willing to follow him, the whites voted against him, to his disgust. (And in their defense, his route would have certainly added six or so days of hard travel to the journey, and they were starting to run low on rations at this point.) He noted in his autobiography that Navajos had raided the settlements north of St. George and had driven off "twelve or fifteen hundred head of animals," and if Hamblin's group had taken the Crossing of the Fathers, they might have recovered the cattle that had been stolen.[55]

I have not yet been able to document this raid Hamblin refers to. The closest thing to it is a raid that took place on October 30, after Jacob's company arrived at Kanab. John D. Lee, in his diary, states that the Navajos raided Beaver, Paragoonah, Parowan, Summit, Cedar City, Hamilton's Fort, Kanarraville, and New Harmony, driving off a thousand horses and mules. According to Lee, Coal Creek John led a band of friendly Indians that routed a group of Navajos and recovered two hundred animals.[56] These figures were wildly exaggerated; actually, fifty-two head were lost and twenty-one recovered.[57] Hamblin's numbers were certainly greatly exaggerated also.

At noon the expedition set out and camped at Hatch's Wells. On the twentieth, in the morning, one of the horses "gave out"—a grim, common feature of these trips across the Colorado. The horses seemed to be able to make the journey to Oraibi, but the trip back was too much for them. The forty-mile stretches without water did not help, and they probably also did not get regular, substantial feed in the desert or in mountain areas in the late fall or winter.

Some of the Indians, led by Coal Creek John, followed the route that they had taken coming to Oraibi, but the Mormons took a different trail, which started by running somewhat southwest. Two more horses collapsed on this day. That night, after dark, George Whitmore discovered some "good water in rock hole[s] and good grass and wood," and they named the pool Whitmore Lake in his honor.[58]

On the twenty-first, they rode eleven miles and came to a "mountain" that lay south of Lee's Ferry, probably Echo Cliffs. Jacob Hamblin and John R. Young searched for water, without success. As the company tried to find a way down the mountain,

> some of the Indians found an Indian wickeup with an old squaw in it. She was very badly scard and cried. The Indians eat up most of the food that they could find and wanted to take her blanket away fm her but some of the boys came up and shamed them out of that. Jacob Hamblin s[t]opped with her till the Indians left. She told him where the water was.

This is an action very typical of Hamblin.

After drinking some of this water, they continued on, and had to make a dry camp that night.

The next day, they came to Mineral Springs again, where they found the Coal Creek John contingent of the company, then rode to Navajo Springs and camped. On the way, John R. Young's horse gave out, but he was able to coax it to camp. In addition, the horse of Indian George, which had been struggling for several days, finally lay down and refused to move. After the expedition reached a camping site with water, two Indians had to backtrack and take water to the horse, then were able to bring it to camp.

The next day the company arrived at the Colorado, at modern Lee's Ferry, and found their previous raft still usable. They began ferrying men and horses over. Two horses that the Indians had been riding drowned, probably as a result of exhaustion. John R. Young arrived with his nearly "given out" horse, who was able to cross—he got "mired down" on the north side of the river, but the missionaries were able to pull him out to solid land.[59]

It took five trips to get all of the men across, and John Young worked hard all day on the raft, his lower legs constantly in the cold water.[60] The missionaries moved down the river to a camping place as quickly as they could. "Here J Hamblin dug up some lead that he had cached on a previous trip," wrote Morrill. "The last of the boys got here about dark. They report one Indian horse that cound [could] not be got to the river. This was the one that layed down yesterday."

On October 24, John Young's horse could go no farther, so Young took him back to the river and left him. The company arrived at Jacob's Pools an hour past sunset. "Ashton Nebakers pack horse gave out and was left also another Indian horse was left," writes Morrill. With this grim sentence, his journal ends.

Apparently, at about this time, Young "was seized with cramping colic"—probably severe intestinal pain, accompanied by intense cramping—as his exertions crossing the Colorado caught up with him. But in the morning they had to move on, as they were out of provisions. "It hurt me to ride on horseback, but I had to do so or be left to die," Young wrote. Finally they reached Kanab, probably on the twenty-fifth or twenty-sixth. They did not have adequate resources for treating Young, so they fixed a kind of hammock and some of the men carried him home to Washington.[61] There, he was given up for dead by his friends, but eventually pulled through and survived.

As this was Hamblin's eighth trip across the Colorado, one might expect that this journey would be getting easier for the Mormons, but judging from the horses dropping like flies on the road back, it wasn't. John Young wrote, "The trip was fraught with hardship and danger," and also mentions that, as usual, the expedition had run out of food on the way back, so forced marches were necessary. While the large size of the expedition gave them more security, this undoubtedly made it more difficult to transport the food necessary for such a large company.[62]

As was stated earlier, soon after Hamblin returned home, in late October and early November, Navajos raided settlements north of St. George and drove off a number of horses. Iron County military leaders sent James Andrus out with a company to try to punish the raiders and recover the animals before they could reach the Colorado. Jacob was part of this company.

Edwin G. Woolley kept a diary of the expedition, and wrote that the company, three men on horseback and three in a baggage wagon, set out from St. George on November 4.[63] After traveling through the Pipe Spring and Pahreah area, on the eleventh some of them discovered Navajos with stolen horses close to Warm Creek, between the Paria River and the Crossing of the Fathers, and opened fire on them, apparently wounding two. Woolley wrote: "There are eight (8) of the Navajoes with 12 horses. There are 6 of us, Bro. Jacob Hamblin having got behind."[64]

The six men, after thus opening hostilities against the Navajos, found that they were in a weak defensive position. They exchanged shots with the Indians for fifteen minutes, but as bullets continued to whistle around their heads, they fell back and rode their horses out of range. So the Mormons retreated and, as usual, the raiders were not stopped.

As Hamblin remembers the incident, some of the company fired before the rest of the men were ready, and although two Navajos were hit, this allowed the others to take shelter in an advantageous position. The Mormons tried to approach them but could not. "I was fired at several times, as also were several of the other brethren," Hamblin wrote. "Once, as I was secreted behind a cedar tree, a Navajoe crawled up behind a sand drift, fired at me, and the bullet just missed my head." He records that they recovered one horse, while the Navajos retained ten horses but lost three of their party.[65]

The Andrus company returned on November 18,[66] leaving Jacob Hamblin, Lyman Hamblin, John Mangum, Hyrum Judd, Jehiel McConnell, and the Paiutes "to watch the frontiers," as they had done through the winter.[67] However, Jacob came to St. George on the twentieth and reported to Erastus Snow, who in turn wrote to Brigham Young: "Col Andrus and Jacob Hamblin have returned from their last expedition—they report about 50 to 60 Navajos engaged in the late raid with a few Moquis—They had many rifles and some good coats and other clothing supposed to have come from Fort Lyons in exchange for our stock—Jacob thinks from the trails that near 200 head have been taken within a month."[68]

Snow then talked Indian policy with Young:

> Our military men think Jacob and the Paiutes are insufficient to defend the frontiers—though willing to try while Jacob feels a little jealous of too much interference by the military,—and owing to his feelings—and former instructions about Jacob's mission—I feel delicate in attempting to build and garrison forts farther east with whites—and especially as facilities are few and expenses great—We will second Jacob and his Pahutes or take the lead and let them second us—whichever you think best—but something more thorough and effective seems necessary to defend our frontier.

Hamblin, in his autobiography, wrote that he and his fellow watchmen endured a winter of "great hardship," for "they suffered with the cold, and passed many sleepless nights." They crossed the Kaibab Plateau several times, traveling through snow that was waist deep in some places.

Hamblin confessed that "this Navajoe war caused me many serious reflections. I felt that there was a better way to settle matters, and I made up my mind to go and see the Navajoes, and have a talk with them as soon as circumstances would permit."[69] Hamblin must have suddenly realized that he had somehow returned to his military role, before his conversion in Tooele. It is surprising, but beyond Spaneshanks and his band, Hamblin had never talked to Navajo chiefs, to the best of our knowledge, though he may have talked to some Navajos at the Hopi Mesas through an interpreter. As we have seen, there were good, practical reasons for this, notably the Navajo Wars with the U.S. government, the Mormons' ties with traditional Navajo enemies, the Hopis; the death of George A. Smith Jr.; Kit Carson's devastating campaign against the Navajos in 1863; the fact that the more aggressive Navajos refused to turn themselves in, lived in the Four Corners region of the southwest, and became allies with Black Hawk in the Black Hawk War.[70]

However, after the failure of the Navajo Reservation at Bosque Redondo, Barboncito gave a famous speech requesting that the Navajos be allowed to return to their traditional lands. This was granted, and a new treaty was signed on June 1, 1868.[71] The Navajos at Bosque Redondo were able to return to their territory. And though some outbreaks of violence would continue after the return, the full-fledged "Navajo wars" with the U.S. Army would not reoccur.

The Black Hawk War had inclined the desperate Navajos to ally with Ute outlaws rather than Mormons whom they did not know. But the Black Hawk War had been winding down. The last major raid of the war, which had been a disastrous failure for Black Hawk, occurred in June 1867, and the war chief agreed to a peace a month later.[72] Though the war dragged on a few years more, and some raiding continued, the Utes' most talented and effective leader was gone.

So circumstances were indeed starting to look favorable for a talk and treaty with Navajo leaders. Nevertheless, Navajo raids into southern Utah continued.

Black Hawk, in fact, began to travel from settlement to settlement, preaching peace. On December 5, he and his brother Mountain spoke at the St. George sacrament meeting, and Jacob interpreted for them.[73] Charles Walker wrote that they spoke "meaningly to us and if they carry out their talk it will be well for them and us." After this meeting, a prayer circle was held, a more elite and ceremonial gathering, and, with Erastus Snow acting as "mouth," the group laid hands "on the Head of Br Jacob Hamlin and blessed him and set him apart to labor among the Lamanites."[74] Though details about this ceremony are lacking, it seems Jacob was being asked to start some new chapter in his mission to Indians.

Erastus Snow wrote to Brigham Young two days later, mentioning the talk of Black Hawk and Mountain, and then wrote, "I have sent this day U. Miller—and Major A. P. Hardy and ten 10 other men with Jacob Hamblin and ten 10 indians to establish an Indian farm on the Pahreer and a guardhouse near the Colorado ford."[75] So began the rebirth of Pahreah, at Paria creek, called Rockhouse or Pahreah (I), located in a beautiful valley with "painted" cliffs to the west and east. In later years, around 1872, floods and irrigation difficulties caused the settlers to abandon this location, and some moved five miles north to found Pahreah (II), while others moved five miles south to found Adairville (named after Thomas Adair). Both settlements, as well as Rockhouse/Pahreah (I), are now ghost towns.[76]

After Jacob and his friends started this Indian farm, William Meeks was put in charge of it, though Jacob often visited and worked there, and Jacob appointed one of the Indians to act as "bishop" of the Paiute workers.[77] Meeks was a fifty-five-year-old Indiana native who, with his wife Betsy, had converted to Mormonism in 1842. The Meeks family was called to Dixie in 1862, and settled in Pine Valley before relocating in Pahreah.[78] Pahreah was sometimes called Fort Meeks during this period.

When Brigham Young and his party visited the Pahreah farm in early September 1870, they found two Mormons and about fifty Paiutes living there.[79] John D. Lee, in the same company, wrote that the Paria stream lay

> between two high Bluff[s] of purpendicuelar Rocks about a 1000 feet high, the bottom from 50 to 300 yards in witdth, the Banks low & sandy, water Rily, gren [green?] cottonwood & squaw bushes, the latter Bending with Berries....The Missionaries & Natives had some 35 or 40 acres in corn, turnips &c.[80]

Both Lee and Musser described Peter Shirts's stone house, which shows that this location, at the time called Pahreah, was what had previously been called Rockhouse. The Shirts' house was located near a large sandstone ridge.[81]

Hiram Judd was called to act as bishop in the "Kanab and Pahreah Indian Mission" on December 26, "under Jacob Hamblin, President."[82] So Jacob was serving as a sort of mission president, with local leaders such as Judd and Meeks beneath him.

During this year, Jacob was constantly on the move, marshalling Paiutes to try to track and punish Navajos; leading a difficult expedition to the Hopis to try to strengthen them in their opposition to the Navajos; guiding the Kanab Indian farm and founding another on the Paria; and he even served in a military expedition to regain livestock.

But during these activities, Jacob became increasingly troubled by the violence and enmity with the Navajos. Aside from the obvious losses of property to the Navajos, he was deeply troubled by the Navajo deaths.

In the following year he would try to convince his leaders to authorize an expedition to talk to Navajo leaders, and stop the raids and the retaliatory killing.

21

"We Will Now Ack Knowlage but One Father Suck the Milk of One Mother"

With Powell among the Uinkarets, and Treaty at Fort Defiance, 1870

In 1870, Jacob continued to preside over Paiute Indian farms at Kanab and Pahreah, and he witnessed Brigham Young, pursuing his "southern strategy," turn Kanab into a substantial Mormon town and Pipe Spring into a fort. Jacob continued to work with the Paiutes to deter Navajo raids. But later in the year changing circumstances would allow him to talk with Navajo leaders at Fort Defiance in eastern Arizona and make a treaty that would bring the Navajo raids to an end. One of these fortunate circumstances was the mutually beneficial relationship between Jacob and John Wesley Powell that began this year.

In the early days of 1870, a group of about a hundred Navajos made a raid into Mormon territory, successfully rounding up cattle and horses from the Beaver and Pinto areas. One of the Navajos' slaves, a Hispanic from New Mexico, escaped to the Mormons and identified the leader of the raid as "Barow-azeta," the brother of "Spanishaunk [who] was killed about ~~the time~~ the time the Berry boys were murdered."[1] It is possible that the death of his brother in 1866 at the hand of Mormons led this Navajo leader to have a special antagonism toward the Saints.[2]

Jacob and his Paiutes would have been trying to deter just such raiding, by keeping watch on the Crossing of the Fathers and the mouth of the Paria, at modern Lee's Ferry. On January 13, Jacob left Kanab with three Paiutes, apparently planning to meet some Mormons at the mouth of the Paria then continue on to the Crossing of the Fathers. After twelve miles' journey, they made camp. "Slep[t] cold," wrote Hamblin. "Thought of home and its comforts. I had hurd of the blews but I knew not a thing of it unles it was that knight."[3] Beneath the public Hamblin—Indian missionary and explorer—we see the loneliness and melancholy of the private Hamblin on an expedition, missing his family, missing a normal bed in a house.

The next day the four men climbed to the top of the snow-covered Kaibab Plateau and camped. Jacob again thought of home and family as he drifted into sleep, and soon had a comforting dream:

> I found my self at home with my Family. I asked them how they ware and if they kneeded any thing. One of them said they needed a Dollar very mutch. I went to my purse saying I hav one raged [ragged] green back. When I took hold of it it was heavy .2. or 3 pounds weight. On examining it I found it was gold coin from small coin up to 50 slugs. I asked is this a dream or not. So I shook the money it sounded like gold. I said I am not deceivd. It is not a dream. I a woak and it was a dream.

However, then Hamblin wrote, in superscript, "I thought I was not deceived." In other words, the dream had a literal reality somehow. He continued: "I was cold and wet. I hav written this because I know it has a meaning. It comforted my hart."

On the fifteenth, Jacob and the Paiutes traveled twenty miles, to the foot of what Jacob called "Purple Mountain." It began to rain, the rain turned to snow, and Jacob again endured "a cold wet sleeples night." When dawn broke, he woke up drenched and chilled through. "It was with mutch dificulty that I could get warm," he wrote. To add insult to injury, the horses had disappeared and had to be tracked down.

Jacob's group arrived at the mouth of the Paria on the seventeenth and made a warm, pleasant camp under a rock. Apparently, Jacob was waiting for his friends to arrive, so now it was time to rest and relax. The Paiutes killed "a larg Beaver fat and fine," while Jacob read his Book of Mormon and wrote a letter to Erastus Snow.

No one showed up at the Paria crossing, so about a week later, on the twenty-third, Jacob, possibly accompanied by one or two Paiutes, started for the Crossing of the Fathers. "Past a cold nite. Little wrest," he wrote. The next day he came to Warm Creek, about five miles from the crossing, but his friends had not made an appearance. "What is the reason?" he asked.

The next day, he turned back to the Paria and endured another "cold lonesome night." He reached Pahreah on the twenty-fifth, at eight p.m., and found Hiram Judd there at a guard house, waiting to go build a guard house at the Colorado, presumably at the Crossing of the Fathers. The next day, Hamblin sent four whites and five Indians "to watch on the Pass," then worked on the "sleeping department" of one of the buildings.[4]

On the twenty-ninth, he set out to "the ford on the Colerado"—the Crossing of the Fathers—and met "the white and Read Brotheren" at Warm Creek; they had seen no Navajos. He talked with the group, and they decided that this would be a good place to watch for raiders. They moved camp a couple times to find a situation where they could make a fire without being seen, then stayed there a few days, the Paiute hunters bringing in rabbits for meals, Jacob reading the Book of Mormon. On February 1, he had a pain in his head and symptoms of the mumps. "I hope it will not be very sever[e] on me," he wrote. This wasn't the ideal place to recover from illness, but fortunately it was a comparatively mild winter, and there was a stretch of warmish, pleasant days in early February.

"Indian Charly" brought letters from St. George on the fifth stating that Navajos had taken "all the horses from little Pinto to Minersville." Jacob wondered what route they had taken back to Arizona, because they hadn't passed their lookout spot. (Possibly they had forded Lee's Ferry.) The next day, Jacob took his bedding and food and traveled down to the Crossing of the Fathers. Indians met him, climbing down the rocks by moonlight—"rather dangerous," Hamblin remarked. They did not dare light a fire, and "past [passed] a sleeples night."

Examining tracks the next day, Jacob saw that two groups of Navajos had met and held a council, then one group had gone back over the river. He returned to the encampment—presumably the lookout spot at Warm Springs—arriving there late at night, with "boath feet badley blisterd." He called this hike the most "miserables days journey I ever performed."

On the eighth, a Brother Potter started for Fort Meeks (Pahreah) to ask for a horse for Hamblin, as he could scarcely walk. Two men with horses came the next day, bringing news that some forty-five Navajos were in the area. Jacob set out for Pahreah, arriving on the eleventh.

He was back in Kanab on the fifteenth. The next day he wrote, "Talked with the Indians. They think thare mite be some trety made with the Navajose."

Life at Kanab was uneventful until February 22, when Hiram Judd and the other men arrived with a beef. The following day three wagons with supplies arrived from St. George, and they also had a message: "Hyram Judd and my self mite manag the frontier to sutt ourselves."

Jacob and some Indians started for "the Pahrier" on the twenty-fourth, but it was so stormy that apparently they turned back, and the following day, they started "for Parier" again, traveling by very muddy paths, reaching the fort after dark the following day. On the twenty-seventh, some unnamed brethren "left 20 lbs of dried meet 40 lbs of pork," then apparently turned back westward.

The next day, Hamblin "pild and burnt brush with the Ind. all day with my rifle strapt to my back." This is a vivid image showing the real danger Hamblin felt at Pahreah. He wrote that three Paiute men, two women, and four children arrived, after he had sent for them. These were apparently Kaibab Paiutes who wished to live at Pahreah.

Jacob cut brush on March 2, and two days later, brought water on to the farmland. However, "fifty feet of earth slid in to the ditch." Irrigating in southern Utah was never an easy matter, and severe floods would often complicate circumstances on the Paria. The next day, Hamblin writes, they again worked with guns on their backs.

On the fifteenth, he and the Indians mended a water ditch, and the next two days they watered the land.

Hamblin wrote, on the twentieth, "finished one mild [mile] and a half of water ditch. That is we let in the water." The next day, one of the Paiutes' dogs barked, and they thought that Navajos might be nearby, so "gethered up the horses in the darkness of the night."

They sowed wheat on the twenty-second. The following day was clear and warm, but that was not entirely a blessing, for it brought "musketoes." That night, Indian Charly arrived with startling news: "Pres. Young was on his way to cross the Colerado River at the mouth of the Virgin and then visit kanab." Such a visit shows Young's keen interest in the Dixie frontier. He could easily have been content with a visit to St. George and the small towns near to it, but he wanted to see Kanab and assess it as a possible colonizing area.

On the twenty-fourth, Hamblin and his helpers finished sowing six acres of wheat, and the next day were faced with an unromantic task: "Helpt cleer the corell [corral] of manure the Indian Women halling the wagons by hand from the corell to the yard," he wrote.

Hamblin was in Kanab by March 27 and wrote a letter to Erastus Snow:

> I have just returned from Pahreah. All well there. Business prospering finely under the Presidency of William Meeks. There is a safe GuardHouse and small corral there where men can cook and lodge safely with 20 or 25 horses; one outside gate only for houses [horses] and corral. We have finished there one mile and a half of water ditch. I consider it permanent, as we need no dam. We have put in 6 acres of wheat and some garden seeds. We have eight laboring native men there, two women and six children. I took them in on condition that they subsist on half rations, depending on roots and their former diet for the balance. They have a large breadth of land ready for the plow and were still clearing off, when I came away, at the rate of one acre and a half a day. There is no lack of water [f]or the very best of land on the stream.
>
> We have not been able to discern any sign of Navajos since Bro. Miller was there. We have 800 yards of good fence newly put up at Kanab, we expect to finish the fencing this week; which will secure to us great advantages in stock raising and farming.[5]

On March 28, Hiram Judd started for home, and some Paiute women brought in some baskets to sell. Jacob apparently returned to Pahreah.

On March 31, Jacob received a note that Brigham Young would be at Kanab on April 2, and the Indian missionary set out west immediately. He met Young, traveling with George A. Smith and Erastus Snow, twenty men, and five or six wagons, at Pipe Spring that day, and traveled with the company to Kanab.[6]

At Kanab, they had cleaned up the fort to prepare for their visitors. "The Piutes," Hamblin wrote, "seventy in number, washed off the dirt and paint which usually besmeared their persons, and put on a fair appearance for Indians."[7] At the fort, Hamblin assigned Paiutes to take care of the company's horses, as usual, though Young at first balked at the idea. However, Jacob convinced him that the animals would be safe, and Young agreed.

A meeting was held, in which

> Pres. Young Blest the People of kanab dedicated the Land unto the Lord Blest it and set it a part for the getheren of the Saints. Told me I should not lack any thing I needed to cary on the Mision among the Lamanites. Held a council. Concluded to stok the country this season and make arangements to setle Familys in the land of Canion [Canaan] as he caled the kanab country.[8]

Young, in his ongoing power struggle with the federal government, and non-Mormons in Utah, was beginning to see southern Utah and Arizona as a place of refuge, a Canaan. So he indeed wanted to make Kanab a solid, permanent outpost. He solidified Kanab in two ways: first, he apparently directed the missionaries already at Kanab to bring their families to the town; second, he would assign a group of Saints in northern Utah to resettle there.

Hamblin had a private interview with Young, who firmly approved his "labors and policy on the frontiers." Then Hamblin told him of his wish to bring an end to the Navajo conflict through negotiation:

> I told him that I desired to visit the Navajoes, and have a talk with them; that there had been a number of raiders killed, and I never saw a Navajoe's bones on the ground, the flesh having been eaten off by wolves and vultures, but what I felt sorrow for the necessity of such things; that I always abhorred the shedding of blood, and desired to obtain peace in some better way.[9]

Young evidently did not reply to Hamblin immediately, but when he arrived at Toquerville, he sent him a letter supporting his desire to end the bloodshed. He directed Jacob

> to do all I could to prevent the shedding of blood; not to let the Indians have any firearms or ammunition if I thought they would use them for killing

21.1. Kanab fort on January 25, 1872, with a number of early settlers, many of them children. The large building may be the meetinghouse in the northwest corner of the fort, while the building on the right looks like one of the typical cabins in the fort. Photograph by E. O. Beaman, of the Powell survey. Courtesy LDS Church History Library.

miners or other travelers; and, if it were possible, he wished the people to get along without the killing of any more Navajoes.[10]

The stage was set for Hamblin's visit to Navajo country later in the year.

Jacob was immediately obedient to Young's injunction to bring families to Kanab: "Started for home," he wrote.[11] There he must have dropped what, according to family traditions, was a bombshell. Priscilla and Louisa would have to give up their comfortable rock house, leave the comparatively civilized Santa Clara, and move to the ragged edge of the frontier again. Priscilla, reportedly, was extremely reluctant to leave Santa Clara at first, but finally acquiesced.

Louisa and her son Walter would return to Kanab with Hamblin immediately, along with two of Rachel's sons, Joseph and Benjamin. Hamblin wrote in his diary: "April 12th 1870 started for canian [the Kanab area] with wife Louesa hur son Walter 2 years old Joseph my son and Benjiman driving some stock."[12] Census records entered on June 1, 1870, confirm this exactly: on that date, Jacob was living at Kanab (occupation "farmer"), accompanied by Louisa with her three-year-old, Walter, and also Joseph, fourteen, and Benjamin, eleven.[13] According to family tradition, one of the older children—possibly Joseph—was herding the cows behind the wagons, and as they traveled mile after weary mile, he objected to the monotony of the landscape. "When we climb over one hill there is always another damn hill to climb," he said.[14]

When Louisa and her children arrived at Kanab, they found about six men, some with families, living there, as well as the Paiutes.[15] Louisa would have moved into a crude, mud-chinked log cabin, probably with an earth floor, built on the northeast wall of the fort. According to a map of the old Kanab fort, its west, north, and east walls all had cabins, while on the south there was a wall of cedar posts tied with cedar strips—essentially a stockade fence. A major gate faced east at the northeast corner.[16] Dellenbaugh called the fort a "stockaded square of log houses," rather than a fort proper. A combination schoolhouse, meeting house, and ballroom, built of stone, was situated at one of the corners.[17] All cabins faced an enclosure about 112 feet square. The cabin roofs were made of willows covered over with a thick layer of dirt, and one of the occupants of the fort remarked, dryly: "When it rained water outside, it often rained mud inside."[18]

Brigham Young, after visiting Kanab, called a trusted leader, businessman Levi Stewart, to lead a party of settlers to Kanab, and this new infusion arrived in May and June, with Stewart's family occupying cabins in the northwest part of the fort.[19] Stewart, a fifty-eight-year-old native of Illinois, had converted to Mormonism in 1836 and moved to Far West, Missouri, in June 1838—just in time to be driven back to Illinois after considerable loss of property. He served as storekeeper in Winter Quarters, and later in Salt Lake City, and performed a number of missions for church leaders. He eventually married five wives and had twenty-nine children.[20] In 1865, Young asked him to move to Big Cottonwood Canyon, Salt Lake County, to start a paper mill, and Stewart put down solid roots there. However, when the call to Kanab came, in typical Mormon fashion, he accepted this mission to one of the frontier outposts of Utah without hesitation, and selected a number of families, mostly from Cottonwood, who also accepted the call. This group, amounting to seven wagons and fifty-two people, arrived at Pipe Spring on June 1, stayed there for a couple weeks, then moved on to Kanab, arriving on the fourteenth.[21] The old residents of Kanab "kindly welcomed us," wrote William Thomas Stewart, one of Levi's sons, who would soon become Jacob's son-in-law. "They felt willing to divide the scanty supply of water with us." We are reminded at once that this was the arid West, and Kanab's water supply was very limited. According to one early report, Kanab was more suited to ranching than farming, due to scarcity of water.[22] The Stewarts mostly became ranchers in the upcoming years, as did Jacob's sons Lyman and Walter, and his brother Frank.[23]

The newcomers quickly planted corn, constructed corrals, and laid up hay.[24] When Brigham Young visited Kanab in September, there were sixty whites and a hundred Paiutes living in the town.[25]

For Jacob, it was the old pattern starting again: he had settled Kanab as an Indian farm, a frontier outpost. A few whites had coalesced around him. But now, with a sizable infusion of settlers sent by Brigham Young, it would become a town, and he would no longer be the leader—that role would be taken over by Levi Stewart. Instead, he would become the Indian expert for a new community, whose residents would be focused on farming and ranching rather than on missionary work. In addition, while before there had been an emphasis on Indian farming at the town, now the new residents would be focusing on their own economic concerns.

On May 16, Hamblin started for Fish Lake (modern Panguitch Lake) with two Indians, and they arrived three days later. He found about a hundred Indians there—Red Lake Utes—"living off fish." Jacob stayed about a week, talking with the Indians. He stocked the lake with three quarts of fish eggs he had brought, and also talked with some Mormons there—a few Parowan residents, led by Silas S. Smith, heard he was at the lake and came out to visit him, arriving on the twenty-second.[26] Joseph Fish wrote that they came "to consult [him] upon the best methods of protecting our stock and settlements, and upon our Indian policy." After this consultation, and a bit of fishing, the Parowaners started back, crossing the mountain on the twenty-third. "Bro. Hamblin came with us this far where we camped," Fish wrote. The next morning, they traveled west, and Jacob returned to the lake.[27]

In Little, Jacob wrote: "I visited the Red Lake Utes, spent some time at Fish Lake, east of Parowan, and visited the Indians along the Sevier. I had many long talks with them, and believe I accomplished much good, in inspiring them with the spirit of peace."[28]

On the thirtieth, Jacob returned to what was now no longer the ragged edge of the frontier—St. George and Santa Clara.[29] He attended a conference of the southern mission in St. George on June 3, where he was sustained as "president of the Indian Missions east and southeast of the Rio Virgen,"[30] and after this traveled to Santa Clara and had a homecoming with Priscilla and the family still at the stone house.

On June 7, he left for Kanab, stopping by St. George to buy numerous items for Louisa. He must have arrived at Kanab just a little before the Stewart company came on June 14. The very next day, Jacob set out for Fish Lake again, "to see the chief and lurn of the whareabouts of a Hostile band of Eutes." However, there were no Indians at the lake, so he crossed over to Parowan, where he obtained two more quarts of fish eggs, and added them to the lake on his way home.[31]

At Kanab, on the eighteenth, he planted corn in his garden, and went to explore Hog Canyon, extending east from Kanab Canyon, about two miles north of Kanab. The next day, the Kanabans held Sacrament meeting, after which Jacob "prepared ground for turnips." He apparently gave "Indian Frank" some ammunition. This may be the young Kaibab chief Chuarumpeak[32] or, according to A. Milton Musser, "Naraquats, *alias* Frank,"[33] who might be our old friend, the Kaibab headman Naraguats, who guided Hamblin over the Colorado for the first time in 1858. However, I suspect

21.2. Chuarumpeak, "Frank," headman of the Kaibab Paiutes, and his family, near a brush shelter. Chuar was a friend of Jacob and John Wesley Powell and his men. Note baskets (often used for gathering seed), and mano and metate (mortar and rock), used for grinding seed, in foreground. Photograph by John K. Hillers, 1873. Courtesy National Anthropological Archives, Smithsonian Institution, GN-01597.

that Musser was simply confused. John Wesley Powell later regarded "Chuar" most highly; Frederick Dellenbaugh, in the second Powell company, wrote that he was "a remarkably good man. He had been constantly devoted to the safety and welfare of the whites. A most fluent speaker in his native tongue, he would address his people with long flights of uninterrupted rhetorical skill."[34]

Toward the end of July, Jacob reportedly accompanied Levi Stewart and the Indian Mose on a journey of exploration northward to find a wagon road over the "Divide" and down the Sevier River, but unfortunately they could find no likely road.[35] On August 1, Jacob conferred with Anson Winsor and Levi Stewart, and they decided to explore the south end of the Buckskin Mountain–Kaibab Plateau, to "see what was thare."

Jacob continued to spend time at Pahreah. William Thomas Stewart wrote that in summer or fall 1870, he visited Pahreah and stayed a few weeks, along with Jacob, William W. Meeks, his father, and a David Brinton.[36]

21.3. Jacob Hamblin and John Wesley Powell in a parley with Paiutes beneath Utah junipers, near Kanab, Utah. Hamblin worked closely with Powell, supporting his 1871–1872 second Colorado expedition and his geological and anthropological surveys. The Paiute in the center may be Kaibab headman Chuarumpeak. Photograph by John K. Hillers, 1873. Courtesy National Anthropological Archives, Smithsonian Institution, GN 01621.

Jacob Hamblin's life story now intersects with the saga of another extraordinary man, John Wesley Powell. Like Hamblin, Powell was a fearless explorer; like him, he was sensitive to Indian culture; like him, he had been a farm boy in Walworth County, Wisconsin. Unlike Hamblin, he was not deeply religious, and was a man of science, a well-educated geographer and anthropologist.[37] Despite any differences in outlook they may have had, Powell and Hamblin worked well together, and the Mormon was instrumental in helping Powell prepare for his second trip down the Colorado in 1871–1872, and in providing for the logistics of this trip. Powell was undoubtedly the

21.4. Detail from figure 21.3 showing Jacob Hamblin and John Wesley Powell on the right.

first man to methodically explore the upper Colorado and Grand Canyon. Nevertheless, Hamblin had been exploring sections of the Colorado, and the lands north and south of the Colorado, since 1858, and had been learning the language and culture of the Indians of southern Utah and Arizona since 1854. He had much experience and knowledge that Powell would lean on in the upcoming years.

Powell, born in 1834 in New York, obtained a good education at three different colleges, though he never received a formal advanced degree, and was especially attracted to the natural sciences. He fought on the Union Side during the Civil War, losing his right arm during the Battle of Shiloh in April 1862. After the war, he taught geology at Illinois Wesleyan University and helped found the Illinois Museum of Natural History. However, his intense interest in exploring the American West caused him to give up permanent employment at these places to spend years in exploration and the practical preparations for exploration, such as fundraising.

In 1869, while Hamblin was laboring at the Kanab Mission, Powell made his famous first expedition down the Colorado, leading a group of nine men with four boats down the Green and Colorado Rivers and through the Grand Canyon. Three of Powell's men, Oramel G. Howland, Seneca Howland, and William Dunn, faced with a difficult stretch of rapids, left him at "Separation Rapid," south of the Shivwits Plateau and St. George. They struck out overland for St. George and were never seen again, by whites.

Powell and his reduced party continued to the confluence of the Virgin and the Colorado, where they were able to make contact with the Mormons in the Muddy River settlements. The Muddy settlers fed the famished men and helped them return to civilization, via St. George.

Though it is not well known, Hamblin was instrumental in helping Powell finish the 1869 expedition, even before the two men met. The only part of Powell's journey that had been explored by boat before him was the stretch of river between Grand Wash and the Virgin River confluence, which, as we have seen, Hamblin, with Jesse Crosby and Henry Miller, explored by boat in April 1867. When Powell was in Salt Lake City in 1869, someone gave him a diary record of Hamblin and company's journey, and he had it with him during the 1869 expedition. "Three men—Hamblin, Miller, and Crosby— ...went on down the river to Callville, landing a few miles below the mouth of the Rio Virgen," Powell wrote in his published diary. "We have their manuscript journal with us, and so the stream is comparatively well known."[38] When the Howlands and Dunn tried to convince Powell to end the 1869 expedition just south of St. George, Powell knew from the 1867 diary that if he could get to Grand Wash, the rest of the voyage would be comparatively easy and he could follow the Virgin back to St. George. Thus he refused to end the expedition at Separation Rapids, and was able to traverse the Grand Canyon fully.[39]

The 1869 expedition made Powell famous, and he immediately began to prepare for another, better funded and better organized, trip down the Green and Colorado Rivers in 1871 and 1872. He planned to make preparations in Utah in 1870, arranging for food and supplies to be waiting for the expedition at various points on the Colorado. A further goal was to discover what he could about the fate of the three missing men from his 1869 voyage (he had heard that Shivwits Indians had killed them). He would also try to meet with Indians that lived near the Colorado and make sure that they were well disposed to him and his men. In addition, since he was interested in Indians purely from an anthropological standpoint, he wanted to visit the Hopi mesas.[40] Just about all of this activity would take place in territory that Jacob Hamblin had made his own, so it is not surprising that the two men would end up working together.

Powell arrived in Salt Lake City in late August, and headed south. Brigham Young was in southern Utah, on another of his tours of Dixie, and was planning to visit Kanab again. Powell met Young at Parowan in early September and joined the presidential party, which also included Jacob Hamblin and John D. Lee. Young recommended that Powell enlist Hamblin as a guide and Indian interpreter, and the explorer hired Jacob for fifty dollars per month.[41] This would be the start of a long relationship between the Indian missionary and Powell, and between Jacob and the members of Powell's party, such as the young artist Frederick Dellenbaugh; Walter Clement "Clem" Powell, the explorer's cousin, who acted as photographer; John "Jack" Hillers, who eventually became a skilled photographer; and Powell's brother-in-law and second-in-command, Almon Thompson, the "Professor," a geographer.[42]

Brigham's party of about forty-three men—including many leading men of southern Utah, such as Apostle Erastus Snow, St. George mayor and stake president Joseph W. Young, Willam H. Dame of Mountain Meadows fame, Daniel D. McArthur, and Lorenzo Roundy—"roled out" of Parowan on September 5.[43] They probably traveled north of Paragonah, then took a road through Little Creek Canyon and Three-mile Creek Canyon that led them to the long, often broad upper Sevier River valley.

Powell lunched with Jacob Hamblin and John D. Lee that day, part way to Panguitch, high on the plateau. It was a curious conjunction of three men who became famous in radically different ways. In the evening, the company camped at the deserted town of Panguitch, and the following day, they traveled "up the Severe River over the Summit to the head waters of the Kannab," through "pine vys. [valleys] & a meadow lande," as Lee wrote.[44] They traveled south through the Sevier River valley into upper Long Valley, with the Markagunt Plateau looming to the west and the pink cliffs of the Paunsaugunt Plateau to the east.

The "Summit," at modern Long Valley Junction, a few miles north of modern Alton (formerly Upper Kanab), is the drainage divide between the Sevier, which flows into the Great Basin, and the East Fork of the Virgin, which flows through southern Utah and into the Colorado. The headwaters of Kanab Creek, another tributary of the Colorado, are nearby. A. Milton Musser, a record keeper for the group, described this area as "a paradisaic country...a valley gently undulating, covered with grass, and dotted with springs and 'seaps,' which form a small stream that courses through the valley and empties into the Sevier River."[45] The remarkable trio, Powell, Lee, and Hamblin, selected the camping place that evening. After dinner, President Young gave Lee "some kind Fatherly council"—he advised him to gather his family and relocate in Arizona, in the San Francisco Mountains.[46] Lee had increasingly become a legal and public relations liability, and Young wanted him out of sight. Lee would subsequently join Hamblin in settling southeastern Utah and northern Arizona.

Young and company decided that they would now turn east, visit the Indian farm Pahreah, then travel southwest to Kanab—a remarkable itinerary for this large party with wagons and carriages. It shows Young's intense interest in southern, frontier Utah.

On the seventh, the company started off southeast toward Pahreah, following the Sink Valley Wash to "Skutumpah Valley," which led into modern Johnson Canyon. Passing "cañon-like vales with high walls of white and red sand rock," they descended "over sandy mounds" and stopped for the night at "Rock Springs," which in a year or two would become the town of Johnson.[47] The next day, the group emerged from Johnson Canyon to travel northeast "over barren, Roling, cedar Ridges covered occasionally with Petr[i]fied wood."[48] Their route probably followed modern Highway 89. They reached the Paria River where it cuts through the Cockscomb, at or near what would become the second location of Pahreah. Then they turned south. Musser described the horses and wagons having to make "abrupt and difficult" crossings of the Paria Creek some twenty-one times before they finally reached the first Pahreah, the Indian farm, in the upper Paria Basin near modern Rock House Cove.

Musser and Lee recorded two Mormons at Pahreah, along with fifty Kaibab Paiutes. Musser described these as "the wildest and most untutored [Indians] I have ever met with in all my travels." The company feasted on local corn, gave the Paiutes some presents, had them tend their animals, and camped for the night.

The next day, the ninth, the company retraced their steps up the Paria, then southwest along the route of modern Highway 89 toward Kanab. At this time, the road must have been primitive at best as it passed over the mud and sand of the Chinle formation. It could accommodate a carriage, but at one point, as the carriage of Lorenzo Roundy, the driver, and R. Ashby negotiated a narrow turn of the road, one of the carriage horses got its hoof stuck between two rocks, and the carriage and two horses made "a fearful plunge down [a] bank" before the outfit stopped just short of a sheer cliff. Roundy and Ashby were able to leap from the carriage, according to Musser, but Lee says that Roundy still was thrown forty feet down a cliff. Fortunately, he was not hurt, the horses and carriage were preserved, and the company continued on its way. Powell, who witnessed the accident, was amazed that there was no loss of life, human or equine.[49]

Young's party arrived at Kanab just after sunset. The next morning, the church president and other leading brethren rode around the area to select the site for the city of Kanab; they chose a place northeast of the fort, on an elevated point, out of the path of canyon winds. A surveyor, Jesse W. Fox, laid out the city in blocks and Arza Hinckley located places where wells could be dug. This was a typically organized Mormon city foundation. Jacob baptized a native of Nashville, Tennessee, John Henry Stone, and Dimick Huntington—the legendary Indian interpreter from northern Utah—confirmed him and ordained him an elder.[50] In the evening Fox and Powell "took observations."[51] Thus the modern town of Kanab, where it is presently located, was founded.[52]

It is likely that Powell's meeting with Hamblin and the Kaibabits occurred now, at Kanab. "Jacob Hamblin, who has been a missionary among the Indians for more than twenty years, has collected a number of *Kai'-vav-its*, with *Chu-ar'-ru-um-peak*, their chief, and they are all camped with us," wrote Powell. "They assure us that we cannot reach the river [the Colorado], that we cannot make our way into the depths of the canyon, but promise to show us the springs and water pockets, which are very scarce in all this region, and to give us all the information in their power."[53]

On September 11, after Fox laid out a few more blocks, there was a public meeting, and Brigham ordained Levi Stewart to be bishop of Kanab branch, and Jacob "to continue to Presd over the Indian Mission &c." He instructed Stewart to organize a cooperative herd and store "& let the Poor own it & keep out speculators."[54] This presages the Mormon United Order, a communitarian experiment that would sweep southern Utah and the early Little Colorado settlements in Arizona in a few years.

At two p.m., Young's company, with Hamblin and Powell, set out for Pipe Spring, where Young laid out a fort, which Anson Perry Windsor (or Winsor) would be in charge of, as he supervised "the church Stock." This house fort would be called Winsor's Castle and still stands in the Pipe Spring National Monument.[55] Pipe Spring, in 1858 a Paiute campground, had become a key site on the road from Utah to Arizona, as its supply of water controlled passage from St. George to the Kaibab and Lee's Ferry, and as its plentiful surrounding grass offered rich cattle country. It would be important for Young's southern strategy.[56]

The Young company departed for St. George on the twelfth, but Powell and Hamblin stayed at Pipe Spring, where the rest of Powell's party met them in the afternoon. Francis Marion Bishop, in Powell's company, wrote, "Was glad to meet Mr. Jacob Hamblin, our interpreter, and the Maj. at Pipe Springs, and find our plan is somewhat changed, to wit the wagon goes on to Kanabe while our party, (Maj. Powell, myself, Walter, Mr. Hamblin, Charlie Benn, Mr. A. [Ash] Nebeker, and the Indian guides) with the pack animals will go on south for the Colorado."[57]

Bishop, a topographer, was a former student of Powell, a devout Christian, and a Civil War veteran. As a member of Powell's 1871 expedition, he would often express distaste for the religion of the local Mormons. Logically enough, he soon thereafter converted to Mormonism, married one of Orson Pratt's daughters, and lived the rest of his life in Utah, teaching science for a time at the University of Deseret.[58] Walter Graves was an assistant topographer from the Midwest.

Among the Mormon contingent, Ashton Nebeker was a seventeen-year-old Toquerville resident who would work extensively with Powell and his parties.[59] Charlie Benn remains obscure. One of the Indian guides was Chuarumpeak, and the other was Shuts, a "one-eyed, bare-legged, merry-faced pigmy," in Powell's words. Chuarumpeak rode a pony during the upcoming journey to the Colorado, but Shuts preferred to walk, often taking shortcuts, then sitting and waiting, "always meeting us with a jest."[60]

Powell, after talking with Hamblin and local Paiutes, realized that he could easily have supplies sent to the Crossing of the Fathers or Lee's Ferry (though they were close enough together that he would only need to cache at one of these points). He wanted to discover another supply point farther west, so decided that his group with pack train would set out immediately to seek a new route to the Colorado southwest of Pipe Spring. In addition, this route would bring him close to the area where the Howlands and Dunn had disappeared, and he hoped to learn more about their fate. The Kaibab Indians debated all day which route to take to the Colorado—a longer route with sure water or a shorter route with less certain water—but decided that the shorter route would probably have water at this time of year so decided to risk it.[61]

They set out on September 14: "Here we go for the Colorado, or bust," wrote Bishop.[62] They were venturing into the modern Mount Trumbull Wilderness area, on the Uinkaret Plateau in the Arizona Strip. The poetic geographer Clarence Dutton,

Powell's protégé, described a journey from Pipe Spring to Mount Trumbull in 1880, and the first part was a trek through a barren, sandy, burning desert: "The air is like a furnace, but so long as the water holds out the heat is not enervating." Eventually, he left the sand and could travel faster on firm soil. Plants were not plentiful: "Several forms of cactus are seen looking very diseased and mangy, and remnants of low desert shrubs browsed to death by cattle." For Dutton this desert was "not without charms, however repulsive [it might be] in most respects."[63]

The Hamblin–Powell–Chuarumpeak company, traveling through this furnace, reached the expected water pocket at five p.m., and to their great relief, it was not dry.

The next day they worked their way toward a towering mountain. "These mountains are of volcanic origin," wrote Powell, "and we soon come to ground that is covered with fragments of lava. The way becomes very difficult. We have to cross deep ravines, the heads of canyons that run into the Grand Canyon."[64] They reached a water pocket near dusk, "in a deep gorge on the flank of this great mountain"—soon to be named after Powell's friend and patron, Illinois senator Lyman Trumbull. They camped here that night.[65]

On the sixteenth, they came to a village of Uinkaret Paiutes, living in a mountain valley which had a good spring.[66] Before they reached the village, Powell sent his men on and climbed a small peak to get his bearings: "I can see the Indian village... in a grassy valley," he wrote, "embosomed in the mountains, the smoke curling up from their fires; my men are turning out their horses and a group of natives stand around. Down the mountain I go and reach camp at sunset." After dinner they threw some juniper boughs on the fire, and the whites and Paiutes sat round it, smoking and talking. Powell explained that he wanted to descend to the Colorado. The Uinkaret Paiutes told him that there used to be a way down, but it was very difficult, and no one had been down there for years. Powell also said that he would like to talk to some Shivwits, and the Indians told him that they lived thirty miles away, and that they would send a runner to them immediately. Then Powell prevailed on the chief of the village, To-mor'-ro-un-ti-kai, to relate myths to them, even though this was not the winter season, the usual time for tales.

I presume that Hamblin was acting as Powell's interpreter in all these conversations, though Powell in his memoir gives the impression that he was communicating with Paiutes directly. Powell's most recent biographer, Donald Worster, concludes that Powell knew some Paiute words, since he had made large lists of closely related Ute vocabulary. But he clearly was not fluent in Paiute or Ute; Hamblin was much more familiar with it.[67]

They added a Uinkaret guide to their company at this point—"a blear-eyed, weazen-faced, quiet old man, with his bow and arrows in one hand and a small cane in the other"[68]—leaving Chuarumpeak and Shuts (along with their gear and pack animals) at the village. The next morning, they made a steep descent down the mountain, then dropped farther into side canyons.

Three days later, on the nineteenth, they made an approach to the Grand Canyon.[69] As they descended a side canyon, Bishop was overwhelmed: "To one not familiar with such wild scenery, the first sight is awfully grand," he wrote. "We stood for a while gazing down into the awful gulf below, then looking around us upon the dizzy heights above, and until a sense of the superlative littleness of man seemed to hide us, even from ourselves." They had not even reached the north rim yet.

Powell describes the company leading their ponies along a narrow ledge, "a wall upon our left; unknown depths on our right." The path was so narrow or sloping that "I ache with fear lest a pony should make a misstep and knock a man over the cliffs with him," he wrote. "Now and then we start the loose rocks under our feet, and over the cliffs they go, thundering down, down, the echoes rolling through distant canyons."[70]

After winding their way through these subsidiary canyons, they reached the edge of the Grand Canyon. "The effect here was grand indeed," wrote Bishop. "Before us yawned a fearful gulf dropping down some 1500 feet in one threatening cliff. To the left one immense bed of lava, black and threatening. The lava appears at one time, to have filled the cañon and side cañons for 43 miles and then to have washed out again, giving a beauty to the scene unparalleled in any country."

But there seemed to be no way down that vast cliff. Powell wrote, "Our withered guide, the human pickle, seats himself on a rock and seems wonderfully amused at our discomfiture." After letting the whites consider the impossibility of descent for a while, the guide rose, beckoned them to follow, then pointed out a narrow sloping shelf to the right, which was a path of sorts. "It leads along the cliff for half a mile to a wider bench beyond," wrote Powell, "which, he says, is broken down on the other side in a great slide, and there we can get to the river. So we start out on the shelf; it is so steep we can hardly stand on it, and to fall or slip is to go—don't look to see!"[71]

After reaching the wider bench, the party rested; then Jacob and the Uinkaret Paiute left to try to find a route down to the Colorado that animals could traverse. Bishop, an experienced climber, decided to descend to the Colorado by himself, as a joke on the other men. He accomplished the deed, reached the bottom, in the darkness, and quenched his thirst at the cool Colorado. After building a bonfire, he started to climb back up in the dark with a torch in one hand. "I lighted my torch and committing my life to the Mercy of God, began the ascent, which proved to be of no ordinary danger and peril," he wrote.[72]

Jacob and the Paiute quickly realized that horses could not descend to the river here, and returned to the main company. The little group of men left their mounts on a shelf with bushes, then started the dangerous descent to the Colorado in the twilight and dark. After following a gulch, often passing huge boulders in their way, they reached a dropping off point that seemed to hang over a sheer cliff. They contemplated having to wait there till morning, but the Uinkaret found some branches and made a torch. Then they were able to make out a way down. Eventually they met

Bishop with his torch, and he was able to lead them down to the river fairly easily.[73] There they made a camp and slept, utterly exhausted.

Up early the next morning, they decided that this point—which Worster concludes was near the Lava Falls Rapid, some sixty miles upstream from Separation Rapids—would work as a supply depot. They could take pack horses as far as possible, then hire Indians to carry supplies down to the river. Having reached this conclusion, they now faced the daunting task of climbing up the side of the Grand Canyon—a "mile of altitude." Fortunately, they found a faint trail up the canyon wall with occasional stairs, a much easier route than the one they had taken in the night. They came to the top of the first cliff, then led their exhausted horses up to the top of a second. There they came to a "stinking water pocket" that their ponies had refused to drink at coming down; now, after thirty hours without water, they each drank two or three gallons, and the men strained "loathsome, wriggling larvae" out of it to make coffee.[74] They reached the Uinkaret village at sunset, again exhausted.

For Hamblin, it was one more descent to the Colorado.

The next day, September 21,[75] they rested in the village of the Uinkaret Paiutes, and Powell in his "diary" left a perceptive, if slightly paternalistic, description of the people in the village. "Altogether, these Indians are more nearly in their primitive condition than any others on the continent with whom I am acquainted," he wrote. They had had almost no contact with whites at all and wore little clothing in the hot climate. He described the fruits and seeds they ate, and how they collected and prepared them; how they varied this diet with rabbits, grasshoppers, and (rarely) a mountain sheep. Babies were carried in "wicker boards" on mothers' backs, "and the little brown midgets are ever peering over their mothers' shoulders," he wrote. He was pleased that he had been able to get them to share their myths with him, as that showed trust.

That night, the Shivwits arrived, and the whites and Indians held a long council after the evening meal. "A blazing fire is built, and around this we sit—the Indians living here, the *Shi'-vwits*, Jacob Hamblin, and myself," wrote Powell. Now he gives his famous description of Hamblin:

> This man, Hamblin, speaks their language well and has a great influence over all the Indians in the region round about. He is a silent, reserved man, and when he speaks it is in a slow, quiet way that inspires great awe. His talk is so low that they must listen attentively to hear, and they sit around him in death-like silence. When he finishes a measured sentence the chief repeats it and they all give a solemn grunt. But, first, I fill my pipe, light it, and take a few whiffs, then pass it to Hamblin; he smokes, and gives it to the man next, and so it goes around.[76]

Powell then told the Paiutes that he wanted to be a friend while spending time in their country for the next year, and tried to explain that he was not a trader or a miner, and did not want their land. "Heretofore I have found it very difficult to make the natives understand my object, but the gravity of the Mormon missionary helps me much," he wrote. He told the Indians that "all the great and good white men" wanted to know many things, "the mountains and the valleys, the rivers and the canyons, the beasts and birds and snakes." Then he told them about other Indian tribes, and moved on to describe European nations, China, and Africa—certainly a challenge in perspective for these Paiutes. He explained that he wanted to learn about "their canyons and mountains, and about themselves." He tried to explain photography, and that he wanted to capture their images to show others.

> Then their chief replies: "Your talk is good, and we believe what you say. We believe in Jacob, and look upon you as a father. When you are hungry, you may have our game. You may gather our sweet fruits. We will give you food when you come to our land. We will show you the springs and you may drink; the water is good. We will be friends and when you come we will be glad. We will tell the Indians who live on the other side of the great river that we have seen *Ka'-pu-rats* ["arm off," the Indians' name for Powell], and that he is the Indians' friend. We will tell them he is Jacob's friend. We are very poor. Look at our women and children; they are naked. We have no horses; we climb the rocks and our feet are sore. We live among rocks and they yield little food and many thorns. When the cold moons come, our children are hungry. We have not much to give; you must not think us mean. You are wise; we have heard you tell strange things. We are ignorant. Last year we killed three white men. Bad men said they were our enemies. They told great lies. We thought them true. We were mad; it made us big fools. We are very sorry. Do not think of them; it is done; let us be friends. We are ignorant—like little children in understanding compared with you. When we do wrong, do not you get mad and be like children too.
>
> When white men kill our people, we kill them. Then they kill more of us. It is not good. We hear that the white men are a great number. When they stop killing us, there will be no Indian left to bury the dead. We love our country; we know not other lands. We hear that other lands are better; we do not know. The pines sing and we are glad. Our children play in the warm sand; we hear them sing and are glad. The seeds ripen and we have to eat and we are glad. We do not want their [the whites'] good lands; we want our rocks and the great mountains where our fathers lived. We are very poor; we are very ignorant; but we are very honest. You have horses and many things. You are very wise; you have a good heart. We will be friends. Nothing more have I to say.

The whites and Indians shook hands, "a few presents were given," and the council broke up.

According to Powell, Hamblin then took one of the Shivwits aside and asked in more detail about the death of the Howlands and Dunn. The Indian said they had fed the explorers and sent them on their way to the Mormon settlements, but then an Indian from across the river (possibly a Hualapai) had arrived, and told them about miners who had killed an Indian woman, and that the Howlands and Dunn were these miners. Miners had begun to explore the territory south of the Grand Canyon in the late 1860s, so this story is entirely credible.[77]

In addition, the whites' story that they had boated down the Colorado seemed obviously false; no one had ever done that. "In this way, he worked them into a great rage." They then followed Powell's men and ambushed them at the foot of Mount Dellenbaugh, killing them with arrows.[78]

Hamblin, in his autobiography, emphasized that the Indians south of the river thought that Powell's men were miners. They said "that miners on their side of the river abused their women," and in addition, "if they found any mines in their country, it would bring great evil among them."[79] Therefore, the death of the Howlands and Dunn could be seen as a result of miners exploring Arizona and Utah at this time.[80]

"That night I slept in peace," Powell concluded, "although these murderers of my men, and their friends, the *U-in-ka-rets*, were sleeping not 500 yards away. While we were gone to the canyon, the pack train and supplies, enough to make an Indian rich beyond his wildest dreams, were all left in their charge, and were all safe; not even a lump of sugar was pilfered by the children."[81]

This account is remarkable because some have accused Powell of taking undue credit for his exploring accomplishments, instead of sharing it with his companions on the expeditions down the Colorado. Nevertheless, in this account, Powell stresses the importance of Hamblin's help in this murder investigation and peace treaty. The Paiutes liked Powell, clearly, but accepted him in part because he was "Jacob's friend." Powell describes them as understanding his mission in large part because of Jacob's prestige and power of communication with them.

According to an alternative theory of the death of the Howlands and Dunn, they actually reached the Mormon settlements, but the Mormons took them for spies and killed them secretly in Toquerville, spreading the story that they had been killed by Indians. An 1883 letter from William Leany to John Steele speaks of three persons being killed in the Toquerville ward building, and by this theory the three persons were the Howlands and Dunn. In this scenario, Hamblin knew that Mormons killed the men, and was engaged in an elaborate cover-up, possibly including Brigham Young, to convince Powell otherwise.[82] Powell's biographer, Donald Worster, convincingly argues against this theory.[83] He points out that Powell had a background in the Ute/Paiute language, and apparently could follow Paiute speech to a significant extent. Therefore, Hamblin could not have simply made up a false story as he translated. In addition, there would be no logical reason for the Shivwits to confess to the murder of the Howlands and Dunn, as they did, unless they had actually carried out the killings. Also, Worster quotes Hamblin's September 30, 1870, letter to Young as showing no conspiratorial tone or content. Don Lago, in an important article, supplies more convincing candidates for the three persons killed in Toquerville.[84] On May 10, 1872, Almon Thompson wrote to John Wesley Powell that he had looked for Shivwits in their territory and found that they "feared we were in to punish them for the murder of Howlands & Dunn and so fled to the St George & Santa Clara Indians for protection."[85] This would not have happened if they had no responsibility for the killings. All the best evidence suggests that the theory of Mormons killing the Howlands and Dunn in Toquerville is flatly wrong.[86]

Powell and his company returned to Kanab.

Soon after this Jacob must have received a letter from Brigham Young and Daniel H. Wells, dated September 13. Young directed Hamblin to "seek to obtain access to the Navajoes as well as the Red Lake Utes at the earliest opportunity to conciliate them and promote friendship towards the inhabitants [of Utah]." He advised against supplying them with arms; instead, Jacob should encourage them "to resort to the more peaceful avocation of life" such as farming and ranching.[87]

This may have been the permission or orders that Hamblin felt he needed to visit the Navajos. Powell had decided to travel to the Hopi Mesas and Fort Defiance, in Navajo country, and from there continue east to Santa Fe. Their needs and intents had combined as if directed by fate. Powell asked Hamblin to accompany him, and he readily agreed.[88]

But first, he needed to bring the rest of his family to Kanab, so he turned west toward Santa Clara and Priscilla. He was in Santa Clara by September 30, when he wrote a letter to Brigham Young in which he reported briefly on the recent journey to the Colorado:

> I have been to the Colorado, with Maj. Powel, found a place where we can get supplies to the River for his exploreing Party annother season, yet it will be with concidrable difficulty. This point is sixty miles south of Pipe Springs or Windsor Castle, two watering places. [*letter blotted here*] abundence of grass, & dwarf sage, the most of the way. We visited the small band that killed two or three of Maj. Powels men, last season. I gathered them together & explained to them, Maj. Powels business, sent one of them over the River to visite the remainder of the band, and left our Horses, & most of our lugage with them while we climed down to the River. The Maj. expressed some anxiety about

his goods & horses, found on our return, that every thing was right being absent nearly two days.[89]

Jacob told Young his immediate plans: first he would take a portion of his family to Kanab the next day. Then he would pick up John Henry Stone, whom he had baptized in Kanab, from Pahreah, and travel to the Hopis and Navajos, leaving John Mangum in charge at Pahreah "to superintend the sowing of fall wheat & to keep a friendly influence with the Red Lake Utes while I am gon to the Navijos." He would also travel with Powell and two or three of his men to Navajo country. A small flatboat was being built at the mouth of the Paria (modern Lee's Ferry), at Powell's expense, to cross the Colorado.

Hamblin also mentioned that there was a superb place for a stock ranch southwest of Buckskin Mountain, and that Lewis Greeley, who we last met in Hamblin's spring 1863 trip across the Colorado, might be interested in settling there. Apparently Greely had stayed in Utah, and was now living in Fairfield, near Camp Floyd, in Utah County.

Jacob apparently brought Priscilla and her part of the family to Kanab starting on October 1, 1870. This must have been a bittersweet moment for the family. "With regrets," Priscilla later remembered, "we left the big rock house in Santa Clara.... Death, sickness, childbirth, fear and loneliness, and many other things had happened to us here. It had seemed that we were finally realizing something from our hard labors. At last, we had our home, garden, and orchard. But duty called and we gladly answered."[90] The Santa Clara neighbors held a party for the Hamblins a few nights before they left. "We will always consider this our home," Jacob told the group.[91] He reportedly sold the house to the widow of James Whitmore, who moved in with Mrs. McIntyre, presumably the widow of Robert McIntyre.[92]

Jacob must have stopped in St. George and conferred with the local leaders, including Joseph W. Young, for Young, with his counselors in the stake presidency, wrote out a certificate attesting to Jacob's good character on October 1.[93]

We have one anecdote from the move with Priscilla and her children. Priscilla's youngest, two-year-old Ella, had been given a marvelous new porcelain doll, a rarity on the frontier. During the journey to Kanab, Ella accidentally left the doll beside a stream, and only remembered it after miles of travel. As she wept inconsolably, Priscilla tried to explain why they must leave the doll where it was. "The trip was so long; and I could not ask her father to wait while someone went back for it.... An hour lost in those days of travelling was a great loss." But Jacob heard his daughter's sobbing, and when he discovered why she was crying, rode back himself in search of the doll. Priscilla wrote, "After a time, he came back into sight with his head down and his hands behind him, just as he always walked." Ella began to weep, assuming he hadn't found the doll, but he handed it up to her and said, "'Now you hang on to it, my Little One. I can't go back for it again.' She held it clutched in her arms all the rest of the way to Kanab."[94] Jacob always had a soft spot in his heart for children.

Powell, in his quasi diary, writes, "It is our intention to explore a route from Kanab to the Colorado River at the mouth of the Paria, and, if successful in this undertaking, to cross the river and proceed to Tusayan."[95] This gives the impression that Powell was now blazing a trail from Kanab to Lee's Ferry for the first time; actually, Hamblin had been crossing the Colorado at Lee's Ferry since 1864, and had first traveled to the Paria crossing in 1858! Powell was simply following Hamblin's lead all the way to the Hopi mesas, along a route that had been traveled many times, both by Hamblin and by other Mormons.

At this point, the puzzle pieces of history present us with a number of variant chronologies and scenarios, deriving from conflicting reminiscences of Hamblin, Powell, and Ammon Tenney.[96] The first solid date we have is Hamblin writing in Santa Clara on September 30, planning on returning to Kanab starting the next day.

So the party must have left Kanab for the Colorado and Hopi Mesas on about October 1. It split up, with Powell, Hamblin, and Chuarumpeak traveling south to explore the Kaibab Plateau, and the rest of the party—Ammon Tenney and Ash Nebeker, as well as Francis Bishop, Walter Graves, and Walter Dunn—following the regular trail to modern Lee's Ferry, carrying lumber to make a boat to cross the Colorado. "From here to the mouth of the Paria it [the boat lumber] must be packed on the backs of mules," Powell wrote. "Captain Bishop and Mr. Graves are to take charge of this work, while with Mr. Hamblin I explore the Kaibab Plateau."

Powell wanted to find another place to descend to the Colorado to drop off supplies. However, they were unable to find such a place on the North Rim south of the Kaibab.[97] Nevertheless, he and Hamblin discovered some unforgettable views of the surrounding country. One night, after they camped at a spring, Powell wrote, "The Indian goes out to hunt a rabbit for supper, and Hamblin and I climb the cliffs. From an elevation of 1,800 feet above the spring we watch the sun go down and see the sheen on the Vermilion Cliffs and red-lands slowly fade into the gloaming; then we descend to supper."

The next day they climbed a promontory which gave them an unforgettable view of the Grand Canyon. "Its deep gorge can be seen to the westward for 50 or 60 miles, and to the southeastward we look off into the stupendous chasm, with its marvelous forms and colors," Powell wrote. He considered this the most beautiful view of nature in the west: "The scene before me was awful, sublime, and glorious—awful in profound depths, sublime in massive and strange forms, and glorious in colors."[98]

According to Ammon Tenney, the group building the boat at Lee's Ferry became more and more anxious when Powell and Hamblin did not show up when expected. Finally, they despaired and Tenney and Graves were going to return to Kanab to report that their leaders may have been killed by Indians, but to their joy, met them on the way back.[99] (Powell's account seems entirely different: he and Hamblin separated from the group temporarily, then met with the party, as expected, at Jacob's Pools.)

The trip with Hamblin and Chuar to the North Rim is the last time Powell mentions Hamblin in *Canyons of the Colorado*, published in 1895. This is curious, as Hamblin and his Indian friends would be important guides to Powell in the difficult journey to the Hopi Mesas, and Powell played an important part in Hamblin's talk with the Navajos at Fort Defiance.[100]

At the mouth of the Paria, Hamblin, Powell, and company used the crude boat that Tenney and friends had built to ferry their baggage across the Colorado while swimming their horses—the standard method Hamblin had used since 1862.[101] Hamblin lists the company as himself, Powell, three members of Powell's company (actually, there were probably only two, Bishop and Graves), Tenney, Ash Nebeker, Nathan Terry, and Elijah Potter, also "Frank, a Kibab Indian," Chuarumpeak.[102]

On the other side of the river, the group spent the day surmounting Lee's Backbone and made a dry camp at night. Powell next described what might have been Hamblin's standard route from modern Lee's Ferry to the Hopis.[103] The party went south along the Echo Cliffs for a day and a half, then turned westward at a cedar ridge, east of the Shinumo Altar. There is a Cedar Ridge on the maps today, about eight miles southeast of the altar.

There they climbed a cliff, possibly Echo Cliffs, which led to a route eastward over an expanse of sandstone, whose pockets were fortunately filled with water—one point near the cedar ridge Powell called Thousand Wells. Then they rode laboriously over sand dunes. Toward night, they climbed a cliff and, as Indians with them promised, found water—in fact, a lake—in a cave there. They had a somewhat unsatisfactory parley with local Indians, so left very early the next morning to avoid trouble.

In the morning they came to Moenkopi Wash.[104] "Before us, two or three miles, was the meandering creek, with a little fringe of green willows, box-elders, and cotton-woods," wrote Powell. "From these, sage plains stretched back to the cliffs that form the walls of the valley. These cliffs are rocks of bright colors, golden, vermilion, purple and azure hues."[105] They probably came to Quichintoweep, but Powell, a non-Mormon, does not mention it. Lizards of all sorts were everywhere, along with an occasional rattler.

They camped early in the day, and Powell and Jacob rode north to visit "an artificial wall extending across the country for many miles," which Mormons had told the easterner about. As they had described it, it was made of blocks that appeared to have been brought from another area. "We were well mounted and rode across the country at a good gallop," wrote Powell. The wall turned out to be an "igneous dike, the blocks composed of columnar basalt." There was even whitish material between the blocks that looked like mortar but was, in fact, an accumulation of a white mineral. This was Wildcat Peak, rising five hundred feet above the surrounding area, whose "dikes" extending north and south looked uncannily like man-made structures.[106]

That night, some Navajos showed up at the camp, "fine-looking fellows, tall and lithe, with keen eyes, sharp features, and faces full of animation," wrote Powell.[107] Tempted by the smell of coffee and biscuits, they camped with the American-Mormon-Paiute party that night. Powell described how well they communicated with the Kaibab Paiutes, using maps in the sand and sign language. "They made gestures, struck attitudes, grunted, frowned, laughed, and altogether had a lively time."[108]

The following morning a Navajo boy volunteered to guide the party to Oraibi, according to Powell (once again, Powell seems reluctant to admit that Jacob and Ammon Tenney had been to the mesas many times). They descended from the tableland they had been traversing, crossed a deep valley—probably Dinnebito Wash, which modern maps call Dry Creek—and then ascended a steep rock mesa which turned into a "slope terraced by rude masonry"—probably Hotevilla, where a number of Hopis were harvesting vegetables.[109] These would have greeted Hamblin with pleasure, and in fact feasted the company on melons. At sundown Hamblin and Powell came to Oraibi, probably on about October 16.

Powell and Hamblin stayed among the Hopis for about two weeks.[110] Powell visited each of the Hopi towns and talked extensively with the Hopis: "Professor Powell took much interest in their festivals, dances, religious ceremonies and manner of living," Hamblin wrote.[111] The Indian missionary's previous ties with the Hopis, and Tenney's Spanish, would have been an invaluable help to the explorer arriving for the first time at the mesas.

Toward the end of October, Hamblin, Powell, and company made the dangerous journey to Fort Defiance. One traveler called this stretch of land "a dismal, deserted landscape, the embodiment of dreadful monotony."[112] Hamblin, Tenney, and Powell would have passed by elevations covered by pine, as well as desert canyons, plateaus, and mesas of yellow and red sandstone, filled with sagebrush, juniper, and low grasses. According to Tenney, he, Powell, and a Hopi interpreter traveled together, to make arrangements for a parley with Navajo leaders, then the rest of the company, led by Hamblin, came later. Tenney tells of meeting with two Navajos covered with silver ornaments, who rode with Tenney and Powell, apparently to protect them. However, as the whites could not speak Navajo, they could not talk with them, and could only hope that they were friendly. Midway through the journey, two other Navajos appeared, gave a war whoop, and rode down toward Powell, Tenney, and the Hopis. The two friendly Navajos rode up to intercept the attacking Indians. Tenney drew his gun, but Powell told him to put it away, and reached into his pack for tobacco. "He walked over to the two men and slapped each on the shoulder, then with a loud and hearty laugh handed them the tobacco."[113] Powell and Tenney were able to travel on and reached Fort Defiance the next day. Hamblin appeared soon after.

21.5. A group of Navajos standing with William F. M. Arny, left, Navajo agent in 1874. Fort Defiance, eastern Arizona, can be seen in the background. Courtesy Wikimedia Commons/National Archives.

Powell and Hamblin reached Fort Defiance on November 1, according to a November 5 letter by Frank Tracy Bennett, Navajo Indian agent.[114] Bennett was one of the Indian agents who dealt with Navajos justly and sympathetically; their affectionate name for him was "Big Belly."[115] He appears to have been helpful to Jacob Hamblin, also, a welcome contrast to other Indian agents who were openly anti-Mormon. Bennett immediately sent out messages to Navajo leaders that he, Powell, and Hamblin wished to have a talk with them on the fifth. Powell's prestige undoubtedly helped Hamblin in this meeting with U.S. officials and Navajo chiefs.

Fort Defiance, founded in 1851, now served as an agency for the Navajos; it had not been used as a military post since 1864. Situated on an elevation at the mouth of the striking sandstone canyon Bonito, it was not an imposing sight—in 1882, one traveler described it as a number of "low, decayed buildings and adobe sheds—in addition a large, stone schoolhouse."[116]

Hamblin met with "Delgeto one of the Navajo chiefs" on November 2.[117] This would be Delgadito ("Te na al so se ae"), a brother of the dominant Navajo leader, Barboncito; Delgadito is known for having convinced the Navajos to go to Bosque Redondo reservation in 1863. In his journal, Hamblin describes his conversation with this Navajo:

> Told him I had come along way to talk with the Navajoes as they had stolen meny horses and some other stock from our setlements. Many of our young

21.6. Barboncito, main spokesman for the Navajos when Jacob Hamblin, John Wesley Powell, and Navajo agent Frank Bennett met leading Navajos in 1870 at Fort Defiance, eastern Arizona, and agreed to a peace treaty. This ended the four-year Navajo War in southern Utah. Courtesy National Anthropological Archives, Smithsonian Institution, OPPS NEG 55766.

> Men and middle aged wanted to get together and follow their trail and take all the horses sheep they could find [and] kill all the Navajos they could come to but our hed chief s[t]opt it and told me to come and hav a talk with their wise Men and see if they would not try and stop the rading and live in pees and stop rading ~~in pees and friendship.~~ He said he liket that ~~he said he wanted to and from what he had hurd~~ and would doe all he could to stop it and from what he had hurd all the chiefs was in favor of it. He the[n] told the Mans name that got up thos rades. Said he was ded ~~thot~~ thought thare would be no more rading.

The main talk with the Navajo chiefs occurred on November 5. According to Tenney, twenty-nine Navajo headmen met with Hamblin and Powell in a spacious room in the fort, while some six to eight thousand Navajos were gathered outside.[118]

Barboncito was the principle spokesman for the Navajos. Known as "Tah gan is" or Hastiin Dagha, "Man with the Whiskers," he had for many years been a prominent raiding and war leader. With Manuelito, he had led the attack on Fort Defiance in 1860, and had always resisted white incursions in Navajo territory. Aside from his political and military leadership, he was known as a religious leader, who would chant long ritual ceremonies such as the Blessing Way. He had been the last major Navajo leader to surrender and go to Bosque Redondo, but in 1868 he gave a famous, eloquent speech that convinced General William Tecumseh Sherman to allow the Navajos to return to their homeland. He was the first signer of the 1868 peace treaty that recorded this agreement, and was recognized by Navajo agents as the head chief of all the Navajos—a leadership office foreign to Navajos before this, but influential in the early reservation period of Navajo history.[119]

Navajo agent Frank Bennett began the meeting by saying, "I have called you together to talk upon a subject that concerns every man, woman and child of your nation. I want you to listen to what is said—and then we will listen to what you say."

Powell spoke next, saying that he was "glad to meet this people." He reminded the Navajos that "the white people from one ocean to the other, are one people," that they all paid taxes to support the government and the Navajos. People in Utah paid taxes, and "the Great Father at Washington sends troops to protect the Mormons as well as others." He warned that the U.S. government would declare war on the Navajos for "depredations committed upon Mormons as well as upon others." He asked the Navajos "to hear what the Mormon Captain says."

Jacob spoke:

> I can also say, as the American Captain said,—that I am glad to see you. I have come a long way for that purpose and feel to rejoice at the prospect of forming a Treaty to live at peace with the Navajos. I do not like to talk of war. Your people have stolen a large amount of horses, mules, and some other stock from the Mormons. Our young men and middle aged, gathered together to make war upon the Navajos, determined to cross the river and follow the trail of the stolen stock and lay waste the country. Many people were compelled to leave their homes to escape the raids of the Navajos.
>
> Our head Chief—Brigham Young was a man of Peace; and stopped his people from raiding, and wanted us to make peace; this is my business here, and they are anxiously waiting for one to bring your answer. Your Agent says you are men of truth.
>
> I believe what he has told me.

"Barbancito—Head Chief" replied, expressing his support for "the Americans," the government "that has saved them from hunger and death."[120] Next he gave a remarkable evaluation of the Navajo raids, stating that they were not an organized Navajo war, but the work of "some thieves" who had never been to Bosque Redondo, who had "gone out as between their fingers or legs, and committed depredations." Moreover, "Piutes have had trouble with the Mormons, and...some of the Navajos were induced to join them in committing depredations upon the Mormons. Have done so several times." In fact, Paiutes had often led Navajos to Mormon stock. So Barboncito was stating that the Navajo raids were in fact part of the Black Hawk War conflict—Paiutes or Utes had even "induced" Navajos to join them.

Nevertheless, Barboncito mentioned one chief who had a relative (Spaneshanks?) who had been killed by the Mormons, and conducted raids in Utah. When he was told that this chief was on a Utah raid, Barboncito "said if they were killed he should not mourn for them." When he returned, Barboncito told him that in any future raids, "they should not keep their stolen property." He said he had stopped a raid.

He said he could not promise that the raids would stop entirely, "but he as well as the Agent will use their best endeavors to stop all raids in the future," and if any raids were made, they would return all stolen stock.

He strongly suggested that Jacob keep a guard on the two crossings of the Colorado, to assist him and Indian agents with information, and so that Paiutes would not make thefts and blame the Navajos.

He said that he looked upon "Capt. Hamblin as his father, and is pleased to see him." He said that from this time the Navajos would "be at peace with the Mormons, as with the Great Father at Washington. I cannot bear to talk of war."

Jacob replied: "I am glad to hear it. I love peace, and have spent much time to preserve peace between the white man and the indian, and for that reason I am now sent on the frontier." Here Barboncito arose and embraced the Indian missionary "with a genuine Indian Hug."

Bennett then asked Barboncito how he would stop future raids. The headman replied that the Navajos would try to stop the raids, and ask for government help to arrest the thieves, if necessary. He said he would turn raiders over to the government.

Jacob then told of the Pipe Spring incident, in which Navajos led by three Paiutes had killed the two Mormons, and then the Mormons had killed seven local Paiutes, "the wrong Indians," not the guilty Paiutes. But Jacob had visited Brigham Young, and he had ordered no retaliatory raids.

Then Barboncito, in response to a question, said that the governor of New Mexico had told them that they could keep the stock from recent raids, but should stop raiding hereafter. (This is an odd statement; how would the governor of New Mexico be involved in regulating Navajo raids upon Mormons?) Jacob responded that he would talk to the federal government about this. He liked the way that "Navajos talk, but does not like the talk of the Governor of New Mexico."

Bennett also said he was pleased with Barboncito's parley. He emphasized that the Navajos must obey him and "they must put a stop to this raiding. If they do not it will bring war upon them, not only from the Mormons, but from the Government." He told them they had broken the treaty at Bosque Redondo by raiding in Utah; and "although they broke their treaty ignorantly, they cannot do so now; and they must so understand it."

Powell stated, "Today Peace and Friendship is planted, but it will not grow unless the Navajos cultivate it." Barboncito agreed. Jacob affirmed that he was a "warm friend" of the Navajos now. Barboncito asked if the Navajos could visit Utah and trade for horses with a pass, and Jacob said they could. Without a pass, they would be treated like enemies.

According to Tenney, some of the Navajos were contemptuous of the Mormons, and openly rode horses stolen from Mormon herds.[121] However, Barboncito was conciliatory and desired peace, and was very influential. Tenney felt that one of the crucial agreements made at this parley was that Navajos would not carry out further raids on the Mormons, but that the Navajos could keep stock they had already taken.[122]

After this council, Hamblin and Powell parted company. Powell traveled east to Santa Fe, while Hamblin, leading Powell's pack train, returned to the Hopi mesas, where he traded for Hopi artifacts that Powell wanted to place in museums in the East.[123]

On November 9, Hamblin and Ammon Tenney, at the Hopi village Hano (Tewa), on the First Mesa, "met 4 of the principal Men of the Navajo nacion,"[124] in a large room supplied by the leader of the village. These were Navajo headmen who had not been at the main council at Fort Defiance because they lived so far west of the fort. Therefore, Barboncito had summoned them to agree to the treaty.[125] The dominant leader of this group was, according to Hamblin, "the principal chief of the raiding band."[126] The chief Hastele was also present; he would later become a good friend of Hamblin.[127] Hamblin felt that this meeting was even more "interesting" than the parley at Fort Defiance. Tenney says that the chiefs were impressed by the possibilities of trade with the Mormons, exchanging blankets for horses. Hamblin wrote:

> They had not come to alter anything that was agreed on at the trety but would like to talk...with me. [They] wanted nothing but Pease and their childrin after them. I told them I was a man of Pees...Hoapit we would liv in Peas and our children after us then we would all hav enough with out stealing. Come over and visit our setelments...and see what a people does that does not steal but labors for aliving. We had ben ~~thare~~ but a few years at the plase. You herd me talk but you doe not know until you see. Then one of the chiefs[128] embrast me and said I love Pees I never stole. The other chiefs pointing to him said he was all wa[y]s was [*sic*] a good Man is now and allways would be. You can trust your self with him and believe what he sais. [We] Talked mutch about the past. I said I had spent mutch time and anxiety of mind to preserve Pees ~~among~~ with the white Man and the Indians. The Principal chief then [said:] Now liston to what I say. We hav a father at Fort Defiance that givs us food and clotheing but we hold you as our Sun Father the Father of Peas. We will now ack knowlage but one Father suck the milk of one Mother set by one fire smoak one segeret eat at one Table and cover with one blanket and teach our childrin to doe the same after us.[129]

Hamblin broke down in tears at these words. Tenney, acting as interpreter, asked how he should respond, and Hamblin asked him to say what seemed best to him. "I began to speak along the same lines that they had in regards to teaching our children," wrote Tenney. "I taught them the gospel and the pursuits of peace and happiness, and within a few minutes these noble sons of father Lehi were all weeping, until they had no control of themselves."

Seized by a feeling of ecstatic joy, two of the leaders came forward, picked Tenney up, and danced all over the room with him, singing and shouting. Then they came to Jacob and embraced him. Gradually their ecstatic shouts quieted to normal speech and handshakes. "As for me," wrote Tenney, "never before had I felt the demonstration of the spirit and power of God as on that occasion."[130]

One of the Navajo leaders asked Jacob to help him recover a flock of sheep that had been stolen by a Hopi in a nearby town. Jacob talked to the owner of the sheep, an acquaintance of his, and though the Hopi was at first surly and reluctant, he eventually gave up the sheep to the Navajo.[131]

While at the mesas, Hamblin convinced the Hopi Tuuvi and his wife, Talasnimki, to visit Utah. He wrote to Erastus Snow on November 21, "We also brought a head man & wife of the Moquich who are going to stay here one year to make blankets and learn our ways."[132] Thirteen Paiutes from east of the Colorado also accompanied him,[133] including Patnish, the San Juan Paiute-Navajo whom Jacob believed was the mastermind of the Whitmore raid and murders.

Before crossing the Colorado, Hamblin also had a peace talk with about thirty Paiutes east of the Colorado who had joined with the Navajos in their raids on Mormon communities.[134] He also tells an odd story about being struck down by some supernatural manifestation while descending a difficult cliff as they approached the Colorado—"suddenly, what appeared like a flash of lightning came over me"—and he could breathe only with great difficulty. He regained his strength only when Nathan Terry administered to him.

At the Colorado, presumably at the Paria Crossing, Tuuvi requested that Hamblin join with him in celebrating a Hopi ritual before crossing this imposing river. Hamblin agreed, and after Tuuvi's prayer, the two men took the contents of Tuuvi's medicine bag and scattered it into the air, on the land, and into the river. "To me, the whole ceremony seemed humble and reverential, I felt that the Father has regard to such petitions," wrote Jacob.[135] Thus he, and other Indian missionaries, created a kind of private synthesis of Christian and Indian religion.

The group crossed over the great river in safety.

Hamblin was at Kanab by November 21.[136] He checked the Hopi artifacts he had brought in Powell's pack train, and sent him a report.[137] He obtained rooms for Tuuvi and Talasnimki in the fort, and they became a part of the Kanab community for the following year, developing deep ties of friendship with many Mormons.[138]

In early December, Patnish showed up at Kanab, and at first said that he simply wanted to ratify Jacob's treaty with the Navajos at Fort Defiance. However, in a few days he began to make demands of cattle and horses. In a December 7 letter to Erastus Snow, Jacob and John R. Young, at Pipe Spring (now called Winsor Castle), reported that Patnish "told Bro. Jacob that, if he would give him a horse and other things he (Patnish) would go back and preach peace, but, if not, he would preach more raids and perhaps blood." Hamblin refused to give him the horse on those terms. Young and Hamblin wrote, "We would like to be able to put a quietus on Patnish, if he attempts to drive off stock." This is the closest Hamblin came to seeking the death of an Indian, to the best of my knowledge, after his "conversion" to pacifism in Tooele. And of course, this language is probably Young's, though Hamblin signed the letter.

Young and Hamblin stated that Patnish's "spirit is anything but good, and it is evident that he would like to break up the treaty Bro. Hamblin has just effected with the Navajos." They referred to Patnish and his companions as "renegade" and "lawless," and thought that the thirteen San Juan Paiutes might try to raid Mormon stock before returning east of the Colorado, so asked Snow for extra men to help guard the Crossing of the Fathers.[139]

Perhaps because of Patnish's threats, the Indians at Pahreah had retreated to Kanab, and did not want to return without several whites, so Jacob was at Pipe Spring trying to recruit men for that mission.[140]

At one point late in 1870, Zadok Knapp Judd remembered that about thirty Navajos came to Kanab and "seemed very hostile, making heavy demands upon us for provisions, of which we had a very small supply." They began to make threatening actions, tinkering with their bows. Jacob Hamblin and a few others gathered with the Judds, and some asked, "What shall we do?"

"Let's give them their breakfast," suggested Mary Minerva Judd, Zadok's wife.

"That's a very sensible idea," Jacob replied. "Will you feed a few of them?"

"Yes, I can feed four or five."

Jacob went to the group of Navajos and brought four or five to the Judd camp (apparently, a number of Saints were new arrivals and had not yet built a house), and other Navajos to other families. Mary Judd fed her guests a hearty breakfast of mush and roasted ears of corn. "This seemed to satisfy them, and after trading a little with us, they went off and left us," wrote Zadok. "Thus a peaceful policy avoided trouble."[141]

This is quite similar to events that took place in 1871, so it is possible that Judd simply got the year wrong; however, it is also possible that during this transition period a number of similar events occurred.

Jacob visited John D. Lee's new mill at Skutumpah, on the upper Kanab, on December 1.[142] Lee had followed Brigham Young's counsel and had begun to sell out his Harmony property and relocate near Kanab to work as a sawyer for the outlying communities in Kane County. On November 17, however, he had received devastating news: he, along with Isaac Haight, had been excommunicated from the church.[143] So he had suddenly become a religious as well as a physical exile. From this point, Lee and his family located farther and farther from substantial settlements—on the Arizona strip, at Lee's Ferry, and in Hopi-Navajo country southeast of the Colorado. Despite the excommunication, Lee would continue to associate with Mormons, and Jacob would continue to work in close alliance with him until the eventual bitter rupture of their friendship.

One of the notable tragic events of early Kanab history took place this December. Bishop Levi Stewart was storing ten gallons of kerosene and five gallons of turpentine in his home (or, according to another account, two kegs of powder and ten gallons of coal-oil), and on the thirteenth, the containers exploded without warning in the middle of the night. There must have been a sudden, horrific inferno within the cabin, and its dirt roof collapsed on the sleepers, a number of Stewart's sons. One of Stewart's plural wives, Margery Wilkerson Stewart, mother of three of the boys in the room, rushed into the bedroom, and she and five of Levi Stewart's sons were killed.[144] It was a devastating blow for the surviving members of the family, as well as for the other Kanab pioneers, many of whom had not yet lived half a year in their new town on the far frontier.

Jacob Hamblin regarded the fire as fulfillment of a prophecy by a Kaibab Paiute headman, Choog, who predicted that because the devil had been frustrated east of the Colorado by Jacob's peace efforts, he would attack the Mormons in the form of fire west of the Colorado.[145] It was typical of Jacob to interpret a troubling event from a religious perspective, combining Mormon and Indian apocalyptic vision.

On December 23, Jacob came to St. George with Tuuvi and Talasnimki and met with President Young and George A. Smith, who were visiting. On the twenty-fifth, George noted that Jacob gave them an interesting account of his mission to the Navajos and Hopis.[146] Jacob said that "the Navago Chief promised that his People should not make any more raids upon the Saints and wished to have peace between us and them."[147]

Evaluations of Hamblin's November 1870 talks with the Navajos vary. Clearly, he felt it was one of the significant accomplishments in his life, and some historians agree. Stewart Udall regarded the Fort Defiance agreement as Jacob's "crowning achievement."[148] Historian of the Little Colorado Charles Peterson writes that Hamblin "successfully negotiated an agreement with the Navajos opening the route to Arizona and ultimately to Mexico, with eventual if distant prospect of a seaport there."[149]

P. T. Reilly, with his typical worm's-eye view of Hamblin, suggests that the Indian missionary had accomplished very little due to his ignorance of the Navajo culture, and that he naively believed that Barboncito was an authoritarian leader of all the Navajos, after the pattern of Brigham Young, when in fact he was simply one of many loosely confederated chiefs. According to Reilly, Hamblin, in making the Fort Defiance treaty, was talking only with the eastern Navajo leaders, not the western leaders who were responsible for the raids into Utah.[150]

Reilly does not take into account the fact that Barboncito had enormous prestige as a spokesman for the Navajo people.[151] He was not representing only the eastern Navajos; though he was associated with Canyon de Chelly, some fifty miles east of the Hopi mesas, he had close ties with Navajos in northwest Navajo territory. Hamblin states that "all the principal chiefs but one, and all the sub chiefs but two were there."[152]

In addition, Reilly inexplicably ignores the November 9 meeting with four western Navajo headmen, including a raiding chief. Tenney states that Barboncito summoned these chiefs to sign the Fort Defiance treaty, which shows that Hamblin dealt directly with western Navajo leaders, and that Barboncito had considerable influence with the western Navajo headmen.

Hamblin, though he respected Barboncito's prestige, did not view him as an all-powerful leader. The chief frankly stated that he did not have control of all the Navajos, and Hamblin understood this. Barboncito could not promise Hamblin "immunity from raids"; therefore, he and the other Navajo leaders wished Hamblin "to keep a guard [at the Crossing of the Fathers], to assist him by information."

Contrary to Reilly, the evidence suggests that Jacob's accomplishment in his Fort Defiance treaty was substantial. It is typical of Hamblin that, in the middle of a war with the Navajos, he sought to visit them, talk over their conflicts, and seek for peace—this in itself was a risky business, not to mention the plodding boredom and difficulty of these trans-Colorado trips from Utah to Arizona. The Fort Defiance visit did not bring an immediate and complete end to the Navajo-Mormon conflict, but it certainly was a significant step toward eventual peace.

22

"I Was Not Happy Unless I Was Miserable, For I Knew Nothing Except Hardships"

Rituals and Trials of a Missionary Family, 1870

The journey of Jacob Hamblin and Ammon Tenney to Fort Defiance and back gives us an opportunity to stop and consider the price their families paid during such long absences. Louise Udall, a granddaughter of Jacob and Louisa, described the Hamblin family ritual observed when Jacob left on a trip across the Colorado. An older son would reshoe the horses or mules that Jacob would be taking, and Jacob would put new soles and heels on his boots. His wives might knit new socks and mend his shirts and underclothes. "Then, early some morning, with pockets and saddlebags filled with parched corn and jerkey (lean meat cut in strips and dried), he would ride southward, to return weeks later."[1] Preparing for Jacob's departure was a family event. And surviving without papa would undoubtedly put burdens on his wives and older children.

Jacob's return would be a joyful family occasion. Family traditions say that Melissa, Priscilla's second child, was often the last to see him as he left, and the first to spy him out when he returned.[2] Then there would be the mutual sharing of news, the family meal, Jacob and family relaxing around the fire. He probably treated himself to a bath with hot water, and a change of clothes, at the first opportunity.

Melissa remembers one of Jacob's returns—after he met with the Navajos in the wake of the Grass Valley massacre in 1874—in which he was in such a hurry to share news with church leaders that he did not even change his clothes, to Melissa's dismay, but went straight to a council of the brethren in Kanab. "Oh father, why didn't you at least put on a clean shirt before going to that meeting," Melissa asked when he returned. "Melissa," he replied, "my dirty shirt did not disturb my friends nearly as much as did my absence. Time was precious. Learn to value this gift. Time, my girl, time is the material with which we build."[3]

On one return home, Priscilla presented Jacob with a new daughter. On other returns, as we have seen, Jacob received the shattering news of the loss of children.

Stewart Udall, a great-grandson of Jacob, has written, "Jacob Hamblin played a prominent role in western settlement, and his zeal for this was so all-consuming that he put an inordinate burden on his wives." In addition, Jacob was a polygamist; it was always more difficult to care for two or three families than one.

Udall's great-grandmother, Louisa Bonelli, was known to her children as a "dutiful wife and mother," but Jacob's absences made her life a constant struggle. She told a granddaughter, "I was not happy unless I was miserable, for I knew nothing except hardships." Long after Jacob's death, a preacher in church pointed out Louisa as Jacob's widow one Sunday, and praised him as a great peacemaker. Later that day, with her family at lunch, Louisa "wryly observed, 'He should have said Jacob Hamblin's squaw.'"[4] She probably said this with a smile; but it shows that her life as Jacob's spouse, from her viewpoint, was not ideal.

Udall writes that after Brigham Young died in 1877, Jacob promised Priscilla and Louisa that he would live more of his life at home, spending time with the children and making their lives more comfortable. "But his promises were not kept. Hamblin's yearnings to see new country, not calls from church officials, led him to uproot his wives and children three more times in the last eight years of his life."

Though this comes from a direct descendant, it is not entirely fair to Jacob. If we look at his expeditions and moves in his later years on a case-by-case basis, we find that many of them were the result of calls by the brethren. In addition, Jacob was a prominent Mormon who was a polygamist, and was increasingly fearful of arrest and imprisonment. Family traditions state that Priscilla became reconciled to the move from Kanab to the Little Colorado because she knew that prosecution of Jacob as a polygamist was becoming more and more likely in Utah. In addition, the main motivation for the Mormon colonization of old Mexico was to provide a polygamous haven; there is no reason to suspect that Jacob's motivations for moving there were any different.

Nevertheless, Udall's main point was correct. His calling as Indian missionary and explorer, which caused frequent absences, and the polygamous nature of the Hamblin household, put enormous strains on his wives.

Amarilla Hamblin Lee, Jacob's last child, told an interviewer in 1970, "As [a] missionary he [Jacob Hamblin] didn't spend much time on his family.... Lots of em have felt bad about that."[5] She had no direct memories of Jacob, as she was just two years old when he died, but clearly she had heard stories from her siblings.

Another of Jacob's children, Inez Hamblin Lee, wrote:

> Since my father was an Indian missionary, called for life, it seemed, he was away from home the greater part of the time. He seemed to take no thought as to what his family should eat nor what they should be clothed with, but went happily on his life's work of trying to help his chosen people to a higher standard of thought and living.[6]

According to John D. Lee in his 1873 diary, one of Jacob's wives was planning to leave him, but Lee, before the days of the Lee-Hamblin feud, talked her out of it. According to Lee,

> Many kindness that I have done for him, & when his wife was ready to give up & leve him on account of his neglect to her, I reasoned with her till She wept, & reconciled to him; told her that he was one of the best Men in the world, that his whole life was devoted to this cause & to stand by him without a Murmur & her [reward] would be great &c.[7]

While Lee does not name which wife he refers to, it is hard to imagine Priscilla, in her position as senior wife, considering leaving Jacob, so it is probable that the wife referred to here is Louisa. If so, she at one point experienced what she felt was "neglect" as part of Jacob's family—either because of Jacob's frequent absences, or because of her status as a plural wife, or a combination of the two.

The trials of an Indian missionary's family were compounded by the missionary's standing, or lack of it, in the wider, nonmissionary social fabric. Ammon Tenney, in his writings, left us some striking evaluations of the status of the early Mormon Indian missionary in his community, and the plight of the missionary family during the husband's absences. As we have seen, he apparently felt that his contributions as Indian missionary were not sufficiently recognized. Though the results the Indian missionaries achieved were highly valued by more sedentary Mormons, the missionaries' constant travels caused them to be gone from their families and agricultural or ranching work on a regular basis, and they often felt that their families were not adequately supported in their absences. According to Tenney, the appreciation of their community did not translate into actual support in daily necessities of life.

In his late life, Tenney wrote to his niece, "I was neglected. I served the People in Maintaining Peace for 15 years, & Never received in that entire time to exceed 175 dollars ... [we, the Indian missionaries, were] being used to Protect the People while the People were in the main unable to aid us in Maintaining our Poor families."[8]

When Tenney was traveling to Fort Defiance with Jacob in 1870 to protect his fellow Saints from Navajo raids (and his services as a Spanish speaker were a crucial part of the 1870 treaty's accomplishment), his family was living in the fort at Kanab, in a single room with no chimney. Bishop Levi Stewart, to his credit, saw that Tenney's family needed help and arranged for a few men to put a chimney in their room. However, when Ammon returned, "Brother Farnsworth called on me for his Pay before I had been Home 24 Hours, notwithstanding I had then been gone three months & made a journey of 2000 Miles, & furnished My self, every-thing—all for the People."[9]

Supplying provisions for one of these expeditions, along with a horse and a mule, was expensive, and as Tenney writes, the expense was often borne by the missionary himself. In addition, months of labor and economic improvement at home were lost. In the face of this, a chimney would be only a minor recompense for someone like Tenney, but at least one of Tenney's neighbors did not feel this way.

This anecdote also shows vividly the difficulties faced by the wives and children of these early Indian missionaries, when the head of the household was often absent.

Undoubtedly, Jacob experienced these same pressures, lack of financial support, and occasional disillusionments with the communities he worked for. The sacrifices he made—often sleeping in the open, often in the rain and snow, instead of in a bed, often being absent during joyful family events, or missing daily life with his family—were sacrifices that his wives and children also made, in different ways.

23

"A Slow-moving, Very Quiet Individual, Who Said He Was Jacob Hamblin"

Exploring the Escalante; Navajos in Kanab; at Lee's Ferry, 1871

In early 1871, Hamblin, Tuuvi, and Talasnimki visited the cotton factory in Washington. After seeing three hundred spindles in motion, Tuuvi said that he would never think of spinning yarn with his fingers to make blankets again. Talasnimki was equally impressed with a flour mill, as she reflected on the great labor it required for Hopi women to produce just a little cornmeal.[1]

Hamblin wrote to Brigham Young on February 11, "It is continually on my mind, that as early as practicable a settlement should be located on the 'Moancoppy,'" and he pointed out that it was on the route to the San Francisco Mountains, and that Hopis were eager to unite with Mormons to build a town there. It had a good water supply, about eight or nine springs, and good grazing country nearby. He mentioned that Tuuvi talked of a Mormon-Hopi Moenkopi settlement continually—"the last thing at night, and the first thing in the morning." Hamblin was not just an explorer for Brigham Young the colonizer; he himself sometimes actively encouraged settlement in Indian territory.

Hamblin then requested some "church horses" to trade for sheep south of Fort Defiance. One horse could be traded for twenty-five to fifty sheep, and such sheep could be put in the care of a Hopi or Navajo, which would strengthen the Navajo-Mormon peace initiative.[2] As it turned out, Young evidently allowed Hamblin to have seventy-five horses at some point—perhaps at this time.[3]

A major Mormon migration was now taking place that would impact Kanab and Jacob. When the Muddy River settlements in modern Nevada were legally declared to actually be in Nevada, state authorities demanded back taxes, and with Brigham Young's blessing, the Muddy River settlers decided to leave Nevada and return to Utah. Most of them moved to Long Valley, just north of Kanab, in February and March, resettling former towns and founding other towns. (The cessation of Navajo raiding made the resettling of Long Valley possible.) Some Muddy Mission veterans, including Jacob's brother-in-law Zadok Knapp Judd, relocated in Kanab.[4] Long Valley would become an important part of Kanab's cultural environment.

On March 20, Hamblin was considering starting a settlement both at Moenkopi and in Navajo country, at a place called "Cañon Benita," about a hundred miles from the Colorado.[5] He told Brigham Young that he was planning to visit Navajo territory as soon as he could get his family comfortably situated in Kanab, but that a Navajo chief was expected to visit Kanab soon, and if he came, this would make his trip unnecessary.[6]

In late April Hamblin was in Salt Lake City, possibly to confer with Indian agents there, for earlier in the year, he had been formally appointed as an Indian subagent for southern Utah.[7]

Powell was back in Utah by early May, and began his second trip down the Green and Colorado Rivers on May 22. He was counting on Jacob to bring supplies to the company at various points in the journey. First, he hoped Jacob could meet him with supplies at the mouth of the Dirty Devil, so he asked him to travel down the Devil to its mouth to see if this was practicable. In June Jacob enlisted Isaac Haight to accompany him. Haight had been excommunicated at the same time Lee had been and, like him, was now living on the southeastern Mormon frontier as a quasi exile.[8]

On June 12, the two men left Kanab, accompanied by William Crosby, Fred Hamblin, and "Frank," presumably Chuarumpeak; these three would travel with Hamblin and Haight only to Panguitch. Powell had given Hamblin rough instructions and maps on the location of the Dirty Devil, from the perspective of a traveler on the Colorado River—that is, the mouth was forty miles below the junction of the Green and Colorado Rivers, eighty miles above the mouth of the San Juan River.

The party crossed the divide into the Sevier Valley the next day and stayed at Panguitch for a few days. Jacob went to Panguitch Lake to see the Indians who were there, received a group of "Church horses," and preached at church on the eighteenth, giving "much good instructions" on dealing with Indians.[9] After the meeting, Hamblin and Haight left for the Dirty Devil, while Crosby, Fred Hamblin, and Chuar returned to Kanab. Haight recorded, somewhat ominously, "Br Hamblin failed in getting a suitable guide to Dirty Devil River."

Hamblin and Haight passed through the mining town of Marysvale, in Piute County, then continued on and reached Glencove (modern Glenwood, about twenty-five miles northeast of Marysvale) on the twenty-first. There they engaged a Bishop B. Cannon and Frank King to help them find the river.[10] Hamblin then decided that he could not continue: "I started home as I had little time [to] get redy for packing the suplys to Mag Powel." So Haight continued eastward, while Hamblin departed for the south.

He passed by Circleville, where some of the worst events of the Black Hawk War had taken place, and brooded darkly on that conflict. "Her[e] I reflected of the deeds of cruelty perpetrated bothe by the Intians and brotheren," he wrote. He did not see simply "depredations of Indians," but "deeds of cruelty" carried out by Mormons also.[11]

On the twenty-fourth he reached Panguitch, and in two more days was in Kanab. He started for Salt Lake City on July 6, traveling with Tuuvi and Talasnimki, but the following day he was overtaken by Haight, who had not been able to find a route to the mouth of the Dirty Devil (as he thought) that had sufficient water for travelling in this lonely and dry country. Local Indians confirmed that it would be impossible to reach the mouth of the river. Actually, the river that Haight started to explore might have been the San Rafael River.[12] So Haight had arrived back at Skutumpah on the sixth, discovered Jacob's travel plans, and was able to overtake him on a borrowed horse and report on his findings.

On the eleventh, Hamblin and friends came to Beaver and then continued north, arriving at Salt Lake City six days later.[13] Powell had been in the city checking on the health of his pregnant wife, but had just departed to reunite with his crew. Jacob sent a messenger to him stating that he and Haight had found no trail to the mouth of the Dirty Devil.[14]

In Salt Lake, Jacob must have met Captain Pardyn (or Pardon) Dodds, a Civil War veteran who served as Indian agent for the Utes on their reservation in Uintah County, eastern Utah.[15] Powell had already sent Dodds on a first unsuccessful mission to find the Dirty Devil mouth.[16] (Powell himself evidently made a brief, futile attempt to locate the Dirty Devil mouth along with Marion Shelton, our old friend from the 1859 visit to the Hopis.)[17] Now Powell asked Jacob and Dodds to make another attempt to get supplies to the Colorado via the Dirty Devil.

Tuuvi and Talasnimki were probably given extensive tours of Salt Lake City; at some point, Brigham Young gave Tuuvi a suit of clothes.[18] Hamblin, Tuuvi, Talasnimki, and perhaps Dodds left Salt Lake City for southern Utah on July 25.[19]

Back in Kanab, Jacob and Dodds decided that, instead of traveling east from Glencove as Jacob had done with Haight, they would try a route northeast from Kanab, then would follow the Dirty Devil east to the Colorado. As it turned out, in this expedition, Hamblin again engaged in a remarkable adventure and accomplished a significant feat of exploration. He and Dodds and two companions became the first whites to explore the Escalante River and experience the otherworldly beauty of its canyons.

As Powell Survey geographer Almon Thompson later wrote, this was a most difficult and dangerous job:

> The perilous character of the journey of Mr. Hamblin and party was apparent. For eighty miles they traveled in a cañon, finding, in all that distance, but two

> places where the walls could be scaled. They crossed, recrossed, waded, and sometimes swam a rapid stream, that often filled the gorge from wall to wall. A single shower, on the rock land above, would have changed the stream to a raging torrent, that would have swept them into the Colorado, or imprisoned them in some rock walled alcove, with no possible way of escape.[20]

This accomplishment is all the more remarkable in that it was technically a mistake—Hamblin and Dodds thought they were following the Dirty Devil to its confluence with the Colorado. While some authors have implied that Hamblin was an incompetent explorer to mix up two major rivers,[21] in fact he made a logical mistake, based on the information that he had been given by Powell.[22] Walter Clement Powell, Major Powell's cousin, wrote in his diary that Hamblin explored the wrong river because "Major Powell had stated that the Dirty Devil was the only stream of any size between the San Raphael and the Pahria; hence the error."[23] In fact, by the time the Escalante reached the Colorado, it was barely recognizable as the mouth of a major river.

On August 15, Hamblin began a diary of this second expedition to find the Dirty Devil: "Started to explore a rout to Durty Devel in co with Bro Walter Winsor and [*illegible*] Dodds. And a gurman Doct."[24] Walter Winsor was the twenty-seven-year-old son of Anson Winsor, builder of Winsor's Castle at Pipe Spring. The identity of the German doctor remains a mystery.

Hamblin and this group traveled northeast, passing by Pahreah, then came to Potato Valley, east of the Escalante Mountains near the modern town of Escalante, on the nineteenth. The following day they evidently started down the Escalante River canyon, traveling "4. or 5 mles down a narow canion. Dificuilt traviling. High virticil rocks on eathr [either] side," Jacob wrote. "The seeniary in this canion is grand and sublime." This was a most difficult exploration; they were entering one of the last great unexplored, unmapped areas in America. Sometimes they had to climb twenty to forty feet from the ground to proceed; at other times they traveled along the bottom of the canyon, at the level of the river, the Escalante not helping matters by "shooting from one side to the other obliegeing us to clime in and out often." The river, usually about twenty yards wide and fifteen inches deep, had occasional dangerous deep holes and patches of quicksand. The bottom land near the river was covered with brush and vines, which the party had to cut through to proceed. It was very slow going.

On August 22, they climbed a high rock to see the surrounding country: everything they saw looked like "nearly naked sand rock," with some juniper and patches of grass.

Hamblin decided at this point that their pace was so slow, traveling at the bottom of the canyon, that they had no chance of reaching the Colorado in time to meet the Powell party. He sent Dodds, Winsor, and the doctor to "hunt a rout on the rock on the west side of the creek." The three men came back the next day and reported that they had indeed found a good route to travel, but apparently felt that it would not finally reach the mouth of the river.

Hamblin now abruptly wrote in his diary, "started for home." Almon Thompson later wrote, "It seems that Captain Dodds succeeded in getting in to the mouth of the Dirty Devil, or so near that he saw the mouth and knew there was no travel, and went back for Hamblin."[25] The report of Dodds, Winsor, and the German must have convinced Jacob that they could not get to the mouth of the river, so they immediately turned back. That same day, an uncomfortable accident befell Jacob, as his horse fell in the creek and rolled over, thoroughly dousing him and his blankets. He took some medicine he had with him, but was nevertheless sick all night.

On the night of August 24, the party camped near the head of the Escalante, and two days later were traveling down the Paria Canyon. They presumably arrived at Kanab on August 27 or 28, where they received a message from Powell to bring supplies to the Crossing of the Fathers by September 25.[26] Hamblin knew he could get to the Crossing in a few days, so he could now spend a few weeks in his normal pursuits at Kanab.[27]

After the treaty with the Navajos at Fort Defiance the previous year, Navajos had begun to visit the Mormons peacefully. However, while some came in complete friendship, other groups had agreed to the treaty reluctantly and were inclined to continue raiding.

Hamblin, in his autobiography, emphasized the positive contacts. He mentions that in early 1871, he returned to Kanab and found eighty Navajos there on foot, with blankets to trade. There were women in the group, which was a sign of a peaceful expedition, and one of the leading men was named Comiarrah. According to Hamblin, they received fifty horses in Kanab, then traded for others in St. George, and returned home "quite satisfied."[28]

Other sources seem to report tensions in this encounter that almost escalated into conflict. Apparently Erastus Snow invited about eighty Navajos to meet with him in Kanab in early September.[29] Erastus Snow arrived in Kanab on the seventh.[30] On the eighth, Jacob was in Washington, obtaining supplies for his family in preparation for his upcoming trip to Arizona.[31]

By September 9, seventy-nine Navajos, led by thirteen headmen, had come to Kanab, and met with Snow and leading Mormons. Chief among them were Pe-o-caan (first listed), Ko-mi-gezze, and Ketchene, aka Muerto Deambro (the chief spokesman). Ira Hatch and Tuuvi acted as translators—Hamblin is not mentioned, and he may not have been present.[32] Ketchene, whose name may be a transliteration of Táchii'nii,

"Red Forehead Clan,"[33] and Peokon were headmen from the Inscription House area on the Shonto Plateau in northeast Arizona.[34]

At first, Snow's talk with Ketchene was positive and friendly, both men expressing firm desires for peace. "Ketchene said he wanted his people to be as brothers and sons among us. They were at peace with the neighboring tribes and wished to cultivate peace with us; they did not want war.... They brought four women along with them to show that they meant peace. Their whole talk was peace." Snow and Ketchene both said they wanted Navajos and Mormons to be able to travel safely through each other's country. The council finally ended with "the usual token of a satisfactory Agreement—an Indian Embrace," and Snow returned to St. George.[35]

The eighty Navajos stayed at a camp near Kanab for a few days after the council, and were fed by the Mormons. But on the eleventh, something went seriously wrong. The Navajos on that day "threw off [their] friendly mask" and demanded seventy horses, seventeen cattle, "and other smaller things."[36] This put Kanab in a dangerous position, as three-fifths of the men of that community, not too populous in the first place, had gone north for some reason.[37]

Why had the Navajos suddenly turned menacing? Was there a power struggle within the group, in which antagonistic chiefs gained the upper hand over peace chiefs? Without the Navajo side of this story, it is impossible to tell.

The Mormon response was quick. Erastus Snow sent a message asking for help from Utah governor George L. Woods, who reportedly simply ignored it.[38] Snow then sent for all available able-bodied Mormons in southern Utah to hurry to Kanab. Enough arrived that on the eleventh or twelfth, the Navajos, "finding an accession to the numbers of Kanab, had moderated their demands and were willing to trade for horses."[39] At some point Jacob also came to Kanab.

Just after this possible tinderbox, on the thirteenth, Jacob wrote to Snow, saying that "after talking with the Navajos the third time and counciling with Bis[hop] Stewart and other[s]," he, Stewart, and others felt it would be wise that some of the Navajos be given permission to visit St. George so that they "could then form some eyedie [idea] of the advantage of Sivlesacion," and Snow granted this.[40] In the same letter, Jacob recommended that the mouth of the Paria be settled by ten to fifteen Indian missionaries "to inshure safty to this country."[41] Jacob saw the crucial strategic value of the Paria crossing, and possibly now nudged Snow to begin a Mormon settlement there.

Also on the thirteenth, Indian-fighter James Andrus left Short Creek for Kanab and sent instructions for more men from Washington and St. George to follow him.

In a note that Ira Hatch wrote to Snow three days later, he stated that the leading Navajos, many of whom had walked to Kanab, "expected to get horses to carry them home, and if they cannot get them, it will jeopardise Jacob and Company that are going to the Navajo Nation." Hatch mentioned that Patnish and three of his men were at Virgen City and sixteen Navajos were at Shunesburg, another town on the

Virgin.[42] The presence of Patnish was an ominous sign, as he had previously attempted to extort stock from Hamblin. Had he influenced the Navajos to try to do likewise?[43]

A telegraph message from Kanab suggests that Hamblin was gone for some time, then came back with forty horses.[44] This thoroughly anti-Navajo report suggests that the Indians simply appropriated these horses then departed, but the writings of the Powell company show that evidently the Navajos traded blankets for horses, though on terms extremely advantageous to the Navajos.[45] Walter Clement Powell, on October 6, writes:

> The Navajo Indians, 116 [*sic*] strong, have been over among the Mormons "trading" (?), that is, a "Red" would take a horse and give Mr. Mormon a blanket for it and then make him throw in vegetables, melons, fruit, &c. to boot. After getting all they wished, came back, crossing the river at this point [the Crossing of the Fathers] 2 or 3 days ago, and now they have gone to Fort Defiance to receive their present from the government.[46]

Thus, apparently, the Navajos, after the trading, passed back over the Colorado at the Crossing of the Fathers on October 3 or 4.[47]

It is possible that the Powell men were exaggerating the situation for humorous effect. Hamblin later, in 1874, described the confrontation thus: "I asked if they remembered of 80 of their men coming to Kanab after our peace talk & telling me that they were cast out like hungry wolves naked without any thing to help themselves with & my giving them 30 horses for just what blankets they pleased to leave."[48] This does not portray the exchange as a trade forced by the Navajos, as the Powell men recorded it, but as generosity on the part of Hamblin and the Mormons.

One of the most contemporary reports of this incident from Kanab, the diary of James Bunting, has no mention of any threats or extortion by the Navajos. Instead, he wrote, "They desired our Friendship & wished to trade blankets for horses." He mentions that a group of the Navajos visited St. George, "where they were treated very kindly & retnd feeling well pleased with their visit."[49]

Moses Farnsworth describes a confrontation that may be a different version of the same story, though it could be an entirely different but similar incident. He dates it in November 1871, and says that a group of 129 "renegade Utes, Navajos and Shivwits" appeared, led by "Patnish, a very ugly chief," and made very unreasonable demands.[50]

Another version of the story comes from a 1929 interview with longtime Kanab resident, Nathan H. Adams, who, with Ben Hamblin, worked for the Powell geographic survey parties for some seven years.[51] He stated that hostile Navajos camped near Kanab, and the Kanabans immediately sent to Long Valley for reinforcements, and to Jacob in Santa Clara. Jacob arrived with Andrew Gibbons, and soon he, Gibbons, and Ira Hatch rode out to meet the Navajos. The Kanab residents watched nervously as these three men disappeared into the middle of the many Indians, but were then relieved when they saw the whites smoking a pipe with them. Then Jacob, Gibbons, and Hatch returned to the fort with the Navajos accompanying them, picked out a fat steer, slaughtered it, and barbecued it. According to Adams, after this feast, the Navajos "filed out and went back to their land, with the understanding that they could come back any time they wanted to trade with the whites in safety, and thus peace was established."

If all of these are different accounts of the same event, the story, like most accounts of Mormon-Indian relations, has variant traditions. Often pro-Indian and anti-Indian accounts of an incident are told very early after it occurred, creating parallel, dueling traditions. However, it is possible that two different events occurred, with one group of Indians led by Patnish, more hostile and renegade than the Ketchene group.

Despite these early, tense confrontations, smaller groups of friendly Navajos began crossing the Colorado and bringing blankets to trade for horses or cattle. For example, Hamblin mentions four "Navajoe Braves" visiting Kanab in his February 11 letter to Brigham Young.[52] On October 14, Walter Clement Powell's diary recorded a small group of Navajos led by Agua Grande, apparently the prominent headman Ganado Mucho, on their way to trade in Utah, with a pass signed by the Navajo agent and Jacob.[53] On October 28, we will see, nine Navajos with extraordinarily beautiful blankets crossed Lee's Ferry with Jacob Hamblin. A half a month later, on November 18, four Navajos encamped at Navajo Wells, just east of Kanab.[54] This is a striking contrast to the period of the raids from 1866 to early 1870.

Meanwhile, Jacob had to keep the important appointment with Powell at the Crossing of the Fathers, and he planned to continue on from there with Tuuvi and Talasnimki to the Hopi Mesas and into Navajo country. Hamblin, his Hopi friends, and Pardyn Dodds left Kanab with a supply pack train on September 15 and arrived at the Crossing of the Fathers a week later, three days before their September 25 appointment. However, the twenty-fifth came and no boats arrived. Jacob, with Dodds and some non-Mormon miners, waited impatiently, becoming more and more anxious about Powell's party. They travelled upstream on the Colorado for a ways to see if they could meet the explorers, but found no one. Finally, Jacob decided to leave Dodds with the supplies and continue on to the Hopi mesas and Fort Defiance.

Powell's party finally reached the Crossing of the Fathers on October 6 and were extremely relieved to find Dodds waiting there with the supplies. They had been running short of food, and two of their company were in bad health.

Jacob, in this trip to the Hopi mesas and Fort Defiance, took with him Tuuvi and Talasnimki, Isaac Haight, George Washington Adair Jr., and Joe Mangum.[55]

Adair, a thirty-four-year-old native of Alabama, was one of the few men indicted for the Mountain Meadows Massacre.[56]

The diary of Jack Hillers, who later became the Powell company photographer, gives us our earliest and most detailed account of the purpose of the trip. On October 6, he wrote that the Powell party had expected to find Jacob at the Ute ford,

> but Mr. Hamblin had gone to Ft. Defiance, Arizona, on a Mormon mission, to obtain indemnity from the Government—the Navajos having been down to Kanab and forced the people to give up their stock and everything else they wanted. They submitted rather than have war with them. The Navahoes receive an annuity from the Government. Hamblin hopes to stop some of it.[57]

As was mentioned above, this may distort the transaction slightly—the Navajos traded valuable blankets for the horses, which the Mormons had already set aside to give them.

Stephen Vandiver Jones wrote, on October 28, 1871, "Ham[b]lin and his party had been over to make a treaty with the Indians and put a stop to raiding if possible."[58] Clearly, the 1870 peace treaty had not made a complete halt to the raiding.

While Hamblin's company was negotiating some steep cliffs, some of their horses bruised their legs and one fell from a cliff and was killed instantly. The company was able to lower a man over the cliff with a rope and he was able to salvage the precious baggage from the dead animal.

Hamblin also mentioned that he visited Navajo ranches on the way out and on the way back. This was an entirely different atmosphere from that which had prevailed in previous trips to Navajo country.

On arriving at Fort Defiance, Jacob found that two of his firm allies were gone. Barboncito had died on March 16 of that year, and Frank Bennett was no longer the Navajo agent. In his autobiography Hamblin mentions no attempts to negotiate or make a treaty with the Navajos, or receive indemnification for the horses that had been given to the Navajos at Kanab. (And it is doubtful that he was able to make any progress on this with Barboncito and Bennett gone.) He merely says that he attended a Methodist meeting on a Sunday morning and was allowed to preach to the Indians in the afternoon. The subject he chose was "the coming forth of the Book of Mormon, and about the ancient inhabitants of the American continent," which would not have warmed the Methodist minister's heart.[59]

However, apparently Jacob somehow reinforced his previous treaty with the Navajos, and one account speaks of him making a treaty with the Navajos on this trip. Jacob and company, along with some Navajos, arrived back at the Paria crossing on October 28, as we will see. On that day, Stephen Vandiver Jones wrote that Jacob "had succeeded [in making a treaty and putting a stop to raiding] to his entire satisfaction, and had opened trade with them [the Navajos]."[60]

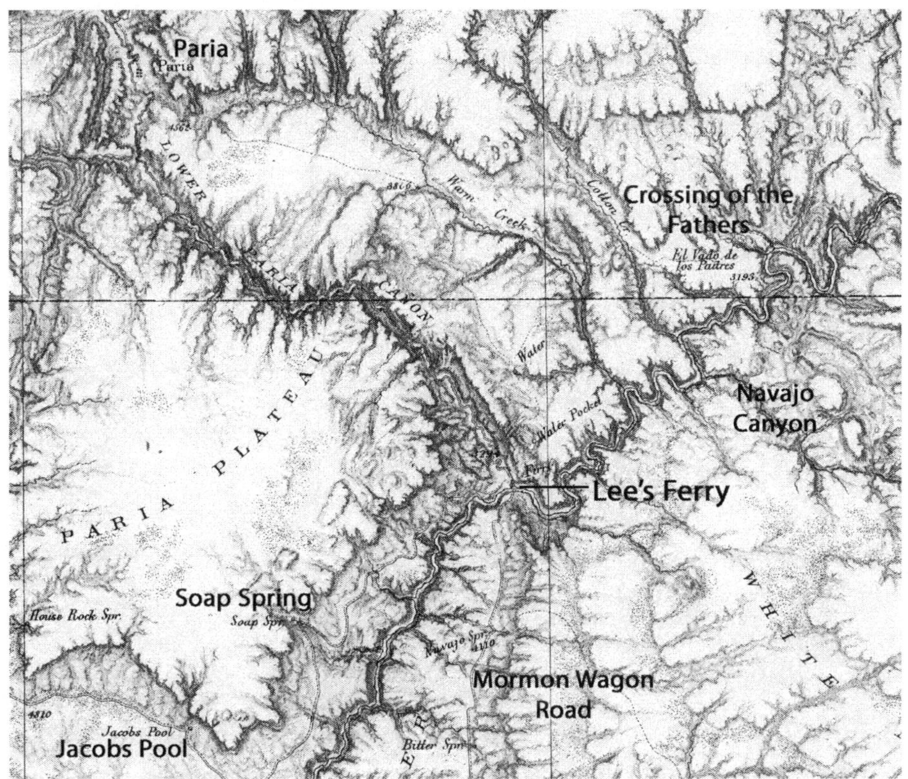

23.1. Lee's Ferry area. The Utah-Arizona road descended to the mouth of the Paria (later Lee's Ferry), crossed the Colorado, surmounted Lee's Backbone, then led south, west of the Echo Cliffs. The earlier crossing, "El Vado de los Padres," the Crossing of the Fathers, is northeast. Detail from Wheeler, *Topographical Atlas*, Map 67, courtesy David Rumsey Historical Map Collection.

According to Navajo historian Raymond Friday Locke, Navajo leaders Manuelito and Ganado Mucho came to realize that continued raiding by younger or more aggressive Navajos was undermining the very existence of the Navajo nation. They felt that one of the prominent raiders, a headman named Dichin Bilqéhe, was a witch, and was using sorcery that might endanger the more law-abiding Navajos. Therefore, Manuelito, Ganado Mucho, and their followers rounded up forty witches or raiders and executed them after a short trial. American authorities reprimanded those who carried out the execution, but this action nevertheless "put an end to Navajo raiding—except for a few isolated incidents—for all time."[61]

In early to mid-October, Powell had left his party at the Crossing of the Fathers and traveled to Kanab. The party at the Colorado, led by "Prof" Almon Thompson, continued their river trip again on October 14, and reached the mouth of the Paria, modern Lee's Ferry, on the twenty-third, where they made a camp.

Five days later, at about nine a.m., the Powell group heard an "Indian yell" from across the Colorado, and saw what looked like three mounted Indians on the edge of the canyon wall, fairly low at this point. Artist and assistant topographer Frederick Dellenbaugh, who later wrote a number of books about the Colorado,[62] wrote that the Powell men prepared a boat to cross and investigate,

> when a fourth figure joined the group, and in good English came the words, "G-o-o-d m-o-r-n-i-n-g," long drawn out. On landing we were met by a slow-moving, very quiet individual, who said he was Jacob Hamblin. His voice was so low, his manner so simple, his clothing so usual, that I could hardly believe that this was Utah's famous Indian-fighter and manager.[63]

It is remarkable that, as early as 1871, Hamblin had become legendary, even among non-Mormons. Of course, Dellenbaugh's reference to Jacob as an "Indian-fighter" is not correct.

Hamblin's party, four whites and nine Navajos, was crossed over in the usual fashion, men and supplies on the boat, horses being swum over. Repeated trips were necessary to cross everyone. Some of the Navajos, who had never seen the Colorado, were amazed at its size. This process took all day, and when the whole party was safely over, Jacob camped with the Powell party that night.

A description of a rollicking gathering around the campfire follows, in which for a moment it seems that the culture gap between white and Indian was briefly bridged by music and humor. Dellenbaugh wrote, "The Navajos were found to be a very jolly set of fellows, ready to take or give any amount of chaff, and perfectly honest.... Their spirits ran high, they sang their wild songs for us, and we had the liveliest evening we had seen in many a month." While their chief, Koneco, drummed on one of the camp kettles with a willow root, the celebration became general. Clem Powell wrote:

> All of us, white and red, joined hands and danced around the fire, the Indians singing war songs. We had a gay time and lots of fun. The Navajos seem to be a free hearted, social, chatty, intelligent set and instead of being the stoics that popular tradition makes the Indian, it is the reverse. They laughed as heartily at our blunders in the war dance as we did at them.[64]

"They are *the* Indians of the West," Clem wrote of the Navajos—"a fine looking set of fellows, tall, well-built and intelligent."[65]

The Navajos retired to rest, but Hamblin and his companions stayed up with the Powell men a little longer to sing them some Mormon hymns.[66] One imagines the strains of "Come Come Ye Saints" or "Redeemer of Israel" echoing through the vast, lonely canyon at Lee's Ferry.

Either that day or the next, the Navajos showed the Powell men some of their blankets, which impressed them greatly. They were "the finest blankets I ever saw," wrote Stephen Vandiver Jones.[67] Bishop mentioned one especially beautiful blanket, made of black wool with other colors interwoven, that had taken a Navajo woman seventy days to make. Jacob traded for it, and if he gave the woman her asking price, paid her a mare and a colt. The blanket was later placed in a Salt Lake City museum.[68]

Jacob and his party left the next morning, after he shared some beans with the Powell men, and made arrangements for more supplies to be brought to them and a wagon to come and take their sick men back to Kanab.[69]

In Kanab, Jacob found that a pack train had left on October 23 to take provisions to the Powell men at Lee's Ferry. One of the non-Mormon miners who had been at Crossing of the Fathers, George Riley, was the leader of the group, John Mangum was guide, and Jacob's son Joseph, now seventeen, was also part of the company.[70] Concerned that he had not seen the party, Jacob sent Isaac Haight and Charles Riggs to take food to the Powell company at the mouth of the Paria and help find the missing pack train, then departed for St. George.

As it turned out, the Riley-Mangum party had become lost, with Riley and Mangum accusing each other of misleading the party. The Powell group and the Mangum-Riley party met on November 3, and Haight and Riggs arrived at the ferry with welcome supplies the following day.[71]

In St. George, Jacob attended a conference, at which Brigham Young and George A. Smith were also present. It lasted from November 3 to 9, and was an important conference for the Saints, as the St. George temple site was dedicated at this time.[72]

Jacob counseled with Young, Smith, and Snow, talking about the projected guard presence at the Paria crossing. Either Young, Snow, or Hamblin had an idea: that location, far from civilization, would be a perfect place for John D. Lee to settle and avoid arrest.

Returning to Kanab on the thirteenth, the Indian missionary found Almon Thompson and some members of the Powell expedition already there.[73] From this point, the diaries of the Powell company document life in Kanab, from the viewpoint of observant non-Mormons who were generally friendly, occasionally slightly caustic. Clem Powell, on reaching Kanab on December 8, wrote that it was "only a small collection of houses and a log fort."[74] Dellenbaugh, who estimated that about a hundred families were living in the town, gave a more appreciative and expansive description. The town "was laid out in the characteristic Mormon style with wide streets and regular lots fenced by wattling willows between stakes." Streets with houses of adobe or sun-dried brick were shaded by shade trees and fruit trees, and gardens were filled with vines, corn, and potatoes. Water ditches, located on both sides of every street,

23.2. Kanab, which Jacob helped found, and where his family lived for many years. Sketch by Albert Tissandier, 1886. Courtesy Utah Museum of Fine Arts.

allowed water to reach any lot. Dellenbaugh noted the absence of establishments typical of many Western towns: grog shops, gambling saloons, and dance halls.

On arriving in Kanab, Dellenbaugh rode to the fort and found Clem Powell and E. O. Beaman, a photographer, in a cabin they had set up as their photography lab, "with a swarm of children peeping through every chink and crevice of the logs to get a view of the 'Gentiles,' a kind of animal they had seldom seen."[75]

At this point, Hamblin's story intersects with that of John D. Lee, and Lee's diary often records Hamblin's doings, from Lee's perspective and range of interest. At the same time, Lee was entering an increasingly troubled and tragic period in his life, in which the church and church leaders he had served so faithfully and energetically gradually withdrew their support for him, until he was tried for his actions in the Mountain Meadows Massacre in 1875 and 1876, and executed in 1877. There are many cries of anguish in Lee's remarkable diaries as he saw friends, as well as some wives and family members, turning against him.

Hamblin is part of this story of gradual loss and betrayal, from Lee's perspective, and Lee's attacks on Hamblin are expressed in detail, and with passion, in Lee's diaries and letters. Some historians, such as P. T. Reilly, have unabashedly taken the

23.3. John Doyle Lee, a leading pioneer in southern Utah, was the only man convicted and executed for the Mountain Meadows Massacre. For years he and Jacob Hamblin were allies, but in 1874, there was a bitter falling out between the two men. Used by permission, Utah State Historical Society, all rights reserved.

side of Lee in this dispute. But, as Juanita Brooks has written, we often do not have Hamblin's side of the story. Lee, as is often the case with diarists, writes with extreme partisan emotion, from his own point of view. He became bitter toward nearly every Mormon leader during this period.

Nevertheless, as was stated earlier, I believe that the Mountain Meadows Massacre left few Mormons unscathed, including Brigham Young, Jacob Hamblin, and other leading Mormons. In the years following the massacre, they generally acted to hide Mormon involvement in the event.[76] In addition, trying and executing Lee, unaccompanied by other equally culpable Mormon leaders, such as Haight and Dame, was not fair to Lee, despite his undoubted guilt in perpetrating the massacre.

Thus, the Mountain Meadows Massacre, because it had not been admitted and its Mormon perpetrators had not been punished by the Mormon church internally until years after the event, continued to overshadow southern Utah.

In mid-November, John D. Lee was in hiding, as a writ had been served on him, and Hamblin occasionally visited him with messages and food.[77] On November 16, Hamblin had a historic meeting with Lee, who wrote that Hamblin "gave Me a pass word to Make My way to the Lonely Dell by way of the Hogon Wells,[78] & Join a company & make a Road to the crossing of the Colerado River near that point. There is a good place for setlement & you are invited to take it up & occupy it with as Many good Ranches as you want & can secur, that is, if you fel to do so; & I would like to have a small interest in it.... So if you have a woman that has Faith enough to go with you, take her along & some cows."

"How many should I take?" Lee asked.

"Suit yourself," Hamblin replied, "the more the better. There is feed enough on the [Paria] Creek to keep 200 head without putting them on a Ranch."

Jacob offered to supply Lee with seeds and fruit trees, but requested that Lee repay him "in propo[r]tion to what I furnish or do." He also stated that there were possible mining opportunities near the mouth of the Paria. "Now take due Notice & govern your self accordingly," he said.[79] As Reilly notes, it is unlikely that Hamblin would make this offer on his own authority, though Hamblin's September 13 letter to Snow suggests that a settlement at the crossing was his idea;[80] Snow and Young probably agreed that Lee should be allowed to settle there. This would keep Lee far from settlements where he ran the risk of being arrested; in addition, it would give the Saints a Mormon presence at the crucial Paria crossing of the Colorado.

Lee decided to accept this offer, which opened a new chapter in his eventful life. Toward the end of November, he started for what would eventually be Lee's Ferry, with a herd of fifty-seven cattle. On the thirtieth, when he was already on the road, Jacob met him and told him that the regular route, which he was taking, would not have sufficient water for his herd. Instead, he advised him to travel east to the Pahreah settlement (recently augmented by a few new settlers), then follow the Paria River down to the Colorado.[81] Lee, traveling with a young son, took this advice, but found the journey down the Paria with his cattle herd enormously difficult. Two men from the Pahreah settlements, John Mangum and Thomas Adair, were fortunately able to accompany him. Lee arrived at the mouth of the Paria with the cattle in mid-December, an epic accomplishment, then returned with much of his family on Christmas day. A new settlement had begun.[82]

On December 21, Jacob took a stab at proselyting Major Powell's cousin: "While there Jacob had a long talk with me about Mormondom, xtolling its virtues, &c. &c. Told me about the life of Joseph [Smith] and showed me a Mormon bible [Book of Mormon]," Clem Powell wrote. Clem was not ripe for conversion, but the next day he wrote, "Jacob paid us a visit; I like him."[83] On the day before Christmas Jacob and Ammon Tenney dropped by the Powell camp and told Clem stories of Hopis and Navajos. The day after Christmas, Jacob departed for Long Valley.

In the midst of all his activity in 1871, Jacob at least claimed a ranch at House Rock Springs, just east of the Kaibab Plateau.[84] Though Jacob never developed this property in a substantial way, it shows that he was thinking of settling down and becoming a rancher.[85]

Dellenbaugh's writings give us a good snapshot of the Hamblin family at this time. He wrote that Jacob's Kanab home "was simple but it was comfortable. He was a poor man for he did his work for the people with very slight compensation."[86] At some point in his Kanab residence, Jacob had two houses, one for each of his white wives. Dellenbaugh praised Louisa, writing, "Sister Louisa was the one I came to know best and she was a good woman. [On January 15, 1872] We had an excellent dinner with rich cream for the coffee which was an unusual treat."[87] He praised Louisa as "a very nice, sensible woman—English [*sic*]."[88]

Priscilla also had dealings with the Powell company; she remembered hosting Major Powell, and sewing him a special pair of white buckskin gloves, which had gauntlets that partially covered his missing arm.[89]

Dellenbaugh's portrayal of Jacob as poor was an overstatement. Though he was not wealthy, by any objective standards, he was solidly middle class by Kanab standards. In 1874, he owned the third biggest herd of cattle in Kanab.[90] He took part in many of Kanab's collective business and financial ventures, such as the "Kanab Association" and the Kanab Tanning & Manufacturing Company.[91]

Kanab Ward records contain many accounts of him speaking in church meetings. One day he spoke in Paiute to the Indians attending the meeting.[92]

Dellenbaugh wrote that Jacob, "was 'sealed' to two Pai Ute women when I knew him."[93] This is a remarkable statement; if it is correct, Jacob had two Paiute wives about whom we know very little, his sixth and seventh wives. Dellenbaugh is a credible witness who knew Jacob and Louisa Hamblin well. However, Dellenbaugh apparently wrote this note in 1921, and, in his 1908 memoir of the Powell expedition, he is less certain, writing that Hamblin was "'sealed' to one or two Pai Ute women."[94] One might argue that Dellenbaugh, not a Mormon insider, could have misunderstood Jacob's marital arrangements, but it is also possible that Dellenbaugh's outsider status allowed him to touch on a topic that was taboo for many southern Utah Mormons of that era.[95]

Jacob's sons were increasingly important presences in Kanab. Dellenbaugh admired Joseph's cowboy skills: "'Joe' was an expert on horseback and with the lasso and was with our land parties constantly," he wrote.[96] Lyman also became a good friend of the Powell men.

The Hamblin family gained a child and lost one this same year. Louisa's second child, Inez Louisa, had been born on April 4,[97] but Jacob and Priscilla's eight-year-old Lucy was very ill through the winter. She had been infested by tapeworm for some two years, and though Jacob and Priscilla had taken her to Salt Lake City for treatment, and had tried numerous medications, none worked. On December 28 "she died in Jacob's arms," wrote Priscilla. "This was a sad time, but we were relieved to see her rest from her pain."[98]

24

"They Died Off So Fast That There Were Hardly Any Left in a Short Time"

The Fate of the Santa Clara Paiutes, 1871

On June 22, 1871, Jacob's friend, Tutsegabits, died in Santa Clara. "He was a man of peace," James Bleak wrote, "and a wise counselor to his people."[1] When he heard the news, Jacob would have grieved for the Paiute headman. Unfortunately, after the death of Tutsegabits, Paiutes in Santa Clara, Beaver Dam, and the Muddy reportedly took the opportunity to raid stock from Mormon settlements.[2]

The death of Tutsegabits, the most prominent representative of the Santa Clara Paiutes, perhaps gives us a chance to look back at this group briefly.

When Jacob Hamblin arrived at Toquerville, the Virgin, and Santa Clara in 1854, there had been many Paiutes living and farming on the banks of creeks and rivers, though at certain times of the year traveling to different parts of southern Utah to harvest seeds and hunt. These Indians had received the early Mormon missionaries with the utmost hospitality, sharing their limited food with them. Certainly, their situation was not ideal, and they were seeking an alliance with whites who might help them raise their standard of living. They hoped that their farming would improve with such help, and that the Mormons would help prevent the raids of the Utes for Paiute women and children. These idealistic early Indian missionaries wanted to help the Paiutes in these practical ways, as well as convert them to the Mormon faith and many aspects of white culture, especially western farming.

At first, Paiute farming seemed to benefit. On June 30, 1857, George Armstrong, an Indian agent, wrote, "'Tot-sag-gabots,' the principal chief of seven bands on the river, has under cultivation about sixty acres, and expects to raise a sufficiency for himself and band, and a surplus to trade to emigrants.... 'Captain Jackson,' another of the chiefs on this river, has about twelve acres in corn and squashes."[3] This records successful and extensive farming operations among the Santa Clara Paiutes. The Santa Clara was a population center.

However, when William Palmer wrote his early survey of the Utah Indians in 1928, he wrote of the "Tonoquint-its," those who dwelled on the Tonoquint (Santa

Clara): "Of this tribe only one survives. His name is Tamalots, and he is living with the Shebits at St. George."[4] Isabel Kelly, in 1935, also speaks of one survivor of what she calls the St. George band of Paiutes, living on both the Santa Clara and Virgin Rivers.[5]

Angus Woodbury, in 1950, recorded that the Virgin River Paiutes, originally estimated to have a population of a thousand, had been reduced to one survivor, named Peter Harrison, partly as a result of disease.[6]

Much earlier, on February 2, 1878, Augustus P. Hardy, who had been called as bishop of Indians near St. George in 1866, stated that some twenty-five Shivwits families were living near St. George. But aside from these "immigrants" from south of St. George, local Indians had disappeared. When Jacob and his friends arrived in Dixie in 1854, there were, Hardy estimated, three to four hundred Paiutes living on the Santa Clara. Now, only two Santa Clara Paiutes remained—named Quan-tun and Tutsegabits Charley.[7] In 1878, this group of Paiutes, which had probably accounted for the bulk of the Paiute population in Dixie, had virtually disappeared.

It is worth asking how this occurred.[8] There were a number of significant factors and steps that must have brought about this disastrous population collapse.

First, competition for water resources as a result of white settlements must have increasingly limited Paiute agriculture. The Santa Clara was more a creek than a river, and at times it simply dried up. Even before the settlement of St. George, there were water disputes between the early Mormon settlers and the Santa Clara Paiutes. These early disputes were tempered by the fact that Indian missionaries were the leaders in the Mormon settlements.

The major influx of Mormons in late 1861, some three hundred heads of families to St. George and ninety Swiss to Santa Clara, followed by two hundred more families called to St. George the following year, undoubtedly brought increased competition for resources.[9] St. George immediately became the largest town in southern Utah, and the settlers needed water from the Santa Clara as well as from the Virgin. The sudden advent of these settlers in the Virgin River Basin area—perhaps twelve hundred to three thousand persons—was a typical Brigham Young colonizing operation—suddenly and miraculously successful from one point of view. But from the Paiute point of view, it was enormously disruptive to their way of life.[10]

As early as spring 1862, the St. George residents began farming near the Santa Clara and using its water.[11] In the succeeding years, the St. George residents, who had planned to use the plentiful waters of the Virgin as their primary water source, found that its quicksand bottom, frequent floods, and heavy silt loads made it a difficult source for irrigation. In 1867, apostle Erastus Snow and other St. George leaders decided to shift focus from the Virgin field to the Santa Clara field, as the Santa Clara River, despite its small size, was much easier to use as a source of irrigation.[12] As a result, there was intense competition between St. George and Santa Clara for the water of the Santa Clara through the years (with the St. George leaders, led by a resident apostle, having the final say in how the water was apportioned).[13]

After the 1861–1862 arrival of the large population of Mormons, what is striking about the record of St. George–Santa Clara water disputes is that the Tonaquint Paiutes do not seem to have even been a factor in the competition, as they had been previously.

In addition to the sheer number of Mormons who arrived in that period, the focus of the new arrivals was no longer on Indian relations or encouraging Indian agriculture. While the early Santa Clara settlements had been dominated by Indian missionaries, the Swiss and St. George Saints (now led by Apostle Erastus Snow, not an Indian missionary) had a primarily economic focus—which included the typical Mormon emphasis on agriculture and stock raising. The agriculture needed the Paiutes' creek, the Santa Clara; the stock needed not only the creek but the grasses and grass seed that the Paiutes depended on at certain times of the year for food.[14] In addition, St. George had been settled primarily as part of the "Cotton Mission"—and cotton needed a great deal of water to grow successfully.

Jacob Hamblin understood these conflicts quite clearly. In 1863 he wrote to Apostle George A. Smith, his friend and a close friend of Brigham Young, that it looked as if Young had intended for St. George to take the water of the usually quite small Santa Clara River, and thus deprive the Santa Clara Paiutes and white Santa Clara residents of it. He asked Smith to take the letter to Young. On November 3, George A. wrote to Jacob, in response:

> I have [*illegible*] idea that it was over the design or council of the Prest to deprive[15] the original settlers on the Santa Clara, or the Indians of the water,[16] or to build up St. George, at the sacrifice of that place.... I must acknowledge I hated to present the thing [Jacob's letter] to the President at all, and would rather have come down myself if I had the time and pacified the matter, than to have presented it to the President at all.[17]

Yet Brigham and George A. must have realized that sending so many settlers to the Dixie basin, and requiring them to focus on such a water-intensive crop as cotton, would have required the Santa Clara and Virgin Paiutes to cede much of their already limited water resources. It is remarkable that Jacob should write a letter to Young that George A. must have found so offensive, given Jacob's friendship and loyalty to both Smith and Young.

In Little, published in 1881, Jacob pinpointed 1861 as the time when Mormons began to transform the ecosystem of the Paiutes in southern Utah, and thus disrupt Mormon-Paiute relations. Naturally, we can see this as the beginning of their precipitous decline. He wrote:

> At this time [1863] a considerable change had taken place in the spirit and feelings of the Indians of Southern Utah, since the settlement of the country

24.1. Moapat Paiute Wunuvai gathering seed. An important staple for Paiute survival was seeds, gathered in baskets, as seen here. Livestock owned by whites often overgrazed in key Paiute seed-gathering areas, destroying the plants. Photograph probably by John K. Hillers, 1870s. Courtesy Wikimedia Commons/National Archives.

in 1861–62. Up to that time, our visits among them and our long talks around their camp fires, had kept up a friendly feeling in their hearts.

After the settlement of St. George, the labors of the Indian missionaries, from force of circumstances, became more extended and varied, and the feelings of the Indians toward the Saints became more indifferent, and their propensity to raid and steal returned.

The great numbers of animals brought into the country by the settlers, soon devoured most of the vegetation that had produced nutritious seeds, on which the Indians had been accustomed to subsist.[18] When, at the proper season of the year, the natives resorted to these places to gather seeds, they found they had been destroyed by cattle. With, perhaps, their children crying for food, only the poor consolation was left them of gathering around their camp fires and talking over their grievances.

Those who have caused these troubles have not realized the situation. I have many times been sorely grieved to see the Indians with their little ones, glaring upon a table spread with food, and trying to get our people to understand their circumstances, without being able to do so. Lank hunger and other influences have caused them to commit many depredations.

> When our people have retaliated, the unoffending have almost invariably been the ones to suffer. Generally those that have done the stealing have been on the alert, and have got out of the way, while those who have desired to be friends, from the want of understanding on the part of our people, have been the sufferers. This has driven those who were before well disposed, to desperation.
>
> The Navajoes and other Indians east of the Colorado River have taken advantage of these circumstances to raid upon the settlements, and drive off many hundreds of cattle and valuable horses and mules.[19]

Though Hamblin does not say it explicitly, overgrazing land was an ecological disaster that devastated land for both Indian and white man.[20] Cattle overgrazing, for instance, aside from destroying seeds that Indians had harvested as a staple of their diet, also destroyed vegetation that deer normally browsed on. The population of deer declined, and Indians who partially depended on deer for survival lost both grasses and deer.[21] In addition, overgrazing in mountain meadows was an important factor that helped produce floods that ravaged towns and farms in southern Utah from the mid-1880s through the late 1930s, causing Paiute farming to further decline.[22]

Given Jacob's earlier criticism of Brigham Young for suddenly introducing hundreds of settlers into a situation where they would compete for the already minimal Santa Clara water, this passage in the autobiography can be interpreted as another muted criticism of Young. Given Jacob's intense Mormonism, and his loyalty to Young throughout his life, it is a remarkable critique.

Jacob also wrote directly to Brigham Young about this issue in 1873, though here he omitted the 1861 date as a watershed:

> I have noticed that the first natives in southern Utah live mostly on seeds & roots. The first seeds commence to ripen about the 10th of June. This harvest continues till the weather gets cool on the high lands. They then take to the valleys, living on Rabits & the seeds they have carefully preserved.[23] When the white man settles the country, as a matter of course it is where it is the most productive, the same where the red man and his forefathers have subsisted for generations unnumbered.

Many observers have noted this: clearly, whites would settle at places with the most water, the most fertile land. So white towns in southern Utah were often founded on places that had been Indian farms or camping grounds.

> The white man's cattle crop the vegetation that produces the seed from early spring to late winter, from valley to mountain, following up as the season puts forth the Indian's bread, which year after year's cropping causes to grow

> less. The game also disappears, grievances are talked over at the camp fire, the women & children beg at the door of the white man, necesity drives the Indian to steal, the white man wants to bring the Indian to his standard of civilization, they are both driven to desperation, all for the want of a little understanding. All these evils we have had to contend with, from the early settling of this Territory.
>
> At an early day I herd a white man bost [boast] of fattening his horses on seeds taken from an Indian cache. This called my attention to listen to both sides of the question—the Indian's and white man's.[24]

This is a remarkably sympathetic and insightful account of the plight of the Native American in southern Utah. When Hamblin writes that "Necesity drives the Indian to steal," he is a far cry from the anti-Indian propagandist who characterizes the Indian as preferring theft to work.

In addition, as was noted earlier, the 1862 flood must have been a major disaster for the Tonaquint Paiutes. It probably swept away much of their hereditary farmland.[25]

As a result of these two events, some Paiutes literally starved to death. As we have seen, Jacob Hamblin, in his September 19, 1873, letter to Brigham Young, described the increasing lack of food that faced the Utah Paiutes after 1861. In 1866, a Utah Indian agent described the fate of the Paiutes south of Corn Creek:

> These Indians are all extremely poor. For the past two years, the new settlements made in their country have taken up much of the arable land; the miners have taken nearly all the balance, and these influences, with the constantly increasing concourse of freighters passing to and fro from this [Salt Lake] City to Southern California, and the Colorado River, have driven off what little game there ever was in the country. *Many Indians have perished of starvation, within the past six or eight months*....Some of these Indians, to save themselves from actual starvation, have occasionally stolen stock from the miners and settlers. This has led to acts of retaliation.[26]

As a result of lack of water, and increasing competition for resources with whites near Santa Clara, Washington, and St. George, it is possible that some Santa Clara Paiutes moved to different areas and were absorbed into other bands. As Paiutes saw their subsistence plants and animals reduced, they became increasingly dependent on white help.[27]

In addition, many Santa Clara Paiutes died from diseases introduced by the whites. This is a story that, surprisingly, has long been untold, both in Utah and elsewhere in the history of Indians in America, but in recent years historians have begun to piece together these tragic events.[28]

We have seen that the Paiutes were burning their wickiups because of death (presumably by disease) even before the 1862 flood.[29] Santa Clara resident John Stucki wrote that, a few years after the Swiss arrived in late 1861, the Santa Clara Paiutes endured a horrific epidemic:

> They had their Wigwams along the sides of the South hill and the edge of the Santa Clara Bench close to our town. They had the habit of burning their wigwams whenever anyone died. I remember that we could see wickiups burning every day for a while. I remember well one day when I went along what we called the South Ditch. I came to a place where there were four Indian men lying dead side by side and as I went a little farther up, there were two more lying there dead on the ground. They died off so fast that there were hardly any left in a short time and the white brethren went in mass one day to bury dead Indians. Although Santa Clara Valley seemed to be almost alive with Indians [previously], afterwards there were hardly any to be seen.... Although the Indians lived on both sides of our town, none of the white people caught the disease.[30]

This appears to be a classic case of the indigenous people having no resistance to the germs carried by the whites and their domestic animals. Historian Jared Diamond, in his book *Guns, Germs, and Steel*, provides exhaustive documentation for diseases from Europeans decimating native peoples, in the Americas and elsewhere. He writes that before 1492, there were an estimated twenty million Indians in North America; this number declined by ninety-five percent in the century or two following the advent of whites, primarily as the result of "Old World germs," especially smallpox, measles, typhus, and influenza, as well as diphtheria, malaria, mumps, pertussis, plague, tuberculosis, and yellow fever.[31] According to Diamond's analysis, these germs were often carried by European livestock. Whites' political cohesion, numbers, guns, and aggressive settlement patterns were also a significant factor in the decline of the Indians.

Modern historians view these epidemics in terms of scientific causality. However, early Mormons often saw them through the lens of religious ideology. Stucki tells the story of the final epidemic of the Santa Clara Paiutes in the context of divine judgment. Jacob Hamblin had prophesied that if the Santa Clara Paiutes did not "quit stealing the time would come when God would punish them with a severe disease, until they would die off like diseased and rotton sheep."[32] Stucki felt that the local Indians had not listened to this warning, and had been visited with destruction by a God reminiscent of the God of judgments found in the Old Testament.[33]

While there is no direct documentation for how the Santa Clara Paiutes viewed the disastrous epidemic that decimated them, general Paiute views of sickness suggest that they would have felt that powerful enemies, inimical shamans—possibly

Mormons viewed as having supernatural power—had sent "bad medicine" against them.[34] John A. Peterson notes that Black Hawk, when his Shiberetch Utes were dying of a smallpox epidemic, "believed that Mormons used supernatural powers to punish them by sending evil spirits who brought death in the form of diseases."[35]

The first historian I know of who has considered the tragic enigma of the Santa Clara Paiutes is Edward Leo Lyman, though other authors have treated epidemics among the Paiutes and Utes more generally.[36] He notes that it is striking that this epidemic that destroyed the once-flourishing Santa Clara Paiute community was not described in standard histories of the area—for instance, in James Bleak's "Annals of the Southern Utah Mission." Lyman records an 1877 epidemic, either smallpox or measles, among the Chemehuevi Paiutes on the lower Colorado, in which sufferers were "abandoned in panic by their own people…as they lay dying in the streets of some towns."[37] According to ethnobotanist Edward Palmer, there was apparently a smallpox epidemic among the Southern Paiutes previous to 1877.[38] Since Palmer did much of his work in the St. George area of southern Utah, he may have been referring to the epidemic that Stucki describes.

One Indian explained the depopulation of the Dixie Paiutes matter-of-factly: "When white man come, lotsa Injuns here…Injuns heap *yai-quay* [meaning lots of them die]; maybe so six, maybe so five, maybe so two in night. Purty soon all gone. White man, he come; raise'm pompoose. Purty soon lotsa white man."[39] This is clearly referring to an epidemic, perhaps of smallpox or measles.

There are also reports of epidemics among Nevada Paiutes, a cholera plague,[40] and, a little before 1860, an epidemic of diarrhea and "passage of blood" (which may be cholera again) in Muddy Valley, in which deaths were so numerous that bodies were "dumped into a near-by gully."[41] This reminds us of Stucki's description of the end of the Santa Clara Paiutes, and also of the smallpox epidemic among the Hopis in 1853 and 1854. Northern Paiutes were also affected by devastating attacks of disease.[42]

Though I have not made the Utes a central focus in this book, there are some indications that they endured similar epidemics. On June 23, 1858, Indian translator Dimick Huntington talked to some Utes at Spanish Fork in Utah County, northern Utah, and the chief of this group was furious with the Mormons: "He said that Brigham and the Mormons had made bad medicine, which was killing the Indians, before the Mormons came here, the Indians were healthy and numerous, now they were sickly and few."[43]

I believe, then, an epidemic of smallpox quite possibly caused the final downfall of the Santa Clara (and Virgin River?) Paiutes, perhaps in the early 1870s, though the settling of St. George and Santa Clara in 1861 and 1862 by Mormon colonists had already caused a precipitous decline in the Paiute way of life. While Mormons obviously did not intentionally cause any of these epidemics, decrease in the Paiute quality of life, including intense hunger and near starvation, would have made the Indians increasingly susceptible to disease. Malnourished children would have died more easily than adults. And there might have been lower conception rates among malnourished survivors.[44]

In 1865, Tutsegabits, with other Paiute leaders, met with the U.S. Indian agent and signed a treaty agreeing that Paiutes would move to the Uintah Reservation with the Utes in northeastern Utah. As it turned out, nothing came of this treaty, because the U.S. Senate failed to ratify it, and also because the Paiutes finally refused to move into a reservation with their traditional enemies and persecutors, whom they regarded, in fact, as malevolent sorcerers. Powell and Ingalls wrote that the Paiutes insisted that "the Utes of Uintah...had stolen their women and children; had killed their grand-fathers, their fathers, their brothers and sons, and, worse than all, were profoundly skilled in sorcery, and that under no consideration would the Pai-Utes live with them."[45]

In 1869, Indian agent Reuben N. Fenton, after a visit to Tutsegabits and his people near St. George, described Paiute agriculture in terms very different than the description of Armstrong in 1857: "The Pi-Utes are a very destitute tribe," he wrote. "A few around the settlements engage in farming to a limited extent. They raise a small quantity of wheat, corn and melons, using sticks to plant and knives to harvest with; therefore, the crops raised amount to almost nothing."[46] While Fenton is reporting on Paiutes in Nevada as well as in Utah, if the Santa Clara Paiutes had been pursuing remarkably successful agricultural operations, he probably would have commented on them.[47]

Tutsegabits died in 1871. In 1873, Powell and Ingalls, in their recommendations for moving Utah Indians to reservations, spoke of "Mo-ak-Shin-au-av, chief of the U-ai-Nu-ints, who live in the vicinity of Saint George."[48] In their table, they list the U-ai-Nu-ints, in the St. George area, but give no listing for Paiutes in Santa Clara.[49] The U-ai-Nu-ints might include both the Santa Clara and Virgin River Indians, but it is possible that Powell and Ingalls were speaking exactly, and there was no significant community of Paiutes at the Santa Clara anymore.[50]

The Virgin and Santa Clara Rivers had been "the riverine core of the Paiute homeland and its center of densest population."[51] White disease, white appropriation of water resources, and overgrazing from the whites' cattle had reduced this Paiute homeland to a few scattered bands, for whom the extensive Tonaquint villages that Jacob Hamblin had encountered when he came to the Santa Clara River in 1854 were only a memory. The few Santa Clara Paiutes who survived the plague described by Stucki were apparently absorbed into other Paiute bands, into Shivwits and Kaibab and Cedar City groups. As we have seen, by 1878, there was no Santa Clara or St. George band of Paiutes, beyond a few Shivwits who had migrated near St. George.[52]

25

"Jacob Whiled Away the Evening 'Yarning'"

Helping Powell and Lee, 1872

After John D. Lee, with his wives Rachel and Emma, took up residence at Lonely Dell (modern Lee's Ferry) in December 1871 and January of the new year, he waited anxiously for help that Jacob Hamblin had promised, but it did not arrive, and there were no visitors from the Mormon settlements. Finally, Lee traveled to Pahreah on March 3 and met Jacob, who had come to organize a branch of the church there. Jacob laid the blame for his long delay on Isaac Haight, a J. M. H. (possibly John M. Higbee, a reputed Mountain Meadows Massacre participant), and Jehiel McConnell "for not handing Me his letter of instructions & expressed his deep regret at their inhuman treatment towards us in our Isolation &c."[1] Satisfied with this explanation, Lee stayed to witness the branch organization, at which Allen Smithson was called to preside and John Mangum was selected as a counselor. However, when Jacob advised the settlers to store up grain and vegetables in Shirts's fort, Lee, always one to speak his mind, strongly advised against it, as he felt the fort was in a bad strategic position.

Hamblin and Lee stayed at Pahreah till about March 6. The Pahreah Saints generously divided their seeds with Lee, and Hamblin informed him that he had hired Joseph Mangum to help him at the Dell for a month or two. However, Mangum did not show up to work.

Hamblin sent the vineyard and orchards supplies that he had promised—2,000 grape cuttings, 120 apple trees, and more garden seeds.[2] Later, he sent 300 pounds of flour to Lee via Pahreah, but John Mangum reportedly appropriated it there.[3] Lee and Hamblin at this point had become entirely disillusioned with the Mangums.

In early May, Lee decided to relocate his cattle at Jacob's Pools, twenty miles away, halfway between the Kaibab Plateau and the Colorado, and installed his wife Rachel there.[4] As it soon became well known (to non-Mormons) that Lee had settled at Lonely Dell, and as he was avoiding the law (and vengeful Gentiles), he often spent time at Jacob's Pools. As Stephen Vandiver Jones wrote on August 8: "Here John D. Lee has built a willow shanty and here lives Rachel, one of his wives. Keeps about 40 cows."[5] This left the heroic Emma Lee running the ferry alone at the Dell, dealing with miners and Navajos by herself.[6]

25.1. John D. Lee's residence, the "willow shanty," at Jacob's Pools, an important stopping place east of the Kaibab Plateau on the Utah-Arizona wagon road. With Lee are three of his children, Joseph Willard, William Franklin, and Amorah Lee Smithson. Photograph by E. O. Beaman, June 3, 1872. Used by permission, Utah State Historical Society, all rights reserved.

In mid-May, Hamblin wrote to Lee and commended him for his work securing ranches at Jacob's Pools and Lonely Dell. Should the ferry slip into the hands of non-Mormons, he wrote, he, Hamblin, would be blamed, so he was grateful for Lee's efforts.[7] However, Lee continued to feel that Hamblin did not provide adequate support for him in his isolated position. The two men next met on August 24, as Hamblin was en route to Pahreah. "He apologised for neglect of duty," Lee wrote, "& yet he Said that he was not all togeather in fault," as he had sent supplies to Lee that Mangum had stolen. Again, Hamblin praised Lee for his faithfulness in his mission at the Pools and Lonely Dell. Though he had been treated badly, he said, Lee "had done more on this Mission than all the rest & as a reward for My integrity, I [Lee] have the promise of triump[h] & that I Shall never be captured by My Enemies & that I Shall come fourth in the resurrection of the Just & no Power Shall hinder &c."[8] Clearly, despite Lee's excommunication, Jacob still valued him. The two men would continue to work as firm allies until their final bitter parting of the ways.

John Wesley Powell had two major objectives in 1872: first, continue boating down the Colorado, from Lee's Ferry onward. There was no need to go all the way to the mouth of the Virgin River, but Powell wanted to travel through the Grand Canyon again, more slowly, for scientific purposes. Second, Powell and his party would continue the Powell Survey, mapping the Grand Canyon and surrounding areas.

The Powell boating group left Lee's Ferry on August 17.[9] After successfully navigating Marble Canyon and a good stretch of the Grand Canyon, they arrived at the mouth of Kanab Creek on September 7, where they heard a halloo on the north bank of the river. It was George Adair, with Nathan Adams and young Joe Hamblin, the company's "faithful packers," with provisions and mail. Stephen Vandiver Jones wrote that the Mormons brought news of general Indian troubles, from the Utes in the north[10] to the Shivwits at St. George, who, after an altercation with the Mormons, had retreated to their normal territory in the mountains south of the Mormon settlements, "threatening vengeance on the whites."[11] Jones wrote that Jacob had "started across the river to try and keep the Co-ho-ne-nee's from joining the Shivwits. Hamblin and Bishop [Stewart?] both send word that it will be unsafe for us to go farther."[12]

In the letter to Powell, Jacob explained,

> Our home Indians Say the Sevits [Shivwits] hav found the bodys of the Family they suspected ware murderd ner [near] Mt Troumble. That and the Indian that was kiled in St George has raised their feelings towards the whites to that extent they hav sworne vengance on the setlers. They wanted the clary Inds. to go over river [?] and help them. They refused to goe. The Sevits hav moved their Familys all over the Colerado and want to get help of the Cohoneneys and other bands to help them.[13]

I have found nothing substantial about the Shivwits family that was killed near Mount Trumbull, but Mormons were believed to be responsible for the deaths. Therefore, Clem Powell wrote, the Shivwits, who naturally associated the Powell company with Jacob Hamblin and the Mormons, were "on the lookout for our party for revenge."[14]

The Indian killed in St. George is better documented. In June several hundred Indians, apparently Shivwits, began to camp near St. George and reportedly helped themselves to the crops of the Latter-day Saints, which the Mormons found to be a "heavy tax." On August 3, some Mormons shot and severely wounded a Paiute. "Our boys were hasty and not altogether justified in shooting," wrote Erastus Snow to Brigham Young. The Indian was brought into town and his wound was treated, but he died about a week later, on August 11. The Mormons gave the Paiutes presents and they dispersed, but still felt angry at the killing.[15]

Therefore, Jacob advised Powell, "My feelings is that it would not be [advisable] for you to send them [your men] into their [the Shivwits'] country until we lurn more about it." He stated that he was on his way to Moenkopi, and would try to talk to "the Cohononeys" while there to judge their views on the conflict. The term

"Cohononeys" was derived from the Hopi name for the Hualapai and Havasupai Indians.[16]

Powell conferred with Almon Thompson and they decided that it would be wise to discontinue their boat voyage and return to Kanab, both because the river was abnormally high for that time of year and because of the danger from Indians. As the group turned up Kanab Canyon on the ninth, this marked the end of Powell's second Colorado expedition.

Jacob's trip across the Colorado to consult with the Hualapai and/or the Havasupai is not documented anywhere but in Jones's diary and in Jacob's August 27 letter to Powell and Thompson. He said he was planning on being gone from ten days to two weeks. He must have left Kanab on about August 27 and returned by September 12, for when the Powell company arrived at Kanab on that date, Jacob was there.[17]

Fred Dellenbaugh, exhausted after the trek up Kanab Canyon, went to the Powell storehouse, a log cabin in Jacob's corral, gathered a number of blankets, laid them out in Jacob's garden, and instantly fell asleep. He slept dreamlessly, and when he returned to consciousness Jacob was bidding him good morning. After washing, he breakfasted on peaches and melons at "Sister Louisa's."[18]

Not long after this, Jacob's fifteenth biological child, Priscilla's sixth, Mary Elizabeth, was born, on September 25.[19]

John Wesley Powell next turned to a substantial geographical survey of the Grand Canyon area. The Powell Survey, though less dramatic than the adventurous boat trips down the Colorado, was equally significant, as Powell and his men mapped southern and southeastern Utah and northern Arizona, taking photographs, making geological and anthropological notes, and collecting plant specimens.[20] Wallace Stegner characterized the Powell company as scientific amateurs, which was technically true;[21] nevertheless, some of them, notably Almon Thompson, were talented men who learned fast, and their accomplishment was significant. Powell's survey differed from its competitor surveys in its anthropological focus, the result of Powell's intense interest in Indians.

Jacob was a key support for this effort. Historian Herbert Gregory writes, "To no small degree the success of the [Powell] land surveys [was] due to the skill and knowledge of Utah men employed as guides and packers—particularly William D. [Derby] Johnson, George Adair, Jacob Hamblin, Fred Hamblin, George Riley, and Nathan Adams."[22] (I would also add Jacob's sons, Lyman and Joseph.) Jacob clearly was the leader in this group; of all Mormons, he knew the territory east of St. George and Kanab, and the Colorado, especially from the Crossing of the Fathers to the lower Colorado, better than anyone. While he lacked the thoroughgoing scientific outlook of Powell's group, he contributed significantly to their scientific accomplishments.

Kanab would continue to be a major meeting place for the Powell survey. Though the Powell men generally lived in camps outside the town, they sometimes lived in town itself, and often visited one another. When her husband left on an expedition, Almon Thompson's wife, Ellen (John Wesley Powell's sister), resided in a large tent in the corner of Jacob's garden and ate her meals with Louisa.[23] When Fred Dellenbaugh was convalescing with a leg injury in September and October 1872, he stayed in Kanab and also ate with Louisa.

Traveler and journalist John Beadle visited Kanab in 1872, and stayed two days in the Hamblin home. Jacob evidently was not shy in his proselyting: "Hamlin ... struck it on the subject of Mormonism the first meal," Beadle wrote. "But as I was once more in the land of beef and biscuit, hot coffee and other luxuries, I could stand up to any amount of argument." Whatever they were arguing about, Mormon religion or Utah politics, the discussion did not stop after that first meal. "We had it hot for two days, but parted friends," according to Beadle.[24] Jacob Hamblin's home served as a locus for hospitality in Kanab.

Hamblin's contributions to the Powell survey were varied. First, as we have already seen, he was an invaluable guide through the forbidding country of southern Utah and northern Arizona. In addition, he served as a guide for Powell in his dealings with the local Indians. He acted as interpreter, and also introduced Powell and his men to important Paiute, Hopi, and Navajo gatherings and headmen. Stegner correctly writes of Powell among the Uinkarets and Shivwits, "His introduction by Jacob gave him great status."[25] Jacob helped facilitate any number of transactions with Indians. On May 20, Almon Thompson simply wrote, "Distributed goods to Indians. Jacob helped."[26] On August 5, Jacob acted as interpreter as Powell tried to convince chief "Frank" and the Kaibab Paiutes that they needed to live on a reservation.[27]

One of the key accomplishments of the Powell Survey was photography, and Hamblin often helped arrange for the Indians to be captured on film. A diary entry from Clem Powell gives his view of the Paiutes around Kanab, and shows Hamblin's involvement in a photography session:

> An Indian pow-wow was again in order. For some time the Kaibab Indians have been hanging about in ever-increasing numbers. Having heard that goods were on the way for them, they have carelessly inquired, "How many sleeps (days) blankets come?" They are always hungry, firmly believing that a feast is vastly better than enough. Andy makes them rustle sage-b[r]ush and pack water in part payment of the biscuit they consume.... We have them make moccasins for us; they are the easiest shoes to travel in [that] the world can produce. While making these notes, squaws, papooses, and braves have gathered about, squatting in a circle. "Prof." told them that the Big Chief at Washington wanted very much to see them. I accordingly took their pictures. Ham[b]lin acted as interpreter. This is Frank's band.[28]

Whites often characterized the Paiutes of this era as beggars, but this passage shows that, when given the opportunity, they were very willing to work in exchange for food and clothes.

On Oct. 4, Clem recorded another frontier "sitting": "After breakfast Maj., Jacob, Jack, and I drove over to the Pa[i]ute camp to picture it; were at [it] nearly all day. Braves, squaws and pampooses were done up in the most artistic fashion, as also was the Ancient Arrow Maker."[29] This entry shows that the Powell photographers were not photographing Paiutes realistically, by the generally accepted anthropological standards of our day. In fact, Powell sometimes even gave buckskin clothes and Ute garments to Paiutes to wear, to make especially striking pictures, instead of the minimal clothing they normally wore.[30] Despite this, many of these photographs are anthropological treasures. For example, they document how the Paiutes harvested seeds, and the baskets and grinding implements they used to do so.[31]

Jacob also served as a supply master for the survey. The journals of the Powell men are full of references to buying food, animals, and other material from him.[32]

Almon Thompson, the chief cartographer of the survey, often consulted Jacob, and the Mormon explorer's experience helped Thompson work out geographical problems. On July 21, he journalized, "Talked with Jacob. I am certain from Jacob's talk and Ives map, that the Cataract Creek of Ives and Coenina Canon of Frank are the same, and Ives has made a big mistake in placing the little Colorado as far west as he has. It is too far by 60 miles."[33] When Thompson led a company (including Pardyn Dodds and Dellenbaugh) to the Escalante River and the real Dirty Devil River in May, June, and July, he was continuing the explorations of Hamblin and Dodds the previous year.[34]

Hamblin's twelfth journey across the Colorado took place because of his Powell company work. It included only a small group, himself and three Powell men, photographers Jack Hillers and Clem Powell, and cook Andrew Hattan.[35] Powell and Hillers would take photographs of the Hopis and of the territory along the way, and they would try to obtain more Hopi cultural items for Powell's museums in the east. In addition, as usual, there would be trade.

By 1872, the journey to the Hopi Mesas had almost become a matter of course for Jacob. Indeed, there were now Mormon settlements all the way from St. George to the mouth of the Paria, and the Mormons were close to creating a usable if primitive road to Lonely Dell. It was a far cry from the first trips to the Hopis, when these early adventurers would nearly starve to death northwest of the Colorado on their return journeys. The crossing of the Colorado was much easier, and Lonely Dell would soon become a full-fledged ferry. On the other side of the Colorado there were still uncertainties regarding water sources, but now that the Navajos were generally peaceful and often friendly, that part of the journey was much less dangerous.

While this was not an especially dramatic trip to the mesas, the diaries of Powell and Hillers give a good idea of what it was like to travel and camp with Jacob Hamblin. The four men left Kanab on October 9 with ten horses and mules and a wagon.[36] Jacob's journey to Lonely Dell was interrupted at the first camp, Navajo Wells, when Fred Dellenbaugh and Charley Riggs rode in at dawn on the tenth with news that Navajos had driven off seventy-five horses and mules from "Summit Creek"; Jacob and Charley rode off to intercept the thieves at the Crossing of the Fathers, or at a narrow passage leading to the Crossing. However, at the Pahreah settlement Jacob apparently received information that led him to doubt the report, or caused him to think that the thieves were Utes and not Navajos, so he turned south and came directly to Lonely Dell. He was there on the twelfth, with John D. and Emma Lee, when Hillers, Clem Powell, and Hattan arrived.[37]

The five men sought to resurrect the *Nell*, a sunken Powell boat that had been left there. Having no success, they spent a few days and made a new skiff.

On the sixteenth, the little company finished crossing the Colorado at sunset and surmounted "Lee's Backbone" by moonlight. They "skirted the base of the cliffs to the southwest, climbed and descended one steep dangerous cliff safely," Clem Powell wrote. At about ten o'clock at night they camped at "Ten Mile Spring."[38]

Part of Jacob's function in the group was entertainment around the campfire. "Jacob whiled away the evening 'yarning,'" wrote Clem on October 17. In this part of the trip, the company passed by "a wilderness of sand, with here and there lying scattered about a rocky butte or a distant range of cliffs."

As was typical of the trip from Lee's Ferry to the mesas, water was a perpetual worry. On the nineteenth, Hillers described a waterless day; in the evening, after climbing a cliff, they traveled till nine p.m. Then, "Jacob took a few canteens, knowing that water was in the neighborhood. He returned with them filled. Had supper and rolled up in blankets." Clem tells us that at this camp, "Jacob entertained us with a history of his past life."[39]

On the twentieth, after finding large quantities of water in pockets of stone, Hillers wrote, "Hamblin mistook his direction and another dry camp was the result." However, Clem describes Jacob shooting a rabbit, which tasted good when cooked at Whitmore's Pool.[40]

The next day the company met a group of nine Navajos, led by an elderly headman, Ko-neko, on their way to trade in the Mormon settlements. "Hamblin is well acquainted with Quinico," wrote Hillers, "and they two set up a regular pow-wow." This was the chief we last met in October 1871, drumming on a camp kettle for the night of uproarious dancing at Lee's Ferry. Jacob and friends continued on, camping at Quichintoweep, near the Moenkopi Wash, where Jacob told Hillers of the death of George A. Smith and how the rest of the company had escaped.[41] That night, Jacob became ill.

The little company reached Oraibi on the twenty-third, and Jacob visited Tuuvi's home, where Talasnimki invited them to dine on piki, "cano," and melons, which they ate thankfully. "Wandered about town looking at things in general," wrote Clem. "The Moquis all knew Jacob."[42]

That night Jacob and Jack Hillers were invited to a Hopi home to eat, and the main course was a corn and mutton soup eaten with fingers. Hillers "sailed in with my digits and pulled forth a dumplin," but Jacob told him not to eat it, as it had been prepared by the virgin of the house "to arouse the animal passion of the young warior and so hasten her marriage." Hillers took a leg of mutton instead.[43] So Jacob served as cultural adviser to another white on his first introduction to a very alien culture.

The company then visited a number of Hopi towns, traveling to Sichomovi (which Clem called Moquis) on the First Mesa the next day, and spending a few days photographing the towns of the First Mesa. Jacob spent his time trading and herding the group's troublesome animals.

They came to Mishongnovi on the Second Mesa on the thirtieth, then the next day returned to Oraibi, where they had an open invitation to stay at Tuuvi's home. The following day, as they faced the end of their stay, Jacob evidently made a final effort to obtain materials that Powell wanted for his museum back east. Clem wrote, "To day Jacob had hard work in getting the rest of the stuff and finally could only get part, the Moquis looking on us with distrust. Got a couple of looms with blankets partly woven by paying big prices." Tuuvi was going to Moenkopi the next day, and Jacob and the photographers decided to go with him.[44]

They left Oraibi on November 3 and reached Moenkopi the following day. Clem described it as cottonwoods scattered along a creek, near which were about six Hopi houses. The Hopis raised corn, melons, beans, and cotton in a large garden watered from springs. There the four men were able to bathe thoroughly and change their clothes on a raw, chilly, overcast day. At dinnertime, Tuuvi invited the men to spend the night in his "cabin," and as rain looked imminent, Clem and Jacob accepted the invitation. The three men ate piki, melons, and onions for dinner, then smoked.[45]

On the fifth, Jacob, Powell, Hillers, and Hattan set out for home, with a Paiute who lived in the area for a guide; they came to Tuuvi's cotton field, probably Moenave, after eight to ten miles, and reached the Paiute's farm fifteen miles after that.[46] Now they faced the long, dry stretch northward with Echo Cliffs to the east. Clem left a poignant expression of how tedious these seemingly adventurous journeys could be: "The thoughts of the long dreary rides are perfectly sickening," he wrote.[47]

They ascended and descended Lee's Hill on the seventh and in the twilight came to the Colorado. They shouted across the river, and soon Emma and twelve-year-old Billy Lee were coming for them in their boat. The four men left most of their baggage, crossed north of the Colorado, and then enjoyed a warm supper cooked by Emma. Clem and Jacob browned and ground a supply of coffee for Emma, and she agreed to cook bread for their trip to Kanab. Clem was quite impressed with Mrs. Lee: "She told us of the trouble she had in crossing the Navajos. She certainly is a woman of pluck," he wrote. Jacob made a rat-trap for her as she boiled a pot of beef, then he and his companions spread out their blankets on corn husks inside the house—a luxury after days of sleeping under the stars.[48]

They left the following day and arrived at Jacob's Pools at sunset on the ninth, where they met John D. Lee. "The 'elder' [Lee], of course, gave us a warm greeting and invited us to a supper of mush and milk with his 'Happy Family,'" wrote Clem Powell. "Gave him the gun. Jacob slept at the house; I slept alone."[49]

Jacob wanted to spend the day at the Pools, but the three non-Mormons were anxious to get to Kanab, so the group pushed ahead, reaching the town just after sundown on the eleventh.

On the tenth, Jacob and his group had met some of Wheeler's Survey, another geographical expedition, who told them that Ulysses Grant had been re-elected president, "which made Jacob draw a fearful long face," Clem wrote.[50] The legal pursuit of leading Mormons by Republican appointees in Utah would continue. On October 2, 1871, Young had been arrested for polygamy. The real name of this case, Judge James McKean famously said, is "Federal Authority versus Polygamic Theocracy."[51] And on January 2, 1872, Young had been indicted for murder, resulting from the accusations of Mormon enforcer Bill Hickman. Judge McKean put Young under house arrest and refused bail. Young was released from these charges on legal technicalities in April, as a result of the Englebrecht decision in the Supreme Court (which also gave a "get out of jail free" card to men recently prosecuted for polygamy under the antipolygamy Morrill Act of 1862).[52] Nevertheless, as Newell Bringhurst writes, these legal conflicts with the federal government "further dramatized the fact that Mormonism's frontier sanctuary was rapidly disappearing." The Mormons would have to learn to live by federal law, a painful period of adjustment that would last well into the next century.[53]

One of Young's responses to this challenge to the Mormon cultural and ideological framework was to renew his search for a place of refuge outside of U.S. federal authority—south of Utah, in Arizona and Mexico.[54] Young's old friend Thomas Kane returned to Utah during the winter of 1872–73, and the two men began planning Mormon colonies south of the Mexican border.[55] And a key way station between Utah and Mexico would be Arizona. A significant barrier to emigration south of Utah was the Colorado, and therefore, Lonely Dell (and the other possible ferry site, at the mouth of the Grand Wash) had great strategic importance for the Mormon prophet. Jacob, as explorer, thus had become an important figure in Young's ongoing chess game with the U.S. government. No one knew the crossings of the Colorado better than he did, and no one knew the area south of the Colorado better.

For Young's plan to succeed, there needed to be a working ferry, with ferryboat, at the mouth of the Paria, and a road from Kanab to the ferry, as well as a road south of the Colorado, and to future Mormon towns in Arizona.

It is remarkable that the man entrusted with the ferry would be an excommunicant Mormon in grave legal jeopardy due to mass murder charges. Nevertheless, John D. Lee was an energetic, excellent choice for the job—if only the Mountain Meadows charges had not been hanging over his head. Jacob was also a crucial link in the plan to create a ferry and build a road to it. He would often deliver instructions and messages to Lee, as well as workers, equipment, and material.

Jacob visited Long Valley from November 14 to 17, possibly to make arrangements for timber to be sent to Lee for building a ferry boat.[56] At any event, on December 16, a carpenter, "Uncle Tommy Smith," arrived at Jacob's Pools with gunwales and sixteen hundred feet of lumber.[57] After Smith helped Lee with his rock home at the Pools, the two men went to Lonely Dell and began to build a ferryboat. They also assessed the best place for the ferry, and for roads on both sides of the river. They decided that a site a half mile above the Paria mouth would be the best place for the ferry, though Jacob had recommended a site below the Paria, which was easier to reach on the northwest side, but harder to approach on the southeast side, and was submerged in times of high water.[58]

Jacob then sent Lee some spikes for the boat, used to nail the cross-planks to the gunwales, via James Jackson, a young schoolteacher, who arrived on the twenty-third.[59]

The day after Christmas Jacob sent Lee a message by Indian runner that Lee summarized in his diary:

> He [Jacob] was Notified by Telegraph to be at St. George by the 28 inst., as Prest. B. Young & Suite, also The Hon. Thomas L. Kane & Lady, to hold a two days Meeting. Gen. Kane has rentd a Room for the winter. That the Destrict Judges [as opposed to the Mormon judges] were all quiet, waiting for congress to appro[pri]ate Money. There is doubtless a Storm gathering; the Message of Pres. Grant Strongly indicates it. The Ferry Boat Must be in & the Road Made preparitority for the Emergency. Jacob Said the [President, i.e., Young?] would likely be in to the River within 15 to 20 days. Wanted me to feed Jackson & the Indian (Tocotaw). Jackson was to Stay at the Dell & assist in growing vines &c.[60]

A storm was gathering—apparently Young felt that intolerable legal persecution of the Mormons was approaching, and another major Mormon exodus, south of Utah to Arizona and Mexico, might be necessary.[61] Therefore, a ferry across the Colorado must be ready.

Jacob thus apparently spent the last days of 1872 conferring with Brigham Young, Thomas Kane, and, doubtless, St. George stake president Joseph W. Young who, despite his bad health, would be in charge of the mission to Arizona the following year (Erastus Snow having been sent on a European mission).

26

"We Wass the First Ones That Ever Crosed the Cilored with Wagons"

Mormons to Arizona, 1873

To carry out their plans for a Mormon colony in Mexico, Brigham Young and Thomas Kane decided that Kane would leave in the spring to look into the Sonoran land grant. Young, in turn, would build a road to Lee's Ferry, send an exploring party to the Little Colorado in Arizona in January and February, then would boldly send a group to settle on the Little Colorado later in the year.[1] In both these expeditions, Jacob would serve as a guide. In addition, Jacob, under the influence of Tuuvi, had been enthusiastic about Moenkopi-Moenave as a place of settlement for some time, and now wanted to establish a Mormon presence at that oasis.

On January 22, 1873, Jacob wrote in his diary: "I started for Ft Defiance and to goe with a company to form a setelment or start a colony in Arzoni."[2] Our other two early sources for this expedition (called The Arizona Exploring Company) say nothing of a possible settlement as the purpose of this expedition but instead talk only of exploration. Bleak wrote that the company planned to "explore the San Francisco Mountain country, in Arizona."[3] Lee also referred to the group as "explorers" going to the San Francisco Mountains, which would be "the Probably Rout for the rail Road from Salt Lake into Arazona."[4] Young wrote to his counselor Daniel Wells that the company would explore the area south of the San Francisco Mountains, and the rivers "flowing there from, with the view of learning the character of the country and to ascertain its capabilities for settlement."[5] If this was an exploring expedition, it was preparing for a settlement in Arizona soon after.[6]

A letter of instruction, apparently a letter from Young summarized or quoted by Bleak, tells more about the exploring company's purposes. They were instructed to go "to the East of the San Francisco Mountain until they intersect the head waters of the Rio Verde"—a geographical impossibility, as the Verde River is actually southwest of the San Francisco Mountains, so Young presumably means the Little Colorado—"then to travel down the river till they are satisfied as to the character of the country, the nature of the soil, facilities for irrigation, timber, stock-range &c &c." Jacob was directed to "organize a corps of Indian scouts" to take reports to Kanab and bring instructions—a unique and overly optimistic communications plan.[7]

Jacob had received a telegram from Brigham asking him to take "some trusty Indians" and travel with the company,[8] which was organized at Toquerville on the twenty-second.[9] Lorenzo Roundy, bishop of Kanarraville, who had come south as a missionary with Jacob in 1854, led the company, while Jacob served as "captain of the Indians," as Lee put it.[10] Aside from Jacob and Roundy, the members of the company included a number of veterans from previous trips across the Colorado: Jehiel McConnell (historian or clerk), Andrew Gibbons and Ira Hatch (interpreters), Isaac Riddle, and Mosiah L. Hancock. Also in the group were William J. Flake, Gideon A. Murdock, Barnard "Barney" Greenwood, Myron Roundy (Lorenzo's son), James Brigham Thompson, Heber J. Mulliner, Pahreah resident Lehi Smithson, and a Paiute, To ka tann (aka Tocotaw).[11]

Jacob rode ahead of the company with his fourteen-year-old son, Benny, and met John D. Lee at Jacob's Pools on the twenty-sixth, informing him of the exploring company that was following. After this, Jacob and Lee engaged in an elaborate trading session, in preparation for Jacob's trip to the Hopi mesas. Lee came to Lonely Dell on January 28 and found Allen and Lehi Smithson waiting there for Jacob—Lehi to come on the expedition, Allen to help build the road.

Jacob and Benny arrived the following day, and Lee showed Jacob the route to what he felt would be the best ferry location. Smithson quickly agreed with Lee's choice. On the thirtieth, Jacob admitted that Lee's location was better than his own, according to Lee, but apparently still wanted his route considered. Jacob spent a couple days of rest regulating his packs and doing more trading.

The exploring company arrived at Lonely Dell on February 1, and Lee transported nine men, fifteen horses, and their baggage across the river on that day. The men then crossed back over to spend the night at Lee's home. After dinner, they had a formal meeting, giving talks, singing, and reading the letter of instruction from Brigham Young.

The next morning, Lee crossed three baggage wagons over the Colorado. The only mishap occurred when one of Jacob's horses, which was carrying a heavy pack, fell overboard. They were able to save the horse and pack, but Lee criticized Jacob for overpacking his horse as it was being ferried.

Jacob left Benny with Lee and led the company south. They stopped at Moenkopi, where Jacob and apparently Ira Hatch split from the group and came to Oraibi on the seventh. Jacob wrote that he found the Hopis "in ill youmer onacount of the Americans comeing thare to give them presants." The Hopis may have felt that accepting such presents would obligate them to an alliance with the government in some way.

The following day, Hamblin and Hatch hired a multilingual Hopi as a guide for the exploring party.[12] Then they linked up with the main company at Black Falls on the Little Colorado. Roundy was not impressed with Hamblin's Indian negotiations, and in his report to Brigham, he groused, "Jacob came to us with one Oriba gide. The Indian Department was a failure. Would not [have] got any [Indian guide] if I had not sent Br Hatch."[13] This statement is somewhat enigmatic, as it does not make clear who brought the guide, Hamblin or Hatch.

Then for a day and half the company "explord up the little Colorado," as Jacob wrote. He described this area in glowing terms: it had "larg furtile bottams coverd with heavy groves of cotton wood serounding rich ~~and~~ lu[x]erant groth of grass."[14] They apparently traveled as far as the area near modern Winslow.[15]

When the company turned toward the San Francisco Peaks, the Hopi guide refused to go any farther and left them, saying that they were going into Apache country, and the Apaches would kill them. Roundy offered him a horse if he would act as Indian interpreter for the company, to no avail.[16]

On the tenth, Roundy's company ascended the bench of the San Francisco Peaks. "Mutch grass some cedar volcanic peaks on eather side," Jacob wrote. They camped in the San Francisco forest, and the next day rode through territory in which the snow touched the bellies of their horses.[17] They followed the Beale Road, passing south of the San Francisco Mountains.[18]

Apparently Jacob departed from the main group now, accompanied by Lehi Smithson. "I left Bro Roundy's Company in the San Francisco forrest," he wrote to Brigham Young in March. "Capt Roundy thot it advisable under the circumstances for me to do so and visit the Moquis & Navajo Indians."[19]

At about this time, Roundy once again took a potshot at Jacob in his report to Brigham Young. "When we got out of the forest"—apparently the forest around the San Francisco Peaks—"we came into a warm country again. Wher Jacob could settle all the Saints in this vacinity ~~of~~ round them mountains I faild to see."[20] Jacob had apparently recommended this area for settlement, in addition to the Little Colorado, but according to Roundy, at least, this would be impossible.

Jacob and Smithson descended the San Francisco Peaks on the thirteenth and the following day camped on the Little Colorado. On the seventeenth, they were in Oraibi, visited Walpi on the First Mesa from February 21 to 24, then returned to Oraibi. They hunted horses, then on the twenty-eighth left for home.[21]

Jacob summarized his reception by the Hopis and Navajos to Young:

> I found these invariably much pleased to see me. The first question generally asked by them was, "When are your people going to come over here to live." I

> generally answered there will be some come pretty soon. They said, we hope so. We want to be one with you—I am satisfied that this is the feeling among 30,000 of the Natives, at least. I did not see that many, but heard from them. Many of the Navajos asked me if I thought there would be a chance for them to get a living among our people by work.[22]

Thirty thousand is a major overestimate! Hamblin also wrote that there was a difference of opinion among the Hopis concerning the Saints: "The Oribe's are divided on the Mormon Question," Jacob wrote. The Oraibi hereditary chief, Lo Le Lama, and Tuuvi headed different parties, the chief arguing that "the Mormons & Americans are of the same spirit, and that their [the Hopis'] Women would be diseased there, as in other towns, if they were to strike hands with the Mormons." Tuuvi, however, argued that the Mormons were "the people spoken of by their forefathers, and instances our rapid increase in the last few years."

Hamblin described Moenkopi:

> Mo-en-cop-pe Wash runs throu a rich grass country for 100 miles no cactus, or sage, but some scrub Cedar. This Mo-en-cop-pe as it is called by the Moquis is a cliff of Rock for about 25 miles, ranging East & West out of the South face of which ooses many springs of pure water, I counted 40...One of them I think yields water enough to turn a small mill.

He wrote that the Hopis at Moenkopi wanted Mormons to live among them to build a strong storehouse (much of their grain had been stolen the previous year).[23]

Lorenzo Roundy, with eleven men, crossed the Colorado on February 25, and Hamblin and Smithson arrived at the river a week later, on March 4.[24]

Jacob stayed at the Dell for two full days. Lee had given him some animals (presumably in a trade) and Jacob had sold them very advantageously for "stocking yarn, Tinware, Flannels, Axes, Blankets &c."—he gave some of this to Lee.[25] One day Jacob and Lee boated up the river five miles to visit an oak grove, where they found a curious artifact, a plough beam with two bolts of iron, which must have drifted down the river somehow over the years. The men loaded up their skiff with oak wood and returned to the ferry site.[26]

Just after lunch on March 7, Hamblin, with Lehi Smithson, Jackson, "litle Benny," and Lee's daughter Amorah, set off on the road north,[27] arriving at Kanab probably on March 8 or 9. Hamblin's newest child, George Oscar, Louisa's third, was born two weeks later, on March 25.[28]

Roundy delivered a report on his explorations at stake conference in St. George on May 2. Like Hamblin, he was essentially positive about the Little Colorado country. The climate was warm and favorable, he said, and he thought "the facilities for settling" along the Little Colorado were "very good." Cottonwood timber was abundant, the land was rich, and there was plenty of grass and water. The river's water was a "little brackish," but not as bad as the Virgin. He had seen timber fifteen to twenty miles away from the river, and he thought the area would prove to be "very excellent" stock country. He said that many Hopis were anxious to settle on the Little Colorado, with Mormons.[29]

The actual colonization company that soon attempted to settle on the Little Colorado would not be as enthusiastic as Roundy. Historian Charles Peterson, in fact, suggests that Roundy knew the country was much worse than he reported, but the ideology of Mormon "manifest destiny" caused him to encourage the upcoming colonization effort. Part of the psychology of Mormon colonization, Peterson suggests, was to pick less fertile places for settlement.[30] (The most famous example of this was Brigham Young choosing Utah, instead of California, as the new Zion for Mormonism, after the Saints left Nauvoo.) Nevertheless, Roundy and Hamblin had explored the Little Colorado in the winter, when the country was at its best. In the summer, the country was drier, less green.[31]

Brigham Young was anxious to establish a colony in mid-Arizona, and even before receiving Roundy's report, he had begun to call settlers in typical Mormon fashion, giving them mission assignments to settle the area. This settlement would be a most difficult undertaking; Mormons on the Little Colorado would be far from Utah, would be in Navajo and Apache country, and would have to create their own roads at many points in their journey. The Little Colorado region, in upper Arizona, was not by any means a fertile crescent. Nevertheless, the settlers were called and asked to "take up their mission." In Brigham's view, an important part of this expedition would be to teach the local Indians: "To hire them to work to make farms plant vinyards, Gardens, build houses, and learn them to read, write, &c. &c. preach the Gospel to them, teaching them every principle that be conducive of makeing them happy and comfortable."[32] For a variety of reasons, this ideal for the Arizona mission was never fully realized.

Horton David Haight, who would be called to lead this colonization effort, was a forty-one-year-old native of New York, and had distinguished himself as a leader of companies traveling overland to Utah. He had also served with Lot Smith in the military groups trying to delay the U.S. Army in the Utah War.[33] In Dixie, Joseph W. Young, the St. George Stake President, would help to guide the expedition.[34]

The new colonizing missionaries traveled in different groups, but in all, the company included some 109 men, six women, one child, 112 animals, and 54 wagons.[35] The first group, under the leadership of John Bennion, set out from northern Utah with about nine wagons on March 26, and its movements are recorded by a spelling-challenged, but perceptive, Norwegian named Andrew Amundsen.[36]

Because of the rapidly approaching Haight expedition, locating the ferry at Lonely Dell and creating a workable road to it became an instant priority, and Joseph W. Young made a trip to Lonely Dell in early April.[37] On the way there, he met Hamblin, who reportedly spoke strongly in favor of his "lower" crossing, which he said was as good as Lee's but which would cost only a hundred dollars to build, while Lee's crossing, Hamblin said, would cost three thousand dollars.[38]

Young arrived at the mouth of the Paria on April 3, and Lee showed him the two possible ferry sites, his and Hamblin's. To Lee's immense satisfaction, Young pronounced Hamblin's location unsafe, and stated that his estimate of one hundred dollars for expenses was unrealistic. "We durst not trust Jacob's Judgement in Such things," said Young.[39] So the road was blazed to the site above the Paria mouth. However, despite Lee's moment of triumph, the competition between the two sites had not been definitively laid to rest. As Reilly notes, if Young had seen the two sites at a different time of the year, he might have chosen differently.[40] Lorenzo Roundy had preferred Hamblin's site to Lee's, and a few years later, a ferry site was created at Hamblin's lower crossing, because at that point, travelers would not have to surmount Lee's Backbone (though a steep dugway was still necessary to leave the canyon). This became the preferred ferry point, even though it was not usable at times of high water.[41]

Having selected the upper crossing, Joseph W. Young began building a road over the hill later called Lee's Hill or Lee's Backbone.

The Bennion-Amundsen company was in southern Utah in early April, reaching Kanab on the thirteenth, and Jacob talked with them that day.[42] He would accompany this group. Brigham Young had directed Joseph W. Young to enlist Jacob Hamblin as Indian expert for the Haight expedition, saying that Jacob "should make it his special business to do all in his power towards bringing the Indians into line, that is, to instruct them to work, to herd the stock, to act as watchmen, to learn our language &c."[43] Joseph W. asked Jacob to guide the company to the Little Colorado, then return to the mesas and Moenkopi and wait for further orders.[44] Jacob decided to take his son Benny, also, so that the young teenager could start to learn the Hopi language.[45]

Jacob started out with the Bennion company on April 16, but the following day, "Brother Hamling tuk very sick," with "the Flux" (diarrhea or dysentery), and continued sick the following day. On the twenty-first, the company reached Jacob's Pools, and Jacob "lay bye" there for two days under the care of Rachel Lee.[46]

The Bennion group crossed the Colorado on April 22 and 23 with no problems.[47] "The Morning wass very calm no wind, and the Rivver still, the Wether pretty and clear, birds singing and all injoyed a good spirit," wrote Amundsen. "We then comenst crosing ouer Wagons, all over sef and sound." That night, a group of men worked on the road up Lee's Backbone, and the next morning, the wagons surmounted the precipitous hill. Amundsen recorded the historic moment:

> In the Morning we started op the hill verry rokky and steep on both sides of the mountain and after gitting down to the foot no track nor road ever made, for we wass the first ones that ever crosed the Cilored [Colorado] with wagons, so we hed to break ouer [our] road all the way, and in som places very rough so that we hed to woke [walk] it.

Jacob, still sick, stayed at the ferry for a couple days more. On the twenty-third, he was "quite feeble," but the next day he was improving. He shared with Lee Brigham Young's instructions to him: "to take as Many of the prestant co. & explore the R[i]o verda Walnut grove & the head waters of the Litle Colerado & report."[48] He was also "to locate Said co. on some of the best territory that he could find." As it happened, he would not serve in this capacity at all, apart from an early exploratory journey up the Little Colorado. "Then direct his labours to the House of Iseral & turn the Indians into line & let them help the Brethren build up cities, Heard [herd], & Farm. Thus we see the Key of Salvation is about to [be] turned to the House of Iseral, as the gentiles reJect it."[49] Young was so intent on colonizing Arizona that this informed his view of the Indian mission—they would "help the Brethren build up cities."

On the twenty-sixth, Lee ferried Jacob and Benny over the great river,[50] and they quickly caught up with the Bennion company, who were continuing to work on creating a rough road south of the Colorado. They experienced typical difficulties finding water during their journey to Moenkopi, a task that was magnified by the need to find adequate drinking water for a large company, and to water its stock. In addition, finding feed for stock would be a pressing concern.

It was only at this time, on April 29, that the main Haight company was officially organized, back at Winsor Castle (Pipe Spring), on which date Joseph Young read an official letter to sixty-six members of the expedition. He officially appointed Horton Haight as president of the settlements on the Little Colorado, and called Ira Hatch to be "a pilot and Indian interpreter and missionary" for them. He gave Jacob an assignment that was not on the Little Colorado proper:

> Bro Jacob Hamlin is instructed to assist the Oribies to establish a farm at the Moencuppy. He has the liberty to ask eight or ten volenteers to stop and labor with him but we donot wish any of our brethren to remain there unless the Oribies manifest a willingness to co-operate with us in this work. Bro Jacob Hamlin will consider himself a missionary at large, and when on the South East side of the river he will be under the counsil and advice of Prest H D. Haight; and he is expected to make it his special business to labor among the Indians and endeavor to get them to fall into line and co-operate with us in herding, watching and taking care of Stock farming &c. &c. &c.[51]

The Bennion company reached Moenave, eight miles southwest of the Hopi settlement of Moenkopi, on May 1.[52] Amundsen described Moenave as a sandy place with a number of springs, a bottom eighty miles long with "plenty of Cottonwood along the creek."

Jacob immediately set out for Moenkopi eight miles away, returning the following day with Tuuvi and another Hopi, two women (probably Talasnimki, Tuuvi's wife, and the other Hopi's wife), two papooses, a Navajo, and two Paiutes. They "hed dinner with os," wrote Amundsen, "and hed a good time." The Indians returned to their settlement on the third. As the company waited at Moenave, they started to farm, plowing and planting seven acres of land. Haight wrote, "Bro Jacob Hamlin located here [at Moenave] at the suggestion of Tuby Chief of the Oribes who gave permission for him to occupy that ground to test our method of farming on."[53]

On Sunday, May 4, a "buetifull" but very warm morning, the company held a Sacrament meeting. "Brother Hamling spoke about som of hiss expirians, his traveles, the Lords goodnes towards his people and them that obey his lawes and keep his comandmends," wrote Amundsen.

The following day Jacob and a William H. Morrell set out on an exploring trip up the Little Colorado. On May 6, Jacob wrote in his journal, "Started to the oribes and to the 3 forks of the little Colorado." After their exploration up the Little Colorado (and to the mesas, apparently), Jacob and Morrell arrived back at Moenave on May 13, accompanied by Tuuvi, Talasnimki, and another Hopi.[54]

Another part of the Haight expedition, including Horton Haight himself, crossed the Colorado on May 11. Jacob traveled back to help this group on the seventeenth and returned with the Haight group two days later.[55]

On the twentieth, the combined companies left Moenave, and Haight addressed them at a meeting in the afternoon. He told them that he had been appointed president of the company, and called two men as counselors, Henry Holmes and John R. Bennion. He then read the letter from Joseph W. Young, which might have been the first time that Jacob learned that he had been called to actually settle at Moenave. Probably unbeknownst to Priscilla or Louisa or Jacob's Paiute wives, his new center of operations would soon be Arizona. Then, Amundsen wrote, Jacob himself spoke "on a good menny poyents,"

> Telling os a litle of his Experience in the Church, about his Travels amongst the Indians, bilding setlements, Forts and soforth, he sead that he herd Joseph Smith speek obout this move, more than 30 years ago. He sead he hed ben in the Church 33 years, and hed allso [always?] the seam Testimony to ber. He was glad to meet with so menny on this pressent Okesion, hoping the Lord wood bless all ov os.

For an insight into Mormon-Indian relations, it is worthwhile to hear what Ira Hatch ("ouer Indian interpreter and gide") and an Indian friend said at the same meeting. Hatch

> sed [he] wass allso glad, to be her[e], alltho the Cuntry [was] luking very rough. But he sead that we would sun [soon] git in to a better Country, if only we would be peashent. By request of [Horton] Hate The Indian Prests, named Sti-ti-a-ny spoke a litle, Inturpreted by Hach. He sed he wass glad to se so menny Mormons, and that he would like os for to Setle in an round their [there], so the[y] could herd ouer Stok. He sead he liked os all, and that he wass ouer Brother, he had a great menny recomends given him by the leeding Oficers of the U. S. Goverment, seaing [saying] that he wass a good man, for the[y] wass all read.

On May 21, Jacob returned to Moenave, and the Haight company went southwest along the Moenkopi Wash, reaching the Little Colorado the next day. In his official report to Young, Haight described the river as "a small amount of salty mineral water with quicksand and mineral bottom."[56] Not exactly flights of ringing praise! Powell's men had described the river as "a loathsome little stream…as disgusting a stream as there is on the continent."[57]

On the twenty-fourth, the company camped at a place they called Camp Utah, about eighty-seven miles from the (big) Colorado, and Haight and an exploring group of fifteen men (including William Morrell, Ira Hatch, Anson Call of Callville fame, and diarist Amundsen) set out down the river to find a suitable place for their colony. To their dismay, they found the Little Colorado country remarkably inhospitable. On May 25, Haight wrote, "Here we saw the only spot of green grass on the whole trip, about one-half acre."[58] The company battled through sandstorms and tried to keep their mounts from sinking into the plentiful quicksand near the river. After traveling five days and 136 miles downriver, they arrived at about the location of present-day Winslow and had seen enough. Amundsen wrote in his diary that, in the territory they had seen, there was "no Plase fit for a humen being to dwell opon"! He delivered a stinging indictment of the territory. Yes, there was water in the Little Colorado, but if the water was high, the bottoms would become flooded. (This was prophetic, as the eventual Little Colorado towns endured many floods and washed-out dams.) Next, there was no place for a dam, and if there was one, it would cause the water to back up six or eight miles up the river. In addition, the local trees were not adequate for building. The cottonwoods were "so scrubby and krukked" that they could only be used for firewood. There was also no rock for building nearby, and no pine timber within fifty or seventy-five miles. "Wher ever you may luck the Cuntry is all broken op," he wrote, one of those typical responses of newcomers to the beauty of desert country in the Southwest. He then closed his peroration with a Biblical fulmination. This was "the moste desert lukking plase that I evver saw, Amen."

In addition, it was fearsomely hot, the Little Colorado had actually dried up in places, and the water that remained was "brackish."[59]

Haight, in his report to Brigham Young, wrote,

> We can See nothing better ahead of us. The river closes in again above the upper bottom, the hills are red and bare, we have had heavy winds nearly every day, at times enveloping us in Storms of Sand.... With the poor feed and bad water our animals are failing and on the 29th we turned back. As we passed down the Stream we noticed the water failing; at the upper falls there was but little; at the lower or black falls it had stopped running.[60]

The exploring party arrived back at Camp Utah on June 1, and Haight sent two messengers, William H. Morrell and E. H. Evans, to President Joseph Young, giving him an account of the limitations of this forbidding country, the lack of water, and mistakes in Roundy's report, and asking for further instructions.[61]

At Moenave, Jacob planted thirteen acres of corn, beans, and other vegetables, watered from a large, pure spring. He later wrote to Brigham Young, "Tuby & some 20 other Oribes came down to farm some 8 miles above where I put in the crop. Tuby & his brethren are anxious to have assistance to build a mill & improve the Moyencoppy, to get out the water on the best of the land."[62] Thus, there was a Mormon settlement, Moenave, in the general Moenkopi area and, eight miles to the east, a Hopi settlement and farm, Moenkopi proper, where Tuuvi and about twenty Hopis worked.[63] Moenave thus became the first Mormon colony in Arizona, with Jacob its founder.

The Haight company reached Moenave on about June 4 and settled in to wait for direction from up north. Two days later, Samuel Rose Parkinson wrote in his diary, "I saw Jace Hamblin pres of the indains. He was traiding for spads howes axes flower or any thing he could get."[64] Haight and company waited, more and more impatiently as the days went by, since they had no adequate forage for their livestock (they eventually started feeding them the flour they'd brought for their own sustenance) and they had to endure typical desert temperatures, upwards of 120 degrees in the shade. Still, they doggedly awaited instructions from Joseph Young or Brigham Young.[65]

Finally, however, some members of the company starting trickling homeward.[66] And on June 22, the company received unsettling news from Morrell and Evans—Joseph W. Young, president of the Arizona mission, had died on June 7.[67] There were problems with telegraph connections in southern Utah, and they had received no response from a telegram they had sent to Brigham Young.

Feed and water for livestock was not sufficient at Moenave, and Haight began to allow settlers to retreat to Navajo Springs, not far from the Colorado.[68] A company including diarist Amundsen set out on the twenty-third, stayed at Navajo Springs for four days, then crossed the Colorado.[69]

On June 25, Haight received a message from Evans, stating that Lorenzo Roundy left an order for the company to retreat to Navajo Springs.[70] The main company traveled there and continued to wait for further instructions. According to Jacob's diary, he planted beans at Moenave two days later, then started for home with another part of the Haight company, leaving an elderly non-Mormon miner, John Winburn, to tend the crops at Moenave, entrusting to him a number of farming implements: plows, axes, picks, scythes, spades, and shovels, many of which the Haight company had donated to the cause in order to lighten their loads.[71]

At Navajo Springs, once again, Haight received no definitive instructions from St. George or Salt Lake City, and he finally decided to cross the Colorado, which the company did from July 4 to 7. Lest we forget the extreme difficulties encountered by these pioneers, Samuel Rose Parkinson states that the temperature at the time was 137 degrees in the shade. On the seventh, Haight formally disbanded the company and they started for their various homes.[72]

It is not known why Brigham Young did not answer Haight's messages promptly and directly. However, sometime before July 26, according to John D. Lee, Jacob received a telegram from Young directing "the A[ri]Zona Missionaries to remain South & recruit ther animals & prepare for another Move, as the Mission was not give up, & that Pres. B.Y. would be down in the Fall."[73] But it was too late. Most of the Haight company had already scattered to their former homes, probably vastly relieved that they had escaped what would have been an enormously difficult colonizing task in the Arizona desert.

Jacob Hamblin, in his 1881 memoirs, blamed the exploring group for not going far enough down the Colorado, and characterized them as having a "demoralizing spirit" and a "want of faith." Just past the area where they stopped, he asserted, were excellent places for settlement.[74] Jacob was especially chagrined that Mormons did not get into these choice areas before Gentiles did. Dan Jones also characterized the Haight company as lacking in faith.[75]

Brigham Young was angry at the retreat of the Haight company, and told a Salt Lake City congregation that if he had been part of the Arizona expedition, "there would have been good places [to colonize] found."[76] At one point, he reportedly said, "we sent a passel of Squaws down there—some of our pets whom we have raised in Salt Lake City. [We have] raised them on a feather pillow with silver spoons in their mouths. Men that don't know anything about a hard day's work or a privation—and they came away because the sun shone hot and the wind blew!"[77]

Members of the Haight expedition have disputed these characterizations sharply. Jacob Miller, a friend of Haight, angrily countered Hamblin and Jones specifically.[78] It is true that the authoritative early accounts by Haight and Amundsen described a horrific situation for the settlers: the heat, lack of water, the brackishness of the water when they could get it, fierce wind, sandstorms, lack of feed for their animals, quicksand that made approaching the river difficult—all of this added up.

Apparently, Jacob was right, technically. An early explanation of the company's failure stated that the Mormons simply had not gone far enough. In a dry year, the Little Colorado sank into quicksand in the valleys where the Haight company came; if they had followed the stream to its headwaters, they would have found "a fine stream of water in the river, large and rich valleys, and other inducements for settlement."[79] Silver Creek, the only tributary of the Little Colorado with consistent year-round flows, lay about fifty miles farther; later, Mormons would found successful towns on it. However, in defense of the Haight company, they had been sent in a dry year and probably at the wrong time of the year.[80] The exploring company traveled some 126 miles up the Little Colorado, until their animals were starting to fail them, and, as Haight wrote, they could see nothing better ahead of them.

Morrell and Ira Hatch, who had previously explored up the Little Colorado, were with the Haight exploratory company, and presumably agreed with his decision to turn back. Hatch, especially, was an able, experienced frontiersman.

In addition, there were disastrous communications failures with St. George and Salt Lake—the company waited for guidance and nothing definitive came in reply. The death of Joseph W. Young was a heavy blow—the company might have received instructions relatively quickly if he had not died. In addition, there were sections of the telegraph that were down in southern Utah, and such repairs often could not be made quickly. And apparently Brigham Young himself delayed in giving the Haight company quick, definitive instructions.

In retrospect, as historian Kevin Folkman has shown, the Haight expedition should be regarded more sympathetically than it was in the rough and tumble of early historical judgments. They had been sent in haste, during the dry season of a dry year, and had not been given reliable information on exactly where, on the forbidding Little Colorado, the best place to settle might be. Jacob Hamblin and Brigham Young should have taken partial responsibility for the difficulties and uncertainties the Haight expedition faced.

As Jacob Hamblin traveled north to Lee's Ferry, on June 27, he unexpectedly met Lee himself, traveling south.

Why was Lee south of the Colorado? On June 16, a windstorm had blown a tree onto the ferryboat at Lonely Dell, loosening it, and it drifted off into the rapids and was destroyed.[81] This was a devastating blow to Lee, who now had only a small skiff to work with in his ferrying operation. Brigham Young sent Lorenzo Roundy to assess the situation, and Roundy arrived at Lee's Ferry on the twenty-third, but decided it would be best to return to Kanab and telegraph to Brigham Young the latest news he had heard from Mormons returning from Arizona. While at the ferry site, he told Lee that a party of U.S. soldiers was coming down to build a fort at the ferry. Apparently,

26.1. John D. Lee's home at Moenave, Arizona. Jacob Hamblin, Lee, and the Hopi Tuuvi helped found the Mormon colonies at Moenave and Moenkopi, near modern Tuba City. Hamblin and Lee had heated words in this structure in 1874. Photograph by George Wharton James, about 1900. Reproduced by permission of The Huntington Library, San Marino, California.

he was repeating hearsay that was completely untrue, but Lee was unsettled by the news.[82]

Two days later two messengers from Kanab came to Jacob's Pools and told Lee that a military force of six hundred men with forty baggage wagons had passed Kanab en route to Lonely Dell, with orders to built a fort at the crossing, and that they were bragging that "they would hang old Lee & every child that had a drop of his Blood runing in its veins." While at Kanab, they had brutally turned their animals loose on the settlement's meager crops.[83] Shocked, Lee's family members immediately set out for Lonely Dell and relayed the message to John D.

None of this proved true, and no troops came to Kanab.[84] In retrospect, it sounds entirely unlikely. Nevertheless, Lee believed the messengers and immediately made plans to follow the Mormon settlers into Arizona. After a tearful parting from his family, he crossed the Colorado on June 25. "I swam My Horse over the foaming Colerado by a skift," he wrote, "& bent My way for the Mowencroppa, there to take up My abode with the House of iseral—Mokies, orabias, Piutes, & NavaJoes."[85]

When he met Jacob on the twenty-seventh and told him the "news," Jacob encouraged Lee to settle at Moenave with the friendly non-Mormon prospector John

Winburn, and tend the gardens there, while Jacob would try to look after Lee's settlements near the Colorado, and if necessary sell them off. So began the Moenave chapter in Lee's eventful life.

Lee reached Moenave that same day and was welcomed by Winburn, Tuuvi, and a local Paiute named Shew (known to the Hopis as "Cuckebur").[86] Industrious as ever, Lee immediately set to work farming. Tuuvi came to like him and respected his industry and his generosity to local Indians. Lee's wife Rachel would join him a month later.[87] Jacob arrived home at Kanab on July 4.[88]

In mid-August, Jacob set out again for Arizona, picking up James Jackson at Lee's Ferry; they arrived at Moenave on August 21.[89] Jacob brought news from north of the Colorado: Emma hoped she and her family would not be separated from John long; Brigham Young sent a message that he wanted Lee to stay at Moenave and take care of the crop there.

That evening there were light showers, but as it rained, Jacob, Lee, and Jackson sang some songs, then Winburn and Jackson slept while Jacob and Lee sat up and talked through the night "in council on the future." Jacob strongly urged John to stay at Moenave and leave the ranch at Jacob's Pools in the hands of some trusted friend. Lee said he would think about it.

The next day Jacob and Winburn traveled to Moenkopi to confer with "Tuby, Taltee & other lead Men" about Jacob's claim to the land and water of Moenave—or Lee's, if they "exchanged places."

Jacob came back the following day with the Hopi agent, William S. DeFrees, and three of his associates, and they dined with Lee.[90] Their talk was most encouraging. They hoped to create an extensive Indian farm for different tribes at Moenkopi, and build a mill and schools at the town. DeFrees unrealistically hoped to bring all the Hopis down from their mesas to live there. He and his colleagues were "much delighted" that Lee was planning to bring his family to Moenave.

On the twenty-fourth, Jacob and Lee made a formal agreement to "trade places": Jacob would take Lee's ranch at the Pools, and Lee would take Hamblin's farm at Moenave. Jacob agreed to care for Lee's cattle at the Pools for a one- to three-year term, and bring Lee's family to Moenave, with his own wagon if necessary. Blythe characterizes this exchange as a sale, and states that Moenave "was sold to John D Lee ~~with~~ and he claimed all that was raised upon it."[91] Reilly observes that this transaction was not formally valid, as no one had formal legal ownership of Moenave, but Tuuvi and DeFrees seemed to approve of it, so for practical purposes it worked. Squatters' rights often were the beginning of legal rights in the West.[92]

The next day Jacob left with Rachel (who was returning to the ranch at Jacob's

Pools to bring her children back to Moenave), Winburn, and Jackson, leaving Lee alone at the farm—though Tuuvi promised to visit frequently and Shew and his family also were living nearby.

Jacob returned to Moenave on September 7, with Rachel and nine Lee children, not to mention two of Lee's older daughters, Amorah and Nancy E. Dalton, and Nancy's husband Heber Dalton.[93] Lee was ecstatic: "We rejoiced together that My Prayers had been heard & answered, & My Family & Effects had been almost Maraculously preserved & brought through in safety, Bro. Hamblin acknowledge[d] the hand of the Lord & power of foreknowledg & said that he had fulfilled a vision or dre[am] that I had related to him 12 Month ago." In the dream, Lee had driven one of his wives in his wagon and team through deep water and to the desert.

This also marks the high-water mark of the alliance of Lee and Hamblin. Though the full-blown break between the two men would not occur till early November of that year, Lee in the following days, as was typical of him, portrayed Hamblin as having poorer judgment than Lee himself, and also as less honest. In November 1873, however, Lee began to write open attacks on Hamblin's character, both in his journals and in letters to Brigham Young.

On September 9, Jacob, Lee, Rachel, Heber and Nancy Dalton, Amorah Lee, and a Navajo chief traveled to Moenkopi where Tuuvi received them "with Marked Frindship." They feasted on melons, piki, and dried meat, then were required to visit another encampment and "feast again until we were ready to bust," wrote Lee. Then there was a talk. According to Lee, Tuuvi turned to Jacob and said:

"Jacob, you lie to us. You come & go."

Jacob replied, "I have brought a man that will not lie to you; he will stay here & be a Father to you."

"I thank you for sending a Man to live amoungst us," returned Tuuvi, "that will not lie to us. We will look to him & if the NavaJoes remain friendly, all right. If not, we will come to geather somewheres for Protection &c."[94]

One wonders about this conversation as reported by Lee. Would Tuuvi forthrightly call Jacob a liar to his face? And would Jacob calmly accept the accusation as valid, as he apparently does here, while recommending Lee as someone who is thoroughly honest—unlike himself? Such an exchange seems unlikely.

The next day two prospectors arrived in Moenave, and Jacob described the rich land near the San Francisco Mountains to them, so they decided to go there and stake out ranching claims before the next wave of Mormon colonists arrived. Lee was furious at Jacob for his "imprudence of talking to strangers & giving them a key to our interests." Jacob agreed that he had spoken thoughtlessly, according to Lee, and promised to talk to the miners and try to convince them to settle elsewhere.

Jacob had also informed Winburn that he would go with him to search for a gold mine that had been reported on the Little Colorado fifty years earlier if Winburn would tend crops at Moenave. However, now Jacob said that he had to return to Utah, and suggested that Lee take Winburn on the expedition instead. Lee grudgingly agreed.[95]

With the mining expedition on the Little Colorado arranged, and after more financial negotiations with Lee relating to the Jacob's Pools ranch and Moenave, Jacob left on the evening of September 12.[96]

Jacob was back in Kanab a little before the nineteenth.[97] In a letter he wrote to Young on that day, he said that he found that the crops, corn, beans, squashes, and melons were doing well at Moenave. As there had been a drought in Arizona, with rains coming twenty days late on July 20, the Hopi corn crop at the mesas—along with many Navajo corn farms—had failed. So the success at Moenkopi was most welcome, and many Hopis came to Moenkopi for corn. While the Oraibi chief, Lo Le Lama, had at first opposed the efforts of Tuuvi and Hamblin, lately he had "come round very goodnaturedly," wrote Jacob.[98]

Then he hinted that he needed to spend time in Kanab: "I find my home & family matters requireing some of my attention. I have spent the last nineteen years of my life mostly attending to Indian matters; have spent more nights under cedar & pine trees than in a house." Jacob was clearly suggesting that he needed to settle down now and tend to his family, but he quickly added that he did not regret his years among Indians and away from home. "I feel that I have been an instrument in the hands of the Lord in doing some little good, in preventing difficulties with our frontier settlements. I always have abhored the shedding of the blood of the ignorant red man especially since I have become more fully acquainted with his character."

In this same letter, he described the plight of the Indian in Utah, and the West, emphasizing how white ranchers encroached on the grasslands Indians depended on at certain times of the year.[99] "I anticipate better results in the future with our Arizona red men," Jacob wrote, "because of our experience and the more industrial habits they have acquired through the necessitous circumstances they have pased through."

At this point, John D. Lee, who had been subtly demeaning Jacob in his journal for some time, now turned against him with open enmity. It is hard to know how to assess Lee's attacks on Hamblin. If one were to accept them unreservedly, one would have to view Jacob as corrupt, manipulative, motivated by private gain, entirely dishonest, lying to Indians apparently as a general policy, and lacking in even minimally sound practical judgment.

We should keep a few points in mind while considering Lee's attacks on Hamblin. First, as Juanita Brooks pointed out, we do not have Jacob's side of the story in many of Lee's accusations.[100] In history, when we have a rich, full diary from only one side of a conflict, it is the path of least resistance for the historian to simply accept it and let it tell the main story.

Second, Lee was charismatic, likable, capable, and a fine writer; but most would agree that he was a profoundly flawed individual. Though it is typical of diaries and autobiographies for the authors to portray themselves in the best light possible (and Hamblin's writings are no exception), one is struck by the powerful egoism in Lee's diary. The force of Lee's personality either attracted people and repelled them, as we have seen in Thomas Brown's instant antagonism to him in Harmony in the 1850s.[101] In the dynamics of the Lee-Hamblin relationship, it is apparent that Lee considered himself the better man.

Finally, Lee often accused Hamblin of dishonesty, but he himself was sometimes not truthful. He often denied participation in the Mountain Meadows Massacre when people asked him about it.[102] He gave Brigham Young the first report on the massacre, evidently portraying it as an Indian affair. He was furious about his excommunication in late 1870 for his participation in the massacre. "I declared my innocence of doeing any thing designedly wrong," he told Brigham Young after his excommunication. The leading men in southern Utah had agreed, after prayer, that the mass killing was the right thing to do. "Our covenants & the love of Righteousness alone prompted the act."[103] He clearly felt no regret for his participation in the massacre.

Keeping these factors in mind, we will now consider Lee's accusations against Hamblin in his diary, but will also try to give Hamblin's side of the story when possible. My intention is not to present a hagiographic view of Hamblin, but to give a balanced view of him as a human being.

On November 5, Lee left Moenave for a trip to Lonely Dell, arriving there the following day.[104] Emma was overjoyed to see him. She had a new baby which she had delivered herself, or with the help of her older girls.

Lee was furious when he found that Emma had delivered the baby without any adult help, for, he said, Hamblin had agreed to send Mrs. Mangum to Lonely Dell as a midwife. Not only this, but as Lee and Emma compared notes, Emma told him that Hamblin, when passing through, had told her that she was wrong to have children by Lee, since he had been excommunicated.

On the first charge, one wonders how Jacob would have responded. Had he made arrangements with the Mangums for them to go to Lonely Dell? Brother Mangum had failed Lee and Hamblin before—had he done it again?

On the second charge, this seems to be a standard attitude among Mormons. If a man was excommunicated, women sometimes were encouraged to leave him, as their eternal marriage bond had been broken. When Lee was excommunicated, one of his wives counseled with Brigham Young, and he encouraged her to leave Lee.[105]

Without Jacob's side of the story, it is hard to know how to definitively assess these charges. But it is certain that John D. and Emma Lee had turned against him at this point.

27

"The Indians... Were Murdered in Cold Blood by One McCarthy and His Employees"

The Grass Valley Murders, Navajo Negotiations, and the Arizona Mission, 1874

In mid-December 1873, four young Navajo men—named Te Pa Gad Lu, Tagla Sa Gad, Te Che Chic Chu and Ne Chic Se Cla[1]—came to the Grass Valley, a long valley running north-south, just north of the East Fork of the Sevier River in south-central Utah, twelve miles east of Circleville, to trade with the Ute chiefs An-guh-teshaep and Joe.[2] Two of the Navajos were sons of Ketchene (the Navajo who had served as spokesman for the eighty or so Navajos who visited Kanab in September 1871), and another was his nephew.[3] After the Navajos completed their trading and began their journey back home, three of them were cold-bloodedly killed by whites led by an A. McCarty; the other Navajo was seriously wounded but somehow was able to make his way across the Colorado and back to Navajo territory.

This event, which acted as a tinderbox that nearly reignited a major Mormon-Navajo conflict, caused Jacob to take three trips across the Colorado in the first half of 1874, as he strove to negotiate with furious Navajos. As is typical of documentation of white-Indian violence in the American West, the actual event has become obscured by a tortured maze of contradictory historical traditions, some sympathetic to the Navajos, others casting the Indians as the aggressors, as well as some late Navajo oral traditions. The historian can only put the puzzle pieces together as logically and reasonably as possible.

Ironically, sincere Mormon attempts to further white-Indian peace precipitated the violence. In June and July of 1873, Brigham Young sent two Indian specialists, George Washington Bean and Bishop Albert King Thurber, to explore central Utah in the Sevier Valley, make peace treaties with local Utes, and find a good location for an Indian farm.[4] The forty-two-year-old Bean, who had lost his arm in a cannon accident twenty-five years earlier, was an experienced Indian interpreter, having dealt with Utes while living in Provo, in Utah Valley. A teacher by profession, he had served many missions for the LDS Church. When he was part of the Las Vegas Indian mission in 1855–1856, he probably knew Jacob.[5] Thurber, a forty-eight-year-old Rhode Island native, had converted to Mormonism as an argonaut. He spoke Ute and had had extensive dealings with the Utes as a resident of Spanish Fork, also in Utah Valley. In the early 1870s, he served as bishop and mayor of that town. He wrote that Brigham Young called him to relocate in Richfield, Sevier County, in 1874 specifically "to use my influence in the interests of peace with the Indians inhabiting and visiting that country."[6]

Bean and Thurber reported favorably on Grass Valley, which had a number of verdant, grassy meadows that would be ideal for farming and ranching.[7] Bean and Thurber planned to move to the general area and situate the Indian farm there. There were several camps of Utes in this vicinity, and they welcomed the Mormon plans.[8]

However, Bean and Thurber's report evidently sparked an interest in Grass Valley, and when they returned to the area in August, they found that a number of whites had quickly moved in and claimed many choice sites. Among them was a non-Mormon rancher, Dr. Alexander McCarty, who had a contract to supply beef to the troops at Fort Cameron, near Beaver.[9] He was accompanied by his sons, William and Tom, and an employee, Thomas Richards. Their ranch was situated in south Grass Valley; James H. Clinger, apparently a friend of the McCartys, lived about twenty-five miles north of them.[10]

Hamblin later wrote that McCarty was the type of white who hated Indians and sought to kill them on the slightest pretext.[11] McCarty notified Thurber in August 1873 that he and his men "had secured the country, and intended to keep it, and would shoot every Indian that came in their reach—not in company with a white man."[12] In addition, they were sometimes on the wrong side of the law. The two McCarty sons, Bill and Tom, later gained notoriety as rustlers and bank robbers. Tom reportedly acted as the criminal mentor of Circleville native Robert LeRoy Parker—more widely known as Butch Cassidy—in his early outlaw days. Bill McCarty was later killed in a botched bank robbery in 1893.[13]

So, as often in western history, the attraction of fertile cattle country had set up an environment in which the possibility of violence, especially directed toward Indians, was heightened. It was into this newly dangerous area that the four Navajos arrived in December 1873. According to a Navajo oral tradition, they were from the Shonto Plateau, south of Navajo Mountain, near the modern Inscription House Trading Post, and had crossed the Colorado at the Crossing of the Fathers.[14]

According to Thurber, the four Navajos were delayed by heavy snows on their way north. Running short of food, they stopped at the McCarty ranch, in the southern part of Grass Valley, and traded for a calf, for which they paid three blankets.[15] They had a portion of this meat with them when they arrived at the Ute camps, after a journey of about twenty-eight miles.

The McCartys, after making this trade, then followed the Navajos northward, an ominous development. They met John Clinger, apparently a Mormon or former Mormon, about three miles from the Ute camps, and he joined their group.[16] Gottfredson says that Clinger was originally from Provo and returned to Provo, which points to a man named James Henry Clinger.[17] His children during this time period were born in Lake View (Provo), Utah, so if he is the Clinger of the killers, he did not stay in Grass Valley long.[18] However, both Bean and Thurber refer to a John Clinger, not James.[19] The wounded Navajo later said that "one of the attacking party was a Mormon with his front teeth out."[20]

Ne Chic Se Cla and his friends visited the Ute camps for two days and traded blankets and bridle bits for about four horses; when these were added to the horses they had ridden, they probably had nine to eleven horses, a substantial herd.[21] They also made a pact with the Utes to visit them again in the upcoming year. According to some accounts, the Utes gave them "plenty" of venison and flour for their journey home.[22] Then the Navajos began traveling south.

When they were about halfway down Grass Valley, heavy snows caused them to take refuge in the empty cabin of a Mr. McCarter, who lived in Beaver.[23] The McCartys, following them, saw that they had stopped in the cabin, then the McCartys passed on to the McCarty ranch briefly, some eight to ten miles away, before returning to the McCarter cabin.[24]

The Navajos had begun to repair their clothes and were roasting venison that they had received from the Utes.[25] According to one account, the McCartys accused the Navajos of killing a cow, and there was a quarrel which erupted into violence.[26] Another possibility is that the McCartys knew that the Navajos had not killed a cow, and were simply seeking a pretext for a quarrel.

However, we should remember that the source of these stories were the whites who carried out the murders—the McCartys or Clinger. The stories of the Navajos killing one of McCarty's calves, or of a quarrel escalating to violence, may be exculpatory stories told by the whites. Bean's June 20 letter also states that the murders took place "according to previous threats"—possibly a reference to McCarty's warning to Thurber that he planned to kill any Indians without a white escort.

Some sources, such as Thurber and Hamblin, seem to portray the McCartys coming upon the Navajos suddenly and opening fire on them. But it seems more likely that the McCartys used their earlier acquaintance with the Navajos to put them at ease, then attacked them without warning.

In the Navajo oral tradition there is a chilling story of the four Navajos staying in the cabin while the McCarty group camped outside. One of the Navajos felt especially uneasy at the presence of the whites and watched them carefully. When the cowboys began shooting at a stump for target practice in the morning, two of the Navajos left the cabin to join them. The two Navajos within the cabin watching from a window suddenly saw their friends drop to the ground, dead.[27] The two surviving Indians immediately went into defensive mode. While the cabin gave them some protection, they were also trapped within it, with little chance of escape.

This story has the support of persistent traditions that the McCartys tried to smoke the Navajos out of the cabin, by rolling a bundle of hay up to the cabin, either already burning or soon to be lit.[28]

Thurber and Bean name four men in the party that killed the Navajos: A. J. McCarty; his son William; John Clinger; and Thomas Richards, an employee of McCarty.[29] However, it is clear that A. McCarty was primarily responsible for the murders.[30] The incident apparently occurred between December 20, 1873, and January 1, 1874.[31]

There is an early account that looks as if it came directly from McCarty that is quite different from these sources, a military report by W. L. Pitcher, second lieutenant at Fort Cameron, to F. S. Adams, first lieutenant, dated January 13, 1874. Pitcher would have known McCarty at Fort Cameron. Pitcher states that he talked with nearly all the sixty settlers of Circle Valley before making his report, which seems to reflect praiseworthy enterprise, but Circle Valley was twelve miles west of Grass Valley, and the only witnesses to the murders were McCarty and his men. For Pitcher, the incident is a straightforward story of Indian depredations, cattle theft, and justified punishment of the criminals. In his retelling, the McCartys found two of their cattle slaughtered, and followed the tracks *northward* to the deserted cabin. (This account reflects no knowledge of the Navajos' trading session with the Utes.) The whites then entered the cabin and found the four Indians eating the meat from the "slain cattle." McCarty attempted, "by signs and words," to explain to the Navajos that they would have to give up multiple horses for each head of cattle they had killed. According to Pitcher, the Indians ran for their weapons, and "one of the Indians was about to shoot McCarty when one of the whites fired at the Indian wounding him severely. Hostilities then commenced in earnest, two Indians being killed outright."

If we accept this as an early story told by McCarty, one crucial discrepancy with the reports by virtually everyone else is that the Navajos killed two cattle while traveling northward. The visit to the Utes—the main focus for the Navajos' journey—has been edited out. Evidently, McCarty did not want the military investigator to know that the Navajos had traded with the Utes for a few days, then traveled south (which might have led to unwelcome questions about how the McCartys showed up at McCarter's cabin). This strongly suggests that the portrayal of the Navajos eating the

McCarty meat they had recently butchered was entirely fictitious. Given these clear fabrications, one is not inclined to trust the McCartys' portrayal of themselves as shooting the Navajos in self-defense. (In fact, McCarty's story was early suspected of being a self-justifying fabrication. James Bunting of Kanab, in August 1874, stated that "Mr. McCarthy, his son and Mr. Clinger were the leaders in this bloody tragedy, and they now seek to screen themselves under the plea of having acted in self-defence.")[32]

Peter Gottfredson, known for his anti-Indian writing, tells another story that places the blame for the incident directly on the Indians.[33] He wrote that the Indians slaughtered one of McCarty's calves, then called at McCarty's main cabin, where the men were making breakfast. The Navajos blocked the men from their guns, insolently ordered them out of the building, and helped themselves to the food. When the "boys" rolled a large bundle of hay toward the cabin, the Indians panicked, and two of them jumped on a large horse belonging to Clinger and the other two mounted "Indian ponies." The "boys" quickly shot the two Indians on ponies, then pursued the Indians on Clinger's horse, killing one and wounding another at about sunset.[34]

This is a late, second-hand account, which seems to lack internal coherency. Gottfredson says that a son of George Washington Bean was his source, but it is striking that two early letters by Bean do not have the "breakfast" story at all—not to mention the Thurber report, Jacob Hamblin's early letters, and even the Pitcher report, which was McCarty's earliest attempt to exculpate himself. (In addition, the son of George W. Bean must have heard the story either from the McCartys or from Clinger, so the McCarty company was the ultimate source of the story.)[35] I regard it as largely fictitious.

When the McCartys rolled the bundle of burning hay up to the cabin, the two Navajos had no choice, and quickly fled from the wooden structure. Their own horses were not close, but one or both of the Navajos were able to jump on a large white horse owned by Clinger. If two rode the horse, one was quickly shot and killed, leaving Ne Chic Se Cla to ride for his life. He was shot and severely wounded also, a bullet hitting him beneath a shoulder blade and passing entirely through his body.[36] Somehow, he was able to continue riding and outdistanced his pursuers.

After reaching mountainous forest country, he abandoned the horse, which was thoroughly worn out, found a hiding place in a cavern, and covered himself with leaves. In the night he heard the whites, who had probably found the horse, searching for him. McCarty and his group did not want witnesses. But Ne Chic Se Cla had hidden himself well, and new snow covered his tracks. The whites finally gave up their search and returned to the cabin to divide their plunder.[37] This was probably their main motivation for the murders, aside from typical hatred for Indians that many Americans held at the time.

Ne Chic Se Cla somehow made his way home in the dead of winter. He "traveled on foot 13 days to reach home with fine cedar bark stufed on the wound," Jacob wrote.[38] This homeward journey was a monumental feat of survival. The Navajo traveled through forbidding territory without blanket or food, sometimes wrapping himself in cedar bark, and sometimes kindling fires with sticks. He believed that Mormons had attacked him, so did not dare to ask for help at any Mormon settlement.[39]

According to Navajo tradition, he ate herbs and tried to self-treat his wounds as he walked to the Ute Crossing, but they became infected. He was able to cross the Colorado only with great difficulty.[40] On the other side of the river, completely exhausted and expecting death soon, he took refuge in a deserted hogan. However, his relatives had performed a divination ceremony for him in Shonto which convinced them that he needed help; they traveled north, found him, and were able to save his life.[41]

Ne Chic Se Cla reached home on about January 14, and immediately sought to rouse the Navajos to a war against Mormons. The young Navajos were soon "clamoring for revenge." A friendly Navajo rode all night to Hopi country to warn John D. Lee and his family, who had been specifically threatened by the wounded man. A Paiute came to Tuuvi's home with the message, and Tuuvi then rushed to Moenave.[42] With Lee at Moenave were Rachel and five children, Winburn, who had been bedridden with an ailing foot for four months, and four prospectors, James Elnathan Smith and his brother Edward, John Pattie, and John D. Boyd.[43] Lee sent a message to Fort Defiance, via Tuuvi, then Lee with his son Ralph started for the Colorado to warn the Mormons. When he got to the ferry, Lee wrote a letter to Brigham Young and sent it ahead. As Brooks notes, Lee deserves great credit for notifying the Mormons so quickly that a Navajo attack on the Mormons was possible.[44]

On January 18, a Paiute messenger sent by the Navajos arrived at Moenave, and Rachel Lee interpreted as he spoke. He said that the young Navajos wanted war, but that the older men did not, and they would wait for Jacob Hamblin to arrive.[45]

Meanwhile, in January, Navajo headman Ganado Mucho, who lived in the Pueblo Colorado area (modern Ganado) west of Fort Defiance, brought the news of the killing of the three Navajos to Navajo agent William Frederick Milton Arny at Fort Defiance, which brings two important characters into our story. Arny, a friend of Abraham Lincoln and a devout Presbyterian, had years of experience with the Indians of New Mexico,[46] but was, at the least, a very judgmental agent—he is known for firing men in the agency who did not live up to his strict standards of moral purity.[47] Historians have been divided on his character; his biographer, Lawrence Murphy, views him as often unwise and extreme, but as sincerely concerned for the welfare of the Navajos. Frank McNitt, historian of the Navajo Wars, regards him as a scoundrel: "a hypocritical rascal, a Bible-pounding moralist who plotted larceny. Within a week of assuming charge [of the Navajo reservation], Arny boldly set in motion a scheme to defraud the Navahos of the best part of their reservation."[48] At a time when the Navajo reservation was much smaller than it is now, he hoped to wrest the San Juan area, which was believed to be rich in ores, from the Navajos, and give them arid southern and western lands in return. And, according to some historians, he felt that he could use the Mormon-Navajo conflict after the Grass Valley killings to further his aims.[49]

Ganado Mucho, Navajo name Totsohnii Hastiin ("Man of the Big Water Clan"), sometimes known as Agua Grande (Spanish for "Big Water"), was a wealthy and influential Navajo headman (his Spanish name means "Much Cattle").[50] Though he probably started his career as a warrior, he became known as a moderate, inclined to negotiate peace with whites.[51] After the Navajos returned from Bosque Redondo in 1868, he, with Manuelito, was a prominent chief who helped Navajos adjust to the early reservation era. He invited John Lorenzo Hubbell to open his trading post in the Ganado area and Hubbell later named the locality after him. Navajo historian David Brugge and P. T. Reilly have identified Ganado Mucho as Hastele, Jacob Hamblin's friend, and this association is very possible, if not yet proven.[52]

Arny accepted the early Navajo account that Mormons had committed the murders,[53] and sent a letter to *The New Mexican* on the supposed Navajo-Mormon war stating that it was certain that Mormons had killed three or four Navajos, and also that Navajos had killed about the same number of Mormons—both statements incorrect.[54]

With a desire for vengeful retaliation raging among some of the younger Navajos, Arny had several long talks with Navajo leaders and convinced them not to attack the Mormons, but instead to demand reparations.[55] He sent Ganado Mucho to the Navajo Mountain area, and when the chief returned, he reported to Arny that the Navajos were generally peaceful, but that the relatives of the dead men were demanding reparations from the U.S. government. Arny replied that he could not pay the relatives because they had been off the reservation—even though the Bosque Redondo Treaty of 1868 allowed Navajos to leave the reservation and even live off the reservation under certain circumstances.[56]

Arny, a confirmed Republican, was thus by definition opposed to the Mormons, and wanted Navajos to stay on the reservation and not trade northwest of the Colorado. Naturally, the Grass Valley killings, as long as the Navajos believed that Mormons had been the killers, would serve to further his purposes.

When Lee's letter reached Brigham Young, with news of the Grass Valley murders and retaliation threatened by some Navajos, Young saw another obstacle to his long-sought-for Arizona colonies. He sent a telegram to Jacob Hamblin, instructing him "to see & talk with the Navajos."[57] Jacob had been in bad health in January, but nevertheless, set out from Kanab.[58] According to Little, soon after he left, Bishop Levi Stewart sent him a message by Jacob's son Joseph asking him to return, as the local

Paiutes said that the mood of the Navajos was extremely violent. But Jacob continued on.[59] He apparently picked up Lehi Smithson at Lee's Ferry, for when John D. Lee met them on January 23, they were traveling together. Jacob also brought news of Brigham Young's plans for Moenave—he had appointed a Scotchman named John Law Blythe as bishop and president of the Arizona Mission, and Blythe was supposed to take ten families and set out for Moenave immediately, where he should build a substantial fort.[60] Brigham had not given up on the Arizona mission, but for the time being was focusing on Moenave.

Blythe had emigrated to American to work in mines in Pennsylvania, but soon traveled west to California in search of gold. In 1854, he was converted to Mormonism by a Mormon woman, whom he eventually married, and they moved to Utah in 1859. He was falsely accused in a controversial murder in Salt Lake City in 1873, and when released from custody, church leaders quickly sent him to Dixie. He had not crossed the Colorado with the Haight company, but had helped build a new ferry boat in fall 1873 to replace the ferry boat that had been destroyed.[61]

When Jacob came to Lonely Dell, Lee confronted him with statements he had made to Lee's wife Emma. "Had some Plain talk with Bro. Hamblin about Matters of a delicate [c]haracter, things that a man in his Position should be ashamed off," wrote Lee. "We, however, agreed to drop it as he pled innocence, still that did not e[xone]rate him in My opinion, but was only one of his old tricks to Evade the Truth." For Lee, Jacob had become the personification of deception, while he portrays himself as practicing forbearance. "I however treated him with the same kind respects as I did before."

Jacob, Lee, Smithson, and Smithson's wife Amorah (a daughter of John D. Lee and Rachel) crossed the Colorado on January 28 and arrived at Moenave the following day.[62] Jacob immediately departed for Moenkopi to send a messenger to the Navajos. However, the Hopi village was mostly deserted, only a few Paiutes, including the lame Paiute Cuckebur-Shew, and a Hopi remaining there.[63] Tuuvi, worried by the long delay of the Mormon party, had gathered his sheep and returned to Oraibi.[64]

Jacob asked a Paiute to bring some of the Navajos to Moenkopi, but the Paiute advised him to go to Ketchene's ranch, which was a day's ride away. The next day, the thirtieth, Jacob set off with Cuckebur as interpreter, and with two non-Mormon prospectors, James and Edward Smith.[65]

They rode fifteen miles, then met the Paiute who had acted as the Navajo's messenger previously; he was delighted to see Hamblin, and asked him to come to Ketchene's camp, which he said was fifteen miles distant. They rode ten miles more than that, according to Smith, through heavy snow, and finally arrived at the camp, which consisted of two circular wood hogans. They arrived at the ranch late at night, and runners were quickly sent out to gather local Navajos for a talk.

Ketchene was not there but was believed to be close by (the Paiute messenger was sent to locate him). Six Navajos were at the camp, three men and three women. A tall, powerful, but aged Navajo welcomed Hamblin and his companions warmly, with "an embrace like the hug of a grizzly bear," according to Smith. After a smoke and a dinner of broiled and boiled goat meat and corn meal mush, they began to discuss the Grass Valley killings, with Cuckebur serving as interpreter. The talk was encouraging: "The Navahoes present expressed themselves anxious that the affair should be settled without further bloodshed and that that was the wish of the principal men of the tribe. They said the Navahoes had long known Hamlin, and they believed he would do what was right." Jacob explained that neither he nor any Mormons were guilty of the murder of Ketchene's sons and nephew, and they wanted a group of Navajos to travel north and investigate the truth of this. This message seemed to resonate, and, "after smoking innumerable cigarettes with our savage friends," wrote Smith, "we retired to rest on a pile of buffalo skins and Navahoe blankets, worth a horse apiece, and slept soundly and well."

The next morning, January 31, Jacob and his friends, after being given a hearty breakfast, waited for the arrival of the chief. The Smith brothers relaxed and wandered around the camp, examining such Navajo items as were novel to them.

Just before noon, however, twelve young Navajo men arrived, fully armed with bows, arrows, and rifles, and the atmosphere in the camp suddenly chilled. They refused to shake hands and demanded tobacco. After a smoke, they moved everything out of one of the hogans, as they said more Navajos were coming. Soon seven more rode up. The three whites, the twenty plus Navajos, and some Paiutes now filled the hogan—Hamblin estimated twenty-four Navajos, plus three to six Paiutes led by a chief.

Hamblin asked when Ketchene would arrive; the answer was, he had gone to Fort Defiance. This was discouraging news.

All smoked in silence for a time. Jacob then started the parley, speaking through a Paiute interpreter, telling the Navajos that "our head chief" had told him that non-Mormons had killed the three Navajos at Grass Valley, and he invited two or three Navajo leaders to come to Utah to learn the facts, and the Mormons would do their best to help punish the murderers. All of this would comply "with our big pease talk at Ft Defiance with their Principle Chief," the late Barboncito.

The owner of the hogan replied, talking in a measured tone for an hour. But then the atmosphere in the hogan turned menacing. A number of Navajos spoke, gesturing wildly, including one old man who frequently drew his hand across his throat. Two Paiute interpreters faltered as they began to talk to Jacob, and the Paiute chief, furious, called another.

This one explained to Jacob that the Navajos had decided that he had lied when he said he and Mormons had not been involved in the Grass Valley killings. All the Navajos present, except for the host and two other old Navajos, voted for his immediate death. They would not kill the Smiths, as they were "Americans," but they would force them to watch Hamblin being tortured, then send them back to Moenave on foot.

The interpreter asked Jacob if he was not afraid. "No. What shal I be afraid of?" he replied.

"Of Navajos."

"I am not afraid of Navajos, I am not afraid of my friends."

"They are not your friends. Navajo's blood has been spiled on your land since the big peace talk."

"Our people did not do it & we want it settled like men & not like brutes."

The Paiute Chief now arose to his feet and said, "I tell you you have lied. It was you folks who kiled the Navajos:...their Father has gone off alone to mourn the loss of his sons: You have caused the breath that he breathes to be like hot ashes to his mouth: the food that he eats like coals of fire. You say you are not afraid: would not you be afraid if he would stretch your bare back on those coals?" He pointed to a large fire in the centre of the lodge.

"It might hurt me," Jacob answered, "but I know no fear. I have come to talk like men, not like children as they had talked during this council. My business is to settle this difficulty...according to our big talk at Ft Defiance."

Jacob continued to speak for a long time, calmly and steadily, though he was rudely interrupted a number of times. He reminded the Navajos of his long history with their people, and challenged them to prove that he had ever lied to them. He drew a map of Utah on the ground and showed how far away Kanab was from Grass Valley, how it was impossible that he had been involved in the killings.

This impressive speech quieted the firebrands in the hogan for the moment. But then a brother of one of the murdered men rose and delivered another angry speech. As his climax he called a man out of the group—it was Ne Chic Se Cla, the survivor. The speaker stripped off his buckskin shirt and displayed the recent bullet wound in his chest and back. He pointed to the fire, and Jacob, and demanded that he be burned alive immediately.

This electrified the crowd. But their host spoke again on behalf of the Indian missionary. Jacob added: "Our peace talk was to prevent such things & I did not want to hear any thing more of that kind if that is the way you talk I have no more to say." He reminded them that eighty Navajos had come to Kanab in 1870 "cast out like hungry wolves naked without any thing to help themselves with" and how Jacob had given them thirty horses for a few blankets. The moderate Navajos now began to remember Jacob's "good deeds" and how he had been a guest friend in their hogans for years.

The Navajos asked Jacob if he knew Hastele (possibly Ganado Mucho), and Jacob said that Barboncito had recommended him "as a man with an honest heart & straight tongue & when any serious difficulty arose to apply to him." Jacob suggested that Hastele and some other good Navajos go home with him. They said that Hastele was far away and could not go now.

But, Jacob wrote, the Piute interpreter informed him that "the Navajos were well pleased with me that I had a sound heart & knew no fear. & that their Chief

Ketchena who was a way from home would meet me at the Moyancoppy in a few days." The Navajos also agreed that John D. Lee was not to blame for the killings, and neither he nor his family would be punished.

Finally, James Smith wrote, "The strain was over and we breathed freely once more. We smoked the pipe, or rather the cigarette of peace, and a roasted goat being shortly produced, we fell to with a will and gnawed ribs together as amicably as if it had not been just previously their benevolent intention to roast us instead of the goat."

It was now past midnight. "I never was so tired in my life," wrote Smith. "Eleven hours in a partially recumbent position, cramped for room with every nerve strained to its utmost tension and momentarily expecting a conflict, which must be to the death, is tolerably hard work."

They agreed that Hamblin and the Smiths would return to Moenave the next day and wait there for Ketchene to arrive. The three whites slept, spelling each other off.

The next day, February 2, they returned to Moenave in safety, arriving after dark, and related their adventures to the Lee family.

While some have interpreted this story as an example of Jacob's heroism—a tradition that started early with the account written by the non-Mormon Smith on February 2—Lee saw it as an example of Jacob's foolishness, his lack of influence with Indians, and his disobedience to church authority. According to Lee, Young had counseled Jacob to invite Navajo chiefs to come to Moenkopi for a talk and not put himself in danger; Lee, before he left, had echoed this advice. "My advise Was not heeded," Lee wrote.[66] In his March 15 letter to Brigham Young, Lee wrote that he told Jacob that "through neglect" he had lost all the influence he ever had with Indians "& that I did not consider it safe for him to go among them."

Not too surprisingly, Jacob rejected this insulting interpretation. "My sugestions by him was treted with indignation," wrote Lee, "[Hamblin] Saying that he was ~~But to my surprise~~ ordain[ed] an apostle to the Lamanites & knew his own buisiness. I then asked the two Mres Smith if they would accompany him which they did & probably was the means of saving his life."[67]

The Smith company was anxious to depart on a mining expedition, with Lee as their guide, and Hamblin felt that the Navajo situation was now stable, but Lee was not yet confident that his family was safe. Again, he emphasized Jacob's bad judgment and lack of influence with Indians. "The Indians have little confidence in Jacob," he wrote in his diary.[68]

On February 6, Ketchene showed up at Moenave, accompanied by some of his sons, four other Navajos, and a Paiute interpreter.[69] Hamblin wrote,

> After arriving at the Moyencoppy Ketchena Father of two & uncle of one of the men kiled came to me & said the bodies of his sons were eaten by the wolves & owls; but it would do no good to spill more blood but thought I

ought to pay for them. I told him I would not pay for what others had done; & that I would report the matter to my people.[70]

Lee's account in his diary, written near the time the exchange occurred, is similar. They asked for four hundred head of horses and four hundred head of cattle (one hundred horses and one hundred cattle for each man killed or wounded), and asked Lee to write to Brigham Young, and for Jacob to take the letter to Brigham "& consult the matter & bring word within 25 days &c." They smoked a pipe of friendship, Lee fed the visitors, "& they Embraced Jacob & I" and then departed.[71]

In many other respects, however, the accounts differ dramatically. Lee asserts that Jacob deliberately led Ketchene to believe that reparations would be made, knowing that they would not, therefore putting Lee's family and Moenave in danger. Both James Smith and Jacob tell an entirely different story, with Jacob continually asserting that the Mormons had not committed the murders, and thus were not going to pay the reparations. In a heated exchange, Lee demanded that Hamblin act as he ordered, while Hamblin "said that he was responsible for his own acts & wished me to mind my own buissness." Lee was outraged: "He spoke verry insulting to me," he wrote.[72] According to Lee, Hamblin and the Navajos then agreed that Jacob would leave in two days' time and return twenty-five days later. So the appointment was set for March 5. As it happened, Jacob left Moenave the next morning, February 7, traveling with the unfortunate Mr. Winburn.[73]

According to Lee, Hamblin had told the Smith group of prospectors that there was gold or silver among the Hualapai or Havasupai, and Lee was now called upon to lead the Smith group to these Indians. There he should tell them "that Jacob said that th[e]y knew where there was oar & wanted th[e]m to show it to these Men; that they were fri[e]nds." Lee, who had met the Cohoninas in a previous exploration, accordingly led the Smiths on a difficult month-long expedition west of Moenave.

However, Lee said that when he gave the Cohoninas Jacob's message, they refused to show their wealth to the miners. Lee also became disillusioned with the Smiths and their companions, as some of them said they would cheerfully kill Indians in order to find and develop a rich lode of ore. Lee returned home on March 7.[74]

The Blythe group, with seven men, and Blythe's wife and adopted son, set out from Kanab on February 7 and camped for a few days at Navajo Wells. There was a snowstorm on the eleventh, and that night Jacob arrived, "wet and cold," on his way to Kanab with the bad news from Arizona. He had found the Navajos "very hostile and agreed to meet them again in 27 days from the time he left and settle the difficulties," William Solomon noted in his diary.[75] Jacob left for Kanab the next morning.

He arrived at Kanab on about February 12, and sent a report to Brigham Young that was dated the thirteenth. "I intend to start tomoroh morning for Ft. Defiance," he wrote to Brigham, "& not return till I get three men I know of in the Navajos Nation to return with me. I think they had better see you first & then take the nescessary steps to be satisfied in regard to the facts in the matter."[76]

Jacob left Kanab to return to Arizona on the seventeenth, staying overnight with Ira Hatch at Johnson Canyon.[77] Exposure to a storm after leaving Hatch's home caused him to become seriously ill, and he wondered if he would die, but found a deserted house with wood and was able to sleep in warmth, which restored him.[78]

The Blythe company was still at Navajo Wells on February 18, and Jacob met them there again on his way back to Arizona. "Jacob Hamblin came into camp from Kanab this afternoon," journalized William Henry Solomon, "he being the Apostle to the Lamanites."[79] The next day, Blythe spared one of his company, John Everett, to travel with Jacob, and later in the day Jacob was at the Pahreah settlement, where he convinced two more men to accompany him to Arizona, James Smith and Nephi Smithson.[80]

At Lee's Ferry, Jacob wrote to Blythe, suggesting that his party come to the ferry and "improve" the land there until they heard from him: "I would have liked to of seen you very mutch but I think it will be the safest to here from the Oriby and Navajos before you cross the River with so small a company."[81]

On March 2 Jacob and his three companions arrived at Lee's house at the Moenave, "expectin a Mesenger from the Navajos on the Morow," as Hamblin wrote in his diary. March 3 would be exactly twenty-five days after February 6. As Brigham Young had refused to pay any indemnity, Hamblin and the Lee family prepared for the worst. "Fixing up the house and arms for defense," Jacob wrote. "7 men 2 women 6 childrin. Anxously wating to see the Mesenger to arrive."[82] When no one arrived on March 3, Jacob traveled to the Hopi mesas.[83]

John D. Lee, in his diary and his March 15 letter to Brigham Young, once again tells a different story. According to Lee, who was still gone on the mining expedition so was not a first-hand witness, Jacob and friends arrived at Moenave on February 27. Lee said that they stayed at Moenave, at the Lee home, until the 25th day—which would be March 3, presumably. On that day, seeing that Ketchene had not arrived, Jacob said that "he would not trouble himself about seeing them—took his guard & went to the Oriba villages to trade with them [the Hopis]." He left at noon, according to Lee, not even staying the whole day. Two days later, Ketchene arrived and was reportedly furious that Jacob was not present, stating that "Hamblin talked out of the back of his head & Each Side of his face," and that he had "no confidence in him." He asked Rachel Lee to send one of her sons to summon Ira Hatch to come to Moenave to talk to him instead of Hamblin. The Navajo chief told her that Lee and his family and cattle need have no fear of retaliation, that he was not angry with them.[84]

On this twenty-five or twenty-seven day controversy, it seems there are two options. One is that Jacob was genuinely confused.[85] Another possibility is that Hamblin intentionally came early in order to avoid putting himself in another life-threatening situation.

Apparently, Jacob had told Rachel Lee that he intended to go to Fort Defiance, and she told Ketchene this, but Ketchene told her this was another of Jacob's lies, as he had seen his tracks leading to the Hopi mesas.[86] In fact, the Hopi mesas were a logical place to stop on the way to Fort Defiance. As Lee tells the story, Jacob took his three companions and wasted their time trading at the Hopi mesas, to Lee's disgust. Lee reports them also complaining that Jacob had "half starved" them "to gratify the whim of a bigot," and would never accompany him to Arizona again.[87]

In Little, Hamblin states that while at the mesas, he asked the Hopis to inform Navajos they met that Jacob had returned on the agreed date, but that no one had met him.[88]

As was noted above, Hamblin intended to visit Fort Defiance and talk to Navajo leaders and the Navajo agent there. However, due to heavy snows, the lack of supplies, and the fatigued state of his horses, he decided not to go.[89]

On March 7, Hamblin, at the village Hano on the First Mesa, wrote to Arny stating the Mormon position on the Grass Valley murders, explaining that Mormons had not killed the three Indians. He suggested that two or three Navajo chiefs cross the Colorado with a Spanish interpreter, "& it can all be satisfactorily arranged." He mentioned that the Mormons had started a settlement at the Moenkopi, which would serve as a springboard for other Mormon settlements.[90]

On March 11, Hamblin, Smith, Smithson, and Everett, with Tuuvi, returned to Moenave, Jacob and Tuuvi arriving near sunset. Lee castigated Jacob for not being present at Moenave on the twenty-seventh day, but Jacob said that the day agreed upon had been the twenty-fifth day, and he had been there on that day.

The next morning a son of Ketchene, a Navajo leader, and a Paiute interpreter arrived before sunrise. Ketchene had heard that Jacob planned to leave for Utah again without talking to him, and wanted to "catch him before he could get away," as Lee put it.[91] According to Lee, the son of Ketchene asked Jacob why he had not arrived at the time appointed. Jacob said he had come on the twenty-fifth day and that Ketchene and his sons had not been there.

Ketchene's son—according to Lee's diary—said that they had agreed to meet on the twenty-seventh day, and Jacob knew this full well, "& that was an other one of his crooked yarns. Why did he not Say that he did not want to Meet then [them] & tell the truth like an honest man instead of lieing like a Dog."[92] He then suggested that Jacob meet with Ketchene at a halfway point, and Jacob agreed.

However, Lee told Jacob that he felt this was a trap, and that if he kept the appointment he would "lose his hair." So Jacob instead made arrangements to meet Ketchene at Moenave in ten days, with Ira Hatch, "a good interpeter." This would be March 22.

Lee felt that Hamblin was once again setting up an appointment which he did not intend to keep and tried to impress on him that if he did not show up this would make matters much worse.[93] But, according to Lee, Hamblin "seemed to treat my views lightly" and told Lee that "he run that shebang [Indian affairs] & not me." A heated exchange ensued, in which Lee accused Hamblin of a number of misdeeds.

Lee said that he would report Hamblin's actions to Brigham Young if he did not mend his ways. "Report & be damned," Hamblin reportedly replied, "& that he had more trouble with these Dam Plugs [his three companions?] then he had with the Indians." This infuriated Lee, who threatened to kick Hamblin out of his house. "It was bad enough to have the lives of my Family endangered, without having to bear his slang & insults." Hamblin then said that if Brigham didn't like the course he had taken, "that he Might apoint some other man. He had Negociated for 20 years between Brigham & the Indians & now he wanted to resign!"

Lee denounced Jacob for criticizing Young to the Smiths, and telling them that "Brigham had never backed you up in any thing that he sent you to do with the Indians & that was the cause that they were mad at you." Lee said that Hamblin's assertion—that Brigham Young never backed him up—was "as false as hell."

Just as Lee promised to send Young a report of Hamblin's misdoings, so he did, and the March 15, 1874, letter to Young is the result. It repeats many of the accusations in the diary.

Meantime, Hamblin had agreed to meet the Blythe company at Lee's Ferry, but when the company arrived there on March 10, they found the note from him instead, which stated that "he thinks that we had better wate until we hear from the Oribes & the Navjoes Indians."[94]

On March 12, Hamblin, his three companions, Lee, his daughter Amorah and son-in-law Lehi Smithson, and the Smith company of prospectors, left Moenave, arriving at Lonely Dell two days later. There they met John Blythe and his company.[95]

Reportedly, Jacob now decided that he could not keep the ten-day appointment he had made with the Navajos, possibly because he felt he needed to visit Brigham Young in St. George, and asked Ira Hatch (part of the Blythe company) if he would keep the appointment for him. According to Lee, Hatch replied, "If you have made an agreement to Meet the NavaJoes, you had better do so yourself in Person, as it is as Much as I can do to fill my own apointments."[96] Lee wrote that Jacob, "knowing that Ira Hatch would not fill that apointment we[nt] on with as Much indiference as [if] nothing was at stake."

However, Blythe, in a letter to Brigham Young, tells an entirely contradictory story: Ira Hatch was not even at Lonely Dell when Jacob arrived, but was obtaining supplies at the Pahreah settlement.[97] Jacob told Blythe that Ira could fulfill the appointment and left the Colorado,[98] but Hatch did not return in time to keep the meeting with Ketchene. In this account, Jacob left Lonely Dell thinking that the appointment might be fulfilled by Hatch.

On the fifteenth, a meeting was held in Lee's house, in which Jacob spoke about the situation with Navajos in Arizona, Solomon wrote, "from which we learned that we, the Arizona mission need not apprehend any particular danger." Even though

Brigham Young would not send the Indians any of the eight hundred animals demanded, Jacob "thought the difficulties would be settled."[99] In Blythe's letter, he wrote that he asked Jacob "if the way was clear and safe, for the company to go," and Jacob replied that "he considered it was, although some of the Indian[s] was a little riled and mad. but [he] did not think these was any particular danger."[100]

Jacob then continued on to Pahreah with the Smith prospectors, describing them to the Mormons as honorable men, which disgusted Lee.

According to Lee, when the Navajos arrived at Moenave on March 22 and found Hamblin absent, they were furious. "Their feelings became so enraged that it was almost beyond controle," he wrote. Rachel Lee told them that she did not know when Jacob would come, but that Ira Hatch was on his way south, and only a few hours away. The Navajos went north to talk to Hatch.

Blythe, Hatch, and their company crossed the Colorado on the nineteenth and started the journey south.[101] They met Ketchene, two of his sons, and a wife who knew some Spanish at Rock Pools, about ten miles from Bitter Springs, on the twenty-fourth, and a parley with Hatch and Blythe ensued. Ketchene and his sons were angry at Hamblin for not keeping his appointment, and demanded that Blythe and Hatch meet them at the home of Peokon in ten days, which the two Mormons agreed to. The Navajos asked for food, and Blythe gave them a yearling steer to eat.[102] "We told them the Mormons were not guilty of the crime," William Solomon wrote, "that we were their friends and Ketcheene and one of his sons looked cheerful and friendly, but the other drew the collar of his coat up around his mouth and looked sad and sullen."[103]

The name Peokon might have been a red flag; he was not a chief given to seeking peace. Peokon had once claimed to be the murderer of George A. Smith Jr., and was no friend of Mormons.[104] We last saw him as a leader of the eighty or so Navajos who visited Kanab in September 1871. He was reputed to be a son of Spaneshanks, Jacob's old friend and eventual enemy.[105]

Blythe and company continued to Moenave, arriving on March 27.[106]

Jacob was in Kanab by March 17,[107] and three days later, he and Bishop Levi Stewart sent McCarty a letter, asking him to return the property of the murdered Navajos and giving a precise catalog of what he should return. The quantity of valuable goods listed is impressive; it increases the likelihood that the McCartys had killed the Navajos in order to appropriate their horses, blankets, saddles, and weapons. Bill and Tom McCarty later had no qualms about stealing from whites; they probably viewed these Navajos as easy targets.[108]

On March 21, Jacob started for St. George to visit Brigham Young. He apparently wanted to secure the help of Ammon Tenney, Ira Hatch, and John Oakley in his upcoming mission; he was concerned that legal right to Lee's Ferry should be secured; and he wanted to obtain the horses that had belonged to the victims of the Grass Valley killings. He also arranged for supplies for the James E. Smith company of prospectors. Brigham Young, with George A. Smith and other Mormon leaders, blessed Jacob on April 4, and set him apart "to minister to the Lamanites."[109]

William F. M. Arny received Hamblin's March 7 letter on March 28. If the Navajo agent had not known it before this letter, he now knew that the Mormons claimed that they had not killed the three Navajos in Grass Valley. This seemed to have no effect on the way Arny reported the confrontation, and on his anti-Mormon biases. Arny's biographer writes, "In much the same way that he had been unwilling to work with Catholics to improve Pueblo education, Arny now refused to cooperate with Hamblin and the Mormons."[110]

Arny replied to Hamblin on the twenty-eighth, stating that he had made three attempts to arrange a meeting between the Mormons and Navajos, but could not get the parties together. He said he had made every effort to restrain the Navajos "from retaliation." He demanded that Hamblin come to Fort Defiance as early as possible, prepared "to do justice to the Indians for the wrong done them." At this meeting, they would discuss how Mormons, miners, and settlers in Navajo lands could be protected, and "define" where such people could make settlements safely. (No doubt, Arny would demand that Mormons stay northwest of the Colorado.) If Hamblin did not come to Fort Defiance, Arny threatened, "I fear I will not be able to restrain my Indians."[111]

Arny gave the letter to Ganado Mucho and John Lorenzo Hubbell, who had interpreted for Jacob at Fort Defiance in 1870, and later became a well-known Navajo trader. Hubbell had come to Utah and worked for John D. Lee at Lonely Dell in April 1873, before visiting Kanab and the towns in Long Valley. He returned to Navajo country later in the year after getting the worst of a fight in Panguitch.[112] Hubbell and Ganado Mucho apparently took the letter to Hamblin, though it is not known when he received it. According to McNitt, Hamblin, "always willing to negotiate when there was a chance of agreement, declined Arny's proposals."[113] Nevertheless, he wanted to meet with Navajo leaders at Fort Defiance.

Arny seemed to reject out of hand the explanation that the three Navajos had met their deaths at the hands of non-Mormons, and felt that the Mormons should and would be willing to pay reparations. On the same day, the twenty-eighth, he wrote to New Mexico Indian Superintendent Colonel L. Edwin Dudley, enclosing a copy of Hamblin's letter, and stated that in the killing of the Navajos, "the Mormon leaders find that some of their followers...made a mistake which they now desire to correct." This is curious, as Hamblin clearly stated that non-Mormons had done the killing. To Arny, a paramount concern was preventing Mormon settlements in Arizona—he felt that the Mormon-Navajo dispute "should be used in a peaceful way to prevent the settlement of the Mormons too near to either the Moquis or Navajo reservations."[114] Arny seemed to be working behind the scenes to keep Navajo-Mormon tensions simmering.

It should be remembered that the Navajo reservation, at that time, did not extend very far west of Fort Defiance.[115] Thus, even the Mormon settlement at Moenave was not legally within Arny's jurisdiction.

However, Arny wanted Protestant missionaries in Navajo country, not the Mormons, and he especially railed against John D. Lee at the Colorado (he did not know he was even closer to the Navajos, at Moenave), telling Dudley that Lee was teaching Indians to steal from Gentiles (a ludicrous accusation). In addition, in his view, neither Hamblin nor Young had any formal authority to deal in Indian affairs.[116]

According to McNitt, Arny, working on behalf of powerful third-party interests, tried to use the Mormon-Navajo tensions to "conceal his real objective: seizure of the fertile and supposedly mineral-rich northern one-quarter of the Navaho reservation."[117] The Navajo chiefs had agreed in February to give up the San Juan area, but the deal needed to be finalized in Washington, and Arny decided that he needed to take the Navajo leaders to the nation's capital to accomplish his purposes. On May 12, he warned his superiors that there would be a border war with the Mormons if this journey to Washington did not take place.[118]

Jacob was still in Kanab on April 14, when he wrote a letter to St. George stake president John Willard Young, but he said that Samuel Knight and Thales Haskell had arrived recently, and he intended to start for Moenkopi soon.[119]

Back in Arizona, the Blythe company, after visiting Moenave, had come to Moenkopi and found it deserted. When Tuuvi arrived the next day, he welcomed the company and invited them to inhabit their "little Huts, or houses" until the Mormons could build better. The Hopis had left Moenkopi due to the threats of the Navajos against Mormons, said Blythe; or perhaps, as Tuuvi told him, bountiful snow that year made it possible to grow ample corn near the mesas.[120] Tuuvi gave them two pieces of land and some water privileges. Blythe and his companions hauled a wagon up to where Jacob had marked a site for a fort.[121]

Blythe and Hatch, with Tuuvi as guide, talked with Navajo leaders at Peokon's camp on April 2.[122] Aside from Ketchene and Peokon, "old Patnish who killed Doctor Whitmore & made such a sweep of his stock, painted & with a feindish Grin upon his countainance came in & took a seat."[123] Not an auspicious entrance! This parley turned out to be another twelve-hour marathon, quite similar to what Jacob and the Smiths had endured previously. Ketchene, a moderate leader, insisted that Mormons provide reparations for the three Navajos' deaths. Hatch and Blythe again explained that Mormons and Americans were different, and that Mormons were not guilty of the deaths. They suggested that Navajo leaders come to Utah to investigate.

At one point the Navajos, angered, said that they "wanted to know if we had come for them to use us up then." Hatch and Blythe replied that they did not fear injury in the house of their friends. Peokon then spoke at length, again threatening to kill the two Mormons. Finally, the Navajos said that unless their demands were met by June 13, they would kill all Mormons in Moenkopi then raid into Mormon settlements and ranches northwest of the Colorado. This was probably not a credible threat, as they were unlikely to risk another Bosque Redondo.

Blythe and Hatch were allowed to depart and arrived back at Moenkopi on April 7.[124] The following day, Blythe wrote to Brigham Young and asked for guidance. "Bro Jacob Hamblyn has not been with us one whole day since we left Kanab," Blythe wrote accusingly. "And the Navijoes are filled with wrath and very bitter toward him at presant accusing him of talking every way but Strait."

On April 18, a horseman arrived in Kanab with Blythe's letter and the demands of the particular group of Navajos that Blythe and Hatch had dealt with.[125] This message was telegraphed to St. George and then to Brigham Young in Salt Lake.

John D. Lee was in Kanab in April, and heard a sensational report that Blythe and Hatch had been physically threatened by Navajos, having buttons cut off their coats.[126] However, this is not found in the Blythe letter.

In any event, this embellished letter to Young was evidently shared with local leaders. Lee reported that Bishop Stewart of Kanab was extremely alarmed by the story and wanted all the Saints brought back to Utah immediately. Lee noted sarcastically: "I must here say that Bishop Stewart is a good faithful Religious man but gets skerred or excited to easy to make a good fronteer captin."[127] Nevertheless, St. George stake president John Willard Young gave John R. Young the assignment to assemble a group of men and bring all Mormons back across the Colorado.[128] John R. selected Andrew S. Gibbons of Glendale in Long Valley, Thomas Chamberlain of Mount Carmel in Long Valley, and Frank Hamblin of Kanab to help him, and they recruited five men each and the company set out for Moenkopi-Moenave.[129] Young and twenty-two men departed from Kanab on April 22.[130]

Lee, when he had heard the alarming news in Kanab, left for Moenave immediately, probably around the twenty-third. Hamblin left Kanab a day later, apparently traveling with Ammon Tenney, trying to overtake the John R. Young company before they reached the Colorado, to tell them that the reports were false.[131] Jacob, with Tenney, passed Lee at Jacob's Pools and told him that he and "five other men" would oppose the removal from Arizona. Surprisingly, Lee agreed. "Said I Jacob I will stand by you in that thing."[132]

Lee suggested that Hamblin visit Fort Defiance and talk with the head chiefs there, through Ammon Tenney. Jacob said that that was their plan, to explain the matter fully to the officials and the leading Navajos at the fort.

Jacob, now traveling with Elijah Potter, met the John R. Young company at Lee's Ferry.[133] Thales Haskell, Sam Knight, and Ammon Tenney arrived at Moenkopi on April 26, and the John R. Young company, with Jacob and probably John D. Lee, arrived three days later.

Jacob and Lee had made no headway with John R. Young, who apparently felt that he was simply fulfilling a mission given him by church leaders. "I found my task a hard and delicate one," wrote Young in his memoirs. "Jacob Hamblin and John L. Blythe were older and more experienced in frontier life than I. Each of them, moreover, was presiding in some capacity over that particular mission, and so they were reluctant to yield to my counsel and suggestions." Frank Hamblin and Ira Hatch served as a sort of counterweight to Jacob and Blythe, however.[134]

Lee, when he reached Moenave, found that his family had heard nothing of any war in the offing. Navajos had been visiting and trading peacefully. Lee came to Blythe, who flatly denied the story that Ketchene had cut off the buttons from his shirt and threatened all the Mormons and their cattle in Arizona. "They showed no signs of hostility towards us," he said. Nevertheless, according to Blythe (as reported by Lee), "They wanted the stock & said that they were made [mad] at Jacob for talking crooked to them & not bringing it; as he told them he would. & that he was no longer a captain to them &c."[135]

Again, Lee wrote, "Bro. Blythes & the Brethrren that was with him = were eaqueally surprised to hear of the reported hostilities = & wondered who could be at the bottom of that mischief."[136] If Lee's report is correct, then it raises the possibility that Blythe's letter to Brigham Young was exaggerated. Solomon's diary describes the parley but without any threats.[137] In addition, Solomon describes how Peokon and an interpreter visited Moenkopi on April 18 and 19; while he at first was suspicious and "a little mad," the next day after gift-giving and breakfast, Peokon actually gave Blythe a Navajo embrace, and he and his interpreter "went away seeming to feel much better than they did last night." This is a different Peokon than the one found in Blythe's April 8 letter.[138]

On April 30, after Jacob, John R. Young, Blythe, and others held a council, they sent a letter to Arny (signed by John R. Young and twenty others, including John Blythe, Ira Hatch, Samuel Knight, James B. Maxwell, Frank Hamblin, and "Joseph Hamblin," probably a copyist's mistake for Jacob), again stating the Mormon position—that they had not committed the murders and therefore would not pay the reparations that the Navajos were demanding of them. They said that the Navajos were boasting that the U.S. government was giving them arms to use in a possible war against the Mormons. They called upon Arny to avert war, and asked that Navajo chiefs come north of the Colorado and investigate the murders. They said they would send this letter by Andrew Gibbons, a former member of the Arizona legislature.[139] Arny's biographer writes, "Once more the Navajo agent rejected the appeal."[140]

Back at Moenkopi, Jacob, Gibbons, and Tenney, with five other men, set out for Fort Defiance on May 1.[141] Two hours after they left, however, a telegram from Brigham Young was brought to Moenkopi, saying that Mormons would pay no reparations for the Grass Valley murders and instructing all Mormons to return northwest of the Colorado. In addition, Young suggested that the Mormons invite the Hopis to come with the Mormons back to Utah—a fond dream of Young's that he apparently refused to give up.[142]

James Maxwell was sent to Hamblin's company to turn them back. However, to his surprise, Hamblin and his companions did not immediately obey. As Lee tells the story, Jacob rejected Brigham Young's counsel, and "said that he would go alone & see the cheives & agency before he would return; that he was satisfied that you [Brigham Young] had been misinformed, with regard to the feelings of the Indians."[143] According to Hamblin, however, Brigham Young had instructed him to talk with some Navajos before returning, so he felt that he would have to continue on to Fort Defiance to fulfill that part of his duties.[144] Ammon Tenney agreed to accompany Jacob.

The members of the company considered the situation, then one by one decided to stay with Jacob and Tenney and continue their journey east.[145]

Maxwell quickly rode back to Moenkopi, and when John R. Young heard the news, he, Ira Hatch, and Frank Hamblin immediately saddled up and set out to talk with Jacob in person.[146] After riding all night, they found Hamblin's party and continued with them to Oraibi. They conferred there, and Jacob still thought it would be best for him to visit Fort Defiance, but finally agreed that it might be "sufficient if he went to see the Government Agent residing at the Wallapi Moqui village."[147] So Young and five or six men returned to Moenkopi, and Jacob with five men traveled to Walpi. Apparently these men included the irreplaceable Ammon Tenney, the ever-dependable Thales Haskell, W. T. Stewart, Thomas Chamberlain, and Elijah J. Potter.[148] There, according to the Stewart-Knight report, two Navajos refused to talk with Jacob and Ammon, and a Navajo chief, "Stiff Arm," spoke severely to them.

Jacob and Tenney reported that the Hopi agent was not present, but his representative, a G. Rawlings, a Mormon who had ended up working for the Hopi agency, was.[149] He talked with Jacob, Tenney, and a Hopi who knew Spanish. This Hopi said that he had been in three Navajo councils, and that the relatives of the men who had been killed were very angry, and a class of Navajos he called Piotes—renegades or thieves—wanted to continue raiding among the Mormon settlements. However, other Navajos said, "No, let's not go to war, for we will lose what we have got." The Hopi said, "All of the chiefs and the Father of the dead sones [were] decli[ni]ng war or raiding upon you."[150] Powerful Navajo headmen did not want another Fearing Time, or another scorched earth campaign carried out by the U.S. military, with another possible Long Walk resulting.

Jacob and his companions learned that a well-respected Navajo headman who lived near Moenkopi was in the area. Hamblin and Tenney sent a messenger and asked for an interview with him. He received them hospitably, but demanded to know why the Mormons had killed the three young men, "who were honorable and honest and not stealing?" He said that the Navajos were mad and were going to raid until they were satisfied.

Jacob and Ammon replied by asking the Navajo if he remembered how Navajos had killed George Smith Jr., the son of a great leader among the Mormons. And if they remembered Navajos killing Mormons in Utah and "taking great heards of stock." He admitted these deeds.

Jacob and Ammon replied, "We never made war on you for that not with standing all this we still reached out our hands for friendship but you demand pay from us for a rong our people never committed. Do you remember all this, when you done rong we did not wage war but we came and made peace and did not demand pay?"

The Navajo replied, "The answer was yes. I know it and remember it all. I dont know what will be done but they are mad now. I want peace but for that I would not be here."[151]

Lee reports more generally that, while traveling, Hamblin and Tenney "had a good talk" with three Navajos. Tenney, the interpreter, told Lee "that he reached their Hearts & made deep impressions upon them = It made the Hair rise on his head while talking with them, & his opinion was that there was nothing searious between them & us."[152]

After talking with this Navajo headman, Jacob and the other Mormons wrote a letter to the leading Navajo chiefs. The signers—Hamblin, Thales Haskell, and Ammon Tenney, W. T. Stewart, Thomas Chamberlain, and Elijah J. Potter—once again stated the Mormon position on the murders. A non-Mormon had perpetrated the killings, and therefore it was futile for the Navajos to demand reparations from the Mormons. "We have tried very hard to satisfy your people of this, but they will not listen to the truth; but demand of us 400 Four Hundred head of Cattle; in payment for a deed our people never committed," they wrote. Therefore, they required that Navajos stay southeast of the Colorado until the matter was resolved. However, Jacob and the others again suggested that a few Navajos, with an interpreter, come to Lee's Ferry to investigate the killings. There, "we will be happy to see you, and satisfy you that what we have said is true."[153] Jacob sent this to Arny, asking him to interpret it to the Navajo leaders.

At Moenkopi, the Mormons received news, or a rumor, that some Navajos had set a date and time for attacking the Mormons there, but had given up the plan when they were discovered.[154]

Jacob apparently was back at Moenkopi on May 4.[155] The following day the evacuation of Moenkopi and Moenave took place. The Mormons, with Tuuvi and Talasnimki, who had decided to visit Utah again, left Moenkopi and came to Moenave;

on the sixth, with Lee's family, they departed for the Colorado.[156] It was a bitter parting for Lee; he had spent over two thousand dollars to reclaim Moenave, he wrote to Brigham Young, "& it was a litle Paradise in Embryo. My wife & myself wept when we left it."[157] Three days later, John R. Young had accomplished his purpose, as the company crossed the Colorado.

Hamblin and Tenney arrived in Kanab on May 13,[158] ahead of the main party, and three days later, they sent a report to John W. Young in which they downplayed the threats of the Navajos. They stated that they felt that if the Navajos really wanted to raid, they would not make threats. Instead, they were threatening in the hope of extorting cattle from the Mormons. "All the Moquis say, it is nothing but talk, in hopes of their demands being met," Hamblin and Tenney wrote. "In all our talks from the beginning, the Spirit testified to us that that what the Moquis said was true."[159] Hamblin and Tenney did recommend keeping a close watch on the three places where the Colorado could be crossed; however, none of these could be traversed before the low-water season in August.[160]

The main Blythe and John R. Young party arrived at Kanab on May 21.[161]

So the Arizona mission and Jacob's colony at Moenkopi-Moenave came to an abrupt end. The circumstances of this occurrence remain somewhat mysterious. Jacob felt that Brigham Young had been given false information, and in his autobiography criticized those responsible for withdrawing the Moenave settlement—probably referring to John Blythe and John R. Young. He later wrote, "I had passed through many perils to establish a mission among the Indians on the east side of the Colorado, but on account of the sayings and doings of unwise brethren, the time came for it to be broken up."[162]

Arny, meanwhile, wrote Commissioner Dudley on May 12, again accusing the Mormons of major complicity in the murders: "McCarty who killed the Indians referred to is a Gentile but he had mormons to help him."[163] This is misleading, and in its plural, factually untrue. McCarty or his sons had the main responsibility for the murders, and apparently only one Mormon, Clinger, was present (in the Hamblin-Navajo scenario for the murders, which I accept as earlier and more reliable). Arny again pled for his trip to Washington with ten Navajos, including two relatives of the Grass Valley victims, as he felt that this would provide a cooling-off period for Navajos still angry about the killings. Though he did not mention it in this letter, it would also allow him to pursue his San Juan land trade.

He also wrote, "Four of the Mormons who have signed the enclosed letters, were engaged in the Mountain Meadows Massacre, and I am fully satisfied that the miners and Gentile settlers will be treated in the same manner, and the crimes committed by

27.1. Delegation of Navajos in Washington, D.C., in December 1874. Jacob Hamblin had dealings with Ganado Mucho (standing, second from left, possibly the same as Hastele), Navajo agent William F. N. Arny (standing, fourth from left), headman Manuelito (sitting, third from right), and interpreter Jesus Arviso (standing, far right). Photograph by Charles Milton Bell. Courtesy Wikimedia Commons/National Archives.

the Mormons will be charged to the Indians, unless they are kept on this reservation." Arny's anti-Mormonism continued unabated.

Instead of Navajos traveling north of the river, Arny felt that he himself should travel to Lee's Ferry, and on June 3 requested that Col. John I. Gregg provide an escort.[164] Gregg apparently ignored the request, and the superintendent of Indian affairs in New Mexico, L. Edwin Dudley, vetoed the idea, a humiliating setback for Arny. On June 19, Dudley wrote to Edward Smith, the commissioner of Indian affairs in Washington, that Arny was definitely not the man to bring about peace in Arizona and Utah, and that a "Special Commissioner" might be required to negotiate a settlement.[165] Dudley apparently then instructed Arny to select this special commissioner, along with a respected Navajo chief, to investigate the McCarty killings. Soon they would be in Utah.

Jacob spoke at quarterly conference in St. George on June 6, stating that the Navajos "as a nation" wanted no war with the Mormons, but that some of the "wayward" Navajos wanted to resume raids in Utah, therefore the crossings on the Colorado should be watched.[166] Jacob attended a meeting on Indian policy after this conference session, presided over by Robert Gardner and Alexander McDonald, counselors in the Stake Presidency (John W. Young was out of town). Also present were Levi Stewart, John R. Young, Andrew Gibbons, Sam Knight, Lorenzo Roundy, James

Leithead, and James Andrus. They decided that two settlements and trading posts would be established on the Colorado, one at Lonely Dell (led by Thales Haskell) and the other at the Crossing of the Fathers (led by Andrew Gibbons). St. George stalwart Daniel D. McArthur was called to help select the locations for the posts, with Jacob as his guide. The St. George leaders decided to send thirty men to build forts at the two sites and leave ten men at each post.[167]

While traveling with McArthur, Jacob again told him that he felt that breaking up the Arizona mission was a mistake, and that there would be no trouble with the Navajos. The party decided that a fort at the Crossing of the Fathers would be unnecessary, as the water was extremely high, but did locate a fort at Lonely Dell. (This building, which was used as a trading post, still stands at Lee's Ferry.)[168] While there, according to Little, Jacob again predicted that a party of investigating Navajos would soon cross the Colorado, then he set out for Pahreah.[169]

When he arrived back at Kanab on about July 14, he found an investigating party already there, on their way to Grass Valley, led by Hamblin's friend Hastele.[170] Hamblin must have been overjoyed to see that moderate Navajo doing what he had suggested for so long, investigating in Utah, at the site of the murders. With Hastele was John D. Boyd, the prospector whom we last met as an associate of the Smith brothers who accompanied Jacob to the parley with the Navajos; now he was an official agent for the government sent to investigate the murders and return the horses and property of the slain Navajos.[171] Boyd was friendly with Hamblin, so this was also a stroke of good fortune.

Two interpreters accompanied Hastele and Boyd, John Lorenzo Hubbell and "Jesus Albiso" (Jesús Arviso), another well-known interpreter.[172] Also in the party was a George Kennedy (whom I have not identified) and another Navajo.

The question of who authorized this investigating company has been debated, as it would seem out of character for Arny to send the moderate Hastele to investigate.[173] Arny disapproved of Arviso and Hubbell, but expert Navajo-English interpreters were not plentiful, so he was often forced to use them. Arny also had had conflicts with Ganado Mucho (if Hastele is Ganado Mucho), who was technically living off the Navajo Reservation.[174]

Nevertheless, it appears that Arny was behind the deputation, though perhaps he sent Boyd, Hubbell, and Arviso with some reluctance. According to Bunting, Boyd was "appointed by the agency at Fort Defiance," which would suggest Arny as the appointer, and Thurber explicitly says that Arny sent Boyd and two interpreters on this mission.[175] Arny had earlier sent Hubbell and Ganado Mucho to Hamblin (which might support the argument that Hastele was in fact Ganado Mucho).

After meeting this party in Kanab, Hamblin wrote that at first, he felt that he had pressing family responsibilities at home, and did not need to travel with the investigatory company, so he sent his trusted lieutenant, Ammon Tenney, instead. But he soon received one of his characteristic spiritual witnesses, a violent pain in his knee as he worked in his gardens, and thought better of not going with the group. He overtook them sixty miles north of Kanab.

He explained to Hastele the geography of the killings, where Mormons and non-Mormons lived in Grass Valley, and where McCarty's ranch was located. He had telegraphed ahead to Albert Thurber, now living in Richfield, and Helaman Pratt, who would be able to explain the crime more thoroughly than Hamblin, to meet them at the lower end of Grass Valley. Pratt, twenty-eight years old, was a son of Apostle Parley P. Pratt, and later became a prominent leader in the Mormon colonies in Mexico.[176]

According to Hamblin, Hastele recognized Thurber and Pratt from a distance, and felt an immediate confidence in them. "Yes, they are good men, men of God," he said, then embraced them "in true Navajoe style." They discussed the crime, and after this talk, Hastele felt he did not need to visit the scene of the murders.

"I am satisfied; I have gone far enough," he said.

> I know our friends, the "Mormons," are our true friends. No other people we ever knew would have taken the trouble they have to show us the truth. I believe they have good hearts. Here is Jacob; he has been traveling about to do good all winter and spring, and is going yet. When I get home I do not intend my tongue to lay idle until the Navajoes learn the particulars of this affair.[177]

Hastele turned south toward Kanab, but Boyd and the interpreters wanted to see the scene of the murder, so the remaining group traveled to the cabin site the next day, guided by Pratt and Thurber. Jacob, Boyd, and the interpreters then returned to Kanab by way of Richfield.[178]

George Washington Bean wrote to Brigham Young on August 20, stating that Jacob felt that the Navajo nation would be satisfied by the report of Hastele and Boyd. He planned to go to Fort Defiance with the group and return with more Navajos, who would reopen trade and intercourse with the Mormons.[179]

As it turned out, Hamblin's feelings were correct. This investigation was a boon to Hamblin and the Mormons. They now could state, both to Navajos and to the officials at the Navajo agency, that Mormons were not to blame for the Grass Valley killings, and they could rely on the prestige of Hastele and an official government investigator when making that claim. It must have been a blow to Arny, and it also worked against the interests of the more militant factions of the Navajos.

At Kanab, Hastele and his companion were apparently staying at or near Jacob's home, and the Navajo chief became good friends with Jacob's children. When he departed, he asked to see the Hamblin family. According to one report, Jacob's numerous offspring gathered around him, and he gave the boys full Navajo embraces, then held out his hand and blessed Jacob and his family collectively. This Navajo ritual must have been an impressive sight.[180]

Hamblin, Ammon Tenney, Thales Haskell, Boyd, and Hastele were at Fort Defiance in mid-August, and Hamblin described the events there in a letter to Brigham Young.[181] After several unsuccessful requests, the Mormons were able to meet with leading Navajo chiefs on August 19. Jared W. Daniels, an "Indian Agent inspector" visiting from Washington, D.C., was also at the meeting, and asked Hamblin why the Mormons had not prosecuted the killers of the three Navajos. Hamblin replied that it was "because of the well known course that the Federal Judges had pursued in Utah." After which, Hamblin wrote, the inspector "treated us with the utmost contempt & did not speak peaceable to us."[182]

Another Navajo had been killed, in New Mexico, and Manuelito, whom Hamblin referred to as the "the principle Chief," and "a tall inteligent good natured appearing Indian," turned to the inspector and demanded compensation for this man, as well as for the three Navajos killed in Utah:

> Now nerve up your mussels & settle this matter: I want it done & off my mind so I can look the relatives of the murdered men in the face: these men have been treachourously murdered: it must be settled. We are under now & rode upon by the white man but it will be our turn next to ride: should I see you at Washington I want you to look me square in the face.[183]

Manuelito may have been allied with Black Hawk in raiding Mormon settlements.[184] Since that time, he had finally surrendered and moved to Bosque Redondo, and signed the treaty that allowed the Navajos to return home in 1868.[185] After Barboncito's death, the Navajo agent had appointed him as a leading chief of the Navajos (a position nonexistent before Bosque Redondo), while Ganado Mucho served as a subchief in western Navajo territory.

Ne Chic Se Cla, the survivor of the Grass Valley murders, spoke, giving what Hamblin believed to be "a straightfo[r]ward testimony of the murderous affair." Hamblin certainly accepted the Navajo version of the Grass Valley killings, rather than the McCarty-Clinger version preserved by Pitcher and Gottfredson.

Boyd, the investigator who had gone with Hamblin to Grass Valley, as well as Hubbell and Arviso, the two interpreters, also spoke, blaming McCarty for the killing and the federal legal system for shielding him. "He told the Council that it was impossible to bring the murderers to justice because the federal judges stood in the way." It is entirely credible that Hubbell and Arviso, whom Arny had offended, would work against his interests in this way. Arny had also antagonized the moderate Ganado Mucho.

So apparently, the Mormons and the investigating party had come a long way to convincing the Navajos that "Americans" and the federal government were to blame for the Grass Valley murders, not the Mormons. This was good for the Mormons, but Inspector Daniels was furious, and forbade the Mormons from trading and talking with the Navajos, as they had done before January 1874.[186]

This rubbed the Navajos the wrong way. According to Hamblin, they "expresed to us indignation that they were not to be permitted to trade with the Mormons: that they were a free people & would trade with whom they pleased & yet have all the land they possessed before the war with the U.S."[187]

After this, Jacob had a private interview with Arny. He seemed more friendly to Jacob than the inspector had been, and said that if Jacob had come at any other time, he could have done something for him:

> I am satisfied that you people have not done the killing but I am in the hands of this Inspector. It will take me months to get things in a running order after he leaves: I will see that this matter is righ[t]ly handled & steps taken to prosecute. I shall leave here in a few days for Washington & take with me some of the principle Cheifs of the Navajos.[188]

After Arny's repeated attempts to blame the Mormons for the Grass Valley killings, this statement to Hamblin seems disingenuous at best.

Arny then informed Hamblin that what he had told him was confidential, and he did not want anyone to know that he had even had an interview with him. "The Navajos run the agency," he said, "& I do not know what will result; I am in fear."[189] He also said that he had withheld arms and ammunition from the Navajos to protect the Mormons, but he would do this no longer. The Mormons must protect themselves.[190] This is hardly an expression of solidarity with the citizens of Utah.

On their way back home, Hamblin, Haskell, and Tenney stopped at the ranch of a Navajo named Garney Monsher, who told the Mormons that they could return to Utah in good spirits.[191] "The Navajos were our friends," he said, "& [he] hoped that we would always be theirs." The Navajos "were making many good Blankets which they wished to trade for Horses."[192] The three missionaries told them that if Mormons did business with Navajos, it would have to be at the river, because Inspector Daniels had forbidden them to trade or talk with the Navajos. Garney answered, "Who is Washington? Tell him to kiss our — —."[193]

A remarkable turnabout had taken place. Navajo anger at Mormons in January and February 1874 had turned to anger at the way the federal officials were handling matters at the Navajo reservation. Some Navajos, at least, were now demanding reparations from the U.S. government.[194]

Jacob arrived home at Kanab on September 2, and could once again deal with his own affairs. However, he found that he had deeply offended Ammon Tenney, who had served as his valued and steady companion for many years. Tenney wrote in his autobiography, "After fifteen years of toil there arose conditions that my 'netly' and irritable organization could no longer bear and I made it known to everybody that I should never go again with Jacob Hamblin." He would try to "forgive and overlook the past," but would not work with him again.[195] Apparently he felt that Jacob had not given him his proper recognition for his efforts as an Indian missionary.[196]

Ammon later said that he regretted that he had not had more understanding of Jacob in 1874.[197] Despite this, his "wounded heart" at the time shows that working with Jacob had been difficult. The Mormon Church's Indian missionaries often felt unsupported and underappreciated; probably Jacob's associates, many of whom were remarkable men in their own right, and pursued similar peace policies with Indians at considerable danger to themselves, felt especially underappreciated working in his shadow.

Ammon would continue on to have a remarkable career as an Indian missionary and leading citizen in the Mormon colonies in Arizona and Mexico.

The diplomacy of Hamblin, Brigham Young, and others such as Tenney and Ira Hatch, must be accounted a major success in the aftermath of the Grass Valley killings. Moore writes, "Arny's role in the matter had been provocative.... A war between the two [Mormons and Navajos] would have served his purposes. A settlement had been reached because the Mormons had been ceaseless in their quest for peace and because the Navajos had used restraint."[198] Jacob, sick when called by Brigham Young, had acted with courage and indefatigable energy, making three dangerous and difficult trips to Arizona.

It is hard to assess Lee's attacks on Jacob during this period objectively. Possibly they are simply the product of a flawed, embittered man; possibly, they show some of Jacob's imperfections. In any event, Jacob's diplomacy, his repeated visits to Arizona, his ability to work with important friends such as Ammon Tenney and Ira Hatch, and his friendship with the important Navajo headman Hastele, worked to ward off major Navajo raids against Mormon settlements. (The unwillingness of leaders such as Manuelito and Ganado Mucho to risk another Bosque Redondo must have been another factor.)

Jehiel McConnell, after spending time on guard duty at the Colorado, returned to Kanab on November 8 and "gave a favorable report of the Navajoes and the spirit of the 'Red men' in general."[199] Though the Mormons remained wary of dissident or outlaw Navajos, and would continue to guard the Colorado crossings, they no longer feared full-scale retaliation from the tribe.[200]

Jacob ended 1874 discussing the Arizona and Navajo question with Brigham Young, Erastus Snow, George A. Smith, and other leaders in Brigham's home in St. George.[201] For Young, the way was open to once again try to colonize Arizona.

28

"The Navajoes Carried on Quite an Extensive Trade with Our People"

At the Colorado Post, 1875

The year 1875 was comparatively uneventful for Hamblin, now fifty-six years old. In fact, his diplomacy after the Grass Valley massacre was the last great dramatic event in his life. After this, he would play a part in the Mormon colonization of Arizona and New Mexico, but while he continued exploring, helping Mormon settlers, and working with Indians, there were a number of other explorers and Indian missionaries working actively at the same time. He was one of many. Nevertheless, he was still a prominent Mormon, and the leading Indian authority in southern Utah and Arizona.

He spent time at Kanab in 1875, and also at the trading post at Lonely Dell, exchanging horses with Navajos for their beautiful blankets.[1] Ketchene visited once, and Jacob introduced one of his sons to him. "He turned away and wept, apparently much dejected," Hamblin wrote. "His friends told me that the loss of his sons was killing him."[2] Two months after this meeting, Ketchene died.

In late December 1874, Brigham Young and George A. Smith had sent three parallel letters to Jacob Hamblin, Ammon Tenney, and Ira Hatch, who probably received them in early 1875. "Dear Brother," Jacob's started. "We wish you to continue your labors as missionary to the Natives; and call upon such of the brethren, from time to time as you feel will render you suitable help." After a paragraph expressing appreciation for Hamblin's labors during the past year, Young and Smith wrote, "We have written to Brothers Tenney and Hatch to meet your calls according to their ability. And it is for you, according to the spirit of your appointment, to determine from time to time when to make moves in crossing the River and continuing your labors in preaching to and teaching the Indians." Young's focus was no longer on Kanab and Pahreah, the Mormons and Paiutes there.

Perhaps sensing that Jacob, and Indian missionaries in general, sometimes felt that they were not sufficiently valued, the letter continued, "We fully appreciate your labors in the past and feel to encourage you to persevere."

Young and Smith wanted Emma Lee and her family to stay at Lonely Dell and run the ferry, "and have the avails of the transient travel"; but they asked Jacob to help her moor the ferryboat in a safe place. They also recommended that Jacob recruit some families to settle and farm at Lonely Dell.[3]

To Tenney and Hatch, Young and Smith wrote: "Dear Brother, It is our wish that you assist Brother Jacob Hamblin, in his labors among the Indians, and answer his call from time to time." They should strive to uphold Jacob "in his councils," and asked "that the Spirit of the Holy Gospel of Peace shall animate you in all your relations with the Indians."[4] Young wanted these three to make sure that diplomacy with local Indians, and especially with the Navajos, was carried out well as he made efforts to colonize Arizona once again.

On January 13, 1875, Jacob, together with Thales Haskell and John Oakley, wrote Brigham Young while they were visiting at the fort that had been built at Lee's Ferry in 1874 (which was now being used as a trading post). They stated that things were going well, that many Navajos were trading. Andrew Gibbons feared a bad spirit among the Mormons more than he did among the Indians. They were awaiting news from the Navajo leaders in Washington.[5]

Oakley would work with Jacob frequently in the upcoming years. Now fifty-six years old, Oakley was a former resident of St. George, known for his expert gardening, who had moved to Kanab in March 1872.[6] After losing the use of his right eye as a child, he had injured his other eye in St. George, so was gradually becoming blind.[7]

Jacob sent a message to Brigham Young and George A. Smith in mid-February, reporting that the Colorado post did not need further supplies, or men, except those men who wanted to "build up and improve the place." He was still planning another trip across the Colorado. "I will take some Pi-utes if necessary and visit the Navajos. Old Patnish will try and post me in regard to the spirit and feelings among the Indians on the other side of the River."[8]

About a month later, on March 14, Jacob and Oakley wrote to Brigham from Kanab, saying that they had heard no news from the Navajos in Washington, but felt that they were so friendly that they could reduce the guard at the Lee's Ferry trading post.[9] Jacob mentioned that some local Paiutes, including Cedar City headman Coal Creek John, felt it would be beneficial to travel with him across the Colorado to talk with the Diné.[10] "In taking some good spirited Indians from here I would feel safe: if there should yet be some crusty Navajos," he wrote. He mentioned that he was collecting "scrub horses" for future trade with the Navajos, and would leave them with William Swap at the "Pools" in House Rock Valley.

The Kanab Indians were fencing fifteen acres of land that Bishop Stewart had "set off" to them, and Jacob had given them a thousand pounds of corn to sustain them while they were fencing.

Jacob asked John Oakley to write about a slight conflict that had arisen at the trading post. "There is some friction between the brethren at the Post & Prest. Jacob

Hamblin," he wrote. "While I would not uphold Bro. Hamblin as a perfect man: I feel that his general aim ... is good & it hampers him to make good Indian Missionaries of persons who have been educated in freight trains & mining camps &c."[11]

He mentioned that Warren Johnson had passed Kanab on his way to "the ferry." The next chapter in the history of Lee's Ferry belongs to this quiet, unassuming, reliable man, now thirty-seven. Reilly justifiably writes that Johnson has stood in the shadow of Lee's Ferry legends Jacob Hamblin and John D. Lee (and, I might add, Emma Lee), but that he deserves to stand fully beside them in the saga of the ferry. Jacob explored Lee's Ferry, Reilly writes, and the Lees settled it, but "Warren Johnson made the place bloom.... Johnson's green pastures, his ready hospitality, and his great faith provided material succor and spiritual courage to the pioneer colonists who ventured into the inhospitable Arizona desert across the Colorado River."[12]

A native of New Hampshire, Johnson had been struck by gold fever in 1866, and as he and some friends were traveling overland to California, an ulcer forced him to stop at the nearest city for medical treatment—as fate would have it, Salt Lake City. His companions went ahead while he convalesced in the home of a Dr. Jonathan Smith in Farmington. He converted to Mormonism and eventually, in 1869, married Smith's daughter, Permelia Jane. Less than a year after his baptism, he was called to the difficult Muddy Mission in Nevada and settled in St. Thomas. There he served as schoolteacher and became a leading citizen of the town.

When most of the Muddy Mission was abandoned in 1870, Warren and Permelia settled in Long Valley, in Glendale, formerly known as Berryville. Johnson taught again and also served as bookkeeper and clerk in a store. He married one of his pupils, Samantha Nelson, as a plural wife in 1872, and was called as a counselor to Bishop Howard O. Spencer in the Long Valley bishopric.

According to Reilly, Spencer asked Johnson to take over Lee's Ferry temporarily, and the job became permanent. He came to the ferry with his first wife, Permelia, on March 30, 1875,[13] and took over the land of James Jackson, who had died. He began to farm, and helped run the ferry and the Lee's Ferry trading post.

Jacob wrote to Young again on March 29, only about two weeks after his previous letter, reporting that he had visited the ferry.[14] Fourteen Hopis had come to Utah to trade, and they all reported that the Navajos were "warm" (friendly) to the Mormons and cold to the Mormons' enemies, presumably the U.S. government in Navajo territory.

One detail from Warren Johnson's first season at the Ferry supports the proposition that the Navajos now were generally peaceful and were not threatening. Between April 1 and November 1, 1875, Johnson ferried 522 Indians, 497 of them Navajos, across the river.[15] Clearly, they found trade with the Mormons to be advantageous and safe.

Lee had written and made an offer to the men at the ferry to rent the land at Lonely Dell to them, but they were not enthusiastic about the offer. He understood that only an acre or two was needed for the trading post. Warren Johnson would stay "& do the best he can," Jacob wrote. "He does not seem absorbed in a greedy trade spirit. I left him in charge of all local matters Farming &c." Young had evidently cautioned the men at the trading post against "a spirit of avarisious trade."[16]

Jacob reported that the ferry had evidently lost some customers because some were crossing at the Crossing of the Fathers, but stated that this could be made impassable "by turning a small rivulet on." There were rumors that Mormons actually dynamited the Crossing of the Fathers between 1870 and 1880.[17]

Jacob stated that Brother Winsor was elated with the prospect of a ranch in House Rock Valley.[18] He ended the letter, "Of necesity I must attend as witness in J. D. L's trial at Beaver. It is my intention to carry out my mission by the blessing of the Lord. Believe me as ever: in the Gosple of truth." The last chapters in Hamblin's tortuous relationship with Lee were approaching. After returning to Utah, Lee had visited his families, and had been arrested by federal marshals on November 7, 1874, while visiting one of his wives in Panguitch. He was imprisoned until the beginning of his first trial, when he was freed on bail for a few months.

This trial took place in Beaver, beginning on July 23, 1875, with U.S. District Judge Jacob Boreman presiding.[19] Though Lee was one of the main targets of the prosecution, Isaac Haight, William Dame, John Higbee, George Adair, and others were also indicted. (Many of these were friends or associates of Jacob.) Philip Klingensmith, who had accompanied Jacob on his 1863 visit to the Hopis, had turned state's evidence and was the star witness for the prosecution. Jacob did not testify as a witness in this first trial. One report states that U.S. Attorney William Carey and Deputy District Attorney Robert Baskin urged him to testify and he declined.[20] However, this is questionable, as they could have simply given him a subpoena if they felt he had important evidence on the massacre.

The case went to jury on August 5, 1875, and the twelve men deadlocked, with the group's eight Mormons voting that Lee was not guilty, one non-Mormon voting with them, and three non-Mormons voting for conviction.[21] This meant that the case had to be tried again. Jacob would figure prominently in the second trial the following year.

John Oakley sent Brigham Young a report on Kanab while Jacob was in Beaver which gives a vivid snapshot of the town at the time. The United Order, Mormonism's communitarian system, was not going well there, as there was a split between Bishop Levi Stewart and order leader John R. Young. "The parties are getting further & further apart," Oakley wrote. Usually the bishop was leader of the order in a town, but not in Kanab, unfortunately.[22]

There was a constant stream of Navajos and Hopis passing through Kanab, intent on trading for horses—sixty-five in the few days before the time of writing, as well as forty Sevier Utes who were then visiting. The local Paiutes were an irritation. When Oakley complained to Chuarumpeak about thefts of wheat, potatoes, and cattle, the headman said that "he could not control some of his people, no more then [than] the Bp. could his."[23] It was an astute comment, given Stewart's problems with the United Order.

Hamblin, meanwhile, was building a "comfortable dwelling house" for either Priscilla or Louisa, and was apparently trying to finish it before going on any major expeditions.[24]

On September 16, the divided order ended, as L. John Nuttall replaced Levi Stewart as Kanab bishop, and John R. Young as president of the United Order, in an attempt to unify the divided town.[25] Though he was an able leader (and later served as private secretary for three church presidents), Nuttall often did not live in Kanab.

As Jacob relaxed in Kanab and Lee's Ferry, Brigham was starting to plan the next attempt at colonizing Arizona. In the fall, he sent a small company of explorers and missionaries to Mexico and Arizona, led by the irascible Daniel Webster Jones, a forty-five-year-old Spanish-speaking Indian interpreter from central Utah. A native of Missouri, he had been orphaned at age twelve, and five years later joined the U.S. Army to serve in the Mexican-American War, from 1846 to 1848. After the war he stayed in Mexico for a few years and learned Spanish. In 1850 he was back in the states, on his way to California, when his gun went off accidentally in its holster, wounding him in the leg and groin. Mormons nursed him back to health in Provo, in northern Utah, and he was baptized a Mormon the following year. Sharp tongued, he had rocky relationships with his fellow Saints, but was nevertheless known for helping and defending Indians, and became a favorite of Brigham Young.[26]

The Jones company was instructed to explore Arizona, including the Little Colorado area, so they are part of the Arizona exploration that Jacob was always so interested in. But their main commission was to visit Mexico and assess it as a place for possible Mormon colonization. This missionary trip was, in fact, the beginning of the saga of the Mormon colonies in Mexico, a chapter in Mormon history that Jacob would play a limited part in.[27] As we have seen, Brigham Young and Thomas Kane had been interested in planting Mormon colonies in Mexico since 1872. They were coming one step closer to this objective.[28]

Jacob's expertise was with American Indians; he did not know Spanish. So Spanish-speakers such as Dan Jones were necessary for this mission to Mexico. In the group of seven men were Ammon Tenney, another Spanish speaker, as well as an Indian missionary, and later a resident of the Mexican colonies; Anthony W. Ivins, eventual president of the colonies and still later an apostle and a member of the First Presidency; and Helaman Pratt, whom we met in Grass Valley in 1874, and who would become a church leader in Mexico.[29]

Jacob and Thomas Chamberlain went with the Jones company during the first part of their journey but were not full-fledged members of this mission, as they intended to go only a limited way with the group. "Bro. Jacob Hamblin and Thomas Chamberlain will accompany us part way," wrote Helaman Pratt in his diary at the beginning of the journey.[30] Chamberlain, a twenty-one-year-old native of Tooele, had served in the Muddy Mission, then moved to Long Valley after that mission's demise. He had been part of John R. Young's expedition to bring home the Blythe company in 1874.[31]

The Jones company left Kanab on October 20, and after passing the by now familiar stops on the journey—Navajo Wells, House Rock Springs, and Jacob's Pools—arrived at Lee's Ferry on the twenty-sixth, where the family of Warren Johnson was living.

They crossed the Colorado on Emma's ferry boat and traveled to Bitter Springs, where they camped the next day. John D. Lee's main defense attorney, "Judge" Wells Spicer, who was also a prospector, now showed up at Bitter Springs, as did three Navajos.[32] Hamblin struck up a friendship with Spicer and suggested that he travel with the group the next day. However, after the party set out the morning of the twenty-eighth, Jones discovered that Spicer was a prospector and absolutely refused to let him travel with the missionaries, "and because Bro Hamblin showed friendship" to Spicer, Anthony Ivins wrote, "Bro. Jones requested them both to leave the company." Attempts were made to reconcile Hamblin and Jones, but to no avail. "Bro Hamblin felt very badly," Ivins wrote, "he said he had always been taught to assist all men when he found them in need and that it was because of this that he proposed to assist Judge Spicer."[33] Ammon Tenney recorded that Jacob even wept copiously because of this conflict: "It caused me to feel somewhat sober for on parting he wept & there was more than his eyes that was wet with tears."

So Hamblin, Spicer, and Chamberlain left the party, turning back toward the Colorado.

In P. T. Reilly's account of the event, Jacob, who had reportedly been previously hired by Spicer, secretly arranged a rendezvous with the attorney at Bitter Springs, intentionally started a dispute with Jones, then, after the Jones company had departed, took up an illicit prospecting expedition with Spicer. This reconstruction does not hold up, however, when we examine the evidence from such sources as Little and Spicer, as well as letters and diaries from a number of people who had firsthand knowledge of the events.[34]

Jacob mentioned the Jones expedition in a November 17 letter to Brigham Young: "I accompanied Bro. Jones a short distance the other side of the River, they all seemed to have the spirit of their Mission and was well united.... The best of feelings prevail, from the best I can learn, among all their ranches [the Navajo ranches]. In talking with Bro. Jones & Tenney I thought it best to return home."[35] So Jacob glossed over Jones's dictatorial treatment of him.

The company, now without Hamblin and Chamberlain, continued south. They explored the Little Colorado again, then visited the Phoenix-Tempe area in the Salt River Valley, and Tucson. Jones later recommended the upper valleys of the Little Colorado as a place for settlement.[36] The company split in January 1876, with the main group going south to Mexico, while Tenney and Robert H. Smith went north to western New Mexico, where they opened up the remarkably successful Zuni mission. Jones and his group returned to Utah in late June.

Brigham was preparing to settle the Little Colorado soon, but before he did so, he sent one final exploring mission to the area. This time he selected an unlikely explorer, missionary, and settlement leader, a one-legged Mormon Battalion veteran and Indian missionary, James Stephens Brown. A native of North Carolina who had converted to Mormonism in 1844, Brown had extensive experience on the frontier; in fact, he had been one of the men who discovered gold at Sutter's Mill.[37] When Young called Brown in a private interview on September 29, he said, "I should like to send you on a mission to those Indians [Navajos]." He told Brown to make a list of a few men to go with him, "But none of your Babies on this mission. I want good men." Brown and seven hand-picked men were formally called on October 9; six more were added later. Brown was set apart "to take charge of the Mission to the Navajos in Arizona and adjacent tribes."[38] On October 28, Brown received a letter from Brigham Young and Daniel H. Wells that did not mention Indians, but emphasized that he would be in charge of new settlements in Arizona:

> Dear Brother:—You are hereby appointed to take charge of the mission about to go south and southeast of the Colorado River. It will become your duty to found settlements in suitable locations, where the brethren can congregate in cultivating the earth to bring forth substance for the families of the brethren who may feel disposed to join you.[39]

Brown immediately began to prepare for this mission, and recruited a group of thirteen men, including three extremely capable Indian missionaries, Andrew Gibbons, Thales Haskell, and Ira Hatch.

In Jacob's November 17 letter to Brigham, he mentioned this "mission called to the Moancopy" and stated that Thales Haskell would be a good Indian interpreter for the group, as he knew Hopi and understood "the Indian character." He said that he thought Haskell would make a "good, safe" settlement at Moenkopi, "which might have been don over a year ago if everyone that was sent there would have paid attention to their own affairs." The 1874 pullout from Arizona still rankled Jacob.

The Brown company left Kanab on November 22, reached Lee's Ferry five days later, then continued on "over a dry, rough, difficult road" till they reached Moenkopi on December 3. This was, wrote Brown, "the pleasantest spot we had seen since before arriving at Kanab. I was impressed to make this place winter quarters, and designated a site for a fort."[40] Arizona was inhabited by Mormons once again.

Haskell visited Oraibi and returned with Tuuvi and Talasnimki, who were delighted to have Mormons come settle in Moenkopi and begin farming in partnership with Hopis.[41] On December 9, Brown led five men, including Ira Hatch, to explore the Little Colorado and the San Francisco Mountains.[42] They arrived back at Moenkopi on the twenty-ninth, and Brown decided to return to Salt Lake immediately and report to Brigham. On New Year's Day, 1876, he set out north with two men, arriving at Kanab on January 6—this speedy, six-day journey being a stark contrast to the plodding, difficult, insecure early expeditions over the Colorado.

On his way northward, Brown met companies of Mormons traveling south to Arizona; Brigham, not waiting for Brown's verbal report, had already called them to settle on the Little Colorado.

A major Mormon migration was now in progress.

Jacob stayed in Kanab and built his new home, but he would periodically visit Lee's Ferry. In the November 17 letter, he wrote, "Good feeling prevails there, with the Navijos, and those having charge of the Ferrey. I would make honorab[l]e mention of Bro. Warren Johnson as being particularly careful of the boat, and making some valuble improvements on the land deeded to him by Sister Emma Lee near the Post." He mentioned that Brigham had asked him to "build up a good place" at the ferry, but he had trouble recruiting settlers: "There were none who felt like making improvements there, excepting Bro. Johnson, under the circumstances."

At this point, the John D. Lee diary attacks Jacob for his work at Lee's Ferry. According to Lee, the wife of John Blythe visited him in prison in February 1876 and told him that Jacob had been running the ferry and pocketing the proceeds. Emma complained about this to the Blythes, and when they visited Young, they relayed Emma's protests; Young reportedly then removed Jacob from his assignment at Lee's Ferry.[43]

As with all of Lee's attacks, without Jacob's response, it is difficult to assess this charge. It would be valuable to have the Blythes' account of the incident also. It is possible that Jacob, responding to Young's call to help Emma with the ferry, ran the ferry at times. (Incidentally, managing the ferry was no easy job: two oarsmen, one experienced, were required to operate the boat.)[44] According to Emma and Lee, Jacob wanted all of the proceeds, but this seems difficult to accept. Juanita Brooks writes that "no evidence has been found...to support Mrs. Blythe's charge against Hamblin."[45] We also should remember that Jacob had had half ownership of the ferry operation at Lee's Ferry.[46]

In addition, Jacob was building a permanent home in Kanab, and his focus was not on Lee's Ferry. He also appears to have been enthusiastic about the presence of Warren Johnson at the crossing (which argues against Lee's accusations that Jacob was trying to muscle in on the ferry business).

When he was at the ferry, Jacob often acted as Indian trader. If Mormons could trade with the Navajos at the Colorado, fewer Navajos would have to travel among the southern Utah settlements, and there would be less risk of trouble.[47]

It was at about this time that the well-known incident occurred in which Jacob's son Jacob Jr. short-changed a Navajo in a trade. According to Jacob Jr.,

> One day my father sent me to trade a horse with an old Navajo Indian chief. I was a little fellow and I went on horseback, leading the horse to be traded. The old chief came out and lifted me down from my horse. I told him my father wanted me to trade the horse for some blankets. He brought out a number of handsome blankets, but, as my father had told me to be sure and make a good trade, I shook my head and said I would have to have more. He then brought out two buffalo robes and quite a number of other blankets and finally, when I thought I had done very well, I took the roll on my horse, and started for home. When I gave the blankets to my father, he unrolled them, looked at them, and then began to separate them. He put blanket after blanket into a roll and then did them up and told me to get on my horse and take them back and tell the chief he had sent me too many. When I got back, the old chief took them and smiled. He said, "I knew you would come back; I knew Jacob would not keep so many; you know Jacob is our father, as well as your father."[48]

From March 19 to 23, there was a mass baptism of Shivwits Paiutes in St. George, in which some 170 Indians were baptized by Daniel D. McArthur, David H. Cannon, and Josiah G. Hardy.[49] This event was captured in stunning photographs by Charles Savage; in one of them, Daniel D. MacArthur baptizes a remarkably unkempt Shivwits, as our old friend Gus Hardy stands on the bank and translates.[50] On the twenty-first, at a Sunday meeting, one of the Shivwits who had been baptized, Mo-ke-ok, spoke, with Hardy translating, and said that he "desired to give his heart to God, as he had given his hands to the man who had baptized him.... He felt glad that some thirty Navajos had lately been baptized by Jacob Hamblin. He expressed his belief that many tribes would listen to God's word and obey it."[51] This is our only testimony to this baptism of Navajos by Jacob. These may have been the earliest Navajos ever baptized into the Mormon faith.[52]

In 1872, gold had been found by the Powell company, especially in Kanab Canyon, and a number of prospectors started a little gold rush in the area. This event, though it brought a number of non-Mormons into southern Utah, was an economic windfall for Mormons, and for Jacob in particular. He wrote in Little, "The winter of 1875–6 I had the privilege of remaining at home. My family was destitute of many things. Some mining prospectors came along, and offered me five dollars a day to go with them, as a protection against the Indians. To go with them could not injure the interests of our people. It seemed like a special providence to provide necessaries for my family, and I accepted the offer. I was gone sixty days, for which I received three hundred dollars."[53] The identity of these prospectors is unknown.

According to an engineer, Frederick Brind, Jacob worked for a geologist named C. S. Dutton between 1870 and 1872.[54] To the best of my knowledge, the only geologist named Dutton working with the U.S. Geological Survey Corps in the Grand Canyon and San Juan areas was the distinguished geologist Clarence Edward Dutton, a protégé of Powell, and author of the classic *Tertiary History of the Grand Canyon District* (1882) and also *Report on the Geology of the High Plateaus of Utah* (1880).[55] However, Clarence Dutton did his field work from 1875 to 1880, not between 1870 and 1872.[56] Assuming that Brind refers to Clarence Dutton, he must have worked with Jacob from 1875 to 1880.

According to Brind, the survey was centered in Kanab; Brind served under an R. U. Goods, in a company that covered the Grand Canyon. Jacob and Jacob's son Benjamin were also part of the company at times. Brind stated that he had been told that Jacob had helped plan the Mountain Meadows Massacre, and decided to investigate his character. From this unpromising beginning, he developed a special friendship with Jacob—whom he described as "a grizzled and comparatively old man"—and the two often walked and camped with each other. He described him as "a good, kindly man, one worthy of mixing with, of emulating." In Kanab, he even asked and was given permission by Jacob to take one of his daughters to a dance.

For Brind, Jacob was "a veritable child of nature, and kindly in disposition toward all human, animal, and insect life." He testified to Jacob's gentleness toward animals, describing him carefully walking around troops of ants in mountain paths, and rebuking his son Ben severely when the boy used the whip and spur on a horse too freely. Once, while the geological company was in Kanab, Jacob took Brind down to the Kanab stockyard, the Big Field, which included a number of horses and cattle. Jacob then called some of the animals by name, and, Brind wrote, "what was my surprise to note a sudden disturbance among the stock...about two or three dozen of which, came galloping toward us and forthwith surrounded him and began nibbling up against him."[57]

Brind stated that he and Jacob "traversed over much hitherto unexplored country together, which he alone knew intimately." Brind's letter also vividly shows Jacob in the milieu of the American Indian. The engineer stated that at night, Jacob would "wander away from the party—build a little fire of his own—and sit down and croon little Indian ditties—he having largely adopted their system of life, having been so much associated with them—almost in preference to intermingling with his own."[58] This description may seem slightly romanticized, as we know that Jacob had strong ties with his Mormon culture. Nevertheless, there is probably some truth in it, as frontiersmen who spent a great deal of time with Indians did tend to acquire some of their traits.[59]

Jacob Hamblin was a man who, I believe, authentically liked Indians. Beginning in Tooele, he was drawn to spend time with them, talking and hunting. He evidently learned some Goshute in Tooele, and later, in southern Utah, came to speak Paiute well. As a result of his frequent visits to Indians, and living in their territory, he came to have a wide knowledge of the Indians of the Southwest, especially Goshutes, Paiutes, Hopis, Navajos, Utes and Shoshoni, and he also "became Indian," as it were—he came to have many of their characteristics.

Martha Cragun Cox, who was a friend of Jacob's daughter Tamar, referred to "his life and manners which were much like those of an Indian—He spoke in gutteral tones, had a sober face, and rarely smiled."[60] Though Cox was making an ethnic stereotype of Indians as solemn and unsmiling, her description of Hamblin is first-hand.[61]

Indian missionaries often did become immersed in the culture of Indians, to the extent that they sometimes felt some discomfort in returning to white society. When Thomas Kane spent a day with Ira Hatch in 1857, he remembered that Hatch, living in the Nevada desert without a white companion, was so used to speaking Indian languages that he could not speak English comfortably.[62]

One of Jacob's children, Inez Hamblin Lee, remembered being left at home during church meeting to tend the younger children, when she was about seven, and having a large group of Navajos call at the house. They spoke no English, but could only say, "Jacob." Inez pointed to the meeting house, which the Navajos seemed to misunderstand; they talked among themselves once again, then once more asked for "Jacob." To the seven-year-old's relief, Jacob and Louisa soon came home, "and the Indians were soon comfortably ensconced in our lane leading to the barn and corral and lying between the two orchards," Inez wrote. Jacob gave them corn from his fields, which they roasted with husks still on. In the following days, the Indians traded blankets and other goods for horses. Inez remembered that Jacob virtually disappeared during this period, except at night: "Father came home only to sleep, eating and spending all his time" with the Navajos.[63]

As we have seen, John Wesley Powell, in his classic description of Jacob that gave the Indian missionary some national fame in 1875, described Jacob as an exceedingly reticent person, who talked slowly and in a low voice, which caused Indians to listen to him in absolute silence.[64] Frederick Dellenbaugh, companion of Powell in his second Colorado expedition, also wrote that Hamblin's habit of talking slowly and calmly helped him create a powerful bond with Indians:

> Jacob Hamblin, I knew very well. He was an extraordinary character and had a great influence over the Indians. He was always fair with them and his slow, quiet way of talking suited their ideas. He never exhibited any fear or excitement, whatever might have been his inner feelings. I never saw anyone so quiet, calm and self-contained as "Old Jacob" as everyone in Kanab called him.[65]

Jacob's well-known guidelines that he used in dealing with Indians, extant both in his diary and in a letter to John W. Young, touch on some of these same qualities.[66] He wrote: "John W Young wanted me to write some maxims or Proverbs to manage Indians."

> first. Never talk any thing but truth to them.
> 2 Never let them see you in a pashion.
>
> 2nd. I think it useless to speak of things they cannot comprehend.
>
> 3 Never shoe show feer. Theis [This] should b[e] observd that you may shoy [show] your self of a sound hart and strong mind.
>
> 4 Never aproach them in an ostier [austere] manner youseing more woords than is nessisary to convey the idie in full[,] nor in a higher tone of vois than to be distinctley hurd.
>
> 5 Allways listen to an Indian when he wishes to tell you his grievances and redress rongs if they can show their is any.[67]
>
> 6 Never youse obseen language or take any cours of that king [kind] before them.[68]
>
> 7 Never submit to any unjust demand or [allow them to] cohure [coerce] anything from you. ther by [thereby] shoeing you are gov erned ~~by the~~ and govern by the rule of wright and not might.

Then, in the letter, Jacob attested to the value of these "rules": "I have tried to observe the above rules for the past twenty years and it has given me a salutary influence where I have met with them....I believe, if the rules, &c., I have mentioned were generally observed, there would be but little difficulty on our frontiers with the Redman."

We see in rule number four that that Jacob consciously kept his voice low while talking to Indians, and rules two and three show that his calmness was also due to a conscious effort and policy.

Jacob became so immersed in Indian culture that he came to have what might be seen as an unusual respect for Indian religion, granted that one of his primary focuses was to convert Indians to the Mormon version of Christianity. Though he disapproved of Paiute shamanistic healing—perhaps because he saw it as being in direct competition with Mormon healings[69]—he participated in and approved of other elements of Indian religion.[70]

Back in late 1857, as we have seen, Jacob, journeying with a party of whites through a dangerous stretch of Nevada, wrote in his diary that when some Indians visited their camp at night, "we made them some mush and I got them to dance by joining with them." As a result, "This begat a good spirit in them." More Indians came to the white camp during the night and the next morning, and also enjoyed the feast and dance, which made it possible for the whites to continue on in safety.[71] Participating in ritual dancing helped defuse a possibly violent situation.

Jacob was particularly sympathetic to Hopi ceremonialism and religion. When he first witnessed a Hopi ceremony in 1858, as we have seen, he wrote, "I have ben to many an Indian dance but this surpased any I ever witnessed."[72] This can be contrasted to some early white visitors to the mesas who regarded Hopi ritualism with open contempt.[73] After this same trip, Hamblin felt that he and other Mormons had visited the Hopis as a fulfillment of prophecies given to the Hopis generations earlier—that is, he accepted Hopi prophecy as valid. On one occasion, at least, he accepted a Paiute prophecy as valid.[74]

In late 1862 and early 1863, on his fifth trip across the Colorado, after witnessing Hopi rain ceremonies followed by a welcome storm, Jacob took this as a literal divine answer to the Hopis' prayers.[75]

In 1870, preparatory to crossing the Colorado at Lee's Ferry, Hopi convert Tuuvi requested that Hamblin join with him in celebrating a Hopi ritual before passing over that imposing river. Hamblin agreed, and after Tuuvi's prayer, the two men took the contents of Tuuvi's medicine bag and scattered it into the air, on the land, and into the river. "To me, the whole ceremony seemed humble and reverential, I felt that the Father has regard to such petitions," wrote Hamblin.[76]

While some Indians, notably Tutsegabits and Tuuvi, accepted Mormonism, Hamblin and some other Mormon Indian missionaries accepted aspects of Native American belief. There was a synthesis of religion from both sides, though neither would be considered a complete conversion.

Thus, Jacob Hamblin was a man who liked to spend time with Indians, hunting with them, talking with them. He apparently married at least two Indian wives, though the marriages did not last or produce children. He would smoke ceremonially with Indians, dance with them, and he accepted the efficacy and beauty of Hopi prayers and ceremonialism. Despite his thoroughgoing Mormon background, he also became part of Indian culture and religion.

29

"If He Had His Choice He Should Desire to Live in Arizona"

Helping to Found the Little Colorado Mission, 1876–1877

After many false starts and setbacks, the first successful Mormon colonization of Arizona began in early 1876. Brigham Young called two hundred men, in four companies of fifty, to found colonies on the Little Colorado.[1] These colonists began straggling into southern Utah in late 1875 and early 1876.[2]

It would be the last major colonizing project of Brigham Young, the great colonizer, who would die not long after the colony was founded. Though Jacob was not a leader or an initial settler in those first four colonies, he was still an important figure who helped facilitate the move. In the winter of 1875–1876, Young sent him to talk with Indians living near the upcoming settlements to ensure that the colonists would not face dangers on that front. Later in 1876, after the difficulties of crossing the Colorado at Lee's Ferry were highlighted by a serious ferry accident and the drowning death of a major Mormon leader, Young sent Hamblin to find a possible alternate route to the colonies via the Grand Wash crossing south of St. George, which would then follow the Beale Road east across northern Arizona. In addition, Young asked Hamblin to leave Kanab and found a new settlement in Surprise Valley, near the Colorado. Finally, after the stunning news of Brigham Young's death in August of 1877, Hamblin was formally called to the Little Colorado mission.

Hamblin's mission to the Indians in Arizona, in winter 1875, was an important, challenging expedition which was unfortunately little documented. Accompanied by John R. Young, Hamblin apparently visited all Indians living near the impending Little Colorado colonies, or near routes to the colonies—Hopis, Navajos, Apaches, Hualapais, even Pimas. The mission may have lasted some three or four months. "I never felt better than I did then while visiting among them," Jacob wrote to Brigham,

29.1. Mormon settlements on the Little Colorado River. The northwestern route to the settlements, starting with Pearce Ferry. From McClintock, *Mormon Settlement in Arizona* (1921).

after returning. "Their hearts seemed almost ready to receive the Gosple. The Navajos Walipies & Moquis expresed that they looked upon me as the Father of peace."[3]

The Hualapais we have met before, in northwestern and north-central Arizona, in 1862 and 1863. The Pima Indians lived on the Gila River in south-central Arizona, and on Salt River to the north. They called themselves "Akimel O'odham," the river people, and became allied with the Maricopa Indians, who called themselves "Tohono O'odham," the desert people, and were formerly known as the Papago Indians. The Pimas were known for their hospitality and kindness to whites traveling through their territory.[4]

The Apaches, of course, are well known as one of the most warlike of the southwestern tribes, and have become a solid part of the mythos of the American West. There were many bands of Apaches; while some of them were peaceful by this time, others were not. Geronimo had been raiding white settlements since 1858, and would not be permanently captured until 1886. The Little Colorado lay near traditional Apache lands, so the early settlers of the Little Colorado, especially upriver, often lived in fear of Apache attacks.[5]

Hamblin and Young, while returning from this mission, met a company of Mormons at Navajo Wells east of Kanab on March 19, 1876. "Young and Hamblin had been out at the request of President Young to make sure that we could settle in safety in Arizona," wrote one of the company, Christian Lyngaa Christensen—who would later become one of Jacob's fellow Indian missionaries.[6] "They returned with the full consent of the Navajo chiefs." According to Christensen, Navajos had had a "tremendous battle" with Apaches on the Little Colorado in 1875, and wanted Mormons as future allies.[7]

Jacob gave the travelers a glowing report of their destination: "Said it was a fine country, abundant grass, fine timber, and plenty of water...friendly Indians. And that if he had his choice he should desire to live in Arizona."[8] He would soon be given this opportunity.

Jacob and Young told Christensen's company that the road across the Buckskin Mountains might be impassable at that time, and advised them to camp at Navajo Wells for a while before traveling on to Arizona. The company crossed the Colorado on April 10, and on May 7 arrived at the Mormon settlements on the Little Colorado.[9]

In 1876, the Mormons founded four settlements in Arizona, with forts: Brigham City (near modern Winslow, south of the Little Colorado, led by Jesse O. Ballenger); Sunset (across the river from Brigham City, led by Lot Smith); Joseph City or St. Joseph (a few miles to the east of Sunset, led by William C. Allen); and Obed (south of the river, just across from Joseph City, led by George Lake).[10] Lot Smith was also in charge of the entire mission, though initially James Brown also claimed that Brigham Young had given him leadership of the colonies. Lot Smith, a forceful leader, was not one to back down, and characteristically treated Brown rather brusquely; furious, Brown retreated to Moenkopi.[11] After this, he became de facto Mormon leader of that important town, and the Indian mission in Mormon Arizona. Smith became the leading figure in the Little Colorado colonization; his autocratic, sometimes abrasive leadership style ruffled many feathers, but he worked hard to make the Little Colorado colonies successful.[12]

Local Indians—a Navajo named Comah and a Hopi named Nahie—reportedly visited the colonies and seemed extraordinarily friendly. Comah "said he was pleased to have us come and live here," wrote Lot Smith. "They came with a white man as interpreter, and went away well pleased."[13] C. L. Christensen remembers learning his first words of Navajo from a group of thirteen Navajos who visited Sunset in these early days.[14]

Only one of these colonies survived—St. Joseph. The others failed due to various factors. First, the land by the "lower" Little Colorado was not ideal for farming—the sites had been chosen for strategic importance. Second, the water of the Little Colorado was at times scarce, but when present, it was also very alkaline. Third, there were periodic devastating floods at these locations. The Indians told the new colonists that if they wanted to live close to the river, they had better fix scaffolding in the trees, "for the river gets very mad sometimes."[15] The colonists would discover the truth of this observation. Another disadvantage the colonies faced was the requirement of living in the United Order. This was difficult under the best of conditions, and was that much more challenging in the Arizona desert. Lot Smith was an expert cattleman, and ran the Sunset economy with great success; still, many of the residents of Sunset were very dissatisfied with his leadership style as a United Order leader.[16]

Nevertheless, these colonies provided the essential foothold that Mormons needed to establish a presence in Arizona. More permanent settlements, such as Snowflake and Taylor, were later founded on Silver Creek, which flowed into the Little Colorado near modern Holbrook; unlike the Little Colorado, Silver Creek flowed continuously all year. In addition, significant Mormon communities arose in non-Mormon towns farther up the Little Colorado, in Round Valley, near the New Mexico border.[17]

In mid-May, a number of high church leaders decided to visit these new settlements, both to encourage the new settlers in their new, bleak inheritance, and to help set up United Orders. In addition, Brigham wanted his son Brigham Jr. to examine Jacob's "lower" ferry site carefully and assess it.[18] Jacob would serve as one of the guides.

The company assembled in Kanab and departed on May 21. Daniel H. Wells, counselor in the First Presidency, led the expedition, accompanied by two apostles, Erastus Snow and Brigham Young Jr., and other church leaders: L. John Nuttall, bishop of Kanab; Daniel D. McArthur, a bishop in St. George; Lorenzo Roundy, bishop of Kanarraville and former Arizona explorer;[19] and Lorenzo Hatch, who would soon be called to be an Indian missionary and leader in Arizona and New Mexico. Now fifty years of age, Hatch had lived in Salt Lake, Lehi, Utah County, and Franklin, Idaho, where he served as bishop, before accepting his call to Arizona and New Mexico on June 20, 1876, just after he returned from this expedition.[20]

Also numbered in the party, besides Hamblin, were Marius Ensign, Lorenzo D. Young, Brigham S. Young (a son of Brigham Young Jr.), William J. Carter, Hanmer Wells (apparently a son of Daniel H. Wells), B. Hull, William Perkins, L. John Nuttall Jr., James Emmett, B. O. McIntire, and E. W. Wiltbank (probably Ellis Whitney Wiltbank).[21] This impressive group of church leaders was accompanied by nineteen horses and ten mules, along with two carriages, five wagons, and a skiff for the Colorado.

They stopped at Navajo Wells, eighteen miles east of Kanab, and Brigham Jr. noted that Jacob had built a rock house there. After camping on the Kaibab Plateau, they organized the company: Roundy was appointed captain, while Brigham Young Jr. acted as recorder and Jacob as "guide & interpreter." The next day, they followed an "exceedingly rough,—rocky & rutty" road, but finally descended the Kaibab to reach the pure water of House Rock Spring in the valley below. On the twenty-third, after traversing a sandy road to Jacob's Pools, Jacob, Nuttall, and Brigham Jr. "climed a rocky eminence," from which Jacob pointed out the San Francisco Peaks far in the distance.

29.2. Place at Lee's Ferry where Bishop Lorenzo Roundy was drowned on May 24, 1876, as the ferry was submerged in high water. Jacob and others were swept into the icy Colorado but swam to safety. Courtesy Special Collections, Sherratt Library, Southern Utah University.

When the group reached the ferry at one p.m. on May 24,[22] they found that the river was extremely high, as was typical for that time of year—sixty feet deep and four hundred yards wide, it had caused the Paria to back up, covering orchards and gardens and forcing some settlers to leave their homes.[23] "The Colorado was then high—a raging torrent," wrote Jacob. "The current shifted from side to side, and the surging of the waters against the rocks caused large and dangerous whirlpools."

According to some reports, ferryman Warren Johnson and John D. Lee's son, Billy, advised against using the ferry to cross the river with the water so high.[24] However, Wells appointed Lorenzo Roundy as captain and ordered that the crossing with ferry begin.[25] The group was able to successfully ferry the horses across the river in two trips. As part of the company was doing this, apostles Brigham Young Jr. and Erastus Snow examined Jacob's proposed crossing, and found it "wholly impracticable"—though they were assessing it at a time of high water.[26]

At about six-thirty p.m., the company loaded the main baggage wagon, which had most of the supplies for the expedition, on the ferryboat, along with Lorenzo Hatch's wagon and Daniel Wells's carriage (also both fully loaded).[27] Wells, Bishops Nuttall, Roundy, and Hatch, Jacob, Warren Johnson, Carter, and Wiltbank were also on the boat. James Emmet, on a horse on land, with a few others, towed it upriver about a mile, so that it would be able to hit the intended landing spot on the southeast bank. When they were nearing the point where the ferry would leave the northwest bank and start across the river, the ferry had to round a point of rock. At this point, "the boat dipped and commenced to fill."[28]

According to Hamblin, the men on board shouted to the men on the bank to slacken the tow rope, but it got caught on a seam of the rock, and the bow of the boat went underwater.[29] "In a moment the rapid current swept the boat clear of its contents," wrote Jacob. "Men, wagons and luggage went into the surging waters."[30]

According to one report, Roundy, the best swimmer on the boat, ran halfway to the rear of the ferryboat, then said, "'Come on boys those who can swim, come on,' and plunged into the water and swam stoutly for about 2 rods...when he threw up his hands and sank instantly." Johnson reports that he rose again, "with one hand and leg above the water, but sank in a few moments out of sight."[31]

The waters were not only surging, they were ice cold—Jacob referred to them as "snow-water." As Jacob was thrown into the water, his right arm immediately cramped, but with his left arm he was able to grasp a large oar. However, Bishop Nuttall grabbed onto the same oar, and Jacob, worried that it would sink with both of them clinging to it, let go to try swimming again. His right arm came to life and he was able to swim to shore.[32] On land, he ran down the bank and leapt into the new skiff with two other men. They knew that dangerous rapids lurked just beyond Lee's Ferry, so directed the skiff out into the water in front of the rapids to try to save whoever they could.[33]

Lorenzo Hatch, when the ferry boat overturned, sank deep into the Colorado, but rose to the surface and was able to cling to the top of Wells's carriage.[34] William Carter, who had managed to climb onto the carriage, reached for him and drew him up on it. They were close to hurtling into the rapids when Hamblin and two others, on the skiff, intercepted them and brought them on board.[35]

The skiff was also able to pick up Warren Johnson, and saved Hatch's wagon, towing it to an island. However, Daniel Wells's carriage and the main supply wagon were swept into the rapids and lost.[36]

As the soaked and chilled survivors of the wreck gathered on the shore, they found that one of their number was missing: Bishop Lorenzo Roundy. Though he was known to be a good swimmer, his body had probably cramped in the icy water.[37]

The party searched the banks of the Colorado until nightfall, but could not find Roundy's body, and were forced to retreat to the Lee home, where Emma did what she could do for them. "It was a sorrowful time," Brigham Jr. wrote. The Colorado had raised several inches since they arrived, and Brigham could "hear its angry waves as they roll upon the sandy and rocky beach what a dismall sound."[38]

Nevertheless, the survivors of the wreck came to feel that their survival was providential, given the violence of the Colorado at that time—Nuttall writes, "This was truly a miraculous preservation."[39] A disaster from one point of view, it became a miracle story of salvation from another.

The next day, Jacob, Marius Ensign, and others were able to rescue Hatch's wagon; the company also continued the futile search for Roundy's body, and ferried the remaining wagons across with the skiff. About half of the party, including Bishop Nuttall, were forced to return to Kanab, because supplies were limited.

Wells, Apostles Snow and Young, and seven more men, including Jacob, continued across the river on the twenty-sixth and traveled on to Arizona.[40] They reached Moenkopi three days later, and the western Little Colorado settlements on June 2.[41] After preaching in the Little Colorado communities for about a week, the Wells company left to return to Utah on about June 8. The Brigham Young Jr. diary records typical problems with runaway mules as the company traveled from spring to spring en route to the ferry. On the thirteenth, Brigham Jr. wrote, "Bro Hamblin followed mules 12 m. Caught them and attempted to ride and was thrown but not hurt." That an experienced rider like Jacob could be thrown shows the cussedness of the independently minded mules. The group of church leaders climbed "the big hill" (Lee's Backbone)—"the worst it ever was my lot to drive a team up," wrote Brigham Jr.—and crossed the Colorado the next day, under "fearfully hot" conditions. They arrived back at Kanab on June 17, and three days later Jacob attended a meeting with Brigham Young, Daniel Wells, Erastus Snow, L. John Nuttall, Levi Stewart, and others. Doubtless Jacob, Wells, and others reported to Brigham on the ferry accident and the status of the Little Colorado mission.[42]

On July 7, Jacob wrote Brigham Young, expressing his desire to visit the Indians of Arizona again, if it met with Young's approval, as "there is a great door opening among the Walipies Apachies & Pemos." However, he was still working on his house, and wanted to finish it before leaving.[43] He wrote, "All the Kanab Pa-re-ah & Long Valley Indians have demanded Baptism at my hands: I counseled with Bp. Nutall & Bro Oakley on the matter & we attended to it on the 5th Inst. We felt that much good will result." Jacob performed eighty baptisms, forty-one males and thirty-nine females, and they were confirmed by Nuttall, Oakley, and a few other men.[44] So Jacob officiated in one of those mass baptisms of Paiutes that periodically occurred in southern Utah.[45] Jacob ended the letter, "A fine rain the first for the summer is now falling. From your brother in the Gosple of peace: faithfully, Jacob Hamblin."

Another commitment kept Jacob in Utah. The second trial of John D. Lee was held in Beaver from September 14 through 20, and Jacob played a major role in it. The atmosphere of this trial was completely different from the previous one. In the first trial, a number of Mormons were targeted; for this trial, the focus was entirely on Lee. In the first trial, Mormons were resistant to convicting anyone of participation in the massacre, as was shown by the eight Mormon jurors voting that Lee was not guilty. In this trial, loyal Mormons worked for Lee's conviction.

Juanita Brooks believed that, behind the scenes, Brigham Young had agreed to help convict Lee, provided that no one else would be pursued, and that legal prosecution of the Mountain Meadows Massacre would end.[46]

In the contorted ethics of the prosecution of the Mountain Meadows Massacre, this would have been unjust to Lee, in one sense; he certainly was not the only person guilty of perpetrating the massacre. One could argue that Isaac Haight, Cedar City stake president, and William Dame, stake president of Parowan and military leader of southern Utah, were more culpable, along with a few other ecclesiastical and military leaders such as Bishop Philip Klingensmith and John Higbee, counselor in Cedar City stake presidency. Lee asserted that he was only following orders;[47] others portray him enthusiastically plotting the massacre with Haight. He also played a major part in the horrifying deception that the Mormons perpetrated on the company as he decoyed them unarmed from their encampment by promising them safety. According to Hamblin's testimony, as we will see, Lee admitted to Hamblin personally killing a young woman.

Haight had gone into hiding; and charges against Dame were dropped. The U.S. attorneys reportedly stated that they did not have enough evidence against Dame to convict[48]—or were they saying this as part of a behind-the-scenes understanding? Indeed, if there was such an understanding, this is the only thing they could publicly say. (And it is hard to imagine that they had sufficient evidence to arrest and convict only Lee, out of all the people involved in the massacre.)

In any event, in this trial, Mormons were no longer holding back. Those who accept there had been a secret agreement will believe that church leaders let witnesses and jurors know, subtly or overtly, that they should no longer protect Lee. (Lee later felt that Daniel H. Wells, second counselor in the First Presidency and the first witness for the prosecution, served this function.)[49] In this scenario, Hamblin, with others, would have conferred with Wells or would have followed his signals.

The prosecution called seven witnesses: Daniel Wells, Laban Morrill, Joel White, Samuel Knight, Samuel McMurdy, Nephi Johnson, and Jacob Hamblin. While Jacob of course had not been present at the massacre, he testified concerning what Lee had told him about the crime while Jacob was traveling south from Salt Lake on September 24, 1857, near Beaver. Jacob also testified that he reported on the massacre to Brigham Young and George A. Smith soon after the event occurred (presumably in June 1858).

Hamblin's description of what Lee told him he did was devastating.[50] Hamblin testified that Lee told him that the Indians forced him to decoy the company, unarmed, out of their encampment, and then the Indians massacred them.

Jacob also said that Lee had admitted that he had personally killed a young woman. An Indian brought two young women out of the brush, where they had been hiding. "Q: Tell just what he said about that. A: The Indian killed one and he cut the other one's throat, is what he said."[51] When Jacob had returned home, he had asked Albert about this incident, and Albert had led him to the corpses of the two young women. This testimony, which forced hearers to visualize the kind of brutal killing that occurs in a massacre, reportedly electrified the audience.[52]

Why had Jacob not spoken out before? he was asked. He reported that he had given Brigham Young a full account of the massacre, everything he knew, not long after it occurred.[53] He stated, "I felt that a great crime had been committed. But Brigham Young told me that 'as soon as we can get a court of justice, we will ferret this thing out, but till then don't say anything about it.'" This is not extremely convincing, as the long delay before Jacob testified is hard to explain, both for Young and Hamblin. This testimony was potentially damaging to Young, as it showed that he knew of Mormon involvement in the massacre very early.[54]

Young often used a legalistic defense for his response to the massacre, stating that he was willing to help fully in any trial, but that anti-Mormon federal attorneys refused his help. Young's supporters even now have portrayed him as having his hands tied by an incompetent United States legal system after the Utah War. However, from an ecclesiastical point of view, after Young learned of Mormon involvement in the massacre, he did not conduct a thorough investigation and give ecclesiastical punishment to those most responsible for the crime. Apparently at first he even approved of Mormon involvement in the massacre.[55] He did not excommunicate Lee and Haight until much later, when a federal trial was being threatened. Dame was never excommunicated.[56]

On September 20, the all-Mormon jury delivered their verdict: Lee was found guilty and was sentenced to death by firing squad.

Lee was livid at Hamblin's testimony. In a letter to his wife Emma, he wrote of Jacob—whom he called "the fiend of Hell"—"The old hypocrite thought that now was his chance to reek his vengeance on me, by swearing away my life."[57] It is interesting that he regarded Jacob's testimony as an extension of their feud. In his autobiography, he referred to Jacob as "dirty-fingered Jake" and told a story of Jacob's involvement in the Dukes-Turner company cattle rustling that strayed considerably from the truth.[58] (Lee had helped massacre a company in no real danger of Indian attack before whites had encouraged the Indians, then had driven off their cattle and other plunder; Hamblin, at worst, had received cattle that had been driven off from a company that was in authentic danger from Indians, but had not been attacked.)

In addition, Lee accused four of the six witnesses of perjury.[59] In his view, everyone had turned against him and was lying. Lee was writing to one of his loyal wives—perhaps he didn't want her to know the full extent of his involvement in the massacre. She had heard him deny involvement in it when visitors came by Lee's Ferry.[60]

Lee was executed at Mountain Meadows on March 23, 1877.

With Lee's trial and execution the Mormons had achieved legal closure for the Mountain Meadows Massacre. Jacob could return to building his house in Kanab. In 1876, his family continued to multiply. Alice Edna Hamblin, Louisa's fourth, and

Jacob's nineteenth biological child, was born on February 9, 1876, and on November 5, Clara Melvina Hamblin, Priscilla's seventh, was born.[61]

The day after Clara's birth, Jacob, in St. George, wrote in his diary, "Worked on the temple lot clering it of rubish."[62] On the twelfth, he received a telegram informing him that his son Joseph, in Panguitch, was extremely sick. Jacob immediately set out to see him, but was delayed three days by heavy winds. "Wind blew so strong it became unreasonable to travil," he wrote. He was able to leave again on the fifteenth and came to Panguitch three days later, when Joseph happily was well on his way to recovery.

On December 13, Jacob wrote in his diary, "Got readdy for to hunt a wagon road south of St George to Colorado then East over 200 mls thro an un explord coun[t]ry." Brigham Young must have received a full report on the dangers of Lee's Ferry and the road from the Colorado, over Lee's Backbone, and to the Little Colorado settlements, and decided to investigate the possibility of bypassing Lee's Ferry altogether by creating a ferry south of St. George, at the conjunction of the Grand Wash and the Colorado, where Jacob and his companions had crossed the Colorado a number of times before. There were two questions that had to be answered: one, was a good ferry practical there, and two, would there be a viable road, with feed and water for animals, extending from the new ferry to the Little Colorado?

Brigham apparently gave Jacob the assignment to answer those questions on December 15, 1876, in a letter he cowrote with Wilford Woodruff, Erastus Snow, and Brigham Young Jr.[63] Young instructed Jacob to find a good wagon road between St. George and the Colorado, then at the Colorado, counsel Harrison Pearce, who was building a ferryboat there, as to where a road to the ferry should be built.[64] "Then proceed South Easterly near to the west end of the Sanfrancisco mountains to what is called the Beal road; thence easterly to what is called sun set crossing on the Little Colorado river." He should keep careful minutes of his journey and draw maps.

Then Brigham and his cosigners dropped a bombshell on the Hamblin family. "When you return home to Kanab we would like you to take your stock and such ones of your family and friends as you would like to have with you and locate and take possession of a little place called 'Surprise Valley,' near the Colorado river, and report to us your success." Surprise Valley is modern Deer Creek Valley, southwest of the Kaibab Plateau, east of Kanab Canyon. Jacob had just been finishing his home for his family in Kanab, and now he would be expected to leave this and pioneer a completely new settlement!

But before Surprise, Jacob had been called to explore the Pearce Ferry route to the Little Colorado.[65] Jacob recruited Wilford Halliday from Kanab, and Joseph Crosby, Calvin Kelsey, Samuel Alger, and Hyrum A. Williams from St. George to accompany him.

Jacob "was ordained an Apostle to the Lamanites on Friday, 15th Dec., 1876, at St. George by President Brigham Young."[66] The party must have left St. George on that day, or soon thereafter.[67]

On this trip, Jacob took a route a little east of his former one, so as to strike the site of the ferry five miles east of the Grand Wash. They reached the Colorado on the twentieth, and Jacob and his men helped Harrison Pearce build a skiff, used it to take their luggage over the Colorado, then forded their animals. They found a good place for fording horses two hundred yards above the new ferry site, but apparently the approaches to this place were barred by rocky banks.

South of the Colorado, Jacob took a new route that lay east of their former route. The first day they came to the north part of Hualapai Valley, between the Cerbat Range on the west and the Peacock Mountains to the east, and found water near their camp, which Jacob thought was "entirely providential" as this was new country to him. His diary speaks of "grass springs," marshy areas and foothills "coverd with luxuerant groath of grass." The next day, they found a rock barrier of granite, which would be a major obstacle for the new route, so they made a two-hundred-yard dugway across it. Jacob's diary states that "the decent from the sumit is steep and dificilt for over half a mile."

The next day—Christmas—they were without water, and Jacob's companions pointedly asked him when they would find it again. Jacob answered that he was following Brigham Young's instructions in following this new, unknown route, and he "felt impressed" that they would find water that night.[68]

They plodded on for thirty thirsty miles. However, in the afternoon, approaching the foothills of a mountain, they found signs of livestock, and rounding the point of a hill, came upon a house and corral, which Williams called "Stevens Ranch"[69] and which Jacob's diary called "a mining camp cald ~~mineral~~ hack bury district"—it was apparently both a ranch and a miners' camp. A silver mine had been located at Hackberry, in the eastern foothills of the Peacock Mountains, in 1874, and a town grew up nearby, twenty-three miles northeast of Kingman.[70]

Fortunately, Jacob and his friends were hospitably received at Stevens Ranch, as Stevens told them to turn their animals into his yard, where there was a pump with good water. He also told Jacob how to find water in his upcoming journey, until he reached country he knew. The water crisis was over.

About eight miles beyond this, the Mormons came to Beale's Road and were able to follow it east to the Little Colorado, merely taking note of places where there would be good feed for animals, and stretches without water.[71] Jacob's diary is filled with cryptic notes about hours of travel and springs—probably to help future travelers find water. On January 31, his diary ends, "Sunday. Started at 8 & stopt at half past 11."

Jacob and his companions reached Sunset on the Little Colorado about sixteen days after leaving Pearce's Ferry.[72] This would place Jacob and company on the Little Colorado on about January 1 or 2. There he found a familiar face: "I was much pleased to see my daughter Louise," he wrote. "One is likely to appreciate friends and relatives when found by traveling in the desert." This is probably Lois Hamblin Burk, Rachel's first, who was living in Sunset with her husband, Hubert Burk.[73]

Jacob decided to send one of his men home quickly, via Lee's Ferry, to report on his company's outward journey. He chose Williams, who had been keeping a journal and thus would have been paying especially close attention to the lay of the land. Jacob wrote a quick note to Brigham Young on the fifth, to help Dan Jones and other explorers, saying that on his group's return trip, he would make "a more thorough exploration to find the best possible route for a practicable waggon route from Pierce's Ferry to Sunset Crossing or to Pres-cot." This route would be longer than the Lee's Ferry road, but would "pass through near two hundred & fifty miles of the best stock country: especially for Sheep that I ever saw." He ended the letter: "Good feelings & good health prevails in our camp. A large flock of Turkeys has just pased over. As ever yours in the Gospel of peace Jacob Hamblin."

Williams arrived at Kanab on January 15, and John Oakley sent a copy of his journal and Jacob's note to Brigham the next day.[74]

Jacob and his party set out west from Sunset, but his plans for a more thorough exploration were dashed when, on the expedition's third night out from the Little Colorado, a tremendous snowstorm hit them, and they could only manage to find the most minimal shelter from it—an unchinked log cabin without a roof. They put a wagon cover over the cabin and had to stay there for two days and two nights.

On the third day the snow stopped, but it was now very deep. They gave up the idea of pursuing their intended journey, but instead turned south to seek forage for their animals. "The third day we got out of the snow," wrote Hamblin—which makes nine days in all since they had left the Little Colorado. They came to the sunny side of a hill and found grass for their animals, but were running out of food for themselves. They had cached food for their return trip, but now had to take a different route home.

They visited Camp Verde, about thirty-five miles south of Flagstaff, on the Verde River, and asked to buy food on credit, but the military would give them no help.[75] William Sanford "Boss" Head ran a sutler's store near there and Jacob asked him for help, but at first Head was equally unhelpful. However, when Head discovered that Hamblin and friends were Mormons, his attitude changed completely.

"'Oh,' said he 'you are Mormons, are you! What do you want to last you home?'" He then gave the Mormons all they needed.[76]

Jacob and his party made it back to Pearce's Ferry, where they counted on flour and meat they had stored for their return trip, but someone had found it and appropriated it, so the men boiled some wheat, and lived on this for the final five days of their journey. They arrived at St. George on February 10.[77]

It was just like the old days—crossing the Colorado, and nearly starving to death in the snow on the way home.

Jacob gave a glowing report of this route to the Little Colorado when he spoke at the St. George Tabernacle on the eleventh. There was a good ford at the Pearce's Ferry when the water was low, and the road had little sand, plentiful grass ("There is only one patch of grass, and that is all the way") and water.[78] This was "one of the best natural roads he ever saw," he said.[79] Subsequent travelers over this route were not so enthusiastic.

Brigham Young was in St. George, and Jacob reported directly to him. In Little, he remembers Brigham saying,

> I know your history. You have always kept the Church and Kingdom of God first and foremost in your mind. That is right. There is no greater gift than that. If there are any men who have cleared their skirts of the blood of this generation, I believe you are one of them, and you can have all the blessings there are for any men in the temple.[80]

It would be their last conversation. The great colonist and his missionary-explorer were both getting old. Founding the Mormon colonies in Arizona would be their last dual accomplishment.

Jacob returned to Kanab and tried to plant some wheat on the land that he had been allotted in the Kanab field. However, he found his share to be "nearly worthless," and the wheat crop did not grow.[81] This report confirms that the Kanab United Order was dysfunctional, as has been abundantly documented; that Indian missionaries were not valued highly, when it came to rewarding them in practical ways; and that Kanab was not a good agricultural site, in general.

In March, Jacob was back in St. George. The temple was nearing completion, but some parts of it were used for rituals before the formal dedication on April 6, and in Jacob's diary, on March 7 and 8, he records performing vicarious baptisms, priesthood ordinations, and endowments for many of his ancestors.[82] On the seventh, he performed an ordinance reserved for elite Mormons: his second anointing, also known as "the fullness of the priesthood." Nuttall recorded it thus: "Second Anointings. Jacob Hamblin & 3 Wives—W. Woodruff anointed. D. H. Cannon held horn & Bro McAllister Recorder." The wives were probably Rachel, Priscilla, and Louisa, the latter two presumably present, with another woman standing proxy for Rachel.

This ordinance gives its recipients a sure affirmation of attaining ultimate salvation, which Mormons refer to as exaltation, in this life and the next life.[83] It was only given to selected Mormons, by invitation and recommendation. Historian David Buerger writes, "The early Mormons who received the second anointing recorded the event in their diaries with great joy."[84] This must have been a spiritual highlight of Jacob's life.

The following day, Jacob talked with Nuttall about "securing the land Known as Dumotts Park by Homestead claims—on Buckskin Mountain."[85] This is De Motte Park, on Kaibab Plateau, about fifteen miles north of the Grand Canyon. Here we have another example of Jacob directing fellow Mormons to good land for ranching or settling. On the ninth, Nuttall arranged for Jacob to transport some soap to Nuttall's wife, and he may have left for Kanab on that day.

Later in the month, Jacob was back in St. George and made a substantial purchase of supplies—flour, oats, salt, bacon, cheese, wheat, barley, potatoes, buns, blankets, shingles, shoes—from a Brother Haycock, which are detailed in his diary.[86] Possibly he was acting as shopkeeper in Kanab.

Surprise Valley (modern Deer Creek Valley), which Brigham Young had asked Jacob to settle, lay southwest of the Kaibab Plateau, about a mile north of the Granite Narrows on the Colorado, some ten miles east of Kanab Canyon.[87] It is a beautiful but remote place. It had been discovered in April 1872, by Elias Olcott Beaman, a photographer in the second Powell expedition, who described it as "a lonely valley, flower-decked and verdant! In its centre stood a grove of young cotton-wood trees, through which flowed a limpid stream of water [modern Deer Creek], fed by a dozen springs gushing from the foot of the mountains."[88]

It is not known how Brigham Young got interested in Surprise Valley—perhaps he read Beaman's account, which had been published in 1874. In any event, Jacob, who had never been to the place, apparently treated this as an exploration assignment. In early April, he traveled through the "Kibab Mountains"—apparently his term for the southwest Kaibab Plateau—and visited it. It was "verry difficult of access: as it took us eight hours to enter it from one terrace to another," he wrote. Geologist Clarence Dutton would visit the valley in 1880, also with great difficulty. He wrote, of one long section of the descent, "A single inadvertence, the slightest accident, sends man or beast to the great unknown."[89] Even now it is not easy of access, if approached by land.[90]

In addition, Hamblin stated that the valley had been misrepresented as perhaps being bigger than it was—in reality it was a short, narrow canyon containing only about a hundred acres of arable land. Aside from that, it was "a romantic place & quite warm as the full grown leaves on the Coton wood trees indicated." Hamblin the scout also reported on its water resources: it had a good stream that might irrigate two thousand acres.

Though Surprise was inaccessible and too small for a settlement, Jacob was enthusiastic about the "Kibab Mountains," which he traveled through to reach Surprise; these were covered with pine and scrub oak, while their foothills and terraces offered richly blooming grasses. On top of the mountains were "open lawns or praries," through which herds of wild bulls roamed. The climate might be cold but Jacob thought that "small grain" might be raised there.

He concludes his report: "I think the timber & farming land on the mountains richly worth securing: but the cañon caled 'Surprise Valley' so difficult of access renders it worthless for ordinary purposes."

The subtext of which letter might be expressed as: no, neither I nor my family will be moving to Surprise Valley. This might be interpreted as one of the few times that Jacob said no to Brigham Young.

Jacob was back in Kanab by April 8, when he wrote his report, with John Oakley acting as scribe.

On about August 27, Jacob took a wagon of grain to be ground at a mill north of Kanab, but on his way there, a messenger came to him with the news that a criminal, Wallace Wilkerson, had escaped from jail in northern Utah, and it was thought that he was traveling south to Arizona.[91] Jacob was asked to start immediately for Lee's Ferry to try to apprehend the fugitive. Jacob unhitched his horses and turned back to Kanab. On the following day, with three other men, including our old friend A. P. Hardy, he set out for Lee's Ferry.[92] They planned to meet "Deputy sheriff Fouts" of Richfield at some point—apparently Joseph Lehi Foutz, who later had a long career as a settler and trader in Arizona and New Mexico.[93]

At the ferry they received stunning news: Brigham Young had died on August 29. All of Mormondom went into mourning. It was the end of an era, and also an end of one of the key relationships in Jacob's life. Much of the missionary work and exploring that he had done were done under Young's direction—including his last two exploring trips, from Pearce's Ferry to the Little Colorado, and to Surprise Valley.

Young's successor, John Taylor, who had not been a favorite of Young, had no special relationship with Hamblin.

There was no sign of Wilkerson at Lee's Ferry, but Jacob and Foutz decided that it would be wise to notify the Hopi Agency that the criminal might show up there, so they continued on to the Hopi Mesas, traveling through the searing heat of September in the Arizona desert.[94] At the mesas, Jacob found the Hopis suffering from lack of rain:

> They scattered corn meal in the paths leading to their fields; the women dressed in white, and sat on the tops of their houses, looking to the ground through an opening in a blanket wrapped around their heads. Others of the people went about with solemn countenances to induce the great Father of us all, as they express it, to send rain. By doing as they did, they believed, He would be more ready to pity them and grant their request.[95]

Some of them asked Jacob to pray for rain, and he did so, exercising all the faith he could.[96] The following night there was a bountiful rainstorm, which allowed the Hopis to harvest corn, squashes, and beans. "We noticed that in and around their towns and fields it had rained very heavily, but on either side the ground was dry and dusty," Jacob wrote. For him, the miraculous was never far away.

Jacob and Foutz arrived back at Kanab on September 13 and reported to bishop Nuttall that the Indians in Arizona were "very kind" and the spirit of the gospel was among them, but that there were dissensions among the Mormons at Moenave.[97]

If Hopi crops had prospered, Jacob's own crop in Kanab was not so fortunate, as drought had entirely destroyed it. Nevertheless, Jacob wrote, "through the blessings of the Lord I was able to provide necessaries for my family."[98]

This is the last anecdote found in Jacob's published autobiography. Presumably Little finished his research on the book in mid-1877 and published it in 1881. James Amasa Little, now fifty-five, was a long-time Southern Utah resident, having been a pioneer in Parowan with George A. Smith in Iron Mission days. After Parowan, he moved to Spring Valley (Eagle Valley), Nevada, and thereafter settled in Kanab. He was a capable writer and editor, and during a mission in England in 1854 and 1855, he had served as editor of the Mormon magazine *Millennial Star*.[99]

We know that Little was paid, though not much, to write the autobiography.[100] He reportedly hounded Jacob in Kanab, asking him questions while he did garden work, and when Jacob was gone, he interrogated Priscilla and Louisa.[101]

At least one friend of Jacob did not feel that Little did his subject justice. In Santa Clara, Martha Cragun Cox, a "friend and chum" of Jacob's Tamar, wrote that Jacob "used to humor my craving to hear the incidents of his life and his experience among the Indians." In her view, there were many important incidents in Jacob's life that did not appear in Little's biography, and once she asked Little about these omissions. His answer was frank: "He told me he was paid but sixty dollars for writing the book and he put into it all that much money was worth. Besides much of the material given him was too visionary and much was really not necessary to make interesting reading." But Cox disagreed: "Viewing it from my stand point we are losers by Bro Little's omissions."[102] If Little left the most visionary material out of what is already a quite visionary book, it would be fascinating to see the material that was rejected![103]

Just as once Kanab had been his home away from home, now Arizona had become Hamblin's home away from home, and soon it would become his home. In October, Jacob was in Salt Lake City to attend General Conference. On the seventh, a number of Saints were assigned missions, a traditional occurrence at conference, and some of them were called to Arizona.[104]

A "meeting of missionaries" was held at the Council House in Salt Lake City the following day, at which seven apostles set apart twenty-five missionaries for various missions throughout the world. In the Arizona portion of this meeting, the first person mentioned is Jacob, and apostles Wilford Woodruff, Orson Hyde, Franklin D. Richards, and Erastus Snow consecrated him for this mission. Next they set apart Joseph Foutz and John Oakley.[105]

Typically, Mormon missionaries left their homes for two or three years to live and preach in the East or in a foreign country, then returned home. However, colonizing calls would require the missionaries to pull up stakes and move to the colony with their families for an indefinite time, and they often ended up living there permanently. This was apparently the kind of call that Jacob had received. The Arizona residence chapter in his career was about to begin.

When Jacob brought the news back to Kanab, according to family traditions, Priscilla, with great reluctance, agreed to accompany Jacob to the Little Colorado, acquiescing partly because she realized that this would help him avoid polygamy prosecution. Through the rest of the year, she and Jacob would have worked to prepare for the move to the Little Colorado. Louisa and her family, on the other hand, would stay in Kanab for some three years.[106] Apparently, in the coming years, Jacob had a dual residence, dividing his time between Kanab and Arizona.

And in fact, there was no immediate move to Arizona. Jacob spoke twice in Kanab church meetings in November, reporting that he had recently visited Pahreah and Long Valley.[107] At the end of the year, on December 30, he spoke at a meeting in St. George with John Willard Young, son of Brigham, an apostle and former member of the First Presidency.[108] This collocation of Jacob and Young points us to Jacob's next journey across the Colorado.

30

"The Watering Places Are All Occupide Buy the White Man"

HAMBLIN, POWELL, AND THE KAIBAB PAIUTES, 1877–1880

As Jacob prepares to leave Kanab, we should look briefly at the Kaibab Paiutes who had worked with him there. Jacob wrote two letters to John Wesley Powell in November 1880, pleading for help for these Indians, using language reminiscent of his September 1873 letter to Brigham Young.[1]

Jacob began the November 19 letter, "As the kibab Inds. are in a very destitute cituacion I thought it would be no more than humanity required of me to call your atencion to it." He mentioned that forty or fifty Paiute families were now living near Kanab, including the Uinkaret Paiutes that Powell and Jacob had visited. Then Jacob incisively outlined the reasons for the Indians' desperate state: "The watering plases are all ocupide buy the white Man,"[2] "thus cutting off all their means of subsistence except game, which you are aware is quite limited."[3] We see here Jacob's dual sympathies, his inner conflict. *He* was one of the white men, as were his fellow Mormons.

He reminded Powell that he, Jacob, had told the Paiutes that Powell had a good heart, and that they now remembered that he had promised to help them. "The grass that produst [produced] mutch seed is all et out." Jacob explicitly referred to stockraising as a cause of the Paiutes' poverty. "The foot hills that yielded hundreds of acres of sunflowers which produced quantities of rich seed, the grass also that grew so luxuriantly when you were here, the seed of which was gathered with little labor, and many other plants that produced food for the natives is all eat out by stock." Then, in the later letter, he wrote, "In fact thare is nothing for them to depend upon but beg and starve." He mentioned that the Paiute crops of corn and squash at Kanab had failed this year because of drought, there were no pine nuts (a former staple) available, and the Indians were living on cactus fruit.[4]

Jacob had a surprisingly astute understanding of how Mormon settlement, control of water, agriculture, and stockraising had destroyed the Paiute way of life, even at this early date. The Mormons had occupied the most fertile places in the area, the land with most water available (usually former Paiute settlement sites, though the Paiutes used them seasonally). In addition, the all-important seeds of grasses and sunflowers had been eaten by cattle and sheep. Jacob movingly portrays the starving Paiutes at their campfires as winter approaches. He closes the November 1 letter, "It being improbable that any appropriation could be made in their behalf at this time, I should esteem it a great favor if you could secure some surplus merchandise for the immediate relief of their utter destitution."

The later letter's language is similar: "If thare could be some asistance rendered this winter and something to incorage them to plant corn another season it would be no more than we could reasonably expect." Hamblin is insistent: "I would like to here from you the earlyest opertunity that I can [and] tell the Inds. what you say."

Unfortunately Powell's Indian policy was entirely bound by the reservation policy he had helped implement in 1873, in which Utah's Indians would be gathered to four reservations, based on their language groups.[5] Therefore, Powell's answer to Jacob, written on February 18, 1881,[6] was simply that the Kaibab Paiutes needed to gather to the southern Nevada Paiute reservation on the Muddy or to the Uinta Ute reservation in northeastern Utah to receive help from the U.S. government. Such policies of throwing different tribes of Indians into collective reservations, requiring many Indians to leave their ancestral territory, was equivalent to asking them to give up their religion and culture.[7] Many Indians understandably were reluctant to move—or were unable to move.

In the case of the Uintah reservation, the Kaibab Paiutes would be forced to live with their traditional enemies and persecutors, the Utes, whom they regarded as evil sorcerers. Therefore this was not a possibility. In the case of the Moapa reservation on the Muddy, at the time white stockmen were driving their livestock freely onto Indian land, and these animals ate anything green, thus making the reservation uninhabitable for Nevada Paiutes. The Indian agent for the Moapa Paiutes wrote in 1880 that the reservation "is entirely deserted by the Indians solely because it is left unprotected from stock owned by herders."[8]

In addition, as Fowler and Fowler write, "Reservations were established, but on land so poor that any real attempt to implement farming on a scale sufficient to sustain the Indian population was futile."[9]

Therefore, the Kaibab Paiutes, despite their desperate situation, chose not to leave, or could not leave, their homelands and go to other reservations.

Powell's letter, taken by itself, seems heartless, especially since he himself understood the religious nature of the Indians' ties to their land. He had written, in another letter in 1880, "The land belonging to an Indian clan or tribe is dear to it not only as a region from which it obtains sustenance but chiefly because it is the locus of its religion. When an Indian clan or tribe gives up its land...everything most sacred to Indian society is yielded up." This is insightful, even eloquent. But he then quickly went on to say, "Such a removal of the Indians is the first step to take in their civilization" and added that the "interests and superstitions of a small number of savages" should not stand in the way of "the progress of civilization and the establishment of homes for millions of civilized people." Nevertheless, Indians should be treated with "strict justice" and "the widest charity."[10] He could not reach the seemingly inevitable conclusion—removal of Indians from their land, if it was central to their culture and religion, was clearly neither just nor charitable.

In other places Powell decried the neglect that the Paiutes suffered at the hands of the U.S. government.[11] Just as Jacob Hamblin had his contradictions and paradoxes in his attitudes toward Indians, so did Powell.

The overgrazing of the grasslands in southern Utah and on the Arizona Strip, which Jacob referred to in his letters to Powell, is one of the environmental tragedies of Utah and Arizona history. Such sites as Pipe Spring, Kanab, and House Rock Springs were originally located close to expanses of grasslands, supplying food for Paiutes, and bountiful feed for horses and cattle. But as early as 1880, much of this was gone.

For example, the LDS Church bought Pipe Spring in 1866, built "Winsor's Castle" directly over the springs, and had introduced one to two thousand head of cattle to the area by 1872. Five years later, there were about two thousand head of cattle at Pipe Spring, but some fifty thousand head of cattle and sheep grazed on surrounding grasslands.[12]

In 1880, Clarence E. Dutton wrote of Pipe Spring,

> Ten years ago the desert spaces outspreading to the southward were covered with abundant grasses, affording rich pasturage to horses and cattle. To-day hardly a blade of grass is to be found within ten miles of the spring, unless upon the crags and mesas of the Vermilion Cliffs behind it. The horses and cattle have disappeared, and the bones of many of the latter are bleached upon the plains in front of it. The cause of the failure of pasturage is twofold. There is little doubt that during the last ten or twelve years the climate of the surrounding country has grown more arid. . . . Even if there had been no drought the feeding of cattle would have impoverished and perhaps wholly destroyed the grass by cropping it clean before the seeds were mature, as has been the case very generally throughout Utah and Nevada.[13]

Visitors to Pipe Spring now can hardly imagine "abundant grasses" spreading southwards of the springs.

Kanab was also once surrounded by grass. On January 3, 1862, John Steele, in an early traversal of Kanab Creek, described it as "a beautiful little stream good land and plenty of grass."[14] Charles Walker, visiting the Kanab Fort in 1869, said that south of it was "a fine open country looking towards the Buckskin Mountains covered with grass in abundance."[15] But in 1874, the Kanab canyon meadow was "thrown open to stock," which caused the loss of both vegetation and water flow of Kanab Creek.[16]

In the same way, House Rock Valley had grass "stirrup high" before cattle were introduced there.[17] One visitor in 1911 wrote, "The range has evidently been overstocked for most of the grass is gone and weeds grow in its place as farther south in Arizona."[18]

Many writers have commented on the tragedy of this overgrazing simply from the viewpoint of white settlers. For example, overgrazing is ruinous for stockmen, ironically enough, as they can no longer graze their cattle in the denuded areas. Overgrazing in higher areas was also a partial cause of the disastrous floods and droughts that continually afflicted Mormon settlements.[19]

We should note that Mormons were no better, and no worse, than non-Mormons in their overgrazing. Much overgrazing on the Arizona strip was the result of the Grand Canyon Cattle Company, the prototype of the demonic cattle company in Zane Grey's western mythos.[20] William Abruzzi, in an important article, "The Social and Ecological Consequences of Early Cattle Ranching in the Little Colorado River Basin," describes how the Aztec Land and Cattle Company destroyed the grasslands in Texas through overgrazing—which was obviously disastrous for Texas stockmen, as well as for the ecological health of the state—then brought their cattle to Arizona and perversely repeated the same process.

In the early days of Mormon settlement of southern Utah, whites moved their cattle into locations that had water and significant vegetation, the same attributes that made these places Paiute campgrounds. Sometimes the whites made trades with the Indians: "In each [site] the white men had purchased the water from the Indians, giving a pony or a gun for the larger springs, and a blanket, a sheep, or some trinkets for the seeps," Juanita Brooks writes. After such questionable exchanges, in which Indians gave up precious resources for gifts of small value, by white standards, the surrounding areas were overgrazed. "In almost every case they moved more cattle to the watering place than the land could support permanently," writes Brooks.[21]

If overgrazing was a short-sighted, ruinous policy for whites, Hamblin's letters show that the disappearance of the grasslands of southern Utah and northern Arizona was an even greater ecological disaster for the local Indians.

And just as the Santa Clara Paiutes had been decimated by disease, it is probable that this took a grim toll among the Kaibabits as well.[22] There are at least two specific records of epidemics among the Kaibab Paiutes. During the 1854 exploration that Jacob was part of, along the east fork of the Virgin through Long Valley up to Panguitch Lake, headed by David Lewis, as the company traveled near the north end of Kaibab Plateau on October 27, Lewis's Paiute guide, Naguts, came up to him "whispering as if afraid to disturb the dead," and confided to him that in this area, the local band of Paiutes had suffered an epidemic: "All of their squaws & many of the indians had died lately, & up there among the rocks they had hid them. The disease from their description must have been vomiting and the bloody flux, only one squaw left among so many men!" One suspects that many children died also, as well as women. As one of the symptoms of this disease was severe diarrhea ("flux") mixed with blood, it may have been cholera or dysentery.[23]

In 1871, Elias O. Beaman, a photographer connected with the second Powell expedition for a limited time, wrote that he visited a valley south of Kanab that had served as a campground for a substantial group of Paiutes; however, after an outbreak of the measles, "a hundred deaths occurred in a very few days. The place was abandoned, and thereafter avoided by the Indians."[24] According to the Powell and Ingalls report, in 1873, there were only 171 Kai-vav-wits, centered at Kanab.[25] If there had been perhaps 300 Kaibab Paiutes in 1870, a hundred deaths would have accounted for the loss of a third of the band.

It is certain that many undocumented deaths resulted from epidemics, which were intensified by hunger and malnutrition.[26] It is virtually certain that the Kaibab Paiute population decreased dramatically after contact with whites, though we do not have precise Indian population numbers in nineteenth-century Utah.[27] One Indian informant said, "After the Mormons came, all the Indians died."[28] This probably refers mostly to disease, but also to malnutrition.

Despite loss of water and food resources, epidemics, and John Wesley Powell's early reservation policy, the Kaibab Paiutes survived, eventually receiving a reservation on the Arizona strip located at Pipe Spring and Moccasin Springs.

In Mormon southern Utah, Paiutes often lived in camps near Mormon towns and villages, where they were sometimes employed as laborers, and were usually paid much less than whites.[29] This occurred at Kanab. But often the Indians were viewed as annoyances, and some townspeople sought to have them removed from close proximity to the town (though other whites liked to have the Paiutes nearby as laborers).

In a priesthood meeting held at Kanab on March 6, 1880, Frank Hamblin, Jacob's brother, reported that Chuarumpeak, "chief Frank," told him that "this was their home and they wanted to live here, but they had nothing to live upon." An unnamed church leader then talked about the best way "to keep the Indians away from the settlements & working for themselves."[30]

In June of that year, Mormon leaders were considering the plan of buying Moccasin Springs, just north of Pipe Spring, and locating all the Kanab and Long Valley Paiutes there.[31] But the Mormon leaders did not follow through on this. The Kanab bishop wrote to the Kanab stake president in 1884, "The Indians feel very bad about not getting the Moccasin Farm," since, apparently, Apostle Erastus Snow had promised them that they would receive it.[32]

Ten years later, in early 1894, Chuarumpeak died, and "Indian George" became the headman of the Kaibab Paiutes.[33]

The LDS Church, as we have seen, obtained Whitmore's ranch after his death, and starting in 1870 used Pipe Spring as a tithing ranch, a ranch for cattle paid to the church as tithing. By 1888, the area had become severely overgrazed, and the LDS Church sold it to local cattlemen,[34] but when it did so, it gave one third of the spring at Moccasin to Kaibab Paiutes, and some of them farmed with that water. In 1907, the U.S. government created a reservation for the Kaibab Paiutes that included Pipe Spring and Moccasin Springs, and despite disputes with local ranchers who had been using this land, the reservation has lasted.[35] Today, some 240 Paiutes live on the 120,431 acres of the Kaibab Paiute Indian Reservation, which includes the Pipe Spring National Monument and Winsor Castle.

31

"He Had Always Led a Frontier Life"

Recircling the Grand Canyon; Counselor to Lot Smith, 1878

John Willard Young may have been Brigham's most charismatic son, and he may have been Brigham's favorite, of his seventeen sons. Brigham ordained him an apostle at the age of eleven (though John never entered the Quorum of the Twelve), and Brigham called him as First Counselor in the First Presidency in 1876. Despite Brigham's partiality for John Willard, and despite the young man's brilliance and charisma, his father often lamented that he seemed fonder of business than of church work. He became a railroad developer, and was often involved in raising money for grandiose schemes and projects.[1] John Willard became interested in Arizona, possibly as a result of Jacob's influence, and he would subsequently raise money for railroads in the area. He decided to claim ranching land near the San Francisco Mountains, so it was decided that Jacob would lead an expedition for John Willard on the Pearce's Ferry–Beale's Road route, which would allow them to spend time at the San Francisco Mountains, then visit the settlements on the Little Colorado. There were two other reasons for the trip. First, acting under John Taylor's direction, John Willard would act as a visiting general authority and organize a stake on the Little Colorado. Second, he would make arrangements to trade for Navajo wool.

The expedition would return via Lee's Ferry, so this would be the first encircling of the Grand Canyon since the winter of 1862–1863.

Hamblin and Young apparently met in Kanab on about December 22, then left St. George eight days later, after speaking in stake conference. Aside from Hamblin and Young, members of the expedition included Bateman Williams of Orderville, Stephen Taylor of Salt Lake City, Mosiah Hancock (who had visited the Hopis with Hamblin in early 1863 and was now residing at Leeds), August Wilchens of Salt Lake, and two nephews of John Willard, Brigham S. Young and Seldon Clawson.[2] These eight men, with three vehicles and thirteen animals,[3] traveled down the Grand Wash, then crossed the Colorado at Pearce Ferry on January 7 and 8. They then traversed Hualapai Valley, the Hackberry district, Truxton Springs (a few miles southwest of Peach Springs), Young's Springs, Spring Valley, and finally came to the San Francisco

Mountains.[4] Though the journey across northern Arizona was "very cold and disagreeable,"[5] and exhausting for the animals, Jacob must have remembered the difficulty of previous journeys and smiled at this one's comparative ease.

John Willard and Jacob met Andrew S. Gibbons—who had just been called to replace James Brown as president of the Arizona Indian mission—on January 23 at San Francisco Wash, where Canyon Diablo meets the Little Colorado.[6] Two days later they were at Ballenger's Camp (Brigham City), and on the twenty-seventh and twenty-eighth, the Arizona Saints held a conference, and John Willard organized the Little Colorado Stake of Zion, selecting Lot Smith as stake president. His counselors were Jacob Hamblin and Lorenzo Hatch[7]—one more sign that Jacob would be required to take up permanent residence in Arizona.

As Reilly correctly observes, Lot Smith was not inclined to take counsel from anyone (except perhaps the church president), so this assignment was probably founded on Jacob's Indian expertise. He and Hatch would presumably handle Indian relations on the Little Colorado, along with Gibbons, while Smith ran the stake. And, in fact, the following were called as Indian missionaries in Arizona at the same conference: Jacob, Ira Hatch, Andrew S. Gibbons, C. L. Christensen, William B. Gardner, Charles Reidhead, and Joseph B. Wakefield.[8]

On the twenty-seventh, Jacob spoke, and the summary of his talk gives us an idea of what his sermons were like at the time, historical retrospectives with visionary touches:

> Brother Jacob Hamblin had experienced some 40 years in a frontier life and since he had been baptized had always been in the U.O. [United Order] in fact but not in form. He gave his experience of some efforts to settle this land which had failed. He felt thankful the settling of this land had become a matter of fact. Spoke of the facilities of this country that everybody would not observe. He thought no man could live in the U.O. without a spirit of inspiration. The U.O. had been talked of for 30 or 40 years, but now it had come to be the word of the Lord unto us. He referred to the great change which had been wrought in the hearts of the Indians in this country within the last 20 years. Told a prophecy which an Indian had told him that a good people from the west would settle on the Little Colorado. This prophecy being a tradition was uttered some 18 or 19 years ago. Spoke of the great number of Indians here and in Mexico and South America. There should be 1,000 elders in Mexico. He told of an Indian that declared he had seen a strange individual that had appeared to the Indians in 1875, giving them good counsel whose name was Nephi. He referred to the increase of water in Utah and said the Lord will send rain here when actually necessary, if an honest man or even an Indian should rely upon Him and exercise his faith for it.[9]

Jacob was set apart for his First Counselor position on January 28,[10] and the following day, he set out for Utah with John Willard. They stopped at Moenkopi and Moenave (where the Joseph Foutz family was residing, along with John D. Lee's son, Joseph Hyrum, who had taken over his father's ranch), then struck out northward. After crossing the Colorado at Lee's Ferry on February 6, they passed through Kanab two days later.[11]

Jacob stayed in Utah throughout February, March, and April, speaking and giving prayers at ward meetings, funerals, and stake conference.[12]

John Willard would return to Arizona and help build railroads in the area; he lived in Moenkopi for a time, and built a large store and a woolen mill factory.[13] Unfortunately, none of these projects really succeeded.

On about April 6, four Paiutes attacked two Hopis near St. George, killing one and wounding the other, and robbed them of two donkeys, seventeen blankets, and some calico. Mormons and local Paiutes apprehended the four Paiutes, and one was committed to trial for murder in Beaver.[14] In 1874, Jacob had seen the diplomatic danger of murders of Arizona Indians in Mormon lands, so must have felt it necessary to return to the mesas quickly to explain to Hopi leaders and relatives of the deceased the status of the case. He left Utah in early May, traveling with John Oakley and possibly John W. Young, and the group arrived at Moenkopi on May 9, bringing a load of fruit trees with them to start a nursery. Jacob then traveled on to Sunset, arriving on the eleventh.[15]

Four days later, he and Andrew Gibbons set out for the "Moqui Agency" and the "Moqui village," probably Sichomovi on the First Mesa. As they traveled, they met one of their Navajo missionaries, William Gardner, at the camp of a man they called Navajo John, and these two men accompanied them to the Hopi agency, now at Keam's Canyon, eleven miles east of the First Mesa.

Since they found three Hopi chiefs and a number of Navajos at the agency, they did not need to go to Sichomovi. Also there was the Hopi agent, William R. Mateer, and "Mr. Keems, Indian Trader"—the well known Thomas Varker Keam.[16] Gibbons explained the Paiute attack to the Hopis, and in the evening Hamblin and Gibbons explained the incident to Navajos, with Keam acting as interpreter. Gibbons noted that Mateer and Keam were gracious and helpful. Hamblin and Gibbons left the mesas on the eighteenth and arrived at Sunset the following day.

A quarterly conference was held the next week, from May 24 through 26. On the second day of the conference, Jacob "said that about the year 1875 a change came over them [Indians in Arizona], caused by the inspiration of the Lord, causing them to be peaceful....He had always led a frontier life and believed if he was faithful in his mission, he would enjoy the society of his family in the world to come. Rejoiced in meeting here and in travelling among the indians."[17] Jacob also gave the closing prayer that day.

In late May or early June, Jacob took the twenty-three-year-old Dane, Christian Lyngaa Christensen, and set out on a mission to the Navajos, Apaches, and Zunis (Christensen called it "our Apache trip").[18] According to C. L., Jacob was searching for Geronimo "to convert him to the pursuit of peace." The Apache chief was then in Mexico, but Jacob and Christensen talked to his brother, Loco, who complained of the abusive treatment Apaches had received at the hands of the U.S. military. The young Dane described the Zuni encounter briefly, writing about Jacob in a tone of unabashed hero worship.[19] Christensen regarded the Zunis as similar to the Hopis: "kind, charitable, never warlike." Their dwellings, in northwestern New Mexico, thirty-five miles south of modern Gallup, were similar to the Hopis,' but not as high; they were raised only enough to avoid floods on the Zuni River, a tributary of the Little Colorado. The Zunis spoke a language related to no other Indian language, and had a complex ritual cycle similar to the Hopi ceremonies.[20]

Mormon missionaries had first visited the Zunis in April 1876, when Ammon Tenney and Robert Smith had preached to the Indians of northeastern Arizona and northwestern New Mexico.[21] They had striking initial success, baptizing about 111 Zunis, including some prominent leaders. Based on this early accomplishment, Lorenzo Hatch was called to settle near the Zunis and continue the missionary effort, and he arrived there in September 1876. Thus an early Mormon New Mexico settlement, eventually called Ramah, in Savoia Valley, was founded.[22]

Llewellyn Harris, who had accompanied Jacob on his visit to the Hopis in spring 1863 as a Spanish interpreter, visited the Zunis in January 1878, and administered to and healed hundreds of them when they were suffering from a smallpox epidemic, in one of the most famous mass-healings in Mormon history.

When Jacob and Christensen came to the Zuni villages, they arranged a talk with prominent Zunis, possibly Zunis who had been previously baptized into the Mormon Church. Christensen evidently knew a language in common with the Zunis—probably Spanish, possibly Navajo. The Zunis told Jacob that though he had never met them, they had heard good things about him, and "the good he had done among the different tribes as a peacemaker."

Jacob told them that Christensen was "of some consequence" as an interpreter, but they laughingly told Jacob that he was just a sapling—he might bear good or bad fruit in time.

Evidently, Jacob then prayed in English, with Christensen translating. It was a prayer "the like of which I had never heard before," wrote Christensen. "It seemed that the one he was praying to, whom he called his Heavenly Father, was so near I actually looked around a time or two to see if He was not present." Christensen emphasized the tremendous impact this prayer had on the Zunis.

They then had a peace talk—to the effect that "all men were brothers and ought not to shed blood but live in peace and honor our government and break no laws, moral or otherwise."

After this, the conversation drifted into history, and the Zunis asked about the history of Tuuvi's wife, Talasnimki, "the queen of the Aztec tribe."[23] They evidently knew the story of Tuuvi killing Rodriguez, and Jacob told them that Tuuvi had married Talasnimki, though they had no children, a special tragedy for Talasnimki, given her reputed royal ancestry. Jacob told how Tuuvi and Talasnimki had crossed the Colorado and visited Utah.

Then Jacob told of the Grass Valley killings, which had disrupted Mormon-Navajo relations, but stated that conditions had improved, and that now Mormons were living on the Little Colorado, and the Navajos "would learn that the whites were friendly and would teach them to farm and would build schools among them."

Jacob asked about Talasnimki's cousin, Lo-lo-tew-sit, who had been taken prisoner while disguised as Talasnimki, and then had ended up in the Zuni villages. They told him her story—she had married and had a daughter "who is our hope of deliverance."

According to Christensen, the Zunis told Jacob,

> We are indeed glad to meet you Ja-co-bea. It makes our hearts glad to know our white brother has a heart of flesh, not stone, who understands our sorrow through the invading of our broad land from the rising sun to where it sits in the western sky, our once mighty people with wise chiefs to guide us to our happy hunting ground. We are an extinct race.

Jacob and Christensen returned from their expedition in June, after five days of travel over a forbidding mountainous desert in which they often had no idea where the next water hole was.

The two men encountered Ammon Tenney in Savoia Valley, and together they traveled back to Arizona, but after they passed Fort Defiance, they turned back to Fort Wingate, near Gallup, New Mexico. There they met an attractive young Navajo woman who had been living as a common-law wife with a Capt. Richard Roe, because he had promised her leather (highly prized at the time), calico, and other valuable articles. After six months he had ordered her from his home after paying her nothing. She came to Jacob asking that he go to Roe and collect the debt he owed her, because Jacob "was a true friend of the Indians." The Indian missionary agreed, but the captain refused to pay anything, feeling that his status as an army officer gave him immunity against requests from Navajos or Mormons. Jacob, however, berated him soundly for his immorality. The three men allowed the Navajo woman to ride west with them in their wagon after they left Fort Wingate, and she became the first Navajo woman to be baptized, according to Christensen, and was instrumental in helping other Navajos convert to Mormonism.[24]

Jacob, with Llewellyn Harris, arrived at Taylor, about five miles south of modern Snowflake, on July 13, and the two spoke at church the following day, with Harris telling of his healing administration to 406 Zunis.[25] On July 29, Andrew Gibbons met Jacob in Moenkopi, traveling with a Brother Gardner (probably William Gardner), on his way to Utah. Gibbons wrote that Jacob seemed "well pleased with trip and success. Reports a good feeling among the portion of the Navajos that he traveled [among] also among the Pueblo Indians of New Mexico."[26]

The following day Jacob left Moenkopi, traveling with a Sister Luce and Sister Sims, and John Oakley, who had been living at Moenkopi for a few months.[27] They reached Kanab on August 10.[28] Apparently Jacob stayed in Kanab at least through November.[29] On December 1, he was sustained again as counselor to Lot Smith, but may not have been in Arizona at the time.[30]

32

"I Am Now Located with a Part of My Family in Round Valley"

Springerville, Arizona, 1879–1882

Before this, despite being called to settle Arizona, and his stake counselor position, Jacob didn't seem to establish permanent residency there, but instead was constantly on the move, sometimes on exploring journeys, sometimes on missionary visits to Indians, and he was often in St. George and Kanab. He had not brought his families to Arizona yet, which drew him constantly back to Utah. In 1879, this would change, as he brought at least one family, Priscilla's, to Arizona (and typically, to one of the most far-flung Mormon settlements). At this point, we might say that Arizona certainly became his place of residence. However, the constant travels continued, partly because one family remained in Kanab. But only partly.

On January 1, 1879, Jacob spoke at a meeting in Woodruff, a little town on the Little Colorado near the mouth of Silver Creek.[1] He was in Snowflake, up Silver Creek a few miles, on the sixteenth, then on the twentieth visited the small town of St. Johns, farther east on the Little Colorado, with Jesse Smith, who had recently been called to be president of the new Eastern Arizona Stake, including the Silver Creek area, St. Johns, and Mormon communities in Round Valley, south of St. Johns.[2] Afterwards, part of the company, possibly including Jacob, traveled on to Springerville, in Round Valley.[3]

By March 1 Jacob had been released from his stake presidency calling in the Little Colorado Stake.[4] He was in Kanab through most of March,[5] then, after March 26, traveled to the upper Little Colorado and settled in Springerville, in a part of Round Valley that later became known as Eagar, a few miles south of Springerville proper.[6]

Springerville, nestled at the base of the White Mountains (the location of the headwaters of the Little Colorado), lies not far from the New Mexico border. It had

32.1. Springerville and Round Valley, in eastern Arizona, from Cemetery Hill, in 1906. Jacob Hamblin and family lived here and in nearby Eagar from 1879 to 1883. By traveling photographer H. T. Shaw. Courtesy Jack Becker's website, www.roundvalleyaz.com.

been settled by non-Mormons in fall 1870, when William Milligan and a few others arrived to create farms to supply Fort Apache (recently set up under the name Camp Ord) and other army posts with grain.[7] A number of Hispanics also settled in the area, many of whom farmed for Milligan; he built a fort which became one of the early landmarks of Springerville.[8]

This was Apache country (in newly created Apache County), though the local White Mountain Apaches, living in a reservation administered by Fort Apache, were not hostile at this time. More dangerous than the Apaches were the outlaws and cattle rustlers that soon infested the area, as Springerville became a cattle town in the early 1880s.

The first Mormons—Jens Skousen, Peter J. Christofferson, and James L. Robertson—reportedly came to the Round Valley area in February 1879. John T. Eagar, who would give his name to the town of Eagar, where the Hamblins would live, arrived in March, as did Jacob; Eagar settled four miles south of Springerville, in Water Canyon.[9]

Jacob was back in Utah in early April, for on April 26 he met apostle Wilford Woodruff while returning from Utah. Woodruff, a senior apostle, lived among the Little Colorado settlements in 1879 and 1880 to avoid polygamy prosecution, and sometimes went on fishing and hunting expeditions with Jacob.[10] On May 15, Jacob was on his way to Utah again.[11]

In the first quarterly conference of the Eastern Arizona Stake, held at Snowflake on June 28 and 29, 1879, Jacob was sustained as "Presiding Elder of the Round Valley Branch."[12] As with his former stake counselor position with Lot Smith, this was a calling that would not last long.

This new stake included 664 Mormons in the towns of Snowflake, Forest Dale (built on what was decided to be the reservation of the Apache Indians, so the Mormons later had to move),[13] Savoia in New Mexico, St. Johns, and Round Valley.

Jacob was also sustained in the conference as an Indian missionary, along with Luther C. Burnham and Ernest A. Tietjen (both living near the Zunis), Llewellyn Harris and Ebenezer Thayne (both in Forest Dale, and thus working with Apaches), Peter J. Christofferson (in Round Valley), and Bateman H. Wilhelm and Ammon Tenney (both near St. Johns).

Jacob brought Priscilla and her family to Springerville in fall 1879.[14] Priscilla remembers weeping as she left Kanab. Jacob turned to her and said, "Now my Pet, I will take you back if you are going to be so depressed and upset. I know it is asking a lot of you to go with me. The trip will be a long, hazardous journey, with many miles of weary travel."

"No, no," I told him, "I'm willing to follow you wherever you want me to go and be by your side. So just drive on!"

When she crossed the Colorado, then went up and down Lee's Backbone, Priscilla wrote, "I felt as though I was going into Dante's Inferno."[15] Going up the "Backbone," C. L. Christensen wrote, there was a four-hundred-foot section of the dugway that "was so close to the ledge that there were scarcely three feet to spare, with the river 3000 feet below, looking like a blue ribbon. Everybody walked but the teamster and he took his chances." After the equally dangerous descent of Lee's Hill, there was at least a well-defined, if difficult, Mormon wagon road stopping at the main Mormon settlements on the Little Colorado. When Priscilla and family arrived in Springerville, the children called it the "tag end" of the world.[16] Priscilla wrote that "we again found the rugged responsibility of pioneering a new state. There were hard times beyond anything so far experienced."[17] Settling Arizona made the southern Utah pioneering experience look comparatively easy. Inez Hamblin Lee called it "the most poverty stricken time of our lives."[18]

Jacob, Priscilla, and family moved into Milligan's Fort, about one mile west of modern Eagar—a square stockade of vertical logs, enclosing a number of dirt-roofed rooms with whitewashed walls, surrounding a central square.[19]

Round Valley was a place of great cultural diversity. According to one local historian, "You had New Mexican sheep men, Anglo Texan cattlemen, Civil War veterans from both sides, friendly White Mountain Apaches, men on the run, farmers, prospectors, European immigrants and finally the Mormon colonists who came to stay." The Mormons in Springerville suddenly found themselves in the middle of this often volatile mix. Many of the Hamblin family's new neighbors were Latinos, and thus confirmed Catholics. Despite the language and religious barriers the Mormons faced in dealing with the Mexicans, Priscilla was appreciative of the gifts and friendship the Latino women shared with them at Christmas. The winter of 1879–1880 was reportedly the coldest in the memory of the previous Round Valley settlers.

If Jacob moved Priscilla to Springerville in early fall 1879, he quickly returned to Utah, for he must have left Springerville for southern Utah in mid-October 1879. On October 30, Joseph Fish met him just southeast of Lee's Ferry, as Jacob was traveling with a Sister Wilhelm—possibly the wife or daughter of Indian missionary Bateman H. Wilhelm.[20] Jacob may have traveled back to Springerville and returned to Utah, for on December 23, he wrote to President John Taylor, "I have just returned from Arizona."[21]

A couple days before this letter, "our old time indian missionary," as James Bleak described him, spoke at the St. George Tabernacle, reviewing his past career, mentioning the towns he had helped found, and stating that he had, "by appointment, lived a frontier life for 30 years." He told of angelic visitations to Indians in Arizona. He said that he "had recently been called to go to Mexico." We have no further details on a visit by Hamblin to Mexico in the early 1880s, if he followed through on this call.[22]

In late December, he was staying in St. George, working in the St. George temple. He wrote to President John Taylor on the twenty-third, again mentioning supernatural messengers that Arizona Indians had reported.[23]

Jacob apparently returned to Springerville after the new year. Perhaps he was present for the birth of Dudley Jabez Hamblin, Priscilla's eighth, on May 5, 1880.[24] Ten days later, Jacob, with Joel Johnson Jr., was on his way to Utah, for he met Stake President Jesse Smith coming the opposite direction, between Grand Falls and Black Falls on the Little Colorado.[25]

Perhaps due to his frequent travels, Jacob was released as presiding elder at Springerville.[26]

He was in Utah in November and December 1880.[27] At this time, he decided to transfer a portion of his Kanab herd of cattle to Springerville, so probably soon after Christmas he took fifteen-year-old Jake Jr. with him and started out with the herd,[28] assisted by Joseph Mangum and accompanied by a few emigrant families.[29] It would be a nightmarish journey.

They arrived at Lee's Ferry on New Year's Day, 1881. Possibly Jacob timed the crossing so that the Colorado level would be low, which would make it easier for the animals to ford the river, but it was unusually cold that year, and after the men drove the cattle across the river, many of the wet animals froze, and had to be killed.[30]

The party began to run low on provisions, and as they traveled south along the Arizona trail, the wind was unusually piercing. When they were about ten miles from Sunset, they had to cross the Little Colorado, and some of the wagons were trapped by the river's treacherous quicksand. One wagon tongue broke, and the wagon bed sank below the water. The men had to carry the women, children, and bedding in the wagon on their backs to shore. That night the water froze, which lowered the water level and made it possible to rescue the wagon. The men carried the wagon box to shore, then had to use three yokes of oxen teams to pull the wagon wheels out, two at a time. One of the oxen sank into the quicksand during this operation, and as they tried to free it, its back became disjointed.

The company was afflicted by lice, and at night took off their underclothes and left them in water overnight to kill the bugs. The next morning they built fires to thaw the blocks of ice that contained their underclothing.

Finally the party reached Springerville. The narrative ends with this abrupt statement: "The next year all the cattle were stolen by outlaws."[31] This is apparently an overstatement, but it does supply a laconic ending to a grim story of pioneer travel.

Jacob's travels between Utah and Arizona continued unabated. On February 3, 1881, he spoke at church in Kanab, and a month later, on March 25, he spoke at a Stake Conference at Snowflake.[32]

The day before this, Willard Otto Hamblin, Louisa's fifth and Jacob's twenty-second biological child, had been born in Kanab.[33] One of Jacob's children said that Willard was nine months old before Jacob saw him, which may show that Jacob's center of gravitation was now Arizona, not Kanab.[34] Don Carlos Hamblin, Priscilla's ninth and last child, and Jacob's twenty-third, was born in Eagar early the next year, on February 16, 1882.[35]

The risk of polygamy prosecution may have been one of the reasons for Jacob's constant travel, and for his having wives in two different states. In the 1880s, anti-polygamy legislation, the Edmunds and Edmunds-Tucker laws, were enacted by Congress; these allowed for easier prosecution of Mormon polygamists because cohabitation was the standard for arrest, rather than proven marriage. Mormons were sent to prison for polygamy, and even Mormon monogamists were disallowed from holding office and voting, in Utah but also in Idaho and Arizona. Many prominent Mormon leaders served jail terms; others had to go into hiding to avoid arrest.[36]

As a result, the Mormons revived Brigham Young and Thomas Kane's plan to found Mormon communities in Mexico, and in coming years, Mormons, including many Little Colorado Saints, among them Jacob himself, would travel to Mexico to try to find refuge from anti-polygamy legal harassment.

In Arizona, non-Mormon polygamy prosecutors were generally not moral crusaders, like the Republicans back east, but anti-Mormon politicians using polygamy prosecution to harass leading Mormons and neutralize LDS political clout.[37] Polygamy gave them the leverage they needed to pursue these goals.

These were dark times for Latter-day Saints. As they continued to hold on to polygamy—proclaiming that it was a practice given by revelation that they could not give up without giving up their religion—they were gradually stripped of political, legal, and financial power.

Jacob, as a polygamist and a prominent Mormon, would now play a small part in the painful saga of the slow decline and eventual demise of authorized Mormon plurality. This losing battle, a struggle of epic proportions, provides the background for the last years of his life. He was on the Mormon underground railroad.[38]

Soon Jacob would move even farther east. But before we leave Arizona, we should look briefly at the story of Mormonism and the Hopis and Navajos there. We have seen that when the Mormons settled the Little Colorado, gaining the permission and help of the local Navajos was a priority. And we have seen that Mormons regularly called missionaries to work with the Navajos, Zunis, Hopis, and Apaches. Some missionaries, including Ammon Tenney, worked with the Pima Indians in south-central Arizona and "Pueblo Indians," such as the Zunis and Isletas in New Mexico.

Nevertheless, though there were many baptisms of Indians, full conversions to Mormonism and western culture were rare. In addition, the practical challenges of settling on the Little Colorado were so great that it was not easy to turn one's focus toward full-time missionary work. Historian Charles Peterson portrays the Mormons in the Little Colorado mission as losing their interest in proselytizing the Indians as soon as they could secure towns and claims to farmland and cattle land in Indian territory.[39]

Remarkably, some sixty-five Hopis left their mesas to farm with the Mormons near Sunset in 1877 and raised a good harvest that year. Even more Hopis came in 1878, but in August, floods on the Little Colorado entirely destroyed their crops, and they retreated to the mesas. Christian Christensen wrote,

> It was a pitiful sight to see these people wading out of the tremendous flood with their small belongings on their backs....They bade us goodbye sorrowfully, and expressed the hope that none of us would die in this display of the Creator's anger, stating that they had left the corn fields and cotton fields of their forefathers' inheritance and this was their reward.[40]

Some Mormons, faced with a lack of widespread Hopi conversions, became disillusioned with them. Apostle Wilford Woodruff wrote of the Hopis (whom Mormons, including Hamblin, had once hoped would become Mormon converts en masse) that they were "very dull and superstitious and hard of understanding compared with the Navajo, Zoonies, Lagoonies and Islatos."[41]

Charles Peterson estimates that no more than a dozen Hopis actually became Mormons, and most of these continued to live the Hopi religion.[42] Only Tuuvi, Talasnimki, and a Hopi named Tom Polacca of Hano seemed to attend church regularly. Polacca was a "progressive" Hopi who advocated government schools; he came down off the First Mesa to manage a trading post, and the town Polacca was named after him as a result.[43] Many of his descendants have become noted Hopi artists.

The story of Tuuvi and Talasnimki provides a fascinating case history of the Hopi in early Mormonism; in one sense, they were Mormonism's chief Indian converts in Arizona. C. L. Christensen described Tuuvi as "a faithful member of the [LDS] church." He and Talasnimki had apparently been baptized Mormons in February 1876,[44] and he was ordained a priest on March 12 of the same year.[45] In 1877, Tuuvi and Talasnimki traveled to St. George with Andrew Gibbons and received their endowments in the newly dedicated St. George Temple on April 10.[46] They also reportedly received a temple marriage for eternity, and presumably they solemnized it at this time.[47]

On September 17, 1878, Apostle Erastus Snow, who was visiting in Arizona, laid out a town site two miles north of Moenkopi, and Mormons and some Hopis and Navajos began to live there. It was called Tuba City, in honor of Tuuvi.[48]

In 1882, Tuuvi accompanied Apostles Brigham Young Jr., Heber J. Grant, and Indian missionary C. L. Christiansen to the Hopi villages, and reportedly strongly denounced the residents of Oraibi for their unwillingness to trust the Mormons.[49]

Despite Tuuvi's participation in Mormon community and even temple ritual, he still retained much of his Hopi religious outlook. For example, at one point he could tell Christensen an elaborately mythological Hopi tale.[50]

In addition, Tuuvi and the Moenkopi Hopis soon came into conflict with local Mormons on familiar issues of land, water, and resource sharing. Just a year after Tuba City was founded, Tuuvi complained to the U.S. Hopi Indian agent, William R. Mateer, about Mormon expansion at Moenkopi, and requested protection against it.[51] This is a remarkable turnabout. He had welcomed the Mormons to Moenkopi for protection against the Navajos; now the influx of Mormons into the area of Moenkopi and Tuba City caused him to turn to the U.S. government to restrain the Mormons.

Six years later, in June 1885, tensions between Mormons and Hopis at Moenkopi and Tuba City were still simmering, and Tuuvi deeply resented Mormon actions at the time, including a Mormon petition to have Hopis removed from Moenkopi.[52] Tuuvi felt that he had agreed with Jacob Hamblin for Mormons to farm only in Moenave, and took the Hopi side when Mormons and Hopis disputed water rights at Tuba City–Moenkopi.[53] On June 15, he told C. L. Christensen that he had "washed him Self against the Mormons and wanted nothing more to do with them. He said he was a Gentile."[54] In December, however, he had another conversation with Christensen, and though Tuuvi still disagreed with the Mormon position on water rights, he said that he hoped the Mormons and Hopis could live in peace, "and we parted in good feeling," wrote Christensen.[55] It is unknown whether he continued to consider himself a "Gentile" or renewed his identity as a Mormon. In any event, the incident shows the ongoing struggle between Mormon and Hopi for precious water and pasture land at Moenkopi,[56] and it also shows the difficulty Mormons had in producing full conversions of Hopis to Mormonism.[57]

The great tragedy of Tuuvi's old age was a separation from Talasnimki, after which she married a younger man. Tuuvi felt that the new husband could not give her happiness either, and "thus we [Tuuvi and Talasnimki] both go down to the grave in mourning."[58] Some sources state that Tuuvi died in 1887, at Moenkopi.[59]

Talasnimki apparently renounced her conversion to Mormonism and joined the "Hostiles" who rejected accommodation with white culture, for she moved to the "Hostile" settlement of Bacavi.[60] Talasnimki and Tuuvi had adopted a Navajo child, Aqawsi, whom they raised as a Hopi.[61] Aqawsi was one of the Hopis who was sent to Alcatraz in 1895, another sign that Talasnimki was aligned with the "Hostiles."[62] Her death date is not known, but in 1911, at age eighty-three, she was living at Bacavi.[63]

Mormons, Hopis, and Navajos continued to dispute water rights and land use at Tuba City and Moenkopi.[64] The U.S. government finally required the Mormons to leave in 1903. Tuba City became a major Navajo community, ironically enough, as it was named after a Hopi.[65]

Just as there were baptisms but few converts among the Hopis, the same was true of the Navajos. In one missionary journey, C. L. Christensen recorded eighty baptisms; his diary mentions a number of Navajos baptized. We have seen that Jacob Hamblin baptized thirty Navajos in 1875.[66] Groups of Navajo chiefs visited Salt Lake City. But full conversions, both to Mormonism and western culture, were rare. One significant convert was Jose Pino, in the Ramah, New Mexico, area, who became an important political leader for his people.[67]

John Taylor, in 1882, referred to the difficulty of full conversions of Indians after baptism:

> The work among the Lamanites must not be postponed if we desire to retain the approval of God. Thus far we have been content simply to baptize them and let them run wild again. But this must continue no longer. The same devoted effort, the same care in instructing, the same organization and priesthood must be introduced and maintained among the house of Lehi as among those of Israel gathered from the gentile nations. As yet God has been doing all and we comparatively nothing.[68]

Many church leaders, such as Taylor, were seriously interested in the Indian mission, but large numbers of Indians, converted to Mormonism and western culture, did not follow. The Tuba City Ward record is probably speaking of Navajos when it records that local Indians were friendly, but "they were in the habit of coming in occasionally for the purpose of being rebaptized and having a feast."[69]

Surprisingly, in 1887 the LDS Church apparently decided to discontinue missionary work among the Indians in Arizona. Between 1875 and 1887, there had been an intense effort to colonize the area and convert the Indians, historian David J. Flake writes, but "eventually the colonization calling won precedence and after 1887 there is little record of preaching to the Indians."[70] Ira Hatch wrote to President John Taylor on March 15, 1886, lamenting that the Indian mission "is almost forgotten."[71]

In December 1887, Apostle Brigham Young Jr., in charge of the mission at the time, came to Ramah, which had become the center of the Indian mission, and formally discontinued Indian proselytizing, reportedly because of "the opposition of the government Indian agents."[72]

Flake gives a number of other possible factors leading to this discontinuation. First, simply enough, cultural disparity between Mormon and Indian was overwhelming; second, language barriers were daunting; third, missionaries were not supported by their communities, but had to fend for themselves in a difficult pioneering situation, so were unable to actually live among Indians and learn their languages well (a continuation of lack of support for Indian missionaries that we saw in Utah); fourth, the legal pressures of polygamy persecution unsettled the Mormon community and caused many Mormon leaders (including Jacob Hamblin) to emigrate to Mexico.[73]

According to Richard G. Oman, a specialist on southwestern Indian art,

> After Tom Polacca was converted, there was little contact between the eastern Hopi and the Church for many years. When Tom became an old man, he called his children around him and told them about the gospel and the Book of Mormon. He made his children promise that they would not join any other Christian church, because the "Mormon missionaries" would come again, and they would have the Book of Mormon.[74]

After 1887, Mormons often had friendly relations with Navajos and Hopis, and a number of Mormons ran trading posts on the Navajo reservation, notably Jacob's friend Joseph Lehi Foutz and his sons—but the LDS Church did not resume its Indian mission in Arizona until some fifty years later, in 1936.[75]

33

"We Found a Nice Farm on the Frisco River"

New Mexico, Old Mexico, 1882–1885

In October 1882, Jacob joined Stake President Jesse Smith, Smith's counselor Lorenzo Hatch, William C. McLellan, and a few other Saints on a tour of Mormon towns in the eastern Gila River area in southeast Arizona and western New Mexico.[1] They departed from Snowflake on October 9, and after visiting Forest Dale and Smithville (modern Pima), they traveled east through ranching and mining country, and crossed the New Mexico border. Traveling north, they climbed the Burro Mountains, then turned northwest and came to Pleasanton, a small town of Saints in Williams Valley on the San Francisco River.[2]

The party held three meetings there and organized a ward, with William Carroll McLellan named as its bishop. Smith wrote, "It was deemed advisable that Elder Jacob Hamblin remove to this place, and in connection with Elder George C. Williams, preach the Gospel in the regions roundabout." Jacob had received his last specific call.[3]

Jacob would thus presumably work in close partnership with George Calvin Williams, the remarkable man who had given Williams Valley its name, in the upcoming years. Now forty-nine years old, Williams was called "Parson" because he had been a Baptist "backwoods preacher" in Tennessee, Texas, and Arkansas before converting to Mormonism.[4] William Bailey Maxwell, Jacob's former son-in-law, who had moved to Pleasanton in 1871, had been instrumental in converting Williams.[5]

The Smith–Hatch–Hamblin party visited the Mormon towns Alpine and Nutrioso, in Arizona, on the way back home, then reached Round Valley in the evening on October 29. We can only imagine Jacob breaking the news of the next family move to Priscilla and the children that night.

The move to Pleasanton has not been precisely documented. Jacob probably waited until spring 1883 to attempt it, but it could have been in late 1882.[6] Whenever the trip was made, it was their last move as a family. Priscilla wrote, "We found a nice farm on the Frisco River, where the land was fertile and rich, and the climate was good. It seemed we could again have our orchard of fruit, and a good garden; we had plenty of water."[7]

33.1. William Bailey Maxwell family, in Pleasanton, Catron County, New Mexico, probably in front of the house of George Calvin "Parson" Williams. This is the only known photograph of pioneer Pleasanton, where Jacob and his family lived from 1883 to his death in 1886. Courtesy Maurice F. Coates.

Jacob returned to Utah at some point, and then moved Louisa to Pleasanton, possibly also in spring 1883.[8]

Jacob bought a "good farm" in Pleasanton for eight hundred dollars, after having sold his farm in Round Valley to Hiram Bigelow for the same price.[9] Eight families moved into Pleasanton with him.[10]

While Jacob's trip to Pleasanton with Priscilla is not recorded, he made a trip back to Round Valley soon thereafter with his fifteen-year-old daughter, Ella Ann, Priscilla's sixth. After collecting some last household items, Jacob and Ella set off for Pleasanton in a wagon, but Jacob was soon very sick with a cramp, so had to lie down in the wagon while Ella drove the team of mules. When they came to the "Silice" River, they found it was running high.[11] Ella urged the mules into the water which covered them until only their ears were above water. Ella looked back at Jacob and saw his lips moving in prayer. But the mules plowed through the water and brought them safe to the other side, though mules, humans, and baggage were all drenched. Ella found a place for a camp and made Jacob some ginger tea. "You are just like your mother, always prepared for anything," Jacob told his daughter.[12] High praise!

As they settled in Pleasanton, the Hamblins had arrived at one of the true hinterlands of the Southwest. Presently a very small community in the Gila National Forest, it was a beautiful location, with plentiful water and excellent farming and ranching land. In addition, it was probably valued because residence in New Mexico

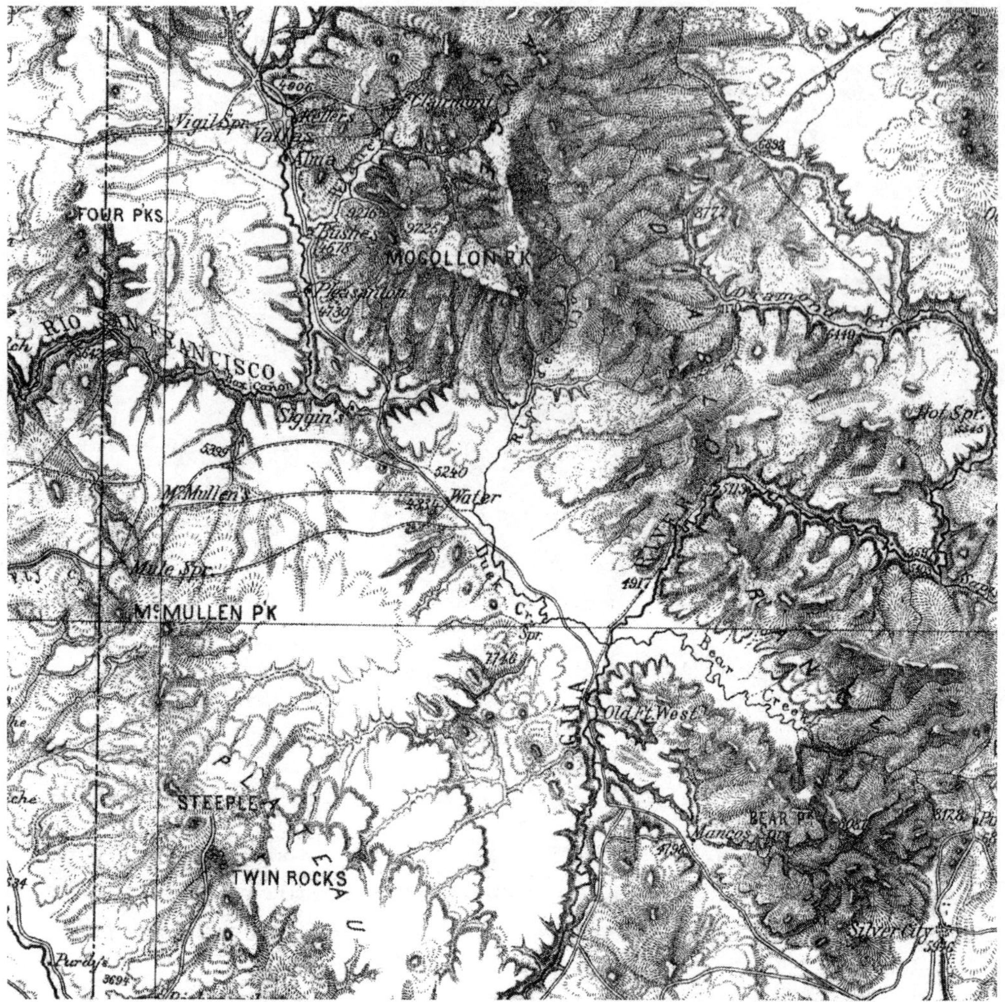

33.2. Southwest New Mexico. This 1883 military map shows Pleasanton on the "Rio San Francisco." Jacob and his sons would freight between the Mogollon mines near Pleasanton and Silver City, in the southeastern part of the map. Courtesy David Rumsey Historical Map Collection.

might have served to shield polygamists such as Jacob and Bill Maxwell from Arizona lawmen.

As in nearly all Mormon towns, irrigation was a central focus, and the settlers created a diversion dam of rocks and brush in the Frisco, and dug ditches from this to land that had been cleared for farming. Pleasanton residents used the Williams' adobe residence as a makeshift fort during Indian scares.[13]

We have little documentation for the precise things Jacob was doing in his Pleasanton years. Priscilla remembered that he was not home much during this time, so he was presumably traveling with other missionaries and visiting Indians.[14] However, at other times he worked to help provide for his family. Pleasanton was in mining country, so often the Mormons freighted between the local mines and Silver City, the major town and railhead in southwestern New Mexico, about forty miles southeast of Pleasanton.[15] At one point Jacob was employed by a local mining company, "taking a contract to get out stalls or timbers used in the mines at Mogollon."[16]

The threat from hostile Apaches was much more real in Williams Valley than in Round Valley, as Apache chiefs, such as Victorio, Geronimo, and Chihuahua, experts in raiding, led bands of Indians who could take cover in the rugged mountainous areas of southwestern New Mexico, and they sometimes killed isolated miners or freighters. Inez Hamblin Lee remembered the bodies of travelers and soldiers, killed by Apaches, being brought in to Pleasanton to be buried.[17] Jake Jr., who freighted between the mines near Pleasanton and Silver City, remembered that a number of his friends and acquaintances were killed by Apaches during 1885 and 1886.[18]

On May 4, 1884, Amarilla, Louisa's sixth child—and Jacob's twenty-fourth and last biological child—was born in Pleasanton.[19]

While Jacob held no formal church position at this time, aside from Indian missionary, he was still one of the leading Mormons in the area. He attended stake conferences in Arizona on September 29–30 and December 8–9, 1883, reporting for Pleasanton.[20] In early 1884, a Mr. Laferre in Silver City invited leading Mormons to come and speak at a hall he owned, and Stake President Jesse Smith agreed. Smith, Jacob, Lorenzo Hatch, and Bill Maxwell, with a few others, traveled to this prominent New Mexico town, where they spoke from January 15 to 19.[21] On the eighteenth, the rabidly anti-Mormon local newspaper recommended the "extermination" of the religious visitors, but the local marshal told the Mormons he would defend them if there was any trouble. Jacob received the assignment to speak on the Mountain Meadows Massacre, which he did "in a masterly manner," wrote Smith, "showing that the leaders of our church had no connection with it whatever."[22] The Mormons were able to return to Pleasanton and Arizona in safety.

In Arizona, a period of anti-Mormon polarization and polygamy prosecutions of Mormon leaders began in earnest in 1884. If you pled guilty to polygamy, you might receive a sentence of six months; but if you fought the charge and were convicted, you could be sentenced to a harsh three-year imprisonment. Ammon Tenney, in fact, was arrested on about June 8, 1884, and stood trial for polygamy in Prescott before a judge, Sumner Howard, who sat in court during the day and gave anti-Mormon lectures at night. Tenney was given a severe sentence: three years in prison in Detroit, Michigan, far from family and friends. He served nearly two years of this sentence before being pardoned and released.

So Jacob would have understood that he ran the real danger of being sentenced to years in prison, far away in the "American Siberia" in Michigan, if he was recognized and arrested by Arizona lawmen.[23]

Because Jacob was a prominent Mormon polygamist, he had to avoid the law, and probably as a result, his reminiscences now record a bewildering series of journeys: "In the winter of 1885 I thought it best to leave home for my owne safty as the feeling in Arazona and Neww Mexico was to arrest allin those Terrys [Territories] that was living in Pligamy and send them to prision," he wrote. "I left my home in New Mexico went back towares [toward] Utah about 200 miles."[24] If Mormon polygamists viewed Utah as safer than Arizona, it shows the level of paranoia among LDS leaders in Arizona.

In January 1885, Jacob traveled back to Arizona and New Mexico.[25] He met President Jesse Smith in Eagar on February 8, and Smith told him "that the first Presidency of the church had aranged and advised a citty of refuge to be built in old Mex[ico] a plase of safty for the oprest."[26] Church president John Taylor had consulted with Arizona church leaders and had decided to found Mormon colonies in Mexico, and Arizona became the staging ground for the Mormon colonies south of the border.[27] Smith was beginning his trip to Chihuahua, and Jacob decided to accompany him.[28]

He thus became part of one of the least known of the Mormon hegiras. Though it has been overshadowed by the early expulsions of the Mormons from Missouri and Nauvoo, this journey was just as heroic and difficult.[29] Mud, snow, bad roads, parched deserts, and steep mountains faced these pioneers traveling from Arizona to New Mexico. And their destination was a foreign country where English was not spoken.

Apparently, Jacob traveled with companies going southeast by way of New Mexico. "I returnd home went in to ~~Shuudh~~ Shauaudh [Chihauhua] old Mexico," he wrote.[30] Some evidence suggests that he traveled with the Joseph Fish group, which split off from the Jesse Smith group. On about the nineteenth they came to Milligan's Hill, between Luna Valley and Baca Plaza, always a fearful descent, but now made terrible by heavy snow.[31] The last part of the hill "was frightful," wrote Sullivan Richardson. After a turn in the road, there was an abrupt drop-off, nearly perpendicular, to the bottom of a canyon, and wheels had to be chained and rough-locked, and twelve men had to help lower each wagon down the steep slope.

Hamblin was driving "a rather antiquated hack" which had no brakes and a high dashboard. He could barely see over it from his seat at the bottom of the hack, as he leaned against a sack of corn. In the first part of the hill, therefore, before the turn, Jacob could see nothing ahead of him, and would "slash with the whip over the dashboard, and say to his team, 'Go on! I know you are there!'" The mules ran at a lope, and Richardson closed his eyes in fear as Jacob approached the drop-off. But he called out "Whoa!" and pulled back on the lines with all his strength, which caused a bit in one of the mules' mouths to break. Despite this potential disaster, the team stopped a few feet from the drop-off.

"While I was between shuddering with horror and rejoicing with thankfulness," Richardson wrote, "Uncle Jacob rose until he could see over the dashboard. He drew up his lines, until the broken bit showed above the mules' neck, its nose out loose, and said, 'We-e-l-l, I've pulled it clear through him!'"[32]

Jacob, with the Fish company, reached Pleasanton on February 22.[33] Fish, a cousin of Priscilla, stayed a few days in the Hamblin home and recorded one of Jacob's visionary predictions. He said that he had heard Joseph Smith, in Nauvoo, say that the Saints would "go down this river (meaning the San Francisco River) and that the Lord and the Devil were playing a game of checkers. The Lord had one move ahead, that the Saints were going into the king row (meaning Mexico and Central America) and when they returned they would sweep the board."[34] Mormons were now intensely disillusioned with the United States and were yearning for an apocalyptic catastrophe that would punish Washington for its anti-polygamy crusade—Wilford Woodruff, for example, in 1879 predicted the imminent downfall of the U.S. government.[35] In their doomed chess match with the federal government, they yearned to go "one move ahead."

Not long after this, Jacob, traveling with his son Lyman, departed for old Mexico. Mormon companies crossed the U.S.-Mexico border in southwestern New Mexico, and came to La Ascensión, in the Casas Grandes River valley, about twenty-five miles south of the border. This was near the eventual LDS colony of Colonia Díaz. A customs house was located at La Ascensión, at which the Mormons had to pay duty. They made a general quasi-permanent camp here, while leading brethren made arrangements to buy land in Mexico.

The Fish company reached La Ascención on March 7,[36] and five days later Fish wrote that Bill Maxwell and Jacob Hamblin rented some land from some Mexicans and moved to the lower end of the town.[37] Jacob spoke at a Sunday meeting on the fifteenth.[38]

The leading brethren were not able to buy land immediately, so the Mormons were forced to rent land to put in crops. This was an extremely difficult time for the Mormon colonists, as they waited month after month for land to be purchased.[39] Of his travel and first weeks in Mexico, Jacob wrote, "On my way down was hur[t] in my brest and side[,] was not able to work mutch in puting in [a] crop as they that was expected to...make the purches made a failyer of [of it] and thought it would take from 3 to 6 months to acomplish the purchase. My son Lyman went home with his team & I was not able to doe mutch."[40]

Jacob apparently returned to Pleasanton, but was back in La Ascención on May 4.[41] Bill McLellan's seventeen-year-old son, Ed, traveled to Mexico with Jacob in the spring of 1885, in what may have been Jacob's third visit to old Mexico. After passing through Silver City and Deming they reached a place where they had to wait for guards to bring them to Ascensión, so they let their horses graze and began to eat their lunch. But soon Ed saw twenty or thirty horsemen approaching and turned to Jacob.

"Uncle Jacob," he said. "These men look like Indians to me." Jacob did not reply. "They are Indians, Uncle. What are we going to do?"

"Nothing," said Jacob.

"But what will you do when they get here?" Ed asked.

"Oh, give them something to eat," said Jacob, as he continued to eat his own lunch.

Ed took a defensive position behind some nearby grass, then realized that the band of men approaching were the Mexican guards they were expecting.

Hatch wrote, "Ed's hasty face-saving pretense that he was just rabbit hunting didn't save him from one of the few hearty laughs ever heard from Jacob Hamblin."[42]

After a stay in Mexico, Jacob wrote, "I then started for utah a journey of 700 miles." It is not known why he suddenly departed to Utah; perhaps land had not been made available for colonists yet. But in America, he would be living on the underground, as marshals were hunting for him in Arizona and Utah.

"On my way I caled to see my Family," he wrote. "One of the little ones asked if I had come home to stay now. I answerd no little [one. She] weept and said 'wh[en] will you come to stay.' I then went to St George in Utah worked in the Temple until it closed for the heat of the season[,] visited many of my old acquantences."[43]

We have some records of these visits to old friends. On July 5, Jacob attended Sunday school in Hebron, about thirty miles north of St. George, and his friend John Pulsipher wrote in his journal, "Jacob Hamblin, our long tried, true & faithful Missionary, pioneer & fronteir man is with us resting from his wicked persecutors, who are determined to fine & imprison every man that has more than one wife."[44]

While Jacob was in southern Utah, Wilford Woodruff, a senior apostle, gave him "a mission to the Lamanite Any whare in the United States or Mexico."[45]

Jacob, after his stay in St. George, came to Kanab, where he spoke at a meeting and blessed a baby on October 1, then left on the eighteenth.[46]

Jacob then "travailed home evading the US Marchals." In Pleasanton, he found that his family "had ben sick with the chils and feaver ware geting mostley over it," an ominous development. The irrigation ditches at Pleasanton probably offered an ideal habitat for the malarial Anopheles mosquito. Jacob and his family, who had endured bouts of malaria in Iowa and Santa Clara, were now about to face a major, lingering onset of the dangerous sickness.

Jacob took seventeen-year-old Walter to Smithville, to learn the blacksmith trade with a Brother Haney, then "travailed 175 miles to asencion chauahuah old M[ex]," as Jacob wrote.[47] There are persistent traditions that Jacob took Louisa to Mexico,[48] and if this is so, this was probably the time he took her.[49]

While in Smithville, the town received the news that "the apaches ware rading and killing some people. 2 of our brotheren ware kiled at Ash Springs on the healy [Gila] river."[50] So Jacob and his company would have been on edge as they traveled southward. The last words in Jacob's last diary are, "I left the Healy in company with 5 wacons 5 of the brotheren for chauah [Chihuahua] old mexico." As these few wagons traveled south, the pioneers were nervous, always on the lookout for Apaches. One day, their fears seemed to be realized: in front of them a line of Indians approached, spread out a long way. The children thought of scalpings and impending massacre; Louisa, holding little one-year-old Amarilla, paled. Jacob, stoic, looked carefully at these Indians. Then one of them made a sign to his men. "Suddenly the grey-haired old chief motioned his warriors to a halt, and galloped forward, shouting, 'Jacob! Jacob!'" It was Hastele, identified by some historians as Ganado Mucho, who had helped defuse the tinder box of the Grass Valley killings in 1874.

Jacob and his old friend exchanged a Navajo embrace. Hastele told him that he and his warriors had assisted the government in driving enemy Apaches out of the area, and as they were returning, they had fanned out to hunt deer and antelope. Jacob's children, far from dying in a massacre, paid their respects to the kindly Hastele and his fellow Navajos.[51]

Jacob and Louisa thus came to Chihuahua, perhaps in November or December 1885. There is no hard data that records how long they stayed, though they both eventually returned to Pleasanton. Perhaps Jacob left Louisa there, and returned to Pleasanton to visit his other family before returning to bring her back again. The details of Jacob's movements at this time are lost in a fog of meagerly documented history.

34

"In a Small Cabin in the High Mountains of New Mexico"

The End of the Trail, 1886

Jacob probably moved Louisa and family back to Pleasanton early in 1886. When he arrived there, however, his son-in-law, Abe Winsor, Olive's husband, made a special trip from Silver City to give him unwelcome news: a federal marshal had specifically targeted Jacob and was searching for him. He would not be able to relax with his families in Pleasanton.

A different son-in-law took Jacob to a sawmill in the Mogollon Mountains, not far from the Cooney mines, where he rented a room from the mill owner, a Mr. Zanders. Somehow Jacob and Zanders recognized each other as masons and exchanged a handclasp of recognition.[1]

A few weeks later Zanders met his brother, a federal lawman, in Silver City, and looked over the list of names of people he hoped to arrest. Seeing Jacob's name there, he quickly returned to the mill and told Jacob that he should leave immediately, as Zanders's brother would be there soon. He helped Jacob mount a mule and Jacob rode all night, reaching his home in Pleasanton in the morning.[2]

He quickly decided to return to old Mexico once more, but he did not stay there long, for he was back in New Mexico by early summer 1886.

He was now sixty-seven years old, not elderly by modern standards, but the constant traveling and exposure to the weather had taken their toll on him. As far back as 1871, Fred Dellenbaugh, in the second Powell expedition, referred to the Indian missionary as an old man. In the past year, the polygamy prosecutions had caused him to visit Mexico perhaps four times, and he had traveled to and from Utah. He had not been able to slow down, and he was wearing down.

After he returned to Pleasanton, malaria, the dreaded chills and fever, struck the town once again, and Jacob was one of the first to contract it. In mid-July, he, Jacob Jr., his nephew, and his daughter-in-law came to Alpine "for their health," as they hoped that the cool mountain air would counter the malaria symptoms.[3]

However, in Alpine, Jacob's health only seemed to decline, "and each chill seemed harder to bear." Finally, in mid-August, Jacob could only think of returning to Pleasanton.[4] According to family traditions, Jacob said to his son, Lyman, "You let me take Old Nell [a horse] and Duane [Lyman's oldest son], he can take me home." So Old Nell was hitched up to a wagon beside Jacob's mule, and Jacob, Lyman, and fourteen-year-old Duane set out on August 18.[5] Jacob promised Duane that they would fish along the way, but Duane didn't think that his grandfather would be able to do much but sit in the wagon and endure the journey.

That night they stayed in Luna Valley, which now had a Mormon settlement, and in the morning Lyman returned to Alpine. After a day of travel, Jacob and Duane slept in a building with only a dirt roof. It rained heavily that night, and Jacob was soaked, which brought about a more intense onset of his chills and fever.

Duane took a cut-off road over Milligan Hill which made the route shorter, though it was very steep. They hoped to arrive at Pleasanton that day, but Old Nell became sick, and they had to camp out again.[6]

The next day they pulled into Pleasanton toward evening.[7] Many members of Jacob's family were also stricken by malaria. Priscilla remembered that on that night, "I couldn't raise my head from the pillow," and her two youngest boys, Dudley and Carl, were also very sick. The two daughters, Mary and Clara, were also ill, but were able to move about some and do things to help the family.[8]

Duane drove the wagon to Priscilla's house, but when he found that the whole household was ill, he went to Louisa's home instead.[9] Louisa

> was standing at the door and recognized the little brown mule. Before Duane was on the ground, she was climbing into the wagon and after a quick survey hurried into the house to get the bed ready. Duane aroused his grandfather and helped him to a sitting position to take the cup of cool water Louisa had brought from the burlap-wrapped jar. Jacob drank long and deep. Duane removed the endgate and climbed back into the wagon to help Jacob to the ground. Jacob finally managed to take the few steps to the house and into the bedroom, where he sank back upon the pillow, exhausted.[10]

Clara, from Priscilla's house, came over and helped Louisa take Jacob's clothes off and get him into bed.[11]

After arriving in Pleasanton, Jacob could only manage short yes and no answers.[12] Elders Johnson and Maxwell were sent for, and administered to Jacob, but to no avail. Priscilla wrote, "I lay in bed not able to go to him, but I prayed for the return of his health."[13] It was not to be.

Emma Coleman, our earliest source, wrote that Jacob died within a few hours of returning home.[14] However, according to his granddaughter Louise Udall, he lived through the night and most of the next day. "The heat of the afternoon found Dudley sitting by Jacob's bedside, fanning his face with a branch to cool him and keep the flies

34.1. Jacob's grave in Alpine, Apache County, Arizona, with his children Mary H. Beeler, Walter Hamblin, Willard O. Hamblin, Clara Hamblin Staley, Amarilla Hamblin Lee, and (pasted in) Dudley Hamblin. This item is reproduced by permission of The Huntington Library, San Marino, California.

away from the semi-conscious man. Jacob lived out the day, but in the wee small hours of night the word passed from house to house: 'Jacob is dead.'"[15] Most sources say that Jacob died on August 31, 1886, but Coleman gives the date of death as August 30.[16]

According to Coleman, one of Jacob's wives—presumably Louisa—"was obliged to prepare him for burial as all the rest of the people of the small place were sick with chills. For the same cause they sent about thirty miles to get a coffin made."[17] Sixteen-year-old Walter, not yet recovered from malaria, had to drive to Alma and sell butter to get funds to pay a carpenter for the coffin. He was able to obtain one, but the problem of digging a grave remained. Coleman wrote that "passing strangers dug his grave. O how hard it seems after having spent his whole life in the interest of the Work, to be deprived of a burial by his brethren!"[18] The gravediggers were two able-bodied young men from Nutrioso, C. S. (Sam) Love and Frank Campbell, who had been working in the Mogollon mines and happened to be passing through Pleasanton. Digging the grave was not easy work, as the ground was very hard, and every blow of a pick could loosen only a small amount of the rocky caliche dirt. After a day's work, they had only dug four feet.

The interment took place on the morning of September 1. Men from surrounding ranches drove in and helped put the coffin on a wagon and transport it from Louisa's house to the grave. Of Jacob's two living wives and two dozen children, only three witnessed the grave ceremony: Jake Jr., Walter, and Dudley.[19] There was no formal funeral.

So ended a "life on the frontier." Priscilla's tribute is one of the best: "On that memorable day, August 31, 1886, with only a small part of his family at his bedside; and in a small cabin in the high mountains of New Mexico, where he had helped blaze enduring trails of peace, my beloved Jacob slipped away to join the prophets in death."[20]

35

"I Could Not Bare the Thought of Killing One of Them"

JACOB HAMBLIN: LEGACY

Richard Slotkin, historian of the mythology of the American frontier, after describing Buffalo Bill's Wild West shows, noted that they expressed ethical truths. He wrote, "The 'moral truth' of the frontier experience, which the Wild West emphasized, was its exemplification of the principle that violence and savage war were the necessary instruments of American progress."[1] When Buffalo Bill and Annie Oakley performed feats of marksmanship, the program gave ideological support with an essay entitled "The Rifle as an Aid of Civilization."

Violence was the tool of Manifest Destiny, and the main opponent of the European rifle was the American Indian. Slotkin wrote,

> The story of American progress and expansion thus took the form of a fable of race war, pitting the symbolic opposites of savagery and civilization, primitivism and progress, paganism and Christianity against each other. Quite early in the history of white-Indian relations, a conception of Indian warfare developed that tended to represent the struggle as necessarily genocidal.[2]

So the American-Indian wars became wars of displacement and extermination.[3] Killing Indians, for some, was seen as a higher good, a religious duty. John Chivington, who commanded the military forces in the infamous Sand Creek Massacre in 1864, was an ordained Methodist minister,[4] and reportedly said, "I have come to kill Indians, and I believe it is right and honorable to use any means under God's heaven to kill Indians."[5]

The "moral truth" of the Jacob Hamblin frontier experience is very different. In Tooele, he probably witnessed five unarmed, innocent Indian prisoners summarily executed by Porter Rockwell, acting as military leader. Not long after this, Jacob was sent by his military and ecclesiastical superiors with the express assignment of killing Indians—who had probably been guilty of theft of livestock. But he had his conversion experience in the mountains near Tooele, and turned from guns and bloodshed to seeking friendship and diplomacy with Indians. In fact, the conversion account is almost comical in its story of a gun that simply would not shoot. The "moral truth" of this story involves *not* shooting, and specifically, not shooting Indians—even though the Mormon leadership at the time felt that those Indians deserved to die.

In addition, as a result of his military experiences in Tooele, Jacob came to regard Indians as fully human, partially as a result of his sensitivity to children and women. In a military expedition before the "conversion" experience, Jacob and his men surprised a small group of Goshutes, only two families, in the mountains, and the women and children ran up the canyon. "When I herd the schreems of the ~~chil~~ chirldin I could not bare the thought of killing one of them," Jacob wrote.[6]

In a subsequent expedition, the Mormons surprised a larger group of Indians, and once again Jacob saw Indian children and women run screaming away from their camp up the mountain, without moccasins, the blood from their bare feet staining the snow, and he felt he wanted to deal with Indians "in a different way."[7]

These early experiences in Tooele shaped the Hamblin of southern Utah and Arizona. In the Southwest, he learned the Paiute language, and lived near Paiutes for the great majority of his subsequent life. As we have seen, some who knew him felt that he "became" an Indian in many ways. If conflicts with Indians arose, Jacob tried to solve them through negotiation, in preference to military means.

After Navajos raided southern Utah in the late 1860s, Jacob, with John Wesley Powell, traveled to Fort Defiance in 1870 to try to confer with Navajo leaders. While his efforts did not bring an overnight solution to the problem, it was a step toward the eventual ending of the trans-Colorado River raids, and it opened up fruitful trading routes for Navajos and Mormons.

In 1874 when four Navajos were attacked by non-Mormons in Grass Valley, Utah, Jacob again traveled to Navajo territory and spoke with angry relatives and friends of the three men who had been killed in Mormon country. Though some Navajos demanded that he be executed in recompense for the Navajos killed in Utah, wiser counsels prevailed, and through his friendship with an influential Navajo leader, Hastele (possibly Ganado Mucho), he was able to convince the Navajos that "Americans," not Mormons, were responsible for the deaths, and for any reparations. Mormon-Navajo relations returned to their previous status quo. This allowed Brigham Young to once again attempt to colonize the Little Colorado in Arizona.

Thus, Jacob was a different kind of hero. It will be worthwhile to look again at the tradition of Hamblin as antihero—coward, serial liar, even one of the architects of the Mountains Meadows Massacre. As Peterson writes, some thought Hamblin was "reckless with the truth, a tireless self-promoter, or a coward."[8] In my research for this book, I have found little support for these melodramatic accusations. To take the charge of cowardice, for example, his missions to Navajo territory in 1870 and 1874 entailed enormous risk.[9] And the result of his dogged negotiations, despite some missteps, was the defusing of the conflict. Simply to travel in the Southwest in the nineteenth century, alone or with a small group of men, was dangerous. If Jacob had been cowardly, he would have stayed in large population centers in Utah.

One of the best defenses of Jacob Hamblin comes from non-Mormon Frederick Dellenbaugh, of the second Powell expedition. When historian Charles Kelly apparently accused Dellenbaugh of having a sentimental view of Jacob, Dellenbaugh pushed back gently:

> Yes, perhaps I have a "soft spot" in my heart for "Old Jacob" as I only think of him as I knew him. He was all right so far as anything occurred while I was in that region. So it is not exactly tolerance on my part in having a somewhat tender regard for him but experience with him and his family over a considerable period.[10]

In other words, Dellenbaugh tells Kelly, I knew him, and for a long time. Dellenbaugh wrote Raymond T. Stites in 1926,

> I think I told you that I knew Jacob very well, also his brothers Fred and Lyman; and his son Joe. The latter was wonderfully expert as a youngster in throwing the lasso. He could catch any animal by any portion of it he chose. The Hamblins were all sterling, reliable men. They were with our outfit a great deal in the 70's and gave us good work.[11]

Nevertheless, Hamblin was human and made mistakes on occasion. He arguably made missteps in his negotiating trips to Arizona in 1874, antagonizing headmen Ketchene and Peokon at one time (and in addition his close ally, Indian missionary Ammon Tenney). He helped church leaders in Salt Lake City and in southern Utah cover up Mormon participation in the Mountain Meadows Massacre, and he gave testimony on the massacre to Jacob Forney in 1858 and army investigator James Carleton in 1859 that was less than the full truth, portraying the event as an Indian massacre with no Mormon involvement.[12] In doing this, he acted as a typical member of his community, and was following Brigham Young's lead, but it was still an ethical misstep, just as the cover-up of the Mountain Meadows Massacre was a collective moral lapse for the Mormon community.[13]

In the second John D. Lee trial, he gave testimony that Lee vehemently characterized as false. However, Lee himself was never forthright about his role in the massacre, at times denying that he participated in the killing at all. (Once again, we are faced with the Lee vs. Hamblin ongoing feud, as well as the conflict in testimony; and it is a mistake to take Lee's side as entirely true and Jacob's as entirely false, or vice versa.) In that same trial, Jacob testified that he had very early given Brigham Young and George A. Smith a full account of Mormon involvement in the massacre, which is a remarkable admission.

Jacob made enemies during his time as a leader in southern Utah—George Hendrix and John D. Lee are two significant examples. They both wrote vitriolic letters to Brigham Young attacking Jacob. Because their partisan enmity is so palpable, one cannot take their accusations at face value, but must in fairness try to understand Jacob's side of the story. Nevertheless, these letters show that he offended and antagonized some fellow Mormons.

The most convincing revisionary view of Jacob comes from historian Charles Peterson, who has argued that Jacob and his fellow missionaries did not really achieve success, if you account success by authentic, full Indian conversions to Mormonism.[14] Jacob and other missionaries generally could not bridge the vast cultural chasm between white and Indian in such a way that would cause Indians to convert to Mormonism as Mormons had hoped. Many Indians were baptized Mormons, but had little understanding of what baptism meant in Latter-day Saint culture. Mormon missionaries were continually puzzled and frustrated by the Indians' non-Western, non-European point of view.

Jacob, for all his sympathy for Paiutes and his knowledge of them, became disillusioned with them, instead turning to the Hopis in 1858 with great hopes for their conversion. But despite the conversion of a few important Hopis, such as Tuuvi, Talasnimki, and Tom Polacca, there was no mass conversion of the Hopis to Mormonism, and Mormons eventually were discouraged by the Hopi response to the Latter-day Saint missionary message.[15] Even Tuuvi seems to have turned against Mormons in 1879 and 1885.[16]

Most seriously of all, however, Jacob acted as Brigham Young's agent in the colonization of southern Utah and Arizona. This was both a triumph and a paradoxical failure.

To treat the triumph first: an important part of Hamblin's work for Young was exploring, as Young often sent him to traverse unknown territory. His work as explorer is one of his undoubted, and underrecognized, achievements. More than a decade before Powell boated down the Colorado, Jacob had begun exploring the territory around the Grand Canyon. In 1858 he became the first white since Domínguez and Escalante in 1776 and Armijo in 1829 to cross the upper Colorado at the Crossing of the Fathers. He was the first to cross the Colorado at Lee's Ferry by boat, in 1860 and 1864. He thus opened up travel between Utah and Arizona, creating the Utah-Arizona road that thousands would use in later years, and parts of which are still in use today.

John Wesley Powell has been called a pathfinder, but Hamblin often guided Powell and his men in their geographic and anthropological exploration and fieldwork. He also apparently served as guide and interpreter for Powell's protégé, geologist Clarence E. Dutton.

Before Powell's 1869 tour de force of exploration, as he boated through the

Grand Canyon, Hamblin accomplished the following enormously difficult and dangerous expeditions:

In March 1858, he traveled to the Lower Colorado.

In October to December 1858, he crossed the Colorado at the Crossing of the Fathers and visited the Hopi mesas. This party returned in two separate companies, and both of them, facing starvation at Pipe Spring, were forced to kill and eat a horse to survive. Hamblin immediately saw that a crossing at the mouth of the Paria (later known as Lee's Ferry) would cut eight or nine days off the journey to the mesas, and in subsequent visits sought ways in which he could cross there.

In October to December 1859, he crossed the Colorado at the Crossing of the Fathers and visited the Hopi mesas again.

In October to November 1860, he crossed the Colorado again, at the Crossing of the Fathers; during this trip his group encountered hostile Navajos, and one of Hamblin's companions was killed. The expedition was forced to give up much of their baggage and retreat back to Utah.

In February to March 1861, Hamblin crossed the Colorado again at the Crossing of the Fathers, to gather the bones of the young man who had been slain the previous November. Once again he and his companions had to travel in hostile Navajo territory.

In November 1862 to January 1863, Hamblin circled the Grand Canyon, crossing the Colorado south of St. George, at the Grand Wash, and returning via the Crossing of the Fathers. Once again, Jacob and his companions often faced dehydration, starvation, and cold while traveling through new territory, deserts, and mountains, without knowledge of the exact whereabouts of rivers, streams, and springs.

In March to May 1863, he crossed the Colorado at the Grand Wash again, turned east, and made one of the early descents, by whites, into the depths of Havasu Canyon (not a task for the faint of heart). After visiting the Hopi mesas, he returned via northern Arizona and the Grand Wash.

In March to May 1864, Jacob and his party successfully crossed the Colorado at Lee's Ferry—a historic moment, as this became the main route across the upper Colorado for decades to come. After a visit to the Hopis, he returned the same way. The Crossing of the Fathers was rarely used by whites again.

In June and July 1864, Jacob probably explored the Colorado near the Virgin River confluence.

In November to December 1864, he visited the Lower Colorado, helping to found Callville, near Black Canyon, then traveled south on the Colorado.

In January to February 1865, Jacob rafted down the Virgin.

In December 1865, he visited the Chemehuevis and Mohaves on the Lower Colorado.

In April 1867, he rode a skiff on the Colorado from the Grand Wash to Callville. Thus he and his companions were arguably the first whites to boat on a portion of the upper Colorado. Powell was given a copy of the diary for this journey, and relied on it while making his 1869 voyage.

While Jacob and John Wesley Powell accomplished different things, and had different talents—they were polar opposites in some ways, and much alike in others—both were important for the exploration of the Grand Canyon country.

One of the reasons Hamblin was able to accomplish these early, enormously difficult journeys across the Colorado was his good relations with Indians, especially Paiutes. They served as guides, told him of water sources, on occasion fed him and his men when they were on the brink of starvation. Thus his Indian mission dovetailed with his exploring mission. We should also emphasize that he had important companions on all these journeys—southern Utah pioneers such as Ira Hatch, Thales Haskell, Samuel Knight, Ammon Tenney, and Dudley Leavitt were his irreplaceable supports on these forays into unknown, unmapped, and often inhospitable places.

Despite this extraordinary accomplishment in opening up the Southwest, it was a success that was fraught with ambiguity, for a man who tried to be a friend to the Indians. The bond between Hamblin and Brigham Young created the great paradox of Hamblin's life. He explored and helped open up new territory for Mormon settlement; but as Mormon towns expanded, fields were claimed for farming, and ranges were used for ranching, Indians were displaced, and the ecosystems they relied on were disrupted. Mormons became powerful competitors for water resources in hot, dry southern Utah and north-central Arizona—one of the best possible geographical examples of the essential aridity of much of the American West.

This was actually a complex process, though the final outcomes were generally the same.

In early stages, Mormons often settled Indian territory at the invitation of the Indians. In 1854, Paiutes welcomed the Mormons as allies against the more powerful "horse-Indians," the Utes, who preyed on their children and women to sell as slaves to Navajos and New Mexicans. In addition, the Santa Clara Paiutes, already experienced riverine farmers, welcomed Mormons with their more sophisticated agricultural tools and irrigation expertise. They also hoped to work for the Mormons and obtain more regular food, and European clothes, as the Cedar City Paiutes had.[17]

Later, in 1869, the Kaibab Paiutes also reportedly requested that Jacob come live with them and direct them in their farming.[18] Even later, Hopis invited Mormons to Moenkopi as a protection against Navajo raids.[19] And when Mormons first settled on the Little Colorado, the Navajos welcomed them as a buffer against the Apaches, with whom they had recently had a bloody battle.

In southern Utah, this process generally started when a few Mormon Indian missionaries moved into Indian territory, and settled near Indian communities, necessarily near water. However, the Mormons built permanent homes and introduced the European tradition of permanent residency when they did so. Often they built forts in these early towns. There was some competition for water and food resources in these early stages of Mormon settlements, but there were not enough whites to make the competition a serious problem.

More and more Mormons trickled into Dixie, but for years Paiutes were still the great majority. However, Brigham eventually "called" settlers on missions to these towns, and then the balance of population gradually shifted to the whites. For example, the two towns that Jacob lived in in southern Utah, Santa Clara and Kanab, started as places where Jacob was helping Paiutes farm.[20] In 1861 and 1862, Brigham Young sent ninety Swiss to Santa Clara and five hundred families (possibly between two thousand and twenty-five hundred people) to St. George and other towns in Dixie; suddenly the Paiutes were a minority, and an impoverished minority with much less political cohesiveness than the Mormons. (The Mormon cohesiveness even exceeded white non-Mormon political unity in the West.) The competition between the *Mormons* in St. George and Santa Clara for the water of the Santa Clara became an ongoing problem; suddenly the Paiutes were not even part of the equation.

In the case of Kanab, in parallel fashion, Brigham called a group of Mormons under Levi Stewart to settle the town in 1870, and suddenly the Kaibab Paiutes who had worked for Jacob had to compete with the new settlers for water and usable farmland in a town in which good farmland was very limited.

In both towns, devastating floods periodically made circumstances worse for both Paiutes and Mormons.

In the case of Moenkopi–Tuba City, the Mormons and Hopis also began to experience severe conflicts over water rights.[21] In 1888, H. S. Welton, an Indian agent, visited Moenkopi, and in a report, stated that there were only sixteen Hopis living at Moenkopi. "Several others formerly came from the Oraibi Pueblo (40 miles east) and planted here in summer. But since the Mormons have taken nearly all the land and Water, they come no more.... While the Indians are still permitted to retain a small piece of land they are deprived of water sufficient to irrigate it. Hence I found the men at work for one Smith who had taken their land from them."[22]

While Welton may have had a bias against Mormons, nevertheless there was undoubtedly some truth in his description. For example, in 1885 the Mormons attempted to have the Hopis removed from Moenkopi![23]

In Santa Clara and Kanab, where before the Indians had to deal with a limited number of Indian missionaries who often spoke their language, now they were facing political leaders and communities whose motivation was primarily economic, and who had no mission to communicate directly with the local Indians. These new leaders often worked with Jacob and his fellow missionaries, but regarded them as Indian specialists, who would help smooth out relations with Indians for the primary good of the new community. The Indians experienced a sudden drop in importance, as did Jacob and his fellow Indian missionaries.

In addition, many of these new settlers were stockmen, bringing herds of cattle, sheep, and horses that often grazed and overgrazed in fields that had formerly supplied seed to the Paiutes. These seeds, ground and prepared in various ways, had been a staple for the Indians at certain times of the year.

Finally, Paiutes often fell victim to the diseases that the whites and their animals brought that the whites had become generally immune to over the centuries. As we have seen, these epidemics had a devastating impact on the population of the Paiutes on the Santa Clara and at Kanab.[24] As a result, the former settlement centers of the Paiutes inevitably declined, while Mormon settlements often arose to replace them.[25]

Jacob was conscious of these issues, and so certainly felt conflicted. He explored for Brigham, sending back reports of good settlement territory in southern Utah and Arizona. He helped found Mormon towns. Though he was generally a settler before Brigham had "called" a much larger group to create a sizable settlement, he still had begun the process that set up bitter struggles for resources between whites and local Indians, struggles that the Indians soon lost.

As a result, especially after the major influx of Mormon settlers into Dixie in 1861, Jacob saw Paiutes increasingly indigent and desperate. Three times he wrote about their plight, once in a letter to Brigham Young, later in a letter to John Wesley Powell, and in the Little autobiography.[26] The seeds the Paiutes had depended on for food were increasingly lost to cattle and sheep. Whites had established large permanent settlements near limited water resources. Some Paiutes actually starved, and many died of white diseases. Witnessing this process, Jacob was not surprised that some Paiutes stole food. While the Santa Clara area had previously been a major gathering point for the southern Paiute, some twenty years after Jacob and his friends had settled Santa Clara, the Santa Clara Paiutes were approaching extinction.

Jacob also understood the perplexities of the whites who could not understand Indians. "The white man wants to bring the Indian to his standard of civilization, they are both driven to desperation, all for the want of a little understanding," he wrote.[27]

Though Jacob was generally profoundly loyal to Brigham Young, he wrote at least one letter to George A. Smith and Young, protesting how the St. George Saints—St. George was central to Young's cotton mission—were taking water from the Santa Clara Paiutes and Mormons. Smith, who gave the letter to Young, apparently found Jacob's accusations offensive, and felt that Young would also.[28]

Given Hamblin's role as explorer and colonizer, and his understanding of the impact of Mormon colonies on Paiutes, he must have felt conflicted. This is the central paradox of Jacob Hamblin's life, the paradox of an Indian missionary.

Nevertheless, one could argue that white expansion into the West was inevitable and, in the case of Utah, Mormon expansion throughout that state and into neighboring states (and into neighboring countries, Canada and Mexico, for that matter). As historian Leonard Arrington points out, there was a constant influx of Mormon immigrants to Utah; outlying Mormon colonies were a necessary means of placing these new arrivals.[29] Given this fact, all that an Indian missionary could do would be to help both Indians and white settlers adjust to the process in a humane and nonviolent way.

Here, Peterson argues, was the real, inarguable, practical success of the southern Utah Indian mission, led by Jacob. It smoothed the way for settlers in southern Utah and Arizona, minimizing conflicts and violent deaths, and arguably preventing massacres of Indians. When conflicts did occur, as in the Black Hawk War and the related Navajo War of southern Utah, Jacob acted as a counterweight to the Mormons who sought for quick, harsh, military solutions to the problems.[30]

After 1861, Jacob surprisingly stated that Indians' hunger sometimes justified them in their thievery.[31] This sympathy is a far cry from the attitude of whites who felt that any theft on the part of Indians was a capital offense, and would immediately send out a military expedition to kill multiple Indians in retaliation.[32]

In contrast, as we have seen, in Tooele, when Jacob was sent out to kill Indians, he surprised a Goshute camp with two families. Despite some errant shots, no one was killed and the screams of the children caused Jacob to have his men stop shooting. Instead of solving the problem with the rifle, Jacob wrote, "We brought them home with us gave them p[r]ovisions blankets and treated them k[i]ndley."

Distinguished territorial historian Howard Lamar, after a summary of Jacob's Indian diplomacy in Tooele, southern Utah, and Arizona among the Hopis and Navajos, writes, "For their quiet and patient labors, Hamblin and his colleagues deserve comparison with Fathers Kino and Serra in their successful relations with the Indians of the Southwest."[33] Despite his cultural limitations and occasional human failings, Jacob Hamblin's antimilitarism, his attempt to solve conflicts through diplomacy, and his view of Indians as fully human, are his final, best legacy.

APPENDIX A

Jacob Hamblin's Families

My sources are generally Miller, *Jacob Vernon Hamblin Family* and Andrews, *The Hamlin Family*, with some modifications from my own research.

Lucinda Taylor. Born on August 24, 1823, in Chardon, Geauga, Ohio. Married Jacob on October 3, 1839, in (modern) Lafayette, Walworth, Wisconsin. Divorced in February 1849. Death date unknown, but after summer 1850.

1. **Duane.** Born on February 11, 1841, in Lafayette, Wisconsin. Married Elizabeth Russell in about 1860 (one child). Died on December 17, 1862, near Santa Clara, Washington, Utah.
2. **Martha Adaline (Crosby).** Born on September 15, 1843, in Lafayette, Wisconsin. Married Taylor Crosby in 1860 (seven children). Died on June 17, 1877, in Kanab, Kane, Utah.
3. **Maryette Magdaline (Young Maxwell Lockwood).** Born on May 17, 1845, in Nauvoo, Illinois. Married John William Young in 1860 (three children, divorce); William B. Maxwell in 1867 (ten children, divorce); and Timothy Lockwood in 1886 (two children). Died on March 1, 1910, in Alma, Catron, New Mexico.
4. **Lyman Stoddard.** Born on March 13, 1848, in Bloomfield, Davis, Iowa. Married Esther Cecilia Burk in 1871 (ten children). Died on September 23, 1922, in Eagar, Apache, Arizona.

Rachel Judd (Page Henderson Hamblin). Born on September 15, 1821, in Jamestown, Greene, Ohio. Married Jacob on September 30, 1849, in Council Bluffs, Iowa. She had previously married John E. Page (divorce) and James Henderson (who died). At the time of marriage to Jacob, she had three Henderson stepchildren, **William Henderson**, **John Henderson**, and **Eunice Henderson**; they lived with Jacob and Rachel until Tooele, then transferred to Henderson relatives. Rachel died on February 18, 1865, in Santa Clara, Utah.

1. **Lois (Burk).** Born on June 15, 1851, in Tooele, Utah. Married Hubert Rosell Burk in 1868 (ten children). Died on August 30, 1891, in Alpine, Arizona.

2. **Joseph.** Born on October 6, 1854, in Tooele, Utah. Married Elsie Albertina Johnson in 1879 (three children). Died on December 3, 1924, in Kanab, Utah.
3. **Rachel Tamar (Stewart).** Born on August 3, 1856, in Santa Clara, Utah. Married William Thomas in 1873 (two children). Died on March 17, 1877, in Kanab, Utah.
4. **Benjamin.** Born on September 29, 1858, in Pine Valley, Utah. Married Della Jane Brown in 1891 (seven children, one adopted). Died on September 27, 1930, in Kanab, Utah.
5. **Araminda.** Born on January 27, 1861(?), and died in 1862, both in Santa Clara, Utah.

Sarah Priscilla Leavitt (Hamblin). Born on May 8, 1841, in Nauvoo, Illinois. Married Jacob on September 11, 1857, in Salt Lake City. Died on July 23, 1927, in Alpine, Arizona.

1. **Sarah Olive (Winsor).** Born on October 15, 1858, in Santa Clara, Utah. Married Abraham Lee Winsor in 1876 (eight children). Died on June 30, 1919, in Safford (or Thatcher), Graham, Arizona.
2. **Melissa (Chesley).** Born on April 25, 1861, in Santa Clara, Utah. Married James Edgar Chesley in 1883 (ten children). Died on May 9, 1933, in Mesa, Arizona.
3. **Lucy.** Born on May 11, 1863, in Santa Clara, Utah. Died on December 28, 1871, in Kanab(?), Utah.
4. **Jacob Jr.** Born on March 21, 1865, in Santa Clara, Utah. Married Sadie Cornelia Lytle in 1885 (fourteen children). Died on April 1, 1939, in Mesa, Arizona.
5. **Ella Ann (Tenney).** Born on June 11, 1867, in Santa Clara, Utah. Married Warren Moroni Tenney in 1884 (thirteen children). Died on March 31, 1947, in Alpine, Arizona.
6. **Mary Elizabeth (Beeler).** Born on September 25, 1872, in Kanab, Utah. Married Edward Beeler in 1896. Died on May 12, 1959, in Mesa, Arizona.
7. **Clara Melvina (Nicoll Staley).** Born on November 5, 1876, in Kanab, Utah. Married Peter Arza Nicoll in 1898 (thirteen children, divorce), then Winthrop S. Staley in 1930. Died on June 27, 1959, in Lakeside, San Diego, California.
8. **Dudley Jabez.** Born on May 5, 1880, in Springerville, Arizona. Married Julia Mae Butler in 1906 (eleven children). Died on July 29, 1968, in Phoenix, Arizona.
9. **Don Carlos.** Born on February 16, 1882, in Springerville, Arizona. Married Ida Lee in 1907 (thirteen children). Died on November 15, 1941, in Phoenix, Arizona.

Eliza (Hamblin). Eliza, a Shivwits Paiute, married Jacob sometime before October or November 1860, according to some sources. She had previously lived in the Hamblin household as an adopted child. On February 14, 1863, at the Endowment House, Jacob was sealed to Eliza for eternity. Eliza's birthdate has been given in genealogical records as 1846, but that date is an estimate. She subsequently left Hamblin and married a Shivwits Indian named Poinkum/Polunkin, or Sussic. I have found no death date for her.

Louisa Bonelli (Hamblin). Born on October 29, 1843, in Weingarten, Canton Thurgau, Switzerland. Married Jacob on November 16, 1865, in Salt Lake City. Died on December 13, 1930, in Thatcher, Graham, Arizona.

1. **Walter Eugene.** Born on April 15, 1868, in Santa Clara, Utah. Married Sara Blanche Robinson in 1897 (six children). Died on January 27, 1950, in Johnson Ranch, Kane, Utah.
2. **Inez Louisa (Lee).** Born on April 4, 1871, in Kanab, Utah. Married John David Lee in 1888 (ten children). Died on March 4, 1933, in Thatcher, Arizona.
3. **George Oscar.** Born on March 25, 1873, in Kanab, Utah. Married Sarah Ida (Doll) Coleman in 1897 (seven children). Died on September 1, 1946, in Mesa, Arizona.
4. **Alice Edna (Brown).** Born on March 3, 1876, in Kanab, Utah. Married Jared Taylor Brown in 1896 (five children). Died on March 1, 1902, in Thatcher, Arizona.
5. **Willard Otto.** Born on March 25, 1881, in Kanab, Utah. Married Lillian Lee in 1901 (eleven children). Died on September 16, 1967, in Eagar, Arizona.
6. **Amarilla (Lee).** Born on May 4, 1884, in Pleasanton, Catron, New Mexico. Married Franklin Lee in 1908 (seven children). Died on March 14, 1982, in Martinez, Solano, California.

Two Paiutes, names unknown. Married to Hamblin during his Kanab period (roughly, 1867–1877), according to Frederick Dellenbaugh, of the second Powell expedition. These marriages have not been confirmed by any other source.[1]

Adopted children:

1. **Albert.** From the White Knife band of Shoshonis, who lived west of Tooele. Hamblin adopted him in February 1853, when he was about ten years old; he died in spring 1863.
2. An **unnamed male child.** Born in approximately 1847.[2]
3. **Susan.**[3]
4. **Ellen.** Died of apparent blood poisoning after stepping on a sharp stick.[4] She was adopted in 1857 or 1858.[5]

5. **Eliza (Hamblin).** Became Jacob's wife, see above.
6. **Fanny (Adair).** Reportedly married Aaron Adair.[6] I have not been able to verify this marriage.
7. **Lucinda (Hatch).** Reportedly married Ira Hatch.[7] I have not been able to verify this marriage.

APPENDIX B

Jacob Hamblin's Trips to and across the Colorado

1858, March 6 to sometime after March 18: Trip to the lower Colorado. Thales Haskell meets Joseph Christmas Ives at Cottonwood Valley.

1858, Oct. 28 to Dec. 4: First trip across the Colorado to the Hopi Mesas, via Crossing of the Fathers. Andrew Gibbons, William Hamblin, Tom Leavitt, and Ben Knell stay longer, arriving back on December 27.

1859, Oct. 4 to Dec. 1: Second trip across the Colorado to the Hopi mesas. Thales Haskell and Marion Shelton stay longer, arriving back on March 27, 1860.

1860, Oct. 10 to Nov. 9: Third trip across the Colorado. George Smith Jr. killed at Quichintoweep. First actual crossing of the Colorado at the mouth of the Paria by raft, but as it is impossible to cross the animals, the company is forced to return to the Crossing of the Fathers.

1861, Feb. 26 to [March 21]: Fourth trip across the Colorado via the Crossing of the Fathers, to gather the bones of George Smith Jr.

1862, Nov. 17, to Jan. 11, 1863: Fifth trip across the Colorado. First encircling of the Grand Canyon, using the Grand Wash, southwest of St. George (the first crossing by boat, swimming horses, on the upper Colorado), on the way out and the Crossing of the Fathers on the way back. The company visits the Hopi mesas, leaves three missionaries, and brings back three Hopis.

1863, March 18 to May 13: Sixth trip across the Colorado to the Hopi mesas, bringing the three Hopis back. Via the Grand Wash crossing both ways; including a visit to the Havasupai Indians at the bottom of Cataract Canyon.

1864, March 10 to April [9?]: Seventh trip across the Colorado, of historical importance as the first successful crossing at Lee's Ferry. After this, Crossing of the Fathers was rarely used. Visit to the Hopi mesas.

1864, June[July?]: Trip to lower Colorado from St. George to the head of navigation on Colorado.

1864, Nov. 25 to Dec. 24: Trip to lower Colorado. The party founded Callville, then traveled farther south on the Colorado.

1865, Jan. 17 to Feb. 8 or earlier: Boat trip down the Virgin River.

1865, [early December] to Dec. 18: Trip to the lower Colorado. Traveled to Las Vegas, the Muddy settlements, and the Chemehuevis and Mohaves on the lower Colorado.

1867, Apr. 10 to [19?]: Boat trip on the Colorado, Grand Wash to Callville; of historic importance as the first well-recorded boating trip on the Colorado. The diary from this expedition was used by John Wesley Powell.

1868 and later: Many trips to the Crossing of the Fathers and Lee's Ferry. Hamblin visited the Crossing of the Fathers and Lee's Ferry multiple times.

1869, Sept. 28 to Oct. [27?]: Eighth trip across the Colorado. Visit to Hopi mesas to check with Hopis on the movements of hostile Navajos.

1870, Sept. 14 to [23]: To the Colorado south of Mount Trumbull with John Wesley Powell to find a drop-off point for supplies. Parley with local Paiutes and Shivwits Paiutes near Mount Trumbull.

1870, Oct. 1 to Nov. [21]: Ninth trip across the Colorado to Hopi mesas and Fort Defiance, with John Wesley Powell. Treaty with the Navajos at Fort Defiance and Hano on the First Mesa.

1871, June 12 to 26: To San Rafael River or the Escalante River. Did not reach Colorado. Jacob was working for Powell, searching for the Dirty Devil River.

1871, Aug. 15 to [27]: To Escalante River. Did not reach Colorado. Jacob was working for John Wesley Powell, searching for the Dirty Devil River.

1871, Sept. 15 to Oct. [29]: Tenth trip across the Colorado to Hopi mesas and Fort Defiance. Used Crossing of the Fathers on the way out (to deliver supplies to Powell's Second Expedition) and Lee's Ferry on the return.

1872, [Aug. 27] to [Sept. 11]: Eleventh trip across Colorado. Jacob travels to Moenkopi, then visits the Hualapais to persuade them not to become allied with the hostile Shivwits.

1872, Oct. 9 to Nov. 11: Twelfth trip across Colorado to the Hopi Mesas with some of the Powell men, for photography, trade.

1873, Jan. 22 to March [8]: To Arizona with the Lorenzo Roundy company. "Arizona Exploring Company," in preparation for settlement on the Little Colorado.

1873, Apr. 13 to July 4: To Arizona with Horton Haight company. First attempted settlement on the Little Colorado; Hamblin to Hopi mesas, Little Colorado, Moenave.

1874, mid. Jan. to Feb. 12: To Arizona for negotiations with the Navajos in response to the killings of four Navajos in Grass Valley, Utah.

1874, Feb. 17 to March 17: To Arizona for follow-up visit. Visits Moenave and the Hopi Mesas.

1874, Apr. 24 to May [9?]: To Arizona, with John R. Young company. Mormons in Arizona are recalled. Hamblin visits Moenave, Moenkopi, and the Hopi mesas.

1874, [mid-July to late August]: To Fort Defiance with Navajo Hastele, John Lorenzo Hubbell, Ammon Tenney.

1874, late, to early 1875 (winter): Jacob at Lee's Ferry—ferrying, trading with Navajos.

1875, Oct. 20 to [early November?]: With Dan Jones expedition to Arizona and Mexico.

Jacob crosses the Colorado with the Jones company, then, on Oct. 28, turns back at Bitter Springs.

1875, [Feb.] to March 19, 1876: Mission to Arizona Indians, Navajos, Hopis, Pimas, Hualapais, and Apaches, to prepare the way for Mormon settlements on the Little Colorado.

1876, May 21 to June 17: Visit to Little Colorado settlements with First Presidency Daniel H. Wells, two apostles, and other high church leaders. Bishop Lorenzo Roundy drowns at Lee's Ferry; Jacob almost drowns.

1876, Dec. 13, to Feb. 10, 1877: Exploration of the "western route," crossing at Pearce's Ferry. The expedition was trying to establish a road from Pearce's Ferry to the Little Colorado settlements.

1877, [early April?] to [before April 8]: To Surprise Valley (modern Deer Creek Valley), near the Colorado. No crossing.

1877, [late August] to September: To the Hopi mesas in search of escaped convict Wallace Wilkerson.

1877, [Dec. 30], to [Feb. 8], 1878: Second circling of the Grand Canyon. Pearce's Ferry on the way out, Lee's Ferry on the return. Jacob and John Willard Young explore northern Arizona, visit the Little Colorado settlements.

Undated: Long trip with Anthony Ivins and Ashton Nebeker. Spilsbury, Autobiography.

After this, Jacob takes up residence in the Little Colorado settlements; there are many trips back and forth between Utah and Arizona. Jacob brought Priscilla and her children to Arizona in 1879, but Louisa stayed in Kanab until early spring 1883, when he had moved to Pleasanton, New Mexico.

Notes

INTRODUCTION

1. LJH, 28; Hamblin, "Autobiography."
2. LJH, 28.
3. This book began when Brooks tried to get film companies interested in a script for a feature film about Jacob Hamblin. Peterson, *Juanita Brooks*, 221–22. As Peterson writes, it is an "uncertain" mixture of history and fiction, slanted toward juvenile readers.
4. For a typical critique of Bailey, William Culp Darrah, a biographer of John Wesley Powell, wrote, "It is to be noted that this latter narrative [Bailey's biography], developed as it is by fictitious conversation, gives a decidedly inaccurate portrait of Major Powell." Darrah, "Major Powell Prepares," 153n11. Jacob's daughter, Amarilla Lee, wrote that Bailey "made up" lots of this book: "He wrote it as that [fiction]." Reilly, interview with Amarilla Hamblin Lee, June 26, 1970.
5. This musical is a mixture of truth and error, historically; Samuelsen, Review of *Utah!*
6. Dellenbaugh, *Romance of the Colorado*, 93.
7. McClintock, *Mormon Settlement in Arizona*, 59; Birney, *Zealots of Zion*, 111–32; Stegner, *Mormon Country*, 145.
8. For the importance of Cooper and his hero in the ideology of nineteenth-century America, see Slotkin, *Regeneration through Violence*, 466–516, and *The Fatal Environment*, 81–106; Smith, *Virgin Land*, 60–70.
9. See White, *"It's Your Misfortune,"* 613–32, on the West's folklore and how men like Buffalo Bill and Kit Carson were turned into legends. Also, Smith, *Virgin Land*, and Slotkin's trilogy, *Regeneration Through Violence*; *Gunfighter Nation; The Fatal Environment*, 51–80. Slotkin shows that one of the key myths of European Americans was western expansion viewed as "civilized" whites subjugating savage Indians. The Indian is dehumanized, becoming merely "a bear in the path, a stone in the field" to colonists, p. 53.
10. Bagley, *Blood of the Prophets*, 305.
11. Peterson, "Jacob Hamblin, Apostle to the Lamanites."
12. Brooks, *On the Ragged Edge*, vii.
13. See chapter 27 (1874), this volume.
14. See Creer, *The Activities of Jacob Hamblin*. While Hamblin's legacy as Indian missionary has been reassessed with a revisionist lens, I believe his accomplishments as explorer have yet to be fully appreciated. For many historians of the West, Jacob Hamblin, as explorer, is just a footnote to the story of John Wesley Powell. For some historians, it is not even a footnote. For example, in map 23, "Routes of American Explorers and Surveyors," of Walker and Bufkin's *Historical Atlas of Arizona*, the route of "Powell 1869" is given, but Jacob Hamblin's epic 1858 journey into northern Arizona is ignored. White, *"It's Your Misfortune,"* 133–34, also highlights "official" explorers.
15. See ch. 29 (1876–1877) of this volume.
16. For the Three Nephites, see chapters 9 (late 1858) and 19 (1866–1868) this volume.
17. I accept that the supernatural exists and impacts our existence. However, I have a complex, ethical, rather than absolutist, view of religion. I would describe myself as a liberal Mormon, which is, of course, a contradiction in terms.
18. My technique follows Richard Bushman in his *Joseph Smith and the Beginnings of Mormonism*, 3, who wrote that he would describe visionary experiences by early Mormons as Mormons experienced them and wrote about them. While non-Mormons would question these experiences, "at least they will have an understanding about how early Mormons perceived the world."
19. For celebratory and revisionist history in southern Utah, see Alder, "Writing Southern Utah History."
20. For Brigham Young as colonizer, see Hunter, *Brigham Young, the Colonizer* (which has a thoroughly Mormon-centered point of view); Campbell, *Establishing Zion* (a more nuanced, scholarly account); and Arrington, *Great Basin Kingdom*, 88–95, 215–22.

21. Dellenbaugh, *A Canyon Voyage*, 167; Udall, *Forgotten Founders*.
22. See Stegner, *Mormon Country* and *The Gathering of Zion*. Stegner also saw problematic sides to Mormonism, but this did not detract from his admiration for many aspects of the culture and history of the Mormon people. Stegner and Etulain, *Conversations with Wallace Stegner*, 101–22. For Mormon cooperation making the difficult Little Colorado mission possible, see also Abruzzi, *Dam That River!*
23. See chapter 4 (1850–1853), this volume.
24. Limerick, *Legacy of Conquest*, 221. While there is a Mormon historiographical tendency to see LDS forefathers as heroic while Indians are mere dangers, this was also a characteristic of a former generation of Western historians. For example, we can point to Frederick Jackson Turner's view of Americans being shaped positively by the West, with Indians relegated to being merely an obstacle for the immigrating Europeans. Lewis, "Still Native," 213; Utley, *The Indian Frontier*, 257–60, 272.
25. Utley, *The Indian Frontier*, 11.

CHAPTER 1

1. It is widely accepted that Jacob's middle name was "Vernon"; however, there is no documentation for this during his lifetime.
2. Hamblin, Autobiography, Jacob Hamblin collection, MS 1951, folder 2, CHL. For the frontier and the West in American history, see Billington and Ridge, *Westward Expansion*; White, *"It's Your Misfortune and None of My Own"*; Limerick, *Legacy of Conquest*; Hine and Faragher, *The American West*; Udall, *The Forgotten Founders*.
3. For Isaiah, see "History of Isaiah Hamblin"; Andrews, *The Hamlin Family*, 288–89; Esshom, *Pioneers*, 910–11; Miller, *Jacob Vernon Hamblin Family*, 40–43. Unless otherwise noted, genealogical information for Jacob and his families is from Andrews, Miller, or Corbett, *Jacob Hamblin*.
4. Andrews, *The Hamlin Family*, 289.
5. See "Daphne Haynes Hamblin."
6. North Hero, VT Deeds (FHL film #0028559), Vol. 3, pp. 1809–1820.
7. Hamblin writes, "My father and two of his brothers emigrated to ohio. They left their famileys in the town of Salam untill they could explore the Contry." Autobiography, 1–2; "History of Isaiah Hamblin."
8. Autobiography, 1–2. *Pioneer and General History of Geauga County*, 258, dates this at "very early in 1819." 1820 U.S. Census, Claridon, Geauga County, Ohio, p. 99.
9. His nickname, "Gunlock," reflects his skill in repairing firearms, and the small town of Gunlock, in Washington County, Utah, was named after him by apostle George A. Smith. Bleak, "Annals," at Aug. 4, 1857, p. 45. See also Jeremiah Leavitt, Autobiography; Joseph Hamblin, "History of Joseph Hamblin"; "William Haynes Hamblin"; Reeve, *Making Space*, 22–29; chapter 16 (1864), this volume.
10. He was reported to be a participant in the Mountain Meadows Massacre. Sexton's Record, Minersville Cemetery; Walker, Turley, and Leonard, *Massacre at Mountain Meadows*, 169–71, 258; Briggs, "Oscar Hamblin (1833–1862)."
11. "Biography of Edwin Hamblin"; Esshom, *Pioneers*, 238, 911; Samuel Miles, letter to editor, Sept. 1, 1880, in *Deseret News*, Sept. 15, 1880.
12. LJH, 9.
13. Corbett, *Jacob Hamblin*, 427, citing a Santa Clara neighbor, Isaiah Cox.
14. Autobiography, 2.
15. Ibid., 2–3.
16. Ibid., 3–4.
17. See Payne, *The Self and the Sacred*; Shea, *Spiritual Autobiography;* Caldwell, *The Puritan Conversion Narrative*.
18. Autobiography, 4.
19. Compton and Hatch, *A Widow's Tale*, 24–27.
20. Autobiography, 4–5.
21. Autobiography, 5.
22. Bressler, *Universalist Movement*.
23. Autobiography, 2.

24. Ibid., 6–7.
25. The Mormon word for Indians.
26. Autobiography, 7.
27. Ibid., 7. LJH, 9. For the lure of Wisconsin for westering Americans, see Wyman, *The Wisconsin Frontier*, 159
28. The county was divided into five towns on January 2, 1838, including Spring Prairie. On March 21, 1843, the "westernmost town was set off as Lafayette." Beckwith, *History of Walworth County*, 1:405, 349.
29. *History of Walworth County*, 316–17.
30. Ibid., 921–22. See also Beckwith, *History of Walworth County*, 1:49, 350.
31. Autobiography, 8; LJH, 10.
32. Autobiography, 8.
33. LJH, 10.
34. Autobiography, 8–9.
35. *History of Walworth County*, 925.
36. William Derby Johnson diary, July 31, 1881; "Oldest Kanab Resident Dies at the Age of 92," an obituary for Rhoda Lay Hamblin, *Kane County Standard*, Sept. 14, 1934, pp. 1, 4.
37. Jepson, "The True Story"; "Incidents in the Life of John Franklin Brown," 3–4.
38. Autobiography, 9.
39. For lead mining in the area, see "The Lead Mines"; Wright, *The Galena Lead District*; Wyman, *The Wisconsin Frontier*, 136–40; Tuttle, *An Illustrated History*, 129–30; Schafer, *The Wisconsin Lead Region*.
40. "Welcome to Scotland's Museum of Lead Mining."
41. LJH, 10.
42. Autobiography, 9–10.
43. Ibid., 10–11; Beckwith, *History of Walworth County*, 1:220; "Wisconsin Marriages, 1836–1930," FHL film no. 1275583.
44. Autobiography, 11.
45. Duane married Elizabeth Russell in about 1861 but died tragically later that year in Santa Clara, Utah. A son was born after his death.
46. U.S. General Land Office Records, Milwaukee Land Office, Certificate 2506.

CHAPTER 2

1. For an introduction to Smith, see Bushman, *Joseph Smith: Rough Stone Rolling*. For general introductions to Mormonism, Arrington and Bitton, *The Mormon Experience*; Quinn, *The Mormon Hierarchy: Origins of Power*; Bowman, *The Mormon People*.
2. For Christian primitivism, see Hughes, *The American Quest*. For Mormonism in this tradition, Hill, "The Shaping of the Mormon Mind," and Alexander, *Things in Heaven and Earth*, 16–17, 91, 341.
3. Smith, *History of the Church*, 4:429.
4. Ward, "1842 Census of Nauvoo," 44; Black, *Membership of the Church*, at "Stoddard, Lyman"; "Died," *Deseret News*, Dec. 28, 1854, p. 3.
5. LJH, 11.
6. Autobiography, 11–12.
7. LJH, 11.
8 Ibid., 12. Bushman, *Joseph Smith: Rough Stone Rolling*, 107; Compton, *In Sacred Loneliness*, 74.
9. Autobiography, 12. For conversion as an important theme in early American autobiography, see Payne, *The Self and the Sacred*; Shea, *Spiritual Autobiography*.
10. LJH, 12.
11. For early Mormons in Wisconsin, see Clark, "The Mormons of the Wisconsin Territory," 59–61, and Clark, "Moses Smith," 159–61.
12. LJH, 13.
13. Ibid.
14. Ibid.
15. Arrington and Bitton, *The Mormon Experience*, 20–43; Harper, "Infallible Proofs."

16. For Mormon apocalypticism, see Ericksen, *As a Thief in the Night*; Underwood, *The Millenarian World*; Hansen, *Quest for Empire*, 3–23; Flanders, "To Transform History." For Jacob Hamblin's apocalyptic mysticism, see Cox, "Biographical Sketch of Martha Cox," p. 103.
17. Sandeen, *The Roots of Fundamentalism*, 42. Brown, "Watchers for the Second Coming"; Cross, *The Burned-Over District*, 287–321; Lienesch, "The Role of Political Millennialism"; Hatch, *The Democratization of American Christianity*, 184–85, 188; Hansen, "The Millennium, the West."
18. See, for example, Popkin, "Rise and Fall of the Jewish Indian Theory"; Ben-Dor Benite, *The Ten Lost Tribes*, 141–42; Cogley, "'Some Other Kinde of Being'"; Huddleston, *Origins of the American Indians*, 33–47, 69–71, 84–88, 128–37; Parfitt, *The Lost Tribes of Israel*, 28–115; Wauchope, *Lost Tribes*, 50–57.
19. Autobiography, 12–13. However, according to LJH, 13, Lyman Stoddard performed the ordination in autumn 1842. Mormon men and young men hold priesthood, which they view as authority from God, and are ordained to priesthood offices by laying on of hands. There are two Mormon priesthoods (both of which are lay, not professional), the Melchizedek and Aaronic, and three grades in both of these. In the higher priesthood (Melchizedek) are elders, seventies (a missionary calling), and high priests (for older men, or men in leadership positions).
20. LJH, 14.
21. Autobiography, 13–15.
22. Ibid.
23. Ibid. For Aaron Smith, see Clark, "Moses Smith," 159–161.
24. Autobiography, 16.
25. She married Taylor Crosby in 1860 (seven children), and died on June 17, 1877, in Kanab, Utah.
26. Autobiography, 16–17: "some time in Sept 1843."
27. Ibid. On the other hand, see LJH, 14.
28. Autobiography, 16.
29. Flanders, *Nauvoo: Kingdom on the Mississippi*; Leonard, *Nauvoo: A Place of Peace.*
30. LJH, 16.
31. Ibid.
32. Ibid.
33. "Setting apart" is a Mormon ritual in which leaders lay hands on a person's head and bless him or her in a church calling or mission.
34. There is a similar prophecy in Bathsheba Smith, "Recollections of the Prophet Joseph Smith," 344. See also "Lost Ten Tribes." Cox, "Biographical Sketch of Martha Cox."
35. Bushman, *Joseph Smith: Rough Stone Rolling*, 514–17; Robertson, "The Campaign and the Kingdom."
36. Autobiography, 18.
37. "Special Conference," *Times & Seasons* 5.8 (April 15, 1844): 504.
38. Hamblin writes that he was "ordained an Elder in the quoram of sevinties," Autobiography, 18. This is a curious phrase, as elder and seventy were entirely separate priesthood callings.
39. For Smith, who became a counselor in the First Presidency in 1868, see Pusey, *Builders of the Kingdom*, 3–126; Quinn, *Mormon Hierarchy: Origins of Power*, 581–83.
40. Autobiography, 18–19.
41. Ibid., 23–24.
42. LJH, 17.
43. Autobiography, 25–27.
44. Ibid., 27. The story is told somewhat differently in LJH, 17, with a different dating.
45. LJH, 17.
46. Autobiography, 27–28.
47. Ibid. Cf. LJH, 20, which has a major dating problem. For Young's succession, see Harper, "The Mantle of Joseph"; Turner, *Brigham Young*, 112–18.
48. LJH, 19.
49. See Hosea Stout diary, September and October 1845 (1:60–88); Flanders, *Nauvoo: Kingdom on the Mississippi*, 322–33; Arrington, *Brigham Young*, 121–26; Hamilton, "From Assassination to Expulsion"; Hallwas and Launius, *Cultures in Conflict*, 241–302.

50. Autobiography, 28–30.
51. Ibid.
52. LJH, 21.
53. Autobiography, 30. LJH, 21, gives the date as April 11.
54. LJH, 21.
55. Maryette later married John William Young (three children), then, after a separation, Mormon Battalion veteran William Bailey Maxwell (ten children), both of whom were extraordinary frontiersman. Maxwell accompanied Jacob on a number of his expeditions. This second marriage also ended in separation, and Maryette then married Timothy Lockwood (two children). She died in 1910 in Alma, New Mexico.
56. LJH, 21.
57. Autobiography, 30–31.
58. Ibid., 31. Hosea Stout diary, Sept. 16–21, 1845 (1:64–70n34); Roberts, *Comprehensive History*, 2:279–81.
59. Autobiography, 31.
60. Arrington, *Brigham Young*, 124.
61. Ibid., 125. Turner, *Brigham Young*, 125.
62. LJH, 21.
63. These rites involved long, semidramatic ritual sequences that mixed the story of the Creation and of the Fall with elaborate ritual actions; baptisms on behalf of the dead; and marriages for eternity. For discussions of these rituals, see Bushman, *Joseph Smith*, 450–52; Prince, *Power from On High*, 135–48; Buerger, *The Mysteries of Godliness*.
64. "Nauvoo Temple Endowment Register," 110. LJH, 21, incorrectly gives a February date. I have not found a record of a temple marriage for Jacob and Lucinda.
65. Autobiography, 32. See also LJH, 21.
66. Hartley, "Introduction," in Black and Hartley, *The Iowa Mormon Trail*, xvii; Brigham Young History, CR 100 102, April 8, 1846 (SC 2).
67. See Kimball, *Historic Sites and Markers*, 27–29; Gentry, "Mormon Way Stations"; Hartley, "Introduction," in Black and Hartley, *The Iowa Mormon Trail*, xxi; Brown and Hilger, "Union County." This settlement began in May–June 1846.
68. LJH, 23. For the location of the death, see Miller, *Jacob Vernon Hamblin Family*, 43; this is consistent with Jacob's autobiography and seems to place the death in spring 1846, not far from Nauvoo. Sources that place Daphne's death in Council Bluffs at a later date are apparently incorrect, for when Jacob reached Council Bluffs on April 11, 1848, his mother was not there; see Autobiography, 35.
69. Autobiography, 32.
70. Ibid., 32–33. For malaria, see Pickard and Buley, *The Midwest Pioneer*, 16–17; Harstad, "Sickness and Disease on the Wisconsin Frontier," 83; Flanders, *Nauvoo: Kingdom on the Mississippi*, 53–54.
71. Autobiography, 33. For glossolalia in Mormonism, see Copeland, "Speaking in Tongues"; Vogel and Dunn, "The Tongue of Angels."
72. Exodus 16:13; Numbers 11:4–14, 31–34. LJH, 22. This event is also documented in the Mormon "poor camps" on October 9, 1846. Thomas Bullock, journal, Oct. 9, 1846, in Bagley, *The Pioneer Camp of the Saints*, 76.
73. Lyman later married Esther Cecelia Burk (ten children). A carpenter by profession, he was widely appreciated for his fiddling at frontier dances. He died on September 23, 1922, in Eagar, Arizona. Death Certificate, copy in author's possession; Golding, *Our Golden Heritage*, 17–21.
74. Autobiography, 35.
75. See Bennett, "Council Bluffs"; *Mormons at the Missouri*.
76. Autobiography, 35–36.
77. Ibid., 37–38.
78. Ibid., 45.
79. Corbett, *Jacob Hamblin*, 29–30.
80. Brooks, *On the Ragged Edge*, 53.
81. Autobiography, 45–46.

82. For Rachel's birth date, see Sexton Records, Santa Clara Cemetery, which records that she was born in Johnston, Canada.
83. See Zadok's *Autobiography* for an account of Rachel's family background.
84. Quinn, *The Mormon Hierarchy: Origins of Power*, 567; Shepard, "Shadows on the Sun Dial," 60–61. Brooks, *On the Ragged Edge*, 53, reporting third-hand an interview with Rachel, incorrectly names Apostle Thomas Marsh as the first husband.
85. Brooks, *On the Ragged Edge*, 53. The children first lived with Jacob and Rachel but ended up with Henderson relatives. Both Brooks and Corbett speak of only two children, but a daughter was also present, according to an 1851 census record from Tooele, Utah, see below.
86. Brooks, *On the Ragged Edge*, 53.
87. Iowa Marriages, 1809–1992, Film No. 0227280, FHL; Andrews, *The Hamlin Family*, 547; Miller, *Jacob Vernon Hamblin Family*, 43.
88. The 1851 Tooele County, Utah, census shows Rachel at household 13–13 with William Henderson, age seventeen, born in Kentucky, John [Henderson], fifteen, born in Indiana, and Eunice [Henderson], thirteen, born in Missouri, and Jacob's four children.
89. Autobiography, 46.

CHAPTER 3

1. Autobiography, 46–47. For this branch, Bennett, *Mormons at the Missouri*, 218.
2. LJH, 24. Thrice-repeated dreams are a common motif in dream lore. Quinn, *Early Mormonism*, 138–41, 266–67.
3. Bennett, *Mormons at the Missouri*, 228.
4. Autobiography, 47; Manwaring, "Aaron Johnson," 322.
5. "From the Valley," *Frontier Guardian*, 8 Jan. 1851, 2, and Elijah Averett, Notebook, 15, in "Mormon Pioneer Overland Travel, 1847–1868."
6. Autobiography, 47.
7. LJH, 24.
8. For the American overland journey generally, see Unruh, *The Plains Across*; Mattes, *The Great Platte River Road*; Faragher, *Women and Men on the Overland Trail*; for the Mormon overland experience, Stegner, *The Gathering of Zion*; Kimball, *Historic Sites and Markers*; Bennett, *We'll Find the Place*.
9. Autobiography, 47.
10. Emma M. Guymon Kearnes, Autobiography, 1921, at "Mormon Pioneer Overland Travel, 1847–1868."
11. LJH, 24.
12. Carter, "'Sometimes When I Hear,'" 154–55.
13. Elijah Averett, in Averett family, Notebook, p. 15, in "Mormon Pioneer Overland Travel, 1847–1868"; Samuel Smith, in Tullidge, *Tullidge's Histories*, 120.
14. "They Came in '50," 443, 423.
15. Autobiography, 48–49.
16. Mattes, *Great Platte River Road*, 83–86, 575. The years 1849, 1850, and 1852 were the worst for cholera on the overland trails. Carter, "'Sometimes When I Hear,'" 146.
17. Cited in Mattes, *Great Platte River Road*, 84.
18. Custer, "Asiatic Cholera in Central Illinois." See also Read, "Diseases, Drugs, and Doctors"; Blair, "The Doctor Gets Some Practice?"; Milikien, "Dead of the Bloody Flux?"; Rosenberg, *The Cholera Years*, 3–4; Rieck, "A Geography of Death." For Mormons and cholera, see Divett, "His Chastening Rod"; Rushton, "Cholera and Its Impact"; Baker, "Illness and Mortality," 83–86.
19. "They Gave Their Lives," in Carter, *Treasures of Pioneer History*, 5:450. "Arrival of the Mail from the Valley," *Frontier Guardian*, 10 July 1850, 2, at "Mormon Pioneer Overland Travel, 1847–1868."
20. Averett family, Notebook, p. 15.
21. LJH, 24. See also "Arrival of the Mail from the Valley," *Frontier Guardian*, 10 July 1850, 2, as cited in "Mormon Pioneer Overland Travel, 1847–1868."
22. Autobiography, 50.
23. Averett family, Notebook, 15.

24. Autobiography, 50.
25. Ibid.
26. LJH, 25.
27. Autobiography, 50.
28. "From the Valley," *Frontier Guardian*, 8 Jan. 1851, 2, accessed at "Mormon Pioneer Overland Travel, 1847–1868." LJH, 25.
29. Mattes, *The Great Platte River Road*, 167–237. Often spelled "Chiles," as Hamblin does here.
30. Autobiography, 51. This is probably Jonathan Ford Jr., the son of Jonathan and Rachel Roberson Ford.
31. Autobiography, 51; George Pectol, diary.
32. Stapley and Wright, "'They Shall Be Made Whole.'"
33. Emma M. Guymon, Autobiography, at "Mormon Pioneer Overland Travel, 1847–1868."
34. The Johnson death was probably twenty-six-year-old Sarah Mariah Johnson, another wife of Aaron Johnson.
35. Autobiography; LJH, 25.
36. LJH, 25.
37. George Pectol, diary. Averett family, Notebook, 15. Oliver Huntington journal, August 4, 1848.
38. Averett family, Notebook, 15.
39. Autobiography, 53. LJH, 25, gives the date of arrival as September 1, as does Edward Bunker, Autobiography.
40. The first companies of Mormons had arrived in Utah in 1847, and there were only about eleven thousand Latter-day Saints living in Utah in 1850.

CHAPTER 4

1. Hunter, *Brigham Young, the Colonizer*; Campbell, *Establishing Zion.*
2. Autobiography, 53.
3. Ibid.; Quinn, "The Practice of Rebaptism," 229–31.
4. Howard Stansbury, November 6, 1849, diary entry in his *Exploration and Survey*, 118; "Memoirs of George A. Smith," July 27, 1847, in George A. Smith Papers, 1834–1875 (MS 1322), bx 1, fd 2 (SC 32); Journal History, July 17, 1849.
5. Quoted in Tripp, "Tooele's First Four Years," 78.
6. Anderson and Brown, "Stansbury Mountain Canyon–Grantsville Division," 479; see also Journal History, February 27, 1849.
7. Jenson, "Tooele Stake History," 3; "Mormon Colonization in the West," 283.
8. Powell, "Cowboys and the Cattle Industry." According to Powell, the Mormons started out with 3,100 head of cattle in 1847, and had 34,000 head by 1860. See also Walker, "The Cattle Industry of Utah," 184; Peterson, "Grazing in Utah." Abruzzi, "The Social and Ecological Consequences," shows the devastating effect overgrazing could have on the ecological stability of a region.
9. For Mormon views of Indians, see Arrington and Bitton, *The Mormon Experience*, 145–46; Bushman, *Joseph Smith: Rough Stone Rolling*, 97–99; Mauss, *All Abraham's Children*, 49–50; Peterson, *Utah's Black Hawk War*, 5–7; Walker, "Toward a Reconstruction"; Whittaker, "Mormons and Native Americans"; Hicks, "Noble Savages"; Murphy, "From Racist Stereotype"; Duffy, "The Use of 'Lamanite'"; Reeve, *Making Space*, 101–10. For white Indian relations in American history generally, the following is a selective listing: Hagan, "How the West Was Lost"; Limerick, *Legacy of Conquest*; Prucha, *The Great Father* and *The Indians in American Society*; Jacobs, *Dispossessing the American Indian*; Utley, *The Indian Frontier*; West, *The Contested Plains*.
10. 3 Nephi 20:10–46; 21:5, 9.
11. For the crucial role of Indians in the Mormon apocalyptic vision, see 3 Nephi 21–22; Ericksen, *"As a Thief in the Night,"* 95–96, 199; Campbell, "Brigham Young's Outer Cordon," 235.
12. Arrington and Bitton, *The Mormon Experience*, 145–60; Arrington, *Brigham Young*, 210–22.
13. Stegner, *Beyond the Hundredth Meridian*, 131. See also Dobyns and Euler, *The Walapai People*, 36; Gilbert, *Westering Man*, 130, 132; Stewart, *The California Trail*, 96, 99.
14. Quoted in Stegner, *Beyond the Hundredth Meridian*, 389n7. For the language of extermination applied to

Indians, see Donovan, *A Terrible Glory*, 23, 27, 29, 35, 90; Trafzer and Hyer, *Exterminate Them*; Svaldi, *Sand Creek*.

15. See chapter 5 of this volume (June 17, 1854).
16. Utley, *The Indian Frontier*, xvi. In Utah, see Campbell, *Establishing Zion*, 100–1, 113. For differences in Indian and white views of religion, Simmons, *Witchcraft in the Southwest*, 136.
17. Arrington, *Brigham Young*, 222.
18. Berkhofer, *Salvation and the Savage*, 160.
19. Ibid., 158. See also Bowden, *American Indians*.
20. For example, see Parley P. Pratt, in Brooks, *Journal of the Southern Indian Mission* (*JSIM*), 34–35, who described the Indians suffering for generations because of the rebellion of their ancestors. A similar statement by Brigham Young can be found in James W. Cummings, "Account of an Excursion to Toole and Other Places," BYOF, bx 73, fd 7. Mormons sometimes associated Indians with the nefarious Gadianton Robbers in the Book of Mormon. Reeve, *Making Space*, 102–4; Murphy, "From Racist Stereotype," 458.
21. Christy, "Open Hand," 235.
22. Brigham Young to D. L. Thomas, May 14, 1870, in *New York Times*, May 30, 1870. For positive views of Brigham Young and the Utah Indians, see Morgan, "The Administration of Indian Affairs in Utah, 1851–1858"; Arrington and Bitton, *The Mormon Experience*, 145–60; Brooks, "Indian Relations on the Mormon Frontier"; Bancroft, *History of Utah: 1540–1886*, 471; Whitney, *History of Utah*, 1:425.
23. I am speaking specifically of massacres, such as the Sand Creek Massacre in Colorado in 1864. Nevertheless, Mormons often were responsible for unduly punitive expeditions against Indians, or unwarranted executions of Indians. Mormon military actions against the Utes in Utah County in 1849 and 1850 are a good example. See Christy, "Open Hand," 221–25; Farmer, *On Zion's Mount*, 70–77.
24. Peterson, *Utah's Black Hawk War*, 7. See also Campbell, *Establishing Zion*, 93–135, 302–4, 330.
25. Christy, "Open Hand and Mailed Fist: Mormon Indian Relations in Utah, 1847–52," 217–35; see also O'Neil and Layton, "Of Pride and Politics," and Christy, "'What Virtue There Is in Stone.'" John Alton Peterson gives Young a mixed review in *Utah's Black Hawk War*, 386: "Young's settlement of his people among the Indians of Utah did not substantially result in bringing the Lamanites to Christ; it did instead substantially contribute to the processes of cultural and physical extermination that Indians experienced throughout North America." See also pp. 7, 12–13, 69–70, 383–86. Equally mixed are Farmer, *On Zion's Mount*, 81–87; Turner, *Brigham Young*, 207–18, 341–49.
26. Walker, "Toward a Reconstruction."
27. O'Neil and Layton, "Of Pride and Politics," 237.
28. Church Historian's Office, General Church Minutes, 1839–77 (CR 100 318), January 31, 1850 (SC 18). See also Church Historian's Office, History of the Church, 1839–ca. 1882 (CR 100 102), January 31, 1850 (SC 2), and the discussion in Christy, "Open Hand," 224.
29. Brigham Young to Daniel H. Wells, February 14, 1850, Territorial Militia Records, 1849–77, Series 2210 (hereafter Territorial Militia Records), No. 1312, Utah State Archives; see also discussion in Christy, "Open Hand," 224n30; Farmer, *On Zion's Mount*, 70–77. For extermination rhetoric in Utah, see Peterson, *Utah's Black Hawk War*, 383 (who notes that the Mormons had earlier faced an extermination order); Turner, *Brigham Young*, 209.
30. Hamblin, Autobiography, 53–54.
31. For introductions to the Goshutes, see Defa, "Goshute Indians" and "The Goshute Indians of Utah"; Allen and Warner, "The Gosiute Indians"; O'Neil, "The Utes, Southern Paiutes, and Gosiutes"; Steward, *Basin-Plateau Aboriginal Sociopolitical Groups*, 132–41; Madsen, *The Shoshoni Frontier*, 9–10. For the Utes, see McPherson, "Ute Indians—Southern"; Duncan, "The Northern Utes of Utah"; Simmons, *The Ute Indians*. For Utah Indians generally, Cuch, *A History of Utah's American Indians*; Tyler, "The Indians in Utah Territory."
32. Parry, "The Northwestern Shoshone"; Madsen, "Shoshoni Indians (Northwestern Bands)."
33. Peterson, *Utah's Black Hawk War*, 86.
34. MacPherson, "Setting the Stage," 17n16; Defa, "Goshute Indians," 228; Steward, *Basin-Plateau Aboriginal Sociopolitical Groups*, 181; Mercer, *History of Tooele County*, 300.

35. Mercer, *History of Tooele County*, 300.
36. Powell and Ingalls, *Report*, 7.
37. James H. Simpson, *Report of Explorations*, May 8, 1859, 51–52. Simpson, a government topographical engineer, explored the Great Salt Lake Desert of Utah and Nevada and visited the Goshutes there.
38. Mormon Indian translator George Washington Bean described the Goshutes as a break-off from the Ute tribe, though "they are little esteemed by the parent tribe." In Simpson, *Report of Explorations*, 54. For Shoshoni Indians, see Madsen, "Shoshoni Indians (Northwestern Bands)," and Peterson, *Utah's Black Hawk War*, 84n17. Bean described their language as a mixture of Shoshoni and Ute. Simpson, *Report of Explorations*, May 9, 1859, 52.
39. Madsen, "Shoshoni Indians," 497; Tripp, "Tooele Indians," 82; Simpson, *Report of Explorations*, 54, at May 9, 1859; Steward, *Basin-Plateau Aboriginal Sociopolitical Groups*, 135. However, sometimes family groups would combine for specific purposes. In addition, they were sometimes allied with Utes, and so might carry out hunts or raids with them occasionally.
40. Woodbury, "Route of Jedediah Smith," 45.
41. Stansbury, *Exploration and Survey*, 202–3.
42. Simpson, *Report of Explorations*, 52; see also Orrin Miller, *History of Tooele County*, 2:49. These were Goshutes living near the present Utah-Nevada border.
43. Simpson, *Report of Explorations*, 52, at May 9, 1859.
44. Ibid., May 9, 1859, 52; for Goshute food, see also Steward, *Basin-Plateau Aboriginal Sociopolitical Groups*, 138–39.
45. Simpson, *Report of Explorations*, 54, at May 9, 1859.
46. Defa, "The Goshute Indians of Utah," 79, 80, 83; Fowler and Fowler, *Anthropology of the Numa*, 250–70.
47. Simpson, *Report of Explorations*, 54.
48. Ibid., 53.
49. Defa, "The Goshute Indians of Utah," 97.
50. From the essay "Thoughts in a Dry Land," in *Where the Bluebird Sings*, 46–47; see also 45–99; Stegner, *The American West as Living Space*, 1–28; Flores, "Stegner, the Environment, and the West," 68. Stegner admired the stability of Mormon settlements, but noted that they were overpopulating an arid country.
51. Arrington and May, "'A Different Mode of Life'"; Alexander, "Irrigating the Mormon Heartland"; Fuller, "Irrigation in Utah"; Simmonds, "Water for the Big Range"; Brooks, "The Water's In!"; Abruzzi, *Dam That River!*; Geary, *The Proper Edge of Sky*, 107–8. For a broader perspective, Worster, *Rivers of Empire*.
52. Worster, *Rivers of Empire*, 77.
53. Article from *Tooele Transcript*, January 30 and February 6, 1903, quoted in Jenson, "Tooele Stake History," 12–14.
54. Garland Hurt to Brigham Young, August 27, 1855, read on *The Nevada Observer* website at http://www.nevadaobserver.com/Reading%20Room%20Documents/Letters%20from%20Nevada%20Indian%20Agents%201855.htm (accessed Nov. 29, 2012).
55. Tripp, "Tooele Indians," 82.
56. Ibid.
57. Journal History, February 27, 1849; Tripp, "Tooele's First Four Years," 71–72.
58. Jenson, "Tooele Stake History," 9; "Valley Journal," *Deseret News*, February 22, 1851, 6; Journal History, February 11, 19, 25, 27, 1851. See also George D. Grant [to Daniel H. Wells], February 22, 1851, Territorial Militia Records, No. 1324; Phineas Wright to Daniel H. Wells, March 19, 1851, Territorial Militia Records, No. 107; "[Auto]Biography of James McBride, 1818–1881."
59. He describes it in his Autobiography, 54–55, leading one to conclude that he was a part of the military company, though not a leading figure.
60. Autobiography, 54–55.
61. Rockwell's report to Brigham Young, Journal History, mistakenly placed at Apr. 23, 1850 (it should be 1851). See also Brooks, *On the Mormon Frontier*, 2:398, April 28, 1851; "Indian Depredations," *Deseret News*, May 3, 1851, 4; Tullidge, *Tullidge's Histories*, 2:83; Schindler, *Orrin Porter Rockwell*, 193–96.
62. Daniel H. Wells to Phineas Wright, April 21, 1851, Territorial Militia Records, No. 111; Schindler, *Orrin Porter Rockwell*, 193–96.

63. Tullidge, *Tullidge's Histories*, 2:83; Autobiography, 54–55; Journal History, April 22, 1851 ("some thirty Utah Indians"); and W. R. Dickinson to "folkes," May 29, 1851, typescript, Utah State Historical Society, Salt Lake City.
64. See Tullidge, *Tullidge's Histories*, 2:83. If the Mormons "mistook the route" of the marauders, the "band of Indians with their families" would have been the wrong Indians.
65. Rockwell to Young, April 23, 1851.
66. Dickinson to "folkes," May 29, 1851; discussed in Schindler, *Orrin Porter Rockwell*, 195. Journal History, April 22, 1851, also records that Custer shot first.
67. Porter Rockwell, in his report to Brigham Young, neglected to mention that Custer fired first, thus shading the narrative to make Custer seem like the victim of an unexpected and unprovoked attack. Later retrospective accounts portray the Indians as even more cowardly. Mary Ann Weston Maughan, "Autobiography and Journal," 381; John Bevan, quoted in Tripp, "Tooele Indians," 83. These accounts conflict with the much earlier and more first-hand Dickinson account, and with the Journal History.
68. Tullidge, *Tullidge's Histories*, 2:84; see also Christy, "'What Virtue There Is in Stone,'" 305 n11. This execution is understandably omitted from some retellings of the story, but the Hamblin autobiography supports it.
69. Special Orders No. 10, February 9, 1850, in Territorial Militia Records, emphasis in original; see commentary in Christy, "'What Virtue There Is in Stone,'" 304.
70. Autobiography, 55.
71. Esaias Edwards, Autobiography, 35.
72. Autobiography, 55–56.
73. Daniel H. Wells to William McBride, June 13, 1851, Territorial Militia Records, No. 120; William McBride to Daniel H. Wells, June 19, 1851, Territorial Militia Records, No. 1327; Tullidge, *Tullidge's Histories*, 2:84.
74. Daniel H. Wells to William McBride, June 20, 1851, Territorial Militia Records, No. 126; William McBride to Daniel H. Wells, June 24, 1851, Territorial Militia Records, No. 1328.
75. McBride to Wells, June 24, 1851.
76. Will Bagley, *Blood of the Prophets*, 110, argues that the tone is serious and that Mormons did poison some of the Indians' wells and meat.
77. William McBride, "Minutes of the Campaigne Against the Hostile Indians in June 1851," 4, Territorial Militia Records, No. 1326. *Deseret News*, as quoted in Allred, *History of Tooele County*, 217; Tullidge, *Tullidge's Histories*, 2:84; Esaias Edwards, Autobiography, 35. According to Richard Warburton, "When the body of men came up there was some shooting done and about 8 Indians made good," including the baby's mother. Richard Warburton, Reminiscences.
78. LJH, 26.
79. Autobiography, 56–58. However, according to LJH, 27, the expedition was Hamblin's idea.
80. Autobiography, 56–58.
81. LJH, 27.
82. Ibid.
83. Autobiography, 58.
84. LJH, 27. On the policy of executing prisoners, see also Christy, "Open Hand," 225; Farmer, *On Zion's Mount*, 74–75. Hamblin's future brother-in-law, Dudley Leavitt, once brought an Indian prisoner to Tooele and refused to allow him to be shot. Brigham Young, contacted by dispatch, "told them to feed the Indian and let him go." Brooks, *On the Ragged Edge*, 46–47, 53. This episode shows the moderate side of Brigham Young's Indian policy.
85. LJH, 27–28.
86. Daniel H. Wells and James Ferguson, Letter to Officers of the Nauvoo Legion, August 1, 1857, quoted in Carter, *Our Pioneer Heritage*, 14:361–62.
87. Autobiography, 60–61.
88. Captain Phineas Wright [with Jacob Hamblin], Military report to James Ferguson, Adjutant General, Salt Lake City, March 15, 1852, Territorial Militia Records, No. 1332. I am indebted to Will Bagley for alerting me to this source. This military report by Wright, Hamblin's immediate military superior, was written on the last day of the three-day expedition. Since Wright was not part of the expedition,

he probably obtained the details directly from Hamblin. This report forms the main framework for my narrative. Also important are Hamblin, Autobiography, 58–61, and LJH, 28–29. Later sources are "Biography of Thomas Atkin," (an autobiography), 29–30, and Bleak, "Annals," 54–57, at Aug. 31, 1886 (a late, inferior account in which Jacob's gun is entirely reliable and he simply lets the defenseless Indian depart). Atkin seems to write as an eyewitness, but he is not listed in the military record mentioned above, although his older brother, George, is. Both Wright/Hamblin's and Atkin's accounts emphasize military aspects of the incident, while Hamblin's autobiography, and the Little and Bleak accounts, have a more religious focus.

89. Autobiography, 58.
90. LJH, 28.
91. Brooks, *On the Ragged Edge*.
92. Wright/Hamblin, Military Report.
93. Atkin, Autobiography, 29–30.
94. Autobiography, 58–59.
95. LJH, 28.
96. Autobiography, 58–59.
97. Wright/Hamblin, Military Report. However, Little states that it was "near a large mountain between Tooele and Skull Valleys," while Atkin recalls it as near "the north point of the stansbury range of mountains."
98. Wright/Hamblin, Military Report.
99. Autobiography, 59. The fact that they were wearing leggings and moccasins shows that this group may have had ties with the more prosperous Utes or Shoshoni.
100. LJH, 28.
101. Wright/Hamblin, Military Report.
102. LJH, 28.
103. Wright/Hamblin, Military Report.
104. Autobiography, 59.
105. The cap, which would be set off by the hammer, contained the priming charge that would explode and set off the gunpowder in the barrel. Chapel, *Guns of the Old West*, 83, 69–71.
106. According to LJH, 28.
107. Autobiography, 59–60. Wright/Hamblin military report, March 15, 1852. Atkin attributes the misfires to the damp weather, not to defective caps.
108. Autobiography, 60.
109. LJH, 28.
110. Wright/Hamblin, Military Report. Atkins, Autobiography, 29–30, also emphasized the military success: "Our short expedition checked their depredations for a while."
111. Autobiography, 60.
112. LJH, 28–29.
113. Ibid.
114. LJH, 29.
115. Ibid., 119.
116. Cox, "Biographical Sketch," 103.
117. LJH, 29–30. Hamblin also mentions this repeated dream in Hamblin to Brigham Young, Oct. 8, 1860, BYOF.
118. "Indian Affairs," in *Deseret News* 3.10, Apr. 2, 1853, p. 2.
119. Carleton, *Special Report*, 6.
120. Hamblin to Young, June 23, 1860, BYOF.
121. See Crum, *The Road on Which We Came*, 2, 18–19; Harris, "The Western Shoshone" and "The White Knife Shoshoni of Nevada."
122. For an account of Albert that is late and second-hand, but from a woman who knew Jacob, see Cox, "Albert Hamblin." This has Jacob healing Albert's mother, and Albert in frequent contact with the Three Nephites.

123. LJH, 30.
124. Bevan, "Events in the Early History of Tooele," 23–25; "Francis Xeveres LOUGY."
125. Arrott, *Sarah Priscilla Leavitt Hamblin*, 24.
126. Ibid. Richard Warburton, Autobiography, as quoted in Tripp, "Tooele's First Four Years," 73.
127. Letter to the Editor, March 25, 1852, in *Deseret News* 2.12, Apr. 17, 1852, p. 1.
128. Tripp, "Tooele's First Four Years," 73.
129. Ibid.; Tullidge, *Tullidge's Histories* 2:100; Jenson, "Tooele Stake History," 31, citing *Deseret News*, May 9, 1855; George A. Smith, Letter to the Editor, May 1, 1855, p. 8. Hartley, "Mormons, Crickets"; Bitton and Wilcox, "Pestiferous Ironclads"; Aird, *Mormon Convert*, 149–50 (locusts).
130. "The result of the August 1st Election . . . ," *Deseret News* 2.21, August 21, 1852, p. 3.
131. Israel Barlow, "Report of the Sixth Quorum of Seventies," report dated April 5, 1853, in *Deseret News* 3.15, June 18, 1853, p. 4; see also George Sims, "Report of the Sixth Quorum," in *Deseret News* 5.4, Apr. 4, 1855, p. 8.
132. Lois would marry Hubert Rosell Burk in 1868, with whom she had ten children. She died on August 30, 1891, in Alpine, Arizona.
133. Tullidge, *Tullidge's Histories* 2:95. Thomas Atkin Jr., Autobiography, p. 28.
134. For the Walker War, see Duncan, "The Northern Utes of Utah," 188; Schindler, *Orrin Porter Rockwell*, 198–99, 203–11; Peterson, *Utah's Black Hawk War*, 63–69; Walker, "Wakara Meets the Mormons"; "Reminiscences of the Early Days of Manti."
135. Autobiography, 62. See also Esaias Edwards, Autobiography, p. 43; Tullidge, *Tullidge's Histories* 2:95.
136. Ibid. Ida Adamson, in "Pioneer Forts of the West," 149. Esaias Edwards, Autobiography, p. 43. Thomas Atkin Jr., Autobiography, p. 28.
137. The date given in Thomas Brown's journal; see Brooks, JSIM, 2. Bleak, "Annals," at year 1853. Hamblin in his Autobiography incorrectly gives the date as "April conference 1854." Bleak notes that the Indian missionaries were part of the fifty families called as missionaries on October 7, "to strengthen the settlements in Iron Co." See "Minutes of the General Conference of the Church of Jesus Christ of Latter-day Saints," *Deseret News* 3.19, Oct. 15, 1853, p. 2.
138. Autobiography, 63.

CHAPTER 5

1. Brown's diary is published in Brooks, JSIM. Lists at 2–3, 6–7. The other main source for this period is Hamblin's own diary, holograph, MS 1951, CHL. Both sources will be cited by date, often given in the text; sometimes page numbers will be included, as an aid to the reader.
2. Brooks, *John Doyle Lee*, 171.
3. Jenson, LDSBE, 1:535; Smart and Smart, *Over the Rim*; Sandberg, *A Million Miles of Faith*.
4. Autobiography; see also Esshom, *Pioneers*, 1004; Brooks, JSIM, 4; Black, *Membership of the Church*.
5. Jenson, LDSBE, 2:750; Brooks, JSIM, 4.
6. Brooks, JSIM.
7. Ibid., 3.
8. Ibid., 6.
9. See Lyman and Reese, *The Arduous Road*; Lyman, *The Overland Journey*.
10. See Lyman and Newell, *A History of Millard County*, 26, 37; Peterson, *The Black Hawk War*, 85n20; Lyman, "Chief Kanosh."
11. Lyman, *San Bernardino*.
12. For Wakara, see Duncan, "The Northern Utes of Utah," 188; Peterson, *The Black Hawk War*, 63–69.
13. William Birdsall Lorton, a forty-niner, as quoted in Lyman and Reese, *The Arduous Road*, 42.
14. For the Iron Mission, see Shirts and Shirts, *A Trial Furnace;* Seegmiller, *A History of Iron County*.
15. Heap, *Central Route to the Pacific*, 90–91.
16. Zadok K. Judd, autobiography.
17. For early Cedar City, see Heap, *Central Route to the Pacific*, 90–91; Carvalho, *Incidents of Travel*, 210.
18. Smart and Smart, *Over the Rim*, 87. For further on Harmony, see Seegmiller, "Ghost Towns," 127; Brooks, "New Harmony."

19. Smart and Smart, *Over the Rim*, 87. "Letter from Elder John D. Lee," Feb. 20, 1852, published in *Deseret News* 2.11, Apr. 3, 1852, p. 3.
20. For Lee, see his diaries, Kelly, *Journals of John D. Lee*, and Cleland and Brooks, *A Mormon Chronicle*; also Brooks, *John Doyle Lee*, and Manderscheid, *Some Descendants of John Doyle Lee*. For the Mormon practice of adopting grown men to church leaders, Stapley, "Adoptive Sealing Ritual in Mormonism."
21. Bleak, "Annals," 17, just before Apr. 22, 1852. Seegmiller, "Ghost Towns," 127.
22. George A. Smith, Letter to the Editor dated Dec. 8, 1852, in "Local Correspondence," *Deseret News* 3.2, Dec. 11, 1852, p. 2; John D. Lee to Brigham Young, March 1, 1853, as quoted in Cleland and Brooks, *A Mormon Chronicle*, 1:134.
23. Brooks, JSIM, May 2, 1854, p. 18.
24. Shirts, "Black Ridge Mountains," 5–7.
25. Brooks, JSIM, 21–22.
26. For Paiutes generally, see Knack, *Boundaries Between*; Tom and Holt, "The Paiute Tribe of Utah"; Holt, *Beneath These Red Cliffs*; Inter-Tribal Council of Nevada, *Nuwuvi*; Martineau, *Southern Paiutes*; Fowler and Fowler, "Notes on the History of the Southern Paiutes"; Stoffle and Zedeño, "Historical Memory"; Manners, *Paiute Indians I*; Kelly, "Southern Paiute Bands" and *Southern Paiute Ethnography*.
27. For the Cedar City Paiutes, see Palmer, "Utah Indians Past and Present," 41; Martineau, *Southern Paiutes*, 160; Matheson and Cooper, "Answers to a Questionnaire"; Knack, "Church and State." For the difficulty of distinguishing between Ute and Paiute, Kelly and Fowler, "Southern Paiute," 368.
28. Palmer, "Utah Indians Past and Present," 41.
29. See Journal History, May 10, 1855. For Young's frequent tours of Utah, see Irving, "Encouraging the Saints."
30. Hamblin has the twenty-seventh, but Brown's chronology seems more reliable.
31. Brooks, JSIM, May 19, 1854, p. 30.
32. Ibid.
33. Ibid., May 21, 1854, pp. 34–35.
34. John D. Lee to Willard Richards, Aug. 7, 1852, printed in "Local Correspondence," *Deseret News* 2.22, Sept. 4, 1852, pp. 1–2.
35. Brooks, JSIM, May 23, 1854, p. 38.
36. Hamblin, diary, June 7 [*sic*]; Brooks, JSIM, May 25–28, pp. 38–39. Brown's dating seems more reliable.
37. Brooks, JSIM, June 7, 9, and 13, pp. 41–42, 50–51, 56–57.
38. Buchanan, *History of Lorenzo Wesley Roundy*; Roundy, "Pioneers of Early Days."
39. Kumen Jones, "Notes On San Juan Mission." For his early life, see Haskell's Autobiography.
40. George A. Smith, "History of the Settling of Southern Utah," 5.
41. Brooks, JSIM, 44.
42. Jacob Hamblin diary, [June 7,] 1854, p. 8.
43. Brooks, JSIM, June 7, 1854, p. 44.
44. For the Southern Paiutes as farmers, aside from the Brown diary, see Escalante diary, October 15, 1776; Warner, *The Domínguez-Escalante Journal*, 95; Roberts, "Settlement and Subsistence Strategies"; Kelly and Fowler, "Southern Paiute," 317; Fowler and Fowler, "Notes on the History of the Southern Paiutes," 101; Stoffle and Zedeño, "Historical Memory," 230–31, 234–39; Manners, *Paiute Indians I*, 37–43; Martineau, *Southern Paiutes*, 162.
45. Stoffle and Zedeño, "Historical Memory," 238; Carroll, "Cultural Affiliation," 65–70.
46. Kelly and Fowler, "Southern Paiute," 393; Tom and Holt, "The Paiutes," 128.
47. Tom and Holt, "The Paiute Tribe," 124–27; Beckstrom and Snow, *"Oh Ye Mountains High,"* 2.
48. Tom and Holt, "The Paiute Tribe," 127.
49. Ibid., 123, 127. For Paiute myths, see Fowler and Fowler, *Anthropology of the Numa*, 76–78; Martineau, *Southern Paiutes*, 22–24; Reeve, *Making Space*, 12.
50. Kelly and Fowler, "Southern Paiute," 384; Martineau, *Southern Paiutes*, 93–105.
51. For one delineation of these groups, based partly on the earlier division by John Wesley Powell, see Kelly and Fowler, "Southern Paiute," 394–96.
52. Fowler and Fowler, *Anthropology of the Numa*, 65–66.

53. Brooks, JSIM, p. 49. Unless otherwise noted, all quotes in the following section are from Brown's diary (Brooks, JSIM) or Hamblin's diary.
54. Austin, Dean, and Gaines, *Yanawant: Paiute Places, Volume Two,* 68; Martineau, *Southern Paiutes*, 188.
55. Bleak, "Annals," after June 5, 1854, p. 25.
56. Richard Robinson to his parents, July 13, 1854, Journal History.
57. Austin, Dean, and Gaines, *Yanawant: Paiute Places* 2:78; Martineau, *Southern Paiutes*, 154, 187. Anthropologist Isabel Kelly refers to the lower Santa Clara Paiutes as the St. George group. Kelly, "Southern Paiute Bands," 552. See also Palmer, "Utah Indians Past and Present," 47–48; Palmer, "Pahute Indian Homelands"; and Martineau, *Southern Paiutes*, 154–70.
58. Brooks, JSIM, June 11, p. 54.
59. See Brooks, "Indian Relations," 41; Snow, "Utah Indians and the Spanish Slave Trade"; Bailey, *Indian Slave Trade*, 144–45; Hafen and Hafen, *Old Spanish Trail*, 259–83; Van Hoak, "'And Who Shall Have the Children?'"; Peterson, *Utah's Black Hawk War*, 63–69; Jones, "'Redeeming the Indian'"; Fowler and Fowler, "Notes on the History of the Southern Paiutes," at nn31–37; Calloway, *One Vast Winter Count*, 283; Sanchez, *Explorers, Traders, and Slavers*, 126–31.
60. Brooks, JSIM, 59.
61. See Walker, "Native Women," for women's place in Ute and Paiute culture.
62. Tullidge, *History of Salt Lake City*, 379; Brooks, JSIM, 61.
63. Lyman, *The Overland Journey*, 153–55.
64. For Mormons' and Indians' different understandings of baptism, see Jenson, "Snowflake Stake. Manuscript History," LR 9236 2, at 1900, CHL; also Flake, "A History of Mormon Missionary Work," 53; O'Neil, "The Mormons, the Indians," 94; Knack, *Boundaries Between*, 67; Reeve, *Making Space*, 75.
65. Brooks, JSIM, 64.
66. Clark, "William Hennefer."
67. For the medicine man or shaman in Paiute culture, see Powell, notes on the shaman in Fowler and Fowler, *Anthropology of the Numa*, 245; Kelly, *Southern Paiute Ethnography*, 133–41 (which focuses on Kaibab Paiutes), and "Southern Paiute Shamanism"; Fowler and Fowler, "Notes on the History of the Southern Paiutes," 101; Whiting, *Paiute Sorcery*, 39–42; Knack, *Boundaries Between*, 25; Reeve, *Making Space*, 140–41; Palmer, "Pahute Indian Medicine." For shamanism in general, Eliade, *Shamanism*.
68. Kelly, "Southern Paiute Shamanism," 162.
69. Ibid., 158; see also 157.
70. LJH, 32.
71. Kelly, "Southern Paiute Shamanism."
72. LJH, 32. Whiting, *Paiute Sorcery*, 39–42. See also Furst, "Introduction," 12.
73. Richard Robinson to his parents, July 13, 1854, Journal History; Brooks, JSIM, June 30, p. 74; Bleak, "Annals," 28, just before summer 1854, which gives the number of baptized Paiutes as fifty.
74. A year later, the Indian missionaries baptized some 350 Paiutes on the Muddy River in modern Nevada, according to Thomas Brown; see his journal at May 31, 1855 (Brooks, JSIM, 129). George Washington Bean gives the number baptized as "about 230," Brooks, JSIM, 129.
75. Brooks, JSIM, June 30, p. 74.
76. Jacob Hamblin diary, July 3, 1854, p. 16.
77. LJH, 33.
78. Thales Haskell, autobiography, in "Thales Haskell," 328.
79. Jacob Hamblin diary, July 17, 1854, p. 17.
80. Brooks, JSIM, July 17, p. 77.
81. See his autobiography, Riddle, "Isaac Riddle Tells His Story"; Esshom, *Pioneers*, 1133.
82. Jacob Hamblin diary, July 26, 1854, p. 17.
83. Ibid., end of Sept., 1854, pp. 18–19.
84. Hamblin, Diary; LJH, 34.
85. Joseph, a rancher, married Elsie Albertina Johnson in 1879 (three children). Elsie died in 1882, Joseph in 1924. Helen Hamblin Burgoyne to Dove Menkes, April 2, 1985, in PTRC, series 1, bx 16, fd 285. Death Certificate, in author's possession; "Biography of Joseph Hamblin."

86. Lewis calls it "the Pangwitch or Fish Lake." Oct. 29, 1854, in Brooks, JSIM, 95. "Panguitch" means "big fish."
87. See Young, "In Memory of Ira Hatch"; Robinson, *The Life of Ira Hatch*; Brooks, JSIM, 21n22; Elkins, *Ira Hatch: Indian Missionary* (an uncritical biography that must be used with care).
88. Shurtz, "History of the Shurtz or Shirts Family," 11.
89. Reilly, "Historic Utilization," 189; Shurtz, "History of the Shurtz or Shirts Family," USHS; Bagley, *Stones, Clubs and Gun Barrels*; Shirts, "Black Ridge Mountains"; Brooks, JSIM, 16n17; Carr, "A Partial List of Church Members," 61; see also chapter 18 (1866), this volume.
90. Excerpted from a Nov. 9, 1854, letter Thomas Brown sent to Brigham Young, see Brooks, JSIM, 93–97. The original, CHL, MS 4598, shows that Brown's version of the diary had been rewritten thoroughly, possibly by Brown and Lewis working together.
91. Lewis diary, in Brooks, JSIM, 93. Thanks to Waldo Perkins for this insight. Nephi Johnson first explored the famous canyon surrounding the north fork of the Virgin in fall 1858, Woodbury, *A History of Southern Utah*, 147–48. John Wesley Powell would traverse the east fork of the Virgin in 1872 (Worster, *A River Running West*, 212) but he was not the first to explore it, as some have assumed—for example, Dellenbaugh, *A Canyon Voyage*, 248.
92. Jacob Hamblin diary, [Oct. 27], 1854, p. 22.
93. Knack, *Boundaries Between*, 41.
94. For Hamblin as Indian trader, see McNitt, *The Indian Traders*, 89–95.
95. Jacob Hamblin diary, [after Nov. 4], 1854, p. 27.
96. Brooks, "Indian Relations," 41. For Mormons purchasing and adopting Indian children, see also Snow, "Utah Indians"; Bailey, *Indian Slave Trade*, 144–45; Van Hoak, "'And Who Shall Have the Children?'"; Peterson, *Utah's Black Hawk War*, 63–69; Jones, "'Redeeming the Indian'"; Cannon, "Adopted or Indentured"; Farmer, *On Zion's Mount*, 51, 84.
97. Brooks, "Indian Relations," 15–16.
98. Jones, "'Redeeming the Indian,'" 229–30.
99. Van Hoak "'And Who Shall Have the Children?'" 17.
100. Carleton, *Special Report*, 7.
101. Van Hoak, "'And Who Shall Have the Children,'" 18.
102. LJH, 34.
103. Ibid. However, see Ivins's account of one of Jacob's Indian wives, chapter 6, this volume. For further on squaw fights, see Powell's notes in Fowler and Fowler, *Anthropology of the Numa*, 51; Palmer, *Notes on the Utah Utes*, 3–4; Knack, "Newspaper Accounts of Indian Women," 88–89; Young, *Memoirs of John R. Young*, 299–304; and chapters 6 (1854–1856) and 11 (1860), this volume.

CHAPTER 6

1. Bleak, "Annals," 29–30, summer 1854.
2. See Cottam, "Brief Sketches"; Briggs, "Samuel Knight (1832–1910)." He was involved in the Mountain Meadows Massacre to some extent. Briggs, "Samuel Knight and the Events Incident"; Bagley, *Stones, Clubs and Gun Barrels*; Turley and Walker, *Mountain Meadows Massacre*, 262–64.
3. For these events, my main source is Hamblin's journal. There are additional details in Thomas Brown, "Home Correspondence. Southern Utah Mission," which quotes from Hamblin's journal, in *The Deseret News* 5.4, April 4, 1855, p. 6. Knight and Hatch came to Santa Clara early in the following year.
4. Before the Black Hawk War, Sanpitch had fairly friendly relations with many Mormons. As an enemy during the war, however, he was captured in 1866 and killed after escaping from jail. See Peterson, *Utah's Black Hawk War*, 135–36, 240; Lyman, "Chief Kanosh," 170, 176–79.
5. Jacob Hamblin diary. This account of Mormon-Ute relations in Utah County is vastly oversimplified.
6. Thomas Brown, in *The Deseret News* 5.4, April 4, 1855, p. 6.
7. Lyman, *The Overland Journey*, 100–1.
8. See Peterson, *Black Hawk War*, 373–74.
9. For this incident, see also the Thomas Brown journal, Brooks, JSIM, 118–19.

10. Unless otherwise noted, quotes in this section are from Jacob Hamblin diary, beginning Jan. 17, 1855.
11. Paiutes barbecued the sweet young flower stalks of the yucca plant. Woodbury, *A History of Southern Utah*, 119; Martineau, *Southern Paiutes*, 146, 199.
12. Palmer, *Notes on the Utah Utes*, 3–4.
13. Ibid.
14. Anthony W. Ivins, Reminiscence, 17–21.
15. Ibid., 21. John W. Young apparently describes this fight, *Memoirs of John R. Young*, 299–304. According to Young, Hamblin subsequently met with local Paiutes in a council "and talked to them until they promised to give up the squaw fights." However, the practice of fighting for brides was so ingrained in Paiute culture that it is doubtful that the practice was completely abandoned.
16. Paiute marriages were somewhat informal, without the legal and cultural formalizations that whites were used to.
17. LJH, 35.
18. Thales Haskell, Autobiography, in Smith, "Thales Hastings Haskell," 22.
19. LJH, 35.
20. Bleak, "Annals," 190–91 (Oct. 31–Nov. 1, 1863); Roberts, "Settlement and Subsistence Strategies," 23; chapters 10 (1859) and 12 (1861), this volume.
21. Joint pain is a symptom of malaria.
22. Bleak, "Annals," 30–31 (1855). For the Cotton Mission in southern Utah, see James McKnight, "Cotton and Its Culture in Utah," *Deseret News* 8.33, Oct. 20, 1858, p. 1; Arrington, "The Mormon Cotton Mission" and *Great Basin Kingdom*, 216–22; Hanson, "A Geographical Analysis"; Larson, *I Was Called to Dixie*, 69, 104–7, 185–234; and chapters 10 (1859) and 12 (1861), this volume.
23. Thales Haskell, Autobiography, in Smith, "Thales Hastings Haskell," 22.
24. Ibid., 22–23.
25. Ibid.
26. See below, this chapter, on Paiute views of sickness and witchcraft.
27. My primary source in this section is the Hamblin diary unless another source is specified.
28. Jacob Hamblin to Brigham Young, circa Dec. 1855, BYOF, bx 24, fd 3.
29. Tooele County Recorder's Book B, A.D. 1855, page 21, as cited in Brooks, *On the Ragged Edge*, 56.
30. Arrington, *Great Basin Kingdom*, 146–48.
31. Dudley, an archetypal Mormon patriarch, would later add three more wives to his family. Brooks, *On the Ragged Edge*.
32. Gates and Whittaker, "The Leavitts," 129; Carnahan, *Sarah Priscilla Leavitt Hamblin*, 12; Arrott, *Sarah Priscilla Leavitt Hamblin*, 25.
33. Zadok Knapp Judd, Autobiography.
34. See Bancroft, *History of Utah*, 478n73; Steward, *Basin-Plateau Aboriginal Sociopolitical Groups*, 229; Peterson, *Black Hawk War*, 60–61; Simmons, *The Ute Indians*, 49.
35. Hamblin to Young, Dec. 1855.
36. Ibid.
37. Ibid.
38. In Hamblin's diary, the name appears to read "L. Snow," but in the earlier December 1855 letter to Brigham Young, the name is definitely "E. Snow."
39. Hamblin to Young, Dec. 1855.
40. Rufus C. Allen to Brigham Young, January 13, 1856, in BYOF, bx 24, fd. 13. Thanks to Michael Landon for alerting me to this letter.
41. See also Bleak, "Annals," 33–34 (winter 1856–57) (who misdates the building of the fort, and is followed by Larson, *I Was Called to Dixie*, 40); Hamblin to Young on May 17, 1856, BYOF, bx 24, fd 20; "Improvements in the South," *Deseret News* 5.52, March 5, 1856, p. 9: "In Washington County John [*sic*] Hamblin and company are building a stone fort on the Santa Clara, and intend entering at once into raising cotton in the warm rich bottoms bordering on that stream." Zadok Judd recalled a longer building period, Autobiography, p. 15.
42. George W. Armstrong, Indian agent, letter to Brigham Young, June 30, 1857, in ARCIA (1858), 597; Brooks, "Indian Relations," 41, and chapters 7 (1857) and 15 (1863), this volume.

43. Jacob Hamblin, diary, March 1856.
44. Crampton, "Utah's Spanish Trail," 19–23; Crampton and Madsen, *In Search of the Spanish Trail*; Lyman, *The Overland Journey*, 5–6; Hafen and Hafen, *Old Spanish Trail*; Sanchez, *Explorers, Traders, and Slavers*.
45. Mary Dart Judd, Autobiography, 11–12.
46. James Bleak to George A. Smith, Jan. 27, 1866, George A. Smith Collection, MS 1322 (SC 33).
47. Beckstrom and Snow, *"Oh Ye Mountains High*,", I, 7.
48. See Isaac Riddle, Autobiography; Larson, *I Was Called to Dixie*, 54–58; Snow and Beckstrom, "Pine Valley."
49. In the American West, whites often required Indians to elect a chief of a large tribe, or appointed one. Hamblin, however, seems to be reporting a political fact, rather than an appointment. The Santa Clara area may have included the largest population of Paiutes, and so Tutsegabits might have been very influential for this reason.
50. Hamblin to Young, May 17, 1856, BYOF, bx 24, fd 20.
51. Bleak, "Annals," 33 (summer 1856).
52. See Gibbons, *Saint and Savage*; Gibbons and Gibbons, *A Gathering of Eagles*, 203–6 (both unscholarly but useful). He served as an Indian missionary for some twenty-five years.
53. Bleak, "Annals," 38–39 (June 2, 1856).
54. Seegmiller, "Ghost Towns," 119–20. Like much of southern Utah, Mountain Meadows later became severely overgrazed.
55. LJH, 37.
56. For this story, see also LJH, 38.
57. LJH, 38.
58. This is further explained later in this chapter.
59. She later married William Thomas Stewart, one of the sons of Kanab bishop Levi Stewart, on September 22, 1873, and bore three children before dying on March 17, 1877, in Kanab, after the birth of her last child. Snow and Beckstrom, "Pine Valley," 182; Beckstrom and Snow, *"Oh Ye Mountains High*," I, 7; William Thomas Stewart, "Personal journal."
60. See Knell, "Pinto"; Bleak, "Annals," 33 (fall 1856).
61. LJH, 43.
62. George Hendrix to Brigham Young, June 23, 1860, BYOF, now in Bigler and Bagley, *Innocent Blood*, 258–61.
63. Hendrix to Young, June 23, 1860.
64. In Hamblin's journal, we read, "he Died ~~Sept~~ Oct 7 1856." See also Isaiah's obituary, "Died," *Deseret News* 7.1, March 11, 1857, p. 12, which gives an incorrect September 7 death date.
65. Jacob Hamblin to Brigham Young, March 2, 1857, BYOF, bx 25, fd 17; Hamblin, diary, 76–79, just after Isaiah Hamblin's death on October 7, 1856; LJH, 38–40. While the diary seems to have Hamblin and Haskell talking to two chiefs together, in Little, Hamblin tells the two stories separately. The letter mentions two chiefs but focuses on the angry one. The earliest source, the letter, entirely leaves out the most miraculous part of the story, the deaths of the chiefs. I have tried to construct a unified story from the three accounts.
66. Hamblin diary.
67. LJH, 38–40. The name "agrarapoots" appears in Jacob's 1854–1858 diaries, MS 1951, CHL, in a list after p. 84, which records that Jacob sold him a shirt.
68. LJH, 38–40.
69. Ibid.
70. Ibid.
71. March 2, 1857, letter; LJH, 38.
72. LJH, 38.
73. March 2, 1857, letter.
74. LJH, 38–40.
75. March 2, 1857, letter.
76. LJH, 38–40. This seems to contradict the letter.
77. March 2, 1857, letter. In the letter, the entire story seems to end here, with Hamblin explaining, "The Lord gav us power over them."

78. LJH, 38–40.
79. Diary. In LJH, 59–60, this first chief dies at Pipe Spring and Hamblin does not find out his fate until he visits there on his first visit to the Hopis, in November 1858.
80. Diary.
81. LJH, 38–40.
82. Diary.
83. Diary, Letter.
84. Diary; LJH, 41.
85. LJH, 41–42.
86. Jacob Hamblin diary, [winter 1856–1857], p. 79.
87. Knack, *Boundaries Between*, 149. Whiting, *Paiute Sorcery*, is useful for understanding Paiute witchcraft in general, though the author focuses on sorcery among Northern Paiutes.
88. Whiting, *Paiute Sorcery*.
89. LJH, 42.
90. Riddle, "Isaac Riddle Tells His Story," 173. See chapter 5 (1854), this volume.
91. LJH, 43–44.
92. LJH, 42.
93. R. A. Morris, interview, as cited in Corbett, *Jacob Hamblin*, 146.
94. Whiting, *Paiute Sorcery*, 12–13, discusses retaliation as a form of social sanction among Paiutes. For retaliation in Indian culture, Simmons, "Kit and the Indians," 79–80; White, *The Middle Ground*, 76–77; John R. Young, *Memoirs*, 298, a generally negative view of Utah Indians. Revenge for injuries inflicted by another band of Indians was viewed as "a culturally prescribed obligation." Utley, *The Indian Frontier*, 11.
95. LJH, 42.
96. For harsh Paiute punishments, see Matheson and Cooper, "Answers to a Questionnaire," Q 26: "Their punishment and discipline were cruel and inhuman by our standards, but to them it was law and was carried out according to their beliefs."
97. R. A. Morris, interview, as cited in Corbett, *Jacob Hamblin*, 146.
98. Yet in other cases, a sexual transgressor might be punished by death. Matheson states that among Paiutes, an illegitimate child might be killed and the mother made an outcast. Matheson and Cooper, "Answers to a Questionnaire," Q 21. For varied reports on Ute and Paiute promiscuity, see Walker, "Native Women," 102.
99. LJH, 43.
100. Ibid., 44.
101. For the difficulties Indians had understanding and adapting to Christianity, see Utley, *The Indian Frontier*, 11–19. Sometimes they compartmentalized, adopting white religious practice and preserving their native beliefs and traditions at the same time.

CHAPTER 7

1. For the Utah War, see MacKinnon, *At Sword's Point*; Bigler and Bagley, *The Mormon Rebellion*; Poll, "The Utah War."
2. For this massacre, basic works are Brooks, *Mountain Meadows Massacre* and *John Doyle Lee*, 199–225; Bagley, *Blood of the Prophets*; Briggs, "The Mountain Meadows Massacre" and "The Tragedy at Mountain Meadows Massacre"; Walker, Turley, and Leonard, *Massacre at Mountain Meadows*. See also chapter 8 (1858), this volume.
3. Dellenbaugh to Charles Kelly, Aug. 16, 1934, in Crampton, "F. S. Dellenbaugh," 242.
4. Alexander, *Brigham Young, the Quorum of the Twelve,* argues that Brigham Young sincerely sought full punishment for Mormons involved in the massacre, but many of Young's actions in the years following the event do not seem to support this perspective. See chapter 8, at June 19, 1858, this volume.
5. Hamblin to Young, March 2, 1857, BYOF, bx 25, fd 17.
6. Arrott, *Sarah Priscilla Leavitt Hamblin,* 33; Corbett, *Jacob Hamblin,* 413.
7. Brigham Young to Jacob Hamblin, April 7, 1857, BYOF (SC 21).

8. See chapter 11 (1860), this volume. Elkins, *Ira Hatch*, 58, with no footnotes, dates the marriage in "mid October 1859."
9. Bleak, "Annals," May 5, 1857, p. 41; Arrington, "The Mormon Cotton Mission," 223; Larson, *I Was Called to Dixie*, 67, and *Red Hills of November*, 14; Alder and Brooks, *A History of Washington County*, 28–29.
10. Arrington, "The Mormon Cotton Mission," 223.
11. Gardner, Autobiography, 13–14.
12. Thales Haskell diary, Oct. 6, 1859.
13. Date from Thales Haskell, "Autobiography," in Smith, "Thales Hastings Haskell," 23.
14. Brooks, *On the Ragged Edge*, 66. Brooks's account, which is semifictionalized and cites no sources, evidently reports Leavitt traditions about the incident.
15. Thales Haskell, "Autobiography," in Smith, "Thales Hastings Haskell," 23.
16. Mary Dart Judd, Autobiography, 15.
17. Juanita Brooks, *On the Ragged Edge*, 67.
18. Brooks, *On the Ragged Edge*, 67.
19. Mary Dart Judd, Autobiography, 16–17.
20. Brooks *On the Ragged Edge*, 68.
21. Thales Haskell, "Autobiography," in Smith, "Thales Hastings Haskell," 23. Isaiah Hamblin had died previously, but his death was somewhat expected.
22. Thales Haskell, "Autobiography," in Smith, "Thales Hastings Haskell," 23.
23. Hamblin, diary, at 79–80. Jacob may not have been in Salt Lake on July 9, the date of a voucher for \$641.50 from Brigham Young (acting as Indian agent) for work he and other missionaries had done the previous year, building dams and irrigation ditches for the Santa Clara Indians. "Voucher No. 1, July 9, 1857," in U.S. Congress. House, *Accounts of Brigham Young*, 77. He possibly picked up the money the next time he was in Salt Lake City.
24. Hamblin, diary, at 80–81.
25. Isaac Haight to Brigham Young, July 25, 1857, BYOF, bx 25, fd 17.
26. Young to Hamblin, August 4, 1857, BYOF (SC 21); reprinted in Brooks, *Mountain Meadows Massacre*, 34–35. See also Young to Rufus Allen, Aug. 4, 1857, and Young to Isaac Haight, Aug. 4, 1857, in Bigler and Bagley, *Innocent Blood*, 103–5.
27. Brooks, *Mountain Meadows Massacre*, 35–40; MacKinnon, *At Sword's Point, Part 1*, 234–37.
28. Church Historian's Office Journal, August 19, 1857 (SC 17).
29. Rachel Lee, diary, August 23, 1857. Allen returned to northern Utah, Ogden, but came back to southern Utah in 1867 to work on the St. George Temple. He died in 1915. "Mormon Battalion Veteran Called Home," *Washington County News* 8, no. 48 (Dec. 16, 1915), 1. For Leavitt and Knight as counselors, Brooks, *On the Ragged Edge*, 72.
30. Carnahan, *Sarah Priscilla Leavitt Hamblin*, 3.
31. We can learn much of Priscilla's personality in her memoirs, written down by a granddaughter; Priscilla's mother also left an autobiography, which communicates clearly that she was a force to be reckoned with, strong-minded and indefatigable, as Priscilla would be. Arrott, *Sarah Priscilla*; Juanita Pulsipher [Brooks], *History of Sarah Sturdevant Leavitt*.
32. Arrott, *Sarah Priscilla*, 25–26.
33. Juanita Brooks, *On the Ragged Edge*, 72, relates the marriage to Hamblin's appointment as president of the Indian Mission, as he would be expected to take a plural wife as a new leader. However, Hamblin's March 2 letter to Brigham Young (see note 5) asked permission to take a plural wife long before he was called as the mission president.
34. Carnahan, *Sarah Priscilla Leavitt Hamblin*, 13–14.
35. Priscilla Hamblin, in Arrott, *Sarah Priscilla*, 26. Kathryn Daynes, *More Wives Than One*, 121, collects examples of men marrying single women, often widows, to give them financial support in pioneer Utah. However, young Priscilla purposefully joins the Hamblin family to help *them.* Furthermore, Rachel suggested the marriage, indicating its origin in the strong ties between the two women. Far from the classic anti-Mormon view of older Mormon men forcing younger wives into unwanted marriages, Hamblin might not have considered proposing to Priscilla without Rachel's initiative. Even

in the Brooks version of the story, Rachel nominated Priscilla as a plural wife "to help some with the chores. She's so full of life and vigor." Brooks, *On the Ragged Edge*, 73.

36. Arrott, *Sarah Priscilla*, 26.
37. Jacob Hamblin and Samuel Knight, testimony, Second Trial of John D. Lee, 1876, Huntington Library.
38. Rachel Hamblin, in Carleton, *Special Report*, 5; Jacob Forney, "Forney's Report," August 1859, quoted in Brooks, *Mountain Meadows Massacre*, 256.
39. George A. Smith, Statement on the Mountain Meadows Massacre, Nov. 1869, MS 1322, bx 11, fd 5 (SC 33).
40. Brooks, *Mountain Meadows Massacre*, 44; Bagley, *Blood of the Prophets*, 106; Walker et al., *Massacre at Mountain Meadows*, 117–18; Historical Department Journal, August 19, 1857, in Bigler and Bagley, *Innocent Blood*, 100.
41. Hamblin, Diaries, 81–82 (1857).
42. Carleton, *Special Report*, 3; LJH, 45; Samuel Knight interview, March 28, 1892, in Turley and Walker, *Mountain Meadows Massacre*, 265–66.
43. For Kanosh, see Lyman, "Chief Kanosh."
44. See chapter 6 (1854–1856), this volume, at November 1855.
45. Dimick Huntington, diary, Sept. 1, 1857; Hamblin diary; Walker et al., *Massacre at Mountain Meadows*, 146.
46. Kenney, *Wilford Woodruff's Journal* (5:88); Journal History, at the date, apparently quoting Woodruff; Historical Department Journal, August 19, 1857, in Bigler and Bagley, *Innocent Blood*, 101. Lyman, *Overland Journey*, 128–29; Bagley, *Blood of the Prophets*, 113; Brooks, *Mountain Meadows Massacre*, 41.
47. Dimick Huntington, diary. This echoes language in Brigham Young's August 4, 1857, letter to Hamblin. For a photograph of the original, see Coates, Review of Bagley, *Blood of the Prophets*, 157.
48. Alexander, Review of Bagley, *Blood of the Prophets*, 168–69.
49. Endowment House Record, film 1,149,514, entry no. 1482, LDS Genealogy Library, Salt Lake City. Thanks to Merlin Compton for checking this.
50. Jacob Hamblin diary, [Sept. 1], 1857, p. "80" [82].
51. Dimick Huntington, Diary, Sept. 10; George A. Smith to William Dame, Sept. 13, 1857, William Dame Papers, MS 2041, CHL, as cited in Walker, et al., *Massacre at Mountain Meadows*, 345; Kenney, *Wilford Woodruff's Journal*, 5:98 (Sept. 16, 1857).
52. Kenney, *Wilford Woodruff's Journal*, 5:75 (Aug. 13, 1857), and 5:109 (Oct. 18, 1857).
53. Jacob Hamblin to Brigham Young, Nov. 13, 1871, BYOF, bx 74, fd 19.
54. Lee said that Samuel Knight and McMurdy drove the wagons with children. Lee, *Mormonism Unveiled*, 243. There is conflicting evidence, Carleton, *Special Report*, 5–6; Bagley, *Blood of the Prophets*, 154.
55. Jacob Hamblin interview, in Carleton, *Special Report*, 3.
56. Brooks, *John Doyle Lee*, 216.
57. Hamblin interview, in Carleton, *Special Report*, 3.
58. Rachel Hamblin interview, in Carleton, *Special Report*, 5; Rebecca Dunlap Evans, "Mountain Meadow Massacre Related by Rebecca Dunlap Evans."
59. Carleton, *Special Report*, 5.
60. Rebecca Dunlap Evans, "Mountain Meadow Massacre Related by Rebecca Dunlap Evans." For another account that incorrectly places Hamblin at the massacre, "'Idaho Bill.' His Story of the Massacre at Mountain Meadows," *Daily [Morning] Call*, San Francisco, May 29, 1877, reproduced at Dale Broadhurst's "Readings in Early Mormon History" website, http://sidneyrigdon.com/dbroadhu/CA/misccalf.htm (accessed Nov. 30, 2010). Idaho Bill claimed falsely to be one of the seventeen child survivors of the massacre.
61. Bagley, *Blood of the Prophets*, 148.
62. For example, Ginn, *The Mormon Mountain Massacre,* 64.
63. In the former group, David Bigler and Will Bagley (with the support of Lee, *Mormonism Unveiled*, 225); those who regard the massacre as primarily a local affair are Juanita Brooks, Ron Walker, Richard Turley and Glen Leonard, and Robert Briggs, though all of these would probably agree that Brigham Young and George A. Smith helped create the psychological environment that made the massacre possible. For the Utah War context for the Mountain Meadows Massacre, see MacKinnon, *At Sword's Point*.
64. Walker et al., *Massacre at Mountain Meadows*, 137–39, 157.

65. Hamblin to Young, Nov. 13, 1871.
66. In LJH, 46, Hamblin says he stayed only a week in Salt Lake City, but this is incorrect. In the second Lee trial, Hamblin estimates that he left Salt Lake City about September 14. "I don't recollect the date, I left the city about the 14th, and came directly there." However, we have seen that the Woodruff diary records Tutsegabits, and probably Hamblin, in Salt Lake City on the sixteenth. In the Carleton report, and his diary, Hamblin says that he arrived at his ranch at Mountain Meadows on September 18. Carleton, *Special Report*, 3.
67. See note 78 below. For the declaration of martial law, Bigler and Bagley, *The Mormon Rebellion*, 148–49. Jesse Smith diary; James Martineau, Journal, Sept. 26, 1857.
68. LJH, 46. Hamblin, Testimony, Second Lee Trial.
69. This is another reason why the "late" dating of Hamblin's trip home must be accepted: Lee journeyed from Harmony to Salt Lake City from September 20 to 29. Rachel Lee diary, Sept. 20, 1857; Brooks, *John Doyle Lee*, 222.
70. LJH, 46. For Lee's story to Hamblin, see also Hamblin's testimony in the second Lee trial. Hamblin told the story of the massacre to army investigator James Henry Carleton in 1859 without any white involvement, Carleton, *Special Report*, 4; however, he knew as early as this that Lee and other whites were involved.
71. Lee, in turn, stated that he had not even had an interview with Hamblin. Brooks, *Mountain Meadows Massacre*, 107.
72. Hamblin to Young, Nov. 13, 1871.
73. Hamblin Testimony, Second Lee Trial.
74. Hamblin to Young, Nov. 13, 1871.
75. Hamblin interview, 1859, in Carleton, *Special Report*, 3.
76. Hamblin Testimony, Second Lee Trial; Hamblin to Young, Nov. 13, 1871.
77. Smith, *Journal of Jesse Nathaniel Smith*, 27.
78. "Military Orders No. 5," Sept. 14, 1857, as cited in Brooks, *Mountain Meadows Massacre*, 106, 121. This includes the notation, "Rec'd Sept. 26/57 fr. Jacob Hamblin." James Martineau, Journal, Sept. 26, 1857.
79. Carleton, *Special Report*, 3.
80. LJH, 46, says he met Knight and Leavitt at Cedar City. Hamblin's 1871 letter to Young also mentions Leavitt and Knight, but at Pinto. Carleton, *Special Report*, 3, says that he met only Leavitt at Pinto Creek. Though some pages are missing at this point, the diary has Hamblin sending more than one person to help the company, presumably Leavitt and Knight, but it mentions only Leavitt coming back and reporting to him.
81. LJH, 46. Other evidence, including Hamblin's own diary, suggests that he sent Leavitt to protect the company but allowed him to drive off cattle.
82. He arrived home on September 29 according to the 1871 letter to Young. However, if he was a day from Parowan on September 25, per the Jesse Smith diary, then reached Parowan on the twenty-sixth and rode to Pinto the same day, a Sept. 27 date seems more likely. Carleton, *Special Report*, 3; diary/reminiscence; LJH, 46.
83. Hamblin interview, in Carleton, *Special Report*, 3.
84. Hamblin Testimony, Second Lee Trial.
85. Hamblin, 1857 diary/reminiscence.
86. Carleton, *Special Report*, 7. This according to some of the child survivors. However, as we have seen, some of the children also testified (incorrectly) that Jacob Hamblin was a participant at the massacre. It is possible that they simply accused people they later came to know.
87. Carleton, *Special Report*, 6–7.
88. For treatments in secondary sources, see Brooks, *Mountain Meadows Massacre*, 121–26; Bagley, *Blood of the Prophets*, 167–68; Bigler and Bagley, *Innocent Blood*, 143–59; Lyman, *The Overland Journey*, 140–41; Turley and Walker, *Mountain Meadows Massacre*, 14, 27, 29, 39, 126–31, and index s.v. Dukes and Turner.
89. Lyman, *The Overland Journey*, 141.
90. "More Outrages on the Plains!! Two Men Wounded!! 320 Head of Cattle Run Off, &C, &C!" *Los Angeles Star* 7.24, Oct. 24, 1857, 2; Lyman, *The Overland Journey*, 140.
91. James Martineau, Journal.

92. Stephen B. Honea, in "More Outrages on the Plains!! Two Men Wounded!! 320 Head of Cattle Run Off, &C, &C!" *Los Angeles Star* 7.24, Oct. 24, 1857, 2. Many of the early California newspaper reports documenting the Dukes-Turner company can be found at Broadhurst, "Readings in Early Mormon History"; see also Bigler and Bagley, *Innocent Blood*, 143–59. The James Martineau journal, Sept. 14, 1857, does not mention payment but makes it sound as if President William Dame sent the guides simply as an act of goodwill.

93. Many sources attest that the road between southern Utah and southern California was notoriously dangerous, and many whites were robbed and killed by Indians there. George Washington Bean, *Autobiography*, 118; "Biography of David Savage," *Daily Journal of Kingston United Order*, CHL, following entry of Dec. 1, 1878, as quoted in Parshall, "'Pursue, Retake and Punish,'" 76.

94. Brooks, *On the Ragged Edge*, 78. As we have seen, some early accounts state that Samuel Knight was with Leavitt, but Knight does not figure in these accounts. Perhaps he played a secondary role.

95. Shirts, "A Report," portrays Nephi Johnson and Ira Hatch as the leaders in the raid. The *L.A. Star* blamed Oscar Hamblin and Ira Hatch. "More Outrages on the Plains!! Two Men Wounded!! 320 Head of Cattle Run Off, &C, &C!" *Los Angeles Star* 7.24, Oct. 24, 1857, 2. See also George Davis, "Letter from San Bernardino," *San Francisco Bulletin* 8:31, Nov. 12, 1857, 2/3; Fish, *Life and Times of Joseph Fish*, 60–61; Brooks, *Mountain Meadows Massacre*, 126; Bagley, *Blood of the Prophets*, 168. For the date, see "The Massacre At Mountain Canon Confirmed–More Indian Outrages, &c," *Daily Alta California*, 9.189, October 27, 1857, p. 1. (Men with news of the robbery of the cattle left the Muddy on October 7 and arrived in San Bernardino on October 17.) For the location of the theft, see the Hamblin diary and Shirts, "A Report."

96. For example, LJH, 46–47. In his earlier diary, he admits, "The missionaries went with the cattle and indians, according to the instructions given br Levett to prevent further out breaks." Hamblin's published autobiography, as usual, smoothes over complexities and edits out problem points. Brooks, *Mountain Meadows Massacre*, 122: "The two accounts are quite typical of the suppressions in Mormon history." And in much of history, one might add! For Leavitt's role in the rustling, see also "More Outrages on the Plains!! Two Men Wounded!! 320 Head of Cattle Run Off, &C, &C!" *Los Angeles Star* 7.24, Oct. 24, 1857, 2. "A man named Lovett, joined us here [on the Virgin River]."

97. Hamblin, diary.

98. BYOF, bx 25, fd 17. Indian agent Jacob Forney wrote, "On my arrival in this Territory [in mid-1858] the Indians were in a feverish excitement, and great energy, and almost incessant traveling among them, and presents, were necessary to calm them down." Jacob Forney to A. B. Greenwood, July 28, 1859, in Buchanan, *Message of the President* (1860), 73.

99. Peterson, *Utah's Black Hawk War*, 114–15; Lyman, *The Overland Journey*, 140.

100. John Aiken, affidavit, Nov. 2, 1857, in "The Late Outrages on the Plains–Further Particulars," *Los Angeles Star* 7.26, Nov. 7, 1857, p. 2.

101. BYOF, bx 25, fd 17.

102. Brigham Young to Jacob Hamblin, March 5, 1858, BYOF (SC 21). See discussion in Brooks, *Mountain Meadows Massacre*, 124. This letter is quoted in LJH, 51–52, with the relevant passage edited out.

103. Jacob Hamblin to Jacob Forney, Dec. 9, 1858, in Jacob Forney, Letterbooks 1857–1859, MS 14278, fd 2, pp. 468–70, CHL; also published in *Kirk Anderson's Valley Tan*, 1.16, Feb. 15, 1859, p. 2.

104. Carleton, *Special Report*, 4.

105. "More Outrages on the Plains!! Two Men Wounded!! 320 Head of Cattle Run Off, &C, &C!" *Los Angeles Star*, Oct. 24, 1857, p. 2.

106. Zadok Judd to George A. Smith, Feb. 10, 1859, in George A. Smith collection, MS 1322, Incoming Correspondence (SC 32). Dudley Leavitt also stated that he helped round up stray cattle to give back to the Dukes-Turner stockowners, Brooks, *On the Ragged Edge*, 78. George F. Hendrix, in his anti-Hamblin letter, also gives a muddled account of the hundred head of cattle, not realizing that Hamblin had been open with Young (and non-Mormons) about controlling the cattle. He accused Hamblin of hiding cattle from Lane's agent. Hendrix to Young, June 23, 1860, BYOF, reprinted in Bigler and Bagley, *Innocent Blood*, 258–61.

107. LJH 47; Carleton, *Special Report*, 4.

108. Bagley, *Blood of the Prophets*, 167.
109. Brooks, *Mountain Meadows Massacre*, 122
110. Lyman, *The Overland Journey*, 140. This might be supported by a Letter by Wm. Webb, Irah Baise, Wm. S. Bledsoe, and Wm. H. Tannehill, Oct. 18, 1857, published in "The late Outrages on the Plains, Another account," *Los Angeles Star* 7.25, Oct. 31, 1857, p. 2. An opposing view appears in "MORE OUTRAGES ON THE PLAINS," p. 2.
111. Lyman, *The Overland Journey*, 140.
112. Hamblin to Young, Oct. 14, 1857, BYOF, bx 25, fd 17.
113. Hamblin to Young, December 26, 1857, BYOF, bx 25, fd 17. Cf. Amasa Lyman, diary, April 16, 1858, "they are a fine looking race of men." For an introduction to the Mohaves, see Kroeber, *Handbook of Indians of California*, 726–80, and Kroeber, *Mohave Indians*.
114. Bean, "George W. Bean," 103. For Mohave agriculture, see Kroeber, *Mohave Indians*, 21. In the Las Vegas Indian mission, see below, the missionaries had met some Mohaves and baptized three of them. Still, they were reputed to be very hostile to whites. Woods, *A Gamble in the Desert*, 149–50.
115. Kroeber, *Handbook of Indians of California*, 754.
116. The Leavitt-Hatch mission to the Mohaves is discussed later in this chapter; also Smith, "Colorado River Exploration and the Mormon War," 212.
117. Hamblin, diary.
118. Rachel Lee, diary. About a week later, on November 3, Brigham Young (as Indian agent) paid Hamblin $370 for two yoke of cattle, two cows, a wagon, and two chains, which Jacob had given to the Santa Clara Paiutes in early August. "Voucher No. 5," U.S. Congress. House, *Accounts of Brigham Young*, 99. Apparently Jacob was not physically present in Salt Lake City when Young made this payment.
119. Hamblin's diary seems to portray the whole company at Pinto.
120. Hamblin, diary. See also Brigham Young to Isaac Haight, Nov. 2, 1857 (SC 21); Isaac Haight, Journal, Nov. 1857; LJH, 47 (who tells the story differently); Brooks, *Mountain Meadows Massacre*, 127.
121. For this company, see the Hamblin diaries, pp. 43–51; LJH, 47–51; Lyman, *Overland Journey*, 144–47; Brooks, *Mountain Meadows Massacre*, 127–31; Bagley, *Blood of the Prophets*, 183–84. Date from John I. Ginn to Kirk Anderson, March 26, 1859, in *The Valley Tan* 1, no. 26, April 26, 1859, p. 2. This letter is mainly focused on the Aiken murders (discussed later in this chapter) but does mention the Bell company in passing. For the number in the company, see MacKinnon, "'Unquestionably Authentic and Correct,'" 337.
122. Ginn, "Mormon and Indian Wars," USHS.
123. Brooks, *Mountain Meadows Massacre*, 127–28.
124. For the Aiken murders, see Bigler, "The Aiken Party Executions"; Schindler, *Orrin Porter Rockwell*, 268–81; MacKinnon, *At Sword's Point, Part 1*, 316–17. Incidentally, the November 25 and 28 dates for the Aiken murders are also a problem for Ginn; why would the party take this long to get from Salt Lake City to Nephi? Unfortunately, Charles Kelly and Hoffman Birney, *Holy Murder*, 173, accept Ginn uncritically and portray Hamblin traveling with the Bell company starting in Salt Lake. They make the sweeping assertion, "There can be no doubt whatever but that Hamblin was fully aware of the nature of the event scheduled to take place at that ford [the Aiken murder]." Actually, neither Hamblin nor the Bell company were anywhere near the Aiken incident.
125. Hamblin reports first being contacted by the Bell party in southern Utah. The Haight diary, a contemporary source, bears this out.
126. McKinnon, "'Unquestionably Authentic and Correct.'"
127. This was a suggestion of Brigham Young; see his Nov. 2, 1857, letter to Haight. Ginn confirms Tutsegabits's enlistment, "Mormon and Indian Wars," 37, but he states that the chief stayed in Utah and sent a "Chief Jackson" to accompany the group into modern Nevada. Ginn, "Mormon and Indian Wars," 50.
128. Hamblin, 1857 diary.
129. LJH, 48.
130. Hamblin, diary. Ginn, "Mormon and Indian Wars," 49, states that at this time "we had about 150 Indians with us" and confirms that they were in a dangerous mood. Little reports only "a few Indians," LJH, 48.
131. Jacob Hamblin diary, MS 14654, CHL, [Sept.–Oct. 1857], p. 43.

132. Ginn, "Mormon and Indian Wars," 50.
133. Hamblin, diary; LJH, 49.
134. Ginn, "Mormon and Indian Wars," 50.
135. LJH, 49.
136. Ginn, "Mormon and Indians Wars," 50.
137. Dialogue from LJH, 49.
138. LJH, 49. The Hamblin diary does not record this early morning meeting.
139. Lyman tentatively identifies Isaac as Chief Tosho of the Virgin River Paiutes, *The Overland Journey*, 183. Hamblin visited a prominent Indian named Thomas in Nevada in 1864; see chapter 16 (1864), this volume, at Nov. 27. He was "Chief of the Indians at the narrows on the Muddy," Bleak, "Annals," 235 (June 4, 1866). Reeve locates him at the Beaver Dam Wash, *Making Space*, 65. Isaac and Thomas had been baptized Mormons during the Las Vegas Mission in 1855 and 1856, hence their Western, biblical names. George Washington Bean, *Autobiography*, 118. Bean describes Thomas as "hostile" in late 1855, and threatening to kill a group of missionaries. Ibid., 122–23.
140. Ginn, "Mormon and Indians Wars," 50–51.
141. Perry Liston, Journal, 1857, USHS, as cited in Brooks, *Mountain Meadows Massacre*, 132. Liston described their mission in this way: "We labored to get the Indians to cease killing the Americans." Hamblin's diary records the opposite. See also William Clark, "A Trip Across the Plains," 217–18. Ginn, "Mormon and Indians Wars," 50–51, confirms that there were two Mormon missionaries with the Indians. See also Brooks, *Mountain Meadows Massacre*, 132, 134; Lyman, *Overland Journey*, 142. Frederick Dellenbaugh, in a letter to Charles Kelly, Aug. 16, 1934 (Crampton, "F. S. Dellenbaugh," 243), remembers Hamblin telling him of a St. George man named Liston desiring to kill a solitary man in the desert, and Hamblin defending the solitary man.
142. Hamblin, diary. This incident is not in Little.
143. Hamblin to Young, Dec. 26, 1857.
144. Hamblin, diary.
145. "Mormon and Indians Wars," 51.
146. Jacob Hamblin diary, [Sept.–Oct. 1857], p. 45.
147. For the early Mormon settlement of Las Vegas, see Dees, "The Journal of George W. Bean"; George Washington Bean, *Autobiography*, 118–26; Jenson, "History of Las Vegas Mission"; Bean, "George W. Bean"; O'Neil, "The Mormons, the Indians"; Lyman, The *Overland Journey*, 115–20; Woods, *A Gamble in the Desert*; Dumke, "Mission to Mining Town."
148. Hamblin, diary. See also LJH, 50; Brooks, *On the Ragged Edge*, 81.
149. "Mormon and Indians Wars," 54.
150. For Hatch and Leavitt among the Mohaves, see Hamblin to Young, Dec. 26, 1857, the Hamblin diaries, LJH, and Dudley Leavitt's reminiscences.
151. Hamblin to Young, Dec. 26, 1857.
152. For Mohave-Chemehuevi relations, which soon became antagonistic, see Stewart, "Mohave Warfare," 258. According to a modern Mohave oral tradition that Stewart reports here, one of the main battles with the Chemehuevi occurred in 1867 when the Mormons in Nevada paid the Chemehuevi to abduct Mohave women for them–not a credible accusation, but it shows the Mormons' reputation. For the Chemehuevi, see Manners, *Paiute Indians I*; Stewart, "A Brief History of the Chemehuevi Indians."
153. Hamblin, diary, 46.
154. Hamblin to Young, Dec. 26, 1857.
155. Possibly September 1, 1857; see C. Kroeber, "The Mohave as Nationalist," 174n10.
156. Stewart, "The Aboriginal Territory of the Mohave Indians," 262; Russell, "Pima Annals," 78–79, and *The Pima Indians*, 47–48; C. Kroeber, "The Mohave as Nationalist," 174; Kroeber, *Mohave Indians*, 230.
157. C. Kroeber, "The Mohave as Nationalist," 174.
158. Ibid., 175.
159. Hamblin to Young, March 2, 1857, BYOF, bx 25, fd 17.
160. Hamblin, diary, 46; Hamblin to Young, Dec. 26, 1857.
161. Hamblin, diary, 46.

162. Ibid., 47.
163. Hamblin to Young, Dec. 26, 1857.
164. Chanawanse, in LJH, 50. Amasa Lyman and his party (including Ira Hatch) met an impressive war leader named "Oat-sen-a-wants" soon after this, Amasa Lyman diary, Apr. 17, 1858 (SC 37), who may be the same person.
165. Hamblin, diary, 48.
166. Brooks, *On the Ragged Edge*, 81.
167. Amasa Lyman diary, April 13, 1858 (SC 37).
168. Jacob Hamblin diary, [Sept.–Oct. 1857], p. 48.
169. Hamblin, diary, 49.
170. Ibid., 49–50.
171. Ginn, "Mormon and Indians Wars," 59.
172. Hamblin to Young, Dec. 26, 1857.
173. Hamblin, diary, 50.
174. Hamblin, diary, 51; James Little and Ira Hatch, "Mission to the Muddy in 1858," *The Deseret News*, June 8, 1870, p. 2.
175. LJH, 51.
176. Hamblin, diary, 55–56.
177. See Hamblin's own near-death experience in chapter 11 (summer 1860), this volume.
178. Arrott, *Sarah Priscilla*, 28.
179. Corbett, *Jacob Hamblin*, 231.
180. Haskell, Autobiography, in Smith, "Thales Hastings Haskell."
181. Brooks, *On the Ragged Edge*, 63–64.
182. Arrott, *Sarah Priscilla*, 39.
183. Jeffrey, *Frontier Women*, 72–73.
184. Brooks, "Indian Relations," 42. Corbett states that a girl named Fanny was Rachel's "personal maid" and Ellen was Priscilla's. Corbett, *Jacob Hamblin*, 227.
185. George W. Armstrong, Indian agent, letter to Brigham Young, June 30, 1857, in ARCIA (1858), p. 597. Brooks, "Indian Relations," 41.
186. Arrott, *Sarah Priscilla*, 35–36 (calling the child Emily); Brooks, "Indian Relations," 41–42; Corbett, *Jacob Hamblin*, 235.
187. Brooks, "Indian Relations," 41–42.

CHAPTER 8

1. Jacob Hamblin to Brigham Young, Dec. 26, 1857, BYOF, bx 25, fd 17.
2. Jacob Hamblin to Brigham Young, Feb. 14, 1858, BYOF, bx 26, fd. 10.
3. Ives, *Report*, 21. For further on the Ives expeditions, see Schubert, *Vanguard of Expansion;* Smith, "Before Powell," "Colorado River Exploration," and "Mormon Exploration"; Dellenbaugh, *The Romance of the Colorado River*, 156–83; Woodward, *Feud on the Colorado;* Goetzmann, *Army Exploration*, 375, 381–89; Stout, *Search for Sanctuary*, 40–43; MacKinnon, "Epilogue to the Utah War," 242, and *At Sword's Point, Part 1*, 425–26.
4. Woodward, *Feud on the Colorado*, Dellenbaugh, *The Romance of the Colorado River*, 156–83.
5. Andrew A. Humphreys to Joseph C. Ives, Nov. 18, 1857, as quoted in MacKinnon, *At Sword's Point, Part 1*, 425–26. See also, Lyman, *Amasa Mason Lyman*, 258.
6. Ives, *Report*, 36.
7. Ibid., 81.
8. Ibid., 87.
9. Amasa Lyman diary, cf. Smith, "Colorado River Exploration," 215. Louisa Barnes Pratt also documents a "Bro' Hamlin," probably Jacob, on his way to the lead mines southwest of Las Vegas in January 1858. He helped this small company (led by Nathan Tenney, father of Ammon Tenney, later a close Hamblin associate) by sending a message to William Crosby, a former San Bernardino bishop, in Santa Clara via

Indian runner. The Tenney company was victimized by Indian thefts, but were also helped and protected by other Paiutes, notably the headman Isaac (possibly Tosho) on the Virgin River. Pratt, *The History of Louisa Barnes Pratt*, 265–67; Lyman, *The Overland Journey*, 183.

10. Amasa Lyman to Brigham Young, January 17, 1858, as quoted in Smith, "Colorado River Exploration," 215.
11. Amasa Lyman diary, cf. Smith, "Colorado River Exploration," 215.
12. Lyman, *Amasa Mason Lyman*, 261.
13. Amasa Lyman diary.
14. Brigham Young to Jacob Hamblin, March 5, 1858, BYOF.
15. Amasa Lyman diary; Smith, "Colorado River Exploration," 215–16.
16. Castetter and Bell, *Yuman Indian Agriculture*, 51; Woodward, *Feud on the Colorado*, 21–29, 46–50.
17. The word is difficult to read, but other sources record a Benjamin Hulse living at the Vegas Fort at that time. Lyman, *Overland Journey*, 182; Knell, "Pinto," 215–16; Woods, *A Gamble in the Desert*, 190.
18. Hamblin's diary, 51–54 (March 6–19, 1858, quite retrospective, though probably worked up from a diary, since it has some dates); LJH, 52–53, and a Thales Haskell autobiography. For Ives's version of the story, see his *Report,* 88–89. The diary of Balduin Möllhausen, the Ives Expedition artist, is discussed in Miller, "The Ives Expedition Revisited: A Prussian's Impressions," and "The Ives Expedition Revisited: Overland."
19. For Patsarump, also known as Joshua, see the George W. Bean diary, Jan. 17 and 26, 1856 (Dees 20–21); Woods, *A Gamble in the Desert*, 215.
20. Jacob Hamblin diary, March 16, 1858, p. 51.
21. Ibid., p. 52.
22. Hamblin, diary. Little has Ives delivering a much more bellicose message to Haskell: the Ives company "exhibited very hostile feelings against our people" and Ives stated "that the expedition had been sent out by the government to examine the river, and learn if a force could be taken into Southern Utah from that direction, should it be needed, to subjugate the 'Mormons.'" LJH, 53. Hamblin's earlier account is preferable; Ives would have hardly tipped his hand this much, even if he had been taken in by Haskell's story.
23. Ives, *Report*, 88.
24. Quoted in Smith, "Thales Hastings Haskell."
25. See also Miller, "The Ives Expedition Revisited: A Prussian's Impressions," 18–21. Balduin Möllhausen, the Ives Expedition artist, seriously felt that their group was in danger of being massacred by local Indians incited by Mormons.
26. This, and following quotes, are from Jacob Hamblin diary, March 18, 1858, pp. 54–55.
27. LJH, 53.
28. "A Brief History of Lieut. Ives' Exploration of the Colorado," *Deseret News* 8:20, July 21, 1858, p. 90.
29. Ives, *Report,* 89.
30. See Miller, "The Ives Expedition Revisited: Overland"; for Hispanic explorers, Crampton, *Land of Living Rock*, 69–76.
31. Lyman, *Overland Journey*, 118–20; Woods, *A Gamble in the Desert*, 151–76.
32. LJH, 54.
33. Brooks, *On the Ragged Edge*, 83.
34. LJH, 55.
35. Ibid., 56.
36. Amasa Lyman Diary; Amasa Lyman to Brigham Young, March 31, 1858, as cited in Smith, "Colorado River Exploration," 221; Lyman, *Amasa Mason Lyman*, 265.
37. Amasa Lyman Diary; Smith, "Colorado River Exploration," 221–22; Lyman, *Overland Journey*, 150; Lyman, *Amasa Mason Lyman*, 269.
38. For Lyman's journey, see Lyman, *Amasa Mason Lyman*, 266–68.
39. Young, *Memoirs of John R. Young*, 110.
40. Jacob Hamblin, testimony, Second Lee Trial, San Marino, Huntington Library.
41. LJH, 56.

42. See Kenney, *Wilford Woodruff's Journal*, 5:102–3 (Sept. 29, 1857). Lee, in a retrospective account, stated that he did tell Young the full story on September 29. *Mormonism Unveiled*, 252. However, the Woodruff evidence is more primary than Lee's later account. Bigler and Bagley feel that Woodruff's journal entry was somehow falsified, *Innocent Blood*, 135–38, but it is hard to prove such a falsification. I believe Lee was entirely capable of lying to hide Mormon culpability in the massacre, especially his own.
43. "Jacob Hamblin, called and had conversation with G. A. S. in regard to the Santa Clara Indians gave and [an] account of the Massacre at Mountain meadows." Church Historian's Office Journal, June 19, 1858 (SC 17). He probably spoke with Young in the same meeting or soon thereafter. Jacob may have also visited Salt Lake City in early November 1857 (see chapter seven), but this is unlikely.
44. Jacob Hamblin, Testimony, Second Lee Trial.
45. LJH, 57.
46. Ibid.
47. Alexander, *Brigham Young, the Quorum of the Twelve*. See later in this chapter at August.
48. Lee diary, 1:314 (May 31[30], 1861), and Kenney, *Wilford Woodruff's Journal*, 5:577 (May 25, 1861); see discussion in Alexander, *Brigham Young, the Quorum of the Twelve*, 24.
49. Juanita Brooks, for example, whose grandfather, Dudley Leavitt, was present at the massacre, grew up believing that the Mountain Meadows Massacre was perpetrated by Indians. Brooks, *Quicksand and Cactus*, 229.
50. Jacob Forney to Charles E. Mix, Aug. 4, 1858, in Jacob Forney, Letterbooks 1857–1859, fd 2, p. 311. For Forney, see Morgan, "The Administration of Indian Affairs," 406–8.
51. LJH, 57.
52. "Report of J Hamblin," June 22, 1858, in Jacob Forney, Letterbooks 1857–1859, fd 2, p. 292.
53. Jacob Forney to James Denver, Jan. 28, 1859, in Buchanan, *Message of the President* (1860), 48.
54. Jacob Forney to Charles E. Mix, June 22, 1858, in Jacob Forney, Letterbooks 1857–1859, fd 2, p. 292. Also in Buchanan, *Message of the President* (1860), 44. Affidavit of James Lynch, July 27, 1859, in Buchanan, *Message of the President* (1860), 81–84, 82–83, reprinted in Brooks, *Mountain Meadows Massacre*, 279–84.
55. Jacob Forney, To Whom It May Concern, Aug. 4, 1858, in Jacob Forney, Letterbooks 1857–1859, fd 2, p. 311.
56. Jacob Forney to A. B. Greenwood, July 25, 1859, in Buchanan, *Message of the President* (1860), 71.
57. Affidavit of James Lynch, July 27, 1859, 82.
58. Forney to Hamblin on August 4, 1858, Jacob Forney, Letterbooks 1857–1859, fd 2, p. 199–200, CHL; see also Brooks, *Mountain Meadows Massacre*, 172. A day before this, Brigham Young had written to William Dame and Isaac Haight asking them to have Jacob gather the children "that were saved from the Indian Masacre at Mountain meadows last fall" and give them to Forney. Brigham Young to Dame and Haight, Aug. 3, 1858, BYOF (SC 21), discussion in Bigler and Bagley, *Innocent Blood*, 239.
59. For example, his Sept. 10, 1858, letter to George A. Smith and his December 9, 1858, letter to Jacob Forney.
60. E.g., Brooks, *Mountain Meadows Massacre*, 102–3, 173. "Jacob Hamblin knew well that no child had ever been in the hands of the Indians."
61. Lee, diary, 1:178–80 (Aug. 3–6, 1858); Brooks, *Mountain Meadows Massacre*, 162–70; Bagley, *Blood of the Prophets*, 212–14; Alexander, *Brigham Young, the Quorum of the Twelve*, 11. Lyman, a junior apostle, apparently followed George A. Smith's lead during this journey, but his biographer suspects that he had reservations about how Smith carried out his investigation, Lyman, *Amasa Mason Lyman*, 273–74.
62. Both conveniently available in Brooks, *Mountain Meadows Massacre*, 242–48. The August 17 report can be found at "History of Brigham Young," CR 100 102, vol. 28, entry for Aug. 17, 1858, pp. 929–37 (SC 3), and at Journal History at Sept. 11, 1857.
63. Alexander, *Brigham Young, the Quorum of the Twelve*, 12.
64. Ibid., 21–22.
65. Cleland and Brooks, *A Mormon Chronicle*, 2:4, 8.
66. Brooks, *Mountain Meadows Massacre*, 165, 170.
67. Brigham Young to Thomas L. Kane, Dec. 15, 1869, CHL, as quoted in Bigler and Bagley, *Innocent Blood*, 229, 469. Young again protested to Kane that Mormons had desired a full trial in a court of law but had been blocked by the federal legal system.

68. Jacob Forney to Charles E. Mix, Aug. 6, 1858, Jacob Forney, Letterbooks 1857–1859, fd 2, pp. 195–97.
69. Jacob Forney to Jacob Hamblin, Aug. 4, 1858, Jacob Forney, Letterbooks 1857–1859, fd 2, pp. 199–200. This letter is dated one day before Jacob arrived in the city.
70. Jacob Forney, To Whom It May Concern, Aug. 4, 1858, in Jacob Forney, Letterbooks 1857–1859, fd 2, p. 311.
71. Report by Thales Haskell, Aug. 29, 1858, in Journal History, Aug. 28, 1858. Also Thales Haskell to George A. Smith, October 6, 1858, George A. Smith collection, CHL (SC 32); Bleak, "Annals," 33 (summer 1856).
72. Lee, diary, 1:149 (Feb. 10–11, 1858). See Seegmiller, "Ghost Towns," 121–22; Harriet Arrington, "Fifty Years Building Utah," 443–44. Tonaquint, at the Santa Clara/Virgin confluence, had been settled in about 1856. Seegmiller, "Ghost Towns," 126. Neither of these towns survived, largely because of flooding.
73. Bleak, "Annals," 40 (Dec. 2, 1856).
74. Hamblin to Forney, Sept. 9, 1858, Jacob Forney, Letterbooks, fd 2, pp. 358–59, CHL.
75. See also Jacob's letter to George A. Smith, Sept. 10, 1858, discussed later in this chapter.
76. Hamblin to George A. Smith, Aug. 29, 1858, George A. Smith collection, MS 1322, bx 5, fd 15 (SC 32).
77. Kelly and Fowler, "Southern Paiute," 380.
78. Smith wrote back to Hamblin, counseling him that the Paiutes should be strongly taught not to kill, but they should not be punished further. Smith to Hamblin, Sept. 22, 1858, Historian's Office Letterpress Copybooks, CR 100 38. Discussion in Lyman, *Amasa Mason Lyman*, 274.
79. Jacob Hamblin to George A. Smith, Aug. 29, 1858.
80. Jacob Hamblin to George A. Smith, Sept. 10, 1858, George A. Smith collection, MS 1322, bx 5, fd 15 (SC 32). Jacob also describes this incident in the September 9 letter to Forney.
81. Jacob Hamblin to George A. Smith, Sept. 10, 1858. Often the Oraibis were viewed as separate from the other Hopis in the second or third mesas, which explains why both "Orabes" and "Moquich" are listed.
82. Ben would marry Della Brown on July 10, 1891, with whom he had seven children (one adopted). He was a rancher in Kanab, Utah, throughout his life and died there on September 27, 1930. Death certificate, copy in author's possession; "Son of Jacob Hamblin Laid to Rest," *Kane County Standard*, Oct. 3, 1930, p. 1.
83. Olive would marry Abraham L. Winsor on November 19, 1876, with whom she had seven children. She died on June 30, 1919, in Safford, Arizona. Death certificate in author's possession.

CHAPTER 9

1. Warner, *The Domínguez-Escalante Journal*; Hafen and Armijo, "Armijo's Journal," 95, at Dec. 6, 1829. For explorers of the Colorado before Powell, see Smith, "Before Powell."
2. "Account of Travels in S. Utah and Ariz."
3. Secondary treatments: Stegner, *Mormon Country*, 145–53; Brooks, *On the Ragged Edge*, 86–89, and "The Arizona Strip"; Reilly, *Lee's Ferry*, 3–5; McClintock, *Mormon Settlement in Arizona*, 63–64; Birney, *Zealots of Zion*, 114–20; James, *Pages from Hopi History*, 86–88; Clemmer, *Roads in the Sky*, 40–42.
4. LJH, 58.
5. Tenney, "Account of Travels." See also "Early Recollections of My Youth."
6. Jacob Hamblin to Jacob Forney, December 9, 1858, Jacob Forney Letterbooks, MS 14278, fd 2, pp. 468–70, CHL. See also Forney to Hamblin, August 4, 1858, in ibid., p. 311.
7. Brooks, *Mountain Meadows Massacre*, 102–3.
8. Ibid., 102, 173; see also Peterson, "The Hopis and the Mormons," 180–81.
9. Tenney, "Early Recollections," 3–4. For Brigham considering different parts of the West as places of retreat, MacKinnon, *At Sword's Point, Part 1*, 440; Stout, *Search for Sanctuary*.
10. Tenney, "Account of Travels"; "Early Recollections," 4. For Mormon interest in this theory, see Dennis, "Captain Dan Jones"; Stegner, *Mormon Country*, 145–53. More generally, Williams, *Madoc: The Making of a Myth*. One Mormon missionary from Wales, Llewellyn Harris, later reported that he did find Welsh words among the Zuni! McClintock, *Mormon Settlement in Arizona*, 64–65.
11. See Dennis, "Captain Dan Jones"; Smart and Smart, *Over the Rim*, 124–26, 227–28; Peterson, "The Hopis and the Mormons," 188.
12. "Minutes of a special conference held by the missionaries of Santa Clara," September 26, 1858, in Journal History.

13. For Tenney, see Smiley, "Ammon M. Tenney: Mormon Missionary," and "Ammon M. Tenney: His Life."
14. Tenney, "Early Recollections," 6.
15. Ibid., 5.
16. Jacob Hamblin to Brigham Young, December 18, 1858, BYOF, bx 26, fd 10.
17. The earliest, best listings of the expedition are the September 26 minutes and Hamblin's December 1858 letter to Young, though no one list is perfect. Incomplete listings are in LJH, 59; Bleak, "Annals"; McClintock, *Mormon Settlement*, 64; and Stegner, *Mormon Country*, 145.
18. Hamblin to Young, Dec. 18, 1858; Tenney, "Account of Travels"; Hamblin to Forney, Dec. 9, 1858.
19. Hamblin to Young, December 18, 1858. According to John Wesley Powell, the Paiute name was Yellow Rock Spring, *Exploration of the Colorado River*, 112, but this is probably incorrect. McKoy, *Cultures At a Crossroad*, ch. 1, at fn 102. For Pipe Spring see Lavender, *Pipe Spring and the Arizona Strip*; Olsen, Jr., "Pipe Spring, Arizona" and "Winsor Castle."
20. "Account of Travels." See also Tenney's "Early Recollections," 6. By fall 1859, Thales Haskell was already referring to the place as Pipe Spring. See his diary, October 18, 1859. Bill Hamblin had gained the nickname Gunlock while crossing the plains, as he frequently cleaned his gun and also cleaned guns for friends and family. Jeremiah Leavitt, Autobiography. Gunlock, Utah, north of Santa Clara, was named after William Hamblin.
21. LJH, 59.
22. Andrew Smith Gibbons Diary, Dec. 18, 1858.
23. LJH, 59.
24. Ibid.
25. Reilly, "Roads across the Buckskin Mountain," 380.
26. Tenney, "Early Recollections," 6.
27. Ibid.
28. Reilly, "Roads across Buckskin Mountain," 382, 386.
29. Tenney, "Early Recollections," 7.
30. Ibid.
31. LJH, 60.
32. Warner, *The Domínguez-Escalante Journal*, 115.
33. Ibid., 116–20.
34. Ibid., November 3, 1776, at p. 116; Hamblin to Young, Dec. 18, 1858.
35. Andrew Gibbons Diary, Dec. 15, 1858.
36. Crampton, *Historical Sites in Glen Canyon*, 6–7, 13. Some ascribe these notches to the 1776 party, others to the Hamblin expeditions. Linford, *Navajo Places*, 289.
37. Stegner, *Beyond the Hundredth Meridian*, 92–93. For this site, see also Frazier, "El Vado de los Padres"; Briggs, *Without Noise of Arms*, 146–47; Topping, "Charles Kelly's Glen Canyon Ventures," 129–30; Crampton, *Ghosts of Glen Canyon*, 28–38.
38. Hamblin to Young, Dec. 18, 1858.
39. Tenney, "Early Recollections," 7.
40. Crampton, *Historical Sites in Glen Canyon*, 9.
41. Ammon Tenney, Autobiography, quoted in Smiley, "Ammon M. Tenney: His Life," 18. See also McClintock, third interview with Ammon Tenney, 5–6.
42. Warner, *The Domínguez-Escalante Journal*, 119–20.
43. Ibid., 125.
44. Ibid.
45. Ibid., 125–26.
46. Tenney, "Early Recollections," 7.
47. Thanks to Kenneth Beesley for his geographical reconstructions of this route.
48. Hamblin to Young, Dec. 18, 1858.
49. Ibid.
50. Tenney, "Early Recollections," 7.
51. James, *Pages from Hopi History*, 14, 86.
52. Hamblin to Young, Dec. 18, 1858.

53. LJH, 60.
54. For the Hopis, see Waters, *The Book of the Hopi*; Whiteley, *Deliberate Acts*; Peterson, "The Hopis and the Mormons."
55. Hamblin to Young, Dec. 18, 1858.
56. Tenney, "Early Recollections," 7.
57. Hamblin to Young, Dec. 18, 1858; LJH, 61.
58. Tenney, "Early Recollections," 7.
59. LJH, 61.
60. Hamblin to Young, Dec. 18, 1858; LJH, 61.
61. Robinson, *The Diaries of John Gregory Bourke*, Oct. 14, 1874, at p. 86; Andrew Gibbons diary, Nov. 22–23, 1858; Kelly, "Journal of Walter Clement Powell," 466, at Oct. 30, 1872.
62. Hamblin to Young, Dec. 18, 1858.
63. Hamblin to Forney, Dec. 9, 1858.
64. Hamblin to Young, Dec. 18, 1858.
65. Ibid.; Hamblin to Forney, Dec. 9, 1858.
66. LJH, 62.
67. Geertz, *The Invention of Prophecy*; Whiteley, *Deliberate Acts*, 270–71; Courlander, *The Fourth World of the Hopis*, 31; Waters, *The Book of the Hopi*, 252; Nequatewa, *Truth of a Hopi*, 30, 48, 130–31n19; Peterson, *Native American Prophecies*, 231–62; Kotchongva, "Where Is the White Brother."
68. LJH, 63. For the Hopi ban on river-crossing, Waters, *Book of the Hopi*, 32–33.
69. LJH, 63–64.
70. Geertz, *The Invention of Prophecy*, 422–40. See also Whiteley, *Deliberate Acts*, 329, and Clemmer, "'Then Will You Rise.'"
71. Whiteley, *Deliberate Acts*, 329n8.
72. As Whiteley notes, *Deliberate Acts*, 329n8: "this version has some different twists."
73. Clemmer, "'Then Will You Rise,'" 38, 43, cites one early mention of Pahana coming from the west.
74. Talayesva, Simmons, and Hine, *Sun Chief*, 88.
75. Courlander, *The Fourth World of the Hopis*, 31.
76. Beadle, *The Undeveloped West*, 585.
77. Kenney, *Wilford Woodruff's Journal*, 6:97.
78. Jacob Hamblin to Brigham Young, May 18, 1863, BYOF, bx 29, fd 9 (not in Jacob's handwriting).
79. See Parmentier, "The Mythological Triangle."
80. Book of Mormon 3 Nephi 28:4–31; Hand, "The Three Nephites"; Fife, "The Legend of the Three Nephites"; Lee, *The Three Nephites*.
81. He told Martha Cox that "the Three Nephites mentioned in the B.M. [Book of Mormon] were his personal directors. When one of them appeared and told him he was needed with some distant or near Indian tribe it became his duty to lay everything aside and go out immediately." Cox, "Biographical Sketch," 103. This is one more example of Hamblin's arrestingly literal Latter-day Saint mysticism.
82. Hamblin, 1858 letter to Young.
83. McNitt, *Navajo Wars*, 342–57.
84. For introductions to the Navajos, see Iverson, *Diné: A History of the Navajos*; Locke, *The Book of the Navajo*; Correll, *Through White Men's Eyes*; Roessel, "Navajo History, 1850–1923." For Mormons and Navajos, Christensen, "Some Experiences Among the Indians" and "Among the Navajos"; Brown, "Navajo Cunning"; Correll, "Navajo Frontiers in Utah"; Lyon, "The Navajos in the Anglo-American Imagination"; McPherson, *Navajo Land, Navajo Culture* and *The Northern Navajo Frontier*; Pavlik, "Of Saints and Lamanites"; Shepardson and Hammond, *The Navajo Mountain Community*; Evans, *Along Navajo Trails*; Flake, "A History of Mormon Missionary Work"; Smallcanyon, "Contested Space."
85. Reichard, *Navaho Religion*.
86. Locke, *The Book of the Navajo*, 58–139; Maryboy and Begay, "The Navajos of Utah," 267–71.
87. Tenney, "Early Recollections," 8.
88. Donaldson, *Moqui Pueblo Indians*, 14–15, 28; Conrad, "The Whipple Expedition," 157; W. B. Truax, Hopi Indian Agent, to E. P. Smith, Aug. 31, 1875, in *Annual Report of the Commissioner of Indian Affairs . . . 1875*,

211 (two-thirds of the Hopi population was decimated by smallpox); Ellis, *The Hopi*, 4 (32). According to Clemmer, "'Then Will You Rise,'" 53, the Hopis also experienced a smallpox epidemic in 1857.

89. Date from Hamblin, Dec. 18, 1858, letter to Young; Andrew Gibbons diary.
90. Tenney, "Early Recollections," 8.
91. LJH, 62.
92. Hamblin to Young, Dec. 18, 1858; Tenney, "Early Recollections," 9.
93. Hamblin to Young, Dec. 18, 1858.
94. Tenney, "Early Recollections," 9.
95. Tenney, "Account of Travels." Tenney, "Early Recollections," 9, adds that one of the guards secretly ate some of the badger and was sick that day.
96. Tenney, "Early Recollections," 9, and "Account of Travels." See also James Bleak diary, March 19, 1864. Hamblin, on the other hand, later stated that the name Soap Creek came from an attempt to boil beans and pork. Horatio Morrill diary, Oct. 8, 1869; Brigham Young Jr. diaries, May 23, 1876.
97. Tenney, "Account of Travels."
98. Hamblin to Young, Dec. 18, 1858.
99. Tenney, "Early Recollections," 10.
100. McClintock, third interview with Ammon Tenney.
101. LJH, 63; Tenney, "Account of Travels."
102. McClintock, third interview with Ammon Tenney.
103. Hamblin to Young, Dec. 18, 1858.
104. Brooks, *On the Ragged Edge*, 88–89; Alonzo Leavitt, Interview with Selena Leavitt concerning Dudley Leavitt, July 24, 1933. Hamblin and Tenney tell the story differently, suggesting that the horse was selected by the group because it was in the best condition. Hamblin to Young, Dec. 18, 1858; Tenney, "Account of Travels."
105. Hamblin to Young, Dec. 18, 1858.
106. Ibid., cf. the 1858 letter to Forney.
107. Our only source for this journey is the Andrew Smith Gibbons diary, Dec. 8 to 26, 1858.
108. For example, in Froeschauer-Nelson, *Cultural Landscape Report*, figure 8, a map showing important early exploration routes in northern Arizona includes Ives (1858) and Powell (1869), but Hamblin (1858) is ignored.

CHAPTER 10

1. George A. Smith to John Bernhisel, January 7, 1859, in *Journal History*; Zadok Judd to George A. Smith, Feb. 10, 1859, in George A. Smith collection (SC 32).
2. Zadok Knapp Judd Jr., Memoirs.
3. Zadok Judd to George A. Smith, Feb. 10, 1859. For early Santa Clara, see also Zadok Judd, "Reminiscence on the Settlement."
4. Amasa Lyman, "Southern Utah," Letter to the Editor, April 14, 1859, *Deseret News* 9.7, April 20, 1859, p. 8; "President Young's Visit South," *Deseret News* 11.15, June 12, 1861, p. 4.
5. Zadok Knapp Judd, Autobiography.
6. Mary Dart Judd, Autobiography, 5.
7. Ibid., 6. The last word is uncertain.
8. Ibid.; Zadok Judd, in Bleak, "Annals," 72, June 1859.
9. Bleak, "Annals," 68, March 7, 1859.
10. Lee journal, Feb. 2, 1859 (1:193).
11. Historian's Office Journal, Aug. 26, 1859 (SC 17).
12. June 23, 1860, letter to Brigham Young; see chapter 7 (1857), this volume.
13. Lucius's sister, Lisania, was married to Hiram Judd.
14. Historian's Office Journal (SC 17).
15. 1870 US Federal Census, Santa Clara, Washington, Utah, p. 3.
16. Forney to Hamblin, Jan. 28, 1859, Jacob Forney Letterbooks, MS 14278, fd 2, p. 496, CHL.

17. Jacob Forney, Letterbooks 1857–1859, MS 14278, fd 2, p. 520, CHL.
18. John D. Lee journal (1:199).
19. "Statement of Mr. Wm. H. Rogers," *The Valley Tan* 2.16, Feb. 29, 1860, pp. 2–3; reprinted in Brooks, *Mountain Meadows Massacre*, 265–78, which I will cite from. Forney to Elias Smith, May 5, 1859, titled "Visit of the Superintendent of Indian Affairs to Southern Utah," *Deseret News* 9.10, May 11, 1859, p. 1.
20. Alexander Wilson to Jacob Forney, March 16, 1859, in Buchanan, *Message of the President* (1860), a section entitled "Condition of Affairs in Utah," 53–55.
21. Jacob Forney to Elias Smith, May 5, 1859, titled "Visit of the Superintendent of Indian Affairs to Southern Utah," *Deseret News* 9.10, May 11, 1859, p. 1(73).
22. Forney's Report, Sept. 22, 1859, *Message of the President*, Senate Document 42 (1860), 87, 89. He also said that the children were "poorly clad"—Forney to General A. S. Johnston, May 1, 1859, *Message of the President*, 8: The children were "contented and happy; poorly clad, however." This is probably because children in pioneer southern Utah were generally "poorly clad" by urban standards.
23. James Lynch affidavit, July 27, 1859.
24. "Captain J. C. Lynch Tells of the Mountain Meadow Horror—Will Ask Congressional Appropriation," *Arkansas Gazette*, June 5, 1908, from typescript in the National Archives. Discussed in Bagley, *Blood of the Prophets*, 219. I am grateful to Will Bagley for sharing this typescript with me, though my interpretation of it differs from his. There is a similar, equally melodramatic account, that does not name Hamblin, but merely a Mormon bishop: "Mountain Meadows," *The Mountain Wave* 1.1 (Marshall, Arkansas), June 17, 1905; consulted at Dale Broadhurst's "Readings in Mormon History" website, at http://www.sidney-rigdon.com/dbroadhu/SO/miscsou2.htm#061705, (accessed on Oct. 21, 2008).
25. Lee diary (1:210–11).
26. Jacob Forney to Charles E. Mix, May 30, 1859, in Buchanan, *Message of the President* (1860), 59–60; Statement of William H. Rogers, 270.
27. Statement of William H. Rogers, 273. The child's name was Joseph Miller.
28. Jacob Forney to General A. S. Johnston, May 1, 1859, in Buchanan, *Message of the President* (1860), 8. In this letter, Forney stated that by interviewing the oldest children, he knew for certain that whites "were mainly instrumental" in the massacre, and hoped that Judge Cradlebaugh would be able to prosecute them soon. In his May 5 letter to Elias Smith, published in the *Deseret News*, he again stated that whites were significantly involved in the massacre.
29. Jacob Forney to Elias Smith, May 5, 1859, a letter entitled "Visit of the Superintendent of Indian Affairs to Southern Utah," *Deseret News* 9.10, May 11, 1859, p. 1; Jacob Forney to Charles E. Mix, May 4, 1859, in Buchanan, *Message of the President* (1860), 57–58.
30. Brooks, *Mountain Meadows Massacre*, 173–78; Bagley, *Blood of the Prophets*, 226–27.
31. Affidavit of Jacob Hamblin, June 3, 1859, in Salt Lake City, included in "History of Brigham Young," 471–72 (SC 4). Published in Brooks, *Mountain Meadows Massacre*, 177n15. Hamblin gave the date as "about May 1," but gives the place as Santa Clara, and the military company did not come to Santa Clara until May 8. Bagley, *Blood of the Prophets*, 227. They left Santa Clara on May 16.
32. Lee diary, Apr. 18, 1859 (1:209).
33. See also an affidavit by Marion Shelton, June 3, 1859, in which he records that Enos described being offered the equivalent of a thousand dollars by military leaders for the head of John D. Lee. If Enos had been intent on killing Lee, he probably would not have mentioned this. In Church Historian's Office Journal, CHL (SC 17).
34. For this aspect of Carleton's career, which would directly impact Hamblin and Mormons in southern Utah, see chapter 16 (1864), this volume.
35. Carleton, *Special Report*, 14.
36. Ibid., 2–8. Marion J. Shelton diary.
37. Brooks, *Mountain Meadows Massacre*, 182–84.
38. Carleton, *Special Report*, 4.
39. Ibid., 15.
40. Ibid., 14; Statement of William H. Rogers, 277.
41. Statement of William H. Rogers, 278.

42. Jacob Forney to General A. S. Johnston, June 15, 1859, in Buchanan, *Message of the President* (1860), 9–10. Judge Cradlebaugh arrived back in Salt Lake City on June 2; see Church Historian's Office Journal (SC 17).
43. Church Historian's Office Journal (SC 17).
44. Affidavit of Jacob Hamblin, June 3, 1859, in Salt Lake City, included in "History of Brigham Young," pp. 471–72 (SC 4). Published in Brooks, *Mountain Meadows Massacre*, 177–78, n15.
45. Kenney, *Wilford Woodruff's Journal*, June 4, 1859 (5:341–42).
46. Historian's Office Journal (SC 17).
47. Historian's Office Journal, June 16, 1859 (SC 17); Journal History. I have not yet identified Major Lyons.
48. Historian's Office Journal (SC 17).
49. Brooks, *John Doyle Lee*, 251, citing records at the General Accounting Office at Washington, D.C.
50. Buchanan, *Message of the President* (1860), 55.
51. Historian's Office Journal (SC 17); LJH, 64.
52. Rachel Lee diary, June 6, 1858; Shelton to George A. Smith, Jan. 22, 1859, George A. Smith collection (SC 32); Historian's Office Journal, June 4, 1859 (SC 17); Tullidge, *Tullidge's Histories*, 2:49.
53. LJH, 64; Brigham Young to Jacob Hamblin, September 18, 1859, BYOF (SC 21).
54. See Brooks, "Journal of Thales W. Haskell." For the 1859 journey to the Hopis, all quotes are from Haskell unless otherwise specified.
55. LJH, 64–65. For the Hamblin-Bullock map, CHL, CR 100 310, fd 2 map 1.
56. Marion J. Shelton to George A. Smith, Nov. 13, 1859; Marion J. Shelton to George A. Smith, Nov. 16, 1859; both in George A. Smith collection (SC 32). I am indebted to Kenneth R. Beesley for sharing his transcription of the Nov. 13 letter with me, and his notes on the letter. See also the Marion J. Shelton diary; Shelton to Brigham Young, April 3, 1860, BYOF.
57. See Haskell diary, October 12. Little, 64, lists Ira Hatch, but this appears to be a mistake.
58. See Gary Young, "Life and Times of William Young." After living in Santa Clara, Young took up residence in Pinto, Kanab, and then in Millard and Piute Counties before dying in Joseph, Sevier County, Utah, in 1891. Some have supposed that John W. Young, as listed in LJH, 64, is Brigham's son, John Willard, but Bleak, "Annals," 78, winter, 1859–1860, clearly identifies him as John William Young.
59. Taylor and Martha had eight children from 1862 to 1876, the last of whom was named Jacob Hamblin Crosby. They lived in Santa Clara, Eagle Valley, Nevada, and Kanab, where Taylor died in 1915.
60. Pearce lived in St. George, then later became part of the Little Colorado mission, founding Taylor, on Silver Creek, in 1878, where he died in 1922. McClintock, *Mormon Settlement*, 96, 167; James Pearce, Interview, 1921; James Pearce, "Early Settler," *Washington County News*, Aug. 24, 1911, p. 1; Briggs, "James Pearce (1839–1922)"; Walker, Turley, and Leonard, *Massacre at Mountain Meadows*, 261.
61. In LJH, 64, Hamblin misdates this as October 20.
62. Ewing, "The Mule as a Factor."
63. "In the Life of Jacob," typescript, in PTRC, series 8.1, bx 6, fd 86; Sides, *Blood and Thunder*, 101.
64. Shelton to George A. Smith, Nov. 13, 1859.
65. Dellenbaugh, *A Canyon Voyage*, 159. See also Powell, *Canyons of the Colorado*, 331; Beadle, *The Undeveloped West*, 654.
66. Shelton to George A. Smith, Nov. 13, 1859.
67. Beesley, "M. J. Shelton to George A. Smith, 13 November 1859." Haskell refers to "quite a large creek emtying into the river" which had "considerable beaver sign."
68. Haskell diary at Nov. 5–6, cf. LJH, 64–65; Shelton to Smith, November 13, 1859.
69. Beesley, "M. J. Shelton to George A. Smith, 13 November 1859," who interviewed Brigham Young University professor Dirk Etzinga.
70. Once again, Hamblin misdates this (as Nov. 6) in his autobiography. The correct date is also in Marion Shelton to George A. Smith, Nov. 16, 1859.
71. Haskell diary; LJH, 65.
72. Marion Shelton to George A. Smith, Nov. 16, 1859. For the identity of the Moquitch Village, see chapter 8 (1858), this volume.
73. Marion Shelton to George A. Smith, Nov. 16, 1859. Shelton to George A. Smith, Nov. 30, 1859, in Brooks,

"Journal of Thales W. Haskell," 97–98. The January 30 date for this letter, as it was written just before Jacob Hamblin departed, appears to be incorrect.

74. Shelton to George A. Smith, November 30, 1859.
75. LJH, 65. The dates in Little are about a week off.
76. Haskell diary, December 18, 1859.
77. One Indian missionary, Christian L. Christensen, said that the name should actually be spelled "Dahnish Yant," which means "He Did Tell the Truth." Christensen to John R. Young, Dec. 16, 1923, MS 4325, CHL. I am grateful to Ken Beesley for his transcription of this. Robinson, *Life of Ira Hatch*, 9. William B. Maxwell named him "Chief Banashaw known as Spanish Shanks by us." William B. Maxwell to George A. Smith, April 12, 1866, George A. Smith collection (SC 33). See also Hamblin to Brigham Young, Nov. 25, 1860, BYOF, bx 27, fd. 14; chapters 11 (1860) and 18 (1866), this volume. Also Peterson, *Utah's Black Hawk War*, 218; McPherson, *Northern Navajo Frontier*, 9. Shepardson and Hammond, *The Navajo Mountain Community*, 28–30, relying on Kildare, "Chief Scarbreast," incorrectly state that Spaneshanks was known as Chief Scarbreast (Navajo name, Todachene Nez) and that he lived until 1911. Spaneshanks was already described as an old man by Haskell in 1859; he would hardly have lived until 1911. Maxwell's identification of the Navajo who died in 1866 as Spaneshanks is probably correct.
78. Christensen to John R. Young, Dec. 16, 1923; Robinson, *Life of Ira Hatch*, 1; Kitchen, "Mormon-Indian Relations in Deseret," 188. See chapter 11 (1860), this volume.
79. Edwin Woolley refers to the snow-capped "Spanny Shank Mountain" on the other side of the Colorado, which appears to be Navajo Mountain. Apparently early Mormons named the mountain after this chief. Diary entry, March 2, 1869, in Crampton and Miller, "Journal of Two Campaigns," 155; Linford, *Navajo Places*, 299–300; Shepardson and Hammond, *The Navajo Mountain Community*.
80. Christensen to John R. Young, Dec. 16, 1923.
81. Lee diary, Nov. 11, 1860 (1:280). For the Elk Mountain Mission, see Firmage, *A History of Grand County*, 73–93; Simmons, *The Ute Indians*, 97–98; Campbell, "Brigham Young's Outer Cordon," 230–31; Gottfredson, *Indian Depredations in Utah*, 84–88.
82. Riddle, "Isaac Riddle Tells His Story," 175.
83. George Snow, "Death of Arapeen," Letter to the Editor, Dec. 9, 1860, *Deseret News* 10.42, Dec. 19, 1860, p. 1. For more on Arapeen, see chapter 6 (1854–1856), this volume.
84. For Tuuvi, see Christensen, "Hopi Legends"; Udall, "Tuba—The Oraibi"; Waters, *The Book of the Hopi*, 291; Johnson, "Echoes from the Past"; Courlander, *The Fourth World of the Hopis*, 192; Levy, *Orayvi Revisited*, 180; Smallcanyon, "Contested Space," passim. Hamblin would take him to Utah in 1870 and 1871.
85. C. L. Christensen to Anthony Ivins, Sept. 30, 1925, USHS, typescript in PTRC, series 1, bx 5, fds 62–63.
86. Haskell diary, March 2, 1860.
87. Whiteley, *Bacavi*, 166; C. L. Christensen, "Hopi Legends," *Times-Independent* (Moab, Utah), Feb. 9, 1933. Hopis received many names throughout their lives, according to religious, ritual, and clan usage; and then often received nicknames and "American" names in addition. Whiteley, *Rethinking Hopi Ethnography*, 105–24.
88. Whiteley, *Bacavi*, 28; Courlander, *The Fourth World of the Hopis*, 192; Clemmer, *Roads in the Sky*, 41. Cf. Whiteley, *The Orayvi Split*, 1:117, 38; Waters, *The Book of the Hopi*, 291.
89. Smallcanyon, "Contested Space," 85. See also William R. Mateer to E. A. Hayt, May 1, 1879, Letters Received by the Office of Indian Affairs, 1824–80, RG 75, M234, reel 24, frames 546–51, NA.
90. Christensen, "Hopi Legends," *Times-Independent* (Moab, Utah), Feb. 2, 1933, p. 1. See LJH, 104; John D. Lee, frequently from July 18, 1873 (2:272) to Jan. 10, 1874 (2:319). Sekaquaptewa, *Me and Mine*, 237–38, says that her nickname was Katsinmana ("Kachina Girl") and her real name was Talasnimka. See also Peter Whiteley, *Deliberate Acts*, 207, *The Orayvi Split*, 117, and *Bacavi*, 86, who suggests that her real name was Puhunimka, citing Andrew Gibbons's 1877–1878 diary. However, Gibbons calls her by her nickname Coehenumon.
91. Whiteley, *Deliberate Acts*, 207, and *Bacavi*, 84–85; Waters, *Book of the Hopi*, 231–34.
92. Courlander, *The Fourth World of the Hopis*, 192; Flake, "A History of Mormon Missionary Work," 50–51; Bright, *Native American Placenames*, 515. By this explanation, the word derives from from *tuuv-*, *tuuva*, "throw." He was "thrown out." There is another explanation of his name—Tuuvi's favorite saying was "Túve!" ("Let's Go!") and this became his nickname. Yava, *Big Falling Snow*, 117n60.

93. Whiteley, *The Orayvi Split*, 115.
94. For Moenkopi and Tuba City, see Christian L. Christensen, diary, 1880–86; Nagata, *Modern Transformations*; Voth, *The Traditions of the Hopi*, 22–23; James, *Pages from Hopi History*, 15; Gregory, "The Oasis of Tuba, Arizona"; Reeve and Fletcher, "Mormons in the Tuba City Area"; Judd, "Tuba City"; Brugge, "The Moencopi Boundary Problem" and *The Navajo-Hopi Land Dispute*; Smallcanyon, "Contested Space," 173–74.
95. LJH, 65.

CHAPTER 11

1. Sides, "Thunderstruck."
2. See Reid, "Principles of Vengeance," 24, who discusses how Indians might not distinguish between different groups or nationalities of whites in seeking vengeance. Also, Simmons, "Kit and the Indians," 79–80. See chapter 18 (1866), this volume.
3. See chapter 21 (1870), this volume.
4. Cleland and Brooks, *A Mormon Chronicle*, 1:233.
5. Church Historian's Office Journal.
6. Lee, Diary, March 10, 1860 (1:242).
7. Little dates this accident to summer 1858, LJH, 57–58, but the "History of Brigham Young" (July 18, 1860, p. 208) and a June 23 letter by Hamblin to Brigham Young make the June 1860 dating certain. Hamblin to Young, June 23, 1860, BYOF, bx 27, fd 14.
8. LJH, 57–58.
9. Example are Albert Hamblin's heavenly visit in 1857 and Jedediah Morgan Grant's visits to heaven and return to earth in the days before his actual death in 1856. Sessions, *Mormon Thunder*, 248–50.
10. Jacob Hamblin to Brigham Young, June 23, 1860.
11. "History of Brigham Young," July 18, 1860, p. 208.
12. LJH, 57–58.
13. Hamblin to Young, June 23, 1860.
14. Lee, Diary (2:262).
15. Jacob Hamblin to Brigham Young, June 23, 1860.
16. Mormon folklore often included visits by demons or the devil. Hafen, *Dixie Folklore*, 14.
17. Church Historian's Office Journal, July 4, 1860 (SC 17).
18. Jacob Hamblin to Brigham Young, Oct. 8, 1860.
19. Hamblin to George A. Smith, Oct. 10, 1860, George A. Smith collection, MS 1322 (SC 32). For Price, Seegmiller, "Ghost Towns," 121.
20. Brigham Young Office Journal, Aug. 17, 1860, p. 130, excerpts in *New Mormon Studies CD-ROM*.
21. Kitchen, "Mormon-Indian Relations in Deseret."
22. Arrott, *Sarah Priscilla Leavitt Hamblin*, 33, see also Corbett, *Jacob Hamblin*, 413; chapter 7 (1857), this volume.
23. Hamblin to Brigham Young, March 2, 1857; chapter 7 (1857), this volume.
24. Kenney, *Wilford Woodruff's Journal*, July 28, 1847 (3:241). See also Kitchen, "Mormon-Indian Relations"; Knack, *Boundaries Between*, 69–71.
25. Kenney, *Wilford Woodruff's Journal*, September 16, 1857 (5:98); Brigham Young to James Brown, June 14, 1855, BYOF (SC 21).
26. Bigler, *Fort Limhi*, 147–48, 162–63.
27. Knack, *Boundaries Between*, 69–71. Mormon women marrying Indian men was almost unheard of. For traders marrying Indian women, see West, *The Contested Plains*, 80–81, 185–86, 189; Utley, *The Indian Frontier*, 29. For eventual cultural rejection of those marrying Indians, West, *The Contested Plains*, 187: "Interethnic marriage, then, changed almost immediately from a proud social asset to the badge of a pariah."
28. Kenney, *Wilford Woodruff's Journal*, July 28, 1847 (3:241); Kitchen, "Mormon-Indian Relations in Deseret," 144.
29. See below.
30. Robinson, *The Life of Ira Hatch*, 5.

31. Ibid., 10. "The wives of Jacob Hamblin and Ira Hatch were with the party of the white men." See also Christian L. Christensen to John R. Young, Dec. 16, 1923, MS 4325, CHL.
32. See below.
33. See chapter 23 (1871), this volume.
34. Anthony W. Ivins, Reminiscence, pp. 11–12, 21–22.
35. There is contradictory evidence. As we will see, Eliza reputedly told Rachel that she was as much a wife of Jacob as Rachel was.
36. Elkins, *Ira Hatch: Indian Missionary*, 69.
37. C. L. Christensen to John R. Young, Dec. 16, 1923, MS 4325, CHL; Robinson, *Life of Ira Hatch*, 10.
38. Amos Tietjen (a grandson of Ira Hatch), "History of Ira Hatch." The chronology of these events, known only from family history, is extremely vague. See chapter 7 (1857), this volume.
39. Tietjen, "History of Ira Hatch"; Robinson, *Life of Ira Hatch*, 2; Elkins, *Ira Hatch: Indian Missionary*, 58.
40. Elkins, *Ira Hatch: Indian Missionary*, 71. She had borne a son the previous year who died after five days. John D. Lee, diary (technically Nov. 5, 1860, but Nov. 11 is mentioned in the entry) (1:279–80).
41. Elkins, *Ira Hatch: Indian Missionary*, 123–24.
42. Endowment House Record, film 1,149,514, entry no. 5680, FHL. Thanks to Merlin Compton for checking this. See also Brooks, "Indian Relations," 42n75, who cites to Book D, page 543, of the Salt Lake Temple Records. In this source, Jacob Hamblin had sealed to him "Eliza, born on the Shivwit Reservation, date unknown, 14 February, 1863." Mormons practice a form of marriage, called a sealing, in LDS temples (or in other places when temples were not available in pioneer Utah), that is believed to unite the couple for eternity.
43. Kelly, "Southern Paiute Bands," 552. See also Palmer, "Utah Indians Past and Present," 47–48; Palmer, "Pahute Indian Homelands," 100; and Martineau, *Southern Paiutes*, 154–70.
44. George W. Armstrong to Brigham Young, June 30, 1857, in ARCIA (1857), 309; Brooks, "Indian Relations," 41.
45. In his May 17, 1856, letter to Brigham Young, Hamblin said he had "redeemed .2. boys and .4. girls or bought them of the Lamanites." See chapter 6 (1854–1856), this volume. Apparently, two of those girls either had been given to other Mormon families or had died by 1857.
46. Davenport, "Biography of John Lee Jones"; Brooks, "Indian Relations," 43–44.
47. Corbett, *Jacob Hamblin*, 215.
48. Bradley, *A History of Kane County*, 60. Adobe was also often used to build buildings inside a fort. See also Roberts and Sadler, *A History of Weber County*, 59.
49. Brooks, "Indian Relations," 43.
50. The primary source for the expedition is George A. Smith Jr. and Jacob Hamblin, diary, MS 1465, CHL. The entire diary from October 10 on is written by Hamblin. Other important sources are John D. Lee, Diary, Nov. 11, 1860 (1:279–80); Jacob Hamblin to George A. Smith Sr., October 10, 1860, George A. Smith collection (SC 32); William L. Warren to George A. Smith, November 21, 1860, George A. Smith collection (SC 32); George A. Smith to Amasa Lyman, November 29, 1860, in "History of the Church," 1860, pp. 396–98 (SC 4); Jehiel McConnell to George A. Smith, Dec. 22, 1860, George A. Smith collection (SC 32); George A. Smith to John L. Smith, January 3, 1861 (telling of an interview he had just had with Thales Haskell), excerpt in "History of Brigham Young," Jan. 3, 1861, pp. 6–7. Jacob Hamblin to Brigham Young, November 25, 1860, BYOF, bx 27, fd 14. Calvin C. Pendleton to William H. Dame, dated November 20, 1860, in the William Dame collection, MS 2041, CHL. "Murder of George A. Smith, jun., by Indians," *Deseret News* 10.40, Dec. 5, 1860, p. 5 (317). Retrospective accounts are LJH, 65–73; Riddle, "Isaac Riddle Tells His Story"; Haskell, in Brooks, "Journal of Thales Haskell," 95–96; Bleak, "Annals," fall 1860, 81–83 (typically dependent on Little); Whitney, *History of Utah*, 4:579–80; McClintock, *Mormon Settlement*, 66. Unless otherwise noted, all quotations are from the Smith Jr./Hamblin diary.
51. John D. Lee, Diary, Nov. 11, 1860.
52. Warren to Smith, Nov. 21, 1860; Calvin C. Pendleton to William H. Dame, Nov. 20, 1860. For more on Enos, see Rich, "Memories of New Harmony"; Workers of the Writers' Program, *Utah: A Guide to the State*, 300; Bagley, *Blood of the Prophets*, 35, 129.
53. McConnell, "Sketch of the Life of Jehiel McConnell."

54. Ibid., 4.
55. Esshom, *Pioneers*, 352, 1212; Bagley, *Blood of the Prophets*, 128; Walker, Turley, and Leonard, *Massacre at Mountain Meadows*, 263.
56. LJH, 65.
57. Smith, "Pioneering."
58. Riddle, "Isaac Riddle Tells His Story," 173–74.
59. George A. Smith Jr./Hamblin diary. McConnell, in McConnell to Smith, Dec. 22, 1860, says that he started the journey on October 10, at Toquerville. The company arrived at Washington the same day. "All in good spirits," John D. Lee wrote.
60. Hamblin to George A. Smith, Oct. 10, 1860. According to the diary, Jacob did not reach Toquerville until the eleventh, but this appears to be incorrect.
61. Hamblin to George A. Smith, Oct. 10, 1860; McConnell to Smith, Dec. 22, 1860. Reports that the company felt forebodings, as in later, retrospective accounts (LJH, 66), are not found in the early sources.
62. George A. Smith Jr./Hamblin diary.
63. McConnell to Smith, Dec. 22, 1860.
64. Reilly, "Roads across the Buckskin Mountain," 384, believes that the main company followed the usual Jacob Canyon trail, while the other part of the company took the boat up LeFevre Canyon.
65. James Pearce, Interview, 1921.
66. Ibid.
67. Powell, *Report of the Explorations in 1873*, 4. Reilly, *Lee's Ferry*, 6, calls this a "partial crossing," but Hamblin, in his diary, writes, "8 of us crosed the River" (the numeral "8" Reilly reads as "3").
68. Pearce, Interview, 1921.
69. Remarkably, this blessing can be found at the beginning of the book containing the George A. Smith Jr./Hamblin diary.
70. McConnell to Smith, Dec. 22, 1860.
71. Warren to Smith, Nov. 21, 1860; Calvin C. Pendleton to William H. Dame, Nov. 20, 1860.
72. George A. Smith Jr./Hamblin diary.
73. Hamblin to Young, Nov. 25, 1860.
74. George A. Smith Jr./Hamblin diary. Cf. Hamblin to Young, Nov. 25, 1860.
75. George A. Smith Jr./Hamblin diary. Hamblin to Young, Nov. 25, 1860, counts four Navajos.
76. Ibid. The George A. Smith Jr./Hamblin diary account is quite similar.
77. George A. Smith Jr./Hamblin diary.
78. John D. Lee, Diary, Nov. 11, 1860.
79. Hamblin to Young, Nov. 25, 1860.
80. See chapters 9 (late 1858) and 10 (1859), this volume, and chapter 14 (1862) at Dec. 23, 1862.
81. For the location in Blue Canyon, in the Moenkopi Wash, see Christian L. Christensen to Anthony Ivins, Jan. 23, 1923, typescript in PTRC, series 1, bx 5, fds 62–63; also Christensen to Ivins, Sept. 30, 1925, p. 9, in Anthony Ivins Papers, bx 9, fd 5, USHS; Clement Powell diary, Oct. 22, 1872 (Kelly 461); Jenson, "Tuba Ward, Snowflake Stake." The fact that Paiutes south of the Colorado had a word for buffalo shows that they were probably connected with the Utes of the Four Corners area, who had been influenced by the Indians of the Plains. See also Steele's 1862–1863 map; and the Nielson D. Dalley diary, May 7, 1879, in Miller, *Hole-in-the-Rock*, 149.
82. Hamblin to Young, November 25, 1860. See also George Smith Jr./Hamblin diary; LJH, 67; Bleak, Annals, March 26, 1864.
83. Warren to Smith, Nov. 21, 1860; John Steele diary, Dec. 23, 1862.
84. George A. Smith Jr./Jacob Hamblin, diary.
85. Ibid.; Riddle, "Isaac Riddle Tells His Story," 174.
86. Hamblin to Young, Nov. 25, 1860.
87. Riddle, "Isaac Riddle Tells His Story," 174. George A. Smith to Amasa Lyman, Nov. 29, 1860. Warren to Smith, Nov. 21, 1860.
88. Discussed later in this chapter.
89. John D. Lee, Diary, Nov. 11, 1860.

90. Hamblin to Young, Nov. 25, 1860; Lee, Diary, Nov. 11, 1860. Thales Haskell dates the incident a little later, at about two p.m., see the poem in Brooks, "Journal of Thales Haskell," 95–96. Brooks, "Journal of Thales Haskell," 95–96. Haskell refers to a spring, though the main location is named after a creek.
91. According to Hamblin to Young, Nov. 25, 1860. As George A. Smith Sr. tells the story to Amasa Lyman, Nov. 29, 1860, the horse darted off during the watering process. Warren to Smith, Nov. 21, 1860; Calvin C. Pendleton to William H. Dame, Nov. 20, 1860.
92. Hamblin to Young, Nov. 25, 1860.
93. Brooks, "Journal of Thales Haskell," 95–96. Warren writes that George "passed round a point." Amos Thornton's horse: John D. Lee, diary, Nov. 11, 1860.
94. LJH, 68.
95. Warren to Smith, Nov. 21, 1860.
96. George A. Smith to Amasa Lyman, Nov. 29, 1860.
97. George A. Smith to John L. Smith, Jan. 3, 1861.
98. Hamblin to Young, Nov. 25, 1860. For the wounds, see also Church Historian's Office Journal, Nov. 27, 1860, CR 100 1 (SC 17), quoted later in this chapter. Hamblin, in Little, incorrectly reverses this, saying that there were three bullet wounds and four arrow wounds. LJH, 68.
99. *Deseret News* report; Haskell, quoted in George A. Smith to John L. Smith, Jan. 3, 1861.
100. Haskell, in George A. Smith to John L. Smith, Jan. 3, 1861. According to Hamblin, in Little, the Navajos removed the shirt, then shot him with the arrows.
101. Christian L. Christensen to Anthony Ivins, Jan. 23, 1923, USHS, typescript in PTRC, series 1, bx 5, fds 62–63. There was a Navajo headman of the Round Rock area named Black Horse (Roessel, "Navajo History, 1850–1923," 16), but he seems to be a different Black Horse.
102. Nielson B. Dalley diary, May 10, 1879, in Miller, *Hole-in-the-Rock*, 149 (May 13) and 31n21, 33n47; also James Davis, "History of the Life of James Davis," in Miller, *Hole-in-the-Rock*, 27; Larsen, "Navajo Chief Peokon." For Peokon and the Mormons, see chapters 23 (1871) and 27 (1874), this volume.
103. Tietjen, *Ernst Albert Tietjen*, chapter 3.
104. Hamblin to Young, Nov. 25, 1860.
105. Warren to Smith, Nov. 21, 1860.
106. Hamblin to Young, Nov. 25, 1860.
107. Ibid.; John Steele Diary, Dec. 23, 1862.
108. Hamblin to Young, Nov. 25, 1860.
109. LJH, 69.
110. McConnell to Smith, Nov. 22, 1860.
111. Hamblin to Young, Nov. 25, 1860. This plundering at the camp is confirmed in John D. Lee, Diary, Nov. 11, 1860.
112. LJH, 68.
113. George Smith Jr./Hamblin diary.
114. John D. Lee, Diary, Nov. 11, 1860. See also George A. Smith to Amasa Lyman, Nov. 29, 1860. Riddle also reports that he was selected because he looked like a captain in the U.S. Army who had killed some Navajo warriors. Riddle, "Isaac Riddle Tells His Story," 175. However, he states that the Navajos wanted Haskell because they knew he was a friend of the Hopis. See also Calvin C. Pendleton to William H. Dame, Nov. 20, 1860.
115. See also LJH, 68–69.
116. These are the last words of Hamblin's addition to the George Smith Jr. diary. In the diary, Hamblin seems to place this incident on November 1, but the other accounts all place it on November 2. See Warren to Smith, Nov. 21, 1860. Warren seems to place it two hours out of Buffalo Creek camp, while Smith, in his letter to Lyman, places it in camp.
117. Lee, Diary, Nov. 11, 1860.
118. Warren to Smith, Nov. 21, 1860; George A. Smith to Amasa Lyman, Nov. 29, 1860.
119. LJH, 67. In Little, this event is placed before the Mormons reached camp. Priscilla agrees that Hamblin took a young Native American woman with him on this trip "to interpret and do the camp cooking," but does not view her as a wife. She calls her Ellen. Arrott, *Sarah Priscilla*, 32.

120. C. L. Christensen to John R. Young, Dec. 16, 1923, MS 4325, CHL.
121. Ibid.; John R. Young, "In Memory of Ira Hatch," 886; Robinson, *Life of Ira Hatch*, 10.
122. C. L. Christensen to John R. Young, Dec. 16, 1923; Robinson, *Life of Ira Hatch*, 10.
123. McConnell to Smith, Dec. 22, 1860.
124. John D. Lee, Diary, Nov. 11, 1860.
125. Warren to Smith, Nov. 21, 1860.
126. Calvin C. Pendleton to William H. Dame, Nov. 20, 1860.
127. John D. Lee, Diary, Nov. 11, 1860.
128. Ibid. George A. Smith, in the letter to Amasa Lyman, tells a similar story, but states that cooking utensils were scattered.
129. Riddle, "Isaac Riddle Tells His Story," 175.
130. John D. Lee, Diary, Nov. 11, 1860.
131. George A. Smith to John L. Smith, Jan. 3, 1861.
132. Warren to Smith, Nov. 21, 1860.
133. Hamblin to Young, Nov. 25, 1860.
134. McConnell to Smith, Dec. 22, 1860.
135. Hamblin to Young, Nov. 25, 1860.
136. Hamblin calls him "the chief of our Friends"; Warren seems to think he *is* Spaneshanks: "one of the three friendly Indians called Yank or some such name." One would think that Hamblin would have named him if he was Spaneshanks. Again, Hamblin is a firsthand witness, while Warren's account is secondhand.
137. Hamblin to Young, Nov. 25, 1860.
138. Warren to Smith, Nov. 21, 1860.
139. Hamblin to Young, Nov. 25, 1860.
140. McConnell to Smith, Dec. 22, 1860.
141. John D. Lee, Diary, Nov. 11, 1860.
142. Hamblin to Young, Nov. 25, 1860. Cf. John D. Lee, Diary, Nov. 11, 1860.
143. Hamblin to Young, Nov. 25, 1860; McConnell to Smith, Dec. 22, 1860; John D. Lee, Diary, Nov. 11, 1860.
144. McConnell to Smith, Dec. 22, 1860. This happened at a place called Cedar Ridge, according to Christensen, and a few cedar branches were placed over the body as it lay beneath a cedar. Christensen to John R. Young, Dec. 16, 1923.
145. Warren to Smith, Nov. 21, 1860. For the Navajo pursuit, see also John D. Lee, Diary, Nov. 11, 1860.
146. John Steele diary, Dec. 23, 1862; see also his 1863 map. There is a George Smith Historical Monument near Tonalea; this may mark the place of Smith's death, but is definitely not the place of shooting.
147. Hamblin to Young, Nov. 25, 1860, cf. LJH, 71.
148. John D. Lee, Diary, Nov. 11, 1860.
149. According to one report, this is exactly what happened: the Navajos scalped George Smith Jr., then had a war dance over him. Jack Hillers diary, Oct. 21, 1872 (Fowler 149). However, according to LJH, 109, in 1871 friendly Navajos told Jacob that one party of Navajos tried to "get up a dance over his scalp" but the majority of the Navajos disapproved of the murder and did not allow the dance. Scalping used to be a part of Navajo culture, The Franciscan Fathers, *An Ethnologic Dictionary*, 438. The scalp of an enemy was a focal point for the Enemy Way sing, in which warriors were purified after battle, though an actual scalp was not always necessary, and eventually fell out of use. Ibid., 367–68, 374–75. Reichard, *Social Life of the Navajo Indians*, 114–19.
150. LJH, 71.
151. Hamblin to Young, Nov. 25, 1860.
152. LJH, 72.
153. Hamblin to Young, Nov. 25, 1860. For soldiers transferred from Utah to Fort Defiance, see later in this chapter.
154. LJH, 72. This is consistent with the background of the Navajo conflicts in early 1860, which took place at or near Fort Defiance.
155. Hamblin to Young, Nov. 25, 1860.

156. LJH, 73.
157. Provided we accept John D. Lee, Diary, Nov. 11, 1860. George A. Smith Sr. said that the company arrived back on November 20. George A. Smith to Amasa Lyman, Nov. 29, 1860. This nine-day disparity is curious; one wonders if Lee's diary somehow misdated the event. Riddle, "Isaac Riddle Tells His Story," 175.
158. Church Historian's Office Journal, CR 100 1 (SC 17). See also Pusey, *Builders of the Kingdom*, 110–11.
159. LJH, 73.
160. Smith, "Pioneering." Lieutenant-Colonel Ruggles is a mystery. There was a Lt. Col. Daniel Ruggles in Utah in the aftermath of the Utah War, whom George A. Smith would have known, and a group of soldiers was transferred from Utah to Arizona in fall 1860. Cullum, *Biographical Register of the Officers*, 1:563; Aird, *Mormon Convert*, 241–42; Moorman and Sessions, *Camp Floyd and the Mormons*, 57, 117. For soldiers sent from Camp Floyd to Arizona, McNitt, *Navajo Wars*, 390. However, Ruggles went on sick leave in 1859, recuperated in Virginia, and apparently did not return to the West before he volunteered for the Confederate Army in 1861, and I have not found Ruggles mentioned in standard books on the Navajo wars, such as McNitt, *Navajo Wars*; Thompson, *The Army and the Navajo*; Altshuler, *Cavalry Yellow* and *Chains of Command;* Bailey, *The Long Walk*. For Ruggles in Virginia, Jones, *Historical Dictionary of the Civil War*, 1:1210. George A. Smith was apparently incorrect in naming him in this context.
161. McNitt, *Navajo Wars*, 365; Bailey, *The Long Walk*, 111–13.
162. McNitt, *Navajo Wars*, 376.
163. Ibid., 382–84; Bailey, *The Long Walk*, 125.
164. McNitt, *Navajo Wars*, 384; Bailey, *The Long Walk*, 126.
165. For Canby, see Heyman, *Prudent Soldier*.
166. McNitt, *Navajo Wars*, 390.
167. Riddle, "Isaac Riddle Tells His Story," 175.
168. Canby, *Prudent Soldier*, 119.
169. McNitt, *Navajo Wars*, 399.
170. Ibid., 403; see also Canby, *Prudent Soldier*, 119.
171. Major Henry H. Sibley to Dabney Maury, Sept. 29, 1860, in Correll, *Through White Men's Eyes*, 3:76–77; Edward Canby to Asst. Adj. Gen., Feb. 4, 1861, and Captain J. A. Whitall to Col. Canby, Feb. 4, 1861, in Correll, *Through White Men's Eyes*, 3:127; Bailey, *The Long Walk*, 133–34.
172. McNitt, *Navajo Wars*, 410.

CHAPTER 12

1. Young to Hamblin, Jan. 8, 1861, BYOF (SC 21).
2. Church Historian's Office Journal, April 7–12, pp. 141–46.
3. Ibid.
4. Ibid. Other important sources are a letter from Hamblin to Brigham Young dated February 26, 1861, quoted in Ward, *Inscription House*, 13–14; Jehiel McConell and William Stewart, oral report in Minutes for the Cedar City Ward Historical Record Book, 1859–1862, CHL, at March 24, 1861, as cited in Ward, *Inscription House*, 14.
5. Church Historian's Office Journal; Hamblin to Young, Feb. 26, 1861. A short biography of John Taylor Lay states that he also went on this journey, Roundy, "John Taylor Lay."
6. Church Historian's Office Journal.
7. Fish, *The Life and Times of Joseph Fish*, 80.
8. Hamblin to Young, Feb. 26, 1861.
9. Church Historian's Office Journal.
10. LJH, 74, says that the chief of the Navajos at Quichintoweep, with his wife, visited and said that if he had known the true character of the Mormons, he would have protected them instead of allowing them to be harmed.
11. Church Historian's Office Journal.
12. LJH, 73–74.
13. Church Historian's Office Journal.
14. Jehiel McConell and William Stewart, oral report.

15. Church Historian's Office Journal. There is a similar description in Minutes for the Cedar City Ward Historical Record Book.
16. Ward, *Inscription House*, 9–11.
17. Ibid., 3–17.
18. Jehiel McConnell, in Minutes for the Cedar City Ward Historical Record Book, 14.
19. Ibid.
20. Church Historian's Office Journal. Jehiel McConnell, in Minutes for the Cedar City Ward Historical Record Book, says that "Spanish Hanks the peacable chief" came with "some 80 others." Perhaps McConnell is counting all the Navajos, not just Spaneshanks's party.
21. I have not yet identified this fort.
22. Church Historian's Office Journal.
23. Ibid.
24. McConnell, in Minutes for the Cedar City Ward Historical Record Book.
25. William Stewart, in Minutes for the Cedar City Ward Historical Record Book.
26. Church Historian's Office Journal.
27. McConnell, in Minutes for the Cedar City Ward Historical Record Book.
28. Joseph Fish, autobiography (Krenkel 80).
29. Ibid.
30. William Stewart, in Minutes for the Cedar City Ward Historical Record Book.
31. Church Historian's Office Journal, April 9, 1861, p. 143.
32. LJH, 75.
33. She would marry James Edgar Chesley in 1883, and die on May 9, 1933 in Mesa, Arizona. Death certificate, copy in author's possession; Beeler, "Life Sketch of Melissa"; West, "Graves In Hubbard Cemetery."
34. BYOF, bx 34 fd 18.
35. See "History of Brigham Young" for this trip.
36. James Martineau diary, Aug. 19, 1857.
37. Brigham Young to Amasa Lyman and Charles Rich, June 13, 1861, in "Correspondence," *Latter-day Saints Millennial Star* 23.32 (Aug. 10, 1861): 509; also Arrington, "Mormon Cotton Mission," 225.
38. Young to Amasa Lyman and Charles Rich, June 13, 1861, and Arrington, "Mormon Cotton Mission," 224–25.
39. Bleak, "Annals," October to December, 1861, pp. 87–99; Larson, *I Was Called to Dixie*, 101; Arrington, "Mormon Cotton Mission," 226. For St. George, see Miller, *Immortal Pioneers*; Logue, *A Sermon in the Desert*; Alder and Brooks, *A History of Washington County*.
40. For Snow (1818–1888), see Larson, *Erastus Snow*; Quinn, *Mormon Hierarchy: Extensions*, 700–1; Olson, "History of Erastus Snow."
41. Arrington, "Mormon Cotton Mission," 226.
42. George A. Smith to Jacob Hamblin, Oct. 16, 1861, FAC 1315 in Jacob Hamblin papers, Huntington Library, San Marino, California.
43. Arrington, *Great Basin Kingdom*, 220–21.
44. See chapter 24 (1871), this volume.

CHAPTER 13

1. For the flood, the most important sources are Daniel Bonelli to Brigham Young, BYOF, bx 28, fd 17 (for context, see Perkins, "From Switzerland to the Colorado River") and Jacob Hamblin to George A. Smith, February 2, 1862, George A. Smith Collection, MS 1322, bx 6, fd 5 (SC 32). See also Harmony Ward Record by John D. Lee, in Cleland and Brooks, *A Mormon Chronicle*, 2:4–7; "The Flood in Washington County," and letters to the editor by Jacob Hamblin, Chapman Duncan, and Jesse W. Crosby, *Deseret News*, February 12, 1862, pp. 4 and 8. The Jacob Hamblin letter to the editor was apparently rewritten and cobbled together by the editor. After these near-contemporary sources, there are many later reminiscences, autobiographies, and family histories. LJH, 75–76; Staheli, "The Life of John and Barbara Staheli"; Gubler, "History of Santa Clara," 164.
2. Staheli, "The Life of John and Barbara Staheli," is an example.

3. Hafen, *Recollections of a Handcart Pioneer*, 31; Erastus Snow to Brigham Young, Jan 5, 1862, BYOF, Box 42 fd 17. Bleak, "Annals," May–June 1861, 85. John Staheli remembered thirty families; see Staheli, "The Life of John and Barbara Staheli." "History of Brigham Young," in "History of the Church, 1839–circa 1882" CR 100 102 (SC 4) at May 25, 1861. The 1860 census for Santa Clara, "Tonaquint," in Washington County, 151–54, lists twenty-five households.
4. Bonelli to Young, January 19, 1862; "Caspar Gubler"; and John R. Young, *Memoirs*, 119.
5. See Bonelli to Young, January 19, 1862; Perkins, "Christen and Samuel Wittwer"; and Bleak, "Annals," 99, who gives the date of arrival as December 22. For the Swiss settlers in Santa Clara, see Tobler, "Heinrich Hug."
6. John Staheli, "The Life of John and Barbara Staheli," 5. Mary Dart Judd, Autobiography, 27; Young, *Memoirs*, 119.
7. Hafen, *Recollections of a Handcart Pioneer*, 32. See also Hafen and Gubler, "Johannes (John) Gubler and Maria (Mary) Ursula Muller"; Bleak, "Annals," Oct.–Dec. 1860, pp. 33, 99. Zadok Knapp Judd, Autobiography; John Stucki, "Autobiography," 12; and Whittaker, *History of Santa Clara, Utah*, 281.
8. Bleak, "Annals," Dec. 22, 1860, pp. 99–100, before Feb. 17, 1862, p. 123D; Hafen, *Recollections of a Handcart Pioneer*, 32–34. Gubler, "History of Santa Clara," 161. John Stucki, Autobiography, 10–11.
9. For the rain starting on Christmas, see Hamblin to Smith, February 2, 1862; Robert Gardner Jr., Autobiography, 20–21; Bleak, "Annals," at December 25, 1861, pp. 113, 123D.
10. Bleak, "Annals," December 25, 1861, pp. 113, 123D; Cleland and Brooks, *A Mormon Chronicle*, 2:6–7.
11. Bonelli to Young, January 19, 1862. Hafen, *Recollections of a Handcart Pioneer*, 33.
12. Young, *Memoirs*, 118; Bonelli to Young, January 19, 1862.
13. Young, *Memoirs*, 118.
14. Bonelli to Young, Jan. 19, 1862.
15. Hamblin to Smith, January 19, 1862, in "Floods in Southern Utah," *Deseret News*, February 12, 1862, p. 8.
16. J. W. [Jesse Wentworth] Crosby, Letter to the Editor, dated January 20, 1862, in *Deseret News*, "Flood in Southern Utah" February 12, 1862, p. 8.
17. Hamblin to Smith, February 2, 1862.
18. Mary Judd, Autobiography, 27.
19. Bonelli to Young, January 19, 1862.
20. Hamblin to Smith, February 2, 1862. See also the Bonelli letter; "The Flood in Washington County," *Deseret News*, February 12, 1862, p. 4; Young, *Memoirs*, 119–20.
21. Young, *Memoirs*, 119–20.
22. Hamblin to Smith, February 2, 1862.
23. Young, *Memoirs*, 119–20.
24. Hamblin to Smith, February 2, 1862.
25. Gubler, "History of Santa Clara," 163.
26. LJH, 76.
27. Corbett, *Jacob Hamblin*, 200.
28. Jacob Hamblin does not give the date, but says that this occurred at night: "when the darkness of the night had set in the southwest corner of the Fort comenced falling." Hamblin to Smith, February 2, 1862.
29. Corbett, *Jacob Hamblin*, 200.
30. Young, *Memoirs*, 119.
31. John Staheli, "The Life of John and Barbara Staheli," 5, remembers it in the middle of the fort.
32. Young, *Memoirs*, 119, portrays the rope being used during all the evacuation. Jacob Hamblin, in his February 2 letter to George A. Smith, and his autobiography, LJH, 77, seems to remember using the rope only for the rescue of Sophia Staheli.
33. Mary Judd, Autobiography, 27.
34. Hamblin to Smith, Feb. 2, 1862.
35. Ibid.
36. Hamblin to Smith, Feb. 2, 1862.
37. Gubler, "History of Santa Clara," 163; "Life Story of Barbara Staheli Graff Stucki"; and Brooks, *On the*

Ragged Edge, 103. This may be a doublet of Hamblin's fall into the Santa Clara described below, in which Albert, an Indian, throws Hamblin the rope.

38. LJH, 77.
39. Walker, "History of Barbara Sophia Haberli Staheli."
40. Mary Judd, Autobiography, 27. This may be a doublet of the incident of Hamblin bringing Sophia Staheli to safety.
41. Juanita Leavitt Brooks, doubtless reflecting Leavitt/Hamblin traditions, wrote that Albert, Jacob's adopted Indian boy, threw him the lasso that saved him. Brooks, *On the Ragged Edge*, 103.
42. Young, *Memoirs*, 120–21, and Zadok Knapp Judd, Autobiography.
43. Bonelli to Young, Jan. 19, 1862.
44. Hamblin to Smith, Feb. 2, 1862.
45. Bleak, "Annals," before Feb. 17, 1862, p. 123D.
46. Ibid.
47. The transition from last day of old year to first day of new year is regarded in many cultures as a time reenacting the destruction of the world and new creation. Eliade, *The Myth of the Eternal Return*, 49–92.
48. Erastus Snow to Brigham Young, March 10, 1862, BYOF, bx 42 fd 17.
49. Quoted in Corbett, *Jacob Hamblin*, 202.
50. Ibid.
51. Robert Gardner Jr., Autobiography, 22–23.
52. Zadok Knapp Judd, Autobiography. Erastus Snow to Brigham Young, March 10, 1862, as quoted in Larsen, *Erastus Snow*, 338–39.
53. Hafen, *Recollections of a Handcart Pioneer*, 34; also John Stucki, "Biography of John S. Stucki," 14; Corbett, *Jacob Hamblin*, 203.
54. Bleak, "Annals," before Feb. 17, 1862, p. 123D.
55. Lee, Harmony Ward Record, Feb. 6, 1862, in Cleland and Brooks, *A Mormon Chronicle*, 2:7.
56. Young, *Memoirs*, 121.
57. John Staheli, "History of John and Barbara Staheli," 6.
58. Frank Staheli, "Johann George Staheli," in Whittaker, *History of Santa Clara*, 348–50.
59. Compton, "Civilizing the Ragged Edge," 180–81; Corbett, *Jacob Hamblin*, 200. Corbett reports that Rachel, when saved from Fort Clara, had an eight-day-old baby, Araminda. However, on p. 460, he gives the date of birth for Araminda as January 27, 1861, which I believe is correct (see Miller, *Jacob Vernon Hamblin*, 54).
60. Larson, *I Was Called to Dixie*, 43.
61. "Church Historian's Office. History of the Church, 1839–circa 1882," CR100 102 (SC 4).
62. See Crosby, "Traveling in the Ministry"; Bleak, "Annals," Oct. 1861, p. 89, and Dec. 1, 1861, p. 101. John Stucki, in a retrospective account, also mentioned the tradition of a prophecy by Young; Stucki, "Biography of John S. Stucki," 13.
63. Bleak, "Annals," Dec. 1859, p. 75.
64. Ibid., winter 1856–1857, p. 34.
65. For Paiute agriculture, see chapter 5 (1854), this volume.
66. John Staheli, "The Life of John and Barbara Staheli," 7. Staheli then lists a few incidents written from the viewpoint of white settlers being troubled by local Indians.
67. Corbett, *Jacob Hamblin*, 198. Burning the wickiup of a dead man to drive his spirit away was a common practice. Whiting, *Paiute Sorcery*, 36, 107. For Paiute death customs, see Thomas Brown diary, June 7, 1854 (Brooks, 42) (cremation and hiding a body among rocks both attested, but burial becoming common in Little Salt Lake Valley); Palmer, *Notes on the Utah Utes*, 4–5 (cremation of the deceased with his possessions, followed by burial, was common, but was changing to simple burial in 1866–1878); Kelly and Fowler, "Southern Paiute," 380; Reeve, *Making Space*, 136–56. For Paiute vulnerability to white disease, see chapter 24 (1871), this volume.
68. Duncan, letter to the editor, Jan. 19, 1862, in *Deseret News*, Feb. 12, 1862, p. 8, in the section, "Flood in Southern Utah."
69. See previous chapter.

70. Hafen, *Dixie Folklore*, 1–2.
71. Bluff in San Juan County also endured some disastrous floods, particularly in spring 1884. McPherson, *A History of San Juan County*, 227. Outside of Utah, settlements in southern Nevada and Arizona were also subjected to dangerous flooding; see Larson, *I Was Called to Dixie*, 367; chapter 29 (1876–1877), this volume.
72. Quoted in Larson, *I Was Called to Dixie*, 367. For floods as causes of abandonment of town sites, see Rosenvall, "Defunct Mormon Settlements," 61–62. For Utah's aridity making it especially vulnerable to flash floods, Honker, "'Been Grazed Almost to Extinction.'"
73. Reeve, "A Little Oasis in the Desert," 233–34.
74. Quoted in Larson, *I Was Called to Dixie*, 365.
75. For Kanab, see Childs, *The Secret Knowledge of Water*, chapter 10, who emphasizes that floods are a paradoxical aspect of living in arid, desert places.

CHAPTER 14

1. "History of David Canfield." The biography now describes a great flood on the Santa Clara, which includes people being drowned. This entire incident seems misdated and incorrect, as no one was killed in the flood. This biography also reports that Jacob was not immediately able to pay Canfield for the home, so Canfield and his family lived in it for two or three years. This also seems unlikely.
2. Juanita Brooks to Aldin O. Hayward, 27 February 1962, in Historic Information, Jacob Hamblin Home, II-D.1/a, Jacob Hamblin Home Records, 1962–1975, Department of Natural Resources, Division of Parks and Recreation, Record Series number 23410, Agency Assigned Box Number 2001–01, Utah State Archives, Salt Lake City, Utah, as cited in Landon, Notes on Hamblin Residences. See also "Life Story of Luke Syphus," 4.
3. Mileski, *Before the Manifesto*, 132.
4. "Life Story of Rosina Brachman," 15–16, as cited in Landon, Notes on Hamblin Residences. Thanks to Michael Landon for these sources.
5. Bleak, "Annals," 136.
6. "Minutes," *Deseret News* 11.41, Apr. 9, 1862, p. 8(328).
7. "Progress of President Young and Company," a letter from J. V. Long, Sept. 14, 1862, in *Deseret News* 12.14, Oct. 1, 1862, p. 4(108).
8. See "The Utah Indian Superintendency," *Deseret News* 10.25, Dec. 18, 1861, p. 2(194). Church Historian's Office Journal, Sep. 30, 1862. For Harding, see Long, *The Saints and the Union*, 75–76.
9. LJH, 77.
10. For the 1862–1863 journey to the Hopis, quotes are from Steele's journal unless otherwise specified. This has two versions: (1) a holograph, MS 1847, CHL, and (2) a more polished version in History of Brigham Young, 33.14–37, at Jan. 8, 1863. The second version is evidently a formal diary-report prepared by Steele from his original holograph diary, and is fuller and more grammatical. This will be my main source, but I will refer to the holograph occasionally. Steele also created a map, MS 15320, CHL. See also: Jacob Hamblin, 1863 Journal, in a Notebook, a photostat of a holograph, Huntington Library, San Marino, California. Woodruff diary, Feb. 3–4, 1863 (6:96–98). LJH, 77–80. Mosiah Hancock, Autobiography, typescript, in author's possession; Autobiography, holograph (MS 570, CHL). I will refer to the typescript unless MS 570 is specified.
11. Mahonri Moriancumer Steele, "Impressions Along Life's Highway." See also Brooks, "Extracts from the Journal of John Steele"; Bate, "John Steele."
12. Brooks, "Extracts from the Journal of John Steele," 28.
13. Steele journal, Thursday, Jan. 5, 1863, see below, also in Brooks, "Extracts from the Journal of John Steele," 28.
14. Samuel Newton Adair, Autobiography.
15. Bleak, "Annals," Oct. 26, 1862, pp. 151–55.
16. Ibid., Nov. 17, 1862, p. 161. Clark was from Washington, see John Steele, diary, Dec. 4, 1862.
17. LJH, 79. Hancock, Autobiography, 63, calls him James Andrews.

18. John Steele, diary, Nov. 26, 1862.
19. Warner, *William B. Maxwell*; Udall, *Forgotten Founders*, 42–48.
20. See McClintock, *Mormon Settlement*, 70–71, 180–81; Hackworth, "Nathan Cram Tenney."
21. Alexander, *Mormonism in Transition*, 258–71.
22. Journal History, Oct. 26, 1862.
23. Steele, diary.
24. Hamblin, 1863 journal, p. 6a.
25. Steele, diary.
26. David P. Kimball, "Distance to Hayden's Ferry," a letter to President John Taylor, Dec. 6, 1878, *The Deseret News*, Jan. 15, 1879, p. 7, and David Kimball, "Arizona Intelligence," a letter to the editor, March 4, 1880, *The Deseret News*, 24 Mar 1880, p. 10(122); Crampton, "Mormon Colonization," 119.
27. Steele, diary.
28. Hancock, Autobiography, 63. On Steele's map, the group passes Rock Spring, Gulch Springs, Cane Springs, and Seven Springs before reaching the Colorado. On a 1913 topographic map of the area, we have Blackrock Spring (just east of Mount Bangs), Cane Spring, and Pakoon Springs.
29. Steele diary, holograph.
30. LJH, 77.
31. Hancock, Autobiography, 63.
32. Steele, diary.
33. Jacob Hamblin to Erastus Snow, Nov. 26, 1862, James Bleak Collection, Box 1, MS 10587, CHL. Summarized in Bleak, "Annals," 162.
34. Knack, *Boundaries Between*, 67.
35. LJH, 77, has the missionaries traveling south up a thirty-mile wash on the first day after crossing, followed by three days "through a rough, bushy country, with some scrub cedar and pine timber." This does not seem to correlate with Steele's journal, unless they are both referring to the same wash, presumably Grapevine Wash.
36. Steele, diary. According to Hancock, they got two guides.
37. Hancock, Autobiography, 63. See also Hancock, Autobiography, MS 570.
38. For further on the Hualapai, see McGuire, "Walapai"; Dobyns and Euler, *Wauba Yuma's People* (pp. 69–71 for the "Walapai War"); Dobyns, and Euler, *The Walapai People* (p. 34 for the Hopis and Hamblin).
39. Steele, diary. Hancock, Autobiography, 63, describes thirty peach trees.
40. Statement of James W. Lesueur.
41. Steele, diary, Dec. 1, 1862.
42. This may be a seep spring that Hamblin refers to in LJH, 77, where they camped the fourth night after the river crossing.
43. According to Steele.
44. LJH, 78; Hancock, Autobiography, MS 570.
45. Steele, diary.
46. Hancock, Autobiography, MS 570.
47. Ibid.
48. Ibid.
49. See also Hancock's typescript Autobiography, 63.
50. Kenney, *Wilford Woodruff's Journal*, Feb. 4, 1863 (6.97).
51. For ancient Pueblo ruins in the San Francisco Peaks area, and near Black Falls on the Little Colorado, see Fewkes, "Pueblo Ruins Near Flagstaff, Arizona."
52. Hamblin remembered reaching it one day after camping at the San Francisco Peaks, LJH, 78. This chronology is wrong, but his identification of the first running water after the San Francisco camp may be correct.
53. Mosiah Hancock, Autobiography, MS 570.
54. Steele, diary.
55. Ives diary, May 2, 1858, *Report*, p. 115.
56. Ives diary, May 6, 1858, *Report*, p. 117. The difficulties of the Ives company as they traveled from San

Francisco Peaks to the Hopi mesas once again suggests that Steele underrated the difficulty of these trans-Colorado journeys to Arizona. In addition, the Ives company, with the backing of the U.S. Army, was probably much better supplied than were any Mormon expeditions.

57. Steele, diary.
58. Ibid.
59. Waters, *The Book of the Hopi*, 154–64; Dorsey and Voth, "The Oraibi Soyal Ceremony."
60. Hancock, Autobiography, MS 570.
61. Steele, diary.
62. Waters, *The Book of the Hopi*, 163.
63. LJH, 78.
64. Lancaster, "Dixie Wine," 97.
65. LJH, 78.
66. Mosiah Hancock, Autobiography, 63; Hamblin to Brigham Young, May 18, 1863, BYOF, bx 29, fd 9. LJH, 78, incorrectly has three Hopis.
67. James Bleak journal, 1864, March 15, 1864. He later converted to Mormonism, see Brown, *Life of a Pioneer*, 459.
68. Church Historian's Office Journal, at Feb. 4, 1863. Tu-wa-wat is sometimes identified as Tuuvi (e.g., Whiteley, *Bacavi*, 29), but this identification is probably incorrect. If Tuuvi had been one of the three, the Mormons, who knew Tuuvi well, would have probably identified him specifically.
69. LJH, 84.
70. See chapter 21 (1870), this volume.
71. LJH, 79; Steele, diary, Jan. 2, 7, 1863; Hancock, Autobiography, 63. Apparently, they were selected because their horses were stronger than the rest.
72. "Pennenshanks"—Hancock, Autobiography, 63.
73. Hancock, Autobiography, 63.
74. LJH, 79.
75. Hamblin incorrectly states that the river was full of ice when the missionaries and Hopis crossed, LJH, 79. Hancock also describes "great blocks of ice" in the river when they crossed. Steele's contemporary diary explicitly says that there was no ice in the river when the missionaries crossed, see below. Also, Hamblin and Hancock incorrectly stated that they crossed the river on New Year's Day. LJH, 79, and Hancock, Autobiography, 63. Hancock also states that he and Hamblin decided to cross the river on the day they came to it—one other detail that Steele's contemporary record contradicts.
76. LJH, 79.
77. Steele, diary. Kenney, *Wilford Woodruff's Journal*, Feb. 4, 1863 (6:98).
78. Kenney, *Wilford Woodruff's Journal*, Feb. 4, 1863 (6:98).
79. LJH, 79, seems to remember only two pioneers, Fuller and Andrus.
80. Hamblin writes that following the crossing of the Colorado, "it occupied a day to bridge a muddy inlet and get on to the bench above." LJH, 79.
81. *Kenney, Wilford Woodruff's Journal*, Feb. 4, 1863 (6:98–99).
82. The Steele map portrays the Mormons as high up the Paria, not visiting the Lee's Ferry site on the way back.
83. Steele, diary. Hancock also seems to describe this, Autobiography, 67.
84. Hancock, Autobiography, 67.
85. Austin, Dean, and Gaines, *Yanawant*, 2:60; Stoffle, Halmo, and Austin, "Cultural Landscapes," 241–42.
86. According to the holograph, the third.
87. Steele diary, holograph.
88. LJH, 79.
89. Steele, diary.
90. LJH, 79.
91. Hancock, Autobiography, 67.
92. Mary Minerva Dart, Autobiography; Bleak, "Annals," 162. In LJH, 80, Hamblin adds the anecdote of him learning in a "dream or vision" that the messenger had been wrong, and that Duane, not Lyman, had been killed. For Duane's death date, see also the Sexton Record, Santa Clara Cemetery.

93. Hancock, Autobiography, 67. For dating, see also Samuel Newton Adair, Autobiography.

CHAPTER 15

1. Brooks, "Indian Relations," 42.
2. Kenney, *Wilford Woodruff's Journal* (6:96); Church Historian's Office Journal (SC 17) on the same date.
3. Kenney, *Wilford Woodruff's Journal* (6:96).
4. Ibid.; George A. Smith to Erastus Snow, Feb. 15, 1863, Historian's Office Letterpress Copybooks, CR 100 38, CHL.
5. Journal History, Feb. 11, 1863.
6. Church Historian's Office Journal (SC 17), at Feb. 14, 1863.
7. Endowment House Record, film 1,149,514, entry no. 5680, LDS Genealogy Library, Salt Lake City. Thanks to Merlin Compton for checking this for me.
8. Brooks, "Indian Relations," 42.
9. George A. Smith to Erastus Snow, Feb. 15, 1863. For the Hopi visit to Salt Lake City, see also Wilford Woodruff to Mr. Blair, Feb. 16, 1863, Historian's Office Letterpress Copybooks, CR 100 38, CHL. "Four of the Moquis accompanied Hamblin Home as embasadors to visit the Mormons to see if they were the people which their Father had taught them for generations would come from the west & bring them the truth in the last days." Also George A. Smith to John Smith, March 10 and 12, 1863, Historian's Office Letterpress Copybooks, CR 100 38, CHL.
10. George A. Smith to Erastus Snow, Feb. 15, 1863.
11. Young to Hamblin, Feb. 16, 1863, typescript, in Journal History. George A. Smith evidently wrote the rough draft for this; see Smith to Jacob Hamblin, Feb. 16, 1863, Historian's Office Letterpress Copybooks, CR 100 38, CHL.
12. George A. Smith to Snow, Feb. 15, 1863.
13. Young to Hamblin, Feb. 16, 1863.
14. George A. Smith to Snow, Feb. 15, 1863.
15. Young to Hamblin, Feb. 16, 1863.
16. George A. Smith to Snow, Feb. 15, 1863. In the Book of Mormon, Ishmael was the father-in-law of Lehi's sons, and Zoram was a servant who accompanied them to America.
17. Young to Hamblin, March 6, 1863, BYOF (SC 21).
18. Hamblin to Young, May 18, 1863.
19. Bleak, "Annals," March 6, 1863, pp. 176–77.
20. For this expedition, see a diary by Hamblin, 1862–63, in two forms: first, a holograph, in Papers of Jacob Hamblin, mssFAC 1307–1325, Huntington Library, San Marino, California. Then a more grammatical typescript: MSS A 567-3, USHS. For the spring 1863 journey to the Hopis, quotes are from Hamblin's holograph journal unless otherwise specified. See also Jacob Hamblin, "Report of a Journey from St. George," and a letter, Hamblin to Young, May 18, 1863, BYOF, bx 29, fd 9.
21. LJH, 81.
22. Hamblin to Young, May 18, 1863.
23. Bleak, "Annals," March 18, 1863, p. 179.
24. See Backus, *Mountain Meadows Witness* (for this journey, 196–97); Briggs, "Philip Klingensmith."
25. McClintock, *Mormon Settlement*, 64–65. See chapter 31 (1878), this volume.
26. Hamblin, "Report of a Journey from St. George," 1.
27. Date from the Hamblin diary, 1862–63.
28. Hamblin, Grammatical diary.
29. For location, LJH, 81. Some accounts locate the ferry one or two miles closer to the Grand Wash than this.
30. McClintock, *Mormon Settlement*, 96; Billingsley, Spamer, and Menkes, *Quest for the Pillar of Gold*, 25. Harrison was father of James Pearce, whom we have met previously, in the 1859, 1860, and 1862 trips to the Hopis. See "Harrison Pearce."
31. Bleak, "Annals," Dec. 17, 1864, p. 251.
32. The grammatical diary has Hamblin refusing to give the Hopis the horses, then letting them have them

only reluctantly, after the expedition voted against him. Little also portrays the Hopis as responsible for taking the animals, *Jacob Hamblin*, 82.

33. LJH, 82.
34. Bolton and Mortensen, *Pageant in the Wilderness*, 5.
35. Ives, *Report Upon the Colorado River*, 105–6.
36. Casanova and Bourke, "General Crook Visits the Supais," 265. See also James, *Grand Canyon*, 171–72.
37. LJH, 82, says that the Mormons deliberated with Hopis and Paiutes before taking a road to the left, but doesn't explicitly say that they knew this would take them to Havasupai Canyon. In this account, the group camped and spent the night halfway down the canyon, though the diary does not seem to record this.
38. For more on the Havasupai, see Schwartz, "Havasupai"; Dobyns and Euler, *The Havasupai People*; Hirst, *I Am the Grand Canyon*.
39. LJH, 83.
40. Hamblin, 1863 diary.
41. Hamblin, 1863 diary, grammatical version; LJH, 83.
42. Hirst, *I Am the Grand Canyon*, 52–53; Braatz, *Surviving Conquest*, 47–48. The Yavapais often had close associations with Apaches, and the Havasupais sometimes called them Apaches, but they actually spoke a language similar to that spoken by the Hualapais and Havasupais. "Euches" may be a degeneration of the name "Apaches." See also LJH, 83.
43. Hirst, *I Am the Grand Canyon*, 54.
44. Cushing, "The Nation of the Willows," 544.
45. Dobyns and Euler, *The Havasupai People*, 6. They give no sources and may have been misled by Hirst. Euler gives a better treatment of Hamblin's visit in Dobyns and Euler, *Havasupai Indians*, 291–92. Lee apparently became friendly with some Havasupai but never entered their canyon (see 294–97).
46. Hamblin, diary. LJH, 84, indicates that the Hopis separated before they emerged from Havasupai Canyon.
47. LJH, 84.
48. Ibid.
49. Hamblin, diary.
50. Waters, *The Book of the Hopi*, 193.
51. Fort Defiance had been evacuated in April 1861, but it would be reoccupied for the Kit Carson campaign in July 1863. McNitt, *Navajo Wars*, 417.
52. Hamblin to Young, May 18, 1863.
53. Ibid.
54. Ibid.
55. Ibid.
56. Hamblin, 1863 diary; LJH, 85.
57. Thompson, *Edward F. Beale and the American West*.
58. Beale, *Wagon Road from Fort Defiance*.
59. Hamblin, diary, grammatical version.
60. Ibid.
61. Conkling and Conkling, *The Butterfield Overland Mail 1857–1869*; Lyman, *Overland Journey*, 170; McClintock, *Arizona*, 271.
62. Hamblin, diary, Apr. 29, 1863.
63. Hamblin, grammatical diary. Or the hooting of an owl, LJH, 85.
64. Hamblin, diary, grammatical version.
65. Simmons, "Kit and the Indians," 79–80.
66. LJH, 85.
67. Ibid., 86.
68. Hamblin, diary.
69. Hamblin, diary, May 9, 1863.
70. LJH, 86; see also Hamblin, diary.
71. Hamblin, diary. Bleak, "Annals," p. 183, reports that they arrived in St. George on May 12.

72. Bleak, "Annals," May 12, 1863, p. 183.
73. Arrott, *Sara Priscilla Leavitt Hamblin*, 31.
74. Corbett, *Jacob Hamblin*, 228.
75. LJH, 86.
76. Corbett, *Jacob Hamblin*, 215. Mary Leavitt, a wife of Dudley, calls Eliza's husband "Old Poinkum." Brooks, *Quicksand and Cactus*, 43.
77. We do not have precise dates for Eliza's birth and death, but she may have been born in approximately 1846. See chapter 11 (1860), this volume.
78. Corbett, *Jacob Hamblin*, 215; Brooks, "Indian Relations," 42.
79. Brooks, "Indian Relations," 47–48; Matheson and Cooper, "Answers to a Questionnaire," Q 18.
80. Rich, "Memories of New Harmony," 13.
81. "Poinkum's Pasture and Native Americans in New Harmony Valley," at http://brentprince.blogspot.com/2008/08/poinkums-pasture-and-native-americans.html (accessed Dec. 3, 2011). There is a "Poinkum" (Indian) in the Grafton cemetery, who died in 1905, along with two other Indians nearby, Wiley (died in 1897) and Puss (no death date). There is a picture of a Poinkum taken by William Palmer in about 1900, no. ph1b5f31446.jpg, Sherratt Library.
82. Jean Hinckley Holbrook, Interview, 1941, as cited in Porter, "A Historical Analysis of Cove Fort Utah," 199.
83. Lucy would turn out to be sickly, and died at the age of eight.
84. Corbett, *Jacob Hamblin*, 227.
85. Jacob Hamblin to Brigham Young, May 18, 1863, BYOF, bx 29, fd 9. This is not in Hamblin's handwriting.
86. He says that this road had been "abandoned in consequence of the Artesian well on the Great Mohave Desert producing salt water." I have not been able to verify this statement.
87. Ibid.
88. George A. Smith to John Smith, July 30, 1863, in Journal History.
89. Bleak, "Annals," Sept. 7, 1863, p. 187.
90. Ibid., Nov. 15, 1862, p. 158.
91. Ibid., June 23, 1863, pp. 185–86.
92. Ibid., pp. 190–91; Perkins, "From Switzerland to the Colorado River," 8.
93. Larson, *I Was Called to Dixie*, 51, 122–23.
94. See chapter 23 (1871), this volume.

CHAPTER 16

1. John Steele diary, Jan. 3, 1863, in "History of Brigham Young," 13.36.
2. Peterson, "'Book A—Levi Mathers Savage,'" 22n7. Bleak, "Annals," before Jan. 22, 1864, p. 200, incorrectly gives the founding date for Kanab as spring 1864. For more on early Kanab, see John Steele to George A. Smith, Nov. 16, 1863, George A. Smith collection (SC 32); a record of an Erastus Snow expedition to the area, March 1865, James Bleak Collection, MS 10587, bx 1, CHL; Levi Savage Jr. to Brigham Young, Feb. 2, 1871, BYOF, bx 34, fd 8; Roundy, "Pioneers of Early Days."
3. McNitt, *Navajo Wars*, 410–29.
4. For Carleton, see Hunt, *Major General James Henry Carleton*; Gibson, "James Carleton"; Altshuler, *Chains of Command*, 24–38, 241–42.
5. Sides, *Blood and Thunder*, 308.
6. Sides, "Thunderstruck." Utley, "An Indian before Breakfast," 98, also sees Carleton as the real scoundrel in the story of the Navajo roundup.
7. General Order No. 15, as quoted in Prucha, *The Great Father*, 147.
8. As quoted in Prucha, *The Great Father*, 147.
9. See Dunlay, *Kit Carson and the Indians*; Sabin, *Kit Carson Days*; Trafzer, *The Kit Carson Campaign*.
10. For the horrors of this forced march, Thompson, *The Army and the Navajo*; Johnson and Roessel, *Navajo Stories of the Long Walk Period*; Iverson, *Diné: A History of the Navajos*, 55; Bailey, *The Long Walk*, 149–75.
11. McPherson, *The Northern Navajo Frontier*, 9–10.

12. Ibid., 11–12, for Navajos allied with Paiutes. For Navajos allied with Utes, Peterson, *Utah's Black Hawk War*, 208–42; McPherson, *The Northern Navajo Frontier*, 13–14.
13. Peterson, *Utah's Black Hawk War*, 208–42.
14. Bleak, "Annals," after March 7, 1864, p. 205. For further thefts from Kanab, ibid., after Feb. 1865, p. 255; at Jan. 5, 1866, p. 294.
15. Erastus Snow to R. N. Fenton, Special Agent of the Indian Bureau, Nov. 17, 1869, in John S. Boyden Papers, MSS 343, Container 2, Exhibit 424, Lee Library. Snow dates this first theft from Kanab in fall 1864; however, Bleak, "Annals," has no record of Navajo thefts from Kanab in fall 1864, but does record such thefts in fall 1863. Snow was probably a year off.
16. See below, this chapter.
17. LJH, 89.
18. James Bleak, journal of the 1864 expedition, at March 24, 1864. See below.
19. Typescript, Ms B 171, fd 6, USHS. For the spring 1864 journey to the Hopis, quotes are from Bleak's diary of the expedition (not to be confused with his "Annals") unless otherwise specified. We also have Hamblin's retrospective account of this journey in LJH, 89–90, which incorrectly dates it to 1865, and Isaac Riddle's autobiography, which also dates the journey incorrectly, to fall 1864. These two sources lead Corbett, *Jacob Hamblin*, 243–46, badly astray here. He has Hamblin and company staying with the Hopis for the winter, from fall 1864 to March 1865. In fact, Hamblin stayed at the mesas only four days.
20. For further on Bleak, see Metcalf, "James G. Bleak"; Addy, "James Godson Bleak."
21. Bleak, in his "Annals," p. 206, adds John S. Woodbury, from St. George, to this list, but the Bleak diary, at March 14, 1864, shows that Woodbury was sent home from Pipe Spring due to a shortage of horses.
22. See "David H. Cannon."
23. See material on Mosiah at "Isaac Behunin Family Archives."
24. Erastus Snow to Elder Jacob Hamblin and company of Missionaries, March 8, 1864, in Bleak, "Annals," March 14, 1864, pp. 206–7.
25. For this historic crossing, see Rusho and Crampton, *Lee's Ferry*, 18; Reilly, *Lee's Ferry*, 7; Crampton, *Historical Sites in Glen Canyon*, 94–97.
26. Bleak diary, March 21, 1864.
27. Riddle, Autobiography, 177.
28. Ibid.; Bleak, diary.
29. Bleak, diary.
30. LJH, 89.
31. Bleak diary.
32. Ibid., 90. Oddly enough, Riddle tells nearly the same story, but with himself as the protagonist. Riddle, Autobiography, 179.
33. Bleak diary.
34. Probably George Washington Adair (1837–1909), who was a participant in the Mountain Meadows Massacre (Walker, Turley, and Leonard, *Massacre at Mountain Meadows*, 256). However, his uncle (1818–1897) had the same name.
35. LJH, 88. I have found no historical context for this story.
36. Bleak, "Annals," May 21, 1864, pp. 222–25, and July 23, 1864, pp. 235–40; Larson, *I Was Called to Dixie*, 159–65; Brooks, *On the Ragged Edge*, 106–9; Hulse, "The Afterlife of St. Mary's County," 241–43; Hulse, *Lincoln County*; Arrington and Jensen, "Panaca: Mormon Outpost"; Reeve, *Making Space*, 21–112.
37. Brooks, *On the Ragged Edge*, 110; Reeve, "Cattle, Cotton, and Conflict" and *Making Space*, 17–20; Anderson, *Desert Saints*, 383–86.
38. LJH, 88–89.
39. Reeve, *Making Space*, 21–22; Joseph Hamblin, "History of Joseph Hamblin."
40. Bleak, "Annals," before June 11, 1864, pp. 224–25; Hulse, *Lincoln County*, 6–7, 26. Apparently, Bill Hamblin and the Mormons did not secure their claims correctly, Perkins, "From Switzerland to the Colorado River," 9.
41. Arrington and Jensen, "Panaca: Mormon Outpost," 209. Erastus Snow to Brigham Young, June 19, 1864, at Bleak, "Annals," p. 228; also pp. 223–24. For early Panaca and mining, see Daniel Bonelli to George

A. Smith, July 18, 1864, George A. Smith collection, MS 1322, Incoming Correspondence (SC 32); Arrington and Jensen, "Panaca: Mormon Outpost"; and Reeve, *Making Space*, 21–112.

42. Bleak, "Annals," before July 23, 1864, pp. 235–36.
43. Hebron Ward Historical Record, vol. 1 (1862–1867), LR 3714 21, at Aug. 21, 1864, pp. 29–30, CHL; Erastus Snow to John Pearce, Meltiar Hatch, and Samuel Lee, August 27, 1864, at Bleak, "Annals," p. 237; also pp. 236–40. Discussion in Reeves, *Making Space*, 70–71. This conflict began, according to Bleak, when a Paiute chief died and the Paiutes demanded a white to be buried with him, which the Mormons of course refused. Bleak, "Annals," pp. 236–37. Demanding a white to be buried with a chief is close to unparalleled in Utah history, to my knowledge. It was more common for Paiutes to kill a relative of a headman, or a slave, to accompany him after death, Kelly and Fowler, "Southern Paiute," 380. However, when Ute Chief Wakara died in 1855, Utes killed four Paiutes and about fifteen horses to bury with him, and sought for two Pahvants and two Mormons to add to this total. David Lewis to Brigham Young, undated letter, in Brooks, JSIM, 162–63.
44. Little has only two Indians killed. Bleak, "Annals," has five Indians captured and killed. The Hebron Ward Record has three Indians killed, then two Indians killed two weeks later.
45. Erastus Snow to John Pearce, Meltiar Hatch and Samuel Lee, August 27, 1864, at Bleak, "Annals," p. 237.
46. Snow to Brigham Young, Aug. 29, 1864, as quoted in Larson, *Erastus Snow*, 365.
47. Erastus Snow to John Pearce, Meltiar Hatch, and Samuel Lee, August 27, 1864.
48. As quoted in Larson, *Erastus Snow*, 365.
49. Bleak, "Annals," p. 240. Reeves, *Making Space*, 71.
50. Peterson, *Utah's Black Hawk War*, 184.
51. Bleak, "Annals," before Sept. 1864, p. 240.
52. Ibid., Nov. 4, 1864, p. 249.
53. Ibid., before Sept. 1864, p. 240.
54. Reeve, *Making Space*, 27; Hulse, *Lincoln County*, 6–7.
55. Reeve, *Making Space*, 95. Excommunication removes a person from church membership, and is Mormonism's most extreme form of discipline. It condemns him or her to a lack of glory in the next life, and a painful removal from the close-knit Mormon community in this life. An excommunicated person can sometimes be rebaptized into the faith.
56. See Campbell, "The Mormon Gold Mining Mission"; Davies, *Mormon Gold*; Walker, *Wayward Saints*, 4–5, 363–64; Reeve, *Making Space*, 195n69.
57. Reeve, *Making Space*, 29.
58. Warrum, *Utah Since Statehood* 4:554.
59. Perkins, "Trailing Cattle"; Lyman, *Overland Journey*, 6, 177; Birney, *Zealots of Zion*, 86. Bleak, "Annals," Nov. 4, 1864, p. 249.
60. For Anson Call, see Call, *The Life Record of Anson Call*; Hartley and Alder, *Anson Bowen Call*, a biography of Anson's son. For Callville, see Fleming, "The Settlements on the Muddy," 150–55; Arrington, "Inland to Zion"; Lyman, *Overland Journey*, 208–9; Hunter, "The Mormons and the Colorado River."
61. Bleak, "Annals," Dec. 17, 1864, p. 250; Larson, *Erastus Snow*, 353.
62. Journal History, Nov. 4, 1864; Bleak, "Annals," Nov. 4, 1864, p. 249.
63. Jacob Hamblin to Brigham Young, Dec. 24, 1864, BYOF, bx 29, fd 20.
64. Anson Call, "Head of Navigation on the Colorado," *Deseret News* 14.16 (Jan. 18, 1865), pp. 4–5(124–25). For this expedition to found Callville, quotes are from this report, unless otherwise specified. See also Bleak, "Annals," Dec. 17, 1864, pp. 250–51.
65. Possibly the Indian mentioned in chapter 7 (1857), this volume, at November.
66. Lyman, *The Overland Journey*, 7–8.
67. Call, "Head of Navigation." Bleak, "Annals," p. 250, incorrectly has Call arriving at the Colorado on December 17.
68. Call, "Head of Navigation."
69. Bleak, "Annals," Dec. 17, 1864, p. 250.
70. Fleming, "The Settlements on the Muddy," 149; see the next chapter.

CHAPTER 17

1. "Home Items," *Deseret News* 14.19, Feb. 8, 1865, p. 4(149); Daniel Bonelli, Letter to the Editor, Feb. 8, 1865, in "Correspondence," *Deseret News* 14.22, March 1, 1865, p. 9(173). For this expedition down the Virgin, quotes are from Bonelli's letter, unless otherwise specified.
2. For Utley, see Esshom, *Pioneers*, 184, 1221.
3. Bonelli, Letter to the Editor.
4. Arrott, *Sarah Priscilla Leavitt Hamblin*, 30; Corbett, *Jacob Hamblin*, 246–47 (though Corbett confuses the journey that kept Jacob away).
5. Arrott, *Sarah Priscilla Leavitt Hamblin*, 30.
6. Corbett, *Jacob Hamblin*, 246–47.
7. Arrott, *Sarah Priscilla Leavitt Hamblin*, 30; Sexton Records, Santa Clara Cemetery.
8. Arrott, *Sarah Priscilla Leavitt Hamblin*, 30; see also Corbett, *Jacob Hamblin*, 246–47.
9. This pattern is found in many polygamous families. Altman and Ginat, *Polygamous Families in Contemporary Society*, 380–83.
10. Sexton Records, Santa Clara Cemetery.
11. He married Sadie Lytle on Dec. 9, 1885, in the St. George Temple (fourteen children). In 1936 the Hamblins became residents of Mesa, where Jacob Jr. died on April 1, 1939. Death certificate in author's possession; "Jacob Hamblin Dies in Arizona," *Kane County Standard*, April 7, 1939, p. 1; "Death Takes Jacob Hamlin at Age of 74," another obituary, source unknown, in PTRC, series 1, bx 16, fd 257; Jenson, LDSBE, 4:596.
12. See Perkins, "From Switzerland."
13. Description from Hamblin and Brimhall, "Biography of Louisa Bonelli Hamblin."
14. Georgia Lewis, a journalist, as quoted in Starr, *Jacob Vernon Hamblin*, 81.
15. Frederick Dellenbaugh, handwritten comments on his copy of LJH, opposite title page, Arizona State Historical Society.
16. Hardy, *Solemn Covenant*, 93–94. In addition, "dynastic" alliances often required that young women marry older men. Alexander, *Things in Heaven and Earth*, 230.
17. Endowment House Record, film 1,149,514, entry no. 8148, LDS Genealogy Library, Salt Lake City (thanks to Merlin Compton for checking on this for me). Andrews, *The Hamlin Family*, 547; Miller, *Jacob Vernon Hamblin Family*, 43; Corbett, *Jacob Hamblin*, 250, states that George A. Smith performed the marriage.
18. Date from the marriage record, see above. However, her death certificate, copy in author's possession, gives October 29, as does Hamblin and Brimhall, "Biography of Louisa Bonelli Hamblin" and "Life Sketch of Louisa Bonelli Hamblin."
19. "Louisa Bonelli Hamblin." At least, statements are quoted as if spoken or written by Louisa. The content of the statements seems reliable to me.
20. Ibid.
21. Hamblin and Brimhall, "Biography of Louisa Bonelli Hamblin." Two family histories of Louisa Bonelli give 1852 as the year of Louisa's baptism. However, the Record of Members collection in the LDS Historical Department gives Dec. 24, 1854, as the date. Waldo Perkins, personal communication. All the Bonellis were baptized in 1854, according to this source.
22. Immigration record for the *George Washington*, arrival date April 20, 1857, copy in author's possession; Perkins, "From Switzerland," 5.
23. Hamblin and Brimhall, "Biography of Louisa Bonelli Hamblin"; "Louisa Bonelli Hamblin," 188.
24. Starr, *Jacob Vernon Hamblin*, 74; Perkins, "From Switzerland to the Colorado River," 5. See also Hafen and Hafen, *Handcarts to Zion*, 153–57. For a memoir that parallels Louisa's, see Mary Ann Hafen, *Recollections of a Handcart Pioneer*.
25. "Louisa Bonelli Hamblin," 188.
26. Georgia Lewis, in Starr, *Jacob Vernon Hamblin*, 81.
27. Memories of Jacob Hamblin, apparently by Amarilla Hamblin Lee, typescript, in PTRC, series 8.1, bx 6, fd 86; Georgia Lewis, in Starr, *Jacob Vernon Hamblin*, 81–82.
28. Memories of Jacob Hamblin, apparently by Amarilla Hamblin Lee, typescript.
29. LJH, 91. Jacob Hamblin to George A. Smith, Dec. 25, 1865, in George A. Smith Collection, MS 1322 (SC

33). Daniel Bonelli, Jacob's new brother-in-law, served as scribe in this letter, and it often seems to be in Bonelli's more educated language and voice.

30. For this settlement, see chapter 16, this volume; Bleak, "Annals," Apr. 22, 1865, p. 257; Perkins, "From Switzerland," 10.
31. For the Muddy Mission, see Bleak, "Annals," Jan. 8, 1865, p. 252; Apr. 21–27, 1865, pp. 257–61; Godfrey, "Colonizing the Muddy River Valley"; Perkins, "From Switzerland," 10–15; Fleming, "The Settlements on the Muddy"; Larson, *I Was Called to Dixie*, 139–54.
32. Fleming, "The Settlements on the Muddy," 149.
33. As it turned out, the Muddy Mission would not survive and was abandoned in 1871.
34. Hamblin to Smith, Dec. 25, 1865.
35. Ibid.
36. Bleak, "Annals," pp. 292–93.
37. Ibid.
38. Arrington, "Inland to Zion," 249–50; Fleming, "The Settlements on the Muddy," 154; Reilly, "How Deadly Is Big Red?" 260n2.
39. Arrington, "Inland to Zion," 250.

CHAPTER 18

1. Sources on the killing of Whitmore and McIntyre and the subsequent Paiute killings are: Daniel McArthur to Richard Bentley, Jan. 21, 1866, in Bleak, "Annals," pp. 299–302; John Steele to George A. Smith, Jan. 22, 1866, in George A. Smith collection, MS 1322 (SC 33); James Bleak to George A. Smith, Jan. 26, 1866, in George A. Smith collection, MS 1322 (SC 33); Johnson and Johnson, "Biographical Sketch of Seth E. Johnson"; Edwin D. Woolley Jr., "A True Indian Story," 11–14, and "Notes on Fathers Life," 7–9; Jensen, "From the Days of '69," 3–4; A. Milton Musser, Journal, Jan. 23, 1866, a secondhand account. Woodbury, *A History of Southern Utah*, 168; Bradley, "The Whitmore-McIntyre Dugout"; Peterson, *The Black Hawk War*, 218–24; Knack, *Boundaries Between*, 82.
2. Bleak, "Annals," after Dec. 18, 1863, p. 196; McKoy, *Cultures at a Crossroad*, n. 78.
3. Whitmore, "Historical Sketch."
4. Bleak, "Annals," at May 28, 1865, p. 266; Lavender, *Pipe Spring*, 16.
5. Whitmore, "Historical Sketch."
6. Bailey and Bailey, *A History of the Navajo*, 38–39.
7. Peterson, *Utah's Black Hawk War*, 218.
8. James Bleak to George A. Smith, Jan. 15, 1866, in George A. Smith collection, MS 1322 (SC 33); Bleak, "Annals," Jan. 5, 1866, p. 294.
9. John D. Lee diary, Sept. 8, 1870 (Cleland and Brooks, 2:137–38); Woolley, "Journal of Two Campaigns," March 1, 1869, p. 157; Elizabeth J. Smith, "Account of the Settling of Paria River"; Thomas Smith, "A Brief History of Early Pahreah Settlements"; Reilly, "Historic Utilization," 189; Peterson, *Utah's Black Hawk War*, 218.
10. Palmer, *Forgotten Chapters*, vol. 2, no. 69, April 27, 1952. William Palmer interviewed local Paiutes, including one of the survivors of the massacre, "Tappie Dick." There is also a short interview with two Paiutes named Robert Pickivit and Johnie on the killings, in the Palmer Collection, bx 35, fd 13, Sherratt Library. For the Paiutes and witchcraft, see chapter 6 (1854–1856), this volume. For belief in witchcraft among the Navajos and Hopis, see Kluckhohn, *Navaho Witchcraft*; Blue, *The Witch Purge of 1878*; Simmons, *Witchcraft in the Southwest*, 135–46; and Malotki and Gary, *Hopi Stories of Witchcraft*.
11. James Bleak to George A. Smith, Jan. 15, 1866; John D. Lee diary, Sept. 5, 1870 (2:137–38); Peterson, *Utah's Black Hawk War*, 218.
12. Cleland and Brooks, 2:255–56; Ward, "A Partial List of Church Members," 63–64.
13. Brigham Young to George Smith and Erastus Snow, March 5, 1866, George A. Smith collection, MS 1322 (SC 33).
14. For Indian views on retribution, see Reid, "Principles of Vengeance," 24; Simmons, "Kit and the Indians," 79–80; chapters 6 (1854–1856) and 11 (1860) this volume.
15. Jacob Hamblin, 1869 Diary, MSS 770, following Sept. 9, 1869, Lee Library. See also Jacob Hamblin to

Erastus Snow, Nov. 21, 1870, as found in Bleak, "Annals," pp. 52–53. "When the raids were first made, five years ago, the Navajos were led by three principal men of the Piutes, this side of the River."

16. For San Juan Paiutes, see Bunte and Franklin, *From the Sands to the Mountain.* For Patnish, pp. 63–65.
17. Dellenbaugh, *A Canyon Voyage*, 167–68. For further on Patnish, see Ivins, "Travelling Over Forgotten Trails," 352; Peterson, *Utah's Black Hawk War*, 217.
18. Anthony Ivins diary, Oct. 29, 1875.
19. McPherson, *The Northern Navajo Frontier*, 13, 15.
20. David Chidester, Statement, in Gottfredson, *Indian Depredations in Utah*, 179–80.
21. John Steele to George A. Smith, Jan. 22, 1866, in George A. Smith collection, MS 1322 (SC 33).
22. LJH, 91.
23. George A. Smith to "Dear Bro Cannon," Feb. 2, 1866 [incorrectly marked as 1865], BYOF, bx 42, fd 7.
24. Palmer, *Forgotten Chapters*, vol. 2, no. 69, April 27, 1952.
25. Martineau, *Southern Paiutes,* 63.
26. One of the Navajo raiders may have been Manuelito, the famous Navajo chief, who, like Black Hawk, refused to go to a reservation and, like Black Hawk, lived by raiding. According to Peterson, he made an alliance with Black Hawk and joined him in raiding Mormon settlements in southern Utah. *Utah's Black Hawk War*, 216–17, 220, 224. For Manuelito (ca. 1818–1893), Navajo name *Naba jihlta* (Warrior Who Grabbed Enemy), see Denetdale, *Reclaiming Diné History*; Hoffman and Johnson, *Navajo Biographies*, 1:80–104; Thrapp, *Encyclopedia of Frontier Biography*, 2:139; Sides, *Blood and Thunder*, 268–69; Williams, *Navajo Political Process*, 5, 9; Correll, *Through White Men's Eyes*, 5:295; McPherson, *The Northern Navajo Frontier*, 10.
27. Erastus Snow to R. N. Fenton, Special Agent of the Indian Bureau, Nov. 17, 1869, in John S. Boyden Papers, MSS 343, Container 2, Exhibit 424, Lee Library.
28. William B. Maxwell, Major, to Daniel D. McArthur, Colonel, Jan. 11, 1866, copied in James Bleak to George A. Smith, Jan. 15, 1866; and Orrin Clark, interview, also in Bleak's Jan. 15 letter.
29. James Bleak to George A. Smith, Jan. 26, 1866. Gardner agrees with Bleak's description, John Gardner to Erastus Snow, Jan. 26, 1866, in BYOF, bx 42, fd 18. See also John Steele to George A. Smith, Jan. 22, 1866.
30. James Bleak to George A. Smith, Jan. 26, 1866; John Gardner to Erastus Snow, Jan. 26, 1866. W. J. Winsor wrote that "they had 16 arrows in their bodys," which presumably means about eight in each body. Letter to Leonard Heaton, as quoted in Heaton, "Historical [*sic*] and Facts," 8. According to Edwin D. Woolley Jr., "A True Indian Story," 12, the bodies were found "about 4 or 5 miles below Pipe in Red Clay Flat." Heaton, "Historical [*sic*] and Facts," 12, says they were passing through some "low grey hills" when they were ambushed and killed. Steele is a minority report, stating that they were killed eight miles from Pipe Spring. John Steele to George A. Smith, Jan. 22, 1866.
31. Henry Lunt to George A. Smith, Jan. 17, 1866, George A. Smith collection, MS 1322 (SC 33). Maxwell to McArthur, Jan. 11, 1866.
32. Heaton, "Historical [*sic*] and Facts," 9, 12; Peterson, *Utah's Black Hawk War*, 229.
33. Edwin D. Woolley Jr. also locates this band at "Bullrush Wash," camped under rocks or ledges. "A True Indian Story," 12.
34. Interview with Robert Pickivit and Johnie, in Palmer Collection, bx 35, fd 13, Sherratt Library.
35. Interview with Tappie Dick, in Palmer, *Forgotten Chapters*, vol. 2, no. 69, April 27, 1952.
36. Interview with Robert Pickivit and Johnie, in Palmer Collection, bx 35, fd 13, Sherratt Library.
37. Roundy, "Pioneers of Early Days"; Heaton, "Historical [*sic*] and Facts," 12.
38. Henry Lunt to George A. Smith, Jan. 17, 1866.
39. William B. Maxwell, Major, to Daniel D. McArthur, Colonel, Jan. 11, 1866, copied in James Bleak to George A. Smith, Jan. 15, 1866, George A. Smith collection, MS 1322 (SC 33).
40. Daniel D. McArthur, Colonel, to Major Richard Bentley, Jan. 15, 1866, in Bleak, "Annals," 298. For McArthur (1820–1908), see an autobiography in Jenson, LDSBE, 1:336–37; Miller, *Immortal Pioneers*, 188. After serving in the Blackhawk-Navajo war, he became St. George stake president for many years.
41. James Bleak to George A. Smith, Jan. 27, 1866, George A. Smith collection, MS 1322 (SC 33).
42. McArthur to Bentley, Jan. 15, 1866; LJH, 91.
43. McArthur to Bentley, Jan. 21, 1866. Steele refers to them as "two runners from the Indian Camp on their way to Grafton."

44. Palmer, *Forgotten Chapters*, vol. 2, no. 69, Apr. 27, 1952. Edwin D. Woolley Jr., "A True Indian Story"; Jensen, "From the Days of '69," 2.
45. Woodbury, *A History of Southern Utah*, 168; Daniel McArthur letter, Jan. 21, 1866.
46. James Bleak to G. A. Smith, Jan. 26, 1866.
47. The Steele letter reports "eight Indians" (evidently males). John Steele to George A. Smith, Jan. 22, 1866. Bleak, in his Jan. 26 letter, counts "six Indians" (males), three women, and "a couple of children." Steele is possibly counting the six male Paiutes found at the camp, plus the two guides.
48. McArthur to Bentley, Jan. 21, 1866.
49. Ibid. George A. Smith and Erastus Snow relate a rumor that several hundred dollars were found in the possession of the Paiutes, which was money that Whitmore had been collecting for a trade venture to San Francisco. George A. Smith and Erastus Snow to Daniel H. Wells, Feb. 7, 1866, Territorial Militia Records, #804, Series 2210, Utah State Archives. However, the primary reports contradict this.
50. John Steele to George A. Smith, Jan. 22, 1866.
51. For the two Paiutes killed at the camp, see James Bleak to G. A. Smith, Jan. 26, 1866; McArthur to Bentley, Jan. 21, 1866; Anson Winsor to Erastus Snow, Jan. 22, 1866, in BYOF, bx 42, fd 18.
52. James Bleak to G. A. Smith, Jan. 26, 1866.
53. Anson Winsor to Erastus Snow, Jan. 22, 1866.
54. Woolley, "A True Indian Story," 12; Jensen, "From the Days of '69," 2. The Jensen account states that the Mormons "commenced firing on the whole group."
55. There are two oral traditions gathered from Kaibab Paiutes, see Martineau, *Southern Paiutes*, 62–63, and Palmer, *Forgotten Chapters* (an interview with the underage survivor). As is typical of all historical sources, and of late, oral traditions, these sources conflict at times. Most importantly, the Martineau sources suggest that the Mormons killed the whole camp, men, women, and children. The earlier oral tradition, collected by William Palmer from the child survivor, makes it clear that the women and children survived, helped tend the wounded men, and eventually helped bury the five men who were massacred.
56. Palmer, *Forgotten Chapters*.
57. McArthur agrees that five Paiutes were brought to the site of Whitmore and McIntyre's bodies, but seems to think that they were all taken prisoner at the camp. McArthur to Bentley, Jan. 21, 1866.
58. James Bleak to G. A. Smith, Jan. 26, 1866.
59. Anson Winsor to Erastus Snow, Jan. 22, 1866.
60. The bodies of Whitmore and McIntyre were brought to St. George on the twenty-third, and buried amid general mourning. John Gardner to Erastus Snow, Jan. 26, 1866, in BYOF, CR 1234/1, bx 42, fd 18.
61. This in fact remained the Paiute tradition, and was accepted by Jacob Hamblin as true. However, the San Juan Paiute Patnish guided the Navajo company, and it is possible that Navajos pressured some local Paiutes to help them.
62. Johnson and Johnson, "Biographical Sketch of Seth E. Johnson," an autobiography, 28–30. Discussion in Knack, *Boundaries Between*, 82.
63. Woolley, "A True Indian Story," 12. Jensen, "From the Days of '69," 2, is also very explicit on this point: "The young boy was lined up and shot with the rest of them."
64. John Steele to George A. Smith, Jan. 22, 1866.
65. Erastus Snow to John D. L. Pearce, Meltiar Hatch and Samuel F. Lee, August 27, 1864, in Bleak, "Annals," p. 237.
66. Gottfredson, *Indian Depredations in Utah*, 180.
67. Martineau, *Southern Paiutes*, 63.
68. Woolley, "A True Indian Story"; "Notes on Fathers Life," 7–8; Jensen, "From the Days of '69," 3–4. Discussion in Peterson, *Utah's Black Hawk War*, 222. For Clark and Ward, see Bleak's list of participants in the Pipe Spring expedition, "Annals," Jan. 30, 1866, p. 304.
69. Johnson and Johnson, "Biographical Sketch of Seth E. Johnson," 28–30.
70. Jacob Hamblin to Erastus Snow, Nov. 21, 1870, as found in Bleak, "Annals," pp. 52–53.
71. John D. Lee to Brigham Young, Feb. 8, 1866, BYOF, bx 31, fd 6. Discussion in Peterson, *Utah's Black Hawk War*, 228.
72. Seth Johnson, Autobiography, 30–31.

73. Knack collects other examples of "casual," extralegal killing of Paiutes by Mormons. One old Paiute was discovered rustling cattle in Kanab. Mormons dug a hole and laid in wait for him: "When he came down we knocked him in the head and threw him in that hole and run the cows over it and we never had any more trouble." Mr. and Mrs. Higbee, interview with Juanita Brooks, Brooks papers, June 19, 1935, USHS; Knack, *Boundaries*, 84. In another case, a camp of Paiutes were attacked by whites (presumably Mormons) after accepting two cows from marauding Navajos in payment for services they had provided the Navajos. Thus, as in the Pipe Spring case, the Navajos committed the crime; Paiutes were blamed because they had received part of the plunder. The Paiutes returned fire but eventually were all killed; only two children escaped to tell the story. Fairley, "Kwagunt."
74. Jacob Hamblin and John R. Young to George A. Smith, September 12, 1869, George A. Smith Collection, MS 1322 (SC 33).
75. Peterson, *Utah's Black Hawk War*, 224; Correll, *Through White Men's Eyes*, 5:344 (despite this report, Manuelito was not killed, though he was severely wounded); 5:347. This wound was one of the factors that eventually caused Manuelito to surrender to the U.S. military and accept the move to Bosque Redondo.
76. William B. Maxwell to George A. Smith, April 12, 1866, George A. Smith Collection, MS 1322 (SC 33).
77. Woodbury, *A History of Southern Utah*, 170. Frank Hamilton, of Harrisburg, quoted in Dalton, *History of the Iron County Mission*, 102. Hamilton's garbled story of the Whitmore-McIntyre killings does not incline one to accept his account. Another late account is Gottfredson, *Indian Depredations*, 181–83, which states that Isabella Berry had been stripped, "outraged and horribly mutilated" (which conflicts with the much earlier Maxwell letter).
78. John Steele to Erastus Snow, Apr. 9, 1866, in "History of Brigham Young," 332–33; James Bleak to George A. Smith, Apr. 13, 1866, George A. Smith collection (SC 33). The earliest report is Nephi Johnson to George A. Smith, Apr. 8, 1866, in Journal History at that date. He writes, "Their bodies were completely perforated with arrows."
79. Kelly, "Journal of Walter Clement Powell," 407–8 (May 21, 1872). "In the year 1868 [1866], a man named [Joseph] Berry occupied the fort. He started [from northern Utah], with his son and daughter-in law [Robert and Isabella], for Long Valley, not anticipating trouble from any of the Lo family [Indians]. Arriving at Short Creek, some 20 miles north of Pipe [Spring], a band of Pah-Utes surprised and fired upon them. The elder Berry, who was driving, fell dead. The woman threw out the load, and young Berry drove furiously away. The Indians, on fleeter ponies, kept heading off the fugitives, until the second driver was slain. The horses gave out from galloping through sage and sand; but the heroic woman tried to unharness one of them, and escape on horseback. She was shot in the endeavor. One Indian only lost his life. Horses and goods were, of course, stolen. A party that went in search of the murdered family, found the dead bodies several days thereafter. The Pah-Utes charged the massacre upon the Navajos, but it is generally believed that the former were the authors of the crime."
80. James Bleak to George A. Smith, Apr. 13, 1866, George A. Smith collection, MS 1322 (SC 33).
81. James Bleak to George A. Smith, Apr. 13, 1866. See also John Steele to Erastus Snow, Apr. 9, 1866.
82. William B. Maxwell to George A. Smith, April 12, 1866. See also Peterson, *Utah's Black Hawk War*, 235.
83. See chapter 16 (1864), this volume.
84. Brigham Young to Erastus Snow, Aug. 15, 1866, BYOF (SC 22). Peterson, *Utah's Black Hawk War*, 235–36.
85. See Palmer, *Forgotten Chapters*, vol. 2, no. 70, May 4, 1952; John M. Berry to A. W. Ivins, March 8, 1916, in Anthony W. Ivins papers, bx 14, fd 11, USHS; also Woodbury, *A History of Southern Utah*, 170; Peterson, *Utah's Black Hawk War*, 235–36; Knack, *Boundaries Between*, 83–84.
86. Woodbury, *A History of Southern Utah*, 170.
87. John Steele to Erastus Snow, Apr. 9, 1866, in "History of Brigham Young," 332–33. Andrus had a reputation for summary killing of Indians that survived for generations in oral traditions handed down by the Paiutes. Martineau, *Southern Paiutes*, 62–65. In an example of partisan polarization of historical perception, Mormons, on the other hand, viewed him as a protector of the Saints and war hero. For further on Andrus, see Peterson, *Utah's Black Hawk War*, 312–14, 325; Miller, *Immortal Pioneers*, 188–89. He became a successful rancher in Long Valley, and a bishop. For a negative Mormon view, Woolley, "Notes on Fathers Life," 7.
88. Frank Hamilton, of Harrisburg, quoted in Dalton, *History of the Iron County Mission*, 102; Knack,

Boundaries Between, 83. As noted above, the Hamilton story of the Whitmore-McIntyre killings is garbled and unreliable.

89. Ivins, notes on a conversation with Nephi Johnson, Sept. 2, 1917, in Anthony W. Ivins papers, bx 14, fd 11, USHS.
90. Esplin, "Massacre of the Berrys"; Knack, *Boundaries Between*, 333n38; Roundy, "Pioneers of Early Days." For Coal Creek John, see chapter 28 (1875), this volume.
91. Peterson, *Utah's Black Hawk War*, 356.
92. Bailey and Bailey, *A History of the Navajo*, 38–39. These historians, in an otherwise valuable review of Navajo raiding in this period, misleadingly state that Mormons also carried out raids on the Navajos. The one piece of evidence they cite is actually a case of Mormons recovering livestock that Navajo raiders had stolen in southern Utah.
93. Chee et al., *Oral History Stories of the Long Walk*, 13. Many informants in this book emphasized Navajo raiding as a cause of the Navajo War and Long Walk, but other informants also mention raids on the Navajos by their enemies. See also Johnson and Roessel, *Navajo Stories of the Long Walk Period*, 23, in which one informant states, of Navajo raiders, "today they would be referred to as gangsters", 79, 156, 200, 229 (there was no one strong leader, so the Navajos had a disorganized leadership and thus had chaotic relations with outsiders); Dunlay, *Kit Carson and the Indians*, 265–66; Iverson, *Diné: A History of the Navajos*, 54. This is not to deny the brutality of the U.S. Army and New Mexican volunteers, which is also frequently mentioned in the oral histories.
94. For Manuelito's desperate situation at this time, see Correll, *Through White Men's Eyes*, 5:295, 347, 352–53, 358, 363, 368; Hoffman and Johnson, *Navajo Biographies*, 1:94–98; MacPherson, *The Northern Navajo Frontier*, 10.
95. Haskell, "Thales Haskell," 331–32.

CHAPTER 19

1. Kidney stones, which can cause vomiting, hematuria, and severe pain in the lower abdomen and groin, and in some cases can be fatal.
2. James Bleak to George A. Smith, Jan. 27, 1866, George A. Smith collection, MS 1322 (SC 33).
3. Journal History, Feb. 23 and March 2, 1866.
4. LJH, 91.
5. "Calienta," Letter to the Editor, Nov. 5, 1866, in "Correspondence," *Deseret News* 15:51, Nov. 21, 1866, p. 6(406). See also Fish, *The Life and Times of Joseph Fish*, at Sept. 17, 1866 (p. 103).
6. Promissory note to Charles B. Taylor, FAC 1314, Jacob Hamblin papers, Huntington Library, San Marino, CA; Corbett, *Jacob Hamblin*, 253–54.
7. John D. Lee diary, May 31, 1858 (1:166), Apr. 7, 1859 (1:206); chapter 8 (1858), this volume.
8. Fish, *The Life and Times of Joseph Fish*, at Sept. 17, 1866 (p. 103). John D. Lee did some freighting for "the Firm of Hamblin & Blair," Lee diary, June 9, 22, 1867 (2:77, 79).
9. FAC 1314 in Jacob Hamblin papers, Huntington Library, San Marino, CA; also in Corbett, *Jacob Hamblin*, 254.
10. Ibid.
11. Fish, *The Life and Times of Joseph Fish*, at Sept. 17, 1866 (p. 103); Corbett, *Jacob Hamblin*, 255, giving as his source an interview with Arland Udell, a Hamblin relative.
12. Corbett, *Jacob Hamblin*, 256. As an example of another business transaction, on March 6, 1868, Jacob sold 2,150 grape cuttings to William Foote, receiving $57.50 in flour and cotton in return. Warren Foote, Autobiography.
13. W. H. Crawford to Second Assistant Postmaster General, March 1, 1868, FAC 1310, in Jacob Hamblin papers, Huntington Library, San Marino, CA; Corbett, *Jacob Hamblin*, 249–56.
14. Henry W. [William] Miller, "Explorations on the Colorado," in "Correspondence," *Deseret News* 16.27, July 3, 1867, p. 1(200). For this expedition on the Colorado, quotes are from this report, unless otherwise specified. See also Bleak, "Annals," April 10–17, 1867, pp. 373–75.
15. Charles Lowell Walker diaries, Dec. 31, 1864 (1:247); Esshom, *Pioneers*, 1039; McClintock, *Mormon*

Settlement, 117. Millersburg, intended to be an important way station between St. George, the Muddy Mission, and Callville, was washed out by a ruinous flood in December 1867. Perkins, "From Switzerland," 10–11.

16. Crosby, "History and Journal."
17. Miller, "Explorations on the Colorado."
18. James White possibly also went through the Grand Canyon, or from Grand Wash to Callville, but not until September 1867. Brune, "Historic River Running."
19. Larson, *Erastus Snow*, 403.
20. See chapter 21 (1870), this volume.
21. Bleak, "Annals," May 1867, p. 377.
22. LJH, 92.
23. Franklin B. Woolley, Military Report, Sept. 21, 1866, in Crampton, "Military Reconnaissance," 149; Peterson, "'Book A—Levi Mathers Savage.'"
24. Jacob Hamblin and John R. Young to George A. Smith, September 12, 1869, George A. Smith Collection, MS 1322 (SC 33). The reference to Indians as "low, degraded" people, which might have been written by Young, shows typical white attitudes toward Indian culture.
25. For the Kaibab Paiutes, see Knack, *Boundaries Between*; Knack, "Interethnic Competition at Kaibab"; Stoffle and Evans, "Resource Competition." This latter article makes some mistakes, but its main argument has validity. Mormons and whites did move into and use the Kaibab homeland, especially the crucial water resources and grasslands used by Mormons for cattle raising. Traditions from Kaibab Paiutes are found in Martineau, *Southern Paiutes*.
26. Stoffle and Evans, "Resource Competition," 175–76.
27. Ibid., 177–78.
28. LJH, 92.
29. Ibid.
30. Ibid.
31. See Lyman, "Caught In Between."
32. For "grasshoppers" in Utah, see chapter 4 (1850–1853), this volume.
33. At age sixteen, on March 4, 1884, Ella married Warren M. Tenney (thirteen children). Known for her interest in education, she served as a Relief Society president in Alpine, Arizona, for twenty-five years, and taught Sunday school for thirty-five years. She died on March 31, 1947, in Alpine. "Sketch of Ella Hamblin Tenney's Life."
34. Walter became a well-known cowboy and rancher in Kanab. He married Sarah Blanche Robinson on January 15, 1898 (six children). He died on January 27, 1950, in Kanab. "Life of Walter Eugene Hamblin"; Death Certificate, in author's possession; "Services for Uncle Walt," *Kane County Standard*, Feb. 3, 1950, p. 1; P. T. Reilly to "Helen," Nov. 10, 1977, in PTRC, series 8.1, bx 2, fd 18.
35. Cox, "Biographical Sketch," 103. For the Three Nephites, see chapter 9 (late 1858), this volume.

CHAPTER 20

1. Henry Eyring, telegraph message, March 8, 1869, in "Items," *Deseret News* 18.6, March 17, 1869, p. 4(64). Eyring gives local Indians, reporting to Jacob Hamblin, as his source. According to "Home Items," "Our Dixie," in *Deseret News*, March 31, 1869, p. 5(89), Navajos were seeking alliances with Hualapais, Shivwits, and Paiutes; Hamblin is again given as a source. Discussion in Lyman, "Caught In Between," 35.
2. Peterson, *Utah's Black Hawk War*, 198–208.
3. Erastus Snow to Young, Jan. 2, 1869, BYOF, bx 42, fd 19.
4. J. Gates to Brigham Young, Feb. 28, 1869, BYOF, bx 33, fd 4. The Navajos had also made a raid, lasting twenty days, in November 1868. Some stock was recovered, mostly through the help of local Indians. John Steele to George A. Smith, March 3, 1869, BYOF, bx 33, fd 10.
5. Dutcher, *Ballard: The Great American Single Shot Rifle*.
6. Historian's Office Journal, June 4, 1869.
7. Erastus Snow to Young, July 20, 1869, BYOF, bx 42, fd 19.

8. Briggs, "James Mangum (1820–1888)" and "John Mangum (1817–1885)"; Walker, Turley, and Leonard, *Massacre at Mountain Meadows*, 260–61; Esshom, *Pioneers*, 1021.
9. Hamblin, journal, MSS 770, Lee Library.
10. Ibid.
11. Erastus Snow to Young, July 20, 1869.
12. For the Red Lake and Elk Mountain Utes, see J. E. Tourtelotte to E. S. Parker, Sept. 20, 1870, ARCIA (1870), 142–43; Franklin H. Head to Dennis N. Cooley, June 21, 1866, ARCIA (1866), 129–30; Peterson, *Utah's Black Hawk War*, 68n, 175, 185, 197n, 314.
13. Erastus Snow to Young, July 22, 1869, BYOF, bx 42, fd 19.
14. Anthropologist Omer Stewart recorded some oral traditions among Kaibab and San Juan Paiutes, and Navajos, in the 1930s, that Jacob Hamblin was a dangerous shaman. "The Indians thought Jacob Hamblin was their friend until the shamans discovered he was sending sickness to kill them off." Stewart, "Culture Element Distributions," 348. This probably reflects Jacob's reputation as a religious leader with supernatural power, combined with epidemics that followed contact with white settlers.
15. John R. Young to Erastus Snow, Aug. 15, 1869, in James Bleak Collection, MS 10587, bx 1, CHL. See also Young, *Memoirs of John R. Young*, 145. "I was called to labor among the Indians, and spent the summer with Jacob Hamblin and John Mangum in cultivating friendly relations with the Kaibab tribes." He seems to date his work with Hamblin in the Kanab area to 1866, but this is apparently incorrect.
16. Hamblin journal, MSS 770, Lee Library.
17. John R. Young to Erastus Snow, Aug. 15, 1869.
18. Jacob Hamblin and John R. Young to Erastus Snow, Aug. 16, 1869, in James Bleak Collection, MS 10587, bx 1, CHL.
19. Hamblin journal, MSS 770, Lee Library.
20. Charles Walker diary, Aug. 22–Sept. 8, 1869 (1:295–98).
21. Ibid., Aug. 28, 1869 (1:297).
22. Ibid., Sept. 5, 1869 (1:297).
23. Moses M. Farnsworth, Journal, June 14, 1870, as quoted in "Settlement of Kanab Region," 25. Woodbury, *A History of Southern Utah*, 179, states that James Wilkins was at the Mountain Meadows Massacre, but I have not found his name in any records of the massacre. A James Wilkin acted as clerk to John D. Lee in his official report of the massacre. Brooks, *Mountain Meadows Massacre*, 153.
24. Jacob Hamblin and John R. Young to George A. Smith, September 12, 1869, George A. Smith Collection, MS 1322 (SC 33). Though Hamblin is the first signer of this letter, and contributed to it, it was undoubtedly written by John R. Young, and Young sometimes speaks of Hamblin in the third person.
25. Hamblin and Young to Smith, Sept. 12, 1869.
26. Robinson, *History of Kane County*, 14.
27. LJH, 94. See also Hamblin and Young to George A. Smith, September 12, 1869.
28. LJH, 94.
29. Hamblin journal, MSS 770, Lee Library, at Oct. 5, 1869.
30. See chapter 13 (early 1862), this volume.
31. See Horatio Morrill, diary. For this 1869 expedition, quotes are from Morrill, unless otherwise specified. Hamblin, journal and reminiscences, MSS 770, Lee Library (which has one entry by Jacob and a diary by an anonymous diarist for the first part of the trip); LJH, 93; George Fawcett, "Memoirs"; Young, *Memoirs of John R. Young*, 145–46 (who apparently misdates the trip to 1866).
32. Joseph Watson Young was a son of Brigham's brother, Lorenzo Dow, see Young, *Memoirs of John R. Young*, 149–51.
33. Erastus Snow and Joseph W. Young to Jacob Hamblin and company, Sept. 24, 1869, in Bleak, "Annals," pp. 493–97.
34. Bleak, "Annals," September 1869, p. 492.
35. Kenney, *Wilford Woodruff's Journal* (6:469).
36. E. Strong is possibly Ezra Strong, one of the early settlers of Kanab; see chapter 16 (1864), this volume. For Ephraim Wilson, see Bleak, "Annals," p. 492.
37. Fawcett, "Memoirs," 12.

38. For Nebeker (1843–1911), see his obituary, *Deseret News*, Sept. 7, 1911, p. 3; Jenson, LDSBE, 3:180; Smallcanyon, "Contested Space," 157–58, 161–71, 202. He participated actively as a boatman in the second Powell expedition and served as sheriff of Kane County from 1873 to 1877.
39. The Shivwits was mentioned in Morrill's diary, at Oct. 18. Quantuquackets was apparently a Paiute from south of the Colorado who had been visiting the Mormon settlements. Hamblin says that twenty-one whites and twenty-one Indians went on the mission; John R. Young lists forty-seven total; Young, *Memoirs of John R. Young*, 145. George Fawcett, "Memoirs," 11, remembered twenty to twenty-four men in the whole company.
40. This sentence is difficult to read, but the general meaning is clear.
41. Jacob Hamblin, journal and reminiscences, MSS 770, Lee Library.
42. Anonymous diarist; Morrill diary.
43. Anonymous diarist.
44. Fawcett, "Memoirs," 11.
45. The anonymous diary ends here.
46. Fawcett, "Memoirs," 11, places "Jacobs' Pools" on the west side of the Kaibab Plateau. It is possible that he was referring to modern Jacob's Lake, which would, if true, be the only early reference to Jacob's Lake that I know of. According to a secondary source, Jacob and John D. Lee built a six-room adobe house with a sod roof here. Woodbury, *A History of Southern Utah*, 189. Azar, "Buckskin Mountain," 53, writes that the house Jacob and Lee raised may have been the first structure built by whites on the Kaibab Plateau. However, Azar incorrectly dates the story to 1860.
47. Morrill diary.
48. Fawcett, "Memoirs," 11.
49. Morrill diary.
50. This location is marked on the map in Powell's "An Overland Trip to the Grand Canyon," 661. It appears to be just north of Moenkopi Wash.
51. Morrill diary. This might have been the Lakon festival, a woman's harvest dance.
52. Fawcett, "Memoirs," 13.
53. LJH, 93.
54. Morrill diary.
55. LJH, 93.
56. John D. Lee, Nov. 2, 1869 (2:124–25); H. Lunt to Brigham Young, November 3, 1869, in Brigham Young collection, CR 1231/1, bx 33, fd 5.
57. Cleland and Brooks 2:254; Bleak, "Annals," Nov. 1, 1869, pp. 497–98.
58. This may be Whitmore Pools, about twenty miles directly north of Tuba City and about ten miles east of Echo Cliffs on modern maps.
59. Morrill diary.
60. Young, *Memoirs*, 145–46.
61. Ibid.
62. Ibid.
63. Published in Wooley, "Journal of Two Campaigns." See also Augustus M. Dodge to Cor. Tourtellotte, Nov. 9, 1869, in Bleak, "Annals," p. 505; Bleak, "Annals," Nov. 16, 1869, p. 508.
64. Wooley, "Journal of Two Campaigns," 173.
65. LJH, 94. In two letters to Brigham Young, written on Nov. 16 and 18, 1869, BYOF, bx 42, fd 19, CHL, Erastus Snow stated that Andrus had killed two Navajos and that sixty head of livestock had been recovered, but the main party of Indians had escaped with a hundred head.
66. Wooley, "Journal of Two Campaigns."
67. LJH, 94.
68. Erastus Snow to Brigham Young, Nov. 20, 1869, BYOF, bx 42, fd 19. For the confusing history of Fort Fauntleroy/Lyon/Wingate (II) (near Bear Springs, seven miles east of modern Gallup) and Wingate (I) (located near the village of San Rafael), see Frazer, *Forts of the West*, 108; James, "The History of Fort Wingate." Erastus Snow and Jacob would have more correctly used the Fort Wingate name. In any event, they were accusing the United States army of actively supporting the Navajos in their raids on the Mormons.

69. LJH, 95. Dellenbaugh, *A Canyon Voyage*, 170, wrote that Jacob, after seeing raiding Navajos killed by Paiutes, "grew heartily sick of this kind of work, and made the resolve to appeal to the Navajos."
70. See chapter 16 (1864), this volume.
71. Iverson, *Diné*, 63–65.
72. Peterson, *Utah's Black Hawk War*, 341–46.
73. The LDS sacrament meeting is held on Sundays in local congregations. In this meeting church leaders share news and conduct business, and members of the congregation, or visitors, give sermons, sing hymns, pray, and partake of communion (which Mormons call the sacrament).
74. Charles Walker, Diary (1:302). For prayer circles, often performed in temples, see Tate, "Prayer Circle"; Quinn, "Latter-day Saint Prayer Circles."
75. Erastus Snow to Brigham Young, Dec. 7, 1869; see also Hamblin to Young, Sept. 30, 1870, discussed in chapter 21 (1870), this volume. P. T. Reilly, *Lee's Ferry*, 15, as usual seems to blame Hamblin for founding Pahreah in a place endangered by floods; however, Snow had asked Hamblin to found the farm there. In addition, Hamblin used a site that had been previously chosen by the Shirts. Pahreah II and Adairville, sites not chosen by Hamblin, also became ghost towns, partially because of flooding.
76. See Jenson, "Pahreah Ward"; Smith, "Account of the Settling of Paria River"; Bradley, *A History of Kane County*, 70; Carr, *Historical Guide*, 126–27; Kelsey, *Hiking and Exploring*, 353–56; chapter 18 (1866), this volume.
77. Jacob Hamblin to Brigham Young, Sept. 30, 1870, BYOF, bx 33, fd 15.
78. Brooks, *On the Mormon Frontier*, 1:150; Nichols and Bracken, "William Meeks."
79. See chapter 21 (1870), this volume.
80. At Sept. 5, 1870 (2:135).
81. Kelsey, *Hiking and Exploring*, 354; Carr, *Historical Guide*, 126.
82. "Pahreah Ward History."

CHAPTER 21

1. "Statement of Mexican Prisoner who deserted the Navajos," Jan. 9, 1870, in James Bleak Collection, MS 10587, bx 1, CHL. For the death of Spaneshanks, see chapter 18 (1866), this volume. Barow-azeta could be the famous Barboncito, probably the most influential Navajo chief, see below, this chapter. Bleak, "Annals," at Jan. 9, 1870, pp. 1–2, reproduces this statement, but gives the name of the chief as "Bar-o-wan-zeta," which even more closely resembles the name "Barboncito." (However, the document in MS 10587 is probably a more primary source.) Historian John Alton Peterson has identified Barboncito as one of the Navajos who raided in Mormon territory during the Black Hawk–Navajo wars, and he has also identified Barboncito as a brother of Spaneshanks, *Utah's Black Hawk War*, 88. On the other hand, Barow-azeta might be an entirely different person. To further complicate the issue, there were multiple chiefs with the names El Barbon or Barboncito. Kelly, *Navajo Roundup*, 145.
2. See chapter 18 (1866), this volume.
3. Jacob Hamblin, diaries and reminiscences, 1868–1870, 1885, MSS 770, Lee Library. The following quotes are also from this source.
4. It appears William Meeks was absent. He was back by Jan. 31, "Pahreah Ward History."
5. Hamblin to Erastus Snow, March 27, 1870, in Bleak, "Annals," pp. 18–20.
6. George A. Smith to Albert Carrington, Apr. 5, 1871, in Journal History at that date; Charles Walker diary, March 28, 1870 (1:309).
7. LJH, 95.
8. Jacob Hamblin, diaries and reminiscences, 1868–1870, 1885.
9. LJH, 95.
10. Ibid. This letter is not extant, to the best of my knowledge. Jacob may have been thinking of Young's Sept. 13, 1870 letter to him, which has some of the same language. See below.
11. Jacob Hamblin, diary.
12. Corbett, *Jacob Hamblin*, 266, incorrectly dates the Hamblin family's move to Kanab in September 1869. Jacob's diary gives the correct date of Louisa's move to Kanab. Priscilla also dated the move to 1870, Arrott, *Sarah Priscilla Leavitt Hamblin*, 40.

13. 1870 Census, Kanab, Kane County, p. 2. Priscilla stayed in Santa Clara till early October. The 1870 Census ("Claratown," Washington County, pp. 1–2) records that on June 25, 1870, Priscilla was living in Santa Clara with Sarah A, eleven; Melissa, nine; Lucy, seven; Jacob, eleven; and Ella, three. See below, Arrott, *Sarah Priscilla Leavitt Hamblin*, 40.
14. Corbett, *Jacob Hamblin*, 267, citing Josephine Bunker, a neighbor.
15. See chapter 20, this volume; John R. Young and Jehiel McConnell were also residents. George A. Smith to Albert Carrington, Apr. 5, 1871, in Journal History at that date.
16. Map of Kanab fort, in PTRC, series 1, bx 10, fd 146. See also Robinson, "History of Kanab," 275–76; Lucinda Stewart, in *Pioneers of Kane County*, p. 213, as cited in "John Mangum, 1817–1881."
17. Dellenbaugh, *The Romance of the Colorado River*, 305; *A Canyon Voyage*, 166–67, 173.
18. Robinson, "History of Kanab," 275–76.
19. William Thomas Stewart, "Personal journal."
20. Ibid.; Arrington, Fox, and May, *Building the City of God*, 225–64.
21. "Settlement of Kanab Region," 24, which lists the family heads; Kanab Ward Historical Record Book A, at June 14, 1870. See also Levi Stewart to Brigham Young, early 1870, typescript in PTRC, series 1, bx 10, fd 147. Stewart, "Personal journal," recalls arriving on July 1. Lucinda Stewart, a daughter of Levi, remembered, "Jacob Hamblin, his wife Louisa, (and) Charlie Riggs from Santa Clara came the same day we did [May 20]." *Pioneers of Kane County*, 213, as cited in "John Mangum, 1817–1881."
22. K. T. L., letter to the editor, Apr. 21, 1871, *Deseret News*, in Journal History at Apr. 21. For a modern agreement, see May, "Utah Writ Small," 172–74.
23. For more on early Kanab, see Reilly, "Kanab United Order"; May, "People on the Mormon Frontier"; Carter, "John Wesley Powell's Headquarters"; Arrington, Fox, and May, *Building the City of God*, 225–64; Bradley, *A History of Kane County*.
24. Stewart, "Personal journal."
25. A. Milton Musser, Letter to the Editor, Sept. 10, 1870, in Correspondence section, *Deseret Evening News*, Sept. 21, 1870, in Journal History, Sept. 10, 1870.
26. Jacob Hamblin, diaries and reminiscences, MSS 770, Lee Library. Fish were an important element for Ute and Paiute subsistence. Farmer, *On Zion's Mount*, chapters 1 and 2. Because Mormons tended to "overfish" former bountiful fisheries they began stocking lakes and streams as early as the 1850s. This overfishing once again endangered a stable food supply for Utes. Sigler and Sigler, "History of Fish Hatchery Development," 584.
27. Fish, *The Life and Times of Joseph Fish*, 126.
28. LJH, 96.
29. Jacob Hamblin, diaries and reminiscences, MSS 770, Lee Library.
30. Journal History, June 3, 1870.
31. For Jacob stocking lakes with fish, see also John D. Lee diary, Sept. 4, 1870 (2:137).
32. See Dellenbaugh, *A Canyon Voyage*, 250; Worster, *A River Running West*, 211.
33. A. Milton Musser, Letter to the Editor, Sept. 10, 1870, in Correspondence section, *Deseret Evening News*, Sept. 21, 1870, in Journal History, Sept. 10.
34. Dellenbaugh, *A Canyon Voyage*, 250. Chuar would die in about 1894. Andrew Jenson, cp., Journal History, Kanab Stake, excerpts in PTRC, series 1, bx 10, fd 147.
35. Kanab Ward Historical Record Book A, at June 29, 1870; Robinson, *History of Kane County*, 21.
36. William T. Stewart, "Personal journal."
37. For Powell, see Worster, *A River Running West*; Stegner, *Beyond the Hundredth Meridian*; Darrah, *Powell of the Colorado*.
38. Powell, *Exploration of the Colorado River*, 102.
39. For the significance of the journal of Hamblin's trip for Powell, see Stegner, *Beyond the Hundredth Meridian*, 105; Worster, *A River Running West*, 191.
40. Darrah, "Major Powell Prepares"; Stegner, *Beyond the Hundredth Meridian*, 124–29; Worster, *A River Running West*, 210–18.
41. LJH, 96; John D. Lee diary, Sept. 3, 1870 (2:135).
42. When Thompson wrote a financial report for the expedition from 1871 to 1873 (Thompson, "Financial

Statement," 2), he listed Jacob in the group of "permanent" employees in 1871 and 1872, with the title "Chief Packer," though his duties as guide and interpreter extended far beyond this job description. Numbered among the "temporary employees" are Jacob's sons, Joseph and Lyman, and his brothers Frederick and Frank. Jacob is not listed among the permanent employees in 1873, though Joseph Hamblin is (with the title "General Assistant"). The Powell men often camped in Jacob's lot in Kanab. For Clem Powell, see Olsen, "Clem Powell."

43. John D. Lee, journal, Sept. 5, 1870 (2:135) and A. Milton Musser, Letter to the Editor, Sept. 10, 1870, in Correspondence section, *Deseret Evening News*, Sept. 21, 1870, in Journal History, Sept. 10. Brigham Young to Horace Eldredge, Oct. 4, 1870, in *Latter-day Saints' Millennial Star* 32.44 (Nov. 1, 1870): 701–2. I follow Eric Olson's reconstruction of the route the Young company took. Those who turn to John Wesley Powell's "diary" for an account of this journey will look in vain, even though it covers the same dates as Lee and Musser. (See Powell, *Exploration of the Colorado River*, 107–12, September 4 to 13.) Powell's "diary" is in fact a memoir in which he injects elements from 1871 and 1872 into his 1869 and 1870 diaries. (He kept a very rudimentary diary during his 1869 trip.) So in reading Powell's September 4–13 "diary," there is no mention of Brigham Young or John D. Lee; instead, Powell makes a trip down the North Fork of the Virgin to Zion's Canyon, a trip he did take, but not until 1872. He does end up at Pipe Spring, and so is historically accurate on that point.
44. John D. Lee, diary. Powell describes a camp, by implication with his men, "by the upper springs of the Kanab," dated before Sept. 5, that is, on Sept. 4 or perhaps 3, and describes a meeting with Hamblin and Kaibab Paiutes there. Powell didn't reach Fort Kanab until the sixth. It seems more likely that Powell's meeting with Hamblin and the Paiutes took place at Kanab.
45. Musser, Letter to the Editor.
46. Lee, diary.
47. Musser, Letter to the Editor.
48. Lee, diary.
49. Ibid.
50. Musser, Letter to the Editor.
51. Lee, diary.
52. The Kanab fort was located west of the present Kanab city center, on the east bank of Kanab Creek (now at the bottom of an expansive ravine). There is a marker for Fort Kanab on Highway 89 (northwest of modern Kanab). Jacob's lot and buildings, in the new town location, were near the historic Parry's Motel.
53. Powell, *Exploration of the Colorado*, 107.
54. Lee, diary.
55. Olsen, "Winsor Castle"; Lavender, *Pipe Spring.*
56. Peterson, "The Last Bastion."
57. Francis Bishop diary.
58. Chamberlain, "Francis Marion Bishop"; Bishop to John Wesley Powell, Jan. 20, 1873, Geological Survey, RG 57, Powell Survey, letters received, M156, Roll 2, NA.
59. See chapter 20 (1869), this volume.
60. Powell, *Exploration of the Colorado*, 113.
61. Ibid.
62. Bishop and Powell both describe this journey, often contradicting each other. Bishop has the more reliable chronology, but Powell is more expansive. See also Jacob Hamblin to Brigham Young, Sept. 30, 1870, BYOF, bx 33, fd 15.
63. Dutton, *Tertiary History of the Grand Cañon District*, 79–80.
64. Powell, *Exploration of the Colorado*, 113.
65. Francis Marion Bishop, diary.
66. Ibid. This was either on Mount Trumbull or on a mountain south of Trumbull.
67. Worster, *A River Running West*, 214–15.
68. Powell, *Exploration of the Colorado*, 122. Remarkably, we have a picture of this Paiute, also. Ibid., fig. 45, just before 123.

69. Francis Marion Bishop, diary. Powell dates the descent to the river on the seventeenth, apparently compressing three days of travel (per Bishop) into one day.
70. Powell, *Exploration of the Colorado*, 123.
71. Ibid., 123–24.
72. Unfortunately, his diary for 1870 ends with this incident.
73. Powell, *Exploration of the Colorado*, 124–25.
74. Ibid. This was a common feature of "frontier water."
75. Assuming that Powell is two days off.
76. Powell, *Exploration of the Colorado*, 128–29.
77. Billingsley, Spamer, and Menkes, *Quest for the Pillar of Gold*, 21. Hualapais specifically were antagonistic to miners, Knack, *Boundaries Between*, 98. Dobyns and Euler, *The Walapai People*, 50, and "The Dunn-Howland Killings"; Casebier, *Camp Beale's Springs*, 21. Miners often caused trouble in their relations with Indian women, Knack, *Boundaries Between*, 107, so that is also a credible part of this story. Prospectors apparently started the "Walapai War," which lasted from approximately 1865 to February 1869, Dobyns and Euler, *The Walapai People*, 36–44; Casebier, *Camp Beale's Springs*, 21. For miners and Indians generally in Utah and Nevada, see Knack, *Boundaries Between*, 100–107; Reeve, *Making Space*. Some historians, such as Belshaw, "The Dunn-Howland Killings," have incorrectly stated that Indians never crossed the Colorado. See Toab, "History of the Three Generations," 2; Dobyns and Euler, "The Dunn-Howland Killings."
78. One Paiute informant, a child at the time of the murders, gave the names of the three Indians who killed the Howlands and Dunn, and located the place of killing. George Brooks to Anthony Ivins, Oct. 17, 1923, in Anthony Ivins Papers, bx 14, fd 11, item 10. See also Dellenbaugh, *A Canyon Voyage*, 269.
79. LJH, 97.
80. Belshaw, "The Dunn-Howland Killings," thinks the story of Indians on the other side of the Colorado inciting the Shiwvits to murder is unlikely; Dobyns and Euler, in "The Dunn-Howland Killings," believe this explanation very credible.
81. Powell, *Exploration of the Colorado*, 131.
82. Larsen, "'The Letter.'" This explanation is taken up by Krakauer in his best-selling book, *Under the Banner of Heaven*, 231–47.
83. Worster, *A River Running West*, 214.
84. Lago, "The Toquerville Myth."
85. Almon Thompson to John Wesley Powell, May 10, 1872, Geological Survey, RG 57, Powell Survey, letters received, M156, Roll 1, no. 124, NA.
86. For more on the death of the Howlands and Dunn, see Ivins, "Traveling Over Forgotten Trails: A Mystery of the Grand Canyon Solved"; Dellenbaugh to Charles Kelly, undated letter, in Crampton, "F. S. Dellenbaugh," 236; Dellenbaugh, *Romance of the Colorado River*, 228–30; Darrah, "The Howland Brothers"; Belshaw, "The Dunn-Howland Killings"; Dobyns and Euler, "The Dunn-Howland Killings"; Barrios, "An Appointment with Death."
87. Brigham Young and Daniel H. Wells to Jacob Hamblin, Sept. 13, 1870, BYOF (SC 22). For the Red Lake Utes, see ch. 20 (1869), above.
88. LJH, 99.
89. Hamblin to Young, Sept. 30, 1870, BYOF, bx 33, fd 15.
90. Arrott, *Sarah Priscilla Leavitt Hamblin*, 40.
91. Corbett, *Jacob Hamblin*, 266.
92. Ibid., 266n8. According to Corbett, the building was later sold to J. T. Graff, then to Samuel Knight Jr., the son of Samuel Knight. Later, it was owned by Hamblins. The LDS Church obtained this building in a trade with the Utah state government in March 1974. Haggerty, "Historic Preservation in Utah," 114; John Hamblin, "Hamblin Home in Santa Clara."
93. Certificate dated Oct. 1, 1870, in James Bleak Collection, MS 10587, bx 1, CHL.
94. Arrott, *Sarah Priscilla Leavitt Hamblin*, 40.
95. Powell, *Canyons of the Colorado*, chapter 13.
96. Ammon Tenney, "Peace with the Navajos." I believe Powell's dates are consistently about seven to ten

days off. Secondary sources, when they have followed Powell, have also gotten the chronology wrong, e.g., Darrah, "Major Powell Prepares," 152. Of course, Hamblin was off by an entire year, dating this expedition to 1871 in Little, LJH 99!

97. Darrah, "Major Powell Prepares," 152.
98. Powell, *Canyons of the Colorado*, chapter 13.
99. Tenney, "Peace with the Navajos." Tenney confuses Powell and Hamblin's trip to the North Rim with the earlier trip to the Uinkarets and Shivwits.
100. He does mention Hamblin on the other side of the Colorado in the 1875 magazine article, "The Ancient Province of Tusayan," 201. *Canyons of the Colorado*, however, was Powell's definitive account of this journey.
101. LJH, 99; Powell, *Canyons of the Colorado*, chapter 13, who dates this on about October 2.
102. LJH, 99. As Hamblin's dating of this expedition is incorrect, it is possible that Nebeker, Terry, Potter, and Chuarumpeak went on the 1871 expedition.
103. In "The Ancient Province of Tusayan," 196, Powell published a map of the journey.
104. In *Canyons of the Colorado*, chapter 13, Powell says that he came to the town of Moenkopi, which was deserted. His memory differs from the map and the earlier article, "Ancient Province of Tusayan," which do not record a visit to the Moenkopi town area.
105. Powell, "Ancient Province of Tusayan," 201.
106. See Gregory, *Geology of the Navajo Country*, 103–4; Linford, *Navajo Places*, 143.
107. Powell, "Ancient Province of Tusayan," 202.
108. Ibid.
109. Ibid.
110. Powell, *Canyons of the Colorado*, chapter 13. In "Ancient Province of Tusayan," 202, Powell states that he stayed with the Hopis for two months!
111. LJH, 99.
112. Kate, *Travels and Researches*, 246–47.
113. Tenney, "Peace with the Navajos."
114. Frank F. Bennett, to "whom it may concern," Nov. 5, 1870, in James Bleak Collection, MS 10587, bx 1, CHL; also in Bleak, "Annals," pp. 46–47. Jacob Hamblin, 1870–1871 diary (CHL, Ms. 14655), dates his parley with the Navajo chiefs on November 5, which correlates exactly with the Bennett letter. Powell, in *Canyons of the Colorado*, chapter 13, says he arrived at Fort Wingate, in New Mexico, on November 1. He does not mention the talk and treaty with the Navajos.
115. Locke, *The Book of the Navajo*, 392–93, 395–96; Moore, *Chiefs, Agents & Soldiers*, 53–74.
116. Kate, *Travels and Researches*, 242; Frink, *Fort Defiance & the Navajos.*
117. Hamblin, 1870–1871 diary, MS 14655, CHL.
118. LJH, 99; Tenney, "Peace with the Navajos." The official transcript of the meeting, dated November 5, 1870, was taken by the Fort Defiance clerk. This is in Jacob Hamblin to Erastus Snow, Nov. 21, 1870, James Bleak Collection, MS 10587, bx 1, CHL, with the signature of Delgadito attached; also in Bleak, "Annals," 48–55. Another copy was made for Powell, MS 834 at the National Anthropological Archives, Smithsonian Institution. I use the Bleak, "Annals," version, but will refer to the Powell copy on occasion. One of the translators was John Lorenzo Hubbell, who later became widely known as a Navajo trader. Tenney, "Peace with the Navajos"; McNitt, *The Indian Traders*, 143; chapter 27 (1874), this volume.
119. For Barboncito (ca 1820–1871), see Brugge, "Barboncito", Hoffman, *Navajo Biographies*, 1:105–28; Mitchell, Frisbie, and McAllester, *Navajo Blessingway Singer*, 25; Thrapp, *Encyclopedia of Frontier Biography*, 1:63.
120. The name is spelled Barboneito in Bleak, but is correctly written Barboncito in the Powell copy, pp. 2, 5.
121. Hamblin said that one of the Protestant missionaries there had a horse that he recognized as belonging to a Mormon, and he shamed him into returning it. George A. Smith diary, Dec. 25, 1870 (SC 32).
122. Tenney, "Peace with the Navajos." See also an interview with Jacob in George A. Smith diary, Dec. 25, 1870 (SC 32).
123. Jacob Hamblin to John W. Powell, Dec. 20, 1870, in Geological Survey, RG 57, Powell Survey, letters received, M156, Roll 1, no. 19, NA.

124. Hamblin's 1870–1871 diary; Jacob Hamblin to Erastus Snow, Nov. 21, 1870, in James Bleak Collection, MS 10587, bx 1, CHL; Tenney, "Peace with the Navajos."
125. Tenney, "Peace with the Navajos."
126. Jacob Hamblin to Erastus Snow, Nov. 21, 1870.
127. LJH, 102. Some have identified Hastele as Ganado Mucho, see chapter 27 (1874), this volume.
128. Possibly Hastele.
129. Hamblin, 1870–1871 diary, cf. Hamblin to Snow, Nov. 21, 1870.
130. Tenney, "Peace with the Navajos."
131. LJH, 102–3.
132. Hamblin to Snow, Nov. 21, 1870; LJH, 104. For Talasnimki, see chapter 10 (1859), this volume.
133. John R. Young and Hamblin to Erastus Snow, December 7, 1870, in Bleak, "Annals," pp. 64–67.
134. LJH, 104–5.
135. Ibid.
136. He wrote the report on Ft. Defiance here, and sent it to Erastus Snow.
137. Hamblin to Powell, Dec. 20, 1870.
138. Udall, "Tuba—The Oraibi," 436. For Tuuvi and Talasnimki in Kanab, see Beaman, "The Cañon of the Colorado," 687.
139. John R. Young and Hamblin to Erastus Snow, December 7, 1870; Levi Stewart to Brigham Young, Dec. 8, 1870, BYOF, bx 33, fd 20.
140. Levi Stewart to Brigham Young, Dec. 8, 1870.
141. Zadok Knapp Judd, Autobiography.
142. John D. Lee, diary (2:148).
143. Ibid. (2:144).
144. James Lovett Bunting, Diaries, Dec. 14, 1870; Levi Stewart, Letter, Dec. 18, 1870, in "The Catastrophe at Kanab," in *Deseret Evening News*, Dec. 22, 1870, in Journal History, Dec. 14, 1870, p. 1; M. F. Farnsworth, Letter, Dec. 18, 1870, in *Deseret Evening News*, Dec. 29, 1870, in Journal History, Dec. 14, 1870, p. 2; John D. Lee, diary, Dec. 13, 1870 (2:149). See also Kanab Ward Historical Record Book A, at Dec. 14, 1870; William Thomas Stewart, "Personal Journal," an autobiography; Robinson, *History of Kane County*, 35–36; Bradley, *A History of Kane County*, 76–77; Udall and Nelson, *Arizona Pioneer Mormon*, 249.
145. LJH, 106–7. Powell and Ingalls, *Report*, 10, list Choog as chief of the Long Valley Paiutes, the Un-ka-ka'-ni-guts, who numbered thirty-six in 1873.
146. George A. Smith diary, Dec. 23, 1870 (SC 32).
147. Charles Walker, diary, Dec. 25, 1870 (1:324).
148. Udall, *Forgotten Founders*, 54.
149. Peterson, "Apostle of the Outposts," 123.
150. Reilly, *Lee's Ferry*, 17.
151. See Williams, *Navajo Political Process*, 8–9, which also gives a good overview of the Navajo political organizations before 1868. Before that time, local groups were organized under peace and war chiefs, though occasionally large ceremonial assemblies of Navajos were called to make important decisions, 4–6.
152. LJH, 99.

CHAPTER 22

1. Udall, "Jacob Hamblin ... Story of His Later Years."
2. Mary H. Beeler, "Life Sketch of Melissa"; Corbett, Jacob Hamblin, 461.
3. Beeler, "Life Sketch of Melissa"; Corbett, Jacob Hamblin, 359.
4. Udall, Forgotten Founders, 56–57.
5. P. T. Reilly, Interview with Amarilla Hamblin Lee, June 26, 1970.
6. Inez Hamblin Lee, Autobiography.
7. John D. Lee, diary, Nov. 5, 1873 (2:306).

8. Ammon Tenney to Pearl Udall Nelson, July 12, 1915, pp. 6–8, Ammon Tenney Collection, Arizona Historical Society, Tucson.
9. Ibid.

CHAPTER 23

1. LJH, 107–8.
2. Hamblin to Young, Feb. 11, 1871, BYOF, bx 34, fd 5.
3. Hamblin to Young, March 20, 1871, BYOF, bx 34, fd 5; John D. Lee, Diary, March 12, 1874 (2:31).
4. Joseph W. Young to Brigham Young, February 24, 1871, BYOF, bx 34, fd 7; Fleming, "The Settlements on the Muddy," 172.
5. This place remains unidentified, unless it is Canyon Bonito, just north of Fort Defiance.
6. Hamblin to Young, March 20, 1871.
7. "Home News," *Deseret News* 20.12, Apr. 26, 1871, p. 8. James Bunting diary, Jan. 26, 1871.
8. See Haight diary, at the date June 22, 1871, in Jacob Hamblin journal, 1871–1874, MSS 1951, CHL. The Jacob Hamblin account, in the same manuscript, is at the date June 12, 1871. For Hamblin and Haight's friendship at this time, see Isaac Haight to ElizaAnn and Annabella Haight, Sept. 8, 1871, in Woolley, *'I Would to God'*, 133–39.
9. Haight diary.
10. Jared Alvin Taylor and Francis Eaton King were prominent settlers in Marysvale and Glenwood. Bishop B. Cannon may be Bishop Archibald Buchanan.
11. Circleville had been the site of a horrific massacre of local Paiutes in 1866. Peterson, *Utah's Black Hawk War*, 246–47; Knack, *Boundaries Between*, 85.
12. Gregory, "Diary of Almon Harris Thompson," July 27, 1871, p. 30; Darrah, *Powell of the Colorado*, 170. Eric Olson feels that Thompson was incorrect, and that Jacob and Haight "were probably probing the Escalante River." Personal communication.
13. Journal History, July 25, 1871.
14. Gregory, "Journal of Stephen Vandiver Jones," July 29, 1871, p. 53; Worster, *A River Running West*, 226.
15. Burton, *A History of Uintah County*, 25, 85, 108, 154.
16. Gregory, "Journal of Stephen Vandiver Jones," July 29, 1871, p. 53.
17. Ibid.; Darrah, *Powell of the Colorado*, 171.
18. LJH, 107–8.
19. *Deseret News*, as cited in Udall, "Tuba—The Oraibi," 437; Journal History, July 25, 1871.
20. Almon Thompson, "Report on a Trip," 138.
21. For example, Reilly, with his usual derogatory view of Hamblin, writes that Thompson "achieved what Jacob Hamblin had twice failed to do." *Lee's Ferry*, 28. He also states that Thompson discovered the Escalante, which is arguably correct, but Hamblin led the first exploring expedition into the canyon. In a similar vein, Kelly, "Journal of Walter Clement Powell," after p. 478n67.
22. The directions Powell gave Hamblin are recorded in Jacob Hamblin diary, 1870–Aug. 1871, section entitled "Maj Powell, Direction to find the Dirty Devil River," Ms. 14655, CHL.
23. June 12, 1872 (Kelly 418).
24. Jacob Hamblin, 1871 journal, Ms. 1951, 3rd notebook, fd 4, CHL.
25. Gregory, "Diary of Almon Harris Thompson," Oct. 6, 1871, p. 56.
26. Gregory, "Journal of Stephen Vandiver Jones," Oct. 6, 1871, p. 99.
27. Darrah, *Powell of the Colorado*, 171, states that Jacob Hamblin, with two of his sons, traveled with Powell to Gray Canyon to meet Powell's company, reaching there on August 29; see also Stegner, *Beyond the Hundredth Meridian*, 138. Actually, Powell traveled to Gray Canyon with Jacob's brother Fred and son Lyman; see the diary of Stephen Vandiver Jones, August 29, 1871, pp. 70–71.
28. LJH, 108.
29. Reilly describes Hatch going south of the Colorado and inviting the Navajos, but unfortunately he does not footnote this section. Elkins, *Ira Hatch: Indian Missionary*, 112–13. Isaac Haight to ElizaAnn and

Annabella Haight, Sept. 8, 1871, in Woolley, *'I Would to God'*, 133–34, refers to eighty Navajos expected in Kanab on September 8.

30. James Bunting, diary.
31. Isaac Haight to ElizaAnn and Annabella Haight, Sept. 8, 1871.
32. Bleak, "Annals," pp. 38–41.
33. Smallcanyon, "Contested Space," 66.
34. Ketchene and Peokon will be major actors in the aftermath of the Grass Valley killings in 1874; see chapter 27, this volume.
35. Bleak, "Annals," Sept. 9, 1871, pp. 39–41.
36. Ibid., p. 42. These same figures are in "Indian Depredation at Kanab," a telegraph message dated Sept. 15, 1871, in *Deseret News*, Sept. 20, 1871, p. 8.
37. Bleak, "Annals," p. 43.
38. Erastus Snow to Governor Woods, Sept. 13, 1871, a telegraph message, BYOF, bx 42, fd 20, CHL; Larson, *Erastus Snow*, 442–43.
39. Bleak, "Annals," p. 42–43; "Indian Depredation at Kanab."
40. Hamblin to Erastus Snow, Sept. 13, 1871, in James Bleak Collection, MS 10587, bx 1, CHL.
41. Ibid. Reilly, in *Lee's Ferry*, 21, implies that Hamblin selfishly laid a personal claim to Lee's Ferry at this inappropriate moment. Actually, Hamblin suggested that a settlement be started, to increase the safety of Mormon towns in southern Utah—an entirely reasonable suggestion. He also refers to others as settlers, not himself.
42. Bleak, "Annals," pp. 43–44.
43. At this point in Bleak's "Annals," the author inserts Jacob Hamblin's account of his 1870 trip to Fort Defiance with Major Powell, which Hamblin misdated as 1871. This makes a hash of the September 1871 story, and Bleak leaves it entirely unresolved. Larson, *Erastus Snow*, 443, follows Bleak's incorrect chronology.
44. "Indian Depredation at Kanab," Sept. 15, 1871, Reilly, *Lee's Ferry*, 21, suggests that Hamblin withheld horses to drive up the price, thereby nearly causing a disaster. I have found no support for such a motivation or scenario in any primary source. Reilly also incorrectly states that Jacob was present at the initial negotiations.
45. Jack Hillers, Diary, Oct. 6, 1871 (Fowler 85).
46. Kelly, "Journal of Walter Clement Powell," Oct. 6, 1871, p. 342. Incidentally, we should not underrate the value of Navajo blankets, even at that time.
47. Reilly, *Lee's Ferry*, 20–21, tells a story of this encounter with many details that I have not been able to confirm from the sources he cites. In addition, Reilly leaves out important elements of the story found in Bleak's "Annals." Reilly describes Hamblin as writing on September 13, "seemingly indifferent to the near debacle." Actually, the moment of danger from the Navajos had ended on the eleventh or twelfth.
48. Hamblin to Brigham Young, Feb. 13, 1874, BYOF, bx 35 fd 6.
49. James Bunting, diary, Sept. 8, 1871.
50. Moses Farnsworth, autobiography, as quoted in Robinson, *A History of Kane County*, 32–33. Possibly this is the December 1870 visit of Patnish to Utah.
51. Adams and Madsen, "Notes from an Interview," 7.
52. See also James Bunting diary, Feb. 11, 1871.
53. Kelly, "Journal of Walter Clement Powell," Oct. 14, 1871, p. 349; Dellenbaugh, *A Canyon Voyage*, 146–48. Agua Grande appears to be a translation of Ganado Mucho's Navajo name. See Canby, "List of Navajo Chiefs, Jan. 13, 1861, in Correll, *Through White Men's Eyes*, 3:120; Kit Carson to J. H. Carleton, Apr. 10, 1864, in Twitchell, *The Leading Facts of New Mexican History*, 3:361; chapter 27 (1874), this volume.
54. John D. Lee, diary (2:176).
55. Gregory, "Diary of Almon Harris Thompson," Oct. 28, 1871, pp. 59–60. Kelly, "Journal of Walter Clement Powell," Oct. 6, 1871, p. 342, wrote, "Jacob Hamblin with a party of Mormons has gone to the fort and is trying to get a settlement with them there." See also LJH, 108; Dellenbaugh, *Canyon Voyage*, 143.
56. Briggs, "George Washington Adair"; Bagley, *Blood of the Prophets*, 298; Walker, Turley, and Leonard, *Massacre at Mountain Meadows*, 256.

57. Jack Hillers diary, Oct. 6, 1871 (Fowler 85). Hillers appears to exaggerate: Jacob and the Kanabans traded "tithing horses" to the Navajos, not their own stock.
58. Gregory, "Journal of Stephen Vandiver Jones," Oct. 28, 1871, pp. 105–6.
59. LJH, 108–9.
60. Gregory, "Journal of Stephen Vandiver Jones," Oct. 28, 1871, pp. 105–6.
61. Locke, *The Book of the Navajo*, 403; Van Valkenburgh, *A Short History*, 47; Bailey and Bailey, *A History of the Navajos*, 33; Young, *The Role of the Navajo*, 48; Allison, "The Navajo Witch Purge of 1878." Blue, *The Witch Purge of 1878*, 30, has a somewhat different interpretation, but she agrees that the witchcraft violence succeeded raiding in this time of transition.
62. For Dellenbaugh, now only seventeen, see Crampton, "F. S. Dellenbaugh"; Darrah, "Beaman, Fennemore." He later became an admiring friend of Jacob Hamblin.
63. Dellenbaugh, *A Canyon Voyage*, 152–53. For this meeting, see also Gregory, "Journal of Stephen Vandiver Jones," Oct. 28, 1871, pp. 105–6, and Bishop, "Letters of Captain F. M. Bishop," 251; Gregory, "Diary of Almon Harris Thompson," Oct. 28, 1871, p. 59; Kelly, "Journal of Walter Clement Powell," Oct. 28, 1871, p. 359.
64. Kelly, "Journal of Walter Clement Powell," Oct. 28, 1871, p. 359.
65. Ibid.
66. Dellenbaugh, *A Canyon Voyage*, 153–54.
67. Gregory, "Journal of Stephen Vandiver Jones," Oct. 28, 1871, pp. 105–6.
68. Bishop, "Letters of Captain F. M. Bishop," 251. For Navajo blankets, see Kent, *Navajo Weaving*; Blomberg, *Navajo Textiles*; Evans, *Along Navajo Trails*, 193–97.
69. Dellenbaugh, *A Canyon Voyage*, 152–53. Gregory, "Diary of Almon Harris Thompson," October 28–29, 1871, p. 60. Kelly, "Journal of Walter Clement Powell," Oct. 28, 1871, p. 359. Darrah, "Journal of John F. Steward," Oct. 30, 1871, p. 249.
70. Gregory, "Diary of Almon Harris Thompson," Nov. 1, 1871, p. 60.
71. Ibid., Nov. 4. Kelly, "Journal of Walter Clement Powell," Nov. 2 [Nov. 3], 1871, p. 361; Dellenbaugh, *A Canyon Voyage*, 155.
72. Bleak, "Annals," pp. 52–67; John D. Lee journal, Nov. 3, 1871 (2:173).
73. Gregory, "Diary of Almon Harris Thompson," Nov. 13, 1871, p. 62. See also Statement by J. F. Steward, an assistant geologist who stayed with Jacob three weeks and whom Jacob then guided to Toquerville. MS 6874, CHL.
74. Kelly, "Journal of Walter Clement Powell," p. 374.
75. *A Canyon Voyage*, 166–67. See also Kelly, "Journal of Walter Clement Powell," Dec. 20, 1871, p. 379; James Bunting, diary, Dec. 15, 1871 (a telegraph to Kanab).
76. See chapter 7 (1857), this volume.
77. Lee diary, Nov. 13, 14, 15, 1871 (2:175–76).
78. This is apparently Navajo Wells, fifteen miles east of Kanab, at the foot of the Kaibab Plateau. McClintock, *Mormon Settlement in Arizona*, 284; Van Cott, *Utah Place Names*, 271; Brooks, *John Doyle Lee*, 303.
79. Lee, diary, Nov. 15 [16], 1871 (2:175–76).
80. Reilly, *Lee's Ferry*, 23.
81. Lee, diary, Nov. 30, 1871 (2:177). For the new settlers, see "Pahreah Ward History."
82. Reilly, in typical anti-Hamblin fashion, portrays him as a sort of dark, Machiavellian plotter, with Lee as his victim. Reilly, *Lee's Ferry*, 22–24. For example, he makes a blanket statement that "Hamblin's promises [to Lee] were not kept"; however, Hamblin helped Lee in many ways in the upcoming years, though at other times Lee felt that he fell short.
83. Kelly, "Journal of Walter Clement Powell," Dec. 21–22, 1871, pp. 379–80.
84. LJH, 110. See also John D. Lee, diary, March 31, 1872 (2:184); Kelly, "Journal of Walter Clement Powell," July 13, 1872, p. 432; William Henry Solomon diary, March 1, 1874. For an overview of House Rock Valley, see Spangler, *Vermilion Dreamers*.
85. See chapter 28 (1875), this volume.
86. *A Canyon Voyage*, 175.

87. Ibid., 174.
88. Handwritten note opposite title page in Dellenbaugh's copy of LJH*: A Narrative of His Personal Experience,* Frederick Dellenbaugh Collection, Arizona Historical Society, Tucson.
89. Arrott, *Sarah Priscilla Leavitt Hamblin*, 41.
90. Stock Appraisal Book for the United Order of Kanab 1874, original, p. 32, CHL, as cited in Reilly, "Kanab United Order," 152.
91. Kanab Ward Historical Record "Book A," at March 18, 1871.
92. Ibid., at Aug. 6, 1876.
93. Handwritten note opposite title page in Dellenbaugh's copy of LJH, Dellenbaugh Collection, Arizona Historical Society, Tucson, quoted in Compton, "Civilizing the Ragged Edge," 197–98.
94. Dellenbaugh, *A Canyon Voyage*, 174.
95. John Mangum had also taken an Indian woman as a plural wife in Kanab; see the James Bunting diary, Jan. 7, 1871.
96. Handwritten note in Dellenbaugh's copy of LJH.
97. As a girl Inez became known for her love of reading and prowess in spelling bees. At age seventeen, she married a widower with three children, John David Lee, known as David, a son of John D. Lee and Lovina Young, and a rancher in Luna, New Mexico. Inez died on March 4, 1933, in Thatcher, Arizona. A number of her descendants became politicians or judges in Arizona and Utah, including Morris and Stewart Udall. See Inez Hamblin Lee, "An Autobiography"; Death Certificate, in possession of author; Brimhall, "Biography of John David Lee"; "Short Life Story of Inez Hamblin."
98. Arrott, *Sarah Priscilla Leavitt Hamblin*, 37.

CHAPTER 24

1. Bleak, "Annals," p. 34.
2. Ibid, pp. 35–36.
3. George Armstrong to Brigham Young, June 30, 1857, in ARCIA (1857), 309.
4. Palmer, "Utah Indians Past and Present," 46–47.
5. Kelly, "Southern Paiute Bands," 552; see also Martineau, *Southern Paiutes*, 163.
6. Woodbury, *A History of Southern Utah*, 122.
7. Bleak, "Annals," p. 6; Lyman, *Southern Paiute Relations*, 17.
8. Two valuable discussions of this issue are Lyman, *Southern Paiute Relations*; Bagley, *Blood of the Prophets*, 341–43.
9. Larson, *I Was Called to Dixie*, 102.
10. See chapter 12 (1861), this volume.
11. Larson, *Erastus Snow*, 338.
12. Ibid., 402; Bleak, "Annals," Sept. 1867, pp. 381–84.
13. Bleak, "Annals," Dec. 9, 1871, pp. 68–70, and July 1, 1874, p. 138; Robert Gardner and James G. Bleak to Brigham Young, July 1, 1874, BYOF, bx 35, fd 6; "Southern News," *Salt Lake Herald*, Oct. 7, 1877, in Journal History, Oct. 2, 1877, "The Santa Clara has been nearly dry since June…"; Larson, *I Was Called to Dixie*, 51–53; Tobler, "Heinrich Hug," 117n37, 122. Also, chapter 15 (1863), this volume.
14. For the importance of seeds in the diet of the Southern Paiute, attested as early as Escalante's diary, see Trudeau, *An Environmental History*, 10–11, 23; John Wesley Powell's notes in Fowler and Fowler, *Anthropology of the Numa*, 41–42; Steward, *Notes on Hillers' Photographs*, 8, 11, plates 1c, 16a, 16b; Palmer, "Plants Used by Indians," 601–6; Knack, *Boundaries Between*, 17, 20. For the importance of cattle in early Utah, see chapter 4 (1850–1853), this volume. The Paiutes were quite aware that the Mormons' cattle were destroying the seed plants they depended upon; Knack, *Boundaries Between*, 93.
15. Word difficult to read.
16. Word difficult to read.
17. Jacob's letter has not been found, but we have George A. Smith's response, Smith to Hamblin, Nov. 3, 1863, copy in Historian's Office Letterpress Copybook, CR 100 38, CHL; discussion in Lyman, *Southern Paiute Relations*, 7.

18. For the surprising variety of plants and seeds which Paiutes depended upon, see Bye Jr., "Ethnobotany of the Southern Paiute Indians"; Palmer, "Plants Used by Indians," which frequently refers to Paiute culture.
19. LJH, 87–88.
20. One historian has written that by 1880, "there was not a single locality west of the Wasatch Mountains from Cache Valley to the basin of the Virgin River that did not exhibit effects of overstocking." Woodfield, "Initiation," 78, as cited in Knack, *Boundaries Between*, 93. Also, Larson, *I Was Called*, 248; Brooks, "The Arizona Strip," 296–97. More generally, White, *"It's Your Misfortune,"* 222–27, who notes that widespread overstocking combined with adverse weather conditions created many disastrous situations.
21. McPherson, *The Northern Navajo Frontier*, 55–56.
22. For overgrazing causing watersheds to deteriorate, which in turn caused floods, see Alexander, "Irrigating the Mormon Heartland," 187; Honker, "'Been Grazed Almost to Extinction.'"
23. In a later hand, "cached" is overwritten.
24. Jacob Hamblin to Brigham Young, Sept. 19, 1873, BYOF, bx 34 fd 18. Caching food was an important part of Paiute culture, John Wesley Powell, notes, in Fowler and Fowler, *Anthropology of the Numa*, 49.
25. The Santa Clara Paiutes had some hereditary land, unlike Indians who were entirely nomadic. All Paiutes had limited, circumscribed homelands. However, the Santa Clara Paiutes would still migrate seasonally, in order to collect seeds and plants when they ripened.
26. Franklin H. Head to Dennis N. Cooley, Aug. 4 1866, RG 75, Letters Received by the Office of Indian Affairs, 1824–80, M234, reel 902, frame 126, NA; discussion in Knack, *Boundaries Between*, 115. My emphasis added. See also Van Hoak, "And Who Shall Have the Children," 18.
27. See White, *The Middle Ground*, 486–92, for Indian dependency triggered by environmental change.
28. For Utah Indians, see Stoffle, Jones, and Dobyns, "Direct European Immigrant Transmission"; Lyman, *Southern Paiute Relations*, 18. For the broader perspective, examples are Fenn, *Pox Americana*; Robertson, *Rotting Face*; Cook, *Born To Die*; Cook and Lovell, *Secret Judgments of God,* especially 213–42; Kunitz, *Disease and Social Diversity*; Diamond, *Guns, Germs, and Steel*; Reff, "The Introduction of Smallpox"; Richter, "The Imperial Virus"; Henige, "When Did Smallpox Reach the New World?"
29. See chapter 13 (early 1862), this volume. Burning the wickiup of a dead man to drive his spirit away was a common practice. Whiting, *Paiute Sorcery*, 36, 107. For Paiute death customs, see JSIM, Thomas Brown diary, June 7, 1854, p. 42; Matheson and Cooper, "Answers to a Questionnaire," Q22; Kelly and Fowler, "Southern Paiute," 380; Reeve, *Making Space*, 136–56.
30. Stucki, "Biography of John S. Stucki," 11–12; see also Corbett, *Jacob Hamblin*, 198. For further on John Stettler Stucki (1850–1933), see Whittaker, *History of Santa Clara, Utah*, 355–57.
31. Diamond, *Guns, Germs, and Steel*, 4, 211–12. The Hopis are an example: their population was estimated to be 29,000 in 1520 AD, and they lived in many cities; when Jacob Hamblin visited them in 1858, they numbered about 2,500 and lived in seven cities. Numerous smallpox epidemics had decimated them, and they were especially vulnerable because they lived in towns. See chapter 9 (late 1858), this volume. We should mention that population estimates of Indians at the time of contact with whites cannot be exact, and some historians are "High Counters" while others are "Low Counters."
32. Stucki, "Biography of John S. Stucki," 11. Brigham Young, and other Mormons, had made similar prophecies, see Peterson, *Utah's Black Hawk War*, 354. See also chapter 18 (1866), this volume.
33. For further on Mormon perspectives on Indian epidemics, Peterson, *Utah's Black Hawk War*, 103, 353–54.
34. See chapter 5 (1854), this volume.
35. Peterson, *Utah's Black Hawk War*, 353.
36. Lyman, *Southern Paiute Relations*. Stoffle, Jones, and Dobyns, "Direct European Immigrant Transmission," give special attention to Utah Indians. This article often works with indirect evidence, citing disease in Mormon communities, then arguing that it must have also been impacting Indians living nearby. Their argument is logical, but direct evidence would be better. See also Stoffle and Evans, "Resource Competition," 188; Woodbury, *A History of Southern Utah*, 122; Holt, *Beneath These Red Cliffs*, 30.
37. Lyman, *Southern Paiute Relations*, 18.
38. Palmer, *Notes on the Utah Utes*, 8; see also Euler, *The Paiute People*, 78.

39. Woodbury, *A History of Southern Utah*, 122.
40. Stoffle, Jones, and Dobyns, "Direct European Immigrant Transmission," 189.
41. Kelly, "Southern Paiute Shamanism," 160; Holt, *Beneath These Red Cliffs*, 30.
42. Canfield, *Sarah Winnemucca*, 59; Zanjani, *Sarah Winnemucca*, 221. For disease and the Kaibab Paiutes, see chapter 30 (1877–1880), this volume.
43. Historian's Office Journal, June 23, 1858, p. 97 (SC 17); Powell and Ingalls, *Report*, 7; Peterson, *Utah's Black Hawk War*, 103–4, 353–54; Farmer, *On Zion's Mount*, 52–53, 98. For disease among the Hopis, see chapter 9 (late 1858), this volume; Donaldson, *Moqui Pueblo Indians*, 10, 28; Beadle, *The Undeveloped West*, 530, 587 (quoting Jacob Hamblin as his informant for a horrific smallpox epidemic at Walpi in about 1867); Reff, "The Introduction of Smallpox"; and Kunitz, *Disease and Social Diversity*, 126, 132. There were well-documented smallpox epidemics among the Hopis in 1853, 1866, and 1899. See also C. L. Christensen, Diary, Feb. 1883, pp. 26–27 (a hundred Hopis and eighty Navajos had died that winter, apparently of measles). Though the Navajos experienced many deaths from disease at Bosque Redondo, their subsequent dispersion saved them from extensive smallpox epidemics, though they suffered a major influenza epidemic in 1918, Russell, "The Navajo and the 1918 Influenza Pandemic"; Mitchell and Frisbie, *Tall Woman*, 247n2. Epidemics also afflicted the Pima (Lewis, *Neither Wolf nor Dog*, 132), the Zunis (see chapter 31 (1878), this volume); the Pueblo Indians (Simmons, *New Mexico: an Interpretive History*, 64–65; Sides, *Blood and Thunder*, 167; White, *"It's Your Misfortune*," 19–33), and Plains Indians (West, *The Contested Plains*, 47; Sides, *Blood and Thunder*, 32–33, 172; Powers and Leiker, "Cholera Among the Plains Indians").
44. White, *"It's Your Misfortune*," 19. For the Ute parallel, see Peterson, *Utah's Black Hawk War*, 103.
45. Powell and Ingalls, *Report*, 7.
46. R. N. Fenton to E. S. Parker, October 14, 1869, in ARCIA (1869), 203.
47. For the Santa Clara Paiutes after 1862, see Lyman, "Caught In Between"; Knack, *Boundaries Between*, 115–17.
48. Powell and Ingalls, *Report*, 7. U-ai-Nu-ints derives from Iuánu (cultivators, planters). Kelly, "Southern Paiute Bands," 558. See also Martineau, *Southern Paiutes*, 162, who writes that both the Virgin River and Santa Clara Paiutes were called "farmers."
49. Powell and Ingalls, *Report*, 10.
50. Ibid., 2. Powell and Ingalls counted eighty Paiutes living near St. George in 1873, but these might have been Shivwits.
51. Tom and Holt, "The Paiute Tribe of Utah," 141.
52. We should mention briefly one impact of the Powell expedition on southern Utah: the reports of Powell and his men starting in the winter of 1870–1871 caused an influx of prospectors into southern Utah in the following years. Crampton, "F. S. Dellenbaugh," 239; Huntoon, "The Opening of Deer Creek" (an estimated five hundred miners invaded the Grand Canyon); Crampton, *Outline History of the Glen Canyon Region*, 16, who describes a post-Powell "gold rush" in the Grand Canyon in 1872, focused on the mouth of Kanab Canyon. While W. Paul Reeve wrote a book about "Mormons, Miners and Southern Paiutes" set in southeastern Nevada (*Making Space*), this same uneasy mixture would occur in southern Utah and northern Arizona—with the southern Paiutes and other Indians usually ending up the worse for the interchange.

CHAPTER 25

1. John D. Lee diary, March 3, 1872 (2:183).
2. Ibid., April 12 [19?], 1872 (2:189).
3. Ibid., May 19, 1872 (2:198).
4. Ibid., May 7, 1872 (2:195). For Jacob's Pools, discovered by Jacob and company on the second trip across the Colorado, see chapter 10 (1859), this volume.
5. Gregory, "Journal of Stephen Vandiver Jones," 142.
6. Brooks, *John Doyle Lee*, 309.
7. John D. Lee, Diary, May 19, 1872 (2:198).
8. Ibid., August 24, 1872 (2:209–10).

9. Gregory, "Journal of Stephen Vandiver Jones," August 17, 1872, p. 144; Kelly, "Journal of Walter Clement Powell," August 17, 1872, p. 438.
10. This was the last gasp of the Black Hawk War. Peterson, *Utah's Black Hawk War*, 362–68.
11. Gregory, "Journal of Stephen Vandiver Jones," 153–54.
12. Ibid.
13. Jacob Hamblin to Major Powell or Prof. Thompson, August 27, 1872, in Geological Survey, RG 57, Powell Survey, Letters Received, M156, Roll 1, no. 94, NA.
14. Kelly, "Journal of Walter Clement Powell," September 7, 1872, p. 449.
15. Erastus Snow to Brigham Young, August 12, 1872, BYOF, bx 42, fd 20. See also Snow to Young, August 3, 1872; Snow to Young, August 4, 1872; Bleak, "Annals," July and August 1872, p. 20. Edwin D. Woolley Jr. tells of a group of slightly drunken young Mormon men shooting a Shivwits; this may or may not be the same incident, as Woolley gives no date. Woolley, "Notes on Father's Life," 9–10, and "A True Indian Story," 4–6. By March 1875, Mormon-Shivwits relations seemed to have stabilized, as there was a famous mass baptism of 166 Shivwits in St. George at that time. See chapter 28 (1875), this volume.
16. Jackson and Stevens, "Hualapai Tradition," 136. *Ko Ho Nin'* meant "The People that Live in the West," that is, west of the Mesas. Hamblin and others referred to the Havasupai as the "Cohonenas," Hamblin diary, Apr. 4, 1863 (see chapter 15, this volume), but the term also included the Hualapai, who use this name (Cohoninas) for themselves in tribal oral accounts. See also Gregory, "Diary of Almon Harris Thompson," July 21, 1872, p. 91, quoted below, and John D. Lee, diary, Aug. 7–10, 1873, and March 9, 1874 (2:281–84, 325–27).
17. Gregory, "Journal of Stephen Vandiver Jones," September 12, 1872, p. 155.
18. Dellenbaugh, *A Canyon Voyage*, 246–47.
19. She married Edward Beeler on September 27, 1896, but Edward, after serving as sheriff of Apache County, was killed by outlaws in 1901. Mary Elizabeth lived a life full of religious and political activity, and tended Priscilla in her old age. She died on May 12, 1959, in Alpine, Arizona. See Rencher, "A Short Sketch of Mary E. Hamblin Beeler."
20. For an overview of geographic surveys in America at the time, see Goetzmann, *Exploration and Empire*; Stegner, *Beyond the Hundredth Meridian*, 125–27; Worster, *A River Running West*, 203–8. For the Powell Survey, Olsen, "The Powell Survey Kanab Base Line."
21. Stegner, *Beyond the Hundredth Meridian*, 124–25.
22. Gregory, "Stephen Vandiver Jones (1840–1920)," 15.
23. Dellenbaugh, *A Canyon Voyage*, 195–96; Gregory, "Journal of Stephen Vandiver Jones," May 15, 1872, p. 125.
24. Beadle, *The Undeveloped West*, 658.
25. Stegner, *Beyond the Hundredth Meridian*, 133.
26. Gregory, "Journal of Stephen Vandiver Jones," 78.
27. John Oakley, Letter to the Editor, August 5, 1872, *Deseret News*, Aug. 21, 1872, p. 12.
28. Kelly, "Journal of Walter Clement Powell," May 20, 1872, pp. 414–15. See also Beaman, "The Cañon of the Colorado," 547.
29. Kelly, "Journal of Walter Clement Powell," 457. For the Arrow Maker, an old Paiute craftsman, see Fowler, *The Western Photographs of John K. Hillers*, 46.
30. Fowler and Fowler, "John Wesley Powell's Anthropological Fieldwork."
31. Steward, *Notes on Hillers' Photographs*.
32. Gregory, "Diary of Almon Harris Thompson," May 11 and July 8, 1872, pp. 77, 89. Kelly, "Journal of Walter Clement Powell," October 4, p. 457. See also Almon Thompson to John Wesley Powell, March 11, 1872, in Geological Survey, RG 57, Powell Survey, letters received, M156, Roll 1, no. 116, NA; Thompson to Powell, March 11, 1872, ibid., no. 117.
33. Gregory, "Journal of Stephen Vandiver Jones," 91.
34. Gregory, "Diary of Almon Harris Thompson," May 29–July 7, pp. 78–89; Almon Thompson, "Report on a Trip"; Dellenbaugh, *A Canyon Voyage*, 196–211.
35. For these men, see Fowler, *Photographed All the Best Scenery?* and *The Western Photographs of John K. Hillers*; Kelly, "Journal of Walter Clement Powell"; Darrah, "Beaman, Fennemore."

36. Jack Hillers diary, in Fowler, *Photographed All the Best Scenery?* 146; Gregory, "Journal of Stephen Vandiver Jones," 162; Kelly, "Journal of Walter Clement Powell," 458.
37. See also John D. Lee, diary (2:215), which records that Lee gave Jacob fifty pounds of flour and other supplies.
38. Kelly, "Journal of Walter Clement Powell," 458.
39. Ibid., 459–60.
40. Ibid., 460. This may be Whitmore Lake, see chapter 20 (1869), this volume.
41. Hillers diary, in Fowler, *Photographed All the Best Scenery?*, 149.
42. Kelly, "Journal of Walter Clement Powell," 461.
43. Fowler, *Photographed All the Best Scenery?*, 150.
44. Kelly, "Journal of Walter Clement Powell," 468.
45. Ibid., 469.
46. See Reilly, *Lee's Ferry*, 31. According to Reilly, "It appears that Hamblin and Tuba had struck some kind of deal regarding future Mormon settlement, and Hamblin was going to examine the prospective area on his way home." Reilly has no actual evidence for this reconstruction. For Moenave, see also Horton Haight to Brigham Young, BYOF, bx 34, fd 18, typescript in Miller, *Journal of Jacob Miller*, at 83; John L. Blythe to Young, Apr. 8, 1874, BYOF, bx 35, fd 3; Reilly, *Lee's Ferry*, 35.
47. Nov. 7, 1872 (Kelly, "Journal of Walter Clement Powell," 470).
48. Ibid.
49. Ibid.
50. For the Wheeler expedition, see Stegner, *Beyond the Hundredth Meridian*, 126–27.
51. See Alexander, "Federal Authority"; Bigler, *Forgotten Kingdom*, 290–91.
52. Bringhurst, *Brigham Young*, 184; Bigler, *Forgotten Kingdom*, 294; Alexander, "Federal Authority," 93. The Supreme Court ruled that juries empanelled by McKean's court during the previous year were illegal.
53. Bringhurst, *Brigham Young*, 184; Alexander, *Mormonism in Transition*.
54. As early as 1858, in the wake of the Utah War, Young began looking to Arizona as a possible route south for the Mormons. See chapter 9 (late 1858), this volume.
55. Grow, *Liberty to the Downtrodden*, 257, 262, 272–75.
56. Kelly, "Journal of Walter Clement Powell," 471. Reilly, *Lee's Ferry*, 32.
57. John D. Lee, diary (2:216).
58. Ibid., Apr. 4, 1873 (2:232); Rusho and Crampton, *Lee's Ferry*, 33; Reilly, *Lee's Ferry*, 32.
59. John D. Lee, diary (2:217); Reilly, *Lee's Ferry*, 32; for Jackson, see pp. 44–45.
60. Cleland and Brooks, *A Mormon Chronicle*, 2:217.
61. Smith, *Journal of Jesse Nathaniel Smith*, March 26, 1881; Arrington, *Brigham Young*, 382; Hammond, "The 1876 Journal," 68–69; Peterson, "The Last Bastion."

CHAPTER 26

1. Peterson, *Take Up Your Mission*, 6.
2. Jacob Hamblin journal, 1871–1874, MSS 1951, 3rd Notebook, Folder 4, CHL.
3. Bleak, "Annals," Jan. 22, 1873, p. 29.
4. John D. Lee, diary, Jan. 26, 1873 (2:222); Feb. 1, 1873 (2:224); Peterson, *Take Up Your Mission*, 6.
5. Brigham Young to Daniel H. Wells, Jan. 8, 1873, BYOF, bx 73, fd 35.
6. Young to Wells, Jan. 8, 1873.
7. Brigham Young to [Lorenzo Roundy], date unknown, in Bleak, "Annals," Jan. 22, 1873, pp. 29–30.
8. Lee, diary, Jan. 26, 1873 (2:222).
9. Bleak, "Annals," p. 29.
10. Reilly writes that Jacob was "piqued" that Roundy was the leader of the company rather than him, *Lee's Ferry*, 33, but the source that Reilly cites, the Lee diary, gives no evidence for this.
11. Lee, diary, Feb. 1, 1873 (2:224); Bleak, "Annals," pp. 29–30. The two lists of participants are slightly different. We know that Smithson met the company at Lonely Dell. See also Brooks, *Emma Lee*, 70. Lee lists James Jackson, but he apparently stayed in the Lee's Ferry area. Reilly, *Lee's Ferry*, 32.

12. There is some evidence that Hamblin and Hatch made the fifty-mile trek to Fort Defiance in search of a guide. See Lee's diary, Feb. 21, 1873 (2:226); Jacob Hamblin journal, 1871–1874 at January 22, 1873. However, both references can be interpreted as showing that Jacob intended to go to Fort Defiance; but he and Hatch may have decided the trip was unnecessary.
13. Lorenzo Roundy to Brigham Young, March 7, 1873, BYOF, bx 34, fd 20. Roundy's dating slightly differs from Hamblin's, who writes this entry for the fifth. Roundy's dating is probably correct, as his diary appears to be contemporary, while Hamblin's has a retrospective tone.
14. Jehiel McConnell described the Little Colorado in similar terms. "In going up little Colo a distance of 75 miles we found some excellent land, good water privilege & abundance of good stock range & some cotton wood timber." Jehiel McConnell to Brigham Young, March 8, 1873, BYOF, bx 34, fd 19.
15. Folkman, "'The Moste Desert Lukking Plase,'" 119.
16. Lorenzo Roundy to Brigham Young, March 7, 1873, at the date Feb. 6; see also Jehiel McConnell to Brigham Young, March 8, 1873.
17. Hamblin diary, 1871–1874.
18. Jehiel McConnell to Brigham Young, March 8, 1873.
19. Hamblin to Young, March 1873, BYOF, bx 34, fd 18.
20. Lorenzo Roundy to Brigham Young, March 7, 1873.
21. Hamblin diary, 1871–1874.
22. Hamblin to Young, March 1873.
23. Hamblin to Young, March 1873.
24. Lee, diary, Feb. 25, 1873 (2:227) and March 4, 1873 (2:228).
25. P. T. Reilly seizes on this bit of trading to once again criticize Hamblin, speaking of Hamblin's "personal trading activity that distracted from his duty to the [Roundy] party." Reilly, *Lee's Ferry*, 34. However, this judgment lacks any support in the historical record. In Roundy's report, there is no reference to it. In fact, Roundy apparently sent Hamblin back to the Hopi mesas. In addition, trading with Indians had been customary for Jacob since his earliest journeys, and there is evidence that he traded fairly with them. Indians often were eager to trade with whites. For example, we remember Spaneshanks's eagerness to trade with Mormons in the third trip across the Colorado; see chapter 11 (1860), this volume. Reilly also suggests that Hamblin might have bought the valuable Moenave settlement from Tuuvi with trade goods and knicknacks, in a deal comparable to the sale of Manhattan Island for trinkets in 1626. Reilly, *Lee's Ferry*, 35. Again, there is no evidence for this; in fact, Tuuvi had always wanted Mormons to settle in the area so they could provide protection for the Hopis against the Navajos and Apaches and instruct the Hopis in their farming methods. See Haskell, "Thales Haskell," March 5, 1860; Andrew Amundsen, Journal, at April 30, 1873; Hamblin to Young, March 1873, and Hamblin to Young, July 19, 1873, BYOF, bx 34, fd 18.
26. Lee, diary, March 6, 1873 (2:228).
27. Ibid., March 7, 1873 (2:228).
28. Oscar married Sara Ida Coleman, daughter of Prime Coleman and Elizabeth Knell, in 1897 (seven children). They lived in Alpine, Arizona, for many years, and Oscar served in church callings and in the Arizona legislature. He died in Mesa, Arizona, on September 1, 1946. See "Sketch of George Oscar Hamblin."
29. Bleak, "Annals," 47–48, and "Minutes," *Deseret News* 22.17, May 28, 1873, p. 10. See also Lorenzo Roundy to Brigham Young, March 7, 1873, BYOF, bx 34, fd 20; Jehiel McConnell to Brigham Young, March 8, 1873; Peterson, *Take Up Your Mission*, 10. In fact, some Hopis did begin farming with the Mormons on the Little Colorado (see chapter 29 [1876–1877], this volume), though their reported "eagerness" to do so may have been an exaggeration.
30. Peterson, *Take Up Your Mission*, 10.
31. Folkman, "'The Moste Desert Lukking Plase,'" 119–20.
32. Brigham Young to Daniel H. Wells, Jan. 15, 1873
33. After his Arizona adventure, he returned to the north, and later became a bishop and stake president in Idaho. Jenson, LDSBE, 1:302; "Captain Horton David Haight—1859."
34. Brigham Young to Joseph W. Young, March 10, 1873, BYOF (SC 22).

35. McClintock, *Mormon Settlement*, 136. For more on the Haight company experience, see Horton Haight to Brigham Young, Aug. 1873, BYOF, bx 34, fd 18, typescript in Miller, *Journal of Jacob Miller*, 81–89; Miller, *Journal of Jacob Miller*, 76–81; Andrew Amundsen, journal, March to June 1873, USHS; "The Arizona Mission," a letter from Henry Holmes to Franklin D. Richards, June 27, 1873, in *Deseret News*, July 23, 1873, p. 14; "The Arizona Mission," a letter from Henry Holmes to Franklin D. Richards, July 14, 1873, in *Deseret News*, Aug. 6, 1873, p. 6; Peterson, *Take Up Your Mission*, 10–14; Reilly, *Lee's Ferry*, 36–40; Folkman, "'The Moste Desert Lukking Plase.'"
36. Andrew Amundsen, journal, March to June 1873. For this expedition, quotes are from Amundsen's journal unless otherwise specified. The number of wagons in the company from John D. Lee, diary, Apr. 20 [21], 1873 (2:236).
37. Brigham Young to Joseph W. Young, March 10, 1873.
38. This is a third-hand report, Lee reporting what Young told him Hamblin said.
39. Young refers to Hamblin's cost estimate, not to his preferred site for the ferry.
40. Reilly, *Lee's Ferry*, 35.
41. Ibid., 34, 92; Rusho and Crampton, *Lee's Ferry*, 56, 165–66.
42. Andrew Amundsen, journal, April 13, 1873.
43. Brigham Young to Joseph W. Young, March 19, 1873, BYOF (SC 22).
44. Jacob Hamblin to Brigham Young, July 19, 1873, in Journal History.
45. Lee, diary, Apr. 26, 1873 (2:236).
46. Andrew Amundsen, journal; Lee, diary, Apr. 20 [21], 1873 (2:236).
47. Andrew Amundsen, journal; Lee, diary, Apr. 22 and 23, 1873 (2:236).
48. Lee, diary. Once again, the Verde River is far south and west of the San Francisco mountains. There is a Walnut Grove some twenty miles southwest of Prescott. Young was apparently unclear on Arizona geography.
49. Lee, diary (2:236).
50. Ibid., Apr. 26, 1873 (2:236).
51. Joseph W. Young to Haight Expedition, Apr. 29, 1873, as quoted in Horton Haight to Brigham Young, Aug. 1873.
52. The early documents confuse Moenave and Moenkopi; technically, these were separate villages. However, Moenave was considered to be part of the general Moenkopi area and was sometimes called Moenkopi. The Hopi village of Moenkopi is now just southeast of modern Tuba City. Moenave is still called by the same name, but is not a village at this time.
53. Haight to Brigham Young, Aug. 4, 1873. Tuuvi was by no means chief of the Oraibi Hopis, but he was the headman of the Moenkopi settlement.
54. For Morrell (1830–1907), see his obituary, "Loa. Demise of W. W. Morrell," *Deseret Evening News*, Jan. 18, 1907, p. 3.
55. Horton Haight to Brigham Young, Aug. 1873.
56. Quoted from Miller, *Journal of Jacob Miller*, 84.
57. As quoted in Peterson, *Take Up Your Mission*, 12. The Little Colorado's water improved the closer one came to its headwaters.
58. Quoted from Miller, *Journal of Jacob Miller*, 84.
59. See Peterson, *Take Up Your Mission*, 11–12; Reilly, *Lee's Ferry*, 38.
60. Haight to Brigham Young, Aug. 4, 1873. The little Colorado was not a year-round water source. Its flow varied from month to month and year to year. Peterson, *Take Up Your Mission*, 11.
61. For more on these two messengers, who reached the Colorado on June 4, see Lee, diary, June 4–23 (2:242–45). E. H. Evans may be Edward Holding Evans (1849–1927). Thanks to Randall Dixon for these identifications.
62. Hamblin to Young, July 19, 1873.
63. Hamblin to Young, Sept. 19, 1873, BYOF, bx 34 fd 18; Hamblin to Young, July 19, 1873.
64. Samuel Rose Parkinson, diary.
65. Ibid., June 25, 1873, also June 4–5.
66. Haight to Young, August, 1873, at June 3.

67. John R. Young, *Memoirs*, 149–51. Helping to build the road over Lee's Backbone had contributed to his death.
68. Haight to Young, August, 1873, at June 23.
69. See also William Henry Solomon, diary, June 22–23, 1873.
70. Haight to Young, August, 1873, at June 28. Young had given Roundy some authority to investigate the problems the Haight company had been facing; Lee, diary, June 23, 1873 (2:245).
71. Hamblin's diary, which has the incorrect date of July 2 for Hamblin's departure. The Lee diary convincingly gives the date as June 27. Haight wrote, "Bros Jacob Hamblin and Milton A Burk have been tending the farm planted by Bro Bennion's Company. They started for Kanab on the 27th." Haight to Young, Aug. 4, 1873.
72. Haight to Young, August, 1873, at July 4–7; Samuel Rose Parkinson, diary, June 5, 6, 1873.
73. Lee, diary, July 26, 1873 (2:277).
74. LJH, 110.
75. Jones, *Forty Years Among the Indians*, 234–35. For a thorough examination of these criticisms of the Haight company, see Folkman, "'The Moste Desert Lukking Plase,'" 139–47.
76. Brigham is quoted in a speech by George Q. Cannon, Aug. 10, 1873, in *Journal of Discourses*, 16:143–44. See also William Henry Solomon, diary, July 24, 1873; Peterson, *Take Up Your Mission*, 10.
77. Biographical Record of Martha Cox, typescript, p. 266, as quoted in Arrington, *Adventures of a Church Historian*, 204. Though Cox applies these remarks to settlers of Phoenix, Young's death in 1877 makes that application impossible, so Arrington and Folkman agree that these remarks were directed at the Little Colorado settlers. Cox wrote them down many years after the speech. Folkman, "'The Moste Desert Lukking Plase,'" 148–50.
78. Miller, *Journal of Jacob Miller*, 79–80.
79. "That Mormon Failure," *Weekly Arizona Miner*, Prescott, Arizona, August 9, 1873, p. 2, as transcribed in John Beck's website, http://www.roundvalleyaz.com/failure.html (accessed on May 5, 2009). For another non-Mormon view, "The Mormons: Failure of the Colonization Scheme—Faith in Brigham Young's Infallibility Shaken," *New York Times*, July 14, 1873, at http://query.nytimes.com/mem/archive-free/pdf?res=9E02EFD71539EF34BC4C52DFB1668388669FDE (accessed on July 20, 2009).
80. See below, this chapter.
81. Lee, diary (2:244).
82. Ibid., June 24, 1873 (2:246).
83. Ibid., June 25, 1873 (2:263).
84. Reilly suggests that Lorenzo Roundy, who disliked Lee, intentionally sent on this false report to drive Lee from Jacob's Pools and Lonely Dell; *Lee's Ferry*, 39.
85. Lee, diary, June 25, 1873 (2:263).
86. Ibid., Sept. 6, 1873 (2:294).
87. Ibid., July 26, 1873 (2:277).
88. Hamblin to Young, July 19, 1873.
89. Lee, diary, Aug. 21, 1873 (2:287–88); William Solomon, diary, Aug. 9, 1873.
90. For DeFrees, see Murphy, *Frontier Crusader*, 208–9.
91. John Blythe to Brigham Young, Apr. 8, 1874, BYOF, bx 35, fd 3.
92. Reilly, *Lee's Ferry*, 41. Navajos would later dispute Hopi rights to the Moenkopi/Moenave area. The Havasupai Indians also felt they had rights to it.
93. Lee, diary, Sept. 7, 1873 (2:295).
94. Ibid., Sept. 9, 1873 (2:295).
95. Ibid., September 10, 1873 (2:296).
96. Ibid., Sept. 12, 1873 (2:297).
97. Hamblin to Young, Sept. 19, 1873, BYOF, bx 34 fd 18. William Henry Solomon, diary, Sept. 21, 1873, where Hamblin speaks in a meeting in Kanab, saying that he did not think that the whites treated the local and trans-Colorado Indians "exactly right."
98. Hamblin to Young, Sept. 19, 1873. Lo Le Lama may be Loololma, a dominant "friendly" Hopi, the Kikmongwi, village headman and priest, at Oraibi, see Whiteley, *The Orayvi Split*, 1:64, 115, 188.

99. This part of the letter is discussed in chapter 24 (1871), this volume.
100. Cleland and Brooks, *A Mormon Chronicle*, 2:342n42.
101. For Lee's strengths and failings, see Brooks, *John Doyle Lee*, 179–80, 258; 276–77; Bagley, *Blood of the Prophets*, 20, 262, 313; Walker, Turley, and Leonard, *Massacre at Mountain Meadows*, 61–62, 65–67.
102. For example, Dellenbaugh, *A Canyon Voyage*, 211.
103. Lee, diary, Dec. 29, 1870 (2:152). It is true that he was not the only person to blame for the massacre, and that local church leaders, especially local stake presidents Isaac Haight and William Dame, also were guilty.
104. Lee, diary (2:306).
105. Ibid., Dec. 19[21], 1870 (2:150).

CHAPTER 27

1. Names from William F. M. Arny to Colonel L. Edwin Dudley, Feb. 16, 1874, RG 75, Letters Received, M234, roll 562, frame 355, NA. According to Navajo Curley Tso (Johnson and Roessel, *Navajo Stories*, 92), there were six Navajos, and two of them were named Atsidíík'áak'éhé (Wounded Hammering or Wounded Silversmith) and Łíí'yilchįįh Biyáázh (Horse Smell's Son). In Tallsalt, "The Lone Survivor," there are five Navajos. According to Thurber, "Statement" (see following note), one of the Navajos was "a sub chief Blacksmith John."
2. LJH, 111. Other important primary sources are Hamblin to Brigham Young, Feb. 13, 1874, BYOF, bx 35 fd 6; George W. Bean to Brigham Young, June 20, 1874, BYOF, bx 35 fd 3; George W. Bean to John Wesley Powell, Feb. 10, 1874, Geological Survey, RG 57, Powell Survey, letters received, M156, roll 2, frame 101, NA; Albert King Thurber, "Statement," ca. August 3rd 1874, RG 75, Letters Received, M234, roll 904, frs. 585–88, NA; W. L. Pitcher, 2nd Lt., to F. S. Adams, 1st Lt., Jan. 13, 1874, RG 75, Letters Received, M234, roll 904, frames 623–25, NA; James L. Bunting, "Prospects of Peace with the Navajoes," July 18, 1874, in *Deseret News*, Aug. 12, 1874, 14(446); James L. Bunting, "More About the Murder of the Navajoes," Aug. 5, 1874, in *Deseret News*, Aug. 19, 1874, 16(464); James Bunting, diary, March 17, 1874; R. W. Young, "A Navajo's Pluck," 282–83; George Washington Bean, *Autobiography*, 173–74; Gottfredson, *History of Indian Depredations*, 330–32 and "Killing of Three Navajo Indians." Remarkably, there are three Navajo oral traditions of the incident: Bert Tallsalt, "The Lone Survivor"; Curley Tso (a grandson of the survivor) in Johnson and Roessel, *Navajo Stories*, 92–102; and John Scott, a twentieth-century descendant of Ketchene, in Golding, *Our Golden Heritage*, 15–16. Secondary treatments of this incident can be found at: McClintock, *Mormon Settlement*, 84; Peterson, *Take Up Your Mission*, 201; Smiley, "Ammon M. Tenney," 92; McNitt, *Indian Traders*, 147; McPherson, *The Northern Navajo Frontier*, 31; Murphy, *Frontier Crusader*, 220–24; Moore, *Chiefs, Agents and Soldiers*, 124–36; Reilly, *Lee's Ferry*, 43; Smallcanyon, "Contested Space," 60–64; Skovlin and Skovlin, *In Pursuit of the McCartys*, 15–20. Rusho and Crampton, *Lee's Ferry*, 43–44, accept the anti-Navajo account found in Gottfredson's *Indian Depredations*, 330; I believe Gottfredson's central incident should be rejected on a number of grounds, which I discuss below.
3. Hamblin to Brigham Young, Feb. 13, 1874.
4. Bean, *Autobiography*, 167–71. These Utes were not on their reservation at Uintah because of dissatisfaction with the agent at the time.
5. Bean, *Autobiography*; Dees, "George W. Bean"; O'Neil, "The Mormons, the Indians."
6. Thurber, autobiographical sketch, 146; Bean, *Autobiography*, 173–74.
7. For this area, see Geary, *The Proper Edge of Sky*, 77–78.
8. For the exploration mission, see George Washington Bean and A. K. Thurber, "Report of an Exploration of a portion of South-Eastern Utah. Made June AD 1873," CHL, typescript in PTRC, series 1, bx 1, fd 15; Bean, *Autobiography*, 167–71.
9. Bunting, "Prospects of Peace." Some sources give the name as McCarthy. For further on the McCartys, see Skovlin and Skovlin, *In Pursuit of the McCartys*, and Charles Kelly, *The Outlaw Trail*, 15–16, who identifies Alexander incorrectly as William. Pitcher to Adams, Jan. 13, 1874, and Thurber, "Statement," refer to A. McCarty as the father of the family. Alexander had been born in Tennessee in 1825; lived in Iowa at least from 1848; served on the Union Side in the Civil War; came to Montana to ranch in 1866; and moved to Utah in 1870. After 1874, he lived in Nevada, Utah and Oregon, where he died in 1894.

For his gravestone and census reports, see "Dr. Alexander G. McCarty," at http://www.findagrave.com/cgi-bin/fg.cgi?page=gr&GRid=72978469 (accessed Aug. 7, 2012). For Fort Cameron, see Alexander and Arrington, "The Utah Military Frontier."

10. Gottfredson, *Indian Depredations*, 330; Bean, *Autobiography*, 179; Bean to Young, June 20, 1874.
11. LJH, 111.
12. Bean to Young, June 20, 1874.
13. Patterson, *Butch Cassidy*, 17, 21–31; Kelly, *The Outlaw Trail*, 17.
14. Tallsalt, "The Lone Survivor," 117. According to Johnson and Roessel, *Navajo Stories*, 92, they came from Tsé'ani'íįhí (Rock Is a Thief), north of Cow Springs.
15. Thurber, Statement. Bunting, "More About the Murder."
16. Thurber, Statement.
17. Gottfredson, "Killing of Three Navajo Indians."
18. For James Clinger (1849–1926), see PTRC, bx 8, fds 117–18.
19. Bean calls him "Johnny Klinger, a Dutchman."
20. Hamblin to Young, Feb. 13, 1874. Bunting, diary, March 17, 1874, says that the perpetrators were "a number of reckless and wicked gentiles or apostate Mormons."
21. Thurber, Statement; Arny to Col. L. Edwin Dudley, Feb. 16, 1874; Bunting, "Prospects of Peace."
22. Thurber, Statement; Bean to Young, June 20, 1874.
23. Bean to Young, June 20, 1874; Thurber, Statement. Other sources, such as Little, say that this was McCarty's cabin, but the early, definite statements of Bean and Thurber, who lived in the Grass Valley area, are convincing.
24. Thurber, Statement. The McCarty ranch was "8 miles below" (that is, south of) the cabin; the cabin was "15 or 20 miles" south of the Ute camps. As the McCarty ranch was about twenty-eight miles south of the Ute camps, the cabin might have been more like ten to twelve miles from it.
25. Thurber, Statement; Bean to Young, June 20, 1874; Hamblin to Young, Feb. 13, 1874. Some accounts, such as Little, Allen, "History of Kingston," 1, and the Navajo John Scott, say that the Navajos had killed a calf belonging to McCarty, but it seems unlikely that the Navajos would have needed extra food so soon after leaving the Ute camp. In addition, it is unlikely that McCarty's cattle would be near McCarter's cabin.
26. Bunting, "More About the Murder." Bean's two early letters, to John Wesley Powell on Feb. 10, 1874, and to Brigham Young on June 20, 1874, also mention a quarrel.
27. Curley Tso, in Johnson and Roessel, *Navajo Stories*, 92.
28. Pitcher to Adams, Jan. 13, 1874; Tallsalt, "The Lone Survivor"; Gottfredson, *Indian Depredations in Utah*, 331.
29. Thurber, Statement; Bean to Young, June 20, 1874. According to Thurber, Richards did not fire any shots during the killing. McClintock, *Mormon Settlement*, 84, adds the name Frank Starr to the group, but this is a comparatively late source.
30. Bunting, "Prospects of Peace"; Arny to Dudley, May 12, 1874, Letters Received, M234, roll 562, NA. John R. Young et al. to the Navajo Agent, April 30, 1874, Arny-Hamblin correspondence, USHS.
31. Hamblin, in his Feb. 13, 1874, letter to Young, says that the wounded Navajo "traveled on foot 13 days to reach home." From Lee's diary, we know he arrived home on about January 14. Bean, in his February 10 letter to Powell, puts it at about December 20 (as also in Bean to Young, June 20, 1874). Gottfredson, *Indian Depredations in Utah*, 331, says the Indian took twenty-one days getting home, which would also put the shooting on about December 23.
32. Bunting, "More About the Murder." The participants of the Mountain Meadows Massacre tended to testify about their actions so as to exculpate themselves and implicate others in the crimes, or to blame the victims. Briggs, "The Mountain Meadows Massacre." The same psychological tendency can be found in whites who participated in Indian massacres.
33. Gottfredson, *Indian Depredations in Utah*, 330–32; Gottfredson, "Killing of Three Navajo Indians."
34. The Navajos jumping on Clinger's horse is paralleled in the Navajo oral traditions. See also Blythe to Young, April 8, 1874, BYOF, bx 35, fd 3; and the Bill of Demands attached to this letter, at Blythe Letters, MS A 1448-1, USHS.
35. According to Gottfredson, Clinger confirmed this account in about 1919, but he did it without restating

it independently, so this is not really solid verification. Gottfredson, "Killing of Three Navajo Indians." Murphy, in his biography of William Arny, *Frontier Crusader*, 221, unfortunately follows the late, second-hand Gottfredson story.

36. Hamblin to Brigham Young, Feb. 13, 1874; John R. Young, *Memoirs*, 153. James Bunting, diary, March 17, 1874; Young, "A Navajo's Pluck," 282. Johnson and Roessel, *Navajo Stories*, 95.
37. Tallsalt, "The Lone Survivor." For the plunder motivation, Bean to Young, June 20, 1874.
38. Hamblin to Brigham Young, Feb. 13, 1874.
39. Young, "A Navajo's Pluck," 282.
40. Golding, *Our Golden Heritage*, 15–16.
41. Tallsalt, "The Lone Survivor," 118–19; Johnson and Roessel, *Navajo Stories*, 99–101.
42. Lee, diary, Jan. 15, 1874 (2:320).
43. James E. Smith, Letter to the Editor, Feb. 5, 1874, in *Pioche [Daily] Record*, as reprinted in *Deseret News*, March 11, 1874, p. 2. For this group of miners, see Lee's diary, Dec. 29, 1873 (2:315–16), and frequently thereafter. They were from Pioche, Nevada, and Lee at first regarded them as "gentlemen in deportment," though he later became disillusioned with them. Also, "Pioche Notes," *Deseret News*, Dec. 31, 1873, p. 15(767).
44. Lee, diary, Jan. 15, 1874 (2:320); James E. Smith, Letter to the Editor; Cleland and Brooks, *A Mormon Chronicle*, 2:342.
45. James E. Smith, Letter to the Editor.
46. Murphy, *Frontier Crusader*; Murphy, *Indian Agent in New Mexico*; Bender, *"New Hope for the Indians,"* 101–45.
47. McNitt, *The Indian Traders*, 144–45.
48. Ibid. Locke, *Book of the Navajo*, 398, entirely agrees with McNitt. Arny "was, beyond a doubt, the worst agent the Navajos ever had to contend with."
49. This was not the first time that desire for mineral wealth had impacted Navajo history. One of the reasons that Carleton had decided to send the Navajos far away to Bosque Redondo was that he was certain that there would be rich mineral strikes in the Navajo territory. Sides, *Blood and Thunder*, 329–31, 361–62.
50. For Ganado Mucho's name, Canby, "List of Navajo Chiefs, Jan. 13, 1861," in Correll, *Through White Men's Eyes*, 3:120; Captain Edward Butler, report, July 28, 1866, in Correll, *Through White Men's Eyes*, 5:358. For his life, Hoffman, *Navajo Biographies*, 1:129–54; Moore, *Chiefs, Agents and Soldiers*; Locke, *Book of the Navajo*, 397–98.
51. Hoffman, *Navajo Biographies*, 1:84–85.
52. Brugge, *Hubbell Trading Post National Historic Site*, 22–23, and personal communication; P. T. Reilly to [Martha] Blue, Apr. 29, 1987, in PTRC, series 1, fd 9. Many details argue for this identification. "Hastele" might be a mispronunciation of the second part of Ganado Mucho's Navajo name, Hastiin. Hastele, like Ganado Mucho, was always inclined toward peace, and Hamblin describes him as a major headman in the western Navajo reservation, like Ganado. Furthermore, Ganado Mucho had definite ties with Utah and Mormons: he visited Southern Utah in 1871 and Salt Lake City in 1877. Kelly, "Journal of William Clement Powell," Oct. 14, 1871 (p. 349); Dellenbaugh, *A Canyon Voyage*, 146–48; Brown, *Life of a Pioneer*, 475–76; chapter 23 (1871), this volume. However, Hastele lived "on the frontier, nearest to the river," per LJH 102, while Ganado Mucho didn't.
53. Arny to Colonel L. Edwin Dudley, Feb. 16, 1874; Murphy, *Frontier Crusader*, 220.
54. Letter to the editor, dated January 24, 1874, reprinted as "The Mormons and the Navajoes" in the *Deseret News*, Feb. 25, 1874, p. 6.
55. Arny to Hamblin, March 28, 1874; Arny to Dudley, May 12, 1874, in Arny-Hamblin correspondence, USHS. Discussed in Murphy, *Frontier Crusader*, 220; Moore, *Chiefs, Agents and Soldiers*, 125–26. Bunting, "Prospects of Peace," stated that the Indian agent at Fort Defiance had tried to make the nation of Navajos believe that Mormons had committed the murder and encouraged them to demand a huge reparation. This is not far off the truth, though at first Arny, relying on the early Navajo reports, did believe that Mormons had committed the murders.
56. McPherson, *The Northern Navajo Frontier*, 31; Kessell, "General Sherman and the Navajo Treaty," 266–6, 271; Arny to Dudley, Feb. 16, 1874; Moore, *Chiefs, Agents and Soldiers*, 126.

57. Hamblin to Brigham Young, Feb. 13, 1874.
58. John Blythe to Brigham Young, Jan. 20, 1874, typescript, in Blythe Letters, MS A 1448-1, USHS.
59. LJH, 111–12.
60. Lee, diary, Jan. 23, 1874 (2:322); John Blythe to Brigham Young and George A. Smith, Jan. 20, 1874, typescript, in Blythe Letters, MS A 1448-1, USHS.
61. For more on Blythe (1829–1893), see his diaries and letters at the USHS; William Solomon, diary, July 15 and 24, 1873; The Mormon Settlements in Arizona Collection, Ms0034, at Special Collections, Marriott Library; PTRC, series 1, bx 2, fds 28–30; Whitney, *History of Utah* 4:523–24; Jenson, *Encyclopedic History*, 887; Reilly, *Lee's Ferry*, 42–88; McClintock, *Mormon Settlement*, 92; Folkman, "'The Moste Desert Lukking Plase,'" 138–39, 146.
62. Lee, diary, Jan. 29, 1874 (2:322). James E. Smith, Letter to the Editor.
63. James E. Smith, Letter to the Editor.
64. Hamblin to Brigham Young, Feb. 13, 1874.
65. Ibid.; James E. Smith, Letter to the Editor. Lee and Smith seem to be a day off in their chronologies. Hamblin's Feb. 13 letter to Young, and the James Smith Letter to the Editor are the sources for Jacob's upcoming negotiations with the Navajos, unless otherwise specified. These letters support each other, despite minor discrepancies. See also Lee, diary, Feb. 2, 1874 (2:323), and LJH, 114–19.
66. Lee, diary, Feb. 2, 1874 (2:324).
67. For Jacob as apostle, see also Lee, diary, March 12, 1874 (2:330) and chapter 29 (1876–77), this volume, at Dec. 15, 1876.
68. Lee, diary, Feb. 5, 1874 (2:324).
69. Ibid., Feb. 6, 1874 (2:326). Lee's March 15, 1874, letter to Brigham Young records two interpreters and six Navajos, counting Ketchene.
70. Hamblin to Brigham Young, Feb. 13, 1874.
71. Lee, diary, Feb. 6, 1874 (2:325).
72. John R. Young felt that it was possible that the Paiute translators mistranslated what Jacob had said.
73. Lee, diary, Feb. 1 and 7, 1874 (2:323, 235).
74. Ibid., Feb. 9, 1874 (2:325–26) (date corrected to March 9 by Cleland and Brooks). One source tells the melodramatic story that Navajos terrorized the Blythe company in Moenkopi daily during the twenty-seven-day period, and took Blythe's wife hostage. Joseph C. Laye, in Gottfredson, "Killing of Three Navajo Indians," 9. However, the Blythe company had not yet arrived at Moenkopi.
75. William H. Solomon, diary.
76. Hamblin to Young, Feb. 13, 1874.
77. Hamblin, 1871–1877 diary, MSS 1951, CHL.
78. LJH, 128.
79. Blythe to Young, March 13, 1874, Blythe letters, MS 1448-1, USHS; William Henry Solomon, diary, February 18–19, 1874.
80. Elizabeth Smith, quoted in Smith, "Brief History of Early Pahreah Settlements." The author confuses this trip with Jacob's trip to the Navajos earlier that year. Lee's diary, March 11 (2:328) and March 24, 1874 (2:332), confirms that Nephi Smithson and James Smith went on this journey, not the earlier one. LJH, 128, on the other hand, has two entirely different men, Thomas Adair and Lehi Smithson, as his companions!
81. Jacob Hamblin to John Blythe, Feb. 26, 1874, typescript in PTRC, series 8.1, bx 2, fd 23.
82. Jacob Hamblin, 1871–1877 diary.
83. LJH, 128, states that Jacob talked with Ketchene at this time, before going to the Hopi mesas. This is apparently incorrect.
84. Lee, diary, March 11, 1874 (2:329); Lee to Young, March 15, 1874.
85. William Solomon's diary records, on February 11, that Hamblin knew the appointment was set for twenty-seven days, however.
86. Lee to Young, March 15, 1874.
87. Lee, diary, March 12, 1874 (2:331).
88. LJH, 128–29.
89. Hamblin to Arny, March 7, 1874, in Arny-Hamblin correspondence, USHS.

90. Ibid. See discussion in Murphy, *Frontier Crusader*, 220–21; Moore, *Chiefs, Agents and Soldiers*, 130–31.
91. Lee, diary (2:329).
92. Lee clearly emphasized and possibly distorted any accusations of Jacob's dishonesty.
93. Lee, diary. The March 15 letter seems to report this conversation on the night before.
94. Blythe to Young, March 13, 1874.
95. Blythe to Young, April 8, 1874; William Henry Solomon, diary; Robinson, *History of Kane County*, 99.
96. Lee, diary, March 15, 1874 (2:333).
97. This is supported by Solomon, "Arizona Mission," March 13, 1874.
98. Blythe to Young, April 8, 1874.
99. William Henry Solomon, diary.
100. John Blythe to Young, Apr. 8, 1874.
101. William Henry Solomon, diary, March 19, 1874; Blythe to Young, April 8, 1874; Lee, diary, March 15, 1874 (2:332–33).
102. William Henry Solomon, diary, March 24, 1874; John Blythe to Young, Apr. 8, 1874; Lee, diary, March 15, 1874 (2:332–33).
103. William Henry Solomon diary, March 24, 1874.
104. See chapter 11 (1860), this volume.
105. Tietjen, *Ernst Albert Tietjen*, chapter 3. This is not an early, primary source, but it does preserve Hatch family traditions, as Ira Hatch's daughter Amanda married Tietjen. Navajo historian David Brugge believed that Peokon was a transliteration of Bii'aghaani, "Backbone," a Navajo who lived in the Big Mountain (Black Mesa) area. Brugge, "The Moencopi Boundary Problem," 13.
106. William Henry Solomon, diary.
107. James Bunting, diary.
108. Hamblin and Levi Stewart to Mr. McCarty, March 20, 1874, typescript, in Juanita Brooks Collection, B-103, bx 28, fd 8, USHS.
109. Bleak, "Annals," Apr. 4, 1874, p. 83.
110. Murphy, *Frontier Crusader*, 221.
111. Arny to Hamblin, March 28, 1874, Arny-Hamblin correspondence, USHS; discussion in McNitt, *The Indian Traders*, 148.
112. For Hubbell (1853–1930), see McNitt, *The Indian Traders*, 142–44; Blue, *Indian Trader*; Albrecht, "John Lorenzo Hubbell"; Farish, *History of Arizona* 6:281–84; Manchester and Manchester, *Hubbell Trading Post*. For his stay in Utah, see Lee, diary, Apr. 3, 1873 (2:231), and Reilly, *Lee's Ferry*, 35.
113. McNitt, *The Indian Traders*, 148.
114. Arny to Dudley, March 28, 1874, Arny-Hamblin correspondence, USHS.
115. See the map at Roessel, "Navajo History," 520.
116. Arny to Dudley, March 28, 1874, Arny-Hamblin correspondence, USHS. Discussions in Murphy, *Frontier Crusader*, 221; McNitt, *The Indian Traders*, 148; Moore, *Chiefs, Agents and Soldiers*, 131.
117. McNitt, *The Indian Traders*, 149. See also Moore, *Chiefs, Agents and Soldiers*, 126.
118. Arny to Dudley, May 12, 1874; McNitt, *The Indian Traders*, 150. Arny had sent a petition for the chiefs to visit Washington on January 2, 1874, Arny to Edward Smith, January 2, 1874, Letters Received, M234, roll 562, NA. On April 8, Arny sent Smith the Articles of Agreement on the proposed change in the Navajo Reservation boundaries, signed by the Navajo chiefs on March 27.
119. Jacob Hamblin to John W. Young, Apr. 14, 1874, in Bleak, "Annals," Apr. 14, 1874, pp. 107–8. This letter includes Hamblin's rules for dealing with Indians.
120. Blythe to Young, April 8, 1874.
121. Solomon, "Arizona Mission."
122. William Henry Solomon, diary, and Blythe to Young, April 8, 1874. See also an interview with Blythe, in "Local and Other Matters," *Deseret News*, July 8, 1874, p. 1.
123. Blythe to Young, April 8, 1874.
124. Date from William H. Solomon's diary and Blythe to Young, April 8, 1874. In Solomon's report of the journey, he does not mention the death threats to the Mormons, but does report the demands for 180 head of horses and 100 head of cattle, and the required date for the fulfillment, June 13.

125. Bleak, "Annals," p. 110.
126. John D. Lee to Brigham Young, May 17, 1874. John R. Young, also, in late secondhand reminiscences, left some melodramatic accounts, "The Navajo and Moqui Mission"; *Memoirs*, 153–54; "In Memory of Ira Hatch." Young gets some of the details wrong; for example, he places the parley at Ketchene's hogan, not at Peokon's. Hamblin to Brigham Young, Feb. 13, 1874. For a less melodramatic account, Stewart and Knight report, in Bleak, "Annals," p. 118. The Navajos blamed the Mormons for not returning the stolen property. But McCarty had refused to give up any property unless the Utah Indian agent required him to do so. Bleak, "Annals," April 22, 1874, p. 111.
127. John D. Lee to Brigham Young, May 17, 1873.
128. Young, *Memoirs*, 153–54; John D. Lee to Brigham Young, May 17, 1873. Young, "The Navajo and Moqui Mission," who (apparently incorrectly) states that the order came from Brigham Young.
129. Young, *Memoirs*, 153–54. For a fuller list, Robinson, *History of Kane County*, 59–60.
130. Bleak, "Annals," p. 111.
131. Ibid.
132. John D. Lee to Brigham Young, May 17, 1873.
133. Robinson, *History of Kane County*, 60.
134. Young, *Memoirs*, 153–54.
135. John D. Lee to Brigham Young, May 17, 1873.
136. Ibid.
137. William H. Solomon, diary, April 7, 1874. This was written just after Blythe and Hatch returned from talking with Ketchene and Peokon. It does mention the reparation demands and the June 13 deadline.
138. John R. Young felt that Peokon was planning an attack on the missionaries at this time; John R. Young to Brigham Young, May 20, 1874, BYOF, bx 35, fd 11. John R. stated that his Navajo informants told him that they had planned to massacre the Mormons at Moenkopi-Moenave, but the arrival of his party caused them to give up the plan. This seems unlikely.
139. John R. Young and others to Superintendant and Agent of Navajo Agency, Apr. 30, 1874, in M234, roll 562, fr 497, NA; also in Arny-Hamblin correspondence, USHS. Gibbons had been part of the Muddy Mission, in modern Nevada, when it was considered to be part of Arizona.
140. Murphy, *Frontier Crusader*, 222.
141. William H. Solomon, diary; Hamblin and Tenney to J. W. Young, May 16, 1874, in James Bleak, Collection, MS 10587, Box 1, CHL; also in Bleak, "Annals," pp. 119–20.
142. John D. Lee to Brigham Young, May 17, 1874. See also Bleak, "Annals," p. 115; Solomon, "Arizona Mission," May 1, 1874
143. John D. Lee to Brigham Young, May 17, 1874.
144. Hamblin and Tenney to John W. Young, May 16, 1874.
145. John D. Lee to Brigham Young, May 17, 1874. This story is also in a report by Levi Stewart and Samuel Knight, May 19, 1874, in Bleak, "Annals," p. 115, who state that Jacob and Ammon Tenney wanted to continue on to Fort Defiance.
146. William H. Solomon, diary.
147. Bleak, "Annals," p. 116.
148. They signed a May 3 letter, see below.
149. For Rawlings, see G. Rawlings to Jacob Hamblin, March 10, 1875, enclosed in John Oakley to Brigham Young, March 26, 1875, BYOF, bx 36, fd 2. Rawlings told Jacob that Arny was entirely unsympathetic to Mormons; Stewart and Knight report, in Bleak, "Annals," p. 117.
150. Hamblin and Tenney to John W. Young, May 16, 1874.
151. Ibid.
152. John D. Lee to Brigham Young, May 17, 1873.
153. Jacob Hamblin et al., "To the Chiefs of the Navajo Nation," May 3, 1874, in M234, roll 562, fr 499, NA; also quoted in Bleak, "Annals," pp. 122–24.
154. Stewart and Knight report, in Bleak, "Annals," p. 117.
155. William H. Solomon, diary. John R. Young, in an undated letter to C. L. Christensen, quoted in Tietjen, *Ernst Albert Tietjen*, chapter 3, states that some Navajos set up an ambush for Jacob at a hollow about

twelve miles east of Moenkopi, but that the Mormons at Moenkopi learned about it from an Indian runner and rode out and prevented the attack, as the mule Jacob was riding, Satan, was able to outrun Jacob's pursuers.

156. For Tuuvi and Talasnimki in Kanab, see Beaman, "The Cañon of the Colorado," 687.
157. John D. Lee to Brigham Young, May 17, 1873.
158. Hamblin and Tenney to John W. Young, May 16, 1874, original in James Bleak collection, MS 10587, bx 1, CHL; copied in Bleak, "Annals," p. 119.
159. Ibid. This flatly contradicts a statement by John R. Young in his May 20 letter to Brigham Young. He says that Jacob went to Walpi, on the First Mesa, and learned that three different Navajo chiefs had "unanimously voted to send strong forces of their young men into our mountains, and agreed never to cease raiding, until they get ample revenge for their alleged, injuries." It is odd to find two good primary sources contradicting each other so flatly. In this case, I tend to believe Jacob, not Young, who may have been trying to dramatize the importance of his mission.
160. Hamblin and Tenney to John W. Young, May 16, 1874.
161. Solomon, "Arizona Mission," May 21, 1874.
162. LJH, 129.
163. Arny to Dudley, May 12, 1874, M234, roll 562, fr 496, NA.
164. Arny to Col. J. Irvine Gregg, June 3, 1874, M234, roll 562, fr 545, NA. Discussed in Murphy, *Frontier Crusader*, 222, McNitt, *The Indian Traders*, 149.
165. L. Edwin Dudley to Commissioner Edward P. Smith, June 19, 1874, M234, roll 562, fr 540, NA.
166. Bleak, "Annals," p. 133–35; LJH, 129–30.
167. Ibid.
168. Ibid., July 31, 1874, p. 139; Rusho and Crampton, *Lee's Ferry*, 45–47, 156.
169. LJH, 130.
170. Ibid. Hastele may be Ganado Mucho; see above, this chapter.
171. Bunting, "Prospects of Peace," who writes, "last Tuesday Mr. Boyde [with Hubbard and interpreters]...arrived here from Fort Defiance on their way to Grass Valley." LJH, 131. Bleak, "Annals," July 31, 1874, p. 140, gives the most complete list of participants. Thurber, Statement. For further on Boyd, see Bean to Young, Aug. 20, 1874, BYOF, bx 35, fd 3; Lee, diary, Dec. 29, 1873 (2:316); Solomon, "Arizona Mission," March 27, 1874; "Pioche Notes," *Deseret News*, Dec. 31, 1873, p. 15(767).
172. LJH, 131; Bleak, "Annals," July 31, 1874, p. 140; Thurber, Statement; Hoffman, *Navajo Biographies*, 1:155–77.
173. Moore, *Chiefs, Agents & Soldiers*, 134, concluded that Navajos were independently behind this investigation. However, Bunting and Thurber state that the investigatory company was sent by Arny, see below.
174. Murphy, *Frontier Crusader*, 205; Moore, *Chiefs, Agents & Soldiers*, 121.
175. Bunting, "Prospects of Peace"; Thurber, Statement.
176. M. D. Allen, "History of Kingston," p. 3, has convincing local details for this meeting.
177. LJH, 130–31.
178. Ibid.
179. Bean to Young, Aug. 20, 1874, BYOF, bx 35 fd 3.
180. James Little, quoted in Robinson, *A History of Kane County*, 64.
181. Hamblin to Young, Sept. 3, 1874, BYOF, bx 35 fd 6.
182. Jared Waldo Daniels (1827–1904) had worked with the Sioux and Dakotas in the Midwest, both as surgeon and agent. Arny mentions his visit in Arny to Edward Smith, Sept. 21, 1874, M234, roll 562, fr 108, NA, and in Arny to Edward Smith, Sept. 24, 1874, M234, roll 562, fr 115, NA.
183. Hamblin to Young, Sept. 3, 1874.
184. See chapter 18 (1866), this volume.
185. Locke, *The Book of the Navajo*, 369–79, 392.
186. Hamblin to Young, Sept. 3, 1874.
187. Ibid.
188. Ibid.
189. Ibid.
190. Hamblin to Young, Oct. 10, 1874, BYOF, bx 35 fd 6.

191. Once again, this could be a transliteration of Ganado Mucho. Ganado Mucho's ranch, in the modern Ganado area, was between Fort Defiance and the Hopi mesas.
192. Hamblin to Young, Sept. 3, 1874.
193. Ibid.
194. According to Navajo oral tradition, Ne Chic Se Cla and one of his relatives made private forays into Utah and slaughtered some Mormon cattle and killed a Mormon family. Golding, *Our Golden Heritage*, 16. Johnson and Roessel, *Navajo Stories*, 101. These stories have exaggerated elements, as are frequently found in oral tradition. But if there is some truth to them, it shows that southern Utah Mormons still paid for McCarty's murders. For Indian views of retaliation, see chapter 18 (1866), at late 1865, this volume. McCarty himself, fearing retribution from the Navajos, retreated to Fort Cameron at Beaver, and later left his Utah ranch and relocated to Nevada. Bunting, Letter to the Editor, July 18, 1874.
195. "Diary of Ammon M. Tenney," as quoted in Smiley, "Ammon M. Tenney: His Life," 43. This is apparently more an autobiography than a diary.
196. Smiley, "Ammon M. Tenney: His Life," 43, citing an interview with Lurlene Tenney Whiting.
197. Ibid.
198. Moore, *Chiefs, Agents & Soldiers*, 136.
199. James Bunting, diary.
200. J. D. Boyd thought there was still danger, "The Navajoes Still Dissatisfied—More Raids Probable," *Deseret News*, Apr. 14, 1875, p. 9. As it turned out, there were no major raids and no further investigation. Arny brought eleven Navajos to Washington in December 1874, but the visit did not result in his desired land swap, nor assessments of reparations from Mormons. Murphy, *Frontier Crusader*, 226–27; Denetdale, *Reclaiming Diné History*, 97–98, 147; Graves, *Thomas Varker Keam*, 73–75; McNitt, *The Indian Traders*, 152–53.
201. Brigham Young Jr., diary, Dec. 28, 1874, CHL, as summarized in PTRC, series 1, bx 13, fd 186.

CHAPTER 28

1. LJH, 134.
2. Ibid.
3. Young and Smith to Hamblin, Dec. 28, 1874, typescript, in Journal History.
4. Young and Smith to Ammon Tenney, Dec. 28, 1874, typescript in Ammon Tenney collection, Arizona Historical Society; Young and Smith to Ira Hatch, Dec. 28, 1874, typescript, in Journal History.
5. Hamblin, Thales Haskell, and John Oakley to Brigham Young, Jan. 13, 1875, BYOF, bx 35 fd 6.
6. James Bunting, diary, March 16, 1872.
7. He would die in Snowflake, Arizona, in 1890. See Fontano, "Life History of John DeGroot Oakley."
8. Message from Hamblin included in J. W. Crosby and Lorenzo Brown, to George A. Smith, Feb. 15, 1875, BYOF, bx 35, fd 14. See also Robert Gardner to Brigham Young and George A. Smith, Feb. 18, 1875, BYOF, bx 35, fd 16.
9. Hamblin and John Oakley to Young, March 14, 1875, BYOF, bx 35 fd 16.
10. For further on Coal Creek John (Paiute name Tau-Gu), see chapter 18 (1866), this volume; "To Whom It May Concern," Feb. 9, 1875, Bleak, "Annals," pp. 20–21; Webb, "William Bailey Maxwell"; Roundy, "Pioneers of Early Days"; Worster, *A River Running West*, 290; Reeves, *Making Space*, 75; Palmer, "Utah Indians Past and Present," 41.
11. Hamblin and Oakley to Young, March 14, 1875.
12. See Reilly, "Warren Marshall Johnson;" and *Lee's Ferry*, 84–144.
13. Reilly, "Warren Marshall Johnson," 9.
14. Hamblin to Brigham Young, March 29, 1875, BYOF, bx 35 fd 16.
15. Bleak, "Annals," at end of 1875, p. 77; Reilly, "Warren Marshall Johnson," 10.
16. Hamblin to Young, March 29, 1875.
17. Linford, *Navajo Places*, 289.
18. See chapter 23 (1871), this volume. According to Walter Hamblin, Jacob sold his House Rock Valley ranch to Orderville for fifty head of cattle and one stallion. Corbett, *Jacob Hamblin*, 518. According to

documents in "Papers pertaining to the Orderville United Order," LR 643 27, CHL, however, Jacob sold it to Ammon Tenney, then Tenney sold it to representatives of the Orderville Order. See also L. John Nuttall, diary, Aug. 6, 1878.

19. Brooks, *Mountain Meadows Massacre*, 191–93; Brooks, *John Doyle Lee*, 338–41; Fielding and Fielding, *The Tribune Reports*, 71–204; Bagley, *Blood of the Prophets*, 291–97; Bigler and Bagley, *Innocent Blood*, 308.

20. Thus the *Salt Lake Tribune*, Sept. 20, 1876, in Fielding and Fielding, *The Tribune Reports*, 235. Judge Jacob Boreman, of the Lee trials, in his "Reminiscences," 43, incorrectly states that Jacob testified in the first trial.

21. Fielding and Fielding, *The Tribune Reports*, 178. Brooks, *Mountain Meadows Massacre*, 193, and Bigler and Bagley, *Innocent Blood*, 308, have slightly different numbers.

22. For the United Order generally, see May, "The United Order Movement"; Arrington, Fox, and May, *Building the City of God*. For Kanab, ibid., and Reilly, "Kanab United Order."

23. John Oakley to Brigham Young, Aug. 1, 1875, BYOF, bx 35, fd 16.

24. Hamblin to Brigham Young, Nov. 17, 1875, BYOF, bx 35, fd 16.

25. James Bunting, diary; Brigham Young to John R. Young, Aug. 30, 1875, in BYOF (SC 22); Reilly, "Kanab United Order," 160. Nuttall was made stake president in April of the following year, ibid., 161. For Nuttall (1834–1905), see Nuttall, *In the President's Office*, xx–xxviii; Jensen, "Leonard John Nuttall."

26. For Jones (1830–1915), see his *Forty Years Among the Indians* (1890); "Daniel Webster Jones (Mormon)"; Tullis, *Mormons in Mexico*, 17. In 1877, he led the company that founded Mesa, Arizona (originally called Jonesville). For Jones's temper and personal conflicts, see Tullis, *Mormons to Mexico*, 17, 22, 28. Ammon Tenney diary, Nov. 2, 1875, and March 16, 1876: "Bro Jones is when vexed a very unreasonable man often giving a way to uncalled for words.... I must confess that I feel better since parting with him."

27. For the Jones expedition and the colonies, see Romney, *The Mormon Colonies in Mexico*, 39–42; Tullis, *Mormons in Mexico*, 17–29.

28. See chapters 25 (1872) and 26 (1873), this volume; also, Arrington, *Brigham Young*, 382; Hammond, "The 1876 Journal," 68–69.

29. For this trip, see Jones, *Forty Years Among the Indians*, chapters 34 and 35; Helaman Pratt, diary; Anthony W. Ivins, diary, Anthony W. Ivins Papers, Oct. 10, 1875, to April 1882 (two versions), and Journal; Ammon Tenney, diary; Daniel Jones to Brigham Young, Nov. 29 and Dec. 14, 1875, BYOF, bx 35, fd 18; Peterson, *Take Up Your Mission*, 15–16; Brooks, *Emma Lee*, 87; Reilly, *Lee's Ferry*, 56–57 (a very problematic interpretation, see below); McClintock, *Mormon Settlement*, 196–98.

30. Helaman Pratt, diary, Oct. 20, 1875.

31. As a young man, in 1877, he became bishop at Orderville and presided over this especially successful United Order until 1884, when he was called as a counselor in the Kanab Stake Presidency and moved to Kanab. A successful farmer and rancher, he had six wives and some fifty-five children. He died in 1918 in Kanab.

32. Anthony Ivins, journal, Oct. 10, 1875, to April 1882, at the date. For this moment at Bitter Springs, see, with caution, Brooks, *Emma Lee*, 87, and Reilly, *Lee's Ferry*, 56–57. Spicer (1831–1887?), apart from his leading part in the trial of John D. Lee, later served as the main judge in the "Tombstone" trial of Wyatt Earp and Doc Holliday in 1881.

33. Anthony Ivins, journal, Oct. 27–28, 1875. See also versions in Ivins diaries, which are not as full.

34. Reilly states that Hamblin was hired by Spicer; but Jacob says he was hired by multiple prospectors at this time, and never mentioned Spicer. Reilly, *Lee's Ferry*, 56; LJH, 134. Reilly states that Spicer and Hamblin colluded dishonestly so Hamblin could leave the Jones party; but, as the Helaman Pratt diary shows, Jacob had always planned on going only part of the way with Jones. Finally, Spicer, in a contemporary letter, states that James L. Tibbetts was his guide, not Hamblin. Wells Spicer, "Arizona. Judge Spicer Heard From ...," *Salt Lake Daily Herald*, March 30, 1876, p. 3, supported by James Brown diary, Nov. 28, 1875.

35. Hamblin to Young, Nov. 17, 1875, BYOF, bx 35, fd 16.

36. Brigham Young to Daniel Jones, Jan. 22, 1876, in Jones, *Forty Years Among the Indians*, 261.

37. For Brown (1828–1902), see his autobiography, *Life of a Pioneer*, also his diary, especially for the years 1875–1876; Kenney, *Wilford Woodruff's Journal*, May 27, 1869 (6:476).

38. Brown, diary, Oct. 9.
39. See Brown, *Life of a Pioneer*, 451. Emma Lee told John D. Lee that Brown had taken Jacob's place; "Jacob Hamblin was droped from the Presidency of the Indian Mission & Brown of Salt Lake City was put in his place." Lee, diary, Jan. 3, 1876 (2:412). There is no actual evidence that Jacob was dropped from any position.
40. Brown, *Life of a Pioneer*, 453–54, and Brown, diary; "The Southern Country," *Deseret Evening News* 9.50, Jan. 21, 1876, p. 3, typescript in PTRC, series 1, bx 3, fd 39.
41. "The Southern Country," p. 3.
42. Peterson, *Take Up Your Mission*, 70.
43. Lee, diary, Feb. 2, 1876 (2:424–25).
44. Reilly, "Warren Marshall Johnson," 9.
45. Cleland and Brooks, *A Mormon Chronicle*, 2:464.
46. Joseph W. Young wrote to Brigham Young, in 1873, "John D. Lee and Jacob Hamblin are owners of the boat, and ferry right. They say that if you want the Church to own and controll this property they will sell to you for that purpose. Or if you will furnish a rope, and other improvements, they will pay for them in ferrying the brethren." Joseph W. Young to Brigham Young, April 17, 1873, BYOF, bx 35, fd 2.
47. Thales Haskell and Andrew Gibbons, report, in Bleak, "Annals," April 8, 1875, p. 36.
48. McClintock, *Mormon Settlement*, 88; see also Corbett, *Jacob Hamblin*, 385–86.
49. Bleak, "Annals," March 19–23, 1875, pp. 24–32, with summary on page 32.
50. See figure 5.3. PH 1401 and PH 1407 in the Lee Library Digital Collection; Slaughter, *Life in Zion*, 61; C. R. Savage, "Dixie In and Out of the Camera," *Deseret News* 24 (Apr. 28, 1875), p. 2 (194).
51. Bleak, "Annals," March 21, 1875, p. 33.
52. Flake, "A History of Mormon Missionary Work," 60, who did not know of this reference, writes that nine Navajos who were baptized in 1882 were the first Navajo converts. For baptisms of Indians generally, see chapter 5 (1854), this volume, at June 17.
53. LJH, 134.
54. Frederick Brind to "Brother Lundwall," undated, quoted in full in Corbett, *Jacob Hamblin*, 330–34. In this section, quotes are from this letter unless otherwise specified. See also Brind to Lundwall, Aug. 20, 1934, FAC 1308, in Jacob Hamblin papers, Huntington Library, San Marino, CA.
55. See Longwell, "Clarence Edward Dutton"; Stegner, *Beyond the Hundredth Meridian*, 158–74; 195–98; Worster, *A River Running West*, 321–28; Geary, *The Proper Edge of Sky*, 49.
56. Longwell, "Clarence Edward Dutton," 136–37; Stegner, *Clarence Edward Dutton*, 10.
57. "Brind" to "Brother Lund-Wall," undated, in Corbett, *Jacob Hamblin*, 331–32.
58. Frederick Brind to "Brother Lundwall," undated, in Corbett, *Jacob Hamblin*, 333.
59. For the tendency of some Western frontiersmen to "become" Indians, see Simmons, *Kit Carson and His Three Wives*, 18; Crampton, *Land of Living Rock*, 71.
60. Cox, "Biographical Sketch," 103.
61. She is definitely not antagonistic; she wrote, just before this, "Hamblin was a great and noble man. I would sharply resent any insinuation made upon his life and manners."
62. Fish, *The Life and Times of Joseph Fish*, 62.
63. Inez Lee, "An Autobiography."
64. Powell, *Exploration of the Colorado*, 128–29.
65. Frederick S. Dellenbaugh, holograph notes on his personal copy of Little, *Jacob Hamblin*, in Dellenbaugh Collection, Arizona Historical Society, Tucson.
66. Hamblin, diary, near Apr. 1, 1874, MS 1951, fd. 6, notebook 5, CHL. Hamblin to John Willard Young, April 14, 1874, in Bleak, "Annals," pp. 107–8.
67. *Letter version:* "6th. Always listen to them when they wish to tell their grievances, and redress their wrongs, however trifling they may be, if possible. If I cannot, I let them know that I have a desire to do so."
68. *Letter version:* "I never allow them to hear me use any obscene language, or take any unbecoming course with them."
69. See chapter 5 (1854), this volume.

70. Some authors have suggested that our term "religion" does not adequately express the all-encompassing nature of Indian culture, which whites have split into "secular" and "religious." See Stoffle et al., "Cultural Landscapes," 232–33; Locke, *The Book of the Navajo*, 45. I would argue that, in describing Indian culture, instead of retreating from the use of the descriptive term "sacred," we might want to expand it.
71. Hamblin, Diary/Reminiscence, MS 14654, pp. 44–45, CHL. For the ritual dance in Indian culture generally, see Laubin, *Indian Dances of North America*.
72. Jacob Hamblin to Brigham Young, December 18, 1858, BYOF, bx 26, fd 10. See chapter 9 (late 1858), this volume.
73. Wyckoff, *Designs and Factions*, 35; Worster, *A River Running West*, 295.
74. LJH, 106–7; see chapter 21 (1870), this volume.
75. LJH, 78.
76. Ibid., 105.

CHAPTER 29

1. Peterson, *Take Up Your Mission*, 15–22.
2. James Bunting, Diary, March 1, 1876.
3. Jacob Hamblin to Brigham Young, July 7, 1876, BYOF, bx 36 fd 13. For this mission, see also C. L. Christensen, "Among the Navajos"; Frihoff G. Nielson, diary excerpts, March 19, 1876.
4. For the Pima, see Cremony, *Life among the Apaches*, 89–90; Fontana, "Pima and Papago: Introduction"; Ezell, "History of the Pima"; Dobyns, *The Pima-Maricopa;* Russell, *The Pima Indians*; Sides, *Blood and Thunder*, 145–46. For the Maricopas, Spier, *Yuman Tribes of the Gila River*. The Pimas offer a remarkable example of how whites callously took over Indian water resources: in the 1880s, whites simply diverted water away from the Pima territory, causing the Gila and Salt Rivers to dry up. Lengthy periods of famine among the Pima resulted. Russell, *The Pima Indians*, 33.
5. For Apaches, see Cremony, *Life among the Apaches*; Debo, *Geronimo: The Man*; Haley, *Apaches*. For Mormons and Apaches, Peterson, *Take Up Your Mission*, 207–11.
6. Christensen (1855–1940) would serve a number of years as a Navajo missionary. See following chapters, and his diary, Lee Library.
7. C. L. Christensen, "Among the Navajos"; Frihoff G. Nielson, diary excerpts.
8. Nielson, diary excerpts.
9. Ibid.
10. Tanner and Richards, *Colonization on the Little Colorado*, 156–64.
11. For Lot Smith, a delightful introduction is Peterson, "'A Mighty Man Was Brother Lot.'" See also Tanner and Richards, *Colonization on the Little Colorado*, 160; Smallcanyon, "Contested Space," 114–50.
12. James Brown, Diary, March 24–27, 1876; Brown, *Life of a Pioneer*, 460–61; Peterson, "'A Mighty Man Was Brother Lot,'" 397–98. Brigham supported Lot Smith's claim; Young to James Brown, May 14, 1876, in PTRC, ser. 1, bx 25, fd 374.
13. Lot Smith to the editor, April 28, 1876, in *Deseret News*, June 21, 1876, p. 4; Lot Smith to the editor, August 28, 1876, in "Local and Other Matters," *Deseret News*, Sept. 20, 1876, p. 1. Discussion in Tanner and Richards, *Colonization on the Little Colorado*, 65.
14. Christensen, "Among the Navajos."
15. Lot Smith to the editor, April 28, 1876, in *Deseret News*, June 21, 1876, p. 4; Brigham Young Jr., diary, June 2, 1876.
16. Peterson, *Take Up Your Mission*, 91–122, and "'A Mighty Man Was Brother Lot.'"
17. For these settlements, see Peterson, *Take Up Your Mission*; McClintock, *Mormon Settlement*; Abruzzi, *Dam That River!*; Tanner and Richards, *Colonization on the Little Colorado*.
18. For this crossing of the Colorado, see Daniel H. Wells, Erastus Snow, and Brigham Young Jr. to Brigham Young, May 26, 1876, in BYOF, bx 43, fd 20, as cited and transcribed in Buchanan, *History of Lorenzo Wesley Roundy*, 73–74; Brigham Young Jr., diary, May 21–26, 1876; L. John Nuttall, letter to Brigham Young, May 29, 1876, as printed in "Further Particulars about the Colorado River Disaster," *Deseret News*, June 7, 1876, p. 1; "Accident on the Colorado," *Deseret News*, May 31, 1876, p. 1; W. D. Johnson Jr., Letter

to the Editor, June 4, 1876, in *Deseret News*, June 28, 1876, p. 346. Retrospective accounts in LJH, 135–36; Anthony Ivins, diary, June 14, 1876, pp. 88–89; Joseph Wright, autobiography, in Jenson, LDSBE, 1:467; Whitney, *History of Utah*, 4:178; James, "Lorenzo Hill Hatch"; Christensen, "Among the Navajos."

19. See chapter 26 (1873), this volume.
20. For Hatch (1826–1910), see Hatch, *Willing Hands*; James, "Lorenzo Hill Hatch." He located in New Mexico and opened up the formal mission to the Zunis (after initial successful efforts by Ammon Tenney and others among those Indians), but was later called as a leader in the Little Colorado settlements from 1877 to 1901. For Wells, see Hinckley, *Daniel Hanmer Wells*.
21. Brigham Young Jr. diary, May 21, 1876. Young says that there were nineteen members of the company. He lists Nuttall twice, but the second Nuttall is probably L. John Nuttall Jr. (1859–1909), who would have been sixteen at the time. See also L. John Nuttall, letter to Brigham Young, May 29, 1876, as printed in "Further Particulars about the Colorado River Disaster," *Deseret News*, June 7, 1876, p. 1; "Accident on the Colorado," *Deseret News*, May 31, 1876, p. 1 (which mentions a "Johnson," presumably Warren Johnson). One account lists a John Porter in the group. A. M. Musser, telegram, June 1, 1876, quoted in "The Story of Telegraphy," in Carter, *Our Pioneer Heritage* 4:569. See also Charles Walker diary, June 1 and 25, 1876 (1:427–28); W. D. Johnson Jr., Letter to the Editor, June 4, 1876, in *Deseret News*, June 28, 1876, p. 346. For Ellis Whitney Wiltbank (1854–1932), who later helped settle Round Valley in Arizona, see McClintock, *Mormon Settlement*, 186.
22. Brigham Young Jr., diary; Nuttall, letter to Brigham Young, May 29, 1876. Hamblin, in Little, has the incorrect date of May 28.
23. Nuttall, letter to Brigham Young, May 29, 1876; Christensen, "Among the Navajos."
24. Reilly, *Lee's Ferry*, 64; Rusho and Crampton, *Lee's Ferry*, 54. See also Brigham Young Jr., diary, May 16 and 24, 1876; John Bushman, diary, May 24, 1876.
25. Thomas G. Lowe, statement on the incident, April 30, 1930, in Journal History, May 24, 1876.
26. Brigham Young Jr., diary; Daniel H. Wells, Erastus Snow, and Brigham Young Jr. to Brigham Young, May 26, 1876.
27. Daniel H. Wells, Erastus Snow, and Brigham Young Jr. to Brigham Young, May 26, 1876, calls the Hatch wagon "Bro Roundy and Hatch's wagon."
28. Nuttall, letter to Brigham Young, May 29, 1876.
29. LJH, 135–36. See also Daniel H. Wells, Erastus Snow, and Brigham Young Jr. to Brigham Young, May 26, 1876. "A knot at the end caught in a crevice of ~~the~~ a rock," writes Brigham Jr.
30. LJH, 135–36.
31. Brigham Young Jr., diary; W. D. Johnson Jr., Letter to the Editor; Daniel H. Wells, Erastus Snow, and Brigham Young Jr. to Brigham Young, May 26, 1876. Young leaves off "swim, come on," as found in Johnson, but the sentence makes sense only when these words are included.
32. LJH, 135–36. Brigham Jr. seems to portray Nuttall clinging to a rope, not an oar.
33. Brigham Jr. refers to two small boats in the water, though Jacob was in the "new boat," which the company had brought with them.
34. LJH, 135–36.
35. James, "Lorenzo Hill Hatch." See also Christensen, "Among the Navajos"; W. D. Johnson Jr., Letter to the Editor; Brigham Young Jr., diary.
36. LJH, 135–36; Brigham Young Jr., diary.
37. LJH, 135–36; W. D. Johnson Jr., Letter to the Editor; Brigham Young Jr., diary. Billy Lee's account of Roundy giving a final wave before disappearing into the rapids seems unlikely. Rusho and Crampton, *Lee's Ferry*, 54; Brooks, *Emma Lee*, 93.
38. Brigham Young Jr., diary. Joseph Wright, autobiography, in Jenson, LDSBE, 1:467.
39. Nuttall, letter to Brigham Young, May 29, 1876. See on Daniel Wells above. Another miraculous assurance of safety in Colvin and Le Baron, "Warren M. Johnson at Lee's Ferry."
40. Nuttall lists Wells, Snow, Brigham Young Jr., McArthur, Hatch, Ensign, Hamblin, L. D. Young, Brigham S. Young, and Hanmer Wells. See also Brigham Young Jr., diary, May 25–26.
41. LJH, 136.
42. Brigham Young Jr., diary.

43. Hamblin to Young, July 7, 1876, BYOF, bx 36 fd 13.
44. L. John Nuttall kept a record of these ordinances, L. John Nuttall collection, Vault MSS 790, Lee Library, as cited in Ray [Taylor?] to P. T. Reilly, July 20, 1972, in PTRC, series 1, bx 10, fd 163.
45. See chapter 28 (1875), this volume.
46. Brooks, *John Doyle Lee*, 358–59.
47. Lee, diary, Dec. 29, 1870 (2:152).
48. Alexander, *Brigham Young, the Quorum of the Twelve*, at n177.
49. Lee, *Mormonism Unveiled*, 32–33. See also Bagley, *Blood of the Prophets*, 298–301. Judge Jacob Boreman wrote of Jacob, "His lips had been opened." Boreman, "Reminiscences," 44.
50. See Brooks, *John Doyle Lee*, 363–64.
51. Jacob Hamblin, testimony, Second Lee Trial, Huntington Library, San Marino, California.
52. Hamblin reportedly once stated that Lee was the main perpetrator of the massacre, and Haight and Dame were not able to understand his plot and stop him in time. Wilford Hamblin to Mrs. Parry, Dec. 19, 1954, p. 4, in Caroline Keturah Parry collection, Special Collections, Sherratt Library, Cedar City, Utah.
53. In his 1871 letter, Jacob stated that both Lee and Dame told him of their involvement in the massacre during his September 1857 trip south from Salt Lake City.
54. And Jacob's explanation did not satisfy non-Mormons. The *Salt Lake Tribune* correspondent, in "The Outlook," *Salt Lake Tribune*, Sept. 23, 1876, p. 2, mocked Jacob's keeping his "guilty knowledge" to himself for nineteen years, and never finding an opportunity to share it with law officers, especially at the previous Lee trial.
55. Brooks, *Mountain Meadows Massacre*, 182–83; Lee, diary, May 30, 1861 (1:313–4); Alexander, *Brigham Young, the Quorum of the Twelve*, 24.
56. Richard Turley, in his forthcoming book on the aftermath of the Mountain Meadows Massacre, may interpret Lee's second trial differently than have previous historians.
57. John D. Lee to Emma Batchelor Lee, Sept. 21, 1876, in Kelly, *Journals of John D. Lee*, 242.
58. Lee, *Mormonism Unveiled*, 269–72.
59. John D. Lee to Emma Batchelor Lee, Sept. 21, 1876.
60. Beadle, *The Undeveloped West*, 650.
61. Alice married Jared Taylor, at Luna, Catron, New Mexico, on February 1, 1896 (five children). She died only six years later on March 1, 1902, in Thatcher, Arizona, soon after bearing twins. Clara married Peter Arza Nicoll on August 19, 1898 in Nutrioso, Arizona (thirteen children). This marriage ended in a divorce, and she married Winthrop S. Staley in 1930. She died on June 27, 1959, in Lakeside, California.
62. Jacob Hamblin diary, notebook 4, MS 1951, CHL. In this section, quotes are from this unless otherwise specified.
63. Young et al. to Hamblin, Dec. 15, 1876, in Hamblin journal, MS 1951, fd 8, CHL; also in Bleak, "Annals," at Dec. 18, 1876, pp. 51–52.
64. For Harrison Pearce (1818–1889) and Pearce Ferry (which was operational from 1876 to 1882), see McClintock, *Mormon Settlements*, 96.
65. For this expedition, see Jacob Hamblin, diary, MS 1951, fd 5, notebook 4, CHL; LJH, 136; John Oakley to Brigham Young, Jan. 16, 1877, including Hamblin to Young, Jan. 5, 1877, including the Hyrum Williams journal, BYOF, bx 36 fd 13.
66. Bleak, "Annals," at Aug. 31, 1876, p. 55. This might have been a reaffirmation of a previous setting apart; see chapter 27 (1874), this volume. See also McClintock, *Mormon Settlement*, 87; Jenson, "Hamblin, Jacob," 100; Quinn, *The Mormon Hierarchy: Extensions*, 659; Corbett, *Jacob Hamblin*, 394.
67. The Hamblin diary has them leaving on the thirteenth. LJH, 136.
68. LJH, 137.
69. Jacob remembered the name as "Stevenson."
70. Hodge, *Arizona as It Is*, 87–88. For Stevens Ranch, *Walapai Papers*, 118; Ida Frances Hunt Udall, diary, April 3–6, 1877, in Marriott, *In Our Own Words*, 146.
71. Hyrum Williams, journal. For Beale's road, see chapter 15 (1863), this volume.
72. Hyrum Williams, journal.

73. Thanks to Larry Burk for identifying Lois.
74. Hamblin to Young, Jan. 5, 1877, included with John Oakley to Brigham Young, Jan. 16, 1877, and also including the Hyrum Williams journal.
75. Jacob calls this "Camp Apache," but it is certainly Camp Verde. The famous Camp Apache/Fort Apache is deep in the White Mountain Apache Reservation, much farther southeast. Camp Verde dealt with the Yavapai and the Tonto Apaches; see Hart, *Old Forts of the Far West*, 159–61.
76. LJH, 138; McClintock, *Mormon Settlement*, 87.
77. L. John Nuttall, diary.
78. Nuttall, diary; Wilford Woodruff, journal (7:327).
79. "Amram," Letter to the Editor, Feb. 13, 1877, in "Correspondence," *Deseret News*, Feb. 28, 1877; Charles Walker, diary, Feb. 11, 1877 (1:449).
80. LJH, 139.
81. Ibid.
82. MS 1951, fd 4, CHL. Mormons, influenced by 1 Corinthians 5:29, perform baptisms and other rituals on behalf of the dead in temples. For endowments, see chapter 2 (1842–1849), this volume.
83. Buerger, "'The Fulness of the Priesthood'" and "The Development of the Mormon Temple," 47; Anderson, *The Development of LDS Temple Worship*, 34–35, 58–63.
84. Buerger, "'The Fulness of the Priesthood,'" 44.
85. Nuttall, diary.
86. Hamblin Diary, March 26, 1877, MS 1951, fd 5, Notebook 4, CHL.
87. I follow the identification of Grand Canyon specialists Peter Huntoon and Drifter Smith; see Huntoon, "The Opening of Deer Creek," and Smith, "Fun with History."
88. Beaman, "The Cañon of the Colorado," 591. Confusingly, the name Surprise Valley was later transferred to a nearby valley to the east that does not fit Beaman's description at all. Huntoon, "The Opening of Deer Creek."
89. Dutton, *Tertiary History*, 160.
90. Huntoon, "The Opening of Deer Creek." It is fairly easy to reach it from the Colorado, which is how Beaman discovered it.
91. See "Local and Other Matters," the section "Prisoner Escaped," *Deseret News*, Aug. 15, 1877, p. 12.
92. Nuttall, diary, Aug. 26–28.
93. Later, Foutz moved his family to Moenkopi, and Foutz families were found there for many years afterward. Six of his thirteen sons became Navajo traders. Hoopes and Hoopes, "Mormon Colonization of Arizona"; Pavlik, "Of Saints and Lamanites," 21; Esshom, *Pioneers*, 876; Evans, *Along Navajo Trails*, 4–6.
94. LJH, 139–40.
95. Ibid.
96. Ibid.
97. Nuttall, diary.
98. LJH, 140.
99. Later he lived in Mexico, from 1890 to 1907, before returning to Kanab, where he died in 1908. George A. Smith diary, Jan. 23, 1871 (SC 32); Esshom, *Pioneers*, 171, 1008; Dwyer, "Introduction."
100. Per Martha Cox, see below.
101. Corbett, *Jacob Hamblin*, 400.
102. "Biographical Sketch of Martha Cox," p. 103.
103. For Martha, see Anderson, "A 'Salt of the Earth' Lady"; Kinkead, *A Schoolmarm All My Life*, 89–102.
104. "General Conference," "Second Day," *Deseret News*, Oct. 10, 1877, pp. 9, 12 (569, 572). Foutz's name is misspelled as Frietz, but in the Journal History clipping, this is corrected. Jacob is not listed here.
105. Minutes of "meeting of Missionaries," Journal History, Oct 8, 1877.
106. See the 1880 census for Kanab, discussed in chapter 32 (1879–82), this volume.
107. Kanab Ward Historical Record Book A, Nov. 18, Dec. 2, 1877.
108. William Nelson, Diary.

CHAPTER 30

1. These letters, dated November 1 and November 19—the first written apparently with a scribe, and the other apparently a holograph—are quite similar to each other. They are available in PTRC, series 8.1, bx 2 fd 23; Fowler and Fowler, *Anthropology of the Numa*, 23; Fowler and Fowler, "Notes on the History," 110.
2. Nov. 19 letter.
3. Nov. 1 letter.
4. For the Paiutes' extensive use of sunflowers and pine nuts, see Palmer, "Plants Used by Indians," 594, 602.
5. See Powell and Ingalls, *Report*; Worster, *A River Running West*, 273–86; Fowler and Fowler, *Anthropology of the Numa*, 11.
6. Quoted in Fowler and Fowler, *Anthropology of the Numa*, 23, and Fowler and Fowler, "Notes on the History," 110.
7. For the Paiutes' religious connection with their lands, see Powell's letter quoted below; also Stoffle, Halmo, and Austin, "Cultural Landscapes"; Reeve, *Making Space*, 11–12.
8. James Spencer, Report for Nevada Agency, Aug. 30, 1880, in ARCIA (1880), 125–26; Stoffle and Evans, "Resource Competition," 188.
9. Fowler and Fowler, *Anthropology of the Numa*, 22; Matheson and Cooper, "Answers to a Questionnaire," Q 25.
10. Powell to Henry Teller, Feb. 1880, as quoted in Worster, *A River Running West*, 270–71; Kirsch, "John Wesley Powell," 565.
11. See Powell's 1875 article, "An Overland Trip to the Grand Cañon," 677, discussed in Worster, *A River Running West*, 284; also p. 285; Holt, *Beneath These Red Cliffs*, 34.
12. Austin, Dean, and Gaines, *Yanawant: Paiute Places*, 2:16–17.
13. Clarence E. Dutton, *Tertiary History*, 78–79.
14. John Steele, diary.
15. Charles Walker, diary, Aug. 28, 1869 (1:297).
16. Herbert E. Riggs, a local Kanab resident, quoted in Davis, *An Excursion to the Plateau Province*, 10–11; see also Austin, Dean, and Gaines, *Yanawant: Paiute Places*, 2:23. A tremendous flood in July 1883 also had a catastrophic effect on Kanab's environmental status; see Riggs, in Davis, *An Excursion to the Plateau Province*, 11.
17. Geary, *The Proper Edge of Sky*, 195.
18. Another visitor in 1917 remarked that previously there had been grass "all over the place" in House Rock Valley, but now it was desert. Both quoted in Trudeau, *An Environmental History*, p. 33.
19. Geary, *The Proper Edge of Sky*, 194–95, 112–13; Austin, Dean, and Gaines, *Yanawant: Paiute Places*, 2:23–24; Worster, *A River Running West*, 353–54; Allen, "Where Have All the Grasslands Gone?"; and chapter 24 (1871), this volume.
20. Geary, *The Proper Edge of Sky*, 195.
21. Brooks, "The Arizona Strip," 295–96; Austin, Dean, and Gaines, *Yanawant: Paiute Places*, 2:17–18, 20. John Willard Young, Brigham Young's son, for a time a counselor in the First Presidency, "bought" the entire Kaibab Plateau from a Paiute for a gun and some ammunition. Trudeau, *An Environmental History*, 41.
22. See chapter 24 (1871), this volume.
23. David Lewis diary, as summarized in Thomas Brown diary (Brooks 94).
24. Beaman, "The Cañon of the Colorado," 593.
25. Powell and Ingalls, *Report*, 10.
26. See also Stoffle and Evans, "Resource Competition," 188, and Stoffle, Jones, and Dobyns, "Direct European Immigrant Transmission."
27. Stoffle and Evans, "Resource Competition," 188, estimate that the Kaibab population dropped from about 1,175 to about 99 between 1863 and 1880. These are very inexact figures, since no actual statistically valid counts of Kaibab Paiutes were taken in those years.
28. Kelly, *Southern Paiute Ethnography*, 24–25.
29. Holt, *Beneath These Red Cliffs*, 27.
30. Kanab Stake Historical Record Book A.

31. L. John Nuttall to William D. Johnson, Bishop at Kanab, June 14, 1880, typescript excerpt, in PTRC, series 1, bx 20, fd 317.
32. William D. Johnson to L. John Nuttall, May 6, 1884, typescript excerpt, in PTRC, series 1, bx 20, fd 317.
33. Kanab Stake Historical Record Book A, at March 5, 1894.
34. Austin, Dean, and Gaines, *Yanawant: Paiute Places*, 2:24.
35. Knack, "Interethnic Competition," 216–17.

CHAPTER 31

1. Compton, "John Willard Young."
2. John Willard Young to John Taylor and the Council of Apostles, Jan. 28, 1878, CHL, typescript in PTRC, series 1, bx 13, fd 192.
3. Reilly, *Lee's Ferry*, 74, citing J. W. Young, 1877 Folder, Box 2, CHL.
4. Young to Taylor, Jan. 28, 1878. For Hualapai Valley, Truxton Springs, and Young's Spring, see Humphreys and Wheeler, *Preliminary Report Concerning Explorations and Surveys*, 66–67.
5. Andrew Gibbons, diary, before Jan. 1, 1878.
6. Ibid., Jan. 1878; Peterson, *Take Up Your Mission*, 84.
7. Minutes of the Little Colorado Stake, pp. 5, 15; John Bushman diary, January 27, 1878.
8. Minutes of the Little Colorado Stake, p. 16. C. L. Christensen is Christian Lyngaa Christensen.
9. Ibid., pp. 14, 15.
10. Ibid., p. 20.
11. William Derby Johnson, Diary, Feb. 8, 1878; Reilly, *Lee's Ferry*, 74, citing J. W. Young, 1878–1879 Folder, Box 2, CHL.
12. Kanab Ward Historical Record Book A; Kenney, *Wilford Woodruff's Journal*, 7:403; William Derby Johnson, Diary, Feb. 9, 10, 14, 17, and 24, March 10 and 24, and Apr. 18 and 19.
13. John Willard Young to John Taylor, June 2, 1878, CHL, typescript in PTRC, series 1, bx 13, fd 189; C. L. Christensen, diary; Brugge, "The Moencopi Boundary Problem," 15–18; Peterson, *Take Up Your Mission*, 126–35.
14. Bleak, "Annals," April 7, 1878, pp. 13–14.
15. Andrew Gibbons, diary, May 2 and 11, 1878.
16. See Graves, *Thomas Varker Keam*, and chapter 27 (1874), this volume.
17. "Minutes of the Little Colorado Stake," pp. 22, 26.
18. Christensen, "Among the Zunis." The following section is from this source, unless otherwise specified.
19. C. L. Christensen, "Pioneer of 1876 Saw Many Things." Christensen dates this encounter in 1876, but this is unlikely, given that the Dane had just arrived in Arizona that year. A "Mr. Cooley and his two Apache wives" served as interpreters. This would be one of the colorful characters in Arizona history, the scout, miner, farmer, and lawman, C. E. (Corydon Eliphalet) Cooley, who married two daughters of Apache chief Pedro. Farish, *History of Arizona*, 6:275–79.
20. For the Zunis, see Eggan and Pandey, "Zuni History, 1850–1970"; Cushing, *Zuni: Selected Writings*; Crampton, *The Zunis of Cibola* (which has a section on the early Mormon mission, 116–18).
21. Jones, *Forty Years Among the Indians*, 260.
22. For the Mormons and Zunis, see Lorenzo Hatch, letter to the editor, Oct. 19, 1877, in "Correspondence," *Deseret News*, Oct. 31, 1877, p. 1; Flake, "A History of Mormon Missionary Work," 64–71; Telling, "Ramah, New Mexico"; Peterson, *Take Up Your Mission*, 204–7; Jensen, "New Mexico, Pioneer Settlements"; Vogt and Albert, *People of Rimrock*.
23. This connection with the Aztecs is doubtful; but it is certain that both Tuuvi and Talasnimki came from prominent families in Oraibi.
24. Christensen, "Addenda—Hopi Article." Slightly different retelling in Christensen, "A True Story and an Experience."
25. William Decatur Kartchner, "Memoirs," at July 13–14, 1878.
26. Andrew Gibbons, diary.
27. Ibid.

28. Nuttall, diary, cf. the William Derby Johnson diary.
29. William Derby Johnson, diary, Aug. 11 and 12, Sept. 1, 12, and 14, and Oct. 1; Kanab Ward Historical Record Book "A.", Nov. 24, 1878; James G. Bleak, journal, Nov. 8, 1878. On April 2, 1878, Bleak and John D. T. McAllister had written a letter to President John Taylor describing "assets & liabilities of the Church in the St. George Stake," and one of the items was "Jacob Hamblin (old A/C Indian Missionary) $918.05." Typescript excerpt in PTRC, series 1, bx 1, fds 16–17.
30. "Minutes of the Little Colorado Stake," p. 66.

CHAPTER 32

1. Lorenzo Hatch, *Journal*, p. 77.
2. John Taylor to Lot Smith, Nov. 27, 1878, in Lot Smith papers, folder 1, Special Collections, Hayden Library, Arizona State University. Minutes of the Little Colorado Stake. Jesse N. Smith, *Journal*, Sept. 30, 1878.
3. Jesse N. Smith, *Journal*, 232–33. For further on St. Johns, see Smiley, "Ammon M. Tenney: Mormon Missionary"; Nelson, *Arizona Pioneer Mormon*, 66–96; 147–59.
4. Minutes of the Little Colorado Stake, p. 75.
5. L. John Nuttall diary, March 8; William Derby Johnson diary, March 8, 10, 26.
6. In the Great Register of 1879, for Springerville, a list compiled in late April through May 12, 1879, Jacob is listed as no. 82. Becker Family Papers—Arizona Historical Society. Consulted at Jack Becker's Round Valley website, at http://www.roundvalleyaz.com/register.html (accessed on July 13, 2010). Many names here are Latino, but there are twelve people born in Utah. See also McClintock, *Mormon Settlement*, 185.
7. For Fort Apache, see Hart, *Old Forts of the Far West*, 162–64.
8. Farish, *History of Arizona*, 6:284–307; Becker, "Round Valley As It Was! 1870–1876."
9. McClintock, *Mormon Settlement*, 185.
10. Alexander, *Things in Heaven and Earth*, 236–38. Kenney, *Wilford Woodruff's Journal*, Aug. 14 and 16, 1879 (7:481–502).
11. Jesse N. Smith, *Journal*.
12. Fish, "History of the Eastern Arizona Stake." Fish, *The Life and Times of Joseph Fish*, 192.
13. See Smith, "Mormon Forestdale"; McClintock, *Mormon Settlement*, 170–73; Peterson, *Take Up Your Mission*, 25–27, 208–11; Tietjen, *Ernst Albert Tietjen*, chapters 3–5.
14. There is no contemporary documentation for this move, but I belief that family traditions for the date are correct. Corbett, *Jacob Hamblin*, 403, 405, 464.
15. Arrott, *Sarah Priscilla*, 43.
16. Corbett, *Jacob Hamblin*, 403.
17. Arrott, *Sarah Priscilla*, 43.
18. Inez Hamblin Lee, "Autobiography."
19. Corbett, *Jacob Hamblin*, 465. For the location of the fort, see Kelly and Lee, *Nutrioso and Her Neighbors*, 79.
20. Fish, *The Life and Times of Joseph Fish*, 198.
21. Hamblin to Taylor, Dec. 23, 1879, holograph, USHS.
22. Bleak, "Annals," Dec. 21, 1879, p. 61.
23. Hamblin to Taylor, Dec. 23, 1879. In another letter to Taylor written on the same day, Jacob asked for his "approval for Second Ordinances in the Temple." This is puzzling, for Jacob had already received this ordinance in March 1877.
24. Jabez Dudley married Julia Mae Butler in 1906 (eleven children). He died on July 29, 1968, in Phoenix, Arizona.
25. Jesse N. Smith, *Journal*, 243.
26. Ibid., 249.
27. See the letters to Powell in chapter 30 (1877–1880), this volume.
28. Kanab Ward Historical Record Book A.
29. Kelly and Lee, *Nutrioso and Her Neighbors*, 79.

30. Ibid., 79–80.
31. Ibid.
32. Kanab Ward Historical Record Book A; Jesse N. Smith, *Journal*, 252.
33. Willard Otto married Lillian Lee, a granddaughter of John D. Lee, in 1901 (eleven children). Willard Otto worked as a farmer in Nutrioso, and died on September 16, 1967, in Eagar.
34. Amarilla Hamblin Lee, 1970 interview with P. T. Reilly.
35. Don Carlos married Ida Lee on March 12, 1907 (thirteen children). He lived in Springerville until 1927, when he moved to Farmington, New Mexico. "Funeral Services for Son of Jacob Hamblin Held in Mesa, Ariz.," *Kane County Standard*, Nov. 27, 1941, p. 1.
36. See Firmage and Mangrum, *Zion in the Courts*, 161–67; Hardy, *Doing the Works of Abraham*, 281–85; Gordon, *The Mormon Question*, 150–55. For the "raid" in southern Utah, Larson, *I Was Called to Dixie*, 624–37; Anderson, *Desert Saints*, 322–23.
37. Bair and Jensen, "Prosecution of the Mormons"; Smiley, "Ammon M. Tenney: Mormon Missionary," 101; Peterson, *Take Up Your Mission*, 227–34; Hardy, *Doing the Works of Abraham*, 335–36.
38. See Hardy, *Doing the Works of Abraham*, 269–341, and *Solemn Covenant*.
39. Peterson, *Take Up Your Mission*, 214–16. See also Pavlik, "Of Saints and Lamanites," 22.
40. C. L. Christensen, "Among the Hopis," *Times-Independent* (Moab, Utah), March 9, 1922; Christensen to Anthony Ivins, Sept. 30, 1925, Anthony Ivins Papers, bx 9, fd 5, USHS; Peterson, "The Hopis and the Mormons," 192.
41. As quoted in Peterson, "The Hopis and The Mormons," 192–93.
42. Ibid., 193–94; also Flake, "A History of Mormon Missionary Work," 50, 52; Reeve and Fletcher, "Mormons in the Tuba City Area," 96–97; Brigham Young Jr. diary, March 6, 1882, typescript notes in PTRC, series 1, bx 13, fd 186.
43. "Notes on Indians," 162. Christensen to Anthony Ivins, Jan. 23, 1923, USHS, typescript in PTRC, series 1, bx 5, fds 62–63.
44. "Local and Other Matters," in the section "News From the South," *Deseret News*, March 8, 1876, p. 8. A different date, probably incorrect, in St. George Temple record, PTRC, series 1, bx 28, fd 406.
45. James Brown, Diary, March 12, 1876; Brown, *Life of a Pioneer*, 459. See also Whiteley, *Deliberate Acts*, 318n5; Flake, "A History of Mormon Missionary Work," 50–51.
46. Andrew Gibbons, Diary; see also Flake, "A History of Mormon Missionary Work," 51; Reeve and Fletcher, "Mormons in the Tuba City Area," 96.
47. Christensen, "Hopi Legends."
48. Jesse N. Smith, *Journal*, September 17, 1878; "SUNSET, ARIZONA TERRITORY," L. John Nuttall to President John Taylor, Sept. 24, 1878, *Deseret News* 27 (Oct. 23, 1878), p. 7 (599); Jenson, "Snowflake Stake: Manuscript History"; Flake, "A History of Mormon Missionary Work," 49; McClintock, *Mormon Settlement*, 158; Reeve and Fletcher, "Mormons in the Tuba City Area," 96; Whiteley, *Deliberate Acts*, 37.
49. Christensen to Anthony Ivins, Jan. 23, 1923, USHS, typescript in PTRC, series 1, bx 5, fds 62–63; Brigham Young Jr. diary, March 6, 1882, typescript notes in PTRC, series 1, bx 13, fd 186.
50. Christensen, "Hopi Legends."
51. William R. Mateer to Ezra A. Hayt, Commissioner of Indian Affairs, May 1, 1879, Letters Received, RG 75, M234, reel 24, frames 546–51, NA. See also Brugge, "The Moencopi Boundary Problem," 15; Wyckoff, *Designs and Factions*, 39. There is an unfortunate ambiguity in this statement, as Tuuvi refers to both Moenave (where Jacob and John D. Lee settled with full permission of Tuuvi, as he notes) and Moenkopi. Nevertheless, this and other sources undoubtedly document that Tuuvi came to resent Mormon settlers at Moenkopi and Tuba City.
52. C. L. Christensen, diary, May 31, 1885 (p. 70). Christensen accused the Hopis at Moenkopi of appropriating water without authorization. Letter to John H. Bowman, July 10, 1885, in C. L. Christensen, diary (p. 20).
53. C. L. Christensen, diary, May 31, 1885 (p. 70).
54. Ibid., June 15, 1885 (p. 76).
55. Ibid., Dec. 22, 1885 (p. 85). Here, Tuuvi stated that the previous summer he had "been beat by his friends until the Blood ran from his head in a Stream." The identity of these "friends" is not known. See

Whiteley, *The Orayvi Split*, 1:188; C. L. Christensen to John Bowman, July 10, 1885, in Christensen's diary (p. 22).

56. See also Minutes of Tuba City Meeting, Feb. 7–9, 1888; Whiteley, *The Orayvi Split*, 1:189; Smallcanyon, "Contested Space."
57. Brigham Young Jr., diary, March 6, 1882; Reeve and Fletcher, "Mormons in the Tuba City Area," 96–97; Peterson, "The Hopis and the Mormons," 193–94. Tom Polacca is the most prominent exception.
58. Christensen, "Hopi Legends," *Times-Independent* (Moab, Utah), Feb. 9, 1933, p. 1. Signs of fissures in the marriage of Tuuvi and Talasnimki are already evident in the 1880s, C. L. Christensen diary, Oct. 17, 1880 (p. 23); Arza Hinckley diary, August 17, 1883; C. L. Christensen diary, June 15, 1885 (p. 76). Whiteley, *The Orayvi Split*, 1:467.
59. Whiteley, *The Orayvi Split*, 1:117, 188; Flake, "A History of Mormon Missionary Work," 53; "Monument Honors Friendly Hopi Indian Chief," in the section, "The Church Moves On," *Improvement Era* 44 (July 1941). Jesse N. Smith, *Journal*, July 24, 1889. Some anti-Mormon rumors hold that Tuuvi died after a Mormon beat him severely, but Hopi historian Peter Whiteley reports that old Hopis told him that Tuuvi died of natural causes. Whiteley, *The Orayvi Split*, 1:188n7.
60. Whiteley, *Deliberate Acts*, 37, 207; *Bacavi*, 86; *The Orayvi Split*, 1:542, 551.
61. Whiteley, *The Orayvi Split*, 1:117. C. L. Christensen calls the Navajo adopted by Tuuvi and Talasnimki "Nan-caw-shey," and reports that some Hopis would not accept him; Christensen, "Navajo Traditions."
62. Whiteley, *The Orayvi Split*, 1:469, 499; 2:880.
63. Ibid., 1:614 (1911 census); Whiteley, *Bacavi*, 85. See also *The Orayvi Split*, 1:563 (a 1908 census); 1:611 (a 1910–1912 census).
64. Reeve and Fletcher, "Mormons in the Tuba City Area," 149.
65. Judd, "Tuba City"; Flake, "A History of Mormon Missionary Work," 81; Reeve and Fletcher, "Mormons in the Tuba City Area," 150–51.
66. Christensen to Anthony Ivins, Sept. 30, 1925, typescript in PTRC, series 1, bx 5, fds 62–63, original in USHS; Flake, "A History of Mormon Missionary Work," 60, 62–63.
67. Flake, "A History of Mormon Missionary Work," 70.
68. John Taylor to Albert Carrington, Oct. 18, 1882, in *Millennial Star* 44:46 (Nov. 13, 1882), 732.
69. Tuba City Ward Record, Manuscript History LR 9236 2, at 1900, CHL. See also Flake, "A History of Mormon Missionary Work," 53.
70. Flake, "A History of Mormon Missionary Work," 79.
71. In Mormon Settlements in Arizona collection, Marriott Library, series XII, fd 3.
72. Flake, "A History of Mormon Missionary Work," 79–80.
73. Ibid., 85–88.
74. Oman, "LDS Southwest Indian Art."
75. Flake, "A History of Mormon Missionary Work," 81; Pavlik, "Of Saints and Lamanites," 21–22. For Mormon Navajo traders, see Evans, *Along Navajo Trails*; Powers, *Navajo Trading*, 12, 15–16.

CHAPTER 33

1. Jesse N. Smith and Lorenzo H. Hatch, "Trip into New Mexico," a letter to the editor dated Nov. 2, 1882, in *Deseret News*, Nov. 12, 1882, p. 12. Reprinted in Smith, *Journal*, 264–66. See also the journal of Lorenzo Hatch for these dates, pp. 98–99. I follow Charles Maxwell's reconstruction of the route of this journey.
2. For Pleasanton, see "Mormons in the Mogollons," in *The New Southwest and Grant County Herald*, March 18, 1882; small interview with William B. Maxwell, *Silver City Enterprise*, Jan. 25, 1884; "The Mogollons," *Silver City Enterprise*, Aug. 22, 1884; N. P. Worden, "Items from New Mexico," a letter to the editor dated Dec. 27, 1884, in *Deseret News*, Jan. 14, 1885, p. 13; Andrew Jenson, Letter to the Editor, March 22, 1894, in "Correspondence" section, *Deseret Weekly* 48.18 (April 21, 1894): 552; Jenson, *Encyclopedic History*, 666; Arrington, "Mormons in Twentieth-Century New Mexico."
3. Smith and Hatch, "Trip into New Mexico"; Hatch, *Journal*, p. 98.
4. Hatch and Hardy, *Stalwarts South of the Border*, 719. Smith and Hatch, "Trip Into New Mexico."
5. Altia Williams Naegle, "Life Story"; George Calvin Williams, "The Life and Religion."

6. An obituary of Jacob Hamblin Jr., a son of Priscilla, states that he and his family came to Pleasanton in 1883. "Death Takes Jacob Hamlin at Age of 74," a clipping, newspaper unknown, in PTRC, series 1, bx 16, fd 257.
7. Arrott, *Sarah Priscilla Leavitt Hamblin*, 46.
8. Louise Udall, "Jacob Hamblin—His Later Years," 253. Udall was a daughter of Inez Louisa Hamblin Lee, Louisa's second child. Louise married Levi S. Udall, who became an Arizona Supreme Court justice, and she was the mother of Morris K. Udall and Stewart Lee Udall, both prominent Arizona politicians.
9. Emma B. Coleman to Eliza R. Snow, Sept. 4, 1886, in "Death of Jacob Hamblin," *Deseret News* 35.36, Sept. 29, 1886, p. 5 (185). For further on Coleman, see Udall and Nelson, *Arizona Pioneer Mormon*, 149; Corbett, *Jacob Hamblin*, 412.
10. Udall, "Jacob Hamblin ... Story of His Later Years."
11. Corbett calls it Salise or Saleese, which seems to be an Anglo rendering of Saliz. This river is probably west of the Saliz Mountains. Julyan, *The Mountains of New Mexico*, 297–98.
12. Corbett, *Jacob Hamblin*, 412–13.
13. Udall, "Jacob Hamblin ... Story of His Later Years."
14. Arrott, *Sarah Priscilla Leavitt Hamblin*, 46.
15. See Corbett's little biography of Jacob Hamblin Jr., at *Jacob Hamblin*, 463.
16. Arrott, *Sarah Priscilla Leavitt Hamblin*, 46.
17. Inez Hamblin Lee, "Autobiography."
18. "Death Takes Jacob Hamlin at Age of 74." For the Apache threat in this area, Faulk, *The Geronimo Campaign*, 73, cf. Twitchell, *The Leading Facts of New Mexican History*, 4:330; Ailman, *Pioneering in Territorial Silver City*, 73.
19. "Rilla" married Franklin Lee, a grandson of John D. Lee, in 1908 in Nutrioso (seven children). Franklin died in 1944 in Los Angeles, California, which left Amarilla a widow for some thirty-eight years. She died on March 7, 1982, in Martinez, California. Amarilla Hamblin Lee, "My Life's Story"; Reilly, Interview with Amarilla Hamblin Lee.
20. "Eastern Arizona Stake Conference," *Deseret News*, Oct. 17, 1883, p. 12; "Eastern Arizona Stake Conference," *Deseret News*, Dec. 26, 1883, p. 13.
21. Jesse N. Smith, *Journal*, 282–84; Lorenzo Hatch, *Journal*, pp. 102–3; *Silver City Enterprise*, Jan. 18, 1884; *Southwest Sentinel* (Silver City, New Mexico), Jan. 19, 1884.
22. This is arguable if you are talking about church leaders in Salt Lake City.
23. Hardy, "The American Siberia"; Bair and Jensen, "Prosecution of the Mormons," 38–39.
24. Hamblin diary, MSS 770, Lee Library.
25. Ibid.
26. Ibid.; Smith, *Journal*, 305.
27. For Arizona as the launching pad for the Mormon colonies in Mexico, see Peterson, *Take Up Your Mission*, 233. More generally, Romney, *The Mormon Colonies in Mexico*; Tullis, *Mormons in Mexico*; Hardy, "Cultural Encystment"; Turley et al., *History of the Mormon Colonies*; Truett, *Fugitive Landscapes*, 125–29; Hatch and Hardy, *Stalwarts South of the Border*; Johnson, *Heartbeats of Colonia Díaz*.
28. Hamblin diary, MSS 770, Lee Library.
29. Hardy, "The Trek South."
30. Hamblin diary, MSS 770, Lee Library.
31. For location, Fish, *The Life and Times of Joseph Fish*, Feb. 19, 1885, p. 273; Jesse N. Smith, *Journal*, Jan. 22, 1884, p. 284.
32. Sullivan Richardson, "journal," as quoted in Johnson, *Heartbeats of Colonia Díaz*, 24–25.
33. Fish, *The Life and Times of Joseph Fish*, 274.
34. Ibid., at March 15, 1885 (278).
35. See Peterson, *Take Up Your Mission*, 228.
36. For the Fish company, aside from the Fish diaries, see the Levi Savage journal, quoted in Johnson, *Heartbeats of Colonia Díaz*, 26–30. I call it the "Fish company" for convenience, as he was a prominent diarist in the group. Technically, they might have been considered stragglers in the overall Snowflake company.

37. Fish, *The Life and Times of Joseph Fish*, 277.
38. Jesse N. Smith, *Journal*, 305; Fish, *The Life and Times of Joseph Fish*, 278.
39. Jesse N. Smith, *Journal*, March 25, 1885; Tullis, *Mormons in Mexico*, 54–55.
40. Hamblin diary, MSS 770, Lee Library.
41. Jesse N. Smith, *Journal*.
42. Hatch, *Colonia Juárez*, 83.
43. Hamblin diary, MSS 770, Lee Library.
44. John Pulsipher, diary, typescript, 2:69. He also visited another veteran, Benjamin Johnson; Johnson, *My Life's Review*, 304.
45. Kenney, *Wilford Woodruff's Journal*, 8:333. Quoted in Corbett, *Jacob Hamblin*, 416–17. Also in Hamblin diary, MSS 770, Lee Library.
46. Hamblin diary, MSS 770, Lee Library. The "18" could be a "13." Kanab Stake Historical Record, Oct. 1, 1885.
47. Hamblin diary, MSS 770, Lee Library.
48. For example, Stewart Udall, a descendant of Jacob and Louisa, in *Forgotten Founders*, 56.
49. The chronology of Johnson, *Heartbeats of Colonia Díaz*, 25, is preferable to that of Corbett, *Jacob Hamblin*, 413–14.
50. Hamblin diary, MSS 770, Lee Library. Two Mormons were killed in the area on December 1, 1885; McClintock, *Mormon Settlement in Arizona*, 254.
51. Johnson, *Heartbeats of Colonia Díaz*, 25–26. See also Corbett, *Jacob Hamblin*, 414; "Life of Walter Eugene Hamblin," with slightly different details.

CHAPTER 34

1. I have found no other references to Jacob's affiliation with freemasonry. However, his father was a "Democrat and Freemason." Miller, *The Jacob Vernon Hamblin Family*, 42.
2. Ella H. Tenney, "Jacob Escapes," as cited by Corbett, *Jacob Hamblin*, 420–21.
3. Coleman to Snow, "Death of Jacob Hamblin." Louise Lee Udall, "Jacob Hamblin ... Story of His Later Years." Louise, a granddaughter of Jacob, was not a firsthand witness, but she probably interviewed Priscilla and Louisa, as well as Jacob's children, as she researched this article.
4. Coleman to Snow, "Death of Jacob Hamblin."
5. Ibid.; Corbett, *Jacob Hamblin*, 421–23. If Coleman's date for Jacob leaving Alpine is correct, then there is a major discrepancy between the family traditions and what actually happened. Family tradition describes only three nights between Alpine and Pleasanton. But if Jacob left on the eighteenth and died on the thirtieth or thirty-first, then there are nine or ten days unaccounted for.
6. Udall, "Jacob Hamblin ... Story of His Later Years." Corbett, *Jacob Hamblin*, 421–23.
7. Udall, "Jacob Hamblin ... Story of His Later Years."
8. Arrott, *Sarah Priscilla Leavitt Hamblin*, 46. According to Udall, "Jacob Hamblin ... Story of His Later Years," however, Dudley was the only healthy person in the family.
9. Udall, "Jacob Hamblin ... Story of His Later Years."
10. Ibid.
11. Arrott, *Sarah Priscilla Leavitt Hamblin*, 46.
12. Coleman to Snow, "Death of Jacob Hamblin."
13. Arrott, *Sarah Priscilla Leavitt Hamblin*, 46.
14. Coleman to Snow, "Death of Jacob Hamblin."
15. Udall, "Jacob Hamblin ... Story of His Later Years." This is also the story found in "Death and Burial of Jacob Hamblin," MS 7704, CHL. Bleak gives an entirely different account, perhaps a folkloric elaboration portraying Jacob as a victim of polygamy prosecution: "He was hounded [by federal marshals] so, that in his last hours he had to leave his home, and breathed his last mortal breath on a high ridge in view of the home of his dear ones." Bleak, "Annals," Aug. 31, 1886, p. 57.
16. Emma Coleman to Eliza R. Snow, "Death of Jacob Hamblin." Corbett, *Jacob Hamblin*, 422, quotes Coleman, but changes the date from August 30 to 31! The death date is given as August 31 in Miller, *Jacob Vernon Hamblin*, 43, and Corbett, *Jacob Hamblin*, 422.

17. Coleman to Snow, "Death of Jacob Hamblin." Actually, Alma was only about fifteen miles away.
18. Ibid.
19. According to Udall, Jake Jr. had been freighting with Oscar and had sensed some need to come back to Pleasanton. Duane and Oscar, however, had to complete the freighting job, so missed the interment. Jacob's body was moved to the Alpine, Arizona, graveyard in July 1889, and a memorial service was held for him on July 28. Udall, "Jacob Hamblin ... Story of His Later Years"; Historical Record, St. Johns Stake, Book A, p. 80.
20. Arrott, *Sarah Priscilla Leavitt Hamblin*, 47. In the weeks after Jacob's death, Priscilla and Louisa were informed that their land titles were not valid, were forced from their homes, and had to leave Pleasanton. For their long widowhoods in eastern Arizona, see Compton, "Civilizing the Ragged Edge."

CHAPTER 35

1. Slotkin, *Gunfighter Nation*, 77.
2. Slotkin, *The Fatal Environment*, 53.
3. Ibid., 61. For the rhetoric of extermination in white-Indian relations, see chapter 4 (1850–1853), this volume.
4. See Stannard, *American Holocaust*, 130–34.
5. Andrist, *The Long Death*, 89.
6. Hamblin, Autobiography, pp. 57–58.
7. LJH, 29.
8. Peterson, "Jacob Hamblin," 23.
9. The first chroniclers of this chapter in the Hamblin saga were non-Mormons, the Smith brothers. It is a curious fact that non-Mormons—the Smiths, John Wesley Powell, and Frederick Dellenbaugh—were among the early proponents of the "Hamblin legend."
10. Dellenbaugh to Kelley, undated letter, in Crampton, "F. S. Dellenbaugh," 235.
11. Dellenbaugh to Stites, Oct. 5, 1926, in Crampton, "F. S. Dellenbaugh," 220. Lyman was actually his son.
12. It is possible, but not certain, that Jacob later opened up to Jacob Forney. See chapter 10 (1859), this volume.
13. See chapters 8 (1858) and 29 (1876–1877), this volume.
14. Peterson, "Jacob Hamblin," 21 and passim.
15. Peterson, "The Hopis and the Mormons," 193–94. See also Flake, "A History of Mormon Missionary Work," 50; and chapter 32 (1879–1882), this volume.
16. Chapter 32, this volume; Clemmer, *Roads in the Sky*, 45.
17. See Alley, "Prelude to Dispossession."
18. Jacob Hamblin and John R. Young to George A. Smith, September 12, 1869, George A. Smith Collection, MS 1322 (SC 33).
19. John D. Lee, diary, Sept. 9, 1873 (2:295–96). See also chapter 10 (1859), this volume.
20. Not counting the early white occupation of Kanab from 1863–1866, before the town was deserted as a result of the Navajo wars. Jacob started an Indian farm there in 1867 or 1868.
21. C. L. Christensen, diary, May–June 1885 (pp. 70–76, see also pp. 20–22); Whiteley, *Deliberate Acts*, 37; chapter 32 (1879–1882), this volume. The Mormon-Indian conflict in Moenkopi–Tuba City ended differently than the settlements in southern Utah, with the Mormons being forced out by the U.S. government in 1903. Whitely, *Deliberate Acts*, 37; Flake, "A History of Mormon Missionary Work," 81.
22. H. S. Welton to CIA, June 16, 1888, NA, OIA, RG 75, LR, 15960/88 and enclosures, as cited in Brugge, "The Moencopi Boundary Problem," 17–18. Smith probably referred to Lot Smith, who in 1892 was killed in a land-water-stock dispute with Navajos; see Smallcanyon, "Contested Space," 114–50; Peterson, "'A Mighty Man Was Brother Lot,'" 412–13.
23. C. L. Christensen, diary, May–June 1885 (pp. 70–85); Peterson, *Take Up Your Mission*, 213.
24. See chapters 13 (early 1862), 24 (1871), and 30 (1877–1880, this volume.
25. Mormon settlements often took the place of former Paiute settlements. Martineau, *Southern Paiutes*, 162. One Cedar City informant, Alva Matheson, said: "The Whites always took their choicest camps for their settlements and crowded the Indian farther out into less desirable spots." Cooper, "Answers to a

Questionnaire," Q 6. Jacob also understood this, see chapter 24 (1871), this volume. In their gradual displacement of Paiutes, Mormons may have practiced what is known as "settler colonialism"—in which settlers take over lands peacefully, but inexorably, at the expense of indigenous peoples.

26. See chapters 24 (1871) and 30 (1877–1880), this volume.
27. Jacob Hamblin to Brigham Young, Sept. 19, 1873.
28. See chapter 24 (1871), this volume.
29. Arrington, *Great Basin Kingdom*, 215.
30. See chapters 18 (1866) and 20 (1869), this volume.
31. Jacob Hamblin to Brigham Young, Sept. 19, 1873.
32. Some of this mindset can be seen in early Tooele, and in the military response to the killing of Whitmore and McIntyre in 1866. And, as I mention in the introduction, I am not arguing that all Indians are victims. Some were violent outlaws; some raided for wealth, not for survival. Wars and raids between tribes caused some Indians to welcome white settlers as allies against stronger, more wealthy, more aggressive Indians (often slave traders).
33. Lamar, *The Far Southwest*, 278. The great geologist Herbert E. Gregory wrote, in a similar vein, "That these murders of Indians by whites and whites by Indians did not develop into a disastrous war with its consequent devastation of all the white settlements in Southern Utah is largely owing to the faith, skill and daring of Jacob Hamblin, who discouraged reprisals and took upon himself the task of visiting hostile bands with a view of establishing peaceful relations." Gregory and Moore, "The Kaiparowits Region," 28.

APPENDIX A

1. Full text of Dellenbaugh's statement in Compton, "Civilizing the Ragged Edge," appendix.
2. Brooks, "Indian Relations," 41.
3. Miller, *Jacob Vernon Hamblin Family*, 54; Ancestral File, www.familysearch.org, lists Susan born "about 1854" in Tooele.
4. Corbett, *Jacob Hamblin*, 234–35, seems to place this death in early 1864; see also Brooks, "Indian Relations," 42. Arrott, Sarah Priscilla Leavitt Hamblin, 35, called this girl Emily.
5. Arrott, *Sarah Priscilla Leavitt Hamblin*, 35.
6. Corbett, *Jacob Hamblin*, 215.
7. Ibid., 213, 215. Corbett says she was the oldest of the Indian girls Hamblin adopted. Brooks, "Indian Relations," 42, gives a daughter of Jacob Hamblin, Mrs. Mary Beeler, as her source. Priscilla mistakenly calls this adopted daughter Ellen but identifies her clearly by saying she later "married a white man and raised a nice family." Arrott, *Sarah Priscilla Leavitt Hamblin*, 33. Arrott also gives her age as "thirteen or fourteen" in about 1863; Ibid., 31.

Bibliography

ABBREVIATIONS

ARCIA: United States. Office of Indian Affairs. *Annual Report of the Commissioner of Indian Affairs.*
Brooks, JSIM: Brooks, *Journal of the Southern Indian Mission.*
BYOF: Brigham Young Office Files.
CHL: Church History Library and Archives, Church of Jesus Christ of Latter-day Saints, Salt Lake City, Utah.
Cline Library: Cline Library, Northern Arizona University, Flagstaff, Arizona.
FHL: Family History Library, Church of Jesus Christ of Latter-day Saints, Salt Lake City.
Jenson, LDSBE: Jenson, Andrew. *Latter-day Saint Biographical Encyclopedia.*
Lee Library: L. Tom Perry Special Collections, Harold B. Lee Library, Brigham Young University, Provo, Utah.
LJH: Little, *Jacob Hamblin.*
NA: National Archives, Washington, D.C.
PTRC: P. T. Reilly Collection, MS 275, Cline Library, Northern Arizona University, Flagstaff, Arizona.
SC: Turley, *Selected Collections.*
USHS: Utah State Historical Society, Salt Lake City, Utah.

Abruzzi, William S. *Dam That River! Ecology and Mormon Settlement in the Little Colorado River Basin.* Lanham, MD: University Press of America, 1993.

———. "The Social and Ecological Consequences of Early Cattle Ranching in the Little Colorado River Basin." *Human Ecology* 23 (1995): 75–98.

Adair, Samuel Newton. Autobiography. Written at Luna, NM, Sept. 15, 1919. At http://home.att.net/~dtadair/samuelnewtonadair.html (accessed via Internet Archive on Feb. 26, 2013).

Adams, Nathan H., and Julius V. Madsen. "Notes from an Interview with Nathan H. Adams at Kanab, Utah Tuesday October 22, 1929. By Julius V. Madsen." Typescript. In Juanita Brooks collection, B-103, Bx 31, fd 24, USHS.

Addy, Caroline S. "James Godson Bleak, Pioneer Historian of Southern Utah." M.A. Thesis, Brigham Young University, 1953.

Ailman, Harry B. *Pioneering in Territorial Silver City: H.B. Ailman's Recollections of Silver City and the Southwest 1871–92.* Edited by Helen J. Lundwall. Albuquerque: University of New Mexico Press, 1983.

Aird, Polly. *Mormon Convert, Mormon Defector: A Scottish Immigrant in the American West, 1848–1861.* Norman, OK: Arthur H. Clark Company, 2009.

Albrecht, Dorothy. "John Lorenzo Hubbell, Navajo Indian Trader." *Arizoniana* 4 (fall 1963): 33–40.

Alder, Douglas. "Writing Southern Utah History: An Appraisal and a Bibliography." *Journal of Mormon History* 20.2 (fall 1994): 156–78.

Alder, Douglas, and Karl F. Brooks. *A History of Washington County: From Isolation to Destination.* Salt Lake City: Utah State Historical Society, 1996.

Alexander, Thomas G. *Brigham Young, the Quorum of the Twelve, and the Latter-day Saint Investigation of the Mountain Meadows Massacre.* Leonard J. Arrington Mormon History Lecture Series 12. Logan: Utah State University Press, 2007.

———. "Federal Authority versus Polygamic Theocracy: James McKean and the Mormons, 1870–1875." *Dialogue* 1 (autumn 1966): 85–100.

———. "Irrigating the Mormon Heartland: The Operation of the Irrigation Companies in Wasatch Oasis Communities, 1847–1880." *Agricultural History* 76.2, Water and Rural History (spring 2002): 172–187.

———. *Mormonism in Transition: A History of the Latter-day Saints, 1890–1930.* Urbana: University of Illinois Press, 1986.

———. Review of *Blood of the Prophets* by Will Bagley. *Brigham Young University Studies* 42.1 (2003): 167–74.

———. *Things in Heaven and Earth: The Life and Times of Wilford Woodruff, a Mormon Prophet*. Salt Lake City: Signature Books, 1991.

Alexander, Thomas G., and Leonard J. Arrington. "The Utah Military Frontier, 1872–1912: Forts Cameron, Thornburgh and Duchesne." *Utah Historical Quarterly* 33 (fall 1965): 330–54.

Allen, Craig D. "Where Have All the Grasslands Gone?" On the "Land Use History of North America Colorado Plateau" website. http://cpluhna.nau.edu/Research/grasslands1.htm (accessed March 17, 2011).

Allen, James B., and Ted J. Warner. "The Gosiute Indians in Pioneer Utah." *Utah Historical Quarterly* 39.2 (spring 1971): 162–77.

Allen, M. D. "History of Kingston (Utah)." Written in 1969. Typescript. MSS A 1675, USHS.

Alley, John R. "Prelude to Dispossession: The Fur Trade's Significance for the Northern Utes and Southern Paiutes." *Utah Historical Quarterly* 50 (spring 1982): 104–23.

Allison, A. Lynn. "The Navajo Witch Purge of 1878." *PaloVerde* 9.1 (May 2001). At http://www.west.asu.edu/paloverde/Paloverde2001/Witch.htm (accessed Feb. 26, 2013).

Altman, Irwin, and Joseph Ginat. *Polygamous Families in Contemporary Society*. Cambridge: Cambridge University Press, 1996.

Altshuler, Constance Wynn. *Cavalry Yellow and Infantry Blue: Army Officers in Arizona between 1851 and 1886.* Tucson: Arizona Historical Society, 1991.

———. *Chains of Command: Arizona and the Army, 1856–1875*. Tucson: Arizona Historical Society, 1981.

Amundsen, Andrew. Journal, 1873. Typescript, MSS A 1482, USHS.

Anderson, Devery S. *The Development of LDS Temple Worship, 1846–2000: A Documentary History.* Salt Lake City: Signature Books, 2011.

Anderson, Janet, and Ella Brown. "Stansbury Mountain Canyon—Grantsville Division." In Carter, *Treasures of Pioneer History* 6:479–83.

Anderson, Lavina Fielding. "A 'Salt of the Earth' Lady: Martha Cragun Cox." In *Supporting Saints: Life Stories of Nineteenth-Century Mormons*, edited by Donald Q. Cannon and David J. Whittaker, 101–32. Religious Studies Center Special Monograph Series, vol. 1. Provo, UT: Religious Studies Center, Brigham Young University, 1985.

Anderson, Michael F., comp. and ed. *A Gathering of Grand Canyon Historians: Ideas, Arguments, and First-Person Accounts: Proceedings of the Inaugural Grand Canyon History Symposium, January 2002.* Grand Canyon, AZ: Grand Canyon Association, 2005.

Anderson, Nels. *Desert Saints: The Mormon Frontier in Utah*. Chicago: The University of Chicago Press, 1942.

Andrews, H. Franklin. *The Hamlin Family: A Genealogy of James Hamlin of Barnstable, Massachusetts, Eldest Son of James Hamlin, the Immigrant, who came from London, England, and settled in Barnstable 1639; 1639–1902.* Exira, IA: by the author, 1902.

Andrist, Ralph K. *The Long Death: The Last Days of the Plains Indians.* New York: Macmillan, 1964.

An Enduring Legacy. 12 vols. Salt Lake City: Daughters of Utah Pioneers, 1978–1989.

Arrington, Harriet Horne. "Fifty Years Building Utah: Joseph Horne's Pioneering Contributions." In Walker and Dant, *Nearly Everything Imaginable*, 431–49.

Arrington, Leonard J. *Adventures of a Church Historian.* Urbana: University of Illinois Press, 1998.

———. *Brigham Young: American Moses.* New York: Knopf, 1985.

———. *Great Basin Kingdom: An Economic History of the Latter-day Saints, 1830–1900*. Cambridge: Harvard University Press, 1958.

———. "Inland to Zion: Mormon Trade on the Colorado River, 1864–1867." *Arizona and the West* 8 (autumn 1966): 239–50.

———. "The Mormon Cotton Mission in Southern Utah." *The Pacific Historical Review* 25.3 (Aug. 1956): 221–238.

———. "Mormons in Twentieth-Century New Mexico." In *Religion in Modern New Mexico*, edited by Ferenc Morton Szasz, and Richard W. Etulain, 101–24. Albuquerque: University of New Mexico Press, 1997.

Arrington, Leonard J., and Davis Bitton. *The Mormon Experience: A History of the Latter-day Saints.* New York: Knopf, 1969.

Arrington, Leonard J., Feramorz Y. Fox, and Dean L. May. *Building the City of God: Community & Cooperation among the Mormons*. 2nd ed. Urbana: University of Illinois Press, 1992. Originally published in 1974.

Arrington, Leonard J., and Richard Jensen. "Panaca: Mormon Outpost among the Mining Camps." *Nevada Historical Society Quarterly* 18 (1975): 207–16.

Arrington, Leonard, and Dean May. "'A Different Mode of Life': Irrigation and Society in Nineteenth Century Utah." *Agricultural History* 49 (1975): 3–20.

Arrott, Mryl Tenney. *Sarah Priscilla Leavitt Hamblin: A Pioneer Midwife*. N.p., n.d., typescript. 49 pages, in possession of author.

Atkin, Thomas, Jr. "Biography of Thomas Atkin." Autobiography, holograph. MSS 341, Perry Special Collections, Lee Library.

Austin, Diane, Erin Dean, and Justin Gaines. *Yanawant: Paiute Places and Landscapes in the Arizona Strip*, volume 2 of *The Arizona Strip Landscapes and Place Name Study*. St. George, UT: Bureau of Land Management, 2005.

Azar, John S. "Buckskin Mountain." In Anderson, *A Gathering of Grand Canyon Historians*, 53–56.

Backus, Anna Jean. *Mountain Meadows Witness: The Life and Times of Bishop Philip Klingensmith*. Spokane, WA: Arthur H. Clark, 1995.

Bagley, Will. *Blood of the Prophets: Brigham Young and the Massacre at Mountain Meadows*. Norman: University of Oklahoma Press, 2002.

———, ed. *The Pioneer Camp of the Saints: The 1846 and 1847 Mormon Trail Journals of Thomas Bullock*. Kingdom in the West series, vol. 1. Spokane, WA: Arthur H. Clark, 1997.

———. *Stones, Clubs and Gun Barrels: Two Lost Accounts of the Mountain Meadows Massacre*. Keepsake for limited edition of Bigler and Bagley, *Innocent Blood*. Norman, OK: Arthur H. Clark, 2008.

Bailey, Garrick, and Roberta Glenn Bailey. *A History of the Navajo: The Reservation Years*. Santa Fe, NM: School of American Research Press, 1986.

Bailey, Lynn R. *Indian Slave Trade in the Southwest*. Los Angeles: Westernlore Press, 1973.

———. *The Long Walk: A History of the Navajo Wars, 1846–68*. Pasadena, CA: Socio-Technical Books, 1964.

Bailey, Paul. *Jacob Hamblin: Buckskin Apostle*. Los Angeles: Westernlore Press, 1948.

Bair, JoAnn W., and Richard L. Jensen, "Prosecution of the Mormons in Arizona Territory in the 1880s." *Arizona and the West* 19.1 (spring 1977): 25–46.

Baker, Shane A. "Illness and Mortality in Nineteenth-Century Mormon Immigration." *Mormon Historical Studies* 2 (fall 2001): 77–90.

Bancroft, Hubert Howe. *History of Utah: 1540–1886*. In *The Works of Hubert Howe Bancroft*, vol. 26. San Francisco: The History Company, Publishers, 1889.

Barrios, Frank M. "An Appointment with Death: The Howland-Dunn Tragedy Revisited." In Anderson, *A Gathering of Grand Canyon Historians*, 145–48.

Bate, Kerry William. "John Steele: Medicine Man, Magician, Mormon Patriarch." *Utah Historical Quarterly* 62 (winter 1994): 71–90.

Beadle, John Hanson. *The Undeveloped West: Or, Five Years in the Territories*. Philadelphia: National Publishing Co., 1873.

Beale, Edward F. *Wagon Road from Fort Defiance to the Colorado River, Letter from the Secretary of War*... House of Representatives, 35th Congress, 1st Session, Doc. 124. Washington D.C.: House of Representatives, 1858.

Beaman, E. [Edward] O. "The Cañon of the Colorado, and the Moquis Pueblos." Chapter 2. *Appleton's Journal* 11.266 (Apr. 25, 1874): 513–16.

———. "The Cañon of the Colorado, and the Moquis Pueblos." Chapters 3–4. *Appleton's Journal* 11.267 (May 2, 1874): 545–48.

———. "The Cañon of the Colorado, and the Moquis Pueblos." Chapters 5–6. *Appleton's Journal* 11.268 (May 9, 1874): 590–93.

———. "The Cañon of the Colorado, and the Moquis Pueblos." Chapter 9. *Appleton's Journal* 11.271 (May 30, 1874): 686–89.

Bean, George Washington. *Autobiography of George Washington Bean and His Family Records*. Compiled by Flora D. B. Home. Salt Lake City: Utah Printing Co., 1945.

———. "George W. Bean." From an autobiography or memoir, relating to the Las Vegas mission. In Carter, *Our Pioneer Heritage*, 18:100–6.

Becker, Jack A. "Round Valley As It Was! 1870–1876." At http://www.roundvalleyaz.com/page1.html (accessed Feb. 26, 2013).

Beckstrom, Elizabeth, and Bessie Snow. *"Oh Ye Mountains High": History of Pine Valley, Utah.* St. George, UT: Heritage Press, 1980.

Beckwith, Albert Clayton. *History of Walworth County, Wisconsin.* 2 vols. Indianapolis, IN: B. F. Bowen & Company, 1912.

Beeler, Mary H. "Life Sketch of Melissa." Jacob Hamblin collection, Huntington Library, San Marino, CA.

Beesley, Kenneth R., ed. "M. J. Shelton to George A. Smith, 13 November 1859." In the possession of the author.

Belshaw, Michael. "The Dunn-Howland Killings." *Journal of Arizona History* 20 (1979): 409–22.

Bender, Norman J. *"New Hope for the Indians": The Grant Peace Policy and the Navajos in the 1870s.* Albuquerque: University of New Mexico Press, 1989.

Ben-Dor Benite, Zvi. *The Ten Lost Tribes: A World History.* New York: Oxford University Press, 2009.

Bennett, Richard E. "Council Bluffs (Kanesville), Iowa." In Ludlow, *The Encyclopedia of Mormonism*, 325–26.

———. *Mormons at the Missouri, 1846–1852.* Norman: University of Oklahoma Press, 1987.

———. *We'll Find the Place: The Mormon Exodus, 1846–1848.* Salt Lake City: Deseret Book, 1997.

Berkhofer, Robert F., Jr. *Salvation and the Savage: An Analysis of Protestant Missions and American Indian Response, 1787–1862.* [Lexington]: University of Kentucky Press, 1965.

Bevan, John Alexander. "Events in the Early History of Tooele." Typescript, probably finished in 1924. MSS A 6019-2, USHS.

Bigler, David L. "The Aiken Party Executions and the Utah War, 1857–1858." *The Western Historical Quarterly* 38.4 (winter 2007): 457–76.

———. *Forgotten Kingdom: The Mormon Theocracy in the American West, 1847–1896.* Spokane, WA: Arthur H. Clark, 1998.

———. *Fort Limhi: The Mormon Adventure in Oregon Territory 1855–1858.* The Kingdom in the West series, vol. 6. Spokane, WA: Arthur H. Clark, 2003.

Bigler, David L., and Will Bagley. *Innocent Blood: Essential Narratives of the Mountain Meadows Massacre.* The Kingdom in the West series, vol. 12. Norman, OK: Arthur H. Clark, 2008.

———. *The Mormon Rebellion: America's First Civil War 1857–1858.* Norman: University of Oklahoma, 2011.

Billingsley, George H., Earle E. Spamer, and Dove Menkes. *Quest for the Pillar of Gold: The Mines & Miners of th Grand Canyon.* Grand Canyon, AZ: Grand Canyon Association, 1997.

Billington, Ray Allen, and Martin Ridge. *Westward Expansion: A History of the American Frontier.* 6th edition, abridged. Albuquerque: University of New Mexico Press, 2001.

"Biography of Edwin Hamblin." Typescript. At http://itsallrelative.cjb.net/histories/EDWIN%20HAMBLIN.pdf (accessed Aug. 30, 2010).

"Biography of Joseph Hamblin." Typescript, 2 pp. Kanab D.U.P. Museum.

Birney, Hoffman. *Zealots of Zion.* Philadelphia: The Penn Publishing Company, 1931.

Bishop, Francis. "Captain Francis Marion Bishop's Journal, August 15, 1870–June 3, 1872." Edited by Charles Kelly. *Utah Historical Quarterly* 15 (Jan., Apr., July, Oct. 1947): 159–237.

Bishop, F. M. "Letters of Captain F. M. Bishop to the Daily Pantagraph 1871–1872." *Utah Historical Quarterly* 15 (Jan., Apr., July, Oct. 1947): 239–53.

Bitton, Davis, and Linda P. Wilcox. "Pestiferous Ironclads: The Grasshopper Problem in Pioneer Utah." *Utah Historical Quarterly* 46.4 (fall 1978): 336–55.

Black, Susan Easton, cp. *Membership of the Church of Jesus Christ of Latter-day Saints 1830–1848.* 50 vols. Provo, UT: Religious Studies Center, Brigham Young University, 1984–1988.

Black, Susan Easton, and William G. Hartley, eds. *The Iowa Mormon Trail: Legacy of Faith and Courage.* Orem, UT: Helix Publishing, 1997.

Blair, Roger P. "The Doctor Gets Some Practice?: Cholera and Medicine on the Overland Trails." *Journal of the West* 36:1 (January 1997): 54–66.

Bleak, James G. "Annals of the Southern Utah Mission." Holograph. MS 318, CHL (SC 19).

———. Diary, March–April 1864. Typescript, Ms B 171, fd 6, USHS.

Blomberg, Nancy J. *Navajo Textiles: The William Randolph Hearst Collection.* Tucson: University of Arizona Press, 1988.

Blue, Martha. *Indian Trader: The Life and Times of J. L. Hubbell*. Walnut, CA: Kiva, 2000.

———. *The Witch Purge of 1878: Oral and Documentary History in the Early Navajo Reservation Years.* Navajo Oral History Monograph Series No. 1. Tsaile, AZ.: Navajo Community College Press, 1988.

Bolton, Herbert E., and Arlington R. Mortensen. *Pageant in the Wilderness: The Story of the Escalante Expedition to the Interior Basin, 1776, Including the Diary and Itinerary of Father Escalante.* Salt Lake City: Utah State Historical Society, 1950.

Book of Mormon: An Account Written By the Hand of Mormon, Upon Plates Taken from the Plates of Nephi. Palmyra: Printed by E. B. Grandin, for the Author, 1830. This first edition is reprinted in *Joseph Smith Begins His Work: Book of Mormon 1830 First Edition*. Salt Lake City: Wilford C. Wood, 1958.

Boreman, Jacob. Reminiscences. In Leonard J. Arrington, ed., "Crusade against Theocracy: the Reminiscences of Judge Jacob Smith Boreman of Utah, 1872–1877." *Huntington Library Quarterly* 24:1 (Nov. 1960): 1–45.

Bowden, Henry Warner. *American Indians and Christian Missions: Studies in Cultural Conflict.* Chicago: University of Chicago Press, 1981.

Bowman, Matthew. *The Mormon People: the Making of an American Faith*. New York: Random House, 2012.

Braatz, Timothy. *Surviving Conquest: A History of the Yavapai Peoples.* Omaha: University of Nebraska Press, 2003.

Bradley, Martha Sonntag. *A History of Kane County*. Salt Lake City: Utah State Historical Society, 1999.

Bradley, Zorro A. "The Whitmore-McIntyre Dugout." *Plateau* 33 (Oct. 1960): 40–45.

Bradshaw, Hazel, ed. *Under Dixie Sun*. Panguitch, UT: Washington County Chapter of the Daughters of Utah Pioneers, 1950.

Bressler, Ann Lee. *The Universalist Movement in America, 1770–1880.* New York: Oxford University Press, 2001.

Briggs, Robert H. "George Washington Adair (1837–1909): Biographical Sketch." At the 1857 Iron County Militia Project webpage http://www.1857ironcountymilitia.com (accessed Feb. 26, 2013).

———. "James Mangum (1820–1888): Biographical Sketch." At the 1857 Iron County Militia Project webpage http://www.1857ironcountymilitia.com (accessed Feb. 26, 2013).

———. "James Pearce (1839–1922): Biographical Sketch." At the 1857 Iron County Militia Project webpage http://www.1857ironcountymilitia.com (accessed Feb. 26, 2013).

———. "John Mangum (1817–1885): Biographical Sketch." At the 1857 Iron County Militia Project webpage http://www.1857ironcountymilitia.com (accessed Feb. 26, 2013).

———. "The Mountain Meadows Massacre: An Analytical Narrative Based on Participant Confessions." *Utah Historical Quarterly* 74 (fall 2006): 313–33.

———. "Oscar Hamblin (1833–1862): Biographical Sketch." At the 1857 Iron County Militia Project webpage http://www.1857ironcountymilitia.com (accessed Aug. 30, 2010).

———. "Philip Klingensmith (1815–1881 or later)." At the 1857 Iron County Militia Project webpage http://www.1857ironcountymilitia.com (accessed Apr. 27, 2010).

———. "Samuel Knight (1832–1910): Biographical Sketch." At the 1857 Iron County Militia Project webpage http://www.1857ironcountymilitia.com (accessed Feb. 26, 2013).

———. "Samuel Knight and the Events Incident to the Utah War, 1857–1858: A Preliminary Study." Unpublished paper, September 2001, in the author's possession.

———. "The Tragedy at Mountain Meadows Massacre: Toward a Consensus Account and Time Line." Juanita Brooks Lecture Series. St. George: Dixie State College, 2002. Available at http://library.dixie.edu/special_collections/Juanita%20Brooks%20lectures/2002%20-%20The%20Tragedy%20at%20Mountain%20Meadow%20Massacre.html (accessed Feb. 26, 2013).

Briggs, Walter. *Without Noise of Arms: The 1776 Domínguez Escalante Search for a Route from Santa Fe to Monterey.* Flagstaff: Northland Press, 1986.

Brigham Young Letterpress Copybooks, CR 1234 1, LDS Church Archives (SC 21).

Bright, William. *Native American Placenames of the United States.* Norman: University of Oklahoma Press, 2004.

Brimhall, Edna Lee. "Biography of John David Lee." In PTRC, Series 8.1, bx 2, fd 17.

Bringhurst, Newell G. *Brigham Young and the Expanding American Frontier.* Boston: Little, Brown, 1986.

Broadhurst, Dale. "Readings in Early Mormon History." Website. The California newspaper section can be found at http://www.sidneyrigdon.com/dbroadhu/CA/misccal1.htm#101257 (accessed Feb. 26, 2013).

Brooks, Juanita Leavitt Pulsipher, ed. *History of Sarah Sturdevant Leavitt*. N.p.: 1919. Note: the author is listed as Juanita Leavitt Pulsipher.

Brooks, Juanita. "The Arizona Strip." *Pacific Spectator* 3 (summer 1949): 290–301.
———. *Dudley Leavitt, Pioneer to Southern Utah*. N.P., 1942.
———. *Emma Lee*. Logan, UT: Utah State University Press, 1984.
———, ed. "Extracts from the Journal of John Steele." *Utah Historical Quarterly* 6 (January 1933): 2–28.
———. "Indian Relations on the Mormon Frontier." *Utah Historical Quarterly* 12 (Jan–April 1944): 1–48.
———. *Jacob Hamblin: Mormon Apostle to the Indians*. Salt Lake City: Westwater Press, 1980.
———. *John Doyle Lee: Zealot–Pioneer Builder–Scapegoat*. Glendale, CA: Arthur H. Clark, 1961.
———, ed. "Journal of Thales W. Haskell." *Utah Historical Quarterly* 12.1–2 (Jan.–Apr. 1944): 68–98.
———, ed. *Journal of the Southern Indian Mission: Diary of Thomas D. Brown*. Western Text Society, no. 4. Logan: Utah State University Press, 1973.
———. "New Harmony." In Bradshaw, *Under Dixie Sun*, 129–41.
———, ed. *On the Mormon Frontier: The Diary of Hosea Stout, 1844–1861*. 2 vols. Salt Lake City: Utah Historical Society/University of Utah Press, 1964.
———. *The Mountain Meadows Massacre*. Palo Alto, CA: Stanford University Press, 1950. 2nd ed. Norman, OK: University of Oklahoma Press, 1962.
———. *On the Ragged Edge: The Life and Times of Dudley Leavitt*. Salt Lake City: Utah State Historical Society, 1973.
———. *Quicksand and Cactus: A Memoir of the Southern Mormon Frontier.* Logan, UT: Utah State University Press, 1992.
———. "The Water's In!" *Harper's Magazine* 182 (May 1941): 608–13.
Brown, Ira V. "Watchers for the Second Coming: The Millennial Tradition in America." *The Mississippi Valley Historical Review* 39 (1952): 451–58.
Brown, James Stephens. Diary, 1875–1876. Typescript. In PTRC, series 1, bx 3, fd 39.
———. *Life of a Pioneer, Being the Autobiography of James S. Brown*. Salt Lake City: Geo. Q. Cannon & Sons Co., Printers, 1900.
———. "Navajo Cunning." *Juvenile Instructor* 12.20 (Oct. 1877): 231–32.
Brown, Robert, and Mary Hilger. "Union County: The Mount Pisgah Experience." In Black and Hartley, *The Iowa Mormon Trail*, 237–44.
Brown, Thomas D. Journal. See Brooks, Juanita, ed., *Journal of the Southern Indian Mission: Diary of Thomas D. Brown*.
Brugge, David M. "Barboncito." In Betz and Carnes, *American National Biography. Supplement*, 26:14–15.
———. *Hubbell Trading Post National Historic Site.* Tucson, AZ: Western Parks Association, 1993.
———. "The Moencopi Boundary Problem: The Final Report." November 1967. At http://www.adwr.state.az.us/Adjudications/documents/HopiContestedCaseDisclosures/Navajo%20Initial%20Disclosure/Images%5CCDV001%5CBROWNBAIN%5CC0090%5CC037.pdf (accessed Feb. 26, 2013).
———. *The Navajo-Hopi Land Dispute: An American Tragedy.* Albuquerque: University of New Mexico Press, 1994.
Brune, Bonnie. "Historic River Running." In Anderson, *A Gathering of Grand Canyon Historians*, 123–28.
Buchanan, James. *Message of the President of the United States*. Senate Document, 36th Congress, 1st Session, Doc. 32 and Doc. 42. Washington, D.C.: U.S. Senate, 1860.
Buchanan, Joseph F. *History of Lorenzo Wesley Roundy.* Available at http://aeb.buchananspot.com/histories/LWRhistory.html (accessed Feb. 10, 2011).
Buerger, David John. "The Development of the Mormon Temple Endowment Ceremony." *Dialogue* 20.4 (winter 1987): 33–76.
———. "'The Fulness of the Priesthood': The Second Anointing in Latter-day Saint Theology and Practice." *Dialogue* 16.1 (spring 1983): 11–44.
———. *The Mysteries of Godliness*. San Francisco: Smith Research Associates, 1994.
Bunker, Edward. Autobiography. Typescript, Edward Bunker Papers, Huntington Library, San Marino, California.
Bunte, P. A., and R. J. Franklin. *From the Sands to the Mountain: Change and Persistence in a Southern Paiute Community.* Lincoln: University of Nebraska Press, 1987.
Bunting, James Lovett. Diaries, 1857–1920. Holograph, Lee Library.

Burton, Doris Karren. *A History of Uintah County: Scratching the Surface.* Salt Lake City: Utah State Historical Society, 1996.

Bushman, John. Diary. 1877–1879. Typescript in PTRC, series 1, bx 3, fd 43.

Bushman, Richard. *Joseph Smith and the Beginnings of Mormonism*. Urbana: University of Illinois Press, 1984.

———. *Joseph Smith: Rough Stone Rolling*. New York: Knopf, 2005.

Bye, Robert A., Jr. "Ethnobotany of the Southern Paiute Indians in the 1870s, with a note on the early ethnobotanical contributions of Dr. Edward Palmer." In *Great Basin Cultural Ecology*, edited by Don D. Fowler, 87–104. Desert Research Institute Publications, vol. 8. Reno, NV: Desert Research Institute, 1972.

Caldwell, Patricia. *The Puritan Conversion Narrative: The Beginnings of American Expression*. Cambridge: Cambridge University Press, 1983.

Call, Anson. *The Life Record of Anson Call*. An autobiography. N.p., n.d.

Calloway, Colin G. *One Vast Winter Count: The Native American West Before Lewis and Clark.* Lincoln: University of Nebraska Press, 2003.

Campbell, Eugene E. "Brigham Young's Outer Cordon: A Reappraisal." *Utah Historical Quarterly* 41 (summer 1973): 221–53.

———. *Establishing Zion: The Mormon Church in the American West, 1847–1869*. Salt Lake City: Signature Books, 1988.

Campbell, Eugene Edward. "The Mormon Gold Mining Mission of 1849." *Brigham Young University Studies* 1–2 (autumn 1959–winter 1960): 19–31.

Canfield, Gae Whitney. *Sarah Winnemucca of the Northern Paiutes.* Norman: University of Oklahoma Press, 1983.

Cannon, Brian Q. "Adopted or Indentured, 1850–1870: Native Children in Mormon Households." In Walker and Dant, *Nearly Everything Imaginable*, 341–57.

"Captain Horton David Haight—1859." In Carter, *Our Pioneer Heritage*, 3:43–44.

Carleton, James Henry. *Special Report of the Mountain Meadows Massacre*. Dated May 25, 1859. Washington, D.C.: Government Printing Office, 1902.

Carnahan, Colleen Arrott. *Sarah Priscilla Leavitt Hamblin: A Pioneer Midwife*. Salt Lake City: self-published, 1997.

Carr, Stephen L. *The Historical Guide to Utah Ghost Towns.* 3rd ed. Salt Lake City: Western Epics, 1972.

Carroll, Alex. "Cultural Affiliation and Historic Memory in the Arizona Strip." In Stoffle et al., *Yanawant: Paiute Places and Landscapes* 1:50–77.

Carter, Kate, cp. *Heart Throbs of the West*. 12 vols. Salt Lake City: Daughters of Utah Pioneers, 1939–1951.

———, cp. *Our Pioneer Heritage*. 20 vols. Salt Lake City, Utah: Daughters of Utah Pioneers, 1958–1977.

———, cp. *Treasures of Pioneer History*. 6 vols. Salt Lake City: Daughters of the Utah Pioneers, 1952–1957.

Carter, Lyndia. "John Wesley Powell's Headquarters at Kanab." Originally published in *History Blazer*, December 1996. At the Utah History to Go website, http://historytogo.utah.gov/utah_chapters/trappers,_traders,_and_explorers/johnwesleypowellsheadquartersatkanab.html (accessed on Feb. 26, 2013).

Carter, Robert W. "'Sometimes When I Hear the Winds Sigh': Mortality on the Overland Trail." *California History* 74.2 (summer 1995): 146–61.

Carvalho, Solomon Nunes. *Incidents of Travel and Adventure in the Far West; with Col. Fremont's Last Expedition*. New York: Derby & Jackson, 1860.

Casanova, Frank E., and John G. Bourke. "General Crook Visits the Supais: As Reported by John G. Bourke." *Arizona and the West* 10.3 (autumn 1968): 253–76.

Casebier, Dennis G. *Camp Beale's Springs and the Hualapai Indians.* Norco, CA: Tales of the Mojave Road Publishing Company, 1980.

"Casper Gubler." Typescript, at http://www.lofthouse.com/history/GublerCa.html (accessed via Internet Archive, Feb. 26, 2013).

Castetter, Edward F., and Willis H. Bell. *Yuman Indian Agriculture: Primitive Subsistence on the Lower Colorado and Gila Rivers.* Albuquerque: University of New Mexico Press, 1951.

Chamberlain, Ralph V. "Francis Marion Bishop, 1843–1933." *Utah Historical Quarterly* 15 (Jan., Apr., July, Oct. 1947): 155–158.

Chapel, Charles Edward. *Guns of the Old West.* New York: Coward-McCann, 1961.

Chee, Patti, et al., collectors and recorders. *Oral History Stories of the Long Walk (Hweeldi Baa Hane)*. Crownpoint, NM: Lake Valley Navajo School, 1990.

Childs, Craig. *The Secret Knowledge of Water: Discovering the Essence of the American Desert.* Seattle, WA: Sasquatch Books, 2000.

Christensen, Christian Lingo [Christian Lyngaa]. Diary. Typescript. Lee Library.

Christensen, C. L. [Christian Lyngaa]. "A True Story and an Experience." *The Times-Independent* (Moab, Utah), Oct. 9, 1924, p. 8.

———. "Addenda—Hopi Article—or Navajo Article." In Anthony W. Ivins Papers, MS B 2, bx 14, fd 12, item 14, USHS.

———. "Among the Hopis." *The Times-Independent* (Moab, Utah), March 9, 1922, p. 4.

———. "Among the Navajos." *The Times-Independent* (Moab, Utah), Feb. 23, 1922, p. 4.

———. "Among the Zunis." *The Times-Independent* (Moab, Utah), June 29, 1922, p. 8.

———. "Hopi Legends." A series. *The Times-Independent* (Moab, Utah), February 2, 9, 16, 23, March 2, 9, 1921.

———. "Hopi Legends." *Improvement Era* 24.6 (Apr. 1921): 516–18. Read in *LDS Library 2006*.

———. "Navajo Traditions. Marriage Ceremonies and Covenants." Anthony W. Ivins Papers, MS B 2, bx 14, fd 12, item 13, USHS.

———. "Pioneer of 1876 Saw Many Things." The [Coconino] Sun, March 29, 1929, clipping in Otis "Dock" Marston Papers, bx 85, fd 1, Huntington Library, San Marino, CA.

———. "Some Experiences Among the Indians." *The Contributor* 16.9 (July 1895): 555–58.

Christy, Howard A. "Open Hand and Mailed First: Mormon Indian Relations in Utah, 1847–52." *Utah Historical Quarterly* 46 (summer 1978): 216–61.

———. "'What Virtue There Is in Stone' and Other Pungent Talk on the Early Utah Frontier." *Utah Historical Quarterly* 59 (summer 1991): 301–19.

Church Historian's Office Journal, CR 100 1, CHL (SC 17).

Clark, David L. "The Mormons of the Wisconsin Territory: 1835–1848." *Brigham Young University Studies* 37.2 (1997–1998): 57–85.

———. "Moses Smith: Wisconsin's First Mormon," *Journal of Mormon History* 21.2 (fall 1995): 155–70.

Clark, Joan. "William Hennefer." In Youngberg, *Conquerors of the West*, 2:1073–74.

Clark, William. "A Trip Across the Plains in 1857." A memoir. *The Iowa Journal of History and Politics* 20.2 (April 1922): 163–223.

Cleland, Robert Glass, and Juanita Brooks, eds. *A Mormon Chronicle: The Diaries of John D. Lee, 1848–1876*. 2 vols. San Marino, CA: Huntington Library, 1955.

Clemmer, Richard O. "'Then Will You Rise And Strike My Head From My Neck': Hopi Prophecy and the Discourse of Empowerment." *American Indian Quarterly* 19.1 (winter 1995): 31–73.

———. *Roads in the Sky: The Hopi Indians in a Century of Change*. Boulder, CO: Westview Press, 1995.

Coates, Lawrence G. Review of Bagley, *Blood of the Prophets*. *Brigham Young University Studies* 42.1 (2003): 153–58.

Cogley, Richard W. "'Some Other Kinde of Being and Condition': The Controversy in Mid-Seventeenth-Century England over the Peopling of Ancient America." *Journal of the History of Ideas* 68.1 (January 2007): 35–56.

Colvin, Elizabeth, and Alice J. Le Baron. "Warren M. Johnson at Lee's Ferry." In Carter, *Heart Throbs Of The West*, 12:137.

Compton, Todd M. "Civilizing the Ragged Edge: Jacob Hamblin's Wives." *Journal of Mormon History* 33.2 (summer 2007): 155–98.

———. *In Sacred Loneliness: The Plural Wives of Joseph Smith*. Salt Lake City: Signature Books, 1997.

———. "John Willard Young, Brigham Young, and the Development of Presidential Succession in the LDS Church." *Dialogue* 35.4 (winter 2002): 111–134.

Compton, Todd M., and Charles M. Hatch. *A Widow's Tale: The 1884–1896 Diary of Helen Mar Kimball Whitney*. Logan: Utah State University Press, 2003.

Conkling, Roscoe P., and Margaret B. Conkling. *The Butterfield Overland Mail 1857–1869*. 3 vols. Glendale, CA: Arthur H. Clark, 1947.

Conrad, David E. "The Whipple Expedition in Arizona 1853–1854." *Arizona and the West* 11.2 (summer 1969): 147–178.

Cook, Noble David. *Born To Die: Disease & New World Conquest (1492–1650)*. Cambridge: Cambridge University Press, 1998.

Cook, Noble David, and William George Lovell, eds. *Secret Judgments of God: Old World Disease in Colonial Spanish America.* Civilization of the American Indian series, 205. Norman: University of Oklahoma Press, 1992.

Copeland, Lee. "Speaking in Tongues in the Restoration Churches." *Dialogue* 24 (spring 1991): 13–33.

Corbett, Pearson. *Jacob Hamblin: Peacemaker*. Salt Lake City: Deseret Book, 1952.

Correll, J. Lee. "Navajo Frontiers in Utah and Troublous Times in Monument Valley." *Utah Historical Quarterly* 39.2 (spring 1971): 145–61.

———, ed. *Through White Men's Eyes: A Contribution to Navajo History: A Chronological Record of the Navaho People from Earliest Times to the Treaty of June 1, 1868*. 6 vols. Window Rock, AZ: Navajo Heritage Center, 1979.

Cottam, Caroline Bunker. "Brief Sketches of the Lives of Samuel Knight and Caroline Beck Knight and Laura Melvina Leavitt Knight." Written ca. 1950. MS 11800, CHL.

Courlander, Harold. *The Fourth World of the Hopis: The Epic Story of the Hopi Indians as Preserved in Their Legends and Traditions.* Santa Fe: University of New Mexico Press, 1987.

Cox, Martha [Nemo]. "Albert Hamblin." *The Latter-day Saints' Millennial Star* 49.49 (Dec. 5, 1887): 774–75. For identification of Cox as the author of this article, see Cox, "Biographical Sketch of Martha Cox," 103ff.

Cox, Martha. "Biographical Sketch of Martha Cox." Finished in 1928, photocopy of holograph. MSS SC 319, Perry Special Collections, Lee Library.

Crampton, C. Gregory, ed. "F. S. Dellenbaugh of the Colorado; Some Letters Pertaining to the Powell Voyages and the History of the Colorado River." *Utah Historical Quarterly* 37 (spring 1969): 214–43.

———. *Ghosts of Glen Canyon: History beneath Lake Powell.* Salt Lake City: Bonneville Books/University of Utah Press, 2009.

———. *Historical Sites in Glen Canyon, Mouth of San Juan River to Lee's Ferry.* University of Utah Anthropological Papers 46. Salt Lake City: University of Utah Press, 1960.

———. *Land of Living Rock: The Grand Canyon and the High Plateaus: Arizona, Utah, Nevada.* New York: Knopf, 1972.

———, ed. "Military Reconnaissance in Southern Utah, 1866." *Utah Historical Quarterly* 32.2 (spring 1964): 145–61.

———. "Mormon Colonization in Southern Utah and in Adjacent Parts of Arizona and Nevada, 1851–1900." Report for U.S. Dept. of the Interior, National Park Service, Capitol Reef National Park, 1965. Available at Arizona Memory Project, http://azmemory.lib.az.us/ (accessed Apr. 6, 2011).

———. *Outline History of the Glen Canyon Region, 1776–1922.* University of Utah Anthropological Papers 42. Salt Lake City: University of Utah Press, 1959.

———. "Utah's Spanish Trail." *Utah Historical Quarterly* 47.4 (fall 1979): 361–83.

———. *The Zunis of Cibola*. Salt Lake City: University of Utah Press, 1977.

Crampton, C. Gregory, and Steven K. Madsen. *In Search of the Spanish Trail: Santa Fe to Los Angeles, 1829–1848.* Salt Lake City: Gibbs Smith Publishing, 1994.

Creer, Leland H. *The Activities of Jacob Hamblin in the Region of the Colorado*. University of Utah Anthropological Papers 33. Salt Lake City: University of Utah Press, 1958.

Cremony, John C. *Life among the Apaches*. San Francisco: A. Roman & Company, 1868.

Crosby, Jeff. "Traveling in the Ministry: The Life of Jesse Wentworth Crosby." At http://www.angelfire.com/ut/jcrosby/history/jesse/jesse.html (accessed Apr. 6, 2011).

Crosby, Jesse W. "The History and Journal of the Life and Travels of Jesse W. Crosby." *Annals of Wyoming* 11.3 (July 1939): 145–218. At http://lincoln.lib.niu.edu/file.php?file=crosby.html (accessed Apr. 6, 2011).

Cross, Whitney R. *The Burned-Over District: The Social and Intellectual History of Enthusiastic Religion in Western New York, 1800–1850*. Ithaca: Cornell University Press, 1950.

Crum, Steven J. *The Road on Which We Came: Po'i Pentun Tammen Kimmappeh a History of the Western Shoshone*. Salt Lake City: University of Utah Press, 1994.

Cuch, Forrest S., ed. *A History of Utah's American Indians*. Salt Lake City: Utah State Division of Indian Affairs, Utah State Division of History, 2000.

Cullum, George Washington. *Biographical Register of the Officers and Graduates of the U.S. Military Academy at West Point, N.Y. from its Establishment, in 1802, to 1890; with the Early History of the United States Military Academy.* 3rd rev. ed. 9 vols. Boston: Houghton, Mifflin and Company, 1891.

Cushing, Frank H. "The Nation of the Willows." Part 2. *Atlantic Monthly* 50 (Oct. 1882): 541–59.

Cushing, Frank Hamilton. *Zuni: Selected Writings of Frank Hamilton Cushing.* Edited by Jesse Green. Omaha: University of Nebraska Press, 1978.

Custer, Milo. "Asiatic Cholera in Central Illinois (McLean and adjoining counties)." *Journal of the Illinois State Historical Society* 33.1 (1930). At http://genealogytrails.com/ill/mclean/asiaticcholera.html (accessed Feb. 26, 2013).

Dalton, Luella Adams. *History of the Iron County Mission and Parowan, the Mother Town*. Parowan: private printer, 1963.

"Daniel Webster Jones (Mormon)." At http://en.wikipedia.org/wiki/Daniel_Webster_Jones_(Mormon) (accessed Feb. 26, 2013).

"Daphne Haynes Hamblin." In *Pioneer Women of Faith and Fortitude*, 2:1203–4. Salt Lake City: International Society Daughters of Utah Pioneers, 1998.

Darrah, William Culp. "Beaman, Fennemore, Hillers, Dellenbaugh, Johnson, and Hattan." *Utah Historical Quarterly*, 17.1–4 (1949): 491–503.

———. "The Howland Brothers and William Dunn." *Utah Historical Quarterly* 15.1–4 (Jan., Apr., Jul., Oct. 1947): 93–94.

———, ed. "Journal of John F. Steward, May 22–November 3, 1871." *Utah Historical Quarterly* 16–17 (Jan., Apr., Jul., Oct., 1948 and 1949): 180–251.

———. "Major Powell Prepares for a Second Expedition." *Utah Historical Quarterly* 15 (Jan., Apr., July, Oct. 1947): 149–53.

———. *Powell of the Colorado.* Princeton, NJ: Princeton University Press, 1951.

Davenport, Clynn L., cp. "Biography of John Lee Jones, 1841–1935." Special Collections, Gerald R. Sherratt Library, Southern Utah University, Cedar City.

"David H. Cannon." A website at http://www.davidhcannon.org/ (accessed Feb. 26, 2013).

Davies, J. Kenneth. *Mormon Gold: The Story of California's Mormon Argonauts.* Salt Lake City: Olympus, 1984.

Davis, William Morris. *An Excursion to the Plateau Province of Utah and Arizona.* In *Bulletin of the Museum of Comparative Zoology, at Harvard College, vol. 42*, Geological Series 6.1. Cambridge, MA: Museum of Comparative Zoology, Harvard College, 1903.

Daynes, Kathryn M. *More Wives Than One: Transformation of the Mormon Marriage System, 1840–1910.* Urbana: University of Illinois Press, 2001.

Debo, Angie. *Geronimo: The Man, His Time, His Place*. Norman: University of Oklahoma Press, 1976.

Dees, Harry C. "George W. Bean, Early Mormon Explorer." *Brigham Young University Studies* 12.2 (1972): 1–12.

———, ed. "The Journal of George W. Bean: Las Vegas Springs, New Mexico Territory, 1856–57." *Nevada Historical Society Quarterly* 15 (fall 1972): 2–29.

Defa, Dennis R. "Goshute Indians." In Powell, *Utah History Encyclopedia*, 228–29.

———. "The Goshute Indians of Utah." In Cuch, *A History of Utah's American Indians*, 73–122.

Dellenbaugh, Frederick S. Annotations in Jacob Hamblin's published Autobiography, in Dellenbaugh Collection, Arizona Historical Society.

———. *A Canyon Voyage: The Narrative of the Second Powell Expedition*. Tucson, AZ: University of Arizona Press, 1996. Orig. published: New York: Putnam, 1908.

———. *The Romance of the Colorado River: the Story of its Discovery in 1540, with an Account of the Later Explorations, and With Special Reference to the Voyages of Powell Through the Line of the Great Canyons...* New York: G. P. Putnam's Sons, 1902.

Denetdale, Jennifer Nez. *Reclaiming Diné History: The Legacies of Navajo Chief Manuelito and Juanita*. Tucson: University of Arizona Press, 2007.

Dennis, Ronald D. "Captain Dan Jones and the Welsh Indians." *Dialogue* 18.4 (winter 1985): 112–18.

Diamond, Jared. *Guns, Germs, and Steel: The Fates of Human Societies.* New York: W. W. Norton, 1997.

Divett, Robert T. "His Chastening Rod: Cholera Epidemics and the Mormons." *Dialogue: A Journal of Mormon Thought* 12.3 (autumn 1979): 6–15.

Dobyns, Henry. *The Pima-Maricopa.* New York: Chelsea House Publishers, 1989.

Dobyns, Henry F., and Robert C. Euler. "The Dunn-Howland Killings: Additional Insights." *Journal of Arizona History* 21.1 (spring 1980): 87–95.

———. *Havasupai Indians*. New York: Garland Publishing, 1964.

———. *The Havasupai People.* Phoenix: Indian Tribal Series, 1971.

———. *The Walapai People.* Phoenix: Indian Tribal Series, 1976.

———. *Wauba Yuma's People: The Comparative Socio-Political Structure of the Pai Indians of Arizona.* Prescott College Studies in Anthropology 3. Prescott, AZ: Prescott College Press, 1970.

Donaldson, Thomas. *Moqui Pueblo Indians of Arizona and Pueblo Indians of New Mexico.* Extra Census Bulletin. Eleventh Census of the United States. Washington, D.C.: United States Census Printing Office, 1893.

Donovan, James. *A Terrible Glory: Custer and the Little Bighorn: The Last Great Battle of the American West*. New York: Back Bay Books/Little, Brown, 2008.

Dorsey, George A., and H. R. Voth. *The Oraibi Soyal Ceremony.* Field Columbian Museum Publ. 55. Anthropological Series III, no. 1. Chicago, 1901.

Duffy, John-Charles. "The Use of 'Lamanite' in Official LDS Discourse." *Journal of Mormon History* 34 (winter 2008): 118–67.

Dumke, G. S. "Mission to Mining Town: Early Las Vegas." *Pacific Historical Review* 22 (1953): 257–70.

Duncan, Clifford. "The Northern Utes of Utah." In Cuch, *A History of Utah's American Indians*, 167–224.

Dunlay, Tom. *Kit Carson and the Indians*. Lincoln: University of Nebraska Press, 2000.

Dutcher, John. *Ballard: The Great American Single Shot Rifle*. [Denver, CO]: J. T. Dutcher, 2002.

Dutton, Clarence E. *Tertiary History of the Grand Cañon District*. Monographs of the United States Geological Survey, vol. 2. Washington, D.C.: Government Printing Office, 1882.

Dwyer, Robert J. "Introduction" to James Amasa Little, "Biography of Lorenzo Dow Young." *Utah Historical Quarterly* 14 (Jan. 1946): 21–24.

Edwards, Esaias. Autobiography. Holograph, written before 1897. Perry Special Collections, Lee Library.

Eggan, Fred, and T. N. Pandey. "Zuni History, 1850–1970." In Sturtevant, *Handbook of North American Indians*, vol. 9, *The Southwest*, edited by Alfonso Ortiz, pp. 474–481.

Eliade, Mircea. *The Myth of the Eternal Return: Cosmos and History*. Translated by Willard R. Trask. Bollingen series 46. Princeton, NJ: Princeton University Press, 1954. Originally published in 1949.

———. *Shamanism: Archaic Techniques of Ecstasy.* Tr. Willard R. Trask. Bollingen series 76. New York, Bollingen Foundation/Pantheon Books, 1964.

Elkins, Richard Ira. *Ira Hatch: Indian Missionary, 1835–1909, Pu-am-ey.* Bountiful, UT: n.p., 1984.

Ellis, Florence Hawley. *The Hopi: Their History and Use of Lands*. New York: Garland Publishing, 1974.

Erickson, Dan. *"As a Thief in the Night": The Mormon Quest for Millennial Deliverance.* Salt Lake City: Signature Books, 1998.

Esplin, Hattie. "Massacre of the Berrys." In Carter, *Our Pioneer Heritage*, 9:204.

Esshom, Frank. *Pioneers and Prominent Men of Utah*. Salt Lake City: Western Epics, Inc., 1966. Originally published in 1913.

Euler, Robert C. *The Paiute People*. Phoenix: Indian Tribal Series, 1972.

Evans, Rebecca Dunlap. "Mountain Meadow Massacre Related by Rebecca Dunlap Evans: The Butchery of a Train of Arkansans by Mormons and Indians." *Fort Smith Elevator*, August 20, 1897, 2. At http://www.legendsofamerica.com/ut-mountainmeadowshistoricaccounts12.html#Mountain%20Meadow%20Massacre%20Related%20by%20Rebecca%20Dunlap%20Evans (accessed Feb. 26, 2013).

Evans, Will. *Along Navajo Trails: Recollections of a Trader, 1898–1948*. Edited by Susan E. Woods and Robert S. McPherson. Logan: Utah State University Press, 2005.

Ewing, Floyd F., Jr. "The Mule as a Factor in the Development of the Southwest." *Arizona and the West* 5.4 (winter 1963): 315–26.

Executive Documents Printed by the Order of the House of Representatives during the Second Session of the Thirty-Seventh Congress, 1861–'62. 12 vols. Washington, D.C.: Government Printing Office, 1862.

Ezell, Paul H. "History of the Pima." In Sturtevant, *Handbook of North American Indians*, vol. 10, *The Southwest*, edited by Alfonso Ortiz, pp. 149–60.

Fairley, Helen. "Kwagunt." *boatman's quarterly review* 10.4 (fall 1997): 15–17. At http://www.gcrg.org/bqr/10-4/kwagunt.html (accessed Feb. 26, 2013).

Faragher, John Mack. *Women and Men on the Overland Trail*. New Haven: Yale University Press, 1979.

Farish, Thomas Edwin. *History of Arizona.* 8 vols. Phoenix, AZ: Filmer Brothers, 1915–18.

Farmer, Jared. *On Zion's Mount: Mormons, Indians, and the American Landscape.* Cambridge, MA: Harvard University Press, 2008.

Farnsworth, Moses. Diary, in General Minutes, Kanab Ward, Kanab Stake, LR 4303 11, vol. 9, microfilm 1, CHL.

Faulk, Odie B. *The Geronimo Campaign.* New York: Oxford University Press, 1969.

Fawcett, George. "Memoirs of George W. Fawcett of Lund, White Pine County, Nevada...." MSS A 350, USHS.

Fenn, Elizabeth. *Pox Americana: The Great Smallpox Epidemic of 1775–82.* New York: Hill & Wang Publishers, 2001.

Fewkes, J. Walter. "Pueblo Ruins Near Flagstaff, Arizona. A Preliminary Notice." *American Anthropologist* 2.3 (1900): 422–50.

Fielding, Robert Kent, and Dorothy S. Fielding, eds. *The Tribune Reports of the Trials of John D. Lee for the Massacre at Mountain Meadows November 1874–April 1877.* Higganum, CT: Kent's Books, 2000.

Fife, A. E. "The Legend of the Three Nephites among the Mormons." *The Journal of American Folklore* 53, no. 207 (Jan.–Mar. 1940): 1–49.

Firmage, Edwin Brown, and Richard Collin Mangrum. *Zion in the Courts: A Legal History of the Church of Jesus Christ of Latter-day Saints, 1830–1900.* Urbana: University of Illinois Press, 1988.

Firmage, Richard A. *A History of Grand County.* Salt Lake City: Utah State Historical Society, 1996.

Fish, Joseph. "History of the Eastern Arizona Stake of Zion and of the Establishment of the Snowflake Stake." Typescript. University of Arizona Library, Special Collections.

———. *The Life and Times of Joseph Fish, Mormon Pioneer.* John H. Krenkel, ed. Danville, IL: Interstate Printers & Publishers, 1970.

Flake, David K. "A History of Mormon Missionary Work with the Hopi, Navaho and Zuni." M.A. thesis, Brigham Young University, 1965.

Flanders, Robert Bruce. *Nauvoo: Kingdom on the Mississippi.* Urbana: University of Illinois Press, 1965.

———. "To Transform History: Early Mormon Culture and the Concept of Time and Space." *Church History* 40.1 (March 1971): 108–17.

Fleming, L. A. "The Settlements on the Muddy 1865 to 1871: 'A God Forsaken place.'" *Utah Historical Quarterly* 35.2 (spring 1967): 147–72.

Flores, Dan. "Stegner, the Environment, and the West." *Montana: The Magazine of Western History* 43.4 (autumn 1993): 67–69.

Folkman, Kevin H. "'The Moste Desert Lukking Plase I Ever Saw, Amen!' The 'Failed' 1873 Arizona Mission to the Little Colorado River." *Journal of Mormon History* 37.1 (winter 2011): 115–50.

Fontana, Bernard L. "Pima and Papago: Introduction." In Sturtevant, *Handbook of North American Indians*, vol. 10, *The Southwest*, edited by Alfonso Ortiz, pp. 125–36.

Fontano, Mildred P. Morgan. "Life History of John DeGroot Oakley." At http://home.earthlink.net/~norm.mcclellan/FamilyHistory/FH/JohnDOakley.htm (accessed Feb. 26, 2013).

Foote, Warren. Autobiography. Typescript in author's possession. Original in CHL.

Forney, Jacob. Letterbooks 1857–1859, MS 14278, CHL.

Fowler, Catherine S., and Don D. Fowler. "Notes on the History of the Southern Paiutes and Western Shoshonis." *Utah Historical Quarterly* 39.2 (spring 1971): 95–113.

Fowler, Don D., ed. *Photographed All the Best Scenery? Jack Hillers's Diary of the Powell Expeditions, 1871–1875.* Salt Lake City: University of Utah Press, 1972.

———. *The Western Photographs of John K. Hillers: Myself in the Water.* Washington D.C.: Smithsonian Institution Press, 1989.

Fowler, Don D., and Catherine S. Fowler, eds. *Anthropology of the Numa: John Wesley Powell's Manuscripts on the Numic Peoples of Western North America, 1868–1880.* Smithsonian Contributions to Anthropology No. 14. Washington, D.C.: Smithsonian Institution Press, 1971. Available online at http://www.sil.si.edu/smithsoniancontributions/Anthropology/ (accessed Feb. 26, 2013).

———. "John Wesley Powell's Anthropological Fieldwork." In *John Wesley Powell and the Anthropology of the Canyon Country.* Geological Survey Professional Paper 670. Washington, D.C.: U.S. Dept. of the Interior, Geological Survey, U.S. Govt. Print. Off., 1969. At http://www.nps.gov/history/history/online_books/geology/publications/pp/670/sec1.htm (accessed Feb. 26, 2013).

"Francis Xeveres LOUGY." A collection of excerpts. At http://www.utahrockhounds.com/mygen/bunn/29.htm (accessed Feb. 26, 2013).

Frazer, Robert W. *Forts of the West: Military Forts and Presidios and Posts Commonly Called Forts, West of the Mississippi River to 1898.* Norman: University of Oklahoma Press, 1965.

Frazier, Russell G. "El Vado de los Padres (The Crossing of the Fathers)." *The Desert Magazine* 3 (July 1940): 3–5.

Frink, Maurice. *Fort Defiance & the Navajos.* Boulder, CO: Pruett Press, 1968.

Froeschauer-Nelson, Peggy. *Cultural Landscape Report: Hubbell Trading Post National Historic Site, Ganado, Arizona*. Santa Fe, NM: National Park Service, 1998.

Fuller, Craig. "Irrigation in Utah." In Powell, *Utah History Encyclopedia*, 276–79.

Furst, Peter T. "Introduction: An Overview of Shamanism." In *Ancient Traditions: Shamanism in Central Asia and the Americas*, edited by Gary Seaman and Jane S. Day, 1–28. Niwot: University Press of Colorado, 1994.

Gardner, Robert, Jr. Autobiography. Holograph, written in 1884. Part of the Robert Gardner collection, MS 1744, CHL.

Gates, Mary Alice, and Joyce W. Whittaker. "The Leavitts—Early Settlers of Santa Clara." In Whittaker, *History of Santa Clara, Utah*, 127–32.

Geary, Edward. *The Proper Edge of Sky: The High Plateau Country of Utah.* Salt Lake City: University of Utah Press, 1992.

Geertz, Armin W. *The Invention of Prophecy: Continuity and Meaning in Hopi Indian Religion.* Berkeley: University of California Press, 1994.

Gentry, Leland. "The Mormon Way Stations: Garden Grove and Mt. Pisgah." *Brigham Young University Studies* 21 (fall 1981): 445–61.

Gibbons, Andrew Smith. Diary, 1858, 1877 and 1878. Holograph. MS 4008 2, CHL.

Gibbons, Francis M., and Daniel B. Gibbons. *A Gathering of Eagles: Conversions from the Four Quarters of the Earth.* Web publication, iUniverse, 2002.

Gibbons, Helen Bay. *Saint and Savage*. Salt Lake City: Deseret Book Company, 1965.

Gibson, Arrell M. "James Carleton." In Hutton, *Soldiers West*, 59–77.

Gilbert, Bil. *Westering Man: The Life of Joseph Walker.* University of Oklahoma Press, 1985.

Ginn, John I. "Mormon and Indian Wars." Typescript, MSS A 77–2, USHS.

———. *The Mormon Mountain Massacre—From the Diary of Captain John I. Ginn.* Edited by Steven E. Farley. Bloomington, IN: 1st Books Library, 2003.

Godfrey, Audrey M. "Colonizing the Muddy River Valley: A New Perspective." *Journal of Mormon History* 22.2 (fall 1996): 120–42.

Goetzmann, William H. *Army Exploration in the American West, 1803–1863*. Yale publications in American studies, 4. New Haven, CT: Yale University Press, 1959.

———. *Exploration and Empire: The Explorer and the Scientist in the Winning of the American West.* New York: Alfred A. Knopf, 1966.

Golding, Lois Hamblin. *Our Golden Heritage: The Duane and Addie Noble Hamblin Family*. [n.p.]: Privately printed, 1977. Available in PTRC, series 1, bx 16, fd 258.

Gordon, Sara Barringer. *The Mormon Question: Polygamy and Constitutional Conflict in Nineteenth Century America.* Chapel Hill: University of North Carolina Press, 2002.

Gordon-McCutchan, R. C., ed. *Kit Carson: Indian Fighter or Indian Killer?* Niwot: University Press of Colorado, 1996.

Gottfredson, Peter. *History of Indian Depredations in Utah*. Salt Lake City: Skelton Publishing Co., 1919.

———. "Killing of Three Navajo Indians in Grass Valley in 1874 and Result." Typescript, MSS A 619b, USHS.

Graves, Laura. *Thomas Varker Keam, Indian Trader*. Norman: University of Oklahoma Press, 1998.

Gregory, Herbert E., ed. "Diary of Almon Harris Thompson." *Utah Historical Quarterly* 7 (Jan., Apr., Jul. 1939): 3–138.

———. *Geology of the Navajo Country: a Reconnaissance of Parts of Arizona, New Mexico, and Utah.* United States Geological Survey Professional Paper 93. Washington D.C.: Government Printing Office, 1917.

———, ed. "Journal of Stephen Vandiver Jones, April 21, 1871–December 14, 1872." *Utah Historical Quarterly* 16–17 (Jan., Apr., Jul., Oct. 1948 and 1949): 19–174.

———. "The Oasis of Tuba, Arizona." *Annals of the Association of American Geographers* 5 (1915): 107–19.

———. "Stephen Vandiver Jones (1840–1920)." *Utah Historical Quarterly* 16–17 (Jan., Apr., Jul., Oct. 1948 and 1949): 11–18.

Gregory, Herbert E., and Raymond C. Moore. *The Kaiparowits Region: A Geographic and Geologic Reconnaissance of Parts of Utah and Arizona.* USGS Professional Paper 164. Washington, D.C.: United States Printing Office, 1931.

Grow, Matthew J. *Liberty to the Downtrodden: Thomas L. Kane, Romantic Reformer.* New Haven, CT: Yale University Press, 2009.

Gubler, Nellie McArthur. "History of Santa Clara, Washington County, 1850–1950." In Bradshaw, *Under Dixie Sun*, 145–76.

Hackworth, R. Allen. "Nathan Cram Tenney: Cowboy Hero." At http://paynegoodegen.iwebs.ws/Nathan%20Cram%20Tenney/NTenney.pdf (accessed Feb. 26, 2013).

Hafen, Arthur Knight. *Dixie Folklore and Pioneer Memories*. 3rd edition. St. George, UT: Published privately, 1964.

Hafen, LeRoy R., ed., and Antonio Armijo. "Armijo's Journal." *The Huntington Library Quarterly* 11.1 (Nov. 1947): 87–101.

Hafen, LeRoy R., and Ann W. Hafen. *Handcarts to Zion: The Story of a Unique Western Migration, 1856–1860.* Spokane, WA: Arthur H. Clark, 1992. Originally published in 1960.

———. *Old Spanish Trail: Santa Fé to Los Angeles; with Extracts from Contemporary Records and Including Diaries of Antonio Armijo and Orville Pratt.* Lincoln: University of Nebraska Press, 1993. Originally published in 1954.

Hafen, Mary Ann. *Recollections of a Handcart Pioneer of 1860: A Woman's Life on the Mormon Frontier.* Lincoln: University of Nebraska Press, 1983. Originally published in 1938.

Hafen, Selina G., and Eliza H. Gubler, cp. "Johannes (John) Gubler and Maria (Mary) Ursula Muller." At http://www.lofthouse.com/USA/Utah/washington/.gubler-johan.html (accessed via Internet Archives on Feb. 26, 2013).

Hagan, William T. "How the West Was Lost." In *Indians in American History*, edited by Frederick E. Hoxie, 179–202. Arlington Heights, IL: Harlan Davidson, 1988.

Haggerty, John W. "Historic Preservation in Utah: 1960–1980." M.A. Thesis, BYU, 1980.

Haight, Isaac. Journal, 1852–62. CHL.

Haley, James L. *Apaches: A History and Culture Portrait*. 2nd ed. Norman: University of Oklahoma Press, 1997.

Hallwas, John E., and Roger D. Launius. *Cultures in Conflict: A Documentary History of the Mormon War in Illinois.* Logan: Utah State University Press, 1995.

Hamblin, Jacob. Autobiography, holograph, MS 1951, folder 2, CHL. Hamblin wrote this in his later life, after 1854 (the last date found in it). Note: Little, *Jacob Hamblin*, is also a sort of autobiography.

———. Diary, 1862–1863. Holograph. In Jacob Hamblin papers, mssFAC 1307–1325, Huntington Library, San Marino, CA.

———. Diary, fifth trip to the Hopis (1863), copy, USHS.

———. Diaries and Notebooks, 1850–1877. MS 1951, CHL.

———. Diaries and Reminiscences, 1854–58, MS 1951 (holograph) and MS 14654 (a copy, with some material missing from the holograph), CHL.

———. "Early Days in Utah's Dixie." *Utah Historical Quarterly* 5.4 (Oct. 1932): 131–34. This is an excerpt from "Home Correspondence. Southern Utah Mission," a Letter from Thomas Brown that quotes from Hamblin's journal. *The Deseret News*, vol. 5, no. 4, April 4, 1855, p. 6.

———. Journal and Reminiscences, 1868–1870, 1885, MSS 770, Lee Library.

———. "Report of a Journey from St. George Washington C.o U.T. to the Moquis Pueblos in New Mexico performed in 1863, compiled from the Journal of Jacob Hamblin." CR 100 397, bx 2, fd 46, CHL.

———. Testimony, Second trial of John D. Lee, Sept. 14–20, 1876. Record of the trial at Huntington Library, San Marino, CA. See also Fielding, ed., *The Tribune Reports of The Trials of John D. Lee*. Available online at the Mountain Meadows Association website, http://www.mtn-meadows-assoc.com/hamblin.htm (accessed Feb. 26, 2013).

Hamblin, John. "Hamblin Home in Santa Clara." Sept. 7, 1978. Typescript in author's possession.

Hamblin, Joseph. "History of Joseph Hamblin, Youngest Son of William Haynes Hamblin and Mary Amelia Leavitt (as dictated to his daughter, Aloha)." On the J. K. Rogers Family website, at freepages.genealogy.rootsweb.ancestry.com/~jkrogers/jhamblin.rtf (accessed Feb. 26, 2013).

Hamblin, Louisa Bonelli, and Edna Lee Brimhall. "Biography of Louisa Bonelli Hamblin." A little autobiography, as dictated to Brimhall. Typescript, undated. In PTRC, series 8.1, bx 2, fd 17.

Hamilton, Marshall. "From Assassination to Expulsion: Two Years of Distrust, Hostility, and Violence." In Launius and Hallwas, *King on the Mississippi Revisited*, 214–30.

Hammond, John J. "The 1876 Journal of Frank Hammond: 'Travailing' to the Little Colorado." *Journal of Mormon History* 33 (spring 2007): 65–120.

Hancock, Mosiah. Autobiography. Holograph. MS 570, CHL.

———. Autobiography. Typescript, in author's possession.

Hand, Wayland D. "The Three Nephites in Popular Tradition." *Southern Folklore Quarterly* 2 (Sept. 1938): 123–29.

Hansen, Klaus J. "The Millennium, the West, Antebellum American Mind." *Western Historical Quarterly* 3.4 (Oct. 1972): 373–90.

———. *Quest for Empire: The Political Kingdom of God and the Council of Fifty in Mormon History.* Lincoln: University of Nebraska Press, 1974. Originally published in 1967.

Hanson, Brooks Kent. "A Geographical Analysis of the Emergence and Subsequent Disappearance of the Cotton Industry in the Virgin River Basin (1856–1910)." MA thesis, BYU, 1967.

Hardy, B. Carmon. "The American Siberia: Mormon Prisoners in Detroit in the 1880s." *Michigan History* 50.3 (Sept. 1966): 197–210.

———. "Cultural Encystment as a Cause of the Mormon Exodus from Mexico in 1912." *Pacific Historical Review* 34 (Nov. 1965): 439–53.

———. *Doing the Works of Abraham: Mormon Polygamy, Its Origin, Practice and Demise.* Norman, OK: Arthur C. Clark, 2007.

———. *Solemn Covenant: The Mormon Polygamous Passage*. Urbana: University of Illinois Press, 1992.

———. "The Trek South: How the Mormons Went to Mexico." *Southwestern Historical Quarterly* 63 (Jul. 1969): 1–16.

Harper, Reid L. "The Mantle of Joseph: Creation of a Mormon Miracle." *Journal of Mormon History* 22 (fall 1996): 35–71.

Harper, Steven C. "Infallible Proofs, Both Human and Divine: The Persuasiveness of Mormonism for Early Converts." *Religion and American Culture: A Journal of Interpretation* 10.1 (winter 2000): 99–118.

Harris, Jack. "The Western Shoshone." *American Anthropologist* 40 (Jul.–Sept. 1938): 407–11. Part of a larger article, Verne F. Ray et al., "Tribal Distribution in Eastern Oregon and Adjacent Regions," 384–415.

———. "The White Knife Shoshoni of Nevada." In *Acculturation in Seven American Indian Tribes*, edited by Ralph Linton, 39–111. New York: D. Appleton-Century, 1940.

"Harrison Pearce." A collection of data, at http://www.familyperkins.com/genealogy/pearce2.htm (accessed Feb. 26, 2013).

Harstad, Peter T. "Sickness and Disease on the Wisconsin Frontier: Malaria, 1820–1850." *The Wisconsin Magazine of History* 43.2 (winter, 1959–1960): 83–96.

Hart, Herbert M. *Old Forts of the Far West*. Seattle: Superior Publishing Company, 1965.

Hartley, William G. "Mormons, Crickets, and Gulls: A New Look at an Old Story." *Utah Historical Quarterly* 38 (summer 1970): 224–39.

Hartley, William G., and Lorna Call Alder. *Anson Bowen Call: Bishop of Colonia Dublán.* Provo, UT: Lorna Call Alder, 2007.

Haskell, Thales Hastings. Autobiography. Holograph, MS 52, CHL.

———. "Thales Haskell." (An autobiography, with an obituary.) In *An Enduring Legacy* 2:321–32.

Haskell, Thales W. Journal. See Brooks, ed., "Journal of Thales W. Haskell."

Hatch, Jo Ann F. *Willing Hands: A Biography of Lorenzo Hill Hatch, 1826–1910.* Pinedale, AZ: Kymera Publishing Company, 1996. Available online at http://www.b13family.com/html/journal-lorenzo_hatch.htm (accessed Feb. 26, 2013).

Hatch, Lorenzo Hill. Journal. Holograph at CHL. Typescript, compiled by Tom Kerr, available at http://hatchfamilyassoc.org/pdfs/Lorenzo%20Hill%20Hatch.pdf (accessed Feb. 26, 2013).

Hatch, Nathan O. *The Democratization of American Christianity*. New Haven, CT: Yale University Press, 1989.

Hatch, Nelle Spilsbury. *Colonia Juarez: An Intimate Account of a Mormon Village.* Salt Lake City, Deseret Book Co., 1954.

Hatch, Nelle Spilsbury, and B. Carmon Hardy, cps. and eds. *Stalwarts South of the Border.* N.p., by the author, 1985.

Heap, Gwinn Harris. *Central Route to the Pacific from the Valley of the Mississippi to California: Journal of the*

Expedition of E.F. Beale, Superintendent of Indian Affairs in California, and Gwinn Harris Heap, from Missouri to California, in 1853. Philadelphia: Lippincott, Grambo, 1854.

Heaton, Leonard. "Historical [*sic*] and Facts Pertaining to Pipe Spring National Monument." Typescript, in possession of the author. Available at Pipe Spring National Monument Visitor Center.

Henige, David P. "When Did Smallpox Reach the New World and Why Does It Matter?" In *Africans in Bondage: Studies in Slavery and the Slave Trade: Essays in Honor of Philip D. Curtin on the Occasion of the Twenty-fifth Anniversary of African Studies at the University of Wisconsin*, edited by Paul Lovejoy, 11–26. Madison: University of Wisconsin Press, 1987.

Heyman, Max L., Jr. *Prudent Soldier: A Biography of Major General E. R. S. Canby, 1817–1873*. Glendale, CA: Arthur H. Clark, 1959.

Hicks, Michael. "Noble Savages." In *Mormons and Mormonism: An Introduction to an American World Religion*, edited by Eric A. Eliason, 180–99. Urbana: University of Illinois Press, 2001.

Hill, Marvin. "The Shaping of the Mormon Mind in New England and New York." *Brigham Young University Studies* 9.3 (spring 1969): 351–72.

Hillers, Jack. Diary. See Fowler, *Photographed All the Best Scenery?*

Hinckley, Arza E. Diary. Typescript, in PTRC, series 1, bx 8a, fd 129.

Hinckley, Bryant S. *Daniel Hanmer Wells and Events of His Time.* Salt Lake City: Deseret News Press, 1942.

Hine, Robert V., and John Mack Faragher. *The American West: A New Interpretive History.* The Lamar Series in Western History. New Haven, CT: Yale University Press, 2000.

Hirst, Stephen. *I Am the Grand Canyon: The Story of the Havasupai People*. 3rd edition of a book first published, under a different name, in 1976. Grand Canyon, AZ: Grand Canyon Association, 2006.

Historical Record, St. Johns Stake, Book A, typescript in PTRC, series 8.1, bx 2, fd 23.

"History of Brigham Young." In "History of the Church, 1839–circa 1882," CR100 102, CHL (SC 4).

"History of David Canfield." Biography, typescript. At http://www.hunthistories.com/Histories/DavidCanfield.html (accessed Feb. 26, 2013).

"History of Isaiah Hamblin." Available at http://www.oocities.org/hamblinancestors/isaiahhamblin.html(accessed Feb. 26, 2013).

History of Walworth County, Wisconsin: containing…its War Record, Biographical Sketches…a History of Wisconsin. Chicago: Western Historical Co., 1882.

Hodge, Hiram C. *Arizona as It Is: or, The Coming Country. Compiled from Notes of Travel During the Years 1874, 1875, and 1876.* New York: Hurd & Houghton, 1877.

Hoffman, Virginia, and Broderick H. Johnson. *Navajo Biographies*. 2 vols. Rough Rock, AZ: Navajo Curriculum Center Press, 1974. Vol. 1 is written entirely by Virginia Hoffman.

Holt, Ronald L. *Beneath These Red Cliffs: An Ethnohistory of the Utah Paiutes.* Albuquerque: University of New Mexico Press, 1992.

Honker, Andrew M. "'Been Grazed Almost to Extinction': The Environment, Human Action, and Utah Flooding, 1900–1940." *Utah Historical Quarterly* 67.1 (winter 1999): 23–47.

Hoopes, Lamro, and Elaine Hoopes. "Mormon Colonization of Arizona." At http://www.angelfire.com/ne/hoopesgenealogy/colonization.htm (accessed Feb. 26, 2013).

Huddleston, Lee E. *Origins of the American Indians: European Concepts, 1492–1729.* Latin American Monographs 11. Austin: University of Texas Press, 1967.

Hughes, Richard T., ed. *The American Quest for the Primitive Church*. Urbana: University of Illinois Press, 1988.

Hulse, James W. "The Afterlife of St. Mary's County: or Utah's Penumbra in Eastern Nevada." *Utah Historical Quarterly* 55 (summer 1987): 236–49.

———. *Lincoln County, Nevada: The History of a Mining Region, 1861–1909.* Reno: University of Nevada Press, 1971.

Humphreys, A. A., and George M. Wheeler. *Preliminary Report Concerning Explorations and Surveys Principally in Nevada and Arizona*. Washington, D.C.: Government Printing Office, 1872.

Hunt, Aurora. *Major General James Henry Carleton: 1814–1873: Western Frontier Dragoon.* Glendale, CA: Arthur H. Clark, 1958.

Hunter, Milton R. *Brigham Young, the Colonizer*. Salt Lake City: Deseret News Press, 1940.

———. "The Mormons and the Colorado River." *The American Historical Review* 44.3 (Apr. 1939): 549–55.

Huntington, Dimick. Diary, MS 1419 2, CHL. Important excerpts in Bigler and Bagley, *Innocent Blood*, 119–22.

Huntington, Oliver. Journal. Lee Library.

Huntoon, Peter. "The Opening of Deer Creek and History of the Thunder River Trail." *boatman's quarterly review* 16.4 (winter 2003–2004): 20–26. At http://www.gcrg.org/bqr/16-4/trail.html (accessed Feb. 26, 2013).

Inter-Tribal Council of Nevada. *Nuwuvi: a Southern Paiute History.* Reno: Inter-Tribal Council of Nevada, 1976.

Irving, Gordon. "Encouraging the Saints: Brigham Young's Annual Tours of Mormon Settlements." *Utah Historical Quarterly* 45 (summer 1977): 233–51.

"Isaac Behunin Family Archives." A website at http://behuninfamily.org/isaac/archives.htm (accessed accessed Feb. 26, 2013).

Iverson, Peter. *Diné: A History of the Navajos*. Albuquerque: University of New Mexico Press, 2002.

Ives, Joseph Christmas. *Report Upon the Colorado River of the West, Explored in 1857 and 1858.* Washington, D.C.: Government Printing Office, 1861.

Ivins, Anthony W. Diary, Oct. 10, 1875, to April 1882. Two versions, in Anthony W. Ivins Papers, bx 1, fds 7 and 8, USHS.

———. Diary excerpt. PTRC, series 8.1, bx 2 fd 24.

———. Journal. Anthony W. Ivins Papers, bx 5, fd 3, USHS.

———. Reminiscence. Anthony W. Ivins Papers, Mss B 2, bx 7, fd 6, Notebook 16, USHS.

———. "Travelling Over Forgotten Trails." Part of a series. *Improvement Era* 19 (Feb. 1916): 350–56.

———. "Traveling Over Forgotten Trails: A Mystery of the Grand Canyon Solved." *Improvement Era* 27 (Sept. 1924): 1017–25.

Jackson, Loretta, and Robert H. ("Hank") Stevens. "Hualapai Tradition, Religion, and the Role of Cultural Resource Management." In *Native Americans and Archaeologists: Stepping Stones to Common Ground,* edited by Nina Swidler, 135–42. Walnut Creek, CA: AltaMira Press, 1997.

Jacobs, Wilbur R. *Dispossessing the American Indian: Indians and Whites on the Colonial Frontier.* Norman: University of Oklahoma Press, 1985.

James, Daryl. "Lorenzo Hill Hatch." At http://members.cox.net/jameshistory/lh_hatch.html (accessed via Internet Archives on Feb. 26, 2013).

James, George Wharton. *The Grand Canyon of Arizona: How to See It*. Boston: Little, Brown & Co., 1910.

James, Harold L. "The History of Fort Wingate." In *Defiance, Zuni, Mt. Taylor Region (Arizona and New Mexico)*, edited by F. D. Trauger. New Mexico Geological Society, 18th Field Conference. New Mexico Geological Society, 1967. At http://nmgs.nmt.edu/publications/guidebooks/downloads/18/18_p0151_p0158.pdf (accessed March 6, 2011).

James, Harry C. *Pages from Hopi History*. Tucson: University of Arizona Press, 1974.

Jeffrey, Julie Roy. *Frontier Women: The Trans-Mississippi West, 1840–1880*. New York: Hill and Wang, 1979.

Jensen, Clarence G. "A Biographical Study of Leonard John Nuttall, Private Secretary to Presidents John Taylor and Wilford Woodruff." M.A. Thesis, Brigham Young University, 1962.

Jensen, Dilworth. "From the Days of '69." [The actual year was 1866.] Typescript. Woolley Family Papers, MSS 1403, Box 1, fd 13. Perry Special Collections, Lee Library.

Jensen, Richard. "New Mexico, Pioneer Settlements in." In Ludlow, *Encyclopedia of Mormonism*, 1010–11.

Jenson, Andrew. *Encyclopedic History of the Church of Jesus Christ of Latter-day Saints*. Salt Lake City: Deseret Book, 1941.

———. "Hamblin, Jacob." In Jenson, *LDSBE*, 3:100–11.

———, cp. "History of Las Vegas Mission." *The Nevada State Historical Society Papers* V (1925–1926), pp. 117–284.

———. *Latter-day Saint Biographical Encyclopedia*, 4 vols. Salt Lake City: Andrew Jenson History Co., 1901–1936.

———. "Pahreah Ward." In Jenson, *Encyclopedic History of the Church*, 627–28.

———, cp. "Tooele Stake History." Available at CHL and FHE.

———, cp. "Tuba Ward, Snowflake Stake: Manuscript History." LR 9236 2, CHL.

Jepson, Emily Hamblin. "The True Story of Frederick Hamblin's Fight With a Bear." At http://www.themorrisclan.com/GENEALOGY/HAMBLIN%20Isaiah%20F116.html (accessed Feb. 26, 2013).

"John Mangum, 1817–1881." Research notes, at http://www.myfamilysearch.net/getperson.php?personID=I1414&tree=2005217a (accessed Feb. 26, 2013).

Johnson, Annie Richardson. *Heartbeats of Colonia Díaz.* Mesa, AZ: Publisher's Press, 1972.

Johnson, Benjamin. *My Life's Review*. Independence, MO: Zion's Printing & Publishing Co., 1947.

Johnson, Broderick, and Ruth Roessel, eds. *Navajo Stories of the Long Walk Period*. Tsaile, AZ: Navajo Community College Press, 1973.

Johnson, Lydia, and Martha Johnson. "Biographical Sketch of Seth E. Johnson." Typescript, MS 13492, 28–30, CHL.

Johnson, S. J., as told to Evelyn Wooster Viner. "Echoes from the Past." *Improvement Era* 53.10 (Oct. 1950): 793, 844–45. Read in *LDS Library 2006*.

Johnson, William Derby. Diary, 1850–1894. Typescript at http://johnson.naflod.com/wdj_journal (accessed Aug. 8, 2011).

Jones, Daniel W. *Forty Years Among the Indians: A True Yet Thrilling Narrative of the Author's Experiences Among the Natives*. Salt Lake City: Juvenile Instructor Office, 1890.

Jones, Kumen. "Notes on San Juan Mission." At http://www.kumenjones.org/HTML/NotesOnSJMission.htm (accessed Feb. 26, 2013).

Jones, Sondra. "'Redeeming the Indian': The Enslavement of Indian Children in New Mexico and Utah." *Utah Historical Quarterly* 67.3 (summer 1999): 220–41.

Jones, Terry L. *Historical Dictionary of the Civil War.* 2 vols. Lanham, MD: Rowman & Littlefield, 2002.

"Journal History." A vast day-by-day compilation of Mormon history. CHL. Available in *Selected Collections* vol. 2.

Judd, B. Ira. "Tuba City, Mormon Settlement." *Journal of Arizona History* 10.1 (spring 1969): 37–42.

Judd, Mary Minerva Dart. Autobiography. Holograph. Huntington Library, San Marino, CA.

Judd, Zadok Knapp. "Reminiscence on the Settlement of the Santa Clara." In James G. Bleak collection, bx 2, fd 6, USHS.

Judd, Zadok, Jr. Autobiography. Typescript, in pamphlet, History of the Judd Family, by Esther Brown Judd. Huntington Library, San Marino, CA.

Julyan, Robert Hixson. *The Mountains of New Mexico.* Albuquerque: University of New Mexico Press, 2006.

Kanab Stake Historical Record, 1877–1901. Typescript excerpts in PTRC series 1, bx 10, fd 147. Original in CHL.

Kanab Stake Historical Record Book A, typescript excerpts in PTRC, series 1, bx 10, fd 149.

Kanab Ward Historical Record "Book A." June 1870–June 1881. Typescript excerpts in PTRC series 1, bx 10, fd 147. Original in CHL.

Kartchner, William Decatur. "Memoirs of William Decatur Kartchner." Finished in 1892, covers years 1878 to 1883. Typescript. At the Kartchner family website, http://kartchner.surnames.com/histories/william_decatur_karchner_memoirs.htm (accessed Feb. 26, 2013).

Kate, Herman Frederik Carel ten. *Travels and Researches in Native North America, 1882–1883.* Translated and edited by Pieter Hovens, William J. Orr, and Louis A. Hieb. Albuquerque: University of New Mexico Press, 2004.

Kelly, Charles, ed. "Captain Francis Marion Bishop's Journal, August 15, 1870–June 3, 1872." *Utah Historical Quarterly* 15 (Jan., Apr., Jul., Oct. 1947): 159–237.

———, ed. "Journal of Walter Clement Powell." *Utah Historical Quarterly* 16/17 (Jan., Apr., Jul., Oct. 1948 and 1949): 257–478.

———, ed. *Journals of John D. Lee, 1846–47 and 1859.* Salt Lake City: Privately printed for R. B. Watt by Western Printing Company, 1938. Republished: Salt Lake City: University of Utah Press, 1984.

———. *The Outlaw Trail: A History of Butch Cassidy and His Wild Bunch.* 2nd ed. New York: Bonanza Books, 1959.

———. "Walter Clement Powell: 1850–1883." *Utah Historical Quarterly* 16/17 (Jan., Apr., Jul., Oct. 1948 and 1949): 253–55.

Kelly, Charles, and Hoffman Birney. *Holy Murder: The Story of Porter Rockwell*. New York: Minton, Balch & Company, 1934.

Kelly, Isabel T. "Southern Paiute Bands." *American Anthropologist* 36.4 (Oct.–Dec. 1934): 548–60.

———. *Southern Paiute Ethnography*. University of Utah Anthropological Papers 78. Salt Lake City: University of Utah Press, 1966. Reprinted in *Paiute Indians II*. New York: Garland Publishing Inc., 1976.

———. "Southern Paiute Shamanism." *University of California Anthropological Records* 2.4 (1939): 151–67.

Kelly, Isabel T., and Catherine S. Fowler. "Southern Paiute." In Sturtevant, *Handbook of North American Indians*, Vol. 11, *Great Basin*, edited by Warren L. D'Azevedo, pp. 368–97.

Kelly, Lawrence C. *Navajo Roundup: Selected Correspondence of Kit Carson's Expedition Against the Navajo, 1863–1865*. Boulder, CO: The Pruett Publishing Company, 1970.

Kelly, Nina, and Alica Wilcox Lee. *Nutrioso and Her Neighbors: The History of a Pioneer Town*. Flagstaff, AZ: by the authors, 2000.

Kelsey, Michael R. *Hiking and Exploring the Paria River*. 5th ed. Provo, UT: Kelsey Publishing, 2010.

Kenney, Scott G., ed. *Wilford Woodruff's Journal, 1833–1898: Typescript*. Midvale, UT: Signature Books, 1983.

Kent, Kate Peck. *Navajo Weaving: Three Centuries of Change*. Santa Fe, NM: School of American Research Press, 1985.

Kessell, John L. "General Sherman and the Navajo Treaty of 1868: A Basic and Expedient Misunderstanding." *The Western Historical Quarterly* 12.3 (Jul. 1981): 251–72.

Kildare, Maurice. "Chief Scarbreast, Master Killer." *The West* 3.6 (Nov. 1965): 20–23, 52–54.

Kimball, Stanley. *Historic Sites and Markers along the Mormon and Other Great Western Trails*. Urbana: University of Illinois Press, 1988.

Kinkead, Joyce, ed. *A Schoolmarm All My Life: Personal Narratives from Frontier Utah*. Salt Lake City: Signature Books, 1996.

Kirsch, Scott. "John Wesley Powell and the Mapping of the Colorado Plateau, 1869–1879: Survey Science, Geographical Solutions and the Economy of Environmental Values." *Annals of the Association of American Geographers* 92.3 (2002): 548–72.

Kitchen, Richard Darrell. "Mormon-Indian Relations in Deseret: Intermarriage and Indenture, 1847 to 1877." Ph.D. Thesis, Arizona State University, 2002.

Kluckhohn, Clyde. *Navaho Witchcraft*. Boston: Beacon Press, 1944.

Knack, Martha C. *Boundaries Between: The Southern Paiutes, 1775–1995*. Lincoln: University of Nebraska Press, 2001.

———. "Church and State in the History of Southern Paiutes in Cedar City, Utah." *Journal of California and Great Basin Anthropology* 19.2 (1997): 159–78.

———. "Interethnic Competition at Kaibab during the Early Twentieth Century." *Ethnohistory* 40.2 (spring 1993): 212–45.

———. "Newspaper Accounts of Indian Women in Southern Nevada Mining Towns, 1870–1900." *Journal of California and Great Basin Anthropology* 8.1 (1986): 83–98.

Knell, Rulon. "Pinto." In Bradshaw, *Under Dixie Sun*, 213–18.

Kotchongva, Dan. "Where Is the White Brother of the Hopi Indian?" *The Improvement Era* 39.2 (Feb. 1936): 82–84, 116–19.

Krakauer, Jon. *Under the Banner of Heaven: A Story of Violent Faith*. New York: Doubleday, 2003.

Kroeber, Alfred L. *Handbook of Indians of California*. Smithsonian Institution, Bureau of American Ethnology, Bulletin 78. Washington, D.C.: Government Printing Office, 1925.

———. *Mohave Indians: Report on Aboriginal Territory and Occupancy of the Mohave Tribe*. New York: Garland Publishing Inc., 1974.

Kroeber, Clifton B. "The Mohave as Nationalist, 1859–1874." *Proceedings of the American Philosophical Society* 109.3 (Jun. 15, 1965): 173–80.

Kunitz, Stephen J. *Disease and Social Diversity: The European Impact on the Health of Non-Europeans*. Oxford: Oxford University Press, 1994

Lago, Don. "The Toquerville Myth." *boatman's quarterly review* 16.3 (fall 2003): 32–33. At http://gcrg.org/bqr/16-3/myth.html (accessed Feb. 26, 2013).

Lamar, Howard Roberts. *The Far Southwest, 1846–1912: A Territorial History*. Rev. ed. Albuquerque: University of New Mexico Press, 2000. Originally published in 1966.

Lancaster, Dennis R. "Dixie Wine." M.A. Thesis, Brigham Young University, 1972.

Landon, Michael. Notes on Hamblin Residences. Unpublished paper, in my possession.

Larsen, Wesley P. "'The Letter': Were Powell's Men Really Killed by Indians?" *Canyon Legacy* (Moab, Utah) 17 (spring 1993): 12–19.

———. "Navajo Chief Peokon: Impediment to the Settlement of the San Juan." *Canyon Legacy* (Moab, Utah) 22 (fall/winter 1994): 26–33.

Larson, Andrew Karl. *Erastus Snow: The Life of a Missionary and Pioneer for the Early Mormon Church.* Salt Lake City: University of Utah Press, 1971.

———. *I Was Called to Dixie: The Virgin River Basin: Unique Experience in Mormon Pioneering.* St. George, UT: The Dixie College Foundation, 1961.

———. *The Red Hills of November: A Pioneer Biography of Utah's Cotton Town.* Salt Lake City: Deseret News Press, 1957.

Laubin, Reginald. *Indian Dances of North America: Their Importance to Indian Life.* Norman: University of Oklahoma Press, 1989.

Lavender, David. *Pipe Spring and the Arizona Strip.* Springdale, UT: Zion Natural History Association, 1984.

LDS Library 2006. CD-ROMs. Salt Lake City: LDS Media and Deseret Book, 2006.

"The Lead Mines." A website at http://www.historyillinois.org/markers/old_markers/181.htm (accessed Oct. 2, 2008).

Leavitt, Alonzo. Interview with Selena H. Leavitt concerning Dudley Leavitt. July 24, 1933. At Western Association of Leavitt Families website, http://members.cox.net/leavittfamilies/H_Dudley%20Leavitt.htm (accessed June 6, 2011).

Leavitt, Jeremiah. Autobiography. At Western Association of Leavitt Families website, http://members.cox.net/leavittfamilies/H_Jeremiah%20Leavitt4.htm (accessed June 6, 2011).

Lee, Amarilla Hamblin. "My Life's Story." Typescript. In PTRC, series 8.1, bx 6, fd 91.

Lee, Hector. *The Three Nephites: The Substance and Significance of the Legend in Folklore.* Albuquerque: University of New Mexico Press, 1949.

Lee, Inez Hamblin. "An Autobiography." Typescript, written in 1923–24. In PTRC, Series 8.1, bx 2, fd 17.

Lee, John D. Journals. See Cleland and Brooks, *A Mormon Chronicle*, and Kelly, *Journals of John D. Lee.*

———. *Mormonism Unveiled; or the Life and Confessions of the Late Mormon Bishop, John D. Lee...* St. Louis: Bryan, Brand & Company, 1877.

Lee, Rachel. Diary. Holograph. In John D. Lee papers, Huntington Library, San Marino, CA.

Leonard, Glen M. *Nauvoo: A Place of Peace, a People of Promise.* Salt Lake City: Deseret Book Company, 2002.

Lesueur, James W. "Statement of James W. Lesueur." Oct. 15, 1920, MS 11914, CHL.

Levy, Jerrold E. *Orayvi Revisited: Social Stratification in an "Egalitarian" Society*. Santa Fe, NM: School of American Research Press, 1992.

Lewis, David. Autobiography. Merrill-Cazier Library, Utah State University.

———. Diary. CHL 4598.

Lewis, David Rich. *Neither Wolf nor Dog: American Indians, Environment, and Agrarian Change.* New York: Oxford University Press, 1994.

———. "Still Native: The Significance of Native Americans in the History of the Twentieth-Century American West." In *A New Significance: Re-envisioning the History of the American West*, edited by Clyde A. Milner and Allan G. Bogue, 213–40. New York: Oxford University Press, 1996.

Lienesch, Michael. "The Role of Political Millennialism in Early American Nationalism." *Western Political Quarterly* 36.3 (Sept. 1983): 445–65.

"Life of Walter Eugene Hamblin." In PTRC, series 8.1, bx 2, fd 17.

"Life Sketch of Louisa Bonelli Hamblin." In PTRC, series 8.1, bx 2, fd 17.

"Life Story of Barbara Staheli Graff Stucki." WPA biography, MSS B 289 box 10, USHS.

"Life Story of Luke Syphus and Christina Long Syphus." At http://reberfamilyhistories.blogspot.com/2010/09/life-story-of-luke-syphus-and-christina.html (accessed Feb. 26, 2013).

Limerick, Patricia Nelson. *The Legacy of Conquest: The Unbroken Past of the American West.* New York: W. W. Norton & Company, 1988.

Linford, Laurence. *Navajo Places: History, Legend, Landscape.* Salt Lake City: University of Utah Press, 2000.

Little, James, ed. *Jacob Hamblin, A Narrative of his Personal Experience, as a Frontiersman, Missionary to the Indians and Explorer, Disclosing Interpositions of Providence, Severe Privates, Perilous Situations and Remarkable Escapes.* The Faith-Promoting Series 5. Salt Lake City: Juvenile Instructor Office, 1881.

Locke, Raymond Friday. *The Book of the Navajo*. 5th ed. Los Angeles: Mankind Publishing Company, 1992.

Logue, Larry M. *A Sermon in the Desert: Belief and Behavior in Early St. George, Utah*. Urbana: University of Illinois Press, 1988.

Long, Everette Beach. *The Saints and the Union: Utah Territory During the Civil War.* Urbana: University of Illinois Press, 1981.

Longwell, Chester R. "Clarence Edward Dutton, 1841–1912: A Biographical Memoir." *National Academy of Sciences, Biographical Memoirs*, 32:132–45. Washington, D.C.: National Academy of Sciences, 1958. At http://books.nap.edu/html/biomems/cdutton.pdf (accessed Apr. 14, 2011).

"Lost Ten Tribes." On the *Mormon Quotes* website, at http://www.mormonthink.com/QUOTES/losttribes.htm (accessed Feb. 26, 2013).

"Louisa Bonelli Hamblin." In *Pioneer Women of Arizona*, edited by Roberta Flake Clayton, 188–91. Mesa, AZ: s.n., 1969.

Ludlow, Daniel H., ed. *The Encyclopedia of Mormonism*. 4 vols. New York: Macmillan Publishing Company, 1992.

Lyman, Amasa. Diary. MS 829, CHL (SC 37).

Lyman, Edward Leo. *Amasa Mason Lyman: Mormon Apostle and Apostate: A Study in Dedication.* Salt Lake City: University of Utah Press, 2009.

———. "Caught In Between: Jacob Hamblin and the Southern Paiutes During the Black Hawk–Navajo Wars of the Late 1860s." *Utah Historical Quarterly* 74.1 (winter 2007): 22–43.

———. "Chief Kanosh." *Journal of Mormon History* 35.1 (winter 2009): 157–207.

———. *The Overland Journey from Utah to California: Wagon Travel from the City of Saints to the City of Angels.* Reno: University of Nevada Press, 2004.

———. *San Bernardino: The Rise and Fall of a California Community*. Salt Lake City: Signature Books, 1996.

———. *Southern Paiute Relations with Their Early Dixie Mormon Neighbors.* Juanita Brooks Lecture Series, 27th Annual Lecture. St. George, UT: Dixie State College, 2010.

Lyman, Edward Leo, and Linda King Newell. *A History of Millard County*. Salt Lake City: Utah State Historical Society and Millard County Commission, 1999.

Lyman, Edward Leo, and Larry Lee Reese. *The Arduous Road: Salt Lake to Los Angeles, the Most Difficult Wagon Road in American History.* Victorville, CA: Lyman Historical Research and Publishing Company, 2001.

Lyon, William H. "The Navajos in the Anglo-American Imagination, 1807–1870." *Ethnohistory* 43.3 (summer 1996): 483–509.

MacKinnon, William P. "Epilogue to the Utah War: Impact and Legacy." *Journal of Mormon History* 29 (fall 2003): 186–248.

———, ed. *At Sword's Point, Part 1: A Documentary History of the Utah War to 1858.* Norman, OK: Arthur H. Clark, 2008.

———. "'Unquestionably Authentic and Correct in Every Detail': Probing John I. Ginn and His Remarkable Utah War Story." *Utah Historical Quarterly* 72 (fall 2004): 322–42.

Madsen, Brigham D. *The Shoshoni Frontier and the Bear River Massacre.* Vol. 1 in the Utah Centennial Series. Salt Lake City: University of Utah Press, 1985.

———. "Shoshoni Indians (Northwestern Bands)." In Powell, *Utah History Encyclopedia*, 497–98.

Malotki, Ekkehart, and Ken Gary. *Hopi Stories of Witchcraft, Shamanism, and Magic.* Lincoln: University of Nebraska Press, 2006.

Manchester, Albert D., and Ann Manchester. *Hubbell Trading Post National Historic Site: An Administrative History.* Professional Papers No. 46. Santa Fe, NM: National Park Service, Division of History, Southwest Cultural Resources Center, 1993. At http://www.nps.gov/hutr/historyculture/index.htm (accessed Feb. 26, 2013).

Manderscheid, Lorraine Richardson, comp. *Some Descendants of John Doyle Lee*. 2nd ed. 2000. At http://www.wadhome.org/lee/index.html (accessed Feb. 26, 2013).

Manners, Robert A. *Paiute Indians I: Southern Paiute and Chemehuevi: An Ethnohistorical Report.* New York: Garland Publishing Inc., 1974.

Manwaring, Winniefred Spafford. "Aaron Johnson." In *An Enduring Legacy*, 3:320–25.

Marriott, Barbara. *In Our Own Words: the Lives of Arizona Pioneer Women.* Tucson, AZ: Fireship Press, 2009.

Martineau, James H. Journal, 1850–circa 1921. MssFAC 1499, Huntington Library, San Marino, CA. I am indebted to Noel Carmack for sharing transcriptions of passages related to Jacob Hamblin.

Martineau, LaVan. *Southern Paiutes: Legends Lore Language and Lineage.* Las Vegas: KC Publications, 1992.

Maryboy, Nancy, and David Begay. "The Navajos of Utah." In Cuch, *A History of Utah's American Indians*, 264–313.

Matheson, Alva, and Inez Cooper. "Answers to a Questionnaire Given Alva Matheson." In the Alva Matheson collection, Special Collections, Gerald R. Sherratt Library, Southern Utah University.

Mattes, Merrill J. *The Great Platte River Road: The Covered Wagon Mainline Via Fort Kearny to Fort Laramie.* Omaha: Nebraska State Historical Society, 1969.

Maughan, Mary Ann Weston. "Autobiography and Journal." In Carter, *Our Pioneer Heritage*, 2:345–420.

Mauss, Armand L. *All Abraham's Children: Changing Mormon Conceptions of Race and Lineage.* Urbana: University of Illinois Press, 2003.

May, Dean L. "People on the Mormon Frontier: Kanab's Families of 1874." *Journal of Family History* 1:2 (winter 1976): 169–88.

———. "The United Order Movement." In Powell, *Utah History Encyclopedia*, 576–79.

———. "Utah Writ Small: Challenge and Change in Kane County's Past." *Utah Historical Quarterly* 53.2 (spring 1985): 170–83.

McBride, James. "[Auto]Biography of James McBride, 1818–1881." Written in 1874. Typescript, Lee Library.

McClintock, James H. *Arizona, Prehistoric, Aboriginal, Pioneer, Modern.* Chicago: S. J. Clarke Publishing Co., 1916.

———. *Mormon Settlement in Arizona.* Phoenix: State of Arizona, 1921.

———. Third Interview with Ammon Tenney. In "Interviews with Arizona Pioneers," MS 18991, CHL.

McConnell, Gladys. "Sketch of the Life of Jehiel McConnell." In Gladys McConnell Collection (Ms. 6), Sherratt Library, Southern Utah University.

McGuire, Thomas R. "Walapai." In Sturtevant, *Handbook of North American Indians*, vol. 10, *The Southwest*, edited by Alfonso Ortiz, 25–37. Washington, D.C.: Government Printing Office, 1983.

McKoy, Kathleen L. *Cultures at a Crossroad: An Administrative History of Pipe Spring National Monument.* Cultural Resources Selections No. 15. Denver, CO: Intermountain Region, 2000. Available at http://www.nps.gov/pisp/historyculture/upload/PISP_adhi.pdf (accessed Feb. 26, 2013).

McNitt, Frank. *The Indian Traders.* Norman: University of Oklahoma Press, 1962.

———. *The Navajo Wars.* Albuquerque: University of New Mexico Press, 1972.

McPherson, Robert. *A History of San Juan County.* Salt Lake City: Utah State Historical Society, 1995.

———. *Navajo Land, Navajo Culture: The Utah Experience in the Twentieth Century.* Norman: University of Oklahoma Press, 2001.

———. *The Northern Navajo Frontier, 1860–1900: Expansion through Adversity.* Logan: Utah State University Press, 1988.

———. "Setting the Stage: Native America Revisited." In Cuch, *A History of Utah's American Indians*, 3–24.

———. "Ute Indians—Southern." In Powell, *Utah History Encyclopedia*, 609–11.

Mercer, Mildred Allred, ed. *History of Tooele County*. Salt Lake City: Tooele County Daughters of Utah Pioneers, 1961.

Metcalf, Brandon J. "James G. Bleak: from London to Dixie." *Journal of Mormon History* 35.1 (winter 2009): 117–56.

Mileski, Melissa Lambert, ed. *Before the Manifesto: The Life Writings of Mary Lois Walker Morris.* Logan: Utah State University Press, 2007.

Milikien, Herbert C. "Dead of the Bloody Flux?: Cholera Stalks the Emigrant Trail." *Overland Journal* 14:3 (autumn 1996): 6–11.

Miller, Albert E. *Immortal Pioneers, Founders of St. George, Utah.* St. George, UT: Privately published, 1946.

Miller, David E. *Hole-in-the-Rock: An Epic in the Colonization of the Great American West*. Salt Lake City: University of Utah Press, 1959.

Miller, David H. "The Ives Expedition Revisited: Overland into Grand Canyon." *Journal of Arizona History* 13 (autumn 1972): 177–96.

———. "The Ives Expedition Revisited: A Prussian's Impressions." *Journal of Arizona History* 13 (spring 1972): 1–25.

Miller, Jacob. *Journal of Jacob Miller*. Ed. Joseph Royal Miller and Elna Miller. [Salt Lake City]: Mercury Publishing Co., 1967.

Miller, Orrin P. *History of Tooele County*, vol. 2. Tooele, UT: Tooele Transcript Bulletin, 1990.

Miller, Vera Leib, cp. *The Jacob Vernon Hamblin Family.* Seal Beach, CA: by the author, 1975.

"Minutes of the Little Colorado Stake [1879–1886]." Typescript by George S. Tanner. University of Arizona Library, Special Collections.

Minutes of Tuba City Meeting, Feb. 7–9, 1888. Typescript in PTRC, series 1, bx 3, fd 38. Original in CHL.

Mitchell, Frank, Charlotte J. Frisbie, and David P. McAllester. *Navajo Blessingway Singer: The Autobiography of Frank Mitchell, 1881–1967.* Tucson: University of Arizona Press, 1978.

Mitchell, Rose, and Charlotte Johnson Frisbie. *Tall Woman: The Life Story of Rose Mitchell, a Navajo Woman, c. 1874–1977.* Albuquerque: University of New Mexico Press, 2001.

"Monument Honors Friendly Hopi Indian Chief." In the section, "The Church Moves On," *Improvement Era* 44.7 (July 1941): 415. Read in *LDS Library 2006*.

Moore, William Haas. *Chiefs, Agents & Soldiers: Conflict on the Navajo Frontier, 1868–1882*. Albuquerque: University of New Mexico Press, 1994.

Moorman, Donald R., and Gene Allred Sessions. *Camp Floyd and the Mormons: The Utah War*. Utah centennial series, vol. 7. Salt Lake City: University of Utah Press, 2005.

Morgan, Dale. "The Administration of Indian Affairs in Utah, 1851–1858." *Pacific Historical Review* 17 (Nov. 1948): 383–409.

"Mormon Colonization in the West." In Carter, *Heart Throbs of the West*, 3:277–325. The section "Tooele County" is on p. 283; its source is given as "Locality History."

"Mormon Pioneer Overland Travel, 1847–1868," Aaron Johnson Company, 1850. At http://history.lds.org/overlandtravels/companyDetail?lang=eng&companyId=170 (accessed Feb. 26, 2013).

Morrill, Horatio. Diary, 1869 mission to Hopi Mesas. Ms B 77, USHS.

Murphy, Lawrence R. *Frontier Crusader—William F. M. Arny*. Tucson: University of Arizona Press, 1972.

———, ed. *Indian Agent in New Mexico: The Journal of Special Agent W. F. M. Arny, 1870.* Santa Fe, NM: Stagecoach Press, 1967.

Murphy, Thomas W. "From Racist Stereotype to Ethnic Identity: Instrumental Uses of Mormon Racial Doctrine." *Ethnohistory* 46 (summer 1999): 451–80.

Musser, A. Milton. Journal. CHL.

Naegle, Altia Williams. "Life Story of Altia Williams Naegle." Typescript. MS 13383, CHL.

Nagata, Shuichi. *Modern Transformations of Moenkopi Pueblo.* Illinois Studies in Anthropology No. 6. Urbana: University of Illinois Press, 1970.

Nauvoo Temple Endowment Register: 10 December 1845 to 8 February 1846. Salt Lake City: The Church of Jesus Christ of Latter-day Saints, 1974. Also available at Family History Library, microfilm 962798.

Nelson, Pearl Udall. *Arizona Pioneer Mormon: David King Udall: his Story and his Family, 1851–1938.* Tucson, AZ.: Arizona Silhouettes, 1959. Available online at http://www.library.arizona.edu/exhibits/davidkudall/mormon/main.html (accessed Feb. 26, 2013).

Nelson, William. Diary. Typescript, 2 vols. Compiled in 1938. Perry Special Collections, Lee Library.

Nequatewa, Edmund. *Truth of a Hopi and Other Clan Stories of Shung-Opovi.* Edited by Mary-Russell F. Colton. Museum of Northern Arizona Bulletin No. 8. Flagstaff: Northern Arizona Society of Science and Art, 1936.

Nevada Observer website. At http://www.nevadaobserver.com/ (accessed Feb. 26, 2013).

New Mormon Studies CD-ROM. Salt Lake City: Smith Research Associates, 1998.

Nichols, Janell, and Patricia Bracken. "William Meeks." In Youngberg, *Conquerors of the West:* 3:1614–15.

Nickel, Ross, and Bambie Reed Zeddis. *Outlaw Trail Adventures*, a website. See especially http://web.me.com/outlawtrailadventur/outlaw/History_Gulch.html (accessed Jan. 4, 2011).

Nielson, Frihoff Godfrey. Diary. Typescript excerpts in PTRC, series 1, bx 20, fd 316. Excerpts also at the Mormon settlements in Arizona collection, Marriott Library, http://content.lib.utah.edu/cdm/ref/collection/UU_EAD/id/1586 (accessed Feb. 26, 2013).

"Notes on Indians." In Carter, *Treasures of Pioneer History*, 6:161–63.

Nuttall, L. [Leonard] John. Diary, 1876–1904. Holograph, CHL. I consulted the typescript excerpts available in the *New Mormon Studies* CD and in PTRC, series 1, bx 20, fd 317.

———. *In the President's Office: The Diaries of L. John Nuttall, 1879–1892*. Edited by Jedediah S. Rogers. Salt Lake City: Signature Books and Smith-Pettit Books, 2007.

Olsen, Robert W., Jr. "Clem Powell and Kanab Creek." *Kiva* 34.1 (Oct. 1968): 41–50.

———. "Pipe Spring, Arizona, and Thereabouts." *Journal of Arizona History* 6.13 (spring 1965): 11–18.

———. "The Powell Survey Kanab Base Line." *Utah Historical Quarterly* 2 (spring 1969): 261–68.

———. "Winsor Castle: Mormon Frontier Fort at Pipe Spring." *Utah Historical Quarterly* 34 (summer 1966): 218–26.

Olson, Joseph William. "History of Erastus Snow." M.A. Thesis, BYU, 1935.

Oman, Richard G. "LDS Southwest Indian Art." *Ensign* 12 (Sept. 1982): 33–48.

O'Neil, Floyd A. "The Mormons, the Indians, and George Washington Bean." In *Churchmen and the Western Indians, 1820–1920*, edited by Clyde A. Milner II and Floyd A. O'Neil, 77–107. Norman: University of Oklahoma Press, 1985.

———. "The Utes, Southern Paiutes, and Gosiutes." In Papanikolas, *The Peoples of Utah*, 27–60.

O'Neil, Floyd A., and Stanford J. Layton. "Of Pride and Politics: Brigham Young as Indian Superintendent." *Utah Historical Quarterly* 46 (summer 1978): 237–50.

"Pahreah Ward History." CHL. Typescript in PTRC, series 1, bx 20, fd 318.

Palmer, Edward. *Notes on the Utah Utes by Edward Palmer, 1866–1877.* Edited by R. F. Heizer. University of Utah Anthropological Papers, No. 17. Salt Lake City: Dept. of Anthropology, University of Utah, 1954.

———. "Plants Used by Indians of the United States." *The American Naturalist* 12.9–10 (Sept.–Oct. 1878): 593–606, 646–55.

Palmer, William. *Forgotten Chapters of History*. 5 vols. A collection of radio talks, typescript. Special Collections, Sherratt Library, Southern Utah University, 1952.

Palmer, William R. "Pahute Indian Homelands." *Utah Historical Quarterly* 6.3 (July 1933): 775–90.

———. "Pahute Indian Medicine." *Utah Historical Quarterly* 10 (Jan.–Oct. 1942): 1–13.

———. "Utah Indians Past and Present." *Utah Historical Quarterly* 1.2 (Apr. 1928): 35–51.

Papanikolas, Helen Z., ed. *The Peoples of Utah*. Salt Lake City: Utah State Historical Society, 1976.

Parfitt, Tudor. *The Lost Tribes of Israel: The History of a Myth.* London: Weidenfield & Nicolson, 2002.

Parkinson, Samuel Rose. Diaries, 1873–1919. Originals at CHL. Transcription at http://srp.parkinsonfamily.org/srp-histories/srp-journal-1831–1876.htm (accessed Feb. 26, 2013).

Parmentier, Richard J. "The Mythological Triangle: Poseyemu, Montezuma, and Jesus in the Pueblos." In Sturtevant, *Handbook of North American Indians*, vol. 9, *The Southwest*, edited by Alfonso Ortiz, 609–22.

Parry, Mae. "The Northwestern Shoshone." In Cuch, *A History of Utah's American Indians*, 25–72.

Parshall, Ardis. "'Pursue, Retake and Punish': The 1857 Santa Clara Ambush." *Utah Historical Quarterly* 73 (winter 2005): 64–86.

Patterson, Richard M. *Butch Cassidy: A Biography.* Lincoln: University of Nebraska Press, 1998.

Pavlik, Steve. "Of Saints and Lamanites: An Analysis of Navajo Mormonism." *Wicazo Sa Review* 8.1 (spring 1992): 21–30.

Payne, Rodger M. *The Self and the Sacred: Conversion and Autobiography in Early American Protestantism*. Knoxville: University of Tennessee Press, 1998.

Pearce, James. Interview. January 9, 1921, at Mesa, Arizona. MS 18476, CHL.

Pectol, George. Diary. CHL.

Perkins, George E. "Trailing Cattle on the Old Spanish or Mormon Trail in 1868." Carter, *Heart Throbs of the West* 12:329–32.

Perkins, Waldo. "Christen and Samuel Wittwer." Typescript in possession of author.

Perkins, Waldo C. "From Switzerland to the Colorado River: Life Sketch of the Entrepreneurial Daniel Bonelli, the Forgotten Pioneer." *Utah Historical Quarterly* 74.1 (winter 2006): 4–23.

Peterson, Charles S. "Apostle of the Outposts." A review of Andrew Karl Larson, *Erastus Snow: The Life of a Missionary and Pioneer for the Early Mormon Church* (1971), in *Dialogue* 6.3–4 (autumn–winter 1971): 120–24.

———, ed. "'Book A—Levi Mathers Savage': The Look of Utah in 1873." *Utah Historical Quarterly* 41.1 (winter 1973): 4–22.

———. "Grazing in Utah: A Historical Perspective." *Utah Historical Quarterly* 57 (fall 1989): 300–19.

———. "Jacob Hamblin, Apostle to the Lamanites and the Indian Mission." *Journal of Mormon History* 2 (1975): 21–34.

———. "The Hopis and the Mormons, 1858–1873." *Utah Historical Quarterly* 39.2 (spring 1971): 179–93.

———. "'A Mighty Man Was Brother Lot': A Portrait of Lot Smith, Mormon Frontiersman." *Western Historical Quarterly* 1.4 (Oct. 1970): 393–414.

———. *Take Up Your Mission: Mormon Colonizing along the Little Colorado River, 1870–1900*. Tucson: University of Arizona Press, 1973.

Peterson, John Alton. "The Last Bastion: Pipe Springs and Its Place in Brigham Young's 'Great Game.'" Talk given at Mormon History Association Conference, St. George, Utah, May 27, 2011.

———. *Utah's Black Hawk War*. Salt Lake City: University of Utah Press, 1999.

Peterson, Levi S. *Juanita Brooks: Mormon Woman Historian.* Salt Lake City: University of Utah Press, 1988.

Peterson, Scott. *Native American Prophecies.* 2nd ed., rev. St. Paul, MN: Paragon House, 1999.

Pickard, Madge E., and R. Carlyle Buley. *The Midwest Pioneer: His Ills, Cures, & Doctors*. New York: Henry Schuman, 1946.

Pioneer and General History of Geauga County: with sketches of some of the Pioneers and Prominent Men. Burton, OH: Historical Society of Geauga County, 1880.

"Pioneer Forts of the West." In Carter, *Our Pioneer Heritage* 9:85–168.

Poll, Richard D. "The Utah War." In Powell, *Utah History Encyclopedia*, 607–8.

Popkin, Richard H. "The Rise and Fall of the Jewish Indian Theory." In *Menasseh Ben Israel and His World*, edited by Yosef Kaplan, Henry Mechoulan, and Richard H. Popkin, 63–82. Leiden: E. J. Brill, 1989.

Porter, Larry C. "A Historical Analysis of Cove Fort Utah." M.A. thesis, Brigham Young University, 1966.

Powell, Allen Kent. "Cowboys and the Cattle Industry." At the website "Utah History to Go," http://historytogo.utah.gov/utah_chapters/pioneers_and_cowboys/cowboysandthecattleindustry.html (accessed Feb. 26, 2013).

———, ed. *Utah History Encyclopedia.* Salt Lake City: University of Utah Press, 1994.

Powell, John Wesley. "The Ancient Province of Tusayan." *Scribner's Monthly* 11 (Dec. 1875): 193–213.

———. *Canyons of the Colorado*. Meadville, PA: Flood & Vincent, 1895. This includes the text of *Exploration of the Colorado River of the West*, but adds a few chapters dealing with Powell and Hamblin's trip to the Hopis and Navajos.

———. *Exploration of the Colorado River of the West and Its Tributaries.* Washington, D.C.: Government Printing Office, 1875.

———. "An Overland Trip to the Grand Cañon." *Scribner's Monthly* 10 (Oct. 1875): 659–78.

———. *Report of the Explorations in 1873 of the Colorado of the West and its Tributaries.* Washington, D.C.: Government Printing Office, 1874.

Powell, John Wesley, and George W. Ingalls. *Report on the Condition and Wants of the Ute Indians of Utah, the Pai-Utes of Utah, Northern Arizona, Southern Nevada, and Southeastern California.* U.S. Congress, House of Representatives, Executive Document no. 157, 43rd Cong., 1st Sess. Washington, D.C.: Government Printing Office, 1874.

Powers, Ramon, and James Leiker. "Cholera among the Plains Indians: Perceptions, Causes, Consequences." *Western Historical Quarterly* 29:3 (autumn 1998): 317–42.

Powers, Willow Roberts. *Navajo Trading: The End of an Era.* Albuquerque: University of New Mexico Press, 2003.

Pratt, Helaman. Diary, 1875–1878. Typescript. Transcribed by Maurine Colgrove and Benson Parkinson. At Jared Pratt Family Association website, http://jared.pratt-family.org/parley_family_histories/list-helaman-pratt.html (accessed Dec. 8, 2011).

Pratt, Louisa Barnes. *The History of Louisa Barnes Pratt: Mormon Missionary Widow and Pioneer.* Edited by S. George Ellworth. Vol. 3, Life Writings of Frontier Women. Logan: Utah State University Press, 1998.

Prince, Gregory A. *Power from On High: The Development of Mormon Priesthood*. Salt Lake City: Signature Books, 1995.

Prucha, Francis Paul. *The Great Father: The United States Government and the American Indians.* Omaha: University of Nebraska Press, 1986.

———. *The Indians in American Society from the Revolutionary War to the Present.* Berkeley: University of California Press, 1985.

Pulsipher, John. Diary. Two volumes, typescript. Book one is called, "Diary of John Pulsipher, Volume 1," transcribed 1936 by Louise Mathews, WPA, Mar. 1835 to Oct. 1874. 178 pp. Volume 2 is titled, "Some of the Life and Doings of John Pulsipher, 1874–1891," typed April 13, 1937, by Claudia Beames. 106 pp. Special Collections, Gerald R. Sherratt Library, Southern Utah University, Cedar City. Copies are available in other libraries.

Pulsipher, Juanita Leavitt, ed. *History of Sarah Sturdevant Leavitt*. See [Brooks], Juanita, ed. *History of Sarah Sturdevant Leavitt*.

Pusey, Merlo J. *Builders of the Kingdom: George A. Smith, John Henry Smith, George Albert Smith.* Studies in Western History and Culture series, No. 1. Provo, UT: Brigham Young University Press, 1981.

Quinn, D. Michael. *Early Mormonism and the Magic World View.* 2nd ed., rev. and enlarged. Salt Lake City: Signature Books, 1998.

———. "Latter-day Saint Prayer Circles." *Brigham Young University Studies* 19 (fall 1978): 79–105.

———. *The Mormon Hierarchy: Extensions of Power*. Salt Lake City: Signature Books, 1997.

———. *The Mormon Hierarchy: Origins of Power*. Salt Lake City: Signature Books, 1994.

———. "The Practice of Rebaptism at Nauvoo." *Brigham Young University Studies* 18 (winter 1978): 226–32.

Read, Georgia Willis. "Diseases, Drugs, and Doctors on the Oregon-California Trail in the Gold-Rush Years." *Missouri Historical Review* 38.3 (April 1944): 260–76.

Reeve, Frank D., ed. "War and Peace: Two Arizona Diaries." *New Mexico Historical Review* 24 (1949): 109–29.

Reeve, Rex C., Jr., and Galen L. Fletcher. "Mormons in the Tuba City Area." In *Regional Studies in Latter-day Saint History: Arizona*, edited by H. Dean Garrett and Clark V. Johnson, 129–75. Provo, UT: Dept. of Church History and Doctrine, Brigham Young University, 1989.

Reeve, W. Paul. "Cattle, Cotton, and Conflict: The Possession and Dispossession of Hebron, Utah." *Utah Historical Quarterly* 67.2 (spring 1999): 148–75.

———. "A Little Oasis in the Desert: Hurricane, Utah, 1860–1920." *Utah Historical Quarterly* 62 (summer 1994): 222–45.

———. *Making Space on the Western Frontier: Mormons, Miners, and Southern Paiutes.* Urbana: University of Illinois, 2006.

Reff, Daniel T. "The Introduction of Smallpox in the Greater Southwest." *American Anthropologist*, New Series, 89.3 (Sep. 1987): 704–8.

Reichard, Gladys. *Navaho Religion.* Bollingen Series XVIII. 2nd ed., in one volume. New York: Bollingen Foundation, 1963.

Reichard, Gladys A. *The Social Life of the Navajo Indians with Some Attention to Minor Ceremonies.* New York: Columbia Press, 1928.

Reid, John Philip. "Principles of Vengeance: Fur Trappers, Indians, and Retaliation for Homicide in the Transboundary North American West." *Western Historical Quarterly* 24 (Feb. 1993): 21–43.

Reilly, P. T. Collection. MS 275. Cline Library, Northern Arizona University, Flagstaff, Arizona.

———. "Historic Utilization of the Paria River." *Utah Historical Quarterly* 45 (1977): 188–201.

———. "How Deadly Is Big Red?" *Utah Historical Quarterly* 37.2 (spring 1969): 244–60.

———. Interview with Amarilla Hamblin Lee. June 26, 1970. MSS A 2756, USHS.

———. "Kanab United Order: The President's Nephew and the Bishop." *Utah Historical Quarterly* 42.2 (spring 1974): 145–64.

———. *Lee's Ferry: From Mormon Crossing to National Park.* Logan: Utah State University Press, 1999.

———. "Roads across the Buckskin Mountain." *The Journal of Arizona History* 19.4 (winter 1928): 379–402.

———. "Warren Marshall Johnson: Forgotten Saint." *Utah Historical Quarterly* 39.1 (winter 1971): 3–22.

"Reminiscences of the Early Days of Manti." *Utah State Historical Quarterly* 6.4 (Oct. 1933): 117–23. Originally published in *The Home Sentinel*, Manti, Aug. 15, 1889.

Rencher, Dora Bigelow. "A Short Sketch of Mary E. Hamblin Beeler." Jacob Hamblin collection, Huntington Library, San Marino, CA.

Rich, Alice Redd. "Memories of New Harmony." At the New Harmony Heritage website, http://www.newharmonyheritage.com/Memories_of_New_Harmony.pdf (accessed Feb. 26, 2013).

Richter, Daniel K. "The Imperial Virus." A Review of Elizabeth Fenn, *Pox Americana: The Great Smallpox Epidemic of 1775–82*. *Common-Place: The Interactive Journal of Early American Life* 2.3 (Apr. 2002). At http://www.common-place.org/vol-02/no-03/reviews/richter.shtml (accessed Feb. 26, 2013).

Riddle, Isaac. Autobiography. Written in 1898. "Life of Isaac Riddle: An Autobiography." Edited by Mark A. Riddle. Unpublished typescript, 1992, in possession of the author.

———. "Isaac Riddle Tells His Story." His autobiography. In Carter, *Our Pioneer Heritage* 11:169–81.

Rieck, Richard L. "A Geography of Death on the Oregon-California Trail, 1840–1860." *Overland Journal* 9.1 (spring 1991): 13–21.

Roberts, Brigham H. *A Comprehensive History of the Church of Jesus Christ of Latter-day Saints: Century I.* 6 vols. Salt Lake City: Deseret News Press, 1930.
Roberts, Heidi. "Settlement and Subsistence Strategies of the Southern Paiute in the St. George Basin, Southern Utah." *Spanish Traces: Old Spanish Trail Association* 8 (fall 2002): 19–25.
Roberts, Richard, and Richard W. Sadler. *A History of Weber County*. Salt Lake City: Utah State Historical Society, 1997.
Robertson, Margaret C. "The Campaign and the Kingdom: The Activities of the Electioneers in Joseph Smith's Presidential Campaign." *Brigham Young University Studies* 39:3 (2000): 147–80.
Robertson, Roland G. *Rotting Face: Smallpox and the American Indian.* Caldwell, ID: Caxton Press, 2001.
Robinson, Adonis Findlay. "History of Kanab." In *An Enduring Legacy*, 9:273–78.
———, cp. and ed. *History of Kane County*. Salt Lake City: Kane County Daughters of Utah Pioneers, 1970.
Robinson, Charles M., III, ed. *The Diaries of John Gregory Bourke*. 3 vols. Denton: University of North Texas Press, 2003.
Robinson, Ezra C. *The Life of Ira Hatch: Famous Indian Missionary and Scout*. N.p., n.d. Copy consulted at Special Collections, Gerald R. Sherratt Library, Southern Utah University.
Roessel, Robert A., Jr. "Navajo History, 1850–1923." In Sturtevant, *Handbook of North American Indians*, vol. 10, *The Southwest*, edited by Alfonso Ortiz, pp. 506–23.
Romney, Thomas Cottam. *The Mormon Colonies in Mexico*. Salt Lake City: University of Utah Press, 1938.
Rosenberg, Charles E. *The Cholera Years: The United States in 1832, 1849, and 1866*. Chicago: University of Chicago Press, 1962.
Rosenvall, Lynn A. "Defunct Mormon Settlements: 1830–1930." In *The Mormon Role in the Settlement of the West*, edited by Richard H. Jackson, 51–74. Provo, UT: Brigham Young University Press, 1978.
Roundy, Jane L. "John Taylor Lay." Carter, *Heart Throbs of the West*, 6:493.
Roundy, Malinda Parker. "Pioneers of Early Days." *Garfield County News*, June 6, 1930, p. 4.
Rusho, W. L., and C. G. Crampton. *Lee's Ferry: Desert River Crossing.* Salt Lake City: Cricket Productions, 1992.
Rushton, Patricia. "Cholera and Its Impact on Nineteenth-Century Mormon Migration." *Brigham Young University Studies* 44.2 (2005): 123–44.
Russell, Frank. "Pima Annals." *American Anthropologist*, New Series, 5.1 (Jan.–Mar. 1903): 76–80.
———. *The Pima Indians*. Washington, D.C.: Government Printing Office, 1908.
Russell, S. "The Navajo and the 1918 Influenza Pandemic." In *Health and Disease in the Prehistoric Southwest*, edited by Charles F. Merbs and Robert J. Miller, 380–90. Anthropological Research Papers no. 34. Tempe: Arizona State University, 1985.
Sabin, Edwin Legrand. *Kit Carson Days (1809–1868)*. Chicago: A. C. McClurg & Co., 1914.
Samuelsen, Eric R. Review of *Utah!*, by Robert Paxton, Reed McColm. Association of Mormon Letter website, July 14, 1997. At http://www.aml-online.org/Reviews/Review.aspx?id=3083 (accessed Feb. 26, 2013).
Sanchez, Joseph P. *Explorers, Traders, and Slavers: Forging the Old Spanish Trail.* Salt Lake City: University of Utah Press, 1997.
Sandberg, Guenavere Allen, cp. *A Million Miles of Faith: the Story of Rufus Chester Allen.* N.p.: Guenavere Allen Sandberg, 2004.
Sandeen, Ernest R. *The Roots of Fundamentalism: British and American Millenarianism, 1800–1930* (Chicago: University of Chicago Press, 1970).
Schafer, Joseph. *The Wisconsin Lead Region*. Madison: State Historical Society of Wisconsin, 1932.
Schindler, Harold. *Orrin Porter Rockwell. Man of God, Son of Thunder*. Salt Lake City: University of Utah Press, 1983.
Schubert, Frank N. *Vanguard of Expansion: Army Engineers in the Trans-Mississippi West, 1819–1879.* Online publication: History Division, Office of Administrative Services, Office of the Chief of Engineers, 1980. At http://www.nps.gov/history/history/online_books/shubert/index.htm (accessed Feb. 26, 2013).
Schwartz, Douglas W. "Havasupai." In Sturtevant, *Handbook of North American Indians*, vol. 10, *The Southwest*, edited by Alfonso Ortiz, pp. 13–24.
Seegmiller, Ella J. "Ghost Towns of Washington County." In Bradshaw, *Under Dixie Sun*, 117–27.
Seegmiller, Janet Burton. *A History of Iron County: Community Above Self.* (Utah centennial county history series.) Salt Lake City: Utah State Historical Society; Iron County Commission, 1998.

Sekaquaptewa, Helen. *Me and Mine: The Life Story of Helen Sekaquaptewa as told to Louise Udall.* Edited by Louise Udall. Tucson: University of Arizona Press, 1969.

Selected Collections: see Turley, *Selected Collections.*

Sessions, Gene. *Mormon Thunder: A Documentary History of Jedediah Morgan Grant.* Urbana: University of Illinois Press, 1982.

"Settlement of Kanab Region, Southern Utah, Kanab State, 1865–1874, Pipe Springs, Jacob Hamblin to Hopi Towns." Complainant's Exhibit No. 621 in *United States vs. Utah*. Typescript. A miscellany of excerpts. Arizona Historical Society, Tucson.

Shea, Daniel B., Jr. *Spiritual Autobiography in Early America.* Princeton, NJ: Princeton University Press, 1968.

Shelton, Marion J. Diary. MS 1412, fd. 1, CHL.

Shepard, William. "Shadows on the Sun Dial: John E. Page and the Strangites." *Dialogue* 41.1 (spring 2008): 34–66.

Shepardson, Mary, and Blodwen Hammond. *The Navajo Mountain Community: Social Organization and Kinship Terminology.* Berkeley: University of California Press, 1970.

Shirts, Morris. "Black Ridge Mountains." Typescript. A talk given to the Iron County Historical Society on Oct. 22, 1970. Sherratt Library.

Shirts, Morris A., and Kathryn H. Shirts. *A Trial Furnace: Southern Utah's Iron Mission*. Provo: Brigham Young University Press, 2001.

Shirts, Peter. "A Report of the Mountain Meadows Massacre." In Bagley, *Stones, Clubs and Gun Barrels.*

"Short Life Story of Inez Hamblin." Jacob Hamblin papers, Huntington Library, San Marino, CA.

Shurtz, Ambrose. "History of the Shurtz or Shirts Family." Typescript, MSS A 1746, USHS.

Sides, Hampton. *Blood and Thunder: An Epic of the American West*. New York: Doubleday, 2006.

———. "Thunderstruck: Q&A with Hampton Sides." *Outside Magazine*, October 2006. At http://outside.away.com/outside/destinations/200610/hampton-sides-interview.html (accessed Feb. 26, 2013).

Sigler, J. W., and W. F. Sigler. "History of Fish Hatchery Development in the Great Basin States of Utah and Nevada." *The Great Basin Naturalist* 46.4 (Oct. 31, 1986): 583–94.

Simmonds, A. J. "Water for the Big Range." *Utah Historical Quarterly* 39.3 (summer 1971): 224–37.

Simmons, Marc. *Kit Carson and His Three Wives: A Family History.* Albuquerque: University of New Mexico Press, 2003.

———. "Kit and the Indians." In Gordon-McCutchan, *Kit Carson: Indian Fighter or Indian Killer?*, 73–90.

———. *Massacre on the Lordsburg Road: A Tragedy of the Apache Wars.* College Station: Texas A&M University Press, 1997.

———. *New Mexico: An Interpretive History*. Albuquerque: University of New Mexico Press, 1988.

———. *Witchcraft in the Southwest: Spanish and Indian Supernaturalism on the Rio Grande*. Omaha: University of Nebraska Press, 1980.

Simmons, Virginia McConnell. *The Ute Indians of Utah, Colorado, and New Mexico.* Boulder: University Press of Colorado, 2000.

Simpson, James H. *Report of Explorations across the Great Basin of the Territory of Utah for a Direct Wagon-route from Camp Floyd to Genoa, in Carson Valley*. Reno: University of Nevada Press, 1983. Orig. Washington, D.C.: United States Government Printing Office, 1876.

"Sketch of Ella Hamblin Tenney's Life." Jacob Hamblin papers, Huntington Library, San Marino, CA.

"Sketch of George Oscar Hamblin." Jacob Hamblin papers, Huntington Library, San Marino, CA.

Skovlin, Jon M., and Donna McDaniel Skovlin. *In Pursuit of the McCartys.* Cove, OR: Reflections Publishing Co., 2001.

Slaughter, William B. *Life in Zion: An Intimate Look at the Latter-day Saints 1820–1995.* Salt Lake City: Deseret Book Company, 1995.

Slotkin, Richard. *The Fatal Environment: The Myth of the Frontier in the Age of Industrialization, 1800–1890*. New York: Atheneum, 1985.

———. *Gunfighter Nation: The Myth of the Frontier in Twentieth-Century America*. New York: Atheneum, 1992.

———. *Regeneration Through Violence: The Mythology of the American Frontier, 1600–1860*. Middletown, CT: Wesleyan University Press, 1973.

Smallcanyon, Corey. "Contested Space: Mormons, Navajos, and Hopis in the Colonization of Tuba City." M.A. thesis, Brigham Young University, 2010.

Smart, William B., and Donna T. Smart, eds. *Over the Rim, The Parley P. Pratt Exploring Expedition to Southern Utah, 1849–50.* Logan: Utah State University Press, 1999.

Smiley, Winifred Whiting. "Ammon M. Tenney: His Life and Where He Lived." Typescript. Arizona Historical Society, Tucson, Arizona.

Smiley, Winn Whiting. "Ammon M. Tenney: Mormon Missionary to the Indians." *Journal of Arizona History* 13.2 (summer 1972): 82–108.

Smith, Albert E. "Thales Hastings Haskell, pioneer–scout–explorer, Indian missionary, 1847–1909." Includes excerpts from Haskell's autobiography. Salt Lake City: Privately printed, 1964.

Smith, Andrea. "Mormon Forestdale." *Journal of the Southwest* 47.2 (summer 2005): 165–208.

Smith, Bathsheba W. "Recollections of the Prophet Joseph Smith." *The Juvenile Instructor* 27 (June 1, 1892): 344–45.

Smith, Drifter. "Fun with History." *boatman's quarterly review* 16.3 (fall 2003): 35–37. At http://www.gcrg.org/bqr/16-3/history.html (accessed Apr. 5, 2011).

Smith, Elizabeth J. "Account of the Settling of Paria River." Typescript, 1949. See research notes on George Adair, http://wc.rootsweb.ancestry.com/cgi-bin/igm.cgi?op=GET&db=kerryap&id=I1837 (accessed Feb. 26, 2013).

Smith, George A. Collection. MS 1322, CHL.

———. Diary. In George A. Smith Collection, MS 1322, CHL (SC 32).

———. "History of the Settling of Southern Utah." In Journal History, Oct. 17, 1861, and History of Brigham Young, 1861, p. 452 (SC 4).

———. "Pioneering." *The Contributor* 4.6 (March 1883). Read in *LDS Library 2006*.

Smith, Henry Nash. *Virgin Land: The American West as Symbol and Myth.* Cambridge, MA: Harvard University Press, 1950.

Smith, Jesse Nathaniel. *Journal of Jesse Nathaniel Smith: The Life Story of a Mormon Pioneer, 1834–1906.* Salt Lake City: Jesse N. Smith Family Association, 1953.

Smith, Joseph, Jr. *History of the Church of Jesus Christ of Latter-day Saints.* 8 vols. 2nd rev. ed. Salt Lake City: Deseret, 1978.

Smith, Melvin T. "Before Powell: Exploration of the Colorado River." *Utah Historical Quarterly* 55.2 (spring 1986): 105–19.

———. "Colorado River Exploration and the Mormon War." *Utah Historical Quarterly* 38.3 (summer 1970): 207–23.

———. "Mormon Exploration in the Lower Colorado River Area." In *The Mormon Role in the Settlement of the West*, edited by Richard H. Jackson, 29–49. Provo, UT: Brigham Young University Press, 1978.

Smith, Thomas W. "A Brief History of Early Pahreah Settlements." Typescript, MS A 494, USHS.

Snow, Bessie, and Elizabeth Snow Beckstrom. "Pine Valley." In Bradshaw, *Under Dixie Sun*, 177–212.

Snow, William J. "Utah Indians and the Spanish Slave Trade." *Utah Historical Quarterly* 2 (July 1929): 67–73. Relevant documents follow this article.

Solomon, William Henry. "Arizona Mission." Feb.–May, 1874. Typescript. MS A 1465, USHS. This is a diary of the Blythe company; Solomon was its clerk.

———. Diary, June 1873–Aug. 22, 1874. Typescript. MS A 1465, USHS.

Spangler, Jerry D. *Vermilion Dreamers, Sagebrush Schemers: An Overview of Human Occupation in House Rock Valley and the Eastern Arizona Strip.* Document prepared by the Colorado Plateau Archaeological Alliance, Ogden, Utah, on behalf of the Grand Canyon Trust, Flagstaff, Arizona. Jan. 30, 2007.

Spier, Leslie. *Yuman Tribes of the Gila River.* Chicago: University of Chicago Press, 1933.

Spilsbury, George Moroni. Autobiography. Dictated in 1935 to Louise Slack. Typescript at Harris Family History site, http://historyharrisfamily.blogspot.com/2010/03/george-moroni-spilsbury_5752.html (accessed Feb. 6, 2013).

Staheli, John. "The Life of John and Barbara Staheli." Typescript. At http://www.algerclan.org/getperson.php?personID=I11097&tree=Alger (accessed Feb. 26, 2013). Original at MS 7832, CHL.

Stannard, David E. *American Holocaust: The Conquest of the New World.* New York: Oxford University Press, 1993.

Stansbury, Howard. *Exploration and Survey of the Valley of Great Salt Lake of Utah, including a Reconoissance of a New Route through the Rocky Mountains.* Philadelphia: Lippincott, Grambo & Co., 1852.

Stapley, Jonathan A. "Adoptive Sealing Ritual in Mormonism." *Journal of Mormon History* 37.3 (summer 2011): 53–118.

Stapley, Jonathan A., and Kristine Wright. "'They Shall Be Made Whole': A History of Baptism for Health." *Journal of Mormon History* 34 (fall 2008): 69–112.

Starr, Helen Cram, cp. *Jacob Vernon Hamblin: Peacemaker in the Camp of the Lamanites*. St. George, UT: Privately printed, 1995.

Steele, John. Diary. Holograph, MS 1847, CHL. A more grammatical version in History of Brigham Young, 33.14–37, at date Jan. 8, 1863.

Steele, Mahonri Moriancumer. "Impressions Along Life's Highway." 1937. Excerpts in a webpage on Steele, at http://homepages.rootsweb.ancestry.com/~fhcnet/835.htm (accessed Feb. 26, 2013).

Stegner, Wallace. *The American West as Living Space*. Ann Arbor: University of Michigan Press, 1987.

———. *Beyond the Hundredth Meridian: John Wesley Powell and the Second Opening of the American West.* Boston: Houghton Mifflin, 1954.

———. *Clarence Edward Dutton: An Appraisal.* Salt Lake City: University of Utah Press, 1936.

———. *The Gathering of Zion: The Story of the Mormon Trail*. New York: McGraw-Hill, 1964.

———. *Mormon Country*. Lincoln: University of Nebraska, 1981. First published in 1942.

———. *Where the Bluebird Sings to the Lemonade Springs.* New York: Random House, 1992.

Stegner, Wallace, and Richard W. Etulain. *Conversations with Wallace Stegner on Western History and Literature*. Salt Lake City: University of Utah Press, 1983.

Steward, Julian H. *Basin-Plateau Aboriginal Sociopolitical Groups*. Smithsonian Institution. Bureau of American Ethnology. Bulletin 120. Washington, D.C.: U.S. Government Printing Office, 1938.

———. *Notes on Hillers' Photographs of the Paiute and Ute Indians taken on the Powell Expedition of 1873 (with 31 plates).* Smithsonian Miscellaneous Collections, vol. 98, no. 18; Smithsonian Institution Publication 3543. Washington, D.C.: The Smithsonian Institution, 1939.

Stewart, George R. *The California Trail: An Epic with Many Heroes*. New York: McGraw-Hill Book Company, 1962.

Stewart, Kenneth M. "A Brief History of the Chemehuevi Indians." *Kiva* 34.1 (Oct. 1968): 9–27.

———. "The Aboriginal Territory of the Mohave Indians." *Ethnohistory* 16.3 (summer 1969): 257–76.

———. "Mohave Warfare." *Southwestern Journal of Anthropology* 3.3 (autumn 1947): 257–78.

Stewart, Omer C. *Culture Element Distributions: XVIII Ute-Southern Paiute.* Anthropological Records 6.4. Berkeley: University of California Press, 1942.

Stewart, William Thomas. "Personal journal from birth to age thirty." (An autobiography.) At http://www.stewartkin.com/histories/stewart_william_thomas_journal.html (accessed Feb. 26, 2013).

Stoffle, Richard W., and Michael J. Evans. "Resource Competition and Population Change: A Kaibab Paiute Ethnohistorical Case." *Ethnohistory* 23.2 (spring 1976): 173–97.

Stoffle, Richard W., David B. Halmo, and Diane E. Austin. "Cultural Landscapes and Traditional Cultural Properties: A Southern Paiute View of the Grand Canyon and Colorado River." *American Indian Quarterly* 21.2 (spring 1997): 229–49.

Stoffle, Richard W., Kristine L. Jones, and Henry F. Dobyns. "Direct European Immigrant Transmission of Old World Pathogens to Numic Indians during the Nineteenth Century." *American Indian Quarterly* 19.2 (spring 1995): 181–203.

Stoffle, Richard W., and Maria Nieves Zedeño. "Historical Memory and Ethnographic Perspectives on the Southern Paiute Homeland." *Journal of California and Great Basin Anthropology* 23.2 (2001): 229–48.

Stout, Clifford L. *Search for Sanctuary: Brigham Young and the White Mountain Expedition*. Salt Lake City: University of Utah Press, 1984.

Stout, Hosea. Diary. See Brooks, *On the Mormon Frontier*.

Stucki, John S. "Biography of John S. Stucki: 'Pioneer and Settler.'" An autobiography. Typescript, MSS A 5074. Utah State Historical Society.

———. "Excerpts from the Journal of John S. Stucki." This is actually an autobiography, not a journal. In Whittaker, *History of Santa Clara, Utah*, 365–84.

Sturtevant, William C., ed. *Handbook of North American Indians*. 17 vols. Washington, D.C.: Smithsonian Institution, 1986–88.

Svaldi, David. *Sand Creek and the Rhetoric of Extermination: A Case Study in Indian-White Relations.* Lanham, MD: University Press of America, 1989.

Talayesva, Don C., Leo W. Simmons, and Robert V. Hine. *Sun Chief: The Autobiography of a Hopi Indian.* New Haven, CT: Yale University Press, 1963.

Tallsalt, Bert. "The Lone Survivor of the Navaho Trading Expedition to Utah Territory." *Western Folklore* 18.2 (Apr. 1959): 117–19.

Tanner, George S., and J. Morris Richards. *Colonization on the Little Colorado: The Joseph City Region.* Flagstaff, AZ: Northland Press, 1977.

Tate, George S. "Prayer Circle." In Ludlow, *Encyclopedia of Mormonism*, 1120–21.

Telling, Irving. "Ramah, New Mexico, 1876–1900: An Historical Episode with Some Value Analysis." *Utah Historical Quarterly* 21 (Apr. 1953): 117–36.

Tenney, Ammon. "Account of Travels in S. Utah and Ariz." 3 pp. typescript. Huntington Library, San Marino, CA.

———. Diaries 1858–1878. Holograph. MS 1484, fd 6, CHL.

———. "Early Recollections of My Youth: My First Mission." Arizona Historical Society, Tucson.

———. Letter to Pearl Udall Nelson, July 12, 1915. Arizona Historical Society, Tucson.

———. "Peace with the Navajos." Typescript, "copied from the original manuscript," at Arizona Historical Society, Tucson. Also in Reeve, "War and Peace."

The Franciscan Fathers. *An Ethnologic Dictionary of the Navaho Language.* Saint Michael's, AZ: The Franciscan Fathers, 1910.

"They Came in '50." In Carter, *Heart Throbs of the West*, 11:377–455.

Thompson, Almon H. "Financial Statement, Colorado River Expedition 1871–1872–1873." Photocopy of original, copy in my possession.

Thompson, Almon Harris. "Report on a Trip to the Mouth of the Dirty Devil River," dated July 30, 1872. Published in Powell, *Exploration of the Colorado River*, 133–45.

Thompson, David, cp. "Letters from Nevada Indian Agents." In the "Reading Room" of the website, "The Nevada Observer," at http://www.nevadaobserver.com/ (accessed Feb. 26, 2013).

Thompson, Gerald. *The Army and the Navajo: The Bosque Redondo Reservation Experiment, 1863–1868.* Tucson: University of Arizona Press, 1976.

———. *Edward F. Beale and the American West.* Santa Fe: University of New Mexico Press, 1983.

Thrapp, Dan L. *Encyclopedia of Frontier Biography*. 3 vols. Lincoln: University of Nebraska Press, 1991.

Thurber, Albert King. Autobiographical sketch. In "History of Spanish Fork," *Tullidge's Quarterly Magazine* 3.2 (Apr. 1884): 145–47.

Tietjen, Amos. "History of Ira Hatch While on his Mission among the Lamanites." "Told by Bro. Andrew Gibbons, Bro. Ira Hatch, E. A. Tietjen and wives, to Bro. Amos Tietjen." John S. Boyden papers, MSS 343, Container 15, Exh. 869, Lee Library.

Tietjen, Gary. *Ernst Albert Tietjen: Missionary and Colonizer.* Reprint edition, 2003. First published in 1992. Online at http://home.comcast.net/~benparkinson/histories/ernst-book-00.htm (accessed Feb. 26, 2013).

Toab, Foster Charles. "History of the Three Generations of My Family by the Shivwit Indian, Foster Charles Toab, Carlyle Graduate." Dictated Feb. 15, 1936. Library of Congress collection of Mormon Diaries. USHS.

Tobler, Douglas F. "Heinrich Hug and Jacob Tobler: From Switzerland to Santa Clara, 1854–80." *Dialogue* 26.4 (winter 1993): 107–27.

Tom, Gary, and Ronald Holt. "The Paiute Tribe of Utah." In Cuch, *A History of Utah's American Indians*, 123–65.

Topping, Gary. "Charles Kelly's Glen Canyon Ventures and Adventures." *Utah Historical Quarterly* 55.2 (spring 1987): 120–36.

Trafzer, Clifford E. *The Kit Carson Campaign: The Last Great Navajo War.* Norman: University of Oklahoma Press, 1982.

Trafzer, Clifford E., and Joel R. Hyer, eds. *Exterminate Them: Written Accounts of the Murder, Rape, and Slavery of Native Americans during the California Gold Rush, 1848–1868.* East Lansing: Michigan State University Press, 1999.

Tripp, George W. "Tooele Indians." In Miller, *History of Tooele County*, 2:81–84.

———. "Tooele's First Four Years 1849–1853." In Miller, *History of Tooele County*, 2:71–81.

Trudeau, Joseph M. *An Environmental History of Kane and Two Mile Ranches in Arizona*. The Grand Canyon Trust, 2006. At http://www.grandcanyontrust.org/kane/documents.php (accessed March 17, 2011).

Truett, Samuel. *Fugitive Landscapes: The Forgotten History of the U.S.-Mexico Borderlands.* New Haven, CT: Yale University Press, 2006.

Tullidge, Edward W. *The History of Salt Lake City and its Founders, Incorporating a Brief History of the Pioneers of Utah.* Salt Lake City: E. W. Tullidge, 1886.

———. *Tullidge's Histories (vol. II), Containing the History of All the Northern, Eastern and Western Counties of Utah; also the Counties of Southern Idaho*. Salt Lake City: Juvenile Instructor, 1889.

Tullis, F. LaMond. *Mormons in Mexico: The Dynamics of Faith and Culture.* Logan: Utah State University Press, 1987.

Turley, Clarence F., Anna Tenney Turley, compilers and writers; Lawrence Benson Lee, Marilyn Turley Lee, editors. *History of the Mormon Colonies in Mexico: (The Juarez Stake), 1885–1980, consisting of Colonia Diaz, Colonia Juarez, Colonia Dublan, Colonia Pacheco, colonies surrounding Colonia Pacheco, Colonia Garcia, Colonia Chuichupa, Colonia Oaxaca (Sonora), Colonia Morelos (Sonora), Colonia San Jose (Sonora)*. [Mexico]: L.B. Lee, M.T. Lee, 1996.

Turley, Richard E., ed. *Selected Collections from the Archives of the Church of Jesus Christ of Latter-day Saints*, 2 vols. (a set of DVD discs). Provo, UT: Brigham Young University Press, 2002. All citations are to volume 1, as volume 2 is the "Journal History."

Turley, Richard E., and Ronald W. Walker, eds. *Mountain Meadows Massacre: The Andrew Jenson and David H. Morris Collections*. Provo: Brigham Young University Press/University of Utah Press: 2009.

Turner, John G. *Brigham Young: Pioneer Prophet.* Cambridge, MA: The Belknap Press of Harvard University Press, 2012.

Tuttle, Charles R. *An Illustrated History of the State of Wisconsin*. Madison, WI: B. B. Russell & Co., 1875.

Twitchell, Ralph Emerson. *The Leading Facts of New Mexican History.* 5 vols. Cedar Rapids, IA: The Torch Press, 1911–1917.

Tyler, S. Lyman. "The Indians in Utah Territory." In *Utah's History*, edited by Richard D. Poll et al., 357–70. Provo, UT: Brigham Young University Press, 1978.

Udall, David King, and Pearl Udall Nelson. *Arizona Pioneer Mormon: David King Udall: His Story and His Family, 1851–1938.* Tucson, AZ: Arizona Silhouettes, 1959. At http://www.library.arizona.edu/exhibits/davidkudall/mormon/main.html (accessed Feb. 26, 2013).

Udall, Louise Lee. "Jacob Hamblin—His Later Years, Death and Burial." In Carter, *Heart Throbs of the West*, 11:253–61.

———. "Jacob Hamblin . . . Story of His Later Years . . . Death and Burial." *Improvement Era* 54 (Oct. 1951): 720–21, 741–45.

———. "Tuba—The Oraibi." In Carter, *Our Pioneer Heritage*, 3:435–38.

Udall, Stewart L. *The Forgotten Founders: Rethinking the History of the Old West.* Washington, D.C.: Island Press, 2002.

Underwood, Grant. *The Millenarian World of Early Mormonism.* Urbana: University of Illinois Press, 1993.

United States. Office of Indian Affairs. *Annual Report of the Commissioner of Indian Affairs, accompanying the Annual Report of the Secretary of the Interior for the Year 1857*. Washington, D.C.: William A. Harris, Printer, 1858.

United States. Office of Indian Affairs. *Annual Report of the Commissioner of Indian Affairs for the Year 1866*. Washington, D.C.: Government Printing Office, 1866.

United States. Office of Indian Affairs. *Annual Report of the Commissioner of Indian Affairs, Made to the Secretary of the Interior for the Year 1869*. Washington, D.C.: Government Printing Office, 1870.

United States. Office of Indian Affairs. *Annual Report of the Commissioner of Indian Affairs to the Secretary of the Interior for the Year 1870*. Washington, D.C.: Government Printing Office, 1870.

United States. Office of Indian Affairs. *Annual Report of the Commissioner of Indian Affairs to the Secretary of the Interior for the Year 1875*. Washington, D.C.: Government Printing Office, 1875.

United States. Office of Indian Affairs. *Annual Report of the Commissioner of Indian Affairs to the Secretary of the Interior for the Year 1880*. Washington, D.C.: Government Printing Office, 1880.

Unruh, Jr., John D. *The Plains Across: The Overland Emigrants and the Trans-Mississippi West, 1840–60.* Urbana: University of Illinois Press, 1979.

U.S. Congress. House. *Accounts of Brigham Young, Superintendent of Indian Affairs in Utah Territory.* 37th Cong., 2d sess., 1862, H. Doc. 29.

Utley, Robert M. "An Indian before Breakfast: Kit Carson Then and Now." In Gordon-McCutchan, *Kit Carson: Indian Fighter or Indian Killer?* 91–98.

———. *The Indian Frontier, 1846–1890.* 2nd ed. Albuquerque: University of New Mexico Press, 2003.

Van Cott, John W. *Utah Place Names: A Comprehensive Guide to the Origins of Geographic Names: A Compilation.* Salt Lake City: University of Utah Press, 1990.

Van Hoak, Stephen. "And Who Shall Have the Children? The Indian Slave Trade in the Southern Great Basin, 1800–1865." *Nevada Historical Quarterly* 41 (spring 1998): 3–25.

Van Valkenburgh, Richard F. *A Short History of the Navajo People*. In *Navajo Indians III.* New York: Garland Publishing, Inc., 1974.

Vogel, Dan, and Scott C. Dunn. "The Tongue of Angels: Glossolalia among Mormonism's Founders." *Journal of Mormon History* 19.2 (fall 1993): 1–34.

Vogt, Evon Z., and Ethel M. Albert, eds. *People of Rimrock: A Study of Values in Five Cultures.* Cambridge, MA: Harvard University Press, 1966.

Voth, H. R. *The Traditions of the Hopi.* Field Columbian Museum, Anthropological Series, Publication 96, Vol. 8. Chicago: Field Columbian Museum, 1905.

Walapai papers: Historical Reports, Documents, and Extracts from Publications Relating to the Walapai Indians of Arizona. Washington, D.C.: U.S. Government Printing Office, 1936.

Walker, Charles Lowell. *Diary of Charles Lowell Walker.* Edited by A. Karl Larson and Katharine Miles Larson. 2 vols. Logan: Utah State University Press, 1980.

Walker, Donald D. "The Cattle Industry of Utah, 1850–1900: An Historical Profile." *Utah Historical Quarterly* 32.3 (summer 1964): 182–97.

Walker, Elizabeth Staheli. "History of Barbara Sophia Haberli Staheli." In Nora Lund, Biographies Collection, 3, MS 8691, microfilm reel 3, CHL.

Walker, Henry Pickering, and Don Bufkin. *Historical Atlas of Arizona.* 2nd ed. Norman: University of Oklahoma Press, 1986.

Walker, Ronald W. "Native Women on the Utah Frontier." *Brigham Young University Studies* 32.4 (fall 1992): 87–124.

———. "Toward a Reconstruction of Mormon and Indian Relations, 1847–1877." *Brigham Young University Studies* 29.4 (fall 1989): 21–42.

———. "Wakara Meets the Mormons, 1848–52: A Case Study in Native American Accommodation." *Utah Historical Quarterly* 70.3 (summer 2002): 215–37.

———. *Wayward Saints: The Godbeites and Brigham Young.* Urbana: University of Illinois Press, 1998.

Walker, Ronald W., and Doris D. Dant, eds. *Nearly Everything Imaginable: The Everyday Life of Utah's Mormon Pioneers*. Provo, UT: Brigham Young University Press, 1999.

Walker, Ronald W., Richard E. Turley, and Glen M. Leonard. *Massacre at Mountain Meadows.* New York: Oxford University Press, 2008.

Warburton, Richard. Reminiscences. (No formal title.) Written in 1907. "Tooele histories," MS 8326, CHL.

Ward, Albert E. *Inscription House: Two Research Reports.* Museum of Northern Arizona Technical Series No. 16. Flagstaff, AZ: Northern Arizona Society of Science and Art, 1975.

Ward, Maurine Carr. "1842 Census of Nauvoo—Identification of Members—Civil Ward One." *Nauvoo Journal* 5.1 (spring 1993): 19–49. At http://mormonhistoricsites.org/publications/ (accessed Feb. 26, 2013).

———. "A Partial List of Church Members Living in Nauvoo." *Nauvoo Journal* 4 (1992): 15–69. At http://www.mormonhistoricsitesfoundation.org/publications/nj_1992/1992.htm (accessed June 28, 2010).

Warner, Alvin C. *William B. Maxwell and Some of His Descendants, 1821–1959*. Kansas City: Eaton-Cunningham Co., 1960.

Warner, Ted J., ed., and Fray Angelico Chavez, trans. *The Domínguez-Escalante Journal: Their Expedition through Colorado, Utah, Arizona, and New Mexico in 1776.* Salt Lake City: University of Utah Press, 1995. First published in 1976.

Warrum, Noble. *Utah Since Statehood, Historical and Biographical.* 4 vols. Chicago: The S. J. Clarke Publishing Company, 1919–20.

Waters, Frank. *The Book of the Hopi.* New York: Viking Press, 1963.

Wauchope, Robert. *Lost Tribes & Sunken Continents: Myth and Method in the Study of American Indians.* Chicago: University of Chicago Press, 1962.

Webb, Charlotte Maxwell. "A Sketch of the Life of William Bailey Maxwell." At Bartmess Family website, http://bartmess.com/williambmaxwellpg2.html (accessed Feb. 26, 2013).

Webster's Revised Unabridged Dictionary. Springfield, MA: C. & G. Merriam Co., 1913. Available online at http://www.dict.org/bin/Dict (accessed June 28, 2010).

"Welcome to Scotland's Museum of Lead Mining." A website for the museum, at http://www.leadminingmuseum.co.uk/index.htm (accessed via Internet Archive, Feb. 26, 2013).

Wells, Daniel H. "Daniel H. Wells' Narrative." Statement, 1884, given for Bancroft's *History of Utah*. Published in *Utah State Historical Quarterly* 6.4 (Oct. 1933): 124–32.

West, Elliott. *The Contested Plains: Indians, Goldseekers and the Rush to Colorado.* Lawrence: University of Kansas Press, 1998.

West, Velma A. Howard. "Graves in Hubbard Cemetery." At http://files.usgwarchives.org/az/graham/cemeteries/hubbard.txt (accessed Feb. 26, 2013).

Wheeler, G. M. *Topographical Atlas Projected To Illustrate United States Geographical Surveys West Of The 100th Meridian Of Longitude*... Washington, D.C.: The Corps, 1873–.

White, Richard. *"It's Your Misfortune and None of My Own": A New History of the American West.* Norman: University of Oklahoma Press, 1991.

———. *The Middle Ground: Indians, Empires, and Republics in the Great Lakes Region, 1650-1815.* Cambridge: Cambridge University Press, 1991.

Whiteley, Peter M. *Bacavi: Journey to Reed Springs.* Flagstaff, AZ: Northland Press, 1988.

———. *Deliberate Acts: Changing Hopi Culture through the Oraibi Split.* Tucson: University of Arizona Press, 1988.

———. *The Orayvi Split: A Hopi Transformation*. 2 parts. Anthropological Papers of the American Museum of Natural History, Volume 87. New York: American Museum of Natural History, 2008.

———. *Rethinking Hopi Ethnography*. Washington, D.C.: Smithsonian Institution Press, 1998.

Whiting, Beatrice Blyth. *Paiute Sorcery.* Viking Fund Publications in Anthropology, no. 15. New York: The Viking Fund Inc., 1950.

Whitmore, Glendon Montgomery. "Historical Sketch of Doctor James Montgomery Whitmore." Typescript in author's possession. This is part of a collection of information on Whitmore available at the Pipe Spring Visitor Center.

Whitney, Orson F. *History of Utah*. 4 vols. Salt Lake City: George Q. Cannon and Sons Co., 1892.

Whittaker, David J. "Mormons and Native Americans: A Historical and Bibliographical Introduction." *Dialogue* 18.4 (winter 1985): 33–65.

Whittaker, Joyce Wittwer, cp. and ed. *History of Santa Clara, Utah: "A Blossom in the Desert."* Santa Clara, UT: Santa Clara Historical Society, 2003.

"William Haynes Hamblin." Available online at http://jorghistory.blogspot.com/ (accessed Feb. 26, 2013).

Williams, Aubrey W., Jr. *Navajo Political Process*. Smithsonian Contributions to Anthropology, vol. 9. Washington, D.C.: Smithsonian Institution Press, 1970.

Williams, George Calvin. "The Life and Religion of George Calvin Williams." An autobiography. Typescript. MS 13382, CHL.

Williams, Gwyn A. *Madoc: The Making of a Myth*. Oxford: Oxford University Press, 1987. Previously published in 1979.

Williams, Hyrum. Journal. BYOF, bx 36, fd 13.

Wixom, Hartt. *Hamblin: A Modern Look at the Frontier Life and Legend of Jacob Hamblin*. Springville, UT: CFI, 1996.

Woodbury, Angus M. *A History of Southern Utah and Its National Parks.* Springdale, UT: Zion Natural History Association, 1997. Orig. *Utah Historical Quarterly* 12 (Jul.–Oct. 1944): 111–209. First published as a booklet in 1950.

———. "Route of Jedediah Smith in 1826 from the Great Salt Lake to the Colorado River." *Utah Historical Quarterly* 4.2 (Apr. 1931): 35–46. This publishes a letter by Smith dated July 12, 1827.

Woodfield, John K. "The Initiation of the Range Cattle Industry of Utah." M.S. thesis, University of Utah, 1957.

Woodruff, Wilford. Diaries. See Kenney, *Wilford Woodruff's Journal.*

Woods, Fred E. *A Gamble in the Desert: The Mission in Las Vegas (1855–57)*. Salt Lake City: Mormon Historic Sites Foundation, 2005.

Woodward, Arthur. *Feud on the Colorado*. Los Angeles: Westernlore Press, 1955.

Woolley, Caroline Keturah Parry. *'I Would to God': A Personal History of Isaac Haight.* Edited by Blanche Cox Clegg and Janet Burton Seegmiller. Cedar City: Southern Utah University Press, 2009.

Woolley, Edwin G. "Journal of Two Campaigns by the Utah Territorial Militia against the Navajo Indians, 1869." Edited by C. Gregory Crampton and David E. Miller. *Utah Historical Quarterly* 29.2 (April 1961): 149–76.

Woolley, Edwin, Jr. "Notes on Father's Life." Typescript, Woolley Family Papers, MSS 1403, bx 1, fd 13. Perry Special Collections, Lee Library.

———. "A True Indian Story." Typescript, Woolley Family Papers, MSS 1403, bx 1, fd 13. Perry Special Collections, Lee Library.

Workers of the Writers' Program of the Work Projects Administration for the State of Utah, cp. *Utah: A Guide to the State*. American Guide Series. New York: Hastings House, 1941.

Worster, Donald. *A River Running West: The Life of John Wesley Powell*. Oxford: Oxford University Press, 2001.

———. *Rivers of Empire: Water, Aridity & the Growth of the American West.* New York: Pantheon Books, 1985.

Wright, James E. *The Galena Lead District: Federal Policy and Practice 1824–1847*. Madison: State Historical Society of Wisconsin, 1966.

Wyckoff, Lydia. *Designs and Factions: Politics, Religion, and Ceramics on the Hopi Third Mesa.* Albuquerque: University of New Mexico Press, 1990.

Wyman, Mark. *The Wisconsin Frontier*. Bloomington: Indiana University Press, 1998.

Yava, Albert. *Big Falling Snow: A Tewa-Hopi Indian's Life and Times and the History and Traditions of His People.* Edited by Harold Courlander. New York: Crown Publishers, 1978.

Young, Brigham. Brigham Young Office Files, CR 1234/1, CHL.

Young, Brigham, Jr. Diaries. MS 1236/1–4, CHL. Typescript excerpts in PTRC, series 1, bx 13, fd 186.

Young, Gary Dean. "Life and Times of William Young—Tennessee Frontiersman, Utah Pioneer." At http://www.lofthouse.com/USA/Utah/washington/history/wmyoung.html (accessed via Internet Archives on Feb. 26, 2013).

Young, John R. "In Memory of Ira Hatch." *Improvement Era* 25.10 (Aug. 1922): 885–87.

———. *Memoirs of John R. Young, by Himself.* Salt Lake City: The Deseret News, 1920.

———. "The Navajo and Moqui Mission." *Improvement Era* 17.3 (Jan. 1914): 247–49. Read in *LDS Library 2006*.

Young, R. W. "A Navajo's Pluck." *Contributor* 1.12 (Sept. 1880): 282–83.

Young, Robert W. *The Role of the Navajo in the Southwestern Drama.* Gallup, NM: The Gallup Independent and Robert W. Young, 1968.

Youngberg, Florence C., ed. *Conquerors of the West: Stalwart Mormon Pioneers.* 4 vols. Salt Lake City: Agreka Books, 1998.

Zanjani, Sally. *Sarah Winnemucca*. Lincoln: University of Nebraska Press, 2004.

Index